Lecture Notes in Computer Science 3305

Commenced Publication in 1973
Founding and Former Series Editors:
Gerhard Goos, Juris Hartmanis, and Jan van Leeuwen

T0074020

Peter M.A. Sloot   Bastien Chopard
Alfons G. Hoekstra (Eds.)

Cellular Automata

6th International Conference on Cellular Automata
for Research and Industry, ACRI 2004
Amsterdam, The Netherlands, October 25-27, 2004
Proceedings

 Springer

Volume Editors

Peter M.A. Sloot
Alfons G. Hoekstra
University of Amsterdam
Informatics Institute, Section Computational Science
Kruislaan 403, 1098 SJ Amsterdam, The Netherlands
E-mail: {sloot, a.g.hoekstra}@science.uva.nl

Bastien Chopard
University of Geneva
Computer Science Department, CUI
24 Rue du Général Dufour, 1211 Geneva 4, Switzerland
E-mail: Bastien.Chopard@cui.unige.ch

Library of Congress Control Number: 2004113647

CR Subject Classification (1998): F.1.1, F.2.2, I.6, C.2

ISSN 0302-9743
ISBN 3-540-23596-5 Springer Berlin Heidelberg New York

Springer is a part of Springer Science+Business Media

springeronline.com

© Springer-Verlag Berlin Heidelberg 2004

Typesetting: Camera-ready by author, data conversion by PTP-Berlin, Protago-TeX-Production GmbH
Printed on acid-free paper   SPIN: 11339403   06/3142   5 4 3 2 1 0

Preface

"What joy to discern the minute in infinity, the vast to perceive in
the small, what divinity!"
Jacob Bernoulli (1654-1705) in Ars Conjectandi (1713)

We are proud to present to you the proceedings of the Sixth International Conference on Cellular Automata for Research and Industry (ACRI 2004), held in Amsterdam, The Netherlands on October 25–27, 2004.

Since the first conference in Italy, ACRI, which is held biennially, has become the premier conference in the field of cellular automata in Europe and beyond, and is still growing in quality and size.

This year's theme was "From Individual to Collective Behavior", emphasizing the capability of Cellular Automata to simulate macroscopic processes from individual, local interactions. Cellular Automata, in spite of their apparent simplicity, represent a very powerful approach to studying spatio-temporal systems in which complex phenomena build up out of many simple local interactions. In the words of Richard Feynman in the Character of Physical Law (1982), "Nature uses only the longest threads to weave her patterns, so each small piece of her fabric reveals the organization of the entire tapestry".

John von Neumann, who is recognized as the father of cellular automata, would have been 100 years old in 2004. ACRI 2004 wanted to commemorate this date by inviting researchers to submit contributions related to von Neumann's work or to the emergence of organization in systems in which collaboration between components wins over the individual behavior.

In view of this commemoration we had two very inspiring memorial plenary lectures on the first day: *"Von Neumann's Century: Too many souls!"* by Prof. Tomasso Toffoli and *"John von Neumann and Cellular Automata"* by Prof. Roland Vollmar

Other invited lectures that were presented in the plenary sessions during the three meeting days were: *"Pattern Discovery and Automated Theory Building"* by Prof. James P. Crutchfield, *"Studying Biological Development and Evolution with Multilevel Particle Systems"* by Prof. Paulien Hogeweg, *"Cell Scale Simulations, the Neglected Link Between Microscopic and Continuum Modeling"* by Prof. James A. Glazier, *"From Cellular Automata to Wetware"* by Prof. Andrew Adamatzky, and *"Structural Design and Optimization Using Cellular Automata"* by Prof. Zafer Gürdal.

We would like to express our sincere thanks to the invited speakers who delivered such inspiring lectures at ACRI 2004.

The conference was organized along the following tracks:

- Methods and Theory
- Evolved CA
- Traffic, Networks and Communication

- Applications in Science and Engineering
- Bio-medical Applications
- Natural Phenomena and Ecology
- Social and Economical Applications

This volume contains peer reviewed original work on the theory and application of Cellular Automata. After peer review by three experts in the field, 40% of the 150 papers submitted were selected for oral presentation and 30% for poster presentation. A total of 30% of the submitted papers were rejected.

This conference would not have been possible without the support of many people and organizations that helped in different ways to make it a success.

First of all we would like to thank the authors for making the effort to submit so many high-quality papers. We thank the Program Committee for their excellent job in reviewing the submissions and thus guaranteeing the quality of the conference and the proceedings. We thank Liesbeth Otte and the conference office of the University of Amsterdam for their practical assistance and support. Many thanks go to Coco van der Hoeven for her secretarial work. Dick van Albada, Berry Vermolen and Jiangjun Cui are acknowledged for their punctuality in preparing the draft of the proceedings.

We thank our sponsors for their financial support: the board of the University of Amsterdam, the Science Faculty and the Institute for Informatics. Finally we thank the Dutch Science Foundation NWO, section Exact-Sciences, as well as the section Computational Life Sciences.

September 2004

Peter Sloot
Bastien Chopard
Alfons Hoekstra

Organization

Scientific Committee

Peter M.A. Sloot, General Chair (University of Amsterdam, The Netherlands)
Bastien Chopard, General Co-Chair (University of Geneva, Switzerland)
Alfons G. Hoekstra, Program Committee Chair (University of Amsterdam, The Netherlands)

Local Organizing Committee

Liesbeth Otte (University of Amsterdam, The Netherlands)
Dick van Albada (University of Amsterdam, The Netherlands)
Berry Vermolen (University of Amsterdam, The Netherlands)
Jiangjiun Cui (University of Amsterdam, The Netherlands)

Program Committee

Albuquerque, Paul, University of Geneva, Switzerland
Bagnoli, Franco, University of Florence, Italy
Ballegooijen, Marijn van, Amsterdam, The Netherlands
Bandini, Stefania, University of Milano-Bicocca, Milan, Italy
Bandman, Olga, Institute of Computational Mathematics and Mathematical Geophysics, Novosibirsk, Russia
Berec, Ludek, Ceske Budejovice, Czech Republic
Cattaneo, Gianpiero, University of Milano-Bicocca, Milan, Italy
Chopard, Bastien, University of Geneva, Switzerland
Emde Boas, Peter van, University of Amsterdam, The Netherlands
Deutsch, Andreas, Technical University of Dresden, Germany
Di Gregorio, Salvatore, University of Calabria, Italy
Dupuis, Alexandre, Oxford University, UK
Dzwinel, Witold, AGH University of Science and Techology, Krakow, Poland
El Yacoubi, Samira, University of Perpignan, France
Green, Frederic, Clark University, USA
Haeseler, Friedrich von, KU Leuven, Belgium
Hoekstra, Alfons (Chair), University of Amsterdam, The Netherlands
Kaandorp, Jaap, University of Amsterdam, The Netherlands
Legendi, Tamas, Hungary
Manoussaki, Daphne, Hania, Greece
Marconi, Stephane, University of Geneva, Switzerland

Mauri, Giancarlo, University of Milano-Bicocca, Milan, Italy
Meyer-Hermann, Michael, Dresden, Germany
Morishita, Shin, Yokohama National University, Japan
Nishinari, Katsuhiro, Ryukoku University, Shiga, Japan
Plapp, Mathis, Palaiseau, France
Serra, Roberto, Centro Ricerche e Servizi Ambientali Fenice, Italy
Sipper, Moshe, Ben-Gurion University, Beer-Sheva, Israel
Sloot, Peter, University of Amsterdam, The Netherlands
Spezzano, Giandomenico, ICAR-CNR, Italy
Talia, Domenico, University of Calabria, Italy
Tempesti, Gianluca, EPFL, Lausanne, Switzerland
Tomassini, Marco, University of Lausanne, Switzerland
Torenvliet, Leen, University of Amsterdam, The Netherlands
Trautteur, Giuseppe, University of Naples Federico II, Naples, Italy
Umeo, Hiroshi, Univ. of Osaka Electro-Communication, Japan
Vollmar, Roland, University of Karlsruhe, Germany
Worsch, Thomas, University of Karlsruhe, Germany
Zomaya, Albert, The University of Sydney, Australia

Sponsoring Organizations

The University of Amsterdam, The Netherlands
The Dutch Science Foundation NWO, section Exact Sciences and section Computational Life Sciences

Table of Contents

Tom Thumb Algorithm and von Neumann Universal Constructor

Joël Rossier, Enrico Petraglio, André Stauffer, and Gianluca Tempesti

Swiss Federal Institute of Technology
Logic Systems Laboratory
CH-1015 Lausanne, Switzerland
j.rossier@epfl.ch

Abstract. This article describes the addition to the von Neumann cellular automaton of the Tom Thumb Algorithm, a mechanism developed for the self-replication of multi-processor systems. Except for the cell construction process, every functionality of the original CA has been preserved in our new system. Moreover, the Tom Thumb Algorithm now allows the replication of any structure within the von Neumann environment, whatever its number of cells may be.

1 Introduction

In the middle of the last century, John von Neumann was interested in the concept of self-replication. During his research, he presented a model for an Universal Constructor (UC) system based on a two-dimensional cellular automaton of 29 states [1]. This UC is divided in two different parts: a tape that contains the description of the cellular machine to construct and the constructor in itself that reads the tape and builds the new corresponding machine with a dedicated cellular arm. Moreover, if the tape contains the description of the constructor and if the constructor, in addition to its building abilities, can also copy the tape information, then the resulting system is a self-replicating one (figure 1).

In spite of the conceptual success of von Neumann's work, the realization of such a system encounters a major problem: with the proposed architecture, the UC in itself needs about 200'000 cells, while the tape containing its description is almost five time greater. Clearly, it is too big for a physical implementation (at least today) and it is a real challenge even for a software simulation. In fact, the UC has not yet been completely specified [2].

In 1995, Umberto Pesavento presented an extension of the transition rules of the standard system [3]. Thus, he drastically reduced the number of cells used in the UC replication and proved the validity of the von Neumann self-replication process by simulating the entire UC. Despite that, once again, there were too many cells for a physical implementation. To solve this problem, we decided to apply to the standard von Neumann system a new kind of self-replicating process that uses a smaller number of cells: the Tom Thumb Algorithm (TTA).

In section 2, we will briefly present the standard von Neumann system. The basic operation of the Tom Thumb Algorithm will be exposed in section 3.

P.M.A. Sloot, B. Chopard, and A.G. Hoekstra (Eds.): ACRI 2004, LNCS 3305, pp. 1–10, 2004.

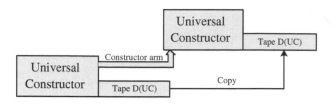

Fig. 1. Universal Constructor self-replication

Section 4 will then introduce the system we have developed for self-replication in the von Neumann environment and in section 5, we will discuss of some potentialities of such a realization from an evolutionary point of view. Finally, we will briefly mention the hardware implementation of our system in section 6.

2   Von Neumann States and Transitions

As mentioned before, each cell of the von Neumann CA possesses 29 states. These states can be divided into several different groups with regard to their "functionality".

The first state is the quiescent one. A cell in this state has no influence on its neighborhood. Every unused cell of the cellular array is in the quiescent state.

Then we find the 16 states responsible for the propagation of excitations through the cellular array. Each of these states has a direction, i.e. one of the four cardinal ones, and can be excited or not. Moreover there are two kinds of transmission states that propagate different types of excitations: the ordinary and the special ones. An ordinary (respectively special) transmission state becomes excited if it receives an ordinary (respectively special) or a confluent (see below) excitation on one of its inputs. Moreover, they introduce a delay of one time unit in the propagation of the excitations and act as OR gates.

A third group contains the confluent states. These are also used for the transmission of excitations. A confluent cell becomes excited only if all of the neighboring ordinary transmission states directed to it are excited. It consequently acts as an AND gate. The confluent states are also used to convert an ordinary excitation into a special one and they permit the splitting of a transmission line, acting as fan-outs. Moreover, they introduce a two time units delay in the propagation of information. Finally, they act as memory units: when none of its neighbours is an outgoing transmission state, if the confluent has been previously excited, it keeps the excitation until it can release this latter through a valid transmission state.

Pesavento's extension of the standard rules provides another type of confluent state that permits the crossing of excitations.

The last group contains the sensitive states that are transitory ones and permit the construction of each specific cell type: when a quiescent state receives an excitation, it goes in the first sensitive state. Then, its state changes at each time unit as seen in figure 2.

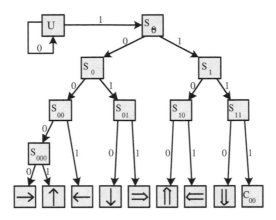

Fig. 2. Sensitive states and construction process

To the construction process corresponds a destructive one: the transition from any state to the quiescent one. When a cell is in an ordinary transmission or in a confluent state and receives a special excitation, it is destructed and becomes quiescent again. The same thing happens when a special transmission state receives an ordinary excitation.

3   Tom Thumb Algorithm

To find an alternative self-replication mechanism for the UC, we define the entire constructor as a two-dimensional *organism* composed of multiple cells. Each cell is defined by two *genes*: the first one corresponds to the cell's state according to von Neumann while the second, as we will see, will be used to direct the construction and replication processes. Using these definitions, we can then apply to the machine a self-replication mechanism known as the Tom Thumb Algorithm (TTA) [4,5].

Without loss of generality, we will present the TTA construction process of a four-cell organism defined by its *genome* showed at the top of figure 3. The numbers correspond to von Neumann states, while the other genes define the directions of the construction path (arrows) as well as the branching directions for the self-replication process (background color of arrows in the figure).

Moreover, although defined by only two genes, each cell of the organism has four memory positions: the two at the right in figure 3 are used to store the cell configuration, i.e. its state and the construction information, while the two remaining ones keep a copy of the genome indefinitely moving around the organism.

The construction process proceeds as follows: when the genome is injected in the cellular array, the first cell receiving it shifts the incoming genes until it has stored its configuration in the corresponding registers (t=4 in figure 3). At that time, the cell knows where to forward the next incoming genome information

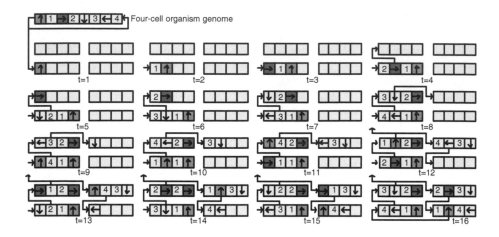

Fig. 3. Genome and first steps of the TTA creation of a four-cell organism

(to the North for the cell of the figure). The next genes arrive in the upper cell which will also shift them to get its configuration and find the way to forward the remaining genes (East, t=8). This process then repeats itself until the organism is fully constructed, i.e. at time t=16 in the figure.

Note that twice the whole genome has been injected for the organism construction: one half of the genes is fixed in the configuration registers while the other half is continuously shifted around the organism, following the construction path.

The self-replication process is started when the first gene of the genome arrives in a cell whose configuration allows branching. In our example, at time t=12, a replication path is consequently initiated to the North. The running genome is duplicated and sent through the replication path. This process obviously starts the construction of a second organism whose genome is the same as for the first one: the organism replicates itself.

Note that when the genome has been transmitted twice through the replication path, the construction of its copy is finished and the branching replication path can be removed. Note also that the construction path of a valid organism has to be a loop; if it were not, the copy of the genome would not have been able to run around the organism and the replication process would have failed.

4   TTA and UC

Our main goal was to add to the von Neumann system an innovative process, in our case a modified version of the TTA, that could drastically reduce the number of cells used for the self-replication. Then, the resulting system had to keep every standard functionality of the original von Neumann CA, as well as implementing the Pesavento crossing ability. Consequently, we have separated our system design in two different layers and we added a new cell type to the system: the *activator*, used to launch the self-replication process.

The first layer (UClayer) contains the von Neumann standard information coded on four bits. The two first bits determine the cell type (quiescent 00, ordinary arrow 01, special arrow 10, and confluent 11). The two remaining ones define the arrow direction or the confluent subtype (memory, crossing or activator). We show in figure 4 the different UC layer codes and their corresponding cell type.

Type	Dir	Cell symbol	
00	$\emptyset$	U	Quiescent
01	00	$\uparrow$	ordinary North arrow
01	01	$\rightarrow$	ordinary East arrow
01	10	$\downarrow$	ordinary South arrow
01	11	$\leftarrow$	ordinary West arrow
10	00	$\Uparrow$	special North arrow
10	01	$\Rightarrow$	special East arrow
10	10	$\Downarrow$	special South arrow
10	11	$\Leftarrow$	special West arrow
11	00	–	not used
11	01	R	activator confluent
11	10	C_+	crossing confluent
11	11	C_{xx}	memory confluent

Fig. 4. UC layer codes

The second layer (TTAlayer) is only used for the construction and replication processes. It's also defined with four bits: the first two give the direction of the replication path, the third bit is a flag that says if the cell is the first one of the organism and, finally, the last bit corresponds to the end-of-organism cell flag.

Moreover, in our TTA version, the path does not have to be a loop, as in the standard algorithm: in our case, the path begins at the start-of-organism cell and then goes through the entire organism, from cell to cell, until it reaches the end-of-organism cell.

4.1   Cell Construction Process

As we have just seen, a TTA-UC cell is fully defined by the eight configuration bits of the two layers. This fact did not obviously permit us to keep the same construction process as in the original von Neumann system, but we maintained the same general idea: a quiescent cell is transformed in another cell when it receives the corresponding (ordinary or special) excitation. To implement the construction process, as shown in figure 5, we added three flags (with the grey background) to the eight configuration bits.

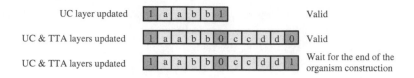

Fig. 5. The different construction pulses

Reading the bits from left to right, the first flag bit is used to start the cell construction process and is always equal to '1'. Then we find the UClayer type on two bits (aa in figure 5), followed by the UClayer direction, on two bits too (bb).

After these, we have the second flag bit: if it is equal to '1', the cell construction process stops. In such a case, the cell has updated its UClayer state, but without modifying its TTAlayer configuration. This could be used to create a new self-replicating organism on a pre-existing TTAlayer, or just to change some cells in a TTA-UC structure without affecting its self-replication ability.

In the other case, i.e. if the second flag is equal to '0', the construction process continues: the two next bits update the TTAlayer direction (cc) and the last two define the TTAlayer type (dd), i.e. start or end of organism.

At the end, we find the last flag bit. While it is equal to '1', it makes the cell wait for the entire organism to be constructed, before being able to act like an usual von Neumann cell. During that time, the cell only forwards every excitation it receives in the direction defined by its TTAlayer.

A cell can then be constructed using a pulse of six excitations, as long as we want to keep the TTAlayer unchanged. Otherwise, the construction pulse needs eleven excitations, with the last being inactive for a single cell creation and active in the case of an organism self-replication.

4.2   Organism Self-Replication

We will now present the self-replication process of a simple organism. For clarity, we will take as example the replication of a two by two cells organism. The two layers of the organism and the configuration bits of its cells (without the construction flags) are shown in figure 6. The start-of-organism cell is in dark grey while the end-of-organism one is in light grey.

Fig. 6. Two layers and configuration bits of the organism

We will first present the emission of the organism genome and then, show how this genome is used in the construction of the new replicated organism.

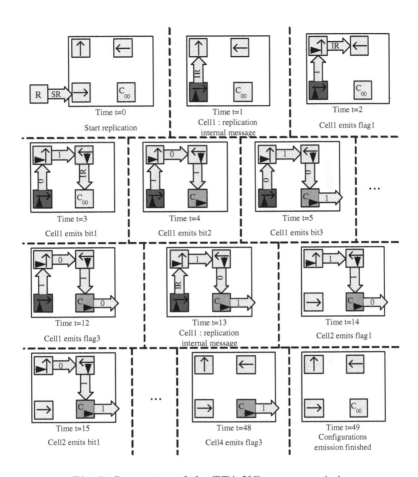

Fig. 7. Some steps of the TTA-UC genome emission

Genome emission: An organism will start its replication process if one of the neighbours of the start-of-organism cell is an excited activator cell (R in figure 7 at time t=0). In such a case, this latter sends a StartReplication message (SR in the figure); the start-of-organism cell then emits to its TTA direction a InternalReplication message (IR) at time t=1. This latter will then be forwarded along the TTA path through the entire organism until it reaches its last cell, making every cell of the organism become in a TTA forwarding state: from that time, they transmit to their TTA direction every excitation they receive.

Just after the InternalReplication message, the start-of-organism cell sends its configuration bits with the appropriate flags during the following 11 clock steps.

As for the first message, these configuration bits are then forwarded through the TTA path until they reach the end-of-organism cell. This latter transmit the configuration pulse to the UC layer of the next cell in its TTA direction.

When the first cell has finished sending its configuration stream, it emits once again a InternalReplication message (t=13) meaning it has finished its replication task. When the next cell on the TTA path receives this InternalReplication message, it goes out of the TTA forwarding state and begin the emission of its own configuration bits.

This process repeats itself in a similar way until the end-of-organism cell has transmitted its last configuration bit: at that time (t=49), the organism has finished its genome emission.

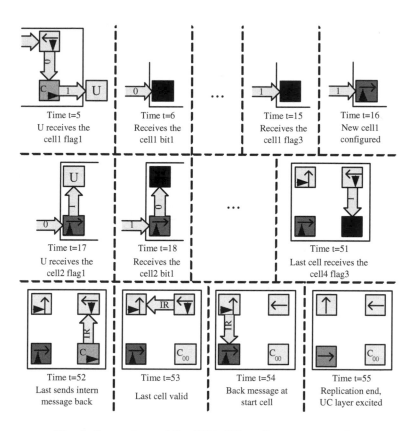

Fig. 8. Some steps of the TTA-UC replicate construction

Construction: We said that the end-of-organism cell transmits the configuration pulses to the UC layer. The excitations then consequently follow the UC layer specifications: they can travel along an ordinary arrows path, if any, until they reach a quiescent cell to configure. In figure 8, that happens at time t=5.

When a quiescent cell has received eleven building excitations, it is fully configured. But, as we have seen, the last configuration bit has to be chosen equal to '1' in the self-replication process. This flag implies that the cell must stay in a TTA forwarding state until the end of the organism construction. Indeed, it has to transmit the next received excitations to its TTA direction in order to pursue the creation of the next organism cells, in the good direction.

When the last configuration bit has reached the new end-of-organism cell (t=51), this latter sends an InternalReplication message back along the TTA path. This message, that notifies the end of the organism construction is forwarded back by each cell of the organism until it reaches the new start-of-organism cell, at t=54 in the figure.

The next time unit, the start-of-organism cell becomes excited in its UC layer and can launch the classical UC behaviour of the new organism: the self-replication process is terminated.

5   TTA-UC and Evolution

As explained before, and unlike the standard Tom Thumb Algorithm, our TTA-UC system does not possess a running genome that keeps unchanged the initial configuration of the organism. In fact, our replication system works by self-inspection [6]: the organism generates the bits configuration that permits to copy its current state (and not the initial one).

Having such an ability should permit a TTA-UC organism to evolve through its replication process: for example if a cell of the organism has got its UCconfiguration modified during its normal behavior, without changing its TTAlayer information, then the organism can still replicate itself but will also copy the modified cell. As a result, this new organism will not be a perfect copy of the initial one: almost every UClayer modification can propagate through the organism generations. An organism population could consequently evolve by the integration of the acquired modifications into the organism configuration of the 'new generations'.

6   Hardware Implementation

The hardware implementation of the TTA-UC uses the BioWall, a two-dimensional electronic wall designed for bio-inspired applications [7]. In order to test the concept, we have realized a simple von Neumann pulser composed of about thirty cells. We were able to verify that the pulser can self-replicate in addition to realizing its usual functionality.

Moreover, due to the huge number of states the TTA-UC design would have used for a standard CA implementation, we realized the system following the Data and Signal Cellular Automaton (DSCA) concept [8,9]. Such a choice permited us to design the TTA-UC almost intuitively and to make the design fit the limited place at disposal.

7   Conclusion

The designed system comes from the unification of the Tom Thumb Algorithm with the standard von Neumann architecture. Its major quality is the great diminution in the number of cells that an organism needs for its self-replication. In fact, with this new TTA-UC system, any von Neumann organism can now be configured in order to possess the self-replication ability. As a result, the concept of Universal Constructor in itself becomes obsolete.

Moreover, we believe that our TTA-UC system is able to emulate all of the precedent von Neumann functionalities. A further interesting work could be to confirm that a Turing Machine can be successfully emulated by our new TTA-UC architecture. Additionally, one should be able to realize this implementation with only small modifications to the original design of the von Neumann Turing Machine, due to the differences in the cell construction process.

References

1. J. von Neumann. Theory of Self-Reproducing Automata. University of Illinois Press, 1996. Edited and completed by A. W. Burks.
2. W.R. Buckley. On the complete specification of a von Neumann 29-state self-replicating cellular automaton. Private communication, wrb@wrbuckley.com, 2004.
3. U. Pesavento. An Implementation of von Neumann's Self-Reproducing Machine. Artificial Life 2(4): pp. 337-354, 1995.
4. E. Petraglio: Fault Tolerant Self-Replicating Systems. PhD Thesis n° 2973, EPFL Lausanne, pp. 79-88, 2004.
5. D. Mange, A. Stauffer, E. Petraglio, G. Tempesti. Self-replicating loop with universal construction. Physica D 191, pp. 178-192, 2004
6. Ibàñez J., Anabitarte D., Azpeitia I., Barrera O., Barrutieta A., Blanco H., and Echarte F. Self-inspection based reproduction in cellular automata. Proc. 3rd Eur. Conf. on Artificial Life (ECAL95), LNCS 929, Springer Berlin, pp. 564-576, 1995.
7. G. Tempesti, D. Mange, A. Stauffer, and C. Teuscher. The BioWall: An Electronic Tissue for Prototyping Bio-Inspired Systems. Proceedings of the 2002 NASA/DOD Workshop Conference on Evolvable Hardware, pp. 221-230, 2002.
8. A. Stauffer and M. Sipper. The Data and Signals Cellular Automaton and its application to growing structures. Artificial Life 10(4): pp. 463-477, 2004.
9. A. Stauffer and M. Sipper. Data and signals: A new kind of cellular automaton for growing systems. Proceedings of the 2003 NASA/DOD Conference on Evolvable Hardware, Los Alamitos CA, pp. 235-241, 2003.

Elementary Probabilistic Cellular Automata
with Memory in Cells

Ramón Alonso-Sanz[1] and Margarita Martín[2]

[1] ETSI Agrónomos (Estadística), C.Universitaria. 28040, Madrid, Spain.
ralonso@est.etsia.upm.es
[2] Bioquímica y Biología Molecular IV, UCM. C.Universitaria. 28040, Madrid, Spain

Abstract. Standard Cellular Automata (CA) are memoryless: i.e., the new state of a cell depends on the neighborhood configuration only at the preceding time step. This article considers an extension to the standard framework of CA by implementing memory capabilities in cells. Thus in CA with memory : while the update rules remain unaltered, historic memory of past iterations is retained by featuring each cell by a summary of all its past states. A study is made of the effect of historic memory on two given sides of the hypercube of *elementary* probabilistic CA.

1 Introduction

Cellular Automata (CA) are discrete, spatially extended dynamic systems composed of adjacent cells or sites arranged as a regular lattice, which evolve in discrete time steps. Each cell is characterized by an internal state whose value belongs to a finite set. The updating of these states is made simultaneously according to a common local transition rule involving only a neighborhood of each cell. Thus, if $\sigma_i^{(T)}$ is taken to denote the value of cell i at time step T, the site values evolve by iteration of the mapping : $\sigma_i^{(T+1)} = \phi\big(\sigma_j^{(T)} \in \mathcal{N}_i\big)$, where ϕ specifies the CA *rule* operating on the neighborhood $(\mathcal{N})$ of the cell i.

This paper deals with *elementary* rules : one-dimensional CA with two possible values $(k = 2)$ at each site $(\sigma \in \{0, 1\})$, with rules operating on nearest neighbors. Following Wolfram's notation, these rules are characterized by a sequence of binary values (β) associated with each of the eight possible triplets $\big(\sigma_{i-1}^{(T)}, \sigma_i^{(T)}, \sigma_{i+1}^{(T)}\big)$:

111	110	101	100	011	010	001	000
β_1	β_2	β_3	β_4	β_5	β_6	β_7	β_8

. The *rule number*,

$R = \sum_{i=1}^{8}\beta_i 2^{8-i}$, of *elementary* CA ranges from 0 to 255. We will restrict our considerations to *legal* rules : rules that are *reflection symmetric* $(\beta_2 = \beta_5,\ \beta_4 = \beta_7)$, and *quiescent* $(\beta_8 = 0)$. These restrictions leave 32 possible *legal* rules.

P.M.A. Sloot, B. Chopard, and A.G. Hoekstra (Eds.): ACRI 2004, LNCS 3305, pp. 11–20, 2004.

2 Memory

Standard CA are ahistoric (memoryless): i.e., no memory of previous iterations except the last one is taken into account to decide the next one. In this paper, a variation of the conventional one-dimensional CA is considered, featuring cells by a summary state in all the previous time steps . Thus, what is here proposed is to maintain the transition rules (ϕ) unaltered, but make them actuate over cells featured by a summary of all their previous states : $\sigma_i^{(T+1)} = \phi(s_j^{(T)} \in \mathcal{N}_i)$, $s_i^{(T)}$ being a summary state of cell i after time-step T . We refer to these automata considering historic memory as *historic* and to the standard ones as *ahistoric*.

A simple way of taking history into account is that of featuring cells by their most frequent (mode) state (in case of a tie, the cell is featured by its last state). Table 1 shows the spatio-temporal patterns of the legal rules affected by such mode memory mechanism when starting from a single site live cell. As long as the latest and most frequent states coincide after the two first time-steps, the *historic* and *ahistoric* evolution patterns are the same till $T = 3$. But after the third time-step, the last and the most frequent states often differ, and consequently the patterns for the historic and ahistoric automata typically diverge at $T = 4$. In the ahistoric context, the deterministic Rule 254 (1111110) progresses as fast as possible: it assigns a live state to any cell in whose neighborhood there would be at least one live cell. Thus, in the ahistoric model, a single site live cell will grow monotonically, generating segments with size increasing two units with every time step. The dynamics is slower in the historic model (see Table 1) : the outer live cells are not featured as live cells until the number of times they "live" is equal to the number of times they were "dead". Then the automaton fires two new outer live cells. Rules 94 and 126 evolve much in the *punctuated equilibrium* manner of Rule 254. The effect of memory on Rule 90 (01011010) is dramatic: after $T = 3$ the most frequent state of all the cells is the dead one, so Rule 90 dies out at $T = 4$. The remaining rules in Table 1 generate period-two oscillators as soon as at T=2.

Historic memory can be weighted by applying a geometric discounting process in which the state $\sigma_i^{(T-\tau)}$, obtained τ time steps before the last round, is actualized to the value: $\alpha^\tau \sigma_i^{(T-\tau)}$ (α being the *memory factor*). This well known mechanism fully ponders the last round, and tends to *forget* the older rounds. After the time step T, the weighted mean of the states of a given cell (i) is :

$$m_i^{(T)}(\sigma_i^{(1)}, \sigma_i^{(2)}, \ldots, \sigma_i^{(T)}) = \frac{\sigma_i^{(T)} + \displaystyle\sum_{t=1}^{T-1} \alpha^{T-t}\sigma_i^{(t)}}{1 + \displaystyle\sum_{t=1}^{T-1} \alpha^{T-t}} \equiv \frac{\omega_i^{(T)}}{\Delta(T)} \qquad (1)$$

The choice of α simulates the long-term or remnant memory effect : the limit case $\alpha = 1$ corresponds to the *full* memory model just introduced, whereas $\alpha \ll 1$ intensifies the contribution of the most recent states and diminishes the contribution of the past ones (*short type* memory). The choice $\alpha = 0$ leads to the ahistoric model. This memory mechanism is *accumulative* in their demand of knowledge of history : to calculate the term $w_i^{(T)}$ of $m_i^{(T)}$ it is not necessary to know the whole $\{\sigma_i^{(t)}\}$ series, while sequentially compute: $w_i^{(T)} = \alpha w_i^{(T-1)} + \sigma_i^{(T)}$.

The rounded weighted mean state (s) will be obtained by comparing its weighted mean (m) to 0.5, so that:
$$ s_i^{(T)} = \begin{cases} 1 & \text{if } m_i^{(T)} > 0.5 \\ \sigma_i^{(T)} & \text{if } m_i^{(T)} = 0.5 \\ 0 & \text{if } m_i^{(T)} < 0.5 \end{cases} \quad \text{In our} $$
two-states scenario, memory is not effectively implemented unless $\alpha > 0.5$ ([4]).

It should be emphasized that the memory mechanism considered here is different from that of other CA with memory reported in the literature[1], which, typically, incorporate memory into the transition rule. Particularly interesting is the second order in time reversible formulation based on the exclusive OR (noted $\oplus$) : $\sigma_i^{(T+1)} = \phi\left(\sigma_j^{(T)} \in \mathcal{N}_i\right) \oplus \sigma_i^{(T-1)}$. *Double* memory (in rule and in cells) can be implemented as : $\sigma_i^{(T+1)} = \phi\left(s_j^{(T)} \in \mathcal{N}_i\right) \oplus s_i^{(T-1)}$, but to preserve reversibility, inherent in the XOR operation, the reversible formulation with memory must be : $\sigma_i^{(T+1)} = \phi\left(s_j^{(T)} \in \mathcal{N}_i\right) \oplus \sigma_i^{(T-1)}$ ([4]) . We have studied the effect of memory on CA in the deterministic scenario in a previous work ([2]-[8]).

Table 1. Legal rules affected by mode memory when starting from a single site live cell up to $T = 8$. Live cells: ■ last ($\sigma=1$), □ most frequent ($s = 1$).

146,218		178,250				222
R 18,90	R 22,54	R 50,122	R 94	R 126	R 150,182	R 254

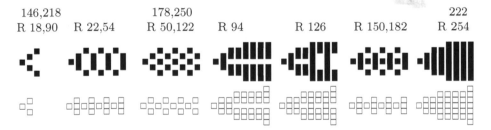

3   Probabilistic Cellular Automata with Memory

So far the CA considered are deterministic. In order to study perturbations to deterministic CA as well as transitional changes from one deterministic CA to another, it is natural to generalize the deterministic CA framework to the probabilistic scenario where the β_i are replaced by probabilities p_i ($0 \leq p_i \leq$

---

[1] See, for example, [1],p.43; or class IMEIMO in [9],p.7. The latter shows an example of 2D CA with memory, but to the best of our knowledge the study of the effect of memory on deterministic CA has been rather neglected.

1). Kinzel [10] and Domany and Kinzel [11] pioneered in the study of these probabilistic CA (PCA for short).

As in the deterministic scenario, memory can be embedded in PCA by featuring cells by a summary of past states s_i instead of by their last state σ_i. A last but not least disclaimer must be done of the use of the term *memory* as entering into the probabilistic scenario. We embed historic memory into the characterization of cells but not directly in the construction of the stochastic transition rules, so we are dealing with probabilities of the generic form $P\big(\sigma_i^{(T+1)} = 1/s_{i-1}^{(T)}, s_i^{(T)}, s_{i+1}^{(T)}\big)$ and not with some form of memory mechanism (of length τ) in which the past configurations $(\underline{\sigma} = \{\sigma_i, i = 1, \ldots, N\})$ determine the transition probabilities : $P\big(\sigma_i^{(T+1)} = 1/\underline{\sigma}^{(T)}, \underline{\sigma}^{(T-1)}, \ldots, \underline{\sigma}^{(T-\tau)}\big)$ as done in the specialized literature when dealing with memory in PCA (e.g.,[12]) .

Legal rules are now of the form $(p_1, p_2, p_3, p_4, p_2, p_6, p_4, 0)$. The five probabilities parameterize a five-dimensional hypercube , where the deterministic rules are placed in the 32 corners. Elementary CA quickly evolve into configurations with a density of non null states fluctuating about a given mean (ρ) so the asymptotic density is considered in the literature as a natural order parameter in the phase space . In this paper we focus on two particular sides of the hypercube, those defined by the structure of probabilities : $i)$ $(0, 0, p_3, 1, 0, p_6, 1, 0)$, with deterministic corners the Rules 18, 22, 50 and 54 , and $ii)$ $(p_1, p_2, p_1, p_2, p_2, 0, p_2, 0)$, with corners 0, 90, 160 and 250. The former is a very interesting subset as including not only Rule 18 (one of the first rules carefully analyzed) but also the *complicated* (to avoid the coined term *complex*) Rules 22 and 54. The rules with the structure $ii)$ are *peripheral* [2] and *totalistic* $\sigma_i^{(T+1)} = \phi\big(\sigma_{i-1}^{(T)} + \sigma_{i+1}^{(T)}\big)$ such as Rule 90 : $\sigma_i^{(T+1)} = \sigma_{i-1}^{(T)} + \sigma_{i+1}^{(T)}$ *mod* 2 . The subset $ii)$ has been very much studied due to the equivalence between *peripheral* PCA and the problem of directed percolation [11]. By the way, Rule 22 in $i)$ is *totalistic* but not *peripheral*.

4   The Simulations

The simulations in this work were run for 1000 time steps on a lattice consisting of 500 sites with periodic boundary conditions. All the simulations start from the same random initial configuration, in which the value of each site is initially uncorrelated, and is taken to be 0 or 1 with probability 0.5 . All the PCA evolve with identical realizations of the stochastic noise. The memory factor α varies from 0.5 (ahistoric model) to 1.0 (fully historic) by 0.1 intervals.

Figure 1 shows the spatio-temporal patterns of four significant deterministic rules affected by memory. Figures 2 and 3 show the asymptotic density (ρ) of the PCA rules of the two subsets just described, when varying the *free* probabilities $(p_3, p_6$, and $p_1, p_2)$ from 0 to 1 by 0.02 intervals. The asymptotic density was taken as the mean density over the last 100 iterations. Table 2 shows the numerical

---

[2] Rules with no dependence in ϕ on the state of the cell to be updated. Some authors feature such rules as rules with *no memory*

values of ρ of the deterministic rules affected by memory. Memory has no effect on in Rules 0, 160, 250 (subset ii)) or has a minimal effect in Rule 50 [3].

Table 2. Asymptotic densities of the deterministic rules affected by memory

$\alpha =$	1.0	0.9	0.8	0.7	0.6	0.5
RULE 18(00010010)	0.120	0.000	0.000	0.012	0.108	0.250
RULE 22(00010110)	0.359	0.038	0.026	0.295	0.357	0.356
RULE 50(00110010)	0.478	0.500	0.500	0.500	0.500	0.500
RULE 54(00110110)	0.461	0.000	0.020	0.412	0.411	0.478
RULE 90(01011010)	0.503	0.521	0.497	0.495	0.507	0.500

Let us first examine the effect of memory on subset i), featured to a great extent by the effect on the deterministic corners. History has a dramatic effect on Rule 18, as is shown in Fig.1 . Even at the low value of $\alpha = 0.6$, the appearance of the spatio-temporal pattern fully changes: a number of isolated periodic structures are generated, far away from the distinctive inverted triangle world of the ahistoric pattern. For $\alpha = 0.7$, the live structures are fewer, advancing the extinction found in $[0.8, 0.9]$. In the fully historic model, only periodic patterns of live cells survive (simpler than for $\alpha = 0.6$). The evolution of the density according to Rule 18 in the ahistoric model yields an asymptotic density $\rho \simeq 1/4$ (a value reached fairly soon). Historic memory induces a depletion of ρ, null for $\alpha = 0.8$ and $\alpha = 0.9$, as quantified in Table 1. The effect of memory on Rules 22 and 54 is similar. Their spatio-temporal patterns in $\alpha = 0.6$ and $\alpha = 0.7$ keep the essential feature of the ahistoric, although the inverted triangles become enlarged and tend to be more sophisticated in their *basis*. A notable discontinuity turns out for both rules ascending in the value of the memory factor: when α is in the $[0.8, 0.9]$ interval, extinction or a few periodic structures surviving is found for both rules. But unexpectedly, the patterns of the fully historic scenario differ markedly from the others, showing a high degree of synchronization. Both rules present notably close values of the asymptotic densities in the ahistoric and full memory scenarios (see Table 2).

The effect of memory on the deterministic corners of the subset i) in reflected in the asymptotic density graphs of Fig.2. Thus, the inhibition induced by memory on Rules 18, 22 and 54 when α is in the $[0.8, 0.9]$ interval is reflected in a clear depletion of the corresponding graphs in Fig.2, in which only the proximities of the corner R50 are not depleted. When α varies in the $[0.6, 0.7]$ interval, the ρ value of Rule 54 is not notably altered, thus depletion in the 0.6 and 0.7 graphs

---

[3] This is unusual but not extremely exceptional in the deterministic scenario. This is case of Rules such as 0, 160 or 32 which early evolve to the null state, or, of Rules 250 and 254 which blacken the space, very soon in the ahistoric model, a little later with memory. Rules which serve as *filters* (Class II), such as Rules 4, 50 72, 76, 200, 204, 232 and 236 are also minimally affected by memory. When dealing with more than two states, memory tends to affect almost every rule ([3])

is restricted only to the R18 corner. The aspect of the full memory graph is fairly particular, with a dominant tendency to the null value in proper probabilistic rules, but not in the fairly deterministic ones (the sides).

The evolution of Rule 90 (subset ii)) is typically featured as chaotic in the ahistoric scenario. The totalistic Rule 90 shows a much smoother evolution from the ahistoric to the historic scenario (Fig.1): no pattern evolves to full extinction nor to the preservation of only a few isolated persistent propagating structures (solitons). In the ahistoric scenario it is $\rho \simeq 1/2$ for Rule 90, independently of the initial density $\rho_0 \neq 0$. When historic memory is taken into account, ρ varies little from this value (see Table 2). Again, the effect of memory on the deterministic corners is reflected in Fig.3. Thus, the gradual effect of memory on Rule 90 is reflected in a smooth effect of memory on the graphs of Fig.3

The results found here starting with an initial density $\rho_0 = 0.5$ regarding the asymptotic density, have been found similar when starting from a high initial density (0.9) and a low one (0.1). We have studied the effect of memory on the damage spreading: the difference between two replicas, which evolve with the same dynamics but from different initial configurations, in both subsets. As a rule, the effect of memory on the difference patterns mimics that on spatio-temporal patterns.

The smooth effect of memory on the peripheral and totalistic subset ii) has been found also for other totalistic but non peripheral subsets, in particular on the important PCA subsets studied by Kinzel [10]: $(p_2, p_2, p_2, p_4, p_2, p_4, p_2, 0)$, $(p_1, p_2, p_2, p_2, p_2, p_2, p_2, 0)$, and $(p_4, p_2, p_2, p_4, p_2, p_4, p_2, 0)$. We have explored the effect of memory in a number of different no totalistic subsets. We expect to report the results of the effect of memory on these subsets in a subsequent work.

5   Other Memories, Other Contexts

A number of alternative average-like memory mechanisms can readily be proposed by writing the components of (1) as : $\omega_i^{(T)} = \sum_{t=1}^{T} \delta_t \sigma_i^{(t)}$, $\Delta(T) = \sum_{t=1}^{T} \delta_t$. Thus, the weighting factor can be implemented in an *exponential* way : $\delta_t = e^{-\beta(T-t)}$, $\beta \in \mathbb{R}^+$ (equivalent to a geometric discount model with $\alpha = e^{-\beta}$), or in an *inverse* way, so that the older rounds are remembered more than the more recent ones, by choosing $\delta_t = \alpha^{t-1}$. Weights such as $\delta_t = t^c$ or c^t, $c \in \mathbb{N}$, allow *integer based* implementation (à *la* CA) by comparing $2\omega^{(T)}$ to $\Delta(T)$ ([3],[6]).

Departing from the weighted mean memory scheme, cells can be featured by the *parity* with the sum of previous states, or by some *neural*-like form: $s_i^{(T)} = \mathcal{H}\left(\sum_{t=\mathsf{T}}^{T} \delta_t \sigma_i^{(t)} - \theta \right)$. A *limited trailing memory* can be implemented by keeping memory of the last τ states. Ahistoric and historic models can be combined by different types of characterizations of the cells of the neighborhood.

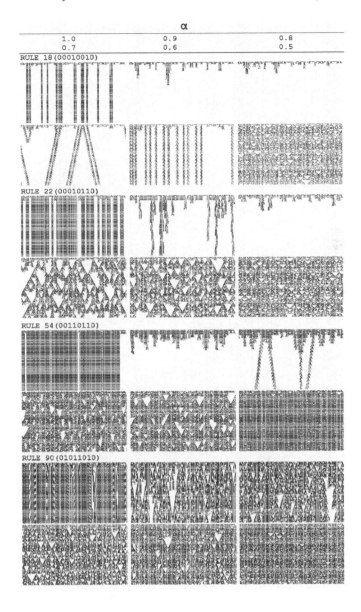

Fig. 1. Spatio-temporal patterns of four legal CA rules affected by memory. The simulation was conducted in a lattice of size 500. The values of sites in the initial configuration are chosen at random to be 0 or 1 with probability $1/2$. The pictures show the evolution of the central band of 250 sites from the initial configuration up to $T = 150$.. The memory factor α is varied from 1.0 (full memory) to 0.5 (ahistoric) by 0.1 intervals.

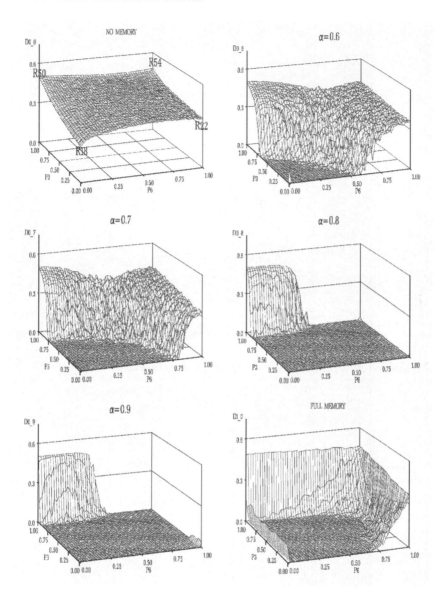

Fig. 2. The asymptotic density of the legal probabilistic CA rules of the form $(0,0,p_3,1,0,p_6,1,0)$ in the scenario of Fig.1. The probabilities p_3 and p_6 are varied from 0 to 1 by 0.02 intervals . The asymptotic density is taken as the mean density over the last 100 of 1000 time steps.

Historic memory can be embedded in *continuous* CA, in which σ ranges in $\mathbb{R}$, by : $\sigma_i^{(T+1)} = \Phi(m_j^{(T)} \in \mathcal{N}_i)$. Memory can be implemented in this way in Coupled Map Lattices, fuzzy CA (see an example in [7]), or Quantum CA.

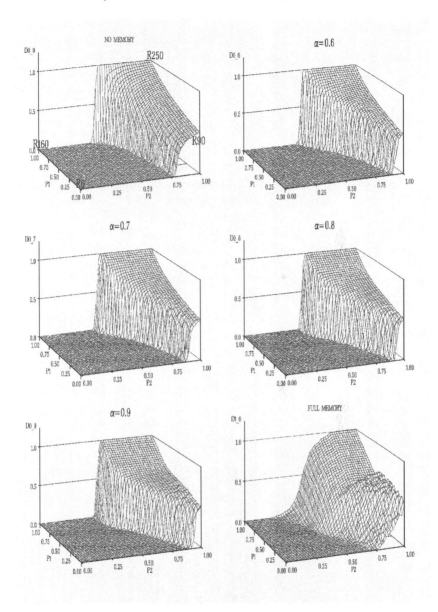

Fig. 3. The asymptotic density of the legal probabilistic CA rules of the form $(p_1, p_2, p_1, p_2, p_2, 0, p_2, 0)$ in the scenario of Fig.2.

We have explored the effect of incorporating memory into *discrete dynamical systems* : $x^{(T+1)} = f(x^{(T)})$ by means of $x^{(T+1)} = f(m^{(T)})$ with $m^{(T)} = \frac{1}{\Delta(T)} \sum_{t=1}^{T} \alpha^{T-t} x^{(t)}$. Thus, [3] deals with the canonical example, the logistic map with memory : $x^{(T+1)} = m^{(T)} + 3.0m^{(T)}(1 - m^{(T)})$. A low level of memory ($\alpha = 0.1$) smooths the characteristic chaotic dynamics of the ahistoric formulation; higher α values generate periodic behaviour, and from $\alpha = 0.4$ the evolution leads to a fixed point ($x = 1$) . From chaos to order, by varying not the parameter of the model ($\lambda = 3.0$) but the degree of memory incorporated.

6   Conclusion

This paper introduces the kind of probabilistic CA with memory in cells (PCA) in the simplest (elementary) scenario by considering two particular sides of the hypercube of elementary PCA. One of the subsets is highly disrupted by memory, the effect of memory on the other subset is fairly smooth. The approach here is mainly *descriptive*. A more complete analysis of the PCA is left for future work. Phase transitions in particular demand a detailed study. Some critics can argue that memory is not in the realm of CA (or even of Dynamic Systems), but we believe that the subject is worth to studying. At least CA with memory in cells can be considered as a extension of the basic paradigm, useful in modeling.

Acknowledgements. Luis Seidel (UPM) contributed to the computer implementation of this work, supported by CICYT AGL2002-04003-C03-02 AGR .

References

1. Ilachinski,A.: Cellular Automata. A Discrete Universe. World Scientific (2000)
2. Alonso-Sanz,R.: One-dimensional, r=2 cellular automata with memory. Int.J. Bifurcation and Chaos **14** (in press).
3. Alonso-Sanz,R.,Martin,M.: Three-state one-dimensional cellular automata with memory. Chaos, Solitons and Fractals **21** (2004) 809-834.
4. Alonso-Sanz,R.: Reversible CA with Memory. Physica D **175** (2003) 1-30
5. Alonso-Sanz,R.,Martin,M.: Elementary cellular automata with memory. Complex Systems **14** (2003) 99-126 .
6. Alonso-Sanz,R.,Martin,M.: Cellular automata with accumulative memory. Int.J. Modern Physics C **14** (2003) 695-719
7. Alonso-Sanz,R.,Martin,M.C.,Martin,M.: One-dimensional cellular automata with memory. Int.J. Bifurcation and Chaos **12** (2002) 205-226
8. Alonso-Sanz,R.,Martin,M.C.,Martin,M.: Two-dimensional cellular automata with memory. Int.J. Modern Physics C **13** (2002) 49-65 and the references therein.
9. Adamatzky,A.: Identification of Cellular Automata. Taylor and Francis (1994)
10. Kinzel,W.: Phase Transitions of CA. Z. für Physics B. **58** (1985) 229-244
11. Domany,E.,Kinzel,W.: Equivalence of Cellular Automata to Ising Models and Directed Percolation.Physical Review Letters. **53** (1984) 311-314
12. Lebowitz,J.L.Maes,C.,Speer,E.: Statistical Methods of Probabilistic Cellular Automata. J. Statistical Physics, **59** (1990) 117-170.

Universal Construction on
Self-Timed Cellular Automata

Yousuke Takada[1], Teijiro Isokawa[1], Ferdinand Peper[2,1], and Nobuyuki Matsui[1]

[1] Division of Computer Engineering, University of Hyogo,
2167 Shosha, Himeji, Hyogo, 671-2201, Japan
takada@comp.eng.himeji-tech.ac.jp, {isokawa,matsui}@eng.u-hyogo.ac.jp
[2] Nanotechnology Group,
National Institute of Information and Communications Technology,
588-2 Iwaoka, Iwaoka-cho, Nishi-ku, Kobe, 651-2492, Japan
peper@nict.go.jp

Abstract. Computation- and construction-universality in cellular automata (CA), first studied by von Neumann, has attracted steady research efforts, over the years, most employing synchronous CA. Asynchronous cellular automata (ACA), though of interest as most interactions in nature are asynchronous, have not been used for this task, other than by the indirect way of simulating a synchronous CA. In this paper, we propose a universal constructor on a self-timed cellular automaton (STCA), a particular type of ACA, in which cells are divided in four partitions, each with four states.

1 Introduction

Biological self-reproduction was first investigated formally in terms of von Neumann's cellular automaton (CA) capable of universal computation and construction [1]. Requiring cells with 29 states, this CA implements a universal constructor able to construct an arbitrary structure on an initially blank space, given its *blueprint*. Follow-ups to this study are the 8-state CA of Codd [2], the 4-state CA of Banks [3], and the 3-state CA of Serizawa [4], all computation- and construction-universal. These investigations have been limited to synchronous systems, while there has been hardly research on asynchronous systems.

In the context of asynchronous systems, Priese [5] investigated computation and construction on a Thue system that resembles CA. Nehaniv [6] implemented self-reproduction on an asynchronous cellular automaton (ACA) based on the method by Nakamura [7], in which a synchronous CA is simulated on an ACA, but this technique suffers from overhead in terms of cell states and number of transition rules. Lee et al. [8], Adachi et al. [9], and Peper et al. [10] studied computation on ACAs, not by this simulation technique, but by directly embedding delay-insensitive (DI) circuits on them, a type of asynchronous circuit in which signals may be subject to arbitrary delays without this being an obstacle to the circuit's correct operation (e.g. see [10,11]). Peper et al. [12] proposed a computation-universal self-timed cellular automaton (STCA), a particular type

P.M.A. Sloot, B. Chopard, and A.G. Hoekstra (Eds.): ACRI 2004, LNCS 3305, pp. 21–30, 2004.

of ACA, in which the state of each cell is partitioned into four parts, each of which corresponds with a neighboring cell. There have been no construction-universal ACAs (or STCAs) proposed, however, by the direct method.

This paper shows that computation- and construction-universality can be implemented on an STCA by the direct method, in a similar way as von Neumann's construction. Our model employs cells with states encoded by 8 bits, and 39 rotation-invariant transition rules.

This paper is organized as follows. We define self-timed cellular automata in Sect. 2, starting with computation-universality, and then move on to construction-universality. The construction arm and the tape unit, each part of the constructor, are described in Sects. 3 and 4, respectively. Sect. 5 gives the basic idea of the universal constructor implementation, and finishes this paper with a discussion and conclusion.

2   Self-Timed Cellular Automata

A self-timed cellular automaton (STCA) [12] is a two-dimensional asynchronous cellular array of identical cells, each of which has a state that is partitioned into four parts in one-to-one correspondence with its neighboring cells. For example, if each part of a cell state consists of 1 bit, a cell can be in one of 16 states encoded by 4 bits, and the cellular space is an array like in Fig. 1. Each cell undergoes transitions in accordance with a transition function f that operates on the four parts of the cell q_n, q_e, q_s, q_w and the nearest part of each of its four neighbors p_n, p_e, p_s, p_w. The transition function f is defined by

$$f : (q_n, q_e, q_s, q_w, p_n, p_e, p_s, p_w) \rightarrow (q'_n, q'_e, q'_s, q'_w, p'_n, p'_e, p'_s, p'_w), \qquad (1)$$

where a state symbol to which a prime is attached denotes the new state of a partition after update (see Fig. 2). We assume that transition rules on an STCA are rotation symmetric, thus each of the rules has four rotated analogues.

In STCA, transitions of the cells occur at random times, independent of each other. Since a transition on a cell may change bits of neighboring cells, two neighboring cells undergoing transitions simultaneously may write different values in shared bits. To prevent such a situation, we assume that neighboring cells never undergo transitions simultaneously.

2.1   Morita's Rotary Element

Morita's *Rotary Element (RE)* [13] is a logic element with four input lines $\{n, e, s, w\}$, four output lines $\{n', e', s', w'\}$, and two states — the H-state and the V-state, which are displayed as horizontal and vertical rotation bars respectively (see Fig. 3). If a signal comes from a direction parallel to the rotation bar of an RE, it passes straight through to the opposite output line, without changing the direction of the bar (Fig. 4(a)); if a signal comes from a direction orthogonal to the bar, it turns right and rotates the bar by 90 degrees (Fig. 4(b)). It is possible

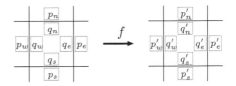

Fig. 1. An example of self-timed cellular space. A filled circle denotes a 1-bit, and an open circle denotes a 0-bit.

Fig. 2. Transition rule in accordance with the function f.

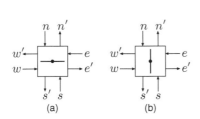

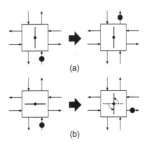

Fig. 3. An RE in (a) H-state and an RE in (b) V-state.

Fig. 4. The operations of an RE: (a) the parallel and (b) the orthogonal case.

to construct a universal Turing machine as a circuit composed of only REs, as shown by Morita [13], implying that an RE is a universal logic element.

An RE can be considered as a kind of a DI circuit. Unlike most DI-circuits in practical applications, however, a circuit constructed entirely from REs — denoted as RE-circuit — contains at most one signal at a time.

2.2   STCA Model Embedding the Rotary Element

Here we explain an STCA model that embeds any arbitrary RE-circuit, whereby each part of a cell state takes 2 bits. The transition rules are depicted in Fig. 5.

Fig. 5. Transition rules to implement a Rotary Element. The resulting STCA is computation-universal. A filled circle denotes a 1-bit; a 0-bit is not shown.

A signal is defined by Rule #1, and is called a *D-signal*. A D-signal is used to conduct ordinary computation. Fig. 6 shows how to transmit a D-signal towards the north on a straight path of continuous cells, all bits of which are 0;

transmitting a signal towards the east, the south, and the west are done in a similar way, due to the rotation-symmetry of transition rules.

A few basic signal routers are defined from Rules #2–4: an *input/output multiplexer (IOM)*, a *merge*, and an *LR-turn for D-signal*. An *IOM* is just a right-turn element for a D-signal that works for signals coming from two directions (see Fig. 7(a)); it has one input path, one output path, and one bi-directional path. An input signal on the input path is output to the bi-directional path (Rule #2), and an input signal on the bi-directional path is output to the output path (Rule #3). A *merge* is an operator with two input paths and one output path (see Fig. 7(b)), which redirects a D-signal arriving from one of the input paths to the output path (Rules #2, 4). An *LR-turn for D-signal* is an operator with two bi-directional paths (see Fig. 7(c)), which redirects a D-signal arriving from one path to the other path (Rules #3, 4). These three elements are realized by a simple pattern on the STCA, a *stable quadruple* that consists of four 1-bits bonded together (see Fig. 7).

A *rotation bar*, realized by a row or a column of two stable quadruples, is introduced in analogy to that of RE (see Fig. 3). A signal coming from a direction orthogonal to the bar will turn right and rotate the bar by 90 degrees (Rule #5).

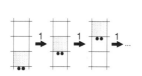

Fig. 6. Signal transmission northwards. The shaded cell in each configuration will be updated according to Rule #1.

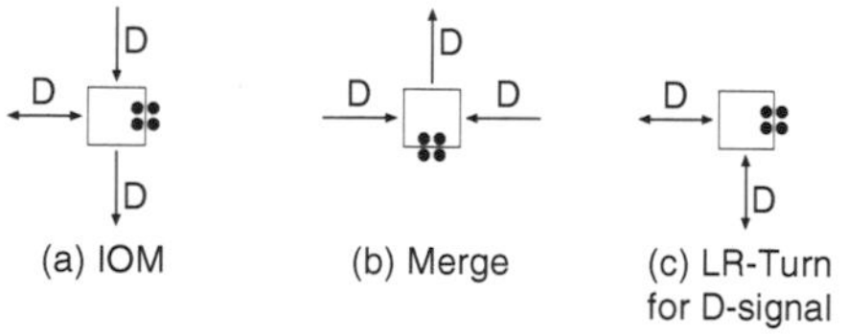

Fig. 7. The operations of a *stable quadruple*, as (a) an IOM, (b) a merge, and (c) an LR-turn for D-signal. Each arrow denotes a signal path, and the character D alongside it denotes the signal's type.

(a) IOM   (b) Merge   (c) LR-Turn for D-signal

An RE can be composed of stable quadruples as shown in Fig. 8. In this implementation, an input/output path pair on each side of an RE is represented by a bi-directional path. By connecting IOMs to the bi-directional paths of the RE in Fig. 8, a regular RE like in Fig. 3 can be constructed. Fig. 9 illustrates the traces of an RE operating on a signal coming from its input line (a) parallel or (b) orthogonal to the rotation bar. The STCA is computation-universal in the sense that a universal Turing machine composed of REs (see [13]) can be embedded on it.

A stable quadruple is the smallest element in circuits implemented on the STCA, since the basic elements such as an IOM, a merge, and an RE can be constructed from it (see Figs. 7 and 8). In this paper, we assume that any circuit on the STCA is represented by a specific configuration of stable quadruples, so that a universal constructor can be regarded as a machine that puts stable quadruples

Fig. 8. Realization of an RE on the construction-universal STCA.

Fig. 9. A signal passing through an RE: (a) the parallel and (b) the orthogonal case.

on desired places. The rules required for this (see Fig. 10) are explained in the remaining sections.

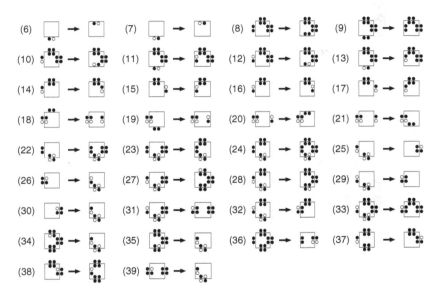

Fig. 10. The transition rules in the STCA, which are used to realize a construction arm and a tape unit. A filled circle denotes a 1-bit and an open circle denotes a 0-bit, but most 0-bits are not shown except when required to avoid ambiguities.

3 The Construction Arm

The *construction arm*, a part of the universal constructor, plays the main role in construction: it moves a writing head over the cell space, and constructs desired structures. In Fig. 11, (a) the initial state and (b) the working state are illustrated. The initial state is composed of only stable quadruples. The I/O path I is used for initialization of the construction arm; L, R and D are used to operate the writing head. The initializing process of the arm is described after we describe how it works.

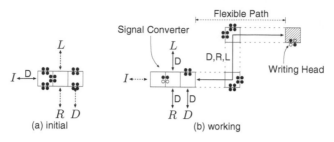

Fig. 11. Configurations of the construction arm in (a) the initial state and (b) the working state. There are four I/O paths I, L, R, and D. Each I/O path is represented as an solid arrow or a broken arrow, the former denoting it is available in the particular (initial or working) state of the arm and the latter denoting it is not. The characters alongside each arrow denote what kinds of signals can be transmitted on it.

A construction arm in the working state (see Fig. 11(b)) can be divided into three parts: a *flexible path*, which is a bi-directional path connecting with the other two parts, a *signal converter*, and a *writing head*. In the construction arm, three kinds of signals, a D-, an R-, and an L-signal, are used to transport information to (from, respectively) the writing head from (to) the signal converter through the flexible path. The *L-signal* and the *R-signal* are each represented by a 1-bit, and transmitted similarly to a D-signal, according to Rules #6 and #7, respectively (see Fig. 10). If a D-signal is input to the I/O path L, R, or D, it is converted into, respectively, an L-signal, an R-signal, or just redirected as is, after which the L-, R-, or D-signal is fed to the writing head through the flexible path. If an L-, an R-, or a D-signal is returned from the head, a D-signal is output to the path L, R, or D, respectively.

On a flexible path, an *LR-turn for all signals* defined by Rules #8–13 (see Fig. 10) is used to change the direction of a path transmitting a D-, an L-, or an R-signal. Unlike an LR-turn for D-signal (Fig. 7(c)), this LR-turn is represented by two stable quadruples, and turns all kinds of signals as well as the D-signal (see Fig. 12(a)).

A signal converter is represented by the combination of a *D-LR multiplexer* and a *D-LR converter* (see Figs. 11(b) and 12(b), (c)). A D-LR multiplexer (Fig. 12(b)) is also an LR-turn for D-signal (Fig. 7(c)), but an L/R-signal arriving from the left path (the right path, respectively) is unaffected by it, and is just output to the right path (the left path) (see Rules #14–17). A D-LR converter (Fig. 12(c)) is an operator that converts a D-signal arriving from the upper path (or the lower path, respectively) into an L-signal (or an R-signal), and outputs it to the right path (see Rules #18, 19). Conversely, an L-signal (or an R-signal, respectively) arriving from the right path is converted into a D-signal and is output to the upper path (or the lower path) (see Rules #20, 21).

A writing head (Fig. 12(d)) can put stable quadruples on its reach. If a D-signal is fed to the writing head, it creates a stable quadruple and returns a D-signal (see Fig. 13(a)i and Rule #22). With more D-signal(s), the writing head

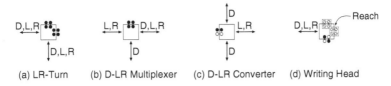

(a) LR-Turn   (b) D-LR Multiplexer   (c) D-LR Converter   (d) Writing Head

Fig. 12. Elements used for the construction arm: (a)–(c) are stable patterns, but (d) a writing head can be moved by an input signal.

creates any combination of stable quadruple(s) on its reach (see Fig. 13(a)ii, iii and Rules #23, 24). If an L-signal is fed to the writing head, the arm is extended, and an L-signal is returned (see Fig. 13(b)i and Rules #25, 26); to change the direction of the arm to the left (respectively, the right), a D-signal (respectively, two D-signals) and an L-signal are subsequently fed to the head (see Fig. 13(a)i, ii, (b)ii, iii, and Rules #26–28). This allows the flexible path to form an arbitrary shape without crossing. Feeding an R-signal to the head results in the withdrawal of the arm, and an R-signal is returned; any configurations written by the head on its reach will be kept intact, however (see Fig. 13(c) and Rules #29–35).

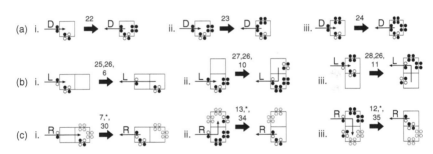

Fig. 13. The operations of a writing head: (a) creation of stable quadruples, (b) extension of the arm, and (c) withdrawal of the arm. Each thin arrow represents an input/output signal. Integers or * above each thick arrow denote the transition rules, where $* \in \{29, 31, 32, 33\}$. In (c) withdrawal, the shaded bits can be all 0-bits or can contain one or two stable quadruple(s).

In the initial state of the construction arm (see Fig. 11(a)), a D-signal first has to be input to the I/O path I, creating a D-LR converter from three stable quadruples (see Fig. 14 and Rule #36). As the path I is only used to initialize the writing head, we leave out I from the figures in the following. After initialization, a D-signal is sent to L to create the head (see Fig. 15(a) and Rule #37). I/O paths D and R are not available until the head is created. Destruction of the writing head is shown in Fig. 15(b): unlike the usual withdrawal, an L-signal is returned due to Rule #38. To *rewind* the extended arm, it suffices to continuously give an R-signal to the head until an L-signal is returned from it, which indicates that the rewind is completed.

Fig. 14. Creation of a D-LR converter from three stable quadruples.

Fig. 15. (a) Creation and (b) destruction of a writing head.

An example of constructing a construction arm is shown in Fig. 16. For this construction, the following command sequence is used:

$$LLDLLLDDLLLDDRRDDDRRDDLLLDDRRDD, \qquad (2)$$

where each character means giving a signal to the corresponding I/O path. The construction arm should be rewound after construction, but this is not shown. It is clear that the arm can construct every structure composed of stable quadruples in this way, as long as an appropriate command sequence is given.

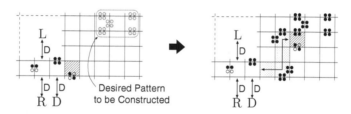

Fig. 16. Example of constructing a construction arm (Fig. 11(a)) by the command sequence in (2). The LHS represents the configuration in which the first command L has already been executed.

4   The Tape Unit

The tape unit operates the *cursor* on the tape, and conducts reading/writing operations on it (see Fig. 17). A tape is represented as an infinite series of bits, each of which is represented by the presence (1-bit) or absent (0-bit) of a stable quadruple. The tape unit resembles the construction arm: the cursor is the same as the writing head, and moves forward and backward by an L- and an R-signal, respectively (see Fig. 13(b)i, (c)i). Note that two L-signals are needed for initialization, i.e., to set the cursor on the left end of the tape (*zero* position).

The reading operation is conducted by executing the command sequence DL. Fig. 18 shows the situation after processing the D-signal. When an L-signal is input, the bit pointed to by the cursor is read and erased: return of an L-signal (respectively, an R-signal) corresponds to a 0-bit (a 1-bit). Reading a 1-bit like in Fig. 18(b) requires a new rule (Rule #39). To return the cursor to the proper state in which it can conduct its next operation, it needs to be

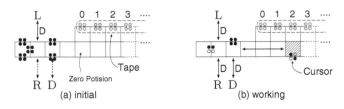

Fig. 17. The tape unit in (a) the initial state and (b) the working state. The presence or absence of a stable quadruple on the tape represents a 1-bit or a 0-bit, respectively.

Fig. 18. Reading operation of the cursor by the command sequence DL, when the bit pointed to is (a) a 0-bit or (b) a 1-bit, resulting in an L- or R-signal, respectively. In (b), the bit is cleared after reading.

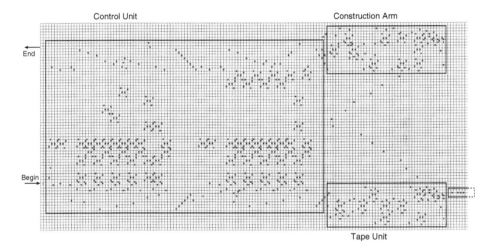

Fig. 19. Implementation of universal constructor on the STCA.

recovered by inputting the sequence R or DR to it (see Fig. 13(a)i, (c)ii). This has the (desired) side effect that a 0-bit or a 1-bit, respectively, is rewritten to the tape position.

5   Discussion and Conclusion

In Sects. 3 and 4, we showed the construction arm and the tape unit implemented on the STCA. By connecting the above two parts and their *control unit* that interprets the tape contents and sends appropriate commands to the appropriate paths of the construction arm, it is possible to construct a universal constructor.

Note that the control unit is a finite state machine, so it can be realized by a RE-circuit (see Sect. 2) in a similar way as in [13]. The implementation of a universal constructor is shown in Fig. 19, in which the construction arm and the tape unit are each equipped with a *microcontroller* realized by a RE-circuit to interface with the control unit, but we cannot describe this implementation in detail due to a lack of space (see the extended version of this paper [14] for details).

The construction-universal STCA presented in this paper requires only 39 rules, and the required configuration is compact, witness the implementation in Fig. 19.

References

1. von Neumann, J.: Theory of Self-Reproducing Automata. University of Illinois Press (1966)
2. Codd, E.F.: Cellular Automata. Academic Press, New York (1968)
3. Banks, E.R.: Universality in cellular automata. In: IEEE 11th Ann. Symp. on Switching and Automata Theory. (1970) 194–215
4. Serizawa, T.: Three-state Neumann neighbor cellular automata capable of constructing self-reproducing machines. Syst. and Comput. in Japan **18** (1987) 33–40
5. Priese, L.: On a simple combinatorial structure sufficient for sublying nontrivial self-reproduction. Journal of Cybernetics **6** (1976) 101–137
6. Nehaniv, C.L.: Self-reproduction in asynchronous cellular automata. In: Proc. NASA/DoD Conf. on Evolvable Hardware. (2002) 201–209
7. Nakamura, K.: Asynchronous cellular automata and their computational ability. Systems, Computers, Controls **5** (1974) 58–66
8. Lee, J., Adachi, S., Peper, F., Morita, K.: Embedding universal delay-insensitive circuits in asynchronous cellular spaces. Fundamenta Informaticae **58** (2003) 295–320
9. Adachi, S., Peper, F., Lee, J.: Computation by asynchronously updating cellular automata. Journal of Statistical Physics **114** (2004) 261–289
10. Peper, F., Lee, J., Adachi, S., Mashiko, S.: Laying out circuits on asynchronous cellular arrays: a step towards feasible nanocomputers? Nanotechnology **14** (2003) 469–485
11. Hauck, S.: Asynchronous design methodologies: An overview. In: Proc. IEEE. Volume 83. (1995) 69–93
12. Peper, F., Isokawa, T., Kouda, N., Matsui, N.: Self-timed cellular automata and their computational ability. Future Generation Computer Systems **18** (2002) 893–904
13. Morita, K.: A simple universal logic element and cellular automata for reversible computing. In: MCU. Volume 2055 of LNCS. (2001) 102–113
14. Takada, Y., Isokawa, T., Peper, F., Matsui, N.: Universal construction and self-reproduction on self-timed cellular automata. in preparation (2004)

Computing Phase Shifts of Maximum-Length 90/150 Cellular Automata Sequences*

Sung-Jin Cho, Un-Sook Choi, Yoon-Hee Hwang, Han-Doo Kim,
Yong-Soo Pyo, Kwang-Seok Kim, and Seong-Hun Heo

Division of Mathematical Sciences
Pukyong National University
Busan 608-737, Korea
sjcho@pknu.ac.kr

Abstract. In this paper, we investigate the study of the sequences generated by maximum-length 90/150 cellular automata(CA) sequences. We propose a method computing the relative phase shifts of all pseudo-noise sequences which have the same characteristic polynomial. As a special case of this method, we give an algorithm to compute relative phase shifts between stages of a CA. This is a very simple and efficient method than the already proposed methods.

1 Introduction

Cellular automata(CA) are mathematical idealizations of physical systems in which space and time are discrete, and each cell can assume the value either 0 or 1. The cells evolve in discrete time steps according to some deterministic rule that depends only on logical neighborhood. For the simplest case, Wolfram [13] suggested the use of a simple two-state, 3-neighborhood one-dimensional CA with cells arranged linearly in one dimension. Each cell is essentially comprised of a memory element and a combinatorial logic that generates the next-state of the cell from the present-state of its neighboring cells(left, right and self). The CA-based scheme for generation of pseudoexhaustive patterns has reported in [1]- [2] and so on. The phase shift analysis of CA([3], [4], [13]), based on 90/150 matrices whose characteristic polynomials are primitive, has been investigated by Bardell [1]. He calculated the phase shifts between the output sequences generated by different stages of a maximum-length 90/150 CA by using discrete logarithms of a binary polynomial. Nandi and Chaudhuri [9] proposed a method for the study of phase shift analysis based on matrix algebra. They showed that every cell position of a maximum-length 90/150 CA generates the same pseudo-noise sequence corresponding to the characteristic polynomial of the CA with a phase shift.

Recently, Sarkar [10] gave an algorithm to compute phase shifts. This was achieved by developing the proper algebraic framework for the study of CA sequences. In this paper, we study the sequences generated by maximum-length

---

* This work was supported by KOSEF:R01-2003-000-10663-0.

P.M.A. Sloot, B. Chopard, and A.G. Hoekstra (Eds.): ACRI 2004, LNCS 3305, pp. 31–39, 2004.
© Springer-Verlag Berlin Heidelberg 2004

90/150 CA sequences. And we apply these to phase shifting of sequences generated by a maximum-length 90/150 CA. From these applications we give an improved method to compute phase shifts, which is different from those methods of Bardell's [1], Nandi and Chaudhuri's [9], and Sarkar's [10].

2   Preliminaries

A CA consists of a number of interconnected cells arranged spatially in a regular manner, where the state transition of each cell depends on the states of its neighbors. The CA structure investigated by Wolfram [13] can be viewed as a discrete lattice of sites (cells), where each cell can assume the value either 0 or 1. The next-state of a cell is assumed to depend on itself and on its two neighbors (3-neighborhood dependency). If the next-state function of a cell is expressed in the form of a truth table, then the decimal equivalent of the output is conventionally called the rule number for the cell.

Neighborhood state	111 110 101 100 011 010 001 000	
Next state	0 1 0 1 1 0 1 0	rule 90
Next state	1 0 0 1 0 1 1 0	rule 150

The top row gives all eight possible states of the three neighboring cells (the left neighbor of the ith cell, the ith cell itself, and its right neighbor) at the time of instant t. The second and third rows give the corresponding states of the ith cell at the time of instant $t+1$ for two illustrative CA rules. On minimization, the truth tables for the rules 90 and 150 result in the following logic functions, where $\oplus$ denotes XOR logic and q_i^t denotes the state of the ith CA cell at the time of instant t, q_{i-1}^t and q_{i+1}^t refer to the state of its left and right neighbors;

$$rule \ \ 90: \qquad q_i^{t+1} = q_{i-1}^t \oplus q_{i+1}^t$$
$$rule \ 150: \qquad q_i^{t+1} = q_{i-1}^t \oplus q_i^t \oplus q_{i+1}^t$$

Let $\mathbb{F}_2$ be the Galois field with cardinality 2 and $\mathbb{F}_2[x]$ the set of all polynomials whose coefficients are members of $\mathbb{F}_2$.

Definition 1. [6] Let $f(x) = c_0 + c_1 x + \cdots + c_{n-1} x^{n-1} + x^n$ be an n-degree primitive polynomial, where $c_0, c_1, \cdots, c_{n-1} \in \mathbb{F}_2$. Then $f(x)$ generates a periodic sequence whose period is $2^n - 1$. This sequence is called a *pseudo-noise(PN) sequence*.

The following definitions and theorem are in [7].

Definition 2. A sequence $\{s_t\}$ is said to be a kth order *homogeneous linear recurring sequence* if

$$s_{t+k} = c_0 s_t + c_1 s_{t+1} + \cdots + c_{k-1} s_{t+k-1} \quad for \ t = 0, 1, \cdots, \qquad (*)$$

where $c_0, c_1, \cdots, c_{k-1} \in \mathbb{F}_2$. The *characteristic polynomial* for the sequence defined in (∗) is defined to be the following polynomial in $\mathbb{F}_2[x]$;

$$f(x) = c_0 + c_1 x + \cdots + c_{k-1} x^{k-1} + x^k.$$

Denote the set of all kth order homogeneous linear recurring sequences whose characteristic polynomials are $f(x)$ by $\Omega(f(x))$.

Definition 3. A homogeneous linear recurring sequence in $\mathbb{F}_2$ whose characteristic polynomial is a primitive polynomial over $\mathbb{F}_2$ and which has a nonzero initial state vector is called a *maximum-length sequence* in $\mathbb{F}_2$.

Maximum-length sequences are of fundamental importance in computer science, cryptology and engineering.

Theorem 1. *Let $f(x)$ be a k-degree polynomial over $\mathbb{F}_2$ and $\{s_t\} \in \Omega(f(x))$. Then $\{s_t\}$ has the maximum-length $2^k - 1$ if and only if $f(x)$ is primitive over $\mathbb{F}_2$.*

3   Computing Phase Shifts

In this section, we study the sequences generated by maximum-length 90/150 CA sequences. Each cell position of the CA generates PN sequences [9].

Consider the following $n \times n$ tridiagonal matrix T_n

$$T_n = \begin{pmatrix} a_1 & 1 & 0 & 0 & 0 & \cdots & \cdots & 0 & 0 \\ 1 & a_2 & 1 & 0 & 0 & \cdots & \cdots & 0 & 0 \\ 0 & 1 & a_3 & 1 & 0 & \cdots & \cdots & 0 & 0 \\ \vdots & \vdots & \vdots & \vdots & \vdots & \vdots & \vdots & \vdots & \vdots \\ 0 & 0 & 0 & 0 & 0 & \cdots & \cdots & 1 & a_n \end{pmatrix},$$

where $a_1, a_2, \cdots, a_n \in \mathbb{F}_2$. We call T_n the state transition matrix for an n-cell 90/150 CA. Hereafter we write the matrix T_n by $T_n = < a_1, a_2, \cdots, a_n >$.

For example, if $T_4 = < 0, 1, 0, 1 >$ is the state transition matrix for a given 4-cell 90/150 CA $\mathbb{C}$, then the characteristic polynomial is $f(x) = x^4 + x + 1$, which is primitive. The following figure shows the structure of $\mathbb{C}$.

Tezuka and Fushimi [12] asserted that for a given primitive polynomial $f(x)$, there exist exactly two maximum-length 90/150 CA whose characteristic polynomials are $f(x)$. If $T_n = < a_1, a_2, \cdots, a_n >$ is a state transition matrix corresponding to $f(x)$, then the other is $T'_n = < a_n, a_{n-1}, \cdots, a_1 >$.

For example, let $f(x) = x^4 + x + 1$. Then $T_4 = < 0, 1, 0, 1 >$ and $T'_4 = < 1, 0, 1, 0 >$ are state transition matrices corresponding to $f(x)$.

For any n-cell 90/150 CA whose state transition matrix is T_n, the minimal polynomial for T_n is the same as the characteristic polynomial for T_n ([11]).

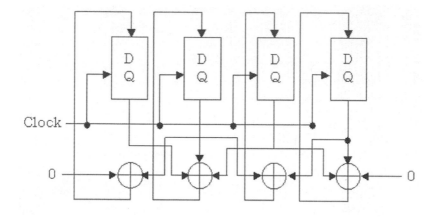

Fig. 1. The structure of 90/150 CA $\mathbb{C}$ with T_4

Theorem 2. *Let T_n be the state transition matrix of an n-cell maximum-length 90/150 CA. Then there exists $p(1 \leq p \leq 2^n - 2)$ such that $I_n \oplus T_n = T_n^p$.*

Corollary 1. *Let T_n be the state transition matrix of an n-cell maximum-length 90/150 CA. Then there exists $k(1 \leq k \leq 2^n - 2)$ such that $T_n^k \oplus T_n^{k+1} = I_n$.*

Example 1. We consider a 4-cell 90/150 CA whose state transition matrix T_4 is as the following :

$$T_4 = \begin{pmatrix} 0 & 1 & 0 & 0 \\ 1 & 1 & 1 & 0 \\ 0 & 1 & 0 & 1 \\ 0 & 0 & 1 & 1 \end{pmatrix}$$

The characteristic polynomial of T_4 is $f(x) = x^4 + x + 1$, which is primitive. We obtain $T_4^{11} \oplus T_4^{12} = I_4$.

From now on, we will simply write T_n by T.

Theorem 3. *Let T be the state transition matrix for a given n-cell maximum-length 90/150 CA. Then the ith row of T^h and T^m are always different, where $0 \leq i \leq n - 1, 1 \leq h < m \leq 2^n - 2$.*

Theorem 4. *Let T be the state transition matrix for a given n-cell maximum-length 90/150 CA and let $w_0 \neq (0, 0, \cdots, 0)$ be the initial configuration of T. Then for any $1 \leq i < j \leq n - 1$, there exists an integer h such that $q_j^{t+h} = q_i^t$ for all $t \geq 0$, where q_i^t denotes the state of the ith cell at the time of instant t.*

Let T be the state transition matrix for a given n-cell maximum-length 90/150 CA and let $w_0 = (1, 0, \cdots, 0)$ be the initial configuration of T. Then we obtain a $(2^n - 1) \times n$ matrix A consisting of n independent PN sequences generated by T as its columns. The sum of some columns of A is also another PN sequence([6]). The number of PN sequences generated by n columns is equal to ${}_nC_1 + {}_nC_2 + \cdots + {}_nC_n = 2^n - 1$. Thus we can get a $(2^n - 1) \times (2^n - 1)$ matrix whose columns consist of all PN sequences generated by A. Such a matrix is referred to as matrix M.

For example, let $T =< 0, 1, 0, 1 >$. Then A and M are given in Table 1.

Table 1. Matrices A and M for $T =< 0, 1, 0, 1 >$

	A	M
0	1000	100011100011101
1	0100	010010011011011
2	1110	111000101110001
3	1111	111100000011110
4	1100	110001111000110
5	1010	101010110101010
6	0001	000100101101111
7	0011	001101111011000
8	0110	011011001101100
9	1011	101110011000101
10	0010	001001010110111
11	0101	010110110110100
12	1101	110101010101001
13	1001	100111001110010
14	0111	011111100000011

For two configurations v and w of T, we define the *row phase shift* k of v with respect to w such that $T^k v = w$. In Table 1 the row phase shift of v with respect to w is 12, where $w = (1, 1, 0, 0)$ and $v = (0, 0, 1, 1)$.

The relative phase shift of one column of M with respect to the other is specified in the following theorems. The PN sequence generated by some cell positions of the CA $\mathbb{C}$ is $\sum_{i=0}^{n-1} a_i q_i$ where a_i is the dependency of q_i.

For example, let $a_0 = a_1 = 1$ and $a_2 = 0$, then $\sum_{i=0}^{2} a_i q_i = q_0 \oplus q_1$. Therefore $q_0 \oplus q_1 = \{q_0^t \oplus q_1^t\} = 1100101 \cdots$ is the 3rd column of M.

Theorem 5. *Let T be the state transition matrix of an n-cell maximum-length 90/150 CA and let $w = \sum_{i=0}^{n-1} a_i w_i$ and $v = \sum_{j=0}^{n-1} b_j w_j$, where w_i^t is the transpose of $w_i = (0, 0, \cdots, 0, \overset{i}{1}, 0, \cdots, 0)$ $(0 \leq i \leq n-1)$. Then there exists an integer r such that*

$$T^r w^t \oplus T^{r+1} w^t = v^t.$$

Proof. We can find β such that $T^\beta w^t = v^t$. By Theorem 2 there exists p such that $(I_n \oplus T) = T^p$. Let $r \equiv \beta - p \ (mod \ 2^n - 1)$. This completes the proof.

Theorem 5 says that $-\beta$ is the row phase shift of v with respect to w of A.

The following theorem gives a method to compute phase shifts.

Theorem 6. *Let T be the state transition matrix of an n-cell maximum-length 90/150 CA $\mathbb{C}$. Let s and u be given two columns of M, where $s = \sum_{i=0}^{n-1} a_i q_i$ and $u = \sum_{j=0}^{n-1} b_j q_j$. If h is the phase shift of u with respect to s, then $h \equiv -(r + p) \ (mod \ 2^n - 1)$, where r and p are in Theorem 5 and Theorem 2, respectively.*

Proof. Let A be the $(2^n - 1) \times n$ matrix consisting of n independent PN sequences generated by T as its columns and let $(1, 0, \cdots, 0)$ be the initial configuration of T. Let $w = \sum_{i=0}^{n-1} a_i w_i$ and $v = \sum_{j=0}^{n-1} b_j w_j$. Since T is symmetric, the phase shift of u with respect to s is equal to the row phase shift of v with respect to w. Therefore $h \equiv -(r + p) \ (mod \ 2^n - 1)$.

Example 2. Let $\mathbb{C}$ be the given CA with $T = < 0, 1, 0, 1 >$ and $(1, 0, 0, 0)$ the initial configuration of T. Then we obtain matrices A and M as Table 1. Since the characteristic polynomial of T is $x^4 + x + 1$, $p = 4$ in Theorem 2. Let $s = (1, 1, 0, 0, 0, 1, 0, 0, 1, 1, 0, 1, 0, 1, 1)^t$ and $u = (0, 0, 1, 0, 0, 1, 1, 0, 1, 0, 1, 1, 1, 1, 0)^t$ in M. If we put $w = (1, 1, 0, 0)$ and $v = (0, 0, 1, 1)$, then by Theorem 5 $r = 14$. Hence $h \equiv -(14 + 4) \equiv 12 (mod \ 15)$. The phase shift of u (which is the sum of the 2nd cell position and the 3rd cell position of $\mathbb{C}$) with respect to s (which is the sum of the 0th cell and the 1st cell position of $\mathbb{C}$) is 12.

Let s be the sequence combined the 0th column with the 1st column and u the sequence combined the $(n - 2)$th column with the $(n - 1)$th column of the matrix A obtained by the given CA rule and the initial vector $(1, 0, \cdots, 0)$. Phase shifts of the sequence u with respect to the sequence s are given in Table 2.

4   Algorithm to Compute Phase Shifts

Now we give an algorithm to find the phase shifts in a given n-cell maximum-length 90/150 CA.

Algorithm FindPhaseShifts

Input: The state transition $n \times n$ matrix T, initial vector $w = (1, 0, \cdots, 0)$.
Output: phaseshift$[n]$.
    Step 1. mark$_{1 \times n}$ by 0; mark$[0]$=1;
       power=1; phaseshift$[0]$=0.
    Step 2. While (all mark $\neq$ 1) do step 3 to step 5.
    Step 3. $w^t = Tw^t$. /* Run the CA */

Table 2. Phase shifts of the sequence u with respect to the sequence s

Degree	CA rule	Phase shift
3	110	3
4	0101	12
5	01111	8
6	000110	23
7	1011001	75
8	01001011	9
9	010011100	44
10	1111000011	994
11	01000011010	1426
12	100101010011	3882
13	0111001110110	7649
14	01000111001111	14568
15	100000011000001	9538
16	0001111001001000	63960
17	10011000110011001	77544
18	110001000000010011	241877
19	1101011101101001011	282318
20	01101011100001010110	314775
21	010010011001010010010	1676666
22	0100011010101101100010	1345981
23	01011010101100101011010	6095661
24	110100111100100111001011	199263
25	1010000011111011100000101	17370017
26	11001101111101111010110011	66236246
27	000110100011000101110101 1000	132625967
28	0101101110000001100111011010	195968798
29	01001000100101111100100010010	205911726
30	101000100111001101101010000101	404894385
31	1111101101100001100011011011111	2015461719
32	00001100010001110000110000000110	25871503

Step 4. If (w contains single 1)
   then mark [position of 1]=1;
   phaseshift[position of 1] $\equiv$ − power (mod $2^n - 1$).
Step 5. power=power+1.

There does not need the Shank's algorithm for the completion of this algorithm any more. The algorithm that we propose does not need any previous phase shifts. Whereas, it is required to compute all previous in Sarkar's method ([10]) which adopted the Shank's algorithm in order to get the phase shifts of the ith column with respect to the 0th cell. So, we can see that this is very practically useful for sufficiently large n.

Table 3. Phase shifts with respect to the 0th cell of the CA whose rule is $<$ 00001100010001110000110000000110 $>$

Degree	CA rule	Phase shifts		
32	0000110001000111	0,	4294967294,	3963262907,	4294967292
	0000110000000110	2182065471,	3478064023,	2842396500
		3797410740,	2636154424,	1477132997
		2453647807,	3833928247,	4122644326
		2445882768,	3715941894,	3131603603
		3781145264,	724531189,	1964528637
		1178642835,	1437488410,	2132417369
		2228497937,	2438002527,	3823282243
		3142683718,	4037203264,	3657430022
		496625232,	3264387886,	25871502
		25871503		

In Table 3 there are all phase shifts with respect to the 0th cell of the CA whose rule is $<$ 00001100010001110000110000000110 $>$.

5   Conclusion

In this paper, we studied the properties of sequences generated by maximum-length 90/150 CA sequences and applied these results to the phase shifting of PN sequences generated by it. From these applications we proposed a method for the study of phase shift analysis. As a special case of this method, we gave an algorithm to compute relative phase shifts between stages of a CA. This algorithm is different from the algorithms of Bardell's [1], Nandi and Chaudhuri's [9], and Sarkar's [10]. Our algorithm is more practical than them.

References

1. P.H. Bardell, "Analysis of cellular automata used as pseudorandom pattern generators", *Proc. IEEE int. Test. Conf.*, pp. 762-767, 1990.
2. S.J. Cho, "Analysis of Pseudo-Noise Sequences Generated by Cellular Automata", *Submitted.*
3. S.J. Cho , U.S. Choi and H.D. Kim, "Analysis of complemented CA derived from a linear TPMACA", *Computers and Mathematics with Applications*, Vol. 45, pp. 689-698, 2003.
4. S.J. Cho, U.S. Choi and H.D. Kim, "Behavior of complemented CA whose complement vector is acyclic in a linear TPMACA", *Mathematical and Computer Modelling*, Vol. 36, 2002, pp. 979-986.
5. A.K. Das and P.P. Chaudhuri, "Vector space theoretic analysis of additive cellular automata and its application for pseudo-exhaustive test pattern generation", *IEEE Trans. Comput.*, Vol. 42, pp. 340-352, 1993.
6. S.W. Golomb, *Shift Register Sequences*, Holden Day, 1967.
7. R. Lidl and H. Niederreiter, *Finite Fields*, Cambridge University Press, 1997.

8. S. Nandi and P.P. Chaudhuri, "Analysis of Periodic and Intermediate Boundary 90/150 Cellular Automata", *IEEE Trans. Comput.*, Vol. 45, pp. 1-12, 1996.

9. S. Nandi and P.P. Chaudhuri, "Additive Cellular Automata as an on-chip test pattern generator", *Test Symposium, 1993., Proceedings of the Second Asian*, pp. 166-171, 1993.

10. P. Sarkar, "Computing Shifts in 90/150 cellular automata sequences", *Finite Fields Their Appl.*, Vol. 42, pp. 340-352, 2003.

11. M. Serra, T. Slater, J.C. Muzio and D.M. Miller, "The analysis of one dimensional linear cellular automata and their aliasing properties", *IEEE Trans Computer-Aided Design*, Vol. 9, pp. 767-778, 1990.

12. S. Tezuka and M. Fushimi, "A method of designing cellular automata as pseudo-random number generators for built-in self-test for VLSI", *Contemporary Mathematica*, Vol. 168, pp. 363-367, 1994.

13. S. Wolfram, Statistical Mechanics of Cellular Automata, *Rev. Mod. Phys.*, Vol. 55, pp. 601-644, 1983.

Cellular Automata Evolution for Distributed Data Mining

Pradipta Maji[1], Biplab K. Sikdar[2], and P. Pal Chaudhuri[1]

[1] Department of Computer Science and Engineering & Information Technology,
Netaji Subhash Engineering College, Kolkata, India 700 152,
pradiptamaji@hotmail.com, palchau@vsnl.net
[2] Department of Computer Science and Technology,
Bengal Engineering College, Howrah, India 711 103,
biplab@cs.becs.ac.in

Abstract. This paper reports design of a pattern classifying machine (PCM) for distributed data mining (DDM) environment. The proposed PCM is based on the computing model of a special class of sparse network referred to as Cellular Automata (CA). Extensive experimental results confirm scalability of the PCM to handle distributed datasets. The excellent classification accuracy and low memory overhead figure establish the proposed PCM as the classifier ideally suited for DDM environments.

1 Introduction

The inter-networked society has been experiencing an explosion of data in many distributed environments. However, the explosion is paradoxically acting as an impediment in acquiring knowledge. The meaningful interpretation of different distributed sources of voluminous data is increasingly becoming difficult. Consequently, researchers, practitioners, entrepreneurs from diverse fields are focusing on development of sophisticated techniques for knowledge extraction, which leads to the promising field of distributed data mining (DDM) [1,2,3].

Due to high response time, lack of proper use of distributed resources, and its inherent characteristics, the conventional centralized data mining algorithms are not suitable for DDM environment. Most DDM algorithms are designed for parallel processing on distributed data. Similar algorithms are applied on each distributed data source concurrently, producing one local model per source. All local models are next aggregated to produce final model.

One of the important problems in data mining is classification. Most distributed classifiers in DDM work in ensemble learning approach, which produces multiple classifiers (base classifiers) at different data sources. Results derived out of multiple classifiers are next combined at a central location to enhance the classification accuracy of predictive models. Majority voting scheme is applied to aggregate base classifiers. Meta-learning framework offers another way to aggregate these base classifiers. So, the most important issues in DDM are the aggregation of the base classifiers and the communication cost from different local data sources to the central location where final classification is performed.

P.M.A. Sloot, B. Chopard, and A.G. Hoekstra (Eds.): ACRI 2004, LNCS 3305, pp. 40–49, 2004.

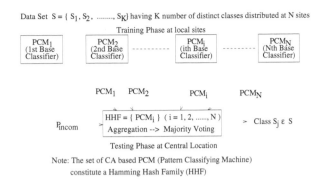

Fig. 1. Architecture of a PCM for distributed data mining (DDM) environment

In the above background scenario, the essential prerequisites of designing a classifier for DDM environment are: (i) base classifier at each local site must have high classification accuracy; (ii) it must be scalable to handle disk resident datasets; (iii) it should have high throughput with less storage requirements; (iv) volume of data transfered from each local to central site should be minimum; (v) aggregation of base classifiers must induce globally meaningful knowledge; and (vi) the algorithm should be simple enough to have a low cost hardwired implementation for on-line operation in the inter-networked society of cyber age.

In this paper, we propose the design of a pattern classifying machine (PCM) to address the problem of DDM. At each local site, we design a CA based PCM as a base classifier. The majority voting scheme is next implemented to aggregate the results of the base classifiers and predict the class of the data element. The architecture of the majority voting scheme is developed around the CA based hamming hash family (HHF) [4]. Each PCM is a member of this HHF. The probability of collision between a pair of patterns varies inversely with their hamming distance (HD) while hashed with HHF. This property of HHF is used to design the majority voting scheme for distributed data mining (DDM).

Next section presents an overview of CA based pattern classifying machine (PCM) for distributed data mining (DDM) environment.

2 PCM for DDM Environment

In this section, we present the architecture (Fig. 1) of a pattern classifying machine (PCM) for distributed data mining (DDM). Let the data which have to be classified into different classes $S = \{S_1, S_2, \cdots, S_K\}$ are distributed among N number of different sites. For a given feature/metric of the dataset, a PCM is generated as a base classifier (PCM_i; where $i = 1, 2, \cdots, N$) at each local data site. The set of PCMs are next copied at a central location. The majority voting scheme is employed to aggregate the results of these PCMs. The property of hamming hash family (HHF) [4] is exploited in majority voting scheme which enhances the classification accuracy at central location. Thus the training phase of the classifier is implemented at a local site to design the PCM, while the testing phase to identify the class of a data element is implemented in the central location. Communication between local site and central location takes place only if data at local site gets updated and a new PCM is generated for classification of updated dataset.

The algorithm of classification for distributed data mining (DDM) environments proceeds as follows. Let the number of PCMs (base classifiers) be N, where each PCM_i has classified a dataset into K number of distinct classes $S = \{S_1, S_2, \cdots, S_K\}$ available at a local site i. Any incoming data $\mathcal{P}_{incom}$ is hashed with each of the PCMs in a central location. At each instance of hashing, $\mathcal{P}_{incom}$ collides with a class $S_j \in S$. Each $S_j \in S$ records the count of the number of times it collides with $\mathcal{P}_{incom}$. Once the process of hashing in all PCMs is completed, the class S_j with which $\mathcal{P}_{incom}$ has collided for maximum number of times is recorded as the class of $\mathcal{P}_{incom}$. The sequential steps of the algorithm follows.

Algorithm 1. Identification_of_the_class_in_a_DDM_environment
Input: An incoming data $\mathcal{P}_{incom}$ input to PCM_i $(i = 1, 2, \cdots, N)$.
Output: Class S_j of the data classes $S = \{S_1, S_2, \cdots, S_K\}$.
begin:
    for $i = 1$ to N
    hash $\mathcal{P}_{incom}$ with PCM_i
    pick S_j with which $\mathcal{P}_{incom}$ collides for maximum number of times
    output S_j.

In rest of the paper we concentrate on the design of hamming hash family (HHF) - a set of pattern classifiers which behave as the base classifiers for different local sites. The classifier design is based on a special class of CA, termed as Multiple Attractor CA (MACA) [4,5]. For the sake of easy reference a brief introduction of MACA follows next.

3   Multiple Attractor CA (MACA)

A Cellular Automaton (CA) consists of a number of cells. In a 3-neighborhood dependency, the next state $q_i(t+1)$ of a cell is assumed to be dependent only on itself and on its two neighbors (left and right), and is denoted as

$$q_i(t+1) = f(q_{i-1}(t), q_i(t), q_{i+1}(t)) \tag{1}$$

where $q_i(t)$ represents the state of the ith cell at t^{th} instant of time. f is the next state function and referred to as the rule of the automata. Since f is a function of 3 variables, there are 2^{2^3} i.e., 256 possible next state functions (rules) for a CA cell. Out of 256 rules there are only 7 rules with XOR logic. The CA employing XOR rule is referred to as linear CA. The pattern classifier proposed in this paper employs a special class of linear CA referred to as MACA [4,5].

The state transition graph of an MACA consists of a number of cyclic and non-cyclic states. The set of non-cyclic states of an MACA forms inverted trees rooted at the cyclic states. The cyclic states with self loop are referred to as attractors. Fig. 2 depicts the state transition diagram of a 5-cell MACA with four attractors {00000(0), 00011(3), 00100(4), 00111(7)}. The states of a tree rooted at the cyclic state α forms the α-basin.

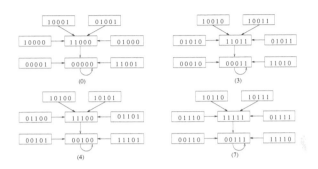

Fig. 2. State transition diagram of a 5-cell MACA. Four cyclic states 0, 3, 4, 7 are referred to as attractors and the corresponding inverted tree rooted on α ($\alpha = 0$, 3, 4, 7) as α-basin.

The detailed characterization of MACA is available in [4,5]. A few fundamental results for an n-cell MACA having k number of attractor are next outlined. Result I:

Definition 1. *An m-bit field of an n-bit pattern set is said to be pseudo-exhaustive if all possible 2^m patterns appear in the set.*

Theorem 1. *In an n-cell MACA with $k = 2^m$ attractors, there exists m-bit positions at which the attractors generate pseudo-exhaustive 2^m patterns.*

Result II: An n-bit MACA with 2-attractor basins can be represented by an n-bit binary string, termed as Dependency Vector (DV). If DV is an n-bit Dependency Vector and $\mathcal{P}$ is an n-bit pattern, then the modulo-2 sum (XOR) of the dependent variables of $\mathcal{P}$ (where DV contains 1's) is equal to zero if $\mathcal{P}$ belongs to zero basin; otherwise 1. That is,

$$DV \cdot \mathcal{P} = \begin{cases} 0, \text{ if } \mathcal{P} \in \text{zero basin} \\ 1, \text{ if } \mathcal{P} \in \text{non-zero basin} \end{cases} \qquad (2)$$

Result III: An n-bit MACA with 2^m-attractor basins can be represented by an n-bit Dependency String (DS). An n-bit Dependency String DS is produced through concatenation of m number of Dependency Vectors of length $n_1, n_2, \cdots, n_m$ respectively (Fig. 3), where $n_1 + n_2 + \cdots + n_m = n$ and $\mathcal{P}$ is an n-bit pattern whose attractor basin is to be identified. For each DV_i (of length n_i), the dependent variables of the corresponding n_i bits of $\mathcal{P}$ (say $\mathcal{P}_i$) gives either 0 or 1, - that is,

$$DV_i \cdot \mathcal{P}_i = \begin{cases} 0, \text{ if } \mathcal{P}_i \in \text{zero basin of } DV_i \\ 1, \text{ if } \mathcal{P}_i \in \text{non-zero basin of } DV_i \end{cases}$$

Fig. 3. An n-bit Dependency String (DS) consists of m number of Dependency Vectors (DVs). Each Dependency Vector (DV) contributes the value of each pseudo-exhaustive bit (either 0 or 1) of an attractor basin.

which indicates the value of ith pseudo-exhaustive bit. Finally, a string of m binary symbols can be obtained from m number of DVs. This m-bit binary string is the pseudo-exhaustive field (PEF) of the attractor basins where the pattern $\mathcal{P}$ belongs. That is, the pseudo-exhaustive field (PEF) of the attractor basin of $\mathcal{P}$ is given by

$$PEF = DS \cdot \mathcal{P} = [DV_1 \cdot \mathcal{P}_1][DV_2 \cdot \mathcal{P}_2] \cdots [DV_m \cdot \mathcal{P}_m] \qquad (3)$$

where DS and $\mathcal{P}$ - both are n-bit vectors. So, the complexity of identifying the PEF of an attractor basin is $O(n)$. This specific result is of significant importance for our design. It enables the scheme to identify the class of an input element with linear complexity.

3.1   Hamming Hash Family

An MACA can act as an effective hash function. The total pool of MACA forms a hash family and exhibits an interesting property: the hash family maintains an inverse relationship between the collision of a pair of patterns while hashed and their hamming distance [4]. The hash family having this property is referred to as hamming hash family (HHF). The concept of HHF imparts an important property to the attractor basin of MACA. Since keys (patterns) that collide lie in the same attractor basin, the keys (patterns) which lie close to each other in terms of hamming distance (HD) belong to the same basin.

3.2   MACA – As a Pattern Classifier

An n-bit MACA with k-attractor basins can be viewed as a natural classifier. It classifies a given set of patterns into k number of distinct classes, each class containing the set of states in the attractor basin. To enhance the classification accuracy of the machine, most of the works [4,5] have employed MACA to classify patterns into two classes (say I and II). The following example illustrates an MACA based two class pattern classifier.

Example 1. *Let, the MACA of Fig. 2 be employed to classify patterns into two classes (say I and II), where Class I is represented by one set of attractor basins (say [I]= {00100 and 00111} in Fig. 2) while Class II is represented by the rest of the basins (say [II] = {00000 and 00011}). All the patterns in the* *attractor basins [I] belong to Class I while rest of the patterns belong to Class II. As per Theorem 1, the pseudo-exhaustive field (PEF) will identify the class of the patterns uniquely. The PEF yields the address of the memory that stores the class information. Therefore, Class I attractors yield the memory address {10, 11}, while Class II will be identified by the memory address {00, 01} (Fig. 4). When the MACA is loaded with an input pattern $\mathcal{P}$, corresponding MACA identifies the PEF of the attractor basin where $\mathcal{P}$ belongs.*

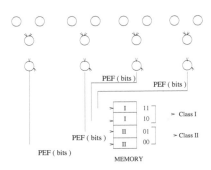

Fig. 4. MACA based classification strategy with 4 attractor basins classifying the elements into two classes. The PEF (Pseudo Exhaustive Field) of the attractor of a basin is extracted to determine the class. Also, the PEF of each attractor points to the memory location that stores the class information.

Genetic Algorithm (GA) formulation to arrive at the desired MACA realizing this specific objective has been proposed in [4] with $O(n^3)$ complexity. The design reported in the next subsection achieves classification with linear complexity. To enhance classification accuracy of the machine, we have refined the approach reported in [4] and report a new CA based classifier. It can classify an n-bit pattern with $O(n)$ complexity. Multi-class classifier is built by recursively employing the concept of two class classifier. MACA based classifier proposed here has two distinct stages and hence referred to as Two Stage Classifier (Fig.5).

3.3   MACA Based Two Stage Classifier

The design of MACA based classifier for two n-bit pattern sets S_1 and S_2 should ensure that elements of one class (say S_1) are covered by a set of attractor basins that do not include any member from the class S_2. Any two n-bit patterns $\mathcal{P}_1 \in S_1$ and $\mathcal{P}_2 \in S_2$ should fall in different attractor basins.

Let, an n-bit 2^m-attractor basins MACA can classify two n-bit pattern sets S_1 and S_2. That is,

$$DS \cdot \mathcal{P}_1 \neq DS \cdot \mathcal{P}_2 \tag{4}$$

where DS is an n-bit Dependency String consisting of m number of Dependency Vectors (Fig. 3). Then, the total number of attractor basins will be 2^m and the

pseudo-exhaustive field (PEF) (Theorem 1) of each attractor basin will be an
m-bit binary pattern/string. Let, k_1 and k_2 be two m-bit pattern sets consisting of pseudo-exhaustive bits of attractors of two n-bit pattern sets S_1 and S_2
respectively. Then, k_1 and k_2 can also be regarded as two m-bit pattern sets for
two class classification. So, we synthesize an MACA based two class classifier
such that one class (say k_1) belongs to one attractor basin and another attractor
basin houses the class k_2. Any two m-bit patterns $p_1 \in k_1$ and $p_2 \in k_2$ should
fall in different attractor basins (while one in zero basin, another in non-zero
basin), - that is,

$$DV \cdot p_1 \neq DV \cdot p_2 \tag{5}$$

where DV is an m-bit Dependency Vector.

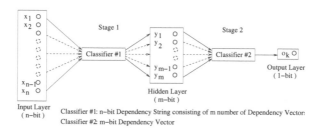

Classifier #1: n–bit Dependency String consisting of m number of Dependency Vector
Classifier #2: m–bit Dependency Vector

Fig. 5. Two Stage Classifier

Fig. 5 represents the architecture of Two Stage Classifier. It consists of three
layers - input, hidden and output layers denoted as x_i $(i = 1, 2, \cdots, n)$, y_j $(j =
1, 2, \cdots, m)$, and o_k $(k = 1)$ respectively. While the first classifier (Classifier#1
of Fig. 5) maps an n-bit pattern of the input layer into an m-bit pattern (PEF)
of the hidden layer, the second classifier (Classifier#2) maps that m-bit pattern
into a single bit (either 0 or 1) of the output layer. That is, Classifier#1 provides
an appropriate mappings of patterns of input layer into PEF (pseudo-exhaustive
field) of the hidden layer and the Classifier#2 implements the classification of
the PEFs rather than the original patterns.

Let, x be an n-bit input pattern whose class is to be identified by MACA
based Two Stage Classifier. At first, x is loaded with the Classifier#1 which
outputs an m-bit pattern y (pseudo-exhaustive field of attractor of the basin
where x belongs). That is,

$$y = DS \cdot x \tag{6}$$

Next, y is loaded with the Classifier#2 which gives a single value o (pseudo-
exhaustive field of attractor of the basin where y belongs) that determines the
class of the input pattern x. That is,

$$o = DV \cdot y \tag{7}$$

In order to evolve MACA based Two Stage Classifier realizing this design objective, we have developed a special type of GA formulation. Next section reports
the performance of MACA based Two Stage Classifier in DDM environment.

4   MACA Based PCM for DDM Environment

The pattern classifying machine (PCM) is designed with a set of Two Stage Classifiers. This section provides a detailed analysis of performance evaluation of MACA based PCM. The major metric to evaluate the performance of the proposed PCM is classification accuracy - the percentage of test data which can be correctly classified into different attractor basins. To evaluate classification accuracy, we perform the experiments on synthetic dataset proposed in [4].

The characterization of MACA basins reported in the Section 3.1 has established following facts: (i) a basin has patterns which are close to each other in terms of HD; (ii) patterns satisfying this criterion have high probability of getting classified into minimum number of attractor basins; and (iii) patterns not covered by the training sets, but satisfying the criteria, will also have high probability of being predicted as the right class.

As a corollary to the above facts, the accuracy of classifying two classes of patterns in distinct attractor basins increases if the average distance between them is high. In this context, to characterize the datasets to be classified in two classes, we introduce two terms D_{min} and d_{max}. D_{min} is the minimum hamming distance (inter-cluster distance) between two patterns $\mathcal{P}_1 \in S_1$ and $\mathcal{P}_2 \in S_2$ in two classes S_1 and S_2 respectively; while d_{max} is the maximum distance (intra-cluster distance) between two patterns within a class. The experimental set up and dataset employed for analysis have been reported in [4]. For the sake of performance analysis, the distributions of patterns in two classes are assumed as shown in Fig. 6.

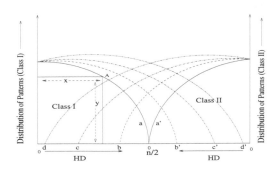

Fig. 6. Distribution of patterns in Class I and Class II (HD denotes hamming distance)

4.1   Experimental Setup

In each of the above distribution, different values of n (number of bits in a pattern) and N (number of sites) are taken. For each value of n and N, 50% of the data are taken to build up the classification model. The rest 50% data are used to test the prediction capability of the classifier. For centralized data mining (DM),

Table 1. Classification Accuracy for Curve $a - a'$ and $b - b'$

No of	Curve $a - a'$				Curve $b - b'$			
Sites	Size	Value	Classification Accuracy		Size	Value	Classification Accuracy	
N	(n)	of m	Centralized DM	DDM	(n)	of m	Centralized DM	DDM
10	200	4	96.12	98.98	200	4	94.49	97.89
	600	5	96.71	98.71	400	5	93.12	97.07
	1000	7	96.87	97.89	1000	7	94.67	96.95
20	200	4	96.12	98.99	200	4	94.49	98.01
	400	5	95.19	98.21	600	5	95.17	98.39
	1000	7	96.87	98.03	1000	7	94.67	97.33
30	200	4	96.12	99.41	200	4	94.49	98.35
	800	7	97.06	99.97	400	5	93.12	97.77
	1000	7	96.87	99.03	600	5	95.17	98.54

Table 2. Classification Accuracy for Curve $c - c'$

No of	Size	Value	Classification Accuracy	
Sites (N)	(n)	of m	Centralized DM	DDM
10	400	5	85.33	98.89
	600	5	86.55	99.07
	1000	7	84.79	98.63
20	200	4	84.25	98.79
	600	5	86.55	99.13
	1000	7	84.79	99.11
30	200	4	84.25	99.17
	800	7	83.94	98.69
	1000	7	84.79	99.16

the PCM is designed based on the 50% of the total dataset centrally available. For distributed data mining (DDM) environment, total dataset is equally distributed to each local site and then same scheme is employed at each local site to synthesize the PCMs. In other words, in each site 50% of available data is used to train the PCM. The MACA based PCMs are next collected in the centralized location where classification accuracy is tested with the remaining set of 50% data not used for training. The classification accuracy of the proposed DDM is evaluated through the majority voting scheme reported in the Algorithm 1 of Section 2. For each values of N and n, 10 different pairs of datasets are taken.

4.2   Classification Accuracy

Tables 1–2 represent the classification accuracy of conventional centralized CA based classifier and that of PCM in distributed environments for the dataset $a - a'$, $b - b'$, $c - c'$. Columns I and II of Tables 1- 2 represent the number of data sites/sources (N) and size of the pattern (n) respectively. Column III represents different values of m (number of pseudo-exhaustive bits), where 2^m is the number of attractor basins of the MACA. Column IV depicts the classification accuracy in centralized and distributed environments. The experimental results confirm the following facts: (i) the accuracy in DDM is better than that of conventional centralized MACA based PCMs; (ii) as the number of sites (N) increases, the classification accuracy for DDM environment significantly increases over centralized classification algorithm; and (iii) the concept of hamming hash family (HHF) is reported in Section 3.1. The scheme of Majority Voting in central location establishes the elegance and efficiency of the scheme of aggregation of classification result of PCMs derived with HHF characterization.

5 Conclusion

This paper presents detailed design of an efficient pattern classifier for DDM environments. The proposed model is built around a special class of sparse network referred to as CA. The excellent classification accuracy and low memory overhead figures establish the CA as an efficient classifier for DDM environments.

References

1. B. Park and H. Kargupta, "Distributed Data Mining: Algorithms, Systems, and Applications," *To be published in the Data Mining Handbook. Editor: Nong Ye*, 2002.
2. H. Kargupta, B. Park, D. Hershberger, and E. Johnson, "Collective Data Mining: A New Perspective Toward Distributed Data Mining," *Advances in Distributed and Parallel Knowledge Discovery, Eds: Hillol Kargupta and Philip Chan. MIT/AAAI Press*, 1999.
3. H. Kargupta and P. Chan, "Distributed and Parallel Knowledge Discovery: A Brief Introduction," *Advances in Distributed and Parallel Knowledge Discovery, Eds: Hillol Kargupta and Philip Chan. MIT/AAAI Press*, pp. xv–xxvi, 2000.
4. N. Ganguly, P. Maji, S. Dhar, B. K. Sikdar, and P. P. Chaudhuri, "Evolving Cellular Automata as Pattern Classifier," *Proceedings of Fifth International Conference on Cellular Automata for Research and Industry, ACRI 2002, Switzerland*, pp. 56–68, October 2002.
5. P. Maji, C. Shaw, N. Ganguly, B. K. Sikdar, and P. P. Chaudhuri, "Theory and Application of Cellular Automata For Pattern Classification," *Fundamenta Informaticae*, 2003.

A Comparative Study of Optimum-Time Synchronization Algorithms for One-Dimensional Cellular Automata – A Survey –

Hiroshi Umeo, Masaya Hisaoka, and Takashi Sogabe

Univ. of Osaka Electro-Communication,
Neyagawa-shi, Hastu-cho, 18-8, Osaka, 572-8530, Japan

Abstract. We present a survey and a comparison of the quantitative and qualitative aspects of the optimum-time synchronization algorithms developed thus far for one-dimensional cellular arrays. Several new results and viewpoints are also given.

1 Introduction

Synchronizing a large scale of cellular automata has been known as the firing squad synchronization problem since its development, and the problem was originally proposed by J. Myhill in order to synchronize all parts of self-reproducing cellular automata [10]. The firing squad synchronization problem has been studied extensively for more than forty years [1-12, 14-15, 16-19]. In the present paper, we firstly examine the state transition rule sets for the famous firing squad synchronization algorithms that give a finite-state protocol for synchronizing large-scale cellular automata. We focus on the fundamental synchronization algorithms operating in optimum steps on one-dimensional cellular arrays in which the general is located at one end. The algorithms discussed herein are the eight-state Balzer's algorithm [1], the seven-state Gerken's algorithm [2], the six-state Mazoyer's algorithm [6], the 16-state Waksman's algorithm [18] and a number of revised versions thereof. Specifically, we attempt to answer the following questions:

- First, are all previously presented transition rule sets correct?
- Do these sets contain redundant rules? If so, what is the exact rule set?
- How do the algorithms compare with each other?

In order to answer these questions, we implement all transition rule sets for the synchronization algorithms above mentioned on a computer and check whether these rule sets yield successful firing configurations at exactly $t = 2n - 2$ steps for any array of length n such that $2 \leq n \leq 10000$. In addition, we construct a survey of current optimum-time synchronization algorithms and compare transition rule sets with respect to the number of internal states of each finite state automaton, the number of transition rules realizing the synchronization, and

P.M.A. Sloot, B. Chopard, and A.G. Hoekstra (Eds.): ACRI 2004, LNCS 3305, pp. 50–60, 2004.

the number of state-changes on the array. With the aid of a computer, the first Waksman's transition rule set is shown to include fundamental errors and the set is shown to contain a considerable number of redundancies. Approximately ninety-three percent of the rules are deleted from the original transition rule set. A number of redundant rules that are not used in the synchronization process are also found in other rule sets. We give the smallest rule set for each algorithm. Finally, we present herein a survey and a comparison of the quantitative and qualitative aspects of the optimum-time synchronization algorithms developed thus far for one-dimensional cellular arrays. We indicate that the first-in-the-world optimum-time synchronization algorithm proposed by Goto [3, 4] and reconstructed by Umeo [12] has a state-change complexity of $\Theta(n \log n)$. Several new results and viewpoints are also given.

2   Firing Squad Synchronization Problem

2.1   A Brief History of the Developments of Optimum-Time Firing Squad Synchronization Algorithms

A finite one-dimensional cellular array consists of n cells, denoted by C_i, where $1 \leq i \leq n$. All cells (except the end cells) are identical finite state automata. The array operates in lock-step mode such that the next state of each cell (except the end cells) is determined by both its own present state and the present states of its right and left neighbors. All cells (*soldiers*), except the left end cell, are initially in the *quiescent* state at time $t = 0$ and have the property whereby the next state of a quiescent cell having quiescent neighbors is the quiescent state. At time $t = 0$ the left end cell (*general*) is in the *fire-when-ready* state, which is an initiation signal to the array. The firing squad synchronization problem is stated as follows. Given an array of n identical cellular automata, including a *general* on the left end which is activated at time $t = 0$, we want to give the description (state set and next-state function) of the automata so that, *at some future time*, all of the cells will *simultaneously* and, *for the first time*, enter a special *firing* state. The set of states must be independent of n. Without loss of generality, we assume $n \geq 2$. The tricky part of the problem is that the same kind of soldier having a fixed number of states must be synchronized, regardless of the length n of the array.

The problem known as the *firing squad synchronization problem* was devised in 1957 by J. Myhill, and first appeared in print in a paper by E. F. Moore [10]. This problem has been widely circulated, and has attracted much attention. The firing squad synchronization problem first arose in connection with the need to simultaneously turn on all parts of a self-reproducing machine. The problem was first solved by J. McCarthy and M. Minsky who presented a $3n$-step algorithm. In 1962, the first optimum-time, i.e. $(2n - 2)$-step, synchronization algorithm was presented by Goto [3], with each cell having several thousands of states. Waksman [18] presented a 16-state optimum-time synchronization algorithm. Afterward, Balzer [1] and Gerken [2] developed an eight-state algorithm and a seven-state synchronization algorithm, respectively, thus decreasing the number of states required for the synchronization. In 1987, Mazoyer [6] developed a six-state synchronization algorithm which, at present, is the algorithm having the fewest states.

2.2   Complexity Measure for Optimum-Time Synchronization Algorithms

• **Time complexity.** Any solution to the firing squad synchronization problem can easily be shown to require $(2n - 2)$ steps for firing n cells, since signals on the array can propagate no faster than one cell per step, and the time from the general's instruction until the firing must be at least $2n - 2$. (See Balzer [1], Mazoyer [5, 6] and Waksman [18] for a proof.) Thus, we have:

[**Theorem 1.**] [1, 5, 6, 18] Synchronization of n cells in less than $2n - 2$ steps is impossible.

[**Theorem 2.**] [1-3, 6, 18] Synchronization of n cells in exactly $2n - 2$ steps is possible.

• **Number of internal states.** The following three distinct states: the *quiescent* state, the *general* state, and the *firing* state, are required in order to define any cellular automaton that can solve the firing squad synchronization problem. The boundary state for C_0 and C_{n+1} is not generally counted as an internal state. Balzer [1] showed that no four-state optimum-time solution exists. In addition, there exists no five-state optimum-time solution satisfying the special conditions that Balzer [1] studied. The question that remains is: "What is the minimum number of states for an optimum-time solution of the problem?" At present, that number is five or six.

[**Theorem 3.**] [1] There is no four-state CA that can synchronize n cells.

[**Theorem 4.**] [1] There is no five-state solution satisfying Balzer's special conditions.

• **Number of transition rules.** Any k-state (excluding the boundary state) transition table for the synchronization has at most $(k - 1)k^2$ entries in $(k - 1)$ matrices of size $k \times k$. The number of transition rules reflects the complexity of synchronization algorithms.

3   Transition Rule Sets for Optimum-Time Firing Squad Synchronization Algorithms

3.1   Waksman's 16-State Algorithm

In 1966, Waksman [18] proposed a 16-state firing squad synchronization algorithm, which, together with an unpublished algorithm by Goto [3], is referred to as the first-in-the-world optimum-time synchronization algorithm. Waksman presented a set of transition rules described in terms of a state transition table. To describe the state transition table in a concise way, Waksman introduced a special symbol γ that matches any state in its right and/or left neighbor. Since Waksman's table cannot be used as is on a computer, we first expand the table *automatically* according to the notation given by Waksman [18]. We thereby

```
----  Q  State ----     036 R1  Q    ->R1      071 R1  B0  P0  ->R1    107 A111 B1  Q   ->P0    141 P1  P0  P0  ->T       ----  A000 State ------
001 Q  Q   Q  ->Q       037 R1  Q   B0  ->R1   072 R1  B0  P1  ->R1    108 A111 B1  B0  ->P0    142 P1  P0  P1  ->T       175 Q  A000 Q   ->Q
002 Q  Q   B0  ->Q      038 R1  Q   B1  ->R1   073 P0  B0  Q   ->B0    ----  R0 State ----      143 P1  P0  www ->T       176 Q  A000 P0  ->B0
003 Q  Q   B1  ->Q      039 P0  Q   Q   ->A010 074 P0  B0  B1  ->B0    109 Q  R0  Q   ->Q       144 A000 P0  P0  ->P0     177 B1  A000 Q   ->Q
004 Q  Q   R0  ->R0     040 P0  Q   B1  ->A010 075 P0  B0  R0  ->R0    110 Q  R0  B1  ->Q       145 A000 P0  A010 ->P0    178 B1  A000 P0  ->B0
005 Q  Q   R1  ->Q      041 P0  Q   R1  ->A010 076 P0  B0  P0  ->P0    111 Q  R0  A111 ->Q      146 A000 P0  www ->P0     ----  A001 State ------
006 Q  Q   P0  ->A000   042 P0  Q   www ->P1   077 P0  B0  P1  ->P0    112 B0  R0  Q   ->B1     147 www P0  Q   ->P0      179 Q  A001 Q   ->Q
007 Q  Q   P1  ->A100   043 P1  Q   Q   ->A110 078 P0  B0  A100 ->P1   113 B1  R0  Q   ->B0     148 www P0  B0  ->P0      180 Q  A001 P0  ->B0
008 Q  Q   A000 ->A110  044 P1  Q   B0  ->A110 079 P0  B0  A011 ->B0   114 P0  R0  B1  ->B0     149 www P0  R0  ->P0      181 B0  A001 Q   ->Q
009 Q  Q   A001 ->A000  045 A000 Q   Q   ->R1  080 P1  B0  Q   ->B0    115 P1  R0  B1  ->B0     150 www P0  P0  ->T       182 B0  A001 B0  ->Q
010 Q  Q   A100 ->A101  046 A000 Q   B0  ->R1  081 P1  B0  B1  ->B0    116 P1  R0  A111 ->B0    151 www P0  P1  ->T       ----  A100 State ------
011 Q  Q   A101 ->A100  047 A001 Q   R1  ->Q   082 P1  B0  R0  ->R0    ----  R1 State ----      152 www P0  A010 ->P0     183 Q  A100 Q   ->R1
012 Q  Q   A010 ->R0    048 A100 Q   Q   ->Q   083 P1  B0  P0  ->P0    117 Q  R1  Q   ->Q       ----  P1 State ----      184 Q  A100 P1  ->R1
013 Q  Q   A110 ->Q     049 A110 Q   B0  ->Q   084 P1  B0  A100 ->P1   118 Q  R1  B0  ->B1      153 Q  P1  Q   ->P1      185 B0  A100 Q   ->P1
014 Q  Q   www ->Q      050 A010 Q   Q   ->A011 085 A001 B0  P0  ->B0  119 Q  R1  B1  ->B0      154 Q  P1  P1  ->P1      186 B0  A100 P1  ->P1
015 B0  Q   Q   ->Q     051 A010 Q   B0  ->A011 086 A011 B0  Q   ->P1  120 B1  R1  Q   ->Q      155 Q  P1  www ->P1      ----  A101 State ------
016 B0  Q   B0  ->Q     052 A010 Q   R1  ->A011 087 A110 B0  Q   ->P1  121 B1  R1  P0  ->B0     156 B0  P1  B0  ->P1     187 Q  A101 R1  ->Q
017 B0  Q   R0  ->R0    053 A010 Q   www ->P0   088 A110 B0  P0  ->P1  122 B1  R1  P1  ->B0     157 B0  P1  P1  ->P1     188 B1  A101 R1  ->P0
018 B0  Q   P1  ->A100  054 A011 Q   Q   ->A010 089 A110 B0  P1  ->P1  123 A101 R1  Q   ->Q     158 B0  P1  www ->P1     ----  A010 State ------
019 B0  Q   A000 ->A001 055 A011 Q   B1  ->A010 ----  B1 State ----    124 A101 R1  P1  ->B0    159 R1  P1  R0  ->P1     189 Q  A010 Q   ->Q
020 B0  Q   A101 ->A100 056 A011 Q   B1  ->A010 090 Q  B1  Q   ->B1    ----  P0 State ----      160 R1  P1  P1  ->P1     190 Q  A010 B1  ->Q
021 B0  Q   A010 ->R0   057 A011 Q   www ->P1   091 Q  B1  B0  ->B1    125 Q  P0  Q   ->P0      161 R1  P1  www ->P1     191 P0  A010 Q   ->B0
022 B0  Q   A110 ->Q    058 A110 Q   Q   ->A111 092 Q  B1  B0  ->B1    126 Q  P0  P0  ->P0      162 P0  P1  P0  ->T       192 P0  A010 B1  ->B0
023 B1  Q   Q   ->Q     059 A110 Q   B1  ->A111 093 Q  B1  R1  ->B1    127 Q  P0  www ->P0      163 P0  P1  P1  ->T       ----  A011 State ------
024 B1  Q   B1  ->Q     060 A111 Q   Q   ->A110 094 Q  B1  A000 ->P0   128 Q  P0  B0  ->P0      164 P0  P1  www ->T       193 Q  A011 Q   ->Q
025 B1  Q   B0  ->R0    061 A111 Q   B0  ->A110 095 Q  B1  A101 ->P0   129 B0  P0  P0  ->P0     165 P1  P1  Q   ->P1      194 Q  A011 B0  ->Q
026 B1  Q   R1  ->Q                             096 B0  B1  Q   ->B1    130 B0  P0  www ->P0     166 P1  P1  B0  ->P1      195 B0  A011 Q   ->Q
027 B1  Q   P0  ->A000  ----  B0 State ----     097 B0  B1  R0  ->Q     131 R1  P0  R0  ->P0     167 P1  P1  R0  ->P1      196 B0  A011 B0  ->Q
028 B1  Q   A001 ->A000 062 Q   B0  Q   ->B0    098 B0  B1  www ->P0    132 R1  P0  P0  ->P0     168 P1  P1  P0  ->T       ----  A110 State ------
029 B1  Q   A101 ->A101 063 Q   B0  R0  ->R0    099 B0  B1  A101 ->P0   133 R1  P0  www ->P0     169 P1  P1  P1  ->T       197 Q  A110 Q   ->R0
030 R0  Q   Q   ->Q     064 Q   B0  P0  ->B0    100 R0  B1  Q   ->B1    134 P0  P0  Q   ->P0     170 P1  P1  A110 ->P1    198 Q  A110 P0  ->R0
031 R0  Q   B1  ->Q     065 Q   B0  P1  ->B0    101 R0  B1  A000 ->P0   135 P0  P0  B0  ->P0     171 P1  P1  www ->T       199 P1  A110 Q   ->R0
032 R0  Q   P0  ->A000  066 Q   B0  A001 ->P1   102 R1  B1  Q   ->Q     136 P0  P0  R0  ->P0     172 A100 P1  Q   ->P1     200 P1  A110 B0  ->P1
033 R0  Q   A000 ->A001 067 Q   B0  A100 ->P1   103 R1  B1  B0  ->Q     137 P0  P0  P0  ->T      173 A100 P1  A110 ->P1    ----  A111 State ------
034 R0  Q   A001 ->A000 068 B1  B0  P0  ->B0    104 A010 B1  Q   ->B0   138 P0  P0  P1  ->T      174 A100 P1  www ->P1     201 R0  A111 Q   ->Q
035 R0  Q   A011 ->Q    069 B1  B0  P1  ->B0    105 A010 B1  B0  ->P0   139 P0  A010 P0  ->P0    140 P0  P0  www ->T       202 R0  A111 B1  ->P0
                        070 R1  B0  Q   ->R1    106 A010 B1  P0  ->P0
```

Fig. 1. USN transition table consisting of 202 rules that realize Waksman's synchronization algorithm.

obtain a transition table that consists of 3208 rules. We implement these rules and examine the validity of the expanded table on a computer. The experiment revealed the following:

[**Observation 3.1.**] For any n such that $2 \le n \le 2000$, the expanded rule set yields successful firings only in the cases of $n = 3, 5$ or 6.

Thus, the firing process fails in most cases.

3.2   USN Transition Rule Set

Umeo, Sogabe and Nomura [15] corrected all errors in Waksman's original transition table. After exploring the Waksman's original transition rule set so that the resultant table yields correct firings for any $n \ge 2$, we get a new transition table consisting of is 3217 rules.

[**Observation 3.2.**] For any n such that $2 \le n \le 10000$, the rule set consisting of 3217 rules yields successful optimum-time firings.

Our computer simulation based on the above list revealed that most of the rules are not used efficiently in the firing process. A histogram-like statistical analysis on the rule set is presented herein and the number of rules valid in the range of $2 \le n \le 10000$ is reduced. Figure 1 is our final, complete list, which consists of 202 transition rules. We refer to this list as the *USN transition rule set*.

In our correction, a ninety-three percent reduction in the number of transition rules is realized compared to Waksman's original list. The computer simulation based on the table of Fig. 1 gives the following observation. Computer simulation shows that 202 rules is the smallest set for the Waksman's optimum-time firing squad synchronization.

[**Observation 3.3.**] The set of rules given in Fig. 1 is the smallest transition rule set for Waksman's optimum-time firing squad synchronization algorithm.

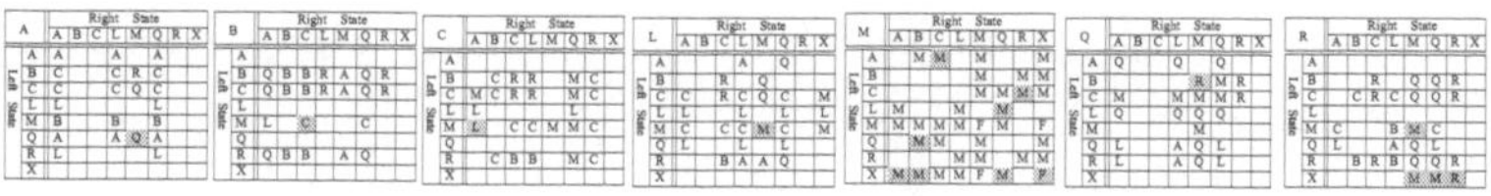

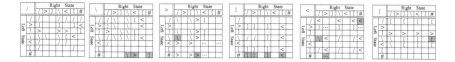

Fig. 2. Transition table for Balzer's algorithm.

Fig. 3. Transition table for the seven-state Gerken's algorithm.

3.3   Balzer's Eight-State Algorithm

Balzer [1] constructed an eight-state, 182-rule synchronization algorithm and the structure of which is completely identical to that of Waksman [18]. Our computer examination revealed no errors, however, 17 rules were found to be redundant. In Fig. 2, we give a list of transition rules for Balzer's algorithm. Deleted rules are indicated by shaded squares, where squares containing letters denote rules included in the original list. In the transition table, the symbols "M", "L", "F" and "X" represent the general, quiescent, firing and boundary states, respectively.

3.4   Gerken's Seven-State Algorithm I

Gerken [2] reduced the number of states realizing Balzer's algorithm and constructed a seven-state, 118-rule synchronization algorithm. In our computer examination, no errors were found, however, 13 rules were found to be redundant. In Fig. 3, we give a list of the transition rules for Gerken's algorithm. The 13 deleted rules are marked by shaded squares in the table. The symbols ">", "/", "..." and "#" represent the general, quiescent, firing and boundary states, respectively.

3.5   Mazoyer's Six-State Algorithm

Mazoyer [6] proposed a six-state, 120-rule synchronization algorithm, the structure of which differs greatly from the previous algorithms discussed above. Our computer examination revealed no errors and only one redundant rule. In Fig. 4, we give a list of transition rules for Mazoyer's algorithm. In the transition table, the letters "G", "L", "F" and "X" represent the general, quiescent, firing and boundary states, respectively.

A

Left State \ Right State	A	B	C	G	L	X
A	A	B	C	B	A	F
B	G	C	C	G	C	
C	A					A
G			C	C		C
L	A	L	G			
X	F		G			

B

Left State \ Right State	A	B	C	G	L	X
A	B	B	L		G	
B	A	B	C	B	G	
C	A			L	L	
G	C		B	G	C	G
L	G	B	L	B		
X						

C

Left State \ Right State	A	B	C	G	L	X
A		B		B	B	B
B			C	G	C	G
C	A	B	C	B	C	
G		B		B	B	B
L	A	G	C	G	C	
X						

L

Left State \ Right State	A	B	C	G	L	X
A	L	L	L	C	G	C
B	L	L	L	L	L	L
C	L	L	L	G	A	G
G	L	L	L	A	C	A
L		L	L	L	L	L
X					L	

G

Left State \ Right State	A	B	C	G	L	X
A		G	G		B	
B		G	G	G	B	G
C		G	G	A	A	A
G		G	G	F	B	F
L	G	G	G			
X		G	G	F	A	

Fig. 4. Transition table for the six-state Mazoyer's algorithm.

3.6 Goto's Algorithm

The first synchronization algorithm presented by Goto [3] was not published as a journal paper. According to Goto, the original note [3] is now unavailable, and the only existing material that treats the algorithm is Goto [4]. The Goto's study presents one figure (Fig. 3.8 in Goto [4]) demonstrating how the algorithm works on 13 cells with a very short description in Japanese. Umeo [12] reconstructed the algorithm of Goto based on this figure. Mazoyer [8] also reconstructed this algorithm again based on the presentation given by Umeo [12]. The algorithm that Umeo [12] reconstructed is a non-recursive algorithm consisting of a marking phase and a $3n$-step synchronization phase. In the first phase, by printing a special marker in the cellular space, the entire cellular space is divided into subspaces, the lengths of which increase exponentially with a common ratio of two, that is 2^j, for any integer j such that $1 \leq j \leq \lfloor \log_2 n \rfloor - 1$. The marking is made from both the left and right ends. In the second phase, each subspace is synchronized using a well-known conventional $(3n + O(1))$-step simple synchronization algorithm. A time-space diagram of the reconstructed algorithm is shown in Fig. 5.

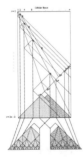

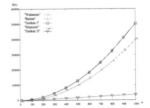

Fig. 5. Time-space diagram for Goto's algorithm as reconstructed by Umeo [12].

Fig. 6. A comparison of state-change complexities in optimum-time synchronization algorithms.

3.7   Gerken's 155-State Algorithm II

Gerken [2] constructed two kinds of optimum-time synchronization algorithms. One seven-state algorithm has been discussed in the previous subsection, and the other is a 155-state algorithm. The transition table given in Gerken [2] is described in terms of two-layer construction with 32 states and 347 rules. The table does not operate as is on a single-layer simulator. In order to obtain an exact transition rule set, we expand this transition table into a single-layer format and obtain a 155-state table consisting of 2371 rules.

4   State Change Complexity

Vollmar [17] introduced a state-change complexity in order to measure the efficiency of cellular algorithms and showed that $\Omega(n \log n)$ state changes are required for the synchronization of n cells in $(2n - 2)$ steps.

[**Theorem 5.**] [17] $\Omega(n \log n)$ state-change is necessary for synchronizing n cells in $(2n - 2)$ steps.

[**Theorem 6.**] Each optimum-time synchronization algorithm developed by Balzer [1], Gerken [2], Mazoyer [6] and Waksman [18] has an $O(n^2)$ state-change complexity, respectively.

[**Theorem 7.**] [2] Gerken's synchronization algorithm II has a $\Theta(n \log n)$ state-change complexity.

Let $S(n)$ be total number of state changes for Yunés-like synchronization algorithms [9, 19] on n cells. We see that $S(n) = \alpha n + 2S(n/2) = O(n \log n)$. Thus we have:

[**Theorem 8.**] Each $3n$−step synchronization algorithm developed by Minsky and MacCarthy [9] and Yunés [19] have a $\Theta(n \log n)$ state-change complexity, respectively.

Based on [Theorem 8] and our description given in subsection 3.6, we can establish the following theorem.

[**Theorem 9.**] Goto's synchronization algorithm as reconstructed by Umeo [12] has a $\Theta(n \log n)$ state-change complexity.

Figure 6 shows a comparison between the state-change complexities in optimum-time synchronization algorithms.

5   A Comparison of Quantitative Aspects of Optimum-Time Synchronization Algorithms

Here, we present a table based on a quantitative comparison of optimum-time synchronization algorithms and their transition tables discussed above with respect to the number of internal states of each finite state automaton, the number of transition rules realizing the synchronization, and the number of state-changes on the array.

Table 1. Quantitative comparison of transition rule sets for optimum-time firing squad synchronization algorithms. The "*" symbol in parenthesis shows the correction and reduction of transition rules made in this paper. The "**" symbol indicates the number of states and rules obtained after the expansion of the original two-layer construction.

Algorithm	# of states	# of transition rules	State change complexity
Goto [1962]	many thousands	—	$\Theta(n \log n)$
Waksman [1966]	16	3216(202*)	$O(n^2)$
Balzer [1967]	8	182 (165 *)	$O(n^2)$
Gerken I [1987]	7	118 (105*)	$O(n^2)$
Mazoyer [1987]	6	120 (119*)	$O(n^2)$
Gerken II [1987]	32(155**)	347(2371**)	$\Theta(n \log n)$

6   One-Sided Versus Two-Sided Recursive Algorithms

Firing squad synchronization algorithms have been designed on the basis of parallel divide-and-conquer strategy that calls itself recursively in parallel. Those recursive calls are implemented by generating many *Generals* that are responsible for synchronizing divided small areas in the cellular space. In Fig. 7, we show two recursive synchronization schemes. If all of the recursive calls for the synchronization are issued by *Generals* located at one (both two) end(s) of partitioned cellular spaces for which the *General* is responsible, the synchronization algorithm is said to have *one-sided* (*two-sided*) recursive property. As for those algorithms discussed, we have the following observation:

[**Observation 6.1**] Optimum-time synchronization algorithms developed by Balzer [1], Gerken [2] and Waksman [18] are two-sided ones. The algorithm proposed by Mazoyer [6] is a one-sided one.

Now we propose a general design scheme for one-sided recursive optimum-time synchronization algorithms that can synchronize any n cells in $2n - 2$ steps. Figure 8 is a time-space diagram for an optimum-time one-sided recursive synchronization algorithm. The *General* G_0 generates an infinite number of signals $w_0, w_1, w_2, ..,$ to generate *Generals* G_1, G_2, .., by dividing the array recursively with the ratio x/y, where x, y is any positive integer such that $2x \le y$. The generated i-th *General* $G_i (i \ge 1)$ does the same operations as G_0 does. When $x = 1, y = 2$, the scheme coincides with the Mazoyer's algorithm [6]. It is noted that, in this case, we need no delay for the generation of *Generals*. We can establish the following theorem.

[**Theorem 10.**] The one-sided recursive scheme given above can synchronize any n cells in $2n - 2$ optimum steps.

7   Recursive Versus Non-recursive Algorithms

As is shown in the previous section, the optimum-time synchronization algorithms developed by Balzer [2], Gerken [3], Mazoyer [6] and Waksman [18] are *recursive* ones. On the other hand, it is noted that overall structure of the recon-

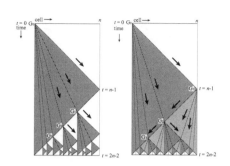

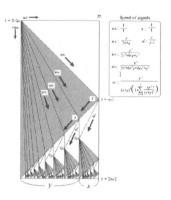

Fig. 7. One-sided recursive synchronization scheme (left) and two-sided recursive synchronization scheme (right).

Fig. 8. Time-space diagram for optimum-time one-sided recursive synchronization algorithm.

structed Goto's algorithm [12] is a *non-recursive* one, however divided subspaces are synchronized by using recursive $3n + O(1)$-step synchronization algorithms.

8 Finite Versus Infinite Number of Signals

Waksman [18] devised an efficient way to cause a cell to generate infinite signals at propagating speeds of $1/1, 1/3, 1/7, .., 1/(2^k - 1)$, where k is any natural number. These signals play an important role in dividing the array into two, four, eight, ..., equal parts synchronously. The same set of signals is used in Balzer [2]. Gerken [3] had a similar idea in the construction of his seven-state algorithm. Thus an infinite set of signals is used in the first three algorithms. On the other hand, finite sets of signals with propagating speed $\{1/5, 1/2, 1/1\}$ and $\{1/3, 1/2, 3/5, 1/1\}$ are made use of in Gerken [2] and the reconstructed Goto's algorithm [12], respectively.

9 A Comparison of Qualitative Aspects of Optimum-Time Synchronization Algorithms

Here, we present a table based on a qualitative comparison of optimum-time synchronization algorithms with respect to one/two-sided recursive properties and the number of signals being used for simultaneous space divisions.

10 O(1)-Bit Versus 1-Bit Communication CA Model

In the study of cellular automata, the amount of bit-information exchanged at one step between neighboring cells has been assumed to be $O(1)$-bit. A 1-bit inter-cell communication model is a CA in which inter-cell communication is

Table 2. A qualitative comparison of optimum-time firing squad synchronization algorithms.

Algorithm	One-/two-sided	Recursive/non-recursive	# of signals
Goto [1962]	—	non-recursive	finite
Waksman [1966]	two-sided	recursive	infinite
Balzer [1967]	two-sided	recursive	infinite
Gerken I [1987]	two-sided	recursive	infinite
Mazoyer [1987]	one-sided	recursive	infinite
Gerken II [1987]	two-sided	recursive	finite

restricted to 1-bit data, referred to as the 1-bit CA model. The next state of each cell is determined by the present state of that cell and two binary 1-bit inputs from its left and right neighbor cells. A precise definition of the 1-bit CA can be found in Umeo and Kamikawa [13]. Mazoyer [7] and Nishimura, Sogabe and Umeo [11] each designed an optimum-time synchronization algorithm on a 1-bit CA model, based on Balzer's algorithm and Waksman's algorithm, respectively. [**Theorem 11.**] [7, 11, 14] There exists a 1-bit CA that can synchronize n cells in optimum $2n - 2$ steps.

11 Summary

Cellular automata researchers have reported that several errors are included in Waksman's transition table. However, the validity of the transition rule sets designed thus far has never been confirmed. This was one of our motivations that we started our study. In the present paper, we have examined via computer the state transition rule sets for which optimum-time synchronization algorithms have been designed over the past forty years. The first transition rule set designed by Waksman [18] includes fundamental errors that cause unsuccessful firings and ninety-three percent of the rules are redundant. In addition, the transition rule sets given by Balzer [1], Gerken [2] and Mazoyer [6] also include redundant rules. The authors think that it is worthy of publishing such smallest transition rule sets for the famous firing squad synchronization algorithms, and they are useful and important for researchers who might have interests in those transition rule sets that realize the classical optimum-time firing algorithms quoted frequently in the literatures. We have presented a survey and a comparison of the quantitative and qualitative aspects of the optimum-time synchronization algorithms developed thus far for one-dimensional cellular arrays.

References

1. R. Balzer: An 8-state minimal time solution to the firing squad synchronization problem. *Information and Control*, vol. 10 (1967), pp. 22-42.
2. Hans-D., Gerken: Über Synchronisations - Probleme bei Zellularautomaten. *Diplomarbeit*, Institut für Theoretische Informatik, Technische Universität Braunschweig, (1987), pp. 50.

3. E. Goto: A minimal time solution of the firing squad problem. *Dittoed course notes for Applied Mathematics* 298, Harvard University, (1962), pp. 52-59, with an illustration in color.

4. E. Goto: Some puzzles on automata. in *Toward computer sciences* (T. Kitagawa ed.), Kyouritsu, (1966), pp. 67-91 (in Japanease).

5. J. Mazoyer: An overview of the firing squad synchronization problem. *Lecture Notes on Computer Science*, Springer-Verlag, vol. 316 (1986), pp. 82-93.

6. J. Mazoyer: A six-state minimal time solution to the firing squad synchronization problem. *Theoretical Computer Science*, vol. 50 (1987), pp. 183-238.

7. J. Mazoyer: On optimal solutions to the firing squad synchronization problem. *Theoretical Computer Science*, vol. 168 (1996), pp. 367-404.

8. J. Mazoyer: A minimal-time solution to the FSSP without recursive call to itself and with bounded slope of signals. Draft version, (1997), pp. 8.

9. M. Minsky: *Computation: Finite and infinite machines.* Prentice Hall, (1967), pp. 28-29.

10. E. F. Moore: The firing squad synchronization problem. in *Sequential Machines, Selected Papers* (E. F. Moore, ed.), Addison-Wesley, Reading MA., (1964), pp. 213-214.

11. J. Nishimura, T. Sogabe and H. Umeo: A design of optimum-time firing squad synchronization algorithm on 1-bit cellular automaton. *Proc. of the 8th International Symposium on Artificial Life and Robotics*, Vol.2 (2003), pp. 381-386.

12. H. Umeo: A note on firing squad synchronization algorithms-A reconstruction of Goto's first-in-the-world optimum-time firing squad synchronization algorithm. *Proc. of Cellular Automata Workshop*, M. Kutrib and T. Worsch (eds.), (1996), pp. 65.

13. H. Umeo and N. Kamikawa: A design of real-time non-regular sequence generation algorithms and their implementations on cellular automata with 1-bit inter-cell communications. *Fundamenta Informaticae*, 52 (2002), pp. 257-275.

14. H. Umeo, J. Nishimura and T. Sogabe: 1-bit inter-cell communication cellular algorithms (*invited lecture*). *Proc. of the Tenth Intern. Colloquium on Differential Equations*, held in Plovdiv in 1999, *International Journal of Differential Equations and Applications*, vol. 1A, no. 4 (2000), pp. 433-446.

15. H. Umeo, T. Sogabe and Y. Nomura: Correction, optimization and verification of transition rule set for Waksman's firing squad synchronization algorithm. *Proc. of the Fourth Intern. Conference on Cellular Automata for Research and Industry*, Springer, (2000), pp. 152-160.

16. R. Vollmar: On Cellular Automata with a Finite Number of State Change. *Computing, Supplementum*, vol. 3(1981), pp. 181-191.

17. R. Vollmar: Some remarks about the "Efficiency" of polyautomata. *International Journal of Theoretical Physics*, vol. 21, no. 12 (1982), pp. 1007-1015.

18. A. Waksman: An optimum solution to the firing squad synchronization problem. *Information and Control*, vol. 9 (1966), pp. 66-78.

19. J. B. Yunes: Seven-state solution to the firing squad synchronization problem. *Theoretical Computer Science*, 127, pp.313-332, (1994).

A Cellular Automaton Model for an Immune-Derived Search Algorithm*

Niloy Ganguly and Andreas Deutsch

Center for High Performance Computing, Dresden University of Technology,
Dresden, Germany. {niloy, deutsch}@zhr.tu-dresden.de

Abstract. Decentralized peer to peer ($p2p$) networks like Gnutella are
so successful because they are robust and require no centralized direc-
tories and no precise control over network topology. In this paper, we
develop an efficient search algorithm for $p2p$ networks with the help of
a 2-dimensional Cellular Automaton (CA) model. The rules followed by
each individual cell of the CA are inspired by concepts of natural immune
systems whereby the query message packets in the network are spread
through opportunistic proliferation. Through a series of experiments, we
compare proliferation with different variants of random walk algorithms.
The detailed experimental results show message packets undergoing proliferation, spread much faster in the network and consequently produce
better search output in $p2p$ networks. Moreover, experimental results
show that proliferation rules are extremely scalable and their performance is largely insensitive to the change in dimension of the CA grid.

1   Introduction

Significant research efforts have recently been undertaken in the development
of peer-to-peer ($p2p$) computing systems. Due to their flexibility, reliability and
adaptivity, $p2p$ solutions can overcome a lot of disadvantages of client-server
systems, and can fit to the dynamically changing Internet environment [7]. This
explains the large popularity of file sharing systems like Gnutella [2], Napster
[1], and Freenet [3].

Among different desirable qualities of a search algorithm, robustness is a very
important property. That is, the performance of a search algorithm should not
radically deteriorate in face of the dynamically changing network. As is known,
the big share of Internet users, consequently participants in $p2p$ networks, leave
the community ($p2p$ network) at very short intervals. Thus in order to give
robustness a high priority, algorithms generally avoid precise routing algorithms
for forwarding query message packets. However, flooding-based query algorithms
used by the networks produce enormous amounts of traffic which substantially
slows down the system. Recently flooding is increasingly replaced with different
variants of more efficient k-random walkers[1] algorithms [5].

---

* This work was partially supported by the Future & Emerging Technologies unit of
the European Commission through Project BISON (IST-2001-38923).

[1] A system where there are k message packets each performing a random walk, independently.

P.M.A. Sloot, B. Chopard, and A.G. Hoekstra (Eds.): ACRI 2004, LNCS 3305, pp. 61–70, 2004.

The goal of this paper is to study more-efficient alternatives to the existing k-random walkers algorithms, which form the base algorithm for a large class of $p2p$ networks. In this respect, we draw our inspiration from the natural immune system. *Our algorithm has been inspired by the simple and well known concept of the humoral immune system where B cells upon stimulation by foreign antigens undergo proliferation generating antibodies. The increasing number of antibodies consequently efficiently track down the antigens.*

In this paper, we develop a 2-dimensional Cellular Automaton model to simulate the $p2p$ environment. Performance by different random walk and proliferation techniques is evaluated with the help of the 2-dimensional CA. Hence in the next section, we detail the CA model used to abstract the $p2p$ environment. The experimental results are noted in *Section 3*.

2   Modeling and Evaluation Methodology

In this section, we elaborate the two-dimensional CA model. Both state definition of each cell of the CA as well as the rules guiding the state transition behavior of the cells are defined. The transition rules can be divided into two parts, rules which are common to both proliferation and random walk techniques and rules which are unique to one of these techniques. In *Section 2.1*, we describe the features common to all the processes, whereas in *Section 2.2*, we explain the unique rules.

2.1 CA Model

It is impossible to model all the dynamics of a $p2p$ system. In this paper, we are not attempting to resolve minor quantitative disparities between k-random walk and proliferation algorithms, but instead are trying to reveal fundamental qualitative differences. While our simple models do not consider all aspects of reality, we hope they capture the essential features needed to understand the qualitative differences.

Each cell of the two-dimensional $(m \times n)$ CA represents a peer/node in a $p2p$ system. Each peer in the network (consequently cells in the CA) can communicate with four neighbors. The peers (cells) host some data which are searched by other peers (cells) during a search operation. For simplification, we have assumed that there are 1024 different types of data present in the network, each of which can be represented by a 10-bit string. Hence, each cell hosts a 10-bit data string (say) P which we also refer to as token.

The search operation is performed with the help of three rules - *Query Initiation Rule (QIR)*, *Query Processing Rule (QPR)* and *Query Forwarding Rule (QFR)*. Next these rules are explained one by one.

Query Initiation Rule (QIR): A query is initiated by a randomly selected peer which requests for some data (say M). To obtain an answer to the request, the peer floods message packets (M) into its neighboring peers. In order to receive these message packets, each cell of the CA maintains a message queue MQ. The length of the message queue is considered as unbounded. Like the tokens, there are 1024 unique query messages (M). The Query Initiation Rule is

Rule 1. QIR: *Form Message Packet M /*Pick an element M from Query Set Q*/*
Flood k message packets(M) into the neighbors.

Data and Query Distribution: The 1024 unique tokens (both data and query) are distributed according to Zipf's law. It is generally believed that the distribution of documents in the Internet follows *Zipf's law* [6]. In Zipf's distribution the frequency of occurrence of some event (here token/message) t, as a function of the rank i, where the rank is determined by the above frequency of occurrence, follows a power-law $t_i \propto \frac{1}{i^a}$. In the experimental setup, the Zipf's exponent (value of a) for both the data and query distribution is 1. The ranking in terms of frequency is the same, for both tokens and messages—for instance, the most popular token in the network is also the most popular query.

Query Processing Rule (QPR): Once the search is initiated, the messages hop from cell to cell in subsequent time steps. Whenever, a cell encounters a message packet, it checks whether the message has earlier visited this cell or not. In this connection, each cell maintains a field named V. If the message has not previously visited the cell, then the message is compared with P. A successful search is reported if $P = M$. A field SS which initially is set to 0 everywhere is updated to 1 in the respective cell to indicate a successful search.

Rule 2. QPR: *If (Message packet(M)) Start*
   $V++;$
   if ((V == 1) AND (P = M)), /*Report a match, V = 1 indicates first
   $SS = 1$ *time visit by a message*/*

Once the queries are processed, the messages have to be forwarded to the neighboring cells through a *query forwarding rule*. Each of the proliferation and random walk techniques has a unique *query forwarding rule* which will be defined in the next section. A summary of the common features is presented.

CA Model - Summary: The states, rules, neighborhood configuration and updation synchrony of each cell of the two dimensional CA is next summarized.

A. States: *Token P:* A 10-bit string which doesn't change over time.

Message Queue(MQ): A queue of messages of unbounded length.

Visit Count(V): A counter to track the number of messages visiting the cell.

Success Indicator(SS): A one bit switch which is set to one if there is a successful search. MQ, SS and V are initialized to 0 at the beginning of each search.

B. Rules: *Query Initiation Rule (QIR):* During every search operation it is executed once only by a cell randomly selected to initiate the search.

Query Processing Rule (QPR) & Query Forwarding Rule (QFR): These rules are executed by all the cells at each time step. QFR differs from process to process, which will be discussed in *Section 2.2.*

C. Neighborhood: Each cell has *four neighbors.* The rules are periodic in nature, that is, in effect, the CA is a two-dimensional toroidal grid.

D. Update Synchrony: The CA is *updated asynchronously;* the sequence in which cells get *updated is random*. The asynchronous update mimics the real-life environment, where peers in the *p2p* network update their states without maintaining any synchrony with the neighboring peers.

2.2   Query Forwarding Rule (QFR)

We here describe two proliferation- based and two random walk based *QFRs*. **Proliferation ($\mathcal{P}$):** In the proliferation scheme, packets undergo proliferation at each cell they visit. The proliferation is guided by a special function, whereby a message packet visiting a node proliferates to form N_{new} message packets which are thereby forwarded to the neighbors of the node.

Rule 3. *$\mathcal{P}$: If(Message packet(M)) Start*
            Produce N_{new} message packets(M)
            Spread the N_{new} packets to N_{new} randomly selected neighbors
of A

The function determining the value of 'N_{new}' ensures that $N_{new} \leq 4$, where 4 is the number of neighbors of any cell. The function is discussed in detail after we elaborate the proliferation rule which imposes restrictions in packet movement. **Restricted Proliferation ($\mathcal{RP}$):** The rule $\mathcal{RP}$, similar to $\mathcal{P}$, produces N_{new} messages. But these N_{new} messages are forwarded only if the node A has $\geq$ N_{new} free neighbors. By 'free', we mean that the respective cells haven't been previously visited by message M. If A has $\mathcal{Z}$ 'free' neighbors, where $\mathcal{Z} < N_{new}$, then only $\mathcal{Z}$ messages are forwarded, while the rest is discarded. However, if $\mathcal{Z}$ = 0, then one message is forwarded to a randomly selected neighbor.

Rule 4. *$\mathcal{RP}$: If (Message packet(M)), Start*
        Produce N_{new} message packets (M).
        $\mathcal{Z}$ = No of 'free' neighbors
        if ($\mathcal{Z} \geq N_{new}$)
            Spread the packets to N_{new} randomly selected neighbors of A
        else if ($\mathcal{Z} > 0$)
            Spread $\mathcal{Z}$ packets to $\mathcal{Z}$ free neighbors of A
            Discard the remaining (N_{new} - $\mathcal{Z}$) packets
        else
            Forward one message packet to a randomly selected neighbor of A
            Discard the remaining (N_{new} - 1) packets

We now elaborate the function used to control the amount of proliferation. **Proliferation Controlling Function:** We choose the proliferation of message packets at any cell A to be heavily dependent on the similarity between the message packet (M) and the token (P) of A. This is in line with the affinity based proliferation mechanism followed by immune systems. In this regard we define p, where $p = e^{-HD} \times \frac{\rho}{4}$, ρ represents the proliferation constant, it is identical for all nodes; HD is the Hamming distance[2] between the message (M)

---

[2] The number of bits which differ between two binary strings

and the information profile (P). With the help of the expression p, we define $P(\eta)$ - the probability of producing at least η packages during proliferation by the following equation.

$$P(\eta) = \sum_{i=\eta}^{4} \binom{4-1}{i-1} \cdot p^{i-1} \cdot (1-p)^{4-i}$$

The significance of the above equation is (a).the number of packets proliferating is ≥ 1 and ≤ 4; (b). when $HD = 0$, for $\rho = 4$, 4 packets always proliferate; (c). the probability of proliferation decreases exponentially if $\eta > \rho$; (d). for $HD > 0$, the probability of proliferation of η packets decreases exponentially for $\eta > 1$.

We now describe k-random walk and a restricted version of it.

k-random walk $(\mathcal{R}W)$: In k-random walk, the cell forwards the message packet to a randomly selected neighbors. The rule$(\mathcal{R}W)$ is represented as

Rule 5. $\mathcal{R}W$: If(Message packet(M)) Start
    Send the packet M to a randomly chosen neighbor peer

Restricted random walk $(\mathcal{R}RW)$: In $\mathcal{R}RW$, instead of passing the message (M) to any random neighbor, we pass on the message to any randomly selected 'free' neighbor. However, if there is no 'free' neighbor, we then pass on the message to any randomly selected neighbor.

Rule 6. $\mathcal{R}RW$: If (Message packet(M)) start
    Send the packet M to a randomly chosen 'free' neighbor peer
    If no 'free' neighbor
        Send the packet M to a randomly chosen peer

The next section describes various metrics used to compare performances of the algorithms.

2.3   Metrics

In this paper we focus on efficiency aspects of the processes solely, and use the following simple metrics in our abstract *p2p* networks. These metrics, though simple, reflect the fundamental properties of the different *query processing rules*. *Success rate:* The number of similar items (say $\mathcal{K}$) found by the query messages within a given time period, that is $\mathcal{K} = \sum_{i=1}^{N} SS_i$, where i represents each cell and N is the total number of cells.

Coverage rate: The amount of time required by the messages to cover a percentage of the network. The network is fully covered when the visit field - $V_i \geq 1$ in each cell of the CA.

Cost per search output: The number of messages required to output a successful search. In some sense, it is the inverse of the success rate, but it also provides different insights into the system, which we will discuss in the next section.

Bad visits (BV): The number of times the same message re-visits the same cell. If a message packet visits the same cell more than once, it amounts to wastage of that packet. $BV = \sum_{i=0,(if V_i \geq 1)}^{N} (V_i - 1)$. So, a good design should minimize the amount of *bad visits*.

3 Simulation Results

The experimental results compare efficiency of different *query processing rules* (rule 3 - 6). The efficiency comparison is carried out with respect to the metrics defined in *section 2.3*. Beside assessing efficiency, we also perform different scalability tests with the QFRs. In order to assess the efficiency of different QFRs, we have also to ensure fairness of 'power' among them which is elaborated next.

3.1 Fairness in Power

To ensure fair comparison among all the QFRs, we must ensure that each QFR ($\mathcal{P}$, $\mathcal{RP}$, $\mathcal{RW}$, $\mathcal{RRW}$) should participate in the network with the same 'power'. To provide fairness in 'power' between a proliferation QFR (say $\mathcal{P}$) and a random QFR (say $\mathcal{RW}$), we ensure that the total number of query packets used is roughly the same in both cases. Query packets determine the cost of the search; too many packets cause network clogging bringing down the efficiency of the system as a whole. It can be seen that the number of packets increases in the proliferation algorithms over the generations, while it remains constant in the case of random walk algorithms. Therefore the number of message packets - k in *Rule 1* is set in a way so that the aggregate number of packets used by each individual algorithm is roughly the same, that is, for $\mathcal{RW}$, $k_{\mathcal{RW}} = \frac{Tot\_Pack[\mathcal{P}]}{Tot\_Step[\mathcal{P}]}$, where $Tot\_Pack[\mathcal{P}]$ is the total number of message packets used by $\mathcal{P}$ to perform a particular experiment, while $Tot\_Step[\mathcal{P}]$ indicates the total number of time steps required to perform that task.

To ensure fairness in 'power' between two proliferation rules ($\mathcal{P}$ & $\mathcal{RP}$), we keep the proliferation constant ρ and the value of k the same for both processes. The value of k is generally set as $k = 4$, where each cell has 4 neighbors.

We are now reporting the major experimental results one by one.

3.2 Experimental Result – Network Coverage

To evaluate the time taken by the message packets to visit all the cells of the CA using different QFRs, we consider a 100×100 two-dimensional CA comprising of 10000 cells and perform the following *coverage* experiment.

Coverage experiment: In this experiment, upon initiation of a search (*Rule 1*) from a randomly selected cell, the CA is allowed to run till the message packets cover the entire network (all cells of CA^3). The experiment is repeated 500 times on randomly selected initial cells. During the experiment, we collect different statistic at every 10% of coverage of the network.

Fig. 1 plots statistic collected through *coverage* experiments. *Fig. 1(a)* shows the network coverage rate of the $\mathcal{RP}$, $\mathcal{P}$ algorithm at $\rho = 3$, as well as $\mathcal{RRW}$ and $\mathcal{RW}$ algorithms. The graph plots the % of network covered (x-axis) vs.the time taken to cover corresponding % of network (y-axis - semilog scale). From the figure, it is seen that the time taken to cover the network is much shorter in $\mathcal{RP}$ followed by $\mathcal{P}$, $\mathcal{RRW}$ and $\mathcal{RW}$.

---

[3] The term 'network' and 'CA' are used interchangeably throughout the section.

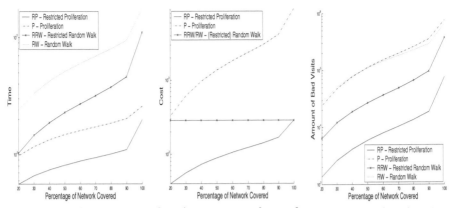

a. Number of time steps   b. Average number of   c. Number of bad visits.
required to cover the grid.   message packets used.

Fig. 1. Graphs plotting network coverage time, average message used, and number of bad visits by $\mathcal{P}$, $\mathcal{RP}$, $\mathcal{RW}$ and $\mathcal{RRW}$ (semilog scale).

Fig. 1(b) plots the average number of packets used by the different $QFRs$ (y-axis) vs. network coverage (x-axis). As expected, the number of packets increase in $\mathcal{RP}/\mathcal{P}$ over the period of network coverage while it remains constant for random walk ($\mathcal{RW}/\mathcal{RRW}$) schemes. Therefore, while performing *coverage* experiments, the value of k for $\mathcal{RRW}/\mathcal{RW}$ is set to the average number of message packets used by $\mathcal{RP}$ to cover 100% of the network. Although the proliferation constant is the same for $\mathcal{P}$ and $\mathcal{RP}$, from the figure it is seen that $\mathcal{P}$ produces enormous amount of messages, almost 10 times more than $\mathcal{RP}$. This happens because $\mathcal{P}$ indiscriminately proliferates. The tendency is further detailed through the next figure (*Fig. 1(c)*).

Fig. 1(c) shows the number of *bad visits* (defined in Sec. 2.3) by $\mathcal{RP}, \mathcal{P}, \mathcal{RRW}$ and $\mathcal{RW}$s (y-axis) vs. network coverage (x-axis). It is seen that execution of both $\mathcal{RW}$ and $\mathcal{P}$ results in a huge amount of *bad visits* due to their indiscriminate behavior. However, even though both $\mathcal{RRW}$ and $\mathcal{RP}$ generally inherently try to avoid already visited nodes, we find that $\mathcal{RP}$ can avoid such visits much more efficiently. (The number of bad visits by $\mathcal{RRW}$ is 10 times higher than $\mathcal{RP}$.) Therefore, we can conclude that $\mathcal{RP}$ by far outperforms all other techniques in terms of network coverage.

3.3   Experimental Results – Search Efficiency

To compare the search efficiency of $\mathcal{RP}$ & $\mathcal{RRW}$, we perform the *time-step* experiment on the 100×100 two-dimensional CA.

Time-step experiment: In the experiment, after initiation of a search (*Rule 1*), the CA is allowed to run for $\mathcal{N}$ ($= 50$) time steps. The search is initiated by a randomly selected node and the number of similar items (n_s) found within 50 time steps from the start of the search is calculated. The search output (n_s) is

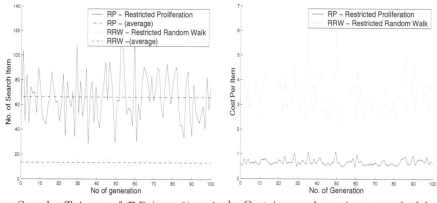

a. Search efficiency of $\mathcal{RP}$ ($\rho = 3$) and $\mathcal{RRW}$.

b. Cost incurred per item searched by $\mathcal{RP}$ ($\rho = 3$) and $\mathcal{RRW}$.

Fig. 2. Graphs showing search efficiency and cost incurred by $\mathcal{RP}$ and $\mathcal{RRW}$.

averaged over one generation (100 different searches), whereby we obtain N_s, where $N_s = \sum_{i=1}^{100} n_s/100$.

The graph of *Fig. 2(a)* displays the average value N_s against generation number for $\mathcal{RP}$ and $\mathcal{RRW}$. The search results for both $\mathcal{RP}$ and $\mathcal{RRW}$ show fluctuations. The fluctuations occur due to the difference in the availability of the searched items selected at each generation. However, on average, the search efficiency of $\mathcal{RP}$ is almost 5-times higher than that of $\mathcal{RRW}$. (For $\mathcal{RP}$, the number of hits ≈ 65, while it is ≈ 13 for $\mathcal{RRW}$.) The fluctuations in the results help us to understand an important aspect about cost which is discussed next.

Fig. 2(b) displays the cost/search item (the number of messages required to produce a search output) each scheme incurs to generate the performance of *Fig. 2(a)*. The cost of $\mathcal{RP}$ is hardly changing (it stays constant at around 0.7) even though the corresponding search output is differing hugely, while in $\mathcal{RRW}$ there is significant fluctuation in terms of cost. This can be easily understood from the fact that $\mathcal{RRW}$ always starts with the same number of packets irrespective of the availability of the items. Therefore, when the search output is low, the cost shoots up sharply. While in $\mathcal{RP}$, the packets are not generated blindly, but are instead regulated by the availability of the searched item. Therefore, if a particular searched item is sparse in the network, $\mathcal{RP}$ produces a lower number of packets and vice versa.

3.4 Experimental Result – Scalability

In this section, we perform two different types of scalability tests. In the first type, we change the shape of the two-dimensional CA so far used, from the square CA (100×100) to a more rectangular shape, and observe the impact it creates on the efficiency of $\mathcal{RP}$ & $\mathcal{RRW}$. In the second case, we increase the dimension of the CA and observe the outcome.

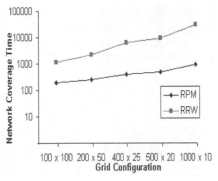
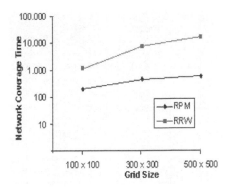

a. Network coverage time taken by $\mathcal{R}P$ and $\mathcal{R}RW$ with different shape of CA, each CA having 10000 cells.

b. Network Coverage time taken by $\mathcal{R}P$ and $\mathcal{R}RW$ at different CA size.

Fig. 3. Graphs illustrating scalability of $\mathcal{R}P$ and $\mathcal{R}RW$ under different conditions.

Shape and Scalability: In this experiment, we consider different two dimensional CAs each having 10000 cells. The dimensions of such CAs are respectively 100×100, 200×50, 400×25, 500×20, 1000×10. Testing the efficiency in all such configurations is particularly important because in real $p2p$ environments, we may not be able to develop exactly square connection among the peers and it is necessary for a proposed algorithm to perform well irrespective of the nature of connection layout. We perform the *coverage* experiments on these differently shaped CA; the experimental results are illustrated in *Fig. 3(a)*.

Fig. 3(a) plots the network coverage time (y-axis) taken by $\mathcal{R}P$ and $\mathcal{R}RW$ against different configuration (x-axis). For each, $\mathcal{R}P$ and $\mathcal{R}RW$, we plot the time taken to cover all the cells of the CA. The figure shows that for both $\mathcal{R}P$ and $\mathcal{R}RW$, as the shape becomes more rectangular, the network coverage time increases. For example, $\mathcal{R}P$ takes 198 time steps to cover the network when the CA is square, whereas it takes 1951 time steps when the CA has the dimension 1000×10. Whereas in case of $\mathcal{R}RW$, the respective figures rise from 1105 to 31025. That is, $\mathcal{R}P$ has a five-fold rise in network coverage time, while for $\mathcal{R}RW$ it increases by a factor of (around) 30.

Size and Scalability: To measure the performance of $\mathcal{R}P$ and $\mathcal{R}RW$ with respect to CAs of different sizes, we consider CAs of dimension 100×100, 300×300 and 500×500. We perform both *time-step* and *coverage* experiments with $\mathcal{R}P$ and $\mathcal{R}RW$ on the three CAs. In case of the *time-step* experiment, a scalable algorithm should ensure that the number of search outputs does not deteriorate with the increase in dimension. And this is indeed confirmed by our experiments for both $\mathcal{R}P$ and $\mathcal{R}RW$ (data not shown).

The more important test of scalability is elaborated through the next result derived by executing a *coverage* experiment and is depicted in *Fig. 3(b)*. *Fig. 3(b)* plots the time (y-axis) taken by $\mathcal{R}P$ and $\mathcal{R}RW$ to cover 100% of the network against different configuration (x-axis). The coverage time in $\mathcal{R}P$ increases from 198 (for 100×100) to 586 (for 500×500). The rate of increase is less than the logarithm of the rate of increase in the number of nodes. Any search algorithm in $p2p$ network with such low rate of increase is considered to be extremely scalable [4]. However, for $\mathcal{RRW}$, the network coverage time increases from 1105 to around 16161, increasing almost linearly with the number of nodes.

4   Conclusion

One of the most important functionalities of $p2p$ networks is *search*. In this paper, we have concentrated on developing efficient search algorithms for $p2p$ networks. We have produced detailed experimental results showing that the simple immune-inspired concept of proliferation can be used to cover the network more effectively than random walk. Moreover, the search efficiency of a rule based on proliferation ($\mathcal{RP}$) is five times higher than that of restricted random walk ($\mathcal{RRW}$) algorithms. The proliferation algorithm is extremely scalable. There is only minor deterioration in network coverage time with respect to changing shape and size. The effectivity of opportunistic proliferation rules we believe is a fundamental result and can be applied beyond the domain of the proposed $p2p$ search application. However, a detailed theoretical analysis to explain these interesting results has to be undertaken in the recent future to explore the full potential of the proliferation algorithm.

References

1. Napster. *http://www.napster.com*, 2000.
2. Gnutella. *http://www.gnutellanews.com*, 2001.
3. I. Clarke, O. Sandberg, B. Wiley, and T. W. Hong. Freenet: A Distributed Anonymous Information Storage and Retrieval System. In *Designing Privacy Enhancing Technologies: International Workshop on Design Issues in Anonymity and Unobservability*, pages 46–59, 2000.
4. A. Deutsch, N. Ganguly, G. Canright, M. Jelasity, and K Monsen. Models for advanced services in AHN, P2P Networks. Bison Deliverable, www.cs.unibo.it/bison/deliverables/D08.pdf, 2003.
5. Q. Lv, P. Cao, E. Cohen, and S. Shenker. Search and Replication in Unstructured Peer-to-Peer Networks. In *Proceedings of the 16th ACM International Conference on Supercomputing*, June 2002.
6. K Sripanidkulchai. The Popularity of Gnutella Queries and Its Implications on Scalability. In O Reilly's www.openp2p.com, February 2001.
7. H. Unger and M. Wulff. Cluster-building in P2P-Community Networks. In *Parallel and Distributed Computing and Systems (PDCS 2002)*, pages 685–690, 2002.

Randomized Computation with Cellular Automata

Bastien Chopard[1] and Marco Tomassini[2]

[1] Computer Science Department, University of Geneva, Switzerland
bastien.chopard@cui.unige.ch
[2] Information Systems Department, University of Lausanne, Switzerland
marco.tomassini@hec.unil.ch

Abstract. This paper exploits the fact that an asynchronous cellular automata naturally provides a randomized algorithm. We study the possibility to repeat many runs over the same problem instance to improve the quality of the answer. We consider the case of the so-called density task and quantify the interest of the approach. In addition we show that almost 100% of success can be achieved provided that the density task is allowed to classify the configuration in three rather than two classes.

1 Introduction

Cellular Automata (CAs) are discrete dynamical systems that have been used for simulating physical, chemical, social, and biological systems that are difficult or impossible to model using differential equations or other standard mathematical methods [3]. Usually, one assumes that the cells of a CA are formally updated simultaneously. However, perfect synchronicity is only an abstraction: if CAs are to model physical or biological situations or are to be considered physically embodied computing machines then the synchronicity assumption is no longer adequate. In fact, in any spatially extended system signals can only travel at finite speeds. Hence, for given dimensions it is impossible for a signal emitted by a global clock to reach any two computing elements at exactly the same time. In biological and sociological environments agents act at different, and possibly uncorrelated, times which seems to preclude a global clock in many cases. In previous work, we have shown that one can evolve asynchronous CAs for computation, in particular for the density task [10]. Although asynchronous CAs proved to be less efficient than their synchronous counterparts, they have the important advantage of being more robust in noisy environments.

A randomized algorithm is a computation whose evolution is driven by random choices. It produces a different output each time it is executed, even if the input data is the same [7,8]. Repeating several time a randomized algorithm on the same problem instance reduces and bounds the possibility of errors. In many cases, randomized algorithms are known to be more efficient than their deterministic counterparts. Here, we apply the principles of randomized computation to improve the performance of an asynchronous CA for the density task.

P.M.A. Sloot, B. Chopard, and A.G. Hoekstra (Eds.): ACRI 2004, LNCS 3305, pp. 71–80, 2004.

The paper is organized as follows. Section 2 briefly describes synchronous and asynchronous CAs. Section 3 describes the density task. In section 4 we describe our randomized computation. Section 5 reports on the experiments and the results. Finally, section 6 presents our conclusions.

2   Synchronous and Asynchronous Cellular Automata

CAs are dynamical systems in which space and time are discrete. A standard CA consists of an array of cells, each of which can be in one of a finite number of possible states, updated synchronously in discrete time steps, according to a local, identical transition rule. Here we will only consider boolean automata for which the cellular state $s \in \{0, 1\}$. The transition rule contained in each cell is specified in the form of a rule table, with an entry for every possible neighborhood configuration of states. The state of a cell at the next time step is determined by the current states of a surrounding neighborhood of cells. The regular cellular array (grid) is d-dimensional, where $d = 1, 2, 3$ is used in practice. For one-dimensional grids, a cell is connected to r local neighbors (cells) on either side where r is referred to as the *radius* (thus, each cell has $2r + 1$ neighbors, including itself). The term *configuration* refers to an assignment of ones and zeros to all the cells at a given time step t. It can be described by $\mathbf{s}^t = (s_0^t, s_1^t, \ldots, s_{N-1}^t)$, where N is the lattice size. The CAs used here are linear with periodic boundary conditions $s_{N+i}^t = s_i^t$ i.e., they are rings.

To visualize the behavior of a CA one can use a two-dimensional space-time diagram, where the horizontal axis depicts the configuration at a certain time t and the vertical axis depicts successive time steps (for example, see figure 1). In the figures state 1 is black, and state 0 is white.

As noted before, asynchronous CA are physically more reasonable than parallel ones. However, there are many ways for sequentially updating the cells of a CA (for a discussion of this point, see [9,10]). The most general and unbiased way is *independent random ordering* of updates in time, which corresponds to a Poisson stochastic process. We use a close approximation to it which consists in randomly choosing the cell to be updated next, with replacement. This corresponds to a binomial distribution for the update probability, of which the Poisson distribution is the limiting case for large N.

It should be noted that because our chosen asynchronous updating is nondeterministic, the same CA may reach a different configuration after n time steps on the same initial distribution of states, which is of course not the case for synchronous CA. This is because the trajectory in configuration space that is followed depends on the evaluation order of the cells for asynchronous CA, while there is a single possible sequence of configurations for a synchronous CA for a given initial configuration of states (see, e.g. figure 1).

3   The Cellular Automata Density Problem

The density task is a prototypical distributed computational problem for CAs. For a finite CA of size N it is defined as follows. Let ρ^0 be the fraction of 1s in the initial configuration (IC) s^0. The task is to determine whether ρ^0 is greater than or less than $1/2$. In this version, the problem is also known as the *majority* problem. If $\rho^0 > 1/2$ then the CA must relax to a fixed-point configuration of all 1's that we indicate as $(1)^N$; otherwise it must relax to a fixed-point configuration of all 0's, noted $(0)^N$, after a number of time steps of the order of the grid size N (if N is odd one avoids the case $\rho^0 = 0.5$).

This computation is trivial for a computer having a central control. Indeed, just scanning the array and adding up the number of, say, 1 bits will provide the answer in $O(N)$ time. However, it is nontrivial for a small radius one-dimensional CA since such a CA can only transfer information at finite speed relying on local information exclusively, while density is a global property of the configuration of states [6].

It has been shown that the density task cannot be solved perfectly by a uniform, two-state CA with finite radius [4], although a slightly modified version of the task can be shown to admit perfect solution by such an automaton [2]. The *performance* P of a given rule on the majority task is defined as the fraction of correct classifications over 10^4 randomly chosen ICs. The ICs are sampled according to a binomial distribution (i.e., each bit is independently drawn with probability $1/2$ of being 0). Clearly, this distribution is strongly peaked around $\rho^0 = 1/2$ and thus it makes a difficult case for the CA to solve.

But the lack of a perfect solution does not prevent one from searching for imperfect solutions of as good a quality as possible. In general, given a desired global behavior for a CA, it is extremely difficult to infer the local CA rule that will give rise to the emergence of a desired computation. Since exhaustive evaluation of all possible rules is out of the question except for elementary ($d = 1, r = 1$) automata, one possible solution of the problem consists in using evolutionary algorithms, as first proposed by Mitchell *et al.* [5,6].

In a recent work [10], we evolved asynchronous CAs for the density task with a genetic algorithm (see 1). Compared with synchronous CAs for the same task, we found that the asynchronous version is slightly less efficient but it has better fault-tolerance capabilities, which is an important feature in noisy environments. Figure 1 shows two executions of the evolved asynchronous CA on the same initial configuration. Its performance on the density task is $P = 67.2\%$. In this work, we do not deal with robustness due to the update mode of the CA, but rather we try to enhance the performance of the asynchronous CA by using a randomized computation scheme.

4   Randomized Algorithms

4.1   General Concepts

Randomized algorithms have become popular in computer science since, in many cases, a randomized algorithm is simpler and faster than a deterministic algorithm [1,7]. For instance, randomized algorithms exist that run in polynomial time, while no polynomial-time deterministic algorithm exist for the problem,

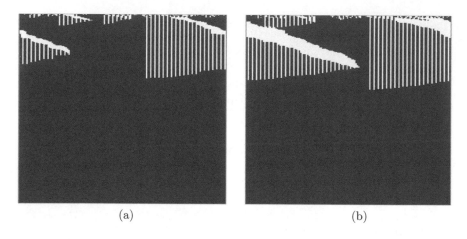

(a)   (b)

Fig. 1. Space-time diagrams of an asynchronous CA for the density task. The density $\rho^0 = 0.55$ in both (a) and (b) and the initial state configuration is the same. The different time evolution is due to the nondeterminism of the updating policy.

like primality testing [8]. But there is a price to pay for that: a randomized algorithm performs random choices during some of its steps and thus, if executed several times, it does not exhibits the same behavior.

The so-called Las-Vegas randomized algorithms are characterized by a completion time that varies from one run to another [1]. Sometimes, a Las-Vegas run may not finish. It this case, a second run, with the same problem instance may well finish in an acceptable time.

In the so-called Monte-Carlo randomized algorithms, given an instance of a problem, the value of the solution should be regarded as a random variable [1]. Randomized Monte Carlo algorithms cannot guarantee that false answers will be avoided. Therefore it is important to estimate the probability p_s that, on a given instance s, the algorithm yields a correct answer. If $p_s > 1/2$, the probability of an error can be brought down to any desired finite level, provided that the experiment is repeated a sufficient number of times. This property is known as stochastic amplification and can be understood as follows. If we call p the probability of computing the correct result in a run, then the probability that the algorithm gives the correct answer on the input i times in k runs is binomially distributed, since the runs are independent Bernoulli random variables:

$$Prob(k, i) = \binom{k}{i} p^i (1 - p)^{k-i}$$

Thus, the probability of answering correctly is:

$$Prob((r_i = r) > k/2) = \sum_{i=k/2+1}^{k} \binom{k}{i} p^i (1 - p)^{k-i}$$

By using a normal approximation to the binomial distribution, one finds for example that, for $k = 42$ runs and with $p = 0.672$, i.e. the performance of the rule, the probability of getting at least $i = 22$ correct answers, and thus of correctly classifying the configuration, is about 0.98. Note that we used $p = 0.672$ in this example because it corresponds to the performance of one run of our asynchronous CA sampled over 10^4 different initial configuration. However, this value is not the average probability of success of the algorithm over the sampled configuration.

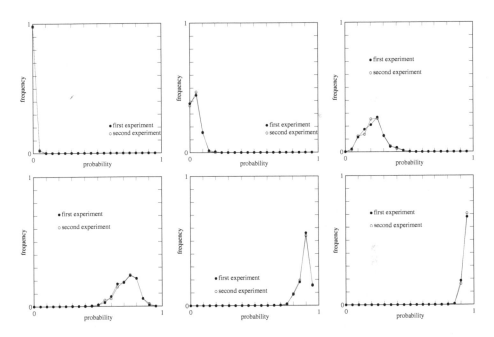

Fig. 2. Histogram of the probabilities that a configuration of given density ρ^0 is evolved by the asynchronous CA to the fixed point $(1)^N$. with all ones. The probability range has been divided in 20 bins. The number of configurations in each bin is normalized by the total number of configurations (1000). System size is $N = 149$ and the number of repetition is $N_r = 100$.

4.2   The Random Behavior of the Asynchronous CA

As described previously, on configuration $\mathbf{s}^0$, the asynchronous CA reaches one of the two fixed points $(1)^N$ or $(0)^N$ in a number t_∞ of site updates. If the algorithm is run only once, the output is $\rho^0 > 1/2$ if configuration $(1)^N$ is reached and $\rho^0 < 1/2$ if the final state is $(0)^N$. Obviously, this is not always the correct answer regarding to the actual density of $\mathbf{s}^0$. Unfortunately, the probability $p_{\mathbf{s}^0}$ that this procedure gives the right answer is not known and varies very much from one configuration to the other.

Note also that the time t_∞ needed to reach one of these two possible fixed points also depends on the updating path. Thus, the asynchronous CA for the density task is a randomized algorithm that behaves as a combination of a Monte-Carlo and Las-Vegas algorithm.

A natural way to improve the performance of the algorithm is to repeat it several time. If one considers N_r repetitions of the asynchronous CA on a chosen configuration s^0, we shall observe that in $N_{\to 1}$ cases, the CA has evolved to $(1)^N$ whereas, in $N_r - N_{\to 1}$ other cases, the final state is the null configuration $(0)^N$.

Therefore, we define $P_{\to 1}$ as the probability that configuration s^0 converges towards $(1)^N$. If the number N_r of repetitions of the algorithm is large, this probability can be estimated by

$$P_{\to 1}(s^0) = \frac{N_{\to 1}}{N_r} \tag{1}$$

This probability of converging to configuration 1 is quite dependent of the problem instance s^0. However, we expect that $P_{\to 1}$ will be small if ρ^0 is small, and large in the opposite case. But, for two initial configurations of same density, the corresponding $P_{\to 1}$ can be quite different, as shown in fig. 2.

Figure 2 shows the histogram of the values of $P_{\to 1}$ for 1000 configurations chosen randomly with various prescribed densities ρ. Practically speaking, these configurations are generated by a random permutation of the cells of a configuration containing the desired number of ones and zeros. The situation depicted in fig. 2 concerns a CA of size $N = 149$. For each configurations, $N_r = 100$ repetitions of the asynchronous CA runs are performed. The situation of fig. 2 corresponds to densities $\rho^0 = 0.35$, $\rho^0 = 0.4$, $\rho^0 = 0.45$, $\rho^0 = 0.55$, $\rho^0 = 0.6$ and $\rho^0 = 0.65$. The case of $\rho^0 = 0.5$ will be shown later on.

In order to evaluate the statistical significance of the curves obtained for 100 repetitions and 1000 configurations, each experiment has been conducted twice, i.e for two sets of 1000 random configurations. We see that, for these parameters, the algorithm gives quite reproducible results.

5   Classification Schemes

The purpose of the present asynchronous CA is to perform the density task, that is to classify each configuration s in different classes, according to the predicted value of ρ^0. In this section, we show how N_r repetitions of the CA evolution can be used for this task. We shall first consider a straightforward extension of the standard case $N_r = 1$ and show that the quality of the classification improves beyond that obtained with the synchronous CA [5] provided that N_r is large enough.

Then, we shall propose a new way to classify the configuration, using three classes instead of two. We show that this methods lead to an almost perfect classification scheme.

5.1   Classification in Two Classes

The natural way to exploit the result of our randomized algorithm is to base the classification process on the value of $P_{\to 1}$. The following pseudocode describes the randomized algorithm we have used to solve the density task:

- choose an initial configuration $\mathbf{s}^0$; set $N_{\to 1} = 0$
- do N_r independent runs of the CA on $\mathbf{s}^0$ and
  for each run, increment N_r if the final configuration is $(1)^N$
- Compute $P_{\to 1} = N_{\to 1}/N_r$
- if $P_{\to 1} > 1/2$ then predict $\rho^0 > 1/2$;
  else predict $\rho^0 < 1/2$;

Following the standard procedure to evaluate the quality of a CA algorithm to perform the density task [5], we consider 10^4 random configurations for which each cell is initialized to 1 with probability $1/2$. The performance α of the algorithm is then the fraction of these configurations that have been correctly classified.

We first give the performance α of our Monte-Carlo CA algorithm as a function of the number of repetition N_r. The result is shown in fig. 3 (a). We observe, as expected, that for $N_r = 1$, we obtain the result of [10], namely $\alpha \approx 0.67$.

Note that we take N_r as an odd number so that $P_{\to 1}$ is never one-half. As N_r increases, α gets larger, showing the stochastic amplification of repeating a Monte-Carlo algorithm several time. However, we observe a saturation of α.

The work done to improve the quality of the prediction increases as the number of repetition N_r increases. Here the work is defined as the average number of site updates that are needed in total to classify one of the 10^4 configurations. It is thus an indication of the average completion time of the algorithm over many instances. This work is proportional to N_r but, it is observed that the proportionality constant increases with the system size N. Table 1 summarizes our measurement of the work.

Table 1. Average normalized work for one run of the asynchronous and synchronous CA. The total work is normalized by the system size. Thus the given figures corresponds to the number of so-called Monte-Carlo steps (asynchronous case) or CA iterations (synchronous case). Data are obtained from an average over 10^4 configurations.

	$N = 149$	$N = 200$	$N = 500$
asynchronous	93	128	340
synchronous	83	112	282

In fig. 3 (b) we compare, as a function of the lattice size N, the work of both the synchronous (1 run[1]) and asynchronous CA (N_r runs) to obtain the same

---

[1] The synchronous CA cannot be repeated since it is deterministic. However random errors could be added to produce a randomized algorithm. This possibility has not been explored here

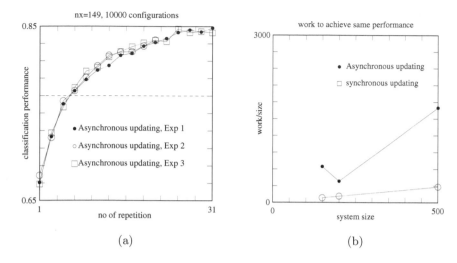

(a)   (b)

Fig. 3. (a) The performance of our Monte-Carlo CA algorithm for the density task, as a function of the number of its repetition on each instance. The lattice size is $N = 149$, and 10^4 configurations have been generated at random. The dashed line indicates the performance achieved with one run of synchronous updating, namely 0.77. **(b)** Work normalized to system size to achieve same performance with the asynchronous and synchronous scheme.

classification performance. We have considered the sizes $N = 149$, $N = 200$ and $N = 500$ for which the performances of the synchronous CA are 0.77, 0.75 and 0.73, respectively.

We see that the ratio work/performance of the synchronous CA is quite good compared to that of the asynchronous one. However, the synchronous CA has a maximum performance that cannot be improved, as opposed to the asynchronous one. In addition, it is argued that a VLSI implementation of an asynchronous CA would run faster than the synchronous version[2]. When $N = 200$, a factor of 4 in the hardware speed of the implementation would be necessary to make the randomized asynchronous CA faster than its deterministic counterpart while keeping the same classification performance.

5.2   Classification in Three Classes

The previous scheme can be improved by using three classes instead of two. Clearly, the configurations whose density is difficult to classify as larger or smaller than one-half are those configurations with a density close to one-half. These configurations turn out to also have a $P_{\to 1}$ spread around 0.5. This is well illustrated in fig. 4 (a) where we show the histogram of $P_{\to 1}$ for densities $\rho^0 = 0.4$, $\rho^0 = 0.5$ and $\rho^0 = 0.6$.

---

[2] A. Stauffer, private communication

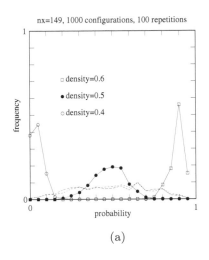
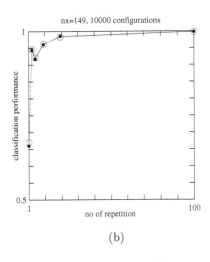

(a)   (b)

Fig. 4. (a) histogram of $P_{\to 1}$ for densities $\rho^0 = 0.4$, $\rho^0 = 0.5$ and $\rho^0 = 0.6$. The two dashed lines gives the histograms when, respectively, 1000 and 10'000 random configurations are visited (each bit generated with probability 1/2). **(b)** Score of the Monte-Carlo CA algorithm for the density task when the classification is made in three classes $\rho < 0.5$, $\rho > 0.5$ and $0.4 < \rho < 0.6$. The number of repetitions is $N_r = 1, 3, 5, 10, 20, 100$.

Figure 4 (a) suggests a new classification scheme. The rule we can extract is the following, for any configuration **s**.

- If $P_{\to 1} < 0.3$ then $\rho^0 < 0.5$
- If $P_{\to 1} > 0.75$ then $\rho^0 > 0.5$
- If $P_{\to 1} > 0.3$ and $P_{\to 1} < 0.75$ then $0.4 < \rho^0 < 0.5$

Note there is a slight asymmetry in the chosen threshold 0.3 and 0.75. These values are those suggested by figure 4 (a) but this issue has not been further investigated here.

It is important to stress that the three regions defined by the above conditions ($\rho < 0.5$, $\rho > 0.5$, $0.4 < \rho < 0.6$ overlap as a configuration can be at the same time in the region $0.4 < \rho < 0.6$ and $\rho < 0.5$ (or $\rho > 0.5$). However, the algorithm will classify each configuration in only one region. The information we get from these three classes is different from that given with the standard approach but not less. The pertinence of this classification depends the actual reason why the density task is performed.

Note that a classification in 3 regions is only possible with the randomized algorithm which gives an output $P_{\to 1}$ with more than two values.

The quality of this scheme is extremely good: over 95%, even for $N_r = 10$. Figure 4 (b) shows the performance we obtain as a function of N_r, for a system of size $N = 149$. It is possible that the thresholds used to define the three regions depend on the lattice size. This question has not been investigated yet.

Finally, the thresholds 0.3 and 0.75 on $P_{\to 1}$ can be adjusted to narrow the middle region ($0.4 < \rho^0 < 0.6$). However, this will decrease the score of the algorithm. More simulations would be required in order to obtain the relation between these threshold values and the algorithm performance.

6 Conclusions

In this paper we showed that an asynchronous CA for a global task can be naturally turned into a randomized, Monte-Carlo algorithm. It gives a different answer each time it is executed, even if it is on the same input data. By repeating it several times we can improve the performance of the classification of initial configuration with respect to their initial densities. The ratio work/performance of this approach is compared with that of the traditional synchronous approach.

We then propose a new way to perform the classification of the initial density ρ^0, using three classes: $\rho^0 < 1/2$, $\rho^0 > 1/2$ and $0.4 < \rho^0 < 0.6$. This possibility is offered by the random nature of the algorithm and yields more than 95% performance for a moderate cost.

Clearly, the combination of asynchronous CA and randomized algorithms offers new perspectives in the framework of global task computations.

References

1. G. Brassard and P. Bratley. *Fundamentals of Algorithms*. Prentice-Hall, 1994.
2. M. S. Capcarrere, M. Sipper, and M. Tomassini. Two-state, r=1 cellular automaton that classifies density. *Physical Review Letters*, 77(24):4969–4971, December 1996.
3. B. Chopard and M. Droz. *Cellular Automata Modeling of Physical Systems*. Cambridge University Press, Cambridge, UK, 1998.
4. M. Land and R. K. Belew. No perfect two-state cellular automata for density classification exists. *Physical Review Letters*, 74(25):5148–5150, June 1995.
5. M. Mitchell, J. P. Crutchfield, and P. T. Hraber. Evolving cellular automata to perform computations: Mechanisms and impediments. *Physica D*, 75:361–391, 1994.
6. M. Mitchell, P. T. Hraber, and J. P. Crutchfield. Revisiting the edge of chaos: Evolving cellular automata to perform computations. *Complex Systems*, 7:89–130, 1993.
7. R. Motwani and P. Raghavan. *Randomized Algorithms*. Cambridge University Press, 1995.
8. C. H. Papadimitriou. *Computational Complexity*. Addison-Wesley, Reading, Massachussetts, 1994.
9. B. Schönfisch and A. de Roos. Synchronous and asynchronous updating in cellular automata. *BioSystems*, 51:123–143, 1999.
10. M. Tomassini and M. Venzi. Evolving robust asynchronous CA for the density task. *Complex Systems*, 13(3):185–204, 2002.

Applying Cell-DEVS in 3D Free-Form Shape Modeling

Pengfei Wu, Xiuping Wu, and Gabriel Wainer

Department of Systems and Computer Engineering
Carleton University
1125 Colonel By Drive
Ottawa, ON, K1S 5B6, Canada
{pfwu, xpwu, Gabriel.Wainer}@sce.carleton.ca

Abstract. Modeling free-form shapes in 3D spaces based on strict physical laws require a considerable amount of computation time. Previous experiences with Cellular Automata demonstrated substantial improvements for these applications. Here, we describe an efficient approach applying the Cell-DEVS formalism to model the deformation of free-form shape objects in a 3D space. The objects are treated as virtual clay, and the values assigned to each cell in the model represent a certain amount of clay in the cell. The clay object is deformed in accordance with the physical conservation laws.

1 Introduction

3D modeling techniques have become increasingly attractive, ranging from CAD systems up to image morphing in computer graphics. The representation of solid 3D objects requires to use restrictive geometrical operations. Different studies on the simulation of such deformations for objects use strict physical models, such as finite element methods, methods based on elasticity theory, and applications of particle systems. All these methods and applications need considerable time for computing deformations according to the laws, and human interactions are not permitted especially for complex shapes.

Instead, imagining the 3D objects as clay that can be freely deformed, we can understand problems on 3D objects. Some of the undergoing efforts considering volume sculpting in a 3D virtual space use a discretization of the space in 2D or 3D cells. In [1], a solution based on Cellular Automata (CA) was presented. A 3D CA is used to simulate plastic deformations of clay, and each cell is allocated a finite state automaton, which is given the simple distribution rules of the virtual clay instead of complicated physical laws. Each automaton repeats state transitions according to the state of their neighbors. This approach tries to avoid the considerable computation time for plastic deformation and make the deformation process natural by showing the behavior of real clay. An extension of this work, presented in [2], includes new repartition algorithms.

We will show how to model a 3D free-form object using Cell-DEVS [3], and we will simulate deformation using the CD++ toolkit [4]. Cell-DEVS is a novel approach

P.M.A. Sloot, B. Chopard, and A.G. Hoekstra (Eds.): ACRI 2004, LNCS 3305, pp. 81–90, 2004.

to represent models of real systems as cell spaces. Cell-DEVS uses the DEVS (Discrete Events systems Specifications) formalism [5] to define a cell space where each cell is defined as a DEVS model. This technique permits to build discrete-event cell spaces, and it improves their definition by making the timing specification more expressive. The Cell-DEVS presented here describes the behavior of each cell in a 3D free-form virtual clay model using the state transition rules presented in [1]. This model describes effectively the behavior of free-form object: compression (from outside) and deformation (from inside).

2 Background

Cell-DEVS [3] is a combination of CA and DEVS [5] that allows the implementation of cellular models with timing delays. A Cell-DEVS model is defined as a lattice of cells holding a state variable and a computing apparatus to update the cell state. This is done using the present cell state and a set of inputs coming from cells in the neighborhood. Cell-DEVS improves execution performance of cellular models by using a discrete-event approach. It also enhances the cell's timing definition by making it more expressive [6]. Each cell, defined as $TDC=< X, Y, S, N, delay, d, \delta_{INT}, \delta_{EXT}, \tau, \lambda, D >$, uses N inputs to compute its next state. These inputs, which are received through the model's interface (X, Y), activate the local computing function (τ). State (s) changes can be transmitted to other models, but only after the consumption of a delay (d). Two kinds of delays can be defined: *transport* delays model a variable commuting time, and *inertial* delays, which have preemptive semantics (scheduled events can be discarded). Once the cell behavior is defined, a coupled Cell-DEVS is created by putting together a number of cells interconnected by a neighborhood relationship.

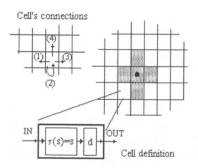

Fig. 1. Description of a Cell-DEVS model.

A coupled Cell-DEVS is composed of an array of atomic cells, with given size and dimensions, defined as $GCC = < Xlist, Ylist, X, Y, n, \{t_1,...,t_n\}, N, C, B, Z >$. Each cell is connected to its neighborhood through standard DEVS input/output ports. Border cells have a different behavior due to their particular locations. Finally, the model's external couplings can be defined in the Xlist and Ylist. Each cell in a Cell-DEVS is a DEVS atomic model, and the cell space is a DEVS coupled model. DEVS is an increasingly accepted modeling and simulation framework. DEVS is a sound formalism based on generic dynamic systems, including well defined coupling of components, and hierarchical modular construction. A DEVS model is described as a composite of submodels, each of them being behavioral (atomic) or structural (coupled). Each atomic model, defined by $AM = < X, Y, S, \delta_{ext}, \delta_{int}, \lambda, ta>$, has an interface consisting of input (X) and output (Y) *ports* to communicate with other models. Every state (S) in the model is associated with a time advance (*ta*) function, which determines the duration of the state. Once this time is consumed, an internal transition is triggered. At that moment, the model generates results through the output ports by activating an output function (λ). Then, an internal transition function (δ_{int}) is fired, producing a state change. Input external events, which are received in the input ports, activate the external transition function (δ_{ext}). Coupled models are defined as a set of basic components (atomic or coupled), which are interconnected through the model's interfaces. The model's coupling defines how to convert the outputs of a model into inputs for the others, and to inputs/outputs to the exterior of the model.

CD++ [4] is a modeling tool that was defined using DEVS and Cell-DEVS specifications. DEVS Atomic models can be incorporated onto a class hierarchy programmed in C++. Coupled models can be defined using a built-in specification language, in which the model is specified by including the size and dimension of the cell space, the shape of the neighborhood and borders. The cell's local computing function is defined using a set of rules with the form: POSTCONDITION DELAY { PRECONDITION }. These indicate that when the *PRECONDITION* is satisfied, the state of the cell will change to the designated *POSTCONDITION*, whose computed value will be transmitted to other components after consuming the *DELAY*.

3 A Virtual Clay Model

In virtual clay models, a 3D object deformation is considered as a physical process that equally distributes the virtual clay to the adjacent areas. A threshold is associated with the deformation of the object [1]: when the density is under the threshold, the object keeps its shape. If a portion receives an external force, its density changes; if the density is above the threshold, the object is deformed, and clay is transported from high-density to low-density portions. However, the total mass of the clay should be conserved. We model the object as a 3D Cell-DEVS. A positive value assigned to each cell represents the mass of clay in the piece. In [1], the authors define the model using a Margolus neighborhood, and the following rules for each block:

[Step A] For each cell i whose state is 1,

$$dm_i = m_i * \alpha;$$
$$m_i = m_i - dm_i;$$

[Step B] For each cell j whose state is 0,

$$m_j = m_j + ((dm_1 + dm_2 + ... + dm_t) / n);$$

where α is a constant rate for distribution ($0 < \alpha < 1$), t is the number of cells over threshold and n is the number of cells under threshold. Here, we denote the state of a cell as 1 if its virtual clay is over the threshold. Otherwise, the state is 0. The value dm_i represents the excessive clay in cell i, which will be distributed to the neighboring cells. From these two steps, we can see that the total mass of virtual clay within a block is conserved during the state transitions. Figure 3 illustrates the transition rules in 2D.

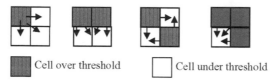

◼ Cell over threshold   ☐ Cell under threshold

Fig. 2. 2D block patterns.

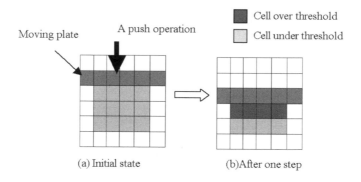

Moving plate   A push operation

◼ Cell over threshold
☐ Cell under threshold

(a) Initial state   (b)After one step

Fig. 3. Push operation by a moving plate.

The deformation of a virtual clay object is based on a push operation. The clay is transported from a cell into the adjacent ones along the direction of pushing. The surface of a virtual clay object can be pushed at most one cell in depth per step.

Figure 3 shows an example of the push operation by a moving plate. This plate is modeled as a set of special cells to which virtual clay cannot be distributed. When the threshold is surpassed as the result of pushing, virtual clay is distributed according to the transition rules. The state transitions are repeated until there are no cells over threshold (a stable state). The number of steps to reach the stable state depends on the total mass of virtual clay, the threshold and the parameter α.

4 Modeling a Virtual Clay Object in Cell-DEVS

We used Cell-DEVS model to simulate the behavior of the deformation of a virtual clay object. Our focus is on a 3D free-form object, using the transition rules presented in the previous section. Figure 4 illustrates the 3D Margolus neighborhood we used, in which the nearest 8 cells make one block. Similarly to the 2D neighborhood, each cell belongs to different blocks in odd and even steps.

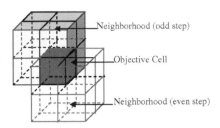

Fig. 4. 3D Margolus neighborhood

The values in each cell represent the density (mass) of that cell. A cell with a value of zero means this cell is out of the object, while a positive value means the cell is within the object. The final state contains the free-form object in stable state after deformation. The transition procedure is done in two stages as follows.

- Deformation: if there are cells with density over the threshold, the deformation transition rules are applied.
- Compression: we assume that there is a moving plate and the virtual clay next to the plate is transferred from a cell into the adjacent cell along the direction of pushing. In the model, this plate is handled as a dummy plate with each cell having a value of zero, staying right on top of the object.

During the transition procedure, each cell has its different neighbors at odd and even steps. The neighborhood of each cell is identified according to its location in the block. Meanwhile, each cell has different transition policies for the deformation and compression stages. Therefore, we used a four-dimensional Cell-DEVS model, in which each 3D hyperplane of (x, y, z) represents a set of state variables and the fourth dimension is a control variable, as follows.

- Hyperplane 0 (x, y, z, 0) represents the free form object.
- Hyperplane 1 (x, y, z, 1) defines the odd or even step so that each cell in Hyperplane 0 can identify its Margolus neighborhood.
- Hyperplane 2 (x, y, z, 2) is a control Hyperplane. Compression will be performed if (x, y, z, 2) = 1, and deformation if cell(x, y, z, 2) =0.

This Cell-DEVS coupled model is defined as follows:

$$Plastic = < Xlist, Ylist, X, Y, n, \{t_1,...,t_n\}, N, C, B, Z >.$$

$X=Y=Xlist=Ylist= \emptyset$; $S = \{s| \ s >= 0, s\in R \}$; $n=4$; $t_1=10$; $t_2=9$; $t_3=12$; $t_4=12$;

$N = \{(-1,-1,-1,0),(-1,0,-1,0),(-1,1,-1,0),(0,-1,-1,0),(0,0,-1,0),(0,1,-1,0),(1,-1,-1,0),$
$(1,0,-1,0),(1,1,-1,0),(-1,-1,0,0),(-1,0,0,0),(-1,1,0,0),(0,1,0,0),(0,0,0,0),(0,1,0,0),$
$(1,-1,0,0),(1,0,0,0),(1,1,0,0),(-1,-1,1,0),(-1,0,1,0),(-1,1,1,0),(0,-1,1,0),(0,0,1,0),$
$(0,1,1,0),(1,-1,1,0),(1,0,1,0),(1,1,1,0),(-1,-1,2,0),(-1,0,2,0),(-1,1,2,0),(0,-1,2,0),$
$(0,0,2,0),(0,1,2,0),(1,-1,2,0),(1,0,2,0),(1,1,2,0),(0,0,0,1),(0,0,0,2)\}$

The definition of this Cell-DEVS coupled model using CD++ is illustrated in Figure 5 below.

```
[plastic]
dim : (10,9,12,3)          delay : transport
border : nowrapped
neighbors:(-1,-1,-1,0)(-1,0,-1,0)(-1,1,-1,0)
(0,-1,-1,0)(0,0,-1,0)(0,1,-1,0)(1,-1,-1,0)
(1,0,-1,0)(1,1,-1,0)(-1,-1,0,0)(-1,0,0,0)(-1,1,0,0)
localtransition : deformation-rule
[deformation-rule]
...
```

Fig. 5. Cell-DEVS coupled model specification in CD++

This Cell-DEVS model that has three hyperplanes of 10*9*12 each. The cell's behavior is defined by the localtransition clause, and it will be discussed in detail in the following sections. We will present the rules at deformation and compression stages and show how the transformation is controlled in Cell-DEVS formalism. The rules can be generalized as follows.

1. Perform deformation if cell (0, 0, 0, 2) = 0 and this cell is on Hyperplane 0.
2. Perform compression if cell (0,0,0,2) = 1 and this cell is on Hyperplane 0
3. Even/odd step alternates if cell (0, 0, 0,1) = 0 and this cell is on Hyperplane 1
4. Deformation/compression control alternates if this cell is on Hyperplane 2

4.1 Deformation Rules in the Cell-DEVS Model

The deformation stage involves the activating different rules at odd and even steps, in which we decide the different neighbors that the objective cell receives clay from or distributes clay to. Only hyperplane 0 (x, y, z, 0) performs the deformation transition, while hyperplane 1 (x, y, z, 1) helps to judge whether the cell in Hyperplane 0 change in odd step or in even step and hyperplane 2 (x, y, z, 2) identify the deformation stage. In each step its neighborhood can be located in a 2x2x2 block. In Figure 6 we show the mechanism to select the Margolus block. The origin cell is colored in gray and its neighbors are defined according to the coordinates shown in the figure. We repeat the procedure for other cells in the same Margolus block to obtain the neighbors of each objective cell in the same hyperplane.

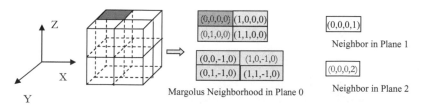

Margolus Neighborhood in Plane 0   Neighbor in Plane 2

Fig. 6. A cell and its neighborhood definition at the deformation stage

The pair < (x,y,z,0), (x,y,z,1) > define the step (odd or even). The neighbor on the hyperplane 0 is described in the figure, and its value, together with the value of all the neighbors in the same Margolus block, can be used to decide which transition rule should be applied. The deformation rules can be generalized as follows (the detailed definition of these rules in CD++ can be found in [7].

- Cells **gain** clay from neighbors on hyperplane $(x,y,z,0)$ if $(0,0,0,2) = 0$, $(0,0,0,0)$ is below the threshold, and at least one neighbor is above the threshold.
- Cells **distribute** clay to neighbors on Hyperplane $(x,y,z,0)$ if $(0,0,0,2) = 0$, $(0,0,0,0)$ is above threshold and at least one neighbor is under threshold.

4.2 Compression Rules in the Cell-DEVS Model

Similar to deformation, the compression only takes place on hyperplane 0. Hyperplane 2 controls when compression occurs: only when cell $(x, y, z, 2) = 1$. During compression the clay in the cells right under the moving plate is transferred into the adjacent cells along the direction of pushing. The moving plate is represented by a set of cells with values of zero sitting on the top of the object. We assume the plate moves down along z-axis as shown in Figure 7. For each cell $(x,y,z,0)$, if all neighboring cells $(-1,-1,2,0)$, $(-1,0,2,0)$, $(-1,1,2,0)$, $(0,-1,2,0)$, $(0,0,2,0)$, $(0,1,2,0)$, $(1,-1,2,0)$, $(1,0,2,0)$, $(1,1,2,0)$ are zero and at least one of neighbor cells $(-1,-1,1,0)$, $(-1,0,1,0)$, $(-1,1,1,0)$, $(0,-1,1,0)$, $(0,0,1,0)$, $(0,1,1,0)$, $(1,-1,1,0)$, $(1,0,1,0)$, $(1,1,1,0)$ is greater than zero, the cell should gain all clay in its neighbor $(0,0,1,0)$. The neighbors of each cell are defined in Figure 7.

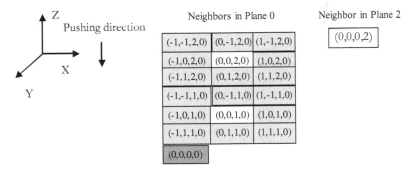

Fig. 7. A cell and its neighbor definition at the compression stage

The definition of these rules in CD++ is as follows:

```
[compression-rule]
%plate moving
rule : {(0,0,0,0)+(0,0,1,0)} 100 {(0,0,0,2)=1 and
cellpos(3)=0 and cellpos(0)>0 and cellpos(0)<9 and
cellpos(1)>0 and cellpos(1)<8 and cellpos(2) <10 and
((-1,-1,2,0)+(-1,0,2,0)+(-1,1,2,0)+(0,-1,2,0)+(0,0,2,0)
+(0,1,2,0)+(1,-1,2,0)+(1,0,2,0)+(1,1,2,0))=0 and
((-1,-1,1,0)+(-1,0,1,0)+(-1,1,1,0)+(0,-1,1,0)+(0,0,1,0)
```

```
+(0,1,1,0)+(1,-1,1,0) +(1,0,1,0)+(1,1,1,0))>0 }
%step 1: add the first row to the second row
rule : 0 100 {(0,0,0,2) = 1 and cellpos(3)=0 and
cellpos(0)>0 and cellpos(0)<9 and cellpos(1)>0 and
cellpos(1)<8 and cellpos(0) < 11 and ((-1,-1,1,0)+
(-1,0,1,0)+(-1,1,1,0)+(0,-1,1,0)+(0,0,1,0)+(0,1,1,0)+
(1,-1,1,0) +(1,0,1,0)+(1,1,1,0))=0 and ((-1,-1,0,0)+
(-1,0,0,0)+(-1,1,0,0)+(0,-1,0,0)+(0,0,0,0)+(0,1,0,0)+
(1,-1,0,0) +(1,0,0,0)+(1,1,0,0))>0}
%step2 :change the first row to 0, the plate has moved
one step further
```

Fig. 8. Cell-DEVS specification of the compression rules in CD++.

4.3 Control Hyperplane in Cell-DEVS Model

Hyperplane 2 controls when the deformation or compression stages occur. The value of each cell on hyperplane 2 switches between 0 (deformation) and 1 (compression). We assume that the transport delay of performing a compression step is 3000 ms, thirty times longer than the delay of a deformation. The 3D free-form object will reach stable state within 3000 ms if deformation occurs.

The transition rule for the control hyperplane is as follows.

- S ←1 if cell (0,0,0,1)=0 and cell (0,0,0,0) =0 and cell itself is on hyperplane 1
- S ←0 if cell (0,0,0,1)=0 and cell (0,0,0,0) =1 and cell itself is on hyperplane 1
- S ← 1 if cell (0,0,0,0) =0 and cell itself is on hyperplane 2
- S ← 0 if cell (0,0,0,0) =1 and cell itself is on hyperplane 2

The specification of these rules in CD++ is illustrated in Figure 9 below.

```
rule : 1 100 {(0,0,0,1)=0 and cellpos(3)=1 and
             (0,0,0,0)=0 }
rule : 0 100 {(0,0,0,1) = 0 and cellpos(3)=1 and
         (0,0,0,0)=1} %alternate Margolus neighborhood
rule : 1 3000 { cellpos(3)=2 and (0,0,0,0)=0 }
rule : 0 100 {cellpos(3)=2 and (0,0,0,0)=1}
%plate moving
```

Fig. 9. Cell-DEVS specification of control rules in CD++

5 Experimental Results

We executed this Cell-DEVS model, and studied the deformation process of a clay object. We studied each cell at different time steps (compression or deformation), and the total mass of the object was examined. We found that the total mass (represented by cells in hyperplane 0) was conserved for every transition.

Some of the results obtained are presented in Figure 10. We show several steps during the transition process, which includes the initial state, first three compression steps and some related deformation steps. Figure (b) shows the immediate result after the first compression step. Figures (c) and (d) show the object deformation. In Figure (d), a stable state is reached. Figure (e) to (i) show the repartition of clay after the second and third compression steps.

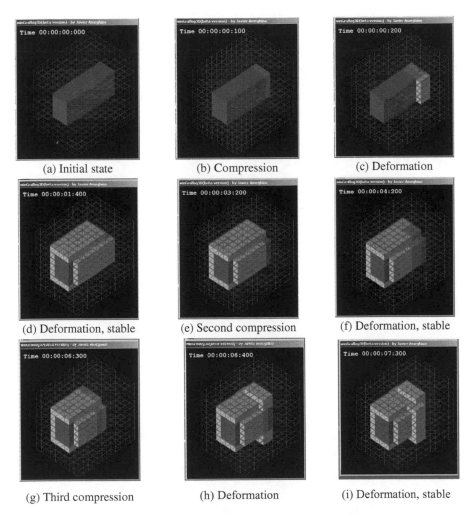

(a) Initial state (b) Compression (c) Deformation

(d) Deformation, stable (e) Second compression (f) Deformation, stable

(g) Third compression (h) Deformation (i) Deformation, stable

Fig. 10. The deformation of the free-form object using Cell-DEVS

6 Conclusion

We have showed how to model the deformation of 3D free-form object using the Cell-DEVS formalism. The total mass of the free-form object is conserved during the stages of deformation. The complex behavior has been simulated using simple and easy-to-understand transition rules. These rules are defined using the specification language in CD++, which is itself is simple and easy to learn. A similar study has been carried out in [1] and [2]. However, in their work, a sophisticated simulation program was developed in order to simulate this complex behavior. The simulation program is application-specific, which can not be applied to general cases. By applying the Cell-DEVS formalism along with the CD++ toolkit support, more generality can be achieved. This allows us to model complex systems in a simple fashion. Likewise, changing parameters for studying simple conditions is straightforward. Cell-DEVS permits defining zones of cells with different behavior, which can be used to analyze objects composed of different materials. Likewise, Cell-DEVS models can be integrated with other DEVS and Cell-DEVS models, permitting defining multimodels interacting with each other, using different modeling techniques.

One of the key aspects to simulate the deformation is to understand the characteristics of the Margolus neighborhood. This has been studied and explored in the model specification. The results, which have been illustrated by a visualization tool have demonstrated the capability of Cell-DEVS modeling approach as well as the tool utilities. The behavior of the deformation is well simulated with a simple, easy-understood mechanism.

References

1. H. Arata, Y. Takai, N. K. Takai, T. Yamamoto: Free-form shape modeling by 3D cellular automata. Proceedings of the International Conference on Shape Modeling and Applications (1999)
2. S. Druon, A. Crosnier, L. Brigandat: Efficient Cellular Automata for 2D / 3D Free-Form Modeling. Proceedings of the 11th International Conference in Central Europe on Computer Graphics, Visualization and Computer Vision'2003 (2003)
3. G. Wainer, N. Giambiasi: N-dimensional Cell-DEVS. Discrete Events Systems: Theory and Applications, Kluwer, Vol.12. No.1 (January 2002) 135-157
4. G. Wainer: CD++: a toolkit to define discrete-event models. Software, Practice and Experience. Wiley. Vol. 32. No.3. (November 2002) 1261-1306
5. B. Zeigler, T. Kim, H. Praehofer: Theory of Modeling and Simulation: Integrating Discrete Event and Continuous Complex Dynamic Systems. Academic Press (2000)
6. G. Wainer, N. Giambiasi: Application of the Cell-DEVS paradigm for cell spaces modeling and simulation. Simulation, Vol. 76. No. 1. (January 2001)
7. P. Wu, X. Wu.: A model of 3D deformation of free-form shapes in Cell-DEVS. Technical Report SCE-03-006. Dept. of Systems and Computer Engineering. Carleton University. (2003)

Universality of Hexagonal Asynchronous Totalistic Cellular Automata

Susumu Adachi, Ferdinand Peper, and Jia Lee

Nanotechnology Group, National Institute of Information and Communications
Technology,
588-2, Iwaoka, Nishi-ku, Kobe, 651-2492, Japan
{sadachi, peper, lijia}@nict.go.jp

Abstract. There is increasing interest in cellular automata that update their cells asynchronously, i.e., at random times and independent of each other. Research, however, has been limited to either models of trivial phenomena, or models that require a global synchronization mechanism to induce nontrivial phenomena like computation. This paper employs local synchronization, a technique in which particular temporal sequences of states are imposed locally on cells and their direct neighbors, while the exact timing of state transitions is left undetermined. A hexagonal asynchronous totalistic cellular automaton is presented that achieves a completely asynchronous way of computation by simulating delay-insensitive circuits, a type of asynchronous circuits that are known for their robustness to variations in the timing of signals. We implement three primitive operators on the cellular automaton from which any arbitrary delay-insensitive circuit can be constructed, and show how to connect the operators such that collisions of crossing signals are avoided. The model requires six states and 55 totalistic transition rules.

1   Introduction

Cellular Automaton (CA) models have been used extensively for studying dynamical systems. Simulations of CAs on computers [15] suggest that the evolution of CAs from disordered initial states can be grouped into four classes:

I.   Evolution leading to a homogeneous state,
II. Evolution leading to a set of separated simple stable or periodic structures,
III. Evolution leading to a chaotic pattern,
IV. Evolution leading to complex localized structures, sometimes long-lived.

This classification has mainly been investigated for synchronous CAs. Most dynamical systems have an overall behavior that appears asynchronous, suggesting that synchronous CA models are not the optimal choice for simulating them. To make matters worse, some of the phenomena observed in synchronous CAs are actually artifacts of the synchronous mode of operation.

P.M.A. Sloot, B. Chopard, and A.G. Hoekstra (Eds.): ACRI 2004, LNCS 3305, pp. 91–100, 2004.

This motivates study into Asynchronously Cellular Automaton (ACA) models. According to [5], asynchronous updating makes it more difficult for information to propagate through ACAs, and thus tends to prevent initial perturbations from spreading. A system whose level of asynchronicity is above a certain threshold, rather tends to converge to a randomly fluctuating steady state [3], suggesting class-I and class-II behavior. How can we induce class-III and class-IV behavior in ACAs? Computation, generally associated with class-IV behavior, has been studied on ACAs, but mainly by simulating a synchronous CA on an ACA [9], after which a synchronous model, like a Turing Machine, is simulated on the synchronous CA. This method suffers from an increased number of cell states required for the ACA. Moreover, the ACA is *de facto* synchronous. ACAs free from these shortcomings have been proposed [1,7,12,13,14], that, rather than relying on global synchronization mechanisms, conduct asynchronous computations directly by simulating *Delay-Insensitive* (DI) circuits (see also [4]). A DI circuit is a type of asynchronous circuit, in which delays of signals do not affect the correctness of circuit operation. Configurations are designed on the ACA of cells in appropriate states that behave like signals in DI circuits and like modules whose operations change the directions or numbers of signals. Put together in appropriate ways, the configurations operating on signals can be used to form DI circuits that conduct computations.

This paper proposes an ACA that conducts its computations in a purely asynchronous way, adopting the same local synchronization method as in [1,7,12, 13,14]. Unlike previous ACAs, however, the proposed ACA assumes a hexagonal neighborhood and totalistic updating—reason to call it *Hexagonal Asynchronous Totalistic Cellular Automaton (HATCA)*. The DI circuits implemented on the ACA are based on a novel set of primitive DI elements that are especially suitable for implementations on hexagonal cellular spaces. Consequently, our ACA is more straightforward than the comparable ACA in [1], which is also totalistic but based on a squared cellular space with Moore neighborhood. Though both the ACA in this paper and the ACA in [1] require 6 states, our ACA requires less transitions rules (55 against 85). It is also less restricted in its asynchronous updating scheme, in the sense that, unlike in [1], two neighboring cells are allowed to undergo transitions simultaneously. In a *totalistic* CA like the proposed ACA, the total numbers of cells in certain states in a cell's neighborhood determine the transitions the cell can undergo. A well-known totalistic synchronous CA is the *Game of Life* [2], which exhibits behavior that is in class-IV. Our results may lead to more realistic CA-based models of physical phenomena and to massively parallel computation models with improved physical realizability.

Section 2 introduces DI circuits. We describe three primitive modules by which any arbitrary DI circuit can be constructed. In Section 3, we define HATCA, and in Section 4, we implement DI circuits on HATCA and describe the transition rules required for this. We show how to implement the signal and the primitive modules on HATCA, and how to connect them in circuits without collisions of crossing signals. We finish with concluding remarks.

2   Delay-Insensitive Circuits

A DI circuit is an asynchronous circuit whose operation is robust to arbitrary signal delays. A DI-circuit needs no central clock since it is driven by input signals; it may thus be called an *event-driven* circuit. The circuit is composed of *paths* (wires) and *modules*. Signals are transmitted along the paths and are processed by the modules.

Any arbitrary Boolean circuit in a synchronous system can be constructed from a fixed set of primitive operators, for example from AND-gates and NOT-gates. Such a set is called *universal*. Likewise, there are universal sets of primitives for DI-circuits, for example [6,11,8]. We use a universal set of primitives that is particularly suited for hexagonal cellular automata. It consists of the following three modules:

- **FORK**: A module (Fig. 1(a)) that, upon receiving an input signal from its input path A, produces one output signal in each of its output paths B and C.
- **MERGE**: A module (Fig. 1(b)) that redirects an input signal from either input path A or B to output path C.
- **Arbitrating TRIA (A-TRIA)**: A module (Fig. 1(c)) with three input paths (A, B, and C) and three output paths (P, Q, and R), which has two functionalities. In the first functionality, it acts like a TRIA module [11]: when it receives one signal from A (B) [C] and one signal from B (C) [A], it sends an output signal to P (Q) [R]. The second functionality is similar, except that the A-TRIA allows *arbitration* when the input paths A, B, and C receive signals at the same time. The A-TRIA then arbitrarily selects two input signals and operates on them as if it were a normal TRIA, while leaving the third input signal *pending*, i.e. holding it as is.

This set of modules is universal, that is, any arbitrary DI circuit can be constructed from them. As an example, a module called a SEQUENCER, is constructed from three FORK, two MERGE and three A-TRIA modules, as shown in Fig. 2. A SEQUENCER arbitrates between two input signals, one on a_i and one on b_i, letting one of them pass whenever there is an input signal from a third path c. If the signal from a_i (resp. b_i) passes, an output signal is produced on a_o (resp. b_o).

3   Hexagonal Asynchronous Totalistic Cellular Automata

A CA consists of identical finite automata arranged as cells in a regular $d(d \geq 1)$-dimensional array, such that they are mutually connected to their neighbors [10, 2,7]. Each cell is in a state from a finite state set. The states in this paper, 0, 1, 2, 3, 4, and 5, are denoted by the symbols in Fig. 3. A cell with state 0, called *quiescent cell*, is commonly used for background. The state of a cell at time t changes to a state at time $t + 1$ in accordance with a local function f, which has the cell's state and the neighboring cells' states as inputs. In a

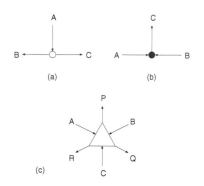

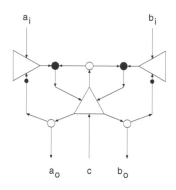

Fig. 1. Primitive modules: (a) FORK, (b) MERGE, and (c) A-TRIA

Fig. 2. A SEQUENCER module constructed from three FORKs, two MERGEs and three A-TRIAs. The two blobs (small filled circles) on the paths denote pending signals

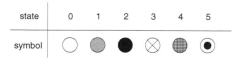

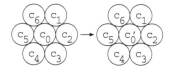

Fig. 3. The symbols by which the cell states are encoded

Fig. 4. Update of a cell by a transition

conventional CA, all cells undergo transitions at the same time; in other words, the CA is synchronous. Consequently, the global states are uniquely determined at all times by the local function f.

If cell transitions occur randomly and not necessarily at the same time, the resulting model is an asynchronous CA. In this paper, we use an asynchronous CA which includes synchronous updating, that is, neighboring cells may undergo transitions at the same time, but not necessarily so. This is a general case of an asynchronously updating scheme [9,7], and it is called *completely asynchronous*. In an asynchronous CA, the global states are not uniquely determined at all times by the local function f, because of the randomness by which transitions are timed.

The model used is a 2-dimensional hexagonal asynchronous totalistic CA, that is, a hexagonal CA in which transitions are timed completely asynchronously according to totalistic transition rules. The transition function is a function of a cell's state and of the numbers of neighboring cells in certain states:

$$c_0' = f(c_0, \{n_k\}) \tag{1}$$
$$n_k = |\{c_i | c_i = k\}|, \tag{2}$$

where, c_0 and c_i are the states of cells located at 0 and i ($i = 1, 2, \ldots, 6$) before the update, and c_0' is the state of cell 0 after the update (see Fig. 4). The variable n_k denotes the number of cells in state k ($k = 0, 1, 2, \ldots, N - 1$), where N is the number of possible states. In a completely asynchronous updating scheme, a transition takes place in a certain cell with a certain probability p, but only so if the local function is defined for the particular combination of a cell's state and its neighboring cells' states. If the local function is undefined, no transition takes place, even if the cell is selected by the scheme. In other words, the updating scheme is as follows:

1. for all i, j:
2.   select the cell at position (i, j)
3.   determine random number $q \in [0, 1]$
4.   if $q < p$ and $f(c_{ij}, \{n_k\})$ is defined:
5.   do transition $c_{ij}' = f(c_{ij}, \{n_k\})$
6. for all i, j: replace c_{ij} by c_{ij}'

4   Implementing Delay-Insensitive Circuits

4.1   Signals

A signal consists of a configuration of cells in certain states that moves in a certain direction over time. We call a continuous area of cells along which a signal propagates a *path*. The propagation of a signal requires rules 1 to 8 in Table 1 and is illustrated in Fig. 5. The signal in Fig. 5(a), composed of the four cells in states 1 and 2, propagates along a path in the eastern direction, using state 3 in the process. In front of the signal configuration, there is a cell in state 0 that has five neighbors in state 0 and one neighbor in state 2. The only rule matching to this situation is rule 1, and applying this rule to the cell changes its state from 0 to 3, yielding configuration (b). After this, configuration (b) is transformed to one of the configurations in (c) by rule 2, and this is followed by the intermediate configuration in (d) due to rule 3. Subsequently, configuration (d) is transformed to (k) via (e)-(f)-(g) or (h)-(i)-(j). A configuration in (e) may also evolve into a configuration in (i), but we leave the arrows out in Fig. 5 for simplicity; similarly (f) may evolve into (j).

Due to the asynchronicity of the model, the order in which the cells in Fig. 5 undergo transitions may vary, and even subsequences of transitions different from those in Fig. 5 may occur. The standard form of the signal in Fig. 5(a), however, will always reoccur. Finally, the transition rules are designed such that successive signals moving along the same path always remain separated by at least one quiescent cell.

4.2   Primitives

To implement the three primitive modules {FORK,MERGE,A-TRIA} in Section 2 on HATCA, we use six states, of which states 4 and 5 are specifically for the modules.

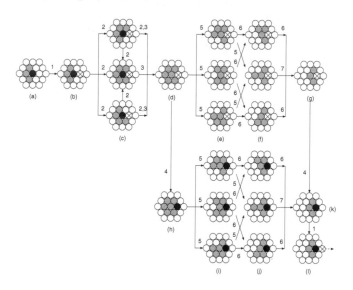

Fig. 5. Development of a signal on HATCA. A *number above an arrow* denotes the applied rule. Signal configuration (a) is transformed to (b) by rule 1 in Table 1; configuration (b) is transformed in one of the configurations in (c) by rule 2; and that configuration is transformed to (d) by rule 3. The intermediate pattern (d) is transformed to (k) via (e)-(f)-(g), (e)-(i)-(j), (e)-(f)-(j), or (h)-(i)-(j)

Table 1. Transition rules for propagation of a signal (No. 1-8), for FORK module (No. 9-22), for MERGE module (No. 23-33), and for A-TRIA module (No. 34-55)

No.	c_0	n_k	c_0'	No.	c_0	n_k	c_0'	No.	c_0	n_k	c_0'	No.	c_0	n_k	c_0'
1	0	501000	3	15	3	310020	2	29	3	310011	0	43	3	310002	4
2	0	311100	1	16	0	301110	1	30	1	210021	0	44	1	300012	2
3	2	050100	1	17	2	030120	1	31	1	310011	0	45	4	301002	5
4	3	330000	2	18	1	120030	0	32	1	410001	0	46	0	112101	1
5	1	330000	0	19	1	130020	0	33	1	500010	0	47	5	212001	3
6	1	420000	0	20	1	310020	0	34	0	401001	5	48	3	131001	1
7	1	510000	0	21	1	320010	0	35	5	401001	0	49	0	221100	1
8	1	600000	0	22	1	410010	0	36	5	400002	3	50	3	041001	1
9	0	301020	3	23	0	301011	3	37	3	300003	5	51	2	040101	1
10	0	211110	1	24	0	211101	1	38	3	500001	5	52	1	310002	0
11	3	130020	2	25	3	130011	2	39	3	600000	5	53	1	320001	0
12	0	201030	2	26	0	201021	2	40	0	300102	1	54	1	400002	0
13	2	031020	1	27	2	031011	1	41	3	030003	5	55	1	500001	0
14	2	010230	1	28	2	010221	1	42	1	300003	0				

The FORK is composed of three cells in state 4. Upon being presented by an input signal, the FORK typically operates like in Figs. 6 (a)-(l). The transition rules required for the FORK are 9 to 22, listed in Table 1.

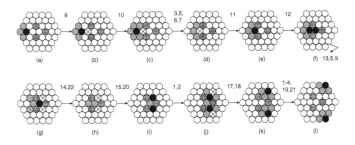

Fig. 6. Configuration and operation of FORK module

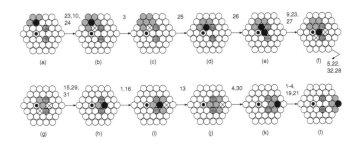

Fig. 7. Configuration and operation of MERGE module

The MERGE is composed of two cells in state 4 and one cell in state 5. Upon being presented by an input signal, the MERGE typically operates like in Figs. 7 (a)-(l). The transition rules for the MERGE are 23 to 33, listed in Table 1.

The A-TRIA is composed of one cell in state 5. Its TRIA functionality is illustrated in Fig. 8: upon being presented by two input signals, these signals are joined such as to produce one output signal. The arbitration functionality of the A-TRIA is illustrated in Fig. 9: upon being presented by three input signals, two of the signals—chosen arbitrarily due to the asynchronous mode of updating—are joined to produce one output signal, while the third input signal is kept pending. The transition rules required for the A-TRIA are 34 to 55, listed in Table 1.

4.3   Crossing Signals

Realizing a particular DI circuit is a matter of connecting the primitives to each other by paths in an appropriate way and laying them out on the CA. Special care is required for paths that cross each other, since the CA lacks a third dimension to cross signals. If crossing signals collide, they need to resolve which of them may pass first. Though most circuits can be designed such that crossings are collision-free, in some circuits it is hard to guarantee this. It is possible to add rules for crossing signals, but there is a more elegant way based on a module specialized in crossings [1,7,12,13] that is similar to a SEQUENCER.

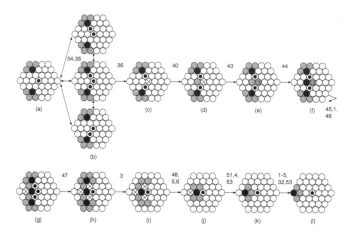

Fig. 8. Configuration and operation of A-TRIA module when being presented by two input signals. The signals are joined, resulting in one output signal

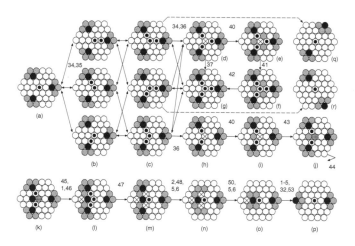

Fig. 9. Configuration and operation of A-TRIA module when being presented by three input signals. Two of the signals are arbitrarily selected, and joined, while the third signal is kept pending. The evolutions into the three possible outcomes are shown fully in (c)–(p) and briefly in (c)–(q) and (c)–(r)

The module is realized using only our primitives and collision-free path crossings. The implementation of the crossing on HATCA is shown in Fig. 10. A signal arriving at a_i (resp. b_i) gives rise to an output signal at a_o (resp. b_o). In case signals arrive at a_o and b_o simultaneously, only one is allowed through by the A-TRIA just left of the center. To this end, the A-TRIA tries to join one of these signals with the control signal, input at its right side. If this fails, i.e., if the A-TRIA rather joins a_o with b_o, a feedback signal is generated that gives rise to a new a_o and b_o. This procedure is repeated until one of a_o and b_o gets

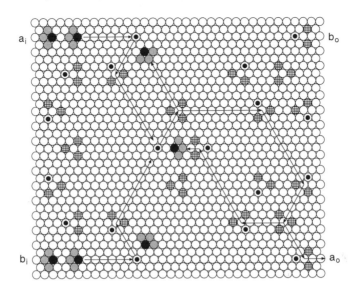

Fig. 10. Implementation of a delay-insensitive crossing module on HATCA. The arrows show a typical example of a signal passing through the crossing from a_i to a_o

through. The crossing module can be used under all circumstances: the order by which the signals arrive at its inputs is irrelevant for its correct functioning.

5 Concluding Remarks

To compute in a purely asynchronous way on an asynchronous hexagonal cellular automaton, we have embedded DI circuits on it. As we can construct any particular DI circuit by connecting the primitives proposed in this paper in appropriate ways, a universal Turing Machine can be build [8]. Other examples on how to build simple circuits on ACAs are given in [1,7,12,13]. A discussion on the implementation of DI circuit-based program structures, such as for-loops, etc., on ACAs can be found in [12]. Since computation is within the reach of the proposed ACA model, it may be considered as belonging to class-IV if Wolfram's classification is extended to asynchronous systems.

In the approach followed in this paper and in [1,7,12,13,14], synchronization is done locally, as opposed to the traditional approach of simulating a globally synchronized CA on an ACA. A cell will only undergo a transition if there is a transition rule that matches the state of the cell and the states of its neighbors. If there is no such match, the transition cannot be accomplished, and the cell will wait until one or more of its neighbors change states such that a match ensues. As this mode of operation is often found in nature, where for example chemical reactions only occur when the right molecules are available in the right positions at the right moments, this approach may lead to improved ways to simulate physical systems by ACAs.

References

1. S. Adachi, F. Peper, and J. Lee: "Computation by asynchronously updating cellular automata", *Journal of Statistical Physics*, Vol. 114, Nos. 1/2 pp. 261–289 (2004)
2. E. R. Berlekamp, J. H. Conway, and R. K. Guy: *Wining Ways For Your Mathematical Plays*, Academic Press, 1982.
3. H. J. Blok and B. Bergersen: "Synchronous versus asynchronous updating in the "game of life"", *Phys. Rev. E*, Vol. 59, pp. 3876–9 (1999)
4. U. Golze and L. Priese, "Petri net implementations by a universal cell space," *Information and Control*, Vol. 53, pp. 121–138 (1982).
5. T. E. Ingersion, and R. L. Buvel: "Structures in asynchronous cellular automata", *Physica D*, Vol. 10, pp. 59–68 (1984)
6. R. M. Keller: "Towards a theory of universal speed-independent modules", *IEEE Trans. Computers*, Vol. C-23, No. 1, pp. 21–33 (1974)
7. J. Lee, S. Adachi, F. Peper, and K. Morita: "Embedding universal delay-insensitive circuits in asynchronous cellular spaces", *Fundamenta Informaticae*, Vol. 58, Nos. 3/4, pp. 295–320 (2003)
8. J. Lee, F. Peper, S. Adachi, and K. Morita: "Universal delay-insensitive circuits with bi-directional and buffering lines", *IEEE Transactions on Computers*, Vol. 53, No. 8, pp. 1034–1046 (2004)
9. K. Nakamura: "Asynchronous cellular automata and their computational ability", *Systems, Computers, Controls*, Vol. 5, No. 5, pp. 58–66 (1974)
10. J. von Neumann: *Theory of self-reproducing automata*, University of Illinois Press, 1966.
11. P. Patra and D. S. Fussel: "Efficient Building Blocks for Delay Insensitive Circuits", *Proc. International Symp. on Advanced Research in Asynchronous Circuits and Systems*, pp. 196–205 (1994)
12. F. Peper, J. Lee, S. Adachi, and S. Mashiko: "Laying Out Circuits on Asynchronous Cellular Arrays: A Step Towards Feasible Nanocomputers?", *Nanotechnology*, Vol. 14, No. 4, pp. 469–485 (2003)
13. F. Peper, J. Lee, F. Abo, T. Isokawa, S. Adachi, N. Matsui, and S. Mashiko: "Fault-tolerance in nanocomputers: a cellular array approach", *IEEE Transactions on Nanotechnology*, Vol. 3, No. 1, pp. 187–201 (2004)
14. L. Priese, "A note on asynchronous cellular automata," *Journal of Computer and System Sciences*, Vol. 17, pp. 237–252 (1978).
15. S. Wolfram: *Cellular Automata and Complexity*, Addison-Wesley, Reading, MA, USA, 1994.

Efficient Simulation of CA with Few Activities

Richard Walter and Thomas Worsch

IAKS Vollmar, Universität Karlsruhe, Germany

Abstract. Motivated by the wish to make large simulations of Bak's sandpile model we investigate a simple method to simulate cellular automata with "few activities" efficiently on a computer.

1 Introduction

Simple ideas are sometimes more useful than complicated ones – if they are noticed. In this paper we pursue a simple idea to simulate cellular automata with small state change complexity [4] on a computer.

Self-organized criticality is a phenomenon which several systems and models of them exhibit. One of the prototype examples is the sandpile model by Bak, Tang and Wiesenfeld [2]. The CA part of this model has the property that most of the time only very few cells change their states even if the lattice is large (which is the interesting case).

In such a situation the straightforward simulation technique of computing the new state for each cell in each global step does a lot of superfluous work: When a cell p and all of its neighbors do not change their states during a global update of a CA one can be sure that p will again not change its state during the next global update. One could at least hope that in such a situation restricting the simulation to cells where a state change might happen would pay off. We call this the *adaptive simulation algorithm*. Depending on how little or how much bookkeeping work is necessary it will be competitive for configurations with relatively many or few "active" cells.

The rest of this paper is organized as follows: In Section 2 we quickly review the definition of CA (thus introducing the notion we will use in the sequel) and explain the sandpile model. In Section 3 we describe the adaptive simulation algorithm, prove its correctness and discuss some implementation issues. In Section 4 results of simulation runs for different CA are reported and evaluated. We conclude the paper in Section 5.

2 Basics

2.1 Cellular Automata

We assume that the reader is familiar with the concept of deterministic synchronous cellular automata. We use the following notations.

P.M.A. Sloot, B. Chopard, and A.G. Hoekstra (Eds.): ACRI 2004, LNCS 3305, pp. 101–110, 2004.
© Springer-Verlag Berlin Heidelberg 2004

By R we denote the regular grid of positions where the cells are located. We assume that R is an additive group with neutral element $\mathbf{0}$. We use x, y, z for the coordinates of cells. The finite set of states is always denoted as Q. Thus a (global) configuration is a mapping $c : R \to Q$, or $c \in Q^R$ for short. We usually write c_x instead of $c(x)$ for the state of cell x. The local neighborhood N is a finite set of differences of coordinates. We write $x + N = \{x + n \mid n \in N\}$ for the coordinates of all neighbors of cell x. Analogously $x - N$ is the set of coordinates of all cells for which x is a neighbor. In general we do not require $\mathbf{0} \in N$, and we write N_0 for the set $N \cup \{\mathbf{0}\}$.

A mapping $\ell \in Q^N$ is a local configuration. Given a global configuration c we write c_{x+N} for the local configuration observed by cell x, i.e. $c_{x+N} : N \to Q :$ $n \mapsto c_{x+n}$. The local transition function is a mapping $\delta : Q^N \to Q$. It induces the global transition function $\Delta : Q^R \to Q^R$ by the prescription that for all $x \in R$ must hold: $\Delta(c)_x = \delta(c_{x+N})$.

2.2   Sandpile Model

The sandpile model by Bak, Tang and Wiesenfeld [2] actually consists of two parts. One is a CA, the other is a sequence of "external events". We will only consider the original simple version.

The CA part works as follows. It is a two-dimensional CA using von Neumann neighborhood of radius 1. The set of states is $Q = \{0, 1, 2, 3, 4, 5, 6, 7\}$. The local rule can be described like that: Each cell is a little bin which contains a certain number $q \in Q$ of grains of sand. In each step each cell does the following:

- If a cell is *critical*, i.e. $q \geq 4$, then "it takes 4 of its grains of sand and puts one in each of its 4 neighboring bins." This is called the *toppling* of a cell.
- If a cell is not critical, i.e. $q \leq 3$, then "the cell does nothing" by itself. (It may still receive one or more grains from its neighbors.)

One does *not* use cyclic boundary conditions. Instead, if for example a cell at the left border tries to put a grain of sand to its left neighbor, the grain simply "gets lost". That way one can always be sure, that no matter what the initial configuration looks like, after a finite number of CA steps one will reach a configuration in which all cells are not critical.

Given such a configuration one repeatedly does the following:

1. Uniformly one of the cells is chosen at random and one grain of sand is added to it.
2. Starting at this cell there may be an *avalanche*. As long as there is at least one critical cell, the CA does one global step.

There are several quantities which could be used as the *size* of an avalanche: the number of global CA steps needed to reach a quiescent configuration, the total number of cells "involved" in an avalanche or total number of cell topplings. For the figures in this paper we have used the number of global CA steps.

The reason why for example geophysicists are interested in this (and similar more advanced) models is that the distribution of frequencies of avalanches of different sizes is similar to the distribution of frequencies of earthquakes of different magnitudes. This is true at least if one has already reached a global state of so-called *self-organized criticality.*

3   Simulation Technique

The conventional algorithm for simulating a CA works with two global configurations c and c'. In c the current states of all cells are stored. By iterating over all cells $x \in R$ for each of them the new state is computed and stored in c'. At the end the roles of c and c' are exchanged to prepare for the simulation of the next global step.

Algorithm 31 (Conventional simulation method for one global CA step).

---

    foreach $x \in R$ **do**
        $c'_x \leftarrow \delta(c_{x+N})$
    od
    $c \leftrightarrow c'$

This algorithm always computes new states for all cells. It does so even for cells which are inside a neighborhood where no actual state changes (from s to some $s' \neq s$) took place recently.

3.1   Abstract Version of the Adaptive Algorithm

The following algorithm tries to be more clever. It maintains a set $A \subseteq R$ of cells, such that whenever $x \notin A$ one can be sure that one need not compute a new state (because c' already contains it).

Here is the algorithm, already extended by a few assertions needed for its verification:

Algorithm 32 (Adaptive simulation method for one global CA step).

    $\boxed{\text{A1}}$ ———————— $\langle\ \forall x \in R : x \notin A \Longrightarrow c'_x = c_x \wedge c_x = \delta(c_{x+N})\ \rangle$
    foreach $x \in A$ **do**
        $c'_x \leftarrow \delta(c_{x+N})$
        if $c'_x \neq c_x$ **then**
            foreach $y \in x - N_0$ **do**
                $A' \leftarrow A' \cup \{y\}$
            od
        fi
    od
    $\boxed{\text{A2}}$ ———————— $\langle\ c' = \Delta(c),\ \text{i.e.}\ \forall x \in R : c'_x = \Delta(c)_x\ \rangle$
    $\boxed{\text{A3}}$ ———————— $\langle\ \forall x \in R : x \notin A' \Longrightarrow c'_x = c_x \wedge c'_x = \delta(c'_{x+N})\ \rangle$
    $c \leftrightarrow c'$
    $A \leftarrow A';\quad A' \leftarrow \emptyset$
    $\boxed{\text{A4}}$ ———————— $\langle\ \forall x \in R : x \notin A \Longrightarrow c'_x = c_x \wedge c_x = \delta(c_{x+N})\ \rangle$

3.2   Correctness

Assume that assertion A1 is correct, and consider an arbitrary $x \in R$ just before the **foreach** $x \in A$ **do** loop is entered.

Case 1: $x \in A$. Then the loop body is executed for x. Obviously one gets $c'_x = \delta(c_{x+N}) = \Delta(c)_x$ as claimed in assertion A2.

Case 2: $x \notin A$. In this case already by assertion A1 one can be sure that $c'_x = \delta(c_{x+N}) = \Delta(c)_x$ holds.

Therefore assertion A2 is true.

Now consider the set A' after the **foreach** $z \in A$ **do** loop has finished and an arbitrary $y \in R$:

Case 1: $y \in A'$. In this case there is no need to prove anything.

Case 2: $y \notin A'$. This can only happen if $\neg \exists x \in R : y \in x - N_0 \wedge c'_x \neq c_x$. This is equivalent to $\neg \exists x \in R : x \in y + N_0 \wedge c'_x \neq c_x$, and this to $\forall x \in R : x \notin y + N_0 \vee c'_x = c_x$.

Since $y \in y + N_0$ one has $c'_y = c_y$.

Furthermore $c'_x = c_x$ holds for all $x \in y + N$, i.e. $c'_{y+N} = c_{y+N}$, and therefore $\delta(c'_{y+N}) = \delta(c_{y+N})$. We already know from A2 that $\Delta(c)_y = c'_y$, hence $\delta(c'_{y+N}) = c'_y$.

Therefore assertion A3 is true.

Assertion A2 tells us that the algorithm really computes $c' = \Delta(c)$.

We note that the **0** is really necessary in the loop **foreach** $y \in x - N_0$ **do** . If a neighborhood does not contain **0** one would otherwise get wrong results in general. One can easily get this detail wrong.

If one uses the above algorithm inside another loop to simulate several global steps of a CA, assertion A1 is an important loop invariant. Because of the statements $c \leftrightarrow c'$ and $A \leftarrow A'$ from assertion A3 one gets assertion A4 immediately. And this is in fact *identical* with assertion A1.

3.3   Implementation in C

For the measurements reported in the next section, we used an implementation of the above algorithm written in C. For the tests we used implementations of local CA rules for a shift and the sandpile model.

In both cases the state of each single cell was stored in **char** variable. Thus global configurations were **char** arrays. Because we wanted to run computations for different R, the memory for them were **malloc**ed one-dimensional **char** arrays and the transformation to two-dimensional coordinates was done by hand.

See Subsection 4.3 below for remarks on different storage schemes.

The most important aspect is an efficient implementation of the (mathematically speaking) *sets* A and A' of active cells. We used the following approach: For A and A' one-dimensional arrays **currActList** and **nextActList** (respectively) of elements are **malloc**ed in which cell coordinates are stored.

- Variables `currActIndex` and `nextActIndex` are both initialized with 0.
- Adding the position p of a cell, its *coordinates* for short, to a list is done by a statement like
  `nextActList[nextActIndex++] = p;`

In order to avoid that the coordinates of one cell are added to the activity list several times, there is an additional `char` array `actArray` which stores one bit of information for each cell:

- If for some index p the bit `actArray` is 0, this means that p has not yet been added to `nextActList`.
- If for some index p the bit `actArray` is 1, this means that p has already been added to `nextActList`.

Therefore `actArray[p]` has to be updated when p is added to `nextActList`. Without going into too many details, the C code basically looks as follows:

```
for (i=0; i<currActIndex; i++) {
    p = currActList[i];
    nextConf[p] = delta(currConf, p);
    if (nextConf[p] != currConf[p]) {
        for all q in p-NO {
            if (!actArray[q]) {
                nextActList[nextActIndex++] = q;
                actArray[q] = 1;
            }
        }
    }
}
swap the pointers currConf and nextConf;
for (i=0; i<nextActIndex; i++) {
    actArray[nextActList[i]]=0;
}
swap the pointers currActList and nextActList;
currActIndex = nextActIndex;
nextActIndex = 0;
```

Already in the conventional simulation algorithm one has to be careful when trying to access "neighbors" $p + n$ of border cells p. Often this problem can be dealt with by allocating additional memory for border "ghost cells" which are set to their proper values outside the global CA step.

In the adaptive algorithm an additional similar problem comes up when looking at the potential cells $p - n$ of which a cell p is a neighbor. In order to avoid lots of `if` statements for testing whether $p - n$ is still within bounds, we used a method inspired by the idea of *localization* suggested in [6]. There is yet another array `localize` with ghost cells holding for each cell the information whether it is within the bounds of the real CA lattice. Indexing it with $p - n$ gives the information whether it should be added to A'.

For meaningful results `currActList` has to be initialized correctly, i.e. assertion A1 has to be satisfied. In the case of the shift we simply included *all* cells in `currActList`. In particular in the case where there usually are only few active cells, this spoils the total running times for a not too large number of global steps.

Figure 1 shows an example. For two initial configurations with 100 and 10 000 ones the average time needed for one global step is determined by making an increasing number k of global steps and dividing the total running time by k.

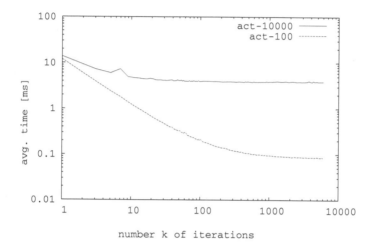

Fig. 1. Average time needed for one global step computes by averaging over an increasing number of iterations for two different initial configurations

Readers may have noticed that the above implementation is memory intensive. It may happen that *all* cells are active during several global steps. Hence `currActList`, `nextActList`, `actArray`, and `localize` all need the same amount of memory as `currConf` and `nextConf`.

In the implementation of the sandpile model we use a pseudo random number generator by L'Ecuyer which his known to be very good [3, p. 280].

4   Simulation Results

In this section we compare the running times of the conventional and the adaptive simulation method for a few example CA.

All actual numbers have been obtained on a Pentium 4 with 3 GHz clock frequency with 2 GB of RAM running Debian GNU/Linux with a 2.6.x kernel. The programs had been compiled with `gcc` version 3.3.3 using option `-O2` (other optimizations didn't help). Running times are taken using the `gettimeofday()`

function. It is called immediately before and after the computations to be bench-marked and the time difference is reported. Thus we only report wall clock times which in general do not exactly represent the running times of the process we interested in but may be spoilt by activities of the operating system and/or other system or user processes.

What we do want to get across in this paper is that there are interesting applications which benefit significantly from the adaptive simulation algorithm. As will be seen below, significantly here means a speedup factor in the range of a few thousands. In the light of this we do not really care whether concrete running times are off by a few percent due to OS activities. (Similarly optimizations of the source code could also affect the speedup factor.)

4.1   Shift

The first CA we investigate simply does a shift of all cells "down one row" in each step. Each state was stored in a variable of type **unsigned char**.

All simulation results reported in this and the next subsection have been obtained for CA with 1000×1000 cells and cyclic boundary conditions. Times were taken for 10 000 global iterations and then divided by this number. This eliminates deviations which are due to operating system activities and the like to a large extent.

Different initial configurations were chosen, where a randomly chosen subset (of the proper size) of cells was set to 1.

For the conventional simulation method the number of ones in a configuration of course has no influence on the time needed for a global step. But for the adaptive method it has. As can be seen in Figure 2 for our implementations of shift down there is a break-even point at about 0.09%. Since the number of active cells in each global step is twice the number of 1-cells this indeed means, that the adaptive algorithm is faster only as long as the number of active cells is really small. At first this looks not very promising. But two important facts have to be taken into account:

1. There are interesting CA like the sandpile model where the number of active cells usually *is* really small.
2. In the case of the shift CA the number of active cells must be small for the adaptive algorithm to be competitive because the conventional implementation of the local rule is extremely efficient; we can use a simple **memcpy()** for it. If in the conventional case the local rule takes more time, then the overhead of the adaptive algorithm becomes less disadvantageous.

4.2   Sandpile Model

In Section 2.2 we mentioned that for the sandpile model to produce results which are relevant for the application one must already have reached a configuration which exhibits self-organized criticality (SOC). To give a vague impression of what this means the following experiment was carried out. We started with a

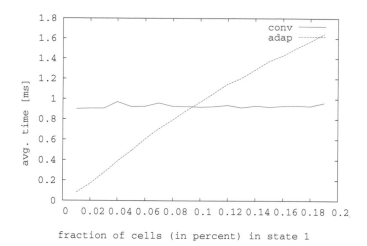

Fig. 2. Average running times of the shift CA depending on the fraction of cells (in percent) in state 1 in the initial configuration for the conventional ("conv" line) and the adaptive ("adap" line) algorithm

completely "empty" configuration where *all* cells were in state 0. Then grains of sand are thrown onto it. For each batch of 1000 grains we record the sum (over all grains) and the maximum (for one grain) of global CA steps and the CPU computation time needed for the batch as well as the relative frequencies of states 0, ..., 3 after it. The results are shown in Figures 3 and 4. There is a quite sharp change of behavior which occurs for 1000 × 1000 arrays after approximately 2 140 000 grains. (For the curious: Experiments with other array sizes indicate that in general the point is at about 2.140 times the number of cells. But these investigations are off-topic in this paper.)

The speedups for the adaptive over the conventional algorithm depend on the type of configuration. when started with an empty array, during the first batches we observed speedups between 7000 and 8000 for a 1000 × 1000 lattice. For a SOC configuration speedups were between 100 and 120.

4.3   Assessing Feasibility and Compatibility with Other Methods

The adaptive simulation method is faster than the conventional one whenever there are relatively few locations with activity. Besides the sandpile model this includes for example the game of life, some Ising models, and models where set of "micro agents" moves around on a lattice, e.g. [1].

There are already some methods known to speed up the simulation of CA. One possibility is parallelization, which may come in different flavors.

If one has several processors, domain decomposition is a standard approach. It gives reasonable speedup numbers as long as the lattice is large. But what one does speed up is only the conventional simulation method (which may be slow as we have seen above).

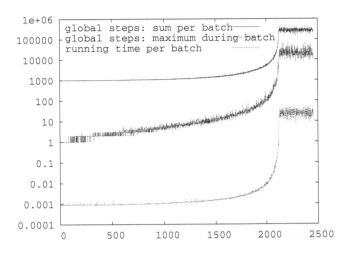

Fig. 3. Sum (top) and maximum (middle) of absolute numbers of global CA steps and CPU running times for the adaptive method (bottom) in seconds per batch: possibly a phase transition during the transient period of the sandpile model before (or when?) reaching SOC.

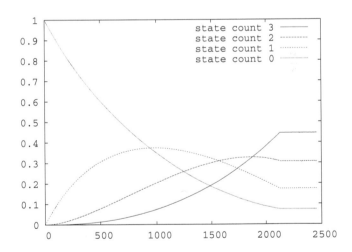

Fig. 4. Relative frequencies of states in quiescent configurations: possibly a phase transition during the transient period of the sandpile model before (or when?) reaching SOC.

Another method to process several cell updates simultaneously is to store several states in each of the native machine word processed by the CPU. For example recently Weimar [5] has reported remarkable results using *multispin coding*.

Concerning the latter it is more or less obvious that the adaptive simulation algorithm can be used together with it and that one can expect some additional savings.

On the other hand, an efficient application of the adaptive algorithm in a setting with a real parallel machine is less trivial. For reasonable results one probably needs a CA where there a few activities and these should be spread out fairly regularly over the whole lattice.

5   Conclusion and Outlook

We have demonstrated that the simple idea of looking only at the active cells and their neighbors for the computation of a global CA step can result in impressive speedups over the conventional simulation method. Of course, this is only the case if there are relatively few active cells.

Most probably other people have used this approach before us. The main contribution here is an elegant description with verification of its correctness. During systematic investigations we also discovered what may be a phase transition during the initialization phase of the sandpile model as a byproduct.

We stress again that there are interesting applications having the required property of few activities in at least most global steps. We have shown a few measurements for the sandpile model. Others will be investigated in the future. We will also have to have a look at efficient parallelization of the adaptive simulation method which is not completely straightforward.

References

1. Paul Albuquerque and Alexandre Dupuis. A parallel cellular ant colony algorithm for clustering and sorting. In Stefania Bandini, Bastien Chopard, and Marco Tomassini, editors, *Proceedings 5th ACRI Conference*, volume 2493 of *LNCS*, pages 220–240, 2002.
2. Per Bak, Chao Tang, and Kurt Wiesenfeld. Self-organized criticality: An explanation of the $1/f$ noise. *Physical Review Letters*, 59(4):381–384, 1987.
3. William H. Press, Brian P. Flannery, Saul A. Teukolsky, and William T. Vetterling. *Numerical Recipes in C.* Cambridge University Press, 1993.
4. Roland Vollmar. Some remarks about the 'efficiency' of polyautomata. *International Journal of Theoretical Physics*, 21:1007–1015, 1982.
5. Jörg Weimar. Translations of cellular automata for efficient simulation. *Complex Systems*, 14(2):175–199, 2003.
6. Thomas Worsch. Simulation of cellular automata. *Future Generation Computer Systems*, 16(2-3):157–170, 1999.

Perturbing the Topology of the Game of Life Increases Its Robustness to Asynchrony

Nazim Fatès[1] and Michel Morvan[1,2]

[1] ENS Lyon - LIP
UMR CNRS - ENS Lyon - UCB Lyon - INRIA 5668
46, allée d'Italie - 69 364 Lyon Cedex 07 - France
{Nazim.Fates,Michel.Morvan}@ens-lyon.fr
[2] Institut Universitaire de France

Abstract. An experimental analysis of the asynchronous version of the "Game of Life" is performed to estimate how topology perturbations modify its evolution. We focus on the study of a phase transition from an "inactive-sparse phase" to a "labyrinth phase" and produce experimental data to quantify these changes as a function of the density of the initial configuration, the value of the synchrony rate, and the topology missing-link rate. An interpretation of the experimental results is given using the hypothesis that initial "germs" colonize the whole lattice and the validity of this hypothesis is tested.

1 Introduction

Cellular automata were originally introduced by von Neumann in order to study the logical properties of self-reproducing machines. Following Ulam's suggestions, the requirements he made for constructing such a machine was the discreteness of space using cells, discreteness of time using an external clock, the symmetry of the rules governing cells interaction, and the locality of these interactions; it resulted in the birth of the cellular automaton (CA) model. In order to make the self-reproduction not trivial he also required that the self-reproducing machine should be computation-universal (e.g., [13]). The resulting CA used 29 elementary states for each cell and updates used 5 neighbors. Later on, Conway introduced a CA called "Game of Life" or simply *Life* which was also proved to be computation universal [2]. This CA is simpler than von Neumann's in at least two ways: the local rule uses only two states and it can be summarized with by sub-rules (birth and death rules).

However, the question remained open to know what is the importance of perfect synchrony on a CA behavior. Indeed, since the first study on the effects of asynchronous update carried out by Ingerson and Buvel [6], many criticisms have been addressed to the use of the CA as models of natural phenomena. Some authors investigated, using various techniques, how synchrony variations changed CA qualitative behavior [6], [10], [3], [5], [14], [8]. All studies agree on the

P.M.A. Sloot, B. Chopard, and A.G. Hoekstra (Eds.): ACRI 2004, LNCS 3305, pp. 111–120, 2004.

fact that for some CA, there are situations in which small changes in the update method lead to qualitative changes of the evolution of the CA, thus showing the need for further studies of robustness to asynchronism. Similarly, some authors investigated the effect of perturbing the topology (i.e., the links between cells) in one dimension [11] by adding links, or in two dimensions with small-world construction algorithms [15], [9]. Here too, the studies showed that robustness to topology changes was a key factor in the CA theory and that some CA showed "phase transitions" when varying the intensity of the topology perturbation.

The aim of this work is to question, in the case of *Life*, the importance of the two hypotheses used in the classical CA paradigm: what happens when the CA is no longer perfectly synchronous and when the topology is perturbed? In Section 2, we present the model and describe the qualitative behavior induced by the introduction of asynchronism and/or topology perturbations. In Section 3.1, we observe that (i) *Life* is sensitive to asynchronism; (ii) robust to topology perturbations and (iii) that the robustness to asynchronism is increased when the topology characteristics become irregular. Section 3.2 is devoted to presenting a rigorous experimental validation and exploration of these phenomena for which a potential explanation based on the notion of "germ" development is discussed and studied in Section 4.

2   The Model

Classically, *Life* is run on a regular subset of $\mathbb{Z}^2$. For simulation purposes, the configurations are finite squares with $N \times N$ cells and the neighborhood of each cell is constituted of the cell itself and the 8 nearest neighbors (Moore neighborhood). We use periodic boundary conditions meaning that all cell position indices are taken in $\mathbb{Z}/N\mathbb{Z}$. The type of boundary conditions does play an important role at least for small configurations as shown in [4].

Life belongs to the outer-totalistic (e.g., [12], [11]) class of CA: the local transition rule f is specified as a function of the present state $q(c)$ and of the number $S_1(c)$ of cells with states 1 in the neighborhood. The *Life* transition function $f(q, S_1)$ can be written:

$$f(0, S_1) = 1 \text{ if } S_1 = 3 \; ; \; f(0, S_1) = 0 \text{ otherwise,} \qquad \text{(birth rule)}$$

$$f(1, S_1) = 1 \text{ if } S_1 = 2 \text{ or } S_1 = 3; f(1, S_1) = 0 \text{ otherwise.} \qquad \text{(death rule)}$$

In the sequel, we consider *Life* as an asynchronous cellular automaton (ACA) acting on a possibly perturbed topology.

There are several asynchronous dynamics: one may, for example update cells one by one in a fixed order from left to right and from bottom to top. This update method is called "line-by-line sweep" [14] and it has been shown that this type of dynamics introduce spurious behaviors due to the correlation between the spatial arrangement of the cells and the spatial ordering of the updates. These correlations can only be suppressed with a random updating of the cells. In this work, we choose to examine only one type of asynchronism which consists in applying the local rule, for each cell independently, with probability α. The parameter α is called the "synchronicity" [5] or the *synchrony rate*; one can also view it as a parameter that would control the evolution of a probabilistic cellular automata (PCA) where the transition function results in applying *Life* rule with a probability α and the identity rule with probability $1 - \alpha$.

We choose to perturb topology by definitely removing links between cells. Let $G_0 = (\mathcal{L}, E_0)$ be the oriented graph that represents cells interactions: $(c, c') \in E$ if and only if c' belongs to neighborhood of c. The graph with perturbed topology $G = (\mathcal{L}, E)$ is obtained by examining each cell $c \in \mathcal{L}$ and, for each cell in the neighborhood of c and removing the link (c, c') with a probability ϵ^-; the parameter ϵ^- is called *missing-link rate*. Note that, as the local function is expressed in an outer-totalistic mode, we can still apply it on neighborhoods of various sizes. The definition we use induces an implicit choice of behavior in the case where a link is missing : the use of S_1 in the local rule definition implies that the cell will consider missing cells of the neighborhood as being in state 0. Other choices would have been possible; for example assuming this state to be 1 or the current value of the cell itself.

3   Observations and Measures

3.1   Qualitative Observations

Figure 1 shows that the behavior of *Life* depends on the synchrony rate α: a phase with labyrinthine shapes appears when α is lowered. Bersini and Detours studied this phenomenon and noticed that the asynchronous (sequential) updating of *Life* was significantly different from the (classical) synchronous version in that sense that a "labyrinth phase" (denoted by LP) appeared (see Fig. 1 below). For small lattice dimensions, they observed the convergence of this phase to a fixed point and concluded that asynchrony had a stabilizing effect on *Life* [3].

The phase transition was then measured with precision by Blok and Berg-ersen, who used the final density (i.e, the fraction of 1's sites) as a means of quantifying the phase transition. They measured the value α_c for which the phase transition was to be observed and found $\alpha_c = 0.91$ [5]. They showed that the type of phase transition is *continuous* (or a second-order transition): when α is decreased from $\alpha = 1.0$ to $\alpha = \alpha_c$, no change is observed in terms of the values of the average density. When we have $\alpha < \alpha_c$ the "labyrinth phase" gradually appears and the average density starts increasing in a continuous way. It is thus *the derivative* of the density that shows discontinuity rather than the function itself.

Figure 2 shows that the removal of links between cells does not qualitatively perturb the aspect of the final configurations attained. So, according to the observation of steady states, synchronous *Life* seems somehow robust to topology perturbations. However, we also noticed that the transients are much shorter in presence of topology errors: for $N = 50 \times 50$, the order of magnitude of transients are $T = 1000$ for $\epsilon^- = 0$ and $T = 100$ for $\epsilon^- = 0.1$.

$\alpha = 1.0$ $\alpha = 0.5$ sequential updating

Fig. 1. *Life* configurations for $N = 50 \times 50$, after $T = 100$ time steps, starting from a random configuration of density $d_{\text{ini}} = 0.5$. In the sequential updating, cells are randomly updated one after another.

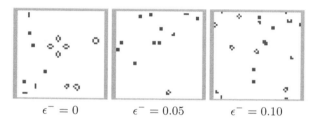

$\epsilon^- = 0$ $\epsilon^- = 0.05$ $\epsilon^- = 0.10$

Fig. 2. *Life* configurations for synchronous evolution ($\alpha = 1.00$) with $N = 50 \times 50$, after $T = 1000$ time steps, starting from a random configuration of density $d_{\text{ini}} = 0.5$.

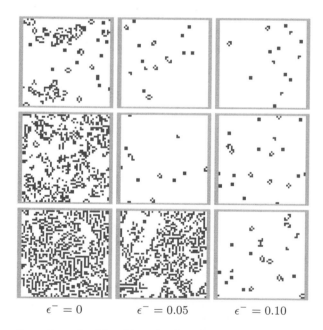

$\epsilon^- = 0$ $\epsilon^- = 0.05$ $\epsilon^- = 0.10$

Fig. 3. *Life* configurations for $N = 50 \times 50$, after $T = 1000$ time steps, starting from a random configuration of density $d_{\text{ini}} = 0.5$: (up) $\alpha = 0.90$ (middle) $\alpha = 0.75$ (bottom) $\alpha = 0.50$. The figure in the upper-left corner shows that the system is still in a transient mode.

Figure 3 shows what happens when both asynchronism and topology perturbations are added. Rows of Fig. 3 display the behavior with a fixed synchrony rate α and columns display the behavior with a fixed missing-link rate ϵ^-. We see that increasing topology errors from $\epsilon^- = 0$ to $\epsilon^- = 0.05$ makes the phase transition occur for a higher value of synchrony rate α_c. With a further increase from $\epsilon^- = 0.05$ to $\epsilon^- = 0.10$, the phase transition cannot be observed any more, at least for the selected values of α.

This demonstrates that both parameters ϵ^- and α control the phase transition between the "inactive-sparse phase" [9] and the "labyrinth phase" (LP). The next section is devoted to quantitatively measure the interplay of these two control parameters.

3.2   Quantitative Approach

To detect the apparition of the labyrinth phase (LP), we need to look at the configurations by eye or to choose an appropriate macroscopic measure. Clearly, a configuration in LP contains much more 1's than a configuration in the "inactive-sparse phase" ([9]). This leads us to quantify the change of behaviour using the measurement of the "steady-state density" (i.e. the average density after a transient time has elapsed). This method has been chosen by various authors (e.g. Blok and Bergersen [5]) and it has been applied to exhaustively study both the dynamics [7] and the robustness to asynchronism [8] of one dimensional elementary cellular automata.

We define the steady-state density $\rho(d_{\text{ini}}, \alpha)$ using the sampling algorithm defined in [8]: Starting from a random initial configuration constructed with a Bernoulli process of parameter d_{ini}, we let the ACA evolve with a synchrony rate α during a transient time $T_{\text{transient}}$ then we measure the value of the density during a sampling time T_{sampling}. The value of ρ is the average of the sampled densities.

The sampling operation results in the definition of a function $\rho(d_{\text{ini}}, \alpha)$ that can be represented in the form of a "sampling surface". This surface contains part of the information on how the behaviour of a CA is affected by asynchronism. Figure 4 shows the experimental results obtained for $N = 50 \times 50$, $T_{\text{transient}} = 1000$, $T_{\text{sampling}} = 1000$. The transient time $T_{\text{transient}}$ is chosen according to the observations made in [1] where equivalent transient times were found for greater lattice sizes.

Let us first look at what happens for $d_{\text{ini}} \in [0.2, 0.8]$ (right column of Fig. 4). The invariance of the surface relatively to the d_{ini}-axis shows that the macroscopic behavior of *Life* does not depend on the value of this parameter within this range. The upper right corner of Fig. 4 shows that for $\epsilon^- = 0$ (regular topology), the phase transition occurs for $\alpha_c \sim 0.90$ as expected [5]. However, when ϵ^- increases, experiments show that α_c also decreases. This means that the settlement of LP becomes more difficult as links are removed; this can be interpreted as an increase of the robustness to asynchrony. We can observe that for $\epsilon^- = 0.10$, the surface is flat and horizontal, which means that the behavior is

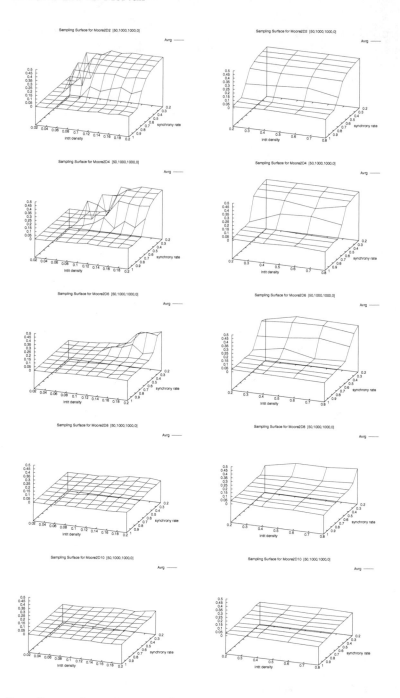

Fig. 4. Sampling surfaces for $\epsilon^- = [0\cdots 0.10]$, $N = 50 \times 50$, $T_{\text{transient}} = 1000$, $T_{\text{sampling}} = 1000$. The left column has a different range for d_{ini} to focus on the behavior for small initial densities.

not anymore perturbed by asynchronism (at least if we consider our observation function).

The left column of Fig. 4 shows the behavior of *Life* for $d_{\text{ini}} \in [0, 0.2]$. We observe two different abrupt change of behaviors. On the one hand, there is a value of $d_{\text{ini}}^{\text{c}}$ which separates the "inactive-sparse phase" and LP. On the other hand, the value of $d_{\text{ini}}^{\text{c}}$ increases as ϵ^- increases. This means that LP becomes more difficult to reach when links are removed; which again can be interpreted as a gain of robustness.

Experiments were held for various lattice sizes and allowed to control that the sampling surface aspect was stable with N; we however observed that when ϵ^- and α are fixed, the value of $d_{\text{ini}}^{\text{c}}$ is a decreasing function of N.

All the previous phenomena may be the consequence of multiple intricate factors. In the next section, we study the evolution of so called "micro-configurations" put in an empty array and propose a first hypothesis in the direction of understanding these behaviors.

4   Micro-Configurations Analysis

4.1   Experiments

The observation of the settlement of LP shows that it can develop from very localized parts of the lattice and then spreads across the lattice until it fills it totally. By analogy with a crystal formation, we call "germs" these particular configurations that have the possibility to give birth to an invasive LP. We investigate the existence of germs by performing an exhaustive study of the potential evolution of *micro-configurations*, i.e. 3×3 configurations that are placed in an empty array. There are 512 such configurations and we experimentally quantify, for each one, the probability that a it becomes a germ. Our goal is to infer the behavior of the whole structure from the evolution of these micro-configurations.

Setting the synchrony rate to $\alpha = 0.5$, we used the following algorithm: For every micro-configuration $i \in I$, (a) we initialize the lattice $N \times N$ with i, and (b) we let the CA evolve until it reaches a fixed point or until it reaches LP. We repeat $S = 1000$ times operations (a) and (b) for the same initial micro-configuration but for a different update histories. We consider that the CA has reached LP if the density is greater of equal than a limit density $d_\infty = 0.1$. Indeed, we observed that if the CA was able to multiply the number of 1's from the micro-configuration to a constant ratio of the lattice, then it will almost surely continue to invade the whole lattice and, asymptotically, reach LP. We experimentally obtain the probability $P_{\text{germ}}[i]$ that a configuration i is a germ. Grouping micro-configurations by the number k of 1's they contain, we obtain an array with 9 entries $P_{\text{germ}}(k), k \in [0, 9]$, displayed in Table 1.

Results show that for $k < 3, P_{\text{germ}}(k) = 0$, which means that all such micro-configurations always tend to extinction. For $n \geq 3$, the probability to reach LP increases as n increases.

Table 1. Probability $P_{\mathrm{germ}}(k)$ for a micro-configuration to be a germ (in %) as a function of the number k of 1's for different missing-link rates ϵ^- (in %).

k	0	1	2	3	4	5	6	7	8	9
$\epsilon^- = 0$	0	0	0	1.28	4.34	7.88	14.52	21.76	29.92	40.90
$\epsilon^- = 2$	0	0	0	0.28	2.17	3.93	7.22	11.18	15.34	21.70
$\epsilon^- = 4$	0	0	0	0.19	0.72	1.24	2.40	3.96	5.52	8.00
$\epsilon^- = 6$	0	0	0	0.02	0.06	0.09	0.24	0.34	0.63	1.30

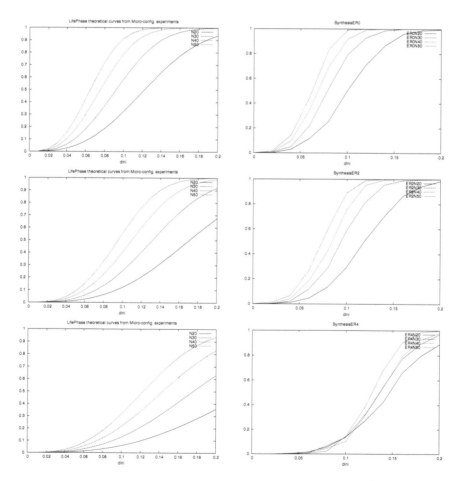

Fig. 5. Probability to reach LP as a function of d_{ini} for different lattice sizes $N \in \{20, 30, 40, 50\}$ and different missing-link rates: $\epsilon^- = 0$, $\epsilon^- = 0.02$, $\epsilon^- = 0.04$ from top to bottom. Left column shows theoretical curves calculated with the independent-germ hypothesis; the right column shows the actual measurements.

4.2   Inferring Some Aspects of the Global Behavior

Our idea is to use the previous results about germs to extend them to a description of the global behavior of *Life*. Unfortunately, we are not able to do that in the exact way. In a first approximation, let us assume that we can infer this global behavior by approximating the probability P_{LP} for a uniformly initialized system to reach LP using an "independent-germ hypothesis": interactions between potential germs are neglected and we assume that LP is reached if and only if there is at least one cell that gives birth to LP. This results in the application of formula : $P_{LP} = 1 - (1 - P_{LP1})^{N*N}$ where P_{LP1} is the probability that one cell gives birth to LP. We have $P_{LP1} = \sum_{k=0}^{9} P_{germ}(k) \cdot P_{app}(k, d_{ini})$, where $P_{app}(k, d_{ini})$ is the probability that a micro-configuration initialized randomly with d_{ini} contains k 1's. It is simply obtained by applying the binomial formula: $P_{app}(k, d_{ini}) = \binom{9}{k} d_{ini}^{k} (1 - d_{ini})^{9-k}$.

Calculated and experimental values of $P_{LP}(d_{ini}, \epsilon^-)$ are given in Fig. 5 and show that this assumption is justified in a first approximation even if the predictions seem more accurate for small values of ϵ^-.

The germ hypothesis allow us to understand better some of the observed behavior. Let us first consider the abrupt change of behavior observed for $d_{ini} \in [0, 0.20]$: this can come from the fact that as d_{ini} increases the probability to observe a micro-configuration that contains more 1's increases thus increasing the probability to find a germ in the initial configuration. We can also understand with this point of view the invariance of the sampling surfaces in the d_{ini}-axis with $d_{ini} > 0.20$ by the fact, observed in Fig. 5 that in this case $P_{LP} \sim 1$, that is the "labyrinth phase" always appears. In the same way, the shift of d_{ini}^c observed in Fig. 4 when varying ϵ^- can be explained by the looking at the variations of $P_{germ}(k)$ with ϵ^- : we see that all probabilities to reach LP decrease when ϵ^- increases. Finally, we are able to qualitatively predict the scaling of d_{ini}^c with the lattice size N from the plots the function $P_{LP}(d_{ini}, \epsilon^-)$: when d_{ini} and P_{LP} are relatively small (i.e., $P_{LP} < 0.1$), we have a linear scaling of P_{LP} with N^2; whereas as P_{LP} is close to saturation, there tends to be no variations with N.

5   Conclusion

Experiments have shown that *Life*'s transition from an "inactive-sparse phase" to a "labyrinth phase" (LP) is a continuous phase transition dependent on the synchrony rate α and whose critical value α_c is controlled by the missing-link rate ϵ^-. As the topology was perturbed (i.e., when ϵ^- increased), the inactive-sparse phase domain extends while the LP domain shrinks. The abrupt change in behavior according to the values of initial density d_{ini} was interpreted with the hypothesis that the settlement of LP results from the development of "germs", i.e. small configurations that are able to "colonize" the whole lattice. The study of the evolution of potential germs from micro-configurations allowed us to start to understand the observations and to give some predictions on the probability to reach LP starting from a random configuration. One interesting question is to examine whether these observations hold for a large class of CA or if they are somehow related to the computational universality of *Life*.

References

1. Franco Bagnoli, Raúl Rechtman, and Stefano Ruffo, *Some facts of life*, Physica A **171** (1991), 249–264.
2. Elwyn R. Berlekamp, John H. Conway, and Richard K. Guy, *Winning ways for your mathematical plays*, vol. 2, Academic Press, ISBN 0-12-091152-3, 1982, chapter 25.
3. H. Bersini and V. Detours, *Asynchrony induces stability in cellular automata based models*, Proceedings of the 4th International Workshop on the Synthesis and Simulation of Living Systems $Artificial LifeIV$ (Brooks, R. A, Maes, and Pattie, eds.), MIT Press, July 1994, pp. 382–387.
4. Hendrik J. Blok and Birger Bergersen, *Effect of boundary conditions on scaling in the "game of Life"*, Physical Review E **55** (1997), 6249–52.
5. _____ , *Synchronous versus asynchronous updating in the "game of life"*, Phys. Rev. E **59** (1999), 3876–9.
6. R.L. Buvel and T.E. Ingerson, *Structure in asynchronous cellular automata*, Physica D **1** (1984), 59–68.
7. Nazim Fatès, *Experimental study of elementary cellular automata dynamics using the density parameter*, Discrete Mathematics and Theoretical Computer Science Proceedings **AB** (2003), 155–166.
8. Nazim Fatès and Michel Morvan, *An experimental study of robustness to asynchronism for elementary cellular automata*, Submitted, `arxiv:nlin.CG/0402016`, 2004.
9. Sheng-You Huang, Xian-Wu Zou, Zhi-Jie Tan, and Zhun-Zhi Jin, *Network-induced nonequilibrium phase transition in the "game of life"*, Physical Review E **67** (2003), 026107.
10. B. A. Huberman and N. Glance, *Evolutionary games and computer simulations*, Proceedings of the National Academy of Sciences, USA **90** (1993), 7716–7718.
11. Andrew Illachinski, *Cellular automata - a discrete universe*, World Scientific, 2001.
12. Norman H. Packard and Stephen Wolfram, *Two-dimensional cellular automata*, Journal of Statistical Physics **38** (1985), 901–946.
13. William Poundstone, *The recursive universe*, William Morrow and Company, New York, 1985, ISBN 0-688-03975-8.
14. Birgitt Schönfisch and André de Roos, *Synchronous and asynchronous updating in cellular automata*, BioSystems **51** (1999), 123–143.
15. Roberto Serra and Marco Villani, *Perturbing the regular topology of cellular automata: Implications for the dynamics*, Proceedings of the 5th International Conference on Cellular Automata for Research and Industry (Geneva), 2002, pp. 168–177.

Local Information in One-Dimensional Cellular Automata

Torbjørn Helvik[1,2], Kristian Lindgren[2,*], and Mats G. Nordahl[3]

[1] Department of Mathematical Sciences, Norwegian University of Science and
Technology (NTNU), NO-7491 Trondheim, Norway
[2] Department of Physical Resource Theory, Chalmers University of Technology and
Göteborg University, SE-41296 Göteborg, Sweden
[3] Innovative Design, Chalmers University of Technology, SE-41296 Göteborg, Sweden

Abstract. A local information measure for a one-dimensional lattice
system is introduced, and applied to describe the dynamics of one-
dimensional cellular automata.

1 Introduction

Cellular automata (CA) are spatially extended dynamical systems. They have
been widely used as models of spatial dynamical processes [1]. They have
also been used as simple systems in which to study the phenomenon of self-
organization, i.e., the ability of a system to build up structure from homogeneous
initial conditions.

In this paper we use concepts from information theory to study the dynamics
of cellular automata. The field of information theory was founded by Shannon
in his 1948 paper [2]. The Shannon entropy introduced in [2] is a global quantity
that measures the average information content per symbol in symbol sequences
generated from a given distribution, when all correlations are taken into account.

Since the work of Boltzmann and Gibbs, entropy has been used in physics
as a measure of the disorder in a system. The connections between physics and
information theory are strong. For instance, in the framework of Jaynes [3], the
entropy of a system with many degrees of freedom quantifies the uncertainty
regarding the microstate of the system. A number of physicists, going back to
Wheeler's vision of "It from Bit", have argued that the concept of information
should be used to describe fundamental physical processes (e.g., [4,5]). One area
where information theory has been particularly important is in the thermodynamics of black holes (e.g., [6]).

In numerical and mathematical studies of self-organizing spatially extended
systems, the microstate of the system may often be known in great detail or exactly. In this case, it is useful to define local versions of entropy or information to
characterize the structure that arises in the time evolution [7,8]. In [8], such local

* This work has been supported by PACE (Programmable Artificial Cell Evolution),
a European Project in the EU FP6-IST-FET Complex Systems Initiative.

P.M.A. Sloot, B. Chopard, and A.G. Hoekstra (Eds.): ACRI 2004, LNCS 3305, pp. 121–130, 2004.

quantities were utilized to describe structure arising at different length scales in continuous spatiotemporal systems. Information flow in spatial dimensions and between length scales was also discussed. A number of other authors have also investigated information transport in spatially extended dynamical systems [9, 10,11,12,13,14].

If the time evolution is reversible, microscopic entropy is a conserved quantity. This is the case both for classical systems viewed in terms of phase space distributions, and in quantum mechanics. An important question is whether we can introduce a local version of the microscopic entropy that is *locally* conserved. In other words, we would like to define a corresponding local information flow so that the system obeys a local continuity equation. Since the information or entropy depends on the degree of correlation in the system, it is not immediately obvious that this can be done.

Several authors have however suggested that such an approach may be possible. This was first proposed in the context of CA by Toffoli [10], who showed the local continuity of information flow in a restricted setting of perturbations around uncorrelated equilibria of particle conserving reversible CA, such as lattice gas automata. The continuity equation for information flow in 1D CA of this paper, which takes correlations into account, was first formulated in [15].

The goal of this paper is to provide a mathematically rigourous foundation for these statements in the case of one-dimensional reversible and surjective CA rules. In Sect. 2 we introduce a local information measure for a 1D lattice system and discuss its properties. In Sect. 3 we define the information flow and derive the local continuity equation.

2   Local Information

The Shannon entropy measures the average information gained by observing a new symbol from an infinite string being read in some direction, given knowledge of the past. The intent of introducing a local information quantity is to measure exactly how much information is contained in each symbol. However, the correlations in a symbol sequence can in general be arbitrarily long. Consequently, it is impossible for information to be completely localized. That is, the local information at a particular position i cannot always be correctly computed merely by looking at the configuration in a finite neighbourhood of i. The natural approach is therefore to define the local information as a limit which converges to a local analogue of the Shannon entropy as more and more distant neighbours are taken into account, and which can be computed locally when the correlations are finite in extent. The speed of convergence depends on the typical length of correlations in the system, which could be quantified as in [16].

In the following, $\mathcal{A}$ is a finite set and $\mathcal{A}^{\mathbb{Z}}$ is the space of all bi-infinite sequences of symbols from $\mathcal{A}$. For a sequence $x \in \mathcal{A}^{\mathbb{Z}}$, we use the notation x_i^{i+k} for the length $k+1$ block $(x_i, x_{i+1}, \ldots, x_{i+k})$. A probability measure μ on $\mathcal{A}^{\mathbb{Z}}$ is defined by a consistent set of block probabilities $\mu(a_i \ldots a_{i+n})$ for all finite blocks $a_i \ldots a_{i+n}$ of symbols in $\mathcal{A}$ and positions $i \in \mathbb{Z}$.

We define the local information in the following way. Let μ be a probability measure on $\mathcal{A}^{\mathbb{Z}}$. Define the left local information at position i of $x \in \mathcal{A}^{\mathbb{Z}}$, conditioned on n past symbols, as

$$S_{\mathrm{L}}^n(x; i) = -\log \mu(x_i | x_{i-n}^{i-1}) \ . \tag{1}$$

Then define the *left local information* at position i by $S_{\mathrm{L}}(x; i) = \lim_{n \to \infty} S_{\mathrm{L}}^n(x; i)$, and define the quantities S_{R}^n and S_{R} in the same way, but conditioned to the right instead, using $\mu(x_i | x_{i+1}^{i+n})$. Finally, define the local information S as $\frac{1}{2}(S_{\mathrm{L}} + S_{\mathrm{R}})$.

The quantity $S_{\mathrm{L}}^n(x; i)$ is the information gained from the symbol at position i when only knowledge of the n left symbols are assumed. If μ is Markov there is an n such that $S_{\mathrm{L}}^n = S_{\mathrm{L}}$. In other cases, correlations are not finite and no such n will exist. The information $S_{\mathrm{L}}(x; i)$ depends on the measure μ. However, in an ergodic case, the correct probabilities of finite blocks can be recovered with probability one from x by estimating the block frequencies. In a numerical simulation, this would normally be the case.

A position i in a sequence has high local information if its symbol is unexpected given knowledge of already observed symbols. We can illustrate this using two examples of CA dynamics. For some CA, the time evolution can after an initial transient be described in terms of domains of some background pattern together with moving domain boundaries. The background pattern typically consists of blocks from a regular language which is invariant under the CA (e.g., [17]). The domain boundaries are local configurations which are often periodic and propagate with fixed velocity (often called particles), or move at random depending on the local context. They may be destroyed, transformed or created during collisions. In terms of local information, the background pattern generated by the CA will have low information, common particles will haver higher information, rarer particles will have even higher and extremely rare events will have very high information.

An example is elementary CA rule 110, using Wolfram's rule numbering system [18], which generates a background pattern of large spatial and temporal periodicity and a large diversity of particles. A space-time diagram and a numerical estimate of the local information for rule 110 is shown in Fig. 1. As can be seen, local information acts as a filter for the space-time diagram and quantifies the structure that is built up.

An example that shows a different type of spatial structure is elementary CA rule 18. Here, domain boundaries (kinks) perform random walks and annihilate pairwise upon collision [19,20]. The background pattern is in this case the regular language consisting of all blocks without consecutive 1's. The CA acts as the additive rule 90 on the background pattern. A space-time diagram for rule 18 along with the corresponding local information is found in Fig. 1. Notice that although the background in this case has non-zero entropy it is still filtered out by the local information. For both rule 110 and rule 18, the probability measure at each time step was estimated from the block frequencies for blocks of length 14 in a CA run with a sequence of length 10^7. The initial measures were iid product measures with the probability of a 1 being respectively 0.5 and 0.2.

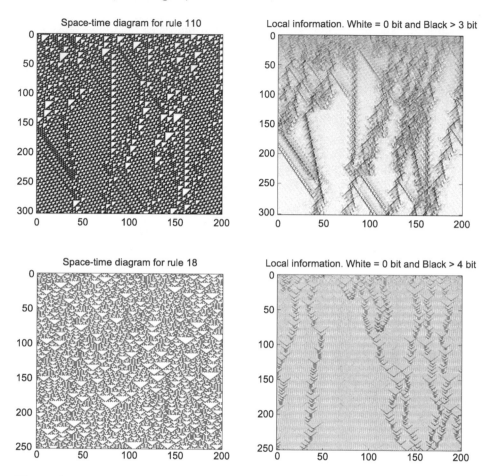

Fig. 1. Space-time diagrams and the corresponding local information S^{14} for elementary CA rules 110 and 18.

For the definition of local information to make sense, we need to check that it converges with n. The convergence of the local information S_L^n to S_L follows immediately from results by Khinchin (Lemma 7.2 and Lemma 7.7) given in connection with a proof of the entropy theorem in [21]. When applied in our setting, these prove the existence of the local information in the following sense: Fix $i \in \mathbb{Z}$. For all n, $S_L^n(\cdot; i) \in L^1(\mu)$, and $S_L^n(\cdot; i) \to S_L(\cdot; i)$ almost everywhere and in the L^1-norm. By symmetry, the same is true for $S_R^n(\cdot; i)$.

Another requirement of a local information measure is that in the case of a translation invariant measure μ the average of the local information should equal the Shannon entropy h. Write $H(X|Y)$ for the conditional entropy of the random variable X given Y. We can then show that $E[S_L^n] = H(x_0|x_{-n}^{-1})$ and $E[S_L] = h$. The same is true for S_R and S.

The first statement is proved by the calculation

$$\int_{\mathcal{A}^{\mathbb{Z}}} S_{\mathrm{L}}^n d\mu = -\sum_{x_{-n}^0} \mu(x_{-n}^0) \left(\log \frac{\mu(x_{-n}^0)}{\mu(x_{-n}^{-1})} \right) = H(x_0 | x_{-n}^{-1}) \ . \tag{2}$$

The second statement then follows from the L^1 convergence of local information and the fact that $H(x_0 | x_{-n}^{-1}) \to h$ [22, Ch. 4.2]. The equality for S_{R} and S follows since $H(x_0 | x_{-n}^{-1}) = H(x_0 | x_1^n)$.

3   Information Flow

We now consider the time evolution of the local information introduced in the previous section. In this paper, we primarily discuss reversible CA rules (e.g., [23]), where the global CA mapping on bi-infinite sequences has a unique inverse. Since microscopic classical dynamics in physics is reversible, this is a very important class of CA for modelling physical phenomena. Some well-known physical CA models are lattice gas automata [24] and CA for simulating spin systems such as the Q2R rule [25]. Simple nearest-neighbour reversible CA have in particular been studied by Takesue (e.g., [26]). The elementary reversible CA rule 26 in [26] can be considered as the simplest known system with plausible thermodynamic behaviour when one interprets its locally conserved quantity as energy.

We also consider the more general class of surjective cellular automata, where the global mapping is onto. In this case, the number of preimages of any infinite sequence is bounded [27]. Since there are interesting examples of surjective rules among the elementary CA (both additive rules, and more complicated examples such as rule 30), but only trivial examples of reversible rules, simple illustrative examples of CA behaviour are often from this class. For surjective CA, and thus also for reversible CA, the global Shannon entropy (as well as all Rényi entropies) is preserved in the time evolution [28,29]. For non-surjective rules, where infinite sequences typically have an infinite number of preimages, the entropy decreases in time reflecting the shrinking phase space.

Our aim is to show that the local information introduced above obeys a local continuity equation under the time evolution of a CA, or in other words, that there is an analogue of the continuity equations which apply to locally conserved physical quantities such as charge or particle density. We show how a flow J_{L} that satisfies a continuity equation can be constructed. We consider the case of a reversible CA F, but the construction can also be carried out for surjective CA (see [30] for details).

Fix $x \in \mathcal{A}^{\mathbb{Z}}$, and let $S_{\mathrm{L}}(t; i) = S_{\mathrm{L}}(F^t(x); i)$. We will show that there is a well-defined function $J_{\mathrm{L}}(t; i) = J_{\mathrm{L}}(F^t(x); i)$ such that

$$\Delta_t S_{\mathrm{L}} + \Delta_i J_{\mathrm{L}} = 0 \ . \tag{3}$$

Here, Δ is the forward difference operator, so that $\Delta_t S_{\mathrm{L}} = S_{\mathrm{L}}(t+1; i) - S_{\mathrm{L}}(t; i)$ and $\Delta_i J_{\mathrm{L}} = J_{\mathrm{L}}(t; i+1) - J_{\mathrm{L}}(t; i)$. With these definitions, $J_{\mathrm{L}}(t; i)$ is the information flow from position $i-1$ to position i in iteration $t+1$ of the CA. Since the flow is associated with a change between two time steps (just like other currents in physics which involve a time derivative), it will naturally involve the state and measure of the CA at $t+1$ as well as t, even though it can be expressed solely in terms of quantities defined at t,

In the following, we consider a reversible CA F with left radius m, right radius r and local map $f : \mathcal{A}^{m+r+1} \to \mathcal{A}$. The inverse of a reversible CA is also a CA [31]. Let the inverse CA $\tilde{F}$ of F have local map $\tilde{f}$ with left radius M and right radius R. Fix $x \in \mathcal{A}^{\mathbb{Z}}$, and let $y = F(x)$.

In general, the measure μ changes in time due to the cellular automaton time evolution, unless we happen to start from an invariant measure for the CA. Let μ^0 be a measure on $\mathcal{A}^{\mathbb{Z}}$ and let $\mu^t = F^t(\mu^0)$. The evolution of μ^t is given by the standard relation (e.g., [29])

$$\mu^{t+1}(y_{i-n}^i) = \sum_{f^{-1}(y_{i-n}^i)} \mu^t(x_{i-n-m}^{i+r}) \tag{4}$$

where $f^{-1}(y_{i-n}^i)$ is the set of all blocks x_{i-n-m}^{i+r} that map to y_{i-n}^i under f. For simplicity of notation, we consider the information flow at spatial coordinate 0 in the first iteration of F, but this can trivially be changed to an arbitrary position i and an arbitrary time step t to $t+1$.

We also define the joint measure ν of two consecutive time steps as the measure on $(\mathcal{A} \times \mathcal{A})^{\mathbb{Z}}$ defined by

$$\nu(x_{-n}^0, y_{-n}^0) = \mu^0(\{z_{-n-m}^r \in \mathcal{A}^{m+n+r+1} | z_{-n}^0 = x_{-n}^0 \text{ and } f(z_{-n-m}^r) = y_{-n}^0\}) . \tag{5}$$

It is easy to show that ν actually is a measure, and furthermore that ν is translation invariant if μ^0 is translation invariant. Note that by summing over all possible y_{-n}^0 or x_{-n}^0 we obtain from the definition $\nu(x_{-n}^0) = \mu^0(x_{-n}^0)$ and $\nu(y_{-n}^0) = \mu^1(y_{-n}^0)$.

From the definition of local information we have

$$\Delta_t S_{\mathrm{L}}(0) = \lim_{n \to \infty} \left(-\log \mu^1(y_0|y_{-n}^{-1}) + \log \mu^0(x_0|x_{-n}^{-1}) \right) . \tag{6}$$

Adding and subtracting the same terms, we can express this change as

$$\begin{aligned}
\Delta_t S_{\mathrm{L}}(0) &= \lim_{n \to \infty} \left(\log \frac{\nu(x_0, y_0|x_{-n+M}^{-1}, y_{-n}^{-1})}{\mu^1(y_0|y_{-n}^{-1})} - \log \frac{\nu(x_0, y_0|x_{-n}^{-1}, y_{-n+m}^{-1})}{\mu^0(x_0|x_{-n}^{-1})} + \gamma_n \right) \\
&= \lim_{n \to \infty} \left(\log \frac{\nu(x_{-n+M}^0|y_{-n}^0)}{\nu(x_{-n+M}^{-1}|y_{-n}^{-1})} - \log \frac{\nu(y_{-n+m}^0|x_{-n}^0)}{\nu(y_{-n+m}^{-1}|x_{-n}^{-1})} + \gamma_n \right)
\end{aligned} \tag{7}$$

where

$$\gamma_n = -\log \frac{\nu(x_0, y_0|x_{-n+M}^{-1}, y_{-n}^{-1})}{\nu(x_0, y_0|x_{-n}^{-1}, y_{-n+m}^{-1})} \tag{8}$$

converges to zero almost everywhere as $n \to \infty$. This can be proved using martingale methods. See [30] for details.

We can now write

$$\Delta_t S_{\mathrm{L}}(0) = \lim_{n \to \infty} \left(-\log \nu(y^0_{-n+m}|x^0_{-n}) + \log \nu(y^{-1}_{-n+m}|x^{-1}_{-n}) \right.$$
$$\left. + \log \nu(x^0_{-n+M}|y^0_{-n}) - \log \nu(x^{-1}_{-n+M}|y^{-1}_{-n}) \right) . \quad (9)$$

Let us show that two of these terms have well-defined limits. The other two can be resolved in the same way. The first term can be written as

$$- \lim_{n \to \infty} \log \nu(y^0_{-n+m}|x^0_{-n}) = - \lim_{n \to \infty} \log \mu^0(x^r_1 \in B|x^0_{-n}) \quad (10)$$

where $B \subset \mathcal{A}^r$ is the set of extensions to the right of $x^0_{-\infty}$ that are compatible with the image sequence $y^0_{-\infty}$. That is, $B = \{z^r_1 \in \mathcal{A}^r | f(x^0_{-m-r} z^r_1) = y^0_{-r}\}$. The right hand side of (10) converges because $\mu^0(x^r_1|x^0_{-n})$ converges for each block x^r_1. This follows from the convergence of local information. If $r > 0$ there is at least one block for which this conditional probability is non-zero, otherwise x will have infinite local information at some position. If $r = 0$ we define $\mu^0(x^r_1 \in B|x^0_{-n})$ to be 1. If we denote by Z_0 the set of all preimages $z^r_{-\infty}$ of $y^0_{-\infty}$ that satisfies $z^0_{-\infty} = x^0_{-\infty}$, (10) becomes

$$- \lim_{n \to \infty} \log \nu(y^0_{-n+m}|x^0_{-n}) = - \log \sum_{Z_0} \mu^0(z^r_1|x^0_{-\infty}) . \quad (11)$$

Using the reversibility of the CA, we have analogously that

$$\lim_{n \to \infty} \log \nu(x^0_{-n+M}|y^0_{-n}) = \lim_{n \to \infty} \log \mu^1(y^R_1 \in C|y^0_{-n}) \quad (12)$$

where $C \subset \mathcal{A}^R$ is the set of extensions of $y^0_{-\infty}$ to the right that are compatible with the preimage $x^0_{-\infty}$. By the same argument as above the right hand side converges. We can also express $\lim_{n \to \infty} \log \nu(x^0_{-n+M}|y^0_{-n})$ purely in terms of x and μ^0. In fact, one can prove that

$$\lim_{n \to \infty} \log \mu^1(y^R_1 \in C|y^0_{-n}) = \log \frac{\sum_{Z_0} \mu^0(z^r_{-R+1}|x^{-R}_{-\infty})}{\sum_{Z} \mu^0(z^r_{-R+1}|x^{-R}_{-\infty})} \quad (13)$$

where Z_0 is as above and Z is the set of *all* preimages of $y^0_{-\infty}$. Since F is reversible and R is the right radius of the inverse, all preimages agree on $z^{-R}_{-\infty}$, but might be different to the right of coordinate $-R$.

Equations (9), (11) and (13) now enable us to define the locally conserved information flow

$$J_{\mathrm{L}}(i) = J^+_{\mathrm{L}}(i) - J^-_{\mathrm{L}}(i) \quad (14)$$

where

$$J^-_{\mathrm{L}}(i) = - \log \sum_{Z_0} \mu^0(z^{i+r-1}_i|x^{i-1}_{-\infty}) , \quad (15)$$

$$J^+_{\mathrm{L}}(i) = - \log \frac{\sum_{Z_0} \mu^0(z^{i+r-1}_{i-R}|x^{i-R-1}_{-\infty})}{\sum_{Z} \mu^0(z^{i+r-1}_{i-R}|x^{i-R-1}_{-\infty})} . \quad (16)$$

Fig. 2. Left: The information $J_L^-(i)$ needed to determine $y_{-\infty}^{i-1}$ which is not found in $x_{-\infty}^{i-1}$ flows to the left across the boundary. Right: The information $J_L^+(i)$ in $x_{-\infty}^{i-1}$ which is not present in $y_{-\infty}^{i-1}$ leaks out to the right across the boundary.

Here, Z are the preimages of $y_{-\infty}^{i-1}$ and Z_0 are those preimages that satisfies $z_{-\infty}^{i-1} = x_{-\infty}^{i-1}$. Both $J_R^+(i)$ and $J_R^-(i)$ are non-negative.

By using these definitions, (9) can be written as the continuity equation

$$\Delta_t S_L + \Delta_i J_L = 0 \tag{17}$$

which is valid at every i and t and for all measures μ^0, not necessarily translation invariant.

The expressions J_L^- and J_L^+ have natural information theoretic interpretations. This is more readily apparent if the flow is written in terms of quantities defined both at t and $t+1$:

$$J_L(1) = J_L^+(1) - J_L^-(1) = \lim_{n \to \infty} \left(-\log \nu(x_{-n+M}^0 | y_{-n}^0) + \log \nu(y_{-n+m}^0 | x_{-n}^0) \right) . \tag{18}$$

The quantity $-\log \nu(y_{-n+m}^0 | x_{-n}^0)$ is the additional information needed to uniquely specify y_{-n+m}^0 when knowing x_{-n}^0. The definitions above can be viewed as a choice of boundary conditions in the definition of the flow. In the case of $\Delta S_L(1)$, we only want the contribution from information flow across the boundary between 0 and 1 and not the boundary at $-n$. Due to the condition on the left boundary of the finite strings (knowing m more symbols of x than of y, see Fig. 2) the left part of y_{-n+m}^0 is uniquely determined by x_{-n}^0, and we avoid the unwanted effect of an information flow across the left border. Therefore, the remaining information needed to determine the right part of y_{-n+m}^0 must come from the coordinates to the right of 0. Consequently, a flow $J_L^-(1)$ from coordinate 1 to 0 is induced. The limit $n \to \infty$ must be taken to ensure that all information contained in $x_{-\infty}^0$ about its left prolongation is taken into account.

The quantity $-\log \nu(x_{-n+M}^0 | y_{-n}^0)$ is the additional information needed to uniquely specify x_{-n+M}^0 given knowledge of y_{-n}^0. Once again the left boundary conditions ensure that the left part of x_{-n+M}^0 is uniquely determined, see Fig. 2. However, not all information about the right part of x_{-n+M}^0 is found in y_{-n}^0. This missing information leaks out to the coordinates to the right of 0 inducing the flow $J_L^+(1)$. Technically, the boundary conditions are obtained by introducing a term γ_n which vanishes in the limit, see (7).

By an argument similar to that used for reversible CA, the existence of a continuity equation can also be extended to a larger class of CA than the reversible CA. The crux of the argument used to find a continuity equation for reversible CA is that all preimages of y_{-n}^0 agree on a central block. This is also the case for those surjective CA where almost all $y \in \mathcal{A}^{\mathbb{Z}}$ have exactly one preimage. These are the CA with $M(F) = 1$ in the notation of Hedlund [27]. In this case $J_L^-(i)$ has the same expression, but in $J_L^+(i)$ R will be changed to the stopping time τ, which is the smallest integer such that all preimages of $y_{-\infty}^{i-1}$ agree to the left of coordinate $i - \tau$. We will present the details of this and other cases as well as examples in [30].

4   Conclusions

We have studied local information quantities S_L and S_R that measure the local information density of a one-dimensional lattice system. These are useful for detecting and quantifying structure in a lattice configuration.

An information flow J_L has been introduced such that a continuity equation $\Delta_t S_L + \Delta_i J_L = 0$ holds under iteration of a one-dimensional reversible CA. We have discussed how the CA generates two different types J_L^+ and J_L^- of information flow satisfying $J_L = J_L^+ - J_L^-$. Moreover, we have sketched how an expression for J_L may be found in other cases by choosing boundary conditions in a suitable way.

The continuity equation is a fundamental property of information transport in reversible systems. But we expect local information in cellular automata to have further interesting properties. In particular, a continuity equation in physics can be viewed as a constraint, rather than an equation that determines the dynamics of the system. In a similar way, one may expect information flow to have different dynamic characteristics in different CA. We have seen examples of CA building up high information in local configurations. Other CA might show diffusive behaviour and smear out initial inhomogeneities in local information. Such properties would give much information about the dynamical behaviour of the CA.

References

1. Wolfram, S., ed.: Theory and Application of Cellular Automata, World Scientific (1986)
2. Shannon, C.E.: A mathematical theory of communication. Bell System Tech. J. **27** (1948) 379–423, 623–656
3. Jaynes, E.T.: Information theory and statistical mechanics. Phys. Rev. (2) **106** (1957) 620–630
4. Wheeler, J.: Information, Physics, Quantum: The Search for Links, in Complexity, Entropy and the Physics of Information. Addison-Wesley, Redwood City, CA (1988)
5. Lloyd, S.: Computational capacity of the universe. Physical Review Letters **88** (2002) 237901.
6. Bekenstein, J.: Black holes and entropy. Physical Review D **7** (1973) 2333–2346

7. Eriksson, K.E., Lindgren, K.: Structural information in self-organizing systems. Physica Scripta **35** (1987) 388–397
8. Eriksson, K.E., Lindgren, K., B.Å.Månsson: Structure, Context, Complexity, and Organization. World Scientific, Singapore (1987)
9. Kaneko, K.: Lyapunov analysis and information flow in coupled map lattices. Physica D **23** (1986) 436–447
10. Toffoli, T.: Information transport obeying the continuity equation. IBM J. Res. Develop. **32** (1988) 29–36
11. Vastano, J.A., Swinney, H.L.: Information transport in spatiotemporal systems. Physical Review Letters **60** (1988) 1773–1776
12. Schreiber, T.: Spatio-temporal structure in coupled map lattices: two-point correlations versus mutual information. Journal of Physics. A. **23** (1990) L393–L398
13. Schreiber, T.: Measuring information transfer. Physical Review Letters **85** (2000) 461–464
14. Lindgren, K., Eriksson, A., Eriksson, K.E.: Flows of information in spatially extended chemical dynamics. To appear in Proceedings of ALife 9 (2004)
15. Eriksson, K.E., Lindgren, K., Nordahl, M.G.: Continuity of information flow in discrete reversible systems. Chalmers preprint (1993)
16. Grassberger, P.: Toward a quantitative theory of self-generated complexity. International Journal of Theoretical Physics **25** (1986) 907–938
17. Hanson, J.E., Crutchfield, J.P.: Computational mechanics of cellular automata: an example. Physica D **103** (1997) 169–189
18. Wolfram, S.: Universality and complexity in cellular automata. Physica D **10** (1984) 1–35
19. Grassberger, P.: Chaos and diffusion in deterministic cellular automata. Physica D **10** (1984) 52–58
20. Eloranta, K., Nummelina, E.: The kink of cellular automaton Rule 18 performs a random walk. Journal of Statistical Physics **69** (1992) 1131–1136
21. Khinchin, A.: Mathematical Foundations of Information Theory. Dover Publications Inc., New York, N.Y. (1957)
22. Cover, T.M., Thomas, J.A.: Elements of information theory. Wiley Series in Telecommunications. John Wiley & Sons Inc., New York (1991)
23. Toffoli, T., Margolus, N.H.: Invertible cellular automata: a review. Physica D **45** (1990) 229–253
24. Frisch, Hasslacher, B., Pomeau, Y.: Lattice-gas automata for the Navier-Stokes equation. Physical Review Letters **56** (1986) 1505–1508
25. Vichniac, G.: Simulating physics with cellular automata. Physica D **10** (1984) 96–115
26. Takesue, S.: Reversible cellular automata and statistical mechanics. Physical Review Letters **59** (1987) 2499–2502
27. Hedlund, G.A.: Endomorphisms and automorphisms of the shift dynamical system. Mathematical Systems Theory **3** (1969) 320–375
28. Lindgren, K.: Correlations and random information in cellular automata. Complex Systems **1** (1987) 529–543
29. Lindgren, K., Nordahl, M.G.: Complexity measures and cellular automata. Complex Systems **2** (1988) 409–440
30. Helvik, T., Lindgren, K., Nordahl, M.: Local information in discrete lattice systems. (Forthcoming)
31. Richardson, D.: Tesselations with local transformations. Journal of Computer and Systems Sciences **5** (1972) 373–388

Diffusion Controlled Cellular Automaton Performing Mesh Partitioning

Jiří Kroc

Mikkeli Business Campus, Helsinki School of Economics
Lönnrotinkatu 5, 50100 Mikkeli, Finland,
kroc@c-mail.cz,
http://www.c-mail.cz/kroc

Abstract. A model performing mesh partitioning into computationally equivalent mesh parts on regular square lattices using a diffusion controlled cellular automaton (DCCA) is proposed and studied in this article. Every processor has assigned a domain seed at the beginning of a simulation. Algorithm works with growth of seeds and migration of domain borders, the later is triggered when the difference of diffusive agents on both sides of a border exceeds a given threshold. The model is built using self-organization principles ensuring convergence. Solutions are dynamically stable configurations achieved from any initial configuration.

1 Introduction

Mathematical formulation of physical, engineering and other scientific problems often leads to a model expressed by a set of Partial Differential Equations (PDE). Numerical formulation of a set of PDE is typically done by the Finite Element Method (FEM). This technique splits a continuous problem – typically without any analytic solution – into a finite number of discrete problems called the finite elements. The whole problem is then solved by this discrete solution above the whole set of finite elements. Fine FE meshes approximates the continuous problem more precisely then coarse meshes. Therefore, the data storage requirement and the computational cost rapidly becomes a 'bottleneck' of a computer simulation. This naturally leads to use of parallel computers to solve extra large FE meshes. One of the most used techniques – splits a mesh into sub-domains where each sub-domain is assigned to different processor – uses large distributed memories, and message passing for inter-processor communication. Among all parallel algorithms dealing with this problem, we could distinguish three main groups of methods: the parallel direct methods, the parallel iterative methods and the domain decomposition methods.

Most of the research had been done on development of mesh partitioning algorithms based on a load balancing approach, see for example the papers [1, 2,3] and references therein. Algorithms with special interest to the aspect ratio of the sub-domains were investigated later on. The most efficient mesh partitioning algorithms are now implemented in program libraries, like [4,5,6,7,8,9].

P.M.A. Sloot, B. Chopard, and A.G. Hoekstra (Eds.): ACRI 2004, LNCS 3305, pp. 131–140, 2004.
© Springer-Verlag Berlin Heidelberg 2004

The partitioning problem is known to be NP-complete in general and there is no single algorithm that is always capable of producing the best solution. Many algorithms are based on heuristics of varying degrees of efficiency, which may fail because of special properties of the partitioning problem being considered. Most of these algorithms are based on graph theory because the topology of the finite element mesh could be represented as a graph.

Cellular automata (CA) are often represented as discrete dynamical systems where space, time and variables are discrete. CA–model discretize space into a given number of dimensions – in our case into two–dimensional (2D) lattice of squares. The elements of this lattice are called cells. A neighbourhood is defined to every cell – a list of the nearest neighbouring cells – that is uniform through the whole lattice. Every cell contains a list of variables, e.g. domain number, amount of a diffusive agent, etc. The evolution of the system is driven by a transition rule that computes new values of variables of an updated cell using old values of variables of cells laying in the neighbourhood and values of the cell itself taken at the previous CA–step. Comprehensive information about the CA can be found in [10,11,12,13], at the web page of the author and at links provided there. A good introduction into CA with examples is provided at web page [14].

We propose a novel diffusion controlled cellular automaton (DCCA) model performing domain decomposition on square lattices – restricted to square lattices – into N computationally equal parts. Algorithm works with growth of domains from domain seeds using migration of domain borders, the later is triggered when the difference of the diffusive agent on both sides of a boundary exceeds a given threshold. The model is built using self-organization principles ensuring convergence. This model performs load balancing only. CA-models of dynamic recrystallization [15] and living cells [16] motivate growth of seeds, and models of dynamic recrystallization and grain boundary migration [17,18] motivate migration of domain boundaries.

2   Cellular Automaton Model

Explanation of the model is done in three subsequent parts in order to make the definition of this model easier to follow. In the first one, the general concept of diffusion controlled cellular automata (DCCA) is proposed. In the second one, all variables used in the proposed model are defined. Finally, all five sub-steps of the DCCA-model are defined.

General Concept of Diffusion Controlled CA. A diffusion controlled cellular automaton is built upon several sub-steps: growth of domains from domain seeds, diffusion of a diffusive agent, and migration of domain boundaries. All starts in domain seeds; the rest of cells is empty. Their number defines the number of domains, which are finally assigned to distinct processors. Every domain seed initially occupy space of just one cell where the initial amount of the diffusive agent – conserved during the whole simulation – is stored.

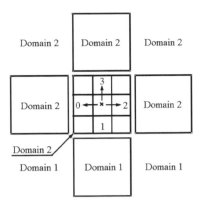

Fig. 1. A figure displaying dispersion of the *growth-factor* into three directions $distr[i]$ for the middle cell under consideration within the first diffusion step

Growth of a domain is allowed only if the difference of the diffusive agent between growing domain and empty cells exceeds a given threshold. If domain borders meet then growth is terminated and the migration starts to operate. When the difference of diffusive agent on one side exceeds a prescribed threshold, a migration event occurs, i.e. domain boundary of domain having a higher content of the diffusive agent migrates into domain having a lower content.

Definition of Variables. The algorithm is relatively complicated because one complete step is composed of five subsequent sub-steps: *growth, migration$_1$, diffusion$_1$, diffusion$_2$, migration$_2$* where the lower index tells that given process is split into two separate parts. One cycle is accomplished only when all five sub-steps in the above defined order is accomplished.

The following variables are used: (a) *domain-number* assigns an unique number to all cells from a given domain or to wall; (b) *growth-factor* stores the amount of growth factor; (c) *ditribution*[0], *distribution*[1], *ditribution*[2], and *distribution*[3] are temporary variables used to store the fractions of *growth-factor* split in four directions: they are defined as relative translations [-1,0], [0,-1], [1,0], and [0,1]; and (d) *protect* protects a given cell – assumed to migrate – from being migrated by other neighbouring cell. A cell under consideration means the cell with the relative coordinates [0,0].

All variables belonging to every cell are initialized to zero values except seeds. Every simulation starts in a number of cells – called *domain seeds* – that is equal to the number of required domains. The amount of *growth-factor* is strictly conserved in every domain.

Rules Defining DCCA. All five rules defining the DCCA algorithm are explained in this subsection.

Growth rule G performs growth of domain seeds until all space that could be occupied is consumed:

(a) All cells from the von Neumann neighbourhood (W, S, E, N) of the cell under consideration are tested against possibility to grow into the place occupied by it. Growth is not allowed into cells marked as the wall cells.

(b) A neighbouring cell with the greatest content of *growth-factor* will be allowed to grow into the position of cell under the consideration. When two or more domains meet, the domain having greatest potential to grow wins.

This sub-step **G** is checked during every cycle even in the case when no empty cell is available to be occupied by growth of a domain. Cells initialized as a wall enables us to insert irregular boundary and holes into the simulated lattice.

Migration rule M1 tests five conditions for a cell under consideration. Variable *protect* could be set to a value that lock the potential migration sub-step against being influenced by other cells until the migration sub-step is finished. A migration threshold is defined. It ensures that migration operates above some difference of diffusive agents of neighbouring domains:

(0) Is the difference of the *growth-factor* of both cells above the threshold?

(a) If *domain-number*s of cells [0,0] and [-1,0] are different $\Rightarrow$ set *protect* = 10.

(b) If *domain-number*s of cells [0,0] and [0,-1] are different $\Rightarrow$ set *protect* = 11.

(c) If *domain-number*s of cells [0,0] and [1,0] are different $\Rightarrow$ set *protect* = 12.

(d) If *domain-number*s of cells [0,0] and [0,1] are different $\Rightarrow$ set *protect* = 13.

Condition (0) has to be fulfilled for all cases. Conditions (a), (b), (c), and (d) are exclusive.

Implementation of the sub-step **M1** before diffusion sub-steps **D1** and **D2** and the sub-step **M2** is fundamental. It is necessary to protect cells that are going to be migrated from diffusion of *growth-factor* inside them. The *growth-factor* belonging to any domain has to be conserved.

Diffusion rule D1 is implemented by use of a modified finite difference scheme of the Laplace operator. One physical diffusion step is split into two distinct sub-steps. In the first one **D1**, the *growth-factor* is deposited into four directions. In the second one **D2**, deposited *growth-factor* is shifted into appropriate neighbouring cells and then one physical diffusion step is finished:

(a) Number of neighbouring cells belonging to the given domain within von Neumann neighbourhood is counted (maximum of four).

(b) The amount of *growth-factor* is equally divided between all neighbouring cells within the von Neumann neighbourhood and the cell itself that belongs to the same domain. Remaining amount of the *growth-factor* after this division stays in the cell under consideration. Therefore, the *growth-factor* is conserved!

(c) *Growth-factor* belonging to a neighbouring cell is dispersed into the variable *distr*[i] that are associated with direction i pointing to this cell.

A schematic figure displaying preparation of dispersion of the *growth-factor* into three directions *distr*[i] for a cell under consideration can be seen in Fig. 1. Data are stored in the cell that disperses the *growth-factor*. Please

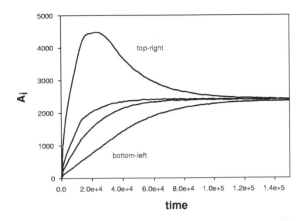

Fig. 2. The resulting time evolution of domain sizes A_i for four domain seeds located in the bottom-left corner where domain sizes belonging to top-right and bottom-left seeds are marked

note that a cell that does not belong to given domain is located in the south. Therefore, the *growth-factor* cannot be dispersed into this direction denoted by the number equal to 1. Hence, the total amount of diffusive agent is divided into four equal parts – three neighbours and the cell under consideration.

Diffusion rule D2 represents the second finalizing part from two subsequent diffusive steps. Diffusive agent is migrated into destination cells selected in diffusive sub-step **D1**:
(a) The amount of *growth-factor* deposited in temporary variables $distr[i]$ of neighbouring cells – i.e. in directions pointing to this cell – belonging to the same domain are added into the *growth-factor* variable.
Remark: When we collect the *growth-factor* from east then we take the *growth-factor* from variable $distr[(0+2)\%4]$. The symbol % denotes modulo operation.

Migration rule M2 is the final sub-step of the whole cycle. It is the second part of migration, $migration_2$. Protected movements of domain border into the cell [0,0] are realized in this sub-step:
(a) If $protect = 10$ then the domain from direction [-1,0] is migrated into.
(b) If $protect = 11$ then the domain from direction [0,-1] is migrated into.
(c) If $protect = 12$ then the domain from direction [1,0] is migrated into.
(d) If $protect = 13$ then the domain from direction [0,1] is migrated into.
(e) The variable *protect* is set to zero.

Those new potential reorientations in the second migration sub-step **M2** leading to creation of disconnected small domains are rejected. The whole simulation cycle is accomplished by the second migration sub-step. Only output from this sub-step can be used as the numerically correct one.

3   Results and Discussion

The properties of the CA-model are studied on several examples working with four and eight domain seeds and a change of the domain shape. Every sub-step of the full simulation step requires different amount of time to be completed. Therefore, optimization of the proposed algorithm should be primarily focused into the most computationally expensive sub-steps of the algorithm. The algorithm of growth sub-step **G** is based on diffusion of the *growth-factor* – let us call it diffusive-growth – that enables us to control achievement of approximately globular shape of domains.

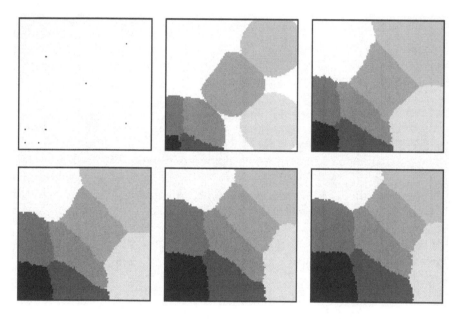

Fig. 3. Snapshots of the evolution of domain shapes taken at six different times in the case of eight domain seeds. The simulation starts at the top-left corner and proceeds in rows (times 0, 1k, 10k, 20k, 60k, and 150k)

Let us assume for a moment that growth is without restriction of diffusion of the diffusive agent – i.e. the pure growth. The good message is that the pure growth without diffusion – i.e. *non-diffusive-growth* – is roughly ten times faster compared to the growth with presence of the *growth-factor*. The bad message about the *non-diffusive-growth* is that it produces rather unrealistic initial domain decompositions – with elongated and narrow domain shapes – requiring much longer migration time. The migration sub-step **M** is much computationally expensive than the growth one **G**. Therefore, the total simulation time is more longer for the *non-diffusive-growth* then for *diffusive-growth*.

There is shown evolution of initial configurations having four domain seeds and two different initial configurations with eight domain seeds. The initial stage of evolution of domains of *four domain seeds* is same as in Fig. 3 with four seeds located at bottom-left corner before impingement them with other seeds. Those seeds located in the bottom-left corner are initial ones, the initial configuration is far away from the ideal one. In other words, one domain – the top-right – is growing too fast and growth of the others is suppressed by growth of this dominant domain. Therefore, simulation spends a long time in migration sub-step **M** and the total simulation time becomes too long. The resulting area A_i evolution with respect to time of all four domain sizes can be seen in Fig. 2 where the top curve belongs to the domain in the top-right corner. The curve having the smallest slope belongs to the domain located in the bottom-left corner, see Fig. 3. More ideal positions of domain seeds diminish the simulation time.

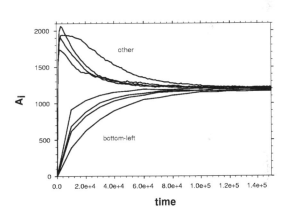

Fig. 4. The resulting time evolution of domain sizes A_i for eight domain seeds located in the area without a hole – for the topology in Fig. 3

A simulation with *eight domain seeds* is displayed in Figs. 3 and 4 where snapshots of the evolution of domain shapes are provided in Fig. 3 and relevant evolutions of the domain sizes in Fig. 4. Not surprisingly, the use of a higher number of seeds for the same total size of the simulated lattice diminishes the total simulation time. It is because domains become smaller. Distances that have to be migrated by domain borders are shorter. The final shapes of all domains except one located in the up-left corner are convex. Non-convex shapes of domains automatically mean longer domain borders.

The initial positions of domain seeds are not distributed homogeneously. Four seeds are located closely in the bottom-left corner and the other four seeds are spread across the rest of the lattice. This initial configuration leads to a distorted growth of seeds. Some are suppressed to grow by others that are growing too fast.

A simulation with *eight domain seeds and a hole* located in the middle of the lower part of the lattice is displayed in Figs. 5 and 6. Diffusive agent serves as a

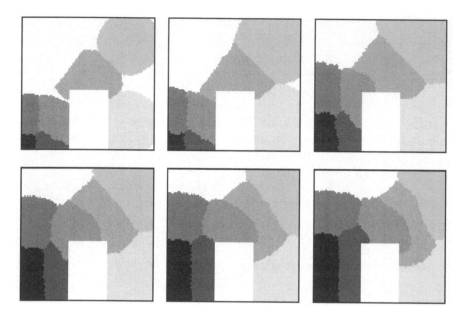

Fig. 5. The evolution of domain shape at six different times in the case of eight domain seeds located in the very same positions as in Fig. 3 and with a hole in the middle of the lower part of the lattice. The simulation starts at the top-left corner and proceeds in rows (times 1k, 2k, 20k, 50k, 80k, and 150k)

compactor of domains, i.e. it helps to keep them together. Nevertheless, presence of holes brings anisotropy into the lattice and slows down the overall diffusivity within the lattice. Hence, the total simulation time is substantially longer than in the case without presence of the hole.

The simulation starts in the similar way as in the case of eight domain seeds without a hole. Growth of domain seeds quickly fills the whole lattice. The problem is that those four domain seeds located in the bottom-left corner are allowed to grow and migrate only upwards contrary to the previous case. Therefore, their movement is substantially slowed down. Induced anisotropy of the lattice leads to production of non-convex domains. One of domains – the second one from the up-right corner – has a quite large curvature.

The CA-model is constructed in such way that domains finally occupy the approximately equal volume, and therefore, processors have the same computational load. This is done by use of self-organization principles in the CA-model. It is easy to see from results that position of the domain seeds at the very beginning of a simulation strongly affects the total simulation time – by at least one order of magnitude – and the final shape of domains. The CA-model proposed in this contribution is formulated for the case of regular square lattices having four neighbours. Generalizations to trigonal lattices having three neighbours and to non-periodic grids is the subject of the future work.

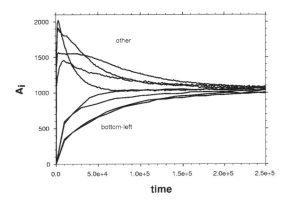

Fig. 6. The time evolution of domain sizes for eight domain seeds located in the area with the hole – for the very same topology as in Fig. 5. Compare it to the case having the very same location of domain seeds but without the hole, Figs. 3 and 4

It is expected that domain decomposition of complicated topologies using DCCA in 3D is too hard for this model. There is development of more sophisticated models, which could be sufficient to solve any problem in 3D. This model should be understood as an introduction into the whole class of new models.

4 Conclusions

A novel diffusion controlled cellular automaton (DCCA) model performing domain decomposition on regular square lattices with special attention to load balancing is proposed and studied in this work. It is recognized that convergence speed is the highest in the case when the positions of domain seeds are estimated closely to their ideal positions. It was found that presence of holes within the lattice leads in the case of bad positions of the initial seeds to a dramatic increase of the total simulation time.

Acknowledgments. This work is dedicated to the memory of my mother Miroslava and to my son Václav who encourage me to work on this research by their presence in my life. The work was done during the first half of the year 2003 when I was recovering from injury of my left leg and from several operations. The author is indebted to J.D. Eckart for his program [14] used to display simulated data. The whole research and conference was sponsored from private funds.

References

1. C. Farhat and M. Lesoinne: Mesh partitioning algorithms for the parallel solution of P.D.E.s. Applied Numerical Mathematics **12** (1993) 443–457

2. D.C. Hodgson and P.K. Jimack: Efficient mesh partitioning for parallel elliptic differential equation solvers. Computing Systems in Engineering **6** (1995) 1–12
3. L. Lammer and B. Topping: Partitioning of computational meshes. In: B. Topping and L. Lammer (edts): High Performance Computing for Computational Mechanics. Saxe-Coburg Publications (2000) 75–104
4. B. Hendrickson and R. Leland: The Chaco users guide - version 2.0. Technical Report SAND93-2339, Sandia Natl. Lab., Albuquerque NM (1995)
5. G. Karypis and V. Kumar: METIS - unstructured graph partitioning and sparse matrix ordering system - version 2.0. Technical report, University of Minnesota, Dept. Computer Science, Minneapolis MN 55455 (1995)
6. R. Preis: The Party partitioning library - user manual - version 1.1. Technical Report SAND93-2339, University Paderborn (1996)
7. F. Pellegrini: Scotch 3.1 user's guide. Technical Report 1137-96, Laboratoire Bordelais de Recherche en Informatique, Université Bordeaux (1996)
8. C. Walshaw, M. Cross, and M.G. Everett: A localized algorithm for optimizing unstructured mesh partitions. Int. J. Supercomputer Appl., **9(4)** (1996) 280–295
9. C. Farhat, S. Lanteri, and H.D. Simon: TOP/DOMDEC - a software tool for mesh partitioning and parallel processing. Journal of Computing Systems in Engineering, **6(1)** (1995) 13–26
10. T. Toffoli and N. Margolus: Cellular Automata Theory. MIT Press, Cambridge (1987)
11. T. Toffoli: Cellular automata as an alternative to (rather than an approximation of) differential equations in modelling physics. Physica **10D** (1984) 117–127
12. G.Y. Vichniac: Simulating physics with cellular automata. Physica **10D** (1984) 96–116
13. Y. Bar-Yam: Dynamics of Complex Systems. Addison-Wesley (1996)
14. D.J. Eckart: Cellular/Cellang environment. Technical report (2002)
15. J. Kroc: Application of Cellular Automata Simulations to Modelling of Dynamic Recrystallization. Lecture Notes in Computer Science, **2329** (2002) 773–782
16. J. Kroc: Simulation of chemically limited growth of cells within living tissues: a case study (to appear)
17. J. Kroc and V. Paidar: Modelling of Recrystallization and Grain Boundary Migration by Cellular Automata. Materials Science Forum, **426–432** (2003) 3873–3878
18. J. Kroc: Influence of Lattice Anisotropy on Models Formulated by Cellular Automata in Presence of Grain Boundary Movement: a Case Study. Materials Science Forum (to appear)

Cellular Automata with Majority Rule on Evolving Network

Danuta Makowiec

Institute of Theoretical Physics and Astrophysics, Gdańsk University,
80-952 Gdańsk, ul. Wita Stwosza 57, Poland

Abstract. The cellular automata discrete dynamical system is considered as the two-stage process: the majority rule for the change in the automata state and the rule for the change in topological relations between automata. The influence of changing topology to the cooperative phenomena, namely zero-temperature ferromagnetic phase transition, is observed.

1 Introduction

Lattice models are the basic instrument in the study of phase transitions in equilibrium statistical mechanics (see, e.g., [1]). The Ising model is the simplest model of nearest-neighbor ferromagnetic interactions where the collective features are studied. Traditionally, the phase transition has been considered in regular lattices. According to the renormalization group theory, detailed structure of interactions as well as the structure of network connections are irrelevant. Therefore, for example, cellular automata have been continuously tested with the hope that these systems can imitate nature [2].

If the cellular automata are considered on a regular lattice and each site i of the lattice is occupied by a binary variable, s_i, which assumes the values ± 1, then referring to these variables as *spins* which point either 'up' (+1) or 'down' (−1), we employ the terminology of the Ising model. The Ising nearest-neighbor interaction in case of cellular automata becomes usually a simple majority rule, it is: if most of the nearest neighbors of i spin point up (down) at time t then the value of the i spin at time $t + 1$ is up (down). This deterministic rule is interpreted as the zero-temperature approximation to the Ising interactions. The research here is aimed on the ergodicity, i.e., on the uniqueness of the final state. Especially, one asks if starting from a random distribution of spins states one ends up with a homogeneous states of *all spins up* or *all spins down*. To mimic the temperature effects one adds a stochastic noise to perturb with some probability the execution of the deterministic dynamics. The research here is focused on properties of the transition from the non-ordered phase to the ordered phase - ferromagnetic phase transition.

Recent research in the structure and topology of real networks [3,4] has shown that social, biological, technological networks are far from being regular. However, they also are being far from a random network. It has been shown that

P.M.A. Sloot, B. Chopard, and A.G. Hoekstra (Eds.): ACRI 2004, LNCS 3305, pp. 141–150, 2004.

networks called *small-world* networks and *scale-free* networks exhibit mixed properties of regular lattices and a random graph [3,5]. This has trigged to study of standard models of statistical mechanics in these networks. The transition from non-ordered phase to the ordered phase in the spin system spanned on the small-world network shows a change in behavior from the regular case to the mean-field characteristics [7,12]. Interesting that, depending on the network construction, the phase transition at the finite temperature exists or not [6]. Moreover, when the scale-free network is employed then the critical properties of the Ising model are different from those ones observed in the regular networks [13,14]. Many authors have considered other problems in these new networks: percolation properties [8], the spread of infection diseases [9] social relations [10], computer organization [11].

Small-world networks are intermediates between regular lattices and the random graph. A small-world network is generated by rewiring with a probability p the links of a regular lattice by long-distance random links [5]. The presence of a small fraction of 'short-cuts' connecting otherwise distant points, drastically reduces the average shortest distance between any pair of nodes in network.

In case of cellular automata such the small-world network means that the cellular automata is no longer homogeneous — inhomogeneity is due to the topology. Sets of nearest-neighbors differ from a site to a site.

There is one important property which is ubiquitous in biological and artificial networks and which is missed in the small-world network — the distribution of the vertex degree does not show wings decaying as a power-law. Two important ingredients have been shown to be sufficient to generate such feature: growing number of vertices and preferential attachment of links. The well established Barabasi-Albert model based on these two mechanisms has been proposed [3]. The distributions of the vertex degree in this network is of the form $P(k) \propto k^{-\gamma}$ where $\gamma \in [2,3]$ and k a vertex degree. Thus adapting the Barabasi-Albert idea to cellular automata one obtains a computing system with the topology that evolves.

In this paper we address the question of the role played by the topology in the zero-temperature ferromagnetic transition considered in the cellular automata of spins. The starting system is the cellular automata on a square lattice. The square lattice used here is strongly clustered in the sense that if j and k are neighbors of i then there is a short path between them that does not pass through i. In order to keep the high clustered property (typical for the small-world network) and reproduce the distribution of the vertex degree with the power-low decay (sign of the scale-free network) we propose the evolution rule for the network. Hence, the cellular automata time step means the change of the spin states and the change of the network topology. It will be shown that with increasing p- the rewiring parameter, the cellular automata work as the solver to the *density classification task* [15], highly accurately, namely our cellular automata converge to a fixed point of all 1's if the initial configuration contains more 1's than -1's by 2%, and, symmetrically, to a fixed point of all -1's if the initial configuration contains more -1's than 1's by 2%.

2   Model Description

We present the model of the spin cellular automata located in N vertices among which there is an explicit integer parameter N_0 fixing the total number of edges. These N spins are located to form a square lattice with the periodic boundary conditions. Hence, if the linear size of the lattice is L then $N = L \times L$ and $N_0 = 4N$. We start with the ordinary nearest-neighbor relations, i.e., for any i site the nearest-neighbor spins are located in the following set of vertex indices: $N(i, 0) = \{i - L, i - 1, i, i + 1, i + L\}$. Initially, each spin state is set up randomly with the probability ρ.

The evolution step consists of the two subsequent steps: (A) the asynchronous stochastic evolution of topological relations and (B) the synchronous deterministic majority rule.

2.1   Evolution of the Lattice

In each time-step t and for each vertex i the following rearrangement of the edges is performed: from the set of neighbors $N(i, t)$ of the vertex i (at the given time t) one element j is chosen at random with the probability p. Thus p relates to the parameter of the small-world evolution [5]. Then, another vertex k is picked up from the set of all vertices $N - \{i\}$ randomly. A new edge is created between i and k independently of the fact that there was or not an edge between them. The edge between i and j is deleted. Hence the total number of edges N_0 is conserved. This evolution we will call stochastic on the contrary to the evolution in which some preferences are applied. The proposed preferences are in the agreement with the basic conviction how to obtain a scale free distribution for the vertex degree: 'the richer you are, the richer you get' — principle [3].

The preferences are as follows: in each time step t and for each vertex i, from the set of neighbors $N(i, t)$ an element j is chosen with the probability modified by the degree of j vertex. Namely, the probability that j neighbor is unlinked is

$$p[1 - \frac{deg(j)}{T}] \tag{1}$$

where $deg(j)$ denotes the degree of j vertex, T denotes the value of the unlink threshold. The degree of a vertex denotes the number of edges attached to the vertex. By (1) if $deg(j) \geq T$ then it is impossible to unlink j. This process will be called the intensional detachment. The edge between i and j is deleted. Then a new vertex is randomly chosen but with the preference to link to a vertex with the high vertex degree. It is, a randomly picked up vertex k is accepted with probability

$$\frac{deg(k)}{T} \tag{2}$$

Thus if $deg(k) \geq T$ then randomly chosen k is certainly accepted. This process will be called the preferential attachment.

In the following we will name:
model 0 : the completely stochastic edge evolution,

model 1 : the intensional detachment and the stochastic attachment,
model 2 : the stochastic detachment and the preferential attachment,
model 3 : the intensional detachment and the preferential attachment.

2.2 Evolution of Spins

Synchronously, in each time step, the majority rule is applied to set the state of every spin in the next time-step. The rule acts on all spins belonging to the the set of nearest neighbors $N(i, t)$ of the given ith spin. In the case when the result of voting is zero, the ith spin does not change the state.

3 Results

The system simulated is a square lattice with $L = 200$ and periodic boundary conditions. We start with a random distribution of spin states with probability ρ to set the spin state to $+1$. In each time step we measure *magnetization* – the sum of all spins states normalized by L^2. If the magnetization is 1 or the time step reaches the limit of the hundredth step, then we stop the evolution and record the following characteristics: magnetization, susceptibility (the variation of the magnetization), vertex degree and number of time steps to reach the stable state. The experiment is repeated 200 times for each p and ρ value. The threshold value for the preferences, see (1), (2), is $T = 8$ in all experiments.

3.1 Final State Characteristic

The sharp change in properties of the final state of cellular automata is observed when ρ is crossing 0.5, see Fig.1, Fig.2. The final state switches between the state of *all spins down* if $\rho < 0.5$ (magnetization $= -1$) to the state of *all spins up* if $\rho > 0.5$ (magnetization $= 1$), Fig.1. Depending on the model of the network evolution this transformation goes fast: model 0, or less rapidly: model 3. The transformation can be estimated by measuring the intervals of ρ around the 0.5- value which lead to the final states with with magnetization close to ± 1, see Fig.1. More accurate marks for these intervals can be found by observing susceptibility, see Fig.2. In case of unperturbed network ($p = 0$) the susceptibility takes the parabola-like shape on the log-plots. With increasing p the suscpetibility becomes the sharply pointed curve with maximum at $\rho = 0.5$. The basic step in ρ in the experiments performed is $\Delta \rho = 0.02$. Therefore the peaks of susceptibilities are recognized within the interval $(0.48, 0.52)$. In the small windows of Fig.2 one can observe how fast and which way the parabola transforms into the sharply pointed curves. The significant qualitative change occurs when p changes from $p = 0.01$ to $p = 0.02$. In particular, if one assumes that the interval of critical changes means the susceptibility greater than 1 (at average this condition is equivalent to the demand of the absolute magnetization being smaller than 0.9), then one finds:
— $\rho \in (0.30, 0.70)$ in case of cellular automata without the network evolution

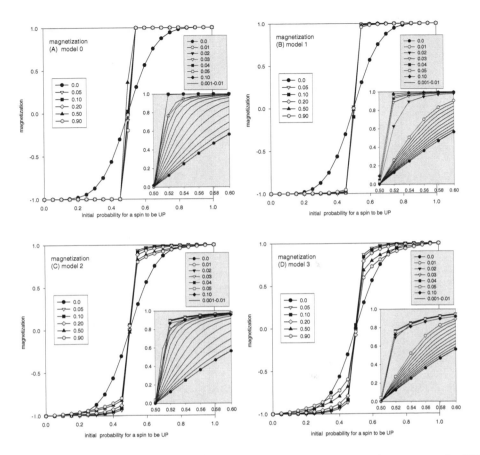

Fig. 1. Magnetization of final configurations vs initial probability for a spin to be UP (ρ) for different values of short-cut edges (p) what is indicated by curve's labels: (A) model 0 – stochastic linking and unlinking, (B) model 1 – intentional unlinking, (C) model 2 – preferential linking to, (D) model 3 – intentional unlinking and preferential linking to. The large frames present the general dependences on p and ρ; the inside frames show the change of magnetization if ρ is close to 0.5 and p is small. The lines without point markers are results for $p = 0.001, 0.002, \ldots, 0.01$ subsequently.

— $\rho \in (0.48, 0.52)$ in case of cellular automata with the network evolving according to the rules of models 0,1,2
— $\rho \in (0.46, 0.54)$ in case of cellular automata with the network evolving according to the rule of model 3.
Because of the observed rapid changes in main characteristics one can say that the cellular automata solve the density classification task. Especially, model 0 solves the density classification problem extremely efficiently: quickly and with the high certainty.

Also time needed to reach the fixed point stabilization changes when p is increasing. If $p > 0.1$ and $\rho << 0.5$ then the time to stabilization is larger than

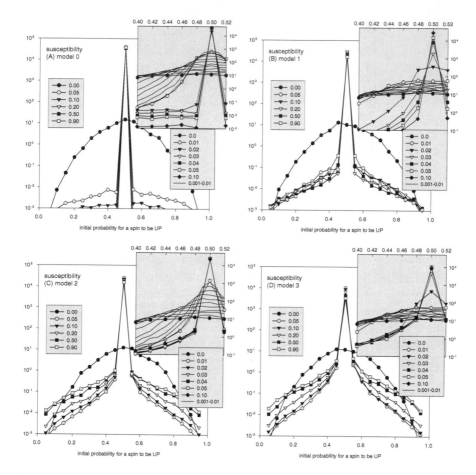

Fig. 2. Log plots of susceptibility of final configurations vs initial probability for a spin to be UP (ρ) for different values of short-cut edges (p) what is indicated by curve's labels: (A) model 0 – stochastic linking and unlinking, (B) model 1 – intentional unlinking, (C) model 2 – preferential linking to, (D) model 3 – intentional unlinking and preferential linking to. The large frames present the general dependences on p and ρ; the inside frames show the change of susceptibility if ρ is close to 0.5 and p is small. The lines without point markers are results for $p = 0.001, 0.002, \ldots, 0.01$ subsequently.

in case of the system with not evolving network. However, the stabilization is reached in less than 40 steps. If $\rho \in (0.4, 0.6)$ and p is small, $p < 0.01$, then the fixed point stabilization is not observed in less than 100 steps. The properties shown in figures collect features found as snap-shots of cellular automata states at the one hundredth step. This limitation does not introduce any important restriction. It is because that when the network does not evolve then, due to the many invariants of the spin-state rule, one observes the stabilizations on configurations which oscillate with some time period. This results in that the stabilization time is read as $t = 100$. Such limit configurations occur also if p is small, i.e., $p < 0.01$. When the rewiring process is stronger the oscillating patterns disappear in less than 100 steps. The stabilization different from the fixed points is not observed if $p > 0.01$.

3.2   Degree Distribution

The vertex degree distributions are presented in Fig.3. The plots collect results recorded when the cellular automata systems arrive to the limit of either a ferro fixed point stabilization or a hundred step of time. Hence the total number of changes in the network depends on the time given to the evolution. However, if $p \geq 0.01$ then after a hundredth steps the average probability for an edge to change is 1. Thus, the difference between a network state after a hundred steps with $p = 0.01$ and after the first step with $p = 1$ consists in the synchronousness of events: with increasing p the edge evolution becomes more synchronous.

All plots of the vertex degree distribution with $p \leq 0.01$ characterize the network configurations that are obtained at the one hundredth step. In case of model 0 the fast convergence to the Gaussian distribution (the parabola shape in the log-plot) centered at $k = 4$ is observed. The significant distinction from the Gaussian shape in cases of other models is due to the preferences introduced. One observes vertices with the degree higher than 20 which in the Gaussian world do not exist. Because of the threshold value considered here, $T = 8$, the vertices with the degree larger than 8 are protected from unlinking and preferred in linking. Therefore the number of vertices with high degree is growing with increasing p. However, the presented distributions do not have wings depending polynomially on the vertex degree, namely, decaying as $k^{-\gamma}$ for some γ and k vertex degree.

4   Concluding Remarks

We have considered properties of spin cellular automata initially spanned on the regular square lattice and then rewired each time step systematically. What we have observed is the final spin state. We have concentrated on the two configurations: *all spins up* and   *all spins down*. It has appeared that only these two configurations are possible as the final configuration for spins. Which one of these two emerges is depended on ρ the density of 1 in the initial configuration. Due to the changes in the network the interval of uncertainty about the final configuration contracts sharply to the small interval around the critical value of $\rho = 0.5$. From the statistical physics point of view main investigations concern the ergodicity problem, i.e. the memory about the initial state properties in the evolving systems. The strong connectivity arisen from the small-world network enhances sharply the solution. The cellular automata considered are ergodic outside the interval $\rho \in (0.48, 0.52)$ what means that the interval of ergodicity is definitely larger than the interval of ρ in case of the ordinary spin cellular automata. Therefore we claim that the systems considered can work as solvers of

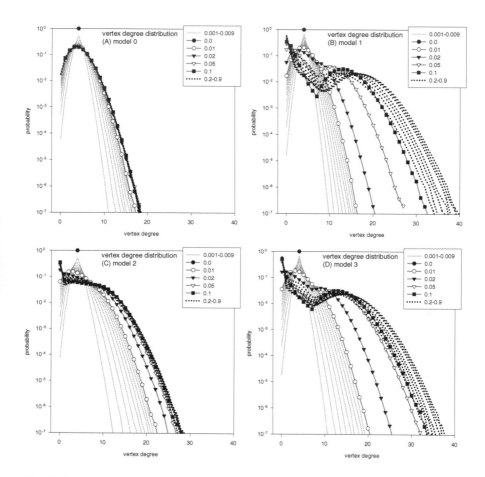

Fig. 3. Log plots of vertex degree in final configurations vs initial probability for a spin to be UP (ρ) for different values of short-cut edges (p) what is indicated by curve's labels: (A) model 0 – stochastic linking and unlinking, (B) model 1 – intentional unlinking, (C) model 2 – preferential linking to, (D) model 3 – intentional unlinking and preferential linking to. The gray lines are results for $p = 0.001, 0.002, \ldots, 0.009$ subsequently; the dotted lines are results for $p = 0.2, 0.3, \ldots, 0.9$ subsequently.

the density task. Moreover, since the analysed properties have been collected at time moments much smaller than the system size, the stated features seem to be universal in the sense that they are size independent.

Our work is only preliminary. The dynamical system considered here needs further investigations. We have studied the zero-temperature Ising problem. Now the study of stochastic spin evolution should be undertaken. Moreover, the networks considered here can bee included into the one thermodynamic ensemble, so-called canonical ensemble, because all networks have the same number of edges [16]. For the canonical ensemble there is a possibility to fix a temperature and associate the energy to every network configuration. Such approach states the new question: how this temperature and this energy relate to the ordinary thermodynamic characteristics of spin system.

Acknowledgments. We wish to acknowledge the financial support of Polish Ministry of Scientific Research and Information Technology : PB/1472/PO3/ 2003/25

References

1. Binney, J.J., Dowrick, N.J., Fisher, A.J., Newman, M.E.J.: The Theory of Critical Phenomena. Oxford University Press, Oxford, 1992;
2. Domany, E.,: Exact Results for Two and Three-Dimensional Ising and Potts Models. Phys. Rev. Lett. **52** (1984) 871–874; Grinstein, G.C., Jayaparash, C., Hu, Ye,: Statistical Mechanics of Probabilistic Cellular Automata Phys. Rev. Lett. **55** (1985) 2527–2530; Hede, B. Herrmann, H.J.: Fast simulation of the Ising model using cellular automata. J. Phys. A: Math. Gen. **24** (1991) L691–L697; Makowiec, D., Gnacinski, P.: Universality Class of Probabilistic Cellular Automata. in Cellular Automata, Bandini, S., Chopard, B., Tomassini, M. (eds.), LNCS **2493**, Springer Berlin (2002) 104–113; Grinstein, G.: Can complex structure be generically stable in a noisy world? IBM J. Res. Dev. **48** (2004) 5–12
3. Albert, R., Barabasi, A.-L.: Statistical mechanics of complex networks. Rev. Mod. Phys. **74** (2002) 47–97
4. Newman, M.E.J.: The structure and function of complex networks. SIAM Review **45** (2003) 167–256
5. Watts, D.J., Strogatz, S.H.: Collective dynamics of 'small-world' network. Nature **393** (1998) 440–442
6. Novotny, M.A., Wheeler, S.M.: On the possibility of Quasi Small-World Nanomaterials. arXiv: cond-mat/0308602 (2003)
7. Gitterman, M.: Small-world phenomena in physics: the Ising model. J. Phys. A: Math. Gen. **33** (2000) 8373–8381
8. Moore, C., Newman, M.E.J.: Epidemic and percolation in small-world networks. Phys. Rev. E **61** (1999) 5678–5682
9. Kuperman, M., Abramson, G.: Small world effect in an epidemiological model. Phys. Rev. Lett. **86** (2001) 2909—2913; Newman, M.E.J.: The spread of epidemic disease on networks. Phys. Rev. E **66** (2002) 016128:1–12
10. Klemm, K., Eguiluz, V.M., Toral, R., Miguel, M.S: Nonequilibrium transitions in complex networks: A model of social interaction. Phys. Rev. E. **67** (2003) 026120:1– 6; Stauffer, D., Meyer-Ortmanns, H.: Simulation of consensus model of Deffuant et al. on a Barabasi-Albert network. Int. J. Mod. Phys. C **15** (2004)to appear; Stauffer, D., Sousa, A.O: Discretized opinion dynamics of Deffuant on scale-free network. cond-mat/0310243 (2003)
11. Kolakowska,A., Novotny M.A.: Algorithmic scalability in globally constrained conservative parallel discrete event simulations of asynchronous system. Phys. Rev. E **67** (2003) 046703:1–13
12. Svenson, P.: Damage spreading in small world Ising models. Phys. Rev. E **65** (2002) 036105:1–7
13. Aleksiejuk, A., Holyst, J.A., Stauffer, D.: Ferromagnetic phase transition in Barabasi–Albert networks. Physica A **310** (2002) 260–266

14. Goltsev, A.V., Dorogovtsev, S.N., Mendes, J.F.F.: Critical phenomena in networks. Phys. Rev. E **67** (2003) 026123
15. Mitchell, P., Hraber, P.T., Crutchfield, J.P.: Revisiting the Edge of Chaos: Evolving Cellular Automata to Perform Computational Tasks. Complex Syst. **7**(1993) 89–130.
16. Farkas, I., Derenyi, I., Palla, G. Vicsek, T.: Equilibrium statistical mechanics of network structures, to appear in Networks: structure, dynamics, and functions (E.Ben-Naim, H.Frauenfelder and Z.Toroczkai, eds) Springer, Berlin (2004)

Searching for Pattern-Forming Asynchronous Cellular Automata – An Evolutionary Approach

Tomoaki Suzudo

Department of Nuclear Energy Systems, Japan Atomic Energy Research Institute,
Tokai-mura, Japan 319-1195
suzudo@clsu3a0.tokai.jaeri.go.jp

Abstract. This paper discuss a class of 2-dimensional asynchronous cellular automata with conservation of mass, for the formation of patterns in groups. The previous study [14] reported a methodology of searching, automatically, for pattern-forming cellular automata using a genetic algorithm; this approach successfully found a few types of pattern-forming rules. The current study is a series of statistical analyses of one of the classes found by the above methodology, with the hope of understanding the mechanisms of the pattern formation. These analyses lead to some basic logic necessary to the pattern formation, but not to enough information to elucidate the whole mechanism of the pattern formation. This result suggests that the existence of unidentified cooperative operations between the different transitions of the cellular automaton rule to carry out the pattern formation.

1 Introduction

Nature produces many kinds of patterns, and the mechanism of such pattern formations are often unknown. Cellular automaton (CA) is a mathematical tool suitable for such studies and has been exploited intensively by many researchers. Because this mathematical tool is especially suitable for visual analyses of the results of calculation, the self-organization of spatial patterns is a very common topic among studies. For instance, the hodgepodge machine[1], and the cyclic cellular automata[2] give intricate patterns and are reminiscent of real phenomena of some chemical reactions. The formation of crystal-like pattern is also studied by a class of CAs [13].

In common CAs, all of the cell states are updated synchronously, and the patterns formed by such CAs are usually heavily dependent on the synchronous timing of the events occurring at each cell. This means that such pattern formations are sensitive to a tiny delay of the events at each cell. Such perturbations always exist in the natural environment, yet self-organization observed in real physical, chemical, or biological systems is robust and not dependent upon synchronous timing. Several scientists have already started questioning the assumption of the synchronous adjustment of random boolean networks[7,3,4] and CAs[8,12,11,16,14].

P.M.A. Sloot, B. Chopard, and A.G. Hoekstra (Eds.): ACRI 2004, LNCS 3305, pp. 151–160, 200

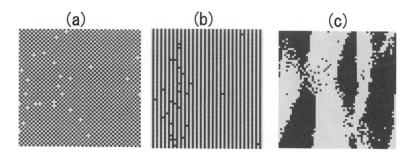

Fig. 1. The three kinds of patterns found by using genetic algorithms: (a)checkerboard, (b)stripe, and (c)sand-like.

Applications of artificial dynamical systems, such as random boolean networks or CAs, to the study of spatial pattern formations are expected to reveal the mechanism of advanced self-organizations frequently seen in biochemical systems and sometimes even in solid-state physical systems such as self-protection, self-replication, self-maintenance, etc. However, the discrepancies, discussed above, between artificial and natural systems may spoil the fruit yielded by such studies.

In this paper, we will consider asynchronous CAs leading to a certain spatial order. As an example we will discuss pattern formations in 2-dimensional CAs defined on a regular lattice, and a genetic algorithm will be applied to searching, automatically, for pattern-forming CAs. Techniques to search for CAs using a genetic algorithm were exclusively studied for the collective behaviors such as a density task[16,10], a classification[6], and a period three behavior[9]. However, few studies have been done for searching for spatial pattern formations. For this purpose, we will consider a kind of interactive particle system (or a kind of lattice gas), in which the total number of non-zero cells is conserved. This mass-conservative condition is essential to the searching methodology, because this eliminates CAs which unnaturally generate and annihilate particles to form spatial patterns; such CAs are meaningless for the study of pattern-forming mechanisms.

In the previous work [14], three types of pattern-forming CAs, *ckeckerboard*, *stripe*, and *sand-like*, were found (See Fig. 1). This paper describes a follow-up study that statistically analyzes the rules found by the above methodology hoping that we can obtain some fundamental mechanism related to pattern formations. The analyses in this paper are focused on the checkerboard type out of the patterns mentioned above; this pattern is already discussed in [14] in depth from the phase transition's point of view.

In Sections 2 and 3, the mathematical structure of the CA applied to this study and the methodology to search for pattern-forming rules are explained, respectively. Section 4 shows the results of the statistical analyses, and some related discussions are given. The conclusion is given in Section 5.

2   Asynchronous Cellular Automata with Mass Conservation

Cellular automata are dynamical systems in which the current state of each cell is determined by the states of its neighboring cells at the previous time step. We consider, in this paper, an interactive particle system modeled by a CA having two kinds of cells, occupied and empty cells. In common cellular automaton schemes, each cell has its own neighborhood and its state is determined regardless of what states its neighboring cells will take. In other words, the update rule of a cell is a many-to-one mapping, which is why the total mass is not conserved in such schemes. One technique employed to realize mass-conservative dynamics within CA is to divide the whole cellular space into many blocks composed of several cells with the states of each block being updated with the total mass in the block conserved. In this case the rule becomes a many-to-many mapping. This technique is called partitioning, and such a rule is called a *block rule*. Margolus neighborhood is a typical method of partitioning and has been applied to various CAs with the above conservation laws [15].

While the partitioning technique has been applied mainly to synchronous CAs, for example Fredkin's Billiard Ball Machine[5], we will, in this study, apply the technique to asynchronous updating schemes: The position of the block, composed of several adjacent cells to be updated, is randomly selected and the states of cells in the selected block are updated while the remaining cells are left unchanged. From now on, we will simply call this block 'neighborhood'. The rule applied to neighborhood is constant over time, just as it is for the common synchronous scheme. See Fig. 2 for a schematic picture of the asynchronous partitioning in the case of von Neumann-type neighborhood being adopted. We will concentrate on this type of the neighborhood throughout this paper.

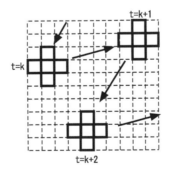

Fig. 2. Asynchronous partitioning cellular automata: A set of 5 neighbpring cells, randomly selected, are updated in the order indicated by the arrows.

Because the influence of a single update to the dynamics is much smaller than that of an update in the common synchronous method, the unit time is newly defined as being composed of $\frac{x_{max} \cdot y_{max}}{N_{neighbor}}$ asynchronous updates, where $N_{neighbor}$ is the total number of neighbor cells, i.e. five for the von Neumann neighborhood; $x_{max}(=100)$ and $y_{max}(=100)$ are the dimensions of the cellular space. With this new definition, a cell is, on average, updated once in a unit time step, which is consistent with the common synchronous updating schemes. Note that some cells may not be updated in a unit time step, while others may be done more than once.

We adopt, in this study, a commonly used torus-type boundary condition in which the top and left edges of the cellular space are connected to the bottom and right ones, respectively. The state of each cell is assumed to take an integer equal to either nil or unity. The nil state denotes an empty cell and is depicted in our graphs as a white cell, while the other state is one occupied by a particle and is depicted in our graphs as a black cell; i.e. the dynamical system is regarded as a mono-particle artificial chemical system or a kind of lattice-gas system. The particles merely move around the cellular space neither separating into two new pieces, nor merging with others to form a new particle. To satisfy this mass conservation law, the update rule must be defined such that the total number of particles in neighborhood does not vary.

The initial condition of each run is given by placing particles randomly on the cellular space with a specified "density", which is the ratio of the number of particles to the total number of cells in the cellular space. We here set the density at 0.5. For the random number generations, a unique randomizing seed is used for each space tried, ensuring that the initial configurations are always different.

3   A Methodology to Search Automatically for Pattern-Forming Cellular Automata

We, in this paper, measure the degree of pattern formation by the spatial entropy of global cellular states. Thus, finding pattern-forming CAs means finding those with the spatial entropy being relatively small. The space of CA rules is discrete and two closely similar rules do not necessarily produce a similar development. The optimization of cellular automaton rules therefore tends to become a messy problem; classical tools such as steepest descent method are not applicable. Genetic algorithms are, however, useful for problems in which the function to be minimized (or maximized) has a rugged surface, and we apply this technique to our problem as described below.

Each rule in consideration is composed of $2^{N_{neighbor}} = 32$ mappings. The graphic patterns of all the 32 entries of the mapping are shown in Fig. 3. Because such graphic patterns can be indexed by integers, the rules of our interest can be represented by the array of 32 integers, say $T[i](i = 0, 1, \ldots, 31)$. This integer array becomes the chromosome of this genetic algorithm. The value of $T[i]$, i.e. the output of i'th entry assumes an integer between 0 and 31, but as described above each transition must satisfy the mass-conservative condition,

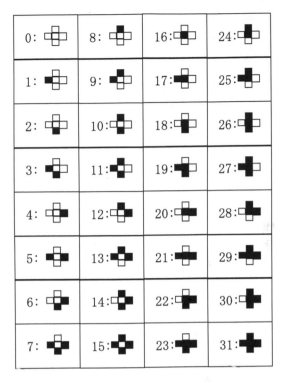

Fig. 3. All the entries of the transitions of the cellular automata.

and the transitions changing the mass inside the neighborhood are prohibited; then the whole rule space is approximately composed of $\sim 10^{14}$ rules, which is much smaller than that of the general rule space of 32^{32} rules.

The algorithm of the searching is:

1. Choose M chromosomes, i.e. mass-conservative cellular automaton rules at random, where M is called a *population*.
2. Run all of these CAs.
3. If at least one of the CAs satisfies a condition of being optimized (see below for the detail of the condition), stop the program; continue otherwise.
4. Calculate the fitness functions (given below) of all the CAs.
5. Choose the $M_e (0 < M_e < M)$ best-fit CAs for the next generation; they are called *elites*.
6. Choose M_n pairs of individuals at random out of the remaining CAs for the next generation so that the total of the elite and non-elite individuals becomes M again in the next generation, i.e. $M = M_e + 2M_n$.
7. Cross over each pair of non-elites at a randomly chosen point with probabilities of P_c, crossover rate.
8. Mutate each non-elites with probabilities of P_m per a transition. Note that new transitions also satisfy the mass-conservative condition.
9. Go to Step 2.

Table 1. The parameters of the genetic algorithms

symbol	explanation	value
M	population	20
M_e	the total number of the elite	6
P_c	crossover rate	0.5
P_m	mutation rate	0.05
H_s^o	the target value of H_s	0.57

The fitness function is defined as:

$$F = \left(\frac{1}{H_s(t_c) - H_s^o}\right) \cdot t_c, \tag{1}$$

where $H_s(t)$ is a spatial entropy of global cellular states at the time step t (A rigorous definition of H_s is given in Appendix A.); H_s^o is the target value of optimization of H_s; t_c is the transition time, that is, the time when the time development of H_s becomes almost steady. The length of t_c is determined by the sequential tests of

$$|H_s(t+1) - H_s(t)| < \epsilon, \tag{2}$$

$$|H_s(t+2) - H_s(t+1)| < \epsilon, \tag{3}$$

and

$$|H_s(t+3) - H_s(t+2)| < \epsilon. \tag{4}$$

The smallest t satisfying all of eqs.(2)-(4) was considered as t_c, where ϵ was empirically set at 0.003. In case a pattern formation occurs, the transition time (i.e. t_c) is long, For this reason, the multiplication by t_c in eq.(1) was added to a simple $\frac{1}{H_s(t) - H_s^o}$, and it was empirically found that this multiplication improved the optimization speed. The condition to stop the program is when at least one of the individual was found $H_s(t_c) < H_s^o$. The parameters for running the genetic algorithm are summarized in Table 1.

4   Statistical Analyses of the Rules Found by the Genetic Algorithm

Many runs of the optimization trial by the genetic algorithm were conducted, and the rules that satisfied the condition were collected. The number of generations needed to reach the condition of being optimized is sometimes less than a hundred, but a few other cases reached 300 generations at which the program gave up the further optimization and went to a next trial. The spatial patterns that the rules found by the searching give are the same as those in [14], i.e. , (a)checkerboard, (b)stripe, and (c)sand-like pattern (see Fig.1). In the following,

Table 2. The Shannon entropy of the selected transitions

entry	entropy	entry	entropy	entry	entropy	entry	entropy
0	0.0	8	0.72	16	0.11	24	0.67
1	0.71	9	0.99	17	0.66	25	0.98
2	0.70	10	1.00	18	0.66	26	0.99
3	0.98	11	0.65	19	0.98	27	0.73
4	0.69	12	0.99	20	0.68	28	0.98
5	0.99	13	0.66	21	0.99	29	0.71
6	0.98	14	0.69	22	0.98	30	0.64
7	0.67	15	0.10	23	0.71	31	0.0

we will concentrate on the analyses only of the rules that develop the checkerboard pattern.

The total number of the collected checkerboard rules is ~ 1000. For these rules, the probability of what transition is selected through the optimization process, say $p_{i,j}$, were calculated, where i and j are indices for the entry and the output of the transition, respectively. Using $p_{i,j}$, the Shannon entropy of $p_{i,j}$ for each entry i was calculated; the results are shown in Table 2.

From the entropy values, it is possible to classify each entry into 4 groups:

I   Entry-0 and Entry-31 (The entropy is exactly nil; each entry has only one possible transition because of the mass-conservative restriction.),

II   Entry-15 and Entry-16 (The entropy is ~ 0.1; the entry pattern already matches the checkerboard pattern and the identical mapping is dominantly selected.),

III   Entry-3, Entry-5, Entry-6, Entry-9, Entry-10, Entry-12, Entry-19, Entry-21, Entry-22, Entry-25, Entry-26, and Entry-28 (The entropy is almost unity, thus the transition is almost randomly selected. From Fig. 3, we can recognize that these entries are not directly related to the creation of the checkerboard pattern.), and

IV   The remaining entries (The entropy is in the range of $0.64 - 0.73$; The further analysis will be given below.).

The key point of the above grouping is whether or not the entry is one of the matching patterns of which the checkerboard pattern is composed, that is, 15th and 16th graphic patterns in Fig. 3.

The most-frequently selected transition for each entry and its probability, $\sup_i p_{i,j}$, were also calculated (See Table 3). From Table 3, we notice that Group IV can be classified into two subgroups:

IVa   Entry-1, Entry-2, Entry-4, Entry-8, Entry-23, Entry-27, Entry-29, and Entry-30 (The value of $\sup_i p_{i,j}$ is around $0.6 - 0.7$; The patterns for these entries are possible to transit to either of the two matching patterns of which the checkerboard pattern is composed, and such transitions are most-frequently selected.), and

Table 3. Transition most-frequently selected by the optimization; the values in the parenthesis is its probability (i.e. . $\sup_i p_{i,j}$.)

$0 \rightarrow 0(1.0)$	$8 \rightarrow 16(0.63)$	$16 \rightarrow 16(0.97)$	$24 \rightarrow 24(0.33)$
$1 \rightarrow 16(0.64)$	$9 \rightarrow 9(0.14)$	$17 \rightarrow 17(0.30)$	$25 \rightarrow 25(0.14)$
$2 \rightarrow 16(0.65)$	$10 \rightarrow 10(0.13)$	$18 \rightarrow 18(0.31)$	$26 \rightarrow 26(0.14)$
$3 \rightarrow 3(0.16)$	$11 \rightarrow 11(0.31)$	$19 \rightarrow 19(0.15)$	$27 \rightarrow 15(0.63)$
$4 \rightarrow 16(0.66)$	$12 \rightarrow 12(0.14)$	$20 \rightarrow 20(0.31)$	$28 \rightarrow 28(0.16)$
$5 \rightarrow 5(0.14)$	$13 \rightarrow 13(0.32)$	$21 \rightarrow 22(0.12)$	$29 \rightarrow 15(0.65)$
$6 \rightarrow 10(0.14)$	$14 \rightarrow 14(0.29)$	$22 \rightarrow 22(0.16)$	$30 \rightarrow 15(0.70)$
$7 \rightarrow 7(0.31)$	$15 \rightarrow 15(0.98)$	$23 \rightarrow 15(0.64)$	$31 \rightarrow 31(1.0)$

(a) t=0   (b) t=25   (c) t=50

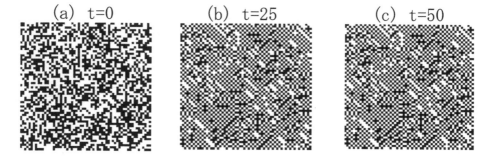

Fig. 4. The time development of the cellular automaton given by the rule in Table 3.

IVb Entry-7, Entry-11, Entry-13, Entry-14, Entry-18, Entry-20, and Entry-24 (The value of $\sup_i p_{i,j}$ is ~ 0.3; The patterns of these entries are close to one of the matching patterns, but the transition to them are prohibited under the mass-conservative condition; the identical mappings in these entries are most-frequently selected.).

Through the above classification, we seem to understand how each transition is selected to achieve the checkerboard pattern. Natural question is then; "Is this all about the tricks of the pattern formation?". If so, a rule created by putting all the most-frequently selected transitions of Table 3 together must have a performance of making the checkerboard pattern as good as that given by the "raw" rules obtained by the optimization. Figure 4 gives the time development of the CA composed of the most-frequently selected transitions. The graph at $t = 25$ has the spatial entropy of ~ 0.72, much larger than 0.57, the optimization target. The configuration of the cellular states at $t = 25$ (Fig. 4b)is almost identical to that at $t = 50$ (Fig. 4c), and the spatial entropy of the cellular states are not improved even in the further time-development. Such a poor performance does not meaningfully vary with the initial condition of the cellular states, so this rule's performance cannot compare with that of the rule composed of a raw set of transitions found by the searching. See Fig. 1(a); this graph is a cellular states developed by a typical rule found by the searching.

Although the statistical analyses given above seem theoretically sound, these are not enough to elucidate the whole mechanism of the pattern formation. In other words, the genetic algorithm selects each transition more cleverly than we can intuitively do. This result is not, however, surprising because complex phenomena such as pattern formations cannot be decomposed into a simple addition of many simple actions, but are organized by combinations or sometimes networks of them.

5   Conclusion

As a study of self-organization, the spatial pattern formation of CAs was studied. Especially, to seek the pattern formation more consistent to Nature, asynchronous CAs under the mass conservation law was explored and the asynchronous partitioning scheme was applied for this purpose. A methodology for automatically searching for the pattern-forming CAs was introduced, and its performance was confirmed. The methodology can be extended to more complicated situations for more realistic simulations of natural phenomena.

In addition, the rules giving the checkerboard pattern were collected by using the searching method for the purpose of their statistical analyses. The probability how often a certain transition is selected by the searching was discussed. It was possible to explain why certain transitions are dominantly selected by the searching, but the success of such analysis was limited because it failed to explain all the mechanisms of the pattern formation. This indicated that the checkerboard-pattern formation cannot be explained by a deduction of a simple addition of the mappings.

A further development of this study is to analyze the interaction between different transitions. For this purpose we perhaps need much more samples of the rules, and therefore it is necessary to drastically improve the searching speed. I hope that this extension could open a wide range of potential studies for approaching the origin of self-organization in Nature.

References

1. Dewdney, A.K.: Computer recreations. Sci. Amer. **August** (1988) 86–89
2. Dewdney, A.K.: Computer recreations. Sci. Amer. **August** (1989) 102–105
3. Di Paolo, E. A.: Searching for rhythms in asynchronous random boolean networks. Alife **VII**, The MIT Press (2000) 73–80
4. Di Paolo, E. A.: Rhythmic and non-rhythmic attractors in asynchronous random boolean networks. BioSystems **59(3)** (2001) 185–195
5. Fredkin, E., Toffoli, T.: Conservative logic. Int. J. Theor. Phys. **21** (1982) 219–253
6. Ganguly, N., et al.: Evolving cellular automata as pattern classifier. In S. Bandini, B. Chopart and M. Tomassini (Eds.), Cellular Automata, Lecture Notes in Computer Science **2493** (2002) 56–68
7. Harvey, I., Bossomaier, T.: Time out of joint: Attractors in asynchronous random boolean networks. Proceedings of the Fourth European Conference of Artificial Life, The MIT Press (1997) 67–75

8. Ingerson, T. E., Buvel, R. L.: Structure in asynchronous cellular automata. Physica D **10** (1984) 59–68
9. Jiménez-Morales, F.: An evolutionary approach to the study of non-trivial collective behavior in cellular automata. In S. Bandini, B. Chopart and M. Tomassini (Eds.), Cellular Automata, Lecture Notes in Computer Science **2493** (2002) 32–43
10. Mitchell, M.: An Introduction to Genetic Algorithms. The MIT Press (1996).
11. Nehaniv, C. L.: Self-reproduction in asynchronous cellular automata. University of Herfordshire, Faculty of Engineering and Information Sciences, Technical Report **368** (2002).
12. Schonfisch, B., de Roos, A.: Synchronous and asynchronous updating in cellular automata. BioSystems **51(3)** (1999) 123–143
13. Suzudo, T.: Crystallisation of 2-dimensional cellular automata. Complexity International **6** (1999) (online journal at http://www.complexity.org.au/).
14. Suzudo, T.: Spatial pattern formation of asynchronous cellular automata with mass conservation. Physica A in press
15. Toffoli, T., Margolus, N.: Cellular Automata Machines - A New Environment for Modeling. The MIT Press (1987)
16. Tomassini, M., Venzi, M.: Artificial evolved asynchronous cellular automata for the density task. In S. Bandini, B. Chopart and M. Tomassini (Eds.), Cellular Automata, Lecture Notes in Computer Science **2493** (2002) 44–55

A   Definition of Spatial Entropy of the Global Configuration of CAs

Consider four adjacent sites of the cellular automaton space such as (i, j), $(i + 1, j)$, $(i, j + 1)$ and $(i + 1, j + 1)$, where i and j are the x-axis and y-axis position of an arbitrary cell, respectively. There are $2^4 = 16$ possible patterns for this local patch if each cell takes either '0' or '1' state. In this paper, we use

$$H_s(\tau) \equiv -\sum_k P_s^k(\tau) log_{16}(P_s^k(\tau)), \tag{5}$$

as the definition of the spatial entropy of global configuration at an arbitrary time step τ, where $P_s^k(\tau)$ is the probability for a particular pattern of the local patch at the time step τ. Note that a base of 16 is used for the logarithmic function as the entropy assumes a real number between nil and unity.

Heredity, Complexity, and Surprise: Embedded Self-Replication and Evolution in CA

Chris Salzberg[1,2] and Hiroki Sayama[1]

[1] Dept. of Human Communication, University of Electro-Communications, Japan
[2] Graduate School of Arts and Sciences, University of Tokyo, Japan

Abstract. This paper reviews the history of embedded, evolvable self-replicating structures implemented as cellular automata systems. We relate recent advances in this field to the concept of the evolutionary growth of complexity, a term introduced by McMullin to describe the central idea contained in von Neumann's self-reproducing automata theory. We show that conditions for such growth are *in principle* satisfied by universal constructors, yet that *in practice* much simpler replicators may satisfy scaled-down — yet equally relevant — versions thereof. Examples of such evolvable self-replicators are described and discussed, and future challenges identified.

1 Introduction

In recent decades, the study of embedded self-replicating structures in cellular automata has developed into one of the main themes of research in Artificial Life[31,32]. A common goal motivates such research: to extract the fundamental organizing principles that govern real-world biological phenomena (and, in a wider sense, life as we know it[13]) from an abstraction of their driving biophysical processes. Central among such processes is self-replication in its variety of forms. The eminent mathematician John von Neumann was the first to suggest that essential features of such biological self-replication, with its many degrees of freedom and complex kinematics, could be usefully represented in a discrete cellular space with uniform local rules[41]. His seminal self-reproducing automata theory, which he situated "in the intermediate area between logic, communication theory and physiology"[41, p.204], set the stage for future research in artificial self-replication[16] and remains among the defining achievements of this field[17].

Following von Neumann's work of the late 1940s and early 1950s, research on CA-based self-replicators split into a number of major trends. Among these, the majority are efforts to implement regulated behavior (universal construction[8, 9,20,38,40], self-replication[5,12,14,18,22,34], self-inspection[11], functionality[7, 19,37]) manually introduced to satisfy pre-defined goals of the designer. Such goal-oriented design is important for resolving theoretical problems (bounds and limitations on self-replicating structures) and for direct application (computation, problem-solving, nanotechnology), yet does little to address the fundamental issue that shaped von Neumann's original theory. This issue centers on the

P.M.A. Sloot, B. Chopard, and A.G. Hoekstra (Eds.): ACRI 2004, LNCS 3305, pp. 161–171, 2004.
© Springer-Verlag Berlin Heidelberg 2004

vague and intuitive concept of "complication"[41, p.78], roughly measured in terms of the number of elementary parts of a machine or organism. Von Neumann observed that natural organisms have a surprising collective tendency to increase such complication over time. Such increases are *unexpected*, resulting from robustness and adaptability of the natural self-replication process rather than from any specific functionality. Von Neumann proved that, *in principle*, such increases are not confined to natural automata but may equally be achievable in artificial ones, in particular by one of his own creation: a complicated universal construction machine embedded in a 29-state CA system. His machine realizes an ingenious separation between static description (tape) and active translation (machine) that has since become synonymous with the concept of self-reproduction[15]. Yet while significant as a defining example, von Neumann's design has been widely critiqued for its reliance on a lengthy set of rules and expansive space. His machine and others like it are so computationally demanding as to be largely unfeasible[1]; hence simpler alternatives with comparable potential are sought.

Considerable disagreement on the topic of such simpler replicating structures has arisen over the fifty years since von Neumann first developed his theory. Such disagreement stems from conflicting definitions of "self-reproduction" and from misconceptions regarding von Neumann's original intent. Most commonly, the "self-reproduction problem"[3, p.xv] has been stated in terms of "non-trivial" self-reproduction, understood to mean reproduction of structures with some minimal level of complexity. First mentioned by Burks[4, p.49], this idea was later adopted by Langton[12] and subsequently incorporated as a guiding principle in CA-based self-replication models[31]. Langton's famous Self-Reproducing (SR) Loop, a model often mistakenly viewed as a *simplification* of von Neumann's machine, embodies a common belief derived from this way of thinking: that minimal *non-trivial* self-reproduction is *explicit* (or *self-directed*[22]) self-reproduction. Such an interpretation is natural when one focuses on engineering aspects of von Neumann's machine design, which indeed embody a highly explicit translation/transcription copy process. Yet it fundamentally overlooks an essential property stressed by von Neumann himself, namely that "self-reproduction includes the ability to undergo inheritable mutations as well as the ability to make another organism like the original"[42, p.489]. Such capacity to withstand *viable heritable mutations* was central to von Neumann's formal theory and to the evolutionary growth of complexity described therein[17,36].

In this paper, we take a new look at the history of self-replication studies in cellular automata. With hereditary variation in mind, Sections 2 and 3 review key concepts underlying von Neumann's original work, highlighting an area of the field that has received little attention. These are the recently de-

---

[1] Von Neumann's machine required 29 states and a highly complex set of transition rules, occupying an estimated 50,000 to 200,000 CA cells[31, p.241]. Pesavento[20] recently simulated a modified version of this CA, yet was unable (due to prohibitive computational demands) to implement even a single complete self-reproduction cycle.

veloped evolvable loop- and worm-shaped self-replicators of *marginal* hereditary and structural complexity[1,6,29,30,35], reviewed in Section 4, that straddle the boundary between von Neumann's powerful yet fragile machine and more robust yet trivial systems. In Section 5, we identify future challenges and relate their importance in the field of Artificial Life to von Neumann's original search for the evolutionary growth of complexity.

2   Embeddedness, Explicitness, and Heredity

A defining property of CA systems of self-replicators, *embeddedness* quantifies the extent to which state information of an individual is expressed in the arena of competition[2]. Taylor[36, p.216] argues that embeddedness is important because it enables "the very *structure* of the individual to be modified"[original emphasis], likely a necessary condition for open-ended evolution. Related to embeddedness is the range of possible interactions that are allowed between objects or structures. Von Neumann's machine is fully embedded; the entire specification of the machine — its various control organs, memory, and construction arm — are expressed in the cellular space itself rather than hidden in auxiliary non-interactive locations. At any time, the construction process may be modified or disrupted via local rules applied to cells adjacent to the machine. This is distinct from e.g. systems of evolutionary computer programs such as Tierra[21], popular and well-studied in Artificial Life, which assume an unlimited number of CPUs existing outside of the arena of evolution, beyond the influence of other individuals. Since CA by their nature do not "hide" any information (with the exception of the transition rules themselves), CA-based replicators are as a rule highly embedded and in general allow for direct and unrestricted interactions among them. This goes some way to explaining their popularity as a medium for the theoretical study of self-replication.

Self-replicators embedded in CA share an important defining property with biological organisms: both are fundamentally built up from — and interact through — a common material structure grounded in physical laws (i.e. CA rules). Unlike other evolutionary systems such as those of computer programs, CA-based models supply no universal structural cues: everything down to the separation between replicator and its environment is distinguished relative to the system observer. This property has the side-effect of making such systems intrinsically "messy" to analyze, yet has the potential to elevate the richness and surprise of their evolutionary dynamics to levels inherently excluded from less embedded systems. Von Neumann never witnessed such dynamics; although his system is *in principle* capable of producing them, it is *in practice* far too computationally demanding and structurally fragile to be useful in this regard. This key difference manifests the importance of developing simpler, more robust models of self-replication imbued with the potential for evolvability.

Since von Neumann's original work, the majority of discussions on such CA-based embedded models of self-replication have focused on the *explicitness* of

---

[2] This discussion of embeddedness is based on an analysis by Taylor[36, p.215-219].

the self-reproduction process rather than any potential *evolvability* contained therein[12,18,22,32]. Langton, who supplied possibly the most well-known argument to this effect, makes the case that

> Von Neumann's work suggests an appropriate criterion, which is all the more appropriate because it is satisfied by molecular self-reproduction: the configuration must treat its stored information in two different manners[...]: *interpreted*, as instructions to be executed (translation), and *uninterpreted*, as data to be copied (transcription).[12, p.137, original emphasis]

Although von Neumann indeed based the design of his construction machine on this translation/transcription process, and although he did emphasize the interpreted/uninterpreted distinction at the heart of his theory, this does not imply that such separations should be considered an appropriate *criterion* for self-reproduction. A criterion based on explicitness alone is, in any case, somewhat arbitrary as the transition rules of the CA will always play some role in enabling structures to copy themselves.

More appropriate as criterion is the issue of *heredity*, on the basis of which simple replicators such as Langton's Loop can be unambiguously distinguished from potentially evolvable machines such as that of von Neumann. Whereas Langton takes the translation/transcription *process* to be of primary interest, von Neumann emphasized static *descriptions*, the importance of which

> is that they replace the varying and reactive originals by quiescent and (temporarily) unchanging semantic equivalents and thus permit copying[,] the decisive step which renders self-reproduction (or, more generally, *reproduction without degeneration in size or level of organization*) possible.[41, p.122-123, emphasis added]

Such non-degenerative reproduction is an immediate consequence of construction universality, an important result recently clarified and strengthened by McMullin[17]. Yet whereas such universality is computationally demanding and biologically implausible, a less stringent yet explicit encoding — one that enables a shift in heredity from *limited* towards *indefinite* — is in fact possible and indeed has already been implemented in a number of models[1,10,26,30,35]. Such a shift enables evolutionary complexity growth, described in the next section.

3   The Evolutionary Growth of Complexity

In his recent re-appraisal of von Neumann's work, McMullin[17] summarizes three principal conditions he deems necessary to solve the problem of what he calls the *evolutionary growth of complexity*. Namely, to do so

> one would need to exhibit a concrete class of machines [...] in sufficient detail to satisfy ourselves that they *are* purely mechanistic; one would need to show that they span a significant range of complexity; and finally, one would have to demonstrate that there are construction pathways leading from the simplest to the most complex[17, p.351, original emphasis]

He goes on to show that von Neumann's machine satisfies these require-ments, that it is thus capable of "incremental, bootstrapping *increases* in complexity"[17, p.354, original emphasis], and moreover that it is arguably the *simplest* machine so far capable of doing so. The proof of this result rests on the construction universality that von Neumann worked so hard to real-ize in his machine. Whereas the concept of complexity is notoriously ill-defined (von Neumann referred to his own understanding of it as "vague, unscientific and imperfect"[41, p.78]), this turns out not to be essential for demonstrating complexity-increasing construction pathways — the central piece of the puzzle.

Having elucidated the above result, McMullin goes on to ask the important question: "what further conditions are required to enable an *actual*, as opposed to merely *potential*, growth in complexity?"[17, p.360, emphasis added]. Von Neumann's machine does not qualify as "actual" primarily due to the fact that its structure is extremely fragile, unable to withstand minimal external pertur-bations. Such fragility would render any interactions — notably those between parent and child immediately following self-reproduction — highly destructive, preventing the coexistence of a population of such machines. In addition, neither current computational resources nor those of the foreseeable future hold much promise for implementing such a complicated system on any significant scale.

There is an added concern, and this relates to the concept of a *Darwinian* — as distinct from *mutational* — growth of complexity. The former entails *actual* growth and requires direction from selection pressures, whereas the latter merely implies *possible* growth and only requires the presence of construction pathways. McMullin notes that, if the former were to occur at all, they would happen "along paths in the genetic network that lead "uphill" in terms of fitness". Yet a fixed genetic network such as that of von Neumann's machines "*may* impose severe limits on the practical paths of Darwinian evolution (and thus on the practical evolutionary growth of complexity)"[17, p.358, original emphasis]. The question of whether or not a population of replicating machines, directly competing and evolving within such a network, would indeed favour increases in complexity is clearly an important one, yet one to which a complicated system such as von Neumann's provides no concrete answers.

One may thus ask: what then are the *practical* alternatives to fragile and complicated universal constructors, and are they capable of any evolutionary growth in complexity? Addressing the latter question, McMullin makes the im-portant admission[3] that the solution he presents "may seem to imply that a *general* constructive automaton (i.e., capable of constructing a very wide range of target machines) is a prerequisite to *any* evolutionary growth of complexity. It is not."[17, p.357,original emphasis] If we are interested in studying complexity-increase during the earliest stages of life, a universal constructive automaton in any case hardly seems like the appropriate model; such a complicated machine would have to be preceded by simpler, less sophisticated replicators. It is to such simpler evolvable replicators that we turn our attention in the following section.

---

[3] McMullin makes this point in the context of a related discussion on genetic rela-tivism/absolutism.

4   Evolvable Self-Replicators in Cellular Automata

A wide array of self-replicating structures have been implemented in cellular automata since von Neumann first introduced his self-reproducing automata theory. Such models are often conceptualized as situated on a linear scale of "complexity", with complicated universal constructors at one end and simple self-replicators at the other. Because the terms "simple" and "complex" are themselves so ill-defined, it is not always clear what properties should be associated with the intermediate region between these extremes. Sipper[31, p.245], for instance, situates self-replicators with added computational and functional capabilities[7,19,37] in this region. Models such as these are indeed interesting from the point of view of achieving *targeted* behaviours, but in terms of studying the evolutionary *process* itself — and in particular that of complexity-increase — they fall short of the requirements stated earlier[4]. In particular, such models lack the "surprise!"[23] element that plays a crucial role in the emergence of complexity-increasing evolution.

Taylor[36, p.200] presents an alternative 2D visualization in which each system is assigned to a point on a plane, with x and y axes representing the copying process (explicit/implicit) and heredity (limited/indefinite), respectively, of self-replicators. The diagram we have drawn in Fig. 1 is based on Taylor's and, like his, is not intended to be quantitatively accurate; rather it is a qualitative tool to better visualize certain key concepts. Von Neumann's machine, which carries out a highly explicit translation/transcription process, is also construction universal and hence appears close to the upper left (indefinite/explicit) portion of the diagram. In contrast, self-reproduction of template-based replicators[10,34] is largely implicit in "physical" rules, allowing any arbitrary string to be replicated; hence they appear close to the upper right (indefinite/implicit) portion of the diagram. Langton's Loop and other minimal self-replicators appear at the same level on the heredity scale as do trivial self-replicators; neither accommodates any hereditary variation, although Langton's CA has a more explicit translation process.

Note that certain evolving self-replicating loops and worms — not yet developed at the time when Taylor produced his thesis — are included at the center of the diagram, far from Langton's Loop along the hereditary axis. It is this central region, representing self-replicators of *marginal* hereditary and structural complexity, that is our focus. Such structures should have the following virtues: they should have some potential for hereditary variability, should be sufficiently robust to self-replicate continuously without self-destruction, and should be sufficiently simple in specification to be realized on a computer.

Chou and Reggia[6] designed the first such system while studying the emergence of CA-based self-replicating loops from a "soup" of components. Initiated with a random distribution of "unbound" cells, the soup is "stirred" (using

---

[4] This represents another interpretation of "complexity", namely that of *computational functionality* (or *universality*). McMullin[17, p.348-349] addresses this perspective and finds it inadequate for describing evolutionary complexity-growth.

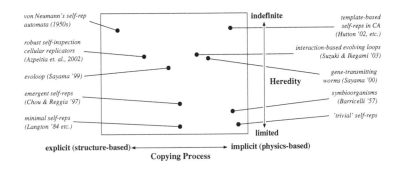

Fig. 1. Categorization of CA-based Self-Replicators.

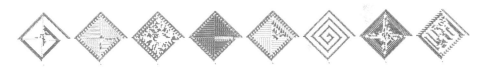

Fig. 2. Pattern formation of some different size-6 evoloop species after 5000 time steps.

only local rules) until a minimal-sized loop appears by chance. This structure is identified by local rules, certain "bound" bits are set to distinguish it, and a self-replicating loop emerges. An evolutionary cycle then commences and continues indefinitely: smaller loops, induced by "growth bits" scattered about the space, become progressively larger until the space cannot accommodate them, at which point smaller ones re-emerge. Chou and Reggia did not aim at studying an evolutionary *process* with this work but rather the *emergence* of self-replicators. Evolution in this model, explicitly induced and somewhat artificial, was not a priority. Heredity was also highly constricted, with each loop "species" defined exclusively by replicator size.

Sayama's "evoloop" model[29], developed shortly thereafter and based on his earlier self-replicating loop called the SDSR Loop[28], differs significantly in these regards. Although it borrows its basic structure from Langton's Loop, the evoloop exhibits more complex and interesting evolutionary behaviour than do earlier minimal self-replicators of its kind — behaviour traditionally assumed to require a more complicated system specification. Within this model occur evolutionary processes (viewed here as variation plus natural selection) that result exclusively from the *local, structural* interaction of embedded self-replicators. Such variation and selection processes are not defined a priori but rather emerge spontaneously from the low-level "physics" of the CA, a distinctly bottom-up feature that distinguishes it from earlier evolutionary models. Initially it was believed that such variation was limited to size only, but extensive and detailed studies[24] have since revealed that the genetic state-space grows *combinatorially* with loop size. Each genotype within this vast possibility space has unique growth patterns (Fig. 2) and genealogical connectivity[27], exerting a demonstrable and decisive pressure on selection and resulting in a rugged fitness landscape[26], producing a limited form of complexity-increase in hostile environments[25].

Evolutionary systems of self-replicating structures with other shapes have also yielded interesting evolutionary potential. Morita and Imai[18] were the first to develop CA-based shape-encoding worms and loops. A variety of different structural patterns can replicate successfully in this model, however collisions leading to mutations are explicitly disallowed. Sayama[30] borrowed this basic shape-encoding worm structure and adapted it to enable gene transmission through structural interaction, enabling worms to change their genotype (and phenotype) in a bottom-up way. Results from experiments with this model showed a tendency of worms to increase their average length over time, hence demonstrating a limited form of complexity-increase.

Suzuki and Ikegami[35] applied the shape-encoding mechanism to study interaction based evolution of loop structures. Although more complicated than the models already mentioned, this CA allows for a variety of different loop-shaped structures (other than the traditional square) to successfully self-replicate, mutate, and evolve, and in this respect it is quite unique. The main thrust of this work is an interaction mechanism between replicating structures that makes use of a hypercycle-like network of collision rules. Using such a network, it was found that larger, more complex loop structures emerged at the boundary between waves of superior and inferior species in a propagating hypercycle formation.

Using a novel CA system incorporating both self-inspection and genetic reproduction strategies, Azpeitia and Ibáñez[1] investigated the spontaneous emergence of robust cellular replicators (self-replicating loops). Emergence in this system is notably achieved without explicit mechanisms (e.g. "bound" or "growth" bits as in [6]). The detailed comparison of self-inspection and genetic reproduction strategies in this study is moreover unique among those we have discussed. In their conclusions, the authors note: "experiments suggest that self-inspection reproduction could be a precursory stage for the genetic one." Yet "despite having a better chance to trigger the reproduction dynamics, self-inspection would be taken over by the evolutinary advantages of genetic reproduction."[1, p.142]

Systems of template-based replicators[10,33,39] aim at simulating the emergence of living (i.e. self-replicating and possibly evolving) structures from a soup of non-living components under virtual physical laws; they hence bear similarities to the models already mentioned. Hutton[10] recently designed such a system in a CA-equivalent Artificial Chemistry (Squirm3) in which strands of "atoms" self-replicate via a set of reaction rules that apply locally throughout the space. No limitations are imposed on this replication process, hence any arbitrary strand, if immersed in a sufficiently large random soup of atoms, will self-replicate. Although the number of different possible "types" is thus quite high in this system, all strands have the same basic behaviour. Hutton discovered the emergence of self-replicators and a limited form of adaptation to the environment, although he concluded that more reactions were necessary to enable complexity growth.

5   Conclusion

The systems we mentioned in the previous section constitute a small sample of the possible marginal self-replicators that could potentially be devised in CA. Results with these models, notably the genetic diversity and complex geneal-ogy recently discovered with the evoloop[24,26], demonstrate that complexity-increase of a limited kind is possible *in practice* using such evolvable explicit self-replicators. In many ways such models constitute the first step towards von Neumann's original goal of complexity-increase in CA, steps that he himself could never take because his model was too fragile and complicated.

Models of the kind discussed here are also important as a teaching tool. For a student who is learning about the principles of evolution, a system such as the evoloop has unique advantages over more complicated systems such as those of evolutionary computer programs. Namely, the basic mechanism for evolution (variation and selection) is in one case *emergent*, in the other case *prescribed*. Whereas the latter case *assumes* certain basic principals of biology, the former allows one to *discover* them. The analysis and insight that ultimately lead to such a discovery are at the heart of scientific thinking.

An immediate future challenge is to incorporate within CA systems of self-replicators the possibility for functional interaction potentially leading to more complex hierarchical relations between organisms. The diversity of multi-cellular life that has evolved in the biosphere is clear evidence that self-replication at concurrent multiple scales plays a critical role in the growth of complexity. Al-though the emergence of self-replication has been shown[1,6,10], self-replication of macro-scale replicators from simpler micro-scale ones has not[5]. The study of self-replication and evolution — and in particular the search for complexity-increasing evolution — would likely benefit from work in this direction.

References

1. I. Azpeitia and J. Ibáñez. Spontaneous emergence of robust cellular replicators. In S. Bandini, B. Chopard, and M. Tomassini, editors, *Fifth International Conference on Cellular Automata for Research and Industry (ACRI 2002)*, pages 132–143. Springer, 2002.
2. N. A. Barricelli. Symbiogenetic evolution processes realized by artificial methods. *Methods*, IX(35–36):143–182, 1957.
3. A. W. Burks, editor. *Essays on Cellular Automata*. University of Illinois Press, Urbana, Illinois, 1970.
4. A. W. Burks. Von Neumann's self-reproducing automata. In *[3]*, pages 3–64, 1970.
5. J. Byl. Self-reproduction in small cellular automata. *Physica D*, 34:295–299, 1989.
6. H. H. Chou and J. A. Reggia. Emergence of self-replicating structures in a cellular automata space. *Physica D*, 110:252–276, 1997.
7. H. H. Chou and J. A. Reggia. Problem solving during artificial selection of self-replicating loops. *Physica D*, 115:293–372, 1998.

---

[5] Barricelli's early work with symbioorganisms[2] is however an important first step in this direction.

8. E. F. Codd. *Cellular automata*. ACM Monograph Series. Academic Press, New York, 1968.

9. J. Devore and R. Hightower. The Devore variation of the Codd self-replicating computer. Original work carried out in the early 1970s though apparently never published. Presented at the *Third Workshop on Artificial Life*, Santa Fe, NM, 1992.

10. T. J. Hutton. Evolvable self-replicating molecules in an artificial chemistry. *Artificial Life*, 8:341–356, 2002.

11. J. Ibáñez, D. Anabitarte, I. Azpeitia, O. Barrera, A. Barrutieta, H. Blanco, and F. Echarte. Self-inspection based reproduction in cellular automata. In F. Morán, A. Moreno, J. J. Morelo, and P. Chaucón, editors, *ECAL'95: Third European Conference on Artificial Life*, pages 564–576, Heidelberg, 1995. Springer-Verlag.

12. C. G. Langton. Self-reproduction in cellular automata. *Physica D*, 10:135–144, 1984.

13. C. G. Langton. Artificial life. In *Artificial Life*, volume IV of *Santa Fe Institute Studies in the Sciences of Complexity*, pages 1–47, Redwood City, CA, 1989. Addison-Wesley.

14. J. D. Lohn and J. A. Reggia. Automatic discovery of self-replicating structures in cellular automata. In *IEEE Transactions on Evolutionary Computation*, volume 1, pages 165–178, 1997.

15. D. Mange and M. Sipper. Von Neumann's quintessential message: genotype + ribotype = phenotype. *Artificial Life*, 4:225–227, 1998.

16. P. Marchal. John von Neumann: The founding father of artificial life. *Artificial Life*, 4:229–235, 1998.

17. B. McMullin. John von Neumann and the evolutionary growth of complexity: Looking backward, looking forward... *Artificial Life*, 6:347–361, 2000.

18. K. Morita and K. Imai. A simple self-reproducing cellular automaton with shape-encoding mechanism. In C. G. Langton and K. Shimohara, editors, *Artificial Life V: Proceedings of the Fifth International Workshop on the Synthesis and Simulation of Living Systems*, pages 489–496, Nara, Japan, 1996. MIT Press.

19. J. Y. Perrier, M. Sipper, and J. Zahnd. Toward a viable, self-reproducing universal computer. *Physica D*, 97:335–352, 1996.

20. U. Pesavento. An implementation of von Neumann's self-reproducing machine. *Artificial Life*, 2:337–354, 1995.

21. T. S. Ray. An approach to the synthesis of life. In *Artificial Life II*, volume XI of *SFI Studies on the Sciences of Complexity*, pages 371–408. Addison-Wesley Publishing Company, Redwood City, California, 1991.

22. J. A. Reggia, S. L. Armentrout, H.-H. Chou, and Y. Peng. Simple systems that exhibit self-directed replication. *Science*, 259:1282–1287, February 1993.

23. E. M. A. Ronald, M. Sipper, and M. S. Capcarrère. Design, observation, surprise!: A test of emergence. *Artificial Life*, 5:225–239, 1999.

24. C. Salzberg. Emergent evolutionary dynamics of self-reproducing cellular automata. Master's thesis, Universiteit van Amsterdam, Amsterdam, The Netherlands, 2003.

25. C. Salzberg, A. Antony, and H. Sayama. Evolutionary dynamics of cellular automata-based self-replicators in hostile environments. *BioSystems*. In press.

26. C. Salzberg, A. Antony, and H. Sayama. Complex genetic evolution of selfreplicating loops. In *Artificial Life IX: Proceedings of the Ninth International Conference on Artificial Life*. MIT Press, 2004. In press.

27. C. Salzberg, A. Antony, and H. Sayama. Visualizing evolutionary dynamics of self-replicators: A graph-based approach. *Artificial Life*, 2004. In press.

28. H. Sayama. Introduction of structural dissolution into Langton's self-reproducing loop. In C. Adami, R. K. Belew, H. Kitano, and C. E. Taylor, editors, *Artificial Life VI: Prodceedings of the Sixth International Conference on Artificial Life*, pages 114–122, Los Angeles, California, 1998. MIT Press.

29. H. Sayama. A new structurally dissolvable self-reproducing loop evolving in a simple cellular automata space. *Artificial Life*, 5:343–365, 1999.

30. H. Sayama. Self-replicating worms that increase structural complexity through gene transmission. In M. A. Bedau, J. S. McCaskill, N. H. Packard, and S. Rasmussen, editors, *Artificial Life VII: Proceedings of the Seventh International Conference on Artificial Life*. MIT Press, 2000.

31. M. Sipper. Fifty years of research on self-replication: An overview. *Artificial Life*, 4:237–257, 1998.

32. M. Sipper and J. A. Reggia. Go forth and replicate. *Scientific American*, 285(2):26–35, 2001.

33. A. Smith, P. Turney, and R. Ewaschuk. Self-replicating machines in continuous space with virtual physics. *Artificial Life*, 9:21–40, 2003.

34. A. Stauffer and M. Sipper. An interactive self-replicator implemented in hardware. *Artificial Life*, 8:175–183, 2002.

35. K. Suzuki and T. Ikegami. Interaction based evolution of self-replicating loop structures. In *Proceedings of the Seventh European Conference on Artificial Life*, pages 89–93, Dortmund, Germany, 2003.

36. T. J. Taylor. *From artificial evolution to artificial life*. PhD thesis, University of Edinburgh, 1999.

37. G. Tempesti. A new self-reproducing cellular automaton capable of construction and computation. In F. Morán, A. Moreno, J. J. Merelo, and P. Chacón, editors, *ECAL'95: Third European Conference on Artificial Life, LNCS929*, pages 555–563, Heidelberg, 1995. Springer-Verlag.

38. J. W. Thatcher. Universality in the von Neumann cellular model. In *[3]*, pages 132–186, 1970.

39. T. Tyler. Crystal 1D: Template-based replication. Online documentation and source code. http://cell-auto.co.uk/crystal1d/.

40. P. Vitányi. Sexually reproducing cellular automata. *Mathematical Biosciences*, 18:23–54, 1973.

41. J. von Neumann. *Theory of Self-Reproducing Automata*. University of Illinois Press, Urbana, Illinois, 1966. Edited and completed by A. W. Burks.

42. J. von Neumann. Re-evaluation of the problems of complicated automata – problems of hierarchy and evolution (Fifth Illinois Lecture), December 1949. In W. Aspray and A. Burks, editors, *Papers of John von Neumann on Computing and Computer Theory*, pages 477–490. MIT Press, 1987.

Unlearning Phenomena in Co-evolution of Non-uniform Cellular Automata

Boaz Leskes and Peter M.A. Sloot

Section Computational Science, Faculty of Science, University of Amsterdam, Kruislaan 403, 1098 SJ, Amsterdam, The Netherlands

Abstract. This paper presents results of a study of a genetic algorithm, designed to evolve cellular automata for solving a given problem. Evolution is performed between the cell's update-rules in a local manner, allowing for easy parallelization. As a case study, the algorithm was applied to the density classification problem: classifying any given initial configuration according to the percentage of 1-valued cells. The main result presented in this paper is an 'unlearning' phenomenon: highly fit solutions are generated by the algorithm, only to be 'unlearned' and completely disappear as the evolutionary run continues.

1 Introduction

Cellular Automata were invented in the late 1940's by von Neumann[1] as simplified models to study self-reproduction. Since then, CA have been widely used to study complex behavior. In such studies, the update rules which dictate the CA behavior are either designed per se or mimic the local behavior of problems at hand. The results and analysis are then based upon global behavior which is apparent (or not) in the computation over time. A well known example of such problem is Conway's Game of Life, which displays complex behavior (and universal computation [11]) using very simple local rules. Other examples such as fluid flow simulation, growth modeling and Ising Spin models can be found in [4]. [4] also includes theoretic analysis of CA and various implementation details and considerations. In all of the above examples, and many other, the CA rules are typically available or are inspired by nature.

On the other side of CA research is the reverse problem: How to decide what rules should be used in order to perform a specific computation? Answering this question is a complicated and crucial issue, both for utilizing and implementing CA as real life tools and for explaining natural phenomena as the result of local interactions.

One approach to this problem involves using Genetic Algorithms in an attempt to 'evolve' a CA for solving a specific task (for example, [2,3,5]). A more extensive description of the field can be found in [8]. In 1996, Moshe Sipper published a Genetic Algorithm designed to co-evolve non uniform CA for performing computational tasks [6,7]. In his papers [6,7], Sipper shows that using that algorithm, Cellular Automata were evolved to performed several complex tasks. However, a study of the algorithm and its parameters is not presented. This paper presents some interesting insights based upon such a study.

P.M.A. Sloot, B. Chopard, and A.G. Hoekstra (Eds.): ACRI 2004, LNCS 3305, pp. 172–181, 2004.

Algorithm 1 Pseudo-code of the cellular programming algorithm

---

Parameters:

- M - How many time steps the evolved CA would be allowed to perform when computing the solution.
- C - How many initial configurations are used for rule evaluation.
- Stopping criteria

1. Initialization:
   a) For each cell i in the CA do (possibly in Parallel)
      i. Initialize rule table of cell i.
      ii. $f_i = 0$ { fitness value }
   b) $c = 0$ { initial configuration counter }
2. while *not done* do:
   a) generate a random initial configuration.
   b) run CA on initial configuration for M iterations.
   c) For each cell i do (possibly in Parallel):
      i. if cell i is in the correct final state then $f_i = f_i + 1$
   d) $c = c + 1$
   e) if $c \bmod C = 0$ then { evolve every C configurations }
      i. For each cell i do (possibly in Parallel):
         A. Compute $nf_i(c)$ { number of fitter neighbors }
         B. if $nf_i(c)$=0 then don't change the rule of cell i
         C. else if $nf_i(c)$=1 then replace the rule of cell i with the fitter neighboring rule, followed by mutation.
         D. else if $nf_i(c)$=2 then replace the rule of cell i with the crossover of the two fitter neighboring rules, followed by mutation.
         E. else if $nf_i(c)$>2 then replace the rule of cell i with the crossover of the two randomly chosen fitter neighboring rules, followed by mutation.
         F. $f_i = 0$

---

2   Algorithm and Methods

This section presents the algorithm designed by Sipper in [6,7,8] for co-evolving a CA for solving a given problem. We will use the same definition of Cellular Automata as in [7], where uniform CA implies that the cells' state is updated using a single update rule. This is in contrast to non-uniform CA where each cell has its own local update rule. A more formal notion of Genetic Algorithms and the related operators (Crossover, mutation etc.) can also be found in that paper. The algorithm studied in this paper is presented in Algorithm 1. At every iteration, the quality of the current CA rules is evaluated over a set of randomly selected initial configurations followed by creation of new rules using the better ones of the previous step. The algorithm is supplied with a method for the correct measurement of the cells' final behavior/value. This can be in the form of an "oracle" able to evaluate the correct result for a given example or by some sort of a criteria to measure the output correctness (for example: correct behavior over time). After a given number of such examples have been presented to the CA and its rules are evaluated, an evolution step is performed. Each cell is compared with its neighboring cells. If the cell is the best cell in its neighborhood, it is left unchanged (this will be further referred to as elitism). If not, its better neighbors are used to create the cell's new rule.

The algorithm is different from the standard GA approaches to CA programing taken, for example, by Mitchel et al., in [5]. In Mitchel's algorithm, the population consists of uniform CA and their evaluation is done independently. Therefore, there is no dependence between population elements of the same generation. However, in the algorithm suggested by Sipper, the GA population are the cell rules and therefore their evaluation is highly interdependent. Due to the way evaluation is done, the cells are highly influenced by their neighbors. A 'bad' neighbor can cause the current cell to be evaluated badly as well. Furthermore, evolution is done in a local manner, since each cell is evolved using only the neighboring rules. This leads to a very local but dependent evolution. Cells' success affects the success of their neighbors and vice versa. In contrast, in Mitchel's Algorithm, every CA (rule) in the population can be crossed over with any other in the population and not only with a very limited neighborhood. On one hand the local evolution used might hinder the algorithm, since it may prevent a good rule from being fully exploited. On other hand, such interrelations lead to fitter groups of rules: rules which are fit for working together. It is this interaction between rules and their effect on each other's evolution process that gives rise to the name co-evolution. This algorithm is similar to the Diffusion Genetic Algorithms[9], where each element is only allowed to 'mate' with its close neighbors. However, in that model, each element of the population is a 'solution' while here, it is the population itself which serves as one.

Note that the Algorithm itself can be viewed as an extended form of (stochastic) Cellular Automata, acting as a non-uniform CA for a fixed number of iterations, followed by a local evolution step. The algorithm can also be described in terms of an Abstract Cellular Genetic Algorithm, a framework for a parallel population based process [12, 13]. This means that most of it can be performed, at least in principal, in parallel.

2.1   Implementation

This section describes the specific implementation used to study the algorithm. The description is divided into two parts, corresponding to the main ingredients of the algorithm: The non-uniform CA being evolved, and evolution related operations.

Non-Uniform CA: The CA studied here are all two dimensional grids of size $N \times N$ (which will be referred to as size N in the rest of the paper). Following the reasoning presented by Sipper, the CA performs a number of iterations equal to the number of cells, N^2. All cells have a value of 1 or 0 and have a von Neumann neighborhood with periodic boundaries. Each cell's rule was stored as 2^5 bits denoting the the cell's value in the next iteration for all possible setting of its neighborhood. In order to map the neighborhood configuration to a bit, the neighborhood cell values were converted into a binary number in the following order of importance: Cell value, Left, Right, Down and Up.

Evolution Operators: The algorithm uses crossover and mutation operators. The implementation of those operators was as follows:

- *Crossover*: To crossover two rules, a point is selected randomly along their lengths (at a corresponding location on both rules). The new rule, or the crossover result would be either the merger of the first part (before that point) of the first rule with the second part of the second rule, or the first part of the second rule with the second part of the first one. This choice was made using a 50%-50% distribution.
- *Mutation*: In order to mutate a rule, each bit of the rule would be flipped with a probability p_m, which is part of the algorithm's parameter-set.

2.2   Solution Quality Assessment

Investigating an algorithm immediately entails running it in various scenarios and comparing the solutions produced by the algorithm. In this case this entails that it is necessary to have a method of comparing the evolved CA. Furthermore, the various CA that emerge during an evolutionary run need also to be compared and assessed. There is no guaranty that the best CA will be the one present at the last step. There exist several ways for defining such a CA fitness score (see [5],[8, page 82]), but here the average fitness of the CA's cells will be used. This fitness assignment is easy to calculate from the data collected by the algorithm during its run and allows to save only the best CA. Note that this fitness does not necessarily depict the global demands of the given problem. This point will be further discussed in Section 4.1.

3   Experiments

As part of this study many experiments have been performed, designed to test the effects of the parameters (and some others criteria) on the learning capabilities of the algorithm. Only two of the results will be presented here. As a test case, we chose the *Density Classification* problem in which the CA is required to detect whether the initial configuration has more then 50% 1-values. If so, the entire CA has to be set to the value 1. Otherwise, all cells should have the value 0. This problem has been proven [10] to be unsolvable for a uniform CA: no uniform CA can classify all initial configurations correctly. However, this does not say anything regarding a non-uniform CA, nor how good a uniform CA can get (apart from never doing perfect). The initial configurations were generated in the following way: First, a desired density was drawn uniformly over [0,1] and then a configuration with such density was chosen randomly. This makes the problem somewhat easier since it spreads the density of the initial configuration uniformly over [0,1] while choosing an initial configuration completely at random would lead to a higher chance of it having a density in the neighborhood of 0.5, a region which have proven hard for CA. This problem has been investigated in detail by Mitchel et al., and Sipper [5,7,6,8].

4   Results

Two aspects of the algorithm will be presented here. In the first part, three fit solutions are presented and analysed. The second part deals with an 'unlearning' phenomenon discovered during the experiments.

4.1   Solution Examples

In this section, three examples of the best evolved solutions to the Density Classification problem are presented. Figure 1 presents and compares the solutions in several aspects. The first row of sub-figures shows the diversity of the rules among the three solutions. Each rule is colored uniquely such that a rule which is present in two separate solutions is colored in the same color in both. The second row of graphs shows the distribution of the rules present in each solution. On the x-axis the rules are ordered in an arbitrary

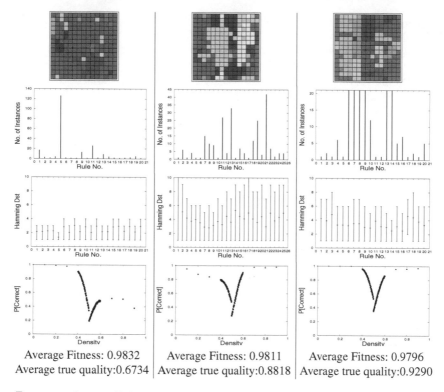

| Average Fitness: 0.9832 | Average Fitness: 0.9811 | Average Fitness: 0.9796 |
| Average true quality:0.6734 | Average true quality:0.8818 | Average true quality:0.9290 |

From top to bottom: Rules (colors are maintained between columns), Rule distribution, Hamming distance (from each rule to others), True solution quality

Fig. 1. Three Density Classification solutions, evolved by the algorithm.

order, which is maintained in the graphs in the third row. These graphs show, for each rule in the solution the average minimum and maximum hamming distance to other rules in the same solution. These quantities serve as a measure of how different the rules are. The fourth row presents a more detailed evaluation of the solutions. The graphs display the probability that the solution would compute a correct answer as a function of the density in the initial configuration. By correct it is meant that *all* cells of the CA display the correct answer (0 or 1). This was evaluated using 5000 initial configurations drawn at random and independently. Last, the solution's average fitness is displayed, along with the solution's true average quality. The true average quality of the solutions was evaluated using 5000 initial configuration as well.

While being almost completely different, the three solutions have an almost equal average fitness. The left solution has the highest score of 0.9832 , followed by the middle one and 0.9811 and the right one with 0.9796. However, looking at the true quality of the solution, or the probability that its output would be correct as defined by the problem, the situation is reversed. The best solution is now the right one, with a score of 0.929. Following is the middle one with a score of 0.8818 and last is the left solution with a score of 0.6734. The graphs showing the solution's quality as a function of the initial density show that the left most solution does not classify well densities larger then 0.5, resulting in its poor performance. These graphs also show that all solution perform poorly for densities in the range [0.4,0.6]. This can be expected since in these domains the difference between the number of 1's and 0's is small and therefore determining which value dominates is harder.

Using two methods to evaluate solutions can be expected to give different results. The first method used is average fitness of the different rules, which is measured independently for each rule along 300 initial configurations. The second measures the entire CA, meaning that in order to achieve a good score all rules must display the correct output. Nevertheless, it was expected that the difference would not prove meaningful and that a solution which is deemed good by the average fitness score would also be good according to the full problem definition. The difference and its effect on correct classification put in doubt the choice of average fitness as a solution measurement. Differences such as the one between 0.98 and 0.67, are too large to be accepted.

The distribution of rules, displayed in the second row of Figure 1, suggests that higher rule diversity produces a better density classifier. The left most solution is dominated by a single rule, and performs the poorest. The right solution is the most diverse one and has the highest quality.

While different, the rules are not far apart. The maximum hamming distance between two rules in all the solutions is 10 (out a maximum possible of 32) and this is reached only for two rules in the middle solution, which has only one instance each. Furthermore, rules that are more common tend to be more central. The averaged distance from those rules to others is relatively low. This is to be expected since the algorithm mutates good rules when they are copied to a different location. It follows that a set of rules which are close-together will result.

4.2   A Look into the 'Unlearning' Phenomenon

In several occasions during the experiments, it became clear that a good solution can be evolved during a run, only to be 'unlearned' or disappear. The good solution would gradually be replaced by a worse one, resulting in a poor quality solution. A clear example of this can be seen in Figure 2, where 10 runs of the algorithm are shown. As the figure suggest, 'unlearning' is not rare, making our reproducible. Another point of interest is that the 'unlearning' runs seem to converge to a fitness of around 0.79 (see Figure 3 as well). In this section this 'unlearning' phenomenon is presented in more detail. All experiments shown here relate to the Density

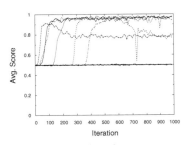

Fig. 2. Unlearning phenomenon

Classification problem with the following parameters: $N = 32$, $C = 300$, $p_m = 0.001$.

One immediate question that arises is whether the unlearning is final: will the algorithm, after loosing the previous good solution, evolve a new one? This can be expected, since as the evolutionary run continues it is likely that a new good solution will emerge. In order to check this, several long evolutionary runs were performed, involving 10,000 evolutionary iterations. Figure 3 shows two such typical runs, one successful and the other displaying 'unlearning'. As can be seen, the 'unlearning' is stable and final. Once a value of ≈ 0.78 has been reached (after a peak of ≈ 0.9) it remains roughly stable for the rest of the run. Note the sharp drop just before the thousandth iteration and the drops after 3500 and 7500 iterations.

A different run where unlearning can be seen is presented in Figure 4. The first three figures display the average fitness and the number of instances of 18 rules. These rules had the most instances during the run[1] and are ordered according to this criteria. The rules are ordered 6 per graph, beginning with rules 1 to 6, followed by 7-12 and 13-18. The rules are tagged with numbers resulting from reading the rule bit string as a binary number. Figure 4 also shows the average fitness of the solution, in similar fashion to previous experiments, to allow comparison and understanding of the run. In comparison, a successful run is displayed in Figure 5.

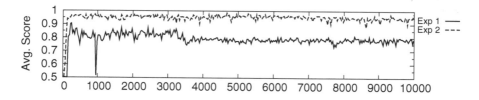

Fig. 3. Successful Learning and Unlearning - long evolutionary runs.

As can be clearly seen in Figure 5, the unlearning beginning is accompanied by a sharp increase and decline in rule 250000192192. This rule first appears at time step 605, where the average CA fitness is fairly high, 0.955. In the next 35 steps, by time step 640, 51 instances of this rule are present with an average rule fitness of 0.97. The rule continues to expand and reaches its peak in time step 662, where it has 171 instances: the maximum number of instances of a rule during the whole run. By this time the rule average fitness has dropped to 0.927 along with the average CA fitness (which is now 0.927 as well). At this point the rule begins to disappear, loosing instances while the average CA fitness continues to decrease. In time step 750, only 1 instance of this rule is present and its fitness is 0.867. Note the behavior of the second rule (186170228192), which is present in the period where the average CA fitness is high and disappears roughly when rule 250000192192 reaches its peak. After the disappearance of rule 250000192192 no other rule is dominant and a mixture of rules is maintained. However, the average fitness does not rise again. These dominant patterns are notably different from the patterns displayed in the successful run, where rule diversity is kept along the run.

This experiments are not sufficient to determine the cause of the unlearning phenomenon, nor to explain the complicated dynamics between rules during the evolutionary processes. However, it seems that the behavior seen in Section 4.1, where rule

---

[1] The 18 rules which had the best $\max\limits_{k} \left(R_k^i \right)$ value, where R_k^i denotes the number of instances rule i had at iteration k

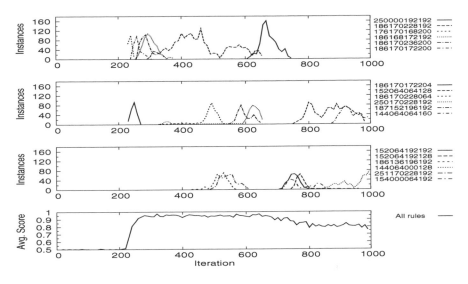

Fig. 4. Unlearning Phenomena

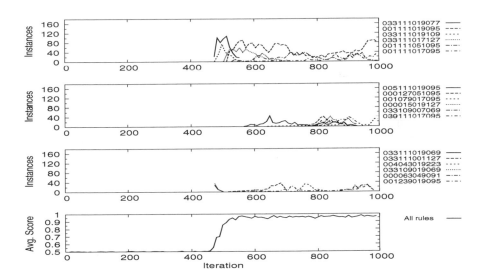

Fig. 5. Successful run

diversity seemed to coincide with better density classifiers, reappears here. Once a rule managed to dominate the lattice, the quality of the CA decreases, causing a decrease in the fitness of the top rule and therefore allowing other rules to take over. The rule could only maintain its high fitness because of the presence of other rules in sufficient quantities. Being the best rule, it quickly multiplies reducing the number of other rule instances, to a point where it has diminished its 'source of power' and it immediately starts to decrease. Since introduction and removal of rules is mainly done at the edges of its continuous domain (inside evolution rarely occurs and if it does the rule would always survive crossover - the main creator of new rules), the process is gradual. Once the rule covered a large part of the lattice, several iterations are necessary for it to shrink back and perhaps disappear.

This can explain the rise and fall of rule number 250000192192, but it does not explain why, after the rule disappeared, the evolutionary process does not manage to generate, once again, a good solution. Further, this might explain the relatively slow declines seen in Figure 3 but it does sufficiently explain the sharp drop and recovery just before the thousandth iteration nor the apparent convergence to a fitness ≈ 0.79. When using the Density Classification as a goal and fitness evaluation, the rules are highly interdependent. This fact makes analysis of rule interaction and understanding of the evolution process difficult. More experiments, and perhaps different measurement methods are needed.

5   Conclusions

This paper presents a study of an algorithm designed by M. Sipper [6,7,8] for programming non-uniform CA. The algorithm uses random examples (and their correct output) to evaluate fitness values of the CA rules and based on these, performs crossover and mutation operations in order to improve the current CA. The algorithm operates in a strictly local fashion, allowing easy parallelisation.

The study investigated the effects of the algorithm parameters, using the 2D density classification problem as a test case. When applied to this specific problem and several other reported by Sipper, the algorithm was successful in producing highly fit solutions. However, what is a fit solution and how it is defined has proven to be a key issue. One possible choice, and the one taken in this study and by Sipper, is to define CA fitness as the average fitness of its rules. This is a natural choice since it can be easily extracted from the fitness values of the rules, which are already calculated by the algorithm. Furthermore, since the algorithm is a genetic one, it is expected or, in some sense, it is the task of the algorithm to evolve a fit *population*[2]. However, due to the local nature of rule fitness evaluation, this has proven to be a problem. When correct problem output is defined in global terms, as in the density classification problem, it is not necessarily the case that a population which is in average locally fit will also be fit in a global sense. There is a large gap between the average fitness of a CA and its true global performance. Furthermore, these two measures are not correlated: CA with small rule diversity tend to be more fit but perform worse in absolute terms. CA using a richer set of rules are slightly less fit but perform significantly better. Since cellular automata are commonly used to produce global behavior, a general rule-fitness function, which is strongly connected to this notion, is needed.

During the experiments it became apparent that the algorithm may sometimes loose a good solution and produce an inferior one. This phenomenon, named here 'unlearning', was briefly adhered and seems to be caused by the interactions between the population members - the CA rules. The decrease in solution fitness coincides with an increase in

---

[2] The typical definition for the goal of a genetic algorithm is to find a highly fit solution, or individual. However, the algorithm is usually measured in terms of average population as well.

the relative representation of a single rule. The rule's portion of the population increases until it has covered almost all cells, followed by a sharp decline. At the end of this decline the rule disappears completely and other rules come in its place. Given the apparent connection between rule diversity and the CA's quality, this might explain the observed slow decrease in CA fitness. However, some of the other observed behavior is yet to be explained: sharp drops in fitness followed by and immediate recovery, apparent convergence to a specific fitness value and the algorithm's failure to generate a new fit solution. In our experiments, 'unlearning' was more common in the larger CA. This suggests that that 'unlearning' is not caused by the finite size of the CA but further research on the effects of the size of the CA should performed. More experiments and new techniques are needed to study this phenomenon.

References

1. von Neumann, J. 1966. Theory of Self Reproducing Automata. University of Illinois Press, Illinois. Edited and completed by A.W. Burks.
2. M. Mitchell, J. P. Crutcheld, and P. T. Hraber. Evolving cellular automata to perform computations: Mechanisms and impediments. Physica D, 75:361 - 391, 1994.
3. M. Mitchell, P. T. Hraber, and J. P. Crutcheld. Revisiting the edge of chaos: Evolving cellular automata to perform computations. Complex Systems, 7:89-130, 1993.
4. P.M.A. Sloot, J.A. Kaandorp, A.G. Hoekstra and B.J. Overeinder: Distributed Cellular Automata: Large Scale Simulation of Natural Phenomena, in A.Y. Zomaya; F. Ercal and S. Olariu, editors, Solutions to Parallel and Distributed Computing Problems: Lessons from Biological Sciences, pp. 1-46. Computer Centre University of Tromso, 2001
5. James P. Crutchfield, Melanie Mitchell, and Rajarshi Das. The Evolutionary Design of Collective Computation in Cellular Automata.
http://www.santafe.edu/sfi/publications/wpabstract/199809080
6. Moshe Sipper. Co-evolving non-uniform cellular automata to perform computations. Physica D 92 (1996) 193-208.
7. Moshe Sipper, Marco Tomassini. Computation in artificially evolved, non-uniform cellular automata. Theoretical Computer Science 217 (1999) 81-98.
8. Moshe Sipper. Evolution of Parallel Cellular Programming Approach. Lecture Notes in Computer Science. Springer. ISBN - 3-540-62613-1.
9. Chrisila C. Pettey. "Diffusion (Cellular) Models", The Handbook of Evolutionary Computation. (Oxford University Press) 1997.
10. Mark Land, Richard K. Belew. No Perfect Two-State Cellular Automata for Density Classification Exists. Physical Review Letters, Volume 74, number 25. 19/6/1995.
11. Robert T. Wainwright. Life is universal!, Winter Simulation Conference, Proceedings of the 7th conference on Winter simulation - Volume 2 Pages: 449 - 459.Washington, DC. 1974.
12. A. Schoneveld; J.F. de Ronde; P.M.A. Sloot and J.A. Kaandorp: A Parallel Cellular Genetic Algorithm Used in Finite Element Simulation, in H-.M. Voigt; W. Ebeling; I. Rechenberg and H-.P. Schwefel, editors, Parallel Problem Solving from Nature IV, pp. 533-542. 1996.
13. P.M.A. Sloot; A. Schoneveld; J.F. de Ronde and J.A. Kaandorp: Large scale simulations of complex systems Part I: conceptual framework, (SFI Working Paper: 97-07-070) Santa Fe Instute for Complex studies, 1997.

Evolving Transition Rules for
Multi Dimensional Cellular Automata

Ron Breukelaar[1] and Thomas Bäck[1,2]

[1] Universiteit Leiden, LIACS, P.O. Box 9512, 2300 RA Leiden, The Netherlands
{rbreukel,baeck}@liacs.nl
[2] Nutech Solutions GmbH, Martin-Schmeisser-Weg, 44227 Dortmund, Germany

Abstract. Genetic Algorithms have been used before to evolve transition rules for one dimensional Cellular Automata (CA) to solve e.g. the majority problem and investigate communication processes within such CA [3]. In this paper, the principle is extended to multi dimensional CA, and it is demonstrated how the approach evolves transition rules for the two dimensional case with a von Neumann neighborhood. In particular, the method is applied to the binary AND and XOR problems by using the GA to optimize the corresponding rules. Moreover, it is shown how the approach can also be used for more general patterns, and therefore how it can serve as a method for calibrating and designing CA for real-world applications.

1 Introduction

According to [6] Cellular Automata (CA) are mathematical idealisations of physical systems in which space and time are discrete, and physical quantities take on a finite set of discrete values. The simplest CA is one dimensional and looks a bit like an array of ones and zeros of width N, where the first position of the array is linked to the last position. In other words, defining a row of positions $C = \{a_1, a_2, ..., a_N\}$ where C is a CA of width N and a_N is adjacent to a_1.

The neighborhood s_n of a_n is defined as the local set of positions with a distance to a_n along the connected chain which is no more than a certain radius (r). This for instance means that $s_2 = \{a_{148}, a_{149}, a_1, a_2, a_3, a_4, a_5\}$ for $r = 3$ and $N = 149$. Please note that for one dimensional CA the size of the neighborhood is always equal to $2r + 1$.

The values in a CA can be altered all at the same time (synchronous) or at different times (asynchronous). Only synchronous CA are considered in this paper. In the synchronous approach at every timestep (t) every cell state in the CA is recalculated according to the states of the neighborhood using a certain transition rule $\Theta : \{0, 1\}^{2r+1} \rightarrow \{0, 1\}, s_i \rightarrow \Theta(s_i)$. This rule basically is a one-to-one mapping that defines an output value for every possible set of input values, the input values being the 'state' of a neighborhood. The state of a_n at time t is written as a_n^t, the state of s_n at time t as s_n^t and the state of the entire CA C at time t as C^t so that C^0 is the initial state and $\forall n = 1, ..., N$ $a_n^{t+1} = \Theta(s_n^t)$. Given $C^t = \{a_1^t, ..., a_N^t\}$, C^{t+1} can be defined as $\{\Theta(s_1^t), ..., \Theta(s_N^t)\}$.

P.M.A. Sloot, B. Chopard, and A.G. Hoekstra (Eds.): ACRI 2004, LNCS 3305, pp. 182–191, 2004.

Because $a_n \in \{0, 1\}$ the number of possible states of s_n equals 2^{2r+1}. Because all possible binary representations of m where $0 \leq m < 2^{2r+1}$ can be mapped to a unique state of the neighborhood, Θ can be written as a row of ones and zeros $R = \{b_1, b_2, ..., b_{2^{2r+1}}\}$ where b_m is the output value of the rule for the input state that maps to the binary representation of $m - 1$. A rule therefore has a length that equals 2^{2r+1} and so there are $2^{2^{2r+1}}$ possible rules for a binary one dimensional CA. This is a huge number of possible rules (if $r = 3$ this sums up to about $3, 4 \times 10^{28}$) each with a different behaviour.

One of the interesting things about these and other CA is that certain rules tend to exhibit organisational behaviour, independently of the initial state of the CA. This behaviour also demonstrates there is some form of communication going on in the CA over longer distances than the neighborhood allows directly. In [3] the authors examine if these simple CA are able to perform tasks that need positions in a CA to work together and use some form of communication. One problem where such a communication seems required in order to give a good answer is the Majority Problem (as described in section 3.1). A genetic algorithm is used to evolve rules for one dimensional CA that do a rather good job of solving the Majority Problem [3] and it is shown how these rules seem to send "particles" and communicate by using these particles [4]. These results imply that even very simple cells in one dimensional cellular automata can communicate and work together to form more complex and powerful behavior.

It is not unthinkable that the capabilities of these one dimensional CA are restricted by the number of directions in which information can "travel" through a CA and that using multiple dimensions might remove these restriction and therefore improve performance. Evolving these rules for the Majority Problem for two dimensional CA using a Moore neighborhood (explained in section 3) is reported in [2] showing that the GA did not clearly outperform random search.

The goal of the research is to find a generalization and report phenomena observed on a higher level, with the future goal to use this research for identification and calibration of higher-dimensional CA applications to real world systems like parallel computing and modelling social and biological processes. The approach is described and results are reported on simple problems such as the Majority Problem, AND, XOR, extending into how it can be applied to pattern generation processes.

2 The Genetic Algorithm

As mentioned before, this research was inspired by earlier work [3,4] in which transition rules for one dimensional CA were evolved to solve the Majority Problem (as defined in section 3.1). The GA is a fairly simple algorithm using binary representation of the rules, mutation by bit inversion, truncation selection, and single-point crossover. The algorithm determined the fitness by testing the evolved rules on 100 random initial states. Every iteration the best 20% of the rules (the 'elite' rules) were copied to the next generation and the other 80% of the rules were generated using single-point crossover with two randomly chosen 'elite' rules and then mutated by flipping exactly 2 bits in the rule.

To be able to compare two dimensional CA with one dimensional CA the GA used in section 3.1 is a copy of the the GA used in [3,4]. The GAs in section 3.2 and 4 on the other hand are modified to fit the different problem demands, as will be explained in these sections.

3   Experimental Results for Two Dimensional CA

The two dimensional CA in this document are similar to the one dimensional CA discussed so far. Instead of a row of positions, C now consists of a grid of positions. The values are still only binary (0 or 1) and there still is only one transition rule for all the cells. The number of cells is still finite and therefore CA discussed here have a width, a height and borders.

The big difference between one dimensional and two dimensional CA is the rule definition. The neighborhood of these rules is two dimensional, because there are not only neighbors left and right of a cell, but also up and down. That means that if $r = 1$, s_n would consist of 5 positions, being the four directly adjacent plus a_n. This neighborhood is often called "the von Neumann neighborhood" after its inventor. The other well known neighborhood expands the Neumann neighborhood with the four positions diagnally adjacent to a_n and is called "the Moore neighborhood" also after its inventor.

Rules are defined with the same rows of bits (R) as defined in the one dimensional case. For a von Neumann neighborhood a rule can be defined with $2^5 = 32$ bits and a rule for a Moore neighborhood needs $2^9 = 512$ bits. This makes the Moore rule more powerful, for it has a bigger search space. Yet, this also means that searching in that space might take more time and finding anything might be a lot more difficult. In [2] the authors discourage the use of the Moore neighborhood, yet in section 3.2 and section 4 results clearly show successes using the Moore neighborhood, regardless of the langer search space.

In a one dimensional CA the leftmost cell is connected to the rightmost cell. In the two dimensional CA this is also common such that it forms a torus structure.

3.1   Majority Problem

The Majority Problem can be defined as follows: *Given a set $A = \{a_1, ..., a_n\}$ with n odd and $a_m \in \{0, 1\}$ for all $1 \leq m \leq n$, answer the question: 'Are there more ones than zeros in A?'.*

The Majority Problem first does not seem to be a very difficult problem to solve. It seems only a matter of counting the ones in the set and then comparing them to the number of zeros. Yet when this problem is converted to the dimensions of a CA it becomes a lot more difficult. This is because the rule in a CA does not let a position look past its neighborhood and that is why the cells all have to work together and use some form of communication.

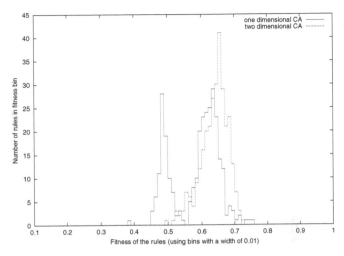

Fig. 1. This figure displays the number of rules that have a certain fitness value in the two dimensional experiment and compares this to the one dimensional experiment. The fitness bins are 0.01 in width and for both algorithm $F_{169,10^3}$ is calculated for 300 rules.

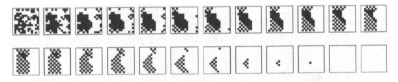

Fig. 2. This figure shows a correct classification of the Majority Problem by a two dimensional CA with both width and height equal to 13 and $\lambda = 84/169$. The transition rule was one of the best tested in the experiment and scored $F_{169,10^3} = 0.715$.

Given that the relative number of ones in C^0 is written as λ, in a simple binary CA the Majority Problem can be defined as: *Find a rule that, given an initial state of a CA with N odd and a finite number of iterations to run (I), will result in an 'all zero' state if $\lambda < 0.5$ and an 'all one' state otherwise.*

The fitness (f) of a rule is is therefore defined as the relative number of correct answers to 100 randomly chosen initial states, where a 'correct answer' corresponds to an 'all zero' state if $\lambda < 0.5$ and an 'all one' state otherwise. In [3] the authors found that using a uniform distribution over λ for the initial states enhanced performance greatly; this is used here as well. The best runs will be tested using randomly chosen initial states with a normal distribution over the number of ones. The relative number of correct classifications on these states is written as $F_{n,m}$ where n is the width of the CA and m is the number of tests conducted.

Preliminary experiments showed that it took much more time to evolve rules for the Moore neighborhood than for the von Neumann neighborhood. The tests that were done with the Moore neighborhood also did not result in any encouraging results, this being in line with [2]. That is why the von Neumann neighborhood was chosen for this experiment. Because this neighborhood consists of five positions, the search space for CA rules is a lot smaller than in the one dimensional experiment. Instead of the $2^7 = 128$ bits in the rule, R now consists of $2^5 = 32$ bits, thus drastically decreasing the serch space. This means that the search space decreased from 2^{128} to 2^{32} and is now $2^{(128-32)} = 2^{96}$ times smaller!

For this experiment we used a CA with width $= 13$ and height $= 13$. This means that these CA have $13 \times 13 = 169$ cells (N) and are $169 - 149 = 20$ cells larger than the one dimensional CA used in the original experiment.

This algorithm was run 300 times and each winning rule was tested by calculating $F_{N,M}$ using $F_{169,10^3}$. These results are plotted agaLints results of our own one dimensional experiment (not reported here, analogue to [3,4]) in Figure 1. The striking difference between this distribution of fitness and the distribution of fitness in the one dimensional experiment is the absence of the peak around $F_{N,M} \approx 0.5$ in the two dimensional results. In those results almost all the evolved rules have a fitness above 0.58. A fitness around 0.66 seems to be average and the best rules have a fitness above 0.7. That is all very surprising taking into account that the von Neumann neighborhood only consists of 5 cells.

The Majority Problem is a good example of a problem that forces cells in a CA to 'communicate' with another. The communication 'particles' can be seen in the one dimensional experiment, but are not easily spotted in the two dimensional experiment. That does not mean there are no 'particles' traveling in the two dimensional CA, because it might be very hard to identify these particles. In a two dimensional CA 'particles' are no longer restricted to traveling in only one direction, but can travel to multiple directions at the same time. Traveling particles in two dimensional CA can therefore look like expanding areas with a distinct border. But there might be multiple particles traveling at the same time, meeting each other and thereby creating new particles. This is why communication between cells in a two dimensional CA is not very visible in the Majority Problem, although results show that this communication is present.

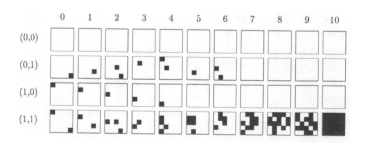

Fig. 3. This figure displays the iterations of a CA solving the AND problem. Every row shows the iteration of the rule using a different initial state. Note that in the first column ($t = 0$) the initial states are clearly visible and in the last column the coloring matches the output of an AND port.

Table 1. Fitness values found in the AND problem.

	Number of runs			
	Neumann		Moore	
Fitness	with crossover	without crossover	with crossover	without crossover
100	0	0	31	21
98-99	0	0	41	54
95-97	0	0	14	25
90-94	77	93	14	0
80-89	23	7	0	0
70-79	0	0	0	0
< 70	0	0	0	0

3.2 AND and XOR Problem

To show the communication between cells in a two dimensional CA a different experiment was conducted. A genetic algorithm was used to evolve rules for two dimensional CA that could solve the simple binary operators AND and XOR. These operators both have two input values and one output value which can only be determined if both input values are known. This is unlike the OR operator for example where the output value is always one if one or more of the input values is one, so if only one input value is known to be one then the value of the other input value is not needed. This may look very trivial, but it is very important in order to force the CA to combine the two values and thereby communicate.

The AND Problem. To show the communications in a CA the information that needs to be combined must be initialized as far apart as possible. The following problem definition takes this into account: *Given a square CA with two 'input cells', one top left and one bottom right: find a rule that iterates the CA so that after I iterations the CA is in an 'all one' state if both the 'input cells' were one in the initial state and in an 'all zero' state otherwise.*

Small two dimensional CA were used with a width and a height of 5 cells and I was set to 10. The borders of the CA were unconnected to allow a larger virtual distance between the two corner cells. This means that the leftmost cell in a row was not connected to the rightmost cell in the same row and the topmost cell was not connected to the bottommost cell as was done with the Majority Problem experiment. Instead every cell on the border of the CA was connected to so called 'zero-cells'. These 'zero-cells' stay zero whatever happens.

When using two input cells, there are four different initial states. These states are written as $S_{(v_1,v_2)}$ where v_1 and v_2 are the two input values. All cells other than the two input cells are initialized with zero.

The fitness of a rule is defined as the total number of cells that have the correct values after I iterations. The number of ones in iteration t is written as $O^t_{(v_1,v_2)}$. The total fitness of the AND problem is defined as $f = (N - O^I_{(0,0)}) + (N - O^I_{(0,1)}) + (N - O^I_{(1,0)}) + O^I_{(1,1)}$. This makes the maximum fitness equal to $4 \times 5 \times 5 = 100$.

In this experiment another variation of the simple genetic algorithm was used. A generation step starts by sorting the rules according to their fitness. Then it selects the top ten% of the rules as 'elite' rules and copies them without changes to the next generation. Every 'elite' rule is then copied nine times or is used in single-point crossover to make the other 90% of the population. Both methods were tested and compared. The generated rules are mutated and also moved to the next generation. Mutation is done by flipping every bit in the rule with a probability p_m. The algorithm stops if it finds a rule with $f = 100$ or it reaches 1000 generations. In preliminary experiments a number of different values of p_m were tested. Setting p_m to a rather high value of 0.05 turned out to be the most effective choice, confirming our insight that with increasing selection strength higher mutation rates than the usual $\frac{1}{l}$ (l beging the the length of the binary string) are performing better [1].

The algorithm was run 100 runs with and without single-point crossover and using both the von Neumann and the Moore neighborhoods. The results are shown in Table 1.

Although rules evolved with the von Neumann neighborhood are not able to solve the problem perfectly, it is already surprising that it finds rules which work for 93%, for such a rule only misplaces 7 cells in the final state. All the other 93 cells have the right value. This suggests that the information was combined, but the rule could not fill or empty the whole square using the same logic.

The Moore neighborhood is clearly more powerful and was able to solve the problem perfectly. The rules that are able to do this clearly show communicational behaviour in the form of "traveling" information and processing this information at points where information "particles" meet.

It is also surprising that using crossover in combination with a Neumann neighborhood does not outperform the same algorithm without the crossover. This may be due to the order of the bits in the transition rule and their meaning. This is worth exploring in future work. Maybe using other forms of crossover might give better results in combination with multi dimensional CA.

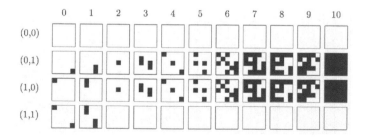

Fig. 4. This figure displays the iterations of a CA solving the XOR problem. Every row shows the iteration of the rule using a different initial state. Note that in the first column ($t = 0$) the initial states are clearly visible and in the last column the coloring matches the output of an XOR port.

Table 2. Fitness values found in the XOR problem.

| Fitness | Number of runs | | | |
| | Neumann | | Moore | |
	with crossover	without crossover	with crossover	without crossover
100	0	0	0	1
98-99	0	0	4	4
95-97	0	0	7	6
90-94	2	1	19	21
80-89	76	96	69	66
70-79	18	3	1	2
< 70	4	0	0	0

Fig. 5. The bitmaps used in the pattern generation experiment.

The XOR Problem. The XOR Problem is not much different from the AND problem. We used the same genetic algorithm and the same CA setup. The only difference is the fitness function. We defined the XOR problem as follows: *Given a square CA with two 'input cells', one top left and one bottom right: find a rule that iterates the CA so that after I iterations the CA is in an 'all one' state if only one of the 'input cells' was one in the initial state and in an 'all zero' state otherwise.* This means that the total fitness of the XOR problem is defined as $f = (N - O^I_{(0,0)}) + O^I_{(0,1)} + O^I_{(1,0)} + (N - O^I_{(1,1)})$.

The algorithm was run with $p_m = 0.05$ for a maximum of 1000 generations for 100 runs with both Neumann and Moore neighborhoods with and without single point crossover. The results are shown in Table 2.

These results support earlier finding in suggesting that single-point crossover doesn't really improve the performance when used in a two dimensional CA. The results show that the algorithm using only mutation has found ways to solve this rather difficult communicational problem. The Neumann neighborhood seemed unable to perform for 100%, yet it came rather close with one rule classifying the problem for 92%. The algorithm found one transition rule using the Moore neighborhood that is able to solve the problem for the full 100%. This rule depicted in Figure 4 shows clear signs of "traveling particles" and is another example of how a local rule can trigger global behaviour.

4   Evolving Bitmaps

Now that it is shown that two dimensional CA's can communicate, it is time to increase the challenge for the CA a bit. The aim of this experiment is to evolve rules for two dimensional CA that generate patterns (or bitmaps).

Table 3. Number of successful rules found per bitmap.

Bitmap	Successful rules (out of a 100)
"square"	80
"hourglass"	77
"heart"	35
"smiley"	7
"letter"	9

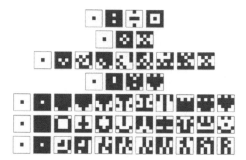

Fig. 6. This figure shows some iteration paths of successful transition rules.

The Bitmap Problem is defined as follows: *Given an initial state and a specific desired end state: find a rule that iterates from the initial state to the desired state in less than I iterations.* Note that this does not require the number of iteration between the initial and the desired state to be fixed.

The CA used in this experiment is not very different from the one used in the AND/XOR experiment (section 3.2). In prelimenary experiments we tried different sizes of CA, but decided to concentrate on small square bitmaps with a width and a height of 5 cells (as done in section 3.2). To make the problem harder and to stay in line with earlier experiments the CA have unconnected borders like in section 3.2. The von Neumann neighborhood was chosen instead of the Moore neighborhood and therefore s_n consist of 5 cells ($r = 1$) and a rule can be described with $2^5 = 32$ bits. The searchspace therefore is $2^{32} = 4294967296$.

After testing different initial states, the 'single seed' state was chosen and defined as the state in which all the positions in the CA are zero except the position ($\lfloor \text{width}/2 \rfloor, \lfloor \text{height}/2 \rfloor$) which is one. For the GA we used the same algorithm as we used in the AND and XOR experiments. Because this experiment uses a Neumann neighborhood and the AND and XOR experiments suggested that the combination between the von Neumann neighborhood and single point crossover was not a good idea, this experiment used only mutation. Like in section 3.2 mutation is performed by flipping every bit in the rule with a probability p_m. In this experiment $p_m = 1/32 = 0.03125$.

In trying to be as diverse as possible five totally different bitmaps were chosen, they are shown in Figure 5. The algorithm was run 100 times for every bitmap for a maximum of 5000 generations. The algorithm was able to find a rule for all the bitmaps, but some bitmaps seemed a bit more difficult than others. Table 3 shows the number of successful rules for every bitmap. Note that symmetrical bitmaps seem to be easier to generate then asymmetric ones.

Although this experiment is fairly simple, it does show that a GA can be used to evolve transition rules in two dimensional CA that are able to generate patterns even with a simple von Neumann neighborhood. Ongoing experiments with bigger CA suggest that they don't differ much from these small ones, although the restrictions on what can be generated from a single-seed state using only a von Neumann neighborhood seem to be bigger when size of the CA increases.

5   Conclusions

This paper shows how two dimensional CA are able to solve the majority problem with similar results compared to one dimensional CA used in [3,4]. Using the same GA as in [3,4] a better average fitness was achieved suggesting that evolving two dimensional CA is easier and more reliable.

The paper shows that two dimensional CA can show communicational behaviour in the form of the AND and XOR problems and that this behaviour can be evolved using a GA. The document also shows that a more generic behaviour can be evolved using a GA by showing how different patterns can be iterated from the same initial state. These results all suggest that a multi dimensional CA is a very powerful tool and in combination with GAs they can be evolved to exhibit specific bahaviour. It is therefore feasible that this combination can be used to solve all sorts of real world problems.

References

1. Bäck, T.: Evolutionary Algorithms in Theory and Practice. Oxford University Press, NY (1996)
2. Inverso, S., Kunkle, D., Merrigan, C.: Evolutionary Methods for 2-D Cellular Automata Computation. www.cs.rit.edu/~drk4633/mypapers/gacaProj.pdf (2002)
3. Mitchell, M., Crutchfield, J.P.: The Evolution of Emergent Computation. Proceedings of the National Academy of Sciences, SFI Technical Report 94-03-012
4. Mitchell, M., Crutchfield, J.P., Hraber, P.T.: Evolving cellular automata to perform computations: Mechanisms and impediments. Physica D, (1994), 75:361 - 391
5. Li, W., Packard, N. H., Langton, C. G.: Transition phenomena in cellular automata rule space. Physica D, (1990), 45:77-94
6. Wolfram, S.: Statistical mechanics of Cellular Automata. Reviews of Modern Physics volume 55 (1983)
7. Wolfram, S.: Theory and Applications of Cellular Automata. World Scientific, Singapore (1986)

Traffic of Ants on a Trail: A Stochastic Modelling and Zero Range Process

Katsuhiro Nishinari[1], Andreas Schadschneider[2], and Debashish Chowdhury[3]

[1] Department of Applied Mathematics and Informatics,
Ryukoku University, Shiga, Japan,
knishi@rins.ryukoku.ac.jp
[2] Institut für Theoretische Physik, Universität zu Köln D-50937 Köln, Germany
[3] Department of Physics, Indian Institute of Technology, Kanpur 208016, India

Abstract. Recently we have proposed a stochastic cellular automaton model of ants on a trail and investigated its unusual flow-density relation by using a mean field theory and computer simulations. In this paper, we study the model in detail by utilizing the analogy with the zero range process, which is known as one of the exactly solvable stochastic models. We show that our theory can quantitatively account for the unusual non-monotonic dependence of the average speed of the ants on their density for finite lattices with periodic boundary conditions. Moreover, we argue that the flow-density diagram exhibits a second order phase transition at the critial density only in a limiting case.

1 Introduction

There has been significant progress in modelling complex systems by using cellular automata (CA) [1,2]; such complex systems include, for example vehicular traffic [3] and biological system [4]. In most cases, particle-hopping CA models have been used widely to study the spatio-temporal organization in systems of interacting particles driven far from equilibrium[2,3]. In the traffic system, the vehicles are represented by particles while their mutual influence is captured by the inter-particle interactions. Usually, these inter-particle interactions tend to hinder their motions so that the average speed decreases monotonically with the increasing density of the particles.

In a recent letter [5] we have reported a counter-example, motivated by the traffic-like flow of ants in a trail [6], where the average speed of the particles varies *non-monotonically* with their density because of the coupling of their dynamics with another dynamical variable. We have discussed the similarity and differences between our ant-trail model (ATM) and vehicular traffic. Our ATM model is a stochatic CA model with two coupled variables, and reduces to the asymmetric exclusion process (ASEP)[7] in special limiting cases.

In [8] we have developed a formalism by introducing the loose cluster approximation and successfully captured the non-monotonicity heuristically with the help of analytical results of ASEP, which is an exactly solvable stochastic model. In this paper, we study the phenomenon in detail by utilizing the analogy

P.M.A. Sloot, B. Chopard, and A.G. Hoekstra (Eds.): ACRI 2004, LNCS 3305, pp. 192–201, 2004.

Fig. 1. Schematic view of the model for ASEP(a) and ZRP(b). The hopping probability of a particle depends on the gap size in front of it in ZRP, while it is constant in ASEP. In both cases, and the hopping to the occupied cell is prohibited.

of ATM with the zero range process (ZRP)[1], which is also known as one of the stochastic models that can be solved exactly [9,10](Fig.1).

The paper is organized as follows: ATM is defined in Section 2 and numerical results are shown in Section 3. Then we discuss the similarity between ATM and ZRP and give analytical calculations based on the analogy in Section 4, including the results in the case of the thermodynamical limit. Concluding discussions are given in Section 5.

2 Ant Trail Model

Let us first define ATM which is a simple model for an unidirectional motion of ants. The ants communicate with each other by dropping a chemical (generically called *pheromone*) on the substrate as they crawl forward [11,12]. The pheromone sticks to the substrate long enough for the other following sniffing ants to pick up its smell and follow the trail.

Each site of our one-dimensional ant-trail model represents a cell that can accomodate at most one ant at a time (see Fig. 2).

The lattice sites are labelled by the index i ($i = 1, 2, ..., L$); L being the length of the lattice. We associate two binary variables S_i and σ_i with each site i where S_i takes the value 0 or 1 depending on whether the cell is empty or occupied by an ant. Similarly, $\sigma_i = 1$ if the cell i contains pheromone; otherwise, $\sigma_i = 0$. The instantaneous state (i.e., the configuration) of the system at any time is specified completely by the set ($\{S\}, \{\sigma\}$).

Since a unidirectional motion is assumed, ants do not move backward. Their forward-hopping probability is higher if it smells pheromone ahead of it. The state of the system is updated at each time step in *two stages*. In stage I ants are allowed to move. Here the subset $\{S(t+1)\}$ at the time step $t+1$ is obtained using the full information ($\{S(t)\}, \{\sigma(t)\}$) at time t. Stage II corresponds to the evaporation of pheromone. Here only the subset $\{\sigma(t)\}$ is updated so that at the end of stage II the new configuration ($\{S(t+1)\}, \{\sigma(t+1)\}$) at time $t+1$ is obtained. In each stage the dynamical rules are applied *in parallel* to all ants and pheromones, respectively.

---

[1] We thank Martin Evans for drawing our attention to this analogy.

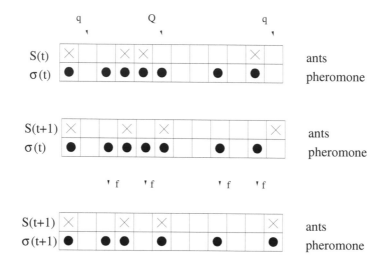

Fig. 2. Schematic representation of typical configurations; it also illustrates the update procedure. Top: Configuration at time t, i.e. *before* stage I of the update. The non-vanishing hopping probabilities of the ants are also shown explicitly. Middle: Configuration *after* one possible realisation of *stage I*. Also indicated are the pheromones that may evaporate in stage II of the update scheme. Bottom: Configuration *after* one possible realization of *stage II*. Two pheromones have evaporated and one pheromone has been created due to the motion of an ant.

Stage I: Motion of Ants

An ant in cell i that has an empty cell in front of it, i.e., $S_i(t) = 1$ and $S_{i+1}(t) = 0$, hops forward with

$$\text{probability} = \begin{cases} Q & \text{if } \sigma_{i+1}(t) = 1, \\ q & \text{if } \sigma_{i+1}(t) = 0, \end{cases} \tag{1}$$

where, to be consistent with real ant-trails, we assume $q < Q$.

Stage II: Evaporation of Pheromones

At each cell i occupied by an ant after stage I a pheromone will be created, i.e.,

$$\sigma_i(t+1) = 1 \quad \text{if} \quad S_i(t+1) = 1. \tag{2}$$

On the other hand, any 'free' pheromone at a site i not occupied by an ant will evaporate with the probability f per unit time, i.e., if $S_i(t+1) = 0$, $\sigma_i(t) = 1$, then

$$\sigma_i(t+1) = \begin{cases} 0 & \text{with probability } f, \\ 1 & \text{with probability } 1 - f. \end{cases} \tag{3}$$

Note that the dynamics conserves the number N of ants, but not the number of pheromones. The boundary condition used in this paper is periodic, that is, we consider an ant trail of a circuit type. The case of the open boundary conditions will be studied in the successive paper[13].

The rules can be written in a compact form as the coupled equations

$$S_j(t+1) = S_j(t) + \min(\eta_{j-1}(t), S_{j-1}(t), 1 - S_j(t))$$
$$- \min(\eta_j(t), S_j(t), 1 - S_{j+1}(t)), \tag{4}$$
$$\sigma_j(t+1) = \max(S_j(t+1), \min(\sigma_j(t), \xi_j(t))), \tag{5}$$

where ξ and η are stochastic variables defined by $\xi_j(t) = 0$ with the probability f and $\xi_j(t) = 1$ with $1-f$, and $\eta_j(t) = 1$ with the probability $p = q + (Q-q)\sigma_{j+1}(t)$ and $\eta_j(t) = 0$ with $1 - p$. We point out that eqs.(4) and (5) reduce to ASEP if we choose p as a constant, i.e., p does not depend on σ. If we further consider the deterministic limit $p = 1$, then this model reduces to the Burgers CA[14], which is also known as an exactly solvable CA.

3   Numerical Results

The ASEP [7] with parallel updating has been used often as an extremely simple model of vehicular traffic on single-lane highways [15]. The most important quantity of interest in the context of flow properties of the traffic models is the *fundamental diagram*, i.e., the flow-versus-density relation, where flow is the product of the density and the average speed. Thus it is interesting to draw the fundamental diagram of ATM to compare ants traffic with vehicle traffic.

The fundamental diagrams of ATM is given in Fig. 3(a). The flow F and the average speed V of vehicles are related by the hydrodynamic relation $F = \rho V$. The density-dependence of the average speed of ATM is also shown in Fig. 3(b). We first know that the diagram does not possess particle-hole symmetry. In the ASEP the flow remains invariant under the interchange of ρ and $1 - \rho$; this particle-hole symmetry leads to a fundamental diagram that is symmetrical about $\rho = \frac{1}{2}$. In ATM, particle-hole symmetry is seen in the special cases of $f = 0$ and $f = 1$ from Fig. 3(a). This is because in the two special cases $f = 0$ and $f = 1$ the ant-trail model becomes identical to the ASEP with parallel updating corresponding to the effective hopping probabilities Q and q, respectively.

Next, over a range of small values of f, it exhibits an anomalous behaviour in the sense that, unlike common vehicular traffic, V is not a monotonically decreasing function of the density ρ (Fig. 3(b)). Instead a relatively sharp crossover can be observed where the speed *increases* with the density. In the usual form of the fundamental diagram (flow vs. density) this transition leads to the existence of an inflection point (Fig. 3(a)).

By a detailed analysis of the spatio-temporal organizations in the steady-state, we were able to distinguish three different regimes of density. At low densities a loosely assembled cluster is formed and propagates with the probability q (Fig.4). The leading ant in the cluster which hops with probability q will determine the velocity of the cluster. Homogeneous mean field theories fail in this region since these theories always assume that ants are uniformly distributed which is not true in the case of ATM [8].

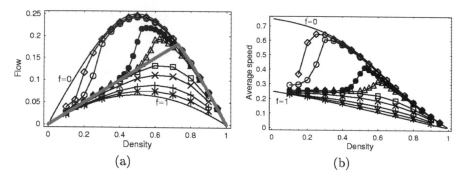

Fig. 3. The average flow (a), speed (b) of the ants, extracted from computer simulation data, are plotted against their densities for the parameters $Q = 0.75, q = 0.25$ and $L = 500$. The discrete data points corresponding to $f = 0.0005(\Diamond)$, $0.001(\circ)$, $0.005(\bullet)$, $0.01(\triangle)$, $0.05(\square)$, $0.10(\times)$, $0.25(+)$, $0.50(*)$ have been obtained from computer simulations; the lines connecting these data points merely serve as the guide to the eye. The cases $f = 0$ and $f = 1$ are also displayed, which are identical to the ASEP corresponding to the effective hopping probabilities Q and q, respectively. The analytical curve corresponds to $f \to 0$ in the thermodynamics limit, which is discussed in Sec.4.2 is also depicted in (a) (the thick curve without ornaments).

In the intermediate density regime, the leading ant occasionally hops with probability Q instead of q, because it becomes possible to feel the pheromone which is dropped by the last ant in the cluster. This arises from the fact that, because of the periodic boundary conditions, the gap size between the last and leading ant becomes shorter as the cluster becomes larger, so that the leading ant is likely to find the pheromone in front of it. This increase of the average speed in this intermediate-density region(Fig. 3(b)), leads to the anomalous fundamental diagram.

Finally, at high densities, the mutual hindrance against the movements of the ants dominates the flow behaviour leading to a homogeneous state similar to that of the ASEP. In this regime we do not have the loose cluster any more and ants are uniformly distributed after a long time. Thus homogeneous mean field theories give a good result in accounting the fundamental diagram only in this regime.

4 Analytical Results

4.1 ZRP and ATM

The ATM is closely related to the ZRP, which is known as one of the exactly solvable models of interacting Markov processes[9,10]. The ZRP consists of the moving particles of the exclusion process. The hopping probability of a particle depends on the number of gaps to the particle in front. In the ATM, the hopping probability u can be expressed as

$$u = q(1 - g) + Qg, \qquad (6)$$

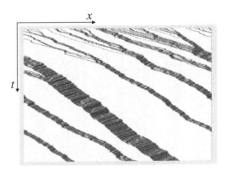

Fig. 4. Spatial-temporal behaviours of loose clusters in the low density case ($\rho = 0.16$). Parameters are $Q = 0.75, q = 0.25, f = 0.005$). We see the loose clusters emerge from the random initial configuration, which will eventually merge after sufficiently long time into one big loose cluster.

where g is the probability that there is a surviving pheromone on the first site of a gap. Assume that the gap size is x and the average velocity of ants is v. Since $g(t+1) = (1-f)g(t)$ holds at each time step, we obtain $g(x) = (1-f)^{x/v}$ after iterating it by x/v times, which is the time interval of between the passage of successive ants through any arbitrary site. Thus, in the ATM the hopping probability u is related to gaps x by [5]

$$u(x) = q + (Q - q)(1 - f)^{x/v}. \tag{7}$$

Using the well known formal mapping between the ZRP and asymmetric exclusion processes [10] we conclude that the steady state of the ATM can well be described by that of the ZRP with parallel dynamics.

By using the results of the ZRP, the average velocity v of ants is calculated by

$$v = \sum_{x=1}^{L-M} u(x)p(x) \tag{8}$$

where L and M are the system size and the number of ants respectively (hence $\rho = M/L$ is the density), and $p(x)$ is the probability of finding a gap of size x, which is given by

$$p(x) = h(x)\frac{Z(L - x - 1, M - 1)}{Z(L, M)}. \tag{9}$$

Since the ATM is formulated with parallel update, the form of $h(x)$, as calculated in (9), is given by [16]

$$h(x) = \begin{cases} 1 - u(1) & \text{for} \quad x = 0 \\ \dfrac{1 - u(1)}{1 - u(x)} \displaystyle\prod_{y=1}^{x} \dfrac{1 - u(y)}{u(y)} & \text{for} \quad x > 0 \end{cases} \tag{10}$$

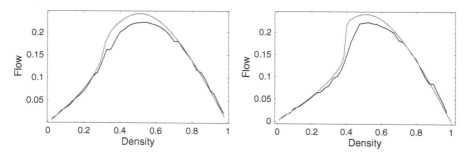

Fig. 5. The fundamental diagram of the ATM with the parameter $L = 100$(left) and $L = 200$(right). Parameters are $Q = 0.75, q = 0.25, f = 0.005$. The smooth thin curve is the theoretical one, while the zigzaged thick one is the numerical data.

The partition function Z is obtained by the recurrence relation

$$Z(L, M) = \sum_{x=0}^{L-M} Z(L - x - 1, M - 1)h(x), \tag{11}$$

with $Z(x, 1) = h(x-1)$ and $Z(x, x) = h(0)$, which is easily obtained by (9) with the normalization $\sum p(x) = 1$.

Next we draw the fundamental diagram of the ATM by using (8) with changing ρ from 0 to 1. In drawing the diagram, we simply put the velocity v in (7) as $v = q$, which is known to be a good approximation for v[17]. In a strict sense v must be determined self-consistently by (7) and (8). Fundamental diagrams are given in Fig.5 with $L = 100$ and $L = 200$. The thick black curve is the numerical data and the smooth thin black one is the theoretical curve in each figure with the specified value of L. We see that the theoretical curves are almost identical to the numerical ones, thus the ZRP is confirmed to describe the steady state of the ATM.

4.2   Thermodynamic Limit of ATM

Next we discuss the thermodynamic limit of the ATM, that is, the case $L \to \infty$. From Fig.5 we see that the curve shows sharp increase near the density region $0.4 < \rho < 0.5$, and the tendency is expected to be strong with the increase of L. Thus it is important to study whether there is a second order phase transition or not in the ATM in the thermodynamic limit.

Following [16], the partition function $Z(L, M)$ is written as

$$Z(L, M) = \sum_{x_1, \cdots, x_M} h(x_1) \cdots h(x_M)\delta(x_1 + \cdots + x_M, L - M), \tag{12}$$

where $\delta(a,b) = 1$ if $a = b$ and $\delta(a,b) = 0$ otherwise. Considering $\rho = M/L$, (12) is rewritten by using the integral representation of the δ function as

$$Z(L, M) = \int \frac{ds}{2\pi i s} \left(\frac{G(s)}{s^{1/\rho - 1}} \right)^M,\qquad (13)$$

where $G(s)$ is the generating function of h defined by

$$G(s) = \sum_{x=0}^{\infty} h(x)s^x.\qquad (14)$$

By the saddle point method, in the $L \to \infty$ limit we have

$$Z(L, M) \sim \exp(M \ln G(z) - (L - M) \ln z)\qquad (15)$$

by keeping $M/L = \rho$ as constant, where z is defined by

$$\frac{1}{\rho} - 1 = z \frac{\partial \ln G(z)}{\partial z}.\qquad (16)$$

Then average velocity v is given in this limit as

$$v = \sum_{x=1}^{\infty} \frac{u(x)h(x)}{G(z)} z^x.\qquad (17)$$

Next we study the properties of the generating function $G(z)$ in detail to consider the phase transition of the ATM model. Since $u(x) \to q$ $(x \to \infty)$ for $f > 0$, the condition that G converges is given by

$$\lim_{x \to \infty} \sup \frac{h(x+1)z}{h(x)} = \frac{1-q}{q} z < 1.\qquad (18)$$

That is, G converges in the range

$$0 < z < z_c = \frac{q}{1-q}.\qquad (19)$$

The critical value of G at $z = z_c$ is given by

$$G(z_c) = 1 - u(1) + \sum_{x=1}^{\infty} \frac{1 - u(1)}{1 - u(x)} \prod_{y=1}^{x} \left(\frac{1 - u(y)}{u(y)} \frac{q}{1-q} \right).\qquad (20)$$

In the case $f > 0$, this sum diverges for the class of $u(x)$ which decays to q more rapidly than the function $q(1 + c/x)$, here $c > 1 - q$. In the ATM, $u(x) = q + (Q - q)(1 - f)^{x/v}$, which decays exponentially to q as $x \to \infty$. Then we conclude that there is no phase transition in the ATM for $f > 0$. This is because from (16), we have $\rho = 1$ when $z = 0$, and $\rho = 0$ at $z = z_c$ if $G(z_c)$ diverges. *Thus, so long as $f > 0$, in the entire density region $0 \le \rho \le 1$ there is no singularity in G and, hence, no phase transition in the ATM.*

The situation drastically changes when we take the limit $f \to 0$. In this case, we can set $u(x) = Q$, and then $G(z_c)$ becomes finite as

$$\lim_{z \to -z_c} G(z) = \frac{Q(1-q)}{Q(1-q) - q(1-Q)} - Q. \tag{21}$$

Then we have the phase transition in the case $f = 0$ and the critical density is obtained from (16) as

$$\rho_c = \frac{Q - q}{Q - q^2}. \tag{22}$$

Since $u(x) \to Q$ in the case $f \to 0$, the average velocity at $z = z_c$ becomes from (17)

$$v_c = \sum_{x=1}^{\infty} \frac{Q}{G(z_c)} \left(\frac{1-Q}{Q}\right)^x z_c^x. \tag{23}$$

Substituting (21) into (23), we obtain $v_c = q$.

It should be noted [8] that (22) is also obtained by the intersection point of the line $F = v_c \rho$ and the ASEP curve[3]

$$F = \frac{1}{2}(1 - \sqrt{1 - 4Q\rho(1-\rho)}) \tag{24}$$

in the flow-density diagram. The fundamental diagram in the thermodynamic limit is given in Fig.3(a). Note that the limit $L \to \infty$ and $f \to 0$ do not commute[17]. If we take $f \to 0$ before $L \to \infty$, then we apparently have (24), which is the case of our numerical simulations. If we take $f \to 0$ after $L \to \infty$, then we have the thick curve in Fig.3(a). Thus, in the latter case, we have proved that the anomalous variation of the average velocity with the density disappears.

5   Concluding Discussions

Several theoretical investigations have been carried out earlier, in terms of CA, to study the emergence of the trail patterns in ant colonies [4]. However, to our knowledge, our work is the first attempt to understand the traffic-like flow of ants on well formed trails using the language of CA. In this paper we have investigated in detail the stochastic cellular automaton model of an ant trail [5]. The model is characterized by two coupled dynamical variables, representing the ants and the pheromone. The coupling leads to surprising results, especially an anomalous fundamental diagram which arises from an unusual non-monotonic variation of the average speed of the ants with their density on the trail in the intermediate regime of the ant density. We had earlier shown that the homogeneous mean-field approximations are not able to capture the non-monotonicity quantitatively in the low density regime. In this paper we have reported our new quantitative results on this model; these results have been derived by utilizing the analogy with ZRP. Moreover we have shown that there is a phase transition in the thermodynamic limit in this model, albeit in a special limit. Extensions of ATM, including counterflow and the case of open boundary conditions, will be reported in the future[13].

It would be interesting to test the predictions of the model, particularly the non-monotonic variation of average speed with density, by carrying out experiments on a circular ant-trail.

References

1. Wolfram, S.: *Theory and Applications of Cellular Automata* (World Scientific, Singapore, 1986)
2. Chopard, B., Droz, M.: *Cellular Automata Modelling of Physical Systems* (Cambridge University Press, 1998)
3. Chowdhury, D., Santen, L., Schadschneider, A.: Statistical physics of vehicular traffic and some related systems. Phys. Rep. **329** (2000) 199–329
4. Chowdhury, D., Nishinari, K. and Schadschneider, A.: Self-organized patterns and traffic flow in colonies of organisms:from bacteria and social insects to vertebrates. Phase Transitions **77** (2004) 601-624
5. Chowdhury, D., Guttal, V., Nishinari, K., Schadschneider, A.: A cellular-automata model of flow in ant trails:non-monotonic variation of speed with density. J. Phys. A:Math. Gen. **35** (2002) L573–L577
6. Burd, M., Archer, D., Aranwela, N., Stradling, D.J.: Traffic dynamics of the leaf cutting ant. American Natur. **159** (2002) 283–293
7. Evans, M.R., Blythe, R.A.: Nonequilibrium dynamics in low-dimensional systems. Physica A **313** (2002) 110–152
8. Nishinari, K., Chowdhury, D., Schadschneider, A.: Cluster formation and anomalous fundamental diagaram in an ant trail model. Phys. Rev. E, **67** (2003) 036120
9. Spitzer, F.: Interaction of markov processes. Advances in Math. **5** (1970) 246–290
10. Evans, M.R.: Phase transitions in one-dimensional nonequilibrium systems. Braz. J. Phys. **30** (2000) 42–57
11. Camazine, S., Deneubourg, J.L., Franks, N.R., Sneyd, J., Theraulaz, G., Bonabeau, E.: *Self-organization in Biological Systems* (Princeton University Press, Prinston, 2001)
12. Mikhailov, A.S., Calenbuhr, V.: *From Cells to Societies* (Springer, Berlin, 2002)
13. Kunwar, A., John, A., Nishinari, K., Schadschneider, A., Chowdhury, D.: Collective traffic-like movement of ants on a trail – dynamical phases and phase transitions. submitted for publication
14. Nishinari, K., Takahashi, D.: Analytical properties of ultradiscrete Burgers equation and rule-184 cellular automaton. J. Phys. A:Math. Gen. **31** (1998) 5439–5450
15. Nagel, K., Schreckenberg, M.: A cellular automaton model for freeway traffic. J. Phys. I **2** (1992) 2221–2229
16. Evans, M.R.: Exact Steady States of Disordered Hopping Particle Models with Parallel and Ordered Sequential Dynamics. J. Phys. A:Math. Gen. **30** (1997) 5669–5685
17. O'Loan, O.J., Evans, M.R., Cates, M.E.: Jamming Transition in a Homogeneous One-Dimensional System: the Bus Route Model. Phys.Rev.E **58** (1998) 1404–1418; see also Europhys. Lett. **42** (1998) 137–142

Cellular Automata and Roundabout Traffic Simulation*

Enrico G. Campari[1], Giuseppe Levi[1], and Vittorio Maniezzo[2]

[1] Scienze dell'Informazione dell'Università di Bologna, sede di Cesena via Sacchi, 3
I-47023 Cesena, Italy,
enrico.campari@unibo.it, levi@bo.infn.it,
[2] Department of Computer Science, University of Bologna, via Mura Anteo Zamboni
7, I-40100 Bologna, Italy,
maniezzo@csr.unibo.it

Abstract. A new software package, named Archirota, for simulating traffic in roundabouts is introduced. Its simulation module is entirely based on cellular automata and is automatically configured for real-world geocoded data. Archirota can be used both as a support for designing new roundabout and for modeling and simulating existing ones. Tests on actual use cases testified the effectiveness of the implemented approach.

1 Introduction

Among the many applications of cellular automata to complex system problems, the study of traffic is getting more and more popular in these very last years. The reason for that is the ease with which the dynamic features of traffic can be simulated with a cellular automata algorithm. With few simple rules the complexity of traffic (transition from free to congested traffic, lane inversion, stop and go traffic, nucleation of jams in correspondence of ramps etc.) can be reproduced in a way which is hardly achieved by models using differential equations ([13],[10],[5],[4]). Being computationally extremely efficient, large scale simulations can be accomplished with low cost computers and traffic forecasts can be envisaged. In order to simulate with cellular automata traffic on a road, the road is divided into cells whose occupation corresponds to the presence of a vehicle in that place at a certain time. A set of rules specify the time and space evolution of the system, that is how each vehicle moves along that road [6].

A slightly more complex problem is that of simulating a roundabout, that is a multiple (at least three) road junction in the form of a circle, around which all traffic has to pass in the same direction. Roundabouts were originally a particular feature of the British landscape, but in the last two decades they have widely spread all over the world. They replace crossroads, contributing to reduce car accidents and to slow down fast cars. Yet, they increase the flow of vehicles in the road because they tend to avoid the complete stop of cars which has as a direct

---

* This work was partially supported by the Future & Emerging Technologies unit of the European Commission through Project BISON (IST-2001-38923).

P.M.A. Sloot, B. Chopard, and A.G. Hoekstra (Eds.): ACRI 2004, LNCS 3305, pp. 202–210, 2004.

effect the formation of jams. The accidents rate at roundabouts is reduced on average to one half of that of signaled junctions [2]. Finally, they offer lower cost and safer operation and are seen as a way to embellish settings with green and floral displays. The increasing number of roundabouts and their importance for the limitation of traffic jams and the reduction of accidents, fostered researchers into creating some instruments to help traffic engineers projecting roundabouts. Different softwares have been designed [3], showing different features and being currently used in many countries.

In this article we describe a new software, named Archirota^{TM}, which can be used to simulate roundabout traffic. Its purpose is mainly to contribute to the proper design of new roundabouts and to the forecast of the traffic conditions which will be present in a given roundabout. A cellular automata algorithm is used in this software. The specific cellular automaton builds on the experience of the authors on cellular automata for environmental ([7], [8]) and specifically for traffic flow ([5]) simulation. Specifically, the algorithm is obtained essentially by modifying that used for modeling traffic on highways. Vehicles of different lengths occupy here from 1 to 9 cells (where each cell corresponds - parametrically - to 2 m length), a feature which offers a wide dynamic range to the simulations. Vehicle speeds depend on the correspondence among cells and actual space. Cellular automaton evolution rules are accordingly defined.

The Archirota^{TM} software is written using the C++ language and its main features include: the capability to create the roundabout directly from a geocoded digital map; a variable number of roads and lanes per road; an average vehicle speed inside the roundabout depending on the radius of curvature of the roundabout; a variable insertion angle for each road; a dynamic and user-definable vehicle generation function and an easy modification of cellular automata rules. Finally, both a 2D and a 3D graphic interface are supported.

Archirota^{TM} has two output types: a visual simulation and a quantitative analysis of the traffic occurring at the roundabout. This includes: capacity of the roundabout, average crossing time for a vehicle along each path'; delay queuing, average speed, vehicle density and flow inside the roundabout.

In the following we will first frame our work in current research on traffic simulation by means of cellular automata (2), then describe the essential features of the Archirota package (3) and finally show some use cases along with the output produced (4).

2   Cellular Automata for Traffic Simulation

In order to simulate traffic, we designed a cellular automata model which provides a simple physical picture of a road system and is easily implemented on computers. Each road is divided into lanes and each lane is divided into cells, which can be either empty or occupied by a vehicle. Each lane starts at cell 1; vehicles, which enter the road at its beginning move in discrete steps in the direction of increasing cell number.

A set of rules, described in details in reference [5], specify the time and space evolution of the system. These rules were derived from those originally developed by Schreckenberg and coworkers [11] and by Nagel and coworkers [12] to implement a multilane highway without ramps and with periodic boundary conditions. The rules specify at each step and for every car: a) the speed with which cars move along the road, b) how faster cars overtake slower ones and c) how cars slow down or accelerate according to the behavior of neighboring vehicles. Cars have a sufficient braking ability to avoid accidents.

In each traffic simulation a starting configuration is chosen. New cars enter the road at a chosen rate as follows. For all on-ramps, at each iteration the program checks if the cell is empty. If empty, a random number is generated in the [0,1] interval and if it is less than the threshold chosen for that simulation, a car is generated in that cell. A number of local and average quantities are regularly recorded. At selected positions, the flow of vehicles and their average speed are collected. Regarding the flow, this is done counting the vehicles passing trough that location in a time interval divided by that amount of time. From these quantities, all other quantities of interest such as density (density=flow/speed) or the average distance between vehicles are computed. The same data are also collected as space averages: counting the number of vehicles present in a segment of the road at a given time provides the density. Their (average) speed allows to compute again the flow (flow= density × speed) and all other quantities.

The use of averages is due first of all to the discreteness of cellular automata models. Cars in the model can only have as speed an integer number, while car speeds are real numbers in nature. Furthermore, experimental data are averages over time and/or space [9,13], so that a proper comparison again requires to average simulated data. As reported elsewhere [5], this model proved to be able to reproduce most of the experimental data available on traffic.

Some additional rules must be introduced when simulating a roundabout. First of all a new object must be considered: the ring which connects the roads. Its on/off ramps are the end/beginning of the lanes connected by the ring itself. While in a simple road a vehicle disappears from the simulation at the road end, now it is passed on to the roundabout. When approaching the roundabout, a vehicle slows down and possibly stops because it has to give way to vehicles already inside the roundabout. A new rule is chosen for the speed limit of vehicles inside the roundabout so that this speed increases with the radius of the ring. Finally there is an impatient delay rule: car drivers at a road end waiting to enter the roundabout get progressively prone (up to a limit) to brake the respect of the rule defining the distance and approaching speed according to which they give way to vehicles already inside the roundabout.

3   Archirota Specifications and Implementation

The Archirota package was conceived to provide simulation support in actual roundabout design practice. Prospect users are decision makers who have to decide whether and how to construct a roundabout for a particular road junction.

Fig. 1. The Ertha selection interface.

The main program specification are therefore:

- Possibility to work on actual digital city maps.
- Possibility to include any relevant driver style.
- Possibility to consider any relevant environmental influence.
- Possibility to derive aggregate simulation data in the format decision makers are used to.
- Possibility to easily define design alternatives and to support consequent what-if analysis.
- Low cost and ease of use for unskilled practitioners.

These specifications lead to the design of a very simple code, based on the cellular automata model introduced in section 2. The cellular automaton itself is of straightforward implementation, simply requiring to compute for each cell the next-iteration state on the basis of the current state of the cell itself and of those of its neighborhood.

More precisely, following the notation introduced in section 2, we associated a geocoded cell vector $\mathbf{c}_j$, $j \in J$, to each entering and exiting lane and one to each lane of the roundabout itself. For each cell c_{ij}, $i \in I_j$ of each vector J we then defined a cell-specific neighborhood $N(ij)$, automatically including all cells which correspond to location that are visible for a driver occupying the lane position associated to ij. Visibilities are computed by simple computational geometric routines working on GIS-derived layers, such as buildings, green areas etc.

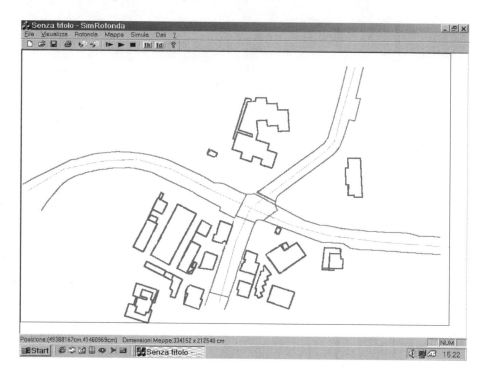

Fig. 2. The Archirota design environment.

The simulation goes on by updating in parallel each cell state at each time instant. An outer loop, time instants, iteratively commands each cell to check its own state and that of its neighbors and to accordingly update its own next-time state. As mentioned, we have defined cell-specific neighborhoods, whereas the state domain is shared by all cells. Basically, each cell can be either free or occupied by a vehicle, in which case the type, portion and speed of the vehicle is recorded. The new state is simply a computation of whether, and by which vehicle, the cell will be occupied on the next time interval. The rules according to which vehicle positions are defined, as mentioned in section 2, are the same as those described in [5] except for the fact that the behavior of all *visible* vehicles is taken into account.

Currently the architecture of the package requires the use of two different applications: a tailored GIS for selecting and exporting all relevant elements and the Archirota package itself.

The GIS activities are currently supported by means of the desktop client of the Ertha GIS [1]. Ertha is an open source project currently under development at the University of Bologna aimed at providing source code for a multi-platform, multi-tier GIS. At the present date desktop, PDA and web browser clients are available, the former of which has been used for supporting the upload of the GIS project of interest, selecting all relevant layers and exporting the selected geocoded data. Figure 1 shows the interface of the tailored Ertha module. The

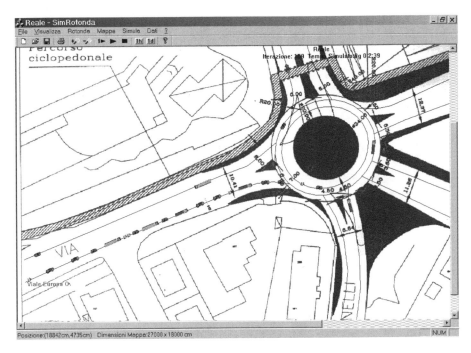

Fig. 3. Simulation of an existing roundabout.

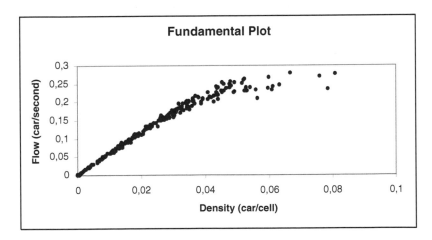

Fig. 4. Fundamental plot under light traffic conditions.

exported layers are later uploaded by Archirota, which is the environment where the actual roundabout design takes place. In Archirota, vectors are automatically defined and dimensioned for each lane reported in the input file and all neighborhoods $N(ij)$ are computed. Figure 2 shows the Archirota design environment.

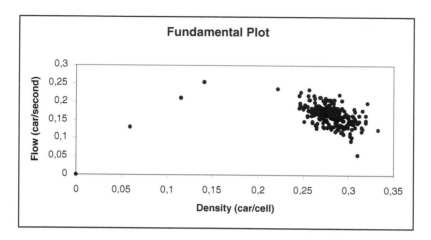

Fig. 5. Fundamental plot under heavy traffic conditions.

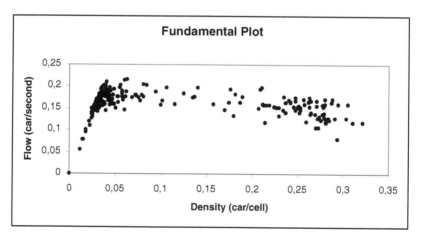

Fig. 6. Fundamental plot under mixed traffic conditions.

4   Computational Results and Use Cases

Archirota was implemented in C++ and runs under windows. Although still under development, the main simulation features are by now stable and have been used to model different real-world cases.

Figure 3 shows the main Archirota interface when a raster image of an existing roundabout is loaded and a simulation is run on it.

In this case we simulated the roundabout efficiency under two different traffic conditions. Specifically, we modified the incoming traffic rate for the roads from the left and from above. Figure 3 shows a snapshot of a congested traffic simulation case.

Quantified results are obtained directly from the cellular automaton by placing "sensors" (i.e., counters) in user-definable roadside locations and recording traffic data for each sensor at each iteration. This data is later processed to obtain reports customized to user needs, even though some output is provided by default, which is the case for example of the traffic fundamental plot.

Figure 4 shows the fundamental plot obtained under light traffic conditions, where traffic flows without developing significant queues. For this result we set a sensor on the road incoming from the left close to the entrance of the roundabout.

Figure 5 shows the fundamental plot for the same roundabout of figure 4 but with much increased incoming traffic. Now vehicle queues are permanent, and this is apparent from the plot since data points are not distributed along a line from the origin but are clustered in a region where a regression line has a definitely downward slope.

Figure 6 finally shows again the same roundabout under mixed traffic conditions, this is a simulation of a time interval when for some minutes traffic was regular but at a certain moment it increases substantially. This could be the case for example of office or school closing hours. From the plot one can see how data point are initially on a line from the origin (regular traffic) and then move toward the congested area.

5   Conclusions

This paper presented the essential features of new a software package, named Archirota, for simulating traffic in roundabouts. The simulation module is extremely simple and based on cellular automata. The neighborhood structure intrinsic to cellular automata supports a great flexibility in simulation conditions and output data, thus an easy adaptation to different use cases.

While the package interface still has to be improved, the simulation module and reporting facilities are by now stable and have been used to simulate real-world cases, both for designing new roundabouts and for modeling existing ones. In all cases the package results were adequate.

References

1. http://astarte.csr.unibo.it/ertha/ertha.htm.
2. www.ksu.edu/roundabouts/.
3. www.rpi.edu/dept/cits/files/soft.ppt.
4. M. Bando, K. Hasebe, A. Nakayama, A. Shibada, and Y. Sugiyama. *Phys. Rev. E*, 51:1035, 1995.
5. E. G. Campari and G. Levi. *Eur. Phys. J. B*, 17:159, 2000.
6. E. G. Campari and G. Levi. *Eur. Phys. J. B*, 25:245, 2002.
7. G. Guariso and V. Maniezzo. Air quality simulation through cellular automata. *Environmental Software*, 7(3):131–141, 1992.
8. G. Guariso, V. Maniezzo, and P. Salomoni. Parallel simulation of a cellular pollution model. *Applied Mathematics and Computation*, 79:27–41, 1996.
9. B. S. Kerner. *Physics World*, 12:25, 1999.

10. W. Knospe, L. Santen, A. Schadschneider, and M. Schreckenberg. *Physica A*, 265:614, 1999.

11. W. Knospe, L. Santen, A. Schadschneider, and M. Schreckenberg. *Physica A*, 265:614, 1999.

12. K. Nagel, D.E. Wolf, P. Wagner, and P. Simon. *Phys. Rev. E*, 58:1425, 1998.

13. D.E. Wolf. *Physica A*, 263:438, 1999.

Acquisition of Local Neighbor Rules in the Simulation of Pedestrian Flow by Cellular Automata

Katsutoshi Narimatsu, Toshihiko Shiraishi, and Shin Morishita

Yokohama National University, Graduate School of Environment and Information Sciences
79-7 Tokiwadai, Hodogaya-ku, Yokohama 240-8501 Japan
{mshin,shira}@ynu.ac.jp

Abstract. Cellular Automata is applied to model the pedestrian flow, in which the local neighbor rules implemented to each person in the crowd are determined automatically in the process of simulation. The collision patterns in the visible area settled around each person is introduced, and each person walks around just avoiding the collision patterns. As the simulation proceeds along the time step, various collision patterns are observed. By being informed the collision patterns to all the pedestrians simultaneously, the pedestrian begins to flow quite smoothly and the column formation is observed.

1 Introduction

Cellular Automata has been considered to be one of strong tools in modeling various kinds of phenomena such as pattern formation of natural system, fluid flow, traffic flow, city logistics or economical activities[1-6]. Especially Cellular Automata is suitable in the simulation of the complex systems. Pedestrian flow is a typical example of the complex systems where one person walks toward the destination, paying attention to the people around him/her, and the pedestrian flow may be observed as assemblage of movement of each person.

In the modeling by Cellular Automata, local neighbor rules and transition rules should be implemented to simulate time evolution of the phenomena to be considered. But these rules have large effects on the simulation results, and careful consideration is required in defining these rules. In such cases as pedestrian flow, we have no standard rules describing the movement of each person in the crowd.

In this paper, Cellular Automata has been applied to the simulation of pedestrian flow, in which local neighbor rules for a person to walk around in the crowd are determined automatically in the process of simulation. The notion of "collision pattern" is introduced in visible area settled around a person, and each person in the crowd is trained to avoid the collision patterns in the movement. Column formation along the pathway is also discussed.

P.M.A. Sloot, B. Chopard, and A.G. Hoekstra (Eds.): ACRI 2004, LNCS 3305, pp. 211–219, 2004.
© Springer-Verlag Berlin Heidelberg 2004

2 Simulation Model and State Variables

As an example model, a long and narrow pathway where people walk along in both directions has been simulated. The pathway is divided into square cells, and state variables are defined corresponding to "pathway floor", "pedestrian", "wall" and "entrance or exit". For the cell whose state variables is "pedestrian" at a certain time step, "direction" and "velocity" are also defined as state variables.

A part of simulation space is shown in Fig.1. A person walking from right to left is indicated as white circle, and from left to right as black one. A person may move in three directions; straightforward, forward to the right and to the left, as shown in Fig.2. Each person on a pathway has four different maximum velocities, which are specific character walking along the pathway from the entrance to the exit.

When the state variable is "pedestrian" on a certain cell, a visible area is settled around the cell depending on the direction as shown in Fig.3. The direction to proceed is chosen in reference to the state of each cell in the visible area.

One side of the square cells is 1 m, and the whole pathway is divided into 17 x 102 cells, which follows that the width of the pathway is 15 m, and the length 100 m. 20 cells from the entrance or exit cells placed at both sides are assumed to the "approach

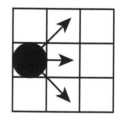

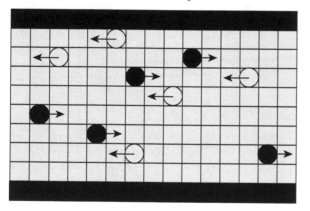

Fig. 1. Simulation space

Fig. 2. Direction of movement

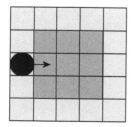
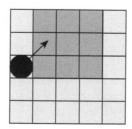
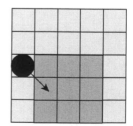

Fig. 3. Visual area of each movement

cells", where the pedestrian flow is not yet in the steady state. The data on the approach cells are excluded in the analysis of simulation results.

As the time step in the simulation is regarded to be 0.1 second in the actual world, the maximum velocities of people are set to 2.5, 1.4, 1.0 and 0.7 m/s, which are based on the measurement data. The difference of velocity is represented in the simulation so that a person can move one cell at every 4, 7, 10 and 14 time step.

The pedestrian is set into the simulation space from the each entrance cell placed at both sides at the probability of 1 % at each time step according to random process. In the simulation, a person is prohibited to move to the cell where the state variable is already "pedestrian", that is, each person cannot overlap each other on the same cell. In case when the cell where a person is going to move has already occupied by the other, the person should stop on the same cell. Further, when a person on the cell where the other are going to move has opposite direction, they are regarded to collide with each other.

3   Acquisition of Local Neighbor Rules

When no local neighbor rule is implemented to each person on the pathway for the movement, the pedestrian flow would not appear and people straggle along the pathway. One of the patterns of movement is shown in Fig.4. In such cases the collision of people can be often seen on the way. This is not the case we always see on the pathway, platform of stations or street.

How to decide the local neighbor rules for pedestrian flow is very difficult, because we don't have the standard rule to describe the movement of each people. Though we can, of course, implement any rules to the movement, they are regarded as reflecting the self-will of the engineer who makes algorithm of the simulation.

The most obvious rule for pedestrian with which almost all the people may agree is just "escape from collision" to each other. In this sense, we would like to propose a new idea to make up the local neighbor rule automatically in the simulation process. In this algorithm, the people on the pathway can acquire the rules for movement automatically without being compelled to obey some given rules. The algorithm is described as follows.

Fig. 4. Example pattern of movement

(1) At first, all the pedestrians are flown into the pathway from the entrance cells without any rules. Each person often collides with each other on the pathway.

(2) When a person collides with other person walking from the opposite direction, the pattern of state variables of all the cells in visible area is memorized as the collision pattern. The pattern of the state variables to be memorized is characterized by the following three parameters;

    (a) existence of wall in visible area (yes:W, no:N)

    (b) the number of people in visible area walking in the same direction

    (c) the number of people in visible area walking in the opposite direction

An example of the pattern is shown in Fig.5. In this case, the pattern is indicated as "N0102". This process is repeated up to 2000 time steps.

(3) A person walking along the pathway sometimes collides with other person on the pattern characterized as the sequence of alphabet and numeric shown above, and sometimes walks smoothly enough without any collision. This is because the memorized pattern consists of mainly the number of specific persons in visible area, and has no information of exact position of other persons. Then, we introduce "collision probability" which is estimated from the simulation results repeated up to 2000 times as follows.

"collision probability" = B / A

A: total number of cases in which all the pedestrian face to this pattern

B: total number of collision all the pedestrian make in this pattern

In this estimation, the probability is regarded to be zero if A is smaller than 100. The collision pattern and its probability are informed to all the pedestrians simultaneously.

(4) A person on the pathway always pays attention to the condition of visible area, and tends to choose the pattern whose collision probability is minimum. If there are several patterns of the same collision probability, the person may choose at random. In case the collision probability of the pattern is zero, the person would continue to walk straight forward.

(5) When collision occurs, back to (2), and then the process continues.

The acquisition process of local neighbor rules described above may be equivalent to choose complementary patterns of the collision patterns.

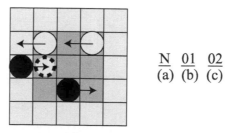

Fig. 5. Example of collision pattern

4 Results and Discussions

4.1 Typical Examples

Typical examples of simulation results implementing the local neighbor rules described in the previous chapter are shown in Fig.6. These are the selected scenes of animation at 2000, 4000, 6000, 8000 and 10000 time steps. As shown in the upper figures, a person on the pathway has no way to step aside to the other persons walk-

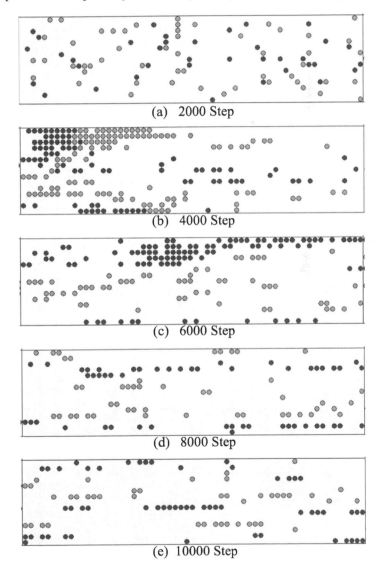

Fig. 6. Typical example of simulation

ing in opposite direction, and tends to collide with each other. As the persons on the pathway are trained to avoid the collision pattern or choose the pattern with minimum collision probability, the pedestrian flow is observed gradually, as shown in Figs.6(d) and (e).

4.2 Degree of Column Formation

As shown in Fig.6, the pedestrian flows in several columns along the pathway, which may be often seen in actual pedestrian flow around us. In this section, a quantitative study of column formation is described.

The column formation is considered to be characterized by the number of columns and the number of people in each column. It is not easy to count the number of column in each scene of animation, because the length and width of a column varies in each time step on the simulation. Then, in reference to Fig.7, we estimate the number of columns and the average number of people in the columns.

At first, a specific point is calculated on each row of cells. Each person walking from left to right corresponds to +1, and the person from right to left to -1. By adding the each point in every row of cells, the total point may be calculated for each row of cells. There may appear some boundaries of total points where the sign of point changes from positive to negative or vice versa. The number of columns in pedestrian flow may be characterized by this number of boundaries in the pathway. There are two columns in the example scene shown in Fig.7.

Next, by adding the absolute value of the specific point of all the row of cells and dividing the number of columns, the average number of people in columns is estimated. As an example shown in Fig.7, the total absolute value is $|+1| + |+5| + |+1| + |-1| + |-5| = 13$. Then the average number of people in columns is $13/2 = 6.5$.

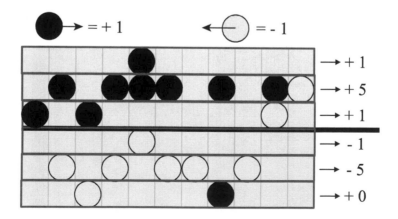

Fig. 7. Number of columns in the example scene

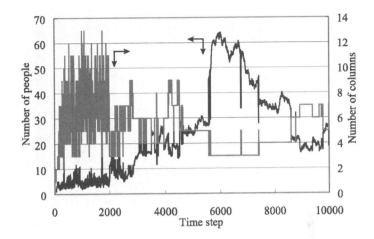

Fig. 8. Number of columns and average number of people

Figure 8 shows the number of columns and the average number of people in columns calculated from the simulation results shown in Fig.6. Though the number of columns varies in wide range at every time step of simulation up to 2000 or 3000 time steps, it gradually converges from 4 to 6 in this case as the people are trained to avoid the collision.

4.3 Collision Patterns and Their Probability

The collision probability corresponding to each pattern is shown in Fig.9. The patterns which are not observed in the simulation, or makes no collision are excluded from Fig.9. The patterns whose collision probability is less than 0.1, are also excluded. The variation of the number of collision which corresponds to the time steps in the simulation is shown in Fig.10. This result is obtained by averaging the number of collision after the repetition of 10 times up to 10000 time steps simulation. During the time steps from 0 to 2000, the number of collision increases, because no training to avoid collision is implemented these interval. Just after 2000 time steps, the number of collision increases suddenly, which is caused by the training algorithm where the number of data for collision is small and almost all the people on the pathway move straight forward. In these state, the typical flow pattern is almost same as the one shown in Fig.6(b), where many people on the pathway cannot move due to collision.

As the training to avoid collision is repeated to all the pedestrian on the pathway, the number of collision decreased dramatically, and almost all the pedestrian walk along the pathway avoiding the collision around 8000 time steps.

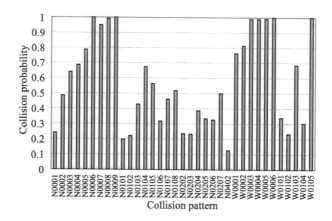

Fig. 9. Collision probability corresponding to each pattern

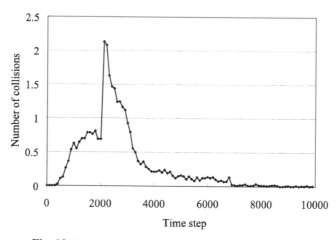

Fig. 10. Average number of collisions in each 100 steps

5 Conclusions

In the present paper, the pedestrian flow on a pathway is simulated by Cellular Automata, in which the local neighbor rules for the pedestrian are implemented automatically. The rule given to each person on the pathway is just to avoid the collision with each other, and this rule may be the way to go through a pathway how we have been all trained from childhood. The collision patterns of state variables in visible area are memorized and are informed to all the people so that they may avoid the collision patterns. These local neighbor rules implemented to the pedestrian may be considered as the complementary rules of the collision rules.

As a lot of previous authors pointed out, Cellular Automata is a strong tool in modeling various kinds of phenomena. But the local neighbor rules implemented in the simulation have definitely large effects on the results. Though in modeling a physical phenomenon we may introduce the rules based on some physical lows, it is difficult to choose the rules in modeling such cases as pedestrian flow. We have no standard rule except for avoiding the collision with each other. In this sense, the algorithm proposed in this paper is one of strong tools to define the local neighbor rules for the "agents" to move on the simulation space autonomously.

References

1. Wolfram, S.: Cellular Automata, Los Alamos Science, Fall (1983) 2-21.
2. Gutowitz, H.: Cellular Automata - Theory and Experiment -, MIT Press (1990) 254-270.
3. Mehta, A.: Granular Matter - An Interdisciplinary Approach - , Springer-Verlag (1994) 85-120.
4. Helbing, D., Farkas, I., Vicsek, T.: Simulating Dynamical Features of Escape Panic, Nature, 407 (2000) 487-490.
5. Shiraishi, T., Morishita, S. and Gavin, H.P.: Estimation of Equivalent Permeability in MR Fuid Considering Cluster Formation of Particles, Transactions of ASME, Journal of Applied Mechanics, 71, 2 (2004) 201-207.
6. Morishita, S. and Nakatsuka, N.: Simulation of Emergency Evacuation by Cellular Automata, Proceedings of 6th International Conference on Complex Systems (2002) 92-97.

Two-Phase Automaton for Porous Structure and Combustion Simulation

Kazuhiro Yamamoto

Department of Mechanical Engineering, Nagoya University,
Furo-cho, Chikusa-ku, Nagoya, Aichi 464-8603, JAPAN
kazuhiro@mech.nagoya-u.ac.jp

Abstract. Although diesel engines have an advantage of low fuel consumption in comparison with gasoline engines, several problems must be solved. One of the major concerns is that diesel exhaust gas has more particle matters (PM) including soot, which is suspected to be linked to human carcinogen. As one of the key technologies, a diesel particle filter (DPF) has been developed to reduce particle matters (PM). Since it is difficult to examine the local flow or temperature field in porous media experimentally, we try to simulate combustion flow. Two-phase Automaton is applied to produce the porous structure based on these particle behaviors. The porosity and tortuosity are freely changed by the profiles of the two-phase interface. Combustion field is simulated in this porous media flow, assuming that soot is attached to the wall surface. Results show that the soot is burned through the reaction with oxygen, similar to the regeneration process of DPF.

1 Introduction

Diesel engines have an advantage of low fuel consumption in comparison with gasoline engines. However, several problems must be solved. One of the major concerns is that diesel exhaust gas has more particle matters (PM) including soot, which are suspected to be linked to human carcinogen. For this reason, more strict exhaust emissions standards such as Euro V in 2008 will be set in many countries. In Japan, the Tokyo municipal government has begun to regulate diesel-powered commercial vehicles that fail to meet the new emission standards.

As one of the key technologies, a diesel particle filter (DPF) has been developed to reduce particle matters (PM) in the after-treatment of exhaust gas. Some filters have been introduced at the Frankfurt Motor Show in 2003. This can be applied to satisfy more strict regulations for diesel emissions, coupled with improvements of combustion conditions. In simple explanation of DPF, it traps the particles when exhaust gas passes its porous structure. Since the filter wall would readily be plugged with particles in a short time, the accumulated particles must be removed. Usually, the filter is heated to burn the particles in combustion. It is called filter regeneration process. However, it is expected that the outer heating with the particle burning may destroy

P.M.A. Sloot, B. Chopard, and A.G. Hoekstra (Eds.): ACRI 2004, LNCS 3305, pp. 220–229, 2004.
© Springer-Verlag Berlin Heidelberg 2004

the porous structure. Then, the thermal durable filter is plausible to maintain the low level of emissions in the long term [1]. So far, the filter has been developed mainly by experiments, and there may not be enough information to observe and understand the phenomena in DPF. For better design of DPF with efficiency and durability, it is necessary to conduct simulation with combustion in porous media. In conventional computational code, it is very challenging to deal with this process, because we need to consider the complex geometry with chemical reaction.

Here, we try to simulate the combustion flow in porous media. The porous inner structure is very complex, which is normally determined by many molecular behaviors when the media is produced or manufactured. However, since the hydrodynamic equations for these complex processes are either unknown or ill-posed, conventional CFD code can not be applied easily [2]. Molecular dynamics (MD) simulation is not practical, because it is impossible to consider the real system due to the huge calculation time and luck of memory. Then, to produce the porous structure, we focus on the Lattice Gas Automata (LGA), which is a kind of cellular automata for fluid simulation. LGA is an idealization of a physical system in which space and time are discrete and the physical quantities (i.e. the states of automaton) take only a finite set of values. It should be noted that sufficiently large cellular automata often show seemingly continuous macroscopic behavior. Frisch et al. [3,4] have proposed a model, where hexagonal lattice is used to succeed in obtaining the correct Navier-Stokes equation by starting from the lattice gas automata. So far, this method has been applied to a large range of scientific problems including diffusion processes and wave propagation.

In this study, we use immiscible lattice gas (ILG) model, which is applied for two-phase flow [5]. When we consider the two-phase interface as porous wall structure, we freely change the porosity and tortuosity of porous media [6,7]. Then, we simulate combustion flow in any porous structure to investigate directly the local heat and mass transfer in DPF. The combustion simulation is conducted by the Lattice Boltzmann method (LBM), which is independent of LG simulation to produce porous structure.

2   Numerical Model

2.1   Porous Structure by Immiscible Lattice Gas

Immiscible Lattice Gas (ILG) model for two-phase is used to produce the porous structure. It consists of a hexagonal (triangular) lattice with particles residing on the node in two-dimensional simulation (see Fig. 1). Two sets of Boolean variables, $r_i(x, t)$ and $b_i(x, t)$ for red and blue particles respectively, are defined to describe the particle presence or absence for each phase. The lattice with unit lattice space, where there are six directions at each node, $i = 1$ to 6, are

$$\vec{e}_i = \left(\cos\left(\frac{(i-1)\pi}{3}\right), \ \sin\left(\frac{(i-1)\pi}{3}\right) \right), \quad (i=1, \ \cdots, \ 6),$$

where e_i is the local velocity vector, and each particle has the same mass and velocity of unity. Properties such as density and velocity are determined by the collective behavior of many particles. As shown in Fig. 1, the local averaging is conducted in sub-domain to obtain the macroscopic quantities.

Starting from the initial state, the configuration of red and blue particles evolves in two sequential sub-steps of collision and propagation. The first step is *collision*.

$$r_i(\vec{x},t^*) = r_i(\vec{x},t) + R_i(r(\vec{x},t),b(\vec{x},t)), \quad (i=1, \ \cdots,6)$$

$$b_i(\vec{x},t^*) = b_i(\vec{x},t) + B_i(r(\vec{x},t),b(\vec{x},t)), \quad (i=1, \ \cdots,6)$$

where, R_i and B_i is the collision operator. This collision occurs just after particles arrive at a node at $t = t^*$. They interact and change their directions according to scattering rules, which preserves mass and momentum. The collision rules for each phase are listed in Ref. [4]. However, in case of collision between red and blue particles, one unique collision is selected so that particles are preferentially moving toward concentrations of same color and away from concentrations of different color, resulting in phase separation [4,8]. Figure 2 illustrates the example where one red particle collides with one blue particle, showing the particle motion before and after collision. Red and blue squares represent the regions of high concentration of each particle.

At the next time step ($t = t +1$), each particle moves to the nearest node in the direction of its velocity, which is called *propagation*.

$$r_i(\vec{x}+\vec{e}_i,t+1) = r_i(\vec{x},t^*), \qquad (i=1, \ \cdots,6).$$

$$b_i(\vec{x}+\vec{e}_i,t+1) = b_i(\vec{x},t^*), \qquad (i=1, \ \cdots,6).$$

Thus, the evolution equation of ILG model is as follows:

$$r_i(\vec{x}+\vec{e}_i,t+1) = r_i(\vec{x},t) + R_i(r(\vec{x},t),b(\vec{x},t)), \quad (i=1, \ \cdots,6).$$

$$b_i(\vec{x}+\vec{e}_i,t+1) = b_i(\vec{x},t) + B_i(r(\vec{x},t),b(\vec{x},t)), \quad (i=1, \ \cdots,6).$$

The total particle density and momentum are defined and given by

$$\rho = \sum_i (r_i + b_i),$$

$$\rho\,\vec{u} = \sum_i \vec{e}_i (r_i + b_i).$$

As already mentioned, physical quantities are obtained by averaging the particle motion in sub-domain. This procedure is needed to eliminate statistical noise. When we take the large sub-domain, the spatial resolution becomes worse. However, there are the large fluctuation exists when the sub-domain size is too small. Here, the sub-domain of 16×16 nodes is used to obtain velocities and density through averaging procedure. The total computational domain has 2,124,081 grid points (3233×657). There are 101×41 sub-domains to determine the physical quantities. As for the boundary conditions, the periodic boundary is adopted both horizontally and verti-cally in this 2D simulation. The initial position of red and blue particles is random, and the velocity field is almost stationary. The particle number ratio of each phase is given to set the porosity. Although the two-phase flow can be simulated by LBM (e.g. particle–fluid suspensions [9]), LG simulation is performed in this study, because the rule for the two-phase interaction is very simple compared with LB equation.

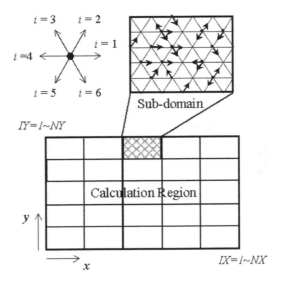

Fig. 1. Calculation region and hexagonal lattice for LGA

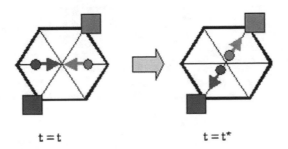

Fig. 2. Collision between red and blue particles in ILG model

2.2 Combustion Simulation by Lattice Boltzmann Method

As for the combustion simulation, we have used the Lattice Boltzmann Method (LBM) [10,11]. For example, the LB equation for temperature is,

$$F_{T,\alpha}(x + e_\alpha \delta_t, \ t + \delta_t) - F_{T,\alpha}(x, \ t) = -\frac{1}{\tau_T}[F_{T,\alpha}(x, \ t) - F_{T,\alpha}^{eq}(x, \ t)] + w_\alpha Q_T$$

where F_T is the distribution function for temperature, τ_T is the relaxation time determined by thermal diffusivity, and $w_0 = 4/9$, $w_\alpha = 1/9$ ($\alpha = 1{:}4$), $w_\alpha = 1/36$ ($\alpha = 5{:}8$) for 9-bit lattice BGK model in two-dimensional square lattice space. The source term, Q_T, is heat release by chemical reaction. As for the soot combustion, we have already tested the real sample of Ni-Cr metal for benchmark study in porous media flow [12]. Here, we apply the same scheme to the porous media formed by ILG model. It is assumed that the soot is homogeneously attached to the wall surface, which is similar situation in the regeneration process of DPF. The over-all reaction by Lee et al. is adopted for soot oxidation [13]. For simplicity, any catalytic effect is not considered. More information on the soot oxidation is found in the review article by Stanmore et al. [14]. In the simulation, the oxygen concentration in inflow is changed. The oxygen concentration is an important parameter in engine operation, because it is easy to control the oxygen concentration by using the exhaust gas recirculation (EGR) [15], in order to prevent an abrupt temperature rise from damaging the local structure of DPF.

Figure 3 shows the coordinate and boundary conditions. The calculation domain is 5 cm × 1 cm, and the inflow velocity, U_{in}, is 20 cm/s. The total number of grids is 201×41, with grid size of 0.25 mm. The porous structure of 100 grid length (L) is placed in the center part in this figure. In the calculation, all equations are non-dimensionalized based on similarity to obtain the temperature and concentration fields. As for the boundary condition, the inflow boundary is adopted at the inlet [16]. The temperature and mass fractions are those of the air at room temperature. At the sidewall, the slip boundary conditions are adopted, considering the symmetry [17]. At the outlet, the pressure is constant, and the gradient of scalar such as temperature is set to be zero. On the surface of the porous wall, the bounceback rule for non-slip boundary condition is adopted.

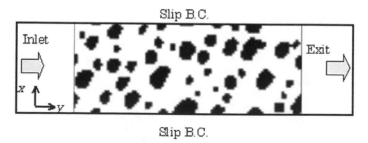

Slip B.C.

Inlet

Exit

Slip B.C.

Fig. 3. Coordinate and boundary conditions in porous media flow

3 Results and Discussion

3.1 Porous Structure

Figure 4 shows time evolution of two-phase automaton. The fraction of red particle is shown. The total density ratio of blue particles to red particles is about three, corresponding to the porosity of 0.75. Time steps are 50, 1000, 10000, and 40000, respectively. The initial position of each particle is random. The average density per node is about 1.5. As seen in this figure, the phase separation is observed. At later time step, the red spot colligate each other to become larger spot. Resultantly, the interface surface is decreased monotonically. The final equilibrium state is full separation with a few large red spots.

Here, we consider the blue phase as volume available for flow and red phase as solid media. The interface of two-phases is regarded as porous wall. The key parameters of porous structure are porosity and total wetted surface. The pore size distribution may be important, but the porosity and total wetted surface are used in the theoretical formula to describe the porous structure [18]. These two parameters are shown in Fig. 5 to see the time dependence. The wetted surface, S, is non-dimensionalized by the porous region length of L. In 2D calculation, the wetted surface corresponds to the wetted perimeter. It is clearly shows that only the wetted surface is decreased as the time step goes. Then, by this model, we can choose any wetted surface of porous media with porosity constant.

Then, we simulate the flow field in created porous structure. We choose three structures with porosity of 0.75, which are cases 1, 2, and 3. The wetted surface of porous media is smaller from cases 1 to 3. These are based on two-phase profiles at the time steps of 1000, 7000, and 30000. Figure 6 shows the distribution of non-dimensional velocity in the x-direction, u_x/U_{in}. It is found that the flow is fluctuated in the porous region and the flow direction is largely changed, even when the flow is

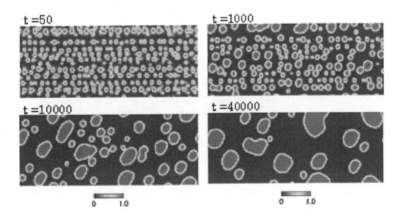

Fig. 4. Time evolution of two-phase automaton, illustrated at representative time steps

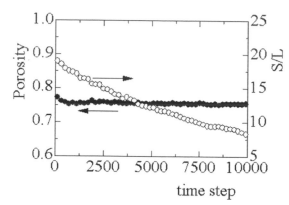

Fig. 5. Porosity and total wetted surface as a function of time step

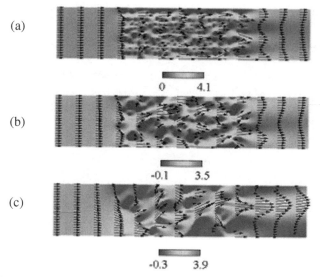

Fig. 6. Flow field in porous media of (a) case 1, (b) case 2, and (c) case 3.

uniform at the inlet. The velocity is locally accelerated in the narrow path, since the obstacle is randomly placed. As a whole, the flow is smooth in case 1. In cases 2 and 3, the negative velocity is observed, which means that the recirculation flow exists. Therefore, with different porous structure, the flow pattern is changed at the same porosity.

The pressure distribution is also examined for the above three cases. Figure 7 shows the averaged pressure distribution along y-direction, which is normalized by the constant pressure at the outlet. In the porous region shown by length of L, the pressure starts to decrease almost linearly, although it slightly fluctuates in cases 2 and 3. After passing this region, the pressure is almost constant. To compare three cases, it is found that the pressure at the inlet is increased as the larger wetted surface, which could be due to the larger effect of shear forces. In future study, our numerical scheme will be extended to produce 3D porous structure to consider the real porous media. Although the simulation is conducted only in 2D geometry, it is demonstrated that the different flow is observed in the produced porous media by ILG.

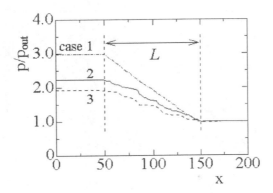

Fig. 7. Pressure distributions in porous media of case 1 to 3

3.2 Combustion Field

Next, the combustion flow is simulated. It is assumed that the soot is homogeneously attached to the wall surface with its mass fraction of 0.1. The mass fraction of oxygen in the air is 0.233. When the porous wall is heated, the soot is burned to react with oxygen. Time, t, is counted after we set the wall temperature for 1200 K. Figure 8 shows the distributions for temperature of T, mass fraction of oxygen and soot of Y_{o2} and Y_c, and the soot reaction rate of W_c. The temperature and reaction rate are non-dimensionalized by inflow temperature and maximum reaction rate. Time step is 5000 after heating, and the porous structure is that of case 2 in Fig. 6. It is found that the oxygen concentration around the wall surface is decreased by the reaction with soot. Then, the maximum temperature is higher than the wall temperature. It is interesting to note that the reaction rate locally varies, simply because the oxygen transport is different by the convection.

Moreover, we change the oxygen concentration in inflow, which is an important parameter to control the reaction rate. Here, nitrogen is added in the air. We set the oxygen concentration (mass fraction) to be 0.233 (air) and 0.1. The total mass of soot is same for both cases. As seen in Fig.8, the reaction rate is locally changed. To make clear the effect of oxygen concentration, the reaction rate is averaged at the wall surface. Results are shown in Fig. 9. The reaction rate is non-dimensionalized by the peak value in case of air. It is found that, as the oxygen concentration is lower, the mean reaction rate is decreased. Then, the reaction of soot is completed at the earlier stage, compared with dilution case. This is very reasonable [12]. We conclude that the combustion simulation in porous media is well demonstrated.

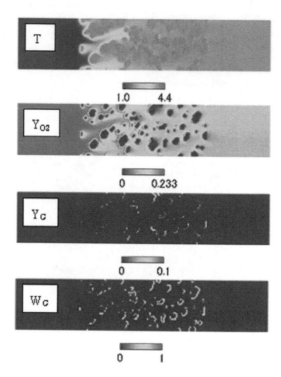

Fig. 8. Distributions of temperature, mass fraction of oxygen and soot, and reaction rate in porous media of case 2

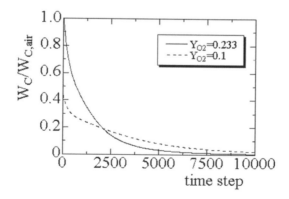

Fig. 9. Mean reaction rate of soot as a function of time after heating

4 Conclusions

Using two-phase automaton of ILG model, we have successfully obtained the porous structure. Setting the ratio of red and blue particles, the porosity is easily given. The tortuosity of the media is determined by the degree of two-phase separation. Then, the flow characteristics are freely changed by choosing the porosity and wetted surface. It has been demonstrated that, using the LBM, the flow is simulated in different porous media structure. For simplicity, the simulation has been conducted only in 2D geometry, but this idea to produce the porous media structure can be extended to 3D simulation. Also, the soot combustion has been well simulated. For example, there are regions where the temperature is locally higher. The effects of oxygen on the reaction rate are clearly recognized. This information is indispensable for the better design of DPF.

References

1. R. A. Searles, D. Bosteels, C. H. Such, A. J. Nicol, J. D. andersson, and C. A. Jemma, F02E310:1-17, *FISITA 2002 World Congress*
2. Chen, S. and Doolen, G. D., *Annual Reviews of Fluid Mech. Vol.30* (1998) 329-364
3. U. Frisch, B. Hasslacher, and Y. Pomeau, *Phys. Rev. Lett.*, 56:1505 (1986)
4. U. Frisch, D. D'humières, B. Hasslacher, P. Lallemand, Y. Pomeau, J. P. Rivent, *Complex Systems*, 1:649 (1987)
5. D. H. Rothman and J. M. Keller, *Int. J. Modern Phys. B,* Vol.52, Nos. 3/4 (1988) 1119-1127
6. Y. Matsukuma, TR. Takahashi, Y. Abe, and H. Adachi, *Trans. Japan Society for Mechanical Engineers*, B64-622 (1998) 1617-1622 (in Japanese)
7. D. Tochio, Y. Matsukuma, Y. Abe, H. Adachi, and H. Nariai, *Trans. Japan Society for Mechanical Engineers*, B68-666 (2002) 325-330 (in Japanese)
8. B. M. Boghosian, *Future Generation Comput. Sys.* 16 (1999) 171-185
9. A. J. C. Ladd and R. Verberg, *J. Statistical Physics*, Vol. 104, Nos.5/6 (2001) 1191-1251
10. K. Yamamoto, X. He, and G. D. Doolen, *J. Statistical Physics*, Vol. 7, Nos.1/2 (2002) 367-383
11. K. Yamamoto, X. He, and G. D. Doolen, *JSME International Journal, Series B,* Vol.47, No.2 (2004) 403-409
12. K. Yamamoto, N. Takada, and M. Misawa, *Proceeding of the Combustion Institute*, Vol.30, in press
13. K. B. Lee, M. W. Thring, and J. M. Beer, *Comb. Flame* 6 (1962) 137-145
14. B. R. Stanmore, J. F. Brilhac, and P. Gilot, *Carbon* 39 (2001) 2247-2268
15. K. N. Pattas, A. M. Stamataelos, K. N. Kougianos, G. C. Koltsakis, and P. K. Pistikopoulos, *SAE Paper* No. 950366 (1996)
16. Q. Zou and X. He, *Phys. Fluids 9 (6)* (1997) 1591-1598
17. T. Inamuro, M. Yoshino, and F. Ogino, *Int. J. Numerical Methods in Fluids* 29 (1999) 737-748
18. R. B. Bird, W.E. Stewart and E.N. Lightfoot, *Transport Phenomena*, Wiley, New York, 1960

Approximation of Continuous Media Models for Granular Systems Using Cellular Automata

Marta Pla-Castells, I. García, and R.J. Martínez

Laboratorio de Simulación y Modelado
Instituto de Robótica, Universidad de Valencia
P.O. Box 2085, 46071 Valencia Spain,
Marta.Pla@uv.es

Abstract. In this paper a new cellular automata model suitable for granular systems simulation is presented. The proposed model is shown to be equivalent to a particularization of the well known BCRE model of granular systems and a correspondence between the parameters of the presented model and the BCRE model is also set, allowing to fit these parameters for a given system. The model has the advantage over other cellular automata models of being more realistic in the behavior of the surface of heaps and slopes. The dynamics of the CA is analyzed in order to confirm that it also has one of the most important features of these systems, $1/f$ noise.

1 Introduction

Granular systems behavior has been widely studied during the last decades, due to its many applications to industry. They show a complex behavior that cannot be easily classified in one of the usual matter states; solid, gas or fluid.

The traditional approach for studying its dynamics has been based in fluids models, describing the flow of granular systems and the formation of heaps. However granular systems show characteristics, such as the appearance of macroscopic patterns or avalanches, that cannot be properly described using this approach. By the other side, Cellular Automata (CA) have also been used for granular systems modelling. Several works have been published that use CA models to study the statistical properties of granular systems [1,2,3]. However the formation of heaps and the way the size of a pile of matter evolves is better described by fluid models.

When simulating the behavior of a granular system in a computer graphics application, the most relevant part is the visualization of the evolution of the external surface of the pile along time [4]. Models based on fluid dynamics do not suit quite well to such applications, since their computational cost makes them difficult to apply to these kind of real-time simulations. In opposite, CA based models describe the granular system as a grid, therefore, as has been shown in [5], they can be solved very efficiently.

In previous works [5,6] some of the CA models found in the bibliography [1,7] were reviewed in order to obtain a more realistic heap and slope formation. The

P.M.A. Sloot, B. Chopard, and A.G. Hoekstra (Eds.): ACRI 2004, LNCS 3305, pp. 230–237, 2004.

main problem of these models is their anisotropy, which is specially notable when a heap is formed by the addition of matter in a single point [6]. The resulting heap has polygonal section, instead of being conic.

Thus, on the one hand continuous models are not suitable for real-time simulation. On the other hand, CA-based models fit well the requirements of this kind of application, but do not show a behavior realistic enough. The objective of this work will be to obtain a CA-based model with a behavior somehow equivalent to that of continuous models. This model fills the need of a realistic and computationally inexpensive model.

In order to achieve this, a model that is shown to be locally equivalent to an existent continuous model is proposed. The model presented by Bouchaud, Cates, Prakash and Edwards [8] (also known as BCRE model) will be used as the starting point, because of its simplicity and its intuitive description.

The BCRE Model. A granular system can be considered as a system with two layers; the standing layer, that forms the slope or the heap of the system, and the rolling layer, that is a thin layer that flows on the surface of the slope [9]. The BCRE model [8] uses this schema and provides a set of equations to describe the evolution of these layers' thickness. The model can be formulated in one dimension as follows: the system has two state variables, the height of the static layer, $s(x, t)$ and the height of the rolling layer, $r(x, t)$. The variation of these variables along time is expressed by the set of equations

$$r_t = vr_x - \gamma(\alpha - |s_x|)r \tag{1}$$
$$s_t = \gamma(\alpha - |s_x|)r$$

where α is the so called angle of repose of the system, γ is a parameter that expresses the rate of matter transfer between layers and v is the speed of the rolling layer that is considered constant.

Equations (1) express that the thickness of both layers will depend on two major processes: on the one hand the transfer of matter from the rolling layer to the resting layer or vice-versa, and on the other hand the exchange of matter at each point of the rolling layer with its surroundings.

This model was extended to 2 dimensions [10] leading to a set of partial differential equations on the variables $r(x, y, t)$ and $s(x, y, t)$

$$r_t = v\nabla(r\nabla s) - \gamma(\alpha - |\nabla s|)r \tag{2}$$
$$s_t = \gamma(\alpha - |\nabla s|)r$$

using the same notation as in equations (1). Equations (2) define the 2-dimensional continuous model that will be used later in this paper.

Following, the update rule that defines the new model will be presented, and the relation between this new model and the BCRE will be explained. In the third section, some properties of the new model will be shown in order to demonstrate that, despite the goal of this work, the main statistical property of most CA models is kept.

2   Description of the Model

In order to define an update rule for a CA model that reflects the behavior of a continuous surface, some simplifications to the two layer description of the granular system that was seen before have to be done.

To define the new model we will work under two main assumptions. The first one is that the thickness of the rolling layer is constant, being $h = r + s$ the height of the system at every point. The second assumption is that the surface of the granular system $h(x, y)$ is a two times differentiable function.

A CA on an $N \times N$ square grid is considered. This grid represents the plane on which the granular system is laying. The value of each cell $h(i, j) \in \mathbb{R}$ will represent the height of the system on the cell's center (x_i, y_j). The set of points $\{(x_i, y_j, h(i, j))\}_{ij}$ is a discretization of the surface $\{(x, y, h(x, y))\}$. Notice that, although the update rule is defined using the derivatives of $h(x, y)$, an expression in terms of the CA variables can be easily obtained.

The update rule is as follows. For each cell, (i, j), the gradient $\nabla h(x_i, y_j)$ is computed. If the angle of the slope $\arctan(|\nabla h|)$ is lower than the repose angle threshold α, the value of cell (i, j) remains unchanged. On the other case, if $\arctan(|\nabla h|) > \alpha$, the height $h(i, j)$ is reduced $z_+ \cdot (h_x + h_y)$, $h(i + 1, j)$ is increased $z_+ \cdot h_x$ and $h(i, j + 1)$ is increased $z_+ \cdot h_y$, that is:

$$h(i, j) \leftarrow h(i, j) - z_+ \cdot (h_x(i, j) + h_y(i, j)) \tag{3}$$
$$h(i + 1, j) \leftarrow h(i + 1, j) + z_+ \cdot h_x(i, j) \tag{4}$$
$$h(i, j + 1) \leftarrow h(i, j + 1) + z_+ \cdot h_y(i, j) \tag{5}$$

where z_+ is a parameter of the model which indicates the velocity of flowing matter, and h_x, h_y are the partial derivatives of $h(x, y)$.

From the assumption that the values of the automata are a discretization of the surface of the system, the value of ∇h can be obtained taking the approximation of the derivatives by differences

$$h_x(i, j) = \frac{\partial h}{\partial x}(x_i, y_j) = \frac{h(x_{i+1}, y_j) - h(x_i, y_j)}{x_{i+1} - x_i}$$
$$h_y(i, j) = \frac{\partial h}{\partial y}(x_i, y_j) = \frac{h(x_i, y_{j+1}) - h(x_i, y_j)}{y_{j+1} - y_j}.$$

This rule is based in the fact that the gradient vector field $-\nabla h(x, y)$ indicates the direction of maximum slope at every point in the surface of the heap. When a cell is updated, if the angle of the slope is higher than the repose angle, the matter flows following the direction of the strongest slope.

2.1   Relation with the BCRE

Once the update rule has been set, the relationship between the behavior of this CA model and the BCRE continuous model will be shown. In order to obtain this relationship the variation of both models at a given point (x_i, y_j), and along a fixed time interval δt, will be obtained. It will be shown that, under certain assumptions, the difference between the models tends to zero if the time interval and the cell size are reduced.

The system evolution after time δt is represented in the CA by an update of the grid using the specified rule. The variation of the height of a cell (i, j) will depend on the update of the cell (i, j) itself, and on the update of cells $(i-1, j)$ and $(i, j-1)$, as they can drop grains into cell (i, j). In a situation in which these three updates are not null, the difference between the height of a cell of the automata, before and after the update, is

$$\Delta h_C = z_+ \left(h_x(i, j) + h_y(i, j) - h_x(i-1, j) - h_y(i, j-1) \right) \tag{6}$$

To see the variation of the BCRE model after time δt, the thickness of the rolling layer r will be considered constant in an open set A including a given point (x_i, y_j). According to equation (2), in (x_i, y_j) the variation of the total height of the system, $h = r + s$, is

$$h_t = r_t + s_t = v\nabla(r\nabla s) \tag{7}$$

that, as r is constant around (x_i, y_j), equals

$$= vr\nabla(\nabla s) = vr\nabla(\nabla h) = vr \left(h_{xx} + h_{yy} \right) . \tag{8}$$

Developing the Taylor series of $h(x_i, y_j, t)$ as a function of time, one obtains

$$\Delta h_B = h(t + \delta t) - h(t) = h_t \delta t + R(\delta t)^2 \tag{9}$$
$$= \delta t\, vr(h_{xx} + h_{yy}) + R(\delta t)^2 .$$

In a similar way, Taylor series of $h_x(\cdot, y_j, t)$ considered as function of x and $h_y(x_i, \cdot, t)$ considered as function of y give

$$h_{xx}(x_i, y_j) = \frac{h_x(x_{i+1}, y_j) - h_x(x_i, y_j)}{x_{i+1} - x_i} + R_1(x_{i+1} - x_i) \tag{10}$$

$$h_{yy}(x_i, y_j) = \frac{h_y(x_i, y_{j+1}) - h_y(x_i, y_j)}{y_{j+1} - y_j} + R_2(y_{j+1} - y_j) . \tag{11}$$

From Equation (9), assuming $x_i - x_{i-1} = y_j - y_{j-1} = d$

$$h(t + \delta t) - h(t) = \delta t\, vr \left(\frac{h_x(x + d, y) - h_x(x, y)}{d} \right. \tag{12}$$
$$\left. + \frac{h_y(x, y + d) - h_y(x, y)}{d} + (R_1 + R_2)d \right)$$
$$+ R(\delta t)^2 .$$

Expressions (6) and (12) give respectively the variation of the proposed CA model, Δh_C, and of the BCRE model, Δh_B, after an interval of time δt. Taking

$$z_+ = \frac{\delta t\, vr}{d} \tag{13}$$

and subtracting equalities 6) and (12) one gets

$$\Delta h_C - \Delta h_B = \delta t \; vr(R_1 + R_2)d + R(\delta t)^2 \tag{14}$$

that represents the difference of the evolution of both models at point (x_i, y_j).

Therefore, considering the situation in which the thickness of the rolling layer in the BCRE model is constant around (x_i, y_j), and in which the three cells (i, j), $(i-1, j)$ and $(i, j-1)$ are effectively updated (i.e. cell (i, j) is in a flowing region), both models converge locally if δt and d tend to zero.

Notice that the assumption of a constant rolling layer implies that the matter flow is not null in a certain region around point (x_i, y_j). In the terms of the CA representation this means that, for d small enough, the update of the four neighbors of cell (i, j) is not null. This is, precisely, which is the assumption made over the CA model to get equation (14).

Thus, as a conclusion, equation (14) expresses that in a point around which the variation of the rolling layer is neglectable, both models lead to the same behavior.

3   Avalanches and $1/f$ Noise

Granular systems are considered a paradigmatic example of systems that evolve to a state called Self Organized Criticality (SOC) [11]. When in this regime, the system remains stable but near to unstable states. When it is perturbated, the system evolves through a set of unstable states until a new stable state is reached. This behavior is usually illustrated by a slope of sand into which grains are dropped randomly. When the slope is higher than a certain angle, the grains start rolling and an avalanche takes place until the system gets relaxed.

Some numerical experiments have been prformed in order to test if one of the most characteristic marks of this behavior, the so called $1/f$ noise, is also present in the model. $1/f$ noise refers to the frequency spectrum of certain events such as avalanches: in a critical system the frequency at which a certain event happens is proportional to the inverse of its magnitude.

Reproducing the tests performed by several authors [1,12,13,14], the frequency of the size of avalanches along a slope, and the correlation between the frequency and the size have been obtained. As a measure of size three values have been chosen; its length as the number of steps that lasts until the system stops again, the area of the avalanche or the number of cells it affects, and the mass displaced, that is the sum of all the matter transfer at every update. Figure 1 shows the power spectra of the measured events.

They have been approximated by a theoretical $1/f^{-\beta}$ function and the correlation of the data have been calculated. The results of this tests are: for the length of the avalanches, $\beta = -6.255718$ with a correlation $r = 0.862181$, for the area, $\beta = -3.375581$ and $r = 0.933205$ and for the displaced mass, $\beta = -7.518815$ and $r = 0.960261$.

The correlation of the measurements of frequency to the theoretical function indicates that the well known behavior of granular systems as critical systems

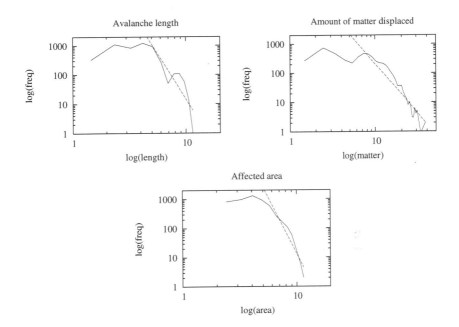

Fig. 1. Frequency spectra for the length, the area and the amount of matter affected by an avalanche, showing the existence of an $i/f^{-\beta}$ relationship. The dashed line shows the regression of the data to a function of that family.

is possible in the presented model. This fact, together with the results obtained in section 2.1 make the model a good tool for the analysis and representation of granular systems.

4   Application of the Model

The integration of the developed model in a more complex application has been done during the development of the Mobile Crane Simulator UVSim, that is currently used in Valencia Harbor. The model presented in this paper is used as a dynamic model for the behavior of bulk material within the complete dynamic model of the virtual environment in the simulator.

In addition to the 3D graphics representation of the system, some interaction modes have been defined in order to allow the manipulation of the bulk material. Further details on the implementation and on the 3D representation of the system using the CA model can be found in [5].

5   Conclusions

In this paper a model addressed to real-time simulation of granular systems that encloses properties of both continuous media models and CA models has been defined. On the one hand, it has been shown that the evolution of the surface of the system is equivalent to the well known BCRE model. On the other hand, some experiments have been done in order to see that the model also keeps at least one of the most characteristic statistical properties of CA.

The evolution of the model has been analyzed at an arbitrary point; it has been shown that the local behavior of the surface is the same that in the BCRE model under the assumption that the rolling layer of the system does not vary substantially near the analyzed point. It has been also stated a relationship between the parameters of both models. The amount of matter displaced z_+ is in equation (13) and the threshold of the automata is set as $\arctan \alpha$. This correspondence allows a direct parameterization of the new model taking as a starting point the parameters of the BCRE model.

Hence, the model fulfills the main requirements stated in Section 1; it behaves as one of the most extended continuous models for granular systems, and has the advantage that the CA implementation is suitable for real-time applications.

Also it has been shown that, although the model behaves locally as a continuous media model, the statistical behavior of the model is consistent with previous CA models. The power spectra of three variables related to avalanches have been obtained, showing that $1/f$ noise, a paradigmatic characteristic of granular systems, can be present in the dynamics of the model.

It can be concluded that the model that has been presented in this work covers the main goals proposed in this paper, providing an improvement of previous CA models.

As future research, the model should be completed to fit the BCRE model in the general case, and perhaps other continuous models should also be translated to a CA model. The analysis of the statistical properties of the model has to be completed in order to determine the different regimes of its dynamics. The possibility of pattern formation can also be studied simulating the experiments usually performed with real granular systems. These works will provide a more robust evidence of the validity of the CA model for granular systems simulation.

References

1. Chen, C. C., den Nijs, M.: Directed avalanche processes with underlaying interface dynamics. Physical Review E. **66** (2002).
2. Prado, C., Olami, Z.: Inertia and break of self-organized criticality in sandpile cellular-automata models. Phys. Rev. A **45** (1992) 6665–6669
3. Nerone, N., Gabbanelli, S.: Surface fluctuations and the inertia effect in sandpiles. Granular Matter. **3** (2001) 117–120
4. Müller, M., Charypar, D., Gross, M.: Procedural modeling and animation: Particle-based fluid simulation for interactive applications. ACM SIGGRAPH/Eurographics Symposium on Computer Animation (2003) 154–159
5. Pla-Castells, M.: Nuevos modelos de sistemas granulares basados en autómatas celulares para simulación en tiempo real. MSc Thesis. Escuela de Ingenierías, Universidad de Valencia. (2003)

6. Pla-Castells, M., García, I., Martínez, R.J.: Visual Representation Of Enhanced Sand Pile Models. Industrial Simulation Conference. Universidad Politécnica de Valencia, Valencia, Spain (2003) 141–146

7. Christensen, K., Olami, Z., Bak, P.: Deterministic $1/f$ noise in nonconservative models of self-organized criticality. Phys. Rev. Letters **68** (1992) 2417–2420

8. Bouchaud, J.P., Cates, M.E., Prakash, J.R., Edwards, S.F.: A Model for the Dynamics of Sandpile Surfaces. J. Phys. I France. **4** (1994) 1383–1410

9. Aradian, A., Raphael, E., de Gennes, P. G.: Surface flows of granular materials: a short introduction to some recent models. Comptes Rendus Physique, **3** (2002) 187–196

10. Hadeler, K. P., Kuttler, C.: Dynamical models for granular matter. Granular Matter.**2** (1999) 9–18

11. Bak, P., Tang, C., Wiesenfeld, K.: Self-organized criticality Phys. Rev. A, **38** (1988) 364–374

12. Kadanoff, L. P., Nagel, S. R., Wu, L., Zhou, S.: Scaling and universality in avalanches. Phys. Rev. A. **39** (1989) 6524–6537

13. Dorso, C. O. , Dadamia, D.: Avalanche prediction in Abelian sandpile model. Physica A: Statistical Mechanics and its Applications. **308** (2002) 179–191.

14. Kertesz, J., Torok, J., Krishnamurthy, S., Roux, S.: Slow dynamics in self-organizing systems. Physica A: Statistical Mechanics and its Applications. **314** (2002) 567–574.

A Topological Framework for the Specification and the Simulation of Discrete Dynamical Systems

Antoine Spicher, Olivier Michel, and Jean-Louis Giavitto

LaMI, umr 8042 du CNRS, Université d'Évry – GENOPOLE
Tour Evry-2, 523 Place des Terrasses de l'Agora
91000 Évry, France
{aspicher,michel,giavitto}@lami.univ-evry.fr

Abstract. MGS is an experimental programming language for the modeling and the simulation of discrete dynamical systems. The modeling approach is based on the explicit specification of the interaction structure between the system parts. This interaction structure is adequately described by topological notions. The topological approach enables a unified view on several computational mechanisms initially inspired by biological or chemical processes (Gamma and *cellular automata*). The expressivity of the language is illustrated by the modeling of a diffusion limited aggregation process on a wide variety of spatial domain: from cayley graphs to arbitrary quasi-manifolds.

1 Introduction

In this paper, we are interested in the modeling of discrete dynamical systems with some internal structure that arises from their evolution function.

Consider the following discrete process: a particle q moves randomly on a square lattice. So, if q is on node (x, y) at time t, then at time $t + 1$ it occupies one of the node $(x + \epsilon_x, y + \epsilon_y)$ where ϵ_x, ϵ_y are randomly chosen in $\{-1, 0, 1\}$ such that $|\epsilon_x| + |\epsilon_y| \neq 0$. The building of a synchronous cellular automata (CA) that simulates this process is not immediate because the update rules change the state of only one node. It will be much more easy to allow rules that update synchronously a entire subset of the nodes. If this kind of rule is allowed, then it would be trivial to define this process as the simultaneous update of two neighbor cells, one empty and the other containing a particle, by the exchange of their state.

The problem of updating a subset of cells defined by some arbitrary conditions is often solved using an asynchronous dynamics: this avoids that two occupied cells decide at the same step to occupy the same empty neighbor. Another solution is the partitioning of the cells into a coarser graph (this is the approach of lattice gas automata [TM87]).

We see here these two approaches mainly as tricks that do not account that a system can be decomposed into subsystems defined by the requirement that

P.M.A. Sloot, B. Chopard, and A.G. Hoekstra (Eds.): ACRI 2004, LNCS 3305, pp. 238–247, 2004.

the elements into the subsystems interact together and are truly independent from all other subsystems parallel evolution.

In this view, the decomposition of a system S into subsystems $S_1, S_2, \ldots, S_n$ is *functional*: the state $s_i(t + 1)$ of the subsystem S_i depends solely of the previous state $s_i(t)$. However, the decomposition of S into the S_i can depend on the time steps. So we write $S_1^t, S_2^t, \ldots, S_{n_t}^t$ for the decomposition of the system S at time t and we have: $s_i(t + 1) = h_i^t(s_i(t))$ where the h_i^t are the "local" evolution functions of the S_i^t. The "global" state $s(t)$ of the system S can be recovered from the "local" states of the subsystems: it exists a function φ^t such that $s(t) = \varphi^t(s_1(t), \ldots, s_{n_t}(t))$ which induces a relation between the "global" evolution function h and the local evolution functions: $s(t + 1) = h(s(t)) = \varphi^t(h_1^t(s_1(t)), \ldots, h_{n_t}^t(s_{n_t}(t)))$.

The successive decomposition $S_1^t, S_2^t, \ldots, S_{n_t}^t$ can be used to capture the *elementary parts* and the *interaction structure* between these elementary parts of S. Cf. Figure 1. Two subsystems S' and S'' of S interact if it exists some S_j^t such that $S', S'' \in S_j^t$. Two subsystems S' and S'' are *separable* if it exists some S_j^t such that $S' \in S_j^t$ and $S'' \notin S_j^t$ or vice-versa. This leads to consider the set $\mathcal{S}$, called the *interaction structure* of S, defined by the smaller set closed by intersection that contains the S_j^t.

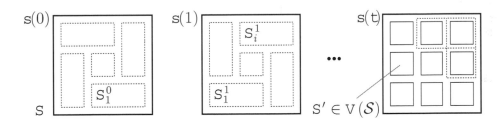

Fig. 1. The interaction structure of a system S resulting from the subsystems of elements in interaction at a given time step.

The set $\mathcal{S}$ has a *topological structure*: $\mathcal{S}$ corresponds to an *abstract simplicial complex*. An abstract simplicial complex [Mun84] is a collection $\mathcal{S}$ of finite nonempty set such that if A is an element of $\mathcal{S}$, so is every nonempty subset of A. The element A of $\mathcal{S}$ is called a *simplex* of $\mathcal{S}$; its *dimension* is one less that the number of its element. The dimension of $\mathcal{S}$ is the largest dimension of one of its simplices. Each nonempty subset of A is called a *face* and the *vertex set* $V(\mathcal{S})$, defined by the union of the one point elements of $\mathcal{S}$, corresponds to the *elementary functional parts* of the system S. The abstract simplicial complex notion generalizes the idea of *graph*: a simplex of dimension 1 is an edge that links two vertices, a simplex d of dimension 2 can be thought of as a surface whose boundaries are the simplices of dimension 1 included in d, etc.

Our proposal is to specify a discrete dynamical system starting from its interaction structure. Our idea is to define directly the set $\mathcal{S}$ with its topological structure and to specify the evolution function h by specifying the set S_i^t and the functions h_i^t. The result is an experimental programming language called MGS. In MGS, the interaction structure $\mathcal{S}$ is defined as a new kind of data structures called *topological collections* and a set of functions h_i^t together with the specification of the S_i^t for a given t are called *transformation*. A transformation is a function defined by the cases S_i^t.

This abstract approach has two main advantages. The first one is that it enables the easy specification of dynamical systems with a dynamical structure $(DS)^2$. In such systems, the phase space cannot be defined *a priori* and must be computed jointly with the state of the system (in other word, the set of states must be an observable of the system itself, see [Gia03]). The second advantage is that this abstract approach enables an homogeneous and uniform handling of several computational models including CA, lattice gas automata, abstract chemistry, Lindenmayer systems and several other abstract reduction systems.

The rest of the paper is organized as follows. We begin with a short introduction to the MGS experimental programming language, through the notions of topological collection and transformation. Then, section 3 illustrates the application of these notions on a simple CA. The same diffusion-aggregation process is considered on two increasingly more complex topologies. Finally, we review some related works and the perspectives opened by this research.

2   A Brief Presentation of the MGS Language

MGS embeds a complete, impure, dynamically typed, strict, functional language. We focus on the notions required to understand the rest of the paper and we only describe here the major differences between the constructions available in MGS with respect to functional languages like OCAML [Ler96].

2.1   Topological Collections

The distinctive feature of the MGS language is its handling of entities structured by *abstract topologies* using *transformations* [GM02]. A set of entities organized by an abstract topology is called a *topological collection*. Topological means here that each collection type defines a neighborhood relation inducing a notion of *subcollection*. A subcollection S' of a collection S is a subset of connected elements of S and inheriting its organization from S.

Topological Collection and the Representation of a (DS)^2 State. A topological collection is used to represent the complex states s of a dynamical system S at a given time t. The elements of the topological collection are the elements S' of $V(\mathcal{S})$ and each element has a value given by s'. In the context of topological collections, the elements of $V(\mathcal{S})$ are called *positions* and we say that s' is the value associated to the position S'. Often there is no need to distinguish between the positions and their associated value. In this case, we use the term "element of the collection".

Collection Types. Different predefined and user-defined collection types are available in MGS, including sets, bags (or multisets), sequences, several grids and arbitrary topologies. We introduce the collection types along with the examples.

For any collection type T, the corresponding empty collection is written ():T. The join of two collections C_1 and C_2 (written by a comma: C_1, C_2) is the main operation on collections. The comma operator is overloaded in MGS and can be used to build any collection by joining its two arguments. To spare the notations, the empty sequence can be omitted in the definition of a sequence: 1, 2, 3 is equivalent to 1, 2, 3, ():seq.

2.2   Transformations

Transformation are used to specify the evolution function of a (DS)[2]. The *global transformation* of a topological collection s consists in the *parallel application* of a set of *local transformations*. A local transformation is specified by a rule r that specifies the replacement of a subcollection by another one. The application of a rewriting rule $\sigma \Rightarrow f(\sigma, ...)$ to a collection s:

1. selects a subcollection s_i of s whose elements match the *pattern* σ,
2. computes a new collection s_i' as a function f of s_i and its neighbors,
3. and specifies the insertion of s_i' in place of s_i into s.

One should pay attention to the fact that, due to the parallel application strategy of rules, *all distinct instances s_i of the subcollections matched by the σ pattern are "simultaneously replaced"* by the $f(s_i)$.

The MGS experimental programming language implements the idea of transformations of topological collections into the framework of a functional language: collections are just new kind of values and transformations are functions acting on collections and defined by a specific syntax using rules. Transformations (like functions) are first-class values and can be passed as arguments or returned as the result of an application.

Path Pattern. A pattern σ in the left hand side of a rule specifies a subcollection where an interaction occurs. A subcollection of interacting elements can have an arbitrary shape, making it very difficult to specify. Thus, it is more convenient (and not so restrictive) to enumerate sequentially the elements of the subcollection. Such enumeration will be called a *path*.

A path pattern *Pat* is a sequence or a repetition *Rep* of *basic filters*. A basic filter *BF* matches one element. The following (fragment of the) grammar of path patterns reflects this decomposition:

$$Pat ::= Rep \mid Rep, Pat \qquad Rep ::= BF \mid BF/exp \qquad BF ::= \text{cte} \mid \text{id} \mid \text{<undef>}$$

where cte is a literal value, id ranges over the pattern variables and *exp* is a boolean expression. The following explanations give a systematic interpretation for these patterns:

literal: a literal value `cte` matches an element with the same value. For example, 123 matches an element with value 123.

empty element the symbol `<undef>` matches an element with an undefined value, that is, an element whose position does not have an associated value.

variable: a pattern variable a matches exactly one element with a well defined value. The variable a can then occur elsewhere in the rest of the rule and denotes the value of the matched element.

neighbor: b, p is a pattern that matches a path which begins by an element matched by b and continues by a path matched by p, the first element of p being a neighbor of b.

guard: p/exp matches a path matched by p if boolean expression exp evaluates to `true`.

Elements matched by basic filters in a rule are distinct. So a matched path is without self-intersection.

Right Hand Side of a Rule. The right hand side of a rule specifies a collection that replaces the subcollection matched by the pattern in the left hand side. There is an alternative point of view: because the pattern defines a sequence of elements, the right hand side may be an expression that evaluates to a sequence of elements. Then, the substitution is done element-wise: element i in the matched path is replaced by the ith element in the r.h.s. This point of view enables a very concise writing of the rules.

2.3   Short Example

We give an example that imply the transformation of a sequence of elements.

Bubble Sort in MGS. The bubble sort consists in (1) comparing two neighbors elements in a sequence and swapping them if they are not in order; (2) repeating the first step until a fixed point is reached. This specification is immediate in `MGS` and can be written:

```
trans bubble_sort = {     x, y / (x > y) => y, x     }
```

The keyword `trans` introduces the definition of a transformation by a set of rules. Here there is only one rule. This transformation can be applied to a sequence `s := 4, 2, 3, 1` until a fixed point is reached: `bubble_sort['iter='fixpoint](s)`. The value of the predefined optional parameter `'iter` indicates that the application of the function `bubble_sort` must be iterated until a fixed point is reached. The results is `1, 2, 3, 4` as expected.

3   (DS)^2 on Complex Topologies

In this section we present the use of `MGS` to model and simulate more complex systems. Our running example will be a diffusion limited aggregation process on different spatial domains. Diffusion Limited Aggregation, or DLA, is a fractal growth model studied by two physicists, T.A. Witten and L.M. Sander, in the 80's. The principle of the model is simple: a set of particles diffuse randomly on a given spatial domain. Initially one particle, the seed, is fixed. When a mobile particle collides a fixed one, they stick together and stay fixed. For the sake of simplicity, we suppose that they stick together forever and that there is no aggregate formation between two mobile particles.

This process leads to a simple CA with an asynchronous update function or a lattice gas automata with a slightly more elaborate rule set. The purpose of this section is twofold. Firstly, we want to show that the MGS approach enables the specification of a simple generic transformation that can act on arbitrary complex topologies. Secondly, we show how to specify MGS topological collections that correspond to standard CAs.

3.1   The DLA Evolution Function in MGS

The transformation describing the DLA behavior is really simple. We use two symbolic values 'mobile and 'fixed to represent respectively a mobile and a fixed particle. There are two rules in the transformation: (1) if a diffusing particle is the neighbor of a fixed seed, then it becomes fixed; (2) if a mobile particle is neighbor of an empty place, then it may leave its current position to occupy the empty neighbor. Note that the order of the rules is important because the first has priority over the second one. Thus, we have :

```
trans dla = {
    'mobile, 'fixed    => 'fixed, 'fixed
    'mobile, <undef>   => <undef>, 'mobile
}
```

3.2   DLA on Uniform Topologies: GBF

Group-based data fields (GBF in short) are topological collections used to define topologies with a *uniform* neighborhood: a position cannot be distinguished only by looking at its neighbors. This implies for example that each position has the same number of neighbors.

A GBF is an extension of the notion of array where the elements are indexed by the elements of a group called the *shape* of the GBF [GMS95,GM01]. For example:

```
gbf Grid2 = < north, east >
```

defines a GBF collection type called *Grid2*, corresponding to the Von Neumann neighborhood in a classical array (a cell above, below, left or right – not diagonal). The two names **north** and **east** refer to the directions that can be followed to reach the neighbors of an element. These directions are the *generators* of the underlying group structure. The r.h.s. of the GBF definition gives a *finite presentation* of the group structure [Sha90]. The list of the generators can be completed by giving equations that constraint the displacements in the shape:

```
gbf Torus2 = < north, east; 12*east = 0, 40*north = 0 >
```

defines a 40×12 torus: if one starts from a position and follows 12 times the
east direction, one finds oneself at the same position. Another example is the
definition of an hexagonal lattice that tiles the plane:

```
gbf Hexa2 = < east, north, northeast; east + north = northeast >
```

Each cell has six neighbors (following the three generators and their inverses).
The equation east + north = northeast specifies that a northeast move is
equivalent to a move following the east direction followed by a move following the north direction.

A GBF value of type T is a partial function that associates a value to some
group elements (the group elements are the positions of the collection and the
the empty GBF is the everywhere undefined function). The topology of T is
easily visualized as the Cayley graph of the presentation of T: each vertex in the
Cayley graph is an element of the group and vertices x and y are linked by an
edge labeled **g** if there is a generator **g** in the presentation such that $x + g = y$.

Figure 2 represents the final state of a DLA process, where each initially
mobile particle has been fixed. The plot at the left is the application, until a
fixed point has been reached, of the transformation dla to a Torus2. The plot
at the right is the fixed point reached by the same transformation dla to a
Hexa2. In this last simulation, particles are initially packed on the right and the
initial static particle was on the left part of the lattice. Particles are constrained
to move on a rhombus. This explains the asymmetries of the figure.

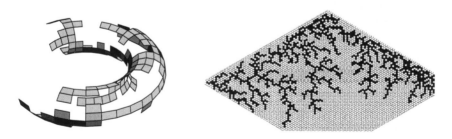

Fig. 2. Example of DLA on two different topologies: a torus (left) and an hexagonal
meshes (right)

3.3 Arbitrary Topology: DLA on Cellular Complexes

Beyond Graphs. The interaction structure of the previous examples can be adequately described by a graph: two positions are connected by an edge if they are
neighbors. Sequences correspond to linear graphs and GBFs provide Cayley's
graphs with regular connectivity. This last family of topologies is convenient to
represent regular spaces where all elementary parts have the same spatial properties, but they cannot be used for instance to model a sphere (there is no regular
graph on a sphere that corresponds to the Cayley graph of some group).

This shortcoming motivates the development of more powerful (arbitrary) topologies. First we would like to represent irregular meshes. However, we also want to represent heterogeneous spaces. As an example, let consider the electrostatic laws. They depend on the geometry of the system and some values must be associated to a dimension: the distribution of electric charges corresponds to a *volumic* density while the electric flux through a surface is associated to a *surface*. Note that *balance equations* often link these values, such as the Gauss theorem for our electrostatic example. See also the work of E. Tonti [Ton74] for an elaboration.

As a consequence, the interaction structure that describes a system S may contains simplices with dimension greater than one. In general, any component of any dimension and their interactions should appear in the description of the system, and we should be allowed to associate some values to them.

Arbitrary Topological Collection as Cellular Complex. The right framework to develop a topological collection type that allows the representation of arbitrary topologies is the *combinatorial algebraic topology* theory.

In this framework, a topological collection is a *cellular complex*: a collection of objects of various dimension called k-*cell*, where k is the dimension. To be more practical, 0-cells are vertices, 1-cells are edges, 2-cells are faces, 3-cells are volumes, etc. To build some arbitrary complex domain, the domain is divided into a cellular partition. Each cell represents a simple part of the domain and the cells are glued together: a k-cell c_1 is incident to a $(k-1)$-cell c_2 if $c_2 \subset \partial c_1$, where ∂c_1 denotes the border of c_1. This boundary relation ∂ can be used to specify the neighborhood relationships in a topological collection: *two k-cells are neighbors if they share an incident $(k-1)$-cell or if they are incident to a same $(k+1)$-cell*. This definition of a topological collection is consistent with the previous one.

G-map in MGS. There are several specializations of the notion of cellular complex. For instance abstract simplical complex evoked in the introduction are special cases of cellular complexes. In MGS one can use *generalized map* or (Gmap) [Lie91] to build arbitrary topologies. The topological objects that can be described by Gmaps are *quasi-manifolds*.

There are several ways to specify and build Gmaps in MGS. A Gmap can be build as the result of construction operations like various products, extrusion, suspension, pasting, gluing, etc. A perhaps simpler way is to edit manually the Gmap in an interactive CAD tool like MOKA[1] and to import the result in MGS.

The figure 3 shows applications of the DLA transformation on different kinds of objects built with Gmaps. As a matter of fact, the change of topological collection doesn't affect the transformation and we still apply the same dla transformation. In these examples, the topological collections have dimension 2 and the values are associated only to 2-cells. The 2-cells are neighbors if they have a common edge on their boundary. In the top of the figure, only the 1-cells are figured, and in the bottom, only the 2-cells that hold a value are represented.

---

[1] http://www.sic.sp2mi.univ-poitiers.fr/moka/

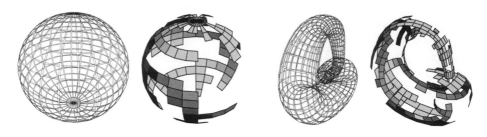

Fig. 3. DLA on complex objects (topology and final state). On the left: a sphere with 18 parallels and 24 meridians. On the right: a Klein's bottle.

4   Conclusion and Perspectives

This paper only focuses on a part of the features available in MGS that can be used to develop computer models of complex discrete dynamical systems that are concise and mathematically well-founded. The approach has been applied successfully to several biological processes (the growth of a tumor, the flocking of birds, colonies of ants foraging for food, the heterocysts differentiation during *Anabaena* growth, etc.) as well as more algorithmic problems (flow on graphs, various sorting algorithms, Hamiltonian path, prime number generation, etc.).

The modeling of $(DS)^2$ through their interaction structure is part of a long term research effort [Gia03]. The topological approach presented here provides a unified description of several computational models. Obviously, Lindenmayer systems [Lin68] correspond to transformations on sequences. Chemical computation, as in Gamma [BFM01], can be emulated using transformations on bags.

There exists strong links between GBF and cellular automata, especially considering the work of Z. Róka [Rók94] which has studied CA on Cayley graphs. However, our own works focus on the construction of Cayley graphs as the shape of a data structure and we develop an operator algebra and rewriting notions on this new data type. This is not in the line of Z. Róka who focuses on synchronization problems and establishes complexity results in the framework of CA.

The perspectives opened by this work are numerous. From the applications point of view, we are targeted by the simulation of developmental processes in biology [GM03,GMM04]. At the language level, the study of the topological collections concepts must continue with a finer study of transformation kinds. Several kinds of restrictions can be put on the transformations, leading to various kind of pattern languages and rules. The complexity of matching such patterns has to be investigated. The efficient compilation of a MGS program is a long-term research. We have considered in this paper only one-dimensional paths, but a general n-dimensional notion of path exists and can be used to generalize the substitution mechanisms of MGS.

The sources of the current MGS implementation, as well as several examples and technical reports, are freely available at http://mgs.lami.univ-evry.fr.

Acknowledgments. The authors would like to thank the MOKA team at the Univ. of Poitier, J. Cohen at LaMI, F. Jacquemard at LSV-Cachan and the members of the "Simulation and Epigenesis" group at Genopole for technical support, stimulating discussions and biological motivations. This research is supported in part by the CNRS, GDR ALP, IMPG, University of Évry and Genopole/Évry.

References

[BFM01]   Jean-Pierre Banâtre, Pascal Fradet, and Daniel Le Métayer. Gamma and the chemical reaction model: Fifteen years after. *Lecture Notes in Computer Science*, 2235:17–??, 2001.

[Gia03]   J.-L. Giavitto. Invited talk: Topological collections, transformations and their application to the modeling and the simulation of dynamical systems. In *Rewriting Technics and Applications (RTA'03)*, volume LNCS 2706 of *LNCS*, pages 208 – 233, Valencia, June 2003. Springer.

[GM01]   J.-L. Giavitto and O. Michel. Declarative definition of group indexed data structures and approximation of their domains. In *Proceedings of the 3nd International ACM SIGPLAN Conference on Principles and Practice of Declarative Programming (PPDP-01)*. ACM Press, September 2001.

[GM02]   J.-L. Giavitto and O. Michel. The topological structures of membrane computing. *Fundamenta Informaticae*, 49:107–129, 2002.

[GM03]   J.-L. Giavitto and O. Michel. Modeling the topological organization of cellular processes. *BioSystems*, 70(2):149–163, 2003.

[GMM04]   J.-L. Giavitto, G. Malcolm, and O. Michel. Rewriting systems and the modelling of biological systems. *Comparative and Functional Genomics*, 5:95–99, February 2004.

[GMS95]   J.-L. Giavitto, O. Michel, and J.-P. Sansonnet. Group based fields. In I. Takayasu, R. H. Jr. Halstead, and C. Queinnec, editors, *Parallel Symbolic Languages and Systems (International Workshop PSLS'95)*, volume 1068 of *LNCS*, pages 209–215, Beaune (France), 2–4 October 1995. Springer-Verlag.

[Ler96]   X. Leroy. The Objective Caml system, 1996. Software and documentation available on the web at http://pauillac.inria.fr/ocaml/.

[Lie91]   P. Lienhardt. Topological models for boundary representation : a comparison with n-dimensional generalized maps. *Computer-Aided Design*, 23(1):59–82, 1991.

[Lin68]   A. Lindenmayer. Mathematical models for cellular interaction in development, Parts I and II. *Journal of Theoretical Biology*, 18:280–315, 1968.

[Mun84]   James Munkres. *Elements of Algebraic Topology*. Addison-Wesley, 1984.

[Rók94]   Zsuzsanna Róka. One-way cellular automata on Cayley graphs. *Theoretical Computer Science*, 132(1–2):259–290, 26 September 1994.

[Sha90]   Igor' Shafarevich. *Basic Notions of Algebra*. Springer, 1990.

[TM87]   T. Toffoli and N. Margolus. *Cellular automata machines: a new environment for modeling*. MIT Press, Cambridge, 1987.

[Ton74]   Enzo Tonti. The algebraic-topological structure of physical theories. In P. G. Glockner and M. C. sing, editors, *Symmetry, similarity and group theoretic methods in mechanics*, pages 441–467, Calgary, Canada, August 1974.

A Basic Qualitative CA Based Model of a Frustrated Linear Josephson Junction Array (JJA)

Claudia R. Calidonna[1] and Adele Naddeo[2]

[1] Istituto di Cibernetica "E. Caianiello"
Dept. Computer Science, National Research Council (C.N.R.)
Viale Campi Flegrei 34 I-80078 Pozzuoli (NA), Italy
c.calidonna@cib.na.cnr.it
[2] Dipartimento di. Scienze Fisiche, Università di Napoli " Federico II"
and Coherentia-INFM, Unità di Napoli
I-80125, Napoli (Italy)
adele.naddeo@na.infn.it

Abstract. Quantum Systems modeling and simulation activity is a challenging research area. Several models and applications were proposed in the past with different approaches. Special purposes models based on Cellular Automata (CA) paradigm were studied as the classical CA present limits in quantum system characterization. In this paper we derive a basic qualitative model, according to the Cellular Automata Network Model version 2 (CAN2), for studying and characterizing a frustrated liner JJA, showing that, when adopting particular system conditions, the corresponding model is extremely simple, and each component characterizing system can be easily individuated.

1 Introduction

Quantum Systems modeling and simulation activity is a challenging research area. Several models and applications were proposed in the past with different approaches. Special purposes models based on Cellular Automata (CA) paradigm were studied [13] as the classical CA present limits in quantum system characterization [18]. An example of special CA quantum models is the Quantum cellular Automata, where each cell is a quantum dot system [13].

In this paper we deal with a particular mesoscopic quantum system: a frustrated linear Josephson Junction Array [9,16]. These JJAs are very challenging solid-state devices: when they are arranged according to a non-trivial geometry at low temperatures, they develop topology order [19,20], allowing for obtaining a qubit [7,8] protected from decoherence [6,10,12]. The JJA devices behavior is often reproduced, according to the underlying physical system, adopting Monte Carlo simulation and exact diagonalization methods. Here we describe our qualitative model, for qubit above, trying to capture the main peculiar aspects for a CAN2 [4] based model reproduction.

This paper is the first but mandatory stage towards the definition of the basic computational building block for the simulation of an ideal quantum computer. The choice of such a system characterization embodies an inner parallelism behavior. In

P.M.A. Sloot, B. Chopard, and A.G. Hoekstra (Eds.): ACRI 2004, LNCS 3305, pp. 248–257, 2004.
© Springer-Verlag Berlin Heidelberg 2004

fact the adopted CA computational model that embodies an inner data parallelism is the inner parallelism level of a more future complex architecture built with an outer quantum parallelism degree.

The challenging future result, which has an intrinsic difficulty, is to combine and synchronize the parallelism levels above.

The paper is organized as follows: Section 2 deals with the phenomenological description of the devices above; Section 3 introduces the Cellular Automata Network v. 2 model that takes into account the classical Cellular Automata (CA) computational model and its modification in order to be used for macroscopic complex phenomena modeling activity; Section 4 deals with the description of a JJA model, obeying to particular conditions, according to a CAN2 computational model; finally some remarks and future works descriptions conclude this paper.

2   Josephson Junction Arrays (JJA): The Physical Model

Josephson junction arrays (JJA) are a very useful tool for investigating quantum-mechanical behavior in a wide range of parameter space. In fact there exists a couple of conjugate quantum variables, the charge and phase ones on each superconducting island, which results in two dual descriptions of the array [2]:
1. through the charges (Cooper pairs) hopping between the islands,
2. through the vortices hopping between the plaquettes.

Furthermore, in the presence of an external magnetic field charges gain additional Aharonov-Bohm phases and, conversely, vortices moving around islands gain phases proportional to the average charges on the islands [1]. Such basic quantum interference effects found application in recent proposals for solid state qubits for quantum computing, based on charge [17] or phase [3,11,14] degree of freedom in JJAs.

"Charge" devices operate in the regime

$$E_C \rangle\rangle E_J$$

where:

- $E_C = \dfrac{e^2}{2C}$ is the charging energy and $E_J = \dfrac{\hbar}{2e} I_c$ is the Josephson coupling energy;
- C is the capacitance of each island, and
- Ic the critical current of each junction;

while "phase" or "flux" devices are characterized by strongly coupled junctions with

$$E_J \rangle\rangle E_C .$$

Recently new kinds of JJAs have been proposed [6,12], with non-trivial geometry, which allow for a novel state at low temperature characterized by a discrete topological order parameter [19,20]. In fact, the Hilbert space of their quantum states decomposes into mutually orthogonal sectors ("topological" sectors), each sector remaining isolated under the action of local perturbations and protected from leakage through a gapped excitation spectrum. If we choose the two qubit states from ground states in different sectors we get a 2^K-dimensional subspace (K is the number of big openings in the array, in general equal to the effective number of qubits) which is *"protected"* from the external noise [10]. Once the protected qubit has been implemented, global operators must be found in order to manipulate its states. Further steps are the implementation of non-trivial two-qubit operations and the construction of a register of qubits. It is evident that such arrays could be promising candidates for a physical implementation of an ideal quantum computer [7,8].

After such a brief account of general features of "protected" JJAs qubits, we focus on the simplest physical array one can devise to meet all the above requests, that is a ring array of N Josephson junctions with half flux quantum ($\frac{1}{2}\Phi_0 = \frac{1}{2}\left(\frac{hc}{2e}\right)$) threading each plaquette [9,16]. The number of plaquettes must be correspond to the number of junctions, so that each plaquette contains two junctions.

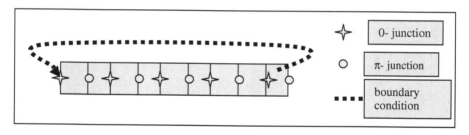

Fig. 1. JJA with N=10 junctions (0 and π) and N=10 loops in a ring geometry.

Such a condition is fulfilled when each plaquette of the ring contains an odd number of so called π- junctions (a π- junction is characterized by a π shift in the phase of the wave function on one side of the junction, so that the current-phase relation is I=Ic sin($\varphi+\pi$)), one in our case.

The array above, sketched in Fig. 1 for N=10, has a ground state twofold degenerate with antiferromagnetic ordering as a result of currents circulating clockwise and counterclockwise in odd and even plaquettes respectively, hence it can be mapped into a linear antiferromagnetic chain of half-integer spins.

3   CAN and CAN2: Two CA Based Computational Models for Micro and Macro Complex Systems Simulation

CA, in the classical model [21,22] based on a regular spatial grid of cells, each cell embedding identical Finite Automata (FA), whose input is the states of neighboring cells; FA have an identical transition function applied simultaneously to each cell. The neighboring cell is defined in terms of a spatial pattern, invariant in time and space. At the time t=0, FA are in an arbitrary state and the CA evolve changing the state of all the FA simultaneously at discrete time steps, according to the FA transition function.

The following informal properties characterize a CA:

- a regular discrete lattice of cells, with a discrete variable at each cell assuming a finite set of states,
- an evolution law, called transition function, that takes place in discrete time steps,
- each cell evolves according to the same rule depending only on the state of the cell and a finite number of neighboring cells; the neighborhood relation is local and uniform.

In implementing CA applications, due to the finite storage and finite computational power of existing machines, many choices about the components of a CA have to be made [21]. Here we give a brief comment on possible choices regarding lattice geometry and neighborhood size:

- lattice geometry i.e. selection of a specific lattice geometry can be one-, two- or three-dimensional;
- neighborhood size i.e. the choice of the neighborhood type for each cell, for instance for a two-dimensional lattice patterns as Von Neumann and Moore types are generally used.

CA proved to be an effective computational model in simulating micro and macroscopic phenomena, although CA are inspired by a-centrism [15] the modeling activity of real macroscopic phenomena requires some extension of classic CA model considering at first the following issues:

1. Dimension of the corresponding cells must be fixed in order to map the elementary portion of the considered region area to each cell grid.
2. Clock unit must be fixed corresponding to the time step considered for each transition function iteration

Our CA model modification, i.e. the CAN [5] model, extends the standard CA model introducing the possibility to have a network of cellular automata, where each automaton represents a component of a physical system and connections among network automata represent a disjoinable evolutive law that characterizes the system to be simulated.

The CAN model can be applied when the construction of complex phenomenon models can be obtained by means of a reduction process in which the main model components are identified through an abstraction mechanism together with the interactions among components. According to the CAN model it is possible to simulate a two-level evolutionary process in which the local cellular interaction rules evolve together with cellular automata connections.

The first version of the model allowed to simulate phenomena composed exclusively by CA component; a novel version CAN2 [4] extends the CAN model allowing for the introduction of global operators as possible nodes of a CAN network.

As in CAN model, it is possible to simulate a two-level evolutionary process according to two different transition step types: a *micro transition*, i.e. the cellular automaton component step; and a *macro transition*, i.e. the whole time step network evolution.

The presence of global operators is necessary when an external influence, to the macroscopic complex phenomena, assumes a control role and allows for expressing any mechanism that could not be expressed in terms of local interaction. Furthermore these mechanisms could not influence the evolution of the phenomenon.

In some cases the introduction of global operators could be useful. Such cases includes: the derivation of **statistics** on the system, i.e. average on global characteristics, or **approximation accuracy,** deriving approximation between the modelled phenomenon and the real one, or **global controls.**

The presence of global operators, introducing another different computational unit, allows to define a renewed CAN model [5] i.e. CAN2 [4]. The original version limits each component to be a a cellular automaton.

According to the network abstraction, a precedence relation must be introduced between each component of the model if some components use variables owned by other ones. More explicitly: a precedence relation, between a global operator and a cellular automaton, occurs if a global operator accesses a state/s values of the cellular automaton; or in an opposite direction a cellular automaton accesses a global variable values, defined in a global operator. A correspondent relation can be derived between cellular automata themselves and global operators themselves, when they access respectively states and global variables.

A network of cellular automata can be represented as a graph, the CAN precedence graph, Figure 2, where:

- nodes represent cellular automata or global operators, and
- edges represent precedence relations between nodes.

Let us now explain with an example the concepts above.

For instance, let **N** be a network composed by three nodes N_1, N_2 and N_3; where respectively N_1, N_2 are cellular automata nodes and N_3 is a global operator.

Let us suppose that: N_1 defines state S_1, N_2 defines state S_2 and N_3 defines global variable **g**. If at each macro step the value S_1 is accessed by N_2 and S_2 is accessed by N_3 the network abstraction, by means of a graph and its precedence relation whose verse is depicted by the dark arrow, is shown in the following figure

Fig. 2. A CAN2 Network abstraction example

4   A Basic CA Based Model for Frustrated Linear JJA

In order to model our physical system some considerations and initialization must be done. In particular different computational approaches can be combined to describe the entire system.

In order to prepare the initial CA variable and parameter input values is necessary to approach the problem according to PDE tools. For our model we choose, as an example, an array with N=10 plaquettes/junctions; a minimum of two elements must be used in order to capture all the interesting physics of such a system [9,16], but we need a large N in order to better and better fulfill the request of a topological protection against local fluctuations [7,8].

Subsection 4.1 deals with this issue, the following Subsection introduce the CA basic model.

4.1 System Model Characterization

In order to obtain a high level system description some abstractions on the physical system must be done:

- lattice grid: is a linear one with N=10 cells
  - the cell dimension must be well defined in order to achieve a good system discretization. The total length of the array L (i.e. the sum of N=10 cells) is to be defined such that the following condition is true: $L \gg \lambda_j$ (where λ_j is the Josephson penetration length) [16], in order to meet "long" total junction requirement;
  - each cell is identified with a Josephson device node of two junctions of different type, regarding the cell center, identifying a right and a left side;
- boundary condition: the topology is annular
- each cell can be characterized by:
  - cell labeling, to identify each array cell;
  - current (we assume to stay in a stable state);
  - spin features, i.e. pseudospin assuming values (-1 o 1);
  - capacitance (equal for each cell);
  - phase_difference, phase shift, assuming different role according to cell side consideration, left (l) or right side (r), it will result phase_difference_r1, phase_difference_l1, phase_difference_r2, phase_difference_l2 (where 1 and 2 are the two possible ground states);
  - a frustration single sawtooth magnetic pulse B.

At the staring point the phases differences are initialized as follows:
The corresponding cell is related to the junctions as follows:
1. odd cells presents 0 junctions to its left and π type at its right
2. even cells presents π type junctions to its left and 0 at its right

At the system definition stage the mapping between cells and initial phase differences can be assigned. In order to explain immediately this mapping we express the relation and correspondence by means of the following table:

Table 1. Mapping between cells and phase differences

phase_difference	even cell	odd cell
r1	0	$+ \pi$
l1	0	$- \pi$
r2	$+ \pi$	0
l2	$- \pi$	0

The phase_differences, in Table 1, obtained after a PDE resolution [16] that involves them, are input values for the corresponding CA model and remain fixed thorough its whole evolution.

The pseudospin state is related to the phase difference behavior: in correspondence to well defined phase difference scheme pseudospinup and pseudospindown are expressed as in the following two tables, table 2 and table 3, for even and odd cells respectively:

Table 2. Mapping for even cells

	phase_diff	pseudospinup	pseudospindown
r1 and l1	0 and + π		X
r2 and l2	0 and - π	X	

Table 3. Mapping for odd cells

	phase_diff.	pseudospinup	pseudospindown
r1 and l1	+ π and 0	X	
r2 and l2	- π and 0		X

This is the initial pseudospin configuration, according to the phase differences above.

4.2 A Basic CA Definition for the System Evolution

According to the consideration in the previous subsection, now we give a formal definition in terms of a CAN2 representation for the basic linear JJA system, under study, as follows:

$$<R,X,S,G,P,Pvar,f,g>$$

- **R** = {x| x $\in$ **N**} is the set of integer points in the finite region, the array, when the system evolves; each point identifies a cell. The lattice grid: is a linear array of with N=10 cells.
- **X**, is the neighborhood set, when it occurs the set includes {x −1,x +1} for each cell x.
- **S**=$S_1 \times S_2 \times S_3 \times S_4$ is the set of state values; it is specified by the cartesian product of the finite sets of values of the three following substates respectively :
  - **Pseudo_S** pseudospin assuming (-1,1) values,
  - **Mp** magnetic pulse for each cell, fixed and invariant for each macro time step.
  - **LABEL** cell label to identify the cell, corresponding to a monotonic enumeration for all cells, itself invariant for each time step.
  - **FLIP** flip state to register if pseudopspin flipping taken.
- **G** is the set of global variables B_{tot} is the total applied magnetic pulse.
- **P** is the finite sets of global constant parameters:
  - **I** current inside the cell
  - **C** capacitance

- **Pvar** is the finite set of CA component variables:
  - **STEP** is the step iterator useful to trigger the evolution.
- **f** $:S \rightarrow S$ is the deterministic state transition for determination of the pseudospin state and values.
- **g:** $S_2 \rightarrow G$ expresses the global operator which controls the total magnetic pulse applied on the system.

In view of the implementation of a system protected form decoherence (see Section 2) boundary condition topology is annular.

In order to have a transition between the two ground states the magnetic pulse period must be related to the CA time step; we have two possibilities:

1. the CA time step is equal to the pulse period, in order to capture the maximum pulse value;
2. the CA time step can be arbitrary, but a pulse value threshold must be chosen.

The first solution is more simple, we adopt this, with a modification.

The flipping procedure between the input and output states implements a tunneling between two ground states which correspond to the physical processes of creation and annihilation of fluxon-antifluxon pairs. In general for N cells, (N\2) double flips are needed to switch from |0> to |1> . In the quantum regime such tunneling processes

```
Operator PULSE
Begin
B_tot := 0
For i := 1 to N
    B_tot := B_tot + Mp(i)
EndFor
If B_tot < N*Mp(1)
            error
EndIF
End
```

```
Function Transition CA
Begin
STEP = STEP + 1
If Mp(i) > 0
    IF (FLIP = 0 and
       (LABEL mod 4) = 0 or
            (LABEL mod 4) = 1))
       IF (Pseudo_S = -1 and

            THEN Pseudo_S = 1

       ELSE
            Pseudo_s = -1
       EndIF
    ELSE
       IF (FLIP = 0 and
          (FLIP (i-1) = 1 or
           FLIP(i+1) = 1)
          IF (Pseudo_S = -1 and
             THEN Pseudo_S = 1
          ELSE
             Pseudo_s = 1
          EndIF
    CALL Function Transition CA
            until STEP not = 2
       EndIF
EndIF
```

Fig. 3. The JJA system components according to a CAN2 vision.

display (N\2)! paths along they can occur. For this reason we choose to use a double step for the CA transition component, with each time step equal to the half of the single sawtooth magnetic pulse period.

The CA component has, as initial condition, the pseudospin configuration obtained in the precedent stage (cfr. Subsection 4.1) since the pseudospin configuration must obey to an antiferromagnetic arrangement and flipping state is zero.

At the initial time, our device is in a steady state, in one of the two possible ground states.

Each parameter is fixed, also the LABEL values are fixed for all transition steps, but the variable STEP is initialized to each macro step T.

The transition function takes into account coupling factor, adding an external frustration, as a single sawtooth magnetic pulse acting on each lattice cell.

The system transition is assumed to be composed by a global operator application followed by a transition function:

$\mathbf{F : S{\times}G{\times}P{\times}Pvar} \rightarrow \mathbf{S{\times}G{\times}Pvar}$ that is the composition of the global operator and transition function of the cellular automata component twice applied.

Let us now describe the system transition, expressed in pseudocode, for the global operator and the transition function as sketched in the boxes of the figure 3.

The net result is the NOT-operator.

5   Conclusions and Future Work

In this paper we describe the first step in building up a model, using the CAN2 computational model, for an elementary "protected" solid state qubit. The adopted boundary conditions allow for obtaining a well defined elementary device: two stable degenerate ground states and the transition between the two ground states. The net result is the NOT operation problem of controlling the amplitude and the relative phase of the superposition between the two ground states will be addressed in a future work. This is the basic building block for the implementation of an ideal quantum computer. For the future we plan to study and simulate the aggregation mechanisms between such basic blocks via CAN2 approach (basic quantum logical gates).

References

1. Aharonov Y., Casher A., Phys.Rev.Lett. 53 (1984), 319.
2. Blanter Y. M, Fazio R., Schon G., Nucl.Phys.B S58 (1997), 79.
3. Blatter G., Geshkenbein V. B., Ioffe L. B., Phys. Rev.Lett. 63 (2001), 174511.
4. Calidonna C.R, The CAN2 model: a CA hybrid model derived by micro and macroscopic complex phenomena empirical observation, submitted to ACRI04.
5. Di Napoli C., Giordano M., Mango Furnari M., Mele F., Napolitano R., "CANL: a Language for Cellular Automata Network Modeling", in Proc. of "Parcella 96" - Seventh International Workshop on Parallel Processing by Cellular Automata and Arrays , Springer Verlag , Berlin, (1996) 16-20.
6. Doucot B., Feigelman M. V., Ioffe L. B., Phys.Rev.Lett. 90 (2003), 100501.
7. Ekert A., Jozsa R., Rev.Mod.Phys. 68 (1996), 733;
8. Galindo A., Martin-Delgado M. A., Rev.Mod.Phys. 74 (2002), 347

9. Goldobin E., Koelle D., Kleiner R., Phys.Rev.B 66 (2002), 100508(R).
10. Kitaev A., Annals pf Physics, 303, (2003), 2.
11. Ioffe L. B., Geshkenbein V. B., Feigelman M. V., Fauchère A. L., Blatter G., Nature 398 (1999), 679.
12. Ioffe L. B., Feigelman M. V., Phys.Rev.B 66, (2002), 224503.
13. Lent S. et al, Quantum Cellular Automata, Nanotechnology 4 (1993) 49.
14. Orlando T. P., Mooij J. E., Tian L., van der Wal C. H., Levitov L. S., Lloyd S., Mazo J. J., Phys.Rev.B 60 (1999), 15398.
15. Petitot J., Centrato/a-Centrato. Enciclopedia Einaudi, vol. 2 Einaudi, Torino, Italy, 894-954. In Italian.
16. Rotoli G., Phys.Rev.B 68 (2003), 052505.
17. Shnirman A., Schon G., Hermon Z., Phys.Rev.Lett. 79 (1997), 2371.
18. T'Hooft G., Can Quantum Mechanics be reconciled with cellular Automata?, Int. Jour. Theor. Phys. 42 (2003), 349.
19. Wen X. G., Niu Q., Phys.Rev.B 41 (1990), 9377.
20. Wen X. G., Phys.Rev.B 44 (1991), 2664.
21. Weimar J.R, Simulation with Cellular Automata, (Logos Verlag, Berlin 1997).
22. Worsch T., Simulation of Cellular Automata, Future Generation Computer Systems 16 (1999), 157.

Cellular Automata Based Encompression Technology for Voice Data*

Chandrama Shaw[1], Pradipta Maji[1], Sourav Saha[1], Biplab K. Sikdar[1],
S. Roy[2], and P. Pal Chaudhuri[3]

[1] Department of Computer Science and Technology,
Bengal Engineering College (DU), Howrah, India 711 103
chandrama_shaw@yahoo.co.in, biplab@cs.becs.ac.in
[2] Department of Computer Sc. and Technology,
Kalyani Government Engineering College, Kalyani, India
samir@kucse.wb.nic.in
[3] Flat E4, Block H30, Murchhana Housing, Kolkata - 94, India
palchau@vsnl.net

Abstract. This paper reports an efficient compression technology for voice data. It is developed around Programmable Cellular Automata (PCA) structure. The program executed on PCA is so designed that it ensures high speed transmission of voice data with desired level of security (encryption). Further, the regular and local neighborhood structure of CA is employed to design high speed low cost implementation of the encompression (encryption + compression) scheme. Comparison with standard GSM (Global System Mobile) technology, in respect of compression ratio, the quality of D'encompressed voice data and the quality of security attained, confirms high potential of the proposed scheme.

1 Introduction

The user community of this cyber age are concerned due to hacker's intrusion into their private messages transmitted as voice data over the public network. Further, the growth of channel bandwidth will always lag behind the demand for transmission of larger volume of voice data from the user community. Efficient and secured voice data transmission demands due attention on following areas:

- an efficient compression technique to reduce the data rate at source,
- an encryption scheme to ensure secured transmission, and
- low cost high speed execution of both the operations.

In this context, we propose an integrated technology referred to as ENCOMPRESSION supporting both ENcryption and COMPRESSION. The objective of this new technology is to ensure high speed secured transmission of voice data with low cost hardware. The major contributions of this research work are:

* This work is supported by AICTE: File No: 8020/RID/TAPTEC-46/2001-2002

P.M.A. Sloot, B. Chopard, and A.G. Hoekstra (Eds.): ACRI 2004, LNCS 3305, pp. 258–267, 2004.

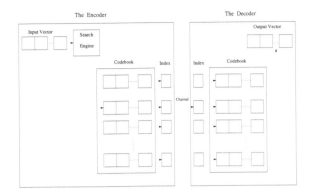

Fig. 1. Encoder and Decoder

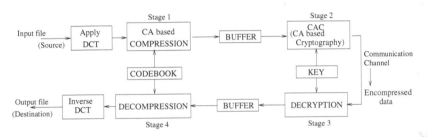

Fig. 2. Basic principle of Encompression

- design of a compression technology for voice data with additional support of security referred to as encompression,
- achieving high speed encompression through hardware implementation,
- design of a VLSI architecture that executes a program on a regulars structure Programmable CA (PCA), to realize the encompression operation.

The compression ratio and quality of encompressed/d'encompressed data are comparable to that of GSM [1], while the security of encompression is comparable to Advanced Encryption Scheme (AES) [2]. An overview of the scheme follows.

2   Overview of Voice Data Encompression

A voice data file, to be compressed, is input in bit serial mode (Fig.2). It is then transformed by DCT (Discrete Cosine Transform) [3]. The transform coefficients are encoded with Cellular Automata (CA) based lossy compression technique (Stage 1). The compressed data enters in streaming mode to Stage 2 and a block (of size same as that of encryption key 'k') gets encrypted with CA based Cryptosystem (CAC). In order to recover the original data, at the receiver end, the encompressed data is first decrypted at Stage 3 and then decoded in Stage 4. The original voice data file is reconstructed through inverse DCT.

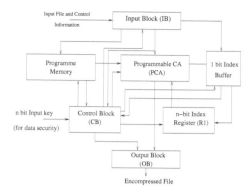

Fig. 3. Architecture of Encompression hardware

2.1   Compression

In the current implementation, the voice data is transformed into frequency domain by DCT. The (lossy) compression of DCT co-efficients is obtained through Vector Quantization (VQ) [4] model. The major components of VQ are -

- An encoder to encode each block of input file with index of a codevector,
- A decoder that retrieves back the representative block from the codebook.

The encoder, as shown in Fig. 1, takes an input vector and outputs the index of the corresponding codevector. The index of the codevector is then sent to the receiver. The decoder, on receiving this index file, replaces each entry with the associated codevector found from the codebook kept in the receiver site. However, the VQ scheme has the inherent drawbacks- difficulty in the generation of codebook to ensure high compression ratio, the high processing overhead at encoding stage.

The proposed CA based design is targeted to overcome the above limitation of VQ. In the current design, rather than developing general compression scheme for any arbitrary class of data files, we concentrate on developing the compression scheme for a specific class of data - that is, voice data. It reduces the problem of designing efficient codebook. We design CA based hierarchical clustering scheme to model the compression operation at each node of VQ binary tree. A set of CA organized as a binary tree is generated. The tree is equivalent to the traditional codebook of VQ in the sense that the centroid of a leaf node cluster represents a codevector.

2.2   Encryption

The encryption process employs a series of reversible CA transforms on the compressed data to arrive at the encompressed data file. Four levels of CA transforms are employed to achieve the desired level of security [5,6]. The operations of CA based voice encompression are realized with a PCA program (Section 5). The architecture is shown in Fig. 3. The CA theory relevant for the work follows.

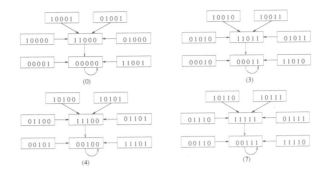

Fig. 4. State transition diagram of a 5-cell MACA $< 102, 60, 204, 204, 170 >$.

3   Cellular Automata (CA)

In a 3-neighborhood dependency, the next state $q_i(t+1)$ of a CA cell $'i'$ depends on itself and on its left and right neighbors, and is denoted as

$$q_i(t+1) = f_i(q_{i-1}(t), q_i(t), q_{i+1}(t)). \qquad (1)$$

$q_i(t)$ represents the state of the ith cell at t^{th} instant of time. $'f_i'$ is the next state function, called rule $\mathcal{R}_i$. There are 2^{2^3} i.e., 256 possible rules. Out of 256 rules, 14 employ XOR/XNOR logic. The CA employing only such rules is called linear/additive CA. In CA based Cryptosystem (CAC), we use reversible linear/additive, and non-linear CA. However, for CA based model of VQ we employ a non-reversible linear CA referred to as MACA.

3.1   Multiple Attractor CA (MACA)

An MACA consists of a number of cyclic and non-cyclic states. The set of non-cyclic states forms trees rooted at the cyclic states. A cyclic state with self loop is referred to as attractor. Fig. 4 depicts the state transition diagram of a 5-cell MACA with four attractors {00000(0), 00011(3), 00100(4), 00111(7)}. The states of a tree rooted at the cyclic state α forms the α-basin. A few fundamental results of MACA are next noted from [7,8].

Defn: An m-bit field of an n-bit pattern set is said to be pseudo-exhaustive if all possible 2^m patterns appear in the set.

Theorem 1. *In an n-cell MACA with $k = 2^m$ attractors, there exists m-bit positions at which the attractors generate pseudo-exhaustive 2^m patterns.*

Theorem 2. *The modulo-2 sum of two states is a predecessor of 0-state (pattern with all 0) if and only if the two states lie in the same attractor basin.*

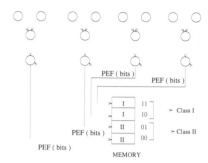

Fig. 5. MACA based pattern clustering strategy

Example. Consider an attractor {00011} and the states {01010, 01011} of the attractor basin. The module-2 sum of the two patterns is {00001} which is a state of 0-basin (Fig. 4).

If a pair of patterns $(\mathcal{P},\tilde{\mathcal{P}})$ fall in a basin of an MACA, the pattern $\mathcal{P}'(= \mathcal{P} \oplus \tilde{\mathcal{P}})$ falls in the 0-basin Theorem 2. $\mathcal{P}'$ is the hamming distance between $\mathcal{P}$ & $\tilde{\mathcal{P}}$.

3.2   MACA for Pattern Clustering

An n-bit MACA with k-attractors can be viewed as a natural cluster (Section 3.1). It distributes a given set of patterns into k distinct groups. The MACA of Fig. 4 can be employed to classify patterns into two clusters. Cluster I is represented by the attractor basins {00100 and 00111} while Cluster II is represented by rest of the basins {00000 and 00011}. As per Theorem 1, the PEF identifies the cluster of a pattern uniquely. The PEF yields the address of the memory that stores the cluster information. Therefore, Cluster I attractors yield the memory addresses {10, 11} while cluster II is identified by the memory addresses {00, 01} (Fig. 5). If the MACA is loaded with an input pattern $\mathcal{P}$ and allowed to run for a number of cycles equal to its depth, it traverses through a number of states and finally reaches to an attractor state. The PEF of that attractor points to the information related to the cluster $\mathcal{P}$ belongs to.

3.3   MACA for Modelling the Conventional Codebook

The MACA based hierarchical clustering technique and the associated hierarchical MACA tree structure (Fig. 6) model a conventional codebook. Each leaf node of the MACA tree represents a cluster of elements - the centroid of this cluster represents a codevector. Binary search for an input vector in the codebook is implemented with the traversal of MACA tree, as illustrated in Fig. 6, till it hits a leaf node. The leaf node represents the best match for the input.

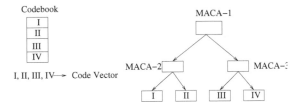

Fig. 6. MACA based hierarchical tree structured pattern clustering technique.

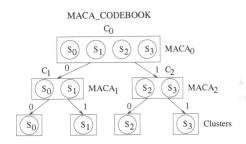

Fig. 7. Structure of MACA based hierarchical clustering scheme

4   CA Based Voice Compression

The MACA based hierarchical clustering scheme is used to design the codebook for lossy compression of voice. The design consists of two steps - design of training set, and generation of codebook.

Training Set: The training set for lossy compression i.e., the 'Wave' files, contains discrete signal value recorded at a sampling frequency of 8KHz. A set of such files are recorded from different speakers. The DCT co-efficients of these sample files, represented as 32-bit floating point numbers, form the training set.

Codebook Generation: Let us consider a codebook is to be generated for the four clusters S_0, S_1, S_2 and S_3 from a training set $C_0 = \{\{S_0\}, \{S_1\}, \{S_2\}, \{S_3\}\}$. At the first level, we generate two clusters $C_1 = \{\{S_0\}, \{S_1\}\}$ and $C_2 = \{\{S_2\}, \{S_3\}\}$ from C_0. An MACA ($MACA_0$) is designed to classify the patterns of C_1 and C_2. The similar process is next repeated for C_1 and C_2 to generate four clusters $\{S_0\}$, $\{S_1\}$ and $\{S_2\}$, $\{S_3\}$ employing two MACA - $MACA_1$ and $MACA_2$ (Fig. 7). A leaf node S_i of the MACA tree is represented by the centroid $\acute{P_i} \in S_i$ of cluster S_i. The MACA tree of Fig. 7 is equivalent to binary VQ tree, representing a codebook.

For test case, we need to identify the codebook entry (i.e., the codeword) closest to the given vector $\acute{P_i}$. At the first stage, the $MACA_0$ is loaded with $\acute{P_i}$ and allowed to run. It returns the desired cluster C_1 or C_2. In next level, $MACA_1$ or $MACA_2$, depending on the results of first stage, is loaded with $\acute{P_i}$ to output the desired cluster S_i and its centroid. The path traversed in MACA tree generates a binary bit string, 0 for left and 1 for right at a node of the tree. For example, 00 represents the leaf node S_0 (Fig. 7). This bit string is the compressed data.

Table 1. Comparison of CA based Voice Compression and GSM

Name of	Compression Ratio		SNR (db)		PSNR (db)		NRMSE	
Voice file	CA	GSM	CA	GSM	CA	GSM	CA	GSM
1.wav	5:1	5:1	10.52	9.13	17.41	14.15	0.30	0.35
2.wav	5:1	5:1	10.43	7.74	17.05	13.25	0.30	0.41
3.wav	5:1	5:1	11.58	8.31	19.13	13.18	0.26	0.38
4.wav	5:1	5:1	11.64	8.79	19.30	13.57	0.26	0.36
7.wav	5:1	5:1	11.49	6.98	18.85	12.68	0.27	0.45

Table 2. Comparative Study of Differential Cryptanalysis for CAC/DES/AES

Input file size (MB)	Avg. Std. Devi^n of XOR distributions for CAC (%)	Avg. Std. Devi^n of XOR distributions for DES (%)	Avg. Std. Devi^n of XOR distributions for AES (%)
1	4.36	31.95	4.2
2	4.30	30.03	4.0
4	4.26	29.05	3.63
6	4.17	28.24	3.62
20	3.59	27.67	3.24

For the experimentation, we have taken samples of 10 male speakers to form the training set. Voice data of 7 other male speakers are used to test the performance of our scheme. A comparison with the GSM [1] algorithm based design in terms of quality of the reconstructed voice, compression ratio, Signal to Noise Ratio (SNR) [9], Peak Signal to Noise Ratio (PSNR) [10] and Normalized Root Mean Square Error (NRMSE) [11] are reported in Table 1. The columns heading 'CA' notes the results of CA based compression scheme, and the heading 'GSM' refers to the performance of GSM. The results of in Table 1 establish that the CA based voice compression achieves higher SNR and comparable speech quality as that of GSM.

5   CA Based Cryptosystem

The details are reported in [6]. A brief overview along with its refinement over that represented in [6], is next provided.

The first level of encryption is a linear transform of the input key and also on plain text, the later one being implemented by rotating each byte of the token. At the second level, an affine transform is introduced with an additive CA [7]. A non-affine transformation is next implemented by employing a non-linear reversible CA [5,6]. Finally, a linear transform (XOR operation) is employed.

The experimental results of Differential cryptanalysis and Shannon's Security Quotient for CAC with the AES [12] and DES [13] are shown in the tables 2 and 3. The results establish that the security level of CAC is better than DES and comparable to AES. Further, the CAC executes faster than the AES (Table 4).

Table 3. Comparative study of Shannon's Security Quotient for CAC/DES/AES

Input file size (MB)	Shannon's Security Quotient (ϑ) of CAC (%)	Shannon's Security Quotient (ϑ) for DES (%)	Shannon's Security Quotient (ϑ) for AES (%)
2	14.1605	14.2374	14.2345
3	11.5527	11.5531	11.5706
7	7.5640	7.9141	7.6014
8	7.1182	7.1468	7.7046
15	5.2097	5.3157	5.5552

Table 4. Comparison of execution time of software version of CAC and AES

Input file size (MB)	AES (in Sec)	CAC (in Sec)
1.06	1.01	0.47
2.78	2.52	1.20
4.46	4.20	2.07
7.68	8.67	4.21
23.76	29.53	14.61

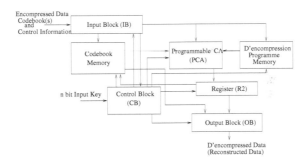

Fig. 8. Architecture of Encompression decoder

6   VLSI Implementation of Encompression Function

The proposed architecture for Encompression, encoder and decoder, are shown in Fig. 3 and Fig. 8. The basic unit of the encoder is Programmable CA (PCA). The encompression function is incorporated in the program stored in the programmed memory. The programmed instruction has the following structure:

– <CA rule vector (Field 1)>, <Number of clock cycles (Field 2)>, <Optional tag field (Field 3)>

The PCA configured with the rule vector (Field 1) runs the specified (Field 2) number of clock cycles. The optional field controls the program flow executing conditional branch. A complete Encompression Program is stored in a

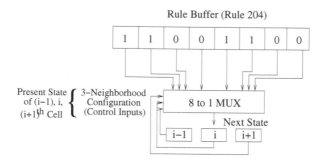

Fig. 9. Universal Programmable CA (UPCA)

programme memory. Each Programme instruction is implemented with the proposed architecture of UPCA (Universal PCA, Fig. 9). A UPCA can be configured with a given rule vector as a linear, additive, and non-linear CA. To execute a program step, the UPCA is configured by the rule vector specified in Field 1 of Programmed instruction. One bit index buffer (Fig. 3) is used to implement the MACA traversal. When the traversal follows next path, the bit value is pushed into the index register. We implement Control Block that generates signals to read the program from memory, to configures the UPCA, and run it for specified cycles.

7   Conclusion

This paper presents a CA based encompression technology of voice data. It ensures efficient transmission of voice data with desired level of security. The modular and cascadable structure of CA provides low cost high speed execution. A hardware architecture has been proposed for VLSI realization of encompression.

References

1. http:\\www.fourmilab.ch \speakfree
2. J. Daemen and V. Rijmen, "Aes proposal: Rijndael;
   http://csrc.nist.gov/encryption/aes/rijndael/rijndael.pdf," June 1998.
3. N. Ahmed, T. Natarajan, K. R. Rao, *"Discrete Cosine Transforms"*, IEEE Trans. Comput. C-23, pp-90-93, Jan 1974.
4. Allen Gresho and Robert M. Gray, *"Vector Quantization and Signal Compression"*, Kluwer Academy Publishers.
5. Subhayan Sen, Chandrama Shaw, Dipanwita Roy Chowdhuri, P Pal Chaudhuri, *"Cellular Automata Based Cryptosystem (CAC)"*, in *Proc.* of 4th *Int. Conf.* on Information and Communications Security (ICICS 2003), Singapore, December 2002.
6. Subhayan Sen, Sk. Iqbal Hossain, Kabirul Islam, Dipanwita Roy Chowdhuri, P Pal Chaudhuri, *"Cryptosystem Designed for Embedded System Security"*, in *Proc.* of 17th *Int. Conf.* on *VLSI* Design, India, pp. 303-314, January 2003.

7. Chaudhuri, P.P., Chowdhury, D.R., Nandi, S., Chatterjee, S.: Additive cellular automata, theory and applications, vol. 1, IEEE Computer Society Press, Los Alamitos, California, No. ISBN-0-8186-7717-1, 1997.

8. Maji, P., Shaw, C., Ganguly, N., Sikdar, B.K., Chaudhuri, P.P.: Theory and Application of Cellular Automata For Pattern Classification. Special issue of Fundamenta Informaticae on Cellular Automata, **58** (2003) 321–354.

9. Lawrence R. Rabiner, Ronald W. Schafer, Digital Processing of Speech Signals. Prentice Hall 1978.

10. Carl Taswell, Speech Compression with cosine and wavelet packet near-best bases, Acoustic, Speech, and Signal Processing, 1996 ICASSP-96. Conference Proceedings. 1996 Vol. 1.

11. S. C. Sivkumar, W. Robertson, W. J. Phillips, On-Line Stablization of Block-Diagonal Recurrent Neural Networks, IEEE Transaction on Neural Networks, Vol. 10, No. 1, Jan. 1999.

12. *www.esat.kuleuven.ac.be/~rijmen/rijndael/rijndael.zip*

13. *ftp://ftp.psy.uq.oz.au/pub/Crypto/DES/libdes-x.xx.tar.gz*

A MCA Motion-Planner for Mobile Robots with Generic Shapes and Kinematics on Variable Terrains

Fabio M. Marchese

Dipartimento di Informatica, Sistemistica e Comunicazione
Università degli Studi di Milano - Bicocca
Via Bicocca degli Arcimboldi 8, I-20126, Milano (Italy)
fabio.marchese@disco.unimib.it

Abstract. In the present work, we describe a fast Motion-Planner for Mobile Robots. Considering robots moving with smoothed trajectories on variable terrains, we have developed an algorithm based on an anisotropic propagation of attracting potentials on a non-Euclidean manifold. The optimal collision-free trajectories are found following the minimum valley of a potential hypersurface embedded in a 4D space. The planner is very flexible: it can be use on a wide class of vehicles with different kinematics and with generic shapes. Because of the latest property, it is also applicable to plan the movements of generic objects (e.g. in assembly workstations in manufacturing industry) as in Piano Mover's problem. Thanks to the underlying Multilayered Cellular Automata (MCA) architecture, it is a distributed approach. This planner turn out to be very fast, allowing to react to the dynamics of the world, evolving toward new solutions every time the environment changes without to be re-initialized.

1   Introduction

The work presented in this paper concerns Mobile Robots Path-Planning exploiting Multilayered Cellular Automata. The Path-planning problem is very important to drive mobile robots avoiding the collisions with obstacles. In our work, we consider robots with different types of kinematics. The realization of a path-planner able to face with different types of motion is quite problematic. Another difficulty arise from the shape of the robot. When a robot moves around obstacles, its real shape and size must be considered to avoid collisions. Most of the work in literature handle this problem substituting the real shape with an equivalent shape, most of the time a circular hull enveloping the robot silhouette. This solution increases the space occupancy of the robot and it is feasible when the robot moves in wide spaces, but not in very cluttered environments. A further complication derives from the space geometry in which the robot is situated. In a flat world, as office-like structured environments, the geometry is quite simple: it is a planar surface (Euclidean 2D space). We want to face different situations, as motion on natural terrains, where the Euclidean metrics is no longer applicable.

P.M.A. Sloot, B. Chopard, and A.G. Hoekstra (Eds.): ACRI 2004, LNCS 3305, pp. 268–277, 2004.

This has an important consequence on the evaluation of the trajectory length, and on the optimality of the solutions: the metric changes from point to point and must be evaluated locally. During the last twenty years, many authors have proposed different solutions, based on geometrical descriptions of the environment (e.g. [7,8]). In the eighties, Khatib in [4] first introduced a new method for the collision avoidance problem in a continuous space for a 6 DOF manipulator robot. This alternative approach is less precise, but more efficient: the Artificial Potential Fields Methods. Jahanbin and Fallside introduced a Wave Propagation algorithm in the discretized Configuration Space (*C-Space*) (*Distance Transform* [3]). Barraquand et al. in 1992 [2] used the Numerical Potential Field technique on the *C-Space* to build a generalized Voronoi Diagram. Zelinsky extended the *Distance Transform* to the *Path Transform* [12]. Pai and Reissel in [10] introduced a Motion Planning algorithm on multiresolution representation of terrains using wavelets. The path finding is based on a variation of Dijkstra's algorithm on a regular 2D lattice. In [5], the authors presented a Path-Planner for outdoor terrain based on the Control Theory and the technique of random trees (RRT). These methods are very precise, but the performances do not allow to use them on real-time systems (about 15 sec to get a path). We used CA as a formalism to merge the grid model of the world (Occupancy Grid) with the *C-Space* of a robot and Numerical (Artificial) Potential Field methods, with the aim to find a simple and fast solution for the path-planning problem for mobile robots with different kinematics. This method uses a directional (anisotropic) propagation of distance values between adjacent automata to build a potential hypersurface embedded in 4D space. Using a constrained version of the descending gradient on the hypersurface, it is possible to find out all the admissible, equivalent and shortest (for a given metric of the discretized space) trajectories connecting two configurations of the robot *C-Space*.

2 Problem Statements

One of the most important types of world models is the Configuration Space [6, 8]. The *C-Space* C of a rigid body is the set of all its configurations $\mathbf{q}$ (i.e. poses). If the robot can freely translate and rotate on a 2D surface, the *C-Space* is a 3D manifold $\mathbb{R}^2 \times \mathbf{SO}(2)$. It can be modelled using a 3D Bitmap $\mathcal{G}C$ (*C-Space Binary Bitmap*), a regular decomposition in cells of the *C-Space*, represented by the application $\mathcal{G}C : C \rightarrow \{0, 1\}$, where 0s represent non admissible configurations. The *C-Potential* is a function $\mathbf{U}(\mathbf{q})$ defined over the *C-Space* that "drives" the robot through the sequence of configuration points to reach the goal pose [2]. Let us introduce some other assumptions: 1) space topology is finite; 2) the robot has a lower bound on the steering radius (non-holonomic vehicle). The latter assumption introduces important restrictions on the types of trajectories to be found.

Cellular Automata are automata distributed on the cells of a Cellular Space $\mathbb{Z}^n$ (a regular lattice) with transition functions invariant under translation: $\mathbf{f}_c(\cdot) = \mathbf{f}(\cdot), \forall c \in \mathbb{Z}^n, \mathbf{f}(\cdot) : \mathbf{Q}^{|A_0|} \rightarrow \mathbf{Q}$, where $\mathbf{c}$ is the coordinate vector identifying a cell, $\mathbf{Q}$ is the set of states of an automaton and $\mathbf{A_0}$ is the set of arcs outgoing from a cell to the neighbors. Robot Path-Planning Problem can be solved with CA in a quite simple way: every cell of the *C-Space Bitmap* $\mathcal{G}C$ is an automaton of a CA. The state of every cell is a vector that contributes to build the *C-Potential* $\mathbf{U(q)}$ through a diffusion mechanism between neighbor cells. The trajectories are found following the minimum valley of the surface $\mathbf{U(q)}$. We used a Multilayered Cellular Automaton [1], where each layer corresponds to a subset of the state vector components. Each subset is evaluated in a single layer and depends on the same attribute of the neighbor cells in the same layer and depends also on the states of the corresponding cell and its neighbors in other layers. In the following section, we describe each layer and the transition function implemented in its cells.

3   Architecture Overview

The Motion-Planner is organized in two major subsystems: an Input Subsystem and an Output Subsystem (Fig. 1.a). They are subdivided in 6 sublayers (4 + 2), some of them are statical and others evolve during the time. The Input Subsystem is thought as an interface with the outside environment. Its layers have to react as fast as possible to the "external" changes: the robot starting pose, the robot goal pose, the elevation map of the terrain and, the most important, the changes of the environment, i.e. the obstacles movements in a dynamic world. The first three layers (*Starting Pose L.*, *Goal Pose L.* and *Terrain L.*) are considered statical, because they are update from the outside at a very low frequency (lower than the internal updating frequency); the *Obstacles L.* is also updated externally, but it evolves testing the movements admissibility as described in section 3.1. In Fig. 1.a, are shown the functional dependencies between layers, and the layers updating order, while in Fig. 1.b, the conceptual hierarchical structure. The Output Subsystem returns the results of the planning, that is the complete set of trajectories from the *Path Extraction L.*, or a single motion step from the *Attraction L.*

3.1   Terrain Layer and Obstacles Layer

The *Terrain Layer* contains the description of the surface on which the robot navigates. It is an elevation map, discretized in correspondence to the cells of the workspace. We consider only 2D continuous (C^1) manifold embedded in a 3D Euclidean space (e.g. Fig. 2.a). On the terrain are placed obstacles the robot has to avoid. The *Obstacles Layer* is used to map both the obstacles and the environmental boundary (Fig. 2.b); the combination of the two layers is shown in Fig. 3. In Regular Decomposition world models, the obstacles are decomposed in cells full or empty (Occupancy Grids) and the robot is often represented as a point (the robot cinematic center) moving from one free cell to a neighbor free one. To take into account of its real extension, the well-known technique of enlarging the obstacles by a given quantity (the robot maximum

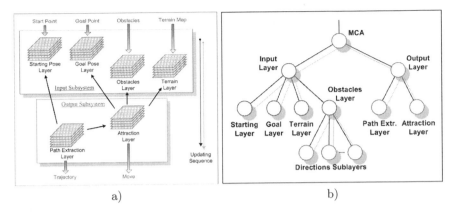

Fig. 1. Layers Architecture: a) layers dependency graph; b) layers hierarchical structure

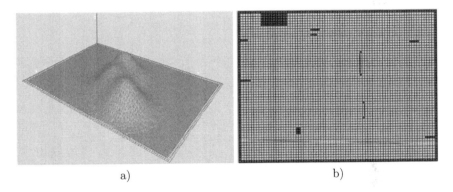

Fig. 2. A simple example of: a) Terrain Layer; b) Obstacles Map Layer

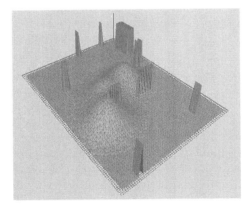

Fig. 3. Combining Terrain and Obstacles Layers

radius) can be used [7]. An anisotropic enlargement [7], i.e. a different obstacle enlargement for each robot orientation, would solve only partially the problem for asymmetric robots: counter-examples can be found where the robot still collides with obstacles due to the sweeping of its silhouette between two consecutive poses (Fig. 4.c). We adopted a different and more precise approach [9] to address this problem, defining a set of admissible robot movements in every cell. The admissibility of each move is influenced: 1) globally, by the specific kinematics of the robot; 2) locally, by the vicinity of an obstacle and by the robot shape. The attribute evaluated in this layer (*Obstacles Attribute*) is a boolean: $Obst_c(\theta, \mu) \in \{True, False\}$, representing the admissibility of each move in each robot pose. Therefore, it is a 4D CA and the transition function is an application: $M \times \mathbb{R}^2 \times \mathbf{SO}(2) \rightarrow \{True, False\}$.

$$Obst_c(\theta, \mu, t+1) = \begin{cases} False \; if \; \exists a \in A_c(\theta, \mu) : \; isObstacle(c + a) \wedge (c + a) \in \mathcal{GC} \\ Obst_c(\theta, \mu, t) \; otherwise \; (keep \; the \; previous \; value) \end{cases}$$

(1)

$\forall t > 0, \forall c \in \mathcal{GC}, \forall \theta \in \mathcal{D}, \forall \mu \in M$, where A_c is the neighborhood of the cell c (e.g. in Fig. 4.d).

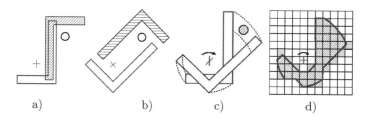

a)   b)   c)   d)

Fig. 4. Silhouette sweeping: a-b) expanded obstacle (hatched) for two robot orientations; c) a counter-example due to a coarse discretization of the orientation; d) a motion sweeping silhouette/cell neighborhood (hatched cells)

As a matter of fact, this layer is decomposed in sublayers, one for each robot orientation and move: it is itself a Multilayered CA on a 2D domain (the space $\mathbb{R}^2$ of positions), as previously shown in Fig. 1.b. It is a particular CA also for another reason: each sublayer has a *non-standard fixed architecture* [11], i.e. the neighborhood does not have the standard square shape. Its shape reflects the motion silhouette of the robot during a movement (sweeping) as in the example of Fig. 4.d. In Fig. 5 is shown the evolution of this layer for a rectangular robot moving in the Occupancy Map of Fig. 3. The grey levels are proportional to the number of admissible moves, ranging from white (all moves are admissible) to black (no move).

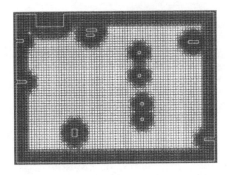

Fig. 5. An example of the *Obstacles Layer* evolution for a rectangular Robot of Fig. 3.a

3.2 Attractive Potentials Layer

This is the core of the entire Path-Planning Algorithm. The *Attraction to Goal Layer* is defined as: $Attr_c(d_{out}) \in \mathbb{N}^8$. It is a vector of eight values corresponding to the eight main directions. It represents the integer distance of the cell c from the Goal cell when the robot moves with the $d_{out} \in D$ direction along a collision free path. It is a digitalized representation of the *C-Potential* function $\mathbf{U}(\mathbf{q})$ defined on the *C-Space Bitmap*. To evaluate the path length, we have introduced a set of costs (called *metric*) for the basic robot movement: (*forward, forward_diagonal, direction_change, stop, rotation, lateral, backward, backward_diagonal*). These basic movements are combined in different ways to obtain different robots kinematics. It is not a metric in the mathematical sense: it has been called metric because it defines the procedure to evaluate the trajectory length in the space. The robot can be subjected to non-holonomic constraints, therefore not every movements can be done (e.g. car-like vehicle). To face with different kinematics, we have introduced a subset of admissible moving directions $D'(c,d) \subseteq D$ depending on the robot position (cell c) and orientation d compiled off-line on the base of the robot kinematics. Given the configuration (c,d), the robot can arrive with a move μ to a configuration $(\gamma, \delta), \forall \gamma \in I'_c(d), \forall \delta \in D'(\gamma, d)$, where $I'_c(d) \subseteq I_c$ is the subset of neighbor cells reachable from the configuration (c,d), and $D'(\gamma, d) \subseteq D$ is the subset of admissible orientations at the destination cell. The transition function is defined as follows:

$$Attr(c,d,t+1) = \begin{cases} 1 & if\ c = goal\_cell \wedge d = final\_direction \\ MinAttr(c,d,\mu,t) & if\ \exists \mu \in M : \neg Obst_\mu(c,d,t) \wedge \\ & \wedge\ Attr(c,d,t) \neq MinAttr(c,d,\mu,t) \\ Attr(c,d,t) & otherwise \end{cases}$$

(2)

$\forall t > 0, \forall c \in \mathcal{GC}, \forall d \in D$, where:
$MinAttr(c,d,\mu,t) \quad = \quad \min_{\forall \mu \in M} \{Attr(\gamma(\mu), \delta(\mu),t) + Cost_\mu(c,d)\}$ and $Cost_\mu(\cdot,\cdot)$ is the length/cost of the move μ from the current configuration (c,d) to the next configuration (γ, δ), and $Obst_\mu(c,d,t)$ is the admissibility

value of the same move generated in the Obstacle Layer. Changing the metric (movement costs), we can realize robots with different types of kinematics. For example, the kinematics $(2, 3, 1, 0, High, High, High, High)$ emulates a car-like kinematics moving only forward (Dubin's vehicle), while the kinematics $(2, 3, 1, 0, High, High, 2, 3)$ emulates a common car-like kinematics moving also backward (Reed's and Shepp's vehicle). A robot also translating in any direction (omnidirectional) has a kinematics like: $(2, 3, 1, 0, 1, 2, 2, 3)$. Two main properties can be demonstrated: the termination of the propagation and the absence of local minima. The later property is very important: it is possible to achieve the goal (the global minimum) just following the negated gradient vector without stalling in a local minimum. The cost function $Cost_\mu(\cdot, \cdot)$ up to now was depending exclusively on the move μ $(cost(\mu))$. The admissibility of the move μ was depending only on the robot pose (c, d), because of the presence of the obstacles distributed around the robot. This is correct on a flat environment (Euclidean space), where the distance between cells does not depend on the position (the space metric is constant), but it is not correct any more for variable terrains, where there is a vertical component too. In this case, the cost must depend on the 3D distance between points on the surface, i.e. on the difference of elevation between two consecutive positions: it is necessary to include the gradient of the surface in the cost function. To make a fast computation, it is usual to approximate the gradient value with the absolute difference, thus obtaining: $Cost_\mu(c, d) = cost(\mu) + |\ Elev(c, d) - Elev(\gamma(\mu), \delta(\mu))\ |$, where the first term is the horizontal component and second is the vertical component of the displacement. The graphical representation of the potential hypersurface (4D) built over the terrain surface is quite difficult. To realize its aspect, we must project it from the 4D space to a 3D space, obtaining the skeleton laying on the hypersurface, which gives an approximate idea of its topology [9]. This skeleton is a tree, with the root in the goal cell, and where the links are the admissible robot movements that connect one cell to each other.

4   Algorithm Properties

This algorithm has the advantage of being computable in an asynchronous way: there is no specific evaluation order of the cells in each layer. Another important property is related to the consistency of the solution found. For a given terrain surface, the solution found (if it exists) is the set of all shortest paths that connect the starting cell to the goal cell. The CA evolution can be seen as a motion from one point to another point of the global state space until an optimal solution is reached. This is a convergence point for the given problem or a steady global state. If we make some perturbations, such as changing the environment (e.g. moving an obstacle) or changing the goal cell, then the point becomes unstable and the CA starts to evolve again towards a new steady state, finding a new set of optimal trajectories. This property is called *Incremental Updating*. The CA spontaneously evolves to a new steady state from the previous one, without to

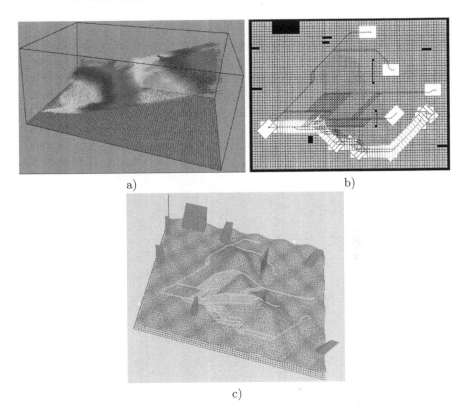

Fig. 6. An example with a car-like kinematics: a) Attraction Potentials Hypersurface (3D skeleton); b) Paths projected on the 2D robot workspace; c) Trajectories on the elevation map

be reset and re-initialized, therefore realizing a *Reactive Path-Planner*: a path-planner that reacts to external changes.

5   Experimental Results

We have generated some synthetic elevation maps and introduced an obstacle distribution to observe the algorithm behavior. An interesting property of this algorithm is the simultaneous computation of trajectories from more than one starting position. We exploit this property to show multiple problems in the same environment. In the example of Fig. 6, the terrain has a group of three "hills" in the middle, and we consider five different starting points of the robot and one goal (bottom-left). From any position, the robot tries to move around the hills, unless the shortest path is to pass over the hills (in any case, at the minimum elevation). In Fig. 7 an U-shaped robot, with omnidirectional kinematics, has to be inserted around an obstacle, with three possible starting positions. To avoid obstacle collision, it has to maneuver around the obstacles in the narrow passages

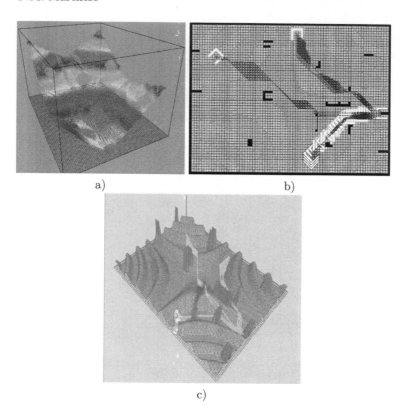

a)   b)

c)

Fig. 7. An example with an omnidirectional kinematics: a) Attraction Potentials Hypersurface (3D skeleton); b) Paths 3D Skeleton; c) Paths projected on the 2D robot workspace; d) Trajectories on the elevation map

to arrive correctly aligned to the final position. In this case, the problem is quite constrained due to the obstacles next to the goal, and quite close to each other.

The performance tests, carried out with an Intel Pentium IV 2.26 GHz PC, gave the following results: 0.18 s (Fig. 6); 0.89 s (Fig. 7). These mean times are evaluated over 100 iterated experiments for each problem and include the initialization phase of each test. The complexity of a path-planning algorithm is always strictly related to the obstacles distribution. It is quite impossible to evaluate it because of the huge number of possible situations. We can find only a good upper-bound estimate. In the worst cases, the longest paths cover nearly $1/2$ of the total number of cells N of the *Workspace Bitmap*, and require nearly $2\frac{N}{2}N$ cells updates to be computed. Thus a realistic upper-bound of the complexity is $O(N^2)$. Taking into account the obstacles enlargement, the result is even better since the number of free cells is lower.

6 Conclusions

In this paper we have described a solution to the Path-Planning Problem for a Mobile Robot with a generic shape (user defined) with a generic kinematics on variable (regular) terrains with a Cellular Automata approach. Some properties of this work can be highlighted: 1) CA is a good formalism when Decomposition Models (as Occupancy Grids) are used to represent the environment; 2) it is complete: it generates all the collision-free trajectories (or determines if no solution exists); 3) the algorithm is quite flexible and can be used with different types of kinematics (just changing a set of weights) and with robots of different shapes on variable terrains; 4) it is reactive: it is fast enough to allow an incremental updating of the trajectories every time environment changes are detected by the sensors.

References

1. Bandini S., Mauri G., Multilayered cellular automata, *Theoretical Computer Science*, **217** (1999), 99-113
2. Barraquand J., Langlois B., Latombe J. C., Numerical Potential Field Techniques for Robot Path Planning, *IEEE Trans. on Systems, Man and Cybernetics*, Vol. **22**, No. 2 (Mar 1992), 224-241
3. Jahanbin M. R., Fallside F., Path Planning Using a Wave Simulation Technique in the Configuration Space in Ccro J. S., Artificial Intelligence in Engineering: Robotics and Processes, Computational Mechanics Publications (Southampton 1988)
4. Kathib O. Real-time Obstacle Avoidance for Manipulator and Mobile Robots, *Proc. of Int. Conf. on Robotics and Automation* (1985)
5. Kobilarov M., Sukhatme G. S., Time Optimal Path Planning on Outdoor Terrain for Mobile Robots under Dynamic Constraints, *Proc. of IEEE/RSJ Int. Conf. on Intelligent Robots and Systems* (2004)
6. Latombe J. C., Robot Motion Planning, Kluwer Academic Publishers, Boston, MA (1991)
7. Lozano-Pérez T., Wesley M. A., An Algorithm for Planning Collision-Free Paths Among Polyhedral Obstacles, *Comm. of the ACM*, Vol. **22**, No. 10, (Oct 1979), 560-570
8. Lozano-Pérez T., Spatial Planning: A Configuration Space Approach, *IEEE Trans. on Computers*, Vol. **C-32**, No. 2 (Feb 1983), 108-120
9. Marchese F. M., A Path-Planner for Generic-shaped Non-holonomic Mobile Robots, *Proc. of European Conf. on Mobile Robots (ECMR 2003)*, Radziejowice (P), (Sept 2003)
10. Pai D. K., Reissell L. M., Multiresolution Rough Terrain Motion Planning, *IEEE Transactions on Robotics and Automation*, **14**(1), (Feb 1998), 19-33
11. Sipper M., Evolution of Parallel Cellular Machines - The Cellular Programming Approach, LNCS **1194**, Springer (1997)
12. Zelinsky A., Using Path Transforms to Guide the Search for Findpath in 2D, *Int. J. of Robotics Research*, Vol. **13**, No. 4 (Aug 1994), 315-325

Simulation of the Dynamics of Pulsed Pumped Lasers Based on Cellular Automata

J.L. Guisado[1], F. Jiménez-Morales[2], and J.M. Guerra[3]

[1] Centro Universitario de Mérida, Universidad de Extremadura,
06800 Mérida (Badajoz), Spain.
jlguisado@unex.es
[2] Departamento de Física de la Materia Condensada, Universidad de Sevilla,
P.O.Box 1065, 41080 Sevilla, Spain.
jimenez@us.es
[3] Departamento de Optica, Facultad de CC. Físicas,
Universidad Complutense de Madrid, 28040 Madrid, Spain.
jmguerra@fis.ucm.es

Abstract. Laser dynamics is traditionally modeled using differential equations. Recently, a new approach has been introduced in which laser dynamics is modeled using two-dimensional Cellular Automata (CA). In this work, we study a modified version of this model in order to simulate the dynamics of pulsed pumped lasers. The results of the CA approach are in qualitative agreement with the outcome of the numerical integration of the laser rate equations.

1 Introduction

A laser device generates or amplifies electromagnetic radiation based on the phenomenon of stimulated emission. It is basically composed of:

1. A *laser medium*: an appropriate collection of atoms, molecules, ions or a semiconductor crystal (we will refer to these elements in general as "atoms").
2. A *pumping process* that excites electrons from those atoms to upper energy levels, due to some external electrical, optical or chemical energy source.
3. *Optical feedback elements* that reflects repeatedly the radiation beam into the laser medium (in a laser oscillator), or allow it to pass only once through it (in a laser amplifier).

The working principle of laser is *stimulated emission*: an excited atom can decay to a lower state stimulated by the presence of a photon with energy equal to the difference between the two energy levels, emitting a second photon with the same frequency and propagating in the same direction. The process of absorption has the same probability, so stimulated emission dominates only when a *population inversion* is induced in the material by some pumping mechanism.

A simplified but still realistic model of many real lasers is the four-level laser system shown in Fig. 1. The population dynamics of a laser (the variation with

P.M.A. Sloot, B. Chopard, and A.G. Hoekstra (Eds.): ACRI 2004, LNCS 3305, pp. 278–285, 2004.

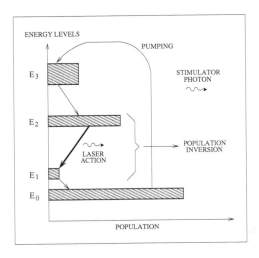

Fig. 1. Schematic view of a four-level laser system.

time in the number of laser photons and in the population inversion, or number of electrons in the upper laser level minus the number of electrons in the lower laser level) is usually described as a system of coupled differential equations called *laser rate equations*.

The rate equations can be put in its simplest form in the case in which the life times of electrons in levels E_1 and E_3 are negligible compared to the life time of electrons in level E_2. Then the electron population of level E_1 is $N_1 \simeq 0$, so the population inversion is approximately equal to the upper laser level population $N(t) = N_2(t) - N_1(t) \simeq N_2(t)$; and the absorption of laser photons by electrons at level E_1 is negligible. Additionally, the pumping into level E_2 can be described by a simple pumping rate R, which is constant for many lasers. For a pulsed laser, the pumping is time dependent, $R \equiv R(t)$.

Under these assumptions, we can take into account only levels E_0 and E_2, and write a simplified form of the laser rate equations including the spontaneous emission process, which is still realistic to describe some dynamic laser behavior -such as relaxation oscillations or gain switching-, as [1,2]:

$$\frac{dn(t)}{dt} = K\,N(t)\,n(t) - \frac{n(t)}{\tau_c} + \varepsilon\frac{N(t)}{\tau_a} \tag{1}$$

$$\frac{dN(t)}{dt} = R(t) - \frac{N(t)}{\tau_a} - K\,N(t)\,n(t) \tag{2}$$

Equation (1) gives the variation with time on the number of laser photons, $n(t)$, which is related to the laser beam intensity. The first term on its right hand side, $+KN(t)n(t)$, represents the increasing on the number of photons by stimulated emission (K is the coupling constant between radiation and the population inversion). The next term, $-n(t)/\tau_c$, introduces the decaying process of laser photons inside the cavity and τ_c is the decay time of the laser photons. The term $+\varepsilon N(t)/\tau_a$ represents the spontaneous emission process, where ε is the fraction of inversion decay processes which are radiative and for which the emited photon has the same frequency and direction of the laser radiation and τ_a is the decay time of the population inversion. This contribution was not taken into account in our previous study [3]. Here, this term has been taken into account in order to get more precise results and to be able to integrate the differential equations (1) and (2) with the initial conditions $n(0) = N(0) = 0$, because otherwise the solution for the number of photons is always $n(t) = 0$.

Equation (2) represents the temporal variation of the population inversion, $N(t)$. The term $+R(t)$ introduces the pumping of electrons with a pumping rate R to the upper laser level. The term $-N(t)/\tau_a$ represents the decaying process of the population inversion with the characteristic time τ_a. Finally, the product term $-KN(t)n(t)$ accounts for the decreasing of the population inversion by stimulated emission.

In this work, the dynamics of a pulsed pumped laser is explored. We suppose that the pumping has a pulsed form of width $2t_p$ which is greater than the life time τ_a of the population inversion. The time dependence of the pumping rate that has been used is:

$$R(t) = \begin{cases} R_m \ \phi(t); & 0 < t < 2t_p \\ 0; & t < 0, t > 2t_p \end{cases} \tag{3}$$

where R_m is the maximum value of the pumping rate at the time t_p and

$$\phi(t) = \frac{1}{2} \left[1 - \cos(\frac{\pi t}{t_p})\right] \tag{4}$$

The value of $R(t)$ is represented in Figure 2 with the legend "Pumping".

The purpose of this work is the study of the CA approach to model the dynamics of pulsed lasers and the comparison with the results obtained by the corresponding laser rate equations.

2 CA Model

We have recently introduced a CA model for simulating laser dynamics, which is described in reference [3]. Further details are discused in references [4,5]. This CA laser model has a similar nature to other models which have been used to describe different reactive phenomena, such as the Belousov-Zhabotinsky reaction [6] or the population dynamics of prey-predator systems [7]. In order to simulate the behavior of pulsed pumped lasers, two main modifications from the original model have been introduced in this work:

i) The pumping probability here is time dependent, whereas in the original model it was constant.

ii) The spontaneous emission process is associated with the decaying of the population inversion. This is more realistic than in the original model, where this was introduced as a random level of noise photons.

The laser system is modeled by a 2-dimensional square lattice of 400×400 cells with periodic boundary conditions. The lattice represents a simplified model of the laser cavity.

2.1   States of the Cells

Two variables $a_i(t)$ and $c_i(t)$ are associated to each node of the lattice. The first one, $a_i(t)$, represents the state of the electron in node i at a given time t. An electron in the laser ground state takes the value $a_i(t) = 0$, while an electron in the upper laser state takes the value $a_i(t) = 1$. A temporal variable $\tilde{a}_i(t) \in \{0, 1, 2, ..., \tau_a\}$ is also introduced, in order to take into account the finite time, τ_a, that an electron can remain in the upper state. If the electron is in the base state $\tilde{a}_i(t) = 0$, otherwise $\tilde{a}_i(t + 1) = \tilde{a}_i(t) + 1$ until the maximum value τ_a is reached and then $\tilde{a}_i(t + 1) = 0$.

The second variable $c_i(t) \in \{0, 1, 2, ..., M\}$ represents the number of photons in node i at time t. A large enough upper value of M is taken to avoid saturation of the system. There is also another temporal variable, $\tilde{c}_i^j(t) \in \{0, 1, 2, ..., \tau_c\}$, which measures the amount of time since a photon $j \in \{1, 2, ..., M\}$ was created at node i. τ_c is the life time of each photon. For a given photon j, $\tilde{c}_i^j(t + 1) = \tilde{c}_i^j(t) + 1$ until the life time τ_c is reached and then $\tilde{c}_i^j(t + 1) = 0$.

2.2   Neighborhood

The *Moore neighborhood* has been used. Nine neighbors are taken into account to compute the transition rules of any given cell: the cell itself, its four nearest neighbors and the four next neighbors.

2.3   Transition Rules

The transition rules determine the state of any particular cell of the system at time $t + 1$ depending on the state of the cells included in its neighborhood at time t. The evolution of the temporal variables $\tilde{a}_i(t)$ and $\tilde{c}_i^j(t)$ was described beforehand. Here we describe only the evolution of $a_i(t)$ and $c_i(t)$.

- **R1.** If $a_i(t) = 0$ then

$$a_i(t + 1) = 1 \qquad \text{with probability } \lambda(t)$$

where $\lambda(t) = \lambda_m \, \phi(t)$ and λ_m is the maximum value of the pumping probability $\lambda(t)$.

- **R2.** If $a_i(t) = 1$ and $\Gamma_i(t) = \sum_{neighbors} c_i(t) > \delta$ then

$$\begin{cases} c_i(t+1) = c_i(t) + 1 \\ a_i(t+1) = 0 \end{cases}$$

where Γ_i is the number of photons included in the neighborhood of the cell i, and δ is a threshold value, which has been taken to be 1 in our simulations.

- **R3.** If $c_i(t) > 0$ and there is one photon j for which $\tilde{c}_i^j(t) = \tau_c$ then

$$c_i(t+1) = c_i(t) - 1$$

- **R4.** If $a_i(t) = 1$ and $\tilde{a}_i(t) = \tau_a$ then

$$\begin{cases} a_i(t+1) = 0 \\ c_i(t+1) = c_i(t) + 1 \qquad \text{with probability } \theta \end{cases}$$

These transition rules represent the different physical processes at the microscopical level in a laser system. Rule **R1** represents the probabilistic electron pumping process. Rule **R2** models the stimulated emission: if the electronic state of a cell has a value of $a_i(t) = 1$ and the number of laser photons in the neighborhood is greater than a certain threshold, then at the time $t+1$ a new photon will be created in that cell and the electron will decay to the ground level. Rule **R3** represents the photon decay. Rule **R4** represents the electron decay in a similar way to rule **R3**: after a time τ_a of the excited electrons, these electrons will decay to the ground level. This rule represents both radiative and non-radiative processes: a fraction θ of the electron decay processes involves creating a new photon in the same cell. This models the spontaneous emission with a probability θ. As in an ideal four level laser the population of level E_1 is negligible, stimulated absorption has not been considered.

3   Results

The expected behaviour of a pulsed pumped laser can be otained by integration of the differential equations (1) and (2). The initial conditions that have been used are: $n(0) = N(0) = 0$ and the values of the parameters are: $\tau_a = 45$, $\tau_c = 3$, $\varepsilon = 10^{-5}$, $K = 6 \cdot 10^{-6}$. The pumping pulse parameters are: $R_m = 8000$, $t_p = 2000$. Here τ_a, τ_c and t_p are measured in *time steps*, K and R_m in $(time\ steps)^{-1}$.

In this study, the values of τ_a, τ_c and t_p have been chosen so that τ_a and τ_c are much smaller than t_p. In this regime, usually referred to as *quasistationary pumped laser*, the solutions of the differential equations consist of a laser emission pulse which follows the pumping pulse, and essentially no relaxation oscillations appear. Figure 2 shows the results obtained by the integration of equations (1)

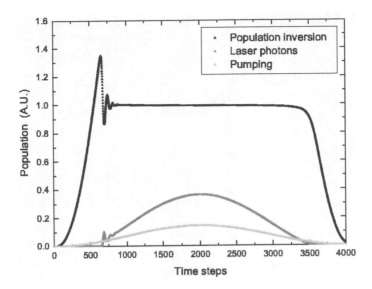

Fig. 2. Evolution of the system obtained by numerical integration of the differential equations, using the values of the parameters indicated in the text. The y-axis values have been normalized relative to the population inversion of the central plateau. The curve with the legend "Pumping" is the value of $R(t)$.

and (2). In the initial phase, the population inversion $N(t)$ increases in response to the pumping, but until a threshold pumping is reached, stimulated emission is not important and very few laser photons are created. When this threshold is reached, the laser process is activated and the number of laser photons $n(t)$ starts to increase. When the pumping is over the threshold value, stimulated emission reduces the population inversion, so $N(t)$ reaches a maximum. After that, in the differential equations solutions $N(t)$ reaches a stable value and $n(t)$ increases towards a maximum, to decrease again, following the pumping pulse. Finally, when the pumping decreases down the threshold value, stimulated emission is no longer important so $n(t)$ decays to zero. After that, $N(t)$ decreases following the tail in the pumping, to reach a zero value when the pumping falls to zero.

For pulsed pumped lasers the dynamics of $n(t)$ and $N(t)$ are strongly dependent on the pumping function $R(t)$. So in order to compare the output of the laser rate equations with the CA we must stress that the pumping process has a probabilistic nature following rule **R1** for the CA, whereas for the laser rate equations the pumping is a smooth function. Then a comparison between both outputs should be made only from a qualitative point of view, because the pumping is not exactly the same.

A typical result by the CA simulation is shown in Figure 3. For this simulation $\lambda_m = 0.1$ and $\theta = 0.01$. Initially there is no laser photon and all

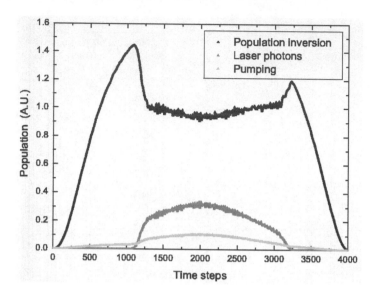

Fig. 3. Evolution of the system obtained by running a simulation using the cellular automata model, for values of the parameters equivalent to those of Figure 2. The y-axis values have been normalized relative to the population inversion of the central plateau. The curve with the legend "Pumping" is the number of electron cells which are pumped by rule **R1** in each time step.

the atoms are in the ground state ($a_i(0) = 0$, $c_i(0) = 0$). The results of the CA simulation reproduce in a qualitative way the behavior exhibited by the solutions of the differential equations. It is remarkable that the CA model reproduces the plateau in the population inversion, which is one of the main features predicted by the equations: after the laser is above threshold, the population inversion remains approximately constant. Another feature which is reproduced by the CA model is the peak in the population inversion when the threshold pumping is reached. A similar -but smaller- peak appears in the CA simulation in the phase in which the pumping is decreasing, after the pumping threshold is surpassed. This peak does not appear in the equations solutions, but has a direct physical interpretation: after the stimulated emission decays to zero, it doesn't contribute to reduce the population inversion, so there is a net increase in $N(t)$, until it decreases again due to the fall in the pumping.

Finally we have found that the results from the integration of equations (1) and (2) are not very sensitive on the values of the parameter ε. By running different simulations changing the value of the equivalent parameter in the CA model (θ), it can be observed that the results are not very sensitive on this value either, in good agreement with the differential equations behavior.

4 Conclusions

Cellular automata models like the one used in this work have an interesting heuristic nature, which helps to understand the physical phenomena being modeled, in a more direct way than the differential equations [8,9]. In addition, this kind of models can be useful as an alternative modeling tool for laser dynamics when numerical difficulties arise, for example in lasers governed by stiff differential equations, with convergence problems. Due to their intrinsic parallel nature, they can be implemented in parallel computers and offer a great advantage in computing time [10,11].

In this work, we report a work in progress involving modifications in a previously introduced cellular automata model of laser dynamics, in order to simulate pulsed pumped lasers. We have compared the results obtained by the numerical integration of the laser rate equations for a quasistationary pulsed pumping, with those resulting from a simulation by a cellular automata model of this type of laser. The results of the CA model reproduce in a qualitative way the behavior exhibited by the numerical integration of the equations. After these preliminary results, more work will be done in order to compare both results in a more quantitative way.

References

1. A.E. Siegman. *Lasers.* University Science Books, 1986.
2. O. Svelto. *Principles of lasers.* Plenum Press, 1989.
3. J.L. Guisado, F. Jiménez-Morales, and J.M. Guerra. A cellular automaton model for the simulation of laser dynamics. *Phys. Rev. E,* 67:066708, 2003.
4. J.L. Guisado, F. Jiménez-Morales, and J.M. Guerra. Application of shannon's entropy to classify emergent behaviors in a simulation of laser dynamics. In T.E. Simos, editor, *Computational Methods in Sciences and Engineering 2003,* pages 213–216, Singapore, 2003. World Scientific.
5. J.L. Guisado, F. Jiménez-Morales, and J.M. Guerra. Computational simulation of laser dynamics as a cooperative phenomenon. *Physica Scripta,* to appear.
6. Barry F. Madore and Wendy L. Freedman. Computer simulations of the Belousov-Zhabotinsky reaction. *Science,* 222(4624):615–616, 1983.
7. S. Bandini and R. Casati. A cellular automata approach to the simulation of a prey-predator system of mites. In Stefania Bandini and Giancarlo Mauri, editors, *ACRI '96, Proceedings of the Second Conference on Cellular Automata for Research and Industry,* pages 135–146. Springer, 1997.
8. B. Chopard and M. Droz. *Cellular automata modeling of physical systems.* Cambridge University Press, 1998.
9. T. Toffoli and N. Margolus. *Cellular automata machines: a new environment for modelling.* The MIT Press, 1987.
10. P.M.A. Sloot, J.A. Kaandorp, A.G. Hoekstra, and B.J. Overeinder. Distributed simulation with cellular automata: architecture and applications. In J. Pavelka, G. Tel, and M. Bartošek, editors, *SOFSEM'99: Theory and Practice of Informatics,* volume 1725 of *Lecture Notes on Computer Science,* pages 203–248, 1999.
11. D. Talia. Cellular processing tools for high-performance simulation. *IEEE Computer,* 33(9):44–52, September 2000.

Surface Roughening in Homoepitaxial Growth: A Lattice Gas Cellular Automaton Model

A. Gerisch[1], A.T. Lawniczak[2], R.A. Budiman[3], H. Fukś[4], and H.E. Ruda[5]

[1] FB Mathematik und Informatik, Martin-Luther-Universität Halle-Wittenberg,
06099 Halle (Saale), Germany, `gerisch@mathematik.uni-halle.de`
[2] Dept. of Mathematics and Statistics, University of Guelph,
Guelph, ON N1G 2W1, Canada
[3] Dept. of Mechanical and Manufacturing Engineering, University of Calgary,
Calgary, AL T2N 1N4, Canada
[4] Dept. of Mathematics, Brock University St. Catharines, ON L2S 3A1, Canada
[5] Dept. of Materials Science and Engineering, University of Toronto,
Toronto, ON M5S 3E3, Canada

Abstract. We study the structural evolution of a growing thin film on time scales in the order of seconds and even minutes. This requires solving the problem of bridging large time and length scale gaps in simulating atomistic processes during thin film deposition. We describe a new simulation approach inspired by lattice gas cellular automata to address this problem. The approach is based on a discrete description of atoms so that the unit length scale coincides with the atomic diameter. For homoepitaxial thin film deposition, the local driving force is the propensity of an atom to establish as many chemical bonds as possible to the underlying substrate atoms when it executes surface diffusion. The interaction between atoms is defined using a coarse-grained approach to boost the computation speed without heavily sacrificing the atomistic details. Simulation results of Si layers deposited on a Si(001) substrate are presented.

1 Introduction

Epitaxial thin film deposition represents a system that has a large number of degrees of freedom. Per unit centimetre, there are about 10^{14} surface atomic sites for deposited atoms to stick to. To deposit one epitaxial layer of atoms onto a substrate, which are in a complete lattice registry with the underlying substrate atoms, deposited atoms perform motions on the substrate's surface in order to find equilibrium (lowest potential energy) sites. Microscopically, these motions can be broken down into elementary hops, from one atomic site to the next, which are driven by the surface energy landscape in addition to energetic barriers separating the initial site from the final site. Various interactions that follow from the ever-changing landscape due to the simultaneous movements of many atoms can be obtained by quantum mechanical simulations. However, the huge number of degrees of freedom involved has so far prevented researchers

P.M.A. Sloot, B. Chopard, and A.G. Hoekstra (Eds.): ACRI 2004, LNCS 3305, pp. 286–295, 2004.

from performing complete multiscale simulations of thin film deposition using quantum mechanics [1].

We know that the collective motion of these atoms gives rise to a macroscopic surface diffusion current and to a surface morphology. It thus remains important to predict the surface morphology based on a reduced microscopic picture. Lattice gas cellular automata (LGCA) are a potential method capable of coarse-graining the microscopic picture of atomic-scale motions to a manageable computational complexity.

This paper describes the formulation of LGCA-based computation to simulate atomistic processes that make up thin film deposition. It is inspired by the LGCA models for chemically reacting systems [2]. The unit length scale for our simulation coincides with the atomic diameter and the unit time scale is matched to the collective diffusion time constant. The LGCA evolution is defined through local rules for the motions of atoms, which are based on the propensity of each atom to make as many chemical bonds as possible in order to attain its equilibrium state.

2 The Lattice-Gas Cellular Automaton Description

Consider an LGCA on a one-dimensional periodic lattice of length L. The lattice sites are denoted by $r = 0, 1, \ldots, L-1$ (mod L) and the discrete time points by $k = 0, 1, \ldots$. The state of a site r at time k is given by the integer-valued variable $h(r, k)$ representing the sites film height, i.e. the number of one atomic-height layers. Periodicity of the lattice implies $h(r + jL, k) = h(r, k)$ for all $j \in \mathbb{Z}$. We initialise the LGCA with values $h(r, 0)$ for all r at time $k = 0$. At time $k = 0$, we also initialise the pseudo-random number generator employed to simulate random events like the determination of landing sites of Si atoms, see Sect. 3.

If $h(r, k) > 0$ then the particle at height $h(r, k)$ is called the adatom at site r at time k; all deposited particles at site r below the adatom are called bulk atoms. If $h(r, k) = 0$ then no adatom is located at site r at time k. We assume that all adatoms and only these, are mobile and can move to neighbouring lattice sites with probabilities to be computed. The rules that govern this motion will be described below. The considerations above imply that the energy of a particle does not dissipate with time and that a particle is always mobile as long as it is not buried by another one. Since adatoms are always mobile we consider them not part of the deposited structure.

The time evolution of the LGCA from time k to time $k + 1$ proceeds in three sub-steps: (i) *particle landing*, (ii) *adatom velocity computation*, and (iii) *adatom motion*. Each sub-step is performed at each lattice site independently from the other lattice sites (distributed execution) and the next sub-step is started only after the previous sub-step has been completed on all sites of the lattice (synchronisation). We introduce the intermediate time steps k' and k'' which are attained when the first and the second sub-step, respectively, are completed. The state of the system can only be observed at times k, i.e. after completion of the third sub-step. We describe the three sub-steps in more detail below.

In order to connect the LGCA model to a real surface growth process, we must relate the simulation time k, i.e. the number of simulation steps performed, to the real time t (in seconds [s]). We assume that each simulation step from simulation time k to $k+1$ corresponds to an *effective time step* Δt_{eff} ([s]) independent of k and this leads to $t = k\Delta t_{\text{eff}}$. A reason for the k-independence and the precise definition of Δt_{eff} is given in the end of this section.

In the description below we make use of the indicator function $1[\cdot]$, where the argument is a logical expression and $1[true] = 1$ and $1[false] = 0$.

Particle Landing. The deposition of particles on the surface is modelled by the particle landing sub-step. We assume a constant and spatially homogeneous particle flux, from which particles are randomly, uniformly in space and time, deposited on the surface, leading to a *growth rate* R_g (in monolayers per second [ML/s]) of the structure. We describe a site- and a lattice-based approach of this sub-step and give reasons why we prefer and use the latter in our simulations.

Site-based approach: Particles land at each lattice site with the *particle landing probability (per unit simulation time and lattice site)* $p_l \in [0, 1]$ derived from the growth rate and the effective time step as

$$p_l = R_g \Delta t_{\text{eff}} .$$

If a particle lands on the surface at site r then the height $h(r, k)$ increases by unity. Let $\{\xi_l(r, k) \,|\, r = 0, 1, \ldots, L - 1\}$ be a set of independent and identically distributed Bernoulli random variables with probabilities $\mathsf{P}[\xi_l(r, k) = 1] = p_l$, then we obtain for all $r = 0, 1, \ldots, L - 1$

$$h(r, k') = h(r, k) + \xi_l(r, k) . \tag{1}$$

Computational concerns regarding the site-based approach: This approach requires L Bernoulli trials for each execution with, in general, a very small landing probability p_l. This raises three concerns.

1. In view of the many time steps necessary for a simulation, the generation of L random numbers for the L Bernoulli trials is computationally very costly.
2. The small probability p_l is often even too small to perform the Bernoulli trials faithfully with the available range of random numbers, see Sect. 3.
3. Additionally, in view of the very small probability p_l, it appears to be a waste of CPU time to perform the Bernoulli trials for each lattice site independently. In fact, the probability that, during one execution of the site-based particle landing sub-step, two or more particles will land on the surface is given by $\mathsf{P}[\text{ two or more particles land }] = 1 - (1 - p_l)^L - Lp_l(1 - p_l)^{L-1}$, and is extremely small for typical values of L and p_l, see Fig. 1 (left).

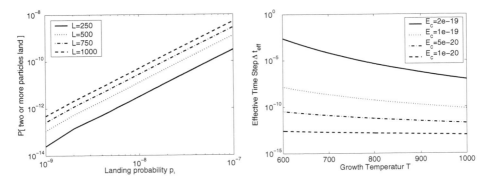

Fig. 1. P[two or more particles land] for various values of the lattice size L and a range of typical landing probabilities p_l (left) and the effective time step Δt_{eff} for typical values of corrugation energy E_c and growth temperature T (right)

Lattice-based (coarse-grained) approach: Based on the concerns and arguments presented, we propose a second approach of defining the particle landing sub-step. This approach is computationally more efficient and for suitable values of L and p_l physically sound. We assume that at most one particle can land on the surface in each execution of the particle landing sub-step. Let $\xi_l(k)$ be a Bernoulli random variable with probability of success Lp_l and $\xi_s(k)$ be a uniformly distributed random variable with range $\{0, 1, 2, \ldots, L-1\}$. Then $\xi_l(k)$ decides whether a particle will land on the surface in the execution of the sub-step and $\xi_s(k)$ selects the particular landing site, i.e.

$$h(r, k') = \begin{cases} h(r, k) + \xi_l(k) : & \text{if } r = \xi_s(k) \\ h(r, k) & : \text{ otherwise} \end{cases} \quad (2)$$

This lattice-based approach requires only the generation of at most two random numbers (improved efficiency), the used probability of success in the Bernoulli trial is larger than p_l (improved reliability), and on average the same number of particles are deposited on the surface (maintained consistency). In the following we consider exclusively the lattice-based particle landing sub-step.

Adatom Velocity Computation. The adatoms on the surface undergo surface diffusion depending on the surface morphology. Therefore we will define for each lattice site r the adatom velocity $v(r, k'') \in \{-1, 0, 1\}$ for the adatom currently located at this site. This velocity determines the motion of the adatom at site r to sites $r-1$, r, or $r+1$, respectively, in the subsequent adatom motion sub-step. Note that we allow for an adatom to stay at its site.

The velocity $v(r, k'')$ is computed as a function of the current height at site r and neighbouring sites. To do this we derive below (diffusion) probabilities $p^-(r, k')$, $p^\circ(r, k')$, and $p^+(r, k')$, with $p^+(r, k') + p^\circ(r, k') + p^-(r, k') \equiv 1$, for the three motion options. This allows to define the set $\{\xi_v(r, k') \mid r = 0, 1, \ldots, L -$

1} of independent random variables with range $\{-1, 0, 1\}$ and corresponding probabilities $p^-(r, k')$, $p^\circ(r, k')$, and $p^+(r, k')$. We then compute

$$v(r, k'') = \mathbf{1}[h(r, k') > 0]\xi_v(r, k'). \tag{3}$$

Eq. (3) implies that the velocity associated with site r is zero if there is no adatom. Hence, we consider in the following the derivation of the *diffusion probabilities* $p^+(r, k')$, $p^\circ(r, k')$, and $p^-(r, k')$ in the case $h(r, k') > 0$. The computation of the diffusion probabilities is based on the number of free bonds which the adatom at site r currently has, $b^\circ(r, k')$, and the number of free bonds it would have if moved one site to the right or left (leaving everything else unchanged), $b^+(r, k')$ and $b^-(r, k')$, respectively. An adatom always has a free bond to the top and possibly free bonds to the left and to the right. We obtain

$$b^\circ(r, k') = 3 - \mathbf{1}[h(r+1, k') > h(r, k') - 1] - \mathbf{1}[h(r-1, k') > h(r, k') - 1],$$
$$b^+(r, k') = 3 - \mathbf{1}[h(r+2, k') > h(r+1, k')] - \mathbf{1}[h(r, k') - 1 > h(r+1, k')],$$
$$b^-(r, k') = 3 - \mathbf{1}[h(r, k') - 1 > h(r-1, k')] - \mathbf{1}[h(r-2, k') > h(r-1, k')].$$

In order to derive the expression for $b^+(r, k')$ (a similar consideration holds for $b^-(r, k')$) denote by $h^{r', +}(\cdot, k')$ the surface profile which is obtained from $h(\cdot, k')$ if the adatom at site r' is moved to site $r' + 1$, i.e.

$$h^{r', +}(r, k') = \begin{cases} h(r'+1, k') + 1 : & \text{if } r = r' + 1 \\ h(r', k') - 1 & : \text{if } r = r' \\ h(r, k') & : \text{otherwise} \end{cases}.$$

Now $b^+(r, k')$ can be expressed as $b^\circ(r+1, k')$ with $h(\cdot, k')$ replaced by $h^{r, +}(\cdot, k')$. Note that the bond counts take the presence of nearby adatoms into account which is an important distinction of the LGCA approach from, e.g., kinetic Monte-Carlo simulations that consider diffusion of only one adatom at any time.

The rate that an adatom with b_1 free bonds at its current site will hop to a site where it would have b_2 free bonds is given by

$$R(b_1, b_2) = \frac{k_B T}{h_P} \exp\left(-\frac{E_c}{k_B T} - \frac{E_d}{k_B T}(b_2 - b_1)\right).$$

In this expression, E_c is the *corrugation energy* (in Joule [J]), E_d is the *unit broken (dangling) bond energy* ([J]), two material properties, T is the *growth temperature* (in Kelvin [K]), k_B is the *Boltzmann constant* (in Joule per Kelvin [J/K]), and h_P is the *Planck constant* (in Joule × second [Js]). We see that if $b_2 - b_1 < 0$, i.e. when the adatom has less free bonds if moved to the new site, that is it achieves a more stable state there, then the rate $R(b_1, b_2)$ becomes large. In particular, $R(b_1, b_2)$ is increasing if $b_2 - b_1$ is decreasing. The expression above allows to define the rates $R^+(r, k')$, $R^\circ(r, k')$, and $R^-(r, k')$ at which an adatom currently at site r is moving to site $r + 1$, staying at site r, or moving to site $r - 1$, respectively, by

$$R^{+, \circ, -}(r, k') = R(b^\circ(r, k'), b^{+, \circ, -}(r, k')).$$

Finally, by normalising these rates with respect to their sum $R^+(r,k') + R^\circ(r,k') + R^-(r,k')$, we obtain the diffusion probabilities $p^+(r,k')$, $p^\circ(r,k')$, and $p^-(r,k')$. Note that the corrugation energy E_c has no influence on the diffusion probabilities; it scales out.

The following observation is important for computational efficiency of the LGCA simulations as it avoids the excessive evaluation of the exponential function. The diffusion probabilities $p^+(r,k')$, $p^-(r,k')$, and $p^\circ(r,k')$ depend on the differences $b^+(r,k') - b^\circ(r,k')$ and $b^-(r,k') - b^\circ(r,k')$ only and these differences only take values in $\{-2,-1,0,1,2\}$. Hence, we define matrices $P^+, P^- \in \mathbb{R}^{5,5}$ such that $p^+(r,k') = P^+_{ij}$, $p^-(r,k') = P^-_{ij}$ and $p^\circ(r,k') = 1 - (P^+_{ij} + P^-_{ij})$, where $i = b^+(r,k') - b^\circ(r,k') + 3$ and $j = b^-(r,k') - b^\circ(r,k') + 3$. These matrices are independent of the simulation time k and, hence, can be set up once and forever at the start of the simulation.

Adatom Motion. The adatoms on the surface are moved to new locations according to the velocities calculated in the adatom velocity computation sub-step. This sub-step guarantees that $v(r,k'') = 0$ if there is no adatom at site r and time k''. The height $h(r,k)$ evolves according to the formula

$$
\begin{aligned}
h(r,k+1) = h(r,k') - \mathbf{1}[v(r,k'') \neq 0] \\
+ \mathbf{1}[v(r-1,k'') = 1] + \mathbf{1}[v(r+1,k'') = -1].
\end{aligned}
\tag{4}
$$

Note that two adatoms may move to a lattice site r in this sub-step. In such a case they will be on top of each other.

The Effective Time Step Δt_{eff}. As pointed out earlier, we relate the simulation time k to the real time t by the *effective time step* Δt_{eff}. The time span Δt_{eff}, equivalent to evolving the LGCA from k to $k+1$, corresponds to the average time taken by adatoms to jump to a nearest atomic site (including the waiting time before the actual jump). Hence, the Δt_{eff} corresponding to simulation step k should depend on the surface morphology *after* simulation step k and therefore can be computed only *after* that step has been completed. However, we need Δt_{eff} within the particle landing sub-step of the kth simulation step. Because of this difficulty (which could be avoided by making the particle landing sub-step the final sub-step of each simulation step) and, more importantly, for computational efficiency we decided to define Δt_{eff} independent of k and with respect to a flat surface as follows. The average time required for an adatom to jump to a nearest atomic site is the inverse of the particle hop rate $R(b_1, b_2)$. Since we assume that the adatom diffuses on a flat surface we have $b_1 = b_2$ and obtain

$$
\Delta t_{\text{eff}}^{-1} = \frac{k_B T}{h_P} \exp\left(-\frac{E_c}{k_B T}\right).
$$

The dependence of Δt_{eff} on growth temperature T and corrugation energy E_c is illustrated graphically in Fig. 1 (right).

3   The Simulation of Random Events

Random events are an integral part of LGCA simulations. We simulate these events using a sequence of uniformly distributed (pseudo-) random integers from the set $\{0, 1, 2, ..., M_{max}\}$, where $M_{max} = 2^{32} - 1$, generated by the pseudo-random number generator described in [3] with an initialisation as in [4]. The generator is a combination generator which combines a subtract-with-borrow generator with a simple Weyl generator. The period of the combination generator is not known but, following [3], should be longer, or at least not shorter, than the period of any of its parts. The subtract-with-borrow generator has a period of about 10^{414}. In the end of this section we will bound the required number of random integers for an LGCA simulation which should be less than the square root of the period of the generator. This condition is satisfied for the simulations to be performed.

The LGCA described requires to simulate three types of random variables

1. a uniformly distributed random variable ξ_M with range $\{0, 1, \ldots, M - 1\}$,
2. a Bernoulli random variable ξ_p with probability of success $p \in [0, 1]$, and
3. a random variable $\xi_{\pm}$ with range $\{-1, 0, 1\}$ and corresponding probabilities $p^+, p^- \in [0, 1]$, and $p^\circ = 1 - p^+ - p^- \in [0, 1]$.

We describe how we simulate these random variables in the following and also discuss further implementation details.

Uniformly Distributed Random Variable ξ_M. We take the next integer n from the sequence of uniformly distributed random integers and define $\xi_M = n$ mod M, which is a good approximation if $M \ll M_{max}$.

Bernoulli Random Variable ξ_p. We take the next integer n from the sequence of uniformly distributed random integers. To determine the success of a Bernoulli random variable with probability of success p, we can check whether $n/(M_{max} + 1) < p$. This computation involves floating point operations (division and comparison) which are computationally more expensive than the corresponding integer operations. Therefore, especially in view of the many Bernoulli trials to be performed with the same probability p, we first and forever define $\mathfrak{p} := \text{round}(p \cdot (M_{max} + 1)) \in \{0, 1, 2, \ldots, M_{max} + 1\}$ and then set $\xi_p = \mathbb{1}[n < \mathfrak{p}]$. This involves only one integer operation for each evaluation of ξ_p.

Here we remark that due to the finite range of random integers provided by the generator we are not able to generate random variables ξ_p with $0 < p < 1/(2(M_{max} + 1)) \approx 1.2 \cdot 10^{-10}$ because all these result in $\mathfrak{p} = 0$. Therefore we recommend to consider only random variables ξ_p with $p = 0$ or $p > 10^{-8}$ which should be faithfully simulated with the available sequence of uniformly distributed random integers (cf. the discussion in the description of the particle landing sub-step in Sect. 2). Similar considerations apply for random variables ξ_p with p close to 1 or if we want to distinguish between random variables ξ_p and $\xi_{\tilde{p}}$ where p and $\tilde{p}$ are very close.

Random Variable $\xi_\pm$. To simulate the random variable $\xi_\pm$ we follow the approach to simulate Bernoulli random variables. We define two integers $\mathfrak{p}^+ := \text{round}(p^+ \cdot (M_{\max} + 1))$ and $\mathfrak{p}^- := \text{round}((p^+ + p^-) \cdot (M_{\max} + 1))$ and take the next integer n from the sequence of uniformly distributed random integers. If $n < \mathfrak{p}^+$ then $\xi_\pm = 1$, otherwise if $n < \mathfrak{p}^-$ then $\xi_\pm = -1$, otherwise $\xi_\pm = 0$.

A Bound on the Required Number of Random Integers. From the discussion above we see that for the simulation of each random variable required in an LGCA simulation we need one number from the generated sequence of uniformly distributed random integers. Hence, per LGCA simulation step, we need at most two for the lattice-based particle landing sub-step and at most L for the adatom velocity computation sub-step. For a simulation up to real time t we perform $t/\Delta t_{\text{eff}}$ simulation steps and, hence, require in total at most $\frac{t}{\Delta t_{\text{eff}}}(L+2)$ uniformly distributed random integers.

4 Selected Simulation Results

In this section we show some typical simulation results of the deposition of Si layers on a flat (i.e. $h(r,0) = 0$) and on a structured Si(001) substrate. The analysis of the deposition on a flat substrate is presented in [5] and on a structured surface is in preparation. The parameters for our LGCA simulation are: lattice size $L = 500$, surface corrugation energy for Si(001) surfaces $E_c = 1.12 \times 10^{-19}$ J (≈ 0.7 eV, [6]), and unit broken bond energy $E_d = 3.68 \cdot 10^{-19}$ J (≈ 2.3 eV, [7]). We consider growth rate values $R_g \in \{0.1, 10\}$ ML/s and deposition temperatures $T \in \{700, 800\}$ K. The number of simulation steps is chosen such that on average $x = 5$ monolayers were grown, i.e. $xR_g^{-1}\Delta t_{eff}^{-1}$ steps. In Fig. 2 we plot snapshots of the LGCA state at different times for one of the simulations. We obtain the expected layer-by-layer growth for the initially flat and also the structured substrate. However, on the initially structured substrate we observe a considerable higher number of small *islands* as opposed to only two big islands on the initially flat substrate. This is the expected behaviour due to the steps of the structured substrate which facilitate aggregation.

As a first qualitative outcome of all our simulations we state that the average height $\bar{h}(k) := (1/L)\sum_{r=0}^{L-1} h(r,k)$ almost perfectly agrees with the expected growth $R_g k \Delta t_{\text{eff}}$ of the structure. Another qualitative measure, used to analyse the roughness of the evolving thin film surface, is the interface width $w(L,k)$,

$$w(L,k)^2 = \frac{1}{L}\sum_{r=0}^{L-1}[h(r,k)^2 - \bar{h}(k)^2],$$

see [5] for plots. For the initially flat surface it is found that $w(L,k)$ behaves independently of the growth temperature for constant growth rate. Furthermore, for constant growth temperature, $w(L,k)$ approaches a smaller value towards the end of the simulation time with increasing growth rate. This behaviour, known as *kinetic stabilisation*, is typical in homoepitaxial deposition. Physically, this

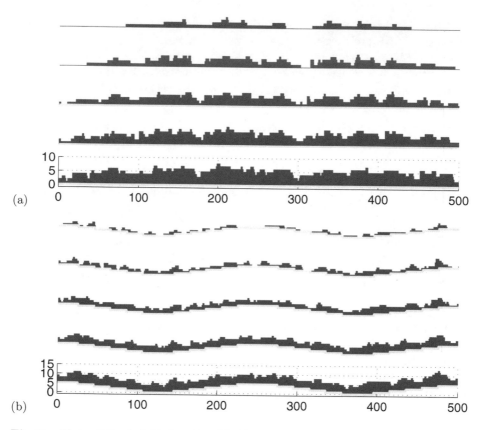

Fig. 2. Plots of the height function $h(r, k)$ for an initially flat, subplot (a), and an initially structured, subplot (b), substrate. In each subplot, the simulation time k corresponds to real times $t = 10, 20, 30, 40, 50\,\mathrm{s}$ (from top to bottom) for a simulation with growth temperature $T = 700\,\mathrm{K}$ and growth rate $R_g = 0.1\,\mathrm{ML/s}$

can be explained by the dominance of the uniformly advancing growth front due to the deposition flux in comparison to the processes that control the adatom diffusion [8]. Further analysis can be performed by considering, e.g. the step density, the height-height correlation of the surface, or island sizes and their distributions. The step density characterises the roughness of the evolving surface morphology by measuring the number of steps. A discussion of this measure, with respect to an initially flat substrate, and its dependence on growth rate R_g and growth temperature T is given in [5].

We conclude this section with some remarks on the computational complexity of the LGCA simulations. The computation time for the simulation of a structure of, on average, x monolayers, is directly coupled to the size of the effective time step Δt_{eff}. As can be seen from Fig. 1 (right), Δt_{eff} decreases, and, hence, the computation time increases, with increasing growth temperature T and decreasing corrugation energy E_c. The most time-consuming sub-steps of the LGCA evolution are the computation of adatom velocities and the motion of the adatoms because these sub-steps depend (linearly) on the lattice size L. In contrast, the lattice-based particle landing sub-step is independent of the lattice size.

5   Conclusions

We have described a spatially one-dimensional LGCA model for the simulation of surface roughening in homoepitaxial growth. In particular, we gave a detailed description of the derivation of the automaton rules based on physical consideration but also taking computational efficiency into account. We discussed our preference of the lattice-based approach for the particle landing sub-step of the LGCA as opposed to the site-based approach. The simulations performed produced results consistent with experimental observations. The presented model should be seen as a starting point for generalisations to higher spatial dimensions and towards more realistic models by incorporating further details of the underlying physical processes. These two directions of future research will clearly increase the computational complexity of the LGCA and, hence, from a computational point of view, interest should be focused on a parallel implementation of the LGCA.

Acknowledgements. The authors acknowledge the financial support of NCE-MITACS and NSERC. Additionally, A.G., A.T.L. and H.F. thank The Fields Institute for support and hospitality.

References

1. Jacobson, J., Cooper, B.H., Sethna, J.P.: Simulations of energetic beam deposition: From picoseconds to seconds. Phys. Rev. B **58** (1998) 15847–15865
2. Boon, J.P., Dab, D., Kapral, R., Lawniczak, A.: Lattice gas automata for reactive systems. Physics Reports **273** (1996) 55–147
3. Marsaglia, G., Narasimhan, B., Zaman, A.: A random number generator for PC's. Comp. Phys. Comm. **60** (1990) 345–349
4. Marsaglia, G., Zaman, A., Tsang, W.: Toward a universal random number generator. Statistics & Probability Letters **9** (1990) 35–39
5. Gerisch, A., Lawniczak, A.T., Budiman, R.A., Ruda, H.E., Fukś, H.: Lattice gas cellular automaton modeling of surface roughening in homoepitaxial growth in nanowires. In: IEEE CCECE 2003-CCGEI 2003, Montréal, Quebec, Canada, May/mai 2003. (2003) 001–004
6. Milman, V., Jesson, D.E., Pennycook, S.J., Payne, M.C., Lee, M.H., Stich, I.: Large-scale ab initio study of the binding and diffusion of a Ge adatom on the Si(100) surface. Phys. Rev. B **50** (1994) 2663–2666
7. Kittel, C.: Introduction to Solid State Physics. Wiley, New York (1996)
8. Pimpinelli, A., Villain, J.: Physics of Crystal Growth. CUP, Cambridge (1998)

Ant Colony System for JSP

Urszula Boryczka

Institute of Computer Science, ul. Bedzinska 39,
41-200 Sosnowiec, Poland
uboryczk@us.edu.pl

Abstract. This paper discusses the application of ACS metaheuristics (based on behaviour of real ants: stigmergy and synergetic effect among ants) for Job-Shop Scheduling problem (JSP). This algorithm is improved by introducing the concept of critical events, in which two new techniques will be applied. Thus, a more flexible heuristic technique is obtained, which improves the performance of ant colony system for JSP.

1 Introduction

The job–shop scheduling problem belongs to the scheduling problems that are the most difficult ones in classical scheduling theory [13]. Note that a well–known problem with 10 jobs and 10 machines formulated in 1963 [20] has been solved optimally only in 1989 [7]. Only some special cases with a small number of jobs or machines can be solved in polynomial times.

For the JSP without setup times branch and bound algorithms and heuristics have been proposed. We may mention algorithms proposed by Carlier and Pinson [7], Brucker et al. [6] and Applegate and Cook [2]. Among heuristics constructive and iterative algorithms have been distinguished. In constructive algorithms priority (or dispatching) rules have been applied [3,14,16,22]. A mixed, dispatching rule has been applied for short–term scheduling problem in [17]. Authors assign different priority rules to the machines. Among iterative algorithms some metaheuristics have been proposed: simulated annealing, tabu search or threshold accepting [18,21]. Also genetic algorithm has been considered as an application for the JSP [23].

The most obvious approach to solving a scheduling problem is a greedy one: whenever a machine becomes available, assign some job to it. A more sophisticated variant of this approach is to give each job a priority derived from the particular optimality criterion, and then, whenever a machine becomes available, assign the available job of highest priority to it. The priority of a job can be determined without reference to other jobs.

The ant colony systems (ACS) were applied to solve several problems, e.g. the travelling salesman problem,vehicle routing problem, coloring graph,shortest common supersequence problem or routing in telephone networks [4]. In this paper, we present how different priority rules improve the performance of the ACS applied to the Job–Shop Scheduling Problem.

P.M.A. Sloot, B. Chopard, and A.G. Hoekstra (Eds.): ACRI 2004, LNCS 3305, pp. 296–305, 2004.
© Springer-Verlag Berlin Heidelberg 2004

Outline. This paper is organized as follows. The considered problem is described in detail in section 2. In section 3 we demonstrate how the variant of the ant colony optimization can be applied to the ACS–JSP. In section 4, we define the extended version of ACS for JSP, where we use critical events memory. Finally the results of our computational experiments are presented and discussed in section 5. We summarize major points and conclusions in section 6.

2   The Job-Shop Scheduling Problem

The Job–Shop Scheduling Problem [15] may be formulated as follows. Let $M = \{M_1, \ldots, M_m\}$ be a set of machines, let $J = \{J_1 \ldots, J_n\}$ be a set of jobs, and let $O = \{u_{ij}\}, (i,j) \in I, I \subseteq [1,n] \times [1,m]$ be a set of operations, where n denotes number of jobs and m denotes number of machines.

For each operation $u_{ij} \in O$ there is a job J_i it belongs to, a machine M_i on which it has to be processed, and a processing time p_{ij}. The set O is decomposed into the chains corresponding to the jobs: if the relation $u_{ip} \to u_{iq}$ is in a chain, then both operations belong to job J_i and there is no u_{ik} such that $u_{ip} \to u_{ik}$ or $u_{ik} \to u_{iq}$.

The problem is to find a starting time $S_{ij}(\forall u_{ij} \in O)$ which minimizes:

$$\max_{u_{ij}} (S_{ij} + p_{ij})$$

subject to

- $S_{ij} \geq S_{ik} + p_{ik}$ when $u_{ik} \to u_{ij}$ (the operation precedence
  constraints on the job chains),
- $(S_{ij} \geq S_{kj} + p_{kj}) \vee (S_{kj} \geq S_{ij} + p_{ij})$ (the machine constraint saying
  that no more than a single job
  can be processed at the same
  time on the same machine).

The value $C_{ij} = S_{ij} + p_{ij}$ is a completion time for the operation $u_{ij} \in O$.

The operations must be assigned to the time intervals in such a way, that once an operation is started it must be completed.

A disjunctive graph

$$D = (V, A, E)$$

where

- V — is a set of nodes,
- A — is a set of conjunctive directed arcs,
- E — is a set of disjunctive, undirected edges,

may be associated with an instance of JSP. In such a case V, A and E are defined as follows (Fig.1.):

- $V = O \cup \{u_0\} \cup \{u_{N+1}\}$, ($\{u_0\}$ and $\{u_{N+1}\}$ are the special dummy nodes which identify the start and the completion of the overall Job–Shop),

- $A = \{(u_{ij}, u_{ij+1}) : u_{ij} \to u_{ij+1}$ is in the chain for job $J_i\} \cup \{(u_0, u_{1j}) : u_{1j}$ is the first operation in the chain for job $J_i\} \cup \{(u_{im}, u_{N+1}) : u_{im}$ is the last operation in the chain for job $J_i\}$, for all i,
- $E = \{(u_{ij}, u_{hj})\}$, for all i.

With each vertex $u_{ij} \in O$, a weight p_{ij} is associated $(p_0 = p_{N+1} = 0)$.

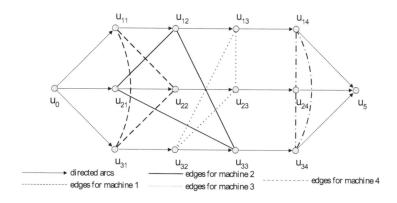

Fig. 1. Graphic representation of the JSP 3×4

The length of a path in the graph is defined as the sum of the weights of the vertices belonging to the path. Thus, solving the JSP corresponds to finding an acyclic orientation of the graph D which minimizes the longest path between u_0 and u_{N+1}. In the algorithm solving the JSP, a data structure based on the approach used by the List Scheduler algorithms is applied. This algorithms comprise two phases. First, a rule for assigning priorities to the still unscheduled operations is defined. Then, the operation with the maximum priority is scheduled. On each step, the algorithm chooses the operations for which all predecessors are already scheduled. As the result the earliest possible starting time with respect to the precedence and machine constraints is assigned to the operation with maximum priority.

3   Application of the Ant Colony System to the JSP

The Ant Colony System (ACS) algorithm has been introduced by Dorigo and Gambardella [11,12] to improve the performance of Ant System [4], which allowed to find good solutions within a reasonable time for small size problems only. The ACS is based on 3 modifications of Ant System:

- a different node transition rule,
- a different pheromone trail updating rule,
- the use of local and global pheromone updating rules (to favour exploration).

The node transition rule is modified to allow explicitly for exploration. An ant k in city i chooses the city j to move to following the rule:

$$j = \begin{cases} \arg \max_{u \in J_i^k} \{[\tau_{iu}(t)] \cdot [\eta_{iu}]^\beta\} & \text{if } q \le q_0 \\ J & \text{if } q > q_0 \end{cases}$$

where q is a random variable uniformly distributed over $[0, 1]$, q_0 is a tuneable parameter $(0 \le q_0 \le 1)$, and $J \in J_i^k$ is a city that is chosen randomly according to a probability

$$p_{iJ}^k(t) = \begin{cases} \dfrac{\tau_{iJ}(t) \cdot [\eta_{iJ}]^\beta}{\sum\limits_{l \in J_i^k} [\tau_{il}(t)] \cdot [\eta_{il}]^\beta} \end{cases}$$

In Ant System all ants are allowed to deposit pheromone after completing their tours. By contrast, in the ACS only the ant that generated the best tour since the beginning of the trail is allowed to globally update the concentrations of pheromone on the branches. The global updating rule is as follows:

$$\tau_{ij}(t + n) = (1 - \rho) \cdot \tau_{ij}(t) + \rho \cdot \Delta\tau_{ij}(t, t + n)$$

where (i, j) is the edge belonging to T^+, the best tour since the beginning of the trail, ρ is a parameter governing pheromone decay, and $\Delta\tau_{ij}(t, t + n) = \frac{1}{L^+}$, where L^+ is the length of the T^+.

The local update is performed as follows: when, while performing a tour, ant k is in city i and selects city $j \in J_i^k$ to move to, the pheromone concentration on edge (i, j) is updated by the following formula:

$$\tau_{ij}(t + 1) = (1 - \rho) \cdot \tau_{ij}(t) + \rho \cdot \tau_0$$

A JSP described by m machines, n jobs and set of operations O can be represented in the context of ACS by a directed weighted graph $F = \langle U, E \rangle$ where:

- $U = O \cup \{u_0\}$,
- $E = \{(u_{ij}, u_{kl}) : u_{ij}, u_{kl} \in O\} \cup \{(u_0, u_{i1}) : u_{i1}$ is the first operation in the chain for job $J_i\}$.

Node u_0 is added to specify which job is to be scheduled first, if more than one job has its first operation to be performed on the same machine.

The graph F has $N + 1$ nodes and $\frac{N(N-1)}{2} + n$ edges. Each node (except u_0) represents an operation performed on a machine, and all the nodes are pairwise connected in both directions (node u_0 is connected only to a first operation of each job).

The arcs of F are weighted by a pair (τ_{ij}, η_{ij}), where τ_{ij} represents the pheromone trail, and η_{ij} relates to the special priority rule. The weights are used to compute the probabilities which tell an ant which operation should be chosen in the next step.

All ants are initially in u_0 and they build a solution by a permutation of the remaining nodes. To cope with this problem transition probability is used and global and local pheromone updating rules have been performed by ants.

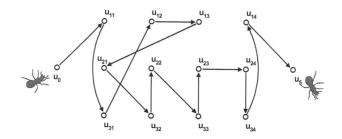

Fig. 2. Visualization of a solution made by an ant in the JSP

4   Critical Events in ACS for JSP

Our work has investigated the use of "iterative repair" search procedures, which start with an infeasible solution and attempt to eliminate conflicts and incorrect solutions. In this paper, we propose a new metaheuristic procedure for solving job–shop scheduling problems. Our approach is somewhat unconventional. We start from a base procedure called ACS for find a critical event in a searching process.

For the JSP examples, we will specify that the critical events of interest consist of solutions, that represent a "local suboptimum" i. e. whose objective function value is worse than that of the solution immediately before and after it. Now we are interested in the effect of restarting the algorithm with a new priority rule. It will be happened after the "critical" solution is found. Then the solutions that correspond to critical events are the initial solution for the next experiment for a special period of time (in our experiments — 50 iterations). To execute a restarting procedure, we penalize the worse solutions, implicitly allowing the penalty function — pheromone updating rules to decay rapidly these values as the number of iterations increases.

For comparison purposes we included various well–known priority rules from job–shop scheduling into our tests, which have been adapted to the considered problems. Among the rules considered in our tests we present computational results for the following rules: SPT, LPT, SRT, LRT, LRM, ECT, FIFO, NINQ [16].

There are different reasons of occurrence of critical events in JSP. Once an operation has been selected to schedule in this problem, it is necessary to check that all the involved constraints are satisfied:

1. The precedence constraints are defined among operations of the same job: it means that the process must guarantee that two operations of a same job are not executed in the same period of time.
2. Checking the consistency of capacity constraints is a difficult process due to the next constraints:
   - When an operation is scheduled and a resource is allocated to the operation, a forward checking process analyzes the set of remaining possible

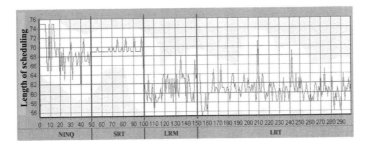

Fig. 3. An example of different priority rules for mt06

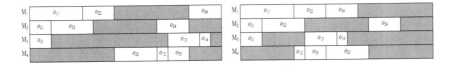

Fig. 4. Gantt chart of the schedule before and after FIND–HOLE procedure

reservations of other operations that requires the same resource, and removes those conflicting reservations.

- We must check if two unscheduled operations that require the same resource are not overlapped. Two operations overlap when both require the same resource at the same time for every start time.
- Before indicating an operation has not any possible execution it is necessary to check the resource usage calendar of the operation. If the shared resource is not used during the entire operation's execution, it can be used in another operation. The FIND–HOLE procedure identifies the two extreme time points of the temporal line in which the resource is available and can be used by another operation. If a hole does not exist, an inconsistency will be detected because the resource is not available. The FIND–HOLE procedure checks if an apparent conflicting situation is actually conflicting.

5 Examining the Efficiency of the ACS in Job–Shop Scheduling Problem

The experimental work consisted of three major phases. First, an efficient and effective parameter settings were determined. Then, ACS–JSP algorithm with different priority rules was run several times using this setting to examine the behaviour of this algorithm (on the problem ABZ6). Finally the results concerning the different JSP problems were compared with results obtained by dynamic tabu Search and Multi PCP [4]. In order to measure the performance of the

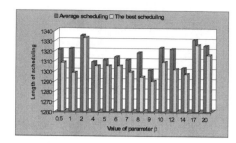
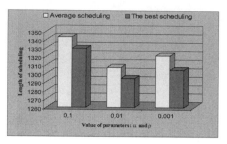

Fig. 5. Value of parameter β for ACS–JSP

Fig. 6. Value of parameters: α and ρ for ACS–JSP

ACS–JSP with two techniques described above, a set of test runs was performed using a selection of the classical job–shop problems [1,19,20].

The main strength of experiment concerning the first version of Ant System (used for JSP) were summarized as follows [10]:

- With the best parameter values algorithm always finds good solutions (the best one about 7% worse from the best–known values.
- The algorithm quickly finds satysfying solutions, nevertheless it does not enter the stagnation behaviour, and the ants continue the search process for new, possibly better, solution.

Our aim is not only to find better results, but also examine the behaviour of this algorithm in finding solutions for such difficult problem. It is known that the good results obtained by the algorithm depend strongly on the parameter setting affecting the computational formulas described in section 3. In the case of presented algorithm β, ρ and α had to be determined. As the starting point for a determination of the role of parameter β the following values of the other parameters were chosen: $q_0 = 0.8$, $\rho = \alpha = 0.01$, $m = 100$. The number of iterations equals to 200.

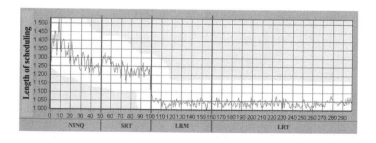

Fig. 7. Different priority rules for ABZ6

Table 1. Makespan results for Job Shop Problems.

Problem	Job × Machine	Optimal value	Multi PCP	Dynamic Tabu Search	ACS_{mod}	Error
LA6	15×5	**926**	**926**	-	**926**	0%
LA7	15×5	**890**	**890**	-	915	2.8%
LA11	20×5	**1222**	**1222**	-	**1222**	0%
LA12	20×5	**1039**	**1039**	-	1047	0.9%
LA17	10×10	**784**	787	**784**	825	3.9%
LA23	15×10	**1032**	1041	**1032**	1089	5.5%
LA26	20×10	**1218**	1272	**1218**	1397	14.6%
LA36	15×15	**1268**	1321	**1268**	1440	13.5%

To consider how ant colony flexible affects scheduling performance, the initial experimental design was repeated for 20 settings of β and three settings for α and ρ. Figures 7 and 8 show the performance results obtained by ACS–JSP for the problem ABZ6 with setting of 0.5, 1 to 20 (for β) and 0.1, 0.01, 0.001 for α and ρ. These parameters occur in global and local updating rules. We adjust experimentally the value of parameter β observing the histogram Fig.5. The experimental results showed that the value 9 for this parameter is the best one (5.4% worse than the optimal schedule $c = 1234$). Also for examining the value of ρ and α the 10×10 ABZ6 was tested with $\beta = 9$. Both values of parameters α and ρ have the same kind (tendency) of fluctuation. Experimental observation has shown that the best value of these constraints equal to 0.01.

Recapitulating the achieved results, the following set of parameters' values were chosen to perform further tests of critical events in ACS: $q_0 = 0.8$, $\rho = \alpha = 0.01$, $\beta = 9$, m depends on the number of nodes.

Next experiment was carried out to find the good result for the ABZ6 problem (10×10) using different priority rules occurred in η. The investigations were performed for the following priority rules: NINQ, SRT, LRM, LRT.

In order to discover which priority rule gives the best result (and in what sequence) we analysed every of the priority rule mentioned in section 4. We cannot point out the best sequence (and its length) unmistakably. All the priority rules influence the results in a similar way. We expect the differences between the priority rules to appear for the greater and more difficult problems.

In order to compare the results found by ACS–JSP for different problems, we perform the next test (see Tab.1). This table shows the best solutions obtained by 3 different algorithms: multi PCP [9], Dynamic Tabu Search [8] and Ant Colony System with critical events. We chose two algorithms for this comparison, interesting from our point of view. Results obtained by ACS_{mod} JSP unfortunately does not outperform the results obtained by other algorithms, but our aim is not to show the best method for JSP. We want to analyse the behavior of ants in such a difficult problem. We must underline that it is our preliminary research and we hope to cope with this problem. According to the presented ta-

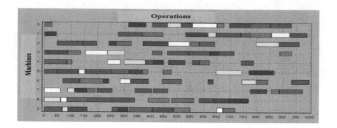

Fig. 8. Gantt chart of the schedule for ABZ6

ble, ants can find the best schedule for small problems (LA6, LA11). Therefore our investigations will be continued.

6   Conclusions

With a rapid increase in creating different hybrid methods we focused on development (or augment) of the ant colony optimisation, which incorporate various forms of repairing methods. In our paper two methods for JSP are proposed and evaluated. The proposed procedure, which we referred as the „critical event" extends the basic algorithm to exploit changeable in time priority rules and re-ordering the operations in order to fill the holes. Our research has investigated a mataheuristic approach with simple priority dispatching rules. Recently these rules are the representative and widely used in different approaches. While the priority rules are extremely fast and easy to implement, there are also drawbacks. The performance of any given rule is typically quite sensitive to problem characteristics, and it is generally quite difficult to find one (or a special sequence of them) that dominates in any particular problem, so in the future work we will try to find the best sequence (and the duration of exploitation) of priority rules. We also try to create more dynamic version of adaptivity to good values of parameters of ACS. The more difficult problem is the more dynamic characteristic of ACS should be examine.

The presented algorithm contains elements of several different approaches used for JSP and in different metaheuerictics (Tabu Search). ACS–JSP is a modified version of ACS with two techniques: FIND–HOLE procedure and by using different priority rules. The results of our experiments tend to be more attractive than those presented in our previous work [5]. ACS–JSP is shown to be interesting among modern metaheuristics in term of using it in such difficult problem as the JSP is. Future research with more experimental work will aim at the motivation for selecting of the ACS for JSP. More generally, the results obtained in these experiments illustrate the difficulty of creating an appropriate version of ACS for Job–Shop Scheduling problems.

References

1. J. Adams, E. Balas, and D. Zawack. The shifting bottleneck procedure for job shop scheduling. *Management Science*, 34:391–401, 1988.
2. D. Applegate and W. Cook. A computational study of the Job–Shop Scheduling Problem. *ORSA J. Computing*, 3:149–156, 1991.
3. J. N. Blackstone, D.T. Philips, and C. L. Hogg. A state–of–the–Art survey of manufacturing job shop operations. *International Journal of Production Research*, 20:27–45, 1982.
4. E. Bonabeau, M. Dorigo, and G. Theraulaz. *Swarm Intelligence. From Natural to Artificial Systems*. Oxford University Press, 1999.
5. U. Boryczka and M. Boryczka. Generative Policies in Ant Systems. In *Proceedings of the Workshop: Intelligent Information Systems V*, Dęblin, 1996.
6. P. Brucker, B. Jurisch, and B. Sievers. A Branch and Bound algorithm for the job–shop problem. *Discrete Appl. Math.*, 49:107–127, 1994.
7. J. Carlier and E. Pinson. An algorithm for solving the job-shop problem. *Management Science*, 35(2):164–176, 1989.
8. J. B. Chambers and J. Wesley Barnes. New tabu search results for the Job Shop Scheduling Problem. *University of Texas*, 1996.
9. Cheng-Chung Cheng and S. F. Smith. Applying constraint satisfaction techniques to job shop scheduling. *Carnegie Mellon University*, 1995.
10. M. Dorigo, A. Colorni, V. Maniezzo, and M. Trubian. Ant system for job shop scheduling. *Belgian Journal of Operational Research, Statistics and Computer Science*, 1994.
11. M. Dorigo and L. M. Gambardella. A study of some properties of Ant–Q. In *Proceedings of Fourth International Conference on Parallel Problem Solving from Nature, PPSNIV*, pages 656–665, Berlin, 1996. Springer–Verlag.
12. M. Dorigo and L. M. Gambardella. Ant Colony System: A cooperative learning approach to the Traveling Salesman Problem. *IEEE Trans. Evol. Comp.*, 1:53–66, 1997.
13. M. R. Garey, D. S. Johnson, and R. Sethi. The complexity of flowshop and jobshop scheduling. *Math. Oper. Res.*, 1:117–129, 1976.
14. W. S. Gere. Heuristics in job shop scheduling. *Management Sci.*, 13:167–190, 1996.
15. R. L. Graham, E. L. Lawler, J. K. Lenstra, and A. H. G. Rinnooy Kan. Optimization and approximation in deterministic sequencing and scheduling: A survey. *Annals oo Discrete Mathematics*, 5:287–326, 1979.
16. R. Haupt. A survey of scheduling rules. *Operations Research*, 25:45–61, 1989.
17. N. Ishii and J. T. Talavage. A mixed dispatching rule approach in FMS scheduling. *International J. Flexible Manufacturing Systems*, pages 69–87, 1994.
18. P. J. M. Van Laarhoven, E. H. L. Aarts, and J. K. Lenstra. Job shop scheduling by Simulated Annealing. *Operations Research*, 40:113–125, 1992.
19. S. Lawrence. Resource constraint project scheduling: an experimental investigation of heuristic scheduling techniques. *Technical Report, Graduate School of Industrial Administration*, 1984.
20. J. F. Muth and G. L. Thompson. *Industrial Scheduling*. Prentice Hall, 1963.
21. E. Nowicki and C. Smutnicki. A fast Taboo Search algorithm for the job shop problem. *TU Wroclav, Preprint, 8/93*, 1993.
22. S. S. Panwalkar and W. Iskander. A survey of scheduling rules. *Operations Research*, 25:25–61, 1977.
23. E. Pesch. *Machine Learning by Schedule Decomposition*. University of Limburg, 1993.

Using de Bruijn Diagrams to Analyze 1d Cellular Automata Traffic Models

René Rodríguez Zamora and Sergio Víctor Chapa Vergara

Centro de Investigación y de Estudios Avanzados del IPN,
Departamento de Ingeniería Eléctrica,
Sección Computación,
Av. IPN 2508, San Pedro Zacatenco, 07360, D.F., México,
renerz@correo.unam.mx, schapa@cs.cinvestav.mx
http://computacion.cs.cinvestav.mx/~rzamora

Abstract. We used de Bruijn diagrams to analyze traffic models based on one-dimensional cellular automata. The first model is the rule 184 which simulates traffic flow with the simplest dynamics. The second model is a rule represented by a cellular automaton of order (4,2), which includes all the configurations that can be presented when the model contemplates two speeds. To this cellular automata we denominated LCA-TRAFFICFLOWVMAX2 which is completely deterministic and we can predict or analyze its behavior still before to carry out simulations in computer using de Bruijn diagrams. We obtained this model taking as it bases the model proposed by Nagel-Schreckenberg to simulate traffic flow in one dimension and one direction.

1 Preliminaries

The cellular automata were conceived at the beginning of 1950's by John Von Neumann, a mathematical brilliant interested in investigating about the required complexity so that a device could be auto-reproductive and the organization of this one to have a correct operation when repairing itself with parts that could have an operation badly. The results were not let hope, all a current of investigation has been developed with a strong interrelation in fields like fractals and dynamic systems, as well as applications in: parallel cellular computing, simulation of dynamic systems and recognition of patterns, and simulation of socio-economical models, for instance.

In general terms, we can say that a cellular automata is defined and operates based on the following elements:

- States, or attributes, e.g., "on" or "off", 0 or 1.
- Containers that store those attributes, e.g., a location in an array, a sector in a computer's memory.
- Behaviors associated with those states; formulated as conditional transition rules (IF, THEN, ELSE) that govern how and when automata react to information that is input to them.

P.M.A. Sloot, B. Chopard, and A.G. Hoekstra (Eds.): ACRI 2004, LNCS 3305, pp. 306–315, 2004.

– Neighborhoods from which the automata draw input, e.g., neighboring locations in an array, databases containing information.
– Temporal domain, through which the evolution of the automata proceeds, e.g., real-time, program cycles.

We can define cellular automata so that it operates in one, two, or more dimensions. Nevertheless, the complexity to analyze them or to implement simulations of these in a computer is exponentially increased with the number of dimensions and states including in its definition.

The mentioned aspect of complexity previously, has oriented some investigators to work with cellular automata that operate in one dimension, since this allows them to analyze with more detail the referring aspects to its behavior. One of the pioneering works about one-dimensional cellular automata made Stephen Wolfram [12] during the decade of 1980's. Professional scientific interest in cellular automata received a considerable impetus from the investigations of Stephen Wolfram, who undertook a computer based search through the properties of one-dimensional automata, guided by some concepts from the realm of nonlinear dynamics and statistical mechanics.

So, according to the Wolfram notation, we can define a one-dimensional cellular automaton of the following way

$$x_i^{t+1} = f(x_{i-r}^t, ..., x_i^t, ..., x_{i+r}^t), f : K^{2r+1} \mapsto K, \tag{1}$$

where r is the neighborhood radius, K is a finite set of states, $i \in \mathbb{Z}$, x is the automaton and $x \in K$. The equation (1) defines the evolution rule φ for a cellular automata of order (k, r), where k is the number of states and $k \in K$.

From the definition of a one-dimensional cellular automaton we can characterize its behavior identifying ancestors, finding cycles, search for the garden of eden - configurations which cannot evolve from any predecessor - or any other pattern of behavior that is of our interest.

A very useful tool which we can use to characterize the behavior of cellular automata is the de Bruijn diagram [9], main tool of shift register theory [1]. Because the cells of one dimensional automata, by denition, form linear chains and the neighborhoods themselves form another kind of chain, wherein they necessarily overlap. The result is an arrangement which has a very close connection with shift register theory, which is a systematic study of the properties of overlapping strings and how the overlaps happen to come about. In particular, the form of graphical representation known as the de Bruijn diagram.

Several papers have used de Bruijn diagrams for representing and analysing the evolution rule of a one-dimensional cellular automata. Masakazu Nasu [8] refers the properties of injective and surjective evolutionary functions to de Bruijn and related diagrams; Wolfram [13] himself used them to express evolutionary properties, and Erica Jen [2] has used them to calculate ancestors. The de Bruijn diagrams are defined as follows:

(i)   The nodes of the diagram are all the sequences of $2r$ cells, i.e. the set K^{2r}.

(ii)   Let a,b be states of K and ξ_1, ξ_2 sequences of K^{2r-1}. Then $a\xi_1$ y $\xi_2 b$ are sequences of K^{2r} representing nodes of the de Bruijn diagram. There is an arc from $a\xi_1$ to $\xi_2 b$ if $\xi_1 = \xi_2$, and it represents the sequence $a\xi_1 b \in K^{2r+1}$ which is a complete neighborhood of the automaton.

(iii) Every arc labelled by the state in which the neighborhood $a\xi_1 b$ evolves according to the evolution rule φ.

In this way, paths in the de Bruijn diagram are sequences of symbols formed in one-dimensional cellular automata. So, the equation that defines a de Bruijn diagram is

$$
BM_{i,j} = \begin{cases} 1 \; j = \begin{cases} ki \\ ki+1 \\ . \\ . \\ . \\ ki+k-1 \end{cases} & (mod \quad k^{2r}) \\ \\ 0 \text{ otherwise.} \end{cases} \tag{2}
$$

Another diagram which we can construct from the de Bruijn diagram is the subset diagram. The subset diagrams was introduced by Edward F. Moore in 1956 [5]. In the subset diagram the nodes are grouped into subsets, note being taken of the subsets to which one can arrive through systematic departures from all the nodes in any given subset. The result is a new graph, with subsets for nodes and links summarizing all the places that one can get to from all the different combinations of starting points. Sometimes, but far from always, the possible destinations narrow down as one goes along; in any event one has all the possibilities cataloged. One point to be observed is that if one thinks that there should be a link at a certain node and there is not, the link should be drawn to the empty set instead; a convention which assures every label of having a representation at every node in the subset diagram.

Let a and b be nodes in a given diagram, S a subset, and $|S|$ the cardinality of S; the formal definition of its subset diagram is

$$
\Sigma_i(S) = \begin{cases} \emptyset & S = \emptyset \\ \{b | link_i(a,b)\} & S = \{a\} \\ \bigcup_{a \in S} \Sigma_i(a) & |S| > 1. \end{cases} \tag{3}
$$

There is another important reason for working with subsets. Labelled links resemble functions, by associating things with one another. But if two links with the same label emerge from a single vertex, they can hardly represent a function. Forging the subset of all destinations, leaves one single link between subsets, bringing functionality to the subset diagram even though it did not exist originally. Including the null set ensures that every point has an image, avoiding partially defined functions.

2   Rule 184

The model that represents traffic flow with the simplest dynamics is that in which
the cars move of left to right by an "artificial highway". This artificial highway
consist of an array of L sites or cells. Each site or cell is either occupied or empty.
In this model we assume periodic boundary conditions. Time is discrete. The
evolution is synchronous, that is, all cars move at same time. At each time step,
each driver moves his car to the right only if the next cell is empty. Therefore,
car at site i can either move to site $i + 1$ this site is empty, or not move if site
$i + 1$ is occupied. Thus, the state of a given cell i depends only on cells $i - 1$, i
and $i + 1$. This model is equivalent to cellular automaton Rule 184 if the state
of an occupied site is 1, whereas the state of an empty site is 0. The Rule table
is

neighborhood	000	001	010	011	100	101	110	111
image	0	0	0	1	1	1	0	1

In the Fig. 1 we showed the generic de Bruijn diagram for the Rule 184, which
is a (2,1) automaton (one having two states per cell with a single neighbor on
each side, according to Stephen Wolfram's notation) has four nodes corresponding to the four two-cell partial neighborhood, with eight links representing the
full three-cell neighborhoods. The still life diagram may be extracted from the
generic diagram by removing all links which do not conserve their central cell
during the automaton's evolution. Loops in the subdiagram composed of the
remain links define sequences, rather than individual cells, which are invariant
to evolution. By reading of such sequences, all the still lifes for the automaton
are automatically determined.

The topological matrix corresponding to the diagram shown in Fig. 1 is

$$BM = \begin{bmatrix} 0 & 0 & . & . \\ . & . & 0 & 1 \\ 1 & 1 & . & . \\ . & . & 0 & 1 \end{bmatrix}$$

Also we can construct subset diagram from de Bruijn diagram. Let $A = 00$,
$B = 01$, $C = 10$, $D = 11$. The subset diagram then has $2^4 = 16$ nodes for the
sixteen subsets, but to save space we show only the part connected to the empty
subset. The destination of each arrow leaving individual nodes is

Node	0 leads to	1 leads to
A	A,B	$\emptyset$
B	C	D
C	$\emptyset$	A,B
D	C	D

Then, form vectors whose elements are the tail nodes and whose components
are indexed by the head nodes; an element is null if there is no incoming link
from any node.

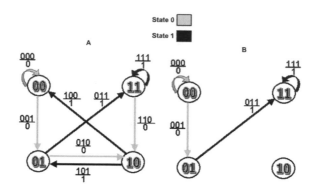

Fig. 1. De bruijn diagrams generated by the Rule 184. (A) The generic de Bruijn diagram. (B) Subdiagrams generated by Rule 184 still lifes.

Node	0 leads to	1 leads to
{ABCD}	(A, A, B+D, ∅)	(C, C, ∅)
{ABC}	(A, A, B, ∅)	(C, C, ∅, B)
{ABD}	(A, A, B, ∅)	(∅, ∅, ∅, B+D)
{D}	(∅, ∅, D, ∅)	(∅, ∅, ∅, D)
{C}	(∅, ∅, ∅, ∅)	(C, C, ∅, ∅)
{AB}	(A, A, B, ∅)	(∅, ∅, ∅, B)
{∅}	(∅, ∅, ∅, ∅)	(∅, ∅, ∅, ∅)

This structure is actually the vector subset diagram; the scalar subset diagram arises by enumerating the non-null indices. We don't care how many incoming arrows there are nor where they originate, as long has there is at least one

Node	0 leads to	1 leads to
{ABCD}	{ABC}	{ABD}
{ABC}	{ABC}	{ABD}
{ABD}	{ABC}	{D}
{D}	{C}	{D}
{C}	{∅}	{AB}
{AB}	{ABC}	{D}
{∅}	{∅∅∅∅}	{∅∅∅∅}

its topological matrix, having indexed the subsets in the order shown, is $S = a+b$ according to

$$
\begin{bmatrix}
. & 1 & 1 & . & . & . & . \\
. & 1 & 1 & . & . & . & . \\
. & 1 & . & 1 & . & . & . \\
. & . & . & 1 & 1 & . & . \\
. & . & . & . & . & 1 & 1 \\
. & 1 & . & 1 & . & . & . \\
. & . & . & . & . & . & 2
\end{bmatrix}
=
\begin{bmatrix}
. & 1 & . & . & . & . & . \\
. & 1 & . & . & . & . & . \\
. & 1 & . & . & . & . & . \\
. & . & . & . & 1 & . & . \\
. & . & . & . & . & . & 1 \\
. & 1 & . & . & . & . & . \\
. & . & . & . & . & . & 1
\end{bmatrix}
+
\begin{bmatrix}
. & . & 1 & . & . & . & . \\
. & . & 1 & . & . & . & . \\
. & . & . & 1 & . & . & . \\
. & . & . & 1 & . & . & . \\
. & . & . & . & . & 1 & . \\
. & . & . & 1 & . & . & . \\
. & . & . & . & . & . & 1
\end{bmatrix}.
$$

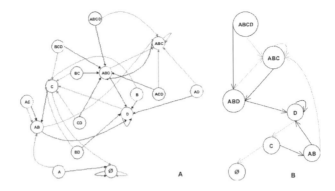

Fig. 2. Subset diagrams for Rule 184. (A) Entire subset Diagram. (B) Subset diagram that shows only the part connected to the empty set.

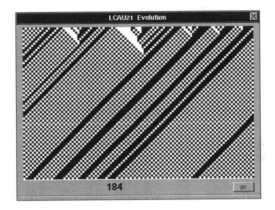

Fig. 3. Space-time diagram that shows the evolution of the Rule 184.

Through subset diagram we can know if cellular automaton it has injective properties finding gardens of eden. In the case of Rule 184 we can observe in the Fig. 2 that 01100 chain or any permutation of this one cannot be generated by any predecessor.

In the Fig. 3 we can observe through the evolution of the Rule 184 that the traffic jams move a site to the left in each time step.

3   LCATRAFFICFLOWVMAX2

This model is based on the Nagel-Schreckenberg traffic model [7]. However, LCA-TRAFFICFLOWVMAX2 is completely deterministic. The road is divided on one-dimensional array of L with periodic boundary conditions. Each site is either ocuppied by one car or empty. Each car has an integer velocity with values between zero and v_{max}. The number of empty sites in front of a car is denoted by *gap*. For an arbitrary configuration, one update of the system consist of the following three consecutive steps, which are applied in parallel for all cars:

1. If $(v \leq gap - 1)$ then $v := v + 1$.
2. If $(v \geq gap + 1)$ then $v := gap$.
3. Car motion: Each car is advanced v sites.

We represented this model with a cellular automaton of order $(4,2)$, where $r = 2$, $K = \{0, 1, 2, 3\}$, and $v_{max} = 2$. The four states have the following representation: state $0 \rightarrow$ empty site, state $1 \rightarrow$ ocuppied site with $v = 0$, state $2 \rightarrow$ ocuppied site with $v = 1$, state $3 \rightarrow$ ocuppied site with $v = 2$. The Rule table is

neighborhood	00000	00001	00002	00003	00010	00011	00012	00013	....	33333
image	0	0	0	0	0	0	0	0	....	1

The de Bruijn diagram of LCATRAFFICFLOWVMAX2 contains $4^{2(2)} = 256$ nodes and $4^{2(2)+1}$ edges which represent the 1024 neighborhoods. In the Fig. 4 we represented the de Bruijn diagram like a tree, where the partial neighborhoods have a decimal representation. These neighborhood are ordered of ascending form according to the number of states and to the possible combinations. With this type of representation it is easier to identify the nodes that form cycles of periodic chains during the evolution of cellular automaton since it is only necessary to take like beginning from the cycle some node from the tree and to follow his ramifications until finding it again. For example, in the Fig. 4 we can see the cycle formed by the nodes $0 \rightarrow 2 \rightarrow 8 \rightarrow 35 \rightarrow 142 \rightarrow 56 \rightarrow 226 \rightarrow 136 \rightarrow 32 \rightarrow 128 \rightarrow 0$. Although we did not show the subset diagram of LCATRAFFICFLOWVMAX2 because its size is too great to this paper -2^{256} nodes- we can say that the chains of 1's form gardens of eden, or in other words, traffic jams.

In the Fig. 5 we showed cycles that form chains in which the cells have a shift of 5 sites to the right in 3 generations during the LCATRAFFICFLOWVMAX2 evolution's.

Finally, in the Fig. 6 we showed the LCATRAFFICFLOWVMAX2 evolution.

4   Concluding Remarks

The behavior of traffic flow represents a difficult problem as far as the analysis that is necessary to make to characterize it. Many works exists in this sense oriented towards different points with the purpose of including the greater number of aspects involved in this complex system. The de Bruijn and subsets diagrams are useful tools to analyze traffic flow models because they contain all the information referring to the behavior and the characteristics of any linear cellular automata. Thus, this kind of tools allow us to know with certainty as the different behaviors that can have the traffic flow models are generated.

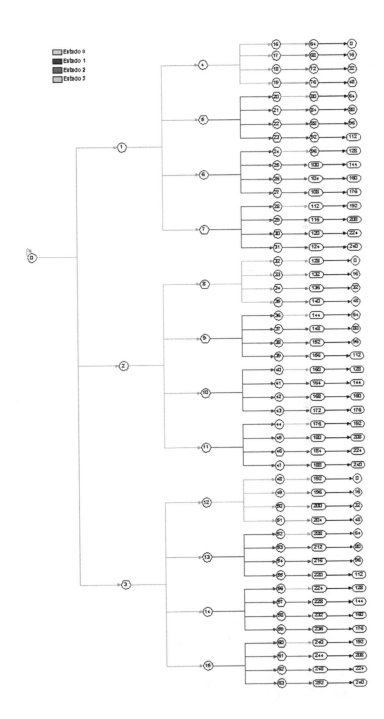

Fig. 4. De Bruijn diagram generated by LCATRAFFICFLOWVMAX2.

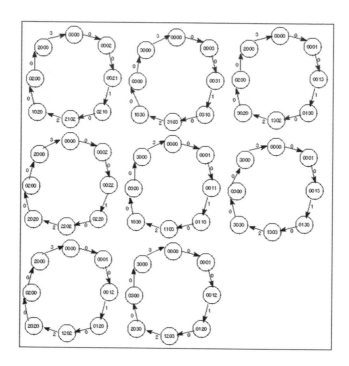

Fig. 5. Cycles that form chains in which the cells have a shift of 5 sites to the right in 3 generations.

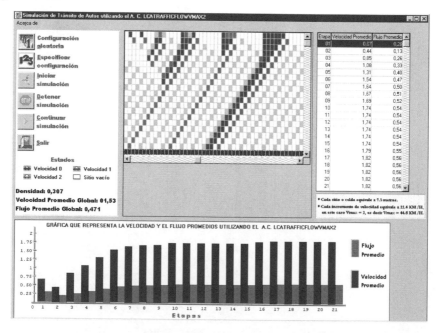

Fig. 6. LCATRAFFICFLOWVMAX2 evolution's.

References

1. Golomb, S.: Shift Register Sequences. Holden Day, Inc., San Francisco (1967)
2. Jen, E.: Scaling of preimages in cellular automata. Complex Systems 1 (1987) 1045-1062
3. Mcintosh, H.: Linear cellular automata. Webpage http://delta.cs.cinvestav.mx/~mcintosh (1990)
4. Mcintosh, H.: Linear cellular automata via de Bruijn diagrams. webpage http://delta.cs.cinvestav.mx/~mcintosh (1992)
5. Moore, E.: Gedanken Experiments on Sequential MachinesScaling, in Automata Studies. C. E. Shannon and J. McCarthy, eds., Princeton University Press, Princeton (1956)
6. Mora, J.: Matrix methods and local properties of reversible one-dimensional cellular automata. J. Phys. A: Math. Gen. 35 (2002) 5563-5573
7. Nagel, K., Schreckenberg M.: J. Phys. I (France) 12 (1992) 2221
8. Nasu M.: Local Maps Inducing Surjective Global Maps of One Dimensional Tessellation Automata. Mathematical Systems Theory 11 (1978) 327-351
9. Ralston, A.: De Bruijn Sequences-A Model Example of the Interaction of Discrete Mathematics and Computer Science. Mathematics Magazine 55 (1982) 131-143
10. Rodriguez, R.: Modelación de flujo de tránsito de autos utilizando autómatas celulares. Graduate thesis, webpage http://delta.cs.cinvestav.mx/~mcintosh (2002)
11. Wolfram, S.: Computation theory of cellular automata. Communications in Mathematical Physics 96 (1984) 15-57
12. Wolfram, S.: Statistical mechanics of cellular automata. Reviews of Modern Physics 55 (1983) 601-644
13. Wolfram, S.: Theory and Applications of cellular automata. World Scientific (1986)

Using Cellular Automata to Determine Bounds for Measuring the Efficiency of Broadcast Algorithms in Highly Mobile Ad Hoc Networks

Michael Kirkpatrick and Frances Van Scoy

Lane Department of Computer Science and Electrical Engineering
West Virginia University
Morgantown, West Virginia, USA
michaelk@csee.wvu.edu

Abstract. The proliferation of mobile computing devices in recent years has produced an increased interest in the development of efficient methods of communication among these devices. As networked mobile devices move, the configurations of the networks of which they are a part change and if the time between these changes is short enough then conventional routing algorithms are no longer useful. This paper describes the use of cellular automata to model message broadcasting among autonomous agents in highly mobile ad hoc networks. The advantages offered by using this method to study the problem are discussed and an upper bound on the time steps required by a "reasonable" broadcast algorithm is derived.

1 Introduction

1.1 The Problem of Message Passing in Highly Mobile Ad Hoc Networks

When networked mobile devices move, the configurations of the networks of which they are a part change. As a result, the best path along which to pass a message from one node in the network to another may change over time. If the changes in topology occur at reasonably well spaced intervals conventional algorithms for determining shortest paths in graphs can be used. But in a more rapidly changing system these methods work less well, if at all.

In this paper we consider networks comprising many nodes which operate independently of each other with no centralized control or global knowledge of the state of the network and in which the topology changes too frequently for conventional routing methods to work. We consider a number of autonomous agents deployed over an area large enough that direct communication between all agents may be impossible at any given time. No individual agent is aware of the location of any other of the agents except those within its communication range.

One agent may be in range of a second agent which, in turn, is in range of – or may move to come in range of – a third agent not in range of the first. The first can send a message to the third by sending it to the second which relays it on. As a starting point for studying techniques for message passing in these networks, we look at broadcast-

P.M.A. Sloot, B. Chopard, and A.G. Hoekstra (Eds.): ACRI 2004, LNCS 3305, pp. 316–324, 2004.

ing a single message from one node to all other nodes by passing the message from any node holding it to any other nodes which come within its communication range. This paper explores the use of cellular automata to model the agents, the messages, and the space in which they move.

1.2 Why Use Cellular Automata to Study This Problem?

Cellular automata lend themselves well to problems which are characterized by elements which assume one of several discrete states and in which the state of an element at any given time depends in some way upon the states of its neighbors at the previous point in time. The use of time steps works well in defining rapidly changing systems because it provides a means of expressing the system state at discrete times.

States can be defined to describe cells with various numbers of agents which, in turn, hold or do not hold the message. By selecting a reasonably descriptive subset of all possible agent/message combinations, the number of states considered can be kept relatively low while at the same time providing a useful description of the system.

Additionally, while a graphic interface is certainly not a required part of a cellular automaton, the nature of the cells – that is, that at any given time, each cell is in one of a finite number of well-defined states – makes graphic display of the system straightforward. Displaying the system state graphically at each time step provides an overview of the activity of the agents and messages which make their movement patterns much more readily observable than they might otherwise be

2 Literature Survey

2.1 Communication in Mobile Ad Hoc Networks

The primary issue in transmitting messages in any network is finding a reasonably efficient path from one node to another. This may mean simply finding the shortest path between the nodes but it often involves consideration of other factors which may effect the time taken to pass the message. When the nodes are mobile, the problem is greater because the connectivity of the networks may change significantly between the time when a path is calculated and when it is used [1]. One way of addressing this is to maintain a routing table at each node listing the nodes it can reach [2]. This table is updated periodically and shared with its neighbors.

In [3] the efficiency of maintaining such tables proactively is compared to that of building them as needed and, in so doing, the overhead of maintaining tables with links to nodes which are no longer in communication is saved. They also use the past history of routes in the ad hoc network to make predictions of the stability of paths and attempt to use more stable paths. A method of taking "snapshots" of a distributed system showing its state at a given point in time is described in [4] and in [5] this technique is adapted for use in delivering messages in an ad hoc network.

Some proposed techniques assign specific tasks to certain nodes [6]. Others assume that the network is always connected and that changes in topology are localized and use this trait to cluster nodes using weakly connected dominating sets of nodes [7]. These approaches, however, present a model different from that being considered in this paper. In particular, the first requires that the agents are homogenous and the second makes assumptions about connectivity that our model does not.

The focus of this paper is to study the ways in which a message moves as it is being broadcast with the goal of discovering ways of fostering this activity while not compromising the autonomy of individual agents. One problem that arises is that the message may be transmitted repeatedly between a given pair of nodes. An interesting method for reducing this transmission redundancy is presented in [8]. It is suggested that delaying the relaying of the message until an agent has had a chance to move out of the area in which it received it can reduce unneeded transmissions.

2.2 Autonomous Agents

This paper discusses the representation of autonomous agents moving in some defined space. A message is broadcast from one of the agents to all of the others. Cellular automata are used to represent the space in which these agents exist and the agents themselves – along with the message if they have it – are represented as states. The idea of the network's nodes being autonomous is an important one because it suggests that each node is free to operate according to some agendum under its control. We are interested in observing the patterns of dissemination that may emerge from letting the nodes (agents) operate in this manner and, ultimately using that to advantage. A discussion of adaptability and self-organization of agents is given in [9] where it is said that autonomy is a necessary and sufficient condition for these to exist. Agent modeling is discussed in more detail in [10] and several possible attributes of agents are listed.

2.3 Cellular Automata

A cellular automaton is an entity which can be in one of a finite number of well-defined states. The state of the automaton at a given point in time is determined by a set of rules based on its state and the states of automata adjacent to it in the automata space at the immediately preceding point in time. The updating of automata states in a space can be done synchronously, in which case the states are changed in some order and the "new" state of a given automaton may depend on the states of some neighbors in the previous time step and the states of others in the current step. Alternatively, updating can be done asynchronously, or in parallel, so that changes of state in neighboring cells do not affect a cell until the following time step. A history of cellular automata and descriptions of several uses for them are given in [11] with further discussion in [12]. Applying cellular automata to the problem of location management in mobile networks is discussed in [13].

3 Simulating Mobile Networks with Cellular Automata

An environment with a mobile network comprises several elements which must be represented by any simulation designed to study message passing in such networks. These elements are the space in which the agents (nodes) exist and move, the messages being passed among agents, and the agents themselves.

Also important is the time required to transmit a message from one agent to another, as is the speed at which the agents can move. The simulator used for this work represents time as discrete steps. The number of steps required for an agent to move from one cell to another and the number of steps needed to transmit the message can be set independently of each other.

3.1   Description of Cells and the Space

The simulation is based on cells that can be in any of several states. The cells used in this simulation are square and the space they occupy is rectangular. Three general cell states are defined as empty, containing one or more agents without the message, and containing one or more agents with the message.

Whenever an agent with the message comes within range of an agent that does not have the message, it passes the message on. Accordingly, if more than one agent occupies a given cell, either they all have the message or none of them does. The total number of possible states for a cell, is $2a + 1$, where a is the number of agents in the system. A given cell can be empty; it can contain up to a agents, none of which hold the message; or it can contain up to a agents, all of which hold the message.

3.2   Definition and Movement of Agents

The number of agents is specified at the beginning of the simulation and is fixed for the entire run. Movement of an agent from one cell to another is modeled by the cell of origin changing state to reflect that the agent is no longer in it and the destination cell changing state to reflect its presence. Since the number of agents in the system is fixed for any given simulation run, if a cell's state is changed to indicate that an agent has moved into it, some other cell's state must change to reflect the movement out.

An agent can move only between adjacent cells. That is, a cell's state can change to reflect the presence of an agent in a given time step only if at least one of the cell's neighbors contained an agent in the previous time step. Consequently, the definition of "neighborhood" is important. The neighborhood of a cell is simply the set of cells defined to be adjacent to it. Two commonly used definitions of adjacency are the *von Neumann* and *Moore* neighborhoods. These are illustrated in Figure 1. A *Rotated von Neumann* neighborhood is also considered in this study. Each of these neighborhoods can be defined either to include or to exclude the cell itself.

One of the defining characteristics of agents is their autonomy. This means that we cannot dictate the detailed movement of agents in the system. Accordingly, there is an element of randomness involved in determining an agent's next location (The randomness is implemented using the C++ *rand* function.) When a simulation is initialized, the dimensions (rows and columns) of the space are defined and the number of agents in the system is set with most of the agents being distributed randomly throughout the cells. An exception to this random placement is made in order to assure that the agent originating the message is in a corner of the space and that at least one other agent is in the diagonally opposite corner.

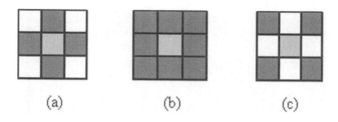

Fig. 1. Neighborhoods: **(a)** Von Neumann. **(b)** Moore. **(c)** Rotated von Neumann

3.3 Passing of Messages

A corner cell is designated to contain an agent which is the message originator and the message is passed from one agent to another whenever an agent holding the message comes within range of an agent not holding it. This is modeled by changing the state of the cell of the agent receiving the message from a cell with one or more agents without the message to a cell with one or more agents with the message.

3.4 Time Steps and Neighborhoods

For this paper, agents could move to a neighboring cell and the message could be passed between neighbors in each time step. The types of neighborhood used for each of these need not be the same and can be used to create a more realistic model; by defining message passing in a Moore neighborhood and agent movement in a von Neumann neighborhood, the agents are restricted to moving around corners while the message can be passed more efficiently.

4 Studies of Message Passing in Highly Mobile Ad Hoc Networks

There are many factors to be considered when studying message passing in highly mobile ad hoc networks. Among these are the patterns of movement of the agents in the network, the rules governing message passing between agents, and the resulting patterns of movement of the messages being passed. Once these factors are well understood, ways of improving the efficiency of the process may be examined. This paper reports results from a series of cellular automata-based experiments designed to establish a practical upper bound on the time required to broadcast a message and thereby serve as a starting point for further investigation.

4.1 Network Simulations

The experiments reported on here are based on a scenario in which many agents can move independently throughout an area. A single agent is initially given a message to be broadcast to the other agents. Cells are updated asynchronously and the simulation is stopped when all agents have received the message.

A set of simulations was run in a 25 x 25 space with different agent densities and the average number of time steps taken to complete broadcast in each case was recorded. The agent initially holding the message is in one corner and there is an agent in the diagonally opposite corner. Otherwise, the agents are randomly distributed throughout the space. Opposing corner cells represent the worst case in terms of distance from other cells and the worst case for time required to complete the broadcast.

As described in Section 3, the number of time steps needed for an agent to move from one cell to another and the number of steps taken to transmit a message between agents can be set independently. For the simulations described in this paper, each of these numbers is set to 1. Increasing the time needed to move relative to message passing produces results similar to those reported here except that, predictably, more total time is required.

Simulations were run using two slightly different rules for agent movement. In one, the agents were required to move to a neighboring cell at each time step. In the other, they were allowed to remain at their current position. In each case, an agent selects a destination cell by choosing from among its neighbors (perhaps including the cell it currently occupies) with equal probability. Whenever an agent with the message comes within range of an agent without the message, the first agent passes the message to the second. Simulations were run for several combinations of neighborhood types.

The results of runs in which agents are allowed to stay in place – that is, when a cell is considered to be part of its own neighborhood – are shown in Figure 2 and are analyzed in the next section. When agents were required to move, the time needed to complete broadcast was somewhat less (for example, 20 to 30 time steps at a density of 10 percent). At higher densities, the times are nearly the same. Note that requiring agents to move is a special case of allowing them to remain in place and the resulting times would be expected to fall between the lower bound time (discussed in Section 4.2.1) and the time needed when they are not required to move.

4.2 Analysis of Simulation Data

In this section the data collected above are discussed in light of existing theory concerning the time required to broadcast in grids. This is then used to establish lower and upper bounds on the broadcast time in order to define the limitations and the potential for gain in broadcast techniques. The simulations above allowed agents to move randomly throughout the space and to pass the message whenever possible. By placing restrictions on the movement or message passing, gains in time may be achievable within the bounds defined here. The potential for these gains is described as future work in Section 5

4.2.1 Lower Bounds for Broadcast Time in a Grid

To analyze the data from the simulations in Section 4.1, it is helpful to consider some underlying theory concerning message passing in fixed networks. In a fixed rectangular network (grid) the worst broadcast time occurs when then message originates in a corner. For a square grid with n nodes on a side this time is $2n - 2$ steps, as proven by Farley's Theorem [14].

When the nodes are allowed to move freely, agents in diagonally opposite corners can move toward each other, cutting this time in approximately half. If we mix neighborhood types, the delivery time can be further improved. If the agents move within

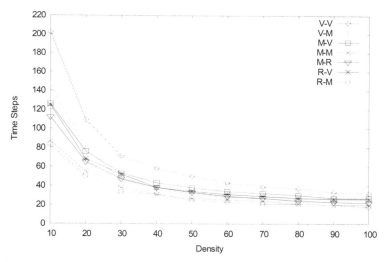

Fig. 2. Time steps to complete broadcast as a function of density for different move/pass neighborhood combinations. In the key, V = von Neumann, M = Moore, and R = rotated von Neumann. The first and second letters refer to the movement and message passing neighborhoods, respectively.

von Neumann neighborhoods, but pass messages within Moore neighborhoods, the best-case time can be reduced to $n - 2$. This scenario is reasonable since the networks being modeled comprise physical agents communicating by radio or some similar medium. A physical agent must move around buildings, walls, or rocks but the radio waves they use to communicate can go through these obstacles.

Finally, if agents move and messages are passed in Moore neighborhoods, the time can be reduced to ceil$(n/2) - 1$. Using these numbers we can establish a lower bound for the number of time steps required to complete broadcasting in a space with given dimensions and neighborhood definitions. When comparing broadcasting techniques, this can be used as a way of measuring their relative efficiency.

4.2.2 The Effect of Neighborhood Choice on Broadcast Time

It is immediately apparent from Figure 2 that, for all choices of movement/passing neighborhoods, the higher the density, the sooner broadcast is complete. It can also be seen that the number of time steps drops dramatically as density is increased to around 40%. Beyond that, the improvement is slight.

The graph also shows the difference in performance resulting from various neighborhood choices. Combinations which include a Moore neighborhood complete broadcasting more quickly than corresponding combinations which do not because a Moore neighborhood allows agents and/or messages to move along the diagonal of the space. It also allows movement in more different directions than either von Neumann or rotated von Neumann neighborhoods, however, decreasing the probability that the message will be disseminated in the most efficient direction.

It is also apparent that the overall most efficient neighborhood choice combines a rotated von Neumann neighborhood for agent movement with a Moore neighborhood for message passing. So the rate of information dissemination depends not only on the relationship of one cell to another but also on the rate at which the message moves away from its point of origin. Movement in a rotated von Neumann neighborhood provides the best chance of moving the furthest from the origin most quickly.

4.2.3 Neighborhoods That Can Cause Broadcast to Fail

As noted in Section 4.2.1, when the von Neumann/Rotated von Neumann and Rotated/Rotated neighborhood combinations are used, broadcast is likely to fail to complete. This is because the two neighborhoods are mutually exclusive. They form, in effect, a checkerboard and the rules for moving among them prevent moving from black to red squares. Agents move, then, on two separated non-overlapping grids, superimposed one over the other.

4.3 Summary of Simulation Results and Comparison with Other Work

The simulation data analyzed here enable us to determine an upper bound for "reasonably efficient" broadcast algorithms for use in highly mobile ad hoc networks. Farley previously proved the lower bound for such algorithms in fixed grid networks. His results are adapted here to ad hoc mobile networks and serve to define that bound.

This paper presents data showing average results for a number of runs under different circumstances. Since these results were obtained without defining any particular movement pattern beyond random selection of a neighboring cell, it is not reasonable to expect that they are optimal. When the density exceeds approximately forty percent, however, the number of time steps needed using this technique differs by nearly fixed amounts from the theoretical best achievable times. This gives us a loose upper bound on what can be considered acceptable.

These results can be used to gauge the efficiency in terms of time steps needed by different algorithms to complete broadcast. The lower bound described is fixed and the closer one can come to it, the better. If that bound is not achieved, the times presented here define an upper bound on what could reasonably be considered to be "close enough."

These results are consistent with work presented in [15] in which information dissemination in mobile ad hoc networks is compared to the spreading of epidemic infections and an analytical model is presented for calculating the time required to reach all nodes under various rates of "infection." They demonstrate that, for a given "diffusion force," as more time passes, the percentage of infected nodes (in other words, agents with the message) increases dramatically to a point and then levels off. This agrees with the results presented Figure 2. In this case the diffusion force is related to the agent density

5 Conclusions and Suggestions for Future Work

Farley's Theorem concerning message broadcast time in fixed grid networks can be adapted to determine the best achievable time in mobile ad hoc networks. This paper shows how to do that and then presents a means for establishing a "reasonable" upper bound.

This paper describes the use of cellular automata for the purpose of analyzing message broadcast time in highly mobile ad hoc networks. This work is intended to serve as a starting point for further research. The simulation method used appears promising as a means of testing a variety of broadcast algorithms. The next step in this process is to study the dissemination patterns produced as agents and messages move throughout the modeled space. Once those patterns are well understood, algorithms can be developed which may improve the broadcast time.

References

1. Tanenbaum, A, and van Steen. M. *Distributed Systems, Principles and Paradigms.* Upper Saddle River, NJ: Prentice Hall, Inc. 2002)
2. Perkins, C. and Bhagwat, P. "Highly Dynamic Destination-Sequenced Distance-Vector Routing (DSDV) for Mobile Computers." SIGCOMM 94, (1994) 234–244.
3. Johansson, P., Larsson, T., Hedman, N., Mielczarek, B., Degermark, M. "Scenario-based Performance Analysis of Routing Protocols for Mobile Ad-hoc Networks." Mobicom '99, (1999) 195–206.
4. Chandy, K. M. and Lamport, L. "Distributed Snapshots: Determining Global States if Distributed Systems." *ACM Transactions on Computer Systems, Vol. 3, No. 1,* (February 1985), (1985) 63–75.
5. Murphy; A. Roman; G-C., Varghese, G. "An Algorithm for Message Delivery to Mobile Units." PODC 97, (1997) 292.
6. Das, S. K., Manoj, B., Ram, C. S., Murthy. "A Dynamic Core Based Multicast Routing Protocol for Ad Hoc Wireless Networks." MobiHoc 2002, (2002) 24–34.
7. Chen, Y. and Liestman, A. "Approximating Minimum Size Weakly-Connected Dominating Sets for Clustering Mobile Ad Hoc Networks," MobiHoc 2002, (2002) 165–172.
8. Peng, W. and Lu, X-C., "On the Reduction of Broadcast Redundancy in Mobile Ad Hoc Networks." MobiHoc 2000, (2000) 129–130.
9. Chantemargue, F., Dagaeff, T., Hirsbrunner, B. "Emergence-based Cooperation in a Multi-Agent System." *Proceedings of the Second European Conference Cognitive Science (ECCS'97),* Manchester U.K., April 9-11, (1997) 91–96.
10. Thangiah, S., Shmygelska, L., Mennell., W., "An Agent Architecture for Vehicle Routing Problems." ACM Symposium on Applied Computing 2001, (2001) 517–521.
11. Sarkar, P. "A Brief History of Cellular Automata." *ACM Computing Surveys,* Vol. 32, No. 1, March 2000. (2000) 80–107.
12. Mukhopadhyay, A. "Representation of Events in the von Neumann Cellular Model." *Journal of the Association for Computing Machinery,* Vol. 15, No. 4, (October 1968) 693-705.
13. Subrata, R. and Zomaya, A. "Evolving Cellular Automata for Location Management in Mobile Computing Networks,." *IEEE Transactions on Parallel and Distributed Systems,* Vol. 14, No. 1, (January 2003) 13–26.
14. Farley, A.,"Broadcast time in communication networks." *SIAM Journal of Applied Mathematics,* No. 39, (1980) 385–390.
15. Khelil, A, Becker, C, Tian, J, and Rothermel, K., "An Epidemic Model for Information Diffusion in MANETs,' Proceedings of The Fifth ACM International Workshop on Modeling, Analysis and Simulation of Wireless and Mobile Systems (MSWiM'02), (2002) 54–60.

From Individual to Collective Behaviour in CA Like Models of Data Communication Networks

A.T. Lawniczak[1], K.P. Maxie[1], and A. Gerisch[2]

[1] Department of Mathematics and Statistics, University of Guelph,
Guelph, ON N1G 2W1, Canada, {alawnicz, kmaxie}@uoguelph.ca,
[2] FB Mathematik und Informatik, Martin-Luther-Universität Halle-Wittenberg,
06099 Halle (Saale), Germany.

Abstract. Understanding the collective behaviour of packets traffic in data networks is of vital importance for their future developments. Some aspects of this behaviour can be captured and investigated by simplified models of data networks. We present our CA like model describing processes taking place at the Network Layer of the OSI (Open Systems Interconnection) Reference Model. We use this model to study spatiotemporal packets traffic dynamics for various routing algorithms and traffic loads presented to the network. We investigate how additional links, added to a network connection topology, affect the collective behaviour of packets traffic. We discuss how some of the network performance aggregate measures reflect and relate to the emergence of packets collective spatio-temporal dynamics. We present selected simulation results and analyse them.

1 Introduction

In recent years data communication networks have experienced unprecedented growth that will continue in the future. The dominant technology is the Packet Switching Network (PSN). Examples of PSNs include the Internet, wide area networks (WANs), local area networks (LANs), wireless communication networks, ad-hoc networks, or sensor networks. The widespread proliferation of PSNs has outpaced our understanding of the dynamics of packets traffics and their dependence on network connection topologies, routing algorithms, amounts and types of data presented to the networks. For the future development of PSNs it is important to understand what effects may have local changes in network connection topologies, changes in operation of single routers, or changes in routing algorithms on the collective behaviour of packets. The further evolution of PSNs and improvements in their design depend strongly on the ability to predict networks performance using analytical and simulation methods, see e.g. [1, 2,3,4] and the references therein. The need to have a simulation model closer to the real packet switching networks than static flow and queueing models in order to study which network features and parameters affect flow, congestion and collective spatio-temporal dynamics of packets in PSNs has motivated our

P.M.A. Sloot, B. Chopard, and A.G. Hoekstra (Eds.): ACRI 2004, LNCS 3305, pp. 325–334, 2004.

research. Our simulation model describes the processes taking place at the Network Layer of the OSI Reference Model. For this layer we have constructed a cellular automaton (CA) like model [5,6]. In order to simulate our CA model of PSNs we developed a C++ simulation tool, called Netzwerk-1 [7]. The benefits of our model are that, like real networks: it is concerned primarily with packets and their routing; it is scalable, distributed in space, and time discrete. Moreover, it avoids the overhead of protocol details present in simulators designed with different goals in mind.

We have applied our model and its further refinements to study, among others, the effects of routing algorithms and network topologies connectivity, size and the addition of extra links with various preferentiality factors of attachment on the phase transition from free flow to congestion, throughput, average packet delay, packet average path length and speed of delivery, see [8,9,10,11]. The presented work is a continuation of our previous investigations. Its goal is to study how the packets collective spatio-temporal dynamics is affected by the network topology. Also, our aim is to isolate aspects of routing algorithms that lead to spatio-temporal self-organisation in packets traffics. We explore, for selected network performance aggregate measures, how they reflect and relate to the emergence of packets collective spatio-temporal dynamics.

The paper is organised as follows. In Section 2 we describe our CA network model. In Section 3 we present selected simulation results and analyse them. In Section 4 we provide our conclusions and outline future work.

2   Packet Switching Network Model

There is vast engineering literature devoted to PSNs, see [3] and the references therein. We limit our discussion to the development of our PSN model. Its detailed construction is described in [6,7]. The purpose of a PSN is to transmit messages from sender to receiver. In a real-world PSN, messages are broken into several equally sized pieces called *packets*. These packets are then sent across a network consisting of connected nodes, known as *hosts* and/or *routers*. In our model we restrict all messages to the length of one packet. Packets contain an information payload along with routing and other header information. Since our concern is strictly with the delivery of packets across the network, the information payload contained within each packet is irrelevant to our discussion. Hence, in the considered models we assume that each packet carries only the following information: time of creation, destination address, and number of hops taken.

As in a real-world PSN, our network model consists of a number of interconnected switching nodes. Each node can perform the functions associated with a *host* and a *router*. The primary functions of the hosts are to generate and receive packets. Routers are responsible for storing and forwarding packets on their route from source to destination. Packets are created randomly and independently at each node. The probability λ with which packets are created is called *source load*. Nodes maintain incoming and outgoing queues to store packets. For this paper we consider one incoming queue and one outgoing queue per switching node. We assume that the outgoing queues are of unlimited length and operate in a first-in, first-out manner. Each node at each time step routes the packet from the head of its outgoing queue to the next node on its route independently from the other nodes. A discrete time, synchronous and spatially distributed network algorithm implements the creation and routing of packets [6, 7,8]. The considered network connection topologies, routing cost metrics and the PSN model algorithm are described in subsections that follow.

Network Connection Topology. In a real-world PSN, while the physical means of communication links may vary, the underlying connection topology can always be viewed as a weighted directed multigraph $\mathcal{L}$. Each switching node corresponds to a vertex and each communication link is analogous to a pair of parallel edges oriented in opposite directions. We associate a packet transmission cost to each directed edge, thus parallel edges do not necessarily share the same cost.

For the presented set of simulations we consider network connection topologies $\mathcal{L} = \mathcal{L}_{l,\square}(L)$ that are isomorphic to two-dimensional periodic or non-periodic square lattices with the number of nodes in the horizontal and vertical directions $L = 16$. We study both unperturbed networks with $l = 0$ additional links and perturbed ones by adding randomly $l > 0$ extra links. The first node to which an additional link attaches is selected with uniform probability from the set of all nodes in the network. The second node is selected randomly from the remaining nodes with bias towards the nodes with higher number of outgoing edges. The bias is called *preferentiality factor (PF) of attachment*. If the bias is equal to zero then the second node is selected with uniform probability. All randomly generated links are added prior to a simulation run. All links in the network are static for the duration of the simulation.

Static Routing and Adaptive Routing. In the network models, packets are transmitted from their source nodes to their respective destination nodes. The path across the network taken by each packet is determined by the routing decisions made independently at each node based on a least-cost criterion. Depending on the costs assigned to each edge of the graph, we consider routing decisions based on the *minimum route distance* or the *minimum route length least-cost criterion* [2,3]. We consider three types of *edge cost functions* called One (ONE), QueueSize (QS), and QueueSizePlusOne (QSPO) [6,7] that are described below. In each considered network model setup it is assumed that all edge costs are computed using the same type of edge cost function.

Edge cost function ONE assigns a value of one to all edges in the lattice $\mathcal{L}$. Applying a least cost routing criterion results in minimising the number of hops taken by each packet between its source and its destination node, *minimum hop routing*. Since the values assigned to each edge do not change during the course of a simulation, this type of routing is called *static routing*. The QS edge cost function assigns to each edge in the lattice $\mathcal{L}$ a value proportional to the length of the outgoing queue at the node from which the edge originates. A packet traversing a network using this edge cost function will travel from its current node to the next node along an edge belonging to a path with the least total number of packets in transit between its current location and its destination. The edge cost function QSPO assigns a summed value of a constant one plus a number proportional to the length of the outgoing queue at the node from which the edge originates. This cost function combines the attributes of the first two functions. Routing decisions made using QS or QSPO edge cost functions rely on the current state of the network simulation. Hence, they imply *adaptive* or *dynamic routing* in which packets have the ability to avoid congested nodes during a network simulation.

Each switching node maintains a *routing table* of least path cost estimates to reach every other node in the network. This type of routing scheme is called *full-table routing*. When the edge costs are assigned by the function ONE the routing tables can be calculated once at the beginning of each simulation and they do not require updating, because edge costs do not change with time. In this case the cost estimates are the precise least-costs. When the edge costs in a PSN model are assigned by the function QS or QSPO, the routing tables are updated at each time step using a distributed version of Bellman-Ford least-cost algorithm [2]. Since only local information is exchanged at each time step, the path costs stored in the routing table are only estimates of the actual least path costs across the network.

Packet Switching Network Model Algorithm. In our model we consider time as given in discrete time units of size one and perform simulations from time $k = 0$ to a final simulation time $k = T$. We can observe the state of the network model at the discrete time points $k = 0, 1, 2, \ldots, T$ only. At time $k = 0$, the network is initialised with empty queues and the routing tables are computed using the centralised Bellman-Ford least-cost algorithm [2].

One step of the discrete time, synchronous and distributed in space network algorithm advances the simulation time from k to $k + 1$. It is given by the sequence of five operations: (1) *Update routing tables:* The routing tables of the network are updated in a distributed manner; (2) *Create and route packets:* At each node, independently of the other nodes, a packet is created randomly with source load λ. Its destination address is randomly selected among all other nodes in the network with uniform probability. The newly created packet is placed in the incoming queue of its source node. Further, each node, independently of the other nodes, takes the packet from the head of its outgoing queue (if there is any), determines the next node on a least-cost route to its destination (if there is more than one possibility then selects one at random with uniform probability), and forwards this packet to this node. Packets, which arrive at a node from other nodes during this step of the algorithm, are destroyed immediately if this node is their destination, otherwise they are placed in the incoming queue; (3) *Process incoming queue:* At each node, independently of the other nodes, the packets in the incoming queue are randomised and inserted at the end of the outgoing queue; (4) *Evaluate network state:* Various statistical data about the state of the network at time k are gathered and stored in time series; (5) *Update simulation time:* The time k is incremented to $k + 1$.

The above described time step from k to $k+1$ of the network algorithm can be repeated an arbitrary number of times. Step (3) of the algorithm simulates a sort of processing delay and ensures that a packet, which arrives at a node in one time step, does not leave the node before the next time step. Further, randomising the incoming queue simulates that the packets arrive at each node in random order.

3   From Individual to Collective Behaviour of Packets in Transit

In this section we present selected simulation results and discuss the emergence of collective behaviour in packets traffic for the described adaptive routing algorithms. We explore how changes in the network connection topology affect critical source load values and packets spatio-temporal collective behaviour. For a discussion of how other network performance aggregate measures reflect and relate to the emergence of packets collective behaviour we refer to [8,9,10,11,12].

Critical Source Load. We classify host source loads λ as *sub-critical, critical,* and *super-critical source loads*. A source load is said to be *sub-critical* if the average number of packets entering the network does not exceed the average number of packets leaving the network. This results in *free flowing traffic* in a network where packets reach their destinations in a timely manner. A *super-critical* source load is just the opposite of this: the average number of packets entering the network exceeds the number of packets exiting the network. The result of applying a super-critical source load is a *congested network*. Finally, the *critical source load* λ_c is the largest sub-critical source load, or the phase transition point from free flowing to congested network states. This phase transition has been observed in empirical studies of packet switching networks [13]. For details concerning the calculation of λ_c for a given PSN model and analysis how various aspects of a PSN affect the critical source load value see [6,7,8,9,10, 11].

We consider how the random addition of links affects the critical source load. The results for periodic (left figure) and non-periodic (right figure) square lattices of size $L = 16$ with $PF = 0$ are displayed in Fig. 1. The lower graphs in both figures correspond to edge cost function ONE, and the upper ones, that almost coincide, to the edge cost functions QS and QSPO. We notice that for a periodic lattice, in the absence of additional links, all three edge cost functions result in similar values for λ_c. For the non-periodic lattice, λ_c for the edge cost ONE is significantly lower than those for QS and QSPO in this case. The reason is that the static minimum hop routing does not route packets around congested regions of the network. The critical source loads for the three edge costs of the otherwise same model setups are significantly lower for the non-periodic lattice without or with relatively small number of extra links than those for the equivalent periodic lattices. We attribute this to the increased average distance between any two nodes in the non-periodic lattice. This implies, that on average many

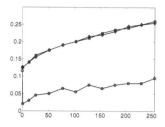 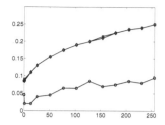

Fig. 1. λ_c versus l for $\mathcal{L}_{l,\square}(16)$ with $PF = 0$. The left figure shows results for periodic lattices, the right for non-periodic lattices. The lower graphs correspond to edge cost ONE, the upper ones to QS and to QSPO. The graphs for QS and QSPO almost coincide

more packets remain longer in transit resulting in faster build up of congestion for lower source load values. Further, many more packets must transit through the centre region of the network, in particular for static routing, i.e. edge cost ONE; in the case of QSPO, see Figs. 2 and 3. For periodic and non-periodic lattices and adaptive routing, i.e. edge cost QS or QSPO, additional links increase the value of λ_c. In fact, for both, QS and QSPO, there is very little difference in the values of λ_c (this may be due to the granularity of the applied source loads). For edge cost ONE (static routing) the addition of a small number of links results in a dramatic drop in the critical source loads. This is likely the result of the local congestion occurring at the ends of these few additional links as is seen in [12]. As more links are added, the critical source loads begin to recover towards their original levels. However, for the periodic lattice the number of additional links needed to fully regain this value is much higher than the one presented in the graph. With regards to the preferentiality factor of attachment of extra links, our study showed that an increase in the PF-value has an adverse effect on the critical source load values [10,11].

Spatio-temporal Packets Traffic Dynamics. Here, we discuss the effects of the lattices periodicity and addition of extra links on the collective spatio-temporal behaviour of packets in transit in PSN models with edge cost function QSPO for connection topology $\mathcal{L} = \mathcal{L}_{l,\square}(16)$. The presented results are for preferentiality factor $PF = 0$ and numbers of additional links $l = 0$, 1, and 51. For the periodic lattices, the source load values λ are 0.125, 0.130, and 0.175, respectively. For the non-periodic lattices they are 0.090, 0.095, and 0.160, respectively. The values of the considered source loads are about 0.005 higher than those of the corresponding λ_c values. For a discussion of results for other cost functions, topologies and source loads, see [12].

In Figs. 2, 3 and 4 the x- and y-axis coordinates denote the positions of switching nodes in $\mathcal{L} = \mathcal{L}_{l,\square}(16)$. The z-axis denotes the number of packets in the outgoing queue of the node at that (x, y) position. In Fig. 2 we present results for periodic lattices and in Fig. 3 for non-periodic ones. In both figures, the left column corresponds to the lattice without an extra link, the right column to the lattice with one extra link. In Fig. 4 we show results for lattices with $l = 51$

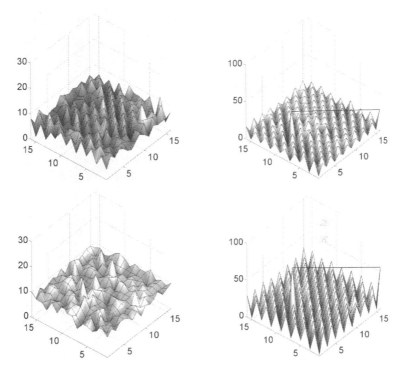

Fig. 2. Evolution of queue lengths for edge cost QSPO, $\lambda > \lambda_c$, periodic lattice $\mathcal{L} = \mathcal{L}_{l,\square}(16)$ without an extra link (left column) and with an extra link (right column), for $k = 1600$ (top row) and $k = 3200$ (bottom row)

extra links; in the left picture for the periodic lattice, in the right picture for the non-periodic one. The distribution of packets is presented for two separate snapshots in time corresponding to $k = 1600$ and 3200 in Figs. 2 and 3, and in Fig. 4 only at $k = 3200$.

The graphs of Fig. 2 demonstrate spatio-temporal self-organisation in packets traffic for periodic lattices with $l = 0$ and $l = 1$ and emergence of wave-like pattern with peaks and valleys in packet distribution for congested networks ($\lambda > \lambda_c$) using adaptive routing with the QSPO edge cost function. As the number of packets in the network model increases, the wave-like pattern emerges in spite the routing scheme attempts to distribute the packets across the network queues evenly. One notices that for each node that is part of a peak (i.e. with a relatively large number of packets in its queue), its directly attached neighbours are part of a trough (i.e. with a relatively small number of packets in their queue). The converse also holds true. The addition of an extra link hastens the formation of the wave-like pattern. The pattern is similar to the one obtained for QS for periodic lattice [12]. However, the addition of many extra links destroys the formation of this pattern, see Fig. 4. Large queues of more or less the same size appear at the ends of the extra links with very small number of packets elsewhere.

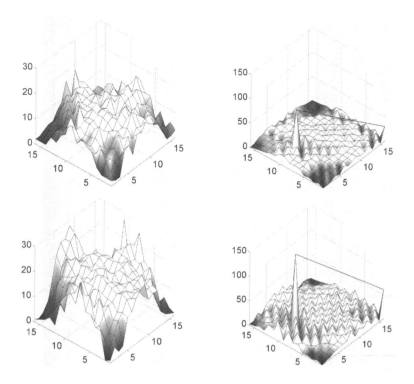

Fig. 3. Evolution of queue lengths for edge cost QSPO, $\lambda > \lambda_c$, non-periodic lattice $\mathcal{L} = \mathcal{L}_{l,\square}(16)$ without an extra link (left column) and with an extra link (right column), for $k = 1600$ (top row) and $k = 3200$ (bottom row)

The graphs of Fig. 3 demonstrate that connection topology periodicity plays an important role in building up of congestion and emergence of packets collective behaviour. For the lattice with $l = 0$ we observe across the network an essentially random distribution of packet queue lengths with their variability increasing over time. The landscape of queue sizes resembles the one observed in the case of the edge cost ONE [12], with the difference that here the queues are significantly larger at the centrally located nodes. That means that, for the QSPO edge cost function, the ONE-part of the cost plays a much more significant role in routing of the packets in the case of non-periodic lattices than in the case of the periodic ones. We observe that the addition of one extra link dramatically changes packets collective dynamics. It destroys the increasing build up of the queue sizes of large variability in the interior of the network. The extra link provides a "short-cut" across the network and plays the surrogate role of the missing links due to the lattices lack of periodicity. The extra link attracts much larger numbers of packets than links elsewhere in the network resulting in local congestion growing at its ends with time. The remaining packets are distributed more evenly among the other queues of the network, then as it was observed for $l = 0$. Initially, the queues are located mostly in the centre of the network. As time progresses this local congestion spreads out almost evenly across the

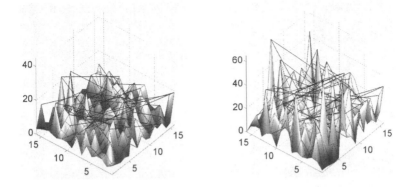

Fig. 4. Packet queue lengths for $k = 3200$, edge cost QSPO, $\lambda > \lambda_c$, lattice $\mathcal{L} = \mathcal{L}_{l,\square}(16)$ with 51 extra links: left picture for the periodic lattice, right picture for the non-periodic lattice

network and a wave like pattern emerges among these queues. The sizes of these queues stay always significantly smaller than that at the ends of the extra link. For times $k > 1600$, the distribution of queue sizes resembles that of the super-position of the distribution of packets for the edge cost ONE with that for QS presented in [12]. The addition of a large number of extra links destroys wave like pattern and packets queue mostly at the ends of the extra links. Fig. 4 shows that the variability of the queue sizes is higher for the non-periodic lattices than for the periodic ones.

4   Conclusions

We described our CA like model of the OSI Network Layer for PSNs. The presented simulation results demonstrate that the network connection topology plays an important role for the amount of traffic that can be presented to the network and for the emergence of packets in transit collective behaviour. For static minimum hop routing, the addition of one extra link decreases drastically the critical source load value and in order for the network to recover its performance many links must be added. For adaptive routing, the critical source load values increase with the increase in the number of extra links. We observe that the addition of one extra link can hasten the spatio-temporal self-organisation in the distribution of packets in transit and lead to the emergence of a wave-like pattern of queue lengths across the network. However, addition of many links destroys this process.

The presented study is a continuation of the authors work in [12]. We plan further investigation into the factors responsible for spatio-temporal self-organisation of queue lengths. Discovering and understanding correlations between the traffic patterns and network parameters has the potential to impact decisions made with regards to topological and routing scheme designs for real-world networks.

Acknowledgements. The authors acknowledge support from the University of Guelph, The Fields Institute and the use of the SHARCNET computational resources. They thank B. Di Stefano and P. Zhao for helpful discussions. A.T.L. acknowledges additional support from NSERC and IPAM.

References

1. Filipiak, J.: Modelling and Control of Dynamic Flows in Communication Networks. Communications and Control Engineering Series. Springer-Verlag Berlin Heidelberg (1988)
2. Bertsekas, P.D., Gallager, R.G.: Data Networks. 2nd edn. Prentice Hall, Upper Saddle River (1992)
3. Stallings, W.: High-Speed Networks: TCP/IP and ATM Design Principles. Prentice Hall, Upper Saddle River, New Jersey (1998)
4. Serfozo, R.: Introduction to Stochastic Networks. Applications of Mathematics Series. Springer-Verlag Berlin Heidelberg New York (1999)
5. Fukś, H., Lawniczak, A.: Performance of data networks with random links. Mathematics and Computers in Simulation **51** (1999) 101–117
6. Lawniczak, A.T., Gerisch, A., Di Stefano, B.: Development and performance of cellular automaton model of OSI Network Layer of packet-switching networks. In: IEEE CCECE 2003-CCGEI 2003, Montréal, Quebec, Canada. (2003) 001–004
7. Gerisch, A., Lawniczak, A.T., Di Stefano, B.: Building blocks of a simulation environment of the OSI Network Layer of packet-switching networks. In: IEEE CCECE 2003-CCGEI 2003, Montréal, Quebec, Canada. (2003) 001–004
8. Lawniczak, A., Gerisch, A., Maxie, K.: Effects of randomly added links on a phase transition in data network traffic models. In: Proc. of the 3rd DCDIS Conf. on Engineering Applications and Computational Algorithms, Guelph, Ontario, Canada, May 15-18, 2003, Watam Press Waterloo (2003) 384–389 Published as an added volume to *DCDIS, Series B, Applications and Algorithms*, ISSN 1492-8760.
9. Lawniczak, A.T., Gerisch, A., Zhao, P., Di Stefano, B.: Effects of randomly added links on average delay and number of packets in transit in data network traffic models. In: Proc. of the 3rd DCDIS Conf. on Engineering Applications and Computational Algorithms, Guelph, Ontario, Canada, May 15-18, 2003, Watam Press Waterloo (2003) 378–383 Published as an added volume to *DCDIS, Series B, Applications and Algorithms*, ISSN 1492-8760.
10. Maxie, K.P., Lawniczak, A.T., Gerisch, A.: Study of a packet average path length and average speed of delivery in data network traffic model. In: IEEE CCECE 2004-CCGEI 2004, Niagara Falls, Ontario, Canada. (2004) 2433–2436
11. Lawniczak, A.T., Maxie, K.P., Gerisch, A.: Effects of network connection topology and routing algortihm on phase transition and throughput in packet-switching network model. In: IEEE CCECE 2004-CCGEI 2004, Niagara Falls, Ontario, Canada. (2004) 2429–2432
12. Maxie, K.P., Lawniczak, A.T., Gerisch, A.: Effects of an extra link and routing on spatio-temporal packet traffic dynamics of network model. In: IEEE CCECE 2004-CCGEI 2004, Niagara Falls, Ontario, Canada. (2004) 2425–2428
13. Tretyakov, A.Y., Takayasu, H., Takayasu, M.: Phase transition in a computer network model. Physica A **253** (1998) 315–322

Agent-Driven Resource Optimization in User Networks: A Game Theoretical Approach

J.C. Burguillo-Rial[1], F.J. González-Castaño[1], E. Costa-Montenegro[1], and
J. Vales-Alonso[2]

[1] Departamento de Ingeniería Telemática
Universidad de Vigo, Spain
{jrial,javier,kike}@det.uvigo.es
[2] Departamento de Tecnologías de la Información y las Comunicaciones
Universidad Politécnica de Cartagena, Spain
javier.vales@upct.es

Abstract. In this paper, we evaluate the feasibility of distributed control of shared resources in user networks. A user network is totally controlled by the users, both at application and transport level. This paradigm has become possible with the advent of broadband wireless networking technologies such as IEEE 802.11. One of the most popular applications in these networks is peer-to-peer file exchange. As a consequence, the "external" access to the Internet (set of links between the user network and the Internet) is a shared resource that can be optimized by node cooperation (i.e., if a node cannot serve its demand with its own external link, it requests help from another node via the high-bandwidth internal user network). We consider cellular automata to model such networks and game theory to model cell behavior. Every cell chooses to behave as a cooperative or defector node. Cooperators may assist in file exchange, whereas defectors try to get advantage of network resources without providing help in return. Simulation results help to understand the conditions for cooperative cells to win the game.

Keywords: Stochastic cellular automata, user networks, complex systems, game theory.

1 Introduction

User networks are totally controlled by the users, both at application and transport level. This paradigm has become possible with the advent of broadband wireless networking technologies such as IEEE 802.11. For applications such as peer-to-peer file exchange, it may be useful to consider the "external" access to the Internet (set of links between the user network and the Internet) as a shared resource that can be optimized by node cooperation (i.e., if a node cannot serve its demand with its own external link, it requests help from another node via the high-bandwidth internal user network). Nodes decide if cooperation requests are granted or not, either by analyzing limited information on their neighbors' states or only based on their own experience.

In this paper, we analyze the conditions that enable cooperation in real user networks. This is not trivial in a realistic scenario. We could impose several conditions leading to

P.M.A. Sloot, B. Chopard, and A.G. Hoekstra (Eds.): ACRI 2004, LNCS 3305, pp. 335–344, 2004.

node cooperation that would never hold considering user behavior in peer-to-peer (P2P) services. Therefore, we have developed a framework that makes it possible to model the real problem and to provide results that explain the conditions for cooperative nodes to win the game, i.e., to become a majority.

In order to hide the complexities of file exchange, we model it as a game where *cells* (i.e. node routers) choose between two different *basic strategies*: *cooperation* and *defection*. Cooperators assist neighbor cells in Internet file exchange, while defectors do not offer help to neighbors (although they request help for their demands). Thus, defectors model non-cooperating users, a typical problem in P2P networks. If we consider the spatial structure of the population, restricting interaction to local neighborhood, a stable spatial coexistence of cooperators and defectors becomes possible under certain conditions.

The context of cooperative games and cooperation evolution has been extensively studied in biological, social and ecological contexts [11], seeking general theoretical frameworks like the Prisoners' Dilemma (PD). In his seminal work, Axelrod has shown that cooperation can emerge in a society of individuals with selfish motivations [10]. For a review of related work in the last twenty years see [12].

The paper is organized as follows: section 2 describes user-managed networks. Section 3 briefly introduces some basic concepts of game theory. Section 4 defines the Cellular Automaton, which is the basic model for the analysis in section 5. Section 6 discusses the results of our simulations. Section 7 presents the conclusions of the paper and suggests future research.

2   User-Managed Networks

User-managed networks have become possible with the advent of wireless technologies such as IEEE 802.11 [2]. They represent one of the last stages in network control evolution [4]. This evolution started with telephone networks. In them, Telcos controlled both transport and applications. Later, the Internet allowed users to control applications. Although Telcos still control transport in most of the Internet, in some scenarios carrier technology is affordable to end-users, and user-managed "islands" appear in a natural way [5,6,7]. For example, this kind of infrastructures is currently being used to provide broadband access in Spanish rural areas, as an expansion of shared asymmetric DVB-S or DVB-T gateways.

A typical *basic node* in a wireless user-managed network is composed by a router, an IEEE 802.11 access point (AP) and/or some IEEE 802.11 cards to set links with other basic nodes. Basic nodes may also be linked to a multi-user LAN (covering a building, for example).

Figure 1 shows a sector of Vigo (Spain) with 46 basic node locations and the corresponding wireless links for near-maximum overall network bandwidth (D-Link DWL-1000 APs, D-Link DWL-650 wireless cards and AP channel cellular planning as in [13], for 50×50 m^2 cells).

A subset of the basic nodes will have cable or DSL access, providing "external" connection to the Internet. For the purposes of this paper and without loss of generality, we will assume that all basic nodes are "externally connected". Additionally, we assume

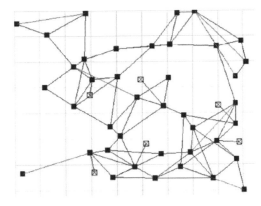

Fig. 1. Network sample: white squares denote isolated nodes

that user network capacity is much larger than external capacity (this holds for reasonable internal and external networking technologies, for example IEEE 802.11b and DSL respectively). Nowadays, peer-to-peer file exchange is a "killer" home application [8]. In a user network, basic nodes can easily share contents, due to the large internal bandwidth. The bottleneck is the set of "external" connections to the Internet. By optimizing their usage, overall performance (and, as a consequence, user satisfaction) can be greatly improved.

By *network stability* we refer to the condition such that external demands (e.g., downloads or uploads at the edges of the user network for peer-to-peer file exchanges) can be satisfied with external capacity, on average. This certainly holds if:

1. The external demand of each basic node can be satisfied with its own external capacity, on average,
2. All basic nodes cooperate via the user network and their combined external demand can be satisfied with their combined external capacity, on average.

Even if the first condition holds (and therefore cooperation is not strictly necessary to guarantee network stability), cooperation minimizes demand service time (nodes with temporarily idle external connections can help neighbors with demand peaks). However, there is no central authority, and -probably selfish- nodes will act either from limited information on their neighbors' state or only based on their own experience. As explained in section 5, cooperation granting/denial with limited information can be modeled as a **game**. The main goals of this paper are (*i*) to demonstrate that cooperative nodes may become a majority in user networks (cooperation may minimize service time) and (*ii*) game players can be implemented as distributed *basic node agents*. In our terminology, an *agent* is the program that implements the *cell* behavior.

3   Game Theory

Game theory [1] provides useful mathematical tools to understand the possible strategies that utility-maximizing agents may follow when choosing a course of action. The simplest type of game is the *single-shot simultaneous-move* game. In it, all agents must choose one action and all actions are effectively simultaneous. Each agent receives a utility that is a function of the combined set of actions. In an *extended-form* game, agents participate in turns and receive a payoff at the end of a sequence of actions. A single-shot game is a good model for many distributed systems, in which encounters require coordination. Finally, many scenarios that seem correctly described by an extended-form game can actually be modeled as a series of single-shot games.

The approach we follow in this paper is a composite game where actions are effectively simultaneous but every agent may interact with several neighbors at a time. Every agent receives a *data throughput* payoff every turn. The better the *strategy* in its context, the better the payoff, i.e., the higher the throughput. After a predefined set of turns d, each agent i chooses a strategy $s_i \in S_i$, where S_i is the set of all basic strategies for agent i. The strategy chosen will be used to interoperate with its neighbors for the next d turns. In our case, we restrict the set of strategies to two basic options: defection $s_i = 0$ or cooperation $s_i = 1$. Note that the payoff of a given agent depends on the choices made by the rest.

4   Defining the Cellular Automaton (CA)

In this section we introduce a model for a cellular automaton (CA) taken from [9], to describe the different nodes of the network (*cells* in the sequel).

In order to specify cell interaction, we adopt a game theoretical approach. Each cell i has two alternative strategies to act in a given situation, defection ($s_i = 0$), and cooperation ($s_i = 1$). Then, $s_i \in S$ indicates whether agent i is a cooperator or a defector. We assume that all agents share the same set of strategies and that the total number of agents N is constant.

For the spatial distribution of the agents we consider a two-dimensional cellular automaton (or a two-dimensional square lattice) consisting of N cells. Each cell is occupied by one agent. Therefore, each cell is characterized by a discrete value $s_i \in \{0, 1\}$, indicating whether it is occupied by a defector or a cooperator. The spatiotemporal distribution of the agents is then described by $\$ = \{s_1, s_2, ..., s_N\}$.

Figure 2 shows a cell i and its neighborhood. In the model in section 5, every cell (i.e. agent) in the square lattice will interact with K closest neighbors to handle external traffic. Thus, there are both local and spatial interactions between neighbor cells.

5   Modeling the Problem

If we let every agent in the system to interact with the remaining $N - 1$ agents, we have a panmictic population. However, in this paper we are mainly interested in the spatial effects of the game. Besides, in real user networks each node interacts with a few neighbors. Therefore, assuming we simplify the typical "mesh-like" user network topology as a pure mesh, we consider that each agent i only interacts with the K agents in its immediate neighborhood.

Interaction is driven by demand service times of externally inbound or outbound data, i.e., when the external service queue of a cell is larger than a particular threshold,

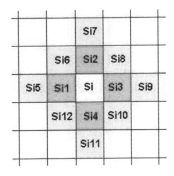

Fig. 2. A two-dimensional cellular automaton. Cell i and two possible neighborhoods.

the agent controlling the cell contacts its neighbors requesting help to handle the files involved. In order to introduce a time scale, the time unit to generate new traffic demands and for neighbors interaction is an hour. The total number of interactions per hour can be $K \times N$ or less.

We decided that, during a 24-hour timeframe (a day), the strategy s_i of an agent does not change. We also decided to consider a day as the time unit for strategy changes, since traffic patterns are similar in the same hour across different days.

After a day passes, s_i can change as described next for two disjoint scenarios:

- *Oracle-based or centralized scenario.* This scenario is unrealistic, because it assumes that every agent knows the strategy of its K neighbors. It can be considered an ideal reference for the distributed scenario below. The agent in cell i mimics the strategy of its "best" neighbor k whose agent offered to i the best worst-case hourly throughput during last day (out of 24 measurements). We decided to compare hourly rather than daily throughput to let user satisfaction be based on a compromise between worst-case and average experience.
  The main interest of this scenario is to determine if cooperation is feasible or not. For this purpose, we consider the best conditions, i.e., when cells share information. Therefore, it allows us to predict the most popular strategy in a game with shared information.
  At the end of every day d, agent i calculates $x = \text{argmax}_{x \in K} (\min_{h \in d}(\text{th}(h, x))$, where $\text{th}(h, x)$ is the throughput of neighbor x during hour h. Then, agent i mimics the strategy of agent x. Obviously, it keeps its previous behavior if the most successful agent followed the same strategy.
- *Realistic or distributed scenario.* In this scenario, each agent is a stochastic automaton with two states: cooperator or defector. Each agent compares its worst-case hourly throughput during the last day (out of 24 measurements) with the average values obtained in previous history by the alternative strategy $\overline{s_i}$. If its throughput is better than the average value achieved by the alternative strategy, then the agent linearly increases the probability of the current strategy s_i (we use the linear reinforcement scheme for stochastic automata in [3]).
  At the end of every day d, agent i calculates $f(i, d) = \min_{h \in d}(\text{th}(h, i))$. Then:

- If $f(i, d)$ is strictly higher than the daily average values of f up to that moment when following the alternative strategy $\overline{s_i}$, then:

$$p_{s_i}[d+1] = p_{s_i}[d] + 0.1(1 - p_{s_i}[d]), \text{ and } p_{\overline{s_i}}[d+1] = 0.9 p_{\overline{s_i}}[d].$$

the strategy for the next day is selected according to probabilities $p_{s_i}(d+1)$ and $p_{\overline{s_i}}[d+1]$.

We assume that, each hour, if the queue length of a cell exceeds a defined threshold, the agent ruling that cell requests help from its neighbors for every pending file (incoming or outgoing). Neighbor agents may grant their external connections or not, depending on their present state and strategy. We implement help transactions using the Contract Net Protocol: neighbors answer with a set of offers and/or refusals. The requesting agent selects the offering cell that provided the best average throughput in the past.

We model defection and cooperation as follows:

- *Defection*: a defector never helps, so it will never grant its external connection. Nevertheless, defectors ask their neighbors for help when they need it. Thus, they use shared resources opportunistically as many users do in P2P networks.
- *Cooperation*: a cooperator helps its neighbors up to a certain credit limit (denoted by CreditLimit in section 6). If cell j reaches its credit limit, cell i does not help j again unless j returns its debt by helping i when requested.

Finally, concerning cell demand distribution, we define two cell types A and B. A cells generate uniformly distributed demand service times (externally inbound or outbound data) during disjoint busy and quiet periods, corresponding to day and night. In B cells, the quiet period takes place during the busy period of A cells, and viceversa.

6 Simulation Results

Diverse interesting characteristics of the spatial game appeared in the simulations. Starting with an initial random distribution of cooperators and defectors, several spatial domains appear, each of them dominated either by cooperators or defectors. Also, we noticed that, in the long run, the percentages of cooperators and defectors become stationary (with minimal changes).

We performed all the simulations with QNet[1]. As previously said, all case studies take place in a completely symmetric user network. Each cell is linked to K neighbors (we have considered $K = 4$ and $K = 8$). The relevant settings for our application are:

- There are ($50 \times 50 = 2,500$) cells in the user network.
- Demand distribution settings are:
  - *Busy period*: the cell generates uniformly distributed demand service times with mean 8 units during 12 hours a day.
  - *Quiet period*: idem, with mean 1 unit during the remaining 12 hours.

---

[1] QNet (Quarter Net) is a Java-based cellular automata simulator that can be requested to J.C. Burguillo, {jrial@det.uvigo.es}

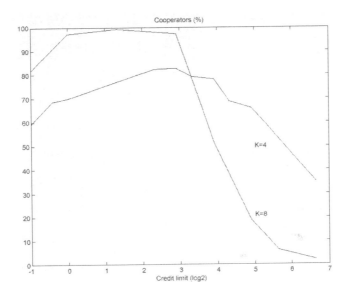

Fig. 3. Percentage of cooperators after 2400 hours, centralized scenario

- External links have a bandwidth of 5 demand units per hour. Note that this is slightly above the average demand ($0.5 \times 8 + 0.5 \times 1 = 4.5$), and therefore external capacity is loaded. For example, for 1 Mbps DSL each demand unit is $\sim$100 MB.
- Cell demand files have a maximum size of two demand units (e.g. 200 MB for 1 Mbps DSL).
- At time origin, node strategies are assigned with equal probability.
- At time origin, cell traffic patterns (A or B) are assigned with equal probability.
- Every cell (including defectors) asks its neighbors for help if it generates over 5 demand units per hour.

Initially, we ran our simulations with a single cell type (A or B). In this case, defectors became a majority. We could have expected this result, since all cells are typically busy at the same time of the day and, as a consequence, cooperation is not rewarding.

When we considered two cell types (A and B), we observed the following:

- Let C and D be the percentages of cooperators and defectors at simulation end, respectively. It happens that $C >> D$ in permanent state if cooperators choose CreditLimit wisely. The larger the value of C, the larger the *global* user network throughput. Roughly, this holds for CreditLimit$\sim$10 in all cases. Figures 3 and 4 show the percentage of cooperating cells after 2400 simulated hours, in the centralized and distributed scenarios respectively. Cooperation success as a function of CreditLimit suggests that, in an agent-based implementation, agents should adjust CreditLimit dynamically, according to the queue lengths in their cells.
- Although cooperators and defectors are completely mixed at simulation start, cooperators tend to form *confederations*. This spatial distribution tends to become

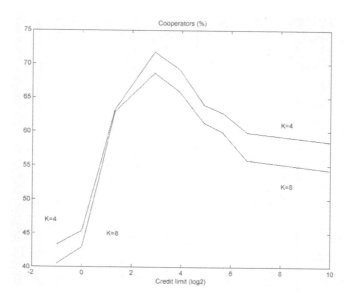

Fig. 4. Percentage of cooperators after 2400 hours, distributed scenario

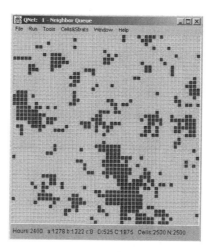

Fig. 5. Spatial distribution (K=4, CreditLimit=7.5, 100 days, centralized scenario)

stable. Figure 5 shows a spatial distribution of the centralized scenario with $K = 4$ and CreditLimit=7.5 after 2400 hours (dark cells represent defectors). Figure 6 shows the evolution of the percentages of cooperators and defectors in two scenarios: centralized (left side) and distributed (right side).

- The choice of CreditLimit is specially critical in the centralized scenario: if cooperators are too conservative (low CreditLimit) or too generous (high Credit-

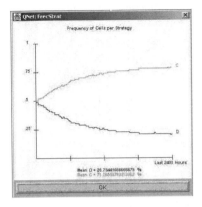 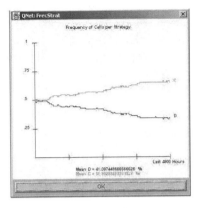

Fig. 6. Percentages of Cooperators vs Defectors (K=4, `CreditLimit`=7.5). a) Left-side: centralized scenario. b) Right-side: distributed scenario. Cooperators win in both cases.

`Limit`), cooperation is less successful than defection. However, in the distributed scenario, this effect is only evident if cooperators are conservative. A possible explanation for the result in the centralized case is that, for `CreditLimit` values around 10, defectors only can fool cooperators at the beginning of the game, since debts have to be promptly returned. If cooperators are too generous, defectors fool them completely. On the other hand, if cooperators are too conservative, their behavior approaches that of defectors.

- The peak of cooperation success is lower in the distributed case. This is logical, since agents do not share information. However, it is surprising to observe the relatively high percentage of cooperators for high `CreditLimit` values in the distributed case, whereas in the centralized case it may be as low as 2% in the same region. We do not have an explanation for this interesting effect yet. In any case, we show that even the simple stochastic automata in the distributed scenario gets close to the cooperation peak in the centralized scenario. Thus, there is plenty of room for further improvements.

7   Conclusions and Future Work

The game presented in this paper is an abstraction of the complex problem of negotiation and resource sharing in user networks. We consider this abstraction reflects the main features of the user network, and we show that under certain conditions (like `CreditLimit` settings) cooperation is the winning strategy, even in case of autonomous node operation. We show that the simple stochastic automata in the distributed scenario gets close to the cooperation peak in the centralized one. This fact encourages us to study more powerful decision algorithms. For example, agents could infer queue occupation peaks and strategies of neighbor cells from local records of past interaction.

We have observed that a user network can obtain benefits from node cooperation if traffic demands are strongly variable during the day, for example in case of several node types with complementary activity periods.

Now that cooperation can be considered a successful strategy in user networks, we plan to adapt the simulator to include real network topologies and to explore more complex strategies.

References

1. Ken Binmore: Game Theory. *Mc Graw Hill*, 1994.
2. IEEE 802.11. [Online]. Available:http://grouper.ieee.org/groups/802/11/.
3. Narendra: Learning Automata. 1989.
4. J. P. Hubaux, T. Gross, J. Y. L. Boudec, M. Vetterli: Towards self-organized mobile ad-hoc networks: the terminodes project. *IEEE Commun. Mag.*, no. 1, pp. 118–124, 2001.
5. Madrid Wireless. [Online]. 2004. Available at: http://madridwireless.net.
6. Wireless Athens Group. [Online]. 2004. Available at: http://www.nmi.uga.edu/research.
7. N. Negroponte: Being Wireless. *Wired Magazine*, 10.10, Oct. 2002.
8. Kazaa news. [Online]. 2004. Available at: http://www.kazaa.com/us/news/index.htm.
9. F. Schweitzer, L. Behera, H. Muhlenbein: Evolution of Cooperation in a Spatial Prisioner's Dilemma, *Advances in Complex Systems*, vol. 5 (2-3), pp. 269-299. 2003.
10. R. Axelrod: The evolution of Cooperation. Basic Books, New York, 1984.
11. F. Schweitzer, J. Zimmermann, H. Muhlenbein: Coordination of decisions in a spatial agent model. *Physica A*, 303(1-2), pp. 189-216, 2002.
12. R. Hoffmann: Twenty years on: The evolution of cooperation revisited. *Journal of Artificial Societies and Social Simulation*, 3(2), 2000.
13. F. Box: A heuristic technique for assigning frequencies to mobile radio nets, *IEEE Trans. Veh. Technol.*, vol. VT-27, pp. 57–74, 1978.

Lattice Boltzmann Modeling of Injection Moulding Process

Jonas Latt[1], Guy Courbebaisse[2], Bastien Chopard[1], and Jean Luc Falcone[1]

[1] University of Geneva, Computer Science Department, 1211 Geneva 4, Switzerland,
Bastien.Chopard@cui.unige.ch,
http://cui.unige.ch/~chopard/home.html
[2] LRPP - ERT 10 - ESP, 85 Rue Henri Becquerel
F-01100 Bellignat, France
courbebaisse@free.fr

Abstract. Polymer injection in moulds with complicated shapes is common in todays industrial problems. A challenge is to optimize the mould design which leads to the most homogeneous filling. Current commercial softwares are able to simulate the process only partially. This paper proposes a preliminary study of the capability of a two-fluid Lattice-Boltzmann model to provide a simple and flexible approach which can be easily parallelized, will include correct contact angles and simulate the effect of the positioning of air-holes.

Keywords: Polymer injection moulding, Hele-Shaw model, mathematical morphology, lattice Boltzmann method, multi-component fluids, numerical simulation.

1   Introduction

In the injection moulding process, as in many other scientific problems, numerical simulations play an important role. Polymer injection pressure, injection points and locations of air evacuation channels all affect the quality of the final object. In particular, the re-attachment of two fronts of matter (weld lines) leads to strong internal constraints and weakens its mechanical resistance.

Commercial softwares, such as MoldFlow, offer powerful tools to simulate the moulding process in the free surface approximation. They provide a quantitative description in which polymer properties can be adjusted. However, they offer little flexibility to combine the simulation with a shape optimization procedure. In addition, the free surface approximation does not allow the designer to study the effect of the location of air evacuation points. Finally, parallelized versions of such softwares are often not available.

There is a need among the practitioners of this field to develop new approaches. In particular, there seems to be a lack of tools offering a pre-modeling of the injection process, with enough flexibility to investigate the impact of geometrical factors. There are several examples in which the mould geometry is dominating in comparison with the fluid rheological properties. For instance,

P.M.A. Sloot, B. Chopard, and A.G. Hoekstra (Eds.): ACRI 2004, LNCS 3305, pp. 345–354, 2004.
© Springer-Verlag Berlin Heidelberg 2004

a recent original method based solely on the propagation of distances demonstrates that the injection process is more driven by the geometry of the mould cavity than by the non-Newtonian features of the polymer. In other words, the crucial hydrodynamic properties are mass conservation, forbidden regions and behaviour at the mould boundaries.

Along this line, the use of mathematical morphology concepts [1,2] for the simulation of the propagation of matter in a cavity, with one or more points of injection [3], is quite promising. The work by G. Aronsson [4] provides an explicit link between the concept of propagation of distances and the spreading of fluids with power-law stress tensors.

The goal of this paper is to exploit the flexibility and simplicity of the Lattice Boltzmann (LB) method [5] to address the mould injection process at a pre-model level. We consider the so-called Shan-Chen model [6] of two immiscible fluids representing the polymer and air respectively. We assume that Newtonian fluids will provide good approximations if geometrical factors are dominant. In this preliminary study we shall not pay too much attention to the actual ratio of densities and viscosities of the two fluids.

We will first test our approach on the so-called Hele-Shaw situation (see for instance [7]) and then consider a more realistic mould cavity. The LB results are compared with MoldFlow simulations. A discussion of the critical features of our approach is finally given.

Note that, at the time of writing, we became aware of a similar work by Ginzburg [8] in which a free-surface LB model is developed and applied to the filling of a cavity. However, this model does not include air behaviour and does not take into account the effect of air evacuation points.

2   The Lattice Boltzmann Model

Lattice Boltzmann (LB) models are historically derived from cellular automata fluid models [9,5]. These models are seen as an alternative to finite element techniques for fluid flow computations. They have been successfully applied to multi-phase and multi-component flows and several other applications. In the present context, we propose to adapt the LB methods to the filling phase of an injection moulding process.

2.1   The Lattice Boltzmann Equation for a Single Fluid

A LB model is built on a discrete space-time universe. The fluid is described by density distributions function $f_k(\boldsymbol{x}, t), k = 0 \ldots z$ containing the amount of fluid that enters lattice node $\boldsymbol{x}$ at time t, with velocity $\boldsymbol{v}_k, k = 0 \ldots z$. The possible velocities are constrained by the lattice topology. Typically, z is the lattice coordination number and the discrete set of velocities is chosen so that, in one time step Δt, the particles travel one lattice spacing Δx in any of the z lattice directions. One also considers a rest population of fluid particles f_0, with velocity $\boldsymbol{v}_0 = 0$.

The usual physical quantities such as local density and velocity are obtained from the f_k by the following relations:

$$\rho = \sum_{k=0}^{z} f_k \quad \text{and} \quad u = \sum_{k=0}^{z} f_k v_k. \tag{1}$$

During time evolution, the fluid density functions are streamed on the lattice, in the direction specified by k. After the streaming, a collision occurs between all the f_k entering the same lattice site. The result of this collision is to redistribute mass and momentum to each lattice directions, thus creating the post collision values of the f_k. It can be shown that, provided that the collision operator is properly chosen, the LB dynamics solves the Navier-Stokes equation [9,5], in the low Mach number regime.

It is also shown that the fluid pressure is related to the fluid density by the ideal gas state equation $p = c_s^2 \rho$, where c_s^2 is the speed of sound. Therefore, in a LB model, there is no need to solve the pressure equation. It is all built-in in the equation of motion for the f_k.

In what follows, we consider a two-dimensional system, with $z = 8$. This corresponds to the so-called D2Q9 model [5]. The collision is obtained by a relaxation with coefficient ω to a truncated Maxwell-Boltzmann local equilibrium distribution function $f^{(eq)}$, which depends only on the current local fluid density ρ and velocity u. This approach is referred to as a LBGK model [9,5].

The following equation summarizes the evolution rule:

$$f_i(x + v_i \Delta t, t + \Delta t) - f_i(x, t) = -\omega \left(f_i - f_i^{(eq)} \right) + \gamma F_{int} \cdot v_i \tag{2}$$

where F_{int} is a term which may account for extra interaction force acting on the particle density distribution. The coefficient γ is a normalization parameter which depends on the chosen lattice topology.

In order to model a system of two immiscible fluids (polymer and air) we use the so-called Shan-Chen model [6]. Two sets of f_k are defined, one for each species. The values corresponding to the two fluids will be distinguished by a supperscript $\sigma \in 0, 1$. Each fluid follows the dynamics of a single fluid system, as given in eq 2. There are only two changes that must be made to describe the interaction between the fluids.

First, the fluids define a common velocity and use it for the computation of the equilibrium distribution in equation 2

$$u = u^{(0)} + u^{(1)} = \frac{\sum_{\sigma, i} f_i^{\sigma} v_i}{\sum_{\sigma, i} f_i^{\sigma}}. \tag{3}$$

Second, the term F_{int} is computed so as to produce a repulsive interaction force between the two fluids. It depends on a parameter W that accounts for the surface tension of the fluids:

$$F_{int}^{(\sigma)}(x, t) = W \rho^{(\sigma)} \sum_{k} \Psi^{(\sigma)}(x + \tau v_k) v_k. \tag{4}$$

In the bulk of the fluid, the quantity Ψ corresponds to the density of the other fluid:

$$\Psi^{(\sigma)} = \rho^{(1-\sigma)}. \tag{5}$$

When one models immiscible fluids, one chooses an interaction force that is sufficiently strong to keep the penetration between the fluids low. The simulated flow field is thus separated in two regions, in each of which one fluid is dominant. In a small range around the interface between those two regions, both fluids coexist symmetrically. In this range, the density variations are large and the approximation for an incompressible fluid is not valid any more. The results must rather be understood as representative of some kind of interface dynamics between the immiscible fluids.

3   Boundary Conditions

On the boundaries of the domain, a specific dynamics is applied on the fluid density distributions f_i^σ in order to produce the desired effect: no-slip on a wall, fixed air pressure on the air-holes and specific contact angle at the interface between air, polymer and solid walls. Finally, polymer injection points also need a special treatment. The boundary conditions we propose are discussed below.

3.1   Bounce Back Boundaries

We implement no-slip boundaries (i.e. boundaries on which the velocity is zero) by assigning bounce back dynamics to the boundary nodes. Thus, the dynamics (2) is replaced by a reflection rule:

$$f_i^{(\sigma)}(\boldsymbol{x}, t + \Delta t) = f_{oppositeOf(i)}^{(\sigma)}(\boldsymbol{x}, t). \tag{6}$$

The index $oppositeOf(i)$ is the index associated with the direction opposite to direction i: $v_{oppositeOf(i)} = -v_i$.

The flow sites next to the boundaries interact with the boundary sites through a wetting parameter $g^{(\sigma)}$. The value of Ψ from equation 4 is thus defined on the boundary nodes by

$$\Psi^{(\sigma)} = g^{(\sigma)} \tag{7}$$

The value of $g^{(\sigma)}$ determines the contact angle of the fluid interface on the wall [10]. In our simulations, we have chosen $g^{(\sigma)} = -g^{(1-\sigma)}$. The situation is explained on Figure 1. On this figure, fluid 1 is wetting, and fluid 0 is non-wetting. This effect is obtained by chosing $g^{(0)} > 0$ and $g^{(1)} < 0$.

3.2   Inlet and Outlet Boundaries

As a boundary condition for the injection spot and the air-holes, we define semi-permeable walls: one fluid is retained by a normal no-slip condition, while the other fluid is injected or evacuated.

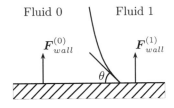

Fig. 1. Bounce back boundaries with a defined contact angle.

Let us consider as an example the case of fluid 0 being evacuated through the semipermeable wall. We chose to perform the evacuation at a constant pressure. This is achieved by applying on fluid 0 the (constant pressure) outlet boundary condition described in the reference [11]. Furthermore, an interaction term $\Psi^{(1)} = \rho^{(0)}$ is defined on the wall. This means that fluid 1 acts like a bulk node (5), rather than a wall node (6).

For fluid 1 we implement a (no-slip) bounce-back dynamics on the wall. Consistently with the presence of this semi-permeable wall, a wetting parameter $\Psi^{(0)} = g^{(0)}$ is defined.

4   Simulation of an Injection in Free Space

A first validation of the numerical model is obtained from a simple simulation with cylindrical symmetry. A polymer is injected at a spot in free space and expands in the form of a disk of increasing radius R. This is the well known Hele-Shaw model [7]. In this case, the boundary conditions have a subsidiary importance. We can therefore verify whether the basic properties of the polymer are properly resolved by the model.

4.1   Assumptions About Material Properties

In the particular case of injection moulding, we consider only very high viscous fluids. In consequence, the inertial and gravitational terms will not be taken into account in the momentum equation. This simplification leads to a well known equation : the Stokes equation (see for instance [7]). During the filling phase, the polymer is assumed to be incompressible. The resulting equations are :

$$\nabla . v = 0 \tag{8}$$

$$- \nabla p + \nabla . \underline{\sigma}_n = 0 \tag{9}$$

where v is the fluid velocity, p the pressure and $\underline{\sigma}_n$ the viscous strain tensor.

4.2   Hele-Shaw Assumptions

The Hele-Shaw model describes the filling of a mould cavity whose thickness can be neglected. The filling fluid flow is modelled according to the Stokes equation between two plates separated by a short distance h.

We consider a cartesian coordinate system where the z-axis is in the thickness direction. The $x - y$ plane is on the mid plane of the cavity and the velocity components u_x, u_y and u_z are respectively taken in the x, y and z directions. The Hele-Shaw flow model consists of the following assumptions [12]:

- The z-component of the velocity is neglected with respect to the other velocity components.
- The pressure is constant across the thickness. It only depends on x and y.
- The velocity gradient in the x and y directions is independent of the z direction.

Applying the Hele-Shaw assumptions to the Stokes equation, one obtains the simplified expressions:

$$\frac{\partial p}{\partial x} = \frac{\partial}{\partial z}\left(\eta\frac{\partial u_x}{\partial z}\right), \frac{\partial p}{\partial y} = \frac{\partial}{\partial z}\left(\eta\frac{\partial u_y}{\partial z}\right), \frac{\partial p}{\partial z} = 0 \tag{10}$$

with η the viscosity.

These equations can be solved explicitly in the case of a disk mould with a constant injection rate Q [7].

Inside the injected polymer, the distribution of the pressure is predicted as follows:

$$p(r) = a + b\ln r \tag{11}$$

where $r < R$ is the distance to the injection point and a and b are constant. The distribution of the velocity is given by

$$\rho(r)v(r) = \frac{Q}{2\pi r} \tag{12}$$

Finally, the expression for the surface growth of the polymer follows directly from the mass conservation in an incompressible fluid:

$$\pi R^2 = Qt \tag{13}$$

4.3   Numerical Result

The geometry of the simulation is a square domain of size 201×201, initially filled with air (fluid 1) at a density (pressure) of 1.0. At the boundary of the domain, the pressure of fluid 1 is kept constant at this value.

Fluid 1 (the polymer) is injected in the middle of the system, on one lattice site, with fixed density (pressure) $\rho_1 = 1.1$. The two fluids have same viscosity (relaxation coeficient $\omega = 1$) and their mutual interaction is defined through $W = -0.3$.

$t = 4000$ $t = 40000$ $t = 80000$ $t = 140000$

Fig. 2. Amount of polymer injected as a function of time, in a free space. In the later stage, the anisotropy is due to the air which cannot escape fast enough out of the boundaries.

The evolution of the system is represented at four chosen time steps in Figure 2. We expect from equation 13 that the radius of the injected disk increases as a square root of the time. This fact is verified on the simulations, both from the program MoldFlow and from the lattice Boltzmann model (see Figure 3).

We have measured the velocity and pressure profile in the simulation at the time step $t = 140000$. The results inside a radius of $r < 30$ are shown in Figure 4. They exclude the domain close to the free boundary that obeys special interface dynamics. Note that the velocity v is the modulus of the velocity (u_x, u_y).

In agreement with the predictions of the Hele Shaw theory (equations 11 and 12), the datapoints are fitted with a logarithmic law for the density and an r^{-1} law for the velocity. The value of Q used to fit the data is the one that is measured in the simulation: our injection boundary condition at a given pressure (density), fills the mould with a constant flow Q.

The above results show that Hele-Shaw model is correctly obeyed by the LB simulation.

5   Simulation of a Realistic Moulding Problem

5.1   Overview

As a second sample application, we consider the moulding of a charge card with integrated chip. In this case, the space taken by the chip is excluded from the moulding domain.

The aim of this application is to show that even somewhat complex geometries can be addressed with the simulations. In general, the implementation of appropriate boundary conditions is a very delicate topic. However, fairly appealing results are obtained already with the simple boundaries we have implemented.

5.2   Results

In the simulation, the surface of the charge card is initially filled with air (at a density $\rho_0 = 1.0$). The polymer is injected on the side opposite to the chip, at a level corresponding to the middle of the chip location.

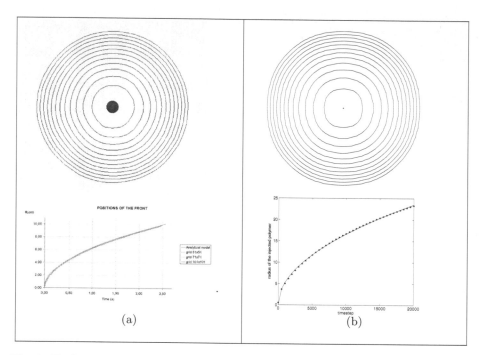

Fig. 3. Evolution of the disk radius during an injection in free space. On the left hand side (a), the results from the program MoldFlow are presented, on the right hand side (b) the results from a lattice Boltzmann simulation. On the upper part of the pictures, the surface of the injected polymer is plotted at successive timesteps. On the lower part, the curves for the time evolution of the radius are fitted with the predictions of the Hele-Shaw theory.

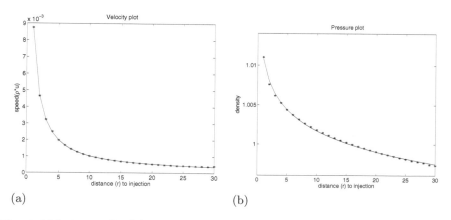

Fig. 4. Velocity profile (a) and pressure profile (b) at $t = 140000$ obtained from the lattice Boltzmann simulation. The solid line shows a fit with the predictions of the Hele Shaw theory.

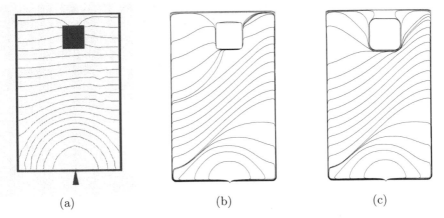

(a)   (b)   (c)

Fig. 5. Mould of a charge card. The curves show the propagation front of the polymer as computed from the program MoldFlow (a) and the lattice Boltzmann method (b,c). In (b), a bounce-back condition is applied on the surface of the chip, whereas in (c), the air is evacuated at constant density on the chip perimeter.

The injection is made at a density $\rho_{in} = 1.01$. The air is evacuated on the right boundary of the card at a constant density $\rho_{out} = 1.0$. All other boundaries implement a bounce-back condition with $g^{(0)} = g^{(1)} = 0$, which produces a contact angle of $\pi/2$. The surface tension is chosen at a value $W = -0.3$.

Figure 5 plots the area occupied by the polymer at successive timesteps, first calculated by the commercial program MoldFlow and, secondly, calculated by the LB method. The difference betweend (b) and (c) consists in the way the boundary conditions are defined on the chip perimeter (see caption). The results of both simulations are very similar in the beginning. In the second part of the simulation, the LB method turns out to be more sensitive to the geometry of the domain than the MoldFlow simulation.

The sensitivity of the flow dynamics to the geometry of the domain that we observe in the LB simulation is due to the pressure of the air on the polymer. Indeed, one of the main advantages of the LB method, the ability to model the influence of the air on the dynamics, also introduces some complications. If, as in our simulations, the air is not evacuated fast enough, this can have a serious impact of the flow dynamics; the resulting flow geometry may disagree with real moulding applications, where the air is much lighter and less visous than the polymer. In this context, some work still needs to be done either on the flow properties of the air or on the boundary conditions.

6   Conclusion

The LB methods brings several interesting elements in the process of injection modeling. The possibility to consider the full system of two fluids (air plus polymers) and to include air traps makes it possible to model how air escapes from the mould as the polymer expands. This feature is not offered by current softwares. In this respect, our preliminary results are relevant. They are especially encouraging in the case of the charge card with a complex geometrical shape.

One assumption of our preliminary study was that both fluids have the same viscosity and density. The simulation shows that although this assumption is sufficient for explaining some geometric properties of the moulded polymer, it is too strong to be able to represent dynamic features such as the detailed polymer front propagation profile. Therefore, future work might include a more realistic model for the different physical properties of the polymer and the air. Our study must be continued in order to give a reliable solution for polymer injection moulding and to include optimization processes where the best injection points and air-holes are determined to minimize weld lines formation.

In conclusion, we think that Lattice Boltzmann methods are promising candidates for the simulation of polymer injection moulding and for the solution of current problems such as melt polymer/mould wall interaction.

References

1. J. Serra. *Image Analysis and mathematical Morphology, Vol. 1.* Ac. Press, 1988.
2. M. Jourlin, G. Courbebaisse, and D. Garcia. Polymer molding simulation : A mathematical imaging approach based on propagation of discrete distances. *Elsevier Computational Materials Sciences*, 18(1):19–23, 1999.
3. G. Courbebaisse, D. Garcia, and P.Bourgin. A way towards optimization of injection molding. ASME Fluids Engineering Division Summer Meeting, 2003.
4. G.Aronsson. On p-harmonic functions, convex duality and an asymptotic formula for injection mold filling. *European J. Applied Mathematics*, 7:417–437, 1996.
5. Sauro Succi. *The Lattice Boltzmann Equation, For Fluid Dynamics and Beyond.* Oxford University Press, 2001.
6. N.S. Martis and H. Chen. Simulation of multicomponent fluids in complex 3d geometries by the lattice Boltzmann method. *Phys. Rev. E*, 53:743–749, 1996.
7. JPH. Sergent J.F. Agassant, P. Avenas. *La mise en forme des matières plastiques.* Lavoisier, 1989.
8. Irina Ginzburg and Konrad Steiner. Lattice boltzmann model for free-surface flow and its application to filling process in casting. *Journal of Comp. Physics*, 185:61–99, 2003.
9. B. Chopard and M. Droz. *Cellular Automata Modeling of Physical Systems.* Cambridge University Press, 1998.
10. Haiping Fang Lewen Fan and Zhifang Lin. Simulation of contact line dynamics in a two-dimensional capillary by the lattice boltzmann model. *Physical Review E*, 63(5):051603, april 2001.
11. Qisu Zou and Xiaoyi He. On pressure and velocity boundary conditions for the lattice botzmann bgk model. *Phys. Fluids*, 9(6):1591–1598, february 1997.
12. P. Kennedy. *Flow analysis of injection molds.* Hanser, 1995.

Cellular Automata Diffusion-Kinetic Model of Dendritic Growth

Andriy Burbelko, Edward Fraś, Wojciech Kapturkiewicz, and Ewa Olejnik

AGH University of Science and Technology, Faculty of Foundry Eng., Reymonta str. 23, 30-059 Kraków, Poland
{abur, edfras, kapt, eolejnik}@agh.edu.pl
http://www.agh.edu.pl

Abstract. A mathematical crystallization model in the meso scale (the intermediate dimension scale between interatomic distance in solids and grain size in metals and alloys) is presented with the use of a kinetic-diffusion cellular automaton model. The proposed model differs from other models by including the diffusion of elements and heat conductivity effects on the physical phenomena at the solid-liquid interface. The model considers the non-equilibrium character of real processes of phase transformation, where the kinetic undercooling of the solid-liquid interface is a measure of this non-equilibrium level. The anisotropy of interface mobility is assumed. The growth of individual dendrites was simulated for different initial conditions and growth parameters. The modelling results are compared to the experimental data.

1   Introduction

Although analytical solutions of dendritic growth tasks are very important, they are only applicable to very simple tasks [1]. They permit the determination of basic dependencies and rules typical of this phenomenon, for instance the tip-splitting effect [2] or morphology diagram of structure patterns in the parameter space of undercooling – surface tension anisotropy [3]. Analytical solutions may also be treated as benchmarks for the verification of numerical solutions.

Numerical simulation is currently used for analysing several specific issues. Most importantly these include the use of phase-field or cellular automation (CA) methods that not only permit the analysis of the steady state but also that of the non-steady state of the solidification processes [4].

The phase-field modelling method [5] permits the precise determination of many parameters related to the creation of a microstructure, e.g. the kinetics of the growth of the dendritic front, the preferred growth orientation, etc. Unfortunately, due to the model physics involved, it is necessary to apply a computation grid step that is smaller than the width of the diffuse interface layer [4] which amounts to several interatomic distances. Despite the use of modern supercomputers, advanced numerical solutions and the multiplication of the diffuse interface width by the arbitrary multiplier of the order of 10-100 [4], the current phase-field model may only be treated as a scientific research instrument to study the solidification phenomenon in the area of one or several dendrites and it cannot be used to model the casting structure.

P.M.A. Sloot, B. Chopard, and A.G. Hoekstra (Eds.): ACRI 2004, LNCS 3305, pp. 355–364, 2004.
© Springer-Verlag Berlin Heidelberg 2004

The order of magnitude of the computation grid step applied in CA technology is between the interatomic distance and the linear size of the microstructure elements. This significantly reduces the modelling time in comparison with the phase-field method and gives an opportunity to apply CA to multiscale-type models in order to model the casting structure.

Already the first attempts to use CA technology in order to model the solidification process showed that this model may be used for analysing dendritic growth [6–8].

In the nineties of past century, the application of a technique of cellular automaton was gaining a wide-spread popularity in simulation of the solidification process [9–14]. Rapid development of computational techniques with easy access to the computation tools favoured even more progress in this field.

Up-to-date publications about solidification modelling with the use of the cellular automation [6-13] do not foresee that the velocity of the phase boundary migration may depend on the value of local undercooling. This possibility was taken into consideration in [15, 16], but only for the front of the primary dendrite arms.

2   Diffusion-Kinetic Model of Dendritic Growth

2.1   Classification of Cells and Capturing Rules

The present model extends further the classification of cells and introduces own set of capturing rules which forecast how the cells of liquid will be absorbed by the growing grains of solid phase. The classification bases on a condition of the nearest neighbouring cells (N, W, S and E in Figure 1) and cells along the diagonal (N-W, N-E, S-E and S-W). The applied rules of classification of the interface cells are compared in Table 1, while some examples of the practical use of these rules are explained in Figure 2. Like in other available models, the division of cells into liquid cells (type Liq), solid cells (type Sol), and interface cells (type Int) was preserved.

Table 1. Classification of interface cells

Type of interface cell and its description		Number of neighbouring cells in solid state	
		neighbouring	along diagonal
Int-1	Nucleus	0	0
Int-2	Planar boundary	1	–
Int-3	Corner	0	1–3
Int-4	Angle	2 (side by side)	–
Int-5	Narrow passage	2 (facing each other)	–
Int-6	Passage bottom	3	–
Int-7	Closed cavity	4	–

The following set of rules is proposed to describe changes in the type of cells and capturing of the liquid cells by interface during solidification:

Rule 1. At the instant when in a nucleus cell of type Int-1 a content of the solid phase $f_s = 1$ appears, the cell changes its type to Sol. The neighbouring cells from its nearest environment (N, S, W and E) still in the liquid state (type Liq) are captured by the growing grain, thus creating type Int-2 with all the attributes of a grain of this type (a number, orientation angle of crystal lattice, and phase type in the case of multiphase growth).

The neighbouring cells along the diagonal (N-W, N-E, S-W and S-E) still in liquid state (type Liq) are also captured by the growing grain, acquiring all its attributes but changing their type to Int-3.

Rule 2. At the instant when a cell acquires type Int-2 (planar boundary) with the solid phase content $f_s = 1$, its type is changed to Sol. The neighbouring cells of type Liq present in the nearest vicinity are absorbed by the growing grain and acquire type Int-2 with all the attributes of a grain of this type.

The neighbouring cells of the type Int-3, belonging to this grain, change their type into Int-2. The neighbouring cells of the type Liq along the diagonal are also captured by the growing grain, acquire all its attributes, but their type changes to Int-3. The attributes of none of the 8 closest cells will change, if the cells have already been captured by other grains.

Rule 3. Rule 2 also applies to cells of types Int-4, Int-5 and Int-6.

Rule 4. Rule 2 is invalid in the case of cells of type Int-3.

Rule 5. At the instant when in a cell of the type Int-7 the content of solid phase $f_s = 1$ is obtained, the type of this cell is changed to Sol.

Rule 6. Other changes in the type of cells result from the count of the neighbouring cells of the type Sol according to Table 1.

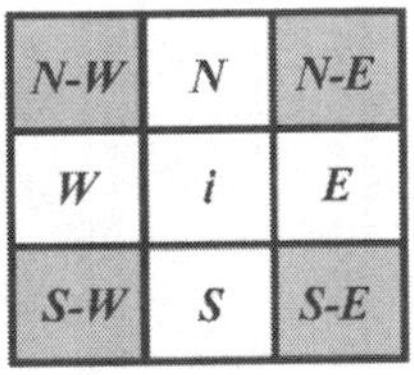

N-W	N	N-E
W	i	E
S-W	S	S-E

Fig. 1. Schematic diagram of classification of the neighbouring cells by cellular automaton

The developed classification and the set of rules describing transformation of the cell type in cellular automaton enable during simulation of solidification minimalising an effect of the computation grid structure with cells of an appropriate size on a preferential orientation of the dendrite arm growth forced by the grid symmetry.

2.2   Heat and Mass Transport

In the presented model, a coupled solution of the non-linear differential equations of diffusion was made on a common mesh of finite differences with square cells and a common time step.

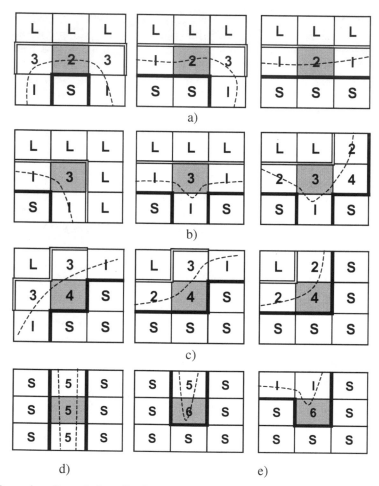

Fig. 2. Examples of practical application of the schematic diagram of interface cells classification : a) planar boundary, b) corner, c) angle, d) narrow passage, e) passage bottom (bold line - solid phase/interface cells boundary, double line - liquid phase/interface cells boundary; broken line - hypothetical true position of the growing grain boundary; S – solid cell (type Sol), L – liquid cell (type Liq), I – interface cell (type Int); numbers –interface cell type according to Table 1)

Since source terms were taken into account, as a solution of model equations an iteration method was proposed, viz. a simple iteration based on the following equations:

$$
T_{n+1} = \frac{\left(k_T^N T_n^N + k_T^S T_n^S + k_T^W T_n^W + k_T^E T_n^E\right) + T_n + \Delta f_S \dfrac{L}{c_v}}{1 + k_T^N + k_T^S + k_T^W + k_T^E},
\tag{1}
$$

$$C_{n+1} = \left(\left(k_C^N C_n^N + k_C^S C_n^S + k_C^W C_n^W + k_C^E C_n^E \right) + \right.$$
$$\left. + C_n \left(1 - (1-k) \cdot f_S \right) \right) / Z , \qquad (2)$$

where: T – temperature; k – coefficient of solute redistribution between the solid and liquid phase; C – true concentration of additional element in liquid (C_L), if the neighbouring cell is of type Liq, or concentration in liquid results from the coefficient of redistribution (C_S/k), if the neighbouring cell is of type Sol; L – heat of phase transformation; f_S, f_S – volume fraction of solid phase and its changes in the last time step, c_v – specific heat volume,

$$Z = 1 - (1-k) \cdot (f_S + \Delta f_S) + k_C^N + k_C^S + k_C^W + k_C^E .$$

In these equations the subscripts n and $n+1$ denote the iteration number, and superscripts – addressing of the neighbouring cells (see: Fig. 1). The values of coefficients k_C and k_T are:

$$k_C = \frac{D\Delta\tau}{\Delta x^2}, \quad k_T = \frac{\lambda\Delta\tau}{c_v\Delta x^2} . \qquad (3)$$

where: λ – thermal conductivity, D –coefficient of diffusion, $\Delta\tau$– time step, Δx –cell size in cellular automaton.

Similar equations of iteration were applied to the cells outside interface, assuming appropriate values of f_S and $\Delta f_S = 0$.

Due to great differences in the coefficient of diffusion of the solid and liquid phase, its effective value in the interface cells was determined as a weighted average.

2.3   Direction and Curvature of Phase Boundary

To determine the direction normal to a surface of the phase boundary, a well-known method based on the determination of vector components joining the centre of a bulk block of the neighbouring cells of the size 3x3 with the centre of a single cell was applied.

The methods of determination of the front curvature based on the cells count [17, 18] cannot always ensure the satisfactory precision. In the case when higher precision was required, in the presented model an approximate computation of the curvature based on its geometrical definition was applied. As an approximate value of the interface curvature one can adopt a quotient of the difference in angles between the directions of the solidification front in the neighbouring cells and the lengths of the front along these segments. In the proposed model, a central difference diagram depicted in Figure 3 was used.

To determine a sign of the front curvature (convex or concave), it is enough to compare the sines of the angles of deviation of side BC and of one of the sides AC or AB in this triangle from the vertical or horizontal direction. The values of the sines of these angles are determined from simple geometrical relations, for example:

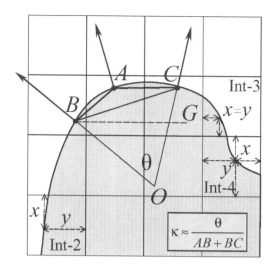

Fig. 3. Schematic representation of designations used for computation of the front curvature

$$\sin(\angle CBG) = \frac{y(C) - y(B)}{\sqrt{(y(C) - y(B))^2 + (x(B) + 1 + x(C))^2}}.$$ (4)

2.4 Migration Rate on Phase Boundary

The velocity of crystal growth depends on the kinetic undercooling ΔT_μ [19]

$$u = \mu \cdot \Delta T_\mu$$ (5)

and is related with the front topography and crystallographic orientation (an anisotropy of the kinetic coefficient in crystals of metals characterised by face-centred lattice amounts to about 17% [20]).

The kinetic undercooling is expressed by equation:

$$\Delta T_\mu = T_{Eq} - T - \Delta T_\kappa,$$ (6)

where T – temperature on the solidification front, T_{Eq} – equilibrium temperature for planar phase boundary with contribution of segregation, ΔT_κ – Gibbs undercooling (the effect of phase boundary curvature), which for the crystals of isotropic surface tension is determined from equation [21]

$$\Delta T_\kappa = \frac{\gamma T_m K}{L},$$ (7)

where: γ – the Gibbs energy falling to an interface unit, T_m – absolute equilibrium temperature for a planar surface, K – front curvature.

It can be assumed that the anisotropy of kinetic coefficient is described by relationship [22, 23]

$$\mu(\theta) = \mu_0 / (1 - \delta_\mu \cos(m_s \theta)),$$ (8)

where: μ_0, δ_m – mean value and amplitude of changes in kinetic coefficient, m_s – fold of crystal symmetry.

Angle θ determines here a deviation of the growth surface direction on a specific section from the selected base crystallographic orientation.

2.5 Transformation Rate

The time t_o, required for the solidification front to cover the entire cell can be defined as a quotient of the cell diagonal projection on vector of the front migration velocity (d_u) and velocity modulus (Fig. 4)

$$t_o = d_u / u .$$ (9)

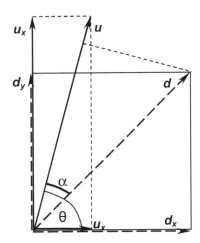

Fig. 4. Schematic diagram to derive relationships between parameters of the solidification rate vector and the phase transformation rate in a cell of cellular automaton

Applying properties of the vectors scalar product, an absolute value of the diagonal projection length on vector of the velocity can be defined as

$$d_u = \frac{d_x |u_x| + d_y |u_y|}{\sqrt{u_x^2 + u_y^2}} .$$ (10)

A relative change in fraction of the transformation products during time interval Δt can be assumed equal to a ratio of this time interval and t_o

$$\Delta f_S = \frac{u\Delta\tau}{d_u} \tag{11}$$

Having substituted to this equation a value of d_u from equation (10), we obtain a formula determining the rate of transformation

$$\frac{\Delta f_S}{\Delta\tau} = \frac{u_x^2 + u_y^2}{d_x|u_x| + d_y|u_y|} . \tag{12}$$

If the mesh of cellular automaton has square cells, the formula can be transformed to a form similar to that proposed in [12]

$$\Delta f_S = \frac{u\Delta\tau}{\Delta x(|\cos\theta| + |\sin\theta|)} . \tag{13}$$

3   Results of Simulation

The results of numerical computations consistent with the presented model are shown as an example in Figure 5, which also shows the growth of a dendritic grain inclined at an angle of about 20° to the axis of coordinates. The computations were made for parameters of a model material (a "succinonitrile – acetone" solution) according to [3], [24] on a mesh of cellular automaton with 800 x 800 cells (the length of a cell side was 0.05 µm). The value of the kinetic coefficient was accepted at a level of 10^{-3} m/(s·K) from 10% anisotropy; the initial undercooling was assumed to be 13.5 K.

As results from   5, the disturbance of the modal value of 8 develops at the initial stage of nucleus growth. The primary dendrite arms are visible growing towards the maximum mobility of the solidification front. The "sea-weed"-type structure develops in the space between them. These arms grow towards the $\mu(\theta)$ minimum value. They are marked with arrows on the picture 5 f and have a specific dense branching morphology (tip-splitting) shape [2]. The structure of a two-dimensional dendrite observed during the solidification of the model substance has similar characteristics (fig. 6). The dendrite arms of the dense branching morphology type are shown on fig. 6d by markers. The shape and positions of these arms are compliant with the modelling results.

4   Conclusions

The virtual structure of dendrites obtained with the help of the developed model is in terms of its quality consistent with the experimental structure of two-dimensional dendrites, formed during the dendritic solidification of "succinonitrile – acetone" solution in thin layers. The results of simulation obtained by means of the model presented in this study are independent of an orientation of the axis of coordinates.

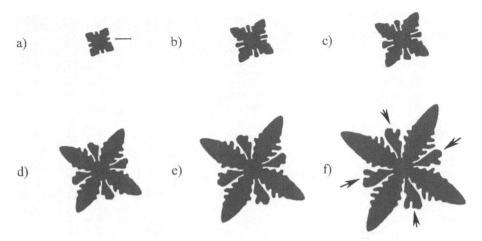

Fig. 5. An example of the two-dimensional dendritic growth - simulation

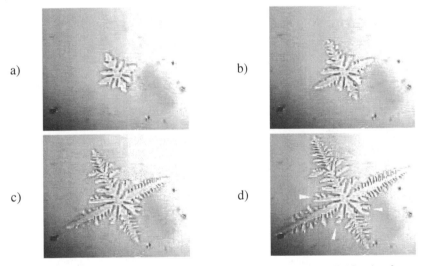

Fig. 6. Change in the structure of two-dimensional dendrite during its solidification from model material ("succinonitrile – acetone")

Acknowledgement. This paper was supported by Polish KBN (Project 4 T08A 041 25).

References

1.   Brener E.A., Mel'nikov V.I.: Pattern selection in two-dimensional dendritic growth. Adv. Phys., Vol. 40, No. 1, (1991) 53-97
2.   Ben-Jacob E., Deutscher G., Garik P., Goldenfeld N.D., Lareah Y.: Formation of a Dense Branching Morphology in Interfacial Growth. Phys. Rev. Lett. Vol. 57 (1986) 1903–1906

3. Brener E., Müller-Krumbhaar H., Temkin D., Abel T.: Morphology diagram of possible stuctures in diffusional growth. Physica A, Vol. 249 (1998) 73–81

4. Boettinger W.J., Coriell S.R., Greer A.L., Karma A., Kurz W., Rappaz M., Trivedi R.: Solidification microstructures: recent developments, future directions. Acta Mater., Vol. 48 (2000) 43-70

5. Ramirez J. C., Beckermann J. C., Karma A., Diepers H.-J.: Phase-field modeling of binary alloy solidification with coupled heat and solute diffusion. Phys. Rev. E, Vol. 69 (2004) 051607

6. Уманцев Р.А., Виноградов В.В, Борисов В.Т.: Математическое моделирование роста дендритов в переохлаждённом расплаве. Кристаллография, Vol. 30, (1985) 455–460

7. Уманцев Р.А., Виноградов В.В, Борисов В.Т.: Математическое моделирование процесса формирования дендритной структуры при кристаллизации переохлаждённого расплава. Заводская лаборатория, Nr 7 (1986) 46–48

8. Уманцев Р.А., Виноградов В.В, Борисов В.Т.: Моделирование эволюции дендритной структуры. Кристаллография, Vol. 31, Nr 5 (1985) 1002–1008

9. Shochet O., Kassner K., Ben-Jacob E., Lipson S.G., Müller-Krumbhaar H.: Morphology transition during non-equilibrium growth. Physica A. Vol. 181 (1992) 136–155; Vol. 187 (1992) 87–111

10. Rappaz M., Gandin Ch.-A.: Probabilistic modelling of microstructure formation in solidification processes. Acta Metall. Mater, Vol. 41, Nr 2 (1993) 345–360

11. Cortie M.B.: Simulation of metal solidification using a cellular automaton. Metall. Trans. B, Vol. 24B, Nr 6 (1993) 1045–1053

12. Zhu P., Smith R.W.: Dynamic simulation of crystal growth by monte carlo method – I. Model description and kinetics. Acta Metall. Mater, Vol. 40, Nr 4 (1992) 683–692

13. Gandin Ch.-A., Rappaz M.A.: Coupled finite element – cellular automaton model for the prediction of dendritic grain structures in solidification processes. Acta Metall. Mater, Vol. 42, Nr 7 (1994) 2233–2246

14. Miller W., Succi S., Mansutti D.: Lattice Boltzmann Model for Anisotropic Liquid-Solid Phase Transition. Phys. Rev. Letter, Vol. 86, No. 16 (2001) 3578-3581

15. Zhu M.F., Hong C.P.: A Three Dimensional Modified cellular Automaton Model for the Prediction of Solidification Microstructures. ISIJ International, Vol. 42 (2002) 520–526

16. Zhu M.F., Hong C.P.: A Modified Cellular Automation Model for the Simulation of Dendritic Growth in Solidification of Alloys. ISIJ International, Vol. 41 (2001) 436–445

17. Nastac L.: Numerical Modeling of Solidification Morphologies and Segregation Patterns in Cast Dendritic Alloys. Acta Mater., Vol. 47 (1999) 4253–4262

18. Zhu M.F., Hong C.P.: A Modified Cellular Automation Model for the Simulation of Dendritic Growth in Solidification of Alloys. ISIJ International, Vol. 41 (2001) 436–445

19. Trivedi R., Franke H., Lacmann R.: Effects of Interface Kinetics on the Growth Rate of Dendrites. J. Cryst. Growth, Vol. 47 (1979) 389–396

20. Hoyt J.J., Asta M.: Atomistic Computation of Liquid Diffusivity, Solid-Liquid Interfacial Free Energy, and Kinetic Coefficient in Au and Ag. Phys. Rev. B, Vol. 65 (2002) Art. 214106, 1–11

21. Woodruff D.P.: The Solid-Liquid Interface. London, Cambridge University Press (1973) 182

22. Xu J.-J.: Stability and Selection of Dendritic Growth with Anisotropic Kinetic Attachment. J. Crystal Growth, Vol. 245 (2002) 134–148

23. Al-Rawahi N., Tryggvason G.: Numerical Simulation of Dendritic Solidification with Convection: Two-Dimensional Geometry. J. Comp. Physics, Vol. 180 (2002) 471–496

24. Muschol M., Liu D., Cummins H.Z.: Surface-Tension-Anisotropy Measurements Of Succinonitrile and Pivalic Acid. Phys. Rev. E, Vol. 46 (1992) 1038–1050

Cellular Automata with Rare Events; Resolution of an Outstanding Problem in the Bootstrap Percolation Model

Paolo De Gregorio, Aonghus Lawlor, Phil Bradley, and Kenneth A. Dawson

Irish Centre for Colloid Science and Biomaterials, Department of Chemistry,
University College Dublin, Belfield, Dublin 4, Ireland. paolo@fiachra.ucd.ie

Abstract. We study the modified bootstrap model as an example of a cellular automaton that is dominated by the physics of rare events. For this reason, the characteristic laws are quite different from the simple power laws often found in well known critical phenomena. Those laws are quite delicate, and are driven by co-operative events at diverging length and time scales. To deal with such problems we introduce a new importance-sampling procedure in simulation, based on rare events around "holes". This enables us to access bootstrap lengths beyond those previously studied. By studying the paths or processes that lead to emptying of the lattice we are able to develop systematic corrections to the theory, and compare them to simulations. Thereby, for the first time in the literature, it is possible to obtain credible comparisons between theory and simulation in the accessible density range.

Complex dynamical processes abound in nature, and their understanding represents one of the great challenges that scientists face as they try to advance our knowledge of the natural universe. The field of 'complexity' in the physical sciences takes a particular view of this endeavor that has been very successful in many arenas of study. In this approach, understanding complex problems is, unlike many areas of physics and chemistry where detail is everything, based on the simplest possible manifestation of the problem. Thus, by stripping away the details that are not responsible for the primary observation, one obtains a simple model that contains the essential features of the problem to be solved.

This approach is sound only when we can be relatively certain that there are striking regularities, or generalities to be learned about the system, for we have learned by our training and experience that such phenomena are rarely determined by a multiplicity of detail. The development of simple models is at its most successful when the phenomena originate in a long length and time scale, for then we have learned, as in problems such as critical phenomena [1], that many of the observations may also be reproduced in a numerically quantitative manner.

The ideas to be discussed in this paper grow from many studies over several decades of assemblies of highly coupled units, each which has a state (for example 'movable' and 'immovable' particles or 'on' and 'off' processors), that depends on

P.M.A. Sloot, B. Chopard, and A.G. Hoekstra (Eds.): ACRI 2004, LNCS 3305, pp. 365–374, 2004.

those of its close neighbors. Thus, the initial state of the system may be highly constrained, with very few opportunities for overall movement. Significant groups of units may require a coherent sequential switching of units, perhaps extending over very large length-scales in the system. This type of problem may also imply an activation barrier, but here we emphasize that the barrier crossing requires movement of many units. Thus long times scales may emerge from not just the intrinsic barrier, but the large number of coherent units required to move along the 'reaction co-ordinate' or direction of 'easy' motion.

The need to work with simplified dynamical models is clear, for often they represent great simplifications of the more realistic dynamical systems that have proven to be difficult to solve by other means. Frequently massive computational effort is directed at such problem, only to find that the key phenomena are still beyond the length and time scales of the physical problem. Those who study such problems as protein folding [2] and the dynamical arrest [3] or glass transition [4] are well aware of the limitations of the direct computational approach. In this paper we will focus on dynamically constrained lattice models [5,6,7,8,9,10], special classes of cellular automat that are proving very important in studying such questions of 'slowed' dynamics. [11,12]. There has been something of a mystery surrounding this class of cellular automata [13] that has lead some to question the value of computational studies at all because of the long history of disagreements between theory and simulations. We are now in a position to clarify this issue, and that is the main purpose of the present paper.

The bootstrap percolation [14,15,16,17,18,19,20,21] problem has attracted considerable interest from a variety of scientific communities. In essence it (or its obvious variants) is a method to analyze the dynamics of such a system of highly coupled units, each of which has a state that depends on those of its close neighbors. In the past such units have been considered particles, processors [22], or elements of a growing population. Units that become active in the underlying dynamics are simply removed in the bootstrap. The ensemble can undergo a transition to an "arrested" state in which all dynamics is quenched, and this is (after bootstrap removal of units) reflected in a transition from an empty to partially filled lattice. This arrest is found to be driven by a long length scale. The change of state of one unit becomes increasingly difficult near arrest, requiring a long sequential string of favorable changes in its surrounding units. Thereby a long length (the size of the surrounding region to be changed) is slaved to a long (relaxational) time scale.

In the well-known conventional "bootstrap model" (in the context of particles) [15,16,23], particles are removed if they are surrounded by c or less neighbors. We study in more detail the modified bootstrap [17,20,24]. In this particles are removed if any two of its vacant nearest neighbors are also second neighbors to each other. The (random bootstrap) transition occurs as a function of c (or the underlying local rule), system size L, and initial particle density ρ and the transition point is defined by the condition that half of the prepared initial states are empty after removal of all movable particles.

The bootstrap-type problems mentioned above fall into two broad "universality" classes of arrest transition [16]. The first (not studied here) a continuous ("critical" point) transition in which progressively more particles lose motion, leading to growing arrested domains whose typical size diverges with a power law.

The second type of transition (of interest to us here) is more reminiscent of a first-order transition, and the theory is more subtle. There, dynamically slowed domains grow near arrest according to an essential singularity. Mobilization of these domains is dependent on rare events (we call these "connected holes" [11, 25]) involving specific units that can "nucleate" motion on this large length. As will become clear, these "nuclei" become rare (highly dilute) near the transition, the typical distance between them being the (diverging) bootstrap length, while the time taken for communication between them, since it involves a diverging number of intermediate units, also diverges.

For such transitions the following conclusions have been drawn by the community. For $c = d$ (the dimension) it is believed that the bootstrap length ξ diverges according to an essential singularity $\xi = \exp^{\circ(d-1)}(-A/(1-\rho))$ where $\exp^{\circ(d-1)}$ is the exponential function iterated $d-1$ times [16,26,27]. For the two dimensional square lattice $c = 2$ and the modified model, theoretical calculations [28] have resulted in an elegant outcome; essentially what are believed to be exact results, $\lim_{\substack{\rho \to 1 \\ \xi \to \infty}} 2(1-\rho)\log \xi = A$, where $A = \pi^2/9$ and $\pi^2/3$ for conventional and modified bootstrap respectively.

Attempts to obtain this asymptotic result by simulation have so far failed, including some of the most extensive calculations to have been applied in statistical mechanics (up to $L = 128,000$). It has been speculated that theory and simulation might agree for system sizes that are far beyond what will ever be possible, or indeed of interest, for Physics to explore [29,28,13]. We will show that this need not be the case. Though the singular behaviour implied by such models is subtle, it can be studied by both theory and simulation.

We will develop a new approach to the theory, and the simulation of the cellular automata under question.

Thus, we identify "holes" on the lattice as spaces (vacancies) into which particles can move [11]. We then identify these holes as either "connected" or caged (disconnected) according to whether the lattice can (or cannot) be vacated by sequentially removing particles beginning from that hole. The relationship to conventional (random) bootstrap simulations (described above) is clear; a given system size and density must contain at least one connected hole for it to be vacated by random bootstrapping processes. Thus, the bootstrap correlation length ξ is related to the connected hole density ν via $\nu = 1/\xi^2$. The bootstrap length is therefore the average distance between connected holes (these representing the growth "nuclei" alluded to in our introductory remarks) that become increasingly rare near arrest. The device of holes allows us to focus on the key "order" parameter, rather than the very populous, but irrelevant particles and vacancies [11]. Here we present some results for $d = 2$.

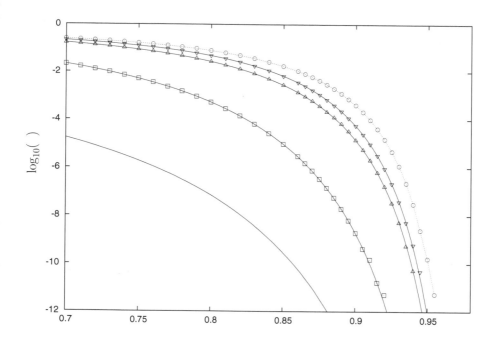

Fig. 1. Modified Bootstrap Model. The (○) points represent the total hole density (the dotted line is a guide to the eye). The symmetrically growing squares (□) are compared with Holroyd's [28] asymptotic result $\exp(-\pi^2/3(1-\rho))$ (lower solid line). Also shown are results for diffusing squares (△) and small-asymmetry rectangles (▽)- in these cases, the lines through the points represent the theoretical result.

In the simulations we begin by creating a hole with the appropriate weight, and then populate ('grow') the configuration with particles and vacancies around this site, checking at each stage to see if that hole is connected, or trapped [11] by identifying cages at that length. Since the typical cage size grows much more slowly $(\log(1-\rho)/\log(\rho))$ than the bootstrap length, we need check only relatively small distances to determine if the hole is connected. This is the imporant difference between studying the simulation model in the usual complete manner. Since the imporant events are so rare, we study only parts of the automata that have them, and then combine the results in an appropriate manner.

The outcome is that the results produced here require only a few hours of time on a personal computer. In Figure 1 and 2 we show results for the total connected hole density in the modified and conventional bootstrap models respectively and these agree, where comparisons are available, with the most extensive conventional simulations. For example, the (◇) points in the uppermost curve of Figure 2 represent the hole density implied by the results in [29,30] (system size $L = 128,000$), while the (○) points on that same curve are from our importance-sampling procedure discussed above (we have simulated up to an effective size of $L = 200,000$).

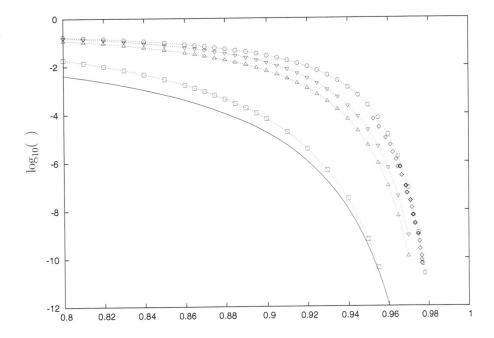

Fig. 2. Bootstrap Model. The ($\circ$) points represent the total hole density (the dotted line is a guide to the eye) and can be compared with the results for $1/\xi^2$ ($\diamond$) for $\xi > 100$ [29,30]. The symmetrically growing squares ($\square$) are compared with Holroyd's [28] asymptotic result $\nu = \exp(-\pi^2/9(1 - \rho))$ (lower solid line). Also shown are results for diffusing squares ($\triangle$) and small-asymmetry rectangles ($\triangledown$).

Theoretical calculations [7,24,28] have approximated the process of simultaneous removal of particles on increasingly large square contours until reaching one that is entirely occupied by particles, and therefore immovable. The hole that originated this process is then termed disconnected. Thus schematically the probability of bootstrap is represented $\Pi_{k=1}^{\infty}(1 - \rho^{ak})^b$, where b represents the number of sides and a the increment on the lattice. In the high density limit one takes the natural logarithm of the product, approximates the sum with an integral and makes the substitution $y = \rho^k$. For $\rho \to 1$ this leads to $-b/(a \ln \rho) \int_0^1 (dy/y) \ln(1 - y) \sim -b\pi^2/6a(1 - \rho)$ [31]. In the modified bootstrap model, $a = 2$ and $b = 4$, one obtains $-\pi^2/3(1 - \rho)$, and it is this result that has been shown to be asymptotically exact [28]. From Figure 1 it is clear that there is no agreement between the simulated results for the total hole density ($\circ$) and the asymptotic result, even for the highest densities we can simulate. We would like to begin by identifying how much of this disagreement is due to the primitive nature of the approximation, and how much is is due to the fact that we are working with an asymptotic result.

To begin with we calculate exactly the probability for removal of concentric squares of particles, a result that includes all corner contributions, and is valid for all densities. Then,

$$P_\infty^{(cs)} = (1 - \rho)\Pi_{k=1}^\infty c_k^{(cs)}(\rho) \tag{1}$$
$$c_k^{(cs)}(\rho) = 1 - 4\rho^{2k+1} + 2\rho^{4k+1}(2 + \rho) - 4\rho^{6k+1} + \rho^{8k}$$

Using $(1 - \rho^{2k+1})^4$ as lower bounds for the coefficients $c_k^{(cs)}(\rho)$ we find a modified asymptotic result for the hole density $(1 - \rho)^{-5}\exp(-A/(1 - \rho))$ [31].

Now we are also able to simulate the same process of simultaneous removal of squares, as a check on the analytical formulae. We find that the modified asymptotic result is almost equal to our numerical solution of Equation 1 and simulation results for the symmetrically growing squares process in the density range of interest. While these are in perfect agreement with each other (see ($\square$) in Figure 1), they are still many orders of magnitude different from the full simulated connected hole density, although there is clearly a considerable improvement over the purely asymptotic result $\exp(-\pi^2/3(1 - \rho))$.

These results indicate that part of the lack of agreement between asymptotic hole density and the simulations is that the asymptotic formulae are simply not appropriate for the density ranges that are accessible. However it also suggests that in the density ranges of interest to physics the theory may also be limited because we have not included enough paths or independent processes of particle removal. Therefore our aim now in development of the theory is to systematically enlarge the possible paths in the calculation, until we approach the full simulated result, at each stage validating the theoretical calculation by simulating the same restricted set of paths.

The problem is simply appreciated. Thus, if we attempt to remove all of the edges of the boundary simultaneously the process will fail if even one of the edges does not contain the appropriate vacancy. Now we can somewhat improve the situation by simultaneous removal of two adjacent edges causing the void to move in the direction of that diagonal. By continuing this process randomly, changing to other pairs of adjacent edges when a given direction is blocked, the expanding void diffuses. This diffusive process therefore confers some improved capacity for the expanding void to avoid being blocked by a continuous line of particles. However, if one included a full set of particle removal paths the voids would be free not just to diffuse but also elongate. This would imply that a blocked edge also elongates, eventually including another vacancy, at which point we are free to remove that edge.

We thus identify two types of movements of the expanding void around a hole that should be taken into account; diffusive motion and elongational fluctuations. We can, again by simulation, estimate the relative importance of these. In Figure 1 we show ($\triangle$) the increase in the connected hole density implied if we allow only this diffusive motion. In the full simulated curve ($\circ$) we admit all diffusive paths, and also all types of elongation, and the difference between the results is therefore due to these shape fluctuations alone. However we may also check the nature of the elongational fluctuations that are required to obtain the full answer. The answer is surprising for we have found that, to obtain the full simulated answer we need never permit paths where the voids exceed an axial ratio of more than 1.4. In fact by far the largest single contribution comes from near-square processes, providing they are permitted to diffuse. Our overall aim of theory is therefore to implement firstly, the diffusive square process, and secondly some degree of elongational fluctuation.

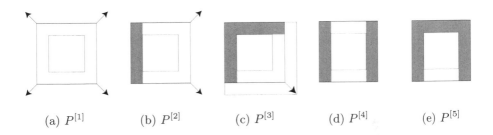

(a) $P^{[1]}$ (b) $P^{[2]}$ (c) $P^{[3]}$ (d) $P^{[4]}$ (e) $P^{[5]}$

Fig. 3. Intermediate configurations arising in evaluation of the sum over 'paths' that may be used to empty the lattice. The inner square from each of these figures is assumed to have been emptied of particles in the previous step, and the next parts to be emptied lie between this and the outer bounding square. Shaded outer regions imply a complete line of particles, blocking further movement in that direction. Unshaded outer regions have at least one vacancy in that part of the perimeter. The arrows on the squares indicate possible transition involving the growth of two adjacent boundary lines by one step. This process restores that local configuration to one of the intermediate states again, with the internal empty square one step larger in two directions. The process terminates when the local configuration makes a transition outside of the class P^1 - P^3 (diffusing squares) or P^1 - P^5 for small-asymmetry rectangles. Note that in P^3 we have given an explicit example of the extension of the boundary implied by the arrow.

We have been able to realize these aims.

We define intermediate states of the system as the squares illustrated in Figure 3, with weight $P_k^{(i)}$. Paths implied by removal of particles map the growing vacant region between only these states, larger by one step at each stage. If we consider only the limited set P^1 - P^3, such processes correspond to growing and diffusing squares. Inclusion of the states P^4 and P^5 permits in addition "fluctuations" of the square by one additional layer. These local intermediate states are related by the coupled equations,

$$P_k^{(i)}(\rho) = \sum_j c_k^{(i,j)}(\rho) P_{k-1}^{(j)}(\rho) \qquad (2)$$

where i, j's range from $1 \to n$, with $n = 3$ in the diffusing squares process, and $n = 5$ in its extended small-asymmetric rectangular version. $c_k^{(i,j)}(\rho)$ defines the probability of migration from class j to i at the kth step. These equations are solved subject to the initial conditions, $P_1^{(i)} = (1 - \rho)\delta_{1j}$.

The choice of these states, and transitions between them, is far from trivial since we must ensure an "ordering" of the removal process if we wish to use a random measure for the particles in calculating the coefficients $c_k^{(i,j)}(\rho)$. For the sake of simplicity, we here present only the coefficients of the process involving diffusing squares,

$$c_k^{(1,1)} = 1 - 2\rho^{2k} + \rho^{2k-1}$$

$$c_k^{(1,2)} = (1 - \rho)(1 - \rho^k)$$

$$c_k^{(1,3)} = (1 - \rho)^2, \qquad c_k^{(2,1)} = 2\rho^k(1 - \rho^{k-1})$$

$$c_k^{(2,2)} = 1 - 2\rho^k + \rho^{2k-2}$$

$$c_k^{(2,3)} = 2\rho(1 - \rho - \rho^{k-1} + \rho^k)$$

$$c_k^{(3,1)} = \rho^{2k-1}, \qquad c_k^{(3,2)} = \rho^k(1 - \rho^{k-1})$$

$$c_k^{(3,3)} = \rho^2(1 + 2\rho^{k-2} - 4\rho^{k-1} + \rho^{2k-3})$$

The total bootstrap probability $P_\infty^{(1)}(\rho)$ may be calculated numerically for any density, limited only by the precision of the computer. The same processes may be simulated on the computer and are in each case identical with the theory. Results for all are given in Figure 1 and for modified bootstrap.

Diffusing squares ($\triangle$), improves the comparison between theory and full simulation, and small-asymmetry rectangles ($\triangledown$) yields results that may (for the first time) begin to be credibly compared to computer simulation of the full simulated hole density.

We may now summarize our results both in relation to the bootstrap problem, and in a more broad context.

The first point is that cellular automata that describe rare events, such as the bootstrap percolation model, and its 'connected holes' may be best simulated by the type of importance sampling we have proposed. That is, rather than simply applying periodic boundary conditions in a square or cubic array we might instead 'grow' the configurations of the automaton around the rare events. In our case this was simple in that in the bootstrap we seek only to identify whether a hole is connected or not, and this is possible by studying successively larger environments around the hole. This is, to our knowledge, a new way of approaching the simulations of such models, and is a theme that might be worth exploring in more detail for this model, and for other examples.

Our second conclusion is that these rare events (the connected holes) confer a rather delicate singular behavior on the correlation length that is not easily dealt with in theory, except in the truly asymptotic limit. It transpires that the system enters this asymptotic limit at such large length scales that it is difficult for simulations to reach them. However, it also transpires that the theory is extendable so that it is a reasonable approximation across a wider range of density, hole density, or bootstrap length. Thereby comparisons between theory and simulations become feasible, indeed systematically improvable as desired.

This is an important point, for these improved theoretical approaches may be shown to share the same leading asymptotic form that has been proposed in the past. However, that leading asymptotic behavior is strongly modified at all but the closest distances to the transition. There is therefore no inconsistency between the theory and simulations, in the density regime where both can be studied. Equally the original theoretical predictions of asymptotic behavior are correct. It seems clear, however, that the length scales at which that leading asymptotic behavior becomes relevant is simply too large to be of interest to simulators, or indeed, to physicists.

Acknowledgements. We acknowledge discussions at various stages with G.Biroli, A. van Enter, S. Franz, A. Holroyd, M. Mezard, A. Robledo, M. Sellitto, D. Stauffer. The work is supported by HCM and DASM.

References

1. Wilson, K.: The renormalization group and critical phenomena. Rev. Mod. Phys. **55** (1983) 583–600
2. Kirkpatrick, T.R., Wolynes, P.G. Phys. Rev. B (1987)
3. Dawson, K.A. Curr. Opinion Coll. Int. Sci **7** (2002) 218–227
4. Mezard, M., Parisi, G., Virasoro, M.A. In: Spin Glass Theory and Beyond. Singapore: World Scientific (1987)
5. Kob, W., Andersen, H.C.: Kinetic lattice-gas model of cage effects in high-density liquids and a test of mode-coupling theory of the ideal-glass transition. Phys. Rev. E. **48** (1993) 4364–4377
6. Jäckle, J., Krönig, A. J. Stat. Phys. **63** (1991) 249–260
7. Jäckle, J., Krönig, A. J. Phys.: Condens. Matter **6** (1994) 7633–7653
8. Krönig, A., Jäckle, J. J. Phys.: Condens. Matter **6** (1994) 7655–7672
9. Jäckle, J. Journal of Physics: Condensed Matter **14** (2002) 1423–1436
10. Sabhapandit, S., Dhar, D., Shukla, P. Phys. Rev. Lett. **88** (2002) 197202
11. Lawlor, A., Reagan, D., McCullagh, G.D., De Gregorio, P., Tartaglia, P., Dawson, K.A.: Universality in lattice models of dynamic arrest: Introduction of an order parameter. Phys. Rev. Lett. **89** (2002) 245503
12. Toninelli, C., Biroli, G., Fisher, D.: Spatial structures and dynamics of kinetically constrained models for glasses. Phys. Rev. Lett. (2004)
13. Gray, L.: A mathematician looks at wolfram's new kind of science. Notices of the AMS **50** (2003) 200
14. Kogut, P.M., Leath, P.L. J. Phys. C. **14** (1981) 3187
15. Chalupa, J., Leath, P.L., Reich, G.R. J. Phys. C. **12** (1981) L31
16. Adler, J.: Bootstrap percolation. Physica A. **171** (1991) 453–470
17. Adler, J., Aharony, A. J. Phys. A. Math. Gen. **21** (1988) 1387
18. Adler, J., Stauffer, D. J. Phys. A. Math. Gen. **23** (1990) L1119
19. Stauffer, D., Adler, J., Aharony, A.: Universality at the three-dimensional percolation threshold. J. Phys. A. Math. Gen. **27** (1994) L475
20. Adler, J., Stauffer, D., Aharony, A. J. Phys. A. Math. Gen. **22** (1989) L297
21. Mountford, T.S. Stochastic Processes and their Applications **56** (1995) 185–205
22. Kirkpatrick, S., Wilcke, W., Garner, R., Huels, H. Physica A **314** (2002) 220
23. Manna, S.S.: Abelian cascade dynamics in bootstrap percolation. Physica A: Statistical and Theoretical Physics **261** (1998) 351–358
24. Schonmann, R. Ann. Probab. **20** (1992) 174

25. De Gregorio, P., Lawlor, A., Bradley, P., Dawson, K.A. in press; Phys. Rev. Lett. (2004)
26. Cerf, R., Cirillo, E.M.N. Ann. Prob. **27** (1999) 1837
27. Cerf, R., Manzo, F.: The threshold regime of finite volume bootstrap percolation. Stochastic Processes and their Applications **101** (2002/9) 69–82
28. Holroyd, A. Probability Theory and Related Fields **125** (2003) 195
29. Adler, J., Lev, U. Brazilian Journal of Physics **33** (2003) 641
30. Stauffer, D. (2004) personal communication.
31. The calculations for growing concentric squares reduce to estimation of the integral $\int_0^\rho (dy/y) \ln(1-y)$ in the limit $\rho \to 1$. A numerical estimate of $-(1-\rho) \sum_1^\infty \ln(1-\rho^k)$ shows that at $\rho = 0.995$ there is still a 1.5% deviation from $-\pi^2/6$. Adding the first correction to the integral in $(1-\rho)$ gives $-\pi^2/6 + \ln \rho \ln(1-\rho)$, already a good estimate at 0.95.

Plastic Deformation Development in Polycrystals Based on the Cellular Automata and Relaxation Element Method

G.V. Lasko[1,2], Y.Y. Deryugin[1], and S. Schmauder[2]

[1]Institute of Strength Physics and Material Science, SB RAS (ISPMS SB RAS),
pr.Akademicheskii 2/1, 634021 Tomsk, Russian Federation
[2]Institute for Material Testing, Material Science and Strength of Materials (IMWF)
Universität Stuttgart, Pfaffenwaldring 32, D-70569, Germany
Galina.Lasko@mpa.uni-stuttgart.de

Abstract. Based on the Relaxation Element Method, the propagation of zones of localized plastic deformation in a polycrystal under loading has been simulated within the framework of continuum mechanics. The model can be referred to the class of geometrical models, known as cellular automata. Plastic deformation is considered to occur under the action of differently scaled stress concentrators. A plastically deformed grain acts as a stress concentrator at the mesoscale level. The involvement of a cell into plastic deformation was determined by the value of the critical shear stress in the cell center along the slip system. This approach allows to analyze the number and interaction of slip systems and accounts for work-hardening on the patterns of the propagation of the bands of localized plastic deformation in aluminum polycrystals.

1 Introduction

Strain localization is one of the most important possible material instability phenomena in solids. In order to describe this phenomenon, many authors [1, 2] introduce gradients either in space or in time into the constitutive equations, that result in the necessity of using a high resolution numerical technique where the accuracy of the solution depends on the number of calculational cells. That is why analytical solutions to resolve such kind of problems are more attractive. It is necessary, therefore, to develop new-basically analytical- calculation methods for determining the zones of localized plastic deformation with gradients. The relaxation element method, initially proposed by Ye. Ye. Deryugin [5] is most suitable to handle the above problem. The necessity of the development of a new modeling method was caused by experimental facts on mechanisms of plastic deformation, having been obtained in the last 10-15 years.

According to experimental investigations by Neuhäuser [3,4], obtained with a videorecorder on the sample surface, the plastic deformation under active loading proceeds at all detectable time scales (from microseconds up to minutes) in form of instabilities, which only from the macroscopic point of view can be considered in terms of a smooth curve of loading. Dislocation theory gives an analogous conclusion: as soon as a dislocation configuration looses its stability due to an increase in

P.M.A. Sloot, B. Chopard, and A.G. Hoekstra (Eds.): ACRI 2004, LNCS 3305, pp. 375–384, 2004.

applied stress, the further development of the shear zone is a rapid dynamic process. Once operated, a shear zone remains during further deformation, as a rule, «frozen». Traditional approaches of continuum mechanics, being justified on the macrolevel, should therefore be completed by other methods when attempting to describe the processes on the level of a separate shear zone. The basis of all approaches of classical mechanics is the assumption about the existence of a local law of plastic flow in one or in another form, i.e. an unambiguous connection between stress and strain (and in generalized theories [5] also the spatial and temporal derivatives of strain). Data on the development of plastic deformation, in form of instabilities in local regions, lead to the conclusion that on the level of a separate shear zone the law of plastic flow in the above sense can not be formulated. Using the relaxation element method [5-10], plastic deformation can be analyzed on such a mesoscopic level.

2   Physical Principles and Algorithm of the Model

The analysis of many experimental data shows, that in real materials the process of plastic deformation occurs not simultaneously over the whole volume of material, but includes separate structural elements. Then a natural reason of grain involvement into this process is the presence of stress concentrators of a definite scale [11]. The stress field in the vicinity of a triple grain junction under tensile loading has been calculated by the relaxation element method [12], when one of the grains undergoes plastic deformation. It was shown, that at high gradients of plastic deformation in front of the boundary of this grain, the corresponding stress concentration can exceed the exernal applied stress by one order of magnitude. However, the influence of such a mesoconcentrator is limited over a very short distance, i.e. only several dozens of interatomic distances. Nucleation of only several dislocations can cause essential relaxation of these microstresses. This means that microconcentrators like dislocations cannot provide a sufficient value and rate of plastic deformation in the neighbouring grain to transfer further rapid propagation of plastic deformation from grain to grain. Hence, an additional concentrator is required, having the region of elevated stress concentration, embracing the region, being commensurable with the dimension of crystallite (mesoconcentrator). A plastically deformed grain besides the peak stresses at the junction creates an elevated stress concentration, embracing the region, commen-surable with grain dimension. The plastically deformed grain acts as a stress concen-trator on the mesoscale level. When simulating on the mesolevel, the plastically deformed grains are represented as a circular site of plastic deformation in a plane isotropic polycrystal. we assume that plastic deformation in the site occurs uniform. To explain the essence of the relaxation element method, consider the following situ-ation: A stress-strained state of a plane with the above-mentioned plastic deformation site with specified boundary conditions on the circular contour. Fig. 1 shows the loading of such a plane schematically. The tensile stress σ is directed along the y-axis. We restrict our attention in what follows to small strains (0,0002%) and the material is characterized in terms of linear elastic constituent relation.

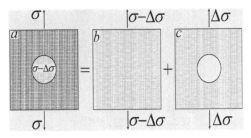

Fig. 1. Schematic representation of the boundary conditions for the plane under loading with a circular site of localized plastic deformation

Taking into account the experimentally discovered fact that plastic shear is accompanied by a stress drop in the local volume of solid [11], let us assume that under plastic deformation, the uniform stress field is decreased by $\Delta\sigma$. Then the stress field inside the site will be described by $\sigma-\Delta\sigma$. According to the superposition law of linear elasticity, the general solution to a boundary problem can be represented by a number of simpler solutions, provided that the resulting boundary conditions shown in Fig. 1 remain the same. This can be simplified as follows: the uniform stress field $\sigma-\Delta\sigma$ (Fig. 1b) is singled out from the general solution. What remains is the solution for a plane under an external load $\Delta\sigma$ (Fig. 1c), if the stresses are zero only in the local region occupied by the plastic deformation site. De Wit showed [13], that absence or reduction of stresses in the given region is the result of plastic deformation. In our case this comparative plastic deformation ensures a displacement of the circular contour under the external stress $\Delta\sigma$, when there is no stress inside the contour. The boundary conditions, according to Fig. 1, are those of a flat testpiece with a circular opening subjected to the uniaxial $\Delta\sigma$.

According to the Kirsh's solution [14], the stress field outside a circular contour in the Cartesian coordinates is characterized by the following components: [14,15]:

$$\Delta\sigma_y=\Delta\sigma+\Delta\sigma k_y=\Delta\sigma+\frac{\Delta\sigma R^2}{2r^2}\left[1+\frac{3R^2+10y^2}{r^2}-F+G\right],$$

$$\Delta\sigma_x=\Delta\sigma k_x=\frac{\Delta\sigma R^2}{2r^2}\left[3-\frac{3R^2+18y^2}{r^2}+F-G\right], \qquad \Delta\sigma_{xy}=\Delta\sigma k_{xy}=\frac{\Delta\sigma R^2\,yx}{r^4}\left[3-\frac{2(3R^2+4y^2)}{r^2}+\frac{12R^2y^2}{r^4}\right],$$

(2)

where R – is the grain radius, $r^2 = x^2+y^2$ – is the distance from the center of inclusion to the point with the coordinates (x, y); $F = 8y^2(3a^2+2y^2)/r^4$, $G = 24R^2y^4/r^6$.

The displacements of the arbitrary point (x_0, y_0) on the contour are defined by the relation

$$u_y(x_0, y_0)=3y_0\Delta\sigma/E, \quad u_x(x_0, y_0)=-x_0\Delta\sigma/E, \tag{3}$$

where E – is Young's modulus. The boundary conditions (3) are satisfied by a homogeneous field of plastic deformation with the components

$$\varepsilon_x = -\Delta\sigma/E, \quad \varepsilon_y =3\Delta\sigma/E, \quad \varepsilon_{xy} = 0 \tag{4}$$

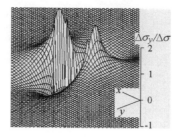

Fig. 2. Spatial distribution of the $\Delta\sigma_y$ component of the internal stress field of the circular relaxation element. (External applied stress σ is directed along the y-axis).

From the performed analysis it follows, that the site of plastic deformation can be considered as a defect of a definite scale with its own field of internal stresses, set by equations (2). Such a defect is called a relaxation element (RE). Shown in Fig. 2 is an example of the component $\Delta\sigma_y$ distribution (2) of the given circular relaxation element. It is seen, that there exists a stress peak on the boundary of the RE. The region of elevated stress is comparable with the dimension of the relaxation element. At a distance not less than 1,3 a from the center of the RE the perturbation of stresses in this region affects greatly the development of plastic deformation in the adjacent grain. Once the grain with the maximum value of shear stress is known, the external stress field needs to be determined under which the resolved shear stress is attained. The calculation mesh was schematically presented by a total of 1250 (50x25) cells shaped as hexagons, playing the role of grains in polycrystal. In each of the grains the slip system orientation with respect to the axis tension was set using random number generator. The second slip system was added at an angle of 60° with respect to the previous one. The involvement of a cell into plastic deformation was determined by the value of τ_{cr}, a critical shear stress in the cell center along the slip system. Plastic deformation initiates on the slip plane of those crystallites, in which the resolved shear stress reaches a critical value along the favorably oriented slip direction. The resolved shear stress was calculated with the following formula [14]:

$$\tau = (\sigma_y - \sigma_x)\sin\alpha\cos\alpha + \sigma_{xy}(\cos^2\alpha - \sin^2\alpha). \qquad (5)$$

The action of the element transition from the elastic into the plastic deformed state was defined by placing of an RE of round shape inscribed into the hexagon in its center. It changes the stress-strain state of the polycrystal aggregate as a whole and the region of operation of maximum shear stress. The act of grain involvement into plastic deformation is accompanied by a stress drop within the local region (in our case within the circular region) and the stress perturbation beyond this region. The problem now consists in designing a cycle that can, according to certain criterion, determine the sequence of grain involvement into plastic deformation after the first RE has appeared.

2.1 Calculational Procedure

In what follows we represent the process of plastic deformation as a sequential chain of elementary acts of stress relaxation in the different crystallites. Suppose the specimen is subjected to tensile loading along the y-axis and the external applied stress is equal to $\sigma_{ext} = \sigma_y$. The external applied stress creates a shear stress in the crystallites:

$$\tau_{ij} = \sigma_{ext} \sin\alpha_{ij} \cos\alpha_{ij.} \qquad (6)$$

where the indices i and j unambiguously define the x,y coordinates of the given crystallite. Having determined the coordinates of the crystallite in the slip system in which the shear stress is maximum, the external applied stress in the formulae is obtained as:

$$\sigma_{ext} = \tau_{ij}/\sin\alpha_{ij} \cos\alpha_{ij} \qquad (7)$$

According to the condition that the critical shear stress equals $\tau_{cr} = 50$, we obtain σ_{ext} =50/$\sin\alpha_{ij}$ $\cos\alpha_{ij}$. With known external applied stress and given coordinates of the crystallite, in which the maximum shear stress is attained, a relaxation element is placed in this crystallite. The relaxation element creates a field of stresses , the compo-nents of which are represented by equations 2. Instead of $\Delta\sigma$ we take 1, ½, ¼, of the minimum external applied stress defined at the previous step. Such values of $\Delta\sigma$ were chosen with taking into account the fact that the stress drop inside the region of relaxation should not exceed the external applied stress. Because the total shear stress in the centers of each crystallite is expressed by the formulae:

$$\tau_{ij} = \sigma_{ext} \sin\alpha_{ij} \cos\alpha_{ij} + (\sigma^*_{y\,ij} - \sigma^*_{x\,ij}) \sin\alpha_{ij} \cos\alpha_{ij} + \sigma^*_{xy\,ij}(\cos^2\alpha_{ij} - \sin^2\alpha_{ij}), \qquad (8)$$

the external applied stress can be calculated in each crystallite is defined by the formula:

$$\sigma_{ext\,ij} = (50 - (\sigma^*_{y\,ij} - \sigma^*_{x\,ij}) \sin\alpha_{ij} \cos\alpha_{ij} + \sigma^*_{xy\,ij}(\cos^2\alpha_{ij} - \sin^2\alpha_{ij}))/\sin\alpha_{ij} \cos\alpha_{ij} \qquad (9)$$

So we have an array of external applied stress in each crystallite under which the critical shear stress $\tau_{cr} = 50$ MPa is attained in each crystallite. Apparently the lowest value of external applied stress matches the maximum shear stress. Physically that means that at the given step of calculation among all of the crystallites the only one will be involved into plastic deformation in which the maximum shear stress is at-tained and that is why the lowest external applied stress is necessary to bring it into action.

We look for the coordinates of those crystallites with the lowest external applied stress. In such a way the coordinates of the crystallite and the external applied stress in this crystallite define the values, necessary for the beginning of a second cycle of calculations. In the present case the equation (9) can be written in the following form:

$$\sigma_{ext\,ij} = \frac{50 - (\sum_{ij}\sigma^*_{y\,ij} - \sum_{ij}\sigma^*_{x\,ij}) \sin\alpha_{ij} \cos\alpha_{ij} - \sum_{ij}\sigma^*_{xy\,ij} \cos 2\alpha_{ij}}{\sin\alpha_{ij} \cos\alpha_{ij}}, \qquad (10)$$

where the sign of sum means the summation of the components of the stress tensor from RE at each step of the calculation. In the given example calculations of plastic deformation localization are performed only for one slip system in each crystallite.

Consider the presence of two slip systems in each crystallite. The second slip sys-tem is oriented at an angle of 60° with respect to the first slip system. The orientation of the first slip system is put at random in each crystallite. The minimum external applied stress in each of the slip systems is defined separately and the minimum one is selected. In this way, the external applied stress and the coordinates of the crystallite with maximum shear stress (and minimum external applied stress) are known. Now the next cycle of calculations can be performed.

Let us next introduce the coefficient of work-hardening. For each crystallite let us introduce the coefficient K_{ij}, which is equal to 0 when the crystallite ij is not involved into plastic deformation and each time it is increased by 1 when the crystallite is involved into plastic deformation, so that $K_{ij} = K_{ij}+1$. Let the resolved shear stress on the slip system in each crystallite follow the formulae: $\tau_{ij} = 50(1+K_{ij})$, where K_{ij} is equal to zero for all crystallites not involved into plastic deformation. Now (10) reads

$$\sigma_{ext\ ij=} \frac{50(1+K_{ij}) - (\sum_{ij}\sigma_{yij}^* - \sum_{ij}\sigma_{xij}^*)\sin\alpha_{ij}\cos\alpha_{ij} - \sum_{ij}\sigma_{xyij}^*\cos 2\alpha_{ij}}{\sin\alpha_{ij}\cos\alpha_{ij}}. \tag{11}$$

There are two possibilities in accounting for work hardening in each crystallite. First, the acting of one slip system doesn't depend on the acting of another one and the crystallite, once involved into plastic deformation according to achieving the critical shear stress in one slip system, can be involved into plastic deformation due to achieving a critical shear stress in another slip system. In other words, we set the two coefficients of work-hardening K_1 and K_2 for each of the two slip systems in each crystallite. Following the above-mentioned procedure we separate the calculation of minimum external applied stress in each of the two slip systems with separate arrays of K_{ij} for each of them, i. e. K_{1ij} for the first slip system and K_{2ij} - for the second one. And secondly, the repeated involvement of the same grain into plastic deformation depends on the involvement of the crystallite into plastic deformation on the first slip system, i.e. we have only one coefficient of work-hardening for two slip systems in each crystallite. We consider two cases of work-hardening: 1) with interaction of two slip systems and 2) without interaction between them. Interaction between two slip systems means, that when one of the grains has been involved into plastic deformation when achieving the critical resolved shear stress in one slip system, it cannot be involved again because a critical shear stress in another slip system needs to be achieved. Hence we put $K_{1ij}=0$ before selecting the grain with minimum external applied stress in the second slip system. Along with accounting of linear dependence of work-hardening on the number of grains involved into plastic deformation an attempt to take work-hardening into account with the help of the power law expression for the stress-strain relationship $\sigma = K\varepsilon_{pl}^n$, where K was chosen, e.g., equal to 250 and n=0.2.

3   Results and Discussion

Using the above approach, the simulation of propagation of the sites of localized plastic deformation has been performed with accounting for work-hardening. The patterns of propagation of the bands of localized plastic deformation with work-hardening and the presence of only one slip system in each crystallite are shown in Fig. 3. The coefficient of work hardening was taken to be $K=4$. As can be seen from the picture the bands quasi-homogeneously fill all the cross-section of the specimen with preferred (60°) direction of their propagation. The loading curve has a clearly pronounced increasing character. Because of the presence of only one slip system in each of the crystallites the repeated involvement of the same grain requires an increase in the external applied stress K times higher than the critical shear stress and that practically exclude the repeated involvement of the same grains into plastic deformation. More and more grains are involved into plastic deformation, which gives he pattern a scattered appearance: Localization is even observed at the first steps of simulation.

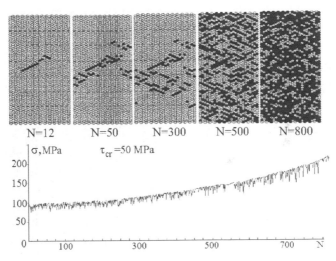

Fig. 3. The evolution of the sites of localized plastic deformation in a polycrystal under tensile loading with one slip systems in each crystallite and with accounting for strain hardening (the value of relaxation is equal to 0.5 of external applied stress).

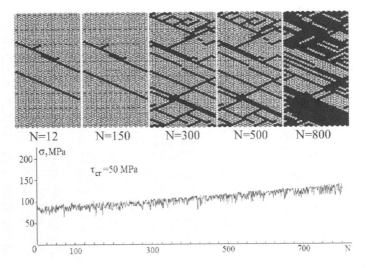

Fig. 4. The evolution of the sites of localized plastic deformation in a polycrystal under tensile loading with two slip systems in each crystallite and with accounting for strain hardening (the value of relaxation is equal to 0.5 of external applied stress), the slip systems in each crystallite are dependent on each other.

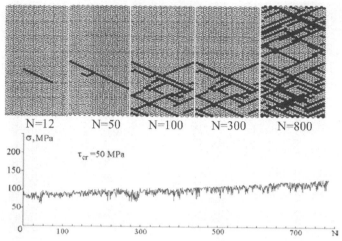

Fig. 5. Patterns of propagation and loading diagram of hardening polycrystal with two slip system in each crystallite with strain hardening coefficient $K=4$, the value of relaxation is 0.5 from the external applied stress, the slip systems in each crystallite do not depend on each other.

In previous papers [5-9], strain-hardening was accounted for only by prohibition of the repeated involvement of grains into the process of plastic deformation. Such an approach resulted in the limited case of work-hardening. Here we account for work-hardening by introducing the coefficient of work-hardening, when calculating the external applied stress. That means that each repeated involvement of the same crystallite into plastic deformation is possible only when achieving the critical shear stress (50 MPa in our case) multiplied by the coefficient K. The critical shear stress is equal to 50 MPa. Setting the K being equal to 4 mean, that after the grain is involved into plastic deformation for the first time, at 50 MPa, its repeated involvement is possible only at $\tau = 200$ MPa. That gives the possibility to other grains, which have not been involved yet into plastic deformation, to be involved, as the resolved shear stress attains the critical value.

Another pattern of the propagation of the bands of localized plastic deformation is obtained by accounting for the presence of two slip systems in each crystallite, Fig. 4. At this stage the sites of localized plastic deformation become more localized. They represent systems of intersecting bands, propagating across the cross-section of the specimen. At the N=50th step of grains involvement into plastic deformation the two parallel bands appear. Then another band propagates from these initial ones, forming the system of intersecting bands. Fragmentation of the specimen by the band of localized plastic deformation is clearly pronounced here. Starting approximately from step number 600 the involvement of new grains takes place, making impossible the repeated involvement of the same grain into plastic deformation, because in the given approach we set the increasing value of the external applied stress for all the grains, once involved into plastic deformation, independently on which system plastic slip occured. The loading diagram has increasing character but the average level of external applied stress goes somewhat lower, because two slip systems can act in the same crystallites. Shown in Fig. 5 is the case of the operation of two sliding systems in each of the crystallites. As opposed to Fig. 4 here we take into consideration the slip systems independently. This means that the same grain may be involved into plastic deformation according to the acting of two slip systems, first on one sliding system, then on another one, where involvement according to achieving the critical shear stress in one sliding system doesn't depend on the acting of another one. The resulting deformation pattern possesses a pronounced localized character. The loading diagram has increasing character, but the stress remains less than in the previous case, depicted in Fig. 4. The patterns of LPD band propagation, accounting of work-hardening with power law dependency are represented in Fig. 6. This is the case of operating of two independent slip systems in each crystallite and the value of relaxation (stress drop) was taken to be equal to 0.2 of external applied stress. Because of the smaller magnitude of stress relaxation (0.2 instead of 05 of external applied stress), the amplitude of oscillations are smaller and it results in less pronounced localization. The curve increases significantly and at the N=801 (ε^p = 0.0002%) it reaches the value 296 MPa. Fragmentation of the specimen by the LPD bands occurs here as in the case of accounting for linear work-hardening, depicted in Fig. 6.

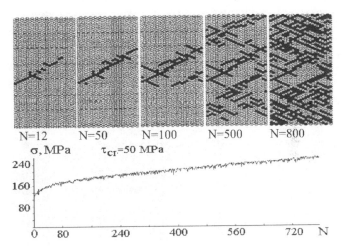

Fig. 6. Loading diagram of hardening polycrystal with two slip systems in each crystallite with the power law hardening, the value of relaxation is 0.2 from the external applied stress, the slip systems in each crystallite are independent on each other.

4 Conclusions

The propagation of the LPD bands and influence of work-hardening on the patterns of development of the sites of plastic deformation has been analyzed within the framework of a meso-mechanical model of plastic strain localization. The model allows to simulate both non-hardening and hardening behavior of the polycrystal material under loading. Work-hardening was accounted for the case of interacting slip systems in each crystallite and not interacting ones. The comparison of the patterns of development of the sites of localized plastic deformation and loading curves for the case of accounting of interaction of two slip systems and non accounting for ones shows, that in the latter case the pattern of plastic strain propagation has more pronounced localized character. The number of slip systems in each crystallite and the non-accounting of the interaction of the slip systems result in the enhancement of the localization, that is accompanied by a lower average level of external applied stress. The bands of localized plastic deformation proceed at an angle of 60° with respect to the tensile axis, is in agreement with the experimental findings [11,12], theoretical descriptions [5] and the results of calculations of Cleveringa et. al [15].

Acknowledgements. One of the authors (G.V. Lasko) expresses gratitude to the Alexander von Humboldt Foundation for the financial support of the work.

References

1. Aifantis, E.C., *Int. J. of Engineering Science.* 30(10) (1992) 1279-1285
2. Hähner, P., *Scripta Metallurgica* et *Materialia.* 29 (1993) 1171-1181
3. Neuhäuser, H. and Hampel, A. *Scripta Metallurgica.* 29 (1993) 1151
4. Neuhäuser, H. Plastic instabilities and the deformation of metals. In patterns, Defects and Material Instabilities, Eds. D.Walgraef and N.M. Ghoniem, Kluwer Academic Publishers (1990)
5. Deryugin, Ye. Ye. Relaxation Element Method, Novosibirsk, Nauka, 1998:253.
6. Deryugin, Y.Y., Lasko, G.V., Schmauder, S. *Computational Materials Science.* 11 (1998) 189-193.
7. Deryugin, Y.Y., Lasko, G.V., Schmauder, S. *Computational Materials Science.* 15;89:99.
8. Lasko, G.V., Deryugin, Ye.Ye., Schmauder, S., Saraev, D., *Theoretical and Applied Fracture Mechanics.* 34 (2000) 93-100
9. Deryugin, Ye.Ye. Proc. Int. Conf. MESOMECHANICS 2000: Role of Mechanics for Deve-lopment of Science and Technology, Tsinghua University Press, Beijing, China, 1; (2000) 455
10. Deryugin, Y.Y., *Computational Materials Science.* 19 (2000) 53-60
11. Panin, V.E. (Ed.), Physical Mesomechanics of heterogeneous Medium and Computer Aided Design of Materials, Cambridge International Science Publishing, (1997)
12. Deryugin Ye.Ye., Lasko G.V., Smolin Yu.E., *Russian Physician J.,* 38 (5) (1995) 15-18
13. de Wit, R., Continuum Theory of disclinations, Mir, Moscow (1977)
14. Timoshenko, S.P., Goodier, J.N., Theory of elasticity, 3d edn. New York:McGraw-Hill, (1970)
15. Cleveringa, H.H.M., E. van der Giessen, Needleman, Proceed. of the 19th Risø International Symposium on Material Science, Carstensen J.V.et.al.(Eds), 7-11 September, (1998) 61-69.
16. Ohring, M., Engineering Materials Science, Academic Press, London (1995)

Predicting Wildfire Spreading Through a Hexagonal Cellular Automata Model

Giuseppe A. Trunfio

Center of High-Performance Computing,
University of Calabria, Arcavacata, 87036 Rende, CS, ITALY
trunfio@unical.it

Abstract. As it is well known forest fires can present serious risk to people and can have enormous environmental impact. Therefore researchers and land managers are increasingly interested in effective tools for use in scientific analyses, management and fighting operations. On the other hand forest fires are complex phenomena that need an interdisciplinary approach. In this paper the paradigm of Cellular Automata was applied and a model was projected to simulate the evolution of forest fires. The adopted method involves the definition of local rules, mainly based on fire spread relationships originally developed by Rothermel in 1972, from which the global behaviour of the system can emerge. The preliminary results show that the model could be applied for forest fire prevention, the production of risk scenarios and the evaluation of the forest fire environmental impact.

1 Introduction

Cellular Automata (CA) are good candidates for modelling and simulating complex dynamical systems whose evolution depends exclusively on the local interactions of their constituent parts [6]. A CA involves a regular division of the space in cells, each one characterised by a state that represents the actual conditions of the cell. The state changes according to a transition function that depends on the states of neighbouring cells and of the cell itself; the transition function is identical for all the cells. At time $t=0$, cells are in states, describing initial conditions, and the CA evolves changing the state of all the cells simultaneously at discrete times, according to the transition function.

The CA features (i.e. locality property) seem to match the "forest fire" system; the parameters, describing globally a forest fire, i.e. propagation rate, flame length and direction, fireline intensity, fire duration time etc. are mainly depending on some local characteristics i.e. vegetation type (live and dead fuel), relative humidity, fuel moisture, heat, territory morphology (altitude, slope), wind velocity and direction, etc.

The fundamental studies of Rothermel [12], [13] point out these characteristics; his forest fire spread model is based on dynamic equations, that allow the forecast of the rate of spread and the reaction intensity knowing certain properties of the fuel matrix (fuel particle, fuel arrangement) and environmental conditions (slope, wind, fuel moisture) in which the fire occurs.

P.M.A. Sloot, B. Chopard, and A.G. Hoekstra (Eds.): ACRI 2004, LNCS 3305, pp. 385–394, 2004.

Some models were previously developed in terms of CA: Green [9] considered a two-dimensional square CA, where each cell is identified by fuel content and its combustion duration. The fire-spread mechanism is briefly the following: each burning cell generates an ellipse with a focus at the cell centre; the ellipse dimension and orientation depends on the wind direction and strength. If a cell with fuel content is inside an ellipse, it will burn in the next steps. Gonçalves and Diogo [8] developed a more complex probabilistic CA model based on the Rothermel's equations of fire rate spread. A burning cell determines, according to the fire rate spread toward the direction of neighbouring cells, an ignition probability. Karafyllidis and Thanailakis [10] developed a two-dimensional square CA which was only tested with hypothetical forests. Malamud and Turcotte [11] developed a statistical model of comprehensive effects in a forest for the two opposite phenomena of trees taking root in free areas and trees burnt by the fire.

The proposed CA model is deterministic, it is related to Rothermel's studies [12] and is partially based on the method described in [6] that may be applied to some macroscopic phenomena in order to produce a proper CA model.

In the next section this paper illustrates the basic equations; the CA model formalization is described in the successive section; the fourth section treats the model implementations and preliminary results of applications; at the end comments conclude the paper.

2 Fire Spread Prediction

The majority of fire models in use today are mainly based on fire propagation relationships experimentally developed in the U.S. by Rothermel [12], [13], Albini [1], Anderson [2]. Fire geometry models were proposed by Anderson [3] and many other researchers.

Rothermel's equations require a description of fuel which includes depth, loading, percentage of dead fuel, moisture of extinction, heat content, surface area to volume ratio, mineral content, silica content, and particle density. Required environmental variables include wind speed at half-flame height, slope and fuel moisture content (live and dead). Models based on Rothermel's equations usually perform adequately in predicting the detail of fire physics.

Rothermel's model leads to the fire maximum spread rate vector. To obtain a bi-dimensional description of fire behaviour it is generally assumed that the fire spread area is an ellipse [3] in which the source lies at one focus and the major axis is parallel to the maximum spread rate direction (which is influenced by local wind and slope).

2.1 Basic Equations

It is known that fires show a higher propagation velocity when they climb up an upward slope, whereas fires show a smaller velocity when they descend a downward slope. Also, wind speed and direction greatly affect forest fire propagation. Therefore, according to the Rothermel's fire study [12], maximum spread rate occurs in the direction of the resultant wind-slope vector:

$$\phi = \phi_w + \phi_s \qquad (1)$$

where ϕ_s is in direction of maximum slope and its module is the *slope effect*, ϕ_w is in wind direction and its module is the *wind effect*. Slope and wind effect are respectively expressed as:

$$\phi_s = 5.275\beta^{-0.3}\tan\omega^2, \text{ and}$$

$$\phi_w = C\ (3.281\ v)^B (\beta / \beta_{op})^{-E} \qquad (2)$$

where v is the wind speed, β is the packing ratio of the fuel bed, β_{op} is the optimum packing ratio, ω is the slope (radians), C, B and E coefficients are functions of the fuel particle size in the fuel bed [1], [2], [12], [13].

The maximum fire spread rate (m min^{-1}), which accounts for local fuel characteristics, slope and wind effect, is computed as:

$$R_{max} = R_0(1+|\phi|), \quad R_0 = I_R \xi /(\rho_b\ h\ Q_{ig}) \qquad (3)$$

where R_0 is the spread rate on flat terrain and without wind; I_R is the reaction intensity; ξ is the propagation flux ratio; Q_{ig} is the heat of pre-ignition; ρ_b is the ovendry bulk density; h is the effective heating number.

The spread rate in an arbitrary direction is obtained assuming an elliptical shaped local spread (see fig. 1a):

$$R = R_{max}\frac{1-\varepsilon}{1-\varepsilon\ \cos\theta} \qquad (4)$$

where the eccentricity ε of the ellipse increases as a function of the effective midflame windspeed v_e according to the Anderson's empirical relation [3] as modified by Finney [7]:

$$\varepsilon = \frac{\sqrt{l_w^2-1}}{l_w}, \qquad l_w = 0.936\ e^{0.2566 v_e} + 0.461\ e^{-0.1548 v_e} - 0.397 \qquad (5)$$

The effective midflame windspeed v_e, defined as the virtual windspeed that by itself would produce the combined effect of slope and wind on fire spread rate, can be derived from eq. (3).

It is worth noting that when $v_e = 0$ (i.e. no slope and no wind) the eccentricity is zero and the ellipse reduce to a circle of radius R_0.

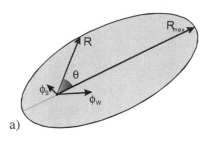
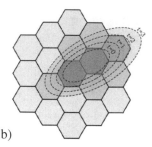

Fig. 1. a) Elliptical fire spread area in which the source lies at one focus and the major axis is parallel to the maximum spread rate direction; b) Neighbourhood pattern and fire propagation in the proposed model: the cells inside the ellipses are burning and each ellipse represents a successive CA step

3 The Cellular Automaton

In order to avoid the spurious symmetries of the square cells, which characterize some previous CA based fire models [8], [9], [10], [11], the proposed model is based on a hexagonal lattice. The neighbourhood pattern includes the double order of hexagons around the cell, as shown in fig. 1b. The further main points of the proposed model are described by the following:

1. The state of the cell must account for all the characteristics, relevant to the evolution of the system and relative to the space portion corresponding to the cell; e.g. the altitude. Each characteristic must be individuated as a substate. The substate value is considered constant in the cell.
2. As the state of the cell can be decomposed in substates, the transition function may be also split in many components. We distinguish two types of components: *internal transformation*, depending on the substates of the cell and *local interactions*, depending on the substates of the cells in the neighbouring (e.g. fire propagation).
3. Special functions must supply the history of "external influences" overall on the CA cells and direction.
4. Some cells represent a kind of input from the "external world" to the CA; it accounts for describing an external initial influence, which cannot be described in terms of rules; e.g. the fire starting points.

3.1 The Model Formalization

We now give a formal description of the model which is a two-dimensional CA with hexagonal cells defined as:

$$CA = <K, X, S, P, \sigma, I, \Gamma>$$

where:

- **K** is the set of points with integer co-ordinates in the finite region, where the phenomenon evolves. Each point identifies a hexagonal cell.

- The set $\mathbf{X}$ identifies the geometrical pattern of the cells, which influences the change in the state of each one (the full second order neighbourhood, see fig. 1b).
- The finite set $\mathbf{S}$ of the states of the cell is:

$$\mathbf{S} = \mathbf{S}_A \times \mathbf{S}_V \times \mathbf{S}_T \times \mathbf{S}_H \times \mathbf{S}_C \times \mathbf{S}_D \times \mathbf{S}_{WD} \times \mathbf{S}_{WR} \times (\mathbf{S}_{FS})^{18}$$

  - $\mathbf{S}_A$, substate "altitude", takes the altitude value of the cell;
  - $\mathbf{S}_V$, substate "vegetation", specifies the type of vegetation, relative to the properties of catching fire and burning. Fuel bed characteristics are specified according to the 13 format of fire behaviour fuel models used in BEHAVE [5].
  - $\mathbf{S}_T$, substate "temperature", takes the temperature value of the cell;
  - $\mathbf{S}_H$, substate "humidity", takes the relative humidity value of the cell;
  - $\mathbf{S}_C$, substate "combustion" for the two possible fire types in the cell: "surface fire" and "crown fire"; it takes one of the values "non-flammable", "inflammable", "burning" and "burnt" for each type.
  - $\mathbf{S}_D$, substate "duration", takes the value of the duration rest of the fire in the cell;
  - $\mathbf{S}_{WD}$, substate "wind direction", takes the values of the wind directions (the eight directions of the wind rose) at ground level (that could be different from the free wind direction);
  - $\mathbf{S}_{WR}$, substate "wind rate", takes the values of the wind rate (Km 0-60) at ground level (that could be different from the free wind rate);
  - $\mathbf{S}_{FS}$, substate "fire spread", accounts for the fire spread from the central cell to the other neighbouring cells;
  - $\mathbf{S}_{FA}$, substate "fire acquire", is just a renaming of $\mathbf{S}_{FS}$ and individuates the fire propagation to the central cell from the other neighbouring cells.
- $\mathbf{P} = \{p_e, p_s, p_t, p_{wd}, p_{wr}, \mathbf{P}_w, \mathbf{P}_v\}$ is the finite set of global parameters, which affect the transition function; they are constant overall in the cellular space:
  - p_e, is the apothem of the cell.
  - p_s, the time corresponding to a single step.
  - p_t, the current time (month, day, hour and minute),
  - p_{wd}, the free wind direction
  - p_{wr}, the free wind rate;
  - $\mathbf{P}_w$, the set of weather condition parameters, varying during the day according to the season (currently $\mathbf{P}_w$ contains the reference values of humidity and temperature). Such parameters are correct considering the type of vegetation, the wind and in the case of a previous rain episode as far as a month
  - $\mathbf{P}_v$, the set of parameters concerning catching fire and burning, depending on the type of vegetation; they are also constant in time.

Note that the function γ_1 keeps p_t up-to-date, the function γ_2 supplies the history of $\mathbf{P}_w$, p_{wd} and p_{wr} at each CA step.
- $\sigma: \mathbf{S}^{19} \rightarrow \mathbf{S}$ is the transition function, that will be sketched in the next section; it accounts for the following aspects of the phenomenon: effects of combustion in surface and crown fire inside the cell, crown fire triggering off; surface and crown fire spread, determination of the local wind rate and direction.
- $\mathbf{I} \subset \mathbf{K}$ individuates the cells where the fire starts.

- $\Gamma = \{\gamma_1, \gamma_2, \gamma_3, \gamma_4\}$ is the set of functions representing an external influence. They are computed at each step before the application of σ.
- γ_1 determines the current time of the CA step;
- γ_2 supplies the weather conditions related to sun, the external wind direction and rate, for each CA step;
- γ_3: $\mathbf{N} \times \mathbf{I} \rightarrow \mathbf{S}_C$ accounts for external setting fire to cells of $\mathbf{I}$ at prefixed steps, where $\mathbf{N}$ is the set of natural numbers;
- γ_4: $\mathbf{N} \times \mathbf{K} \rightarrow \mathbf{S}_C$ accounts for firemen intervention at prefixed steps.

3.2 The Transition Function

The transition function is defined as:

$$\sigma = \sigma_{13} \otimes \sigma_{12} \otimes \sigma_{11} \otimes \sigma_{T1}$$

First the following internal transformation, concerning the effects of combustion in surface and crown fire inside the cell, is computed:

$$\sigma_{T1}: \mathbf{S}_V \times \mathbf{S}_T \times \mathbf{S}_H \times \mathbf{S}_C \times \mathbf{S}_D \times \mathbf{S}_{WD} \times \mathbf{S}_{WR} \rightarrow \mathbf{S}_T \times \mathbf{S}_H \times \mathbf{S}_C \times \mathbf{S}_D.$$

Then the following local interactions are applied:

- $\sigma_{11}: (\mathbf{S}_A)^{19} \rightarrow \mathbf{S}_{WD} \times \mathbf{S}_{WR}$
- $\sigma_{12}: (\mathbf{S}_{FA})^{18} \times \mathbf{S}_C \rightarrow \mathbf{S}_C$
- $\sigma_{13}: (\mathbf{S}_A)^{19} \times \mathbf{S}_V \times \mathbf{S}_C \times \mathbf{S}_H \times \mathbf{S}_T \times \mathbf{S}_D \times \mathbf{S}_{WD} \times \mathbf{S}_{WR} \rightarrow (\mathbf{S}_{FS})^{18}$

where σ_{11} computes the wind direction and rate at the cell altitude, σ_{12} computes the change of combustion conditions in the current cell and σ_{13} computes the fire spread toward the neighbouring cells.

Internal transformation T1
When the substate $\mathbf{S}_C$ is not "burning" it doesn't change the substate $\mathbf{S}_D$, while the substates $\mathbf{S}_H$ and $\mathbf{S}_T$ vary their previous values on the basis of the weather change ($\mathbf{P}_w$), the day hour (p_t), the wind ($\mathbf{S}_{WD}$ and $\mathbf{S}_{WR}$) and the vegetation type ($\mathbf{S}_V$ and $\mathbf{P}_v$). When the substate $\mathbf{S}_C$ is "burning", then the substates $\mathbf{S}_T$, $\mathbf{S}_H$, $\mathbf{S}_C$ and $\mathbf{S}_D$ depend on the previous values of $\mathbf{S}_H$, $\mathbf{S}_D$ and $\mathbf{S}_T$. The value 0 for $\mathbf{S}_D$ determinates the change of $\mathbf{S}_C$ to "burnt". The conditions for the ignition from fire surface to crown fire are applied in the internal transformation T_1.

Local interaction I1
The computation of the substates $\mathbf{S}_{WD}$ and $\mathbf{S}_{WR}$, "wind direction and rate" depends on p_{wd} and p_{wr} that represent the values of the free wind. Such values are reduced in relation to the altitude of the cell according to an empirical table of Rothermel [13], obtaining the wind vector, related to the cell altitude. A corrective vector wind is computed, considering the angle between the slope relative to the cell and the free wind direction. It accounts for the absence of free wind, convective currents form along the maximum slope directions; their rate depends also on the weather and the hour of the

day. Some empirical tables of Rothermel [13] indicate the value of such vector. The new values of S_{WD} and S_{WR} are obtained adding the altitude vector to the corrective vector.

Local interaction I2
This function tests if the fire is spreading toward the central cell from the other cells of the neighbouring. If the combustion substate S_C is "inflammable", then it changes to "burning".

Local interaction I3
If the state S_C is "burning" the following computation steps, depending on substates S_V, S_H, S_T, S_D, S_{WD}, S_{WR} and the set of parameters P_v, are considered:
a) First, using equations (1) and (2), the maximum spread vector is determined as the sum of slope effect ϕ_s and wind effect ϕ_w ;
b) Using equation (3) the maximum spread rate R_{max} is computed.
c) An ellipse with a focus in the centre of the cell whose area depending on R_{max}, is calculated using equation (5); the time corresponding to the CA step p_s also affects the area of the ellipse (see fig. 1);
d) The fire can propagate towards the neighbouring cells inside the ellipse, i.e. S_{FS} (which is an alias of S_{FA}) takes the value "true".

4 Implementation and Preliminary Applications

The implementation was developed in the programming language C++ using the OpenGL library for visualization. The main input are the DEM (Digital Elevation, Model) of the area, the gridded land cover (e.g. fuel kind) and the weather conditions.

A first validation was tested on a real case of forest fire (fig. 2) in the territory of Villaputzu, Sardinia, on August 22nd, 1998. This forest fire was a case treated and monitored in the milieu of European Research Program SALTUS, Environment and Climate [15]. The fire began at 12.30 and lasted less than 9 hours. The wind was in direction SE at a rate 20-30 Km/h. The burnt area was approximately 3 Km². The forest fire area in fig. 2 is illustrated by a legend specifying the different type of burnt vegetation. The dotted lines indicate the roads. The roads on the left and on the right of the initial area of the fire represent a barrier, because the human intervention to limit the fire spread is easily performed in the areas adjacent to roads.

The simulated area (fig. 3 A, B, C, D) is visualised at each simulation step by a matrix with 170 rows and 130 columns; the hexagonal cell apothem is about m 20; the parameter p_s is 2.5 min (as a result of a performed calibration procedure). The forest fire started in the area on the top left of fig. 2. In the simulation matrix, a barrier is introduced in the flat area to the right of the fire beginning area, as an easy human intervention was performed there. Step 30 of the simulation (fig. 3-A, 75 minutes) represents the first cells burning. In the step 90 of the simulation (fig. 3-B, 3.75 hours), the fire is rapidly reaching the mountain peaks. The fire is propagating according to the wind direction and the positive slope also allows the fire to expand towards E, NE. Then the propagation towards the wind direction is almost exhausted and its rate slows with the negative slope (fig. 3-C, almost 7 hours). The only propagation direction is now SW and the fire proceeds very slowly (fig. 3-D, 8.3 hours).

Fig. 4 represents the superimposition of the real fire of simulated fire. The result of simulation looks good, few areas of the real fire don't appear to be burnt in the simulation and few areas, which were not burnt, are computed to be "burnt" in the simulation.

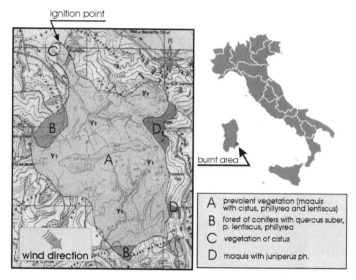

Fig. 2. The forest fire of Villaputzu, August 22nd, 1998

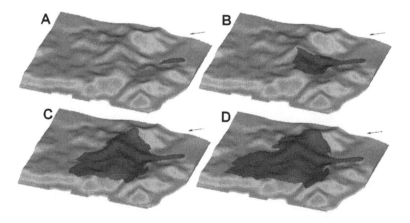

Fig. 3. Sequence of four simulation steps for the test case in fig. 2: figures A, B, C, D correspond respectively to steps 30, 90, 170, 200

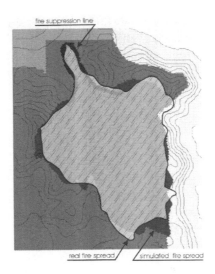

Fig. 4. Simulated vs. real fire spread for the test case in fig. 2

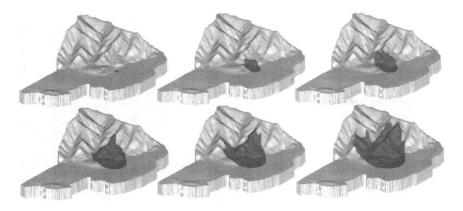

Fig. 5. CA model outcomes in a complex morphology

Many other simulations have been performed (see fig. 5 for example) and currently we are comparing the outcomes with those of a non CA based wildfire simulator (i.e. FARSITE simulator whose spread prediction is based on Huygen's principle [7]).

5 Conclusions

The results of the simulations show a phenomenon development that fits significantly with real data. Because of the use of hexagonal cells, the proposed model does not present the spurious symmetries of the square lattice, which characterizes some previous CA based fire model and which can affect negatively the simulation, especially in flat areas. Nevertheless it is necessary to stress that validation of fire spread models is difficult because usually standard fire records don't account for all the data necessary for simulation (e.g both the collected vegetation and weather data are often incomplete). Future work needs to concentrate on both including a more sophisticated fire description (e.g. spotting phenomena) and validating the model using observed fire growth patterns in a number of fuels, morphology and weather conditions.

References

1. Albini, F.A. Estimating wildfire behavior and effects. USDA For. Serv. Gen. Tech. Rep. (1976) INT-30.
2. Anderson, H.E. Aids to determining fuel models for estimating fire behavior. USDA For. Serv. Gen. Tech. Rep. (1982) INT-122.
3. Anderson, H.E. Predicting wind-driven wildland fire size and shape. USDA For. Serv. Res. Pap. (1983) INT-305.
4. Bendicenti E., Di Gregorio S., Falbo F.M., Iezzi A. – Simulations of forest fires by Cellular Automata modelling - in "Emergence in Complex, Cognitive, Social, and Biological Systems", pp 31-40 (2002) Kluwer Academic P.
5. Burgan, R.E. and R.C. Rothermel. BEHAVE: Fire behavior prediction and fuel modeling system - FUEL subsystem. USDA For. Serv. Gen. Tech. Rep (1984) INT-167.
6. Di Gregorio, S., and Serra, R. An empirical method for modelling and simulating some complex macroscopic phenomena by cellular automata, Fut. Gen. Comp. Systems **16** (1999) : 259-271.
7. Finney, M. FARSITE: Users Guide and Technical Documentation. Missoula. MT, Systems for Environmental Management. (1996)
8. Gonçalves, P., and Diogo, P. Forest Fire Modelling: A New Methodology Using Cellular Automata and Geographic Information Systems, In Proc. of 2nd Int. Conf. on Forest Fire Research, Coimbra 21/24 Nov. 1994
9. Green, D.G., Shapes of simulated fires in discrete fuels, Ecol. Modell. **20** (1983): 21-32.
10. Karafyllidis, I. & Thanailakis, A. (1997) A model for predicting forest fire spreading using cellular automata. *Ecological Modelling*, 99 (1997) : 87-97
11. Malamud, B.D., and Turcotte, D.L. Cellular Automata models applied to natural hazard, Computing in Science and Engineering, **2**,3 (2000): 43-51.
12. Rothermel, R. A Mathematical Model for predicting fire Spread in Wildland Fuels, Res. Pap. (1972) INT-115. Ogden, UT, U.S. Dep. of Agr., Forest Service, Intermountain Forest and Range Experiment Station.
13. Rothermel, R. How to Predict the Spread and Intensity of Forest Fire and Range Fires, Gen. Tech. Rep. (1983) INT-143. Ogden, UT, U.S. Dep. of Agr., Forest Service, Intermountain Forest and Range Experiment Station.
14. SALTUS Reports, from Europ. Res. Prog. SALTUS, Env. and Climate (1998-2000)
15. Trunfio, G.A., Bendicenti, E. - Simulations of Forest Fires by Cellular Automata - Geophysical Research Abstracts, Volume 6, 2004

Modelling Wildfire Dynamics via Interacting Automata

Adam Dunn and George Milne

School of Computer Science & Software Engineering
The University of Western Australia
35 Stirling Highway 6009, WA, Australia
(adam, george)@csse.uwa.edu.au

Abstract. The modelling of wildland fire spread across a heterogeneous landscape is significant because fire dynamics are sensitive to local spatial characteristics. The development of accurate fire models and simulations is important due to the economical and social losses wildland fire can cause and the resulting need to better understand, predict, and contain fire spread. We present a methodology for encoding the spread of wildland fire in a set of interacting automata. The Circal formalism is used to explicitly describe the transmission of fire as an interaction between discrete cells of landscape. We demonstrate the potential for the methodology to accurately model spatial dynamics by giving results of our implementation of a fire spread model that includes a heterogenous environment.

Keywords: Modelling wildfire spread, cellular automata, Circal.

1   Modelling Fire Spread

Fire spread is a phenomenon that deserves attention from scientists; not just because it is socially and economically important, but also because the phenomenon is complex, difficult to model, and computationally expensive to simulate. Indeed, there does not exist a verifiable method for better-than-real-time simulation of the phenomenon. The heterogeneity of a landscape is a specific problem of fire spread simulation. The landscape comprises the heterogeneous variables fuel (including fuel load, fuel type, moisture), slope of terrain, and wind direction and strength. In Section 2, we describe our method for capturing the heterogeneities of the landscape in the state of finite automata and for building a structure of connected automata as depicted in Fig. 1. We then describe a method for describing the interaction of these automata that is also heterogenous; the next-state transitions depend on the features of the landscape.

Throughout the world, and specifically in Australia where the climate is dry and hot, wildland fire is a significant problem because it causes loss of life and property. The scientific challenge is to produce accurate, spatially dependent models and tractable, powerful simulations that can be used to investigate 'what if' questions, containment strategies, and to develop training tools for firefighters.

P.M.A. Sloot, B. Chopard, and A.G. Hoekstra (Eds.): ACRI 2004, LNCS 3305, pp. 395–404, 2004.

Rothermel's research on understanding the physics of fires [1], forms the basis for many approaches to modelling the behaviour of fires in wildland environments. Some approaches to modelling fire spread are discussed in Section 1.1.

1.1   Related Research

Previous approaches to modelling the fire spread phenomenon can be categorised as either empirically-based, physically-based, or a combination of both of these. The techniques used to implement these models include cellular automata techniques (such as Cell-DEVS and other formalisms that involve discretisation) [2, 3,4,5], numerical implementations of differential equations [6,7,8,9], fractal geometry [5], and artificial neural networks [10]. In this section, we highlight the problems faced by researchers when trying to deal with the heterogeneous nature of real landscapes in fire spread simulations using cellular automata techniques.

Bossert et al. [11] validate their simulation against a real scenario where the turbulence of wind (the turbulence is affected by wind speed and the fire itself) caused a marked increase in the spread of the fire due to convection. Research by Linn et al. [8,9] clearly demonstrates the notion that a heterogeneous environment produces phenomena that cannot easily be predicted by extrapolating fine-scale experimental data.

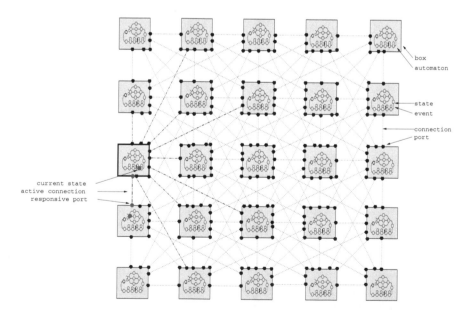

Fig. 1. This figure shows the structure of a simple homogeneous landscape of 25 cells. The state of the centre-left cell (burning) causes a synchronisation of actions/events between the automaton of the centre-left cell and the automaton of the cell below it.

Clarke et al. [5] uses a cellular automaton to implement a model based on fractal geometry. The research is significant because historic data is used to calibrate the model. The argument is presented in support of the fractal nature of wildfire spread; the spread of wildfire is highly sensitive to the heterogeneities of the landscape and initial conditions, and fire is self-replicating. One of the distinct differences between the implementation by Clarke et al. and ours, is that we use heterogeneous wind and fuel and we do not use weighted, random processes to simulate the influence of heterogeneity of the landscape.

Muzy et al. have developed several implementations of a semi-physical model of fire spread [2] based on Rothermel's model [1]. They compare the different approaches to implementing the semi-physical model (namely DEVS and Cell-DEVS approaches [12,13]) and conclude that a more rigorous method of quantisation is required for more accurate and computationally less expensive simulations [4]. Muzy and Wainer [3] have developed such an approach using Cell-DEVS quantisation techniques and they conclude that they have reduced the time taken to run a simulation and increased the accuracy of the results. The discrete, event-based implementation of a model based on Rothermel's original work has accounted for the time and space sensitivities of the fire spread simulation problem.

Our approach to modelling the fire spread phenomenon is different to the approaches described in this section because we explicitly describe the interactions between each discrete cell in the simulation landscape. We discretise the landscape in a way that is typical to cellular automata but then we encode the spatial information of that cell as input of the state of an automaton and use the interactions between the automata of different cells to determine the behaviour in a process algebra way.

In their Cell-DEVS approach, Wainer and Muzy [3] discretise Rothermel's equation for fire spread by the state of the fire (heating, burning, and burnt), but they use continuous arithmetic to describe the heat exchange between cells. We avoid the use of continuous arithmetic for heat exchange by defining a discrete propagation delay (detailed in Sect. 2) that is discrete in both space and time, and relies on a discrete addition operator instead of a continuous multiplicative one. In Sect. 3 we show that we can achieve good results in the simplified homogeneous case using this technique.

2   Modelling Spatial Dynamics via Interacting Automata

Our approach for modelling the fire spread phenomenon is to use interacting automata. This approach requires the discretisation of the landscape into (usually) equally sized cells. The discretisation of the spatial information that determines the spread on a cell-by-cell basis is encoded within each cell's automaton in terms of state and a next-state transition function.

The automaton that corresponds to a specific cell is a finite automaton (deterministic or probabilistic) with a set of states S, alphabet Σ, a next-state transition function δ, and an initial state i. In this section we present an argument for this approach and show how to encode the fire spread model in a set of interacting automata.

How is the information encoded in the automaton? The state of the automaton captures the spatial features of the particular cell to which it belongs. The state $(s \in S)$ of the automaton is defined by the set comprising slope gradient, slope orientation, wind, and fuel as follows:

$$\text{state} \quad s : S = F \times T \times W, \text{where}$$
$$T = S\ell \times O,$$
$$S\ell = \{flat, slight, mid, steep\},$$
$$O = \{n, s, e, w\},$$
$$W = \{f, n, nw, w, sw, s, se, e, ne\}, \text{and}$$
$$F = \{unburnt, burning, burnt\}.$$

The above sets refer to the gradient (slope $S\ell$), the aspect (orientation O) of the terrain T, the wind direction W, and the state of the fuel F at the location of each cell. Figure 2 shows the deterministic finite automaton in which this information is encoded for the example where the slope is mid-ranged (mid), the orientation of the slope is northerly (n), the wind is easterly (e), and the fuel is not yet burnt ($unburnt$).

The state of an automaton captures the spatial information of the cell to which it belongs, and this encoding is therefore a heterogeneous description of the landscape. Figure 2 depicts the state and labelled transitions of the finite automaton where the cell slopes upwards towards the north and has an easterly wind direction. We have used a similar discretisation of fuel as Wainer and Muzy [3], but we also use discrete values for the description of wind and terrain. The result of this approach is a set finite automata that are encoded with information describing the landscape as a combination of terrain, wind, fuel, and fire.

2.1   The Significance of the Circal Formalism

To allow the automata to interact, we need to capture explicit, non-homogeneous interaction between automata. For this, we use Circal [14,15,16], a process algebra that has been used for describing and verifying complex systems such as digital hardware including asynchronous logic and communication protocols. In this section, we detail the use of the Circal formalism as a *specification language* for encoding the spatial dynamics of fire spread as a set of connected and interacting automata, after the landscape has been discretised using the cellular automata paradigm.

Circal is an appropriate formalism for this approach because it has the necessary constituents to permit these modelling concepts to be well-captured [17,18]. Circal is a rigorous formalism and allows concurrent communication between an arbitrary number of processes. We use Circal to explicitly describe the interactions between automata and encode the spatial information of each cell in the states of each automaton.

How do the automata interact? We impose a structure on the landscape as we discretise it; defining areas where fire communication may occur. The adjacent neighbours of a cell can see an abstracted view of the automata because of the way the structure is built. Below, we describe the terminology of the structure, and the procedure for determining the next state transition function.

The communication of fire spread between cells is captured by the actions of each automaton in conjunction with automata that it connects itself with. The *actions* (or transitions) of each automaton are the alphabet set Σ. We say that two automata are *connected* if their associated cells are neighbours as depicted in Fig. 1. In the case of the simulations described in this paper, neighbours will always include the area of cells within a radius (in the cellular automata sense of the word) of two from the cell in question, but two automata could be connected arbitrarily within the landscape using the methodology. This is equivalent to the neighbourhood term used in cellular automata based simulations. Figure 1 shows a landscape of size five by five and depicts all the cells that make up the neighbourhood of the centre cell. The centre-left cell and its connections are highlighted in the figure. The specific terms used in the figure are defined in the following paragraphs.

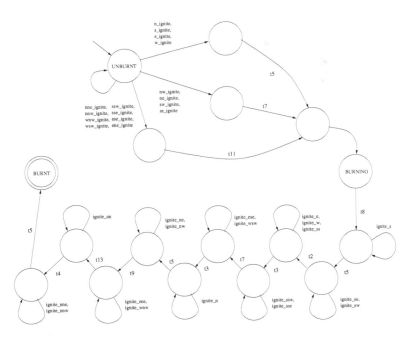

Fig. 2. This figure depicts the state and transition actions of a deterministic finite state automaton that encodes the slope, terrain, and fuel information of a cell in a landscape. This cell slopes upwards towards the north, has a midranged gradient, and has an easterly wind direction.

In the Circal formalism, the *composition operator* [18] uses similarly labelled actions to 'wire together' structures such as the cells in Figure 1. The dashed lines in Figure 1 are *connections* between connected automata are built using the composition operator. This is called the *synchronisation-of-actions* technique.

Cerone and Milne [19] describe a process for the hierarchical description of interacting automata in their research into asynchronous micropipeline digital electronics. The connections between cells are the medium for the spread of fire from one cell to another and are built between similarly labelled ports. The *ports* are associated with the actions in the automaton that are not abstracted as a part of the procedure described below:

1. All actions are *relabelled* to have the same name as the port they are connected to or to an anonymous name if they are not connected to a port.
2. The separate cells are *composed*; similarly named ports are 'wired up' with connections.
3. The actions inside each cell that are not connected to a port cannot be seen from outside the box and are *abstracted*.

Figure 1 shows an example of the structure that has been connected using the process described above. In this case, each of the actions in an automaton's alphabet Σ have been relabelled to reflect the coordinates of the associated cell in the landscape. The automata are composed to build connections using the Circal formalism's composition operator and the alphabet is reduced (abstracted) to remove the actions that are not visible from outside the cell.

The synchronisation-of-actions corresponds to the next state transitions function δ in the automata with the actions taken from the alphabet Σ. In this case, the transition function δ becomes a function that determines the next state of each automata based on a current set of enabled actions and hence indirectly on the state of the automata in the connected cells. An action is *enabled* if it can synchronise with the other similarly labelled actions through a *responsive* port. A port becomes responsive when all the associated actions emanate from the current states of the automata that they are associated with.

Why is it good to do it this way? We have developed a method for describing heterogeneous landscapes using finite automata and using a rigorous formalism to describe the interactions between the automata. The methodology couches the structure and operation of simulations in the paradigm of cellular automata.

Unlike the cellular automata approach, we define heterogeneous landscapes by encoding the spatial information as the state of each automaton. Like the classical cellular automata approach, the state information of the neighbours of a cell determines the next state of the cell. Although we use cellular automata principles to discretise the time and space of the model, the interactions between the cells are defined explicitly as a set of actions using the synchronisation-of-actions technique rather than as a homogeneous update.

3   Experiments and Results

We have identified heterogeneity of landscape as an important feature of modelling the fire spread phenomenon. In this section, we describe the experiments we have carried out using an implementation of the fire spread model. The main aim of these experiments is do demonstrate the effect of the abstractions we have made on the shape of the fire spread and to show the effect of simulating the heterogeneous landscape explicitly using interacting automata. All of the experiments conducted use a landscape with homogeneous fuel.

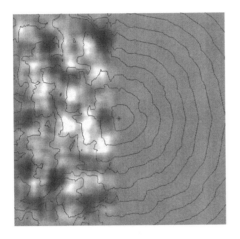

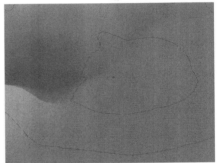

Fig. 3. This figure shows the effect of terrain on fire spread. The contours indicate the position of the fire front at regular intervals. The topography is indicated by darker colours at lower elevations.

Fig. 4. This figure views a section of the simulation results presented in Figure 3 from a different position, highlighting the effect of terrain on the rate of spread of the fire. The fire front spreads more quickly on the uphill slope at the middle-top of the figure and less quickly on a the downhill slope on the middle-left of the figure.

Hargrove et al. describes how the shape of a fire front approximates an ellipse after it has burned for a period of time [20]. In the case of a homogeneous environment (homogeneous wind, flat terrain, and no wind), the ellipse degrades to a circle. Figure 3 demonstrates the difference between a near-flat terrain and a hilly terrain in a scenario that uses a homogeneous fuel landscape and no wind. More detail is shown in Fig. 4, which is a different view of a section of the results presented in Fig. 3. The results show the circular contours on flat terrain (the right hand side of Fig. 3) and the effect of terrain on the rate of spread of the fire.

Balbi et al. and Santoni et al. describe the effect of slope on wildfire spread [21,22] and the shape can be approximated by a double ellipse. From visual inspection of the results, we can conclude that the results of our experiment give a reasonable approximation to both the circular shape we expect in the case where the terrain is relatively flat and the elliptical shape we expect on a hilly terrain. Figure 4 gives a clearer view of the effect of slope on wildfire spread in our experiment that corresponds to the shape described by Balbi et al. and Santoni et al.

When wind is introduced into the scenario described above, the results show that the effects of both wind and terrain on the shape of a spreading fire front are captured by the implementation that uses the interacting automata approach. The shape produced in Fig. 5 is a good approximation of the ellipse expected for a northerly wind direction on a relatively flat terrain. The effect of both wind and terrain can be seen in Fig. 6 where the effects of wind and terrain are captured together, giving a much more irregular spread pattern, as would be expected from knowledge of actual fire spread.

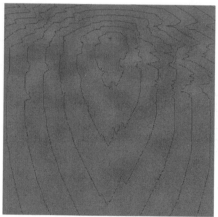

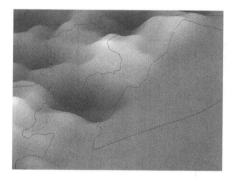

Fig. 5. This figure shows the effect of wind on a relatively flat terrain. An asterisk marks the ignition point, and the wind is homogeneous and its direction is from the top to the bottom of the figure. The contours represent the front edge of the spreading fire at regular intervals. The topography is indicated using a darker colour for lower elevations.

Fig. 6. A view of two types of terrain is presented in this figure. The top-left half of this figure represents a hilly terrain and the bottom-right of this figure represents a flat terrain. The wind is approaching from the top-right corner of the figure and the topography is indicated using a darker colour for lower elevations.

4   Discussion

In this paper, we have discussed the significant problem of wildfire spread modelling and introduced a methodology that can be used to capture spatial heterogeneity via state encoding and explicit actions given by current state. A method for capturing spatial heterogeneity within automaton state has been presented and utilised in a simulation environment. The suitability of the interacting automata approach to wildfire spread modelling has been demonstrated using the implemented simulator.

The results demonstrate the ability of the methodology to capture spatial heterogeneity of a landscape and simulate the spread of wildfire on a landscape that is regular and non-uniform. We have not validated the model against factors such as fuel loads, topography, and varying wind strength. The experiments detailed in the previous section are centred on the demonstration of the interacting automata approach and have shown that it can be used for heterogeneous environments, reproducing the elliptical shape expected of a simulation of wildfire spread. The approach effectively captures the information about the landscape as the state of an automaton, and uses explicit communication between cells to describe the change in state over the landscape as the fire spreads.

Acknowledgements. The authors would like to acknowledge the support by the Centre for Complex Systems Science, CSIRO, Australia and Fabio Boschetti, Division of Exploration and Mining, CSIRO. George Milne is a member of the Bushfire Cooperative Research Centre, Australia.

References

1. Rothermel, C.: A mathematical model for predicting fire spread in wildland fuels. Technical report, United States Department of Agriculture, Forest Service (1972) INT-115.
2. Muzy, A., Marcelli, T., Aiello, A., San-toni, P., Santucci, J., Balbi, J.: An object oriented environment applied to a semi-physical model of firespread across a fuel bed (2001) DEVS Work-shop.
3. Muzy, A., Wainer, G.: Cell-DEVS quantization techniques in a fire spreading application. In: The 2002 Winter Simulation Conference. (2002) 542–549
4. Muzy, A., Wainer, G., Innocenti, E., Aiello, A., Santucci, J.F.: Comparing simulation methods for fire spreading across a fuel bed. In: AIS. (2002)
5. Clarke, K.C., Brass, J.A., Riggan, P.J.: A cellular automaton model of wildfire propagation and extinction. Photogrammetric Eng. and Remote Sensing **60** (1994) 1355–1367
6. Viegas, D.X., Ribiero, P.R., Maricato, L.: An empirical model for the spread of a fireline inclined in relation to the slope gradient or to wind direction. In: Fourteenth Conference on Fire and Forest Meteorology. Volume 1. (1998) 325–342
7. André, J.C.S., Viegas, D.X.: An unifying theory on the propagation of the fire front of surface forest fires. In: Fourteenth Conference on Fire and Forest Meteorology. Volume 1. (1998) 259–279
8. Linn, R., Reisner, J., Colman, J.J., Winterkamp, J.: Studying wildfire behaviour using FIRETEC. International Journal of Wildland Fire **11** (2002) 233–246
9. Linn, R., Winterkamp, J., Edminster, C., Colman, J., Steinzig, M.: Modeling interactions between fire and atmosphere in discrete element fuel beds. Technical report, Los Alamos National Laboratory, Los Alamos (unknown)

10. McCormick, R.J., Brandner, T.A., Allen, T.F.H.: Towards a theory of meso-scale wildfire modeling — a complex systems approach using artificial neural networks. Technical report, University of Wisconsin-Madison (unknown)
11. Bossert, J.E., Linn, R.R., Winterkamp, J.L., Dennison, P., Roberts, D.: Coupled atmosphere-fire behaviour model sensitivity to spatial fuels characterization (unknown)
12. Zeigler, B.P., Vahie, S.: DEVS formalism and methodology: Unity of conception/diversity of application. In: Winter Simulation Conference. (1993) 574–579
13. Wainer, G.A., Giambisi, N.: Application of the Cell-DEVS paradigm for cell spaces modelling and simulation. Simulation **76** (2001) 22–39
14. Milne, G.J.: CIRCAL: A calculus for circuit description integration. VLSI Journal **1** (1983)
15. Milne, G.J., Milner, R.: Concurrent processes and their syntax. ACM **26** (1983)
16. Milne, G.J.: Circal and the representation of communication, concurrency and time. ACM Trans. on Programming Languages and Systems **7** (1985) 270–298
17. Milne, G.J.: The formal description and verification of hardware timing. IEEE Transactions on Computers **40** (1991) 711–826
18. Milne, G.J.: Formal Verification and Specification of Digital Systems. McGraw-Hill International (1994)
19. Cerone, A., Milne, G.J.: A methodology for the formal analysis of asynchronous micropipelines. In: Proceedings of the Third International Conference on Formal Methods in Computer-Aided Design, Springer-Verlag (2000) 246–262
20. Hargrove, W.W., Gardner, R.H., Turner, M.G., Romme, W.H., Despain, D.G.: Simulating fire patterns in heterogeneous landscapes. Ecol. Mod. **135** (2000) 243–263
21. Balbi, J.H., Santoni, P.A., Dupuy, J.L.: Dynamic modelling of fire spread across a fuel bed. International Journal of Wildland Fire **9** (1999) 275–284
22. Santoni, P.A., Balbi, J.H., Dupuy, J.L.: Dynamic modelling of upslope fire growth. International Journal of Wildland Fire **9** (1999) 285–292

Sympatric Speciation Through Assortative Mating in a Long-Range Cellular Automaton

Franco Bagnoli[1,2,3] and Carlo Guardiani[3]

[1] Dipartimento di Energetica, Università di Firenze, Via S. Marta 3, I-50139 Firenze, Italy

[2] INFN, sez. Firenze

[3] Centro Interdipartimentale per lo Studio delle Dinamiche Complesse, Università di Firenze, Via Sansone 1, I-50019, Sesto Fiorentino, Italy

Abstract. A probabilistic cellular automaton is developed to study the combined effect of competition and assortativity on the speciation process in the absence of geographical barriers. The model is studied in the case of long-range coupling. A simulated annealing technique was used in order to find the stationary distribution in reasonably short simulation times. Two components of fitness are considered: a static one that describes adaptation to environmental factors not related to the population itself, and a dynamic one that accounts for interactions between organisms such as competition. The simulations show that both in the case of flat and steep static fitness landscape, competition and assortativity do exert a synergistic effect on speciation. We also show that competition acts as a stabilizing force preventing the random sampling effects to drive one of the newborn populations to extinction. Finally, the variance of the frequency distribution is plotted as a function of competition and assortativity, obtaining a surface that shows a sharp transition from a very low (single species state) to a very high (multiple species state) level, therefore featuring as a phase transition diagram. Examination of the contour plots of the phase diagram graphycally highlights the synergetic effect.

1   The Problem of Sympatric Speciation

The notion of *speciation* in biology refers to the splitting of an original species into two fertile, yet reproductively isolated strains. The *allopatric theory*, which is currently accepted by the majority of biologists, claims that a geographic barrier is needed in order to break the gene flow so as to allow two strains to evolve a complete reproductive isolation. On the other hand, many evidences and experimental data have been reported in recent years strongly suggesting the possibility of a *sympatric* mechanism of speciation. For example, the comparison of mythocondrial DNA sequences of cytochrome b performed by Schlieven and others [1], showed the monophyletic origin of cichlid species living in some vulcanic lakes of western Africa. The main features of these lakes are the environmental homogeneity and the absence of microgeographical barriers. It is thus

P.M.A. Sloot, B. Chopard, and A.G. Hoekstra (Eds.): ACRI 2004, LNCS 3305, pp. 405–414, 2004.
© Springer-Verlag Berlin Heidelberg 2004

possible that the present diversity is the result of several events of sympatric speciation.

The key element for sympatric speciation is *assortative mating* that is, mating must be allowed only between individuals whose phenotypic distance does not exceed a given threshold. In fact, consider a population characterized by a bimodal distribution for an echological character determining adaptation to the environment: in a regime of random mating the crossings between individuals of the two humps will produce intermediate phenotypes so that the distribution will never split. Two interesting theories have been developed to explain the evolution of assortativity. In Kondrashov and Kondrashov's theory [2] *disruptive selection* (for instance determined by a bimodal resource distribution) splits the population in two distinct echological types that are later stabilized by the evolution of assortative mating. The theory of *evolutionary branching* developed by Doebeli and Dieckmann [3] is more general in that it does not require disruptive selection: the population first converges in phenotype space to an evolutionarily attracting fitness minimum (as a result of common echological interactions such as competition, predation and mutualism) and then it splits into diverging phenotypic clusters. For example [4], given a gaussian resource distribution, the population first crowds on the phenotype with the highest fitness, and then, owing to the high level of competition, splits into two distinct groups that later become reproductively isolated due to selection of assortative mating.

In the present paper we will not investigate the evolution of assortativity that will be treated as a tunable parameter in order to study its interplay with competition. In particular we will show that: (1) assortativity alone is sufficient to induce speciation but one of the new species soon disappears due to random fluctuations; (2) stable species coexistence can be attained through the introduction of competition; (3) competition and assortativity do exert a synergistic effect on speciation so that high levels of assortativity can trigger speciation even in the presence of weak competition and *vice versa*; (4) speciation can be thought of as a phase transition as can be deduced from the plot of variance versus competition and assortativity. The use of a *simulated annealing* method enables us to find stationary or quasi-stationary distribution in reasonably short simulation times.

2   The Model

We consider a constant population of N haploid individuals modeled as binary strings. Each bit represents a locus and the Boolean values it can take on represent alternative allelic forms, namely, $g_i = 0$ represents the wild-type allele and $g_i = 1$ is the least deleterious mutant. In agreement with the theory of quantitative characters [5] we assume that the effects of genes are small, similar and additive, so that the phenotype can be expressed by the sum of the bits of the genotype.

The environment is modeled as a probabilistic cellular automaton with a large number of states, one for each different genotype. All the cells of the lattice are occupied by organisms and the population size remains constant throughout the simulation. The evolution of the automaton is given by the application of three rules: recombination, reproduction and mutation.

The recombination rule is implemented as follows, adopting the point of view of an individual of phenotype x located in a cell of a lattice.

Recombination. Each invividual looks for a potential partner within its mating range (dependent on the phenotypic distance) in a given neighborhood of radius ρ. For each partner found, uniform recombination is applied so as to produce an offspring with phenotype z. $A(z)$ copies of the recombinant offspring are then stored in a temporary offspring.

Reproduction. As the population size must remain constant, an individual is randomly chosen from each offspring array which then replaces the parent.

Mutation. For each individual of the new generation, flip a randomly chosen bit with probability μ.

As the model is very complex we will study it using a mean-field approximation that enables us to disregard the spatial structure. The approximation becomes accurate in the limit of a very large radius of the neighborhood so that the neighborhood will extend on all the lattice.

In order to perform the mean-field analysis, let us first define the mating range Δ as the maximal phenotypic distance between two individuals, still compatible with mating; we also define assortativity as $\mathcal{A} = L - \Delta$. In a more formal way, the mating preference function can be defined as:

$$m_\Delta(y, z) = \begin{cases} 0 & \text{if } |y - z| > \Delta, \\ 1 & \text{otherwise}, \end{cases}$$

Once an organism has chosen a suitable partner we apply uniform recombination *i.e.* for each *locus* the offspring might receive an allele from either parents with equal probability. Uniform recombination therefore implies absence of linkage which is a reasonable approximation only in the case of a very long genome distributed on many independent chromosomes.

We illustrate the most important features of the model in the mean-field approximation. Let us introduce the overlap q between two genotypes $(g_1, g_2, \dots)$ and $(h_1, h_2, \dots)$ as the number of loci i for which $g_i = h_i = 1$. For a pair of phenotypes $x \leq y$, it can be shown [6] that the overlap must always be in the range $\max(0, x + y - L) \leq q \leq x$. The probability $Q_{xy}(q)$ is

$$Q_{xy}(q) = \frac{\binom{x}{q}\binom{L-x}{y-q}}{\binom{L}{y}}.$$

Due to the property of binomial coefficient that $\binom{a}{b} = 0$ if $b < 0$ or $b > a$, $Q_{xy}(q) \neq 0$ only for $\max(x + y - L, 0) \leq q \leq \min(x, y)$. Notice that using this property we can freely sum over q obtaining $\sum_q Q_{xy}(q) = 1$.

If phenotype y belongs to the mating range of phenotype x, it can be proven [6] that the phenotype z of the offspings must lie in the range $q \leq z \leq x + y - q$. The probability $R_{xy}^q(z)$ that two phenotypes x and y with given overlap q originate a phenotype z is

$$R_{xy}^q(z) = \binom{x + y - 2q}{z - q} \frac{1}{2}^{x+z-2q}.$$

Again, due to the properties of binomial coefficients, $R_{xy}^q(z) \neq 0$ for $q \leq z \leq x + y - q$. Summing over z one has $\sum_z R_{xy}^q(z) = 1$.

Finally, let us define $A(z)$ as the number of offsprings with phenotype z generated in each suitable crossing. Using this quantity, the selection step will be implicitly performed within the reproduction step. $A(z)$, in fact can be thought of as a quantity related to the probability that an individual with phenotype z may survive till the reproductive age.

We can now compute the number of individuals with phenotype z in the offspring generation:

$$n'(z) = A(z) \sum_x \sum_y \frac{n(x)n(y)m_\Delta(x, y)}{M(x)} \sum_q Q_{xy}(q) R_{xy}^q(z), \tag{1}$$

where the factor

$$M(x) = \sum_k m_\Delta(x, k)n(k)$$

is just the total number of individuals in the mating range of phenotype x.

If N is the constant size of the population, we must now introduce a normalization factor C such that $\frac{1}{C}\sum_z n'(z) = N$. If we introduce the quantity $\tilde{M}(x) = \sum_k m_\Delta(x, k)p(k)$, it can be noticed that $M(x) = N\tilde{M}(x)$ and the normalization factor can be expressed as:

$$C = \sum_z A(z) \sum_x \sum_y \frac{p(x)p(y)m_\Delta(x, y)}{\tilde{M}(x)} \sum_q Q_{xy}(q) R_{xy}^q(z) \tag{2}$$

The new frequency of phenotype z after the normalization procedure, which corresponds to the **reproduction** step of the microscopic model can be therefore computed as: $n''(x) = \frac{n'(z)}{C}$.

Finally we can implement the mutation step that does not affect the total size of the population as

$$n'''(z) = (1 - \mu)n''(z) + \mu \left(\frac{L - z + 1}{L} n''(z - 1) + \frac{z + 1}{L} n''(z + 1) \right), \tag{3}$$

where L is the genome lenght and μ is the *per bit* mutation rate. It is therefore clear that $\frac{L - z + 1}{L}\mu$ is the probability that an individual of phenotype $z - 1$ undergoes a mutation on a bit 0 while $\frac{z + 1}{L}\mu$ is the probability that an individual with phenotype $z + 1$ mutates a bit from 1 to 0. The structure of Equation 3 therefore reflects the fact that in our model we implement only *short range* mutations allowing an individual with phenotype x to turn only in one of the neighbouring phenotypes $x - 1$ and $x + 1$.

As the fitness is related to the survival probability, it is defined as the exponential of the fitness landscape: $A(x,t) = e^{H(x,t)}$. An important feature of our model is that we consider two components of fitness. The static component describes the adaptation to environmental factors not related to the population itself such as climate or temperature, while the dynamic component relates to the interactions with other members of the population and therefore it changes in time as a function of the phenotype frequencies. In our model we consider only competition. The static component of the fitness landscape is defined as a function of the phenotype x:

$$H_0(x) = e^{-\frac{1}{\beta}\left(\frac{x}{\Gamma}\right)^{\beta}}$$

This function becomes flatter and flatter as β is increased: for $\beta \to 0$ the function becomes a sharp peak at $x = 0$; when $\beta = 1$ the function is a declining exponential whose steepness increases with Γ. Finally for $\beta \to \infty$ the fitness landscape is constant in the range $[0, \Gamma]$ and zero outside. The dynamic part of the fitness has a similar expression, with parameters α and R that control the steepness and range of competition among phenotypes. The complete expression of the fitness landscape is:

$$H(x,t) = H_0(x) - J\sum_{y} e^{-\frac{1}{\alpha}\left|\frac{x-y}{R}\right|^{\alpha}} p(y,t) \tag{4}$$

The parameter J controls the intensity of competition with respect to the arbitrary reference value $H_0(0) = 1$. If $\alpha = 0$ an individual with phenotype x is in competition only with other organisms with the same phenotype; conversely in the case $\alpha \to \infty$ a phenotype x is in competition with all the other phenotypes in the range $[x - R, x + R]$, and the boundaries of this competition intervals blurry when α is decreased.

In the limit of an infinite range of neighborhood $\rho \to \infty$, for the sake of computational efficiency we implemented our model as follows. The initial population is chosen at random and stored in a bidimensional matrix with $L + 1$ rows and N columns. Each row represents one of the possible phenotypes; as the whole population might crowd on a single phenotype, N memory locations must be allocated for each phenotype. Each generation begins with the reproduction step. The first parent is chosen at random; in a similar way, the second parent is randomly chosen within the mating range of the first one.

The offspring is produced through uniform recombination, *i.e.*, for each *locus* it will receive the allele of the first or second parent with equal probability; the recombinant then undergoes mutation on a random allele with probability $\mu(t)$. The newborn individuals are stored in a second matrix with $L + 1$ rows and N columns. The reproduction procedure is followed by the selection step. As we consider a constant size population, a cycle is iterated until N individuals are copied back from the second to the first matrix. In each iteration of the cycle, an individual is chosen at random and its relative fitness is compared to a random number r uniformly distributed between 0 and 1: if $r < A(x)/\bar{A}$ the individual survives and is passed on to the next generation, otherwise a new attempt is made.

In order to speed-up simulations in computer time, we adopted a simulated annealing technique: the mutation rate μ depends on time as

$$\mu(t) = \frac{\mu_0 - \mu_\infty}{2} \left(1 - \tanh\left(\frac{t - \tau}{\delta} \right) \right) + \mu_\infty,$$

which roughly corresponds to keeping $\mu = \mu_0$ (a high value, say $10/N$) up to a time $\tau - \delta$, then decrease it linearly up to the desidered value μ_∞ is a time interval 2δ and continue with this value for the rest of simulation.

In the present work we also studied the behaviour of mean fitness $\bar{H}$ during evolution. According to Fisher's fundamental theorem of natural selection [7] and Holland's schemata theorem [8], in fact, the average fitness should always increase. However,according to the modern interpretation of Fisher's theorem by Price [9] and Ewens [10] the total change in mean fitness is the sum of a partial change related to the variation in genotypic frequencies (operated by natural selection) and a partial change related to environmental deterioration, and Fisher's theorem predicts that the first contribution only is always non-negative. The schemata theorem on the other hand, states that schemas with higher than average fitness tend to receive an exponentially increasing number of samples in successive generations. As a consequence, the average fitness of the population is expected to increase as time goes by. Holland's theorem, how-ever, is not general in that it is based on the assumption of fixed fitness for each phenotype. In realistic situations, fitness is frequency dependent, so that as the population becomes richer and richer in fitter individuals the intensity of competition also increases therefore counteracting a further increase in the fre-quency of the best adapted phenotypes. This increase in competition intensity is exactly what was meant by *deterioration of the environmental conditions* in Price and Ewens's reformulation of Fisher's theorem [9,10]. In our formalism, the *deterioration* is explicitly introduced by the competition term.

3   Simulations

The simulations we performed clearly show the synergistic effect of competition and assortativity in inducing speciation. As an example consider the case of a flat static fitness landscape. In a regime of random mating ($\Delta = 14$ or, equiv-alently, $\mathcal{A} = 0$) speciation is never possible however high the competition level may be chosen. Even choosing an extremely high competition intensity $J = 16$ and competition range $R = 7$ (we chose a genome lenght $L = 14$ so that the phenotype can only take on values in the range $[0, 14]$) the frequency distribution only becomes trimodal without splitting because the crossings between the two extreme humps always reproduce the intermediate phenotypes. This shows that while competition was sufficient to induce speciation in non-recombinant population (see Bagnoli [11]) when sexual reproduction is introduced this is no longer true. The missing ingredient for the speciation of recombinant populations is assortativity. If we choose a very high level of assortativity such as $\Delta = 1$ ($\mathcal{A} = 13$), speciation is indeed possible even in the absence of competition ($J = 0$) but one of the newborn species soon disappears due to random fluctuations and the final distribution shows only a single delta peak. It can be therefore concluded that assortativity allows speciation but not the stable coexistence of the new species. We found that competition acts as a stabilazing force: in fact if we keep a very high level of assortativity $\Delta = 1$ ($\mathcal{A} = 13$), but we introduce a weak competition ($J = 1$, $R = 2$), the final distribution will be characterized by the stable coexistence of two or three species represented by delta-peaks located in the phenotypic space so as to minimize the inter-specific competition. The stabilizing effect of competition can be easily explained if we recall that competition decreases with the phenotypic distance between the interacting species and becomes maximal between organisms with the same phenotypes. Consider a frequency distribution with two delta peaks: there will be intra-specific competition within each peak and inter-specific competition between the peaks. Suppose the two peaks at the beginning were equally populated and then due to random fluctuations the frequency of the first peak decreases while the frequency of the second one increases. In the first peak there will be a decrease in intraspecific competition and thus an increase in fitness leading to an increase in frequency whereas in the second peak the decrease in fitness due to the higher intraspecific competition lowers the frequency. As a consequence the frequency of both peaks will oscillate around 50% and none of them will be eradicated.

The simulations also show the synergistic effect of competition and assortativity. Speciation in fact, is possible also in the presence of a very large mating range such as $\Delta = 4$ ($\mathcal{A} = 10$) if we set a sufficiently strong competition: $J = 2$, $R = 4$. For the sake of comparison, consider that with $\Delta = 1$ ($\mathcal{A} = 13$) it is sufficient to set $J = 1$, $R = 2$. The evolutionary dynamics of the simulation with $\Delta = 4$ ($\mathcal{A} = 10$), $J = 2$, $R = 4$ can be followed if we plot mean, variance and mean fitness of the distribution. At the beginning of the run the initial distribution (we chose a delta peak in $x = 0$ but the results are not dependent on the initial distribution) splits in two bell-shaped distributions at the opposite ends of the phenotypic space. This corresponds to an abrupt increase of the mean and variance as well as of the average fitness: if the population is distributed over several phenotypes, the competition pressure is relieved. After $t = \tau$ the mutation rate decreases and the bell-shaped distributions are narrowed first in the regions pointing towards the center of the space (which leads to a further little increase in variance and mean fitness) and then in the regions pointing towards the ends of the space (so that the variance decreases again). The final distribution is represented by two delta peaks each accounting for about 50% of the population. The plots of mean, variance and mean fitness are shown in Figure 1.

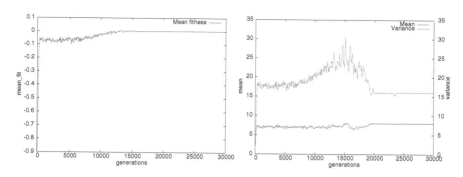

Fig. 1. Average fitness, variance and mean of the population distribution in a regime of weak assortativity ($\Delta = 4$ or $\mathcal{A} = 10$), high competition intensity and long competition range ($J = 2$, $\alpha = 10$, $R = 4$). Annealing parameters: $\mu_0 = 10^{-1}$, $\mu_\infty = 10^{-6}$, $\tau = 10000$, $\delta = 3000$. Total evolution time: 30000 generations.

In order to perform systematic simulations in a wide range of values of competition and assortativity, a suitable parameter must be chosen to monitor the speciation process. We chose the variance of the distribution: $var = \sum_i (x_i - \bar{x})^2 p(x_i)$. The simulations, in fact, show that, as competition and/or assortativity is increased, the frequency distribution first widens, then it becomes bimodal and eventually it splits in two sharp peaks that move in the phenotypic spaceso as to maximize their reciprocal distance: each of these steps involves an increase in the variance of the frequency distribution.

As the simulations discussed so far refer to a flat static fitness landscape, for the sake of completeness, we will now show the plot of variance as a function of competition and assortativity in the case of steep static fitness. We graphically illustrate the synergistic effect of competition and assortativity on speciation in the contour plots shown in Figure 2.

The contour plots divide the J, $\mathcal{A}$ plane in two regions: the area on the left represents the state with a single quasi-species whereas the area on the right represents the state with two or more distinct quasi-species. If a point, owing to a change in competition and/or assortativity, crosses these borderlines moving from the first to the second region, a speciation event does occur. It should be noted that in the high competition region, the contour plots tend to diverge from each other showing a gradual increase of the variance of the frequency distributions. This is due to the fact that, even if competition alone is not sufficient to induce speciation in recombinant populations, it spreads the frequency distribution that becomes wider and wider, and splits into two distinct species only for extremely high assortativity values. In this regime of high competition only the ends of the mating range of a phenotype x are populated and the crossings between these comparatively different individuals will create once again the intermediate phenotypes preventing speciation until assortativity becomes almost maximal. The down sloping shape of the contour plots is a strong indication of a synergistic interaction of competition and assortativity on the speciation

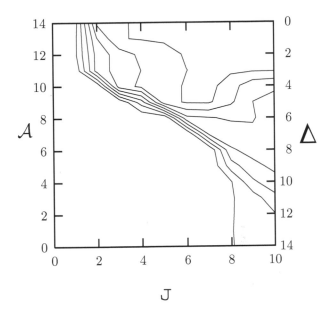

Fig. 2. Contour plots $var = 5, 10, 15, 20, 25, 30, 35$ for steep static fitness land scape. Parameters: $\beta = 1$, $\Gamma = 10$, $\alpha = 2$, $R = 4$, $p = 0.5$. Annealing parameters: $\mu_0 = 10^{-1}$, $\mu_\infty = 10^{-6}$, $\tau = 10000$, $\delta = 3000$. Total evolution time: 30000 generations. Each point of the plot is the average of 10 independent runs.

process. The contour plots show that for moderate competition there is a synergistic effect between competition and assortativity since a simultaneous increase of J and $\mathcal{A}$ may allow the crossing of the borderline whereas the increase of a parameter at a time does not. On the other hand, for larger values of J the phase diagram shows a reentrant character due to the extinction of one of the species that cannot move farther apart from the other and therefore cannot relieve competition anymore. It can also be noticed that for $J = 0$ the contour plot shows a change in slope due to extinction of one species owing to random fluctuations.

4   Conclusions

We presented a microscopic model to investigate the evolution of sympatric speciation. The model is equivalent to the mean field approximation of a probabilistic cellular automaton with a very large number of states. The simulations were speeded up through the use of a simulated annealing technique. We showed that assortativity alone is sufficient to induce speciation, but competition is necessary for the stable coexistence of the new species. Moreover, competition and assortativity influence speciation in a synergystic way as is evident from the down sloping contour lines of the plot of variance as a function of competition and assortativity. The contour plots also show that speciation can be seen as a phase transition and the system shifts from a state with a single species to a state with two or several species as a threshold of competition and assortativity is crossed. Finally, it is quite interesting to observe the behavior of the average of the fitness landscape $\bar{H}$ with respect to time in the various simulations. In general there is a large variation in correspondence of the variation of the mutation rate. One can observe that there are cases in which $\bar{H}$ increases smoothly when decreasing μ, while others, in correspondence of weak competition and moderate assortativity exhibit a sudden decrease, often coupled to further oscillations. At the microscopic level, this decrease corresponds to extinction of small inter-populations that lowered the competition levels.

As explicitely declared, the present work focuses on the mean-field approximation of a Cellular Automaton. Simulations of the CA with finite neighborhood are currently in progress, and the first results will be presented elsewhere. It is also our intention to study the evolutionary dynamics in the case of randomly chosen connections between interacting individuals.

References

1. Schlieven, U., Tautz, D., Pääbo, S.: Sympatric speciation suggested by monophyly of crater lake cichlids. Nature **368** (1994) 629–632
2. Kondrashov, A., Kondrashov, F.: Interactions amon quantitative quantitative traits in the course of sympatric speciation. Nature **400** (1999) 351–354
3. Dieckmann, U., Doebeli, M.: Evolutionary branching and sympatric speciation caused by different types of ecological interactions (2000) IIASA Interim Report IR-00-040, July 2000.
4. Dieckmann, U., Doebeli, M.: On the origin of species by sympatric speciation. Nature **400** (1999) 354–357
5. Falconer, D., Mackay, T.: Introduction to Quantitative Genetics. Addison-Wesley Publishing Company (1996, 4th Edition)
6. Doebeli, M.: A quantitative genetic competition model for sympatric speciation. Journal of evolutionary biology **9** (1996) 893–909
7. Fisher, R.: The genetical theory of natural selection. Clarendon Press, Oxford (1930)
8. Holland, J.: Adaptation in natural and artificial systems. MIT Press (1975)
9. Price, G.: Fisher's fundamental theorem made clear. Annals of human genetics **36** (1972) 129–140
10. Ewens, W.: An interpratation and proof of the fundamental theorem of natural selection. Theoretical population biology **36** (1989) 167–180
11. Bagnoli, F., Bezzi, M.: Speciation as pattern formation by competition in a smooth fitness landscape. Physical Review Letters **79** (1997) 3302

A Cellular "Blocks" Model for Large Surface Flows and Applications to Lava Flows

Maria Vittoria Avolio and Salvatore Di Gregorio

University of Calabria, Dept. of Mathematics & High Performance Computing Center,
Arcavacata, 87036 Rende (CS), Italy
{avoliomv, dig}@unical.it

Abstract. A Cellular Automata methodological approach for modelling large scale (extended for kilometres) surface flows (e.g. lava flows, debris flows etc.) is here presented. It represents an improvement to previous empirical approaches, in order to obtain a more physical description of the phenomenon and a more accurate control of its development. The flows are described as interacting "blocks" individuated by their mass centre position and velocity inside each cell. Such an approach was applied to lava flows; an event of the last (2002) Etnean eruption was simulated with relevant results.

1 Introduction

Cellular Automata (*CA*) applications to fluid-dynamics generated two important computational paradigms: lattice gas automata models [1] and hence the more robust lattice Boltzmann method [2], [3]. This latter is based on microscopic models and mesoscopic kinetic equations, which rule a discrete world, where the fluid is compound by "fluid particles" moving in a regular lattice. This idealised representation has been shown to be sufficient to recover complex features of the fluid-dynamics in many phenomena. Nevertheless many complex macroscopic fluid-dynamical phenomena seem difficult to be modelled in these *CA* frames, because they take place on a large space scale. Therefore, they force to use a macroscopic level of description that could involve the management of a large amount of data, e.g., the morphological data. Moreover, they could even imply complicated transition functions.

Many attempts were made in the past for simulating surface flows with *CA* by our research group. Three-dimensional *CA* (cubic cells) models with few states were developed for lava flows [4]; they gave qualitatively sounding simulations, but applications to real cases were effective only for simplest cases, also regarding the longest computation duration (at that time).

In order to overcome these difficulties, advantage was taken by the superficial nature of the lava flows: quantities concerning the third dimension, the height, may be easily included into the states of the *CA*, permitting models in two dimensions. It involves a large amount of states, which can be formally represented by means of substates: the Cartesian product of the sets of all substates constitutes the set of states. Here a substate specifies an important characteristic (e.g. altitude, temperature etc.) to

P.M.A. Sloot, B. Chopard, and A.G. Hoekstra (Eds.): ACRI 2004, LNCS 3305, pp. 415–424, 2004.
© Springer-Verlag Berlin Heidelberg 2004

be attributed to the state of the cell and necessary for determining the *CA* evolution. Furthermore, an empirical algorithm was developed in this context in order to determine the outflows from a cell toward the remaining cells of its neighbourhood, giving rise to the model SCIARA and permitting first simulations of complex Etnean lava flows [5].

This empirical method was formalised in [6] introducing new features; the good results encouraged further applications to the debris/mud flows [7], [8], [9] and to the soil erosion by water flows produced by rain [10].

This approach has a significant restriction, because it doesn't permit to make velocity explicit: a fluid amount moves from a cell to another one in a *CA* step (which corresponds usually to a constant time), it implies a constant "velocity" in the *CA* context of discrete space/time. Nevertheless, velocities can be deduced by analysing the global behaviour of the system in time and space. In such models, the flow velocity emerges by averaging on the space (i.e. considering clusters of cells) or by averaging on the time (e.g. considering the average velocity of the advancing flow front in a sequence of *CA* steps). Note that such a restriction is typical of the *CA*, including lattice gas automata and lattice Boltzmann models.

Constant velocity could be a limit for modelling finely macroscopic phenomena, because it is difficult to introduce physical considerations in the modelling at a local level. Furthermore, the time corresponding to a step of the *CA* is often deduced "a posteriori" by the simulation results and parameters of the transition function must be again verified when the size of the cell is changed.

A solution is here proposed in the *CA* transition function: firstly, moving flows toward the neighbour cells are computed, they are individuated by their mass and mass centre (i.e., the barycentre), to whom a velocity is attributed; secondly, the resulting new mass, mass centre and velocity are computed by composition of all the "interacting blocks inside the cell", defined as all the inflows from the neighbours and all the outflows, whose mass centre is inside the cell.

Such a method is presented in the second section, the third section defines the applications in modelling lava flows, the simulation results of the 2002 Etnean lava flows are shown in the fourth section, some conclusions are reported at the end.

2 The Methodological Approach

Classical (homogeneous) *CA* [11] are based on a regular division of the space in cells, each one embedding an identical finite automaton (*fa*), whose state accounts for the features attributed to the cell; *S* is the finite set of its states. The *fa* input is given by the states of neighbouring cells. The neighbourhood conditions are determined by a pattern of *m* cells, which is invariant in time and space. The *fa* have an identical state transition function $\tau : S^m \to S$, which is simultaneously applied to each cell. At time *t=0*, *fa* are in arbitrary states and the *CA* evolves changing the state of all *fa* simultaneously at discrete times (the *CA* steps), according to the transition function of the *fa*.

CA formalisation must be further specified in order to account for some features of large scale surface flows (at least metres for the width, kilometres for the length).

2.1 Global Parameters

Additional specifications need for permitting a correspondence between the system with its evolution in the physical space/time, on the one hand, and the model with the simulations in the cellular space/time, on the other hand.

Primarily, the size of the cell p_s (e.g. specified by the cell side) and the time correspondence to a *CA* step p_t must be fixed. These are defined as "global parameters", as their values are equal for all the cellular space. They constitute the set P together with other global parameters, which are commonly necessary for simulation purposes.

2.2 Substates

The state of the cell must account for all the characteristics, relative to the space portion corresponding to the cell, which are assumed to be relevant to the evolution of the system (e.g. the altitude). A substate is attributed to each characteristic. The possible values of the substate, referred to a characteristic *ch* (e.g. the possible values of the altitude), constitute the finite set S_{ch}.

The set S of the possible states of a cell is given by the Cartesian product of the sets of values $S_1, S_2, ..., S_n$ of the substates: $S = S_1 \times S_2 \times ..... \times S_n$.

When a characteristic (e.g. a physical quantity) is expressed as a continuous variable, a finite, but sufficient, number of significant digits are utilised, so that the set of permitted values is large but finite.

The substate value is considered always constant inside the cell (e.g. the substate temperature). It implies a constraint for the global parameter p_s "cell size" that must be chosen small enough so that the approximation to consider a single value for all the cell extension may be adequate to the features of the phenomenon to be modelled.

The movement of a certain amount of fluid from a cell toward another cell is described introducing substates of type "outflow quantity", "outflow mass centre", "outflow velocity".

The substate "outflow velocity" impose a constraint on the global parameter p_t because the shift, determined by the maximum possible velocity of the outflow in the time corresponding to a *CA* step, should not exceed the neighbourhood boundaries.

2.3 Cellular Space

The cellular space is two-dimensional because quantities concerning the third dimension, the height, may be included among the substates of the cell in a superficial phenomenon (e.g. the substates altitude, lava thickness). A regular hexagonal tessellation is chosen, because it minimises the spurious symmetries effect in comparison with triangular and square tessellation.

2.4 Elementary Processes

The state transition function τ must account for all the processes (physical, chemical, etc.), which are assumed to be relevant to the system evolution, which is specified in terms of changes in the states values of the CA space. As well as the state of the cell can be decomposed in substates, the transition function τ may be split into "elementary" processes, defined by the functions $\sigma_1, \sigma_2 ... \sigma_p$ with p being the number of the elementary processes.

The elementary processes are applied sequentially according a defined order. Each elementary process involves the update of the states of the cells. The application of all the elementary processes constitutes a CA step.

Different elementary processes may involve different neighbourhoods; the resulting CA neighbourhood is given by the union of all the neighbourhoods associated to each process.

2.5 External Influences

Sometimes, a kind of input from the "external world" to the cells of the CA must be considered; it accounts for describing an external influence which cannot be described in terms of local rules (e.g., the lava alimentation at the vents, i.e.the craters) or for some kind of probabilistic approach to the phenomenon. Of course special and/or additional functions must be given for that type of cells.

2.6 Outflows Computation

Outflows computation is performed in two steps: determination of the outflows minimising the "height" differences in the neighbourhood [6] and determination of the shift of the outflows.

The neighbourhood of a cell (the "central" cell) is considered. It consists of the central cell (index 0) and its six adjacent cells (indexes $1, 2 ... 6$).

A height quantity, that involves substates concerning the third dimension, is defined for each cell according to the particular type of phenomenon (e.g., altitude plus lava thickness).

The height of the central cell is divided in two parts: the fixed or bound part ($b[0]$) and the movable part ($m[0]$). The movable part represents a quantity that could be distributed to the adjacent cells (e.g., the lava in terms of thickness), whilst the bound part cannot change value (e.g., the altitude). There is no movable part for the adjacent cells ($m[i]=0, 1 \leq i \leq 6$, $b[i] \neq 0, 1 \leq i \leq 6$) because only the mobile part of the central cell may be distributed.

The flow from the central cell to the i-th neighbouring cell will be denoted by $f[i]$, $0 \leq i \leq 6$, where $f[0]$ is the part of $m[0]$ which is not distributed. Let $b'[i]=b[i]+f[i]$, $0 \leq i \leq 6$ be the sum of the content of a neighbouring cell, plus the flow from the central cell, and let b'_min be the minimum value for $b'[i]$.

Thus, the determination of outflows, from the central cell to the adjacent cells, is based on the local minimisation of the differences in "height", given by the following expression:

$$\sum_{i=0}^{n-1} (b'[i] - b'\_min) \tag{1}$$

The "minimisation" algorithm, i.e. the algorithm for the minimisation of differences, guarantees the mass conservation; its complete specification and correlated theorems can be found in [6].

The minimisation algorithm guarantees indeed the maximum possible equilibrium in the neighbourhood when the outflows will reach the adjacent cells, but the velocity of the outflows could be different because they also depend on gravity, slope and friction forces.

A velocity is computed for each minimising flow $f[i]$ according to the following equations (deduced in sequence and similar to the Stokes equations) where F is the force, m is the mass of $f[i]$, g is the acceleration of gravity, v is the velocity of $f[i]$, t is the time, v_0 is the initial velocity, θ is the angle of the slope between the central cell and the neighbour i, α is the friction parameter.

$$F = mg\,sin\theta - \alpha m v$$
$$dv/dt = g\,sin\theta - \alpha v \tag{2}$$
$$v = (v_0 - g\,sin\theta/\alpha)\,e^{-\alpha t} + (g\,sin\theta/\alpha)$$

These equations describe a motion, which is depending on the gravity force and is opposed by friction forces. An asymptotic velocity limit is considered because the effect of the friction forces increases as the velocity increases.

This formal apparatus permits to describe the outflow from a cell c' towards its neighbour c'' as the shift of a "block" (i.e. $f[i]$), individuated by its mass, mass centre position and velocity. Such a shift couldn't be sufficient to locate the new position of the block mass centre outside the central cell c': so more than one step could be necessary for a transfer of the block to the cell c''.

3   The SCIARA γ2b Model for Lava Flows

Navier-Stokes equations represent a good, but perhaps not completely exhaustive approach in terms of systems of differential equations for accounting of physical behaviour of lava flows, moreover such equations become more complicated because lava flows can range, rheologically, from nearly Newtonian fluids to brittle solids by cooling [12]. Numerical methods look difficult to be applied efficaciously. So different *CA* approaches were followed by our research group [4], [5], [6], [13] and by other research groups:

Young and Wadge [14] presented a clever simulation *CA* model, but applicable only to simple flow fronts.

Miyamoto and Sasaki [15] developed a *CA* model for non-isothermal laminar Bingham flows and validated it on real lava flows at Mt. Miyakejima; they solved the problem of the spurious symmetries with a probabilistic method, obtaining positive results in their simulations.

3.1 Main Specifications of the Model SCIARA γ2b

SCIARA γ2b is the last version of the family of *CA* models for lava flows SCIARA (**S**imulation by **C**ellular **I**nteractive **A**utomata of the **R**heology of **A**etnean *lava flows*; the acronym was devised by the word used for the solidified lava path in Sicilian), it improves the previous versions introducing outflows as blocks.

$$\text{SCIARA } \gamma 2b = <R, V, X, S, P, \tau, \phi> :$$

$R = \{(x, y) \mid x, y \in N,\ 0 \le x \le l_x,\ 0 \le y \le l_y\}$ identifies the set of regular hexagons covering the finite region, where the phenomenon evolves. N is the set of natural numbers;

V is the set of cells, corresponding to the area of craters;

X is the hexagonal neighbourhood;

S is the finite set of states of the *fa*; $S = S_a \times S_{th} \times S_x \times S_y \times S_T \times S_{Fth}{}^6 \times S_{Fx}{}^6 \times S_{Fy}{}^6 \times S_{Fv}{}^6$:

  S_a is the cell altitude;

  S_{th} is the thickness of lava inside the cell;

  S_x, S_y are the lava mass centre co-ordinates x and y, referred to the cell centre;

  S_T is the lava temperature;

  S_{Fth} is the lava flow, expressed as thickness (six components);

  S_{Fv} is the velocity of the flow attributed to the mass centre (six components);

  S_{Fx}, S_{Fy} are the co-ordinates x and y of the flow mass centre (six components);

P is the set of the global parameters; $P = \{p_a, p_{step}, p_{TV}, p_{TS}, p_{adhV}, p_{adhS}, p_{cool}, p_{vl}\}$;

  p_a is the apothem of the hexagonal cell;

  p_{step} is the temporal correspondence of a step of SCIARA;

  p_{TV}, p_{TS} are the lava temperature at the vent and the solidification temperature;

  p_{cool} is the cooling parameter;

  p_{vl} is the "asymptotic limit of velocity" for lava flows;

  p_{adhV}, p_{adhS} are the adherence value at the vent and at the solidification temperature (the adherence is the lava thickness, that may not be removed)

$\tau{:}S^7 \to S$ is the transition function, composed by four "elementary" processes:

  σ_{fl} determinates the lava outflows by application of minimisation algorithm;

  σ_{sh} determinates the lava outflows shift by application of velocity formulae;

  σ_{mix} computes the mixing of the blocks: remaining lava and inflows inside the cell;

  σ_{cool} computes the lava cooling by radiation effect and solidification effects;

$\phi{:}S_{th} \times N \to S_{th} \times S_T$ specifies the emitted lava from the V cells at the step $t \in N$.

3.2 The SCIARA γ2b Transition Function

At the beginning of the simulation, the S_a substates assume the morphology values and all the remaining substates are initialised to zero.

At each step, the function ϕ is applied to the cells of V, determining the new lava thickness and attributing the value p_{TV} to the substates S_T, then the four elementary processes are applied in sequence, each one updates the states of all the cells in R.

The "elementary" processes are specified in terms of equations, where names of parameters and substates are derived by the lower indexes specified in the section 3.1: the parameter p_{name} is indicated as *name*; *name* and *nname* are respectively referred to the substate of S_{name} and its new value; when the specification of the index i of a neighbourhood cell is necessary, the notation $name[i]$ is adopted; an index pair $<i,j>$ is specified, if necessary, for the substates of type flow: $Fname[i,j]$ means the value of the flow substate $name$ from the cell i toward the cell j in the neighbourhood ($i=0$ for the outflows, $j=0$ for the inflows, whose values are trivially deduced by the outflows).

Determination of the Lava Flows. The resistance of lava increases as temperature decreases. Because of complexities which are inherent in specifying lava rheology and its variation with temperature [12]; rheological resistance was modelled in terms of an "adherence effect", measured by adh, which represents the amount of lava (expressed as a thickness, as discussed above) that cannot flow out of a cell because of rheological resistance. adh is assumed to vary with temperature T according to a simple inverse exponential relation $adh=ce^{-kT}$, where c and k are positive constants such that $adhV=ce^{-kTV}$ and $adhS=ce^{-kTS}$.

The minimisation algorithm is applied with the following specifications [5], [13]:
$m[0] =th[0] – adh$, $b[0] = a[0] +adh$, $b[i] = a[i] + th[i]$, $1≤i≤6$.

Determination of the Lava Outflow Shift. Etnean lava flows are of "aa" type [16]; therefore, their behaviour may be considered purely gravitational, so there is no dependence on the previous velocity: $Fv[0,i] =vl·\sin\theta$, where the velocity limit $vl=g/\alpha$ and the angle θ is computed according the slope of the ideal path that a flow could follow from the point with co-ordinates ($x[0]$, $y[0]$, $a[0]+th[0]$) of the central cell to the point with co-ordinates (0, 0, $a[i]+th[i]$) of the neighbour i.

The projection of the shift of the flow mass centre on the plane x-y is given by: $shift= vl·\sin\theta·\cos\theta· p_{step}$, it determines $nFx[0,i]$ and $nFy[0,i]$. If the shift is so long that the flow mass centre exceeds the boundary of the cell 0, the flow is attributed to the cell i, otherwise it remains in the cell 0.

Interaction of Blocks inside the Cell. Interaction of blocks inside the cell consists in mixing of lava components i.e. inflows and lava remaining in the cell. The resulting new thickness is obtained by the summation of the thicknesses of all components, while the resulting new temperature and new co-ordinates x and y of mass centres are computed by the weighted average of these quantities on the thickness. Note that the outflows, whose mass centre remain inside the cell are considered as lava remaining in the cell, while those with mass centre outside the cell (i.e. inside the neighbour cell i) belong to the inflows of the neighbour cell i.

Lava Cooling and Solidification. It is always assumed here that different flows in a cell can be thermally well mixed, although this approach involves sometimes a rough approximation. The physical formula applied with the same considerations of the other versions of SCIARA [5], [13] :

$$nT = T/\sqrt[3]{1+\left(T^3 \cdot cool \cdot step/th\right)} \tag{3}$$

4   Simulation of the Lava Flows of 2002 Etnean Eruption

The event which occurred in the autumn of 2002 at Mount Etna (Sicily) involved two main lava flows. The former started on the NE flank of the volcano, with lava generated by a fracture between 2500 m a.s.l and 2350 m a.s.l., near the 1809 fracture and pointed towards the town of Linguaglossa and was exhausted after 8 days.

Such real event (fig. 1) was generated by numerous vents originated from the "fracture of 1809" [17]; simulations were actually carried out by considering two major emission points, neglecting the others, since there was no significant interaction between these flows and the main lava stream.

Fig. 1. The maximum extension of the 2002 Etnean lava flow of NE flank, menacing the town of Linguaglossa.

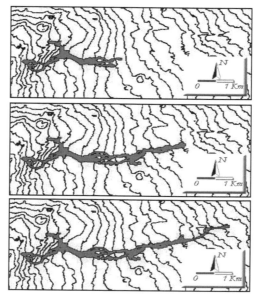

Fig. 2. Simulation steps of 2002 Etnean lava flows in the NE flank, corresponding to the lava fields of the first, fourth and ninth day; maximum extension was reached before the ninth day.

The Linguaglossa lava flow was chosen for validating SCIARA $\gamma2b$ for the more precise (but not optimal) available morphological data. Positions of craters are considered indisputable data, but lava flow rates are considered approximate for obvious known reasons, i.e., the difficulty of measuring flow rates and evaluating eventual rapid changes.

Many simulations with different values of global parameters were performed in order to obtain the better agreement between real and simulated event in terms of surface covered by the lava flows and of the lava flows advancing front.

The following values obtained the best simulation (fig 2): p_a=2.5m, p_{step}=5s, p_{TV}=1373°K, p_{TS}=1123°K, p_{cool}=7.5·10^{-17} s^{-1}·m·°K^{-3}, p_{adhV}=0.9m, p_{adhS}=6m, p_{vl}=2m/s.

The simulation captures the major features of the real event, both in terms of lava extent and in terms of covered distance; moreover field data concerning the advancing flow front fits well with the corresponding steps of simulation.

Other simulations were made just doubling and halving p_{step}. Results were interesting because simulations were strictly similar: it shows that explicit velocity permits time scalability. This feature was not permitted in previous SCIARA models, where time was deduced "a posteriori" on the evaluation basis of the simulation goodness. The same tests for p_a were not performed because of the imprecision of the available DEM (Digital Elevation Model).

Improvements of this model concern two major aspects. Even if in the previous model the overall lava covered distance reflected the real event, the new model has permitted a time correspondence between lava extents at intermediate timings. The second improvement concerns the areal extent of the simulated lava flow. The evaluation of the goodness of a given simulation is performed by a evaluation function, e, simply comparing the extent of actual and simulated events (in terms of affected area). Let R and S be the regions affected by the real and simulated event, respectively; let $m(A)$ denote the measure of the set A. The function e is defined as:

$$e = \sqrt{\frac{m(R \cap S)}{m(R \cup S)}} \tag{4}$$

Note that $e \in [0,1]$. Its value is 0 if the real and simulated events are completely disjoint, being $m(R \cap S)$=0; it is 1 in case of perfect overlap, being $m(R \cap S) = m(R \cup S)$.

Regarding the simulation here presented, e=0.689, while the e value didn't exceed 0.65 in the best simulation of previous SCIARA models.

5 Conclusions

SCIARA γ2b is not a sophisticated model from a physical viewpoint: formulae for explicit velocity are simple, they express the velocity limits, but they could be improved in order to capture better the rheological features of lava flows. The model permits also mixing of lava flows at very different temperatures, rotational effects are reduced to simple displacements between couples of cells, but it is more physical and less empirical in comparison with the previous versions of SCIARA.

Simulations are valuable and developments are being planned for simulating more complex physical phenomena concerning lava flows (e.g. tunnel effects, lava layers at different temperature, etc.) or for extensions to other types of lava.

Acknowledgement. This research has been partially funded by the Italian Ministry of Instruction, University and Research, project FIRB n° RBAU01RMZ4 "Simulazione dei flussi lavici con gli automi cellulari" (Lava flow simulation by cellular automata).

References

1. Frisch, U., D'Humieres, D., Hasslacher, B., Lallemand, P., Pomeau, Y., Rivet, J.P.: Lattice gas hydrodynamics in two and three dimensions. Complex Systems 1 (1990) 649-707
2. Chopard, B, Luthi, P.O.: Lattice Boltzmann Computations and Application to Physics. Theoretical Computer Science 217 (1999) 115-130
3. Succi, S.: The Lattice Boltzmann Equation for Fluid Dynamics and Beyond, Oxford University Press, Oxford (2001)
4. Crisci, G.M., Di Gregorio, S., Pindaro, O., Ranieri, S.A.: Lava flow simulation by a discrete cellular model: first implementation. Int. J. of Modelling and Simulation, 6, (1986) 137-140
5. Barca, D., Crisci, G.M., Di Gregorio, S., Nicoletta, F.: Cellular Automata for simulating lava flows: a method and examples of the Etnean eruptions. Transport Theory and Statistical Physics, 23, 1 3, (1994) 195-232
6. Di Gregorio, S., Serra, R.: An empirical method for modelling and simulating some complex macroscopic phenomena by cellular automata. Future Generation Computer Systems, 16 (1999) 259-271
7. Di Gregorio, S. Rongo, R., Siciliano, C., Sorriso-Valvo, M., Spataro W.: Mount Ontake landslide simulation by the cellular automata model SCIDDICA-3. Physics and Chemistry of the Earth (A) 24 (1999) 97-100
8. Avolio, M.V., Di Gregorio, S., Mantovani, F., Pasuto, A., Rongo, R., Silvano, S., Spataro W.: Simulation of the 1992 Tessina landslide by a cellular automata model and future hazard scenarios. JAG (International Journal of Applied Earth Observation and Geoinformatics) 2 1 (2000) 41-50
9. D'Ambrosio, D., Di Gregorio, S., Iovine, G.: Simulating debris flows through a hexagonal cellular automata model: SCIDDICA S_{3-hex}. Natural Hazards and Earth System Sciences 3 (2003) 545-559
10. D'Ambrosio D., Di Gregorio S., Gabriele S., Gaudio R.: A Cellular Automata Model for Soil Erosion by Water. Physics and Chemistry of the Earth, EGS, B 26 1 (2001) 33-39
11. Worsch, T.: Simulation of Cellular Automata. Future Generation Computer Systems 16 (1999) 157-170
12. McBirney, A.R., Murase, T.: Rheological properties of magmas. Annual Review on Earth and Planetary Sciences, 12, (1984) 337-57.
13. Crisci, G. M., Di Gregorio, S., Rongo, R., M, Spataro, W.: The simulation model SCIARA: the 1991 and 2001 lava flows at Mount Etna. Journal of Volcanology and Geothermal Research 132/2-3 (2004) 253-267
14. Young, P., Wadge, G.: Flowfront: simulation of a lava flow. Computer & Geosciences 16 8 (1990) 1171-1191
15. Miyamoto, H., Sasaki, S.: Simulating lava flows by an improved cellular automata method. Computers & Geosciences 23 3 (1997) 283-292
16. Kilburn, C.R.J., Lopes, R.M.C.: General patterns of flow field growth: aa and blocky lavas. Journal of Geophysical Research 96 19 (1991) 721-32
17. Calvari, Sonia: Personal Communication, 2003

Cell-Oriented Modeling of *In Vitro* Capillary Development

Roeland M.H. Merks[1,2], Stuart A. Newman[2], and James A. Glazier[1]

[1] Biocomplexity Institute
Department of Physics
Indiana University
Bloomington, IN 47405
post@roelandmerks.nl, glazier@indiana.edu
http://biocomplexity.indiana.edu
[2] Cell Biology and Anatomy
New York Medical College
Valhalla, NY
newman@nymc.edu
http://www.nymc.edu/sanewman

Abstract. We introduce a Cellular Potts model (a cellular-automaton-based Monte-Carlo model) of *in vitro* capillary development, or angiogenesis. Our model derives from a recent continuum model, which assumes that vascular endothelial cells chemotactically attract each other. Our discrete model is "cell based." Modeling the cells individually allows us to assign different physicochemical properties to each cell and to study how these properties affect the vascular pattern. Using the model, we assess the roles of intercellular adhesion, cell shape and chemoattractant saturation in *in vitro* capillary development. We discuss how our computational model can serve as a tool for experimental biologists to "pre-test" hypotheses and to suggest new experiments.

1 Introduction

A detailed understanding of capillary blood vessel formation, or angiogenesis, is essential to understand and control physiological and pathological processes from wound healing to tumor growth and angiogenesis-related pathologies such as advanced diabetic nephropathy. Capillaries develop in two main ways: through the aggregation of endothelial cells into capillary cords, and through sprouting from existing capillaries.

In vitro culture of human umbilical vascular endothelial cells (HUVEC) in Matrigel is a popular experimental model of capillary development (see *e.g.* [2]). Matrigel is an extracellular matrix product obtained from murine tumors. The extracellular proteins and growth factors in the gel stimulate HUVEC cells to form networks (Fig. 1) resembling vascular networks *in vivo*. HUVEC-Matrigel cultures and related HUVEC cultures in collagen [3] and fibrin [4] gels are standard models in biomedical research to identify the key molecular players in

P.M.A. Sloot, B. Chopard, and A.G. Hoekstra (Eds.): ACRI 2004, LNCS 3305, pp. 425–434, 2004.

pathological and physiological angiogenesis, to unravel the role of cell growth and apoptosis in vasculogenesis and to probe potential anti-angiogenic pharmaceuticals.

The biophysical mechanisms by which endothelial cells form such networks are poorly understood. Several computational studies have suggested that endothelial cells, behaving according to a small set of rules, could suffice to explain network-formation. Most hypotheses assume that either chemotaxis [5,6] or tractional forces relayed through the extracellular matrix [4,7,8] drive cell aggregation. Partial differential equation models of both mechanisms generate patterns that resemble *in vitro* networks, so which of them most closely parallels the biological mechanism remains unclear.

These continuum approaches implicitly assume that the endothelial cells that construct the pattern are much smaller than the length-scale of interest, namely that of the "cords" and "nodes." *In vitro*, however, at most a dozen elongating cells form the cords, which are one to a few cell-diameters thick (see Fig. 1). Thus, we expect the scale of the endothelial cells to play an important role in patterning. The properties of individual cells, such as their shape, their mutual adhesion and their adhesion to the extracellular matrix may also affect the pattern resulting from their interaction.

This paper develops a *cell-oriented* approach to modeling *in vitro* vasculogenesis, based on the Gamba-Serini chemotaxis model [5,6]. We construct computational models of individual HUVEC cells which mimic experimentally-observed cell phenomenology, including response to external chemical signals, cell elongation, cell adhesion, chemotaxis, haptotaxis, *etc.* We then release these simulated cells in a "virtual Petri-dish" and quantitatively compare their macroscopic, collective behavior to experiments. We attempt to recover minimal sets of physicochemical properties and behavioral rules for the cells which reproduce the experimentally-observed tissue-level pattern.

Our focus on cell phenomenology may seem crude compared to large-scale, post-genomic, systems-biology initiatives whose aim is to model *ab initio* and in detail the internal structure and genetic regulation of individual cells, and even-

Fig. 1. HUVEC culture on Matrigel, 4x magnification, 2h (left) and 9h (right). To improve contrast, we have applied an Opening Top-Hat transform [1] with a small-disk structuring element.

tually collections of interacting cells (see *e.g.* [9,10]). However, the cell-oriented approach allows us to distinguish a) how genomic information determines cell phenomenology (using detailed, single cell models) from b) how collections of cells exhibiting a particular phenomenology interact during biological morphogenesis (using a "cell-oriented" approach). The cell-oriented approach has been successful in the study of biological morphogenesis. In particular, it can simulate the entire developmental life cycle of the cellular slime mold *Dictyostelium discoideum* [11,12], convergent extension in early vertebrate embryos [13], tumor invasion [14] and pattern formation in vertebrate limb cell cultures [15].

The Cellular Potts model (CPM) [16,17], a cellular-automaton-based Monte-Carlo method, is a convenient cell-oriented simulation framework. Early CPM studies of differential-adhesion-driven cell rearrangement in cell aggregates quantitatively reproduced cell sorting experiments [16]. An energy-minimization philosophy, a set of energy constraints and auxiliary conditions determine how cells move. Connections between cells determine a cell-cell contact (or bond) energy. favoring stronger over weaker bonds and shortening of the boundary length. An energy constraint regulates cell volume or area. Further constraints or auxiliary conditions easily extend the CPM to include chemotaxis [11], cell growth, cell death [18] and cell polarity [13].

The remainder of this paper introduces our hybrid CPM/PDE model and extensions to the CPM motivated by HUVEC phenomenology. We then study patterning in the CPM/PDE version of the Gamba-Serini chemotaxis model. Finally, we discuss the biological and computational relevance of our results.

2   Methods

2.1   Hybrid Cellular Potts Model

We use a hybrid Cellular Potts (CPM) and partial differential equation (PDE) model (see [11,12,17]). The CPM models endothelial cells, while the PDEs model the chemoattractant. Experimentally-confirmed cell behaviors, which we include in the model are, 1) secretion of chemoattractants, 2) chemotaxis of cells up chemical gradients, and 3) progressive elongation of cells.

The CPM represents biological cells as patches of lattice sites, x, with identical indices $\sigma(x)$, where each index identifies, or "labels" a single biological cell. Connections between neighboring lattice sites of unlike index $\sigma(x) \neq \sigma(x')$ represent membrane bonds, with a characteristic *bond energy* $J_{\sigma_x,\sigma_{x'}}$, where we assume that the types and numbers of "cell adhesion molecules" (CAMs) of the interacting cells determine J. An energy penalty increasing with the cell's deviation from a designated target volume A_σ imposes a *volume constraint* on the biological cells. To mimic cytoskeletally driven membrane fluctuations, we randomly choose a lattice site, x, and attempt to copy its index σ_x into a randomly chosen neighboring lattice site x'. To ensure isotropy, we use the twenty, first- to fourth-order neighbours on a square lattice. On average, we attempt an update at each lattice site once per Monte-Carlo step (MCS). We calculate how much the Hamiltonian would change if we performed the copy, and accept the attempt with probability:

$$P(\Delta H) = \{\exp(-(\Delta H + H_0)/T), \Delta H \geq -H_0; 1, \Delta H < -H_0\}, \qquad (1)$$

where $H_0 > 0$ is an energy threshold which models viscous dissipation and energy loss during bond breakage and formation[18]. We then define the Hamiltonian as:

$$H = \sum_{\boldsymbol{x},\boldsymbol{x}'} J_{\sigma_{\boldsymbol{x}},\sigma_{\boldsymbol{x}'}}(1 - \delta_{\sigma_{\boldsymbol{x}},\sigma_{\boldsymbol{x}'}}) + \lambda \sum_{\sigma}(a_\sigma - A_\sigma)^2, \qquad (2)$$

where λ represents resistance to compression, and the Kronecker delta is $\delta_{x,y} = \{1, x = y; 0, x \neq y\}$. The cells reside in a "medium" which is a generalized CPM cell without a volume constraint and with $\sigma = 0$. In most simulations, we use a bond energy $J_{cc} = 5$ between the endothelial cells, and $J_{cM} = 20$ between the endothelial cells and the medium. We further define a *surface tension* $\gamma_{cM} = J_{cM} - J_{cc}/2$, which enables us to determine whether the cells cohere ($\gamma_{cM} > 0$) or dissociate ($\gamma_{cM} < 0$) [16] in the absence of chemotaxis. Our default cellular adhesion setting is adhesive, *i.e.* $\gamma_{cM} > 0$. We define a special, high *cell-border energy* $J_{cB} = 100$ to prevent cells from adhering to the boundaries. The viscous dissipation H_0 and all terms in the Hamiltonian, *i.e.* the bond energies J, and the prefactors to the additional energy terms, such as λ, scale with the temperature T; *i.e.* if we multiply T by a factor τ, we can multiply the H_0 and the Hamiltonian by the same factor and obtain the same simulation results.

In analogy to the Gamba and Serini PDE model [5,6], we set the diffusion and secretion of the chemoattractant c to:

$$\frac{\partial c}{\partial t} = \alpha \, \delta_{\sigma_{\boldsymbol{x}},0} - (1 - \delta_{\sigma_{\boldsymbol{x}},0})\epsilon \, c + D\nabla^2 c, \qquad (3)$$

where $\delta_{\sigma_{\boldsymbol{x}},0} = 1$ inside the cells, α is the rate at which the cells release chemoattractant, and ϵ is the decay rate of the chemoattractant. Thus, every site within the cells secretes the chemoattractant, which decays only in the medium. We solve the PDEs numerically using a finite difference scheme on a lattice matching the CPM lattice, using 20 steps per MCS with $\Delta t = 0.2$. For these parameters the chemoattractant diffuses much more rapidly than the cells, enabling us to ignore the advection that occurs as the cells push the medium forward.

Chemotaxis. We implement preferential motion of the cells along gradients of the chemoattractant c by defining [11]:

$$H' = H - \sum_i \chi \, \frac{c(\boldsymbol{x},\boldsymbol{t})}{s \, c(\boldsymbol{x},\boldsymbol{t}) + 1}(1 - \delta_{\sigma_i,\sigma_j}), \qquad (4)$$

where χ is the strength of the chemotactic response, and the saturation s sets the Michaelis-Menten constant of the chemotactic response, for which we use $s = 0.01$ by default. For $s = 0$ the cell's response to gradients does not level off at higher concentrations, as in the original method of Savill *et al.* [11], while for large s the cells become unresponsive. Because the chemical field biases cells' boundary copying, each cell moves with an velocity $v \propto \sqrt{(\mu)} \sum_j \sum_i P_j(d_i)$, where the sums run over the sites of the cell and the twenty lattice directions respectively, and $P_j(d_i)$ denotes the probability that site j copies in lattice direction d_i. The prefactor $\sqrt{\mu}$ has units of force, but we can also interpret it as the chemotactic strain field [19].

Cell elongation. The HUVEC cells in our cultures elongate progressively as the vessel-like pattern develops. To study how cell elongation affects the pattern, we add a cell-length constraint to the Hamiltonian:

$$H'' = H' + \lambda_L (l - L)^2, \tag{5}$$

where l is the length of the cell along its longest axis, L is its target length, and λ_L is the strength of the length constraint. Larger values of λ_L result in more elongated cells. Following Zajac *et al.* [20], we calculate the short and long axes of the moments of inertia as:

$$
\begin{aligned}
I_{xx} &= \sum_i (y_i - \bar{y})^2, \\
I_{xy} &= -\sum_i (x_i - \bar{x})(y_i - \bar{y}), \\
I_{yx} &= I_{xy}, \\
I_{yy} &= \sum_i (x_i - \bar{x})^2,
\end{aligned}
\tag{6}
$$

where the sum is over all the sites $x = (x_i, y_i)$ in the cell. We determine the length l from the largest eigenvalue of I as $l = 2\sqrt{\lambda_b}$, where:

$$\lambda_b = \frac{1}{2}(I_{xx} + I_{yy}) + \frac{1}{2}\sqrt{(I_{xx} - I_{yy})^2 + 4I_{xy}^2}. \tag{7}$$

We can update the inertia tensor locally after each cell extension or retraction, by constructing it from the first and second order moments of the positions of the sites the cells occupy:

$$
\begin{aligned}
I_{yy} &= \sum_i x_i^2 - \frac{1}{a}\left(\sum_i x_i\right)^2, \\
I_{xy} &= -\sum_i x_i y_i - \frac{1}{a}\sum_i x_i \sum_i y_i, \\
I_{xx} &= \sum_i y_i^2 - \frac{1}{a}\left(\sum_i y_i\right)^2,
\end{aligned}
\tag{8}
$$

with a the cell area. Thus Eq. 7 determines l without lengthy calculation.

The length constraint can cause cells to split into disconnected patches. We prevent this artifact by introducing a connectivity constraint. To check whether an index copy into site x will change local connectivity, we count how many of its neighbors x'_i have equal index to x while the next in cyclic order has unequal spin. If this quantity $\sum_i \delta_{\sigma(x),\sigma(x'_i)}(1 - \delta_{\sigma(x),\sigma(x'_{i+1})}) > 2$, with the sum running in cyclic order, changing the site will destroy the local connectivity. We have currently only implemented this algorithm for second-order neigborhoods (*i.e.* 8 neighbours). This test for connectivity loss gives "false positives" for non-convex patches, which occur in our simulations when cells suddenly shrink, for example during "apoptosis" [18]. Instead of introducing a very expensive ($O(N^2)$) global connectivity test, we tolerate temporary violations of connectivity for large energy drops. The bond energies ensure that the lifetime of disconnected patches is short. We assume that cell fragmentation is energetically costly, and set a high energy threshold H_0 (typically $H_0 = 500$) *iff* the attempted update would change the local connectivity.

2.2   Simulation Set-Up and Initialization

In our partial differential equations (PDE), we set boundary values to zero (*i.e.* the boundaries absorb the chemoattractant), while for the CPM we implement repellent boundary conditions by setting the cell-boundary binding energy to $J_{cB} = 100$. We use a 500×500 lattice, where each lattice site represents an area of about $4\mu m^2$. Cells have actual areas of around 45 lattice sites, equivalent to a typical endothelial cell area of around $150\mu m^2$ [21]. To diminish boundary effects we initially disperse n cells randomly within a centered 333×333 square. For $n >= 3000$ we disperse the cells all over the field to minimize cell overlap. After each Monte Carlo Step (MCS) we update the PDE 20 times with $\Delta t = 0.2$.

2.3   Morphometry

We characterize the patterns by measuring the average size $\bar{La}$ of the open spaces which the vessel-like structures enclose (*lacunae*). $\bar{La} = 1/N \sum_i La_i$, with N the number of lacunae and La_i the size of each lacuna, which we identify using a standard connected-component labeling algorithm [1].

3   Results

Figs. 2 and 3 review our results. Fig. 2a reproduces the results of the Gamba and Serini PDE model [5,6] in our cell-oriented model. The cell-adhesion settings are strongly adhesive ($\gamma_{cM} = 17.5$). The cells aggregate into cords and nodes, typical of HUVEC Matrigel cultures (Fig. 1) and the Gamba-Serini model. As the cell density increases, we find a percolation transition as in the Gamba-Serini model [5]; for low densities, $n < 1000$, the cells do not form a connected network, while for high densities, $n > 1000$, all cells interconnect (see Fig. 2a).

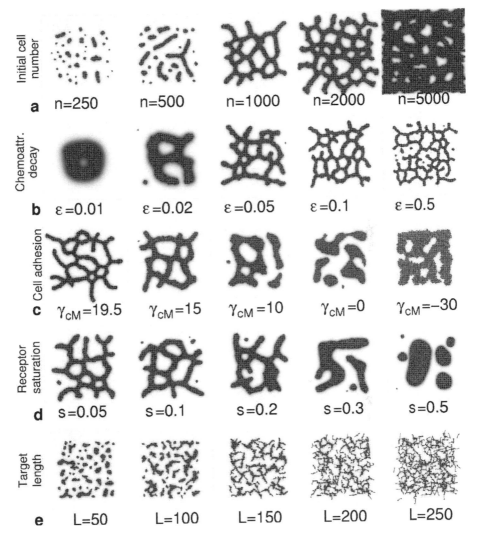

Fig. 2. Overview of parameter sweeps. Typical cell patterns after 5000 MCS. Lattice size 500 × 500, $n = 1000$ scattered within inner 333 × 333 subfield (e: $n = 555$). Parameters were $T = 50$, $\lambda_A = 50$, $A = 50$, $\gamma_{cM} = 17.5$, $s = 0.01$, $\chi = 2000$, $\alpha = 0.01$, $\epsilon = 0.05$, $D = 1$, $\lambda_L = 0$ (e: $\lambda_L = 1.0$), unless indicated otherwise.

Also, as in the Gamba-Serini model, the size of the lacunae depends on the rate of chemoattractant decay, as Fig. 2b shows.

In Figs. 2c-e, we systematically modify the Gamba-Serini model by changing the biophysical properties of the individual cells. First, we study the role of intercellular adhesion. In our model, cell adhesion is essential. If we reduce the adhesivity of the endothelial cells, a network no longer forms and the cells aggregate into "islands" (Fig. 2c). Like the Gamba-Serini model, our model can

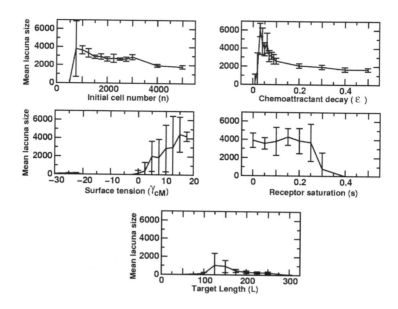

Fig. 3. Dependence of lacuna size on model parameters, after 5000 Monte Carlo steps. Parameters as in Fig. 2. Error bars indicate standard deviations ($n = 5$)

also form networks without cell adhesion, but these networks are unstable and decay into an "island-like" pattern (results not shown).

Fig. 2d shows the effect of changes in s, the threshold for chemotaxis saturation (sensitivity) (see eq. 4). Up to around $s = 0.1$ vessel-like patterns form, while for larger values more amorphous patterns with larger clusters and few lacunae form. The lacuna size becomes more variable for larger values of s (see Fig. 3d).

In the *in vitro* culture experiments, the endothelial cells elongate during vessel-like patterning. Although elongation is not necessary for vessel-like patterning in our model, cell elongation is one of the first observable signs of vessel-like patterning in HUVEC cultures. In Fig. 2e and Fig 3e we investigate the effect of cell elongation on patterning at low cell densities ($n = 555$). Cell elongation facilitates the interconnection of isolated parts of the pattern (see Fig. 3e). For very large length constraints ($L > 300$) the cells fragment, after which the vessel-like pattern no longer interconnects. At higher densities, when the pattern already fully interconnects even for round cells, cell elongation has no effect on lacuna size, but affects the shape of the lacunae (results not shown).

4   Discussion and Conclusions

Computational screening of the parameter dependence of patterning may help to direct experiments to identify the key regulators of vascular development and suggest new hypotheses. If chemotaxis drives vascular development, as in the

Gamba-Serini model, our simulations suggest that endothelial cell adhesion is essential to form stable vascular networks. Furthermore, our simulations suggest that pattern formation changes qualitatively when the receptors saturate at lower concentrations of chemoattractant. We could test this effect experimentally by specifically inhibiting the production of receptors, in which case the remaining receptors would saturate at lower concentrations, or by adding receptors with higher affinity. Cell extension also strongly affects the multicellular pattern, reducing the cell density network formation requires. Biological experiments might attempt to specifically target the elongation of the endothelial cells. Preliminary results also show that cell motility above a mininum required velocity does not significantly affect patterning (not shown). Continuous models have great difficulty assessing the role of these parameters, in particular of intercellular adhesion and cell morphology.

In our ongoing work we are refining and validating our computational model by obtaining experimentally derived values for the model parameters and by comparing our simulation results quantitatively to time-lapse videomicroscopy experiments. We are analyzing the dynamics of patterning in HUVEC cultures under different physiological and pathological conditions and comparing these to the computational model's dynamics for similar simulated conditions. Gradual cell elongation, rather than the instantaneous elongation that we employed here, may change the model's dynamics. We also plan to model the interaction of the individual cells with the viscoelastic extracellular matrix, which experiments and theory [4] suggest is crucial to *in vitro* vasculogenesis. These studies may lead to better understanding of the biophysical mechanisms of vascular development, which will suggest new experimental tests of the genetic and biophysical regulation of vascular development.

Acknowledgments. This material is based upon work supported by the National Science Foundation under Grants MRI-0116050 and IBN-0083653, a Pervasive Technologies Laboratories Fellowship (Indiana University Bloomington), an IBM Innovation Institute Award and NASA NAG 2-1619, the Indiana University Biocomplexity Institute, and the Indiana University AVIDD program. We thank Dr. Sergey Brodsky and Prof. Michael Goligorsky of the Dept. of Medicine at New York Medical College for help with Fig. 1. R.M. developed parts of the simulation software during work with Prof. Paulien Hogeweg at Utrecht University, The Netherlands.

References

1. Dougherty, E.R., Lotufo, R.A.: Hands-on Morphological Image Processing. Volume TT59 of Tutorial Texts in Optical Engin. SPIE Press, Bellingham, WA, USA (2003)
2. Segura, I., Serrano, A., De Buitrago, G.G., Gonzalez, M.A., Abad, J.L., Claveria, C., Gomez, L., Bernad, A., Martinez-A, C., Riese, H.H.: Inhibition of programmed cell death impairs in vitro vascular-like structure formation and reduces in vivo angiogenesis. FASEB J. **16** (2002) 833–841

3. Chen, J., Brodsky, S., Li, H., Hampel, D.J., Miyata, T., Weinstein, T., Gafter, U., Norman, J.T., Fine, L.G., Goligorsky, M.S.: Delayed branching of endothelial capillary-like cords in glycated collagen I is mediated by early induction of PAI-1. Am. J. Physiol.-Renal **281** (2001) F71–F80

4. Namy, P., Ohayon, J., Tracqui, P.: Critical conditions for pattern formation and in vitro tubulogenesis driven by cellular traction fields. J. Theor. Biol. **227** (2004) 103–120

5. Gamba, A., Ambrosi, D., Coniglio, A., De Candia, A., Di Talia, S., Giraudo, E., Serini, G., Preziosi, L., Bussolino, F.: Percolation morphogenesis and burgers dynamics in blood vessels formation. Phys. Rev. Lett. **90** (2003) 118101

6. Serini, G., Ambrosi, D., Giraudo, E., Gamba, A., Preziosi, L., Bussolino, F.: Modeling the early stages of vascular network assembly. EMBO J. **22** (2003) 1771–1779

7. Manoussaki, D., Lubkin, S.R., Vernon, R.B., Murray, J.D.: A mechanical model for the formation of vascular networks in vitro. Acta Biotheor. **44** (1996) 271–282

8. Manoussaki, D.: A mechanochemical model of angiogenesis and vasculogenesis. ESAIM-Math. Model. Num. **37** (2003) 581–599

9. Takahashi, K., Ishikawa, N., Sadamoto, Y., Sasamoto, H., Ohta, S., Shiozawa, A., Miyoshi, F., Naito, Y., Nakayama, Y., Tomita, M.: E-cell 2: Multi-platform e-cell simulation system. Bioinformatics **19** (2003) 1727–1729

10. Silicon cell project. (**http://www.siliconcell.net**)

11. Savill, N.J., Hogeweg, P.: Modelling morphogenesis: from single cells to crawling slugs. J. Theor. Biol. **184** (1997) 229–235

12. Marée, A.F.M., Hogeweg, P.: How amoeboids self-organize into a fruiting body: Multicellular coordination in *Dictyostelium discoideum*. P. Natl. Acad. Sci. USA **98** (2001) 3879–3883

13. Zajac, M., Jones, G.L., Glazier, J.A.: Model of convergent extension in animal morphogenesis. Phys. Rev. Lett. **85** (2000) 2022–2025

14. Turner, S., Sherratt, J.A.: Intercellular adhesion and cancer invasion: a discrete simulation using the extended Potts model. J. Theor. Biol. **216** (2002) 85–100

15. Kiskowski, M.A., Alber, M.S., Thomas, G.L., Glazier, J.A., Bronstein, N.B., Pu, J., Newman, S.A.: Interplay between activator-inhibitor coupling and cell-matrix adhesion in a cellular automaton model for chondrogenic patterning. Dev. Biol. **271** (2004) 372–387

16. Glazier, J.A., Graner, F.: Simulation of the differential adhesion driven rearrangement of biological cells. Phys. Rev. E **47** (1993) 2128–2154

17. Izaguirre, J.A., Chaturvedi, R., Huang, C., Cickovski, T., Coffland, J., Thomas, G., Forgacs, G., Alber, M., Hentschel, G., Newman, S.A., Glazier, J.A.: COMPUCELL, a multi-model framework for simulation of morphogenesis. Bioinformatics **20** (2004) 1129–1137

18. Hogeweg, P.: Evolving mechanisms of morphogenesis: on the interplay between differential adhesion and cell differentiation. J. Theor. Biol. **203** (2000) 317–333

19. Jiang, Y., Swart, P.J., Saxena, A., Asipauskas, M., Glazier, J.A.: Hysteresis and avalanches in two-dimensional foam rheology simulations. Phys. Rev. E **59** (1999) 5819–5832

20. Zajac, M., Jones, G.L., Glazier, J.A.: Simulating convergent extension by way of anisotropic differential adhesion. J. Theor. Biol. **222** (2003) 247–259

21. LaRue, A.C., Mironov, V.A., Argraves, W.S., Czirók, A., Fleming, P.A., Drake, C.J.: Patterning of embryonic blood vessels. Dev. Dynam. **228** (2003) 21–29

Neuropercolation: A Random Cellular Automata Approach to Spatio-temporal Neurodynamics[*]

Robert Kozma[1], Marko Puljic[1], Paul Balister[1], Bela Bollobas[1], and
Walter J. Freeman[2]

[1] Department of Mathematical Sciences, University of Memphis,
Memphis, TN 38152-3240, USA
rkozma@memphis.edu, http://cnd.memphis.edu
[2] Division of Neurobiology, University of California at Berkeley
Berkeley, CA 94720-3200, USA
wfreeman@socrates.berkeley.edu, http://sulcus.berkeley.edu

Abstract. We outline the basic principles of neuropercolation, a generalized percolation model motivated by the dynamical properties of the neuropil, the densely interconnected neural tissue structure in the cortex. We apply the mathematical theory of percolation in lattices to analyze chaotic dynamical memories and their related phase transitions. This approach has several advantages, including the natural introduction of noise that is necessary for system stability, a greater degree of biological plausibility, a more uniform and simpler model description, and a more solid theoretical foundation for neural modeling. Critical phenomena and scaling properties of a class of random cellular automata (RCA) are studied on the lattice $\mathbb{Z}^2$. In addition to RCA, we study phase transitions in mean-field models, as well as in models with axonal, non-local interactions. Relationship to the Ising universality class and to Toom cellular automata is thoroughly analyzed.

1 Introduction

Information encoding in the form of oscillatory patterns has advantage compared to fixed-point (static) memories. A number of researchers acknowledged the limitation of static approaches, and have worked around it. Grossberg has proposed adaptive resonance theory network which is a sophisticated topological arrangement of components [1]. Hopfield proposed his famous associative memory network, which is a recurrent system [2]. Elman uses processing elements with feedback as memory devices [3]. Cellular nonlinear neural network (CNN) represent another paradigm showing great promise by implementing cellular automata theory in the form of a programmable memory device [4]. In a separate development, KIII nets have been introduced which represent a prototype of dynamic memory devices based on information encoding in aperiodic (chaotic) attractors [5].

---

[*] This research has been funded in part by NSF BITS Grant #0130352.

What distinguishes brain chaos from other kinds is the filamentous texture of neural tissue called neuropil, which is unlike any other substance in the known universe [6, 7]. Neural populations stem ontogenetically in embryos from aggregates of neurons that grow axons and dendrites and form synaptic connections of steadily increasing density. At some threshold the density allows neurons to transmit more pulses than they receive, so that an aggregate undergoes a state transition from a zero point attractor to a non-zero point attractor, thereby becoming a population. Such a property has been described mathematically in random graphs, where the connectivity density is an order parameter that can instantiate state transitions [8, 9].

Information processing in the proposed chaotic dynamical memories is closely related to percolation phenomena [10, 7, 11]. For about forty years now, percolation theory has been an active area of research at the interface of probability theory, combinatorics and physics [12]. Interest in various aspects of standard percolation remains high, including estimates of critical probabilities [13, 14]. There has been much work on the family of processes know as bootstrap percolation [15 - 19]. Many percolation problems exhibit phase transitions, where for p less than some critical probability p_{crit} only finite clusters exist, and for $p > p_{crit}$ infinite clusters almost surely exist. We propose to apply the mathematical theory of percolation in lattices to analyze dynamical neural systems and their related phase transitions. First the basics of bootstrap percolations are described. This is followed by the introduction of several generalizations of standard percolation, which we call neuropercolation. Generalizations include the biologically motivated activation and deactivation functions, random transition rules, and non-local interactions. Non-local interactions mean a rewiring of the connections, which is related to small-world phenomena [20]. Related work on percolations in small-world models is described in [21, 22].

First we describe theoretical results on mean field models, and critical behavior observed in local RCAs. This is followed by the analysis of non-local models and the comparison of their behavior with Ising universality class and Toom automata [23]. Finally, we discuss the directions of combining populations of nonlinear processing elements to multi-layer architecture, in order to describe dynamic processes in cortices.

2   Model Description and Activation Density

Here we introduce the mathematical formalism of neuropercolation. A key parameter of the system is the probability p, which characterizes the stochastic nature of the transition rule. We will see that the random initialization is of secondary importance when having random transition rule. I the following considerations we describe effect related to this probability p.

Let Λ be a finite subset of $\mathbb{Z}^d$ containing the origin $\mathbf{0} = (0, \ldots, 0)$ and let $p: 2^\Lambda \to [0, 1]$ be a function that assigns for each subset $S \subseteq \Lambda$ a probability p_S. We define a stochastic process as a sequence of subsets $X_t \subseteq \mathbb{Z}^d$ by including each $\mathbf{x} = (\mathbf{x_1}, \ldots, \mathbf{x_d})$ in X_{t+1} independently with probability p_S where $S =$

$\Lambda \cap (X_t - \mathbf{x})$ and $X_t - \mathbf{x}$ is the translate of X_t by $-\mathbf{x}$. We start the process with X_0 given by some specified distribution. We call such a process a *random cellular automaton* on $\mathbb{Z}^d$. Usually we define Λ to be the closed neighborhood of $\mathbf{z}$, consisting of all points unit distance from $\mathbf{z}$ together with $\mathbf{z}$ itself. Similarly we can define random cellular automata on the d-dimensional torus $\mathbb{Z}_{n_1} \times \ldots \times \mathbb{Z}_{n_d}$, or on the corresponding finite grid (with suitable boundary conditions imposed). We start by considering p of a certain special form. Assume p_S depends only on the cardinality of S and whether or not the site itself is active ($z \in S$). We write $p_r^{(0)}$ in place of p_S when $|S| = r$ and $z \notin S$ and $p_r^{(1)}$ when $|S| = r$ and $z \in S$. We shall call these models *isotropic*. Isotropic models are substantially more restrictive than the general case, but they still have complex behavior. We call the model *fully isotropic* if $p_r^{(0)} = p_r^{(1)} = p_r$ for all r. In this case, the site itself is treated on the same basis as its neighbors. By complementing the sets X_t we obtain a new model with $p'^{(i)}_r = 1 - p^{(1-i)}_{|\Lambda|-i}$ (or more generally, $p'_S = 1 - p_{\Lambda \setminus S}$). We call the model *symmetric* if it is the same as its complement, so $p_r^{(1)} = 1 - p^{(0)}_{|\Lambda|-r}$ for all r (or $p_S = 1 - p_{\Lambda \setminus S}$ for non-isotropic models). For symmetric models, there is a further symmetry. If we complement every other X_t, then this is equivalent to a new symmetric model with p_S replaced by $p_S^* = 1 - p_S$. We call this new model the *dual* model of a symmetric model (p_S). Phases in the original model with density not equal to 0.5 will give oscillating phases in the new model with period two [24]. Random cellular automata generalize deterministic cellular automata such as Conway's game of life. Given the complexity of deterministic automata it should not come as a surprise that random automata display extremely complex behavior.

3   Mean Field Models

On a finite grid or torus, we can compare random automata with the corresponding *mean field* model over $\mathbb{Z}^2$. In the mean field model instead of taking $|\Lambda| - 1$ specified neighbors, we take $|\Lambda| - 1$ elements of the grid at random (with replacement). It is clear that the mean field model does not depend on the topology of the grid, and the only information of relevance in X_t is given by its cardinality $|X_t|$. We define x_t to be $|X_t|/N$ where N is the size of the finite grid or torus. Thus $x_t \in [0, 1]$ gives the density of points in X_t. Let us consider the symmetric fully isotropic model $p_0 = p_1 = p_2 = p$. It can be shown that for the mean field model, this has one fixed point at $x = 0.5$ for $p \in [\frac{7}{30}, \frac{1}{2}]$, but for $p < \frac{7}{30} = .2333$ the fixed point $x = 0.5$ is unstable and there are two other fixed points which are stable [24]. Figure 1 illustrates the average density and its variance for various p values.

Our real interest lies in random cellular automata on $\mathbb{Z}^2$ rather than the mean field models. So one question is how well do the mean field models approximate the corresponding random automata? Unfortunately, the answer is 'not very well in general'. Since the mean field model is equivalent to that of a fully isotropic model, the best we could hope for is that it approximates fully isotropic models. However, even fully isotropic models can exhibit behavior that is richer than that of the mean field models. The theoretical analysis of local RCA is extremely difficult. Recently, a rigorous mathematical derivation of properties of phase transitions in RCA with very small $p \approx 0$ has been given by [25]. Phase transitions near the critical point are not tractable by rigorous mathematical tools at present. Accordingly, we rely on computer simulations with local and non-local RCAs in the following considerations.

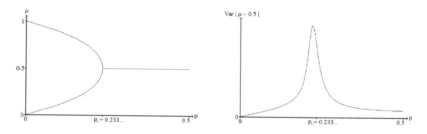

Fig. 1. Activiation density ρ of the mean field with $p_c = 0.233$. The variance of $|\rho - 0.5|$ has a sharp increase as p approaches p_c.

4   Simulation of RCA on Finite Lattices

4.1   Phase Transition in Local RCA

The simulation was run on a 2-dimensional torus with noisy majority rule with $4 + 1$ local neighbors. All the sites are updated simultaneously at a certain time t. In this section we use the statistical physics methodology of finite size scaling that has been developed for Ising systems and consecutively applied to various cellular automata, including Toom automata [26, 23, 27]. Here we summarize the major results and conclusions; for details, see [28]. We define the activation density across the torus as follows:

$$x_t = \frac{X_t}{N_{total}}, \tag{1}$$

where, X_t denotes the number of active sites at time t, and N_{total} is the total number of sites in the torus. The average density over n iterations is defined as:

$$\rho = \frac{1}{n} \sum_{t=1}^{n} x_t. \tag{2}$$

We define the parameter of magnetization as the distance to the known fixed point $\frac{1}{2}$

$$\langle |m| \rangle = \frac{1}{n} \sum_{t=1}^{n} |x_t - \frac{1}{2}|. \tag{3}$$

The system exhibits three basic behaviors depending on p. For p values below the critical probability p_c, the system is of ferromagnetic type, see Fig. 2a (left panel). For p values greater than p_c, the system is like the paramagnetic state in Ising model, Fig. 2c (right panel). When p approaches the critical probability, large clusters are formed in the lattice; see Fig. 2b (center panel). In order to obtain a quantitative charaterization of these observations, we have conducted a detailed analysis of critical exponents using finite size scaling theory.

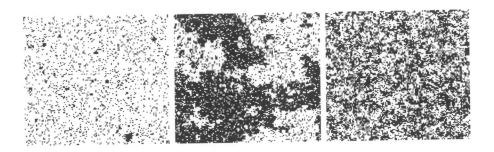

Fig. 2. Illustration of the three regimes. They correspond to the following states in Ising models: (a) $p = 0.11 < p_c$ - ferromagnetic; (b) $p = 0.13423 \approx p_c$ - critical; (c) $p = 0.20 > p_c$ - paramagnetic.

4.2 Estimation of Critical Probability and Critical Exponents

In addition to the magnetization, we introduce the susceptibility χ and the correlation length ξ. In the infinite-size limit, the following power laws are expected to hold:

$$m \sim (p - p_c)^\beta \ for \ p \geq p_c \tag{4}$$

$$\chi \sim |p - p_c|^{-\gamma} \ for \ p \to p_c \tag{5}$$

$$\xi \sim |p - p_c|^{-\nu} \ for \ p \to p_c \tag{6}$$

Finite size scaling theory tells us that the fourth order cumulants of the magnetization are expected to intersect each other at the unique point which is independent of lattice size L. The intersection of the curves determines the critical probability. For example, the fourth order cumulants are defined as

$$U(L,p) = \frac{\langle m^4 \rangle}{\langle m^2 \rangle^2} \tag{7}$$

where "$\langle \ \rangle$" means to take the average over all runs. We calculate $U(L,p)$ for several probabilities and for lattice sizes 45, 64, 91, 128. The critical probability estimated from their intersection points is 0.13423 ± 0.00002. For each RCA configuration, simulations run for $10^8 \sim 10^9$ steps, until they produced a steady

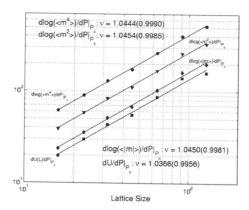

Fig. 3. The exponent of the correlation length is estimated by using finite size scaling theory. The correlation coefficient is displayed in the parenthesis followed the estimated exponent.

estimation of the fourth order cumulants. The critical exponent, which corresponds to the correlation length ξ, is estimated according to finite size scaling theory [26]:

$$\frac{dU_L}{dp}(p_c) \propto L^{\frac{1}{\nu}} \tag{8}$$

To estimate numerically the derivatives in Eq. 8, we fit four adjacent points with cubic interpolation. This approach has shown numerically precise and stable results [27]. The graphs are depicted in Fig. 3. The exponent were estimated using $\frac{dU}{dP}|_{P_c}$, $\frac{dlog(\langle|m|\rangle)}{dP}|_{P_c}$, $\frac{dlog(\langle m^2\rangle)}{dP}|_{P_c}$, and $\frac{dlog(\langle m^4\rangle)}{dP}|_{P_c}$. In the calculations, the previously determined value $p_c = 0.13423$ is used. The average value over all estimations has been used to obtain the final estimation of $\nu = 1.0429$. To estimate the remaining two exponents β and γ, we again apply finite size scaling theory. The results are given in Table 1. Finally, we evaluate the consistency of the estimation of the critical parameters. It is known that the identity function $2\beta+\gamma = 2\nu$ holds for Ising systems. Let us denote the difference between the left hand side and right hand size of the above equation as $I_{error} = 2\beta+\gamma-2\nu$. Table 1 includes calculations with Toom cellular automata TCA [27] and coupled map lattices CML [29].

Table 1. Comparison of RCA and several other models

	β	γ	ν	I_{error}
RCA	0.1308	1.8055	1.0429	0.02
TCA	0.12	1.59	0.85	0.13
Ising(2D)	0.125	1.75	1	-
CML	0.115	1.55	0.89	0.00

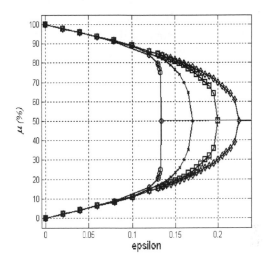

Fig. 4. Magnetization as the function of the noise level for various non-local topologies; circle - local; dot - 25% of sites have 1 nonlocal: 25%(1); square - 100%(1); diamond - 100%(4).

Table 2. Critical exponents for various connection patterns

	p_c	β	γ	ν	I_{error}
Local	0.1342	0.1308	1.8055	1.0429	0.02
25%(1)	0.1702	0.2262	1.4687	0.9760	0.03
100%(1)	0.2052	0.3943	1.0981	0.8780	0.13
100%(4)	0.2247	0.4141	0.9800	0.8759	0.06

5   Critical States in Non-local Random Cellular Automata

The introduction of non-local interaction is strongly biologically motivated. The neurons have most of their connections in their direct neighborhood, but they have also axonal links with other neurons outside of their surround. Clearly, axonal conductance plays an important role in actual neuronal circuits. We approximate long-range axons by replacing several local (direct neighbor) connections with new neighbors randomly selected from the whole lattice. During this rewiring process, each site maintains the same number of connections (4). Therefore, each time a site get a non-local neighbor, we cut out (randomly) one of its local neighbors. In the extreme case, when we cut out all 4 local neighbors of every site, we get an architecture that represents a mean field model.

Figure 4 shows the effect of non-local connections on the critical behavior. We observe critical p in models with non-local links. However, in accordance with the intuition, p_c becomes larger as the proportion of remote connections increases. The curves in Fig. 4 belong to models: local (circle), 25% of sites having one non-local link (dot), 100% of sites have one remote link (square), and all sites have all 4 connections remote (diamond). Table 2 includes the critical exponents obtained by the finite size scaling method for each model structure. It is interesting that the various exponents drastically deviate from the values represented by the Ising universality class. At the same time, the hyperscaling relationship remains valid to a significant degree.

6   Discussion and Conclusions

In this paper we have introduced the biologically motivated neuropercolation model. We have identified two critical parameters: the noise level, and the non-locality. Noise modeled the self-sustaining, randomized, steady state background brain activity is the source from which ordered states of macroscopic neural activity emerge, like the patterns of waves at the surfaces of deep bodies of water. Neural tissues, however, are not passive media, through which effects propagate like waves in water. The brain medium has an intimate relationship with the dynamics through a generally weak, subthreshold interaction of neurons. The synaptic interactions of neurons provide weak constraints on the participants, and the resulting covariance appears in the form of spatiotemporal pattern. In the framework of this research we use mathematical tools of percolation theory to explore the information processing mechanisms in brains as the randomized activity of myriads of neurons that provides the basis for self-organization and higher brain functions. The present works belong to the basic building block of our neurodynamic model based on K sets [30, 31]. This is the single KI layer of homogenous elements. A higher complexity level is represented by the KII model which has interacting excitatory and inhibitory populations. KII may exhibit nontrivial limit cycle and aperiodic oscillations. The interaction of several KII sets produces the KIII system with aperiodic spatio-temporal dynamics. KIII has the potential of spontaneous phase transitions propagating in space and time. Research in this direction is in progress.

References

1. Grossberg, S. (1988), Nonlinear Neural Networks: Principles, Mechanisms, and Architectures, Neural Networks, 1, 17-61
2. Hopfield, J.J., (1982), Neural networks and physical systems with emrgent collective computational abilities, Proc. National Academy of Sciences, USA, 79, 2554-2558
3. Elman, J.L. (1990), Finding structure in time, Cognitive Science, 14, 179-211
4. Chua, L.O., Hasler, M., Moschytz, M., Neirynck (1995) Autonomous cellular neural networks - A unified paradigm for pattern formation and active wave propagation, IEEE Trans. Circ. Syst. I - Fund. Th. Appl., 42, 559-577
5. Freeman, W.J. (1992) Tutorial on neurobiology - From single neurons to brain chaos, Int. J. Bifurcation & Chaos, 2(3), 451-482
6. Freeman, W.J. (1995) Societies of Brains, Mahwah, N.J., Lawrence Erlbaum.

7. Freeman, W.J. (1999) Noise-induced first order phase transitions in chaotic brain activity, Int. J. Bifurcation and Chaos, **9(11)**, 2215-2218.
8. Erdos, P. and Renyi A. (1960). On the evolution of random graphs, Publ. Math. Inst. Hung. Acad. Sci. **5**: 17-61
9. Bollobas, B., 1985, Random Graphs, 1985, London, Orlando, Academic Press
10. Freeman, W.J., Kozma, R., and Werbos, P. J., (2001). Biocomplexity - Adaptive Behavior in Complex Stochastic Dynamical Systems, BioSystems, **59**, 109-123
11. Kauffman, S. A. (1990), Requirements for evolvability in complex systems: orderly dynamics and frozen components, Physica D, **42**, 135-152
12. Grimmett, Geoffrey (1999) Percolation in Fundamental Principles of Mathematical Sciences, Spinger-Verlag, Berlin
13. Balister, P.N., Bollobas, B., and A. M. Stacey (2000) Dependent percolation in two dimensions, Probability Theory and Related Fields, **117(4)**, 495-513
14. Balister P., Bollobas, B., and A. Stacey (1993) Upper bounds for the critical probability of oriented percolation in two dimensions, Proc. Royal Soc., London Sr., A., **400**, no 1908, 202-220
15. Aizeman and Lebowitz (1988) Metastability effects in bootstrap percolation, Journal Phys. **A, 21**, 3801-3831.
16. Duarte, A.M.S. (1989) Simulation of a cellular automaton with an oriented bootstrap rule, Physica A, 157, 1075-1079
17. Adler, J., van Enter and J. A. Duarte (1990) Finite-size effects for some bootstrap percolatioin models, J. Statist. Phys, 60 322-332
18. Schonmann, R. (1992) On the behavior of some cellular automata related to bootstrap percolation, Ann. Probability, **20(1)**, 174-193
19. Cerf, R. and Cirillo, E.N., (1999) Finite size scaling in three-dimensional bootstrap percolation, Ann. Probab., **27(4)**, 1837-1850
20. Watts, D.J., Strogatz, S.H. (1998) Nature, **393**, 440
21. Moore, C., Newman, M.E.J. (2000) Epidemics and percolation in small-world networks, Phys. Rev. E, **61(5)**, 5678-5682
22. Newman, M.E.J., Jensen, I., Ziff, R.M. (2002) Percolation and epidemics in a two-dimensional small world, Phys. Rev. E, **65**, 021904, 1-7
23. Toom, A.L., N.B. Vasilyev, O.N. Stavskaya, L.G. Mityushin, G.L. Kurdyumov and S.A. Prigorov (1990) Discrete local Markov systems in Stochastic cellular systems:ergodicity, memory, morphogenesis; eds. R.L.Dobrushin, V.I.Kryukov and A.L.Toom, Manchester University Press
24. Balister., P., Bollobas, B., Kozma, R. (2003) Mean filed models of probabilistic cellular automata (revised, submitted)
25. Balister, P., Bollobas, B., Johnson, R., Walters, M. (2004) Majority percolation (submitted)
26. Binder, K. (1979) Monte Carlo Methods in Statistical Physics, Springer Verlag, Berlin Heidelberg
27. Makowiec, D. (1999) Stationary states of Toom cellular automata in simulations, Phys.Rev.E **60(4)**, 3787-3786
28. Kozma, R., Balister, P., Bollobas, B., Chen, H., Freeman, W.J. (2003) Analysis of scaling laws in local random cellular automata (submitted)
29. Marcq, P., Chate, H., Manneville, P. (1997) Universality in Ising-like phase transitions of lattices of coupled chaotic maps, Phys. Rev. E, **55(1)**, 2606-2629
30. Freeman, W.J. (1975) Mass action in the nervous system, Academic Press, N.Y.
31. Kozma, R. and Freeman, W.J. (2001), Chaotic Resonance - Methods and applications for robust classification of noisy and variable patterns, Int. J. Bifurcation & Chaos, **11(6)**, 1607-1629

The Use of Hybrid Cellular Automaton Models for Improving Cancer Therapy

B. Ribba[1,2], T. Alarcón[3,4], K. Marron[1], P.K. Maini[3], and Z. Agur[1]

[1] Institute for Medical BioMathematics, 10 Hate'ena Street, P.O.B. 282, 60991 Bene Ataroth, Israel
agur@imbm.org
[2] Present address: EA 3736 - Clinical Pharmacology Unit, Faculty of Medicine Laennec, Paradin Street, P.O.B. 8071, 69376 Lyon, France
b.ribba@upcl.univ-lyon1.fr
[3] Centre for Mathematical Biology, Mathematical Institute, University of Oxford, 24-29 St. Giles', Oxford OX1 3LB, United Kingdom
maini@maths.ox.ac.uk
[4] Present address: Bioinformatics Unit, Department of Computer Science, University College London, Gower Street, London WC1E 6BT, United Kingdom
t.alarcon@cs.ucl.ac.uk

Abstract. The Hybrid Cellular Automata (HCA) modelling framework can be an efficient approach to a number of biological problems, particularly those which involve the integration of multiple spatial and temporal scales. As such, HCA may become a key modelling tool in the development of the so-called integrative biology. In this paper, we first discuss HCA on a general level and then present results obtained when this approach was implemented in cancer research.

1 Introduction

Traditionally, mathematical modelling of biological problems has focused on the integration of the most crucial properties of the phenomenon under study into a model formulated in terms of continuum ordinary differential equations (ODEs) and/or partial differential equations (PDEs) [23]. However, these methods impose a significant restriction on the modelled system's time-scales.

Physiologically-structured models [11,6] are one of the many approaches proposed to cope with this problem. In this paper we will focus on the hybrid cellular automata (HCA), a multiple scale individual-based framework for modelling biological processes.

The paper is structured as follows. In Section 2, biological complexity and complexity in cancer are introduced as limitations to the traditional modelling approach. In Section 3, we give a general introduction to the HCA framework and its uses in biology, focusing on its integrative capabilities. In Section 4, we focus on a particular application of the HCA framework, namely evaluation of the efficiency of CHOP chemotherapy on non-Hodgkin's lymphoma.

P.M.A. Sloot, B. Chopard, and A.G. Hoekstra (Eds.): ACRI 2004, LNCS 3305, pp. 444–453, 2004.

2   Biological Complexity and Complexity in Cancer

Biological complexity has been recognized as a limitation to the current mathematical research approach, particularly in areas such as physiology, molecular biology and genetics [29]. Complexity in pathophysiology and therapeutics may be due in part to the diversity of the levels of our knowledge: gene, molecular, cellular, tissue, organ, body and population. All entities of a living organism interact through quantitative functional relations with time scales varying from nanoseconds to the organism's lifespan. This observation has led to the development of so-called systemic or integrative biology [16] and to the exploration of new methodologies [21], which might be more appropriate for studying complex and heterogeneous diseases such as cancer.

It is necessary to understand the many intricacies of cancer in order to design efficient treatment. Many approaches to anticancer treatment have had limited success. Certain biological properties of cancer render it even more problematic than other complex diseases. One fundamental obstacle to cancer therapy is acquired tumor "robustness", i.e. a self-organizing system which builds resistance to treatment [17]. Another feature is the multitude of intricate pathways for signal transduction. Though intermediates of multiple signalling pathways have been identified, understanding their function has proved to be an extremely difficult task [18]. The increasing evidence of cross-talk between pathways via signal transactivation adds an additional degree of complexity which is difficult to incorporate into traditional modelling approaches. Only fully integrative descriptive methods, capable of dealing with multiple scales, may assess disease and afford reliable treatment prediction. In this context, HCA models possess such capabilities.

3   HCA Modelling of Biological Processes

Cellular automata (CA) models have been applied to many areas of biology (see [14,22,1,4] for an overview). In recent years, a modification to the classic definition of CA has been introduced, yielding the so-called HCA.

The classic definition of CA involves only local rules for the evolution of the state of a given element: the transition rules that define the site dynamics depend only on the configuration of its spatial neighborhood. However, many biological processes depend upon non-local signalling cues or nutrients. Chemical cues and nutrients are usually diffusive substances, smaller than the typical cell.

Nutrient spatial distribution and various signalling processes play a fundamental role in tumor growth [12,24,5], as well as in developmental processes [20]. Therefore, in order to obtain an appropriate description of these processes in CA modelling, it is necessary to expand the original setup to incorporate these non-local effects. This expansion is the essence of the HCA framework, which constitutes a first step towards an integrative (multiple scale) approach to biology.

Given that molecules such as chemical cues and nutrients are usually small when compared to the size of a cell, they can be described in terms of continuous fields that evolve according to appropriate reaction-diffusion equations (RDEs). Signalling cues are secreted by the cell's internal machinery in response to either internal or external stimuli and feed back at the population level, altering the observed macroscopic pattern. The macroscopic structure of the vascular system affects the nutrient supply to the cells. In turn, nutrient levels modulate internal cellular processes such as cell division [6]. The HCA concept has recently been expanded to take into account such intra-cellular processes [6,25].

The HCA approach has been adopted to study various aspects of tumor growth. The model proposed in [12] is formulated as a two-dimensional HCA (or, more precisely a lattice-gas model) and reproduces many of the features of avascular tumors *in vitro*, e.g. their layer structure. In [24], a hybrid CA model of tumor growth in the presence of native vasculature is proposed to analyze the role of host vascular density and tumor metabolism on tumor growth. It seems that unlike normal cells, which use aerobic metabolism, tumor cell metabolism is glycolytic. One by-product of glycolysis is increased acidity. Since tumor cells are more resistant to acidity than their normal counterparts, it appears that cancer uses the glycolytic phenotype (which produces H^+ ions) in order to increase its invasiveness. Several results regarding the interplay between vessel density, increased acidity, and tumor progression were obtained in this study. One of the most significant conclusions is the existence of a sharp transition between states of initial tumor confinement and efficient invasiveness when H^+ production passes through a critical value. This phenomenon has been observed in the clinic [15]. Finally, studies proposed in [7,8] use HCA in order to obtain realistic models for blood flow dynamics.

Recently, HCA has been applied to study the effect of blood flow heterogeneity on tumor growth [5]. Oxygen reaches the tissues via the vascular system. Due to the highly complex nature of blood flow and its interaction with the structure of the vascular system, which is also affected by the metabolic needs of the surrounding tissue, blood flow appears to be highly heterogeneous. Consequently, the spatial distribution of blood-borne nutrients and drugs is also heterogeneous. This heterogeneity has significant implications on tumor growth [5] and therapy, as we will observe in the following sections.

In the next section, we will discuss a particular example of the application of HCA in order to evaluate the efficiency of current clinical protocols for CHOP therapy of non-Hodgkin's lymphoma.

4   CHOP Therapy for Non-Hodgkin's Lymphoma: Insights from an HCA Model

In this section, we present an application of HCA for assessing chemotherapy treatment for non-Hodgkin's lymphoma (NHL) [25].

NHL patients are currently treated with CHOP chemotherapy (Cyclophosphamide, Doxorubicin, Oncovin, Prednisone) in which Doxorubicin and Cyclophosphamide are the more active drugs [19]. CHOP is usually administered over a total of 6 to 8 cycles separated by 21-day intervals [10]. The relationship between this dosing interval and the efficiency of NHL CHOP treatment has not been systematically analyzed. However, theory suggests that the success of cancer chemotherapy is primarily determined by the frequency of drug administration [2,3].

4.1   Methods

A two-dimensional HCA-based mathematical model aimed at simulating the effect of Doxorubicin on NHL was developed. The model takes into account two key factors which influence the efficiency of drug delivery:

- coupling of NHL growth to the vascular network [31], which affects the structure of the blood vessels;
- blood flow heterogeneity which results from this diverse construction.

The domain corresponds to a 2 mm square tissue initially filled with NHL cells forming a random pattern, and composed of 110 vessels whose radii are subject to adaptation through vessel structural modification processes [5].

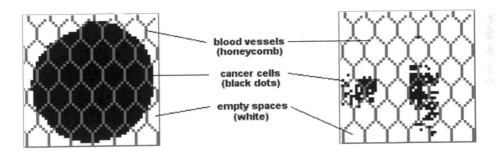

Fig. 1. Representation of NHL cells and the honeycomb-like vascular network on the computational domain (see [5]).
Left: a fully populated domain; Right: the domain following significant cell depletion.

The blood flow in each vessel is assumed to be laminar steady Poiseuille flow. For the dynamics of nutrient and drugs, the adiabatic approximation is applied, according to which chemicals (nutrient and drug) can be considered instantaneously in steady state. For drug pharmocokinetics (PK), i.e. decay of the blood-borne drug, a one-compartment model, in which the drug concentration in plasma over time declines exponentially, is considered. For drug pharmacodynamics (PD), i.e. effect of the extracellular concentration of drug on NHL cells, a simple logit relation is used for determining the probability for a cell to survive the drug. See the Appendix for the continuous model equations and [25] for further details.

The initial cell colony is composed of NHL cells divided into two categories: proliferative and quiescent cells.

To model cell division, a simple cell-cycle model is considered in which the duration of each phase of the cell-cycle was set according to various NHL-kinetic studies [9,13,27]. Each cell is assigned an age, which increases at each iteration. Thus, the cells progress through the different stages of the cell-cycle. Normal progression through the cell-cycle may be disrupted by lack of nutrient, leading to quiescence or cell death, or cells may be killed by the drug. A significant attribute of this model is the ability of the cell colony to influence vascular morphology. Normal vasculature is known to be well organized and endowed with smooth muscle cells and pericytes. This allows the vessels to adapt their structure to various mechanochemical stimuli [28]. Due to neovascularisation, cancer vessels are immature and therefore lack this structure. Consequently they are not able to undergo structural adaptation. Furthermore, cancer cells can destabilize established, mature vasculature, rendering it immature [31]. Therefore, in the model presented in [25] whenever a vessel is engulfed by cancer cells it is assumed that it loses its ability for adaptation and its radius is fixed at random. Vessels not surrounded by lymphoma cells retain the structural adaptation mechanism [5]. The status of all vessels (mature and immature) is updated at each time step.

The following CA rules hold for each cell and at each time step of the model.

- The probability of cell death is determined by the drug concentration and PD;
- If the cell is not killed by the drug, it advances one time step in its cycle phase;
- Between G1 and S-phase, the cell can either die, be arrested, or continue progressing through the cell cycle according to its local environment, i.e, local concentration of nutrient and over-crowdedness.
- If the environmental conditions are appropriate, the cell enters into G2 and divides, daughter cells moving towards higher nutrient concentrations.

4.2   Results

When the dynamics of a simulated NHL cell colony under CHOP chemotherapy were examined [25], a significant phenomenon was observed. After the initial effect of a drug application, the tumor begins to regrow at a steady and rapid rate. However, beyond a certain point, the cell colony's growth ceases to be stable and begins to display unpredictable oscillations of significant amplitude (see Figure 2). Blood flow heterogeneity appears to be a key factor in this result and its effect is illustrated in Figure 3, which compares cell recovery from a chemotherapy cycle when the vessel maturation/destabilization process is taken into account, compared to a case in which this assumption is relaxed [25]. Consequently, one of the conclusions from this study is that in order for treatment to be efficient, additional drug cycles must be administered before the tumor can enter the unstable stage of its regrowth. Note that we have considered a

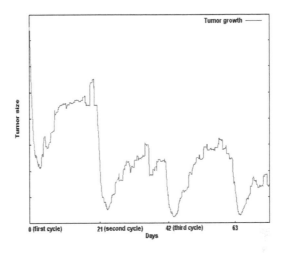

Fig. 2. Model prediction of tumor growth with Doxorubicin chemotherapy treatment cycles separated by 21 days.

regular hexagonal array of blood vessels which is unrealistic, in actual tumors the vasculature is very heterogeneous so we would expect the effects of blood flow heterogeneity to be even more pronounced.

The HCA framework has also been used to describe tumor structures in two pathophysiological settings in a study of which the purpose was to predict the efficacy of two different conventional strategies for chemotherapy intensification [26]. Results suggest the existence of a critical drug regimen intensity (CI) value, i.e. the ratio between the total dose administered and the duration of the treatment. If the regimen intensity is lower than CI, the tumor succeeds in recovering to its initial size over the duration of the dosing interval.

5   Conclusion

HCA can be viewed as an effective means of dealing with some of the problems raised by biological complexity. Through its ability to integrate different temporal and spatial scales, it constitutes a promising investigative tool for analyzing complex biological systems such as cancer and cancer therapy. In the example we presented, an HCA model has been used for investigating the efficacy of current and potential therapies of non-Hodgkin's lymphoma. Within the context of certain model assumptions, our results have raised relevant and interesting conclusions on the issue of treatment efficacy.

Acknowledgements. This work was carried out at the Institute for Medical Biomathematics, and was supported by the EU Research Training Network (5th

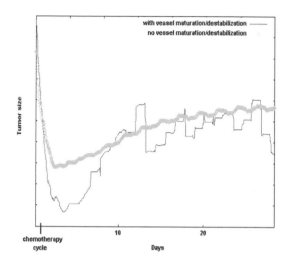

Fig. 3. Model prediction on the effect of vessel maturation/destabilization process on cell population recovery following a 10 mg/m^2 Doxorubicin administration.
Thin line: with vessel maturation/destabilization; Empty circles (thick line): no vessel maturation/destabilization is assumed.

Framework - HPRN-CT-2000-00105): "Using mathematical modelling and computer simulation to improve cancer therapy" and by the Chai Foundation. We wish to acknowledge particularly Prof Jean-Pierre Boissel for useful discussion regarding cancer complexity, Nitsan Dahan, Dr Vladimir Vainstain, Yuri Kogan and Vera Sleitzer for advices, Dr Helen Byrne for her involvement in the initial stages of the modelling and Dr Filippo Castiglione for valuable advice regarding the model implementation and exploitation.

References

1. Agur, Z.: Fixed points of majority rule cellular automata applied to plasticity and precision of the immune response. Complex. Systems. **5** (1991) 351-356
2. Agur, Z.: Randomness, synchrony and population persistence. J. Theor. Biol. **112** (1985) 677-693
3. Agur, Z., Arnon, R., Schechter, B.: Reduction of cytotoxicity to normal tissues by new regimens of phase-specific drugs. Math. Biosci. **92** (1988) 1-15
4. Mehr, R., Agur, Z.: Bone marrow regeneration under cytotoxic drug regimens: behaviour ranging from homeostasis to unpredictability in a model for hemopoietic differentiation. BioSystems. **26/4** (1991) 231-237
5. Alarcón, T., Byrne, H.M., Maini, P.K.: A cellular automaton model for tumour growth in inhomogeneous environment. J. Theor. Biol. **225** (2003) 257-274
6. Alarcón, T., Byrne, H.M., Maini, P.K.: A multiple scale model for tumour growth. SIAM Multiscale Modelling and Simulation. (2004) In press

7. Artoli, A.M.M, Hoekstra, A.G., Sloot, P.M.A.: Simulation of a Systolic Cycle in a Realistic Artery with the Lattice Boltzmann. BGK Method, International Journal of Modern Physics B, vol. 17, nr 1&2. World Scientific Publishing Company (2003) 95-98

8. Artoli, A.M.M, Hoekstra, A.G., Sloot, P.M.A.: Mesoscopic simulations of systolic flow in the Human abdominal aorta. Journal of Biomechanics. (2004)

9. Brons, P.P.T., Raemaekers, J.M., Bogman, M.J., van Erp, P.E., Boezeman, J.B., Pennings, A.H., Wessels, H.M., Haanen, C.: Cell cycle kinetics in malignant lymphoma studied with in vivo iodeoxyuridine administration, nuclear Ki-67 staining, and flow cytometry. Blood. **80** (1992) 2336-2343

10. Couderc, B., Dujols, J.P., Mokhtari, F., Norkowski, J.L., Slawinski, J.C., Schlaifer, D.: The management of adult aggressive non-Hodgkin's lymphomas. Crit. Rev. Oncol. Hematol. **35** (2000) 33-48

11. Crampin, E.J., Halstead, M., Hunter, P., Nielsen, P., Noble, D., Smith, N., Tawhai, M.: Computational physiology and the Physiome project. Exp. Physiol. **89** (2004) 1-26

12. Deutsch, A., Dormann, S.: Modelling of avascular tumour growth with a hybrid cellular automaton. In Silico Biol. **2** (2002) 1-14

13. Erlanson, M., Lindh, J., Zackrison, B., Landberg, G., Roos, G.: Cell kinetic analysis of non-Hodgkin's lymphomas using in vivo iodeoxyuridine incorporation and flow cytometry. Hematol. Oncol. **13** (1985) 207-217

14. Ermentrout, G.B., Edelstein-Keshet, L.: Cellular automata approaches to biological modeling. J. theor. Biol. **160** (1993) 97-133

15. Gatenby, R.A., Gawlinski, E.T.: A reaction-diffusion model of cancer invasion. Cancer. Res. **15** (1996) 5745-53

16. Kitano, H.: Systems biology: a brief overview. Science **295** (2002) 1662-4

17. Kitano, H.: Opinion: Cancer as a robust system: implications for anticancer therapy. Nat. Rev. Cancer. **3** (2004) 227-35

18. Lee, A.V., Schiff, R., Cui, X., Sachdev, D., Yee, D., Gilmore, A.P., Streuli, C.H., Oesterreich, S., Hadsell, D.L.: New mechanisms of signal transduction inhibitor action: receptor tyrosine kinase down-regulation and blockade of signal transactivation. Clin. Cancer. Res. **9** (2003) 516S-23S

19. Lepage, E., Gisselbrecht, C., Haioun, C., Sebban, C., Tilly, H., Bosly, A., Morel, P., Herbrecht, R., Reyes, F., Coiffier, B.: Prognostic significance of received relative dose intensity in non-Hodgkin's lymphoma patients: application to LNH-87 protocol. The GELA. (Groupe d'Etude des Lymphomes de l'Adulte). Ann. Oncol. **4** (1993) 651-6

20. Maree, A.F.M., Hogeweg, P.: How amoeboids self-organize into a fruiting body: Multicellular coordination in Dictyostelium discoideum. Proc. Nat. Acad. Sci. **98** (2001) 3879-3883

21. McCulloch, A.D., Huber, G.: Integrative biological modelling in silico. 'In silico' simulation of biological processes. Novartis Foundation Symposium 247. Ed Bock G & Goode JA. John Wiley & Sons, London (2002) 4-19

22. Moreira, J., Deutsch, A.: Cellular automaton models of tumour development: a critical review. Adv. Complex Sys. **5** (2001) 247-267

23. Murray, J.D.: Mathematical Biology. Springer, New York (2003)

24. Patel, A.A., Gawlinski, E.T., Lemieux, S.K., Gatenby, R.A.: A cellular automaton model of early tumour growth and invasion: The effects of native tissue vascularity and increased anaerobic tumour metabolism. J. theor. Biol. **213** (2001) 315-331

25. Ribba, B., Marron, K., Alarcón, T., Maini, P.K., Agur, Z.: A mathematical model of Doxorubicin treatment efficacy on non-Hodgkin's lymphoma: Investigation of current protocol through theoretical modelling result. Bull. Math. Biol. (2004) In press

26. Ribba, B., Dahan, N., Vainstein, V., Kogan, Y., Marron, K., Agur, Z.: Doxorubicin efficiency in residual non-Hodgkin's lymphoma disease: towards a computationally supported treatment improvement. In preparation.

27. Stokke, T., Holte, H., Smedshammer, L., Smeland, E.B., Kaalhus, O., Steen, H.B.: Proliferation and apoptosis in malignant and normal cells in B-cell non-Hodgkin's lymphomas. Br. J. Cancer. **77** (1988) 1832-1838

28. Pries, A.R., Secomb, T.W., Gaehtgens, P.: Structural adaptation and stability of microvascular networks: theory and simulations. Am. J. Physiol. **275** (1998) H349-H360

29. Wheng, G., Bhalla, U.S., Iyengar, R.: Complexity in biological signaling systems. Science. **284** (1999) 92-6

30. Willemse, F., Nap, M., de Bruijn, H.W.A., Holleman, H.: Quantification of vascular density and of lumen and vessel morphology in endometrial carcinoma. Evaluation of their relation to serum levels of tissue polypeptide-specific antigen and CA-125. Anal. Quant. Cytol. Histol. **19** (1997) 1-7

31. Yancopoulos, G.D., Davis, A., Gale, N.W., Rudge, J.S., Wiegand,S.J., Holash, J.: Vascular specific growth factors and blood vessel formation. Nature. **407** (2000) 242-8

A   HCA Model Equations

A.1   Blood Flow

Assuming Poiseuille flow, the flow rate $(\dot{Q})$ and resistance (Z) in each vessel are given respectively by:

$$\dot{Q} = \frac{\Delta P}{Z} \tag{1}$$

$$Z = \frac{8\mu(r,H)L}{\pi r^4} \tag{2}$$

where ΔP is the pressure drop between two points of the network, L, r, and H are respectively the resistance, length, radius, and hematocrit. μ is the radius and hematocrit dependent viscosity [5].

A.2   Vessel Structural Modification

We assume that the radius of each immature vessel (r_{im}) is modified at each time step according to the equation:

$$r_{im} = r_{mat} \cdot (1 + \epsilon) \tag{3}$$

where r_{mat} is the initial radius of the mature vessels, and ϵ is a random number uniformly distributed in the interval $(0,3)$ according to [30].

A.3   Nutrient and Drug Diffusion

Assuming adiabatic conditions, the diffusion equation for the concentration $(C(x, y, t))$ of nutrient or drugs is given by:

$$K\nabla^2 C(x, y, t) - q(x, y) \cdot C(x, y, t) = 0 \tag{4}$$

where K is a diffusion coefficient and $q(x, y)$ the uptake coefficient at position (x, y).

On the vessel walls, we impose the boundary conditions:

$$- K\mathbf{n_w} \cdot \nabla C(x, y, t) = P \cdot (C_b - C) \tag{5}$$

where $\mathbf{n_w}$ is the unit vector, orthogonal to the vessel wall, C_b is the drug or nutrient concentration in the blood, and P the permeability of the vessel.

On the edges of the computational domain we impose no-flux boundary conditions:

$$n|_{\partial\Omega} \cdot \nabla C(x, y, t) = 0 \tag{6}$$

where $n|_{\partial\Omega}$ is the unit outward vector, orthogonal to the boundary of the domain.

A.4   Doxorubicin PK/PD

The decline of drug concentration in plasma (C_b) is given by:

$$\frac{\partial C_b}{\partial t} = -k \cdot C_b(t) \tag{7}$$

with initial condition:

$$C_b(0) = \frac{dose}{V_d} \tag{8}$$

where V_d is the volume of distribution of the drug, and k the fraction of drug which is eliminated from the compartment per unit time, inversely related to the half-life $t_{1/2}$:

$$k = \frac{ln(2)}{t_{1/2}} \tag{9}$$

The survival fraction SF (percentage of cells that survives the drug at each time step) is given by:

$$SF = \frac{a \cdot C_b(t)}{C_b(t) + Ec_{1/2}} \tag{10}$$

where $C_b(t)$ is the relevant drug concentration and a, $Ec_{1/2}$ are constants. See [25] for model parameters and further details.

A Stochastic Model of the Effector
T Cell Lifecycle

John Burns[1,2] and Heather J. Ruskin[1]

[1] School of Computing, Dublin City University, Dublin 9, Ireland
[2] Department of Computing, Institute of Technology Tallaght,
Dublin 24, Ireland
jburns@computing.dcu.ie

Abstract. The dynamics of immune response to initial infection and
reinfection by the same pathogen sometime later, are considerably different. Primary response, which follows initial infection, is characterised
by relatively slow precursor cell activation and population growth rates,
with a consequent elongated pathogen clearance profile, typically extended over six days or more. On the other hand, secondary response (to
reinfection by the same pathogen some time later) is notable for short
effector activation time, high specificity of response, rapid pathogen elimination and high degree of memory cell participation. In this paper, we
present a seven state non-deterministic finite automata (NFA) of the effector T cell lifecycle, which is encoded as a set of states and state transitions. Our objective is to study the degree to which variable infection
outcome is dependent on the accumulation of *chance* events. Such chance
events may be represented as the consequence of premature, delayed or
even failed state transitions. We show how small variation in crucial state
transitions probabilities during the lifecycle can induce widely variable
infection outcomes. This model is implemented as a spatially extended,
concurrent two-dimensional stochastic cellular automata, executing on a
MPI-based Linux cluster.

1 Introduction

Cellular Automata (CA) have been applied to numerous areas of complex physical systems modelling [1]. CA have several important characteristics which make
them amenable to efficient computational implementation, including ease of representing (in the form of n-dimensional arrays), discrete nature of the underlying computations, simplicity of rules or laws which are programmed into the
CA, and the highly repetitive nature of the processing steps. However, cellular automata posses additional fascinating properties, for example, patterns of
self-organisation of a complexity which cannot be derived numerically from the
rules on which the underling cellular automata is based. As a result of this complexity, [2] has postulated that some form of CA must underlie many complex
physical phenomena visible in nature. Furthermore, with the application of non-
deterministic (*stochastic*) cellular automata, the idea of randomness in CA site

P.M.A. Sloot, B. Chopard, and A.G. Hoekstra (Eds.): ACRI 2004, LNCS 3305, pp. 454–463, 2004.
© Springer-Verlag Berlin Heidelberg 2004

selection and update rule enforcement has yielded further insight into modelling stochastic natural systems such as molecular motion, turbulence in water flow and various biological processes, especially models of the human immune system [3,4,5,6,7]. In this paper we present an approach that seeks to avoid a computational modelling process exclusively influenced by current experimental immune system research trends. We propose a *relaxation* of the deterministic assumptions inherent in earlier work [8], and explore the dynamics of a more stochastic system. Stochastic events appear to play a crucial role in certain immune system functions [9]. The contribution of this work is as follows: (i) an extended non-deterministic state transition model of the effector T cell lifecycle is introduced. This model successfully reproduces time-realistic effector and pathogen population dynamics during primary and secondary response, and during repeated reinfection, (ii) we identify three stages in the effector T cell lifecycle model which are critical in regulating the course of primary and secondary response, and (iii) the model is implemented as a spatially extended two-dimensional cellular automata lattice executing concurrently on a MPI-based Linux cluster. This allows us to scale the model to cell density levels in the order of 10^6 CTL cells - which approaches levels typically observed in *in-vivo* murine experiments. This work is arranged as follows: section 2 is a brief overview of some key features of the adaptive immune response which we model, and serves as an introduction to some specific terminology. Section 2 is intended for readers who may be unfamiliar with general principles of immunology. Section 3 discusses the model structure and explains the motivation and implementation of the underlying non-deterministic cellular automata. Section 4 presents results of the simulation, and in particular, some interesting features which emerge. Finally, section 5 is a discussion of the results, and an outline of further enhancements.

2   Adaptive Immune Response

Common to all immune systems is the principal of sensing of localised space for the purposes of intrusion detection. Intrusion, in this case, is the appearance of a bacteria, viral particle or infected cell which may be classified as *non-self*. Any non-self genetic material discovered must be eliminated in order to prevent infection (or even death), of the host. Broadly speaking, the means by which the non-self intruder gained access to the blood stream or lymphatic compartments is not of interest[1]. There are a great variety in the pathogen challenge and immune response course (not all of which are a concern here). One such scenario arises as follows: when a viral particle has been taken up by an antigen-presenting cell (APC), such as a dendritic cell, it is degraded into one or more peptide chains within the cytosol region of the APC, and is then bound to the major histocompatible complex (MHC) class I molecule (a process known as *antigen processing*) before finally being presented on the surface of the APC as

---

[1] Some viruses, for example, the influenza and corona viruses, enter the host through the air passages and not through tissue damage.

an MHC:peptide complex, a process known as *antigen presenting*. APC will recirculate through the lymphatic system in order to alert the immune system to an infection. Sensing of the lymphatic compartments (of which there are many) for antigen-presenting cells, is a systematic function of immune cell (lymphocyte) recirculation. Cytotoxic lymphocyte (CTL) precursor cells constantly recirculate and sample their environment in the search for foreign pathogens. The process of sampling involves two cells binding for some small time period, during which the immune cell senses the receptor of the bound cell to determine if the bound cell is an invading pathogen (or not). If the bound cell *is* an invading pathogen, the immune cell may be stimulated to produce clones of itself in order to attack and remove other cells bearing the same genetic material. Under normal circumstances, the production of clones ceases after some fixed period of time, and once the infection has been cleared, most CTL cells will undergo programmed death (apoptosis). A small subset of the clone population will remain activated indefinitely, and this population represents effector memory. In the presented here, we do not model free antigen, but only antigen epitopes which have been bound to the surface of an antigen presenting cell.

3   The Model

Our model runs in discrete 30-minute timesteps, and all entities in the model act asynchronously at each timestep (τ). As primary response normally consists of 4 days of cell replication (clonal expansion), the cells in our model will stop dividing at $\tau = 192$. The recirculation space of the lymphatic compartment is modelled as a two dimensional stochastic cellular automata lattice of length $L = 10^3$, with periodic boundary conditions and neighbourhood radius $r = 1$ (in two-dimensions), with a maximum of 8 neighbours. Each site is selected at random for update during the timestep. Not every site is will be visited at each timestep, but each site can be updated at most once in any given timestep. At $\tau = 0$ some 5000 antigen entities are introduced into randomly selected sites on the lattice (following a uniform distribution), and the model executes until $\tau = 3000$ (62.5 days of elapsed time). The CTL population grows exponentially in response to APC stimulation, with a clonal expansion rate which is a function of the *affinity* between the CTL and APC. The dynamics of affinity are modelled using shape space [10,11]. The stimulation rate never exceeding 0.036, which yields a population of daughter clones of ~ 1000 after 4.5 days of clonal expansion. Each lattice site may contain only one entity at any given timestep. The set of entities and states supported is shown in Table 1, which also introduces some important notation used throughout this paper.

3.1   Non-deterministic Finite Automata

To allow the study of a *distribution* of possible outcomes, we identify a subset of the CTL lifecycle state transitions, and replace the certainty of a transition from state w to state v on event e with some probability (< 1) of state transition.

Let us start by defining what is meant by state transition relaxation: If X is a discrete random variable (drv) representing the transition from state w to state v, and e is some event linking wv, the relaxed state transition X_r is:

$$P(X_r|e) = 0 \leq \psi \leq 1 \tag{1}$$

The choice of value for ψ will naturally depend on the wv in question. In contrast to earlier models [2], Eq. (1) implies *duality* in the presence of event e: transition on e (X_r) or not $(\bar{X}_r)$. This extension results in a *non-deterministic finite automaton* (NFA) [12]. Fig. (1) is a non-deterministic finite automata model of the lifecycle of the CTL (and follows notation explained in Table 1). E is the set of events the model, and consists of both deterministic and non-deterministic elements. We define a subset of three critical non-deterministic events $S \subset E$ as: $S = \{e_{2,8}, e_3, e_5\}$. Each $e_i \in S$ is defined as follows:

e_2, e_8 An infected antigen presenting cell will be destroyed by a bound cytotoxic lymphocyte cell which recognises it. Recognition is a function of the distance between the two cells in shape space.

e_3 An activated proliferating immune cell (state $ctl^{+\star}$) will normally end clonal expansion on the event $\langle e_3 : age(ctl^{+\star}) > 192 \rangle$.

e_6 The fraction of effector T cells entering the long-lived memory pool. Normally the majority of activated effector cells undergo programmed cell death (apoptosis) at the end of primary response. However, recruitment to the memory pool consumes around $5 - 10\%$ of activated CTL [13,14, 15], thus, a further stochastic transition occurs on e_6, with of $ctl^{+\dagger}$ enter $ctl^{+\bullet}$ on event $\langle e_6 : age(ctl^{+\dagger}) \geq 192 \rangle$.

e_{rpt} Repeated reinfection events, resulting in repeated doses of infected antigen presenting cells introduced into the simulation, at timestep $\tau + 300n, n = 0, 1, ..., 9$.

Each of the above events (e_n) has an associated probability ψ_n. The set $\{\psi_1, \psi_2, \psi_3, \psi_4\}$, therefore fully describes each simulation configuration of the model (all other parameters being kept constant). In the results presented in the following section, we define the following four experimental onfigurations of $\mathcal{P}$:

1. $\mathcal{P}_1 : \{0.9, 0.9, 0.9, 0.0\}$
2. $\mathcal{P}_2 : \{0.9, 0.9, 0.95, 0.0\}$
3. $\mathcal{P}_3 : \{0.9, 0.9, 0.9, 1\}$
4. $\mathcal{P}_4 : \{0.9, 0.9, 0.95, 1\}$

The first two configurations of $\mathcal{P}$ test the fidelity of the model response when confronted with a singular secondary infection event some 30 days after the initial infection. The first configuration represents a normal response and is intended to calibrate the model for near optimal conditions. For $\mathcal{P}_1$, we would expect to see CTL production levels broadly characterised by low, elongated peak for primary infection, followed by an increase in memory CTL. Another expected observation

---

[2] in that $P(X_r|e) = 1$

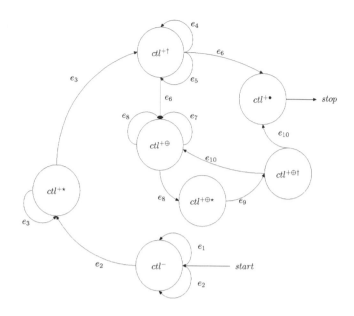

Fig. 1. A seven-state non-deterministic finite automata of the cytotoxic lymphocyte cell lifecycle. Transition events (e_n), which carry the same label, are *non-deterministic*.

is APC clearance: over some $6 - 10$ days for primary response, and significantly faster during secondary response. The second configuration is an increase in ψ_3 from 0.9 to 0.95 and is intended to test the impact of a 5% decline in the number of cells which transition to the effector memory state $(ctl^{+\dagger} \rightarrow ctl^{+\oplus})$. Some viral infections are known to case damage or loss of the memory pool [16], and we test to see the impact this has on our model. We test repeated reinfection with normal and depleted memory cell production ($\mathcal{P}_3$ and $\mathcal{P}_4$, respectively). Many pathogens are known to lead to acute and persistent viral infections, and we test the importance of memory cell production in these cases. Again we deplete the memory production by 5% and study the consequences of this loss. Section 4.1 examines the results of persistent infection in our model.

4   Results

The model is initially executed with parameter set $\mathcal{P}_1$ and $\mathcal{P}_2$ (with no repeat reinfection), and the results are shown in Fig. 2. In (a), the initial infection is visible at $\tau = 0$ with pathogen density $p_d = 5000$, (the broken line) and consequent effector response reaching a maximum value at $\tau = 300$, with $e_d = 8.2 \times 10^3$. Fig. 2(b) shows the antigen presenting cell population level (only). No memory cells are present during primary response, and as such, the effector cell population is made up entirely of clones produced by stimulated precursor cells. To the right of each effector cell peak is a plateau of memory cells. The slope of the CTL density peak is extreme, indicating that the state transitions

Table 1. Notation and definition of model entity states

Notation	Definition
ctl^-	naive recirculating effector precursor
$ctl^{+\star}$	proliferating lymphocyte
$ctl^{+\bullet}$	dead activated lymphocyte (apoptosis)
$ctl^{+\oplus}$	activated memory effector
$ctl^{+\oplus\star}$	activated proliferating memory effector
$ctl^{+\oplus\dagger}$	activated memory effector
$ctl^{+\dagger}$	armed activated effector
apc^+	active infected antigen presenting cell
$apc^{+\bullet}$	dead infected antigen presenting cell

from $ctl^{+\star}$ to $ctl^{+\dagger}$ to $ctl^{+\oplus}$ (or $ctl^{+\bullet}$) occurring with a high degree of certainty. At time $\tau = 1500$ (day 31), secondary exposure to the same pathogen occurs, and the model exhibits following general behaviour: (i) the secondary immune response is preceeded by a pool of committed CTL memory cells which have already been primed to respond to the re-appearing pathogen, (ii) the activated CTL density is some 10 times higher than primary response, and does not last as long, and (iii) the pathogen is reduced to half its original level much more rapidly than during primary response. With $\mathcal{P}_1$, the model exhibits efficient detection and clearance behaviour associated with a healthy immune system. From Fig. 2, it can be seen the advantage in both time and infected cell clearance which is conferred on a response based largely on memory: the half life of the virus during primary response is around 3.25 days, with 90% pathogen clearance achieved at around $\tau = 480$, or 10 days of simulation time. Compared to secondary response on reinfection we see an infected cell half life of $\tau \approx 60$ or 1.25 days - an efficiency of around 87%. Effectively, this is because memory cells, having already been primed by a previous encounter with the specific pathogen, undergo expansion with lower death rates than during primary response: they therefore accumulate more quickly [17]. The results for $\mathcal{P}_2$ are shown in Fig. 2(c) and (d). Here, the probability of entering apoptosis is increased from 0.9 to 0.95. This means that the memory cell population would be around 5% of that activated effector population post-primary response. Recent work (notably [17]) has shown that some $\approx 90\%$ of activated effector undergo apoptosis after primary response. Therefore, $\psi_3 = 0.95$ would represent an unusually high suppression of memory function. Clearly, the reduction of memory effector production should not effect primary response, and this is borne out by CTL density levels prior to $\tau = 1500$ (c). We see a normal 10-day clearance regime (d) during primary response, but a less effective response during reinfection: in fact, the memory cell pool in the time range $500 \leq \tau \leq 1500$ has fallen to ≈ 500. Once reinfection occurs, the APC

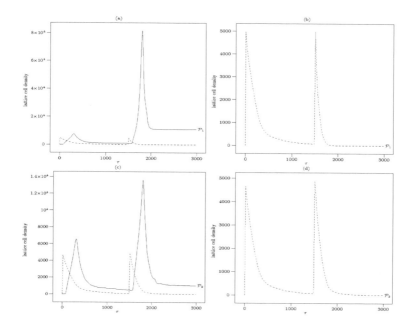

Fig. 2. CTL and pathogen lattice density levels (a),(c) over a simulated 62.5 day period, with an initial infection at time $\tau = 0$ and a reinfection by the same pathogen occurring at $\tau = 1500$, for 3 values of $\mathcal{P}$. Antigen presenting cell (APC) density is shown by the broken line, with the solid line indicating levels of effector memory and activated cells combined. For clarity, (b),(d) show population levels for APC for each $\mathcal{P}$.

population is cleared some 31% more effectively than during primary response. The APC half life is $\tau = 108$, 90% clearance is achieved after reinfection at $\tau \approx 1788$ (or some 5.9 days of simulated time). However, the characteristics of $\mathcal{P}_2$ are significantly degraded compared to that observed in $\mathcal{P}_1$.

4.1   Persistent Reinfection

Some viral pathogens are capable of persistent reinfection, in that, although population levels of infected antigen presenting cells may decline in response to clearance pressure by a specific CTL response, over time, the number of infected cells rises to chronic and sometimes acute levels. Examples of such viruses are HIV, HTLV, hepatitis C (HCV), hepatitis B virus, CMV EBV and rubella [16]. Such persistent reinfection pathogens have been associated with normal immune function suppression. In this section, we simulate persistent reinfection by randomly scattering a repeat 'dose' of the pathogen, introduced at $\tau + 300n, n = 0, 1, ..., 9$. This reinfection pattern is a represents a resurgence of infected cells every 6.25 days, in discrete bursts. The results of this simulation are shown in Fig. 3.

With respect to Fig. 3 (a), the response to the first reinfection is clearly strong: some 3.8×10^5 lymphocytes are generated and the reinfection is rapidly

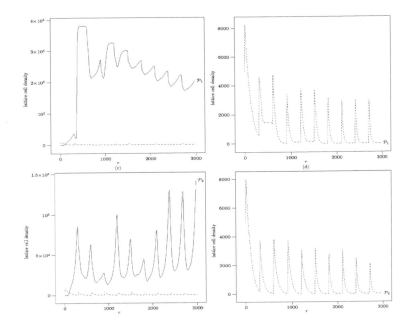

Fig. 3. The model is exposed to repeated infection events, arising at time $\tau = 300n, n = 0, 1, ..., 9$, equivalent to an infection every 6 days.

eliminated. As further infections arise starting at $\tau = 600$, the existing memory pool never falls below 1.8×10^5, and is critical in bringing the repeated reinfections under control in time periods (b) which rarely exceed 130 timesteps (or 2.8 days of simulated time). We also see from (a) that slightly lower responses are sufficient in order to effect optimal clearance. Results from (a) and (b) support the clinical findings that the memory cell levels tends to be higher after secondary and tertiary infections [17], which in turn, supports the clinical practice of vaccination boosting. Finally, when the simulation is executed with diminished memory cell creation and repeatedly stressed with reinfection ($\mathcal{P}_4$), average primary and secondary response levels are similar (around 1.2×10^4). Each response is characterised by rapid expansion and reduction of effector lymphocyte clones. There are no memory cells to confer clearance advantage, and each response is initiated from low levels (around 1.2×10^2).

5   Discussion and Conclusions

The approach taken in this research was to construct a stochastic model of the effector T cell lifecycle, in order to study a distribution of possible simulation outcomes. We have shown how the model reproduces well the time and space dynamics of initial and secondary infection. In addition, we believe the research is valuable in modelling the relationship between repeated reinfection and effector cell transition to memory or apoptosis. We have demonstrated how repeated reinfection can be controlled only within a limited range of ψ_3: too much memory causes the lymphatic compartment to fill-up, too little memory induces the need for clonal expansion from naive precursor cells, and a elongated APC clearance profile. When the ratio of apoptosis to memory is 'just right' ($0.88 \leq \psi_3 \leq 0.92$), antigen presenting cell levels (during repeated reinfection) are brought under control in increasingly rapid time frames. The next steps in this research are to test the homeostasis of our model: where does the model break down, and what insight does this provide. Very recent clinical work [16] suggests that the immune system must periodically preferentially eliminate some memory cells which exhibit poor cross-reactivity. One of the benefits of the the stochastic effector T cell lifecycle model presented here is the relative ease with which this theory could be investigated. The benefits of selective memory cells reduction may form the basis of further work with this model.

References

1. Wolfram, S.: Cellular Automata as Simple Self-Organizing Systems. Nature **1** (1982) 1
2. Wolfram, S.: A New Kind of Science. Wolfram Media (2001)
3. Stauffer, D., Pandey, R.B.: Immunologically motivated simulation of cellular automata. Computers in Physics **6** (1992) 404
4. Castiglione, F., Bernaschi, M., Succi, S.: Simulating the Immune Response on a Distributed Parallel Computer. Int. J. Mod. Phys. **8** (1997) 527
5. Mannion, R., Ruskin, H., Pandey, R.: Effect of Mutation on Helper T-cells and Viral Population: A Computer Simulation Model for HIV. Theor. in Biosci. **199(2)** (2000) 145–155
6. dos Santos, R.M.Z., Coutinho, S.: Dynamics of HIV Infection: A Cellular Automata Approach. Phys. Rev. Lett. **87** (2001) 168102
7. Bernaschi, M., Castiglione, F.: Design and implementation of an immune system simulator. Computers in Biology and Medicine **31** (2001) 303–331
8. Burns, J., Ruskin, H.J.: Network Topology in Immune System Shape Space. In Sloot, P., Gorbachev, Y., eds.: Computational Science - ICCS 2004. Volume 3038 of Lecture Notes in Computer Science., Berlin Heidelberg, Springer-Verlag (2004) 1094–1101
9. Germain, R.N.: The Art of the Probable: System Control in the Adaptive Immune System. Science **293** (2001) 240–245
10. Perelson, A.S., Oster, G.F.: Theoretical Studies of Clonal Selection: Minimal Antibody Repertoire Size and Reliability of Self-Non-Self Discrimination. J.Theor. Biol. **81(4)** (1979) 645–70
11. Burns, J., Ruskin, H.J.: Diversity Emergence and Dynamics During Primary Immune Response: A Shape Space, Physical Space Model. Theor. in Biosci. **123(2)** (2004) 183–194
12. Hopcroft, J.E., Ullman, J.D.: Introduction to Automata Theory, Languages and Computation. Addison Wesley (1979)
13. Murali-Krishna, K., Lau, L.L., Sambhara, S., Lemonnier, F., Altman, J., Ahmed, R.: Persistence of Memory CD8 T Cells in MHC Class I-Deficient Mice. J. Exp. Med. **286** (1999) 1377–1381

14. De Boer, R.J., Oprea, M., Kaja, R.A., Murali-Krishna, Ahmed, R., Perelson, A.S.: Recruitment Times, Proliferation, and Apoptosis Rates during the $CD8^+$ T-Cell Response to Lymphocytic Choriomeningitis Virus. J. Virol. **75(22)** (2001) 10663–10669
15. Badovinac, V.P., Porter, B.B., Harty, J.T.: CD8+ T cell contraction is controlled by early inflammation. Nat. Immunol. **5** (2004) 809–817
16. Kim, S., Walsh, R.: Comprehensive early and lasting loss of memory CD8 T cells and functional memory during acute and persistent viral infections. J. Immunol. **172(5)** (2004) 3139–3150
17. Grayson, J., Harrington, L., Lanier, J., Wherry, E., Ahmed, R.: Differential Sensitivity of Naive and Memory CD8+ T cells to Apoptosis in Vivo. J. Immunol. **169(7)** (2002) 3760–3770

A Cellular Automata Model of Population Infected by Periodic Plague

Witold Dzwinel

AGH Institute of Computer Science, Al. Mickiewicza 30, 30-059 Krakow, Poland
dzwinel@agh.edu.pl

Abstract. Evolution of a population consisting of individuals, each holding a unique "genetic code", is modeled on the 2D cellular automata lattice. The "genetic code" represents three episodes of life: the "youth", the "maturity" and the "old age". Only the "mature" individuals can procreate. Durations of the life-episodes are variable and are modified due to evolution. We show that the "genetic codes" of individuals self-adapt to environmental conditions in such a way that the entire ensemble has the greatest chance to survive. For a stable environment, the "youth" and the "mature" periods extend extremely during evolution, while the "old age" remains short and insignificant. The unstable environment is modeled by periodic plagues, which attacks the colony. For strong plaques the "young" individuals vanishes while the length of the "old age" period extends. We concluded that while the "maturity" period decides about the reproductive power of the population, the idle life-episodes set up the control mechanisms allowing for self-adaptation of the population to hostile environment. The "youth" accumulates reproductive resources while the "old age" accumulates the space required for reproduction.

1 Introduction

The cellular automata paradigm is a perfect computational platform for modeling evolving population. It defines both the communication medium for the agents and the living space. Assuming the lack of individual features, which diversify the population, the modeled system adapts to the unstable environment, developing variety of spatially correlated patterns (see e.g. [1-3]). Formation of patterns of well-defined multi-resolutional structures can be viewed as the result of a complex exchange of information between individuals and the whole population.

Another type of correlations - correlations in the feature space - emerges for the models of populations in which each individual holds a unique feature vector evolving along with the entire system [4]. The aging is one of the most interesting puzzles of evolution, which can be investigated using this kind of models.

It is widely known that the aging process is mainly determined by the genetic and environmental features. The most of computational models of aging involving genetic factor are based on the famous Penna paradigm [5,6]. This model uses the theory of accumulation, which says that destructive mutations - which consequences depend on the age of individual - can be inherited by the following generations and are accumu

P.M.A. Sloot, B. Chopard, and A.G. Hoekstra (Eds.): ACRI 2004, LNCS 3305, pp. 464–473, 2004.

lated in their genomes. The Penna model suffers from the following important limitations.

1. The location of the individuals in space is neglected, thus the system evolves in spatially uncorrelated environment with unbounded resources.
2. Only two episodes of life are considered, i.e., the "youth" and the "maturity". The durations of the two are the same for each individual. The "old age" is neglected.

In this paper we propose a new model, complementary to the Penna paradigm. It does not consider genetic mutations. Instead, it allows for studying the influence of environmental factors on the aging process.

The paper is constructed as follows. First, we describe our algorithm, its principal assumptions and implementation details. In the following section we discuss the results of evolution and self-adaptation of population to the hostile environment represented by periodic plaques. Finally, our findings are summarized.

2   CA Model of Evolution

Let us assume that an ensemble of $S(t)$ individuals is spread on 2D $N{\times}N$ mesh of cellular automata (CA). The mesh is periodic. Each individual, residing in (i,j) node, is equipped with a binary chain – the "genetic code" - of length L. The length and the number of "1"s in the chain correspond to the maximal and actual life-time of individual, respectively. Only "1"s from "genetic codes" of each individual are read one by one along with the evolution while "0"s are skipped. Afterwards the last "1" has been read, the individual is deleted from the lattice. The individuals are treated as independent agents, which can move and reproduce according to recombination (*cross-over*) operator from the genetic algorithms. The code chain consists of three sub-chains corresponding to three episodes of life: the "youth" **y**, the "maturity" **m** and the "old age" **o**. They do not represent biological age of individuals, but reflect their reproduction ability. Only the "mature" individuals from the Moore neighborhood [7] of an *unoccupied* node of CA lattice are able to reproduce. Every individual can move randomly on CA lattice if there is a free space in its closest neighborhood.

Let $\mathbf{A} = \{a_{ij}\}_{N{\times}N}$ is the array of possible locations of individuals on the 2D $N{\times}N$ lattice of the cellular automata. The value of $a_{ij} \in \Re$, $\Re=\{0,1\}$, where "0" means that the node is "*unoccupied*" and "1" that it is "*occupied*". An individual is defined by corresponding "genetic code" $\alpha_{ij} \in \Re^L$ such that:

---

if $(a_{ij} = 1)$ then $(i,j) \rightarrow$ '*is occupied*';

$\alpha_{ij} \rightarrow [\mathbf{y}_{ij}, \mathbf{m}_{ij}, \mathbf{o}_{ij}]$;

$\mathbf{y}_{ij} \rightarrow [y_{ij}^1, y_{ij}^2, ..., y_{ij}^l]$, $\mathbf{m}_{ij} \rightarrow [m_{ij}^1, m_{ij}^2, ..., m_{ij}^m]$, $\mathbf{o}_{ij} \rightarrow [o_{ij}^1, o_{ij}^2, ..., o_{ij}^n]$,

$\wedge\; y_{ij}^k, m_{ij}^k, o_{ij}^k \in \{0,1\}, L=n+m+l$

else

$(i,j) \rightarrow$ '*is unoccupied*' and $\alpha_{ij} \rightarrow \mathbf{0}$

In Fig.1 we show the sequence of instructions describing the process of evolution. The binary vectors $\mathbf{y}_{ij}$, $\mathbf{m}_{ij}$, $\mathbf{o}_{ij}$ represent the subsequent episodes of individual life: the "youth", the "maturity" and the "old age", respectively. The values of l,m,n are the maximum lengths of each of the episodes while their actual durations are equal to the number of "1"s in the corresponding vectors $\mathbf{y}_{ij}$, $\mathbf{m}_{ij}$, $\mathbf{o}_{ij}$. The symbol Ω denotes the classical recombination operator from the genetic algorithms, t is the number of generation cycle (time), $p(\alpha_{ij})$ is the unitation operator, (i.e., it returns the number of "1"s in α_{ij} chain) and the function $p_k(\ )$ is the "counter" operator defined as follows:

$$\forall\ (a_{ij} = 1 \wedge p(\alpha_{ij}) \geq k);\ p_k(\alpha_{ij}) = k.$$

```
while t<MAX do begin                           // Initialize the following generation g.
  for i = 1 to N do begin                      // Go through every lattice site.
    for j = 1 to N do begin

      if aᵢⱼᵍ = 0 then                          // If lattice site (i,j) is unoccupied
                                                // find two different "mature" individuals
          m=find_two_mature_neighbors (i,j, α₁, α₂)   // in the Moor neighborhood of aᵢⱼ
                                                //If they do not exist m=0, otherwise m=1
          if (m=1) then
            aᵍ⁺¹ᵢⱼ → 1,
            (β₁, β₂) → Ω (α₁, α₂)               // Reproduce them.
            αᵢⱼ → (β₁, β₂|pr),                  // pr- a probability for selection of
                                                // one out of two offspring (β₁, β₂)
            kᵢⱼ → 1
      else                                      //If a site (i,j) is occupied
        if pₖᵢⱼ(αᵢⱼ) = p(αᵢⱼ) then              //delete it if its life-time passed
          kᵢⱼ → 0, aᵍ⁺¹ᵢⱼ → 0
        else
          kᵢⱼ → pₖᵢⱼ(αᵢⱼ); kᵢⱼ → kᵢⱼ + 1        // or make it older
    end
  end
end.
```

Fig. 1. The pseudo-code describing evolution rules.

We assume that, the population can be attacked by a plaque represented by "seeds". The "seeds", which are generated periodically in time, are scattered randomly on the CA lattice. The strength of the plague is defined by ε_0 - the ratio between the number of "seeds" and the total number of individuals. If a "seed" is located at the same place as the population member, both are removed from the lattice. Otherwise, the "seed" moves randomly on the CA lattice until it "annihilates" with the first encountered individual. The "seeds" cannot reproduce.

Our system consisting of elements with "genetic codes" evolves not only on CA lattice but also in the abstract multi-dimensional feature space $\mathfrak{R}^L$ represented by the coordinates of binary chains α_{ij}. As shown, e.g., in [4], the clusters of similar individuals are created both on the mesh and in the feature space $\mathfrak{R}^L$ due to the genetic drift. These clusters can be extracted using clustering algorithms [8,9] and then visualized in 3-D space by employing multidimensional scaling (MDS) algorithms [8,9].

3   Results of Modeling

The parameters assumed for a typical run are shown in Tab.1. The periodic lattice of cellular automata 200x200 and 100x100 were considered as optimal ones balancing well adequate representation and computational requirements. These parameters are also sufficient to obtain stable populations and partly eliminate boundary effects.

Table 1. The parameters for typical simulation.

Lattice size (N×N)	100×100, 200×200	Mobility factor $\in(0,1)$	1
Initial density (P0)	0.2 – 0.5	Probability of reproduction	1
"Youth" - length	32	Probability of mutation	0
"Mature" - length	32	Plague period	50
"Old age" - length	32	Dose (ε_h)	0.4

At the start of evolution, the population is generated randomly with P0 density (P0$\in(0,1)$, see Tab.1). Because all individuals are initially "young", the evolution scenario depends strongly on P0 (see Fig.2). For both too large and too small P0 values, after some time, the number of offspring can become marginal in contrast to massive extermination of "old" individuals from the initial population. This may lead to fast extinction of the whole population. This effect can be considerably reduced by increasing mobility factor of individuals, their life-time and initial diversity of population.

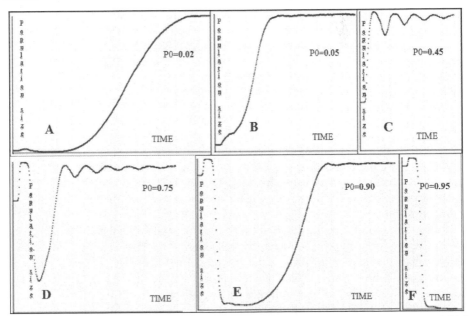

Fig. 2. Various scenario of the growth of population size in time for increasing P0 (initial population size). The simulation was started assuming that all the individuals are "young". The CA lattice of size 100x100 was simulated.

We have assumed additionally that:

- the length L of the vector representing the "genetic code" is equal to 96,
- the lengths of vectors **y, m, o** are identical, i.e., $l=m=n=32$ (see *Definition* 1).

The value of L was selected intentionally to have more compact representation (thus more efficient code) of individual, whose "genetic code" can be implemented then as three *float* values. The value of L cannot be too small due to statistical validity (the number of "1"s in various episodes of individual's life has initially the Gaussian distribution) and due to high sensitivity of the system on various simulation conditions. Other configurations and vector lengths were also examined. The first conclusion is that, the individuals, even those with the same life-time lengths L, can behave in various ways depending on the lengths of subsequent life-episodes **y, m, o**. On the one extreme, the population with too short "maturity" period will die quickly. On the other, the populations with greater reproduction potential (defined by the length of **m** vector) will tend to fill the **m** part of vector α with "1"s. This is due to the population members who are "mature" for a longer time, have a greater chance to reproduce and pass their "genetic code" to other generations. One can expect that the similar behavior will be observed for "idle" episodes of individual's life i.e., the "youth" and the "old age", i.e., the individual's life-time will increase due to the evolution to the maximum length L. However, the situation is completely different.

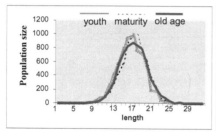 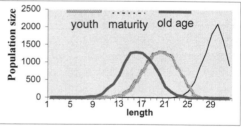

Fig. 3. The histograms representing the number of individuals with various lengths of **y, m, o** life-episodes. For initial generation of individuals the distributions are similar (the plot on the left), but after g=2000 steps they diversifies considerably (the plot on the right).

Let us assume that initially the distribution of "1"s in each of the three episodes of life is Gaussian and there are in average 16 "1"s in each of **y, m** and **o** vectors. These initial conditions are shown in Fig.3a. After t=2000 time-steps, the situation considerably changed. The distributions of "1"s for each period of life undergo strong diversification (Fig.4b).

As displayed in Fig.4, the distribution of individuals both on the CA lattice and in the feature space, changed also dramatically. Instead of initially chaotic configuration of individuals populating 2D lattice, they form distinct clusters. The individuals belonging to the same cluster are similar according to the Hamming distance in the L-D feature space. As shown in Fig.4b there exist four distinct "families" of individuals in the feature space. In Fig.4a we show them projected onto the CA lattice.

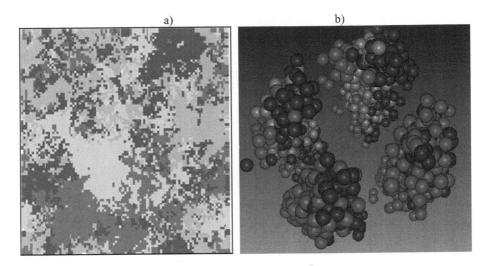

Fig. 4. Clusters of individuals on 2D lattice (a) and in the feature space (b). Single plate in Figs.4b corresponds to a group of individuals with identical "genetic codes". Fig.4b shows the result of *k-mean* clustering in the L-D feature space transformed by using multi-dimensional scaling to 3-D space. Various colors in b) indicate the spurious clusters obtained using *k-means* clustering scheme. While colored 2-D clusters on the CA lattice in Fig.4a represent the four clusters recognized visually from Fig.4b.

The continuation of the evolution from Fig.4 produces a stable attractor, which consists of four "families" of individuals, which have exactly the same "genetic codes". The codes differ between clusters only on two bits positions. Therefore, the offspring generated due to recombination belong to one of the existing clusters. We did not obtain any global solution with only one large cluster of individuals having the same genetic code. It means that the fitness factor for the populations of individuals with the three life periods is not a trivial, increasing function of the length of life. This is unlike for populations, which are "mature" and ready for reproduction during the whole life-time ($L=m$, $l,n=0$). In this case the attractor of the evolution process would consist of individuals with "genetic codes" filled exclusively by "1"s.

The most basic features of attractors resulting from modeling are collected in Tab.2. As shown in Tab.2, where apart from the "natural" elimination - resulting from the limited life-time inscribed in the "genetic code" - there are not any other lethal factors, the "maturity" period fills with "1"s after relatively small number of evolution cycles t. This is obvious because longer ability of reproduction gives a greater chance for passing the genetic code to the offspring. By extending the evolution time about threefold, also the "youth" vector will be filled with '1's. Surprisingly, even much longer simulation does not affect the "old age" vector. It remains the mixture of "1"s and "0"s. This observation confirms also for:

- variable lengths of **y,m.o** ($l{\neq}m{\neq}n$),
- long "old age" period ($n=64$),
- much shorter remaining episodes ($l=16$, $m=24$, respectively).

Table 2. Number of "1"s in the average "genetic chains" of different lengths for corresponding episodes of individual's life after 50,000 time-steps. *"mix"* - the mixture of "0"s and "1"s, *"perished"* - the population deceases quickly.

		YOUNG	MATURE	OLD
1	No plague			
	(32,32,32)	32	32	mix
	(16,16,16)	16	16	mix
	(8,8,8)	8	8	mix
2	No plague			
	(16,24,64)	3	24	mix
	(8,32,64)	1	30	mix
	(0,40,64)	0	perished	perished
3	Plague period < L			
	(32,32,32)	0	32	mix
	(32,32,0)	0	32	0
	(0,32,32)	0	32	mix
4	Plague period >L			
	(32,32,32)	0	32	0
5	Plague period < L			
	(8,8,8)	0	8	mix
6	Plague period >L			
	(8,8,8)	mix	8	0

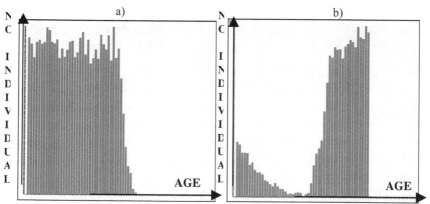

Fig. 5. The histograms of individuals vs. their age for a) stable (*l=32, m=32, n=32*), and b) unstable (*l=0, m=40, n=64)* populations.

Surprisingly, further decrease of the "youth" episode (*l=8, m=32, n=64*) with respective extension of the "maturity" episode weakens considerably the population. For (*l=0, m=40, n=64*) it dies eventually. This behavior shows that the "youth" period accumulates reproductive ability of the population. If released too fast it will cause non-uniform aging (see Fig.5b), which may result in fast extinction of the whole population.

As depicted in Fig.6, the population attacked by the periodic plague dies if the strength (*"Dose"* in Tab.1) of the plague ε_0, defined as the ratio of the number of "seeds" to the number of individuals, and/or its period exceeds a certain threshold.

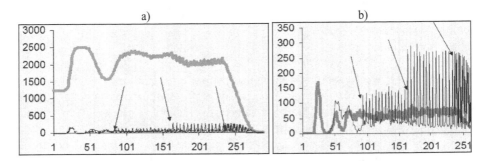

Fig. 6. a) The influence of periodic plague (thin line) on the number of individuals (thick line). b) The number of individuals (thick line) eliminated by the periodic plague (thin line) in time.

The attractors (i.e., the non-evolving populations of individuals with similar "genetic codes" obtained due to the long evolution) in a stable environment die very quickly due to the lack of adaptation ability represented by diversification in the "genetic codes" of individuals. For example, a uniform population (e.g., see Tab.2 for $l=m=n=32$) obtained after long evolution (t=50,000 time-steps) and attacked then by the plague extincts during the following 100 steps. The same population, but this time infected at the early stage of evolution (after t=200 steps) survives. The "genetic codes" of individuals self-adapt to the unstable environment. As shown in Tab.2, the "genetic codes" of attractors of attacked population are different than those obtained for the stable environment. Moreover, they differentiate depending on the period of the plague.

For the outbreak with a period shorter than the average life-time of individuals, the "youth" episode, as the obstacle for fast reproduction, is eliminated completely (all "0"s in vector **y**). Surprisingly, the "old age" period remains relatively long. Because the population can have not enough time for reproduction between subsequent plaques, it has to elaborate sophisticated control mechanism of growth. Let us assume that:

1. the "old age" is inhibited ($n=0$) and the population consists of only "mature" individuals,
2. the majority of individuals are eliminated by the plaque from the lattice in a very short time.

At the very moment when the plaque ceases, <u>all</u> survivors will produce many newborns due to plenty of free space on the lattice. Therefore, after some time, the individuals of a <u>similar age</u> and approximately <u>the same life-time</u> will dominate in the population. Their simultaneous death will weaken the population (see Fig.5b). Thus, the number of "mature" individuals, which survive after the following disasters, may be too small to initiate new generations and the population may extinct eventually.

Assuming that the "old age" episode is greater than 0 ($n>0$), post-plaque demographic eruption (resulting in demographic catastrophe after some time) can be much smaller than for $n=0$. It is easy to remark that the demographic eruption will be monotonically decreasing function of n because only the "mature" survivors have reproductive ability. Moreover, the existence of "old" individuals will decrease the probability of reproduction. The replacement of "old" individuals with newborns will be also postponed and possible only after their death. All of these demographic inhibitors cause that the post-plaque reconstruction of the population takes more time than in the previous ($n=0$) case. Instead, the age distribution in the population is more stable (see Fig.5a). Thus the population allowing the "old age" episode is stronger and has a greater chance to survive in unstable environment than that consisting of only "mature" individuals. We can conclude that the "old" individuals accumulate the environmental resources (free space) for stable growth eliminating dangerous post-plaque effects such as demographic eruptions.

When the plague period is greater than the average life-time of individuals and simultaneously the "strength" of the plague increases, the "old age" is also eliminated due to evolution. This is because the population has enough time for reproduction and demographic minimum does not coincide with the plaque.

4   Concluding Remarks

We have discussed the influence of the lengths of three life-episodes: the "youth", the "maturity" and the "old age" on population evolution. Of course, their duration of depends on the biological construction of individuals. The organism requires a minimum time to grow-up and be ready for reproduction. However, the terms "youth", "maturity" and "old age" used in this paper have not only biological meaning. Environmental factors influence both reproduction ability and the life-time. They may cause that the same organism can be treated as "young", "mature" or "old" independently on his age.

Summarizing our findings, we can conclude that "maturity" period decides about the reproductive power of the population and its survival ability. Thus the population increases its length to a maximum value allowed. The idle episodes of life, i.e., the "youth" and the "old age" play the role of accumulators of the population resources and control their growth. The "youth" accumulates reproductive resources while the "old age" accumulates the space required for reproduction. The idle life-episodes develop the control mechanisms, which allow for self-adaptation of the population to unstable environment.

1. In the case of a stable growth the reproductive resources are accumulated in the "youth" episode of life. The "old age" remains the secondary control mechanism.
2. For periodically infected populations with the period longer than the average length of the life-time L the population is biased only for reproduction, eliminating idle episodes of life.
3. For strong enough and frequent pests the „old age" remains non-zero accumulating additional space required for burst-out of population just after the plague vanishes.

Many aspects of the model have not been explored yet. For example, the influence of lethal mutations and other hostile environmental factors on the survival ability of the population. However, our model can be an interesting complementary constituent to the Penna paradigm of aging.

Acknowledgements. The research is supported by the Polish Committee of Scientific Research KBN, Grant No. 3T11C05926. Thanks are due to dr Anna Jasi ska-Suwada from Cracovian University of Technology, Institute of Teleinformatics, for her contribution to this paper.

References

1. Hermanowicz SW: A Simple 2D Biofilm Model Yields a Variety of Morphological Features. *Mathematical Biosciences* **169**(1)(2001):1-14
2. Lacasta AM, Cantalapiedra IR, Auguet CE, Penaranda A and Ramirez-Piscina L: Modeling of spatiotemporal patterns in bacterial colonies. *Phys. Rev. E* **59**(6)(1999):7036-7041
3. Krawczyk K., Dzwinel W: Non-linear development of bacterial colony modeled with cellular automata and agent object, *Int J. Modern Phys. C* **10**(2003):1-20.
4. Broda A, Dzwinel W: Spatial Genetic Algorithm and its Parallel Implementation, *Lecture Notes in Computer Science,* **1184**(1996): 97-107.
5. de Almeida RMC, de Oliveira S Moss, Penna TJP: (Theoretical Approach to Biological Aging. *Physica A* **253,** (1997):366-378
6. de Menezes MA, Racco A, Penna TJP: Strategies of Reproduction and Longevity, *Int J. Modern Phys. C.* **9**(6) (1998):787-791
7. Chopard B, Droz M: *Cellular Automata Modeling of Physical Systems*, Cambridge Univ. Press, London, (1998)
8. Jain D, Dubes RC: *Algorithms for Clustering Data*, Prentice-Hall, Advanced Reference Series (1998).
9. Theodoris S, Koutroumbas K: *Pattern Recognition*, Academic Press, San Diego, London, Boston (1998)

Mining Ecological Data with Cellular Automata

Alexander Campbell, Binh Pham, and Yu-Chu Tian

Centre for Information Technology Innovation
Queensland University of Technology
GPO Box 2434, Brisbane QLD 4001, Australia
ab.campbell@qut.edu.au

Abstract. This paper introduces a Cellular Automata (CA) approach
to spatiotemporal data mining (STDM). The recently increasing interest
in using Genetic Algorithms and other evolutionary techniques to identify CA model parameters has been mainly focused on performing artificial computational tasks such as density classification. This work investigates the potential to extend this research to spatial and spatiotemporal
data mining tasks and presents some preliminary experimental results.
The purpose is twofold: to motivate and explore an evolutionary CA
approach to STDM, and to highlight the suitability of evolutionary CA
models to problems that are ostensibly more difficult than, for example,
density classification. The problem of predicting wading-bird nest site
locations in ecological data is used throughout to illustrate the concepts,
and provides the framework for experimental analysis.

1 Introduction

Space-time dynamics are ubiquitous in both real-world and artificial systems.
The recently emerging field of spatiotemporal data mining (STDM) opens up a
number of possibilities for the integration of previously distinct research areas.
Cellular Automata (CA) techniques, in particular the use of Genetic Algorithms
and other evolutionary approaches to learn the transition rules from given patterns, show great potential to be combined with data mining techniques in order
to tackle problems of previously prohibitive complexity. They can also give insight to improve on previous approaches.

In order to illustrate our approach, we use a classic problem in spatial data
mining - the prediction of nest site locations in a wading bird ecology - and
examine the merits and difficulties of applying an evolutionary CA approach.
The data consists of nest site locations and environment variables (e.g. vegetation
type, water depth). Given a set of spatial patterns (the training data), the aim is
to construct a CA neighbourhood and transition rule such that they will predict
the locations (or significantly aid prediction) of nest sites on unseen data sets
consisting of the environment variables only.

Genetic Algorithms have been used to discover CA rules that will perform
computational tasks such as density classification (complete cellular grid to become one of two states depending on which had the higher initial density) [1],

P.M.A. Sloot, B. Chopard, and A.G. Hoekstra (Eds.): ACRI 2004, LNCS 3305, pp. 474–483, 2004.

synchronisation (all cells to flash on and off in synchrony) and most recently period three and quasiperiod three behaviours [2]. They have also been applied to identifying the neighbourhood and transition rules that will recreate spatiotemporal patterns generated by CA [3]. The closest in nature to our work is that of Richards et al. [4] who also look at extracting cellular automata rules directly *from experimental data.* In their case the data relate to the dendritic solidification of NH_4Br. The key theme here is to expand this concept to more complex multivariate scenarios.

Section 2 introduces spatiotemporal data mining through a formal treatment of the location prediction problem. In section 3 we motivate and present our evolutionary CA model. Section 4 details the experimental setup and contains preliminary results and analysis. Finally, section 5 concludes and discusses future work.

2   Spatiotemporal Data Mining

Spatiotemporal data mining is a relatively recent expansion of data mining techniques to take into consideration the dynamics of spatially extended systems for which large amounts of data exist. Given that all real world spatial data exists in some temporal context, and knowledge of this context is often essential in interpreting it, spatial data mining is inherently STDM to some degree. Although time series and spatial data mining have existed as research fields for a number of years independently, they have been growing towards a synthesis that is inherently multi-disciplinary.

2.1   The Location Prediction Problem

This multi-disciplinary nature is borne out by the fact that a well known and thoroughly researched spatial data mining application is that of predicting nest site locations in an ecological data set. A particular data set was first considered by Ozesmi [5] in an ecological modelling context, and then taken up as a spatial data mining problem by Shekhar et. al. [6].

Following [6], the problem is defined as follows: Given

- A spatial framework S of sites $\{s_1, ..., s_n\}$ for an underlying geographic space
- A collection X of explanatory functions $f_{X_k} : S \to \mathbb{R}^k, k = 1, ..., K$. $\mathbb{R}^k$ is the range of possible values for the explanatory functions
- A dependent class variable $f_C : S \to C = \{c_1, ..., c_M\}, c_m \in \{0, 1\}$

Find: Classification Model $\hat{f}_C : \mathbb{R}^1 \times, ..., \times \mathbb{R}^k \to C$

In [6], a number of approaches are compared both theoretically and experimentally. In order to gain insight regarding spatially dependent multivariate processes, and to motivate the use of an alternative technique, these approaches are also briefly reviewed here in order of increasing sophistication.

Linear Regression. The classical linear regression equation does not attempt to model spatial dependence. It is defined as

$$y = X\beta + \epsilon \qquad (1)$$

where $\beta = (\beta_0, ..., \beta_m)^T$, y is an n-vector of observations and X is an $n \times m$ matrix of explanatory data. This is then transformed from a real-valued variable to binary via the logistic function, $Pr(c_i|y) = e^y/(1+e^y)$. When the samples are spatially related, the residual errors reveal a systematic variation over space.

Spatial Autoregressive Models. In order to model spatial dependence, a spatial contiguity matrix is used. The essential idea is that spatial locations which are neighbours are coupled through an entry in the matrix. The simplest form is a binary matrix where entries are either 1 or 0 depending on a Euclidean adjacency metric, however 'neighbours' can be defined in any fashion and non-zero elements are often scaled to sum to unity in each row. Figure 1 shows an example spatial framework and figure 2 a corresponding row-normalised contiguity matrix where cells that share an edge have double the weighting of cells that are diagonal neighbours. The modified regression equation is

$$y = \rho W y + X\beta + \epsilon. \qquad (2)$$

The dependence on neighbouring classes is exerted in a static fashion through the contiguity matrix. The fact that it is at heart a logistic regression model means there is an assumption that the class conditional distribution belongs to the exponential family.

Markov Random Fields. A more sophisticated approach is to model the data as a Markov Random Field (MRF). A MRF-based Bayesian classifier is a non-parametric model which, unlike logistic regression, is not bound to make assumptions that the class conditional distribution belongs to a particular family. A MRF explicitly models the relative frequencies in the class prior term. Conceptually it is therefore more suited to the real-world nonlinearity of this

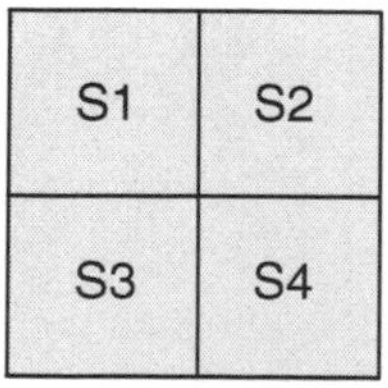

	S1	S2
	S3	S4

	S1	S2	S3	S4
S1	0	0.4	0.4	0.2
S2	0.4	0	0.2	0.4
S3	0.4	0.2	0	0.4
S4	0.2	0.4	0.4	0

Fig. 1. An example spatial framework

Fig. 2. Row-normalised contiguity matrix for the spatial framework shown in figure 1

problem and accordingly has the best experimental performance in the study in
[6].

MRFs consist of a set of random variables with an interdependency relationship represented by an undirected graph which is analogous to the spatial
contiguity matrix. The Markov property contends that a variable depends only
on its neighbours and is independent of all other variables. For this problem,
that means random variable l_i is independent of l_j if $W(s_i, s_j) = 0$, where W is
the neighbourhood relationship contiguity matrix.

Using Bayes rule it is possible to predict l_i from feature value vector X and
neighbourhood class label vector L_i as follows:

$$Pr(l_i|X, L_i) = \frac{Pr(X|l_i, L_i)Pr(l_i|L_i)}{Pr(X|L_i)} \tag{3}$$

Where L_i is the label vector for the neighbourhood of i.

2.2   The Curse of Dimensionality

Despite its theoretical ability to encode complex probabilistic relationships involving multiple variables without reliance on any assumptions about the distributions of class variables, the actual solution procedures for MRFs require
large amounts of training data and/or a number of limiting assumptions on
$Pr(X|l_i, L_i)$. This is because the graph of a Markov field must connect all pairs
of variables that are conditionally dependent even for a single choice of values
of the other variables [7]. In other words, it is hard to encode interactions that
occur only in a certain context and are absent in all others. An example would
be that the probability of a nest site occurring in a location with a certain combination of environment variables is very different when there happens to be
three or more birds within a certain distance of that location. In many situations these assumptions may be acceptable, however if there is a high degree of
attribute interaction this is not necessarily the case. Attribute interaction is a
crucial theme in data mining [8] and is common in many complex real-world systems. The 'curse of dimensionality' is the situation where there is a high degree
of attribute interaction over a sparse amount of data.

3   Evolutionary CA for Data Mining

The importance of approaching analysis of complicated systems with the goal
of *understanding rather than prediction* is becoming more widely acknowledged.
This places the emphasis on dynamic process rather static pattern, as noted by
[9]. A model that has such a characteristic is Cellular Automata. CA are well
suited to a high degree of attribute interaction and sparse data because they are
not a statistical model of the system which requires a large amount of data to
give 'support' to the probability distributions. Instead they are a model that can
map every state of the environment to a state of the dependent variable. The

penalty for such flexibility however is that it is required to search a potentially massive parameter space for the correct rules.

Evolutionary methods are highly suited to such a problem and have been used to evolve CA transition rules for a number of computational tasks. The key theme of evolutionary approaches is that the behaviour of the system is defined implicitly by a fitness function measuring the difference between the candidate solution and the desired solution. No explicit knowledge is needed to show the system *how* to perform the task.

The line between a *forward* CA approach - conscious programming of CA rules with a resultant behaviour in mind - and a backward or *inverse* approach where no *a priori* knowledge is used and the desired behaviour is the only guide, is inherently indistinct. The nature of the relationship mirrors closely the mining-modelling one mentioned previously. In the CA literature this type of problem seems to have been predominantly approached in a forward sense. Examples of this abound especially in urban modelling [10,9] and, perhaps closer in form to our problem, in vegetation dynamics [11].

The problem is approached here in an inverse sense because from a data mining perspective this means there is no explicit requirement for prior domain knowledge. It also ensures the possibility to discover rules that are counter-intuitive and/or too complex to program consciously. Thus it is both more flexible and more general. In the evolution of a complex, high-dimensional system, it is often the case that there are only a relatively small number of degrees of freedom which contribute (above a certain threshold, which is indistinguishable from noise) to the dynamics, such that the attractor of such a system can be reconstructed in a greatly reduced state space. We see these two characteristics as analogous which motivates us to look for a parsimonious rule-set that will represent the important factors in nesting behaviour. Having said that, the immense size of state space is still a huge obstacle, and the method proposed here is intended only as a complementary approach: in combination with domain knowledge and other data mining techniques it offers the chance to discover nonlinear spatial and spatiotemporal relationships, even in the face of sparse data.

3.1   Cellular Automata Model Definition

The model we propose is a synchronous two-dimensional Cellular Automata where data belonging to each grid-cell is the basis for the state of a cell in the cellular lattice. More precisely, each cell's state can be split into two parts. The first is the three independent variables: distance to open water, vegetation durability, and water depth; these remain constant for the duration of each simulation run. The second state denotes the presence or absence of a nest site - this state will be more typical of a CA in that it will be recalculated at each time step according to the current rules. The first state can be collectively thought of as the landscape in which the simulations take place. The second can be thought of as the progressive spatial distribution of the birds as they are drawn towards the attractor which characterises their nest site behaviour.

Our CA can initially be defined as: $\mathbf{CA} = \langle \Omega, Q, N, I, f \rangle$

Where:

- $\Omega = \{(i,j)|1 \leq i \leq L_x, 1 \leq j \leq L_y\}$ is the $L_x \times L_y$ lattice of cell sites
- Q is a finite set of cell state values
- N is a neighbourhood template
- $I : \Omega \to Q$ is the initialisation function
- $f : Q \times Q^{|N|} \to Q$ is the transition function

Incorporating the two-part cell state values we have $Q = \{Q_l, Q_n\}$, where:

$$Q_l = \{DOW, V, WD\}, Q_n = \{0, 1\} \tag{4}$$

Where Q_l is the state of the landscape consisting of DOW - distance to open water, V - vegetation durability, and WD - water depth. Q_n is the presence or absence of a nest site.

The transition function becomes:

$$f : Q_l \times Q_n \times Q_l^{|N_l|} \times Q_n^{|N_n|} \to Q_n \tag{5}$$

Where N_n is the neighbourhood for nest sites and N_l is the landscape neighbourhood. We may additionally wish to have different sized neighbourhood for each individual landscape variable depending on domain knowledge that certain variables have a larger influence.

3.2   Genetic Algorithm Model Definition

Similar to a number of evolutionary CA papers we use a standard CA-GA model of $\mathbf{GA} = \{P, T, \rho, G, E\}$, where P is population size of candidate rules, T is the number of CA time steps, ρ is the mutation rate, G is the number of generations and E is the number of elite rules. However, unlike the artificial computational tasks tackled by other evolutionary CA methods which aim to converge to a particular target configuration, we are looking to learn a complex probability distribution that represents the nest location 'behaviour' of the wading birds. In order to realistically rate the ability of a CA rule to do this, it is necessary to run the GA on a number of training configurations (of target nest site locations) which follow some predetermined probability distribution. Also, the number of CA time steps before the fitness is measure is nonstandard, and is discussed in the next section.

The fitness function of a rule is perhaps the most crucial ingredient in a successful GA. Our fitness function takes into account spatial accuracy so that configurations which are spatially near the target configuration are still rewarded. This may be crucial given the many potential sources of noise and uncertainty in spatiotemporal data sets, and also highly appropriate for discovering qualitative relationships. A modified version of the Spatial Accuracy Measure (SAM) outlined in [6] is used.

$$SAM = TPR - FPR = \frac{AnMPn}{AnMPn + AnMPnn} - \frac{AnnMP}{AnnMPn + AnnMPnn} \tag{6}$$

Fig. 3. Distance to Open Water, DOW **Fig. 4.** Water Depth, WD

where TPR is the true positive rate, FPR is the false positive rate, $An[i] = f_C[s_i]$ and $Pn[i] = \hat{f}_C[s_i]$ are boolean vectors representing actual nest locations and predicted nest site locations respectively, and $Ann[i] = 1 - An[i]$ and $Pnn[i] = 1 - Pn[i]$ are their inverses. The spatial weighting is applied through $M = W + I$, the matrix addition of contiguity matrix W and identity matrix I.

4   Experimental Setup, Preliminary Results, and Analysis

In [12], high fidelity colour images of the three spatial data sets from the study in question are provided, along with a colour-intensity scale. Due to a number of factors, including: a desire to operate on the same data set for future comparisons, the qualitative nature of our approach at this initial stage, and an unavailability of other suitable data, we have used these images (rather than raw data) for our experiments. The relative values of the variables were preserved by creating a colour map based on the provided intensity levels, and the spatial integrity of the data was preserved by reducing the number of cells (pixels) in the image down to the corresponding number of data grid points in the original study.

In the Spatiotemporal Data Mining section it was shown that both regression and MRF models may be forced to make limiting assumptions, especially when there is a high degree of attribute interaction. Our first goal was to show that an evolutionary CA approach is highly suited to problems that are nonlinear in this way.

In order to investigate this in a experimental fashion, synthetic nest site locations were generated using a nonlinear generalisations of equation (2):

$$y_{syn1} = (I - \rho W)^{-1} \times (\beta \times cos(X) + c \times random(\epsilon)) \qquad (7)$$

$$y_{syn2} = (I - \rho W)^{-1} \times (\beta \times cos(X) + W \times cos(X) \times \gamma + c \times random(\epsilon)) \quad (8)$$

where W is an equally weighted, row-normalised 7×7 neighbourhood, X is the DOW explanatory variable, ρ is an arbitrary spatial weighting of 0.6, c is a relatively small noise weighting of 0.5, $\epsilon = N(0,1)$, and β, the weighting on local explanatory data, has been set arbitrarily at 0.3. In equation (9), γ represents the dependence of the dependent variable on neighbouring explanatory data; this has been set high (relative to β) at 0.25 to generate a significantly more nonlinear problem.

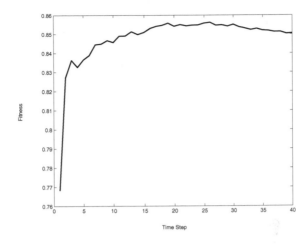

Fig. 5. Gradual fitness increase over CA time steps

Rule Types and Transients. The CA model defined above is very general and is likely in most situations to have a prohibitively large state space. In order to reduce this state space a number of different simplifications have been used. Firstly the the explanatory data has been quantised so that $Q_l = \{0, 1, 2, ..., 16\}$. The level of quantisation should be partly determined by the specific domain. More importantly, a number of rule types have been considered. Initially it was thought that an outer-totalistic rule would be sufficient to capture the extent of the nest-site location interactions, however in looking for a rule that produced an increase in fitness over a number of CA time steps (ie one that reached a higher 'equilibrium' fitness) it was discovered that symmetric rules tend to oscillate between fitness levels in a more extreme fashion. More complex rule types, while when averaged over a large number of specific rules may not have performed any better (plenty decreased in fitness over the CA time steps), seemed to produce a larger number of rules that purely increased in fitness. The mechanism behind this phenomena is more complex rules' greater propensity for *information transfer* across the spatial lattice. In order to retain this property, while increasing the state space as little as possible, reflection symmetric (rather than rotation symmetric or completely symmetric) rules were preferred. Figure 5 shows the increase in fitness over a number of time steps for a von Neumann reflection symmetric rule on a single arbitrary target nest location data set. An empirical study of the transient behaviour of a large number of CA rules led to the requirement that at least Te CA time steps elapse before the spatial accuracy is measured, at which point it is averaged over at least the next Tav time steps, and $T = \{Te, Tav\}$.

Nonlinear Generalisation Capabilities. Thus far a reduced complexity version of the model outlined above has been implemented where the landscape

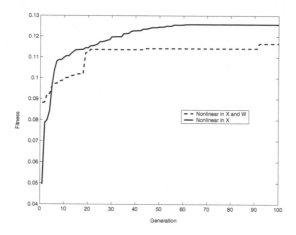

Fig. 6. Fitness of GA for two scenarios: one nonlinear in the local explanatory data only, the other additionally nonlinear in neighbouring explanatory data

consists only of the distance to open water variable. Although we have not yet performed enough experiments for statistical significance, so far results are encouraging. Figure 6 is a typical graph of fitness vs. generation where for both experiments: $\mathbf{GA} = \{P, Te, Tav, \rho, G, E\} = \{100, 30, 5, 0.01, 100, 20\}$. Each candidate CA rule is matched against 10 synthetically generated target nest site locations according to equation (8) for the first experiment and (9) for the second.

Both populations are performing at similar reasonable fitness levels, especially given the difficulty of the task. Secondly and more interestingly, in the population with the more nonlinear probability distribution to learn, the fitness increases take longer to come, but are larger when they do. Intuitively this matches our perceptions about the nature of the tasks and the GA's ability to learn nonlinear relationships for a CA model.

5   Conclusion and Future Work

We have used an analysis of statistical spatial models to give insight into the nature of attribute interaction and as the basis for experimental metrics. We have explored the potential for an evolutionary CA approach to STDM and presented some encouraging, though preliminary, experimental results.

Of the two goals set out at the beginning, more emphasis has been placed on the suitability of CA to nonlinear problems. Hopefully this has provided an experimentally justified foundation for the application of CA to a broader range of problems. The suitability of this technique for data mining specifically has been given less attention due to space constraints and future work will be needed to develop the interpretation of CA rules for data mining purposes in greater depth. Also, the issue of sensitivity to noise needs to be investigated, possibly through the application of a probabilistic CA model.

Acknowledgements. This project is supported by an Australian Research Council Linkage grant in collaboration with the Built Environment Research Unit (BERU), Queensland Department of Public Works.

References

1. Jimenez-Morales, F., Crutchfield, J., Mitchell, M.: Evolving two-dimensional cellular automata to perform density classification: A report on work in progress. Parallel Computing **27** (2001) 571–585
2. Jimenez-Morales, F.: An evolutionary approach to the study of non-trivial collective behaviour in cellular automata. In Bandini, S., Chopard, B., Tomassini, M., eds.: ACRI 2002. Volume 2493 of LNCS., Geneva, Switzerland, Springer (2002) 32–43
3. Billings, S., Yang, Y.: Identification of probabilistic cellular automata. IEEE Transactions on Systems, Man and Cybernetics - Part B: Cybernetics **33** (2003) 225–236
4. Richards, F.: Extracting cellular automaton rules directly from experimental data. Physica D **45** (1990) 189–202
5. Ozesmi, U., Mitsch, W.J.: A spatial habitat model for the marsh-breeding redwinged blackbird (agelaius phoeniceus l.) in coastal lake erie wetlands. Ecological Modelling **101** (1997) 139–152 TY - JOUR.
6. Shekhar, S., Schrater, P., Vatsavai, R., Wu, W., Chawla, S.: Spatial contextual classification and prediction models for mining geospatial data. IEEE Transactions on Multimedia **4** (2002) 174–188
7. Fridman, A.: Mixed markov models. Proceedings of the National Academy of Sciences **100** (2003) 8092–8096
8. Freitas, A.: Understanding the crucial role of attribute interaction in data mining. Artificial Intelligence Review **16** (2001) 177–199
9. Cheng, J., Masser, I.: Cellular automata based temporal process understanding of urban growth. In Bandini, S., Chopard, B., Tomassini, M., eds.: ACRI 2002. Volume 2493 of LNCS., Geneva, Switzerland, Springer (2002) 325–336
10. O'Sullivan, D., Torrens, P.M.: Cellular models of urban systems. In Bandini, S., Worsch, T., eds.: ACRI 2000, Karlsruhe, Germany, Springer (2000) 108–116
11. Bandini, S., Pavesi, G.: Simulation of vegetable populations dynamics based on cellular automata. In Bandini, S., Chopard, B., Tomassini, M., eds.: ACRI 2002. Volume 2493 of LNCS., Geneva, Switzerland, Springer (2002) 202–209
12. Chawla, S., Shekhar, S., Wu, W., Ozesmi, U.: Modeling spatial dependencies for mining geospatial data: An introduction. In Miller, H., Han, J., eds.: Geographic data mining and Knowledge Discovery. Taylor and Francis (2001) 338

Reconstructing Forest Savanna Dynamics in Africa Using a Cellular Automata Model, FORSAT

Charly Favier[1,2] and Marc A. Dubois[1]

[1] SPEC, CEA Saclay Orme des Merisiers, France
[2] LODYC, Université Paris VI, France

Abstract. Large areas of savannas are found in Africa in climatic zones favourable to humid tropical forests: they are relicts of past dry periods and forest domains are naturally expanding. Men have influenced the transgression, especially by starting savanna fires. FORSAT is a stochastic cellular-automaton model dedicated to the forest-savanna mosaic on a landscape scale, taking into account savanna fires, vegetation succession cycle (vegetation types are discriminated by their ecological function: herbs, pioneer seedlings, pioneer adults, forest) and pionneer seed dispersal and recruitment. The model is validated by comparison between its emergent behavior and biogeographical field studies. Two parameters (an environmental factor and a man-related fire frequency) control an van-der-Waals-like phase transition between forest and savanna. This brings to three types of evolution: progression or regression of forest edge, formation and coalescence of clumps in savanna and global afforestation of savanna. These results explain the mainlines of ecosystem distribution in tropical Africa and the gap between the transgression rates inferred from paleostudies and currently measured.

1   Introduction

We know now that current climatic conditions make it possible for the tropical forest to expand over the periforest humid savannas, especially in Africa [1, 2, 3, 4]. In most regions, this trend is balanced by savanna fires, that are the most significant man-induced disturbance (although some are natural) [5]. The balance between these two processes, one favorable – the forest succession – and the other unfavorable – the fires – results in a pattern of evolution in a particular zone.

The evolution displays some similarities throughout the world. First, savanna fires are common in the whole tropics [5]. Secondly, the forest succession happens as follow [6,7]. Light-demanding forest pioneer species disperse seeds and settle in savanna (at the forest edge or further). Provided they do not burn, they grow, shadow the soil and attract forest seed-dispersers. Other forest trees settle beyond and so the edge progresses or a grove appears.

However, if the processes that come into play are identical, there are regional particularities in their parameters and details. The pioneer species that first settle in open-land vary and each of them has its own characteristics (ability for

P.M.A. Sloot, B. Chopard, and A.G. Hoekstra (Eds.): ACRI 2004, LNCS 3305, pp. 484–491, 2004.

their seeds to travel far, ability to resist fire...). Then, in zones of homogeneous vegetation, there can be great changes in how often savannas experience fires (savannas near villages usually burn every year, the other more or less often). This results in differences especially in the rate of edge progression, in the number and shape of clusters of forest trees in savanna. The few existing studies (e.g. [2, 4]) fail to reconstruct the relation between the ecological and ethnological characteristics and the observed emergent behavior. That can be done with a mechanistic model, incorporating the key processes and taking the differences into account. It allows to check the effects of the virtual tuning of the parameters, their effects on the emergent behavior and then check using field studies. Moreover, such a model allows to generalize the knowledge acquired in some spots to the whole ecologically homogeneous region, where differences can appear, for example, in the man-induced disturbance.

2   The FORSAT Model

2.1   Modelling the Key Processes

The FORSAT model [8] is designed in the cellular automata framework: the space unit is a 5-meter-sided square cell which can take four states of vegetation : 'Herbs', 'Young Pioneers', 'Adult Pioneers' and 'Forest'. These states correspond to vegetation stages different in their constitution and their fire sensitivity. 'Herbs' represents grasses and herbs (either savanna grasslands with a sparse shrubby vegetation or low understory vegetation in forest clearings). 'Young pioneers' represents seedlings or bushes of forest woody pioneer species: it is the first stage in the colonization by the forest. 'Adult pioneers' is dominated by seed producing pioneer trees with crowns above understory species. 'Forest' corresponds to patches of dense forest where the herbaceous cover is low and the structure, if not the species cohort, has reached an equilibrium. This choice brings compatibility with remote sensing data: the spatial scale is of the order of the resolution of satellite data and NDVI data can help discriminate between the different states of vegetation. What we here call stages of vegetation are similar to Plant Functional Types (PFTs), in the sense that trees are defined by their roles, which are played by different species in different parts of the tropics.

A simulated year consists in the succession of two processes, modelled stochastically (figure 1): the evolution following the succession cycle with yearly probabilities to for each cell to switch to the next state and the fire propagation in savanna. The choice for stochastic modelling is motivated by the need of restraining the numbers of parameters involved in processes poorly known in detail.

During the succession processes, each cell is assigned a probability to turn into the next state in the succession cycle. These probabilities are related to biological processes and properties: rates of seed dispersal and sprouting, growth, mortality... For the transitions from 'Young Pioneers' to 'Adult Pioneers' (growth) and from any stage to 'Herbs' (death), the probabilities of transition are uniformly distributed. The transitions from 'Herbs' to 'Young Pioneers' (recruitment) and

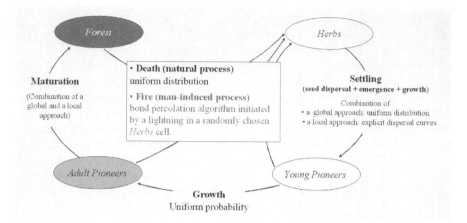

Fig. 1. Synopsis of the processes modelled by FORSAT

from '*Adult Pioneers*' to '*Forest*' (maturation) involve a spatially structured sub-process: seed dispersal. Each seed producer – represented by '*Adult Pioneers*' and '*Forest*' cells for the recruitment transition and by '*Forest*' cells for the maturation transition – confers to other cells a probability of transition depending on their relative distances. The function relating the probability of successful seed dispersal events at the distance from the parent tree is termed seed shadow. Short-distance seed shadow is considered explicitly, whereas far seed dispersal is considered to confer an additional background uniform probability.

Savanna fires are modelled by an iterative bond-percolation-type algorithm, similar to that used in [9]. Each cell in the direct neighborhood of a burning one is conferred a probability to be ignited, that depends on wind and on its vegetation stage (the four vegetation stages have decreasing susceptibility to burn).

Two parameters influence these processes: an environmental factor (modifying the transition probabilities and representing how environmental conditions as climate or soil facilitate the succession cycle) and the frequency of lightning of fires in savannas.

2.2   Model Analysis

The first step of the model analysis consisted in choosing realistic parameters (although not explicitly based on field studies) to check whether the processes chosen are able to reproduce qualitatively the real patterns of transgression. The initial state is a 180×200 cell landscape of forest savanna interface displaying two savanna gulfs.

Then, we studied the quantitative effects of both parameters. For different fire frequencies, we investigated the equilibrium for varying environmental factors with two kinds of initial conditions: savanna (only '*Herbs*') and forest (only '*Adult Pioneers*'). The other parameters 1 have been taken as simple as possible

Table 1. Summary of the parameters used for the different simulations. (1): parameters used for exploring the qualitative emergent behavior. (2): parameters used for the forest-savanna phase transition study.

State	Probability of transition to the next state	Burning probability (1,2)
'Herbs'	(1) Global: 0.02 Local: Gaussian probability $p = 0.1 \cdot \exp(-0.1x^2)$ up to 10 cells near seed cells (2) Global: 0.05 Local: $p = 0.1$ next 'Adult Pioneers'	1
'Young Pioneers'	Global: 0.2	0.5
'Adult Pioneers'	(1) Local: 0.2 next forest cells (2) —	0.2
'Forest'	—	0.005
Other parameters:	(1,2) Death probability: 0.005 (1) Fire frequency: 0.5 (1) Environmental factor: 1.0	

to investigate the phenomenological effects (pioneer and forest seed shadows restricted to the nearest neighbors).In both case, the map contains 256×256 cells, of which the 200×200 cell central region is considered to avoid edge effects.

3 Emergent Behavior

3.1 Phenomenological Behavior

FORSAT proved able to reproduce the qualitative patterns of forest transgression observed in field studies (figure 2): (i) the linear progression of the forest edge, (ii) the filling of savanna gulfs – that is a faster edge progression in the curved edges –, (iii) the creation of clusters of forest in savanna, (iv) their coalescence or incorporation in the forest domain starting by a vegetation bridge between the two entities.

Two aspects, more or less independent, need to be considered: the evolution of the forest edge and the evolution of clusters of forest trees in savanna.

3.2 Savanna Phase or Forest Phase

With the simplified model, two kinds of equilibrium can be reached: a forest, where the region is dominated by 'Adult Pioneers' cells or a savanna, dominated by 'Herbs' and 'Young Pioneers' cells. In reference to the statistical physics theory, these two equilibria can be considered as two phases of the dynamical system. A given state can be characterized by the proportion of space occupied

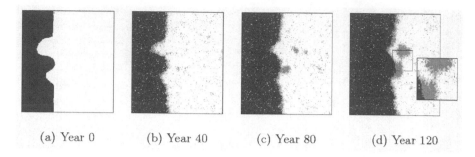

(a) Year 0   (b) Year 40   (c) Year 80   (d) Year 120

Fig. 2. Phenomenological emergent behaviour: progression of forest edge, filling of savanna gulfs, nucleation, growth and incorporation of clusters. Zoom: bridge of vegetation between the forest and the cluster. (maps: 180 × 200 cells)

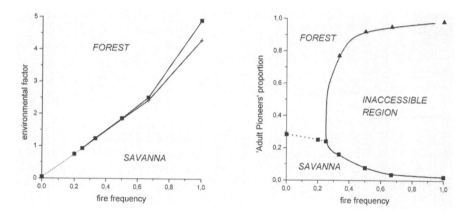

Fig. 3. Left: critical line in the parameters space separating the regions for which the equilibrium is forest or savanna. Right: phase transition diagram. For low fire frequencies, the transition is continuous: all tree covers can be reached. For more frequent fire frequencies, the transition is discontinuous: only very low (for low envorinmental factors) or very high tree covers (for high environmental factors) can be rached.

by the largest cluster of '*Adult Pioneers*' cells: this order parameter (analogous to that for percolation systems) is near zero for the savanna phase (a continuous herbaceous layer with scattered trees) and positive for the forest phase (continuous tree cover possibly interspread with herbs).

The two parameters control a van-der-Waals-like phase transition (figure 3). In the parameter space, the critical line is increasing: the greater the environemental factor is, the greater the fire frequency must be to maintain a savanna. Moreover, the transition is continuous for low environmental factors/fire frequency but discontinuous for higher values. This discontinuity is characterized by an hysteresis: there is a range of parameters for which both savanna and forest can be stable.

3.3   Phase Transition Dynamics

The relative dynamics of forest and savannas can be derived from classical considerations about phase transitions dynamics.

First, in the region of parameters for which savanna is stable, 'Adult Pioneers' cells organize in small clusters that grow and disappear but whose size distribution is fixed, leading to the constant proportion described in the former paragraph. In this situation a forest edge recedes.

In the region where forest is the stable phase, clusters of forest appear, grow over savanna and finally coalesce until total invasion. Once the cluster is big enough, the 'Young Pioneers' and 'Adult Pioneers' cells at the border protect the centre from fire. The number of clusters and their growth rate of course depend upon the values of the control parameters of the transition. Near the threshold, there are few clusters that can emerge and they grow big before they merge and coalesce. As the parameters get farther from the threshold, the time of coalescence decreases: the rate of cluster creation and the rate of growth of the clusters both increase. For values very far from the threshold, the dynamics is so rapid that no spatial structure really appear: there is a global afforestation. This cluster formation is accompanied by a forest edge expansion.

In the hesteresis region, no cluster grows in savannas. Forest expansion is only mediated by the forest edge progression over the savanna.

4   Discussion

When dealing with the emergent behavior of the FORSAT model, the concept of phase transition naturally arises. It is of recent application in ecological studies [10] and the challenge is to make the correspondence between the theoretical results and the ecological and sociological data. We bring here some tracks.

First, the van-der-Waals-like transition brings an explanation for the minlines of the tropical ecosystems repartition in Africa. There, open savannas (with nearly no tree cover) come in between the humid dense forest in the equatorial climatic zones and the wooded savannas or open forests in the dry tropical ones [11]. This paradoxical phytogeographical hiatus is easily explained in the framework described here. In the most humid regions, the environmental factors are high and the transition is discontinuous. Only dense forests and open savannas can exist. Intermediate formations with various tree density can only persist for less favourable environmental conditions (e.g. in arider regions).

Moreover, four kind of dynamics emerge from the FORSAT model that relate to observations:

1. a global afforestation of savanna [12, 13];
2. a progressive encroachment of savannas by apparition, growth and coalescence of clusters of pioneer trees [1, 14];
3. a progression of the forest edge over a preserved savanna [15, 14];
4. a recession of the forest edge [16].

The four of them can happen in one ecologically homogeneous region – where species involved are the same. It is the combination of soil, climate and human pressure (fire) that determines which kind of dynamics takes place. For example, an historical change in climate or human disturbances can help cross the threshold between two dynamics. Spatial changes can also modify locally the dynamics – savannas next to a village burnt more often than those farther away, heterogeneity of soil conditions.

A correlation can be established with field experiments to explain why current measured transgression rates can be so much weaker than those that have been inferred from paleoenvironmental reconstruction. In the past, anthropogenic pressure was weaker than it is now and potentially weak enough to pass the stable coexistence/invasion threshold. In included savannas, afforestation of the zone has taken place at a fast pace. In open landscape, however, dispersal should be assumed to be distance-dependent, and it decreases with distance from the forest edge. Therefore, forest clumps are created in savanna near the forest front. These clumps are progressively incorporated and can also grow.

Paleoenvironmental patterns of forest-savanna dynamics can be interpreted within this framework. One scenario is that gallery forests constituted microrefuges of dry epochs, from which the dense forest could have expanded. Once favorable environmental conditions are met, dense forest clusters would have formed in savanna, and would have been progressively included in the forest zone, creating included savannas that would in turn be rapidly filled. With the increase of human pressure (fires), the system switched to the other regime of a slow linear progression scenario that has been observed in most present studies [17].

Acknowledgments. This work is part of ECOFIT program (Intertropical forest ecosystems and paleoecosystems, CNRS-IRD-CEA program).

References

1. Gautier, L.: Contact forêt-savane en Côte d'Ivoire centrale: évolution de la surface forestière de la réserve de Lamto (sud du V-Baoulé). Bull. Soc. Bot. France, Actual. Bot. **136** (1989) 85–92
2. Schwartz, D., de Foresta, H., Mariotti, A., Balesdent, J., Massimba, J., Girardin, C.: Present dynamics of the savanna-forest boundary in the Congolese Mayombe: a pedological, botanical and isotopic (^{13}C and ^{14}C) study. Oecologia **106** (1996) 516–524
3. Ratter, J.: Transitions between cerrado and forest vegetation in Brazil. In et al., F., ed.: Nature and dynamics of forest savanna boundaries. Chapman & Hall, London (1992) 417–429
4. Youta Happi, J.: Arbres Contre Graminées : La Lente Invasion de la Savane Par la Forêt Au Centre-Cameroun. PhD thesis, Université Paris IV (1998)
5. Schmitz, A., Fall, A., Rouchiche, S.: Contrôle et utilisation du feu en zones arides et subhumides africaines. (1996) http://www.fao.org/docrep/T0748F/t0748f00.htm.

6. Ratter, J.: Ecological processes at the forest-savanna boudary. In et al., F., ed.: Nature and dynamics of forest savanna boundaries. Chapman & Hall, A. Hopkins (1992) 21–34

7. Letouzey, R.: Etude Phytogéographique du Cameroun. Encyclopédie Biologique LXIX, Editions P. Lechevalier, Paris (1968)

8. Favier, C., Fabing, A., Chave, J., Schwartz, D., Dubois, M.: Modelling forest-savanna mosaic dynamics in anthropogenic environments: effects of fire, climate and soil heterogeneity. Ecological Modelling 171 (2004) 82–104

9. Hargrove, H., Gardner, R., Turner, M., Romme, W., Despain, D.: Simulating fire patterns in heterogeneous landscapes. Ecological Modelling 135 (2000) 243–263

10. Li, B.: A theoretical framework of ecological phase transitions for charaterizing tree-grass dynamics. Biotheoretica 50 (2002) 141–154

11. Aubréville, A.: Les lisières forêt-savane dans les régions tropicales. Adansonia 6 (1966) 175–187

12. Eden, M., McGregor, D.: Dynamics of the forest-savanna boundary in the Rio Branco-Rupunumi region of northern Amazonia. In et al., F., ed.: Nature and dynamics of forest savanna boundaries. Chapman & Hall, London (1992) 77–89

13. Louppe, D., Ouattara, N., Coulibaly, A.: Effet des feux de brousse sur la végétation. Bois et Forêts des Tropiques 245 (1995) 59–74

14. Favier, C., de Namur, C., Dubois, M.: Forest progression modes in littoral Congo, Central Atlantic Africa. Journal of Biogeography 31 (2004) 1445–1461

15. de Foresta, H.: Origine et volution des savanes intramayombiennes (R. P. du Congo). ii. apports de la botanique forestière. In Lanfanchi, R., Schwartz, D., eds.: Paysages quaternaires de l'Afrique centrale atlantique. Editions de l'ORSTOM, Paris (1990)

16. Puyravaud, J., Pascal, J., Dufour, C.: Ecotone structure as an indicator if changing forest-savanna boundaries (Linganamakki Region, southern India). Journal of Biogeography 21 (1994) 581–593

17. Guillet, B., Achoundong, G., Youta Happi, J., Kamgang Kabeyene Beyala, V., Bonvallot, J., Riera, B., Mariotti, A., Schwartz, D.: Agreement between floristic and soil organic carbon isotope ($^{13}C/^{12}C$, ^{14}C) indicators of forest invasion of savannas during the last century in Cameroon. Journal of Tropical Ecology 17 (2001) 809–832

Learning What to Eat: Studying Inter-relations Between Learning, Grouping, and Environmental Conditions in an Artificial World

Daniel J. van der Post and Paulien Hogeweg

Department of Theoretical Biology and Bioinformatics, Utrecht University,
Padualaan 8, 3584 CH, Utrecht,
D.J.vanderPost@bio.uu.nl,
http://www-binf.bio.uu.nl

Abstract. In this paper we develop an artificial world model to investigate how environmental conditions affect opportunities for learning. We model grouping entities that learn what to eat in a 2D environment. We study diet development and focus on the social consequences of individual learning in relation to different environmental conditions.
We find that homogeneous and patchy environments have opposite effects on learning. Homogeneous environments lead to diet differentiation, while patchy environments lead to diet homogenization among the members of a group. In patchy environments, grouping results in a social influence on individual learning and could be the simplest way to achieve social inheritance of information. Moreover, diet differentiation can affect group cohesion, leading to group fragmentation along dietary lines. This suggests that if social learning leads to diet homogenization, it could play a role in maintaining group cohesion.

1   Introduction

Social learning and foraging cultures appear to have considerable impact on the foraging behavior of non-human primates. Different food extraction techniques are employed by different groups of chimpanzees [1] and orang-utans [2], and to lesser extent in, for example, capuchin monkeys [3]. These, together with differences in diet that cannot be attributed to ecological factors, constitute evidence for foraging cultures. Social learning constitutes a non-genetic means of information transfer and seems to be an important addition to genetic evolution of behavior.

The discussion on social learning centers mainly around the underlying cognitive mechanisms [4] and its adaptive value [5,6]. Social learning is thought to be adaptive because it reduces the costs of trial and error learning. It is clear, however, that there are many more factors that determine whether social learning and culture can occur. For example, given sufficient cognitive abilities, the emergence of culture depends on the need for sophisticated food extraction or

P.M.A. Sloot, B. Chopard, and A.G. Hoekstra (Eds.): ACRI 2004, LNCS 3305, pp. 492–501, 2004.

processing [7], group size [8,9] and tolerance within a group [2,10]. From this perspective, Coussi-Korbel and Fragaszy [11] have developed a speculative framework where they relate social learning opportunities to primate social dynamics (from egalitarian to despotic). Their main tenet is that despotism increases directionality and reduces the scope for social learning.

In our study we focus on the environmental opportunities for individual and social learning. We aim to gain an understanding of the types of interactions and feedbacks that arise when groups of individuals forage and learn in a given environmental background. We have developed an artificial world where foraging individuals have to learn what to eat. We model individuals which form groups and interact with their environment in a way that is sufficiently representative for primates, yet remains simple enough to understand. An important aspect of our model is the flexibility of interaction between model components, allowing for self-organizing processes to arise. In the present study we look only at individual learning, but we relate our results to social learning and social information inheritance.

2   Model

Our artificial world is a 2D environment with a high number of resource types in which individuals forage in groups. The model is constructed using a combination of a multi-layer cellular automata for the environment and an individual-oriented component for entities that learn to forage. Unlike most ecological models, predator-prey relations are not predefined. Individuals must learn what to eat, so defining their own ecological dynamics.

Local ecological and social context, and individual internal state, determine individual behavior. In this way foraging is dependent on the ecological and social opportunities that arise. Therefore learning is not a default strategy, but depends on who and what individuals can see. Furthermore, learning is linked to genetically determined gastro-intestinal digestive capacity, thus determining the types of resources that can be digested. The model, as used in this study, is described below.

2.1   Environment

The environment is a 20 layer cellular automata (CA) where each layer represents space for resources. The ecological dynamics are limited by single seasonal influxes of resources and subsequent depletion through foraging. A varying number of resource types (species) are modeled and each can have varying degrees of 5 nutrients, bulk and toxicity ($\sum(R_i) + R_{tox} + R_{bulk} = 1$), i.e. all resources have equal unit size.

Resources can be found on the CA grid points and the maximum number of resource items per location is equal to the number of layers. When items are eaten they are removed from the field.

2.2   Individuals

We model individuals which forage in groups using an event-based formalism. Their behavioral repertoire involves moving, searching for food, eating and doing nothing. Furthermore, individuals digest food and learn. Individuals move in a continuous 2D space and can learn during foraging when they find unknown resources. Movements are determined by grouping tendency and food availability.

When modeling foraging we have taken into account that selectivity is an important aspect of primate foraging [12,13]. We model foraging motivation (probability) as a decreasing sigmoid function of an individual's stomach contents. Parameters are set to ensure that an individual's stomach becomes full considerably before digestion has taken place, increasing the importance of selectivity. Furthermore, we model individuals to form estimates of environmental conditions to enable them to adjust their selectivity to changes in the environment. However, the adjustment occurs with sufficient delay to ensure selectivity in a heterogeneous environment. We assume that expectations play a role in primate foraging and believe them to be important for the learning process. For the present model we use individuals that do not evolve, reproduce or die.

Grouping. In contrast to many models of flocking and schooling (e.g. [14]), grouping in our individuals is mediated by foraging. In this way resource availability or distribution can affect grouping. The exact individual motivation for grouping is not important for the model, however our grouping rules are inspired by the idea that primates form groups to avoid predation [15].

We achieve grouping by modeling individuals to require a minimum number of neighbors $(= 3)$ within SAFERADIUS $(= 5)$. Individuals check for safety with a certain probability and if they are not safe they move towards the largest part of the group. They do this by moving to the nearest neighbor of the fullest of four randomly oriented quadrants about themselves within MAXVIEW $(= 50)$. When individuals rejoin the group in this way, they adjust their direction to average group direction.

Foraging. Hungry individuals search for food if they are safe or haven't checked for safety. To avoid crowding, they only search for food if there are no more than a given number of eating neighbors $(= 1)$ within REACHRANGE $(= 0.9)$. They search within SEARCHRADIUS $(= 2)$ and SEARCHANGLE $(= \pi)$ in the direction the individual is facing. A random resource location (grid point on CA) within view is chosen and each resource item at that location is assessed for consumption in a random order. Searching stops when an item is chosen, but can continue up to a maximum of 20 items. If this maximum is not reached, searching continues at another random resource location in view. The maximum number of items defines the time constraints for searching during a search event.

If a food item is selected it is consumed in a subsequent EAT event. If in addition it was beyond REACHRANGE, the individual first moves towards it. If no food is selected an individual can use cues from other individuals within NEIGHAWARERANGE $(= 50)$ to find food; they move towards the part of the group where the density of feeding individuals is highest. Otherwise the individual can search again, move forward or do nothing.

Food Choice: Individuals use preferences and a preference expectation to make food choice decisions ($prob = pref_i/pref_{exp}$). Preferences are formed after digestion of a resource (see Sect. 2.3). Preference expectation is updated when a resource with a higher preference than preference expectation is eaten. Preference expectation then attains the value of that preference. If resources are less preferred than preference expectation, preference expectation decays with time. Preference expectation reflects an individual's estimate of the quality of food presently available in the environment. Resources with a negative preference are avoided. Those with preference zero are unknown.

2.3 Digestion

Digestion capacity is modeled as a normalized function over digestion for 5 nutrients (see Sect. 2.1) and a detoxification capacity: $\sum D_i + D_{tox} = 1$. Digestion takes place periodically (every 100 time steps) and the quality of a resource is equal to the energy an individual gains from it:

$$E_r = \sum_{i=1}^{5}(R_i D_i) - R_{tox}D_{tox} \tag{1}$$

Total energy over all resources eaten is equal to $\sum(E_r N_r S)$, where N_r is the number of items of resource r eaten and S is a scaling factor.

2.4 Learning

In this model there are two components to learning: (1) eating a novel resource (learn events) and (2) forming resource preferences.

Learn events: Learn events occur when individuals eat unknown resources. This occurs with a fixed probability (PROBEXP ($= 0.001$)) if there are unknown resources available. The probabilities of learning are encoded genetically and reflect learning propensity. In the current version, learn events depend only on learning opportunities in the environment and not on any previous learning.

Preference Updates: Individuals form and update resource preferences due to a feedback from digestion. Updates are equal to an update factor times the difference between the average energy gained from digestion and the average expected energy (preference) for all resources eaten:

$$Pref_i = Pref_i + (C\frac{S_i}{S_T}(E_{avg} - Pref_{avg}) \tag{2}$$

where S_i is the number of items of resource i in the stomach, S_T is the total number of items in the stomach and C is an update constant.

Since learning resource preferences depends on digestion time intervals, it is a delayed process. It is sensitive to interference when a mixture of resource types is digested simultaneously, because preference updating is averaged over all resources. Feedbacks on preferences from digestion have been shown for rats [16] and primates [17] and interference has been demonstrated in goats [18].

3 Experiments

In this paper we report on baseline experiments where we study individual learning in different environmental conditions by looking at diet development. We compare homogeneous and patchy environments and test the effect of differences in individual learning propensities.

We use a 800 by 800 field with 100 resource types. Field size is hereby large enough to avoid global resource depletion and resource diversity is high enough to allow for divergence of individual diets. For homogeneous conditions, resources are spread evenly, but not all resources are present at each location. For patchy conditions, patches don't overlap and have empty space in between (see Fig. 4). Resources are initialized simultaneously on an empty field at the beginning of each "season" ($= 10^5$ time steps) and are depleted by foraging.

When comparing different environmental conditions we ran simulations with 20 naïve individuals for 3 seasons and observed diet development, behavior and group cohesion. To test for effects of grouping we ran simulations with solitary individuals. When comparing different learning propensities we ran simulations with 20 explorative (neophilic) and 20 non-explorative (neophobic) individuals.

4 Analysis

We visualize and analyze diets using clustering techniques [19] on data matrices of feeding frequency of each individual over all resources. We display dendrograms and sorted data matrices.

On the one hand we cluster individuals to determine which individuals share dietary components and the extent of dietary overlap in a foraging group. On the other hand we cluster resources to determine which resources share patterns of foragers. In the latter case it is informative to compare distributions of feeding over resources with a randomized feeding distribution. For this we randomize individual foraging patterns over resources before clustering. This means that we randomize the feeding distributions of each individual.

For the clustering, Manhattan distances are used. When clustering individuals, we search for groups of individuals with similar diet and use average distance linkage. When clustering resources, we use single linkage focusing on the distance to the nearest resource. If these nearest neighbor distances center around a certain value, this indicates that there is no common preference for any of the resources and that feeding is over-dispersed over resources.

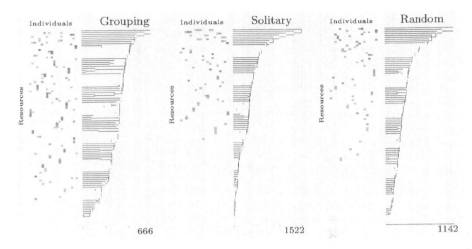

Fig. 1. Dendrograms and data matrices for 100 resources eaten in the 3rd season by 20 individuals in an homogeneous environment: grouping individuals, solitary individuals, and randomized feeding distributions. We use Manhattan distances and single linkage for clustering. Resources eaten by grouping individuals are clearly over-dispersed compared to random and solitary feeding distributions.

5   Results

5.1   Minimal Diet Overlap in Homogeneous Environments

In homogeneous environments we find that foraging groups structure the environment locally through depletion and thereby shape the opportunities for learning. Each individual tends to feed on and learn from resources not eaten by others. Thus each individual develops its own unique diet. This is revealed in cluster analysis which shows that individual diets are over-dispersed over resources types. In comparison, the distribution of resources used by solitary foragers has a closer resemblance to a randomized distribution (Fig. 1).

5.2   Large Diet Overlap in Patchy Environments

In patchy environments we find that foraging in groups has a social influence on individual learning and leads to large within-group diet overlap (group-level diets). In patchy environments foraging groups develop considerably more uniform diets than either solitary individuals in the same environment, or foraging groups in homogeneous environments (Fig. 2 a,b vs Fig. 1). In patchy environments, individuals in groups visit the same patch, therefore any learning taking place is shared with group members. As a consequence, homogenized diets develop.

Diet overlap is not perfect, especially if foraging groups can fragment and each sub-group follows different paths in space. Each sub-group encounters different resources and develops a different diet. However, comparing diets by clustering individuals from separate simulations, results in two main clusters along simulation lines (Fig. 2 c). This illustrates that groups from each simulation form their

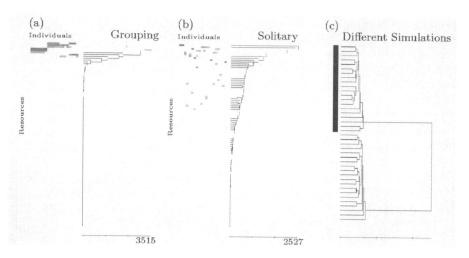

Fig. 2. Dendrograms and data matrices for 100 resources eaten in the 3rd season by 20 individuals in a patchy environment: (a) grouping and (b) solitary individuals and (c) dendrogram showing clustering of 40 individuals from two simulations (black bar indicates one simulation) according to diet. For clustering we use Manhattan distances and single linkage, except for (c) where we use average linkage. Grouping clearly results in homogenized diet development, and groups in different simulations clearly develop their own diets.

own unique diet despite encountering the same number and quality of resources. This implies that grouping in space can shape the context for individual learning, ensuring what is learned is similar to what would be learned under social learning. Thus even without social learning group-based diets emerge.

5.3   Learning Rates, Individual Variation, and Group Cohesion

In previous simulations individuals were identical and our main interest was in environmental differences. Now we study within-group differences in learning propensity (neophobic vs neophilic). Our primary result is that differences in learning cause differences in diet, reducing foraging group cohesion. In turn, diet differentiation in enhanced. How this occurs depends on the environment.

In homogeneous environments neophobia results in better quality diets (results not shown). Neophilic individuals mix more resources while learning and develop less distinguished preferences due to interference during preference updating. This reduces their selectivity during foraging. Being more selective, neophobic individuals move on sooner, thus finding more preferred and better resources and depleting these before neophilic individuals arrive. Neophobia therefore appears advantageous.

Higher movement rates in neophobic individuals brings them to the group periphery. Under present parameter settings this spatial organization does not lead to group fragmentation, but it could under less stringent grouping tendencies.

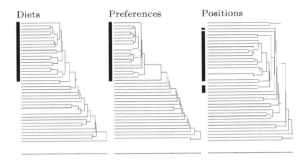

Fig. 3. Dendrograms of 20 neophilic (black bar) and 20 neophobic individuals in a patchy environment clustered on diets (over 3rd season), preferences (at end of 3rd season) and spatial positions (over 3rd season). We use average linkage and Manhattan distances, except for spatial positions where Euclidean squared distances are used. Neophilic individuals are more clustered in all cases.

In patchy environments neophilic individuals develop more homogeneous diets than neophobic individuals. This occurs because neophilia increases the rate of knowledge acquisition and the likelihood of sharing knowledge with group members. As a consequence, neophilic individuals more often stop together at patches. In contrast, neophobic individuals try to move on and end up on the group periphery. This stretches out the foraging group and increases the likelihood of group fragmentation. Fig. 3 illustrates these effects in a foraging group without fragmentation. Neophilic individuals are clearly more similar in diet and resource preferences than neophobic individuals. They are also more cohesive in space, as indicated by the shorter distances between neophilic individuals after clustering on spatial positions. Underlying these results are intricate interrelations between learning, foraging and the spatial organization of a group. This spatial organization shapes learning and foraging opportunities, yet is at the same time a product of differences in learning and foraging interests. This feedback reinforces within-group differences.

In both environments, individual differences lead to group stretching causing stress on group cohesion. In homogeneous environments this occurs because neophobic individuals are more selective foragers. In patchy environments neophobic individuals move to the group periphery because they don't share foraging interests. Whether group fragmentation actually occurs depends on the interplay between the environment and the strength of grouping tendencies. We further tested the effects of individual differences on group cohesion by running simulations with individuals initialized with different diets in a patchy environment. Results show that groups fragment clearly along dietary lines (Fig. 4).

6 Discussion

The results we present are preliminary and reflect only baseline experiments, yet they clearly demonstrate interesting inter-relations between learning, foraging

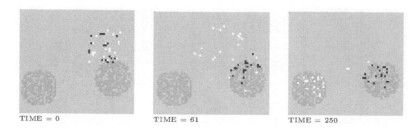

TIME = 0   TIME = 61   TIME = 250

Fig. 4. Snap shots of simulation with 2 diets (black and white individuals have different diets). From left to right: initialization together, splitting due to different feeding interests and eventual feeding on different patches

and an environment with many different resources. In our simulations, resource distributions have a large impact on how diets develop mainly as a consequence of learning opportunities per location and a structuring of the environment through depletion. Depletion leads to a reduction and bias of learning opportunities, but the way this occurs depends on the environment.

Given that competition for resources exists in a foraging group, minimal diet overlap seems a good strategy. As seen above, such diets develop automatically in a homogeneous environment. However, this stands in contrast to the group-level diets that we see in most grouping animals; nevertheless it forms an interesting baseline with which to compare diet development.

In contrast, patches allow grouping in space to assert a social influence on individual learning, resulting in group-level diets. This could be the simplest way to inherit foraging information. However, group fragmentation occurs more easily in a patchy environment and since sub-groups can develop different diets, this leads to diet diversification. Moreover, individual variation within groups stimulates group fragmentation. This is seen for individuals with different diets, but also for individuals with different learning propensities.

Social learning is mostly considered in terms of diet improvement. However, we have seen that individual learning in patchy environments leads to homogenization of diets in a way expected for social learning (see Fig. 2). Moreover, individual variation in learning rates endangers group integrity. Therefore, we suggest an alternative role for social learning, namely that it could be important in reducing individual differences in order to maintain a group's spatial cohesion.

We conclude that insights into the intricacies arising between learning, foraging and environmental conditions are important for understanding learning, diet formation and group cohesion. These intricacies cannot be studied by ethological observation in the wild, foraging experiments, nor by using minimalistic models, however they are demonstrated in the baseline simulations of this artificial world model.

Acknowledgements. This research was funded by the Netherlands Organization for Scientific Research (NWO) through grant number 051-12-040 of the Evolution and Behaviour program.

References

1. Whiten, A., Goodall, J., McGrew, W.C., Nishida, T., Reynolds, V., Sugiyama, Y., Tutin, C.E.G., Wrangham, R.W., Boesch, C.: Culture in Chimpanzees. Nature **399** (1999) 682–685

2. van Schaik, C.P., Knott, C.D.: Geographic Variation in Tool Use on Neesia Fruits in Orangutans. Am. J. Phys. Anthropol. **114** (2001) 331–342

3. Panger, M.A., Perry, S., Rose, L., Gros-Louis, J., Vogel, E., MacKinnon, K.C., Baker, M.: Cross-site Differences in Foraging Behaviour of White-faced Capuchins (Cebus capucinus). Am. Journal of Phys. Anthropol. **119** (2002) 52–66

4. Heyes, C.M.: Imitation, Culture and Cognition. Anim. Behav. **46** (1993) 999–1010.

5. Boyd, R., Richerson, R.J.: An Evolutionary Model of Social Learning: The Effects of Spatial and Temporal Variation. In: Zentall, T., Galef, B.G., Jr. (eds.): Social Learning, Erlbaum, Hillsdale, New York (1988)

6. Laland, K.N., Richerson, P.J., Boyd, R.: Animal Social Learning: Toward a New Theoretical Approach. In: Bateson, P.P.G., et al.: Perspective in Ethology **Vol 10**. Plenum Press, New York (1993) 249–277

7. Yamakoshi, G.: Dietary Responses to Fruit Scarcity of Wild Chimpanzees at Bossou, Guinea: Possible Implications for Ecological Importance of Tool Use. Am. J. Phys. Anthropol. **106** (1998) 283–295

8. Diamond, J.: Guns, Germs and Steel: the Fates of Human Societies. W. W. Norton & Company, New York (1997)

9. Diamond, J.: The Third Chimpanzee. The Evolution and Future of the Human Animal. HarperCollins publishers (1992)

10. van Schaik, C.P., Deaner, R.O., Merrill, M.Y.: Conditions for Tool Use in Primates: Implications for the Evolution of Material Culture. J. of Hum. Evo. **36** (1999) 719–741

11. Coussi-Korbel, S., Fragaszy, D.M.: On the Relationship between Social Dynamics and Social Learning. Anim. Behav. **50** (1995) 1441–1453

12. Altmann, S.A.: Foraging for survival. The University of Chicago Press (1998)

13. Chapman, C.A., Fedigan, L.M.: Dietary Differences between Neighbouring Cebus capacinus Groups: Local Traditions, Food Availability or Responses to Food Profitability? Folia Primatological **54** (1990) 177–186

14. Couzin, I.D., Krause, J., James, R., Ruxton, G.D., Franks, N.R.: Collective Memory and Spatial Sorting in Animal Groups. J. theor. Biol. **218** (2002) 1–11

15. van Schaik, C.P.: Predation, Competitive Regimes and Female Social Relationships among Gregarious, Diurnal Primates. Primate Eye **35** (1988) 10–11

16. Garcia, J., Ervin, F.R., Koelling, R.A.: Learning with Prolonged Delay of Reinforcement. Psychonomic Science **5** (1966) 121–122

17. Hasegawa, Y., Matsuzawa, T.: Food-aversion Conditioning in Japanese Monkeys (Macaca fuscata): A Dissociation of Feeding in two Separate Situations. Behavioural and Neural Biology **33** (1981) 252–25

18. Duncan, A.J., Young, S.A.: Can Goats Learn About Foods through Conditioned Food Aversions and Preferences when Multiple Food Options are Simultaneously Available? Journal of Animal Science **80** (2002) 2091–2098

19. Vilo, J.: EPCLUST, Expression Profiler, http://ep.ebi.ac.uk/Docs/EPCLUST.html

Cellular Automata in Ecological and Ecohydraulics Modelling

Arthur Mynett and Qiuwen Chen

WL | Delft Hydraulics, P.O. Box 177
2600 MH Delft, The Netherlands
{arthur.mynett, qiuwen.chen}@wldelft.nl

Abstract. Cellular Automata are discrete dynamical systems in which many simple components act together locally to produce complex patterns on a global scale, which may exhibit "self-organising" behaviour. Owing to the ability to model local interactions and spatial heterogeneity, cellular automata have been applied to very broad fields. This paper presents the application of cellular automata to modelling (i) a confined ecosystem, (ii) prey-predator population dynamics, where evolution rules are defined entirely by geometric relations, and (iii) open aquatic ecosystems where external forcings are accounted for in the definition of cell state transitions. The results indicate that cellular automata could be a valuable paradigm in ecological and ecohydraulics modelling.

1 Introduction

Cellular automata (CA) constitute a mathematical system in which many simple components act together to produce complicated patterns of behaviour. CA models define interactions between species at a local level. Complex interactions emerge on a global scale through the evolution of relatively simple local rules. Such global behaviour may be very difficult – perhaps even impossible – to describe by a set of deterministic equations due to complicated temporal and spatial relationships. The 'self-organising' property of CA implies that a randomly distributed population can generate ordered structures through a process of irreversible evolution (Chen, 2004).

Cellular automata have been applied in very broad fields, such as lattice gas hydrodynamics, urban dynamics and forest fire spreading. Owing to the ability to deal with local interactions and spatial heterogeneity, cellular automata may provide a viable approach in ecological modelling. This paper presents the capabilities of cellular automata for modelling ecological and ecohydraulics systems through several case studies. Applications include macrophyte vegetation dynamics (Chen, et al., 2002), population dynamics (Chen and Mynett, 2003) and harmful algal bloom prediction (Chen and Mynett, 2004). The model results indicate that CA could be a valuable alternative for differential equations in ecological / ecohydraulics modelling.

2 Cellular Automata for Modelling Prey Predator Dynamics

Modelling population dynamics is of increasing interest in ecological research. These kinds of ecological models are used either for qualitative estimates about species extinction or for more quantitative estimates of spreading and interaction of multiple

P.M.A. Sloot, B. Chopard, and A.G. Hoekstra (Eds.): ACRI 2004, LNCS 3305, pp. 502–512, 2004.

species under various environmental conditions. They also provide decision support to natural resources management like sustainable harvesting strategies in fishery industries. Population dynamics, however, is not very easy to describe mathematically due to the high complexity of the spatial and temporal relationships. Conventional population dynamics models are mostly aggregated, lumping species into biomass and formulating the dynamics by means of ordinary or partial differential equations. One of the simplest paradigms is provided by the predator-prey equations of Lotka-Volterra (LV). However, these models may fail to produce realistic results when individual properties and local interactions play a significant role in determining the relationships between populations and between species and its surroundings.

An alternative approach is to apply individual-based modelling techniques or spatially explicit modelling paradigms. In this paper, a cellular automata based prey-predator model (EcoCA) is developed and compared with the Lotka-Volterra model.

2.1 Development of EcoCA

EcoCA is a stochastic cellular automata based computer simulation model that was developed to approximate a simple prey-predator system (Chen, 2004). It is a two-dimensional CA model which has up to three possible cell states: empty, prey and predator. The boundary conditions are fixed in such a way that the neighbourhoods are completed with cells taking the state of empty. The state of each cell is exclusive; namely that at each time step only one of the three states can exist in one cell. The evolutions for each cell (i, j) are based on cell current state $S^t_{i,j}$, the number of its neighbouring cells occupied by prey, N^t_{py}, and the number of its neighbouring cells that are occupied by predator, N^t_{pd}, as given by

$$p = f(S^t_{i,j}, N^t_{py}, N^t_{pd}) \qquad (1)$$

where f are evolution rules defining the transition probability p that a cell will become either prey or predator dominated or empty at the next time step. These evolution rules take into account reproduction, mortality, predation, loneliness and overcrowdedness. Snapshots of a random initial condition and the spatial pattern at $t = 600$ of a demonstrated run are presented in Fig 1.

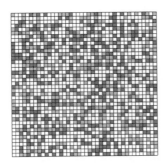
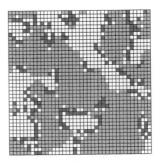

Fig. 1. Snapshots of initial condition ($t = 0$) and population dynamics ($t = 600$)

Several runs of this system with various starting conditions all lead to very similar patterns and results as exemplified by the plot of the population dynamics and phase dynamics (Fig 2).

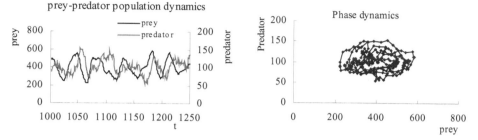

Fig. 2. Population dynamics of prey and predator (left), and phase trajectory (right)

Table 1. Statistical descriptors of EcoCA model output

	Mean	Standard deviation	Skewness
Prey	389	72.2	0.11
Predator	106	18.4	0.11

2.2   Quantification of Model Results

The model is tested to be trend-free, and it also passes the F-test that the variance is constant as well as the t-test that the mean is constant, by using split-record tests. This means that the system is stationary and the simple statistical descriptors given in Table 1 can describe the outputs from the CA model.

Using this way to quantify and visualise the performance of the CA model, it becomes possible to compare the CA model results with real and measured data. As a starting point it was decided to produce a test data set based upon the classical spatially homogeneous LV prey-predator model. This simple deterministic model provides a continuous description of a two-species competition system and may be described in terms of the following ordinary differential equation system:

$$\frac{dG}{dt} = aG - bG^2 - \alpha GH \tag{2}$$

$$\frac{dH}{dt} = -cH + \beta GH \tag{3}$$

where G represents the population of prey, H represents the population of predators, a is the intrinsic growth rate of prey, b is the carrying capacity limit, c is the mortality rate of predator, α is the functional response of prey on predator, and β is the functional response of predators to prey. Each and every organism in the prey population (G) and in the predator population (H) is considered only in relation to the total quantity of its functional type. The effect of the predators upon the prey population is only measured by the 'functional response' term GH.

These equations are highly non-linear. A 4th order Runge-Kutta method was applied to solve these equations numerically, using a time step of 0.2 days. In order to examine whether the CA model output was at all representative for the population dynamics described by the LV equations, the LV model was first calibrated to minimise the mean square error between the CA model output and the LV model output. The population dynamics and phase trajectory of the LV model is given in Fig 3.

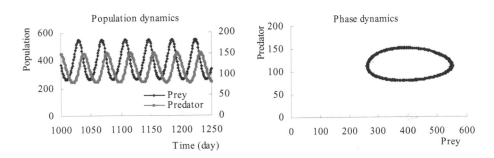

Fig. 3. Population dynamics of prey and predator (left), and phase trajectory (right)

The LV model obviously displays a more uniform and regular periodicity. This is of course a result of the purely deterministic nature of the governing equations, such that the period of oscillation is largely determined by the parameters of the model and the amplitude is determined solely by the initial conditions. Although severe reservations can be expressed about the realism of the LV model for modelling natural systems, the resulting stable limit cycle is an observable property of real populations (May, 1976). Nevertheless, in the absence of real data, the results for the LV model do provide us with a set of data that can be used to perform a quantitative comparison with the CA model. Using the methodologies described above we can quantify the magnitudes of the trend and the periodic components. Once more, the time series was tested for the absence of trend and the invariability of the mean and variance. Having satisfied these tests, the statistical properties of the LV time series were then calculated. These properties are summarised in Table 2.

Table 2. Statistical descriptors of LV model output

	Mean	Standard deviation	Skewness
Prey	389	55	0
Predator	112	14	0

Comparing the values of the statistical descriptors in Table 2 with those in Table 1, it is seen that the means of the two populations are very similar in both cases. The variance of the CA model, however, is significantly larger than the LV model and, of course, the LV model results are completely uniform and thus have a skewness of zero. The differences in the CA model can be explained by the stochastic component in the CA model, which is entirely absent in the LV model.Based on the results of this analysis, it seems fair to say that the mean field results of the CA model quite closely match the population dynamics represented by the classical LV model output.

3   Cellular Automata for Modelling Macrophyte Dynamics

Clearly, the dynamics of Conway's "Game of Life" and the EcoCA model introduced in section 2 is still purely dependent on geometric relations between neighbouring cells, and does not account for physical or biological processes. Therefore, the approach followed here is to extend the conventional cellular automata paradigm by incorporating external forcing. The CA model dynamics are thus not solely governed by the geometric relations of the particular stencil that was chosen, but also by external factors (Chen, et al., 2002a), as illustrated in Fig 4. The first case study involves a CA based model developed to simulate the competition and succession of two macrophyte species in the eutrophic Lake Veluwe, the Netherlands.

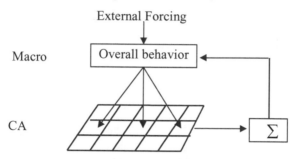

Fig. 4. Diagram of CA model coupling with other models

3.1   Description of Study Area

Lake Veluwe is an artificial isolated part of the larger Lake IJssel in the centre of the Netherlands. The total water surface is around 3300 ha, with an averaged depth of 1.4m. It was formed by the construction of dams in the Southeast part of Lake IJssel in 1952 (Fig 5). According to long-term documentation, the submerged vegetation of the lake has experienced a great change after its formation due to the change in nutrient loading. Before 1968, the water in the lake was clear, with diverse macrophyte vegetation. Due to discharge of wastewater from some small cities, the lake was eutrophicated, and blue-green algae became dominant. Some restoration measures were taken in late 1970s, which resulted in the increase of *P. pectinatus*. The increase of *P. pectinatus* provided the precondition for the return of *C. aspera*. After 1990, *C. aspera* colonised steadily and gradually replaced the dominance of *P. pectinatus*.

From an ecological point of view, it seemed that *P. pectinatus* would outcompete *C. aspera* in this lake system. However, *C. aspera* outcompeted *P. pectinatus* and replaced it gradually in Lake Veluwe. Analysis of long-term observations indicated a self-reinforcing ability of *C. aspera* during eutrophication. *C. aspera* returned at a lower phosphorus level (0.1 mg/l) than the level at the time of their disappearance (0.3

mg/l), a phenomenon known as hysteresis, therefore phosphorus is not a key factor in this case. It is supposed that the competition of dissolved inorganic carbon HCO_3^{-1} and competition of light are the two main factors of the succession. However, the replacement process remained unclear, and triggered the demand for model simulation. In view of the environmental heterogeneity and the local interactions, this research selected a CA approach to simulate the competition of light and HCO_3^{-1} in order to explain the essential features of the replacement process.

Fig. 5. The study area Lake Veluwe

3.2 Model Development

In this CA model, deterministic evolution rules obtained through laboratory and field experiments are applied. The model is designed to contain two partly interacting parallel submodels, one for *P. pectinatus* and the other for *C. aspera*. The processes considered in each submodel include shading, attenuation, HCO_3^{-1} competition, photosynthesis, respiration, morality and spreading. A conceptual framework of the model can be found in Chen, et al., (2002). General aspects of the model include: (1) germination of *P. pectinatus* and *C. aspera* from propagules; (2) initialisation with exponential growth rate; (3) growing and spreading; (4) production of propagules. The deterministic evolution rules used in this CA model are based on laboratory experiments and are calibrated against field observations. The algorithms involved are presented in some detail in Chen et al. (2002).

3.3 Results and Discussion

The simulations of the model are presented in two ways: by visualisation of the growing and spreading patterns of the two species in the lake, and by time series of biomass density averaged over sampled cells. Two graphs (Fig 6) show the changes of biomass density of *P. pectinatus* and *C. aspera* in each cell and the colonisation process resp. As shown in Fig 6, the colonisation is from the Northeast to the Southwest, and it is faster in longitudinal direction than in transverse direction. Besides, the colonisation of *C. aspera* is faster than that of *P. pectinatus*. Several simulation scenarios were carried out to test the governing factors. The results showed that the light intensity and HCO_3^{-1} are two major factors to the competitive growths of *C. aspera* and *P. pectinatus* in Lake Veluwe. Thus, shading and competition of HCO_3^{-1} become two important processes. The scarcity of HCO_3^{-1} has a great negative effect on the growth of *P. pectinatus*, while it has a indirect positive effect on the growth of *C. aspera*, which is advantageous to the replacement of *P. pectinatus* by *C. aspera*. These results are compatible with the field observations of Marcel (1999), who explored an individual based model to study the effects of changing environmental conditions on the dynamics between *C. aspera* and *P. pectinatus*. It can be concluded that a CA model with deterministic local interaction rules proved to be a good modelling paradigm where other methods had failed so far.

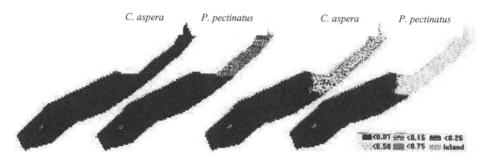

Fig. 6. Germination of both species (*P. pectinatus* germinates earlier than *C. aspera*) at the left, and colonisation pattern by the end of the second year (*P. pectinatus* spreads slower than *C. aspera*) at the right

4   Fuzzy Cellular Automata for Modelling Harmful Algal Blooms

The EcoCA and the macrophyte models use either stochastic rules or deterministic rules. However, there are many systems, in particular ecosystems such as harmful algal blooms, where the detailed mechanisms and their statistical behaviour remain unclear. For that reason, a fuzzy logic technique is introduced into the cellular automata paradigm for rule formulation, denoted as Fuzzy Cellular Automata.

4.1   Description of the Study Area

The Dutch coast receives outflow from the rivers Rhine and Meuse and is one of the most productive fishing areas in the world. In the past 20-50 years, the increase in nutrient discharged by the rivers has led to eutrophication of the coastal zones. Spring algal blooms occur frequently in Dutch coastal waters. The blooms, defined as chlorophyll *a* concentration $\geq$ 30 µg/l, are usually non-toxic, but they may be harmful because the dead algae can lead to anoxia and result in massive mussel mortality.

Algal blooming is a multidisciplinary and complex problem where hydrodynamic, chemical and biological processes take place simultaneously. The blooms usually occur very locally and show strong patchy dynamics. Some of the processes such as the hydrodynamics can be simulated numerically in detail, while a lot of biological mechanisms remain unclear. Besides, water quality and biological data are usually sparse and uncertain for detailed analysis.

Therefore, in this research an integrated numerical and fuzzy cellular automata model was developed to predict phytoplankton biomass and hence algal blooming in the Dutch coastal waters. The numerical Delft3D-WAQ (water quality) module simulates the flow and transport conditions. The fuzzy logic module was transferred from the one that was developed on the basis of Noordwijk 10 data (Chen and Mynett, 2004a) and was used to predict algal biomass on the basis of the computed abiotic factors. In order to take into account the spatial heterogeneity and local behaviour and to capture patchiness dynamics, a cellular automata paradigm was implemented in the developed model where the local evolution rules f are defined by fuzzy logic.

The study focuses on the near shore area of the Dutch coast (Fig 7). The water depth is between 0 and 30 m, and water temperature varies from 5 to 22 °C, and the irradiance is between 132~1700 Whm^{-2}day^{-1}. The concentrations of inorganic nitrogen and phosphorus are between 0.007~1.246 mg/l and 0~0.073 mg/l respectively. The biomass concentration (in chlorophyll a) is from 0.1 ~ 90.2 µg/l. The discharge from the River Rhine at the Maassluis station (including tidal effects) is between -2744~4649 m^3/s, with a mean of 1382 m^3/s. The water is usually well mixed except for temporary weak stratification caused by salinity.

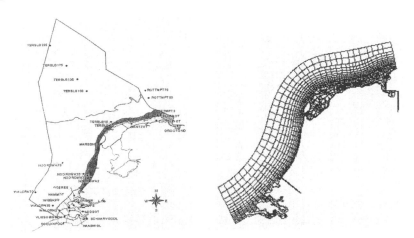

Fig. 7. Study area of Dutch coast of the North Sea and computational grid (right)

4.2 Model Development

A curvilinear grid is used for the computations with Delft3-WAQ (Fig 7), totalling 1157 computational cells in the studied area. Following the computational approach as outlined in Chen (2004), the nitrogen, phosphorus and the transport are calculated first. Since the studied area is usually well-mixed with only temporary and weak stratifications, the mean water column irradiance is used.

The fuzzy logic model was introduced to predict algal biomass on the basis of the calculated nutrient concentrations. The membership functions of Chla and dissolved inorganic nitrogen are shown in Fig 8. The other variables include Julian date, water temperature and concentration of dissolved inorganic phosphorus. There are in total 72 inference rules in the rule base that come both from ecologists' experience and from the data learning process. The simulation time step for nutrients is 1 hour and that for algal biomass is 7 days, therefore a time aggregation is made before initiating the fuzzy cellular automata module. The cellular automata module is directly implemented on the topological connectivity of the curvilinear grid. The Moore neighbourhood configuration is applied in the CA model and the local evolution rules constructed by fuzzy logic techniques follow the general formula:

$$S_{i,j}^{t+1} = f(S_{i,j}^{t}, {}^{*}S_{i,j}^{t+1}, \sum S_{N}^{t}) \tag{4}$$

where $S_{i,j}^{t+1}$ is the state of cell (i, j) at time step $t+1$, ${}^{*}S_{i,j}^{t+1}$ is the state of the cell (i, j) at time step $t+1$ which is preliminarily predicted by the fuzzy logic model, and $\sum S_{N}^{t}$ are the states of the eight neighbouring cells at time step t, while f represents the local fuzzy evolution rules.

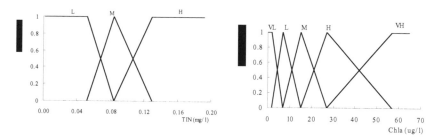

Fig. 8. Membership functions of model variables and output (left: TIN; right: Chla)

4.3   Results and Discussion

The model results for dissolved inorganic nitrogen, inorganic phosphorus and chlorophyll *a* concentrations in 1995 are given at the left of Fig 9 while the figure at the right shows a satellite image at the peak-bloom period.

The modelled peak value of chlorophyll *a* at station Noorwijk 10 is 48 μg/l which appeared on 30th April. By examining the observations of 1995, it is found that the algal bloom initiated by the end of April and the first peak at station Noorwijk 10 appeared on May 3rd with a chlorophyll *a* concentration of 58.2 μg/l. The modelled bloom timing and intensity from the fuzzy cellular automata module are seen to be somewhat close to the observations. In the spatial domain, the algal biomass is higher in the estuaries than in the coastal waters since it affected by the residual flow from the River Rhine. For comparison, the satellite image of algal bloom at the beginning of May 2003 along Dutch coast is shown in Fig 9 (right). It is difficult to quantitatively compare the modelled algae concentrations with the satellite image

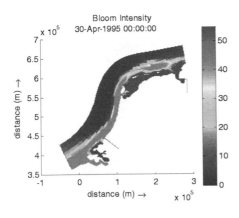
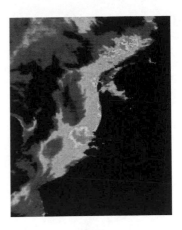

Fig. 9. Concentrations of modelled algal biomass (left) and remote sensing image (right) at peak-bloom period.

observations. However, the modelled spatial patterns are shown to be comparable with the observation. It is particularly important to point out that the application of the cellular automata paradigm has enhanced the capability of capturing patchy dynamics which can be observed from Fig 9. The case study demonstrated that this way of integrated modelling seems a promising approach indeed.

5 Discussions

It becomes apparent from the research that in ecological modelling, cellular automata exhibit good flexibility in realising local interactions and spatial heterogeneity. In order to model practical aquatic ecosystems, it is imperative to extend the purely geometrically-determined rules to include external factors. The selection of cell size and time step is determined by the governing physical and biological processes. Based on these ideas, the CA model successfully simulated the competitive growth and succession of two underwater macrophytes in a eutrophic lake, where previous efforts using PDE models failed and had to be replaced by an individual based model.

However, in aquatic ecosystems, there are usually many mechanisms remaining unclear and their statistical behaviours are difficult, if not impossible, to be defined due to limited data. Neither deterministic nor stochastic description alone is enough under such conditions. The study presented in this paper demonstrated that, although still at the initial stage, the potential to integrate different paradigms (CA and PDEs) and different techniques (fuzzy logic and numerical simulation) in ecosystem modelling. Their strength lies in the fact that (1) some processes can be simulated in detail numerically; (2) some irregular and sparse data, and the empirical knowledge from experts can be encapsulated by fuzzy logic; (3) the spatial heterogeneity, local interactions and emergence of patchiness are captured through cellular automata.

References

1. Chen, Q., Mynett, A.E., Minns, A.W., 2002. Application of cellular automata to modelling competitive growth of two underwater species *C. aspera* and *P. pectinatus* in Lake Veluwe. Ecological Modelling, 147: 253-265
2. Chen, Q., Mynett, A.E., 2003. Effects of cell size and configuration in cellular automata based prey-predator modelling. Simulation Modelling Practice and Theory, 11: 609-625
3. Chen, Q., 2004. Cellular Automata and Artificial Intelligence in Ecohydraulics Modelling, PhD thesis, Taylor & Francis Group Plc, ISBN: 90 5809 696 3
4. Marcel, S., 1999. Charophyte colonisation in shallow lakes. PhD thesis, University of Amsterdam

Chaos in a Simple Cellular Automaton Model of a Uniform Society

Franco Bagnoli[1,2,4,5], Fabio Franci[2,4], and Raúl Rechtman[3]

[1] Dipartimento di Energetica, Università di Firenze,
Via S. Marta, 3 I-50139 Firenze, Italy. bagnoli@dma.unifi.it
[2] Centro Interdipartimentale per lo Studio delle Dinamiche Complesse,
Università di Firenze, Italy. fabio@dma.unifi.it
[3] Centro de Investigacíon en Energía, UNAM,
62580 Temixco, Morelos, Mexico. rrs@teotleco.cie.unam.mx
[4] INFM, Sezione di Firenze
[5] INFN, Sezione di Firenze.

Abstract. In this work we study the collective behavior in a model of a simplified homogeneous society. Each agent is modeled as a binary "perceptron", receiving neighbors' opinions as inputs and outputting one of two possible opinions, according to the conformist attitude and to the external pressure of mass media. For a neighborhood size greater than three, the system shows a very complex phase diagram, including a disordered phase and chaotic behavior. We present analytic calculations, mean fields approximation and numerical simulations for different values of the parameters.

1 Introduction

In recent years there has been a great interest in the applications of physical approaches to a quantitative description of social and economic processes [1, 2,3,4,5,6,7,8,9,10,11,12]. The development of the interdisciplinary field of the "science of complexity" has lead to the insight that complex dynamic processes may also result from simple interactions, and even social structure formation could be well described within a mathematical approach.

In this paper we are interested in modeling the human society in order to understand the process of opinion formation applied to political elections. We know well that an extremely simplified model can not be able to catch all the possible behaviors of people in the society. Nevertheless we believe that the first step of modeling social phenomena should be a very simple model of the single person, in order to see whether the interaction among such simple individuals is already able to produce some non-trivial, complex behavior. When the simple model is well understood, one can add more ingredients and see what effects are generated by these new ingredients.

Many different approaches have been taken by scientists in this matter. The simplest choice is to consider a uniform society, where all the persons are considered equal and have the same influence on all the others. The second choice

P.M.A. Sloot, B. Chopard, and A.G. Hoekstra (Eds.): ACRI 2004, LNCS 3305, pp. 513–522, 2004.

is to consider a society divided into two groups, a group of normal people and a group of leaders (see Ref. [13]).

Another possibility is to consider all the individuals different from one another. This can be modeled using a version of the Kauffman model, where every individual has different (randomly generated) features and interacts randomly with a certain number of other individuals. Despite its simplicity, this model is able to exhibit very complex behaviors, including chaos, which can be ascribed either to the presence of disorder and asymmetric coupling, or to frustrations.

In this paper we start exploring the behavior of a model of an uniform society. By uniform we mean that everybody is exactly like the others, except for the expressed opinion (that may vary with time). All other parameters are exactly the same.

We use a simple neural network model to approximate the process of opinion formation taking place in a society. With this approximation, the individual is represented by an automaton that receives some external inputs, elaborates them using a certain function, and elaborates a response.

As a first step, we study the behavior of the simplest, one-dimensional neural network, composed by binary perceptrons. Such a model has been successfully applied to anticipate personal preferences on products (see Ref. [14]). The inputs for each perceptron are given by the opinions expressed by other persons in a local community, whose size is R.

The parameters of the model are the influence of the mass-media (H), the weight J assigned to the the local community (that can be thought as the result of education), and the conformist threshold Q. This last parameter models the empirical fact that even a strong mass-media campaign or a strong anti-conformist attitude cannot modify an opinion if it is supported by a strong majority in the local community. If the local majority is outside the thresholded intervals, the evolution rule is that of a Monte-Carlo simulation of an equilibrium system with heat-bath dynamics.

The system may be trapped into one of the two absorbing states (uniform opinion), or exhibit several kinds of irregular behavior. Technically, it is an extension of a probabilistic cellular automata with a very rich phase diagram [15], whose mean-field approximation was described in Ref. [16]. A detailed investigation of its behavior will be illustrated elsewhere [17].

This model can also be seen as a Cellular Neural Network [18,19,20], since it is made up of simple non-linear processors which are locally connected.

In Sec. 2 we present this probabilistic cellular automata model and present the main results. In Sec. 3 we extend the concept of Lyapunov exponents to probabilistic cellular automata and present the results obtained for our model. Finally, in Sec. 4, we summarize our work and draw some conclusions.

2   The Model

Let x_i^t be the opinion assumed by individual i at time t. As usual in spin models, only two different opinions, -1 and 1, are possible. The system is composed by L individuals arranged on a one-dimensional lattice with periodic boundary conditions. Time is considered discrete (corresponding, for instance, to election events). The state of the whole system at time t is given by $x^t = (x_0^t, \ldots, x_{L-1}^t)$ with $x_i^t \in \{-1, 1\}$.

The individual opinion is formed according to a local community "pressure" and a global influence. In order to avoid a tie, the local community is made up of $R = 2r + 1$ individuals, including the opinion of the individual himself at previous time. The average opinion of the local community around site (person) i at time t is denoted by $m = m_i^t = \sum_{j=-r}^{r} x_{i+j}^t$.

Let J be a parameter controlling the influence of the local field in the opinion formation process and H be the external social pressure. One could think of H as the television influence, and J as the educational effects. The "field" H pushes toward one opinion or the other, and people educated toward conformist will have $J > 0$, while non-conformists will have $J < 0$.

The hypothesis of alignment with an overwhelming local majority is represented by the parameter Q, indicating the critical size of local majority. If $m < 2Q - R$, then $x_i^{t+1} = -1$, and if $m > R - 2Q$, then $x_i^{t+1} = 1$.

For simpler numerical implementation and plotting, the opinions $(-1, 1)$ are replaced by $(0, 1)$. Let us denote by S the sum of opinions in the local community using the new coding. The "magnetization" can by expressed as $m = 2S - R$, and the probability $P_S = P(1|S)$ of expressing opinion 1 given S neighbors with opinion 1 is:

$$P_S = \begin{cases} 0 & \text{if } S < Q; \\ \dfrac{1}{1 + \exp(-2(H + J(2S - R)))} & \text{if } Q \leq S \leq R - Q; \\ 1 & \text{if } S > R - Q. \end{cases} \quad (1)$$

For $Q = 0$ the model reduces to an Ising spin system. For all $Q > 0$ we have two absorbing homogeneous states, $x = 0$ and $x = 1$, corresponding to an infinite plaquette coupling in the statistical mechanical sense. With these assumptions, the model reduces to a one-dimensional, one-component, totalistic cellular automaton with two absorbing states.

The order parameter is the fraction c of people sharing opinion 1[1]. It is zero or one in the two absorbing states, and assumes other values in the active phase. The model is symmetric since the two absorbing states have the same importance.

The quantities H and J range from $-\infty$ to ∞. For easy plotting, we use the parameters $j = [1 + \exp(-2J)]^{-1}$ and $h = [1 + \exp(-2H)]^{-1}$ as control parameters, mapping the real axis $(-\infty, \infty)$ to the interval $[0, 1]$.

The fraction c of ones in a configuration and the concentration of clusters ρ are defined by

$$c = \frac{1}{L} \sum_i S_i \quad \text{and} \quad \rho = \frac{1}{L} \sum_i |S_i - S_{i+1}|.$$

---

[1] The usual order parameter for magnetic system is the magnetization $m = 2c - 1$.

In the mean-field approximation, the order parameters c and ρ are related by $\rho = 2c(1-c)$. Both the uniform zero-state and one-state correspond to $\rho \to 0$ in the thermodynamic limit.

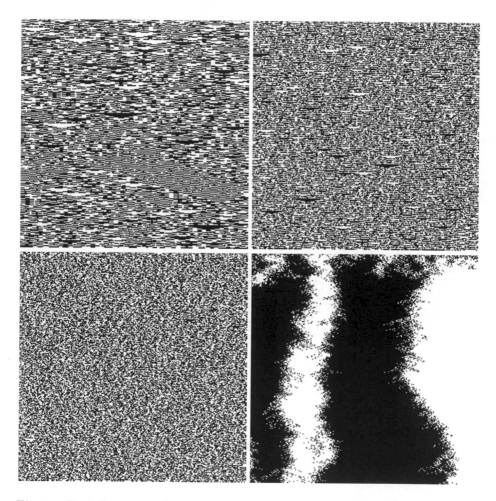

Fig. 1. Typical patterns (256×256 pixels) for $R11Q1$ and $H = 0$, starting from a disordered initial condition with $\rho_0 = 0.5$. (A) [top left, $j = 0.056250$]: "chaotic" phase. One can observe rare "triangles" with "base" larger that R, corresponding to the unstable absorbing states, and other metastable patterns, corresponding to additional absorbing states for $J \to -\infty$. (B) [top right, $j = 0.421875$]: active phase, the only absorbing states are 0 and 1. (C) [bottom left, $j = 0.478125$]: disordered phase. (D) [bottom right, $j = 0.562500$]: quiescent phase. In this phase the only stable states are the absorbing ones. The boundaries separating the phases move randomly until coalescence.

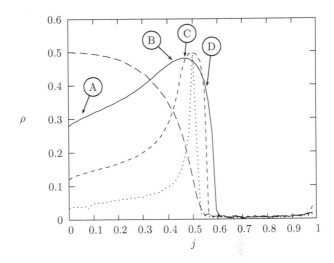

Fig. 2. Behavior of ρ for $H = 0$. $R3Q1$ (long dashed), $R11Q1$ (solid), $R41Q1$ (dashed) and $R81Q1$ (dotted). Letters correspond to patterns in Fig 1.

Typical patterns for $H = 0$ are shown in Fig. 1. Roughly speaking, for ferromagnetic ($J > 0$) coupling, the only stable asymptotic states are the absorbing ones. The system quickly coalesce into large patches of zeroes and ones (Fig. 1-D), whose borders perform a sort of random motion until they annihilate pairwise. For $J < 0$ the stable phase is represented by an *active* state, with a mixture of zeroes and ones. For $J \to \infty$ the automaton become deterministic, of "chaotic" type (for R=3 it is Wolfram's rule 150).

As illustrated in Fig. 2, when R is greater than 3, the quantity ρ is no more a monotonic function of j, and a new, *less disordered* phase appears inside the active one for small values of j. This phase is characterized by a large number of metastable states, that become truly absorbing only in the limit $J \to -\infty$. For reasons explained in the following, we shall denote the new phase by the term *irregular*, and the remaining portion of the active phase *disordered*. By further increasing R, both transitions become sharper, and the size of the disordered phase shrinks, as shown in Fig. 2. By enlarging the transition region one sees that for $H = 0$ (Fig. 3) the transitions are composed by two sharp bends, which are not finite-size or time effects. As shown in Fig. 1-C, in this range of parameters the probability of observing a local absorbing configurations (i.e. patches of zeroes or ones) is vanishing. All others local configurations have finite probability of originating zeroes or ones in the next time step. The observed transitions are essentially equivalent to those of an equilibrium system, that in one dimension and for short-range interactions cannot exhibit a true phase transition. The bends thus become real salient points only in the limit $R \to \infty$.

The origin of the order-disorder (II) and disorder-irregular (I) phase transition is due to the loss of stability of the fixed point $c^* \neq 0, 1$ given by the mean

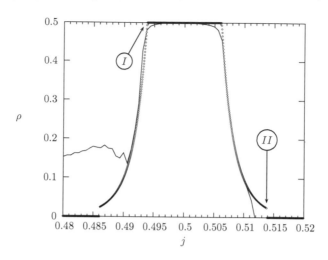

Fig. 3. Comparisons between numerical (thin line) and mean-field (thick dotted line) results for $R81Q1$ and $H = 0$ ($h = 0.5$). The estimated critical values are $j_I^* \simeq 0.493827$ and $j_{II}^* \simeq 0.51384$.

field approximation (in the limit of large R)

$$
c' = \begin{cases}
0 & \text{if } c < \tilde{Q}, \\
1 & \text{if } c > 1 - \tilde{Q}, \\
\dfrac{1}{1 + \exp(-2(H + \tilde{J}(2c - 1)))} & \text{otherwise.}
\end{cases}
\tag{2}
$$

where $\tilde{J} = JR$ and $\tilde{Q} = Q/R$. More details can be found in [17].

For $H = 0$, the mean field approximation (Fig. 4) gives essentially three possible scenarios: a stable value of c intermediate between 0 and 1, or a final absorbing state either due to ferromagnetic ($J > 0$) or strongly antiferromagnetic ($J < 0$) coupling. In a field-theoretic interpretation, the first scenario is reflected by the disordered pattern of Fig. 1-c, the second by the randomly-moving absorbing patches of Fig. 1-d, and the third one by Fig. 1-a. In this latter case, the locally absorbing patches are disposed in a checkboard-like pattern, and are essentially unstable by boundary perturbations. This essentially corresponds to the dynamics of a Deterministic Cellular Automata (DCA) of *chaotic* type, i.e. a system which is insensitive of infinitesimal perturbations but reacts in an unpredictable way to *finite* perturbations.

3   Chaos and Lyapunov Exponent in Cellular Automata

State variables in cellular automata are discrete, and thus the usual chaoticity analysis classifies them as stable systems. The occurrence of disordered patterns and their propagation in stable dynamical systems can be classified into two main groups: *transient chaos* and *stable chaos*.

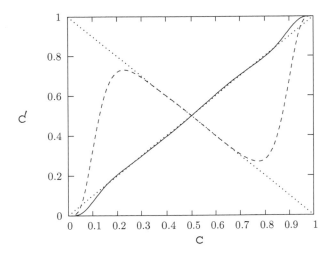

Fig. 4. Mean field map Eq. (2) in the neighborhood of transition I (solid) and II (dashed).

Transient chaos is an irregular behavior of finite lifetime characterized by the coexistence in the phase space of stable attractors and chaotic non attracting sets – namely chaotic saddles or repellers [21]. After a transient irregular behavior, the system generally collapses abruptly onto a non-chaotic attractor. Cellular automata do not display this kind of behavior, which however may be present in systems having a discrete dynamics as a limiting case [22].

Stable chaos constitutes a different kind of transient irregular behavior [23, 24] which cannot be ascribed to the presence of chaotic saddles and therefore to divergence of nearby trajectories. Moreover, the lifetime of this transient regime may scale exponentially with the system size (supertransients [23,24]), and the final stable attractor is practically never reached for large enough systems. One is thus allowed to assume that such transients may be of substantial experimental interest and become the only physically relevant states in the thermodynamic limit.

The emergence of this "chaoticity" in DCA dynamics, is effectively illustrated by the damage spreading analysis [25,26], which measures the sensitivity to initial conditions and for this reason is considered as the natural extension of the Lyapunov technique to discrete systems. In this method, indeed, one monitors the behavior of the distance between two replicas of the system evolving from slightly different initial conditions. The dynamics is considered unstable and the DCA is said chaotic, whenever a small initial difference between replicas spreads through the whole system. On the contrary, if the initial difference eventually freezes or disappears, the DCA is considered non chaotic.

Due to the limited number of states of the automata however, damage spreading does not account for the maximal "production of uncertainty", since the two replicas may synchronize locally just by chance (self-annihilation of the dam-

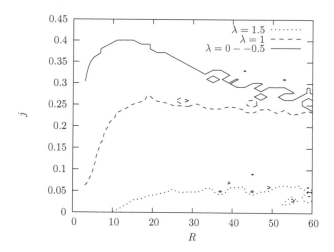

Fig. 5. Contour plot of the maximum Lyapunov λ exponents for different values of neighborhood size R and conformist parameter j. The solid line represent the boundary between the $\lambda \geq 0$ phase and the $\lambda = -\infty$ one.

age). Moreover, there are different definitions of damage spreading for the same rule [27].

To better understand the nature of the active phase, and up to what extent it can be denoted *chaotic*, we extend the finite-distance Lyapunov exponent definition [28] to probabilistic cellular automata. A similar approach has been used in Ref. [29], calculating the Lyapunov exponents of a Kauffman random boolean network in the annealed approximation. As shown in this latter paper, this computation gives the value of the (classic) Lyapunov exponent obtained by the analysis of time-series data using the Wolf algorithm.

Given a Boolean function $f(x, y, \dots)$, we define the Boolean derivative $\partial f / \partial x$, as

$$\frac{\partial f}{\partial x} = \begin{cases} 1 & \text{if } f(|x-1|, y, \dots) \neq f(x, y, \dots), \\ 0 & \text{otherwise,} \end{cases}$$

which represents a measure of sensitivity of a function with respect to its arguments. The evolution rule of a probabilistic cellular automaton may be thought as a Boolean function that depends also by one or more random arguments. In our case

$$f(x_1, x_2 \dots; r) = f(S; r) = [r < P_S],$$

where $S = x_1 + x_2, \dots$, P_S is defined by Eq. (1) and [statement] is the truth function, which gives 1 if the statement is true and 0 otherwise. In this case the derivative is taken with respect to x_i by keeping r constant.

For a cellular automaton rule, we can thus build the Jacobian $J_{ij} = \partial x_i^{t+1} / \partial x_j^t$. This Jacobian depends generally on the point in phase-space (the configurations) belonging to a given trajectory. In the case of a probabilistic automaton, the trajectory also depends on the choice of the random numbers r.

Finally, the maximum Lyapunov exponent λ is computed in the usual way by measuring the expansion rate of a "tangent" vector $\boldsymbol{v}(t)$, whose time evolution is given by

$$\boldsymbol{v}(t+1) = \boldsymbol{J}\boldsymbol{v}(t).$$

As explained in Ref. [28], a component $v_i(t)$ of this tangent vector may be thought as the maximum number of different paths following which any initial $(t = 0)$ damage may reach the site i at time t, without self-annihilation. When all components of $\boldsymbol{v}$ become zero ($\lambda = -\infty$), no information about the initial configuration may "percolate" to $t = \infty$, and the asymptotic configuration is determined only by the random numbers used. This maximum Lyapunov exponent is also related to the synchronization properties of automata [30].

A preliminary numerical computation of λ for our model is reported in Fig. 5. It can be noticed that the boundary $j_c(R)$ of $\lambda \geq 0$ is not monotonic with R, reaching a maximum value for $R \simeq 11$. By comparisons with Fig. 2, one can see that the chaotic phase is included in the irregular one.

4 Conclusions

We have investigated a probabilistic cellular automaton model of an uniform society, with forcing local majority. The phase diagram of the model is extremely rich, showing a quiescent phase and several, active phases, with different dynamical behaviors. We have analyzed the properties and boundaries of these phases using direct numerical simulations, mean-field approximations and extending the notion of finite-distance Lyapunov exponent to probabilistic cellular automata.

References

1. H. Haken, Synergetics. An Introduction, Springer-Verlag, Heidelberg, New York, 1983; Advanced Synergetics, Springer-Verlag, Heidelberg, New York, 1983.
2. Weidlich, W.; Haag, G., Concepts and Methods of a Quantitative Sociology: The Dynamics of Interacting Populations, Berlin: Springer (1983).
3. Dendrinos, D. S.; Sonis, M., Chaos and Socio-spatial Dynamics, Berlin: Springer (1990).
4. Weidlich, W., Physics and Social Science - The Approach of Synergetics, Physics Reports 204, 1-163 (1991).
5. Vallacher, R.; Nowak, A. (eds.), Dynamical Systems in Social Psychology, New York: Academic Press (1994).
6. G. A. Cowan, D. Pines, D. Meltzer (eds.), Complexity. Metaphors, Models, and Reality, Addison-Wesley, Santa Fe, 1994.
7. Gilbert, N.; Doran, J. (eds.), Simulating societies: The computer simulation of social processes, London: University College (1994).
8. Helbing, D., Quantitative Sociodynamics. Stochastic Methods and Models of Social Interaction Processes, Dordrecht: Kluwer Academic (1995).

9. Hegselmann, R. H.; Mueller, U.; Troitzsch, K. G. (eds.), Modeling and simulation in the social sciences from the philosophy of science point of view, Dordrecht: Kluwer (1996).
10. Mantegna, R.N. & Stanley, H.E. An introduction to econophysics. Correlations and complexity in finance. *Cambridge University Press* (2000).
11. D. Stauffer, D. Sornette, Physica A 271 (1999) 496.
12. H.W. Lorenz, Nonlinear Dynamical Equations and Chaotic Economy, Springer, Berlin, New York, 1993.
13. Holyst, J.A., Kacperski, K, Schweitzer, F.: Physica A 285 (2000) 199
14. F. Bagnoli, A. Berrones and F. Franci, Physica A 332 (2004) 509–518
15. F. Bagnoli, N. Boccara and R. Rechtman, Phys. Rev. E **63**, 46116 (2001).
16. F. Bagnoli, F. Franci and R. Rechtman, in *Cellular Automata*, S. Bandini, B. Chopard and M. Tomassini (editors), (Springer-Verlag, Berlin 2002) p. 249.
17. F. Bagnoli, F. Franci and R. Rechtman, in preparation.
18. Chua, L.O., Yang, L. (1988) Cellular Neural Networks: Theory. IEEE Trans. Circ. Syst. CAS-35 1257-1272.
19. Chua, L.O., Roska, T. (1993) The CNN Paradigm. IEEE Trans. Circ. Syst. CAS-I-40 147-156.
20. Harrer, H., Nossek, J.A. (1992) Discrete-time Cellular Neural Networks. Int. J. of Circ. Th. Appl. 20 453-467.
21. T. Tel, *Proceedings of the 19th IUPAP International Conference on Statistical Physics*, edited by Hao Bai-lin (World Scientific Publishing: Singapore 1996)
22. F. Bagnoli and R. Rechtman, Phys. Rev. E **59**, R1307 (1999); F. Bagnoli and F. Cecconi, Phys. Lett. A **260**, 9-17 (2001) and references therein.
23. J.P. Crutchfield and K. Kaneko, Phys. Rev. Lett. **60**, 2715 (1988), K. Kaneko, Phys. Lett. **149A**, 105 (1990).
24. A. Politi, R. Livi, G.-L. Oppo, and R. Kapral, Europhys. Lett. **22**, 571 (1993).
25. P. Grassberger, J. Stat. Phys. **79**, 13 (1995).
26. F. Bagnoli, J. Stat. Phys. **79**, 151 (1996).
27. H. Hinrichsen, J. S. Weitz and E. Domany J. Stat. Phys. **88**, 617-636 (1997).
28. F. Bagnoli, R. Rechtman and S. Ruffo, Phys. Lett. A **172**, 34 (1992).
29. B. Luque and R.V. Solé, Physica A 284 (2000) 33–45
30. F. Bagnoli and R. Rechtman, Phys. Rev. E **59**, R1307 (1999).

Replication of Spatio-temporal Land Use Patterns at Three Levels of Aggregation by an Urban Cellular Automata

Charles Dietzel[1] and Keith C. Clarke[2]

[1] University of California, Santa Barbara, Department of Geography, 3611 Ellison Hall,
Santa Barbara, CA 93106, USA
dietzel@geog.ucsb.edu
[2] National Center for Geographic Information Analysis, University of California,
Santa Barbara, Department of Geography, 3611 Ellison Hall, Santa Barbara, CA 93106, USA
kclarke@geog.ucsb.edu

Abstract. The SLEUTH urban growth model [1] is a cellular automata model that has been widely applied throughout the geographic literature to examine the historic settlement patterns of cities and to forecast their future growth. In this research, the ability of the model to replicate historical patterns of land use is examined by calibrating the model to fit historical data with 5, 10, and 15 different land use classes. The model demonstrates it robustness in being able to correctly replicate 72-93% of the land use transitions over an eight-year time period, in both space and time.

1 Introduction

The logic and mechanisms of cellular automata (CA) allow linking the local to the global, not just through simulation and model forecasting, but also in the sense that global patterns and forms can be illustrated through local processes [2]. While there is a difficulty in simulating large systems at the micro-scale, understanding the processes and evolution of form at the smallest level allows for a better understanding and modeling of process taking place on the next hierarchical scale. The idea of cellular automata-like geographic models, simulating change at the local scale can be traced to Tobler [3], but a more formal outline of CA models and their possible use in simulating urban systems was made by Couclelis [4]. The use of CA for urban systems was slow to catch on, taking nearly a decade before there was a broad body of literature. Adaptation, experimentation, and application of these models to urban systems has been quite prolific in more recent years. One of the lures of these models is as a metaphor for urban growth and change [4], [5], but the models have the ability to at least attempt to simulate real-world systems, if not accurately mirror them [2], [7], [8], due to several advantageous properties of CA.

There are certain properties of two-dimensional CA that make them especially advantageous to use in the modeling of geographic systems. The most obvious is that

P.M.A. Sloot, B. Chopard, and A.G. Hoekstra (Eds.): ACRI 2004, LNCS 3305, pp. 523–532, 2004.
© Springer-Verlag Berlin Heidelberg 2004

CA models are spatial in the same manner that an urban or any other geographic system is. This treatment of space in an absolute manner is an advantage over other urban and regional models (spatial interaction, gravity, econometric and location-allocation) where the treatment of space is relative. The spatial aspect of CA is a natural link to geographic and remotely sensed data; much of which is used as input for these models. The raster structure of GIS and remotely sensed data sources is the same lattice structure as that present in CA models, making them ideal sources for regular grid data.

The process of simultaneous computation in CA allows for modelers to view urban systems growing over time in increments instead of just the beginning and end points. This is not to say that CA model a system at a continual temporal scale, just that the increments between time periods can be set to such a small temporal period that the result is a model that appears to be continuous in time. The flexibility in temporal dynamics that a CA model provides allows the simulation of events that occur at various timeframes; from pedestrian behavior to the growth of cities. CA act within a localized neighborhood, creating micro-scale dynamics; but when the overall micro-scale behavior of the system is taken collectively, there emerges macro-scale pattern. These dynamics are typical of complex systems where the local elements are allowed to interact, creating the macro-scale perspective.

The lattice structure and link to geographic and remotely sensed data makes CA models highly visual – giving modelers and model users the ability to visualize the results of model forecasts. This is especially helpful when models are being simulated for multiple scenarios and analysis is done within the results. Incorporating the temporal dynamics of CA with visualization, CA models allow users to view the dynamic growth process as it takes place within the model. With such advantages, the capabilities of CA for modeling urban systems are powerful. CA models easily incorporate common forms of geographic data, enables processes to take place at multiple scales, and produce outputs that are highly visual, increasing the understanding and appeal.

The SLEUTH urban growth model [1] has capitalized on these advantages to be successfully applied to a wide variety of geographic areas [9], [10], [11]. Yet the accuracy of the model in evaluating different quantities of land use classes has not been rigorously evaluated. The goal of this research is to examine the ability of the SLEUTH model to replicate the spatio-temporal patterns of land use change over an eight year period with the same dataset classified into 5, 10, and 15 land use classes. The purpose is to test the sensitivity of SLEUTH as a typical CA model to land cover class aggregation.

2   The SLEUTH Model

The SLEUTH model has the ability to model urban/non-urban dynamics as well as urban-land use dynamics, although the latter has not been widely used; presumably due to the limitations of gathering consistently classified land use data. The dual ability has led to the development of two subcomponents within the framework of the model, one that models urban/non-urban growth, the urban growth model (UGM) [1] and the other that models land use change dynamics (Deltatron). Regardless of whether each of these components is used, the model has the same calibration routine. The input of land use data during calibration activates the Deltatron part of SLEUTH.

SLEUTH is a moniker for the data required to calibrate and forecast this urban growth model. The model requires topographic data in the form of Slope and Hillshade maps, although the hillshade is used only for visualization purposes, and does not play a role in determining model outputs. Land use with consistent classification for two time periods are needed to implement the Deltatron submodel, they are not necessary to simulate urban growth, but are recommended. An Exclusion layer is used to place constraints on urban growth. Through the Exclusion layer, a user can specify where urban growth is allowed to occur, or where it is prohibited. This layer can also be a weighted layer so that 'resistances' against growth can be put in place in an attempt to slow or alter the rate of urbanization. Urban extent data is critical and necessary for this model. Four different temporal layers are needed, showing the extent of urban areas at different points in time. These maps serve as the control points, against which the model is calibrated, and a goodness of fit is determined. The last layer required for using SLEUTH is Transportation. The creation of these input maps is typically done within a geographic information system (GIS), and then they are converted to GIF format files which are the actual data used in the model.

For this model, the transition rules between time periods are uniform across space, and are applied in a nested set of loops. The outermost of the loops executes each growth period, while an inner loop executes growth rules for a single year. Transition rules and initial conditions of urban areas and land use at the start time are integral to the model because of how the calibration process adapts the model to the local environment. Clarke et al. [1] describe the initial condition set as the 'seed' layer, from which growth and change occur one cell at a time, each cell acting independently of the others, until patterns emerge during growth and the 'organism' learns more about its environment. The transition rules that are implemented involve taking a cell at random and investigating the spatial properties of that cell's neighborhood, and then urbanizing the cell, depending on probabilities influenced by other local characteristics [1]. Five coefficients (with values 0 to 100) control the behavior of the system, and are predetermined by the user at the onset of every model run. These parameters are:

1. *Diffusion* – Determines the overall dispersiveness nature of the outward distribution.
2. *Breed Coefficient* – The likelihood that a newly generated detached settlement will start on its own growth cycle.
3. *Spread Coefficient* – Controls how much contagion diffusion radiates from existing settlements.
4. *Slope Resistance Factor* – Influences the likelihood of development on steep slopes.
5. *Road Gravity Factor* – An attraction factor that draws new settlements towards and along roads.

These parameters drive the four transition rules which simulate spontaneous (of suitable slope and distance from existing centers), diffusive (new growth centers), organic (infill and edge growth), and road influenced (a function of road gravity and density) growth. By running the model in calibration mode, a set of control parameters is refined in the sequential 'brute-force' calibration phases: coarse, fine and final calibrations [9].

2.1 Deltatron Dynamics Within SLEUTH

Three types of land use transitions are assumed to take place in the Deltatron model. First are state changes where land makes a transition from one use to another (e.g. Forest to Agriculture). The Deltatron assumes that urbanization is the driver of change within the system, and that once a cell has become urbanized, it is not possible for it to transform to another state. Neighborhood transitions are also assumed where if one cell is transformed into another land use class, that similar surrounding cells have a higher probability of changing to that land use class as well. The last transition that is assumed to take place is the discrete location change, where a particular cell, while influenced by neighborhood change, changes land use on an individual level. This may be from water to wetlands or vice versa. Thus land use changes in the model are assumed to have spatio-temporal autocorrelation. This violates the "classical" CA assumptions because changes have a "memory" beyond one time cycle, albeit localized.

Three types of change influence transitions. The first is a simple Markov transition matrix that calculates the annual probability of change between all pairs of land uses. The matrix is calculated by differencing the two input land use datasets and is normalized by the number of years between the control years. Topography is also assumed to influence land use change, with slope being a factor in determining where land use classes may occur within the landscape. Urbanization will occupy the flattest land available, while areas with steep slopes are better fit for other classes such as forests and natural vegetation. The driver of change is urbanization. As the amount of urbanization increases, so too does the model's attempts at land use changes, with urban land cover consuming land that is currently in use by other land uses.
Clarke's [12] paper provides the initial outline of the Deltatron model and its primary assumptions:

1   That land transitions be considered to take place on a uniform spacing grid.
2   That transition is between and among a finite set of states, where the number of states is small
3   That the transition matrix accurately estimates land use state transition probabilities from observed counts.
4   That an external model be used to change the state of the dominant or driving class.
5   That there should exist considerable spatial autocorrelation in land transitions.
6   That there exists temporal correlation between land transitions.
7   That specific land transitions are influenced by context.

8   That land transitions happen to some degree at random, i.e. independent from the driving force.

Deltatrons themselves are defined as bringers of change within land use change space; they are the successful culmination of forces of change within the system and have their own life cycles. Deltatrons are born out of land use change between time periods. In proceeding years the likelihood of similar conversion is still high due to the assumption of spatial autocorrelation between land use transitions, and the Deltatron has the ability to affect and promote similar transitions in its neighborhood. Yet when a new land use class has been established, the probability of an immediate transition to another land use class is low. When this is the case, a Deltatron acts as a placeholder or memory and prevents subsequent transition of the land class for the duration of its lifetime. How many cycles, or years, a Deltatron lives may be able to be used as a modifiable parameter to fine-tune the model per application. Due to their sensitivity to local influences, and ability to modify behavior over time, Deltatrons are critical to the spatio-temporal autocorrelation of the land transitions. This process of Deltatron land use change is initiated within the model through two distinct phases. The first is the creation of change within the landscape, and the second is spreading the change throughout it. The result has been described as the dropping of a pebble in pool of water and then the diffusion of ripples throughout the remainder of the pool.

2.2 Creation of Landscape Change

The creation of landscape change is driven by the number of cells that were newly urbanized in the UGM. The change cycles are initiated by choosing a cell at random and then testing if it is suitable for change. There are four conditions that are enforced which prevent some cells from changing: (1). the cell contains no data. (2). the cell is already urban. (3) the cell is in some land use class that has been determined by the user to be incapable of change, water for example. (4). a Deltatron is already present at that location. When a suitable (not meeting the four conditions) cell is found, then two land use classes are randomly chosen, and the class that has the average slope value closest to the selected cell is selected, allowing topography and land cover to both play a role in the transition process. The probability of transitioning between the initial class and the randomly chosen class is calculated, and if a randomly drawn number is greater than the probability of change, then the cell does not change states, and the next random cell is selected. On the other hand, if the randomly drawn number is less that the probability of transition between the two classes, the transition takes place and is encouraged to randomly spread to its neighbors, creating a cluster. At the end of this first phase of growth, several clusters of land use transitions have been made, and a deltaspace is created, tracking the locations of changes in space and time, from which Deltatrons are 'born,' and their ages monitored. This process is summarized in Figure 1.

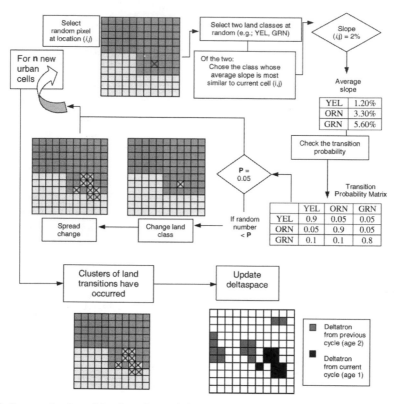

Fig. 1. Summarization of the first phase of the Deltatron model, creation of land use change.

2.3 Proliferation of Landscape Change

In the second phase of the Deltatron model, existing Deltatrons attempt to initiate change on available land within their local neighborhood. The rules for initiating this change are quite simple (Figure 2). If a suitable cell is neighbored by two or three Deltatrons that were created in a previous time step, then an attempt is made to create a transition within that cell. The requirement of two or three neighbors is randomly enforced. If a cell is selected for transition, then the neighboring Deltatrons are queried to determine the land use change that is being proliferated. As is done in the creation of land use change, the probability of land use transition is tested, and a random draw is made to determine if the cell maintains its current state or it is transformed, creating a new Deltatron. Once the process of proliferating change is completed, the deltaspace is updated, and the Deltatrons are either aged or killed.

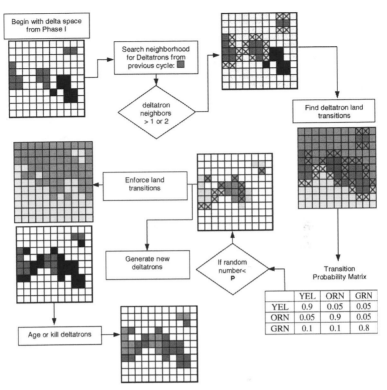

Fig. 2. Summarization of the second phase of the Deltatron model, proliferation of land use change.

The calibration process is done in three stages: coarse, fine, and final. The coarse calibration begins with parsing the parameter space into five areas and using the values of 1, 25, 50, 75, and 100 for each of the five parameters. This gives 3,125 different parameter sets that are tested to determine which range of parameters the one parameter set that best describes the data is located within. Results from the coarse calibration are examined to determine the goodness of fit for each of the parameter sets based on a set of spatial metrics. Narrowing of the parameter set can be based on a variety of different goodness of fit measures and there is not one sole metric that has been shown to be the most effective. For this research a metric that was the product of four individual metrics was used. The four individual metrics looked at the models ability to model the urban area in each of the input dataset, replicate the spatial shape of the input datasets, and replicate the patterns of land use in space and time.

3   Land Use Data

Land use data for San Joaquin County (California, USA), from 1988 and 1996 was downloaded from the California Department of Water Resources webpage. Data were converted from polygons to raster (100m resolution) in a GIS. The data originally consisted of 20 classes that were reclassified to 5, 10, and 15 land use classes as shown in Table 1. Urban extent data were obtained for 1988, 1992, 1994, and 1996 as described in [13].

Table 1. Reclassification scheme of the land use data from San Joaquin County (California, USA) into data sets aggregated into 5, 10, and 15 land use classes

Land Use Class	Reclassified	Code 5	Code 10	Code 15
Citrus and Subtropical	Fruit, Nut, & Vegetables	1	1	1
Deciduous Fruits & Nuts	Fruit, Nut, & Vegetables	1	1	2
Field Crops	Field Crops	1	2	3
Grain and Hay	Field Crops	1	2	4
Idle	Field Crops	1	2	5
Pasture	Pasture	1	3	6
Rice	Field Crops	1	2	7
Truck, Nursery, and Berry	Fruit, Nut, & Vegetables	1	1	8
Vineyards	Vineyards	1	4	9
Barren and Wasteland	Barren	2	5	10
Riparian Vegetation	Riparian	3	6	11
Native Vegetation	Native Vegetation	3	7	12
Water Surfaces	Water	4	8	13
Semi Agricultural	Feedlots	1	9	14
Urban	Urban	5	10	15
Commercial	Urban	5	10	15
Industrial	Urban	5	10	15
Landscape	Urban	5	10	15
Residential	Urban	5	10	15
Vacant	Urban	5	10	15

4   Calibration Results

Results from the calibration show that SLEUTH was able to accurately replicate 93% of the land use changes for the dataset with five land use classes, and 77% and 72% for the dataset with ten and fifteen land use classes (Table 1).

SLEUTH was exceptionally good at modeling the total number of urban pixels in the last year of input data as indicated by the *compare* statistic. It also performed well in replicating the overall urbanization of the input time-series as shown in the *population* statistic, which is a least squares regression score (r^2) for modeled urbanization compared to actual urbanization for the time series. The Lee-Sallee metric [14] was used to evaluate the ability of the model to spatially match historical data; that is, how good was the model at replicating the number of urban pixels and their location in space. The model was able to accurately replicate 74% of these patterns. Not surprisingly, the model's performance with regard to these three statistics was very similar since they all used the same urban extent data over the same time period. The most stringent measure of ability of the model to accurately reproduce land use patterns was measured by the F-match statistic.

The F-match statistic measured the proportion of goodness of fit across land use classes[14]. SLEUTH was able to accurately replicate 93% of the land use changes for the dataset with five land use classes, and 77% and 72% for the dataset with ten and fifteen land use classes.

Table 2. Results from calibrating the SLEUTH urban growth model to replicate land use change patterns of datasets with 5, 10, and 15 land use classes between 1988 and 1996. Four spatial statistics (all scaled 0 to 1, with 1 being perfect replication of data) were used as measure of the models ability to replicate the input data. Details on these statistics are described in [14]

Land Use Classes	Goodness of Fit Measures				
	Compare	Population	Lee-Sallee	F-Match	Composite
5	1	0.83331	0.74278	0.92973	0.575471
10	0.99152	0.83802	0.74427	0.76968	0.475989
15	0.99429	0.83768	0.74267	0.72439	0.448084

5   Conclusions

This research has shown the robust ability of the SLEUTH urban growth and land use change model to replicate land use patterns in both space and time. While the model was better able to replicate the evolution of land use patterns with less detailed data, it was to be expected since the Deltatron submodel has a stochastic component that decreases the probability of picking the correct land use transition as more classes are added. In its current format the model is only capable of handling land use transitions between two time periods. With the increasing availability of multi-temporal spatial data, it may be possible to alter the Deltatron model to handle land use data for multiple time periods. If possible, it will be interesting to reevaluate the robustness of the model in handling multiple classes of land use data.

While previous use of this model has focused on the implementation and application of this model to specific case studies [10], [11], this research is the first to evaluate the ability of the land use model to replicate numerous land use patterns. This has been largely due to two reasons, one that is strikingly concerning. First, the public availability of multi-temporal land use data is not widespread, and there is a significant time lag between when imagery (the basis of most classifications) is taken, and when it is classified by land use and released. The other reason that this has not been done is the general attitude in the geographic modeling community that if a model works and gives credible results, then it should be accepted without further poking and prodding. While the results of this research show the robustness of the model for simulating a variety of different land use classes, it is somewhat disturbing that other researchers [10], [11] have not tested the sensitivity of the model's performance to the number of land use classes. Hopefully this research will encourage other modelers to make strides in their work to further test the mechanics and sensitivity of their models.

References

1. Clarke, K. C., Hoppen, S., Gaydos, L.: A self-modifying cellular automaton model of historical urbanization in the San Francisco Bay area. Environment and Planning B 24 (1997) 247-261
2. Batty, M., Xie, Y.: Modelling inside GIS: Part 1. Model structures, exploratory spatial data analysis and aggregation. International Journal of Geographical Information Systems 8 (1994) 291-307
3. Tobler, W.: Cellular Geography. In Gale, S., Olsson, G. (eds): Philosophy in Geography. D. Reidel Publishing Company, Dordrecht Boston London (1979) 379-386
4. Couclelis, H.: Cellular worlds: a framework for modeling micro-macro dynamics. International Journal of Urban and Regional Research 17 (1985) 585-596
5. Torrens, P., O'Sullivan, D.: Cellular automata and urban simulation: where do we go from here? Environment and Planning B 28 (2001) 163-168
6. Couclelis, H.: Of mice and men: What rodent populations can teach us about complex spatial dynamics. Environment and Planning A 29 (1988) 99-109
7. Batty, M., Xie, Y.: Possible urban automata. Environment and Planning B 24 (1997) 175-192
8. White, R., Engelen, G.: Cellular automata and fractal urban form: a cellular modelling approach to the evolution of urban land-use patterns. Environment and Planning A 25 (1993) 1175-1199
9. Silva, E.A., Clarke, K.C.: Calibration of the SLEUTH urban growth model for Lisbon and Porto, Portugal. Computers, Environment and Urban Systems 26 (2002) 525-552
10. Yang, X., Lo, C.P.: Modelling urban growth and landscape change in the Atlanta metropolitan area. International Journal of Geographical Information Science 17 (2003) 463-488
11. Jantz, C.A., Goetz, S.J., Shelley, M.K.: Using the SLEUTH urban growth model to simulate the impacts of future policy scenarios on urban land use in the Baltimore-Washington metropolitan area. Environment and Planning B 31 (2004) 251-271
12. Clarke, K.C.: Land use modeling with Deltatrons. The Land Use Modeling Conference, Sioux Falls, South Dakota. June 5-6 (1997) http://www.ncgia.ucsb.edu/conf/landuse97/
13. Dietzel, C.: Spatio-temporal difference in model outputs and parameter space as determined by calibration extent. In: Atkinson, P., Foody, G., Darby, S., Wu, F. (eds): Geodynamics. Taylor and Francis, London (2004)
14. Project Gigalopolis Webpage. www.ncgia.ucsb.edu/projects/gig

Perturbation in Genetic Regulatory Networks: Simulation and Experiments

A. Semeria [1], M. Villani [1], R. Serra [1], and S.A. Kauffman [2]

[1] Centro Ricerche e Servizi Ambientali Fenice Via Ciro Menotti 48 48023 Marina di Ravenna, Italia
{asemeria, mvillani, rserra}@cramont.it
[2] Department of Cell Biology and Physiology, MSC084750, 1 University of New Mexico, Albuquerque N.M 87131
stu.kauffman@worldnet.att.net

Abstract. Random boolean networks (RBN) have been proposed more than thirty years ago as models of genetic regulatory networks. Recent studies on the perturbation in gene expression levels induced by the knock-out (i.e. silencing) of single genes have shown that simple RBN models give rise to a distribution of the size of the perturbations which is very similar in different model network realizations, and is also very similar to the one actually found in experimental data concerning a unicellular organism (S.cerevisiae). In this paper we present further results, based upon the same set of experiments, concerning the correlation between different perturbations. We compare actual data from S. cerevisiae with the results of simulations concerning RBN models with more than 6000 nodes, and comment on the usefulness and limitations of RBN models.

1 Introduction

The wealth of data nowadays available in molecular biology calls for new methods and ideas to make sense out of them. One approach which seems very promising is the ensemble approach to the study of genetic networks, pioneered several years ago by one of us [1],[2]. According to this line of research the interest is focussed on the typical properties of networks which are supposed to capture some characteristics of real biological systems, instead of upon the study of specific cases.

Random boolean networks (RBN) have been proposed as a model of genetic regulatory networks, precisely with the aim of devising a model which should be manageable enough to draw conclusions about its generic behaviours, which should be compared with experimental data. Many excellent presentations of the model exist [2], [3], and we will very briefly outline it below (section 2).

Models are useful if they guide our intuition and if they can be compared with some actual data. Comparison has been considered between i) the scaling of the number of attractors and of typical attractor length with the total number N of nodes, on the modelling side, and ii) the scaling of the number of different cell types and typical cell cycle length with the total DNA content in biological organisms [2].

P.M.A. Sloot, B. Chopard, and A.G. Hoekstra (Eds.): ACRI 2004, LNCS 3305, pp. 533–542, 2004.
© Springer-Verlag Berlin Heidelberg 2004

Although this comparison has been criticized [3], it has remained for some years the only experimental test of the model.

Three of us [4], [5] have recently shown that the availability of DNA microarray data allows further testing of the model, by analyzing a set of experiments in S. Cerevisiae [6]. In each experiment a single gene is silenced, and the expression levels of the other genes are compared to those of the wild type, i.e. the cell without knock-out. These experiments can be simulated in silico. In the spirit of the ensemble approach, we have investigated the statistical properties of these nets, introducing the notions of avalanches and susceptibilites (see section 3). Studying networks with two input connections per node (the simplest possible choice leading to non trivial behaviour), it was found that, provided that non-canalyzing functions are excluded, the distributions of avalanches and susceptibilities turn out to be very similar in different network realizations (different connection topology, different boolean functions on a single node). This should be contrasted to most dynamical properties (attractor number and length) which show a high variance. Moreover, the distribution of avalanches and susceptibilities are very similar to those actually found in experimental data, thus suggesting that these might actually be suitable candidate as generic properties, not severely affected by the details of a model or of a specific network. We have therefore decided to investigate further the properties of these perturbations, by looking at correlations between the expression patterns of different genes and between expression profiles of different knock-out experiments. Also in this case a comparison between experimental and simulated data has been performed.

In section 2 a very brief discussion of RBN is given, while in section 3 we review the experimental procedure. In section 4 the major results concerning the simulation of avalanches and susceptibilities are summarized. Useful measures of similarity between gene expression patterns and between knock-out experiment profiles are defined in section 5, where the major results for real and simulated networks are also presented. These results are analyzed in section 6, where comments and indications for further work are also given.

2   Random Boolean Networks

Let us consider a network composed of N genes, or nodes, which can take either the value 0 (inactive) or 1 (active). Let $x_i(t) \in \{0,1\}$ be the activation value of node i at time t, and let $X(t)=[x_1(t), x_2(t) \dots x_N(t)]$ be the vector of activation values of all the genes.

In a classical RBN each node has the same number of incoming connections k_{in}, and its k_{in} input nodes are chosen at random with uniform probability among the remaining N-1 nodes. The output (i.e. the new value of a node) corresponding to each set of values of the input nodes is determined by a boolean function, which is associated to that node, and which is also chosen at random, according to some probability distribution [2]; the simplest choice is that of a uniform distribution among all the possible boolean functions of k_{in} arguments. However, a careful analysis of some known real biological control circuits has shown that there is a strong bias in favour of the so-called canalyzing functions [9]. A boolean function is said to be canalyzing if at least one value of one of its input nodes uniquely determines its output, no matter what the other input values are. Both the topology and the boolean function associated to each gene do not change in time. The network dynamics is discrete and synchronous.

In order to analyze the properties of an ensemble of random boolean networks, different networks are synyhesized and their dynamical properties are examined. The ensembles differ mainly in the choice of the number of nodes N, the input connectivity per node k, and the choice of the set of allowed boolean functions. While individual realizations may differ markedly from the average properties of a given class of networks, one of the major results is the discovery of the existence of two different dynamical regimes, an ordered and a disordered one, divided by a "critical zone".Several observations, summarized in [2], [10], indicate that biological cells tend to be found in the ordered region. The scaling properties of the average number of attractors and average cycle length with the number of nodes N, in the ordered regime near the edge of chaos, have been compared to actual data concerning the dependence, upon the total DNA content, of the number of different cell types (which should correspond to the number of attractors) and of the duration of the cell cycle (which should correspond to the typical length of the attractor cycle). The agreement appears satisfactory for data which span several orders of magnitude, over different organisms belonging to different phyla.

3 Gene Knock-Out Experiments

Useful data from cDNA microarray measurements of gene expression profiles of *Saccharomyces cerevisiae* subject to many different perturbations are available [6]. We will briefly summarize here some features of the experiments, referring the interested reader to the original references for further details.

In a typical knock-out experiment, one compares the expression levels of all the genes in cells with a knocked-out gene, with those in normal ("wild type") cells. In this way, all the experimental data can be cast in matrix form E_{ij}, i=1 ... 6312, j=1... 227. E_{ij} is the ratio of the expression of gene i in experiment j to the expression of gene i in the wild type cell.

Microarray data are noisy, therefore, in order to make precise statements about the number of genes perturbed in a given experiment, it is required that a threshold be defined, such that the difference is regarded as "meaningful" if the ratio is greater than the threshold θ (or smaller than $1/\theta$) and neglected otherwise. Here we limit our analysis to the case of a threshold equal to 4, which is the most stringent value among those examined in [11]. See also [5] for further discussions on this choice.

Let Y be the boolean matrix which can be obtained by E by posing $y_{ij}=1$ if $E_{ij}>\theta$, or $E_{ij} <1/\theta$; $y_{ij}=0$ otherwise ($y_{ij} =1$ means that the modification of the expression level of gene i in experiment j is accepted as "meaningful"). In order to describe the global features of these experiments, two important aggregate variables are then the following. An <u>avalanche</u> is the size of the perturbation induced by a particular experiment (in experiment j, $A_j = \Sigma_i\, y_{ij}$) while the <u>susceptibility</u> of gene *n*, S_n, is equal to the number of experiments where that gene has been significantly affected ($S_n= \Sigma_j\, y_{nj}$). The reader is referred to [5] for data concerning the actual distribution of avalanches and susceptibilities.

4 The Simulation of Gene Knock-Out: Avalanches and Susceptibilities

In order to take into account the dynamical features of gene regulatory networks, dynamical networks with a high number of genes (6300, close to the number of genes of *Saccharomyces Cerevisiae* analyzed in [6]) were computer-generated and several simulations were performed, aimed at reproducing the experimental conditions.

For reasons outlined above the study concentrated upon networks with input connectivity k_{in} =2, which lie in the ordered phase, and particular attention was paid to networks where the non-canalyzing functions are not allowed. For a description of the way how the knock-out has been simulated is referred to [4], [5]. The main results can be summarized as follows

- the distributions of avalanches and susceptibilities are very similar in different networks. This property does not hold in the case where all the boolean functions (including those which are not canalyzing) are allowed. This robust behaviour is in sharp contrast with most properties of these networks (eg number and length of attractors) which vary largely in different networks
- the average distribution of avalanches in synthetic networks is definitely close to the one observed in actual experiments, except for the smallest avalanches, i.e. those of size 1 which are overestimated in synthetic networks.
- the average distribution of susceptibilities in synthetic networks is even closer (than that of avalanches) to the one observed in the experiments.

These results are indeed surprising, even more so if one realizes that there are no adjustable parameters here (there is indeed one parameter in the data preparation, i.e. the threshold; for a discussion see [5]).Let us also note a point which will be important in the discussion of the next section: the avalanches are rather small, as they involve at most a few tens of genes out of 6300. There are only two "anomalous avalanches" observed in the experiments which involve about 200 different genes. The susceptibilities are even smaller, so a gene is modified in just a few experiments.

Table 1. Some features of the real and synthetic data distributions. The latter is the average of the corresponding values of the different synthetic networks

	Mean aval.	Max aval.	Mean susc.	Max susc.	Unaffected nodes
S.Cervisiae	12.9	219	0.46	33	4964
Synthetic	12.5	266	0.45	9.6	4766

5 Distances

Note that the good results obtained, for the distribution of avalanches and susceptibilities, with the simplest possible RBN model (i.e. the one with k=2) are rather surprising, therefore it is important to perform further and more stringent statistical analyses of the response of gene expression levels to the knock-out of single genes, in order to compare the behaviour of model and real networks.

Let us recal that E_{ij} is defined as the ratio between the expression level of gene i in experiment j and the expression level of the same gene in the wild type. In the following we will use, as it is standard practice in DNA microarray studies, the (base 10) logarithm of this ratio for real networks

$$x'_{ij} = \log_{10} E_{ij} \tag{1}$$

In the S.cerevisiae data, due to the properties of the measuring device, $x'_{ij} \in [-2,2]$. Log-ratio values which might correspond to larger values are "saturated" and they are given the values ± 2. In synthetic networks the zero level must of course be excluded: we therefore modify E_{ij} in synthetic networks, by substituing 0.01 to 0, or to any number smaller than 0.01 (E_{ij} in synthetic networks is the average of the level of gene i in experiment j, taken over the attractor cycle with the largest basin of attraction). By using 0.01 as the smallest possible activation level in synthetic networks, since 1 is the maximum, we have the same range for E_{ij} (i.e. [-2,2]) both for real and synthetic networks. Therefore, in syntehtic networks

$$x'_{ij} = \log_{10} E^*_{ij} \tag{2}$$

where E^*_{ij} is the value of E_{ij} renormalized as described above.

As a control, a set of random values was generated according to a gaussian distribution, with the constraints that the average is zero and that the number of data points which lie beyond the [-2,2] interval matches the number of data which are "saturated" in the actual data, and this distribution was compared to the actual distibution of experimental log-ratios: the two distributions are clearly different, thus ruling out the possibility that the distribution of the actual data is the result only of white noise affecting the measurement procedure. For reasons mentioned in section 4, a threshold θ has been applied to the real data (and not to the synthetic ones). Therefore we will consider in the following, for biological data, the values x_{ij} defined as $x_{ij}=x'_{ij}$, if $|x'_{ij}|>\log\theta$, $x_{ij}=0$ otherwise ($\log\theta\cong0.6$). For synthetic networks $x_{ij}=x'_{ij}$.The (non-binarized, see below) distance between experiment j and experiment k , D^E_{jk}, and the distance between gene p and gene q, D^G_{pq}, are defined as follows

$$D^E_{jk} = \sqrt{\sum_{i=1}^{N} (x_{ij} - x_{ik})^2} \tag{3}$$

$$D^G_{pq} = \sqrt{\sum_{i=1}^{M} (x_{pk} - x_{qk})^2}$$

where N is the number of genes and M the number of experiments which are retained for analysis, after removing from any subsequent analysis all those genes and experiments where all the values have become 0. In our case the surviving data for the biological system concern 1357 genes and 213 experiments. A similar pre-processing is applied also to the different synthetic networks.

Note also that in some cases the value of the log ratio is not given, because the quality of the spot on the microarray is poor. In this case the value is "not available". In these cases the distances have been renormalized by i) calculating D with the previous formulae, using only the available data (suppose that these are L) and ii) renormalizing the calculated distances by multiplying the previous value times √(N/L) (for experiments) or √(M/L) (for genes).

The (non-binarized) distances between experiments are shown in fig. 1 for real and synthetic networks, while those concerning genes are shown in fig. 2. In these figures (as well as in figs 2 below) the comparison is between biological data on one side, and the mean of synthetic data (taken over 10 different network realizations) on the other side. A histogram is computed for both real and simulated data; in the figures, the number corresponding to the number of pairs which fall in a given interval are plotted in correspondence to the midpoint of the interval. Note that a bin equal to 2 has been used for distances between experiments (figs. 1 and 2 on the left), while in the case of distances between genes, since there were fewer points, a smaller bin equal to 1 has been used (figs. 1 and 2 on the right).

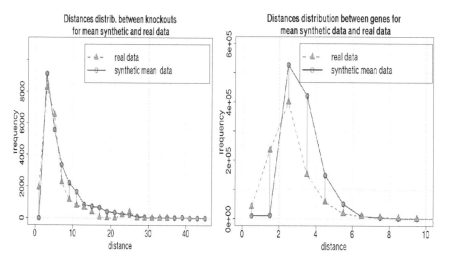

Fig. 1. On the left distances D^E between pairs of experiments (bin=2) and distances D^G between pairs of genes (bin=1) on the right.

The quantities considered so far represent a natural measure of the distances between genes and of the distances between experiments. For the sake of definiteness let us focus on the former: if two genes are uncorrelated, their squared distance will be the sum of M entirely random terms; if they are positively correlated, they will tend to be simultaneously overexpressed, or underexpressed, in a number of tests, thus providing a small contribution to the overall distance. On the contrary, if they are negatively correlated, the contribution to the distance will be high.

A different question might also be asked, which is in the spirit of the previous studies on avalanches: we may be interested in knowing whether two genes tend to "change together", no matter whether they are positively or negatively correlated. In this case it is appropriate to use the variables y, defined in section 4, instead of the x's used above. These variable are binary, and they convey only the information concerning the fact that a gene has changed its expression level in a given experiment, without distinguishing whether it has increased or decreased. The (binarized) distances B^E_{jk} and B^G_{pq} are defined as

(4)

$$B^E_{jk} = \sqrt{\sum_{i=1}^{N} (y_{ij} - y_{ik})^2}$$

$$B^G_{pq} = \sqrt{\sum_{i=1}^{M} (y_{pk} - y_{qk})^2}$$

Note here that the term under square root is equal to the number of genes which take different values in two experiments, in the case of B^E, and is equal to the number of experiments where a gene takes different values, in the case of B^G.

The distances B^E and B^G are shown in fig. 2

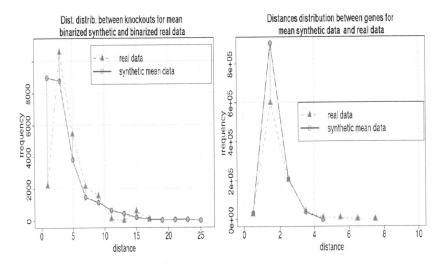

Fig. 2. On the left binarized distances B^E between pairs of experiments (bin=2) and binarized distances B^G between pairs of genes (bin=1) on the right

6   Conclusions and Suggestions for Further Work

As it can be seen, there are some important similarities between the distributions of biological and simulated data; there are also some visible differences, which require comments and further analysis.

As far as fig. 1 (right) is concerned, the agreement between actual and simulated distances between experiments D^E appears satisfactory, excluding the first bin where there are many more points in the real case. This might be explained as follows: in many cases, avalanches in synthetic networks involve just a single gene, i.e. the one which has been knocked out, which is very often a constant one (non oscillating genes are by far the most frequent ones). In this case the ratio jumps from 1 to 0.01, and the log ratio change is 2. Now compare the experiment with just such a single change with another one of the same kind, where the only gene which has changed is of course another one. The squared distance between the two experiments would be $2^2+2^2=8$, and the corresponding distance would be $2\sqrt{2}$, which is larger than the upper limit of the first bin. Of course, if more genes are involved the distances are even greater. That's why the number of small distances (i.e those in the first bin) between experiments in synthetic networks is smaller than that in real networks.

Looking at fig. 1 (right) the difference between real and simulated data appears to be greater, but this is largely a visual effect, due to the fact that in this case a bin equal to one has been used (otherwise the number of points would have been extremely low), so that there are now two points which are almost zero in the synthetic case. But the reason for the difference is exactly the same given above, i.e. that, excluding rare cases which involve oscillating genes, synthetic networks cannot display distances smaller than $2\sqrt{2}$.

Let us now consider the "binarized" distances B. In fig. 2 (left) the most striking difference is that the first bin of the synthetic data is much more crowded than that of the experimental data. This might be tentatively explained as follows. Let us first consider the case where two experiments refer to two avalanches of dimension one, where only the knocked-out gene has modified its value (just as we did in the discussion of figs. 1). Let us suppose that gene has been modified in experiment 1, and that gene g has been modified in experiment 2. There are four possibilities: the value of gene h in experiment 2 is the same as the new value of h in experiment 1 (i.e. 0, in this case), and the value of gene g in experiment 1 is the same as the new value of g in experiment 2: in this case the distance between the two perturbed states would be 0. The two genes might otherwise have different values in both perturbed states, thus providing a distance of $\sqrt{2}$, or there might be one gene with the same value and another with a different value (this can be achieved in two different ways). If all the combinations have the same probability, then the expected value for the distance is

$$< d_{12} >= \left(\frac{1}{4}\sqrt{2} + \frac{2}{4} \right) \cong 0.85 \tag{5}$$

Due to the way distances are computed in the binarized case, this value now falls into the first bin. A similar analysis shows that also cases where an experiment corresponding to an avalanche of size 2 is compared with one of size 1, the distance is higher likely to fall in the first bin, and the same analysis can be applied to the case where two avalanches of size two are compared. That's why the first bin in the binarized case tends to be pretty crowded in the synthetic case.

By looking at the data on avalanche size, one can see that the frequency of small avalanches (of size 1) is definitely higher in the synthetic cases than in the experimental one, so this effect is much more pronounced in synthetic data rather than in biological data. Another way to phrase this remark is that in the simulations only networks with k=2 were used, which is certainly not a biologically plausible assumption. This is likely to lead to a larger number of small avalanches than in the biological case, where higher connectivities might appear, and this might be responsible for the difference in binarized data.

Note also that the curve of biological data shows a (relatively small) peak at fairly high distance values, i.e. 15, corresponding to a number of positions where two experiments differ of more than 200. These are due to the two anomalous avalanches which have been noticed in the previous study on avalanches and susceptibilities; it is interesting to observe that, while there is no such peak in average simulated data, this peak appears in a number of individual simulations of synthetic networks (and is washed away by the averaging procedure).

Finally, in fig. 2 (right) the major differences between the two cases appears to be i) that the height of the peak at the second point is larger in simulated networks and that ii) the tails of the distribution of experimental data are longer than those of synthetic data. The former difference can be explained by considering that a given gene is likely to be in the same state in most knock-out experiments; when that gene is knocked-out, it changes value: if we compare two experiments, each of them involving one gene only, the difference will be $\sqrt{2}$ in the synthetic case, while in real data the difference can be different. Since in this case a bin = 1 has been used, the overcrowding effect of synthetic networks is observed in the second bin. As far as the observation of longer tails in biological data is concerned, this is related to the fact that S. Cerevisiae data have some gene with a much higher susceptibility than those of synthetic networks (see Table 1); these highly susceptible genes, in the binarized case, present high distances from the other more common genes.

By considering the results of section 5, together with the above comments, one is therefore led to the conclusion that the distributions of distances between experiments and genes present important common features in S. Cerevisiae and in random boolean models. The major differences seem to be related to the facts that

- simulated networks present a much higher fraction of small avalanches of size 1 (roughly 30% of the total) than those which are found in real data (15%)
- the maximum value of the susceptibility is smaller in synthetic than in real networks.

It can be conjectured that the difference between the number of small avalanches in the two cases is related to the fact that the number of incoming connections, k, is held fixed to the value 2 in the simulations. This is certainly not a biologically plausible assumption, since it is well known that there are some genes whose expression can be influenced by a higher number of other genes. It would be therefore interesting to explore the behaviours of networks with higher connectivities, although in this case the computational load associated to the simulation of a network with 6000 nodes would be much greater.

Moreover, the presence of unusually highly susceptible genes in biological networks suggests the opportunity to test models where the constraint that all the genes have the same number of input is removed. It would be interesting to analyze the behaviour of random boolean models with exponential or scale-free connectivities.

Acknowledgments. Several helpful discussions with David Lane, Annamaria Colacci, Elena Morandi, Cinzia Severini and Massimo Andretta are gratefully acknowledged. This work has been supported in part by the Italian Ministry for University and Research (Miur) under grant FISR 1509 (2002).

References

[1]   Kauffman, S.A.: *Gene Regulation Networks: A Theory of their Global Structure and Behavior*. Curr. Top. Dev. Biol **6** (1971), 145-182
[2]   Kauffman, S. A.: *The origins of order*. Oxford University Press (1993)
[3]   M. Aldana, S. Coppersmith, L. P. Kadanoff, *Boolean Dynamics with Random Coup*lings, in E. Kaplan, J.E. Marsden, K.R. Sreenivasan (eds), *Perspectives and Problems in Nonlinear Science*. Springer Applied Mathematical Sciences Series (2003). Also available at http://www.arXiv:cond-mat/0209571
[4]   Serra, R., Villani, M. & Semeria, A. (2003): *Robustness to damage of biological and synthetic networks*. In W. Banzhaf, T. Christaller, P. Dittrich, J.T. Kim & J. Ziegler (eds): *Advances in Artificial Life*. Berlin: Springer Lecture Notes in Artificial Intelligence **2801**, 706-715
[5]   Serra, R., Villani, M. & Semeria, A. (2004): *Genetic network models and statistical properties of gene expression data in knock-out experiments*. J. Theor. Biol. **227** (1): 149-157
[6]   Hughes, T.R. et al.: *Functional discovery via a compendium of expression profiles*. Cell **102** (2000) 109-126
[7]   Serra, R. & Villani, M.: *Modelling bacterial degradation of organic compounds with genetic networks*. J. Theor. Biol. **189** (1) (1997) 107-119
[8]   Serra, R., Villani, M. & Salvemini, A.: *Continuous genetic networks*. Parallel Computing **27** (5) (2001) 663-683
[9]   Harris, S.E., Sawhill, B.K., Wuensche, A. & Kauffman, S.A.: *A model of transcriptional regulatory networks based on biases in the observed regulation rules*. Complexity **7** (2002) 23-40
[10] Kauffman, S.A.: *Investigations*. Oxford University Press (2000)
[11] Wagner, A.: *Estimating coarse gene network structure from large-scale gene perturbation data*. Santa Fe Institute Working Paper 01-09-051 (2001)

A Hybrid Discrete-Continuum Model for 3-D Skeletogenesis of the Vertebrate Limb

R. Chaturvedi[1], C. Huang[2], J.A. Izaguirre[2], S.A. Newman[3], J.A. Glazier[4], and M. Alber[1*]

*Author for correspondence: malber@nd.edu.
[1] Department of Mathematics, University of Notre Dame, Notre Dame, IN 46556.
[2] Department of Computer Science and Engineering, University of Notre Dame, Notre Dame, IN 46556-5670.
[3] Department of Cell Biology & Anatomy, New York Medical College, Vallaha, NY
[4] Biocomplexity Institute and Department of Physics, Indiana University, 727 East 3rd Street, Swain Hall West 159, Bloomington, IN 47405-7105.

Abstract. We present a dynamic, three-dimensional, composite model framework for vertebrate development. Our integrated model combines submodels that address length-scales from subcellular to tissues and organs in a unified framework. Interacting submodels include a discrete model derived from non-equilibrium statistical mechanics (Cellular Potts Model) and continuous reaction-diffusion models. A state diagram with associated rules and a set of ordinary differential equations model genetic regulation to define and control cell differentiation. We apply the model spatiotemporal bone patterning in the *proximo-distal* (from body towards digits) direction of developing avian limb.

1 Introduction

The volume of information modern molecular biology provides on genetics and biochemistry can obscure dynamical processes underlying the generation and function of complex biological phenomena. Predictive models and simulations can aid our understanding of such phenomena, particularly if they take into account experimentally-determined cellular and molecular details and treat the complex interactions between various natural scales of biological objects and processes.

In previous papers [1, 2] we described a systems-biology approach to integrating *discrete* and *continuous* models of biological developmental mechanisms to build a reduced, 2-dimensional (*2D*) model of vertebrate limb development. We used *discrete* models to describe cell movement and division, interactions between individual cells, and *differentiation* (changing of fundamental sets of behaviors by turning on or off clusters of genes) from multipotent cells into specific cell types, and continuous models to describe extracellular signaling molecules. Simulations reproduced the proximodistal increase in the number of skeletal elements over time in the developing limb. This paper presents a 3-dimensional (*3D*) multiscale framework for modeling *morphogenesis* (structural development of an organism or its organs) during embryonic development in vertebrates. At subcellular and molecular scales,

P.M.A. Sloot, B. Chopard, and A.G. Hoekstra (Eds.): ACRI 2004, LNCS 3305, pp. 543–552, 2004.
© Springer-Verlag Berlin Heidelberg 2004

morphogenetic molecules are secreted, diffuse and interact. At the scale of cells, morphogenesis involves cell growth, proliferation, differentiation, migration and death. At larger scales, bulk changes in the shapes of tissues produce the dramatic patterns of tissues and organs. We develop submodels for this hierarchy of scales, and combine them into an integrated multiscale model. Specific differences from the 2D model are detailed when dealing with submodels. While 2D simulations can serve as a guide to model building, an adequate understanding of 3D biological phenomena can only be achieved with 3D simulations.

Genes specify products necessary for morphogenesis, but not their distribution or physical effects. Generic physical mechanisms (mechanisms common to living and nonliving materials) organize the materials the genetic mechanisms provide [3]. Experiments on initiation and arrangement of individual skeletal elements in chicken and mouse embryos suggest that the secreted morphogens TGF-β, FGF-2 and FGF-8 are key molecules of a core patterning process, as is the extracellular matrix (ECM) adhesive protein *fibronectin* (reviewed in [4]). Cells differentiate from multipotent stem cells into specialized cell types of the developed organism. Cells diversify into distinct *differentiation types* during development. Differentiation from one cell type to another is a comprehensive qualitative change in cell behavior, generally irreversible and abrupt (*e.g.*, responding to new sets of signals, turning on or off whole genetic pathways). Cells of the same type can exist in different states; but different states typically differ less in their behavior than cells of two different types. The concept of cell types is used to model the major behavioral groups of cells.

Our earlier 2D model for spatiotemporal regulation of *chondrogenesis* (cartilage development) of the vertebrate limb reproduced the biological generation of a sequence of increasing numbers of parallel cartilage elements in proximo-distal sequence (for figures, see [1]). In an avian (chicken) forelimb, the numbers and identities of the main elements are 1 (humerus), 2 (radius+ulna) and 3 (digits). Bones at different proximo-distal levels differ in size and shape (*e.g.*, the humerus is longer and thicker than the ulna). Differences between elements (*e.g.*, different fingers) in the anterior-posterior direction are subtler. Bone replaces the cartilage elements later in development.

Organogenesis depends on the 3D rearrangement of cells. Although 2D simulations provide helpful qualitative insights and require less computing time to run, symmetries and symmetry-breaking during organogenesis differ qualitatively in 3D. This paper treats issues specific to 3D and describes both normal and pathological limb development. Our model framework for organogenesis includes three major submodels: the discrete stochastic Cellular Potts Model (CPM) for cell dynamics, continuum reaction-diffusion (RD) partial differential equations (PDEs) for morphogen production and diffusion, and a state automaton for cell type transition (TT) to model differentiation. The extra degree of translational freedom in 3D CPM relaxes 2D constraints on producing specific structures (*e.g.*, cylindrical condensations of cells in real chondrogenesis). In organisms, patterns of diffusing morphogens, which serve both as *inductive* signals (altering cell type) and *chemotactic* signals (inducing cell movement along chemical gradients), must be stable for time scales of interest. Our earlier 2D simulations [1] used the Schnakenberg RD equations (see [5]) as a specific continuum RD example. We introduced additional cubic terms modifying cells' morphogen production based on our analysis of bifurcations of the Schnakenberg equations in 3D. Parameters associated with these terms also make 3D equations structurally more complex.

2   Biological Background: Multiple Scales in Organogenesis

Hentschel *et al.* [4] outline the biological basis of the model of chicken limb development considered here (see also [1] and [2]). An initial tissue mass, the paddle-shaped *mesoblast*, contains pre-differentiated mesenchymal cells. During successive stages of chondrogenic patterning in the chick limb, cells divide and cluster (condense) at increasingly distal locations and differentiate into chondrocytes, forming the cartilage template for limb skeleton. We consider two main secreted components--the morphogen TGF-β and the ECM molecule fibronectin. The former diffuses through mesoblast; the latter is a larger molecule that accumulates at secretion sites. We assume that the bulk of the ECM provides a medium for diffusion of TGF-β and a hypothesized inhibitor of TGF-β production, action or the action of its downstream effectors [6; 7], and for fibronectin accumulation. Cells diffuse and undergo hatptotaxis in response to fibronectin, *i.e.*, they move up gradients of fibronectin. TGF-β diffuses through the mesoblast and is positively autoregulatory [6]. TGF-β also induces cells to produce fibronectin and upregulates cell-cell adhesivity [8], which recruits neighboring cells into chondrogenic condensations. We make the simplifying assumption that the fibronectin signal upregulates cell-cell adhesion, thus reinforcing accumulation of cells at high fibronectin zones. The three zones in a developing limb are- *apical* where cells only divide; *active* where cells rearrange locally into precartilage condensations; and *frozen* where condensations have differentiated into cartilage and patterning ceases. Cell division continues in both active and frozen zones. Certain FGFs emanating from the apical ectodermal ridge (AER) a band of cells along the anteroposterior margin at the tip of the limb bud have concentration-dependent effects on the underlying cells and thus define the zones [4]. For simplicity, we assume the zones *a priori*.

3   Physical and Mathematical Submodels and Their Integration

Modeling Cellular and Tissue Scales: The CPM Framework
Cell-scale processes underpin the complexity of multicellular organisms. The simplest cell-cell interaction is adhesion, which allows cells to form stable clumps and, combined with cell motility, allows different types of cell with different adhesivity to sort into clusters of like type [9]. Differences in adhesivity result from differences in the quantity and identity of cell adhesion molecules (CAMs) on cell membranes. Modeling variations in cell-specific adhesivity, rather than modeling individual CAMs, suffices to explain cell sorting and clustering in experiments. CPM, our *framework* for modeling cells and their dynamics, describes cell behaviors using an effective energy, E, comprised of real (*e.g.*, cell-cell adhesion) and effective (*e.g.*, the response of a cell to a chemotactic gradient) energies and constraints [10]. CPM dynamics uses imposed fluctuations and strong dissipation to rearrange cell configuration to minimize E. E includes terms to model (i) haptotaxis (ii) variations in cell adhesivity (iii) cell growth, and (iv) division (*mitosis*). CPM uses a lattice to describe cells. Each lattice site (*voxel*) has an associated integer index (*spin*). Value of index at a lattice site is σ if the site lies in cell σ. *Domains* (collections of lattice sites with the same index) represent cells. A cell is thus a set of discrete components that can rearrange, resulting in cell shape changes and motions. A voxel interacts locally

with voxels within an *interaction range*. Each cell has an associated type. ECM is modeled as a generalized cell of distinct type. In [11], quantitative justification of the CPM is provided.

CPM is an efficient and convenient phenomenological framework for modeling the behavior of groups of cells. It uses a minimal number of parameters which have clear physical meanings. Models using molecular-scale chemical reaction-kinetics or intermediate scales (*e.g.* at the level of the cytoskeleton or membrane) are feasible for at most a few cells. M-Cell and VirtualCell[1] are successful examples of such detailed models. In our simulations, where tens or hundreds of thousands of cells differentiate and organize into tissues, completely microscopic approaches are computationally exorbitant and unnecessary. We do introduce micro-scale modeling of mechanisms when appropriate.

The phenomenological parameter T, an *effective temperature*, drives cell-membrane fluctuations. Fluctuations follow the Metropolis algorithm for Monte-Carlo Boltzmann dynamics. A proposed change in lattice configuration produces a change in effective energy, ΔE. We accept it with probability:

$$P(\Delta E) = 1, \Delta E \leq 0; \qquad P(\Delta E) = e^{-\Delta E/kT}, \Delta E > 0, \qquad (1)$$

where k is a constant converting T into units of energy and E includes terms to describe each mechanism we wish to model, *e.g.*,

$$E = E_{contact} + E_{volume} + E_{chemical}. \qquad (2)$$

$E_{contact}$ describes the net adhesion/repulsion between two cell membranes.

$$E_{contact} = \sum_{(i,j,k)(i',j',k')} J_{\tau(\sigma)\tau'(\sigma')}(1-\delta(\sigma(i,j,k),\sigma'(i',j',k'))), \qquad (3)$$

$J_{\tau,\tau'}$, the binding energy per unit area depends on types of interacting cells, τ and τ'. *Kronecker delta*, $\delta(\sigma,\sigma')=0$ if $\sigma\neq\sigma'$ and $\delta(\sigma,\sigma')=1$ if $\sigma=\sigma'$. Sum is over the interaction range.

A cell of type τ has a prescribed target volume $v(\sigma,\tau)$ and surface area $s(\sigma,\tau)$. The actual volume and surface area fluctuate due to changes in osmotic pressure, pseudopodal motion of cells, *etc*. Changes also result from the growth and division of cells. E_{volume} enforces these targets by exacting an energy penalty for deviations. E_{volume} depends on four model parameters: *volume elasticity*, λ, *target volume*, $v_{target}(\sigma,\tau)$, *membrane elasticity*, λ', and *target surface area*, $s_{target}(\sigma,\tau)$:

$$E_{volume} = \sum_{all-cells} \lambda_\sigma(v(\sigma,\tau)-v_{target}(\sigma,\tau))^2 + \sum_{all-cells} \lambda_\sigma'(s(\sigma,\tau)-s_{target}(\sigma,\tau))^2. \qquad (4)$$

Cell Growth and Division: Cell growth results when $v_{target}(\sigma,\tau)$ and $s_{target}(\sigma,\tau)$ increase with an increasing number of *CPM steps* (time). We model cell division by starting with a cell of average size, $v_{target}= v_{target,average}$, causing it to grow by gradually increasing v_{target} to $2v_{target,average}$, and splitting the cell into two cells, each with a new target volume: $v_{target}/2$. One daughter cell assumes a new σ. A modified breadth-first search selects

---

the voxels which receive the new spin; the split is approximately along the cell diameter. For cell death we set the cell's target volume to zero.

Cells can respond to chemical signals by moving along concentration gradients. A chemotaxis/haptotaxis model requires a description of the evolving, spatially-varying chemical *concentration field* for each chemical, and an *interface* to connect the field to the CPM framework for cell and tissue dynamics. $C(\vec{x})$ is the local concentration of the molecule. An effective chemical potential, $\mu(\sigma)$ translates the effect of the chemical on cell motion into the CPM energy formalism. We use the simplest possible form of this coupling:

$$E_{chemical} = \mu(\sigma)C(\vec{x}).$$
(5)

In the above, $\vec{x}$ is the position vector; when we match the grid to the (i,j,k) in the CPM model we approximate it to the voxel it lies in.

Modeling Molecular Scales: Reaction-Diffusion Equations

In [12], Turing introduced the idea that interactions of reacting and diffusing chemicals (at least one autocatalytic *activator* species and one *inhibitor* species which represses the activator) could produce self-organizing instabilities that might explain biological patterning. To model the behavior of TGF-β in the limb, we use RD and chemotactic coupling to the cells, but no back-coupling from the cells to the chemical field [5; 4]. Thus, the response of cells to TGF-β depends on the RD *pre-pattern* of TGF-β. Assuming isotropic diffusion:

$$\frac{\partial u}{\partial t} = D\,\nabla^2 u + \gamma F(u),$$
(6)

where $u=(u_1,u_2)^T$ and $D=diag(d_1,d_2)$, u_1 is an activator (TGF-β in the chicken limb) and u_2 is a hypothetical inhibitor [6; 7].

We are also working on removing the above simplification of having no back-coupling (equivalent to assuming a non-biological source term in the RD equations), see "Work In Progress" below. The modified RD equations include this back coupling and the resulting feedback from cells.

The 2D model in [1] used the Schnakenberg equations, *i.e.*, $F=(F_1,F_2)^T$ with $F_1=a-u_1+u_1^2u_2$ and $F_2=b-u_1^2u_2$. Here, for the *growing* limb bud we seek 3D solutions cylindrically elongated in z (distal) direction. For these patterns to be stable in 3D, we needed to circumvent the observation that stability of stripes and spots is mutually exclusive for the Schnakenberg equations (see [13]). Accordingly, we modified the forms of F_1 and F_2 [13] to:

$$F_1 = a - u_1 + u_1^2u_2 + k_1(u_1 - u_{01})^3$$
(7)
$$F_2 = b - u_1^2u_2 + k_2(u_2 - u_{02})^3.$$

The cubic terms do not change the behavior in an essential way as long as u is close to u_0, where u_0 is a stable solution of $F(u)=0$. Thus, Equation 6 becomes:

$$\frac{\partial u}{\partial t} = \gamma(a - u + u^2 v + k_1(u - u_*)^3) + (D_x \frac{\partial^2 u}{\partial x^2} + D_y \frac{\partial^2 u}{\partial y^2} + \frac{\partial^2 u}{\partial z^2}), \tag{8}$$

$$\frac{\partial v}{\partial t} = \gamma(b - u^2 v + k_2(v - v_*)^3) + d(D_x \frac{\partial^2 v}{\partial x^2} + D_y \frac{\partial^2 v}{\partial y^2} + \frac{\partial^2 v}{\partial z^2}).$$

We solved Equations 8 using an explicit finite-difference scheme over a rectangular domain. Separately, or in combination, the set of parameters γ (relative strength of production vs. diffusion), the ratio l_x/l_y and diffusion coefficients of activator and inhibitor control the number of cylinders and their geometry (mathematically, these changes are equivalent). For instance, decreasing the diffusion coefficient (which is mathematically equivalent to changing the aspect ratio of the domain) in the x-direction by a factor of m^2 increases the number of spots in the x-direction by a factor of m. We use the no-flux boundary conditions. Field values are initialized to a uniform distribution perturbed randomly by a small value.

Modeling Macromolecular Scales: Fibronectin
We assume that cells respond to the TGF-β signal by producing a substratum adhesion molecule (SAM), which we identify with fibronectin, and CAM, which we identify with N-cadherin. We treat fibronectin as a non-diffusing chemical field, which results in slower computations, but is simpler than treating it as a generalized cell within the CPM framework. Cells undergo haptotaxis in the direction of increasing SAM [14]. In addition, the fibronectin signal upregulates cell-cell adhesion, which enhances the accumulation of cells. Hence cells tend to cluster in regions of high fibronectin concentration and reinforce this tendency by secreting more fibronectin within those regions.

Although the Turing-instability-generated TGF-β prepattern initiates fibronectin patterning, self-enhancing *positive feedback* of SAM secretion and CAM upregulation consolidates subsequent patterning. Our model represents an extension of the original CPM introduced by [10] insofar as we introduce a SAM term governing cell haptotaxis (Equation 5), and we allow the strength of CAM-dependent interaction to vary based on morphogen concentration (Equation 3).

Cell Types and the Type Transition Model
All cells of a particular differentiation type share a set of parameters describing their state, while two different cell types (*e.g.*, muscle and bone) have different parameter sets. Cells of the same type exist in different states, corresponding to a specific set of values for the cell-type's parameters. A cell's behavior depends on its state. Genetic and external cues influence both cells' type and state. We model differentiation using a *Type Transition Model* (TT). Each type in this model corresponds to a cell differentiation type (with a defined parameter set) that exists during limb chondrogenesis. Change of a cell from one type to another corresponds to cell differentiation. The type-change map models regulatory networks by defining the rules governing type change, *e.g.*, accounting for the intra- and inter-cellular effects of chemical fields. In the avian limb, one cell type of interest is the initial *precartilage mesenchymal* cell, which can translocate, divide, and produce various morphogens and ECM molecules. All cell types in chick limb undergo mitosis. We assume that

cells in the active zone represent a cell type distinct from those in the apical zone. Specifically, unlike the apical zone cells, *active zone cells* respond to activator, inhibitor, and fibronectin. When a responsive cell in the active zone senses a threshold local concentration of activator, its type changes to *fibronectin-producing*. A fibronectin-producing cell can upregulate its cell-cell adhesion (the parameter $J_{cell,cell}$ in the CPM decreases). Cells that have not experienced local threshold levels of activator can respond to, but not produce, fibronectin. This model of genetic regulation captures the formal, qualitative aspects of regulatory interactions (reviewed in [15] and [4]).

The Scale of the Organ: Integration of Submodels
We must integrate the CPM (stochastic, discrete), RD (continuum, PDEs) and TT (rule based state automaton) submodels while maintaining their modularity, *e.g.* by: (i) Matching the spatial grid for the continuum and stochastic models and (ii) Defining the relative number of iterations for RD and CPM evolvers. The SAM and CAM submodels form a positive feedback loop (of SAM secretion and CAM upregulation) providing the *biologically-motivated* interface between the RD-based TGF-β prepattern and the CPM-based cell dynamics. The RD engine uses an explicit solver, based on forward time marching. We store these calculations as *fields*, *e.g.*, the TGF-β concentration. The CPM simulator implements the lattice abstraction and the Monte Carlo procedure. Acceptance probability function is Metropolis by default. We can view the CPM as an operation on a field of voxels. Various fields can evolve under their own set of rules—Metropolis dynamics for the field of voxels, RD for the field of morphogens. A chemical like fibronectin, which cells secrete and which then remains in place, is another concentration field, the corresponding evolver rule is reaction dynamics with no diffusion. A description of genetically determined response of the cells controls the TT evolver governing cell differentiation. Other sub-modules implement different cell responses, *e.g.*, cell growth and mitosis. Criteria for interfacing the various grids and time scales specify the simulation protocol. In the simulations we present in this paper, we keep the CPM and RD grids identical, but the software framework can also handle different sized rectangular grids. The CompuCell web site[2], distributes the Open Source software.

4 Brief Discussion of Simulation Results

The combined behavior of morphogens, cell dynamics and cell differentiation results in a biologically realistic, roughly periodic pattern of the major chondrogenic elements. The model demonstrates global emergent phenomena resulting from local interactions as well as nonlocal coupling. Sources of nonlocal coupling are present in both the RD and CPM submodels. While reaction is local, diffusion introduces a nonlocal interaction on the scale of the diffusion length and limited to the domain of the diffusion. CPM is non-local because of the volume and area constraints, which connect sites across a cell diameter. However, the emergent pattern of bones has structures much larger than the RD and CPM interaction lengths. We first present the *normal* pattern of precartilage condensation in the chick forelimb: one followed by

---

[2] http://www.nd.edu/~lcls/compucell

two and then three primary (*i.e.*, excluding the wrist bones) elements successively in the proximodistal direction. The SAM concentration and cell condensation patterns follow the activator prepattern. Figure 1 shows simulations of the full 3D chick-limb chondrogenesis model, where the cells have condensed into the chondrogenic pattern of a chick forelimb.

Fig. 1. Normal development of chondrogenic condensations: Cell con-densation into humerus, ulna +radius, and digits in 3D simulation.

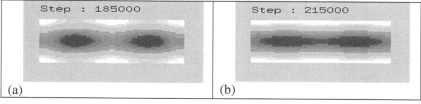

(a)   (b)

Fig. 2. (a) and (b) show transverse sections of TGF-β concentration, with no cubic stabilizing term for activator ($k_1=0$, $k_2=0.375$). Stripes rather than spots are stable, corresponding to fused digits (Apert Syndrome).

We also study the effect of parameter changes affecting the cubic terms describing the production of the activator and inhibitor and relate it to both normal and abnormal growth. The relative effect of the activator and inhibitor cubic terms is of interest. Figures 2 (a) and (b) show TGF-β concentrations in transverse sections of the simulated chick limb in the distal region at successive times , for $k_1=0$ (no cubic term for the activator). Patterning in the proximal region proceeds normally, up to the bifurcation of the solution into two cylindrical elements (two spots in cross-section). As time progresses, the two elements fuse into one long stripe in the transverse section, equivalent to the pathology of fused elements (Apert syndrome in humans [16]). The results were similar for small positive values of k, $0<k_1\approx k_2<0.1$. Figure 3 shows results for $k_2=0$ (no cubic term for the inhibitor). The normal pattern of bone elements is seen. Thus the activator cubic term suffices to stabilize the spots in transverse section. We can interpret the four intermediate spots in Figure 3 as carpal (i.e., wrist) bones.

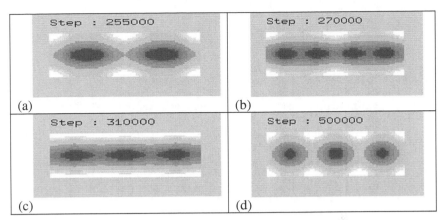

Fig. 3. Transverse sections of TGF-β concentration with no cubic stabilizing term for inhibitor ($k_2=0$, $k_1=0.125$). We obtain the normal pattern, indicating that the activator's cubic stabilization is crucial for generating the bone element pattern. The intermediate stage of four spots resembles the many carpal bone elements.

In summary, normal-looking patterns of the major chondrogenic elements were obtained for a relatively robust range of parameter changes. The correct stable pattern, especially the formation of distinct digits, requires the cubic terms in the equations describing the production of activator and inhibitor, with the activator cubic term more important. This may be justified, in part, by results described in [13] and references therein, showing this to be a general result for the kind of RD systems we consider- i.e., with only the first order terms for reactions, it is not possible to get both "stripes" and "spots" in a stable pattern. Other forms may stabilize the solution; for example, the assumption that fibronectin diffuses a short distance stabilizes [17] the biologically-motivated system of equations for skeletal development studied in [4]. These possibilities can motivate experimentation to determine whether this class of models is viable and if so, how stabilization is actually achieved.

Work in progress: We are extending the model to make the production of TGF-β as realistic as that of fibronectin, to include secretion at cell boundaries, rather than modeling secretion at the domain level. We will incorporate and extend the work of [4], which uses a continuum model of interaction between limb cells and gene products to obtain a more realistic set of RD equations. We are extending our simulation geometry module to incorporate the limb domain's moving boundaries. To incorporate the AER we are introducing two additional cell types, both *epithelial* (cells that cover the outer surface of the limb and give rise to skin) apical epithelial cells which secrete a mixture of FGFs characteristic of the AER, and epithelial cells that secrete a different mixture of FGFs [18].

Acknowledgements. We acknowledge support from NSF grants IBN-0083653, IBN-0090499, and ACI-0135195, NASA grant NAG 2-1619, an IBM Innovation Institute Award and a IUB Pervasive Technologies Laboratories Fellowship.

References

1. Chaturvedi, R., Izaguirre, J. A., Huang, C., Cickovski, T., Virtue, P, Thomas, G., Forgacs, G., Alber, M., Hentschel, G., Newman, S. A., and Glazier, J. A., Computational Science - ICCS 2003: International Conference Melbourne, Australia and St. Petersburg, Russia, June 2-4, 2003. Proceedings, Part III, P. M. A.Sloot, D. Abramson, A. V. Bogdanov, J. J. Dongarra, A. Y. Zomaya and Y. E. Gorbachev editors (LNCS Volume 2659, Springer-Verlag, New York), (2003) 39-49.
2. Izaguirre, J. A., Chaturvedi, R., Huang, C., Cickovski, T., Coffland, J., Thomas, G., Forgacs, G., Alber, M., Hentschel, G., Newman, S. A., and Glazier, J. A., CompuCell, a multi-model framework for simulation of morphogenesis, Bioinformatics 20 (2004) 1129-1137.
3. Newman, S. A.. and Comper, W. D., 'Generic' physical mechanisms of morphogenesis and pattern formation, Development 110 (1990)1-18.
4. Hentschel, H. G. E., Glimm, T., Glazier, J. A., Newman, S. A., Dynamical mechanisms for skeletal pattern formation in the vertebrate limb, to appear in Proceedings R. Soc. Lond: Bio. Sciences (2004).
5. Murray, J. D., Mathematical Biology, Springer, Berlin, 2nd edition (1993).
6. Miura, T. and Shiota, K., Tgf Beta2 acts as an activator molecule in reaction-diffusion model and is involved in cell sorting phenomenon in mouse limb micromass culture, Dev. Dyn. 217 (2000) 241-249.
7. Moftah, M. Z., Downie, S., Bronstein, N., Mezentseva, N., Pu, J., Maher, P., Newman, S. A,, Ectodermal FGFs induce perinodular inhibition of limb chondrogenesis in vitro and in vivo via FGF receptor 2, Dev. Biol. 249 (2002) 270-282.
8. Tsonis, P. A., Del Rio-Tsonis, K., Millan, J. L., Wheelock, M. J., Expression of N-cadherin and alkaline phosphatase in the chick limb bud mesenchymal cells: Regulation by 1,25- dihydroxyvitamin D_3 and TGF-beta1, Exp. Cell Res. 213 (1994) 433- 437.
9. Steinberg, M. S., Reconstruction of tissues by dissociated cells, Science 141 (1963) 401-408.
10. Glazier, J. A. and Graner, F., A simulation of the differential adhesion driven rearrangement of biological cells, Phys. Rev. E 47 (1993) 2128-2154.
11. Upadhyaya, A., Thermodynamic and fluid properties of cells, tissues and membranes, Ph.D. thesis, University of Notre Dame (2000).
12. Turing, A. M., The chemical basis of morphogenesis, Phil. Trans. Roy. Soc. Lond. B 237 (1952) 37-72.
13. Alber, M., Glimm, T., Hentschel, H. G. E., Kazmierczak, B. and Newman, S. A., Stability of n-Dimensional Patterns in a Generalized Turing System: Implications for Biological Pattern Formation, submitted (2004).
14. Zeng, W., Thomas, G. L., Newman, S. A., and Glazier, J. A., A Novel Mechanism for Mesenchymal Condensation during Limb Chondrogenesis in vitro, in Mathematical Modeling and Computing in Biology and Medicine: 5th Conference of the European Society of Mathematical and Theoretical Biology, Milan, V. Capasso and M. Ortisi (ed.) (2002).
15. Kiskowski, M. A., Alber, M. S., Thomas, G. L., Glazier, J. A., Bronstein, N. B., Pu, J., and Newman, S. A.. Interplay between activator-inhibitor coupling and cell-matrix adhesion in a cellular automaton model for chondrogenic patterning. Dev Biol 271 (2004) 372-87.
16. Cohen, M. M., Jr., and Kreiborg, S. Hands and feet in the Apert syndrome. Am J Med Genet 57 (1995) 82-96.
17. Alber, M., Kazmierczak, B., Hentshcel, H.G.E., Newman, S.A., Existence of solutions to a new model of avian limb formation, submitted (2004).
18. Martin, G. R. The roles of FGFs in the early development of vertebrate limbs. *Genes Dev* 12 (1998) 1571-86.

A Cellular Automata Model of Early T Cell Recognition

Arancha Casal[1], Cenk Sumen[2], Tim Reddy[3], Mark Alber[4], and Peter P. Lee[1]

[1] Hematology Division, School of Medicine, Stanford University, Palo Alto, CA 94305, USA
{cas, ppl}@stanford.edu
[2] Center for Blood Research, School of Medicine, Harvard University, Boston, MA 02115, USA
sumen@cbr.harvard.edu
[3] Computer Science Department, Boston University, Boston, MA 02215 USA
treddy@bu.edu
[4] Department of Mathematics and Center for Biocomplexity, University of Notre Dame, IN 46556, USA
malber@nd.edu

Abstract. T cells are key components of the immune system, recognizing the presence of foreign antigens by coming in direct contact with specialized antigen-presenting cells (APCs) and scanning the array of surface molecules presented by the APC. During the first 60 seconds of contact, thousands of molecules on both cell surfaces interact. Based on these interactions the T cell makes a first crucial decision to either sustain contact, eventually leading to activation, or to disengage and move on. This paper presents a Cellular Automata model to study how a T cell integrates a varied array of positive and negative signals into its first activation decision. Our simulations use available biological data and support the notion that complex behaviors, such as the signal processing function of a cell, can emerge from the varied local interactions of many cellular receptors.

1 Introduction

T cells play a central role in orchestrating the adaptive immune response. They are able to distinguish infected or cancer cells from normal cells. To do so, T cells detect abnormal antigens presented on the surface of antigen-presenting cells (APC). During recognition, a T cell comes in contact with an APC and within 60 seconds makes a crucial first decision to either sustain the interaction, potentially leading to activation, or to disengage and resume its patrol. Over this brief period, thousands of homogeneous T cell receptors (TCRs) on the T cell surface interact with thousands of heterogeneous peptide-MHC (pMHC) complexes on the APC surface with a wide range of interaction affinities (binding strength). The T cell quickly integrates this vast array of signals into a first activation decision, which ultimately determines the efficacy of the immune response.

Antigen recognition requires the binding of the T cell receptor to a pMHC complex [1]. This leads to a series of signaling events collectively known as TCR triggering [2]. Despite being the object of intense study, many of the molecular events underlying T cell signaling remain unknown. Some of the early events immediately following engagement with pMHC (notably, phosphorylation of the TCR-CD3

P.M.A. Sloot, B. Chopard, and A.G. Hoekstra (Eds.): ACRI 2004, LNCS 3305, pp. 553–560, 2004.
© Springer-Verlag Berlin Heidelberg 2004

complex) have been well established. Beyond these, it is believed that pMHC engagement leads to functional changes in the TCR that in turn affect the activation signal. However, what these changes are remains the subject of speculation. Several models have been proposed based on various, at times contradictory, experimental observations. One of these models proposes that upon pMHC engagement, activated TCRs begin to cluster with one another [3], [4] as a means of concentrating and enhancing the activation signal in preparation for the formation of a well-observed bulls eye pattern known as the immunological synapse [5]. Our model uses this "TCR microclustering" hypothesis.

Table 1. Categories of peptides

Peptide species	Half-life	Functionality
Strong Agonist	>10 sec	Promote full TCR activation (level 2), and by extension microclustering and T cell activation
Weak Agonist	2-10 sec	Can have the same effects as strong agonists, but only in higher concentrations.
Null	0-1 sec	Do not promote TCR activation by themselves (level 0), but enhance activation in presence of agonists
Antagonist	1-2 sec	Result in partial TCR activation (level 1) and disrupt clustering and T cell activation

Diversity in the T cell response is due to the peptides in the pMHC complex. Table 1 summarizes the different peptide classes and their known functional effect on T cell response. The half-life of interaction is the time the TCR and pMHC remain together, which in turn determines the amount of signaling (as this depends on recruitment and movement of molecules). In our model, when a TCR has interacted with a pMHC it is 'activated' to levels 0-2, thus modeling the different degrees of TCR phosphorylation.

2 Model

We model microclustering of activated TCRs during the first 60s of T cell-APC contact. Molecules move by Brownian motion on a square grid representing the T-APC contact surface and may interact when they collide. Interactions are defined by biologically informed local rules and given a stochastic component. The grid is populated with thousands of molecules, corresponding to a 20% realistic occupancy rate. Despite the low occupancy rate, microclusters can form under the right conditions resulting from an ordered sequence of signal exchanges. Microclustering occurs via a multi-stage process, as illustrated in Figure 1.

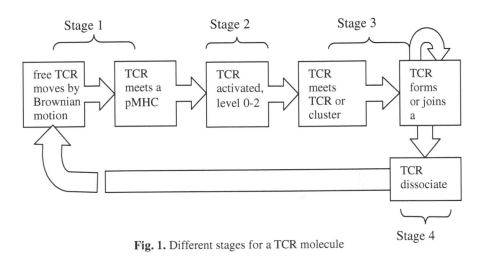

Fig. 1. Different stages for a TCR molecule

Stage 1: Collision of TCR with pMHC. A TCR and pMHC (both moving by Brownian motion) collide. Collisions occur when two particles meet at adjacent locations on the grid.

Stage 2: Activation of TCR by pMHC. The TCR and pMHC stay together for a period of time equal to the half-life, $t_{1/2}$, of interaction (determined by the peptide in the pMHC complex –see Table 1) and move together as a unit by Brownian motion. During this time the TCR gets activated to levels 0-2 (level 0=low activation, level 1=medium activation, level 2=high activation). The activation level reached by the TCR depends on $t_{1/2}$ and a stochastic component. The longer the pair stays together, the higher the likelihood of the TCR achieving a higher activation level by the end of their interaction. Agonists typically lead to level 2, antagonists to level 1 and nulls to level 0 (Table 2).

In order to capture the stochastic nature of TCR signaling [6], every time a TCR-pMHC encounter occurs we use a probability distribution to set the time required to reach the different activation levels. Hence, a half-life of >5 seconds will most likely result in level 2 (full) activation of the TCR, but not always.

Stage 3: Clustering with other TCRs. A TCR may initiate a cluster when it collides with another free TCR, or join an existing cluster when it collides with it. The rules for clustering are as follows. We define six pairwise cluster association probabilities (CAPs), P_{ij}, where i,j=0,1,2 correspond to different activation levels and $P_{ij} = P_{ji}$. The CAPs define the pairwise probability of association between two TCRs at their corresponding activation levels. For example, P_{02} is the probability of association between a level 0 TCR and a level 2 TCR. In our model P_{22} will be the highest probability as it involves two agonist-activated TCRs, and P_{11} the lowest, as it involves two antagonist-activated TCRs. The six CAPs in order of increasing probability (i.e. likelihood of association) are: P_{11}, P_{10}, P_{12}, P_{00}, P_{02}, P_{22}. We choose the CAP values partly by matching experimental data and, once set, their values are stored in a lookup table for use by the simulation.

In the case where the activated TCR collides with another free TCR, the two will join together to form a cluster if the P_{ij} is higher than a threshold. The threshold is a random number, to account for stochastic effects. If the activated TCR collides with an existing cluster, we look at the P_{ij} of the TCR with every other TCR in the cluster and generate a random threshold for every pair. The TCR joins the cluster if any one of the P_{ij} exceeds its threshold.

Table 2. TCR activation levels

TCR Activation Level	Conferred by (highest probability)	Effect on Clustering
0 – low activation	Null peptide	Neutral stability
1 – partial activation	Antagonist peptide	Instability
2 – full activation	Agonist peptide	High stability

Stage 4: Possible Dissociation from Cluster. We want to model instability inside a microcluster due to thermal vibrations and the presence of antagonists. We define six pairwise cluster dissociation probabilities (CDPs), $\underline{P}_{ij}$, where $\underline{P}_{22}$ is the lowest (two agonist-activated TCRs want to stay together), and $\underline{P}_{11}$ is the highest (two antagonist-activated TCRs want to dissociate). The six CDPs in order of increasing (dissociation) probability are: $\underline{P}_{22}$, $\underline{P}_{20}$, $\underline{P}_{00}$, $\underline{P}_{12}$, $\underline{P}_{10}$, $\underline{P}_{11}$. We choose the CDP values partly by matching experimental data and, once set, their values are stored in a lookup table for use by the simulation.

At every time step and for every TCR in the cluster we look up its pairwise dissociation probability P_{ij} with all the other TCRs and generate a random threshold for each pair. A TCR will dissociate from the cluster if any of its P_{ij} exceeds its threshold and it is not physically blocked from falling away by other TCRs.

3   Results

We simulated early T cell recognition under different peptide inputs. We show results corresponding to the tests of Tables 3 and 4. To start the simulation, the APC grid is seeded with a given peptide mix, molecules are allowed to move and interact, and microcluster formation is tracked. We judge the outcome of recognition (or signal strength received by the T cell) by measuring the number of TCRs involved in stable microclusters at 60 seconds. Stable microclusters are defined as lasting >2 seconds with at least 6 TCRs at the end of each simulation. Thus, transient microclusters that may form during the simulation based on random collisions would not be scored.

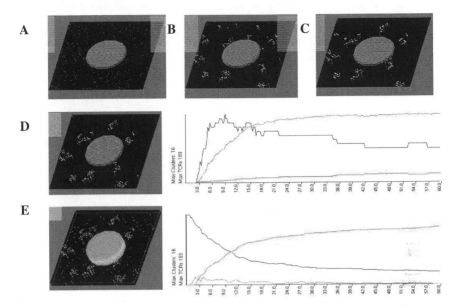

Fig. 2. Microcluster evolution (*A-E*) on contact interface for 100% agonists on APC surface (first test on Table 3). Agonist peptides promote TCR activation and, thus, microcluster formation.

As the results have a stochastic nature, several runs were performed for each peptide repertoire and the results averaged. The initial simulations were performed on a 700 x 700 grid (representing the full 50 μm^2 contact surface). As scaling downward did not qualitatively affect the results, we performed most simulations on a 300 x 300 grid (approximately 1/5 the contact area) to reduce run times, and the results reported below are based on this reduced area. The TCR and pMHC populations on a 300 x 300 grid are approximately 1800 molecules each (~2% occupancy), and the total population for all molecule types is 18,000 molecules (~20% occupancy).

We estimate a minimal activation threshold to be 50-80 TCRs (out of 1800 TCRs) involved in stable microclusters at 60 seconds. These values are based on simulations resulting in stable clustering and are thus far not experimentally measurable, but consistent with previous results [5].

The simulator also includes an animation component to visualize the dynamics and evolution of microclusters during the interaction period. Figures 2 and 3 show serial snapshots of the animations and graphs of the cluster statistics for the first and third tests in Table 3 below. To facilitate clarity in visualization, these animations correspond to a reduced 100 x 100 grid size (all other results below correspond to a 300 x 300 grid).

As a shortform, we use N to denote null peptides, An for antagonists, WA for weak agonists, and SA for strong agonists. For example, 90N:10SA denotes a peptide mixture consisting of 90% Null and 10% Strong Agonist. Unless a distinction is explicitly made between strong and weak agonists, we use the term agonist to imply strong agonist.

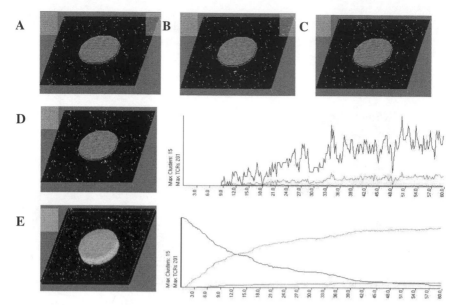

Fig. 3. Microcluster evolution (*A-E*) for 10% agonists and 90% antagonists (third test on Table 3). The high ratio of antagonists prevents the formation of stable (long-lived) microclusters.

3.1 Effect of Agonist and Antagonist Peptides on T Cell Activation

We seeded the APC with the four simple peptide mixtures for which experimental results were available (Sumen C. and Davis M.M., unpublished data). We assume that immune synapse (IS) formation implies, by extension, microcluster formation and we use the data to partially validate our model behavior and estimate parameters. As shown in Table 3, the 100% agonists ($t_{1/2} > 10$ sec) condition produced the largest average number of TCRs involved in stable microclusters (904 on average, out of a total of 1800 TCRs), followed by 10% agonist-90% null, or 10A:90N (512 on average). These data are consistent with biological observations since these two conditions produced IS formation in *in vitro* experiments.

Table 3. Effect of agonist and antagonist peptides on T cell activation. Percentages refer to relative concentrations of each peptide class in the overall pMHC population. The total pMHC population represents 2% of the total population of APC surface molecules. Simulation data represent the total # of TCRs involved in stable (>2 seconds) microclusters at the end of 60 seconds. Data show the mean ± SD of 8 independent simulations of each condition

% Agonist	% Antagonist	% Null	IS observed?	#TCR in microclusters
100	0	0	Yes	904 ± 66
10	0	90	Yes	512 ± 29
10	90	0	No	0 ± 0
1	0	99	No	64 ± 22

Table 4. Effect of weak vs. strong agonists on T cell activation. Different ratios of null, weak agonist, and strong agonist peptides were selected to further validate the model and constrain model parameters based on a relative activation potency ratio of 100:1 strong:weak agonists [8]. Percentages refer to relative concentrations of each peptide class in the overall pMHC population. The total pMHC population represents 2% of the total population of APC surface molecules. Simulation data represent the total # of TCRs involved in stable (>2 seconds) microclusters at the end of 60 seconds. Data show the mean ± SD of 8 independent simulations of each condition

% Weak Agonist	% Null	% Strong Agonist	#TCR in microclusters
0	99	1	64 ± 26
90	10	0	2 ± 5
100	0	0	72 ± 51

As expected, the other two conditions which did not lead to IS formation on lipid bilayer experiments produced far fewer stable microclusters in our model. 99% Null-1% Agonist led to only 64 average TCRs involved in stable microclusters, while 90% Antagonist-10% Agonist led to no stable microclusters, replicating the biological effect of antagonist peptides in our model.

3.2 Differential Activation Potential of Weak Versus Strong Agonist

We also tested the differential activation potency of weak versus strong agonists. It has been widely observed that significantly higher amounts of weak agonist peptides ($2 \leq t_{1/2} < 10$ seconds) are needed to bring a T cell to activation than strong agonists ($t_{1/2} \geq 10$ seconds) [7]. The relative differences in activation potency between weak and strong agonists vary widely in the literature. A reasonable consensus is a 100:1 ratio between strong:weak agonists in activation potency, although some reports suggest an even larger difference. We selected three representative mixtures of weak and strong agonist peptides to recreate this relative potency ratio (Table 4) – 99N:1SA, 10N:90WA, and 100WA.

As above, the 99N:1SA mixture is itself non-activating but within the subthreshold range (average 64). The 10N:90WA mixture produced <10 TCRs in stable microclusters. Importantly, a modest further increase of WA to 100WA led to a substantial increase in TCRs in stable microclusters (Table 4). This replicates the 100:1 relative activation potency ratio between weak and strong agonists.

4   Conclusions and Future Work

In this study we employ a cellular automata model to simulate TCR-pMHC interactions in early T cell recognition, focusing on the first 60 seconds when the first activation decision is made. In the context of microcluster formation, this approach allows us to observe the emergent group dynamics resulting from mixing large and diverse peptide populations. The model cannot reflect all the complex molecular events behind T-APC surface dynamics. However, the model is functionally accurate in being able to fit a number of experimental data, it integrates accepted hypotheses of T cell activation and its assumptions are biologically sound. The *in silico* experiments we perform provide the ability to 'mix and monitor' different populations of thousands of pMHCs and to observe their potential effect on T cell activation, something currently impractical *in vitro*.

Our model supports the notion that a T cell recognizes a continuous mosaic of peptides rather than individual peptides in isolation, suggesting that T cell recognition is based on the 'whole picture' presented by the target cell.

As future work, we will incorporate the effects of other surface molecules (co-receptor and co-stimulatory such as CD4, CD28) and seed with more complex peptide mixtures to investigate these processes in greater detail.

References

1. Irvine, D.J., Purbhoo, M.A., Krogsgaard, M, Davis, M.M.: Direct observation of ligand recognition by T cells. Nature **419** (2002) 845-849.
2. van der Merwe, P.A.: The Triggering Puzzle. Immunity **14** (2002) 665-668.
3. Alam, S.M., Davies, G.M., Lin, C.M., Zal, T., Nasholds, W., Jameson, S.C., Hogquist, K.A., Gascoigne, N.R., Travers, P.J. Immunity **10** (1999) 227-237.
4. Reich, Z., Boniface, J.J., Lyons, D.S., Borochov, N., Wachtel, E.J., Davis, M.M.: Ligand-specific oligomerization of T-cell receptor molecules. Nature **387** (1997) 617-620.
5. Grakoui, A, Bromley, S.K., Sumen, C., Davis, M.M., Shaw, A.S., Allen, P.M., Dustin, M.L.: The immunological synapse: a molecular machine controlling T cell activation. Science. **285** (1999) 221-227.
6. Malissen, B.: An evolutionary and structural perspective on T cell antigen receptor function. Immunol. Rev. **191** (2003) 7-27.
7. Lim, D.G,. Slavik, J.M.,, Bourcier, K., Smith, K.J., Hafler, D.A.: Allelic Variation of MHC Structure Alters Peptide Ligands to Induce Atypical Partial Agonistic CD8+ T Cell Function. J. Exp. Med. **198** (2003) 99-109.
8. Saibil, S.D., Ohteki, T., White, F.M., Luscher, M., Zakarian, A., Elford, A., Shabanowitz, J., Nishina, H., Hugo, P., Penninger, J.: Weak agonist self-peptides promote selection and tuning of virus-specific T cells. Eur. J. Immunol. **33** (2003) 685-696.

Simulation of Cell Population Dynamics Using 3-D Cellular Automata

Belgacem Ben Youssef

School of Interactive Arts and Technology
Simon Fraser University
2400 Central City, 10153 K. G. Highway
Surrey, British Columbia, V3T 2W1, Canada
byoussef@sfu.ca
http://www.surrey.sfu.ca/about/people/faculty/benyoussef.html

Abstract. We present the simulation results of a comprehensive model based on cellular automata that describes the dynamic behavior of a population of mammalian cells that migrate and proliferate to fill a three-dimensional scaffold. The model is applied to study how cell migration and the density or spatial distribution of seed cells affect the cell proliferation rates. A large number of system parameters allow for a detailed simulation of the population dynamics of migrating and proliferating cells. This permits the exploration of the relative influence of these parameters on the proliferation rate and some other aspects of cell behavior such as the average speed of locomotion and the collision rate.

1 Introduction

The development of bio-artificial tissue substitutes involves extensive and time-consuming experimentation. The availability of computational models with predictive abilities will greatly speed up progress in this area. Such models will assist researchers in predicting the dynamic response of cell populations to external stimuli, and in assessing the effect of various system parameters on the overall tissue growth rates.

This study reports the simulation results of a three-dimensional cellular automata model that describes the proliferation of migrating mammalian cells. Based on previous experimental observations [6], the developed model can accurately describe the persistent random walks executed by individual migrating cells, as well as the phenomena occurring when cells collide with each other. In addition, the model quantitatively accounts for contact inhibition phenomena occurring during all stages of the proliferation process: the initial stage of exponential growth of cells without contact inhibition; the second stage where cell colonies form and grow with few colony mergings; and the final stage where proliferation rates are dominated by colony merging events [9]. The simulation results will be analyzed to elucidate the competing roles played by contact inhibition and cell motility in determining the proliferation rate.

P.M.A. Sloot, B. Chopard, and A.G. Hoekstra (Eds.): ACRI 2004, LNCS 3305, pp. 561–570, 2004.
© Springer-Verlag Berlin Heidelberg 2004

The rest of the paper is organized as follows: Section 2 and Section 3 present the states and rules of the three-dimensional cellular automata describing cell proliferation and migration, respectively. Section 4 covers the initial cell distribution used for our simulations while Section 5 elaborates on a special rule, known as the collision rule. After discussing the simulation results in Section 6, we present our conclusion in Section 7.

2   Cellular Automata States

Our simulations of cell migration and proliferation are carried out on cellular automata that are three-dimensional networks of computational sites. Each site is an automaton with a finite number of possible states that interacts with a finite number of neighboring sites. Thus, cellular automata networks are dynamic systems evolving with discrete iterations. At equally spaced time instants t_1, t_2, $\cdots$, t_r, t_{r+1}, ... (where $t_{r+1} = t_r + \Delta t$ for all r), the sate x_i of each automaton i evolves through interactions with neighboring sites. To simulate persistent random walks and asynchronous proliferation in a three-dimensional cellular automaton, we must first define an appropriate set of values for the state of each computational site. To this end, the state x_i of an automaton containing a living cell must specify the following set of parameters:

1. The direction in which this cell is moving.
2. The instantaneous speed of locomotion.
3. The time remaining until the next direction change.
4. The time remaining until the next cell division.

By adjusting the time interval Δt between iterations, the average speed of the cell population can be varied and controlled. This is due to the fact that migrating cells cover a fixed distance in each step. Another means of regulating the speed of locomotion is the ability to adjust the transition probability for the stationary state. Therefore, a migrating cell in automaton i must only specify the direction of locomotion and the times remaining until the next direction change and the next cell division in its state x_i. Hence, the state x_i of an arbitrary automaton i takes values from the following set of seven-digit integer numbers

$$\Upsilon = \{klmnpqr \mid k, l, m, n, p, q, \text{and } r \in \mathbb{N}\}, \tag{1}$$

where k is the *direction index* representing the direction in which the cell is currently moving (see Table 1). The *persistence counter* is denoted by the two digits lm. The time t_c remaining until the next change in the direction of cell movement is equal to $t_c = (m + 10l)\Delta t$. The remaining four digits, $npqr$, are the *cell phase counter*. The time t_d remaining before the next cell division is equal to $t_d = (r + 10q + 100p + 1000n)\Delta t$.

The initial value of the persistence counter lm after each direction change is given by the average waiting time computed by applying a Markov chain analysis to the cell trajectory data. At each iteration, the value of this counter

Table 1. Each direction index has a corresponding direction of motion

Direction Index (k)	Direction of Motion
0	Stationary
1	East
2	North
3	West
4	South
5	Up
6	Down

is decremented by one and the cell changes direction when this counter reaches zero. The initial value of the cell phase counter $npqr$ is randomly assigned to each living cell using the cell division time distribution obtained from experiments. Also, the value of this counter is decremented by one at each iteration and the cell divides when this counter reaches zero [6].

For instance, for simulations carried out on a cubic lattice with $N \times N \times N$ sites using a time step equal to $\Delta t = 0.2$ hr, we let the state of an arbitrary site i, with coordinates (x, y, z), be equal to $x_i = 4100119$ at some time t_0. This means that site i is occupied by a cell that is currently moving in a southern direction (i.e., in the negative Y direction whose direction index $k = 4$). Migration in this direction will continue for ten more time intervals (2 hrs), and the cell will divide after 119 iterations (or 23.8 hrs). At time $t_0 + \Delta t$, this cell will occupy site j, provided it is unoccupied, located at $(x, y - 1, z)$ and $x_j = 4090118$. That is, the persistence and cell phase counters have been decremented by one. If no other cell moves into the ith site, $x_i = 0$ at $t_0 + \Delta t$.

3   Cellular Automata Rules

Using an initial cell distribution and seeding density, we start by distributing the seed cells to the computational sites of the cellular automaton. As decribed in the last section, each cellular automaton takes values from a set of integer numbers that code all the required information about cell migration speed, the direction of movement, and the time remaining until the next direction change and the next cell division. Each cell interacts with its six immediate neighbors located to its north, east, south, west, above, and below it. This is the von Neumann neighborhood in three dimensions. We next describe the rules governing the temporal evolution of the states of computational sites which specify cell movement and division.

3.1   Initial Condition

- Select the sites that will be occupied by cells at time $t_0 = 0$ by using the specified cell seeding density and the spatial distribution of seed cells.
- Assign a state to each occupied site by randomly selecting the direction index, by choosing the proper value of the persistence counter, and by setting the cell phase counter according to the experimentally determined distribution of cell division times. This information can be obtained from independent experiments using the locomotion assays developed in [6].

3.2   Iterative Operations

At each time step $t_r = t_{r-1} + \Delta t$, $r = 1, 2, \ldots$

1. Randomly select a site (an automaton).
2. If this site contains a cell and its phase counter is equal to zero (i.e., it is time for it to divide), execute the *division routine* and go to step 5.
3. If this automaton contains a cell and its persistence counter is equal to zero (i.e., it is time for it to change direction), execute the *direction change routine* and go to step 5.
4. Otherwise, try to move the cell to a neighboring site in the direction indicated by the direction index of its current state:
   - If this site is free, *mark* it as the site that will contain the cell at the next time step and decrement the persistence and cell phase counters by one.
   - If this site is occupied, the cell will remain at the present site (thus, entering the stationary state) and execute the *direction change* routine after a prespecified number of iterations.
5. Select another site and repeat steps 2–4 until all sites have been examined.
6. Update the states of all sites so that the locations of all cells are set for the next time step.

3.3   Division Routine

1. Scan the neighborhood of the current site to determine if there are any free adjacent sites. If all adjacent sites are occupied, the cell will not divide. The cell is assigned a new phase counter.
2. If there are free sites in the neighborhood, select one of these sites by using a random algorithm based on the growth probabilities.
3. Mark the selected site that will contain one of the daughter cells in the next time step (once a site has been marked in this fashion, no other cell can move in it during this iteration). The second daughter cell will occupy the current location. Set the direction index as well as the persistence and cell phase counters. Then, return.

3.4   Direction Change Routine

1. Scan the neighborhood of the current site to determine if there are any free adjacent sites. If all adjacent sites are occupied, the cell remains at the present site. The cell is also assigned a new persistence counter.
2. If there are free sites in the neighborhood, select one of these sites by using a random algorithm based on the experimentally determined state-transition probabilities.
3. Mark the selected site that will contain the cell in the next time step (once a site has been marked in this fashion, no other cell can move in it at this iteration). Set the persistence counter to its appropriate initial value, decrement the cell phase counter by one, and return.

4   Initial Cell Distribution

For our computer simulations, we used a *uniform seeding* distribution as the initial seeding mode. Here, the cells were uniformly and randomly distributed in the cellular array as shown in Figure 1. The number of used cells is dependent on the seeding density. This seeding distribution was designed to simulate the growth of three-dimensional tissues.

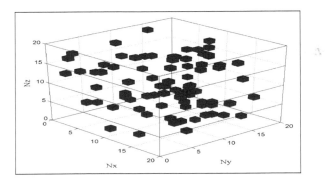

Fig. 1. An example of a uniform cell distribution of 80 cells in a 20 × 20 × 20 cellular array with a 1% seeding density

5   Collision Rule

Our cellular automata model is a good example of a dynamic process where the problem is defined by a set of allowed cell movements and divisions within a defined neighborhood and according to state information. A possible input I is an initial cell population distribution where each occupied site is assigned a state. The corresponding set of possible outputs, O_I, consists of all cell population distributions after simulation of some timesteps according to the defined rules of mammalian cell proliferation and migration. All simulations following these rules are correct solutions. One of the rules is the *collision rule* specifying that no two cells are allowed to occupy the same site (see Figure 2).

Our solution is to avoid any moves or growths to locations already occupied or marked by other cells. In a serial implementation, this does not cause any problems. A single node working on the problem knows exactly about the whole state of the system, for it *owns* the entire cellular space. Before allowing cell movement and division, it can test the cellular array whether such processes are allowed. If so, it *marks* the prospective site. If not, it looks for another unoccupied site within the cell's neighborhood. At the end of each simulation step, it updates the entire cellular array. The crucial point here is the marking of the site. It allows us to handle effectively the collision rule. This is equivalent to a *splitting* of each of the processes of cell division and motion into a *computation* phase and an *execution* phase. The use of cellular automata in our model enforces this concept since updating the cellular array can now be done at once after completing the latter phase.

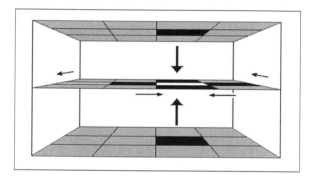

Fig. 2. Illustration of an instance of collision where in this case up to six cells (black) may choose to move or divide into the same empty site (white)

6   Simulation Results and Discussion

Various parameters in the model allow for a detailed study of the population dynamics of migrating and proliferating mammalian cells. The important parameters of our simulations are as follows:

1. Initial volume coverage.
2. Cell motility.
3. Seeding Distribution.

We present the simulation results obtained from the serial implementation of the model. These results were obtained using a $128 \times 128 \times 128$ cellular array.

All simulations have a confluence parameter of 99.99%. The obtained results have significant implications for the design of laboratory experiments aimed at studying the role of the aforementioned parameters on tissue growth rates.

6.1   Effect of Initial Volume Coverage on Tissue Growth Rate and Cell Population Dynamics

The tissue growth rate is represented by the proliferation rate. The proliferation rate and the time to reach confluence are greatly affected by the initial volume coverage. Figure 3 (left) shows the effect of cell seeding density on the proliferation rate and volume coverage, respectively. The cells in these simulations are motile, migrating at a speed of $50\mu m/hr$, and uniformly seeded on the three-dimensional computational grid. For very low seeding densities, the volume coverage curves have a long *induction period* because the slow growth of isolated cell colonies dominates the process after the first few cell divisions. As the initial volume coverage increases, this induction period disappears. At higher cell seedings, the volume coverage increases rapidly as the cells reach confluence within a few divisions and before isolated colonies can form. The time required to reach confluence decreases with increasing initial volume coverage.

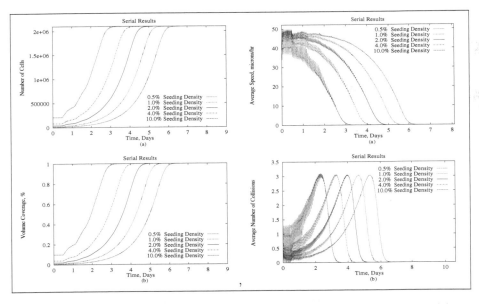

Fig. 3. The effect of seeding density on: (left) (a) the cell proliferation rate and (b) the volume coverage, (right) (a) the average speed and (b) the average number of collisions per hour for initial seeding densities ranging from 0.5% to 10% with a cell migration speed of $50\mu m/hr$

The effects of the initial volume coverage on the average speed of locomotion and on the average number of collisions per hour are also shown in Figure 3 (right) (a) and (b), respectively. The average speed of locomotion decreases faster, as the initial seeding density is increased, reaching zero near confluence. The average number of collisions per unit time is defined as the total number of collisions divided by the total number of cells and time in hours. There is a small number of collisions at the beginning of the simulations due to the fact that cells are initially seeded in a random and sparse fashion. Then, as the volume coverage increases, the average number of collisions also increases due to the increase in the number of cell-cell interactions. When about $70 - 75\%$ of confluence is reached, the average number of collisions reaches its maximum, starts to decrease shortly thereafter due to the merging of small cell colonies, and reduces to zero when confluence is reached. We also observe that increasing the initial seeding density results in a shifting (to the left) of the time at which the maximum number of collisions occurs by a period equal to the decrease in time to reach confluence.

6.2 Effect of Cell Motility on Tissue Growth Rate and Cell Population Dynamics

The growth rate curves, shown in Figure 4, depict the effect of motility on cell proliferation and volume coverage. All of these simulations started with the same cell seeding density of 0.5%, or equivalently with 10, 486 seed cells. We observvve that as the motility of cells increases, the proliferation rate increases and confluence is attained faster. Higher motility of cells decreases the negative impact of contact inhibition on the proliferation rate because it prohibits the formation of cell colonies altogether. We also notice that initially small increases in motility have a large effect on cell proliferation, and the times required to reach confluence decrease rapidly with increasing cell motility. The incremental enhancement of proliferation rates, however, diminishes as the average speed of locomotion reaches values above $10 \mu m/hr$ for such simulations.

Figure 5 (left) shows the temporal evolution of the cell population average speed of locomotion. The average speed of motion remains nearly constant for the first three to four days when cell densities are low. An increase in cell density leads to an increase in the number of cell-cell interactions, which in turn drives the average speed of migration to lower levels.

The same figure (right) also displays the temporal evolution of the average number of collisions for different cell migration speeds. Increasing cell motility increases the average number of cell collisions per hour. Highly motile cells spend more time changing their direction of motion in the pursuit of unoccupied sites in their neighborhoods. However, as volume coverage increases, the number of such empty sites diminishes, thus increasing the likelihood of more cell collisions. Thus, increasing the speed of locomotion results in sustained increases in the average number of cell collisions per hour.

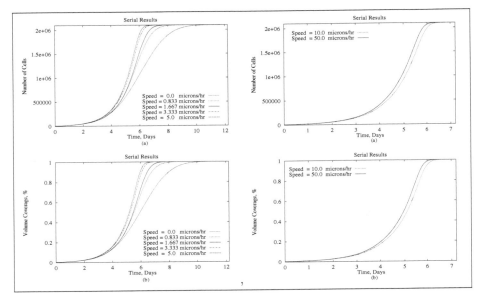

Fig. 4. The effect of cell motility on (a) the cell proliferation rate and (b) the volume coverage for cell speeds ranging from (left) $0.0\mu m/hr$ to $5.0\mu m/hr$ and (right) $10\mu m/hr$ and $50\mu m/hr$ using an initial seeding density of 0.5%

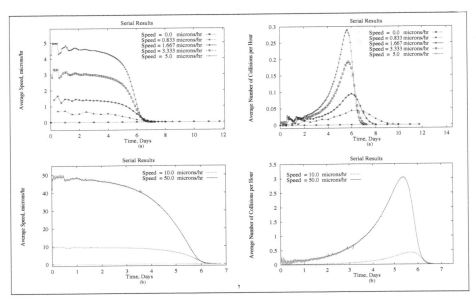

Fig. 5. The effect of cell motility on (left) the population-average speed of locomotion and (right) the population-average number of collisions per hour for cell speeds ranging from (a) $0\mu m/hr$ to $5\mu m/hr$ and (b) $10\mu m/hr$ to $50\mu m/hr$ using an initial seeding density of 0.5%

7 Conclusion

We presented the simulation results of a three-dimensional cellular automata model for cell proliferation and migration. These simulation results were obtained by studying the effects of a uniform seeding distribution, initial volume coverage, and cell migration speeds on the tissue growth rate. Future work involves extending this model to account for mixed cell populations, their organization into different spatial patterns to produce specific tissue architectures, and the implementation of these models on readily available parallel machines such as *Beowulf* clusters to simulate the growth of realizable tissue objects. Through our collaboration with other researchers [2], we anticipate that such results will contribute toward the development of computational tools that can facilitate the research of tissue engineers.

Acknowledgments. This work was initially supported by a National Science Foundation research grant and is currently funded by both a Simon Fraser University start-up grant and a Natural Sciences and Engineering Research Council of Canada (NSERC) discovery grant; the latter under project number 611407.

References

1. Ben Youssef, B.: Cell Proliferation and Migration: 3-D Modeling Using Cellular Automata, Development of a Parallel Algorithm and Its Implementation on an IBM SP2. Ph.D. Dissertation. University of Houston (1999)
2. Ben Youssef, B., Markenscoff, P., Zygourakis, K.: A Computational Model for Tissue Regeneration and Wound Healing. Proceedings of the Third Chemical Engineering Symposium. Athens, Greece, **2** (2001) 1133–1136
3. Bratley, P., Fox, B.L., Schrage, L.E.: A Guide to Simulation. 2nd edn. Springer-Verlag, New York (1987)
4. Chopard, B., Droz, M.: Cellular Automata Modeling of Physical Systems. Cambridge University Press, Cambridge (1998)
5. Langer, R., Vacanti, J.P.: Tissue Engineering. Science. **260** 5110 (1993) 920–926
6. Lee, Y., Markenscoff, P., McIntire, L.V., Zygourakis, K.: Characterization of Endothelial Cell Locomotion Using a Markov Chain Model. Biochemistry and Cell Biology. **73** (1995) 461–472
7. Lehmer, D.H.: Mathematical Methods in Large-Scale Computing Units. The Annals of the Computation Laboratory of Harvard University. Harvard University Press, **26** (1951) 141–146
8. Toffoli, T., Margolus, N.: Cellular Automata Machines: A New Environment for Modeling. The MIT Press, Cambridge, Massachusetts (1987)
9. Zygourakis, K., Bizios, R., Markenscoff, P.: Proliferation of Anchorage-Dependent Contact-Inhibited Cells: I. Development of Theoretical Models Based on Cellular Automata. Biotechnology and Bioengineering. **38** 5 (1991) 459–470
10. Zygourakis, K., Markenscoff, P., Bizios, R.: Proliferation of Anchorage-Dependent Contact-Inhibited Cells: II. Experimental Results and Validation of the Theoretical Models. Biotechnology and Bioengineering. **38** 5 (1991) 471–479

Synchronization of Protein Motors Modeled by Asynchronous Cellular Automata

Ferdinand Peper[1], Kazuhiro Oiwa[2], Susumu Adachi[1], Chikako Shingyoji[3], and Jia Lee[1]

[1] National Institute of Information and Communications Technology (NICT),
Nanotechnology Group, 588-2 Iwaoka, Iwaoka-cho, Kobe, 651-2492 Japan
{peper, sadachi, lijia}@nict.go.jp
[2] National Institute of Information and Communications Technology (NICT),
Protein Biophysics Group, 588-2 Iwaoka, Iwaoka-cho, Kobe, 651-2492 Japan
oiwa@po.nict.go.jp
[3] University of Tokyo, Graduate School of Sciences, Dept. of Biological Sciences,
Hongo, Tokyo, 113-0033 Japan,
chikako@biol.s.u-tokyo.ac.jp

Abstract. Spermatozoa propel themselves in fluids through a rhythmically beating flagellum. Though it is known that the motor protein "dynein" is at the base of such movements, it is unclear how the behaviors of individual elements add up to the coordinated movement of the flagellum. Being single-cell entities, spermatozoa lack nerve systems, so an explanation for their movements ought to be found in a mechanism on molecular scales. This paper aims to clarify part of a possible mechanism in terms of asynchronous cellular automata. The question answered is: "Given a 1-dimensional cellular automaton with von Neumann neighborhood of which each cell—being updated at random times—cycles through three states; how can waves, i.e., patterns of cells in certain states, be formed that on average move in one direction?"

1 Introduction

The mechanisms underlying the motion of living organisms have long fascinated researchers, from the level of muscles to sperm cells and some protozoa, which propel themselves along by rhythmically beating their tail-like flagella or their hair-like cilia. Cells in organisms produce motion by employing *protein motors* (see [1] for an introduction and [11,27] for overviews), which are chemo-mechanical enzymes that generate force and movement along protein filaments (actin filaments and microtubules), using energy from the hydrolysis of adenosinetriphosphate (ATP). Protein motors interact with protein filaments through a *head region* (motor domain). Coupled with ATP hydrolysis, the head carries out a *crossbridge cycle*, in which it successively attaches to the filament, conducts a power stroke through which the head moves the filament along, and detaches from the filament (see Fig. 1(a)), and so on.

The rhythmic beating of flagella may be the result of waves of force-generating dynein molecules, of which the active regions of dynein molecules

P.M.A. Sloot, B. Chopard, and A.G. Hoekstra (Eds.): ACRI 2004, LNCS 3305, pp. 571–580, 2004.
© Springer-Verlag Berlin Heidelberg 2004

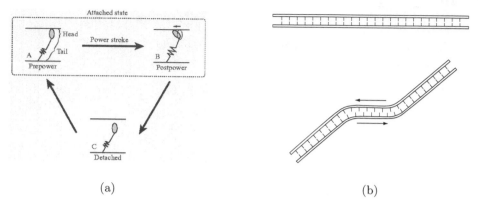

(a)   (b)

Fig. 1. (a) Crossbridge cycle of a motor protein like dynein. The protein consists of a tail (*vertical lever*) with a head (*shaded ellips*). In state A the head, attached to the opposing filament, is about to conduct its power stroke (*prepower* stroke). Due to the power stroke the head moves the filament to the left, after which it is about to detach (state B; *postpower* stroke). The cycle is completed when the head detaches and moves back to the right (state C). (b) Bending of flagellum caused by coordinated attachment and detachment of dynein heads according to their crossbridge cycles. Dynein molecules are located on one filament and they attach to certain sites on the opposing filament. The *bars* perpendicular to the top and bottom filaments are indicator bars, not dynein molecules, to show displacement

gradually shift in phase as a function over space, resembling coordinated up / down swings of supporters' arms during soccer games. Called *metachronal waves*, such waves are thought to underly the concerted bending of a flagellum [23], like in Fig. 1(b).

Metachronal waves may result from a flagellum being composed of elements with self-oscillatory properties [17,18]. Though observations [25] suggest that a single dynein molecule (or at most a few molecules) is capable of oscillations, thereby undergoing the crossbridge cycle around a certain frequency, it is still unknown [6] how multiple dynein molecules are regulated to produce coordinated oscillation. A global mechanism for regulation, like a clock expressed in the form of chemical signals [26], may be a candidate, though it lacks experimental evidence. Alternatively, hydrodynamical couplings [8,28,7] may play a role, or mechanical couplings between individual dynein arms, like tensions [16], the curvature of a flagellum [3,4,9,10], bending [21,24], and the coupling of motor activity to flagellar deformations on local scales [5,6]. Even in the absence of flagellar bending, though, oscillations have been observed in experiments [14,15, 29], be it at higher-than-usual frequencies. This calls for models that inherently exhibit such oscillations due to some subtle local interactions, like the model in [19], in which motors, cycling through three states, have excitable properties with threshold phenomena. This model is restricted to low amplitude motion [8], which is not the case for real flagella. The choice for three states in the model makes sense, though, since it is the minimum required to encode a wave propagating in a certain direction, if the underlying elements have a randomized nature: two states are insufficient, unless certain assumptions are made, like the coupling of motors at remote intervals through a periodic energy landscape [13].

This paper aims to shed more light on mechanisms underlying metachronal waves, using an asynchronous 1-dimensional cellular automaton in which each cell assumes one of three states that cyclically changes at random times. There are up to 27 transition rules underlying such cyclic behaviour. These rules can be classified according to their effects on waves, like creating a new wave front, removing a wave front, biasing a wave to the right, etc. By assigning a weight to each rule relating to the time it takes to update a cell by the rule, the system can be biased such that waves tend to move to the right. Simulations are shown that confirm the effectiveness of this construction.

Asynchronous cellular automata are defined in Section 2 and used to model the crossbridge cycle of protein motors; a simple example is given of a wave moving to the right on the cellular automaton. Section 3 then shows how to turn around waves moving in the wrong direction. Generalizing these results, we show how to create waves out of random patterns by categorizing rules according to the effect they have on waves and weighting them to bias waves to the right. We finish with conclusions and a discussion.

2   Wave Propagation on Asynchronous Cellular Automata

A *cellular automaton* consists of identical finite automata arranged as cells in a regular d-dimensional array (in this paper $d = 1$) [20]. Each cell is in a state from a finite state set, which in this paper is $\{A, B, C\}$. Cell states are updated in accordance with transition rules, which map each cell's state and the neighboring cells' states to the cell's next state.

Synchronous cellular automata, the most commonly used, require all cells to undergo state transitions simultaneously at every time step. If state transitions occur in accordance with some other updating scheme, for example randomly and independently of each other [2,12,22], the resulting model is an *asynchronous cellular automaton*. We use an asynchronous updating scheme in which at each time step cells are ordered randomly, selected one by one in that order with a certain probability, and each selected cell is updated according to a transition rule of which the left hand side matches the states of the cell and its neighbors. A cell's state will remain unchanged if no matches can be made to transition rules, even if that cell was selected.

How can cellular automata help in modeling flagellar beating? In the cross-bridge cycle in Fig. 1(a) we distinguish three states:

A the head is attached, but has not yet done the power stroke (prepower stroke),
B the head is attached, and has done the power stroke (postpower stroke),
C the head is detached and returns to the pre-power stroke position.

A motor cycles through the three states according to the following rules.

$$1: A \longrightarrow B \qquad 2: B \longrightarrow C \qquad 3: C \longrightarrow A$$

The actions of individual motors may depend on those of nearby motors, resulting in cooperative behavior. We model interactions between nearby motors through a 1-dimensional asynchronous cellular automaton in which each cell is able to read the states of the cells directly left and right of it (von Neumann neighborhood). First, we show how to propagate a wave to the right. Such a wave consists of three parts: the front of the wave, encoded by a region of one or more cells in state A, the center part, encoded by a region of cells in state B, and the tail, encoded by a region of cells in state C. A typical wave sequence, read from left to right, is ...$AACCCCCBBAAA$.... This wave propagates to the right accordance to the following transition rules:

$$4:\ BAA \longrightarrow B \qquad 5:\ CBB \longrightarrow C \qquad 6:\ ACC \longrightarrow A$$

When the left hand side of a transition rule matches a pattern in the cellular automaton, the transition may be executed—may, but not necessarily so due to the asynchronous mode of timing. If executed, the transition results in the pattern's center symbol being replaced by the symbol in the right hand side of the transition rule. Note that the rules change the cell states in accordance with the cycle $A \to B \to C \to A$ like with rules 1, 2, and 3. Such rules are called *ABC-cycle preserving*. The waves in the asynchronous cellular automaton with states ...$CCBBBAACBACCC$... then develop for example as follows:

$$...C\underline{CBB}BAACBACCC... \overset{(5)}{\leadsto} ...CC\underline{CBB}AACBACCC... \overset{(5)}{\leadsto}$$

$$...CCC\underline{CBAA}CBACCC... \overset{(4)}{\leadsto} ...CCCCBBAC\underline{BAC}CC... \overset{(6)}{\leadsto}$$

$$...CCCCBBAC\underline{BAA}CC... \overset{(4)}{\leadsto} ...CCCCBBAC\underline{BB}ACC... \overset{(5)}{\leadsto}$$

$$...CCCCBBA\underline{CC}BACC... \overset{(6)}{\leadsto} ...CCCCBBAACBACC...$$

and so on, whereby a label above an arrow indicates the rule applied to the string left of the arrow, and the substring to which the rule is applied is underlined.

3   Turning Waves Around and Creating Waves

The waves in the previous section only propagate to the right. Waves in which the pattern of A-, B-, and C-states is reversed, however, such as ...$AAABBCCCC$... will be unaffected by the above three rules, and will stay static, thus being obstacles to any right-going waves. As our goal is to obtain waves moving in one direction, whatever the initial state of the asynchronous cellular automaton is, we add rules to turn left-going waves around:

$$7:\ CAA \longrightarrow B \qquad 8:\ ABC \longrightarrow C \qquad 9:\ BBC \longrightarrow C$$

Again, the rules are ABC-cycle preserving. Rules 4 to 9, acting on for example a left-going wave (...$CCAABBCC$...) may give rise to a sequence like:

$$...C\underline{CAA}BBCC... \overset{(7)}{\leadsto} ...CCBA\underline{BBC}C... \overset{(9)}{\leadsto}$$

$$...CCB\underline{ABC}CC... \overset{(8)}{\leadsto} ...CCBACCCC...$$

Table 1. ABC-cycle preserving transition rules and their effects. The left-most column contains the rule labels, the second column the rules, and the third column their effects. An arrow to the right ($\rightarrow$) resp. left ($\leftarrow$) in the third colum indicates that the rule effectuates the movement of a wave to the right resp. left; an arrow to the left with a hooked tail ($\hookleftarrow$) indicates the change of a pattern typical of a right-going wave to a pattern typical of a left-going wave; an arrow to the right with a hooked tail ($\hookrightarrow$) indicates the opposite; an upward arrow ($\uparrow$) indicates the creation of a new wave front, effectively increasing the number of waves by one; a downward arrow ($\downarrow$) indicates the deletion of a wave front, decreasing the number of waves by one; and a circle ($\circ$) indicates that the rule is neutral, i.e., that it does not change the number or direction of waves. The fourth column contains a weight related to the speed by which the corresponding transition takes place: roughly spoken, a rule with weight w will be executed w times faster than a rule with weight 1 (see text for details). The particular weight values in the table bias wave propagation towards the right

A_1	$AAA \longrightarrow B$	$\uparrow$	9	B_1	$ABA \longrightarrow C$	$\circ$	6	C_1	$ACA \longrightarrow A$	$\downarrow$	1
A_2	$AAB \longrightarrow B$	$\leftarrow$	2	B_2	$ABB \longrightarrow C$	$\hookrightarrow$	4	C_2	$ACB \longrightarrow A$	$\hookleftarrow$	1
A_3	$AAC \longrightarrow B$	$\hookleftarrow$	3	B_3	$ABC \longrightarrow C$	$\hookrightarrow$	5	C_3	$ACC \longrightarrow A$	$\rightarrow$	1
A_4	$BAA \longrightarrow B$	$\rightarrow$	7	B_4	$BBA \longrightarrow C$	$\hookleftarrow$	1	C_4	$BCA \longrightarrow A$	$\hookrightarrow$	1
A_5	$BAB \longrightarrow B$	$\downarrow$	1	B_5	$BBB \longrightarrow C$	$\uparrow$	1	C_5	$BCB \longrightarrow A$	$\circ$	1
A_6	$BAC \longrightarrow B$	$\hookleftarrow$	1	B_6	$BBC \longrightarrow C$	$\leftarrow$	1	C_6	$BCC \longrightarrow A$	$\hookrightarrow$	1
A_7	$CAA \longrightarrow B$	$\hookrightarrow$	3	B_7	$CBA \longrightarrow C$	$\hookleftarrow$	2	C_7	$CCA \longrightarrow A$	$\leftarrow$	1
A_8	$CAB \longrightarrow B$	$\hookrightarrow$	1	B_8	$CBB \longrightarrow C$	$\rightarrow$	1	C_8	$CCB \longrightarrow A$	$\hookleftarrow$	1
A_9	$CAC \longrightarrow B$	$\circ$	1	B_9	$CBC \longrightarrow C$	$\downarrow$	1	C_9	$CCC \longrightarrow A$	$\uparrow$	1

after which the wave propagates to the right. Another example of a left-going wave turning right is:

$$...CCAB\underline{BB}CC... \overset{(9)}{\hookrightarrow} ...CCA\underline{BB}CCC... \overset{(9)}{\hookrightarrow} ...CC\underline{AB}CCCC... \overset{(8)}{\hookrightarrow}$$

$$...CC\underline{AC}CCCC... \overset{(6)}{\hookrightarrow} ...CC\underline{AA}CCCC... \overset{(7)}{\hookrightarrow} ...CCBACCCC...$$

Rules 7, 8, and 9 work correctly when applied to properly shaped waves, but they fail for arbitrary patterns of states. To make properly shaped waves out of arbitrary patterns, we investigate the effect of transition rules on patterns. Rules 4, 5, and 6 all have the effect of moving a right-going wave further to the right, as already seen. Rule 9, on the other hand, moves part of a wave—a BC wave front—to the left. Rules 7 and 8 have still another effect: they change patterns typical of left-going waves into patterns typical of right-going waves.

To create a set of rules that produces right-going waves out of arbitrary patterns, we list up the effect of each possible ABC-cycle preserving rule with three symbols from the alphabet $\{A, B, C\}$ in its left hand side (see Table 1). Apart from rules like the above that effectuate or change movement to the left or the right, there are also rules that change the number of waves. For example, an AAA pattern is changed by rule A_1 in Table 1 to ABA, thereby introducing the patterns AB and BA, which are typical of left-going and right-going waves, respectively. So, new wave fronts are created. Depending on how the surrounding cells develop, this may (or may not) result in a new wave, to the left or right. Rule A_5 does the opposite: the pattern BAB, which might have developed in a wave, is made homogeneous by replacing the center A by a B, thus decreasing the (potential) number of waves by one. Rule A_9 is neutral. It changes CAC into CBC, keeping the number of wave fronts and directions of waves unchanged.

Will the rules in Table 1 produce right-going waves? In itself they won't, because rules with a certain effect are balanced against rules that do the opposite. This is where the weights right of the rules in Table 1 come into the story: these weights, denoting a speed measure by which the corresponding transitions take place, bias waves to the right. This bias is made stronger by increasing weights of rules favoring right-going waves, and decreasing weights of opposite rules.

There appears to be a weak mechanical interaction between nearby dynein motors when the periods of time they are attached to the opposing filament overlap. Accordingly, motors conducting their power strokes roughly simultaneously may do so at increased speeds; this is reflected in our model by weights in Table 1 with increased values. For example, the large weight (9) of rule A_1 encodes that three motors next to each other conduct their power stroke with increased speed. Rule A_4 implies increased speed as well for the same reason, except that now only two motors next to each other are present, which is the reason for the somewhat decreased weight of 7. In this case the third motor is in state B, i.e., its head is being detached, and this detachment is supposed to hardly slow down the action in one direction. Rule A_2, on the other hand, also has two A's and one B in its left hand side, but in the reverse order: it has a lower weight (2), expressing that the third motor being detached slows down the action more in the opposite direction (this difference may be due to the mechanical difference between dragging and pushing). Similarly, two adjacent A's and one C speed the action up a little. We have (somewhat heuristically) attached weights to the other rules.

In our simulations weights of rules are implemented by an integer counter attached to each cell, counting down from 10 to 1. When a rule is selected for update by the asynchronous updating scheme, the weight belonging to the rule is subtracted from the concerning counter. If the counter stays positive, no update takes place, but if it becomes non-positive, it is increased by 10 and the update takes place according to the rule. Fig. 2 shows the evolution over time from an initial pattern in the asynchronous cellular automaton. Waves have a clear bias to the right: downhill streaks as seen from left to right are much longer than uphill streaks.

To show in a more quantitive way that waves are biased to the right, we introduce a function $U : Q \times Q \to \{-1, 0, 1\}$ defined by

$$U(x,y) = \begin{cases} 1 & \text{if } (x,y) \in \{(B,A), (C,B), (A,C)\} \\ -1 & \text{if } (x,y) \in \{(A,B), (B,C), (C,A)\} \\ 0 & \text{if } x = y \end{cases}$$

This function generates the value 1 for local patterns typical of right-going waves, like BA, CB, or AC, the value -1 for patterns typical for left-going waves, and

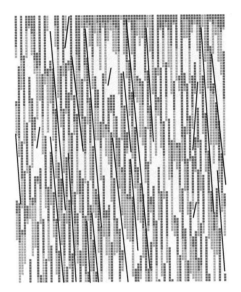

Fig. 2. Development over time of a pattern in an asynchronous cellular automaton with periodic boundary condition. The 1-dimensional cellular space is plotted horizontally (80 cells), and time vertically from top to bottom (100 time steps). One time step corresponds to the update with probability $p = 0.5$ of the 80 cells selected in a random order, which is on average 40 randomly selected but distinct cells. Dark cells have state A, gray cells state B, and white cells state C. Waves tend to the right, as indicated by the streaks going downhill from left to right. Downhill streaks last longer than uphill streaks, which break up almost immediately

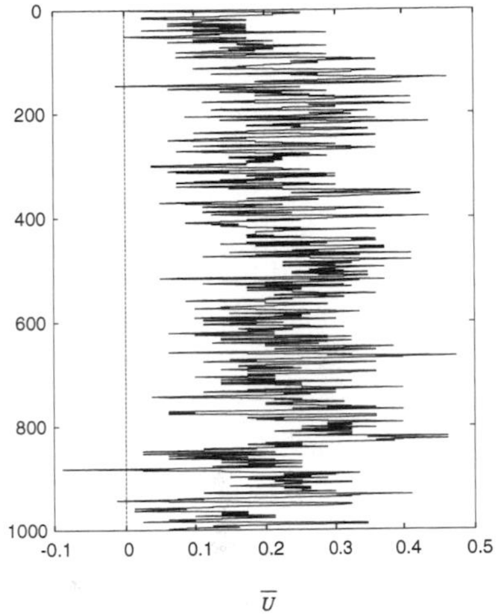

Fig. 3. Development over time of the function $\overline{U}$ in an asynchronous cellular automaton with a periodic boundary condition and 80 cells, that is initialized to a random pattern. $\overline{U}$ is plotted horizontally and time is plotted vertically from top to bottom over 1000 time steps, whereby each time step is defined in the same way as in Fig. 2. The function is positive most of the time, indicating a bias of waves to go to the right

0 otherwise. We then compute the function

$$\overline{U}(t) = \frac{1}{n} \sum_{i=0}^{n-1} U(S_i(t), S_{i+1}(t)),$$

where the n cells in the cellular automaton are numbered 0 to $n-1$ mod n, and $S_i(t)$ is the state of cell i at time step t. The values of $\overline{U}$ lie in the interval $[-1, 1]$, positive values indicating waves going right on average, and negative values waves going left. For an asynchronous cellular automaton of 80 cells a typical graph of $\overline{U}$ over 1000 generations looks like in Fig. 3. The graph exceeds zero except for a few peaks, so there is a clear bias to the right. Stronger or weaker biases are obtained by adjusting weights appropriately. The weight settings that result in realistic waves need to be derived from experimental data not yet available.

4   Conclusions and Discussion

We used a 1-dimensional asynchronous cellular automaton to model metachronal waves of dynein molecules that serve as molecular motors in rhythmically beating flagella. To represent such waves on the cellular automaton, we assumed three states for the cellular automaton: each cell cycles through these states, presumably resembling the dynein crossbridge cycle. Assuming a neighborhood in which each cell has one left neighbor and one right neighbor (von Neumann neighborhood), we classified the 27 possible transition rules according to the effect they have on wave-like patterns, like moving a wave to the right, reversing its direction, creating or deleting a wave, etc. By assigning a weight to each rule that represents the speed by which the corresponding transition is carried out, it is possible to bias waves in a certain direction, as simulation results confirm.

Though this paper shows the possibility of waves emerging in asynchronous cellular automata in which there are asymmetric local interactions between cells, it is too premature to draw definite conclusions with regard to flagella: our model is too coarse for that, and above all, we still lack the experimental data to back up our simulations. Nevertheless, some conclusions may be drawn. The wave lengths observed in our simulations are of the order of a few, say three to ten, cells. This is much less than the wave lengths in beating flagella, which are about a few hundred elements. A flagellum, however, is far more complicated than a simple 1-dimensional array of dynein molecules: it consists of nine microtubule doublets, cilindrically organized at the periphery of a flagellum such that each doublet is connected by dynein arms and flexible passive connections called *nexin* to two neighboring doublets, and this assembly is kept in place by spokes from the doublets to a central filament. It is possible that this arrangement results in mechanical interactions between dynein that extend much farther than the nearest neighbor dynein, thus resulting in larger wave lengths. Some evidence for an inherent shorter wave length in the absence of long-range interactions may be in [14,15,29], in which, as mentioned in the introduction, higher frequency oscillations were experimentally observed when bending of flagella was inhibited.

We have implicitly assumed that flagella have polarity, i.e., that all the dynein heads conduct their power strokes in the same direction. This seems a plausible assumption in the light of the findings in [30] that dynein arms on the peripheral microtubule doublets generate a force that moves an adjacent doublet away from the sperm head and not in the other direction.

References

1. Astumian, R.D.: Making molecules into motors, Scientific American **285**(1), 2001, 57–64
2. Blok, H.J., Bergersen, B., Synchronous versus asynchronous updating in the "game of life", Phy. Rev. E **59**, 1999, 3876-3879
3. Brokaw, C.J.: Bend propagation by a sliding filament model for flagella, Journal of Experimental Biology **55**, 1971, 289–304

4. Brokaw, C.J.: Computer simulation of flagellar movement. I. Demonstration of stable bend propagation and bend initiation by the sliding filament model, Biophysical Journal 12, 1972, 564–586

5. Brokaw, C.J.: Computer simulation of flagellar movement. VI. Simple curvature-controlled models are incompletely specified, Biophysical Journal 48, 1985, 633–642

6. Brokaw, C.J.: Computer simulation of flagellar movement. VII. Conventional but functionally different cross-bridge models for inner and outer arm dyneins can explain the effects of outer arm dynein removal, Cell Motility and the Cytoskeleton 42, 1999, 134–148

7. Camalet, S., Jülicher, F., Prost, J.: Self-organized beating and swimming of internally driven filaments, Physical Review Letters 82, 1999, 1590–1593

8. Gueron, S., Levit-Gurevich, K.: Computation of the internal forces in cilia: application to ciliary motion, the effects of viscosity, and cilia interactions, Biophysical Journal 74, 1998, 1658–1676

9. Hines, M., Blum, J.J.: Bend propagation in flagella. I. Derivation of equations of motion and their simulation, Biophysical Journal 23, 1978, 41–57

10. Hines, M., Blum, J.J.: Bend propagation in flagella. II. Incorporating if dynein cross-bridge kinetics into the equations of motion, Biophysical Journal 25, 1979, 421–442

11. Howard, J.: Molecular motors: structural adaptations to cellular functions, Nature 389, 1997, 561–567

12. Ingerson, T.E., Buvel, R.L.: Structures in asynchronous cellular automata, Physica D 10, 1984, 59–68

13. Jülicher, F., Prost, J.: Cooperative molecular motors, Physical Review Letters 75, 1995, 2618–2621

14. Kamimura, S., Kamiya, R.: High-frequency nanometre-scale vibration in 'quiescent' flagellar axonemes, Nature 340, 1989, 476–478

15. Kamimura, S., Kamiya, R.: High-frequency vibration in flagellar axonemes with amplitudes reflecting the size of tubulin, Journal of Cell Biology 116, 1992, 1443–1454

16. Lindemann, C.B., Kanous, K.S.: A model for flagellar motility, International Review of Cytology 173, 1997, 1–72

17. Machin, K.D.: Wave propagation along flagella, Journal of Experimental Biology 35, 1958, 796–806

18. Machin, K.D.: The control and synchronization of flagellar movement, Proceedings of the Royal Society of London B 62, 1963, 88–104

19. Murase, M., Shimizu, H.: A model of flagellar movement based on cooperative dynamics of dynein-tubulin cross-bridges, Journal of theoretical Biology 119, 1986, 409–433

20. Neumann, J. von: The Theory of Self-Reproducing Automata, edited and completed by A. W. Burks, University of Illinois Press, 1966

21. Okuno, M., Hiramoto, Y.: Mechanical stimulation of starfish sperm flagella, Journal of Experimental Biology 65, 1976, 401–413

22. Schönfisch, B., Roos, A. de: Synchronous and asynchronous updating in cellular automata, BioSystems 51, 1999, 123-143

23. Shingyoji, C., Murakami, A., Takahashi, K.: Local reactivation of triton-extracted flagella by iontophoretic application of ATP, Nature 265, 1977, 269–270

24. Shingyoji, C., Gibbons, I.R., Murakami, A., and Takahashi, K.: Effect of imposed head vibration on the stability and waveform of flagellar beating in sea urchin spermatozoa, Journal of Experimental Biology 156, 1991, 63–80

25. Shingyoji, C., Higuchi, H., Yoshimura, M., Katayama, E., Yanagida, T.: Dynein arms are oscillating force generators, Nature **393**, 1998, 711–714
26. Sugino, K., Naitoh, Y.: Simulated cross-bridge patterns corresponding to ciliary beating in Paramecium, Nature **295**, 1982, 609–611
27. Thomas, N., Thornhill, R.A.: The physics of biological molecular motors, Journal of Physics D: Applied Physics **31**, 1998, 253–266
28. Wiggings, C.H., Riveline, D., Ott, A., Goldstein, R.E.: Trapping and wiggling: elastohydrodynamics of driven microfilaments, Biophysical Journal **74**, 1998, 1043–1060
29. Yagi, T., Kamiya, R.: Novel mode of hyper-oscillation in the paralyzed axoneme of a Chlamydomonas mutant lacking the central-pair microtubulus, Cell Motility and the Cytoskeleton **31**, 1995, 207–214
30. Yamada, A., Yamaga, T., Sakakibara, H., Nakayama, H., Oiwa, K.: Unidirectional movement of fluorescent microtubulus on rows of dynein arms of disintegrated axonemes, Journal of Cell Science **111**, 1998, 93–98

Hybrid Techniques for Pedestrian Simulations

Christian Gloor[1], Pascal Stucki[1], and Kai Nagel[2]

[1] Institute of Computational Science, Swiss Federal Institute of Technology Zürich, Switzerland
{chgloor@inf, stuckip@student}.ethz.ch
[2] Transport Systems Planning and Transport Telematics, Technical University Berlin, Germany
nagel@vsp.tu-berlin.de

Abstract. There is considerable interest in the simulation of systems where humans move around, for example for traffic or pedestrian simulations. Multiple models for pedestrian simulations exist: cell based models are easy to understand, fast, but consume a lot of memory once the scenario becomes larger; models based on continuous space, which are more economical with memory usage, however, use significantly more CPU cycles.

In our project "Planning with Virtual Alpine Landscapes and Autonomous Agents", we simulate an area of 150 square kilometers, with more than thousand agents for one week. Every agent is able to move freely, adapt to the environment and make decisions during run time. This decisions are based on perception and communication with other agents.

This implies a simulation model that is fast and still fits into main memory of a typical workstation. We combined the advantages of both approaches into a hybrid model. This model exploits some of the special properties of the area.

This paper introduces this hybrid system, and presents performance results measured in a real-world example.

1 Introduction

The project "Planning with Virtual Alpine Landscapes and Autonomous Agents" [1] uses a multi-agent simulation to model the activities of tourists (primarily hikers). The goal is to have these agents populate a virtual world, where they are able to evaluate different development scenarios. Such scenarios include the question of re-forestation of meadows, or the summer use of chair lifts and the like. Left to themselves, many areas in the Swiss Alps would be covered by dense forest; it seems, however, that most hikers would prefer a more variable landscape. Many people, in particular families with children or people with health limitations, like mechanical aids to bring them nearer to the top of mountains.

The aim of this project is to implement a multi-agent simulation of tourists hiking in the Alps in order to investigate the achievable level of realism. At the same time, the project is used to explore general computational implementations of mobility simulations.

Such a simulation generically consists of two components: The physical mobility simulation, which moves the hikers through the system and computes their interactions; and the strategy generation module(s), which compute(s) strategic decisions of the agents such as destination or route choice.

P.M.A. Sloot, B. Chopard, and A.G. Hoekstra (Eds.): ACRI 2004, LNCS 3305, pp. 581–590, 2004.

Our approach is adapted from one used in traffic microsimulations. A synthetic population of tourists is created that reflects current (and/or projected) visitor demographics. These tourists are given goals and expectations. These expectations are individual, meaning that each agent could potentially be given different goals and expectations. Next, the agents are given "plans", and they are introduced into the simulation with no "knowledge" of the the environment. The agents execute their plans, receiving feedback from the environment as they move throughout the landscape. At the end of each run, the agents' actions are compared to their expectations. If the results of a particular plan do not meet their expectations, on subsequent runs the agents try different alternatives, learning both from their own direct experience, and, depending on the learning model used, from the experiences of other agents in the system.

A "plan" can refer to an arbitrary period, such as a day or a complete vacation period. As a first approximation, a plan is a completely specified "control program" for the agent. It is, however, also possible to change parts of the plan during the run, or to have incomplete plans, which are completed as the system goes.

After numerous runs, the goal is to have a system that, in the case of a status quo scenario, reflects observed patterns in the real world. In this case, this could, for example, be the observed distribution of hikers across the study site over time.

This paper concentrates on the mobility simulation, i.e. the simulation of the physical system. Sec. 2 discusses the movement model that was selected for our application. An important variable in these movement models is a vector $\mathbf{v}_i^0$, which gives the direction in which the pedestrian wants to move. Obviously, this depends on the destination that the pedestrian wants to reach. Secs. 3 and 4 discuss two different ways of how to obtain $\mathbf{v}_i^0$ when the destination is known but there are obstacles. Sec. 5 then shows how these concepts can be put into use in a simulation of pedestrian behavior in the Zurich main station. The paper is concluded by a summary.

2   Pedestrian Movement

An introduction to possible techniques for pedestrian simulation can be found in [2, 3]. For microscopic simulations, there are essentially two techniques: methods based on coupled differential equations, and cellular automata (CA) models. In our situation, it is important that agents can move in arbitrary directions without artifacts caused by the modeling technique, which essentially rules out CA techniques. A generic coupled differential equation model for pedestrian movement is the social force model [4]

$$m_i \frac{d\mathbf{v}_i}{dt} = m_i \frac{\mathbf{v}_i^0 - \mathbf{v}_i}{\tau_i} + \sum_{j \neq i} \mathbf{f}_{ij} + \sum_W \mathbf{f}_{iW} \qquad (1)$$

where m_i is the mass of the pedestrian and $\mathbf{v}_i$ its velocity. $\mathbf{v}_i^0$ is its desired velocity; in consequence, the first term on the RHS models exponential approach to that desired velocity, with a time constant τ_i. The second term on the RHS models pedestrian interaction, and the third models interaction of the pedestrian with the environment.

The specific mathematical form of the interaction term does not seem to be critical for our applications as long as it decays fast enough. Fast decay is important in order to cut

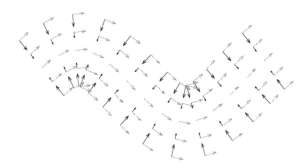

Fig. 1. Path-oriented coordinate system for the computation of the desired velocity and the path forces. The light arrows show the desired velocity, which drives the agent forward along the path. The dark arrows show the path force, which pull the agent toward the middle of the path.

off the interaction at relatively short distances. This is important for efficient computing, but it is also plausible with respect to the real world: Other pedestrians at, say, a distance of several hundred meters will not affect a pedestrian, even if those other pedestrians are at a very high density. We use an exponential force decay of

$$\mathbf{f}_{ij} = \exp\left(\frac{|\mathbf{r}_i - \mathbf{r}_j|}{B_p}\right) \frac{\mathbf{r}_i - \mathbf{r}_j}{|\mathbf{r}_i - \mathbf{r}_j|}, \tag{2}$$

which seems to work well in practice. $\mathbf{f}_{ij}$ is the force contribution of agent j to agent i; $\mathbf{r}_i$ is the position of agent i. Alternative more sophisticated formations are described by [4]. For the environmental forces, $\mathbf{f}_{iW}$, the same mathematical form as for the pedestrian-pedestrian interaction is used.

Ref. [5] introduced a model that uses only sparse information which fits into computer memory, runs efficiently on our scenarios, and has agents follow paths without major artifacts. The model uses a path-oriented coordinate system (see Fig. 1) for the computation of the desired velocity. This model also uses a so-called **path-force**, which pulls the agents back on the path when he moves away from its center (e.g. due to interaction with other agents or obstacles).

A question is what happens when there is no path. This can, for example, be the case in cities or in buildings. The following two sections will discuss implementations of two approaches to this problem when destinations are known. The first approach computes $\mathbf{v}_i^0$ as a function of the spatial location. The second approach first overlays a special graph over the system, and then lets the pedestrian move along the edges of the graph.

3   Potential Field Model

The first approach looked at in this paper is based on a **utility maximization** model [6]. For this model, a potential field is generated for the simulated area, which allows the pedestrians to find their destinations by walking toward the minimal potential.

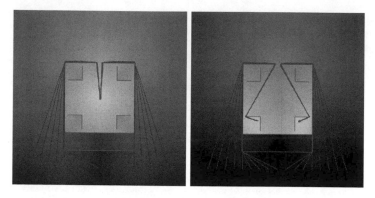

Fig. 2. A potential field generated for one destination in the center of the formation (left) and for two destinations (right). A lighter color means a lower potential (close to the center, the potential is lowest). Some example walking directions derived from this potential field are shown in blue.

Ref. [6] solves partial differential equations (PDEs) on a grid in order to obtain the potential. The computational requirements for this computation are considerable. It turns out that an approximation to the potential can also be generated by a much simpler **flooding algorithm** which starts at the destination and goes backward. The main difference is that the PDE solution treats off-axis distances exactly, while the flooding algorithm uses an approximation. For example, for the knight's movement of chess, our algorithm would obtain a distance of $1 + \sqrt{2} \approx 2.41$, while the exact distance would be $\sqrt{2^2 + 1^2} = \sqrt{5} \approx 2.24$. As a result, a potential field as shown in Figure 2 emerges. Note that for each possible destination a separate potential field needs to be created. However, this field can be used for all agents heading to that destination, regardless of their starting position.

The implementation of the flooding algorithm should use a priority queue, similar to a shortest path algorithm. This is about 2000 times faster than an unoptimized, recursive implementation [7]. Still, an area of 50×50 cells needs approximately $\frac{1}{10}$ seconds.

Before the potential of a new cell can be calculated, a visibility check has to be performed to ensure that the cell is accessible (visible) from the neighbor cell. As the check has to iterate over all obstacles in the simulated area, the calculation time increases linearly with the number of obstacles (Fig. 4, right).

To deduce an agents' desired velocity, or direction, from this potential field is not trivial. The first idea might be to just walk in the direction of the neighbor cell with has the lowest potential, and which is therefore closest to the destination. Using this method, however, yields a zigzagging path, because the possible walking directions are limited by the number of neighbor cells. One possibility to increase the number of possible walking directions is to increase the number of cells looked at. For example, if the 16 cells which are two steps away are considered, 16 directions are possible.

An even more realistic result can be achieved if the algorithm considers more than the neighbor cells. One can follow the minimal potential until the cell can no longer be

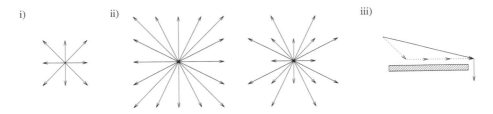

Fig. 3. Possible walking directions $\mathbf{v}_i^0$ are limited by the number of neighbor cells looked at for a lower potential (i and ii). A non-local search can yield in a much shorter path, but is more expensive to compute (iii).

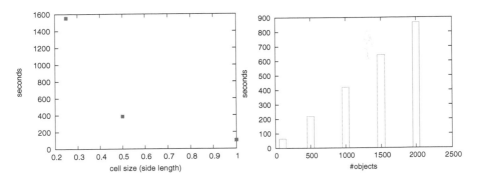

Fig. 4. If we reduce the size of the ground cells (left) or increase the number of obstacles in the scenario (right), the time to precompute the potential field rises.

reached directly from the starting cell and let the agents walk directly into this direction (Figure 3).

A solution that determines the minimum Euclidean distance of any cell to a destination with arbitrary obstacles between them was presented in [8]. It is based on a *visibility graph* and Dijkstra's algorithm

4   Graph Model

For the ALPSIM project, we use a network of hiking paths in the Alps. This network has a resolution of approximately 2m, which is accurate enough for path through forests or meadows. However, inside villages or close to obstacles, a resolution of 25cm is needed to model a realistic behavior of the pedestrians.

One possibility would be to switch to the potential field model (Sec. 3) where needed. Since only $\mathbf{v}_i^0$ is calculated by the potential field, all other aspects of the pedestrian dynamics, as forces between pedestrians or from obstacles, would remain the same.

However, a more intuitive solution is to keep the existing graph, but to add more details where needed. We were looking for a method that generates a graph around a given set of obstacles. This path can then be merged with the global hiking path graph.

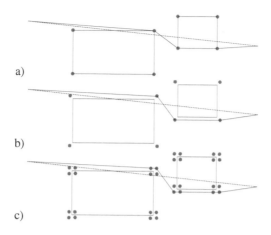

Fig. 5. a) The simplest solution to place nodes would be to add a node to each corner of all objects. b) Since people tend to keep a certain distance to objects, the nodes should be placed at a distance of 25cm to the corner of obstacles. c) It is, however, easier to place 4 or more nodes close to each corner and remove the ones inside an object in a later step.

In a first step, one has to decide where the **nodes** of the new graph should be. There should be enough nodes that an agent is able to circumvent obstacles on a naturally looking path. However, each additional node has to be considered in route choices and adds to path lengths. Paths, which are lists of nodes, are stored in the agents' brains or are transmitted over the network.

It is not that easy to find a simple yet realistic position of a node. The simplest solution would be to add a node to each corner of all objects (see Figure 5a). However, people tend to keep a certain distance to objects. [9] outlines that pedestrians keep an distance of 0.25 m (inside buildings) and 0.45 m (outdoors) to walls, even more to obstacles like fences. The paths would be too close to the objects. This would not be a problem, since agents as well keep a distance to obstacles due to environmental forces, but it is better to avoid the problem in the graph directly.

It was decided to use multiple nodes for each corner of an object. Each of them is in a distance of 0.25 m to the object corner (see Figure 5c). It does not matter in which direction the pedestrian approaches the corner, the distance to the corner is more or less equal. In order to reduce the numbers of nodes, an algorithm is run that eliminates nodes lying inside an object.

Based on these nodes an initial **graph** is constructed. At first, every node is connected to each other node, and each such edge has an weight of the distance between the nodes. We run a visibility check algorithm, known from computer graphics, to determine all the edges that intersect with obstacles. These edges are deleted.

In order to find the **shortest path** through this network, the shortest path algorithm by Dijkstra [10] is used.

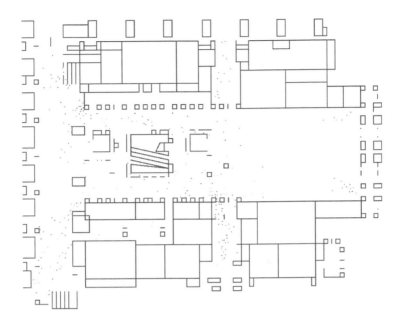

Fig. 6. An evacuation of Zürich Main Station using the potential field model. The pedestrians hurry to the closest exit available. This is a capture of the first of multiple iterations, which means that congestion at a certain exit can occur and is not avoided by the pedestrians.

5   Simulation of Zürich Main Station

As a real-world scenario for testing our models, we chose a simulation of an evacuation of Zürich Main Station (Figure 6). We simulated an area of 700m × 200m with more than 3000 obstacles. Agents were placed randomly within the simulated area (neither inside buildings, nor on the tracks). We considered eight different exit locations, every pedestrian chooses the one closest to him. Note that we did just one iteration, which means that congestion at a certain exit can occur and is not avoided by the pedestrians. It would be possible, however, to run multiple iterations of the scenario to enable the agents lo learn from such a situation (see e.g. [11,12]).

Since Zürich Main Station has more than one exit, we had reflect this in our models. For the potential field model, this is simple: starting the flooding algorithm from all exits simultaneously is sufficient. All the different exits are stored in the same precomputed map, since for every given point in the simulated area, there is exactly one closest exit.

For a pedestrian simulation, two measurements are important: i) how realistic the results are, and ii) how fast the computation is.

A comparison of the presented models is shown in Table 1. The Zürich Main Station scenario was run for 100 and 500 agents using each model.

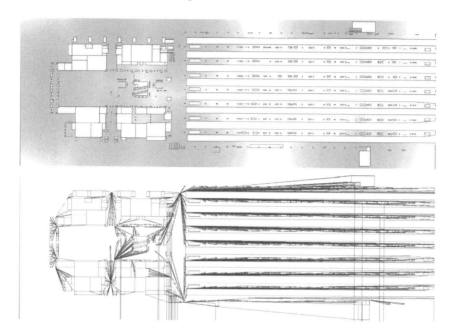

Fig. 7. Potential field and spanning tree for Zürich Main Station, generated for the 8 potential exits. The potential field has to be generated each time the destination changes. This is also necessary for the spanning tree, but here, the underlying nodes do not change.

For the potential field model, the size of the cells that store the potential field affects the time that the pre-computation takes (Fig. 4, left). For our purpose, a cell size of 50cm×50cm was chosen.

To pre-compute the graph in the graph model takes 175 minutes for the full scenario, containing all of the 3000 obstacles. If small obstacles like pillars or benches are removed for the graph generation, the time can be reduced to 35 minutes (Fig. 7). Small objects hardly influence the path of a pedestrian chooses. However, the pedestrians still do not walk through these obstacles, since the 3rd term of the RHS of equation (1) still pushes them away from obstacles.

For the graph model (column c) and d)), the time to simulate the first steps takes longer than the average. This is because the agents are on an arbitrary position that is most likely not on the graph. They have to find an node on the graph and walk into that direction first. Since in the potential field model, the field was calculated for every cell, the direction is available already. The potential field model needs considerable time to load the pre-calculated cells into memory (not shown in Table 1).

6   Summary

This paper describes how a simulation system for large scale pedestrian scenarios can be implemented. The simulation system is developed for the simulation and analysis

Table 1. Time to simulate an evacuation of Zürich Main Station using a) potential field model with minimal neighbor approach (cell size: 0.5m), b) potential field with minimal distances approach, c) graph model ignoring small obstacles and d) graph model. Further the average/maximum time and distance needed to leave the station are shown. This shows that the compared models generate similar results.

	a)	b)	c)	d)
Pre-computation:				
Time to compute the force field or the graph	386s	386s	2134s	10582s
100 walking agents:				
Computing Time Total	139s	75s	290s	525s
Computing Time until end of first step	<1s	<1s	131s	341s
Computing Time per following steps	<1s	<1s	<1s	1s
Walking Time	67.1s	50.9s	70.6s	74s
Max. Walking Time	239s	180s	182s	182s
Walked Distance	73m	51m	80m	77m
Maximal Walking Distance	239m	217m	227m	229m
500 walking agents:				
Computing Time Total	282s	240s	1726s	4617s
Computing Time until End of First Step	2s	1s	664s	1459s
Computing Time per Step	2s	1s	12s	12s
Walking Time	60.3s	67s	69.5s	76.6s
Max. Walking Time	234s	189s	262s	271s
Walked Distance	64m	79.4m	79m	78m
Maximal Walking Distance	236m	245m	247m	233m

of tourist hikers in the Alps, but the design is considerably more general so that it will be possible to apply the simulation system also to related areas such as pedestrian movements in urban areas or in buildings.

Well-known cell-based models for pedestrian crowd simulations are fast, but introduce artifacts. Models based on continuous space allow the agents to move in an arbitrary direction. However, it is necessary to calculate the desired velocity $\mathbf{v}_i^o$ of the agents separately.

We presented two different approaches: the first uses a potential field in order to store the pre-computed values of $\mathbf{v}_i^o$. The second approach is based on a graph, which edges can be followed by the agents.

The two approaches were compared using a real-world example: the simulation of an evacuation of Zürich Main Station. Both fundamental different models show comparable results. However, in order to get quantitative correct predictions, considerably more work will be necessary. Progress will be reported in future papers.

References

1. ALPSIM www page. www.sim.inf.ethz.ch/projects/alpsim/ (accessed 2004) Planning with Virtual Alpine Landscapes and Autonomous Agents.
2. Schreckenberg, M., Sharma, S.D., eds.: Pedestrian and Evacation Dynamics. Springer (2001)
3. Galea, E.R., ed.: Pedestrian and Evacuation Dynamics 2003. Proceedings of the 2nd international conference. CMS Press, University of Greenwich (2003)
4. Helbing, D., Farkas, I., Vicsek, T.: Simulating dynamical features of escape panic. Nature (2000) 487–490
5. Gloor, C., Mauron, L., Nagel, K.: A pedestrian simulation for hiking in the Alps. In: Proceedings of Swiss Transport Research Conference (STRC), Monte Verita, CH (2003. See www.strc.ch)
6. Hoogendoorn, S., Bovy, P., Daamen, W.: Microscopic pedestrian wayfinding and dynamic modelling. In Schreckenberg, M., Sharma, S., eds.: Pedestrian and Evacuation Dynamics. (2002) 123–154
7. Stucki, P.: Obstacles in pedestrian simulations. Diploma thesis, Swiss Federal Institute of Technology ETH (2003)
8. Nishinari, K., Kirchner, A., Nazami, A., Schadschneider, A.: Extended floor field CA model for evacuation dynamics. In: Special Issue on Cellular Automata of IEICE Transactions on Information and Systems. Volume E84-D. (2001)
9. Weidmann, U.: Transporttechnik der Fussgänger. 2 edn. Volume 90 of Schriftenreihe des IVT. Institute for Transport Planning and Systems ETH Zürich (1993) in German.
10. Dijkstra, E.: A note on two problems in connexion with graphs. Numerische Mathematik 1 (1959) 269 – 271
11. Gloor, C., Cavens, D., Lange, E., Nagel, K., Schmid, W.: A pedestrian simulation for very large scale applications. In Koch, A., Mandl, P., eds.: Multi-Agenten-Systeme in der Geographie. Number 23 in Klagenfurter Geographische Schriften. (2003) 167–188
12. Raney, B., Nagel, K.: An improved framework for large-scale multi-agent simulations of travel behavior. In: Proceedings of Swiss Transport Research Conference (STRC), Monte Verita, CH (2004) See www.strc.ch.

A CA Approach to Study Complex Dynamics in Asset Markets

Stefania Bandini[1], Sara Manzoni[1], Ahmad Naimzada[3], and Giulio Pavesi[2]

[1] Dipartimento di Informatica, Sistemistica e Comunicazione
Università di Milano-Bicocca, Italy
[2] Dipartimento di Informatica e Comunicazione
University of Milano, Italy
[3] Dipartimento di Economia Politica
University of Milano-Bicocca, Italy

Abstract. The paper presents first steps in a project that aims at exploring new modelling and simulation tools (e.g. the ones offered by the Cellular Automata approach) in order to study complex systems and phenomena concerning the economic and social contexts. The specific problem we are presenting in this paper concerns the complex dynamics involved in an asset price model with heterogeneous agents. The dynamics of the global asset market can be studied as a result of local interactions that emerges from the autonomous entities that are involved in the market system. The proposed model allows to describe in a unified way both global and local interactions that characterize economic agents involved in financial market trading. Even if experimental work is still ongoing, first performed steps have allowed us to gather some significant results that allowed us to verify the suitability of the proposed approach.

1 Introduction

The application of the Cellular Automata (CA) approach to modelling and simulation of complex systems is diffusing in interdisciplinary researches. It is quite hard work to try to summarize all the researches that, in different contexts, have been experimented and shown interesting results. They, in fact, concern very heterogeneous disciplines like physics, chemistry, biology, social science, and so on (see [1] and [2] for two overview papers).

A research area in which potentialities of the CA approach have been recently recognized due to the complexity that characterizes some studied problems and phenomena is the interaction between economic agents in financial markets [3, 4,5]. Within this area, CA potentialities have already been experimented (see for instance [6], where a stochastic CA is proposed in order to reproduce the volatility clustering, a known phenomenon in this context), but very few of such examples are still presented in the literature (as observed also in [7], a recent work about the application of CA to study the investment behaviors in stock markets).

P.M.A. Sloot, B. Chopard, and A.G. Hoekstra (Eds.): ACRI 2004, LNCS 3305, pp. 591–600, 2004.
© Springer-Verlag Berlin Heidelberg 2004

In this paper, we present our first results in an interdisciplinary research that involves computer scientists and economists. The main aim of this research is to exploit new modelling and simulation tools in order to study complex systems and phenomena concerning the economic and social contexts. The specific problem we are presenting in this paper concerns the complex dynamics involved in an asset price model with heterogeneous agents. Our interest in the application of CA to this problem is motivated by the fact that the dynamics of the global asset market (e.g. global prevailing tendency to buy or to sell) can be studied as a result of local interactions that emerges from the autonomous entities that are involved in the market system.

Our reference model in this experimentation [8] belongs to a new class of economic models that assume price dynamics as an endogenous phenomenon that emerges from the interaction between heterogeneous market traders [9,3,4,5]. Within this class, the model we considered assumes that the global interactions occurring between trading agents is mediated by the asset price, and in particular, it represents a first step towards the integration of global and local aspects that are involved in this problem. In the original model only global interactions were considered, while the here proposed modification represents, according to CA approach, also local interactions occurring among some types of agents. This modifications allow to take into account the heterogeneity of market investors that can not always be assumed to posses the needed knowledge on global asset market parameters (i.e. the expensiveness in terms of time and money to have this knowledge is usually high). Conversely, some investors perform their actions according to the prevailing tendency they observe in the market (i.e. the needed information to behave in this way can be very less expensive; it can be provided, for instance, by newspapers or specialized Internet websites).

The paper is so organized: first, we will outline the model (both its original specification and modifications that are here being presented). We will describe in Section 3 the cellular automaton that have been developed in order to simulate and analyze the dynamics of the market system that the model represents. Section 4 reports first experimentations that have been performed on it. Concluding remarks and future works concerning this interdisciplinary collaboration will end the paper.

2   The Reference Model for Asset Market

Two types of trading agents are involved in the market of a risky asset (i.e. *fundamentalists* and *imitators*). Agents of both types, at each epoch, offer a transaction that can be positive (amount of proposed purchase) or negative (amount of proposed sale). The sum of transactions that are collected and offered by agents of both types is a first index of the prevailing tendency in the market at a given time.

$$q(t) = \sum_{i=1}^{N} q_i(t)$$

where N is the total number of agents involved in the market and $q_i(t)$ the amount of proposed purchase or sale for agent i at time t. In particular, when $q(t)$ is positive the *prevailing market tendency* is to buy, otherwise it is to sell. Moreover, the absolute value of $q(t)$ defines another global index that characterizes the risky asset market: the *intensity of the prevailing tendency* at a given time.

The price adjustment process is regulated by a market–maker that mediates the trading and it is based on demand excess.

$$p(t+1) = p(t) + \beta \cdot q(t)$$

Thus, the asset price in the period $t+1$ is greater than the one in period t, when the total excess demand in period t is positive.

2.1 The Original Specification

Different trading strategies characterize the behaviors of the two types of agents. *Fundamentalists* are supposed to have a reasonable knowledge of the fundamental value of the risky asset (let k indicate this value). This type of agents propose transaction amounts $(q(t+1))$ according to the difference between the fundamental value they perceive (k) and the current *price* of the risky asset $(p(t))$. Thus, fundamentalists buy (or sell) assets when the asset price is below (above) the fundamental value and according to a parameter denoting the strength of fundamentalists demand (let a indicate the fundamental demand).

$$q_i(t+1) = a \cdot [k - p(t)]$$

Conversely, a second type of agents, named *imitators*, are assumed to be unable to acquire autonomously information about the fundamental value of the risky asset. This assumption is motivated by the expensiveness, both in terms of time and cost, of information acquisition. Thus, imitators base their decision on the prevailing tendency they observed in the market. In particular, imitators are trading agents that buy (sell) market assets when the observed prevailing tendency in the market is below (above) a given minimal value.

The behavior of these agents is modelled by:

$$q_i(t) = e \cdot f(q(t) - m)$$

where $q_i(t)$ is the proposed transaction amount of purchase (or sale, according to the sign) at time t, $e > 0$ is a parameter denoting the strength of imitators' demand, $q(t)$ is the global market tendency above defined, and m is the imitators' threshold. If m is positive, agents must perceive a stronger trend to buy, in order to decide to buy themselves, and vice versa if it is negative.

$f(\cdot)$ is a function of the difference between the global market tendency and imitators' threshold that models the dynamics of the prevailing market tendency. Thus, also this second type of agents behave according to their knowledge of the market system they are part. Properties that $f(\cdot)$ function must satisfy are: $f(\cdot) : \Re \rightarrow \Re$, $f(0) = 0$, and $f'(\cdot) > 0$.

With such hypothesis the model has shown to generate planer system of non–linear differential equations that, for some given parameters configurations, show a rich variety of dynamical phenomena: periodic cycles, Hopf bifurcations and chaotic attractors [8].

2.2   The Introduced Modifications

The main model modification that we have introduced concerns the behavior of imitators. As described above, there is an essential distinction between the behavior of the two types of agents: fundamentalists base their decision on a global property of the market system (i.e. the asset price); on the other hand, since imitators do not have knowledge about the price or its variation, they act imitating other agents. Thus, we supposed a suitable and interesting model modification to introduce the assumption that imitators act according solely on local knowledge, for instance estimating asset price according to the local knowledge of their neighborhood. Thus, the assumption of the original reference model that considered the availability of global information also for imitator agents have been removed, and we considered imitators behavior as based solely on information about the behavior of agents that are in their neighborhood.

As sketched above we can in this way take into account in the asset market model the presence of investors that take part to the market system, even not being provided with knowledge on global market parameters (as happens the reality of asset markets). This modification to the original model (that is sub-stantial from the conceptual viewpoint) have been introduced simply defining imitators' behavior as:

$$q_i(t) = e \cdot f(q^n(t) - m)$$

where $q^n(t)$ is the sum of $q_j(t)$ for all cells j belonging to the neighborhood of i (i.e. it represents the tendency in its neighborhood).

In the following we will describe the CA that represents this new model proposal.

3   The Cellular Automaton

We adopted a two–dimensional cellular automaton, whose cells are arranged on a square grid. Every cell of the automaton contains an agent, that can be either a fundamentalist or an imitator. We assume, at least in the basic model, that agents cannot move or change their attitude (they cannot switch from fundamentalist to imitator, or vice versa). Fundamentalists are not influenced in their actions by other agents in the neighborhood but behave according to the global market tendency. On the other hand, imitators try to capture the trend of the market by following the example of their neighbors, regardless of the fundamental price of the asset that they are not able to know.

More formally, the automaton can be defined as:

$$\mathbf{A} = \langle R, H, Q, f, I \rangle$$

where:

1. $R = \{(i,j) | 1 \le i \le N, 1 \le j \le M\}$ is a two–dimensional $N \times M$ lattice;
2. H is the neighborhood, that can be either the von Neumann or Moore neighborhood;
3. Q is the finite set of cell state values;
4. $f : Q \times Q^{|H|} \to Q$ is the state transition function;
5. $I : R \to Q$ is the initialization function.

3.1   Cell State

In particular, the set of cell state values Q is defined as:

$$Q = \{T, q\}$$

where $T \in \{Im, Fu\}$ is the type of agent hosted by the cell (i.e. that can be either Fu Fundamentalist or Im Imitator), and q describes the amount of the asset the agent wants to sell (if negative) or buy (if positive). Thus, at any time, the state of each cell of the automaton describes which type of agent is active in it and the action it wants to perform (when q is equal to zero the agent is *inactive* that is, it neither buys nor sells any asset).

According to the dynamics of the system whose model has been above presented, the evolution of the automaton depends on the current price of the asset $p(t)$, as well as the interactions among neighboring agents. After all the cells have changed their state according to the transition function, the new asset price is recalculated according to the new state of the CA cells.

3.2   State Transition Function

The state transition function f determines the actions of agents according to the type of the agent hosted by the cell. More in detail, let $q_{(i,j)}(t)$ be the value of q of cell state at the grid position (i, j), and $T_{(i,j)}$ its type.

If $T_{(i,j)} = Fu$ we have:

$$q_{(i,j)}(t+1) = e_f \cdot (fundam\_value - p(t))$$

The e_f parameter modulates the agents' response according to the price difference. Within the CA, this parameter can be set as a global parameter, and kept fixed during CA evolution, or it can be updated with the automaton (see Section 4 about experiments). The sign of $q_{(i,j)}(t+1)$ clearly depends on the difference between the fundamental value and the current price. If a fundamentalist perceives that the current asset price is lower than its fundamental value, then it tends to acquire assets (or to sell them vice versa). Moreover, a priori there is no limit on the amount of assets fundamentalists can buy or sell.

On the other hand, let the local trend of a cell (i,j) at time t be indicated by:

$$q^n_{(i,j)}(t) = \sum_{(k,l) \in H(i,j)} q_{(k,l)}(t)$$

Then, if the type of agent is imitator, we define:

$$q_{(i,j)}(t+1) = e_i \cdot \tanh(\gamma(q^n_{(i,j)}(t) - m))$$

where the hyperbolic tangent function modulates the imitator's answer according to the trend of its neighborhood at time t (i.e. $q^n_{(i,j)}(t)$) and the parameter γ defines the steepness of this function (see Figure 1 where functions $\tanh(\gamma x)$ for different γ value are represented).

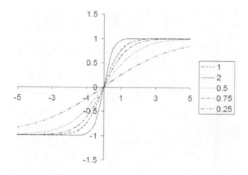

Fig. 1. The function $\tanh(\gamma x)$, according to different values of γ.

Finally, e_i is a parameter that defines the quantity of assets the agents wants to trade according to the trend perceived (it is analogous to the parameter e_f of fundamentalists), while m is the trend threshold value. As with all the other parameters of the automaton, both e_i and m can be defined globally (according to the agent type), locally for each cell, or can be updated at each step of the automaton.

It can be seen that, differently from fundamentalists, the maximum quantity of assets an imitator can trade is limited by e_i, since the hyperbolic tangent function always returns a value between -1 and 1.

3.3   Price Update

As above described, the choices of the different agents influence the evolution of the asset price, that changes according to the overall market tendency. Thus, if $q(t)$ is the sum of the $q_{(i,j)}$ values of the single cells of the automaton at time t:

$$q(t) = \sum_{(i,j)} q_{(i,j)}(t)$$

such that $1 \leq i \leq M$ and $1 \leq j \leq N$, the price of the asset at time $t + 1$ (i.e. $p(t + 1)$) will be:

$$p(t + 1) = p(t) + \beta \cdot Q(t)$$

This means that the prevailing trend is to sell, then $q(t)$ will be negative and the asset price will be decreased; vice versa if the trend is to buy. In the price evolution function, β is a parameters that modulates the price variation according to the trend.

3.4   CA Initialization

The main differences in the initialization of the automaton are in how the agent type of each cell is chosen, and in the initial value of cell states. For the first point, the criterion we adopted is to initialize cells' type probabilistically. In other words, given a p_f value, a cell (i, j) will contain a fundamentalist with probability p_f, and an imitator with probability $1 - p_f$. Concerning the initial $q_{(i,j)}(0)$ values, at the beginning all agents are inactive, that is, $q_{(i,j)}(0) = 0$ $\forall (i, j)$. Also, an initial price value $p(0)$ has to be set and we chose to let it be a parameter to be set during experiments.

At the first step, the fundamentalists determine their new q value according to the current price, while imitators will collect an overall q^n value of 0 from the neighbors. If $m = 0$, that is, no trend threshold is set, then imitators will remain inactive at the first update, waiting for the fundamentalists' influence to spread across the automaton.

4   Experiments

The evolution of the automaton clearly depends, other than the distribution of fundamentalist and imitator agents, on a number of different parameters like the initial price, and all the other parameters we used to modulate the response of agents and price variation.

For all the simulations we employed a small 10×10 grid, and we used a Moore neighborhood with increasing radius. We also set $m = 0$ (thus no trend threshold), and $e_i = 1$. Thus, the imitators follow directly the advice coming from neighbors, and trade a limited amount of assets (never more than one). We also set $\beta = .5$ and $\gamma = .5$, and a Moore neighborhood of radius one.

4.1   Initial Public Offering

In a first series of experiments, we simulated an Initial Public Offering (IPO), where the initial price of an asset is zero, while the fundamental price known by fundamentalists was 100. Also, we chose to modulate the quantities traded by fundamentalists according to the number of fundamentalists present in the CA, that is, we set $e_f = 1/(\#fund)$. In other words, each agent tries to acquire or sell a given amount of assets, but its actions are limited by the behavior of all the other agents of the same type.

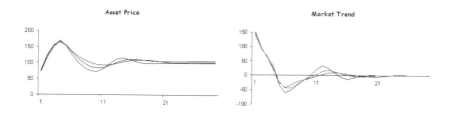

Fig. 2. Trend $q(t)$ and price $p(t)$ evolution with a Moore neighborhood of radius one. After an initial oscillation, the price settles at the fundamental asset value (100).

Even from this simple simulation we can gather some significant information. Figure 2 shows the evolution of the asset price. As we can see, the initial bid of fundamentalists causes imitators to follow the same behavior, with a marked increase on the asset price well beyond the fundamental value. At this point, fundamentalists start to sell, while imitators are still buying and, in a few iterations, the trend (see Figure 2) becomes negative, with a decrease of the price below 100 (i.e. the fundamental asset value). We have another oscillation, but at the end the price settles around the fundamental asset value known by fundamentalists.

It should be noted that this final equilibrium can be reached in two ways: in the first, fundamentalists have their q value around zero, while imitators seem to be split in two halves of buyers and sellers, that keep the price balanced. Otherwise, if we increase the percentage of fundamentalists in the CA, while the overall price variation remains the same (oscillating convergence to a fixed point, i.e. the fundamental value) the equilibrium is reached also by imitators, that are more directly influenced and, at the end, stop trading. Increasing the percentage of fundamentalists up to 50% did not yield any significant change, apart from shorter oscillations at the beginning of the simulation.

4.2   Neighborhood Radius

We performed a second set of experiments in order to evaluate the influence of neighborhood radius on system dynamics. When we increased the Moore neighborhood radius to two cells, in fact, we can observe different evolution dynamics. The result is shown in Figure 3. The enlarged neighborhood puts most of the imitators in direct contact with one or more fundamentalists. Thus, the influence of the latter was perceived immediately, and not indirectly through other imitators. Imitators immediately follow the fundamentalists' behavior, and thus the price keeps oscillating regularly around the fundamental value of 100.

The two scenarios that we just presented reproduce only qualitatively possible real cases. For example, real prices very seldom remain fixed, but rather are subject to continuous fluctuations. We believe that the main cause of this phenomenon is due to the fact that many parameters of the automaton remain fixed throughout the simulation, for example, fundamentalists never change their idea

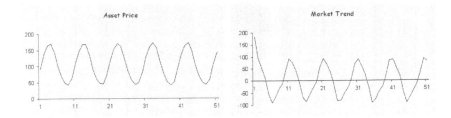

Fig. 3. Trend $q(t)$ and price $p(t)$ evolution with a Moore neighborhood of radius two. Asset price and market trend keep oscillating.

about the real price or imitators never change the response to their perception of the neighborhood. Clearly, the model can (and will be in the future) easily enhanced and improved to take into account further factors, like global market trends (perhaps causing a response of imitator to local tendencies varying in time) or different types of fundamentalists (perhaps disagreeing on the real value of the assets), or fundamentalists changing their perceived real value of the asset, and so on.

5 Concluding Remarks and Future Works

The paper has presented first steps on a interdisciplinary research project involving computer scientists and economists, whose aim is to explore the application of CA approach to study asset price in the market of risky assets. The proposed model describes in a unified way both global and local interactions that characterize economic agents involved in market trading.

First of all, we have presented the introduced modifications to the reference model of this work [8] in order to introduce local aspects. The main difference between the new model specification and the original one concerns the possibility for some agents (named imitators) to be influenced by the tendency of trading agents belonging to their neighborhood.

We have thus described first experimentations that have been conducted on the CA–based simulation system that implement the modified model. First performed steps have allowed us to gather some significant results that positively motivated us in continuing in this research:

- the locality of interactions effects positively the stability to the system behavior (the experiments we conducted incrementing the neighborhood radius suggest this observation);
- when the system behavior described through the asset price converges, it does it to the fundamental value (the same behavior had already been observed in previous analysis performed on the reference model [8]);
- the increase of fundamentalists, contributes to system stability. This point is a clear indication of the suitability of the proposed model (i.e. the stability

of the trading system is strictly related to agents' knowledge about the asset fundamental value and its price).

The started collaboration will continue first, with other experimentations in order to introduce into the model more aspects concerning locality. The assumptions on other global parameters that still characterize the CA–based model will be eliminated and, for instance, individual fundamental values will be introduced for each fundamentalist agent, individual agent thresholds will be considered (e.g. a stochastic value for m could be introduced) and also parameters that now characterize agent types (e.g. a and e parameters) could be set for each agent.

References

1. Bandini, S., Mauri, G., Serra, R.: Cellular automata: From modeling to applications. Parallel Computing **27** (2001) 537–538
2. Hegselmann, R., Flache, A.: Understanding complex social dynamics: a plea for cellular automata based modelling. Journal of Artificial Societies and Social Simulation **1** (1998)
3. Arthur, B., Holland, J., LeBaron, B., Palmer, R., Tayler, P.: Asset pricing under endogenous expectations in an artificial stock market (1997)
4. Brock, W., Hommes, C.: Models of complexity in economics and finance. In: System dynamics in economic and financial models. Wiley (1997) 3–41
5. Lux, T., Marchesi, M.: Volatility clustering in financial markets: a micro-simulation of interacting agents. Int. Journal of Theoretical and Applied Finance **3** (2000) 675–702
6. Bartolozzi, M., Thomas, A.: Stochastic cellular automata model for stock market dynamics. Physical Review E (Statistical, Nonlinear, and Soft Matter Physics) **69** (2004)
7. Wei, Y., Ying, S., Fan, Y., Wang, B.: The cellular automaton model of investment behavior in the stock market. Physica A (2003) 507–516
8. Naimzada, A., Agliari, A.: Complex dynamics in a asset price model with heterogeneous agents. Working Paper at University of Milano-Bicocca (2004) Forthcoming.
9. Westerhoff, F.: Speculative behavior and asset price dynamics. Nonlinear Dynamics, Psychology, and Life Science **7** (2003) 245–262

Modeling the Effect of Leadership on Crowd Flow Dynamics

François Aubé and Robert Shield

Department of Electrical and Computer Engineering, McGill University
3480 University Street, Montreal, Quebec, Canada
{Francois.Aube, Robert.Shield}@mail.mcgill.ca

Abstract. A common problem for both architects and public security officials alike is how best to safely manage large numbers of people enclosed within confined spaces. With the prevalence of large gatherings of people, it is crucial for those ensuring the safety of the public to be able to analyze how best to manage large crowds. This project aims to provide a tool for modeling crowd dynamics factoring in the presence of "leader" individuals who can influence the behaviour of the crowd. This will allow for analysis of the effectiveness of leader placement on crowd control within a defined environment. Mixing in different leader types, placing some in the immediate proximity of the crowd and others scattered around the environment, provides desirable results.

1 Introduction

Ensuring the safety of large crowds of people in constrained environments has ever been both a concern and a challenge for specialists in a variety of fields ranging from security teams and emergency response specialists to architects and building designers. The subject of evacuations in unfamiliar and urgent situations is especially crucial because in some constrained environments, people are highly panicked and uncomfortable with their surroundings, and they end up moving in a suboptimal, disorganized manner that leads to congestion and trampling. Thus some casualties are caused not only by the real threat (be it building collapse, fire, etc.) but by the stampede that follows. On February 2nd 2004, in Saudi Arabia, 251 people died and many more were hurt when people panicked during a crowded religious gathering [1]. On March 25th 2000, 13 people died and 44 were injured in Durban, South Africa, following mass panic when someone released a can of tear-gas in a disco [2].

Previous work concerning crowd flow is often based on the social force model of Helbing and Molnar [3]. For example, Kirkland and Maciejewski[4] used it in their attempts to influence crowd dynamics with robots that acted and influenced others differently than normal agents. Braun et al. [5] modified it to allow for individual parameters and group formation. Helbing, Farkas and Vicsek[6] worked with it to model behaviours specific to escape panic situations. We have built upon the social force model to analyze situations that are most critical: when crowd members have little to no knowledge of the optimal exit strategy to leave their current environment, and they move around in a state of disorganized panic. Since architectural modifications to environments are costly and difficult, using

P.M.A. Sloot, B. Chopard, and A.G. Hoekstra (Eds.): ACRI 2004, LNCS 3305, pp. 601–611, 2004.
© Springer-Verlag Berlin Heidelberg 2004

security personnel or other key persons that can help the evacuation of the crowd is the most practical way to enhance the security of a crowd. This is why we chose to investigate the potential positive effects of the addition of special individuals – or "leaders" – on such evacuation situations, and which parameters affect the success of those effects. Our approach to investigating the effect of leader agents has been the development of a crowd modeling system built as a plug-in to an existing rendering and steering framework called OpenSteer developed by Craig Reynolds from Sony Computer Entertainment America.

Real-world applications of this project are most obvious in the domains of emergency planning services and security training. As real experimentation in those fields are impractical, an effective modeling system is absolutely crucial to ensure people's safety in existing crowded facilities. Additionally, this project's applications also include the study of architectural layouts and their associated critical densities that promote good crowd flow in both the presence and absence of leader individuals.

2   Environment

The environment defined in this simulation is relatively simple allowing us to concentrate primarily on the development of the behavioural aspects of the simulation. It consists of a sequence of straight line walls that can be built up to form complex architectures as well as a number of exit locations. In addition, definable start positions exist for both the leader agents as well as the crowd member agents. At simulation start up time, the environment is taken to be dangerous and the goal of the crowd member agents becomes to reach the exits. The goal of the leader agents is to ensure that as many crowd member agents as possible do.

3   Crowd Member Agents

In order to model the psychology of a person in an escape situation, we use a certain number of behaviours that compete in specific ways. One's route in a crowd is not exclusively a linear sum of competing forces, especially when one is panicking; one can hardly be simultaneously following a group and heading for a specific point in an opposite direction. Neither, however, is a route just a choice among finite options: one can easily be following a group, avoiding contact with a wall and other individuals, and looking visually for a cue. Thus, we built upon the social force model by modeling behaviours as a complex competition among behaviours that are all modulated to a certain extent by the panic level of each agent. The decision algorithm can be described as follows from the point of view of each agent:

```
If I am currently steering toward an exit, keep doing so.
Otherwise,
     If I can see a leader, steer toward him.
     Otherwise,
   If I can see an exit, begin to steer toward it.
     Otherwise, my steering will be a combination of:
```

```
Either flocking with a group OR wandering randomly,
and
Avoiding walls, and
Following a long-term goal if I have one.
```

From the algorithmic description of the model, one can see that some forces are additive in nature, while others are mutually exclusive. For example, an agent tracking towards an exit will avoid all other steering forces. On the other hand, an agent who is neither steering towards an exit nor following a leader will have its steering behaviour result from a combination of different forces. Thus, the following behaviours were implemented: exit seeking, flocking, wandering, wall avoidance, long-term goal formulation and leader following.

4 Leader Agents

Leader agents, unlike the other agents in the simulation, possess global knowledge of their environment. In simulation terms, this translates into leader agents knowing where the exits are and how to get there. The leader agents take advantage of the follow-the-leader nature of the other agents to lead them to safety. The behaviour of a leader agent is to wander towards the nearest large mass of other agents in an attempt to collect a certain number of followers before heading towards the exit. The desired behaviour was that once a leader had accumulated enough followers trailing behind it, the flocking behaviour of other agents would cause a stream or a crowd flow to form which could gradually expand, leading the entire crowd to the exit. As opposed to simple guides or "directional fields" that would act as an external force operating on the crowd members, the leader individuals are themselves part of the crowd and as such are subject to the same basic physical rules as the crowd members themselves. While the leaders have the ability to guide the crowd, they themselves are part of it and are subject to being forced around and having their movement blocked just as much as the regular crowd member agents are.

Several modifiable behavioural parameters, such as the relative movement speed of the leaders versus the crowd members, were included for both the leader type individuals and the regular crowd members. Being able to tweak these parameters at run time allowed for investigation of which factors most influenced any emergent behaviour such as crowd flow.

5 Panic and Its Causes and Effects

In addition to the presence of leader agents, another major factor that influences the flow and general movement patterns of the crowd member agents is panic. Panic is determined on a per-individual basis, thus each crowd member agent has its own level of panic at any given moment in the simulation. Panic can be caused by of the following factors: crowd density, neighbours' panic level, collisions, seeing the exit, and random variations. Panicked agents are more likely to wander than to flock effectively; they tend to forget long-term goals; they have diminished visual ranges; and their wandering is more erratic.

6 Experiment Methodology

In all experiments, four simulations were run with the same initial parameters. At every simulation second, the number of agents that have successfully reached the exit is counted and written to a file. All simulations for which numerical data is presented were obtained in a T-shaped room in the configuration illustrated in Figure 1.

Over the course of experimentation, leader agents were observed to have different effects on the crowd based solely on their initial positions. The observation of the different impact based on the starting point of the leaders led to their classification into three qualitative classes. This classification then provided a basis for numerical analysis of different leader configurations the results of which reaffirmed the initial decision to classify them. A visual description of the positioning of different leader classes is shown in Figure 1. All agents in the configuration shown in Figure 1 start in the gray starting zone and the exit is too far away (not to mention being partially obstructed) for them to see it. The leader classifications are described below.

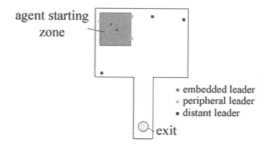

Fig. 1. Default Test Environment And Leader Class Positioning

Embedded Leaders
This class of leader begins the simulation situated in the center of the crowd. These leader agents then serve to guide the core elements of the crowd essentially steering the bulk of the individuals in the desired direction.

Peripheral Leaders
This leader type was placed around the immediate edges of the crowd, essentially forming a border around the crowd starting point. These leaders were then able to influence the crowd as a whole, although not as directly as the embedded leaders.

Distant Leaders
This leader type was placed at some distance from the original crowd starting position. Initially designed to catch the stragglers, they too are able to direct the bulk of the crowd although less efficiently than those leaders that start in closer proximity to it.

Saved Agents with 4 Leaders of Specific Classes (50 agents total)

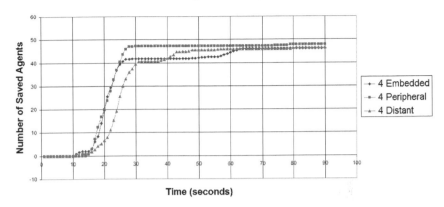

Fig. 2. Experiments Made With Leaders Of A Single Class

Embedded leaders are positioned near the middle of the mass of agents; peripheral leaders are along the border of the zone and distant leaders are positioned in corners to pick up any stragglers. Note that the coloured dots in Figure 1 are intended to be representative of the general starting areas for each leader type and are not designed to show the actual number and position of each leader type for every experiment. The first set of experiments we ran involved attempting to simulate the impacts of employing only one class of leader agents. We ran four simulations in each case and collected the evacuation statistics of the crowd. In this set of simulations, we used a crowd of 50 individuals and 4 leaders of each class (one class at a time).

The second set of experiments involved studying the varying effects of combining different leader classes. In this experiment, we started off with no leaders, then added embedded, then peripheral and finally distant as well to study the impact of adding in additional leaders of different classes. The crowd in this simulation contained 48 individuals and an ever expanding number of leaders as more of different types were added.

Additionally, we tested the impact of using only a fixed number of leaders and arranging them in different configurations to study the optimal placement strategy given only a fixed number of leader agents. Lastly, we varied the relative speed of the leader individuals versus the crowd individuals in order to identify the optimum ratio to promote crowd flow formation.

7 Results

Experiment 1: Employing Only One Class of Leader

The results, shown in Figure 2, obtained demonstrate several points. The first and foremost is that of the three classes of leaders, by themselves peripheral leaders are the most efficient at saving the largest number of people quickly. After 30 seconds, it is the peripheral leaders who have saved the bulk of the crowd. This is expected as the embedded leaders will have a reduced impact on the individuals at the fringes of the crowd and will risk losing those who for whatever reason do not follow along with the core of the crowd. Peripheral leaders are clearly much more capable of preventing this kind of drifting away. The distant leaders are also less efficient at saving the crowd quickly as they must first reach the bulk of the crowd before being able to direct it which results in many more stragglers getting away during that initial interval.

The behaviour of the embedded leaders is also interesting for a couple of reasons. First is the initial hump of people who are saved almost right away (after ten seconds) that occurs even before the peripheral leaders manage to start saving people. This hump is explained by the fact that embedded leaders will begin to drive the core of the crowd towards the exit immediately. This is in contrast to the peripheral leaders for example who must direct the flow of the crowd from the outside resulting in slightly lower immediate returns but, as illustrated, much greater efficiency long-term than the embedded leaders.

Another interesting point when dealing with the different leader classes is that the rate of evacuation is approximately the same during the period over which the bulk of the evacuation occurs (from 15 to 25 seconds for the embedded and peripheral leaders and from 20 to 30 seconds for the distant leaders). This is reasonable as it suggests that during the main evacuation rush, the evacuation rate will primarily be determined by the environment and crowd size rather than by any impact the leaders may have. Thus in this simulation the leaders, while serving to guide the crowd towards the exit, have less influence on the crowd when it reaches the exit.

Experiment 2: Inserting Additional Leaders of Different Classes

In this set of experimental runs, shown in Figure 3, the crowd started off from the same position and we then successively added in more leaders of different classes. This was done to study the varying time delays in evacuating as many people as possible as well as investigating methods to achieve a 100% evacuation rate.

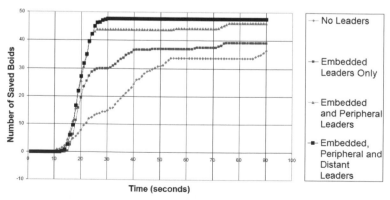

Fig. 3. Experiments Made With Incremental Additions Of Leaders

4 Leaders, 50 Crowd Members

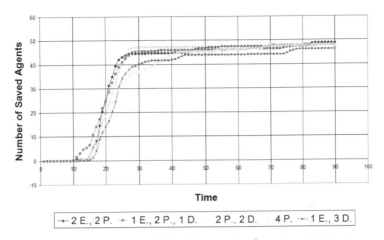

Fig. 4. Experiments Made With Different Configurations Of 4 Leaders

The red data series represents the number of agents, out of 48, that successfully reached the exit in a simulation with no leaders over time. Note that the rate of evacuation is low and varies a lot, as crowd flow forms but with much difficulty. The blue series represent the number of safe agents in a simulation with two embedded leaders. The embedded leaders clearly had a positive effect on saving the majority of the individuals in the crowd as soon as was possible as is illustrated by the steep rise of evacuated individuals early on. There is soon a plateau however, as the individuals that the two embedded leaders were not able to influence have wandered off and only much later in the simulation do some (not all) of them find their way to the exit.

The green data series illustrates what happens when an additional three peripheral leaders are thrown into the situation. After the same steep rise of evacuated individuals, with the experiment displays a much higher plateau indicating that this arrangement can save many more crowd members. However, progress stalls after approximately 25 seconds, showing that even with the addition of peripheral leaders, some crowd members slip through the cracks and are not saved. This is where the distant leaders really come into their own as illustrated by the black data series that achieves a 100% success rate is achieved after 30 seconds. It is important to note in this experiment that the number of people saved was also highly dependent on the fact that we were adding leaders in each set of runs, not just moving them around. Nonetheless, it is highly illustrative of the behaviour achieved using different classes of leaders. Furthermore, not only is the number of crowd members saved important but achieving that 100% evacuation rate is a critical objective. When dealing with people's lives, even one lost is too many. Thus despite the fact that the impact is statistically small, this experiment certainly shows the relevance of employing distant leaders if they are available to always attempt to achieve a complete evacuation.

Number of Agents Saved Out Of 47

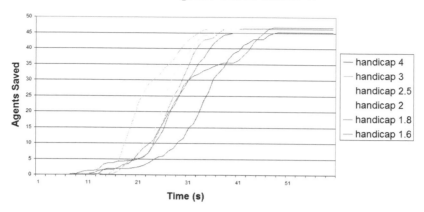

Fig. 5. Experiments made with varying leader speeds

Experiment 3: Configurations with a Fixed Number of Leaders

In this experiment, we employed several different initial leader configurations under the onus of being limited to four leaders in total. Figure 4 illustrates the evacuation results. Although the curves appear relatively similar, useful insight can be derived from them.

First, the deciding factor in getting the crowd out quickly appears to be the combination of embedded and peripheral leaders which is quite intuitive when one considers that with the leaders closer to the crowd, they will be able to react faster to direct it. The trial runs that fared the worst in this experiment (in yellow) are those with only one or two leaders in the immediate vicinity of the crowd.

Another interesting feature is that contrary to the situation in Experiment 1, where only one class of leaders was used in each scenario, here all the trial runs lead to approximately the same results over the long term (around 40 seconds or so). This suggests that as long as one maintains a reasonable mix of leaders, one can still maintain adequate performance within relatively closed environments such as the one described here.

Experiment 4: Varying Leader Speed

Our final experiment attempted to determine the relationship between the velocity difference between the leaders and crowd members and the emergence of good crowd flow leading crowd members to safety. It was discovered that there is an optimal ratio of leader movement speed to crowd member movement speed to attain maximal crowd flow and the peak save rate.

Varying the speed modifier of the leader from 1.6 to 4 times that of the movement rate of the crowd members yielded the discovery that the optimal movement rate of the leader individuals is approximately half the speed of the regular crowd members as illustrated in Figure 5. Leader agents going faster than this outpaced the formation of crowd flow; any slower and while crowd flow does form, the leaders can become crowded with too many crowd members for them to be able to influence. The crowd reaches the exit much slower.

8 Discussion

8.1 Validation of the Model

Before any additional discussion of what the results entail, an important question to answer is whether or not the model we have presented for crowd flow simulations demonstrates a reasonable representation of real-life crowd flow. This validation is very difficult to do in a quantitative fashion for obvious reasons; we must then fall back on a qualitative approach. For example, we can isolate identifiable behavioural components demonstrated by the crowd members and compare them to the existing consensus on crowd behaviour as well as to real-life photos of crowd flow. One example of the kind of crowd flow phenomenon witnessed is the act of "corner hugging", or the tendency of crowd members to slow down and hug corners as they are turning them. This effect is described by G. Keith Still in his PhD thesis "Crowd Dynamics" [9]:

> *"In confined spaces crowd dynamics is a function of the local ge-*
> *ometry and this effect can dominate the crowd flow and behaviour es-*
> *pecially during emergency egress."*

 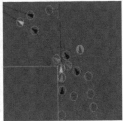

Fig. 6. Effect of Corners on Real and Simulated Crowd Flow. Photo from www.crowddynamics.com

Indeed, the corner effect illustrated in the photograph in Figure 6 can be readily made out in our simulation. This effect is most notable because it was not something that was directly programmed in to the simulation; it is an emergent behaviour resulting from the tendency of the agents to follow the shortest path to their destination. Important to note is that this corner hugging effect slows down the progress of the crowd considerably and his in fact highly undesirable.

Another property that emerged from our system is the spontaneous appearance of sustained crowd flow. While we did introduce flocking in the simulation as a means of replicating the basic following behaviour people do, we were able to consistently witness situations where a flow endured long after leaders had departed toward the exits. This happens to be a very efficient solution to the evacuation of large numbers of people. Additionally, the wall avoidance/following behaviour preventing the agents from ramming directly into walls also contributes to the realism of the simulation. It was most interesting to note the number of factors affecting the emergence of crowd flow. Both the initial placement of the leaders and their relative velocities proved to be most important in determining the formation of optimal crowd flow.

9 Conclusions

The modeling system developed herein has been shown to provide a reasonable approximation of actual crowd flow dynamics and has shown the validity of including leader agents in a crowd control situation, specifically with reference to evacuation situations.

With the aid of the developed modeling system, our experiments have shown that adding leaders with global knowledge of the environment into a crowded area of individuals who are less familiar with their surroundings and are trying to get out can greatly improve the evacuation rate. Realistic emergent phenomena such as corner hugging and sustained crowd flow were also observed in our simulations. Another result of the simulations run with our modeling system is the effect of architectural layout on the results of the simulation, whether under the influence of leaders or not. Sharp corners and bottlenecks are both detrimental to crowd flow and should be avoided in the design of public areas. One interesting avenue for future investigation would be to develop leaders capable of alleviating problems related to such architectural flaws perhaps by standing at a sharp corner and preventing the crowd members from hugging it and compressing as they tend to do now. Given the infeasibility of replacing all existing buildings and installations that possess these sub-optimal architectural characteristics, this observation again supports finding means of alleviating crowd flow problems, of which leader individuals are a prime example.

Furthermore, some useful insights have been gained into optimal layout strategies of leader agents attempting to direct a crowd in an evacuation situation. With the objective always being to ensure evacuation of all crowd members, it has been observed that a mix of leader classes is most desirable. Embedded or peripheral leaders can result in some people slipping through the net, and employing only distant leaders will mean that they will not be able to influence the crowd as rapidly. The optimal approach is to attempt to cover all the bases by employing leader agents of each class. Leaders going about half the speed of other agents lead to the most efficient evacuations, but one suspects variety could be helpful too.

The analysis of the impact of leader individuals remains an interesting and relatively unexplored branch of the study of crowd dynamics. There certainly remains much to be done to continue to develop methodologies and systems to ensure optimal placement and behaviours of leader individuals within crowd control situations. It is our hope that this work will be continued and might one day prove of use to those people responsible for ensuring the safety of people who gather together.

References

1.   Associated Press, "Death toll in hajj stampede rises to 251." International Herald Tribune, February 2nd, 2004. Available at http://www.iht.com/articles/127689.html

2. Associated Press, "Stampede at disco leaves 13 students dead, 44 hurt". Amarillo Globe News, March 25th, 2000. Available at
   http://www.amarillonet.com/stories/032500/usn_LA0756.shtml
3. Helbing, D. and P. Molnar, "Social Force Model For Pedestrian Dynamics," Physical Review E, Vol. 51, No. 5, pp. 4282-4286, May 1995.
4. Kirkland, J. A. and A. A. Maciejewski, "A Simulation of Attempts to Influence Crowd Dynamics," IEEE International Conference on Systems, Man, and Cybernetics, pp. 4328-4333, Washington, DC, Oct. 5-6, 2003.
5. Braun, A., S. R. Musse, L. P. L. de Oliveira and B. E. J. Bodmann. "Modeling Individual Behaviours in Crowd Simulation". In CASA 2003 - Computer Animation and Social Agents, pp. 143-148, New Jersey, May 2003.
6. Helbing, D., I. Farkas, and T. Vicsek, "Simulating Dynamical Features of Escape Panic." Nature #407, 487-490, 2000.
7. Reynolds, C. W., "Steering Behaviors For Autonomous Characters." In the proceedings of Game Developers Conference 1999 held in San Jose, California. Miller Freeman Game Group, San Francisco, California. Pages 763-782, 1999.
8. Still, G.K. "Crowd Dynamics." PhD Thesis, Mathematics department, Warwick University, 2000.

Cellular Automata Application to the Linearization of Stream Cipher Generators

Amparo Fúster-Sabater[1] and Dolores de la Guía-Martínez[2]

[1] Instituto de Física Aplicada, C.S.I.C.
C/ Serrano 144, 28006 Madrid (SPAIN)
amparo@iec.csic.es

[2] Centro Técnico de Informática, C.S.I.C.
C/ Pinar 19, 28006 Madrid (SPAIN)
lola@cti.csic.es

Abstract. A wide family of LFSR-based sequence generators, the so-called Clock-Controlled Shrinking Generators (CCSGs), has been analyzed and identified with a subset of linear cellular automata. In this way, sequence generators conceived and designed as complex nonlinear models can be written in terms of simple linear models. An easy algorithm to compute the pair of one-dimensional linear hybrid cellular automata that generate the CCSG output sequences has been derived. A cryptanalytic approach based on the phaseshift of cellular automata output sequences is sketched too. From the obtained results, we can create linear cellular automata-based models to analyze/cryptanalyze the class of clock-controlled generators.

Keywords: Cellular automata, clock-controlled generators, linear modelling, cryptography.

1 Introduction

Cellular Automata (CA) are discrete dynamic systems characterized by a simple structure but a complex behavior, see [6], [9], [11] and [13]. They are built up by individual elements, called cells, related among them in many varied ways. CA have been used in application areas so different as physical system simulation, biological process such as self-reproduction or test pattern generation. Their simple, modular, and cascadable structure makes them very attractive for VLSI implementations. CA can be characterized by several parameters which determine their behavior e.g. the number of states per cell, the function Φ (the so-called *rule*) under which the cellular automaton evolves to the next state, the number of neighbor cells which are included in Φ, the number of preceding states included in Φ, the dimension, and the geometric structure.

On the other hand, Linear Feedback Shift Registers (LFSRs) [7] are electronic devices currently used in the generation of pseudorandom sequences. The inherent simplicity of LFSRs, their ease of implementation, and the good statistical properties of their output sequences turn them into natural building blocks

P.M.A. Sloot, B. Chopard, and A.G. Hoekstra (Eds.): ACRI 2004, LNCS 3305, pp. 612–621, 2004.

for the design of pseudorandom sequence generators. See [10] for a comprehensive survey on LFSR-based construction of pseudorandom generators and related analysis tools.

CA and LFSRs are special forms of a more general mathematical structure: finite state machines. In recent years, one-dimensional CA have been proposed as an alternative to LFSRs ([1], [3], [9] and [12]) in applications such as cryptography, error correcting codes, and digital signature. In this sense, CA are studied in order to obtain the best rules producing sequences with the properties required in LFSR applications. The results of this study point toward the equivalence between the sequences generated by a subset of CA and those obtained from LFSR-based models.

In this paper, it is shown that a wide class of LFSR-based nonlinear generators, the so-called Clock-Controlled Shrinking Generators (CCSGs) [8], can be described in terms of linear CA configurations. In this way, these automata unify in a simple structure the above mentioned class of sequence generators. Thus, finite *nonlinear* models are converted into finite *linear* models, as well as, all the theoretical background on CA found in the literature can be applied to the analysis and/or cryptanalysis of such generators.

2   Basic Structures

In the following subsections, we introduce the general characteristics of the basic structures we are dealing with: one-dimensional cellular automata, the shrinking generator and the class of clock-controlled shrinking generators. Throughout the work, only binary LFSRs and CA will be considered.

2.1   One-Dimensional Cellular Automata

One-dimensional cellular automata can be described as n-cell registers [6], whose contents are updated at the same time according to a particular rule: a k-variable function denoted by Φ. If the function Φ is a linear function so is the cellular automaton. When k input variables are considered, then there are 2^k different binary neighbor configurations. Therefore, for cellular automata with binary contents there can be up to 2^{2^k} different mappings to the next state. Moreover, if $k = 2r + 1$, then the next state x_i^{t+1} of the cell x_i^t depends on the current state of k neighbor cells $x_i^{t+1} = \Phi(x_{i-r}^t, \ldots, x_i^t, \ldots, x_{i+r}^t)$ $(i = 1, \ldots, n)$.

CA are called *uniform* when all cells evolve under the same rule while CA are called *hybrid* when different cells evolve under different rules. At the ends of the array, two different boundary conditions are possible: *null automata* when cells with permanent null content are supposed adjacent to the extreme cells or *periodic automata* when extreme cells are supposed adjacent. In this paper, all the considered automata will be one-dimensional null hybrid CA with $k = 3$ and linear rules 90 and 150. These rules are described as follows:

$$\begin{array}{cc}
\text{Rule 90} & \text{Rule 150} \\
x_i^{t+1} = x_{i-1}^t + x_{i+1}^t & x_i^{t+1} = x_{i-1}^t + x_i^t + x_{i+1}^t \\
\end{array}$$

<table>
<tr><td>111</td><td>110</td><td>101</td><td>100</td><td>011</td><td>010</td><td>001</td><td>000</td><td></td><td>111</td><td>110</td><td>101</td><td>100</td><td>011</td><td>010</td><td>001</td><td>000</td></tr>
<tr><td>0</td><td>1</td><td>0</td><td>1</td><td>1</td><td>0</td><td>1</td><td>0</td><td></td><td>1</td><td>0</td><td>0</td><td>1</td><td>0</td><td>1</td><td>1</td><td>0</td></tr>
</table>

01011010 (binary) = 90 (decimal)   10010110 (binary) = 150 (decimal)

Remark that the names rule 90 and rule 150 derive from the decimal values of their next-state functions. For an one-dimensional null hybrid cellular automa-

Table 1. An one-dimensional null hybrid linear cellular automaton of 10 cells with rule 90 and rule 150 starting at a given initial state

90	150	150	150	90	90	150	150	150	90
0	0	0	1	1	1	0	1	1	0
0	0	1	0	0	1	0	0	0	1
0	1	1	1	1	0	1	0	1	0
1	0	1	1	1	0	1	0	1	1
0	0	0	1	1	0	1	0	0	1
0	0	1	0	1	0	1	1	1	0
0	1	1	0	0	0	0	1	0	1
⋮	⋮	⋮	⋮	⋮	⋮	⋮	⋮	⋮	⋮

ton of $n = 10$ cells, configuration rules $(90, 150, 150, 150, 90, 90, 150, 150, 150, 90)$ and initial state $(0, 0, 0, 1, 1, 1, 0, 1, 1, 0)$, Table 1 illustrates the formation of its output sequences (in vertical). Within this CA class, it is easy to determine the number of different sequences generated by a particular automaton, the distinct periods and linear complexities [10] of such sequences as well as the number of different sequences associated with each period and linear complexity.

2.2   The Shrinking Generator

The shrinking generator is a binary sequence generator [5] composed of two LFSRs : a control register, called R_1, that decimates the sequence produced by the other register, called R_2, see Fig. 1. We denote by L_j $(j = 1, 2)$ their corresponding lengths and by $P_j(x)$ $(j = 1, 2)$ their corresponding characteristic polynomials [7].

The sequence produced by the LFSR R_1, that is $\{a_i\}$, controls the bits of the sequence produced by R_2, that is $\{b_i\}$, which are included in the output sequence $\{c_j\}$ (the shrunken sequence), according to the following rule P:

1. If $a_i = 1 \Longrightarrow c_j = b_i$
2. If $a_i = 0 \Longrightarrow b_i$ is discarded.

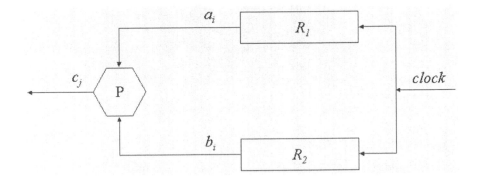

Fig. 1. General scheme of the shrinking generator

A simple example illustrates the behavior of this structure.

Example 1: Let us consider the following LFSRs:

1. R_1 of length $L_1 = 3$, characteristic polynomial $P_1(x) = 1+x^2+x^3$ and initial state $IS_1 = (1,0,0)$. The sequence generated by R_1 is $\{1,0,0,1,1,1,0\}$ with period $T_1 = 2^{L_1} - 1 = 7$.
2. R_2 of length $L_2 = 4$, characteristic polynomial $P_2(x) = 1+x+x^4$ and initial state $IS_2 = (1,0,0,0)$. The sequence generated by R_2 is $\{1,0,0,0,1,0,0,1,1,$ $0,1,0,1,1,1\}$ with period $T_2 = 2^{L_2} - 1 = 15$.

The output sequence $\{c_j\}$ is given by:

- $\{a_i\} \rightarrow 1\ 0\ 0\ 1\ 1\ 1\ 0\ 1\ 0\ 0\ 1\ 1\ 1\ 0\ 1\ 0\ 0\ 1\ 1\ 1\ 0\ 1$ .....
- $\{b_i\} \rightarrow 1\ \underline{0}\ \underline{0}\ 0\ 1\ 0\ \underline{0}\ 1\ 1\ \underline{0}\ 1\ 0\ 1\ \underline{1}\ 1\ \underline{1}\ \underline{0}\ 0\ 0\ 1\ \underline{0}\ \underline{0}$ .....
- $\{c_j\} \rightarrow 1\ 0\ 1\ 0\ 1\ 1\ 0\ 1\ 1\ 0\ 0\ 1\ 0$ .....

According to rule P, the underlined bits $\underline{0}$ or $\underline{1}$ in $\{b_i\}$ are discarded. In brief, the sequence produced by the shrinking generator is an irregular decimation of the sequence generated by R_2 governed by the bits of R_1.

It can be proved [5] that the period of the shrunken sequence is:

$$T = (2^{L_2} - 1)2^{(L_1-1)} \tag{1}$$

and its linear complexity [10], notated LC, satisfies the following inequality:

$$L_2\, 2^{(L_1-2)} < LC \leq L_2\, 2^{(L_1-1)}. \tag{2}$$

A simple calculation, based on the fact that every state of R_2 coincides once with every state of R_1, allows one to compute the number of 1's in the shrunken sequence. Such a number is constant and equal to:

$$No.\ 1's = 2^{(L_2-1)}2^{(L_1-1)}. \tag{3}$$

Comparing (1) with (3), it can be deduced that the shrunken sequence is a quasi-balanced sequence.In addition, the output sequence has some nice distributional statistics too [5]. Therefore, this scheme is suitable for practical implementation of stream cipher cryptosystems and pattern generators.

2.3   The Clock-Controlled Shrinking Generators

The Clock-Controlled Shrinking Generators constitute a wide class of clock-controlled sequence generators [8] with applications in cryptography, error correcting codes, and digital signature. An CCSG is a sequence generator composed of two LFSRs notated R_1 and R_2. The parameters of both registers are defined as those of subsection 2.2. At any time t, R_1 (the control register) is clocked normally while the second register R_2 is clocked a number of times given by an integer decimation function notated X_t. In fact, if $A_0(t)$, $A_1(t)$, ..., $A_{L_1-1}(t)$ are the cell contents of R_1 at time t, then X_t is defined as

$$X_t = 1 + 2^0 A_{i_0}(t) + 2^1 A_{i_1}(t) + \ldots + 2^{w-1} A_{i_{w-1}}(t) \tag{4}$$

where $i_0, i_1, \ldots, i_{w-1} \in \{0, 1, \ldots, L_1 - 1\}$ and $0 < w \leq L_1 - 1$.

In this way, the output sequence of a CCSG is obtained from a double decimation. First, $\{b_i\}$ the output sequence of R_2 is decimated by means of X_t giving rise to the sequence $\{b_i'\}$. Then, the same decimation rule P, defined in subsection 2.2, is applied to the sequence $\{b_i'\}$. Remark that if $X_t \equiv 1$ (no cells are selected in R_1), then the proposed generator is just the shrinking generator. Let us see a simple example of CCSG.

Example 2: For the same LFSRs defined in the previous example and the function $X_t = 1 + 2^0 A_0(t)$ with $w = 1$, the decimated sequence $\{b_i'\}$ is given by:

- $\{b_i\} \rightarrow 1\,\underline{0}\,0\,0\,1\,\underline{0}\,0\,\underline{1}\,1\,\underline{0}\,1\,0\,1\,1\,1\,1\,\underline{0}\,0\,\underline{0}\,1\,\underline{0}\,0\,1\,\underline{1}\,0\,1\,0\,1\,\underline{1}\,1\,1$ .....
- $X_t \rightarrow 2\,1\,1\,2\,2\,2\,2\,1\,2\,1\,1\,2\,2\,2\,1\,2\,1\,1\,2\,2$ .....
- $\{b_i'\} \rightarrow 1\,0\,0\,1\,0\,1\,1\,0\,1\,1\,1\,0\,1\,0\,1\,0\,1\,0\,1\,1$ .....

According to the decimation function X_t, the underlined bits $\underline{0}$ or $\underline{1}$ in $\{b_i\}$ are discarded in order to produce the sequence $\{b_i'\}$. Then the output sequence $\{c_j\}$ of the CCSG output sequence is given by:

- $\{a_i\} \rightarrow 1\,0\,0\,1\,1\,1\,0\,1\,0\,0\,1\,1\,1\,0\,1\,0\,0\,1\,1\,1\,0\,1$ .....
- $\{b_i'\} \rightarrow 1\,\underline{0}\,\underline{0}\,1\,0\,1\,\underline{1}\,0\,\underline{1}\,1\,1\,0\,1\,\underline{0}\,1\,\underline{0}\,1\,0\,1\,1$ .....
- $\{c_j\} \rightarrow 1\,1\,0\,1\,0\,1\,0\,1\,1\,0\,1\,1$ .....

According to rule P, the underlined bits $\underline{0}$ or $\underline{1}$ in $\{b_i'\}$ are discarded. In brief, the sequence produced by an CCSG is an irregular double decimation of the sequence generated by R_2 governed by the function X_t and the bits of R_1. This construction allows one to generate a large family of different sequences by using the same LFSR initial states and characteristic polynomials but modifying the decimation function. Period, linear complexity and statistical properties of the generated sequences by CCSGs have been established in [8].

3   CA-Based Linear Models for the Shrinking Generator

In this section, an algorithm to determine the pair of one-dimensional linear CA corresponding to a given shrinking generator is presented. Such an algorithm is based on the following facts:

Fact 1: The characteristic polynomial of the shrunken sequence [5] is of the form $P(x)^N$, where $P(x)$ is a L_2-degree primitive polynomial and N is an integer satisfying the inequality $2^{(L_1-2)} < N \leq 2^{(L_1-1)}$.

Fact 2: $P(x)$ depends exclusively on the characteristic polynomial of the register R_2 and on the length L_1 of the register R_1. Moreover, $P(x)$ is the characteristic polynomial of *cyclotomic coset* $2^{L_1} - 1$, see [7].

Fact 3: Rule 90 (150) at the end of the array in null automata is equivalent to two consecutive rules 150 (90) with mirror image sequences.

According to the previous facts, the following algorithm is introduced:

Input: A shrinking generator characterized by two LFSRs, R_1 and R_2, with their corresponding lengths, L_1 and L_2, and the characteristic polynomial $P_2(x)$ of the register R_2.

Step 1: From L_1 and $P_2(x)$, compute the polynomial $P(x)$. In fact, $P(x)$ is the characteristic polynomial of the cyclotomic *coset* E, where

$$E = 2^0 + 2^1 + \ldots + 2^{L_1-1} . \tag{5}$$

Thus,

$$P(x) = (x + \alpha^E)(x + \alpha^{2E}) \ldots (x + \alpha^{2^{L_2-1}E}) \tag{6}$$

α being a primitive root in $GF(2^{L_2})$ as well as a root of $P_2(x)$.

Step 2: From $P(x)$, apply the Cattell and Muzio synthesis algorithm [4] to determine the two linear CA (with rules 90 and 150) whose characteristic polynomial is $P(x)$. Such CA are written as binary strings with the following codification: $0 = $ rule 90 and $1 = $ rule 150.

Step 3: For each one of the previous binary strings representing the CA, we proceed:

    3.1 Complement its least significant bit. The resulting binary string is notated S.

    3.2 Compute the mirror image of S, notated S^*, and concatenate both strings

$$S_c = S * S^* .$$

    3.3 Apply steps 3.1 and 3.2 to S_c recursively $L_1 - 1$ times.

Output: Two binary strings of length $n = L_2 \, 2^{L_1-1}$ codifying the CA corresponding to the given shrinking generator.

Remark 1. The characteristic polynomial of the register R_1 is not needed. Thus all the shrinking generators with the same R_2 but different registers R_1 (all of them with the same length L_1) can be modelled by the same pair of one-dimensional linear CA.

Remark 2. It can be noticed that the computation of the CA is proportional to L_1 instead of 2^{L_1}. Consequently, the algorithm can be applied to shrinking generators in, for instance, a range of cryptographic interest (e.g. $L_1, L_2 \approx 64$).

In order to clarify the previous steps a simple numerical example is presented.

Input: A shrinking generator characterized by two LFSRs R_1 of length $L_1 = 3$ and R_2 of length $L_2 = 5$ and characteristic polynomial $P_2(x) = 1 + x + x^2 + x^4 + x^5$.

Step 1: $P(x)$ is the characteristic polynomial of the cyclotomic *coset 7*. Thus,

$$P(x) = 1 + x^2 + x^5 .$$

Step 2: From $P(x)$ and applying the Cattell and Muzio synthesis algorithm, two linear CA whose characteristic polynomial is $P(x)$ can be determined. Such CA are written in binary format as:

$$0\ 1\ 1\ 1\ 1$$
$$1\ 1\ 1\ 1\ 0$$

Step 3: Computation of the required pair of CA.
For the first automaton:

$$0\ 1\ 1\ 1\ 1$$
$$0\ 1\ 1\ 1\ 0\ 0\ 1\ 1\ 1\ 0$$
$$0\ 1\ 1\ 0\ 0\ 1\ 1\ 1\ 1\ 1\ 1\ 1\ 0\ 0\ 1\ 1\ 1\ 0\ \text{(final automaton)}$$

For the second automaton:

$$1\ 1\ 1\ 1\ 0$$
$$1\ 1\ 1\ 1\ 1\ 1\ 1\ 1\ 1$$
$$1\ 1\ 1\ 1\ 1\ 1\ 1\ 1\ 0\ 0\ 1\ 1\ 1\ 1\ 1\ 1\ 1\ 1\ \text{(final automaton)}$$

For each automaton, the procedure in *Step 3* has been carried out twice as $L_1 - 1 = 2$.

Output: Two binary strings of length $n = 20$ codifying the required CA.

In this way, we have obtained a pair of linear CA able to produce, among other sequences, the shrunken sequence corresponding to the given shrinking generator. In addition, for each one of the previous automata there are state cycles where the shrunken sequence is generated by any one of the automaton cells. Moreover, due to the repetitive process followed in *step 3* there are state cycles where the shrunken sequence appears generated by (quasi)periodical automaton cells.

In brief, we have obtained two simple and different linear models describing the behavior of a nonlinear sequence generator.

4   CA-Based Linear Models for the Clock-Controlled Shrinking Generators

In this section, an algorithm to determine the pair of one-dimensional linear CA corresponding to a given CCSG is presented. Such an algorithm is based on the following facts:

Fact 4: The characteristic polynomial of the shrunken sequence [8] is of the form $P(x)^N$, where $P(x)$ is a L_2-degree primitive polynomial and N is an integer satisfying the inequality $2^{(L_1-2)} < N \leq 2^{(L_1-1)}$.

Fact 5: $P(x)$ depends on the characteristic polynomial of the register R_2, the length L_1 of the register R_1 and the decimation function X_t. Moreover, $P(x)$ is the characteristic polynomial of the *cyclotomic coset E*, where E is the distance between the digits of the sequence $\{b_i\}$ corresponding to the same digit of the sequence $\{a_i\}$ when such a sequence is repeated periodically. In fact, for the shrinking generator, this distance is constant and equal to $2^{L_1} - 1$. Now this distance is a function of X_t.

Fact 6: The distance E can be computed taking into account that the function X_t takes values in the interval $[1, 2, \ldots, 2^w]$ and the number of times that each one of these values appears in a period is given by 2^{L_1-w} (except for $X_t = 1$ that appears only $2^{L_1-w} - 1$ times as the initial state identically null in an LFSR is not allowed). Hence the distance E is given by:

$$E = 2^{L_1-w} \left(\sum_{i=1}^{2^w} i\right) - 1 = (1 + 2^w)\, 2^{L_1-1} - 1. \tag{7}$$

From the previous facts, it can be noticed that the algorithm to determine the CA corresponding to a given CCSG is analogous to that one developed in section 3; just the expression of E in equation (5) must be here replaced by the expression of E in equation (7). A simple numerical example is presented.

Input: A CCSG characterized by: Two LFSRs R_1 of length $L_1 = 3$ and R_2 of length $L_2 = 5$ and characteristic polynomial $P_2(x) = 1 + x + x^2 + x^4 + x^5$ plus the decimation function $X_t = 1 + 2^0 A_0(t) + 2^1 A_1(t) + 2^2 A_2(t)$ with $w = 3$.

Step 1: $P(x)$ is the characteristic polynomial of the cyclotomic *coset E*. Now $E \equiv 4 \bmod 31$, that is we are dealing with the cyclotomic coset 1. Thus, the corresponding characteristic polynomial is:

$$P(x) = 1 + x + x^2 + x^4 + x^5 .$$

Step 2: From $P(x)$ and applying the Cattell and Muzio synthesis algorithm, two linear CA whose characteristic polynomial is $P(x)$ can be determined. Such CA are written in binary format as:

$$1\,0\,0\,0\,0$$
$$0\,0\,0\,0\,1$$

Step 3: Computation of the required pair of CA.
For the first automaton:

$$1\,0\,0\,0\,0$$
$$1\,0\,0\,0\,1\,1\,0\,0\,0\,1$$
$$1\,0\,0\,0\,1\,1\,0\,0\,0\,0\,0\,0\,0\,0\,1\,1\,0\,0\,0\,1 \quad \text{(final automaton)}$$

For the second automaton:

0 0 0 0 1
0 0 0 0 0 0 0 0 0 0
0 0 0 0 0 0 0 0 0 1 1 0 0 0 0 0 0 0 0 0   (final automaton)

For each automaton, the procedure in *Step 3* has been carried out twice as $L_1 - 1 = 2$.

Output: Two binary strings of length $n = 20$ codifying the required CA.

Remark 3. From a point of view of the CA-based linear models, the shrinking generator or any one of the CCGS are entirely analogous. Thus, the fact of introduce an additional decimation function does neither increase the complexity of the generator nor improve its resistance against cryptanalytic attacks since both kinds of generators can be linearized by the same class of CA-based models.

5   Sketch of a Cryptanalytic Approach to This Class of Sequence Generators

Since CA-based linear models describing the behavior of CCSGs have been derived, a new cryptanalytic attack that exploits the weaknesses of these models can be also considered. The key idea of this attack is based on the study of the repeated sequences in the automata under consideration and the relative shifts among such sequences. The analysis is composed by several steps described as follows:

- First, the portion of intercepted shrunken sequence is placed at the most right (left) cell of one of the automata.
- Then, the locations of the automaton cells that generate the same sequence have to be detected.
- Finally, the values of the relative shifts among sequences are computed.

Once the previous steps are accomplished, the original shrunken sequence can be reconstructed by concatenating the different shifted subsequences. The procedure can be applied systematically to both automata. In order to carry out this reconstruction, the Bardell's algorithm [2] to phaseshift analysis of CA is applied. Note that we have two different CA plus an additional pair of CA corresponding to the reverse version of the shrunken sequence (the pair associated to the reciprocal polynomial of $P_2(x)$). In each particular case, the most adequate automaton or a combination of the successive automaton can be used.

6   Conclusions

In this work, a wide family of LFSR-based sequence generators, the so-called Clock-Controlled Shrinking Generators, has been analyzed and identified with a subset of linear cellular automata. In fact, a pair of linear models describing the behavior of the CCSGs has been derived. The algorithm to convert a given CCSG into a CA-based linear model is very simple and can be applied to CCSGs in a range of practical interest. The linearity of these cellular models can be advantageously used in the analysis and/or cryptanalysis of the CCSGs. Besides the traditional cryptanalytic attacks, an outline of a new attack that exploits the weaknesses inherent to this class of CA has been introduced too.

Acknowledgements. Work supported by Ministerio de Ciencia y Tecnología (Spain) under grant TIC2001-0586.

References

1. Bao, F.: Crytanalysis of a New Cellular Automata Cryptosystem. In: ACISP 2003. Lecture Notes in Computer Science, Vol. 2727. Springer Verlag, New York (2003) 416-427
2. Bardell, P.H.: Analysis of Cellular Automata Used as Pseudorandom Pattern Generators. Proceedings of the IEEE International Test Conference. Paper 34.1 (1990) 762-768
3. Blackburn, S., Murphy, S., Paterson, K.: Comments on 'Theory and Applications of Cellular Automata in Cryptography'. IEEE Transactions on Computers. **46** (1997) 637-638
4. Cattell K., Muzio, J.: Analysis of One-Dimensional Linear Hybrid Cellular Automata over GF(q). IEEE Transactions on Computer-Aided Design. **45** (1996) 782-792
5. Coppersmith, D., Krawczyk, H., Mansour, Y.:The Shrinking Generator. In: Advances in Cryptology–CRYPTO'93. Lecture Notes in Computer Science, Springer Verlag, Berlin Heidelberg New York. **773** (1994) 22-39
6. Das, A.K., Ganguly, A., Dasgupta, A., Bhawmik, S., Chaudhuri,P.P.: Efficient Characterisation of Cellular Automata. IEE Proc., Part E. **1** (1990) 81-87
7. Golomb, S.: Shift-Register Sequences (revised edition). Aegean press (1982)
8. Kanso, A.: Clock-Controlled Shrinking Generators. In: ACISP 2003. Lecture Notes in Computer Science, Springer Verlag, New York. **2727** (2003) 443-451
9. Nandi, S., Kar, B.K., Chaudhuri, P.P.: Theory and Applications of Cellular Automata in Cryptography. IEEE Transactions on Computers. **43** (1994) 1346-1357
10. Rueppel, R.A.: Stream Ciphers, in Gustavus J. Simmons, Editor, Contemporary Cryptology, The Science of Information. IEEE Press (1992) 65-134
11. Wolfram, S.: Cellular Automata as Models of Complexity. Nature. **311** (1984) 419
12. Wolfram, S.: Cryptography with Cellular Automata. In: CRYPTO'85. Lecture Notes in Computer Science, Springer Verlag, New York. **218** (1994) 22-39
13. Wolfram, S.: Random Sequence generation by Cellular Automata. Advances in Applied Mathematics. **7** 123 (1986)

Agents in Housing Market. A Model for Siena Historical Centre

Francesco Lapiana [1], Giuliano Bianchi [2], and Giovanni Rabino[3]

[1] Via Montanini 132, 53100 Siena. Ph: +39.3339385688
francesco.lapiana@hotmail.com
[2] Dept. of Economic and Social Studies, Faculty of Economics "R. Goodwin",University of
Siena, Piazza S. Francesco, 53100 Siena.
gib.fi@tin.it
[3] Dept. of Architecture and Planning, Politechnic of Milan, Piazza Leonardo da Vinci 32, 20133
Milan, Italy. Ph. +39.02.23994102
giovanni.rabino@polimi.it

Abstract. The goal of the research is to analyse the dynamics and the evolution
of the real estate market of a highly competitive urban centre. An analysis has
been conducted through the definition of a Multi Agents System implemented
on a cellular automata ad hoc. The focus is on the study of the historical city
centre of Siena and behaviours of the agents in this area, namely the students
(six university faculties are located in the historical centre), the professional
working class (the principal actors of the city's tertiary sector) and the tourist
industry (Siena is a well-known pole of international tourist attraction).

1 Introduction

The objective of this paper is to analyse dynamics and evolution of the real estate
market in a highly competitive urban centre, where there is a strong competition on
the demand side for alternative use of the existing buildings. The analysis has been
developed through a Multi Agents System implemented on ad hoc cellular automata.
The study focus is on the historical city centre of Siena and the behaviour of the
agents, which operate in this area, namely: students (six university faculties are
located in the historical centre), professionals (the principal actors of the city's tertiary
sector), and tourist industry (Siena is a well-known international tourism pole). An
expansion of the city's historical centre is impossible, as it is delimited by physical
boundaries (the ancient city wall). So, an increase of real estate supply is unfeasible.
The study assumes that the market should be studied not only with reference to the
supply side (the aggregate bid and the average price), but also, and primarily, with
reference to the effects that are determined on the market by the interactions between
specific groups of agents owing a given operational autonomy.
The analysis is based on a dynamic interpretation of the classical economic theory of
ground rent, applied to the modern urban context (Micelli 2001): the rent is a
diffusive phenomenon that transforms economic values of the real estate system,
through the interaction between pre-existing structural and functional components.

P.M.A. Sloot, B. Chopard, and A.G. Hoekstra (Eds.): ACRI 2004, LNCS 3305, pp. 622–631, 2004.
© Springer-Verlag Berlin Heidelberg 2004

These values are distributed according to contiguity criterions, via local incremental variations, without great leaps. (Sachirollo, 1997).

This model is applied in the paper not for formulating a general law, but in order to identify the qualitative and quantitative processes that are underlying the rent diffusion in the specific urban system of Siena.

Some authors (e.g., Guariso, 1999, Sachirollo, 1997) have analysed, with remarkable results, the housing market by means of cellular automata but without investigating causes that trigger supply evolution and factors that determine the housing prices in a given spatial context. In particular, those studies have used models, where the price change is predetermined according to the market mechanism (AURES, M.O.D.E.), or have assumed that the market evolution depends on its historical trends.

Instead, this analysis starts from the hypothesis that every urban system is intrinsically different, in terms of its structure and of psychological and economic characteristics of its agents (budgets, attitudes and needs, perception of distances, adaptation to change, etc.). So the research aim is to understand the determinants of the demand behaviour.

To this purpose, two analyses have been developed:

1. The first, in order to identify the last decade market trends and their evolutionary trajectories, has been carried out on available statistical documentation;
2. The second, in order to identify the behaviour of each agent category, has been carried out by means of interviews with representative samples of each category.

The results from this dual investigation have allowed establishing two sets of rules:

1. One regarding the operation of the local market;
2. The other regarding the agents' behaviour.

The simulation of the market has been performed through a cellular multi-automata consisting of three automata (one for each category of agents). The transformation rules of have been determined according to the previous couple of rule sets.

Particular attention has been paid to the market evolution. To this aim three scenarios have been hypothesized and analysed:

1. In the first, the trend of housing demand remains constant at its current levels.
2. In the second, the city historical centre specializes into a university city. The university enrolment doubles in number and four new faculties are created, with location in city buildings, taking the place of the present cultural and commercial facilities.

In the third, the city historical centre specializes in tourism. Tourists in the area double in number and residential houses are converted into bed and breakfasts and vacation rental dwellings.

2 The Model

The housing market is broken down in supply and demand. Supply is constant (it is impossible to erect new buildings).

Prices have been grouped into four macro-classes (luxury, high, average, low class) and their historical trend over the past decade (1991-2001) has been ascertained. Each

single building in the city centre has been classified in those macro-classes. The map
(Fig. 1) offers a representation of the present (2001) market bid.

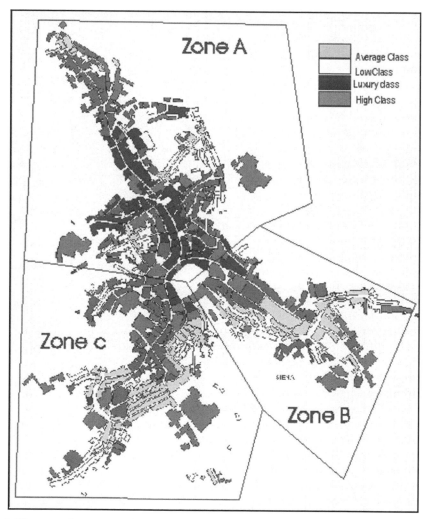

Fig. 1. The map of current market offer (2001). To better clarify the definition of the model and
each simulation, the historical city centre has been divided into three zones (A, B, and C).

Demand has been disaggregated in three components (tourist industry[1], students,
professionals[2]).

---

[1] Bed&Breakfasts (B&B) have been considered as the representative activity of the whole
    tourist sector.
[2] The category "Professionals" include: lawyers, notaries, architects, business experts,
    medicine doctors, and so on.

Information about Bed&Breakfasts (B&B) has been obtained from the numerous studies on tourism that public administrations and private organizations have carried out during the last decade. The analysis of the spatial development of this activity in the historical centre has permitted to identify the areas with the highest concentration of B&B. The growth trend has been determined by computing the average annual increase ratio of this activity. The correlation with the tourism database resulted in tracing the behaviour guidelines of this agent.

In order to recognise the changes that B&B provoke on the real estate market a representative sample of them has been extracted and the impact they have exerted on prices of the contiguous buildings during their birth has been measured.

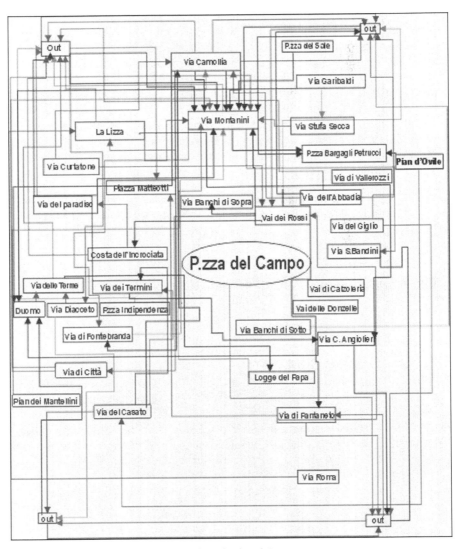

Fig. 2. Map of professionals' movements.

Information about students and professionals have been collected through two distinct investigations:

- One, by means of existing documentation, aimed at quantitative data (members of the various communities, migratory flows, enrolment into or cancellations from various registers, etc.);
- The other in terms of a direct approach (that could be defined as "sociological") aimed at learning the agents' systematic behaviour.

A student population representative sample, within each university faculty, has been interviewed in order to identify their respective domiciles and, hence, their localization needs   (distance from faculty, distance perception, building quality, available income); on this base, an ad hoc coefficient was estimated to evaluate the ability of each faculty to attract the housing supply in its neighbourhood.

Professionals have been classified according to their respective activities and subsequently interviewed to detect their location needs and behaviours. Professionals' demand has revealed to be very diversified as to (i) customer frequency (for example, business experts who continually receive brief visits have a preference for the accessibility and proximity of a parking area; on the other hand notaries who want prestigious offices prefer historical buildings) and (ii) space requirement (architects need large offices, while for a medicine specialist a couple of rooms can be enough). The survey about professionals ascertained also if these agents had changed residence and, if so, for which reasons. So it has been possible to map professionals' movements within the historical centre and to and from the same city of Siena (Fig. 2).

As in the case of tourism, the correlation between behaviour information and market database has led to establishing the role that both students and professionals play on price changes.

3 The Simulation and Its Impact on Real Estate

The model has been run starting with the 2003 real estate scenario and progressively modifying the initial parameters, during the iterations, in order to simulate the changes caused five years later by the ongoing trend, an increase in student population, and a tourism demand growth.

The first simulation has been applied to verify the market evolution, under the conditions that the bid remains constant during the five years and there is no emerging phenomenon.

The second simulation has been applied to verify the market evolution, under the conditions that university students double during the five years, while emerging phenomenon is the creation of four new university faculties. In this way it has been possible not only to evaluate the impact of student population on the real estate market but also to forecast the possible effects on some strategic city structures (contemporary museums, Chamber of Commerce, and two historical residential palaces).

The last simulation has been applied to verify the market evolution, under the conditions that tourism demand increases by 100%, while the emerging phenomenon is the business of "vacation rental houses".
The outcomes are represented at the end of each paragraph.

3.1 Scenario 1. The Consolidation of the Historical Trend

This simulation foresees only minor developments in the housing market. In five model runs (each run represents one "real" year) no significant increases in housing prices or in the number of tertiary activities can be noticed.
The 2008 scenario shows only a fairly small increase in residential housing prices, with respect to the primary residential zones. The increase is diffusive: it stems from the foremost residential zones and slowly spreads to the outer areas.
The simulation predicts an increase of B&B only in the northern part of zone A, where the building value decreases. Zone A is most suitable for professionals and activities requiring prestigious locations. For these reasons, a progressive specialization of this area in professional tertiary sector can be expected.
A significant increase in B&B activity in Zone B occurs in the first year, but with a progressive, even if slow, decrease after the second year (2005).
All in all, the model foresees a global price increase of low and average residential buildings, while the market of luxury residences becomes steadier year after year, with only minimal variations.

3.2 Scenario 2. The City Centre Specialises into a University District

In this simulation, has been hypothesized an annual average increase of 20% in the student population from 2003 to 2008. At the first run, a notable increase in prices of every housing category can be recognized, moving towards Piazza del Campo. This site assumes the role of a major attractor, a sort of merging point of the effects of local increases.
The price increase is most evident in Zone B. In fact, over a two-year time, average and low prices disappear and reach the higher level. Also Zone C undergoes a similar change (although not as intense as Zone B), especially in areas, which are close to the university faculties. The student component, in other words, takes on a protagonist role in the housing market.
If such an increase should occur, it would create a situation of economic disadvantage for the University of Siena. Highest housing prices would induce student depopulation with a decrease in University enrolments: many students would probably transfer to university cities with lower costs, affecting ultimately the city economy and image.

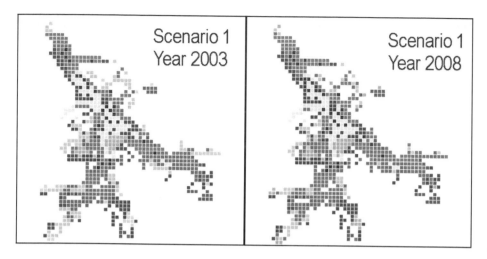

Fig. 3. Scenario 1: Consolidation of the historical market trend.

Luxury Class	Office
High Class	B&B
Average Class	Parking Lot
Low Class	Duomo & P.Campo
University Faculty	

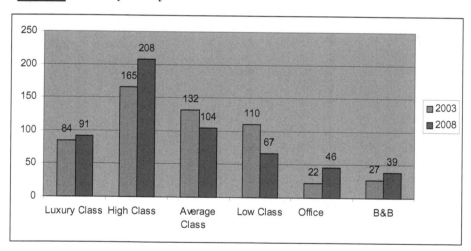

Graph 1. Scenario 1. Share of land-use (Population in 2003 and 2008).

3.3 Scenario 3. The City Centre Specialises into a Tourism District

The outcome of this scenario shows that prices increase throughout the city. In addition, the number of vacation rental houses rises, especially in Zone B, inducing a

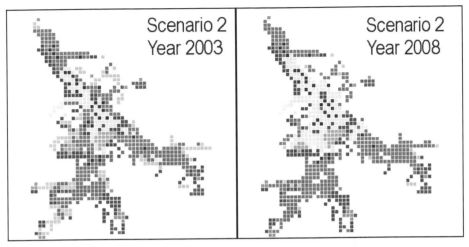

Fig. 4. Scenario 2: Increase in student population.

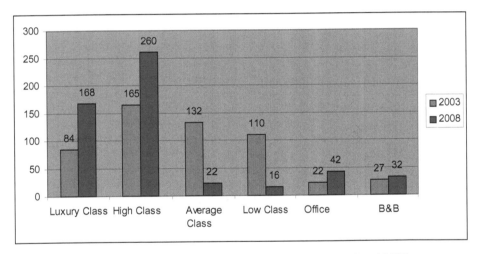

Graph 2. Scenario 2. Share of land-use (Population in 2003 and 2008).

consistent rise in the buildings values. Average and low prices reach those of the higher residential classes. B&B development does not slow down in the five years, so that market saturation can be envisaged. These hypotheses are confirmed by the rapid increase of vacation rental houses. Such phenomena foster the price increase, both at local and global level. The results are similar to those of the second scenario, the only difference being that in Zone C, all prices reach a higher level.

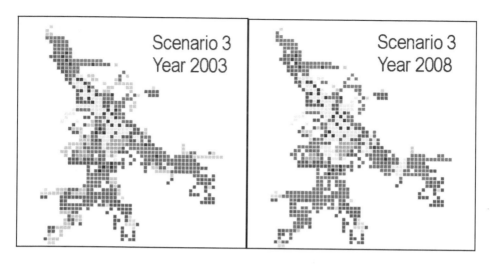

Fig. 5. Scenario 3: Increase in tourist population.

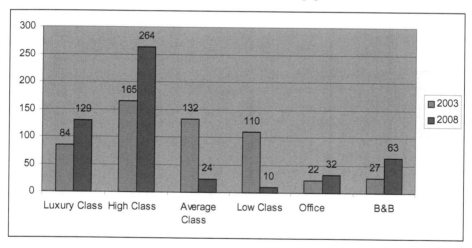

Graph 3. Scenario 3. Share of land-use (Population in 2003 and 2008).

4 Conclusion

The multi-agent analysis of interactions among actors within the real estate market system, has confirmed to be an extremely effective way to simulate the evolutionary dynamics of the housing market.

Direct and first-hand information from the actual market agents have allowed discovering the rationale of their daily decisions. In this way, a systemic knowledge of the agents' "modus operandi" within the system has been attained. On this base it has been possible not only to rationally simulate the evolution scenarios, but also to light up some market dynamics, which had remained in shadow using traditional economic analysis.

Moreover, the simulation of the effects that an emerging or sudden phenomenon might have in the system can be of proper help in generating appropriate strategies for urban planning.

References

Aretze, T.A, Timmermans H.J.P., (2002).Modelling agglomeration forces in urban dynamics: a multiagent   system   approach.   Architecture   and   Urban   Planning.   7th   International Conference on Design & Decision Support Systems.

Camagni, R., (1992). Economia Urbana: principi e modelli teorici. Edz. Nis., Milan

Cavezzali, A., Rabino, G., (2003). Sistemi multiagente e territorio: concetti, metodi e problematiche. In: Input 2003. Papers of 3th National Conference on Computing and Urban Planning, Pisa.

Cecchini, A., Rinaldi, E., (1999). The multi–cellular automaton: a tool to build more sophisticated models. A theoretical foundation and a practical implementation. Proceedings ESIT, Creta.

Cecchini, A., Rizzi, P., (2001). "The reasons why cellular automata are a useful tool in the working-kit for the new millennium urban planner in governing the territory." CUPUM 2001 Proceedings Honolulu.

Deadman, P., (2002). Multi-Agent Systems for the Simulation of Land-Use and Land-Cover Change: A Review. Forthcoming, Annals of the Association of American Geographers.

Gutowitz, H.A., Langton, C., (1988). "Methods for designing Cellular Automata with "Interesting" Behavior". CNLS News Letter. University of Santa Fe press.

Huriot, J.M., Thissie, J.F., (2002). Economics of cities: Theoretical perspectives. Cambridge University Press.

Koomen, E., Burman, JJG., (2002). Economic Theory and Land Prices in Land Use Modeling. In: Papers of 5th AGILE Conference on Geographic Information Science, (Palma Balearic Islands, Spain).

Kurz, H. D., (1999). From classical rent theory to marginal productivity theory: the works of F. B. W. Hermann and J. H. von Thünen.   In: Routledge frontiers of political economy. London: Routledge. p. 145-164.

Lombardo, S. , Petri, M., Zotta, D., (2003). Un approccio multiagente alla simulazione dell'evoluzione delle attività urbane. Alcune sperimentazioni. In: Input 2003. Papers of 3th National Conference on Computing and Urban Planning, Pisa.

Sosa, R., Gero, J.S., (2002). Computational models of creative situations: Towards multi-agent modelling of creativity and innovation in design. Key Centre of Design Computing and Cognition. University of Sydney Press.

On the Omni-directional Emergence of Form in Computation

J.F. Nystrom

University of Akureyri**
IS-602 Akureyri, Iceland
jamesn@unak.is

Abstract. I argue for the use of a specific type of grid and computational style for computational simulation that utilize emergence to produce results that would resemble physical phenomena. Two case studies are presented that highlight the advantages of a grid organization that utilizes tetrahedra and octahedra. Future work in this area is described and this overall computational vision is examined.

1 Introduction

The idea of emergence has a long history in computer science, going back at least to Von Neumann (see, for example, [1]), and reaching a crescendo of sorts in the early 1990's[2]. I assume emergence (e.g., "... emergence occurs when low-level rules generate high-level features"[3]) is one important mechanism for computational simulation, and suggest now that geometrical arrangement is another. The idea that geometrical arrangement is important is of course an idea going back at least to Plato, and has been used more recently to explain the structure of both atomic crystals and DNA.

Herein I make extensive use of the Isotropic Vector Matrix (IVM) grid. Figure 1 shows a small IVM grid containing 55 vertices. I adopt R. Buckminster Fuller's[4] use of the term *omni-directional* when referring to operators that utilize this specific geometrical arrangement of vertices.

I present two case studies highlighting the importance of the geometrical arrangement of vertices in computational simulation. Both case studies utilize the IVM arrangement of vertices. Section II gives an overview of the IVMCEM method[5,6] – a fully discrete computational electromagnetic time-domain solver. Section III gives an overview of a statistical mechanical calculation that utilizes a subset of the IVM arrangement of vertices to produce an exact renormalization group calculation[7] on a two-dimensional tetrahedral fractal. Section IV returns to the topic of emergence in computational simulation, extending the arguments presented in [8] and updating the *computational cosmography* (CC) vision. Therein, we find that the CC gestalt looks ahead and advocates the use of form and structure in computational simulations. The Discussion reiterates the importance of geometrical arrangement and extols the virtue of using emergence for computational simulation that purports to model physical phenomena.

** Formally at Texas A&M University - Corpus Christi.

P.M.A. Sloot, B. Chopard, and A.G. Hoekstra (Eds.): ACRI 2004, LNCS 3305, pp. 632–641, 2004.
© Springer-Verlag Berlin Heidelberg 2004

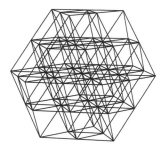

Fig. 1. A small IVM grid of 55 vertices.

2   An Omni-directional Curl Operator

In this section I describe the vector equilibrium (VE) cell and the IVMCEM method. The basic methodology is presented, and I provide comments on IVM grid building and the propagation of electromagnetic solutions within an IVM grid. I also compare the IVMCEM method to a cellular automata (CA). (Note that the IVM grid utilizes the same arrangement of vertices as that found in a face-centered cubic lattice.)

2.1   Methodology Overview

The basic cell of the IVM grid is the VE (which is also known as a *cuboctahedron*). Figure 2 shows the VE cell and the IVM basis vectors: $\mathbf{e}_1$ - $\mathbf{e}_6$. To build an IVM grid, start with a VE and then make the exterior vertices of the VE the center of a new VE cell. We can continue to add new VEs to the outer shell to create very large IVM grids. On inspection, one can see that the VE cell is composed of eight tetrahedra and six one-half octahedra. The twelve exterior vertices of the VE cell form four inter-penetrating hexagonal planes.

The spatial methodology I employ decomposes a vector field into six components at every node within an associated IVM grid, and provides an algorithm whereby the vector calculus curl is obtained. I now refer to this curl algorithm as the *omni-directional curl operator*. In [5,6] it is shown how to calculate the omni-directional curl operator and how to employ the operator for the spatial operations of the IVMCEM method.

In the IVMCEM method, all vector fields are expressed in terms of the basis vectors $\mathbf{e}_1$ - $\mathbf{e}_6$. For example, a vector field $\mathbf{S}$ is written thusly:

$$\mathbf{S} = S_1\mathbf{e}_1 + S_2\mathbf{e}_2 + S_3\mathbf{e}_3 + S_4\mathbf{e}_4 + S_5\mathbf{e}_5 + S_6\mathbf{e}_6 \ .$$

Now, for the four internal hexagonal planes of the VE cell, let a', b', c', and d' be *plane variables* (each evaluated as contour integrals around one of the four hexagonal planes of the VE). The omni-directional curl operator then gives

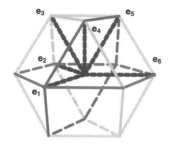

Fig. 2. VE and the IVM basis vectors $\mathbf{e}_1$ - $\mathbf{e}_6$.

$\mathbf{S} = \nabla \times \mathbf{T}$ as[5]:

$$S_1 = (c' + d')/4 , \qquad S_2 = (b' - d')/4 , \tag{1}$$
$$S_3 = (a' + b')/4 , \qquad S_4 = (a' + d')/4 ,$$
$$S_5 = (a' - c')/4 , \qquad S_6 = (-b' - c')/4 ,$$

where it is understood that the plane variables are functions of the vector field $\mathbf{T}$. For example, the plane variable a' is calculated thusly[5]:

$$a' = \frac{\sqrt{3}}{\sqrt{2}\, dA} \, [\oint \mathbf{T} \cdot d\mathbf{l}]_a .$$

From (1), we see that each vector component of $\mathbf{S}$ depends on the contour integrals around two separate hexagonal planes. Figure 3 shows the two hexagonal planes that are used to calculate the S_3 component of the curl ($\nabla \times \mathbf{T}$).

2.2   Electromagnetic Propagation Using the IVMCEM

The IVMCEM method is a fully-discrete time-domain computational electromagnetic solver which utilizes a Runge-Kutta fourth-order integrator to advance

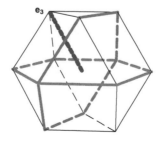

Fig. 3. The $\mathbf{a}$ and $\mathbf{b}$ planes interact to beget the S_3 component of $\mathbf{S}$.

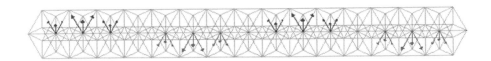

Fig. 4. E-field of TEM wave as traveling tetrahedron.

the electromagnetic solution in time. For initial testing of the IVMCEM method, I model the propagation of a transverse electromagnetic solution discretely in the time domain. I use the Maxwell equations written in terms of the electric field **E** and the magnetic flux density **B** (shown here in SI units for free space propagation):

$$\frac{\partial \mathbf{E}}{\partial t} = c^2 \nabla \times \mathbf{B}, \qquad\qquad \frac{\partial \mathbf{B}}{\partial t} = -\nabla \times \mathbf{E}.$$

For what follows, I seed an IVM grid with the following solution[6]:

$$\mathbf{E} = \mathbf{a}_z \sin(k\,y), \quad \text{and } \mathbf{B} = \mathbf{a}_x \frac{\sin(k\,y)}{c},$$

where $k = 2\pi f/c$ is the wavenumber, f is the frequency, and c is the speed of propagation. Further, I model the frequency at 8 points per wavelength. Figure 4 shows a plot of the **E**-field after it has traveled two wavelengths in a simulation of the wave propagating within an IVM grid[9]. The resulting **E**-field is z-directed; however Fig. 4 shows the vector components equally valued for three of the six IVM basis vector components. By construction, the **E**-field in this simulation is a traveling tetrahedron, oscillating positive and negative

2.3 IVMCEM as Cellular Automata

A CA is a calculation with solution variables located at vertices, and associated rules which advance the solution in time. Typically the rules for a CA base the future value of a solution on the current value and other values in a local neighborhood. With this being the case, we see that the IVMCEM is a CA. The solution, representing the **E**-field and **B**-field, is comprised of 12 real-valued quantities located at each vertex of the IVM. The rules for advancing the solution in time are local rules based on current values and values in a local neighborhood.

3 The Tetrahedral Fractal

The tetrahedral fractal in Fig. 5 is a two-dimensional fractal. The vertices of the fractal can be oriented as to coincide with a subset of the vertices of an IVM. In the remainder of this section I briefly describe an exact two-dimensional Real-Space Renormalization Group (RSRG) calculation[7] that uses this geometry.

Fig. 5. The two-dimensional tetrahedral fractal.

This RSRG calculation is an Ising model calculation with binary spin variables placed at the vertices of the fractal. The orientation of spin variables, $s1 - s10$, is shown in Fig. 6. The spin couplings are shown in Table 1. The Hamiltonian for the base tetrahedron, with spins $s1 - s4$ only, is given as[7]:

$$
\begin{aligned}
-\beta H = {} & 2\,k_0 + m\,(s1s2s3s4) \\
& + k\,(s1s2 + s1s3 + s1s4 + s2s3 + s2s4 + s3s4) \\
& + h\,(1/2)\,(s1 + s2 + s3 + s4) \\
& + p\,(s1s2s3 + s1s2s4 + s1s3s4 + s2s3s4)\ .
\end{aligned}
\tag{2}
$$

A Hamiltonian for the complete fractal (Fig. 6) is given in [7]. The partition functions for the base tetrahedron and the complete fractal are functions of the (respective) Hamiltonians.

Let Z_N be the partition function, and $f_s = (1/N)\ln Z_N$ be the free energy per spin. The magnetization, $\partial f_s/\partial h$, is shown in Fig. 7. Magnetism is the most studied example of *critical behavior*. Here we say that long-range order emerges from local interactions. Thus, magnetism is viewed as an emergent phenomena.

The RSRG calculation is an equilibrium calculation, independent of time, thus we are not concerned with the spin variables in time, but rather the renormalization of the spin couplings. During the calculation of the partition functions we trace over all possible spin configurations, in essence providing a transform from spin space to rule space. The RSRG can thus be viewed as a computation in the *rule space* of the tetrahedral gasket.

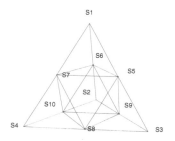

Fig. 6. Spin variables for the tetrahedral fractal.

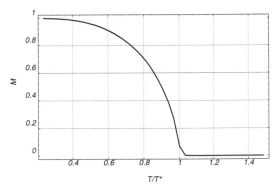

Fig. 7. Magnetization of the tetrahedral gasket.

4   Towards a Computational Cosmography

Cosmography is "the science that deals with the constitution of the whole order of nature" (according to Webster's New Collegiate Dictionary). CC is a computational vision which utilizes emergence and the geometrical system described in Fuller's synergetic geometry to produce simulations whose higher-level behaviors resemble physical phenomena, and whose lower-level interactions are intended to help us understand this Universe better. The remainder of this section will discuss further the IVM geometry and give an overview of the CC.

4.1   Geometrical Basics

I start now with the tetrahedron. If we connect the (neighboring) midpoints of the edges of the tetrahedron, we outline an octahedron (embedded inside the tetrahedron). (This relationship between the tetrahedron and octahedron is the basis for the tetrahedral fractal (§3).) If we connect the midpoints of the edges of the octahedron, we outline a VE (embedded inside the octahedron). This process which takes us from tetrahedron to vector equilibrium is shown in Fig. 8. Another relationship between tetrahedron and the VE is found in the fact

Table 1. Interaction couplings for the tetrahedral fractal.

Coupling	Explanation
k_0	A zero-spin coupling
h	A single-spin (field) coupling
k	A two-spin (nearest neighbor) coupling
p	A three-spin (triangular) coupling
m	A four-spin (tetrahedral) coupling

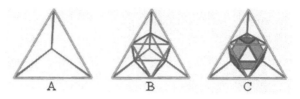

Fig. 8. Finding the vector equilibrium inside the tetrahedron. (Courtesy of R.W. Gray.)

that the IVM basis vectors (of the VE), shown in Fig. 2, are just the six vectors (or edges) of the tetrahedron.

Analysis of the tetrahedron and octahedron finds that there are two geometrical *modules*, the A-module and B-module, each with $1/24^{th}$ the volume of a tetrahedron, that can be used to build up many of the common geometrical forms. It was found that any space-filling polyhedron must in fact have a ratio of 2 A-modules for every 1 B-module. Figure 9 shows A-modules and a B-module as defined inside a tetrahedron and octahedron, respectively. Two A-modules and one B-module combine to form the minimum space-filler, the so-called *mite*.

Potentially, these geometric modules could act as the *atoms* for a geometry; thus answering a query offered in [10]:

> ... the physics of this century has shown us that matter has constituents and the three-dimensional objects we perceive as solids in fact have a discrete underlying structure. The continuum description of matter is an approximation which succeeds brilliantly in the macroscopic regime, but fails hopelessly at the atomic scale. It is therefore natural to ask if the same is true for geometry. Does geometry also have constituents at the Planck scale? What are its atoms? Its elementary excitations? Is the spacetime continuum only a 'coarse-grained' approximation? If so, what is the nature of the underlying quantum geometry.

In a CC computation[1], polyhedra aggregates will act as the *big bits*[11] upon which some of the low-level rules of the simulation act. The big bits will flow, deform, and transform within an active lattice system. Here the big bits may look like particles in a lattice gas automata. The lattice system is based around the geometry of the VE. The chords of the lattice however can take on values representing tensional qualities (used to simulate gravity) and electromagnetic quantities. Here then the background lattice system can be viewed as a type of CA. However, the background lattice of the CC is not a globally fiducial quantity, in that each local VE of the overall IVM-type lattice should be allowed to *jitterbug*[4] slightly. (A sample jitterbug is shown in Fig. 10. Here the eight exterior triangular faces of the VE rotate, passing through an icosahedra phase, to form an octahedron. From the octahedron, the jitterbug can also be maneuvered into a tetrahedron[4].)

---

[1] Although inspired by ideas associated with cellular and lattice gas automata, the CC does not fit snuggly into either category of simulation technique.

Fig. 9. A-modules and B-module combine to form a *mite*. (Courtesy of R. Hawkins.)

4.2 Computational Cosmographical Interplay of Space and Matter

Both the background lattice system and the big bits (or polyhedra aggregates) of a CC computation have restrictions on form resulting from identical embryonic geometrical considerations. It is from the omni-directional lattice system that the form for all entities of a CC computation emerge. The interplay between the big bits and the lattice system creates the need for an active lattice background system, and was described in [8] thusly:

> In this way, we find the lattice tells polyhedra aggregates how to transform, while the polyhedra aggregates in turn tell the lattice how to tense.

The lattice sites can use jitterbug activity to support this interplay. During this interplay, an overall lattice tensegrity will be maintained[8] (and in turn this lattice tensegrity is used as a mechanism for gravity in a CC computation).

Note that when a base VE around a lattice point jitterbugs, we require a virtual VE to be created at each exterior node of the base VE in order to maintain a connected lattice system. As a result of this virtual VE creation, the computational "space" will expand around any lattice point whose base VE jitterbugs. (Here then space expands from with-everywhere [sic].) I contend that this space expansion technique could be a model for what is currently being called *dark energy*. (Dark energy is the physicists term for the mysterious force that seems to be causing the Universe to expand.)

Fig. 10. Jitterbug from VE to octahedron. (Courtesy of R.W. Gray.)

5 Discussion

Herein the premise has been that both emergence and geometrical arrangement are important when constructing a computer simulation that is to model physical phenomena. In this Discussion I examine these premises further, and suggest that a paradigm shift is upon us as it concerns the potential purpose of future computational simulation endeavors.

5.1 Emergence and Geometrical Arrangement

When creating computer simulation, we may be able to learn more about the phenomena being simulated when the phenomena *emerges* in our computation as a result of low-level interactions (if in fact we are able to identify physical significance to the low-level rules). The statistical mechanical calculation in §3 has just such a feature. What we learn from this computation is that magnetism (a high-level feature) emerges from low-level spin interactions. The phenomena that emerges from the low-level rules (which represent spatial and temporal considerations) of the IVMCEM is an accurate representation of macroscopic electromagnetic propagation. Also emerging, as Figure 4 suggests, is the fact that electromagnetic phenomena can indeed exhibit geometric form[8,12]. (That is, the E-field can literally be viewed here as a traveling tetrahedron.)

In the CC vision, I have outlined an interplay between two dynamical pieces of the computation (i.e., the big bits and the active lattice system). We find that from this interplay, we have an emergent spatial expansion, and in this way we can view our CC dark energy as an emergent phenomena[2] resulting from the overall interplay of space and matter in a CC computation.

5.2 Spy Versus Spy

The advance in computational power, currently conforming to Moore's Law for both system performance and simulation size (see, for example, [13], and the references therein), provides an opportunity to fundamentally change our scientific focus. We no longer need be satisfied with only simulating "what" is occurring, but rather now have the opportunity to start to build simulation strategies that can teach us about "how" a particular phenomena occurs (if we are willing to *listen to what the computation has to say*).

The CC vision is all about the "how" of Universe; and is trying to uncover mechanism using the first principles of emergence and geometrical arrangement. For example, above I suggested a "how" for dark energy, and now I can contend that this overall CC interplay, involving an active lattice, may also easily explain the "how" of momentum conservation. Whatever phenomena we want to understand further, more insight will be provided if our computations emerge said phenomena rather than programming it directly.

---

[2] There may be another level of emergent phenomena acting here also. The zero point, or so-called vacuum energy may indeed be the mechanism that drives the lattice jitterbugs. But perhaps this topic is best left to a coffee house discussion.

Acknowledgment. A portion of this work was funded by a United States of America National Science Foundation grant # NSF MII 03-30822 while the author was at Texas A&M University - Corpus Christi, Corpus Christi, TX 78412 USA.

References

1. Burks, A.W., Editor. 1970. *Essays on Cellular Automata*. Urbana, IL: University of Illinois Press.
2. Forrest, S., Editor. 1991. *Emergent Computation*. Cambridge, MA: MIT Press.
3. Stewart, I. and J. Cohen. 1997. *Figments of Reality*. Cambridge, UK: Cambridge University Press.
4. Fuller, R.B. 1975. *Synergetics*. New York, NY: Macmillan.
5. Nystrom, J.F. 2002. The isotropic vector field decomposition methodology. In Proceedings of *ACES 2002*, 257. Monterey, CA: The Applied Computational Electromagnetics Society.
6. Nystrom, J.F. 2003. Grid construction and boundary condition implementation for the isotropic vector field decomposition methodology. In Proceedings of *ACES 2003*, 745. Monterey, CA: The Applied Computational Electromagnetics Society.
7. Nystrom, J.F. 2000. An exact finite field renormalization group calculation on a two-dimensional fractal lattice. *International Journal of Modern Physics* C 11: 257.
8. Nystrom, J.F. 2001. Tensional computation: further musings on the computational cosmography. *Applied Mathematics and Computation* 120: 211.
9. The visualization codes used to create this figure were written by P.I. Wilson while working on a grant funded by the United States of America National Science Foundation grant # NSF MII 03-30822.
10. Ashtekar, A. and J. Lewandowski. 1997. Quantum theory of geometry: I. area operators. *Classical and Quantum Gravity* 14: 55.
11. Huyck, P.H. and N.W. Kremenak. 1980. *Design & Memory*. New York, NY: McGraw-Hill.
12. Nystrom, J.F. 2002. In search of a geometrical basis for the ubiquitous electromagnetic energy. In Proceedings of *PIERS 2002*, 95. Cambridge, MA: The Electromagnetics Academy.
13. Nystrom, J.F. 2003. Moore's law and the visualization of electromagnetic quanta. *PIERS 2003*, 167. Cambridge, MA: The Electromagnetics Academy.

A Flexible Automata Model for Disease Simulation

Shih Ching Fu and George Milne

School of Computer Science & Software Engineering
The University of Western Australia
35 Stirling Highway, Crawley, 6009, WA, Australia
{scfu, george}@csse.uwa.edu.au

Abstract. This paper presents an approach for capturing the behaviour of disease spread in a tractable model. More specifically, by embedding spatial population information into the cells of a cellular automaton, accurate representations of disease spread may be produced. Non-homogeneity is easily introduced into the implicitly discretized landscape of a cellular automaton, contributing to the accuracy of such models and overcoming some of the simplifying assumptions of homogeneity found in earlier models. The need to develop and test more effective disease containment measures inspires the search for new and more accurate models.

1 Introduction

As stated by Ferguson [1], mathematical modelling is the only way to analyse the effectiveness of different disease control strategies. Simulation is the obvious choice since real life experimentation is impractical. An epidemic spread model that provides life-like results and reconfigurable parameters is an invaluable tool for use in developing outbreak contingency plans. Given the costs of outbreaks as foot-and-mouth disease (FMD) in the United Kingdom [2,3], it is desirable to know beforehand whether vaccination or culling interventions are worthwhile.

There have been four recent studies of the spread dynamics of the smallpox virus [1]. Each study set out to determine the best containment strategy for smallpox. Unfortunately, rather than providing a definitive answer, each study recommended a different policy for optimally controlling such outbreaks. This suggests that more research needs to be directed into the field of epidemic modelling and that there may be no general all-purpose containment strategy, rather distinct outbreaks need tailored policies. Virtual simulation of outbreaks therefore provide a practical means to discover and refine these policies. Of particular interest are disease spread models that capture host mobility, spatial population heterogeneity as well as disease biology.

Most existing epidemic models, particularly those using ordinary differential equations (ODEs) assume the host landscape is homogeneous [4]. That is, hosts are taken to be distributed evenly throughout the landscape and mixed in well with one another. This is a major oversight since hosts are rarely found to be

P.M.A. Sloot, B. Chopard, and A.G. Hoekstra (Eds.): ACRI 2004, LNCS 3305, pp. 642–649, 2004.
© Springer-Verlag Berlin Heidelberg 2004

equidistantly spaced and unmoving. Partial differential equation models introduce diffusion terms to model heterogeneous mixing but still treat populations as continuous entities rather than comprising discrete interacting hosts. There is need for models which take into account the spatial conditions of a landscape to improve model accuracy. It is therefore claimed that by using a discretized approach, such as a cellular automaton, we can capture both the local interactions of hosts and the effects of a heterogeneous population landscape into a single more realistic disease spread model.

2   Our Model

The main focus of our model is to capture the effects of geography on an epidemic's emergent behaviour. Of particular interest is the uneven distribution of hosts over the landscape caused by topographic and demographic heterogeneity. In this section, we discuss how we have encoded this heterogeneity into an automaton's cells so as to build a model that more closely reflects nature. We have adopted the widely used SIR framework to describe the disease state of host individuals [5]. In this framework, hosts are designated susceptible, infective, or recovered depending on whether they are healthy, diseased, or immune respectively.

2.1   Cell Definition

In contrast to traditional CA, our model allows each cell to accommodate a variable number of hosts rather than just one static host. This structure is similar to that found in lattice-gas cellular automata [6]. Consequently, the state of each cell is completely defined by its number of susceptible, infective, and recovered hosts. Each cell has another parameter, a maximum *carrying capacity*, which denotes the maximum number of hosts a cell can contain. The landscape is therefore discretized into equal-sized cells whose populations and carrying capacities may vary differentially from cell to cell. The local population density is therefore defined as a cell's population divided by its carrying capacity.

By encoding cell population densities into the cell definition we can use this information to modulate the rate of spread to neighbouring cells. Note that disease spread can be due to both direct disease transmission at cell boundaries and through increased infective host movement between cells. Our CA based model captures both disease and host dynamics.

As implied by the above description, the number of hosts in a particular cell can vary with time; the carrying capacity however, remains constant. Increases and decreases in local cell population which correspond to births, deaths, and movement of hosts over the landscape are also included in the model. Although it is possible to have differing population densities with a neighbourhood of cells, it is assumed that within each cell, the population is well-mixed. That is, during each time step, all the hosts sharing a particular cell will come into contact at least once.

The carrying capacity of a cell is used as a mechanism to limit the movement of hosts between cells. Overcrowding is prevented since the number of newborns per epoch, discussed later, is conditional on a cell not exceeding its carrying capacity. Although the effect of the land's carrying capacity is not directly enforced in nature, carrying capacities are a straightforward way to encourage or discourage the motion of individuals between cells.

The cells are tessellated in a square grid with straight, non-penetrable boundaries. These boundaries are likened to physical boundaries found in nature such as oceans or mountain ranges, or political boundaries over which hosts can 'immigrate' out of the landscape in question. The immigration and emigration of hosts is combined with the increases and decreases in host populations determined by birth and death probability parameters. Such births and deaths are completely independent of disease related parameters such as pathogen morbidity and affect susceptible, infective, and recovered hosts alike. It is assumed that there is no vertical *vectoring* of disease, that is, parents do not pass the disease directly to their offspring at birth.

Our model also uses two distinct neighbourhood radii for host and pathogen movement respectively; both are 8-connected Moore neighbourhoods. In our model, the two ways a cell can become contaminated are if an infective host moves in from an adjacent cell, or the pathogen, by its own spread mechanisms outside a carrier, infects a formerly susceptible host. In this way, we have modelled two kinds of heterogeneity: the spatial heterogeneity of the population due to host movement, and also the biological heterogeneity due to variations in disease presence among hosts.

2.2   Epidemic Spread Parameters

As discussed previously, there are two kinds of epidemic spread factors that we have incorporated into our model: those related to the disease pathogen, and those related to host demographics. Disease parameters include infectiousness, morbidity, and immunity; demographic parameters include population density and host movement. These parameters have featured separately in some earlier epidemic studies [7,8], but we have aimed to capture several key aspects of disease spread into one composite model.

2.3   Cell Update Algorithm

Similar to the LGCA model proposed by Fukś and Lawniczak [6], the cell update algorithm is performed in two phases: the infection phase and the randomization phase. On a cell-by-cell basis, the encoded data relating to factors such as morbidity, mobility, contagiousness, and immunity is used to update the SIR characteristics of the CA lattice. Interleaved between the infection phases are randomization phases which model the movement of hosts between CA cells. Such movement is limited by the size of the CA interaction neighbourhood and cell carrying capacities. The interaction neighbourhood can be of any configuration; we have chosen the traditional 8-connected Moore neighbourhood. Specific information about the interactions between cells, such as cyclic host movement, can be very easily encoded as different interaction neighbourhood [9]. Therefore in contrast to the uniform mixing found in ODE models, we can model localized host movement.

Currently, our model does not take into account other parameters such as latency or incubation time [10]. Latency is the lag between being infected and becoming infective, and incubation is the delay between becoming infected and becoming symptomatic. These times can be implemented by introducing further states, say 'E', to represent those hosts exposed and infected with the pathogen but not yet infective or transmissive. Including this or other states into our model is straightforward since such a change implemented by simply modifying the finite state automata populating the CA lattice.

3   Experimental Scenarios

In this section we describe two experimental scenarios and examine some of the results that our composite epidemic model produced under simulation. The purpose of these scenarios is to show how a cellular automata approach can be used to accurately simulate disease spread, needing only to define localized cell interactions. It is also interesting that due to the intrinsically graphical nature of cellular automata, no further processing of results is needed in order to visualize the resultant disease spread patterns.

3.1   Corridors of Spread

This experiment tries to emulate a real life landscape with imaginary town centres and transport links. Towns and roads are human constructed features and attract high and patterned population densities. Of particular significance is that rather than having flat and uniform population density profiles, settlements around cultural features generally have a directed or linear shape.

In this scenario, each cell has been initialized to have a carrying capacity of 1000, with three 'towns' set to this maximum. Two of these towns, on in the northwest and another in the southeast, start with a 1:9 infective to susceptible ratio. There are also 'transport links' comprising a dense line of susceptibles running between each of the 'towns'. Cells on this line have an initial susceptible population of 100, whilst the cells on either side have an initial susceptible population of 75. The rest of the landscape comprises cells with 10 susceptibles in them. The town in the southwest corner contains 1000 susceptibles and no infectives.

Parameter settings. The primary aim of this scenario is to highlight the fact that disease spread generally occurs faster in regions of high host density. Consequently, to isolate the effects of the heterogeneous landscape, host movement is turned off for this scenario. This is done to preserve the population density profile for the duration of this experiment. The probability of transmission between hosts has been set to one. This means that there is 100% chance of a susceptible host becoming infective after sharing a cell with at least one infective host during a time step. This has been done to accelerate the rate of infection spread and magnify the effect of population density on epidemic dynamics for illustrative purposes.

Results. The results of executing our model with the above-mentioned parameters are presented in the time lag map shown in Fig. 1. The lag map is a series of snapshots taken at $t = 0, 20, 40, 60, 80,$
$100, 200, 300$. Each cell is represented by a square: black squares contain at least one infective host and white squares contain only susceptible and recovered hosts. Figure 1 shows the tendency of the epidemic to follow the lines of population density to produce the 'fuzzy cross' pattern.

After 300 epochs, the top left outbreak has reached all four edges of the map but the bottom right outbreak is yet to reach any. Notice that the epidemic spreads outward along the arms or 'roads' before filling up the space between the roads. This example illustrates how disease spreads over areas of higher population density more rapidly than unpopulated areas, as expected from knowledge of known disease spread. Consequently, we can conclude that we have satisfactorily modelled the relationship between propagation delay of a disease and local population density.

3.2   Barriers to Spread

This experimental scenario depicts how a CA model can used to simulate the effects barrier containment to control disease spread. As seen in the foot-and-mouth disease (FMD) epidemic in Great Britain during 2001, a key to slowing down disease spread is restricting host movement [11]. Culling of livestock to create barrier areas over which FMD cannot spread was the main eradication technique. These measures are simulated by incorporating 'no spread zones' in the initial state of the cellular automaton's lattice.

The starting distribution contains two 'hot spots' which have been segregated from the rest of the landscape. One hot spot has a four square wide barrier surrounding it, whilst the other has a one square wide barrier surrounding it. Barriers are implemented as cells with zero carrying capacity. In Fig. 2, barriers are represented by black squares and all other (blank) squares contain an equal number of hosts. The grey squares depict the two sources of infectives, both of which confined by 'buffers'. The barriers restrict host movement and provide no hosts for pathogens to infect and escape.

4   Conclusion

Accurate disease spread models are necessary for the testing of disease containment measures in the hope of reducing the economic and health impacts of disease outbreaks. We have presented an epidemic model which captures in

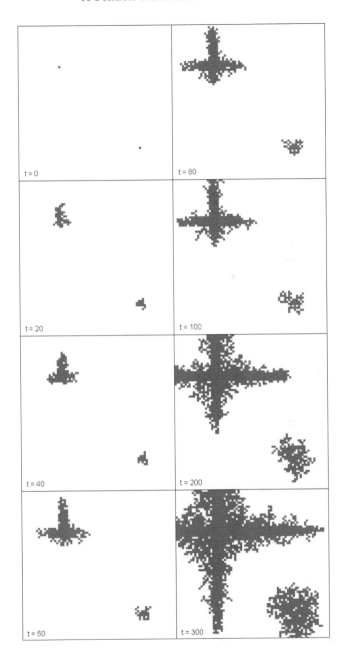

Fig. 1. A lag map showing the state of the epidemic at $t = 0, 20, 40, 60, 80, 100, 200, 300$. Notice that the outbreak to the north-west is able to cover a greater distance than the outbreak in the southeast because it has access to the road link and the population associated with that link. Notice that the spread from $t = 20$ in the top left of the map appears asymmetrical. This is probably an artifact of the stochastic nature of this model.

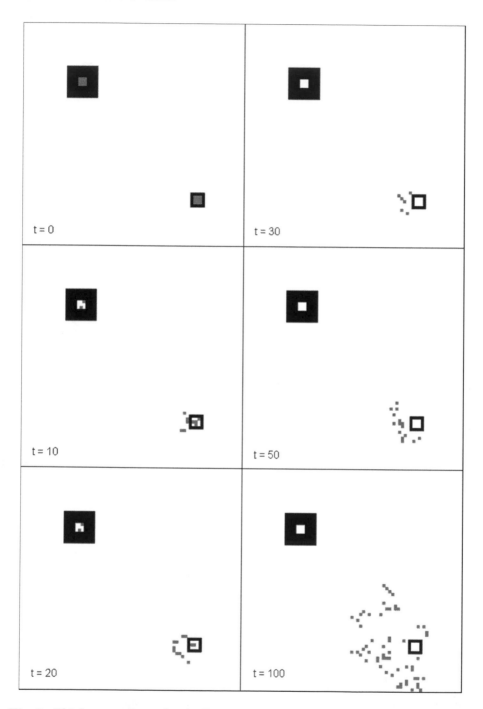

Fig. 2. This lag map shows that buffer zones that are too narrow provide no resistance to the spread of the pathogen.

a CA-like discrete framework, realistic patterns of disease spread. More specifically, a cellular automaton approach has been used to model discrete areas of landscape and non-homogeneous automata states are used to capture the effects of spatial heterogeneity. Such heterogeneity is due to variations in local population density compounded by host movements. Few existing models encode spatial heterogeneity into their mechanics; our approach shows promise for the development of accurate and tractable cellular automata based disease spread models suitable for simulation.

Two scenarios have been presented which demonstrate how a cellular automata model can be initialized with a specific configuration to run hypothetical "what if?" games. The first scenario demonstrated the successful encoding of population density effects into the epidemic model whereby disease spread is accelerated in areas of high density and slowed in sparsely populated regions. The second scenario depicts how our cellular automata model simulates the effectiveness of different disease containment strategies. These two scenarios have reproduced known patterns of spread, and thus contribute to determining the efficacy of a cellular automata modelling approach to disease spread.

References

1. Ferguson, N.M., Keeling, M.J., Edmunds, W.J., Gani, R., Grenfell, B.T., Anderson, R.M., Leach, S.: Planning for smallpox outbreaks. Nature **425** (2003) 681–685
2. Keeling, M.J., Woolhouse, M.E.J., Shaw, D.J., Matthews, L., Chase-Topping, M., Haydon, D.T., Cornell, S.J., Kappey, J., Wilesmith, J., Grenfell, B.T.: Dynamics of the 2001 uk foot and mouth epidemic: Stochastic dispersal in a heterogeneous landscape. Science **294** (2001) 813–817
3. Ferguson, N.M., Donnelly, C.A., Anderson, R.M.: The foot-and-mouth epidemic in great britain: Pattern of spread and impact of interventions. Science **292** (2001) 1155–1160
4. Mollison, D., ed.: Epidemic Models: Their Structure and Relation to Data. Cambridge University Press (1995)
5. Anderson, R.M., May, R.M.: Infectious diseases of humans: dynamics and control. Oxford University Press (1991)
6. Fukś, H., Lawniczak, A.T.: Individual based lattice model for spatial spread of epidemics. Discrete Dynamics in Nature and Society **6** (2001) 191–200
7. Boccara, N., Cheong, K.: Critical behaviour of a probablistic automata network SIS model for the spread of an infectious disease in a population of moving individuals. Journal of Physics A: Mathematical and General **26** (1993) 3707–3717
8. Boccara, N., Cheong, K., Oram, M.: A probabilistic automata network epidemic model with births and deaths exhibiting cyclic behaviour. Journal of Physics A: Mathematical and General **27** (199) 1585–1597
9. Ahmed, E., Elgazzar, A.S.: On some applications of cellular automata. Physica A **296** (2002) 529–538
10. Ahmed, E., Agiza, H.N.: On modeling epidemics. Including latency, incubation and variable susceptibility. Physica A **253** (1998) 347–352
11. Ferguson, N.M., Donnelly, C.A., Anderson, R.M.: Transmission intensity and impact of control policies on the foot and mouth epidemic in Great Britain. Nature **413** (2001) 542–548

A Novel Artificial Life Ecosystem Environment Model

Zhengyou Xia[1] and Yichuan Jiang[2]

[1] Department of computer, NanJing University of Aeronautics and Astronautics, China
zhengyou_xia@yahoo.com
[2] Department of Computing information & technology, Fudan University, China
jiangyichuan@yahoo.com.cn

Abstract. This paper presents information flow model and a novel artificial life grid model to construct artificial life computer ecosystem environment. The life grid model is a three-dimensional information space: (time, artificial life node, and location). The former two dimensions identify the contents or function of artificial life systems, and the third-dimension identifies the location where an artificial life system exists. We depart the artificial life node architecture into four levels: artificial life system application level, engine library level, sensor level, and the connectivity level. In information flow model, we present the ALife information definition, characteristic and four kinds of information communication mechanisms (broad-diffuse, Multi-diffuse, uni-diffuse and any-diffuse).

1 Introduction

Artificial life (ALife) [1] is not a unitary field, but includes several different research programs, which are defined as the following approach: self-reproduction and cellular automata [2][3][4], morph genesis and development processes [5][6], evolution and evolutionary computing [7][8], origins of life [9][10], biochemical synthesis [11][12] and artificial nucleotides [13], collective intelligence [14] and computational life [15][16]. Today, most artificial life models researches are based on technology of the agent [17][18], evolution system [19], neural network [20], Cognitive models [21][22], etc.

The origin of life is how complexity arose in the development of life and how one could construct an artistic interactive system that can model and simulate this emergence of complexity. Many ALife models are designed not to represent known biological systems but to generate wholly new and extremely simple instances of life-like phenomena. The system can show artificial life properties only if the system interacts with and access the information from an open artificial life computer ecosystem environment. The artificial life computer ecosystem environment is composed of different and numerous system nodes, which use the learning, cooperation and evolution mechanism to evolve the system.

Based on the idea that interaction and communication among different artificial life systems are the driving forces for the emergence of higher and more complex structures than its previous architecture. We could imagine an artificial life system

P.M.A. Sloot, B. Chopard, and A.G. Hoekstra (Eds.): ACRI 2004, LNCS 3305, pp. 650–659, 2004.

that can increase its internal complexity as more and more interactions with external artificial life computer ecosystem environment take place. However, nowadays there are few artificial life models that can satisfy these requirements, and there are few researches for constructing artificial life computer ecosystem environment. This paper presents a novel artificial life grid model to construct artificial life computer ecosystem environment, and introduce its construction principles, information flow model and communication mechanisms.

We hope the artificial life computer ecosystem environment based on artificial life grid model could approach the following goals:

1. Environments – We would not be selecting for particular high-level behaviors, but creating artificial life computer ecosystem environment and letting it evolve in any way it likes.
2. Demonstrate the emergence of intelligence in an artificial life system.
3. Learning methods: It is reasonable to assume that adding learning abilities to our artificial creatures can improve their ability to evolve complex behaviors in artificial life computer ecosystem environment based on artificial life grid.
4. The evolution of life is shown as a remarkable growth in complexity. Co-evolution is certainly a very promising technique for developing complex behaviors, especially where these behaviors take the form of a competition between two or more creatures in artificial life computer ecosystem environment based on artificial life grid.

2   The Notion of Artificial Life Grid

The term "Grid" was coined to denote a proposed distributed "cyber infrastructure" for advanced Science and engineering including computational [23], semantic [24] and knowledge grid [25]. A computational Grid forms a closed network of a large number of pooled resources providing standardized, reliable, specialized, and pervasive access to high-end computational resources .The emergence of Semantic Web [24] will result in an enormous of knowledge base (KB) resources distributed across the web. A knowledge grid [25] is a set of well-organized knowledge together with knowledge managements. Nowadays, the notion of grid has been extended. A grid can be computation, data, software, and even people, so a grid can be regarded as an integrated mechanism that enables control sharing of various kinds of resource, evolve among the different grid nodes and demonstrate the emergence of intelligence.

A general grid should have three characteristics:

1. The network ability, i.e. the ability to link the different grid nodes into a grid;
2. The inter-operability, i.e. the ability for any grid nodes participant to use any resources and rules to perform some tasks;
3. The emergence ability, i.e. the ability that grid is more than the sum of its parts (grid nodes).

We extend the notion of the general grid and give the definition of artificial life grid and artificial life computer ecosystem environment as the following.

Definition 1: An artificial life grid can be defined by the following three items:
1. A set of nodes is an artificial life grid, and the nodes can take the form of artificial life or, information transmission, and knowledge, etc.
2. A set (nodes, location) paring together with a set of communication mechanisms constitute a grid.
3. Any artificial life nodes can achieve the complex properties with the **time** using the evolve engine.

Definition 2: Artificial life computer ecosystem environment
1. The artificial life computer ecosystem environment is composed of different and numerous artificial life grid nodes (e.g. artificial life system).
2. Each artificial life grid node is external ecosystem environment in the eye of other artificial life grid nodes.

3   Architecture of Artificial Life Grid

An artificial life grid is a set of well-organized artificial life nodes together with a set of artificial life engine. The artificial life grid node will evolve into new and more complex or intelligent one with time goes in the artificial life computer ecosystem environment. According to the definition of artificial life grid in the above section, the artificial life grid is a three-dimensional information space: (time, artificial life node, and location). The former two dimensions identify contents or function of artificial life systems, and the third-dimension identifies the location that exists an artificial life system. The three dimensional space of artificial life grid is shown in Figure 1.

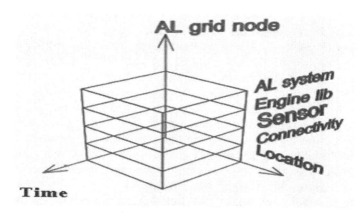

Fig. 1. Space of artificial life grid

Referring to the artificial life node dimension in figure1, we depart the artificial life node architecture into four levels from the high to low: artificial life system application level, engine library level, sensor level, and the connectivity level. The connectivity layer provides communication and authentication service needed to communicate with artificial life ecosystem environment. For example, when the one artificial life node A want to communicate with artificial life node B, the node A uses the connectivity level to authenticate and communicate with the artificial life node B. The function of the sensor level is to process information flow from artificial life computer ecosystem environment or send information flow from the node to artificial life computer ecosystem environment. According to different artificial life system, different rules or algorithms are included in the engine level library. For example, if the artificial life system has self-learning property, the learning rules based on genetics or stochastic search in combination with steepest descent is contained in the artificial life engine level of the artificial life grid. Artificial life system level is defined to the different application of artificial life system. In this layer, research could design the different artificial life application according to different requirement.

In the figure 2, we can see the interaction process between two artificial life grid nodes in artificial life computer ecosystem environment.

The architecture of an artificial life node is shown in the figure 3.

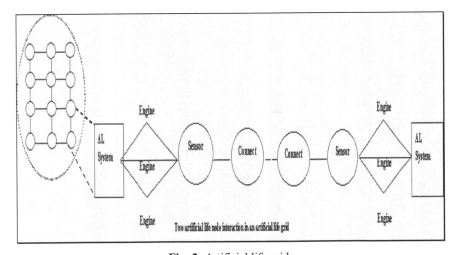

Fig. 2. Artificial life grids

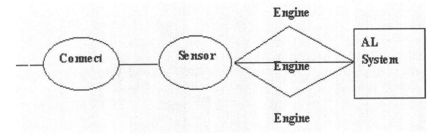

Fig. 3. An artificial life node architecture model

According to figure 3, eng_i denotes the i artificial life engines in the artificial life node. $S(t)$ means the sensor level process the information flow t that comes from external environment. Θ denotes that transmit the information flow coming sensor level to the engine lib level. $F()$ means the process of the artificial life system level. The mathematic model of single artificial life node is shown in equation 1.

$$node = F\left(\sum_{i=1}^{n} eng_i \Theta S(t)\right) \tag{1}$$

Let we consider one node is in the artificial life grid that is shown in figure 2, we can get the following mathematic model.

$$node_k = F\left(\sum_{i=1}^{n} eng_i \Theta S\left(\psi[\sum_{j=1,k=k}^{n} node_j(t)]\right)\right) \quad k \in (1...n) \tag{2}$$

$$\Psi\left[\sum_{j=1,j\neq k}^{n} node_j(t)\right], \text{ i.e. the inputting information flow of the k node from other}$$

n-1 nodes in the artificial life grid.

If we consider the variety of node's status or function along with time, we let $N_{(t+1,i)}$ be status of i node at t+1 time and $N_{(t,i)}$ be status of i node at t time. We can get the following equation.

$$N_{(t+1,i)} = N_{(t,i)} + \phi(\eta_{(t+1,i)}, d_{(t+1,i)}) \quad , (i:1\cdots n) \tag{3}$$

In equation 3, $\eta_{(t+1,i)}$ is information that node i searches in artificial life computer ecosystem environment at t +1 time. $d_{(t+1,i)}$ means node i uses engine to process the collecting information(e.g., it is that the creatures get information by using vision, smell, end feel, etc.) from the external computer ecosystem environment at t +1 time. $\phi(\eta_{(t+1,i)}, d_{(t+1,i)})$ denotes the i node will come into being variable status by using $d_{(t+1,i)}$ and $\eta_{(t+1,i)}$ at t+1 time.

We could get the following properties of artificial life grid from the equation 2 and equation 3.

1. Learning: in the equation 3, if the node uses the learning engine (e.g. $d_{(t+1,i)}$ is learning algorithms or rules), the node will demonstrate the self-learning property.

2. Evolving: similarly, in equation 3, the node uses the evolving engine (e.g. $d_{(t+1,i)}$ is evolving algorithms or rules), the node will develop the complex the system by self-evolving.

3. Emergence and complex: in the equation 2, the node will show the emergence and complex property through learning and evolution mechanisms, if there is enough numerous artificial life node in artificial life computer ecosystem environment.

4 Discussion

In the above section, we have presented the notion model and mathematic model for the artificial life grid. There are some open questions about the ALife grid in the following.

Security trust problems for different ALife systems: The connectivity layer of the artificial life grid may require some or all of the standard security functions, including authentication and authorization. Authentication is an action of securely identifying the user that is requesting a particular service or resource within an artificial life grid. Authentication is a process of verifying an identity of an entity. Usually it is based on public key cryptography that means that each entity presenting a request to ALife node has to have a public/private key pair and a public key certificate. The conception of authorization is access control that governs who may access what and what restrictions are to be placed on those accesses. Authorization is a very important problem in any secure environment. It is an area that governs authenticated entities may access what and what activities they can perform on a resource. There are three major properties of authorization: defining the access restriction types, the components to provide these restrictions and how to deploy these restrictions in the system.

ALife information flow representation: an artificial life information flow is process of artificial life information passing among the nodes in an artificial life grid. It has three crucial attributes: direction, content, and carrier, which respectively determine the sender and the receiver, the shareable life information content, and the media that can pass the content. The content of ALife flow can be described by several kinds: the basic information flow, the rule information flow, and method information flow. The basic information flow includes the basic resource, knowledge and some environment parameters. The rule information flow contains the basic rules and principles of information among the nodes (e.g. it takes form as IF condition THEN conclusion.). The method flow contains the problem-solving methods. The solution can be either a multi-step problem-solving process or simple a one-step solution (e.g. an algorithm).

ALife engine design: We could get different results, when the same artificial life system is implemented by the different ALife engines. The different rules and algorithms are included in the ALife engine Library. (E.g. the rules included evolve, inference, and classifier rules, etc. The algorithms included the Genetic algorithms, ant algorithms, resource search algorithms, and learning algorithm, etc.). An artificial life system may include many ALife engines. We propose that the many ALife engines in the artificial life node are contrived to the ALife engine stack (i.e. as network protocol stack in OS system). It is convenient to update, delete, extend ALife engine by using ALife engine stack method.

ALife system development: the ALife grid is the research platform model for artificial life science, especially for artificial life model at the software level. Since the ALife grid is composed of tremendous ALife nodes, the ALife grid can provide the open and complex artificial life environment for the different artificial life system. We consider that the following properties of artificial life model at software level can success and develop through the ALife grid.

1. Evolving: the artificial life grid is especially well suited for studying the dynamics of natural evolution, because the ALife Grid could provide the complex and extensible evolving environment for the evolving system. In an evolving system's environment can affect the complexity of the organisms that are evolving within the environment. The artificial life system cannot show the life properties, if the external complex environment to the ALife system does not exist. Therefore, we could called it " no complex environment, no complex evolving system."
2. Behavior: The behavior in ALife Grid means that the ALife systems exquisitely adapt to their environment. The behaviors in the ALife grid include social group behavior, combat and territoriality behaviors, etc.
3. Learning: when a particular action is taken, the ALife system in the ALife grid monitors what changes happen in the environment. It uses this information to learn correlations between particular conditions/action pairs and certain result. The research for the learning in ALife grid should include the action selection mechanism, learning method and exploration strategy.
4. Emergence: emergence of ALife is that the whole is more than the sum of its nodes. The ALife grid is compose of the infinite ALife nodes. These nodes create the life properties that are not likely to be produced by detached ALife node.

Standard interface and protocol for connectivity and sensor layer: From the ALife grid model architecture, the connectivity and sensor layer is independent to the ALife system. The interaction with environment is implemented on the two layers. Therefore, the standard interface and protocol for the two layers are very necessary task in our further research.

5   Artificial Life Information Flow Model

Information plays important roles in evolving system. We discuss the information flow definition, characteristic and transmission mechanisms in the artificial life computer ecosystem environment.

5.1   Definition and Characteristic of ALife Information Flow

Definition 1. An artificial life information flow (denoted as ALIF) is a process of artificial life information among the different ALife systems and ALife computer ecosystem environment, which is four dimensions space: content, carrier, direction, time, which respectively determines the information content among senders and receivers, the media that can pass the information content, the direction that the information flow are transferred, and the time that the information flow is generated.

We can use an arrow to denote the direction of an ALife information flow. The carrier can be based on liquid, solid, and gas, etc. In the artificial life computer ecosystem environment, the carrier is based on the network information form.

Definition 2. The field of ALIF is composed of information content field (CF), type field (TF), and timestamp field (SF), denoted as $<ALIF>=<TF, CF, SF>$, where $TF=<t|t$ is information type$>$, $CF=<c|c$ is information content$>$ and $SF=<s|s$ is timestamp of information flow$>$.

Characteristic. Let $<TF_1, CF_1, SF_1>$ and $<TF_2, CF_2, SF_2>$ be the field of ALife information flows $ALIF_1$ $ALIF_2$. We can get the following characteristics.

Union: $<TF_1, CF_1, SF_1> \cup <TF_2, CF_2, SF_2> = <TF_1 \cup TF_2, CF_1 \cup CF_2, SF_1 \cup SF_2>$

Split: An ALife flow can split into more ALife flows, denotes as

$$ALIF \Rightarrow ALIF_1 \cup ALIF_2 \cup ALIF_3 \cdots ALIF_n$$

Connection: two or more ALife information flows form one ALife information flow, denoted as $ALIF_1 \odot ALIF_2 \odot ALIF_3 \Rightarrow ALIF$.

5.2 Information Transmission

In the artificial life computer ecosystem environment, how to transfer information among the different artificial life systems is a very important research. In this paper, the information transmission is defined as the following four mechanisms.

1. **Definition 3 broad-diffuse**: it is communication mechanism that a single artificial life system (e.g. animal) sends information to all artificial life systems all at once, rather than making a separate communication to each artificial life system one at a time in the finite scope of the artificial life computer ecosystem environment.
2. **Definition 4 Multi-diffuse:** it is communication mode allowing multiple artificial life systems (e.g. animals) of the same colony to simultaneously receive the same transmission information or a single animal communicate with multiple animals of the same colony in the artificial life computer ecosystem environment.
3. **Definition 5 uni-diffuse:** it is communication between a single animal and a single animal in the artificial life computer ecosystem environment.
4. **Definition 6 any-diffuse:** it is communication between a animal sender and the nearest of several animal in narrow scope of artificial life computer ecosystem environment.

6 Conclusion

The complex self-organizing behavior of the Life would never have been discovered without the simulation of thousands of generations for millions of sites. The artificial life system cannot show the life properties, if the external complex environment to the ALife system does not exist. Therefore, We could called it " no complex environment, no complex evolving system." The system will show artificial life properties, only if the system can interact with an open and complex artificial life computer ecosystem environment and access the external information from it. In this paper, we present a novel artificial life grid model to construct artificial life computer ecosystem environment, which is a three-dimensional information space: (time, artificial life node, and location). The former two dimensions identify contents or function of artificial life systems, and the three-dimension identifies the location that exists an artificial life system. We depart the artificial life node architecture into four levels from the high to low: artificial life system application level, engine library level, sensor level, and the connectivity level. In information flow model, we present information flow definition and the four kinds of information communication mechanisms (broad-diffuse, Multi-diffuse, uni-diffuse and any-diffuse).

References

1. C.G. Langton, Artificial life, in Artificial life SFI studies in the sciences of complexity, vol.VI, edited by C.G. Langton,Addison-Wesley,1989.
2. J.von Neumann, Theory of self-Reproducing automata, Urbana, University Illinois presses.
3. C.G. Langton, Life at the edge of chaos, in artificial life II ,SFI studies in the sciences of complexity ,vol.//x, edited by V.G.Langton , E.Taylor,J.D.Farmer,S.Rasmussen,Addison-Wesley.
4. S. Wolfram, Theory and application of cellular automata,Singapore, world scientific,1986.
5. Lindenmayer, P. Prusinkiewicz, Developmental models of multicellular organisms, in artificial life, SFI studies in the sciences of complexity, vol. VI, edited by C.G.Langton, Addison-Wesley,1989.
6. R. Dawkins, The evolution of Evolvability, in artificial life, SFI studies in the sciences of complexity, vol. VI.edited by C.G.Langton, Addison-wesley, 1989.
7. J. Holland, Adaptation in natural and artificial systems. Ann arbor university of Michigan Press,1975.
8. D.E. Goldberg, Gentic algorithms in search, Optimization and Machine learning, Addison-Wesley, 1989.
9. M. Eigen, P.Schuster, The hypercycle:A principle of natureal self-organization, new york, Springer verlag,1979.
10. R. Baglev, J.F. Farmer, Emergence of Robust autocatalytic network, in artificial life II, SFI studies in the sciences of complexity, vol. X .edited by C.G. Langton, C.E. Taylor, J.D. Farmer, S. Rasmussen, Addison-wesley,1991.
11. G. North, Expanding the RNA repetrtoire, Naturen.345, 1990.
12. M. Zeleny, Precepiation membrances, Osmotic Growths and Synthetic Biology, in artificial life, SFI studies in the sciences of complexity, vol. VI, edited by C.G.Langton, Addison-Wesley,1989.
13. E. Schrodinger, What is life?, Cambridge university press, Cambridge, 1994.
14. J.L. Deneubourg, S. Gross, Collective Patterns and Deciscion making ,Ethology ecology&evolution n.1,1989.
15. T.S. Ray, An approach to the synthesis of life, in artificial life II, SFI studies in the sciences of complexity, vol. X. edited by C.G langton, C.E.taylor, Rasmussen, Addison-Wesley, 1991.
16. E.H. Spafford , Computer Virus, A Form of artificial life? , in Artificial life 77, SFI studies in the science of complexity, vol.X.edited by C.G.Langton, S.Rasmussen, Addison-wesley,1991.
17. Martin Wildberger, Introduction & Overview of "Artificial Life" Evolving Intelligent Agents for Modeling & Simulation, Proceedings of the 1996 Winter Simulation Conference ed. J. M. Charnes, D. J. Morrice, D. T. Brunner, and J. J. Swmn.
18. Bates, J. The role of emotion in believable agents. *Commun. ACM 37,* 7 (July 1994), 122–125.
19. Luc Steels, Evolving grounded communication for robots, TRENDS in Cognitive Sciences Vol.7 No.7 July 2003.
20. Costas Neocleous1 and Christos Schizas, Artificial Neural Network Learning: A Comparative Review, I.P. Vlahavas and C.D. Spyropoulos (Eds.): SETN 2002, LNAI 2308, pp. 300–313, 2002.

21. Funge, J., Tu, X., and Terzopoulos, D. Cognitive modeling: Knowledge, reasoning, and planning for intelligent characters. In *Proceedings of SIGGRAPH' 99* (Los Angeles, Aug. 8–13, 1999); see also Funge, J. Representing knowledge within the situation calculus using IVE fluents. *J.Reliable Comput. 5,* 1 (1999), 35–61.

22. Funge, J. AI for Games and Animation: A Cognitive Modeling Approach.A.K. Peters, Natick, Mass., 1999.

23. Ian Foster, Carl Kesselman Jeffrey M. Nick Steven Tuecke, An Open Grid Services Architecture for Distributed Systems integration, www.globus.org/research/papers/ogsa.pdf.

24. Heflin, A portrait of the semantic web in action, vol, 16,no.2, 2001

25. H. Zhuge, A Knowledge Flow Model for Peer-to-Peer Team Knowledge Sharing and Management, Expert Systems with Applications, 23 (2002) 23-30.

Cellular Automata Evolution for Pattern Classification

Pradipta Maji[1], Biplab K. Sikdar[2], and P. Pal Chaudhuri[1]

[1] Department of Computer Science and Engineering & Information Technology,
Netaji Subhash Engineering College, Kolkata, India 700 152,
pradiptamaji@hotmail.com, palchau@vsnl.net
[2] Department of Computer Science and Technology,
Bengal Engineering College, Howrah, India 711 103,
biplab@cs.becs.ac.in

Abstract. This paper presents the design and application of a tree-structured pattern classifier, built around a special class of linear Cellular Automata (CA), termed as Multiple Attractor CA (MACA). Since any non-trivial classification function is non-linear in nature, the principle of realizing the non-linear function with multiple (piece-wise) linear functions is employed. Multiple (linear) MACAs are utilized to address the classification of benchmark data used to evaluate the performance of a classifier. Extensive experimental results have established the potential of MACA based tree-structured pattern classifier. Excellent classification accuracy with low memory overhead and low retrieval time prove the superiority of the proposed pattern classifier over conventional algorithms.

1 Introduction

Data classification forms one of the most important foundation stone of modern knowledge extraction methodology [1]. Applications of classification include medical diagnosis, performance prediction, selective marketing, etc. Solutions based on bayesian classification [2], neural networks [3], decision trees [4,5,6,7], etc., have been proposed. But in most of the cases [2,4,5,6,7], the algorithms require a data structure proportional to the number of tuples to stay memory resident. This restriction puts a hard limit on the amount of data that can be handled by these classifiers. In other words, the issue of scalability is the source of major concern.

In this background, design of pattern classifier based on a special class of CA termed as Multiple Attractor CA (MACA) has been explored in a number of papers [8,9]. In [8,9] a design of two class classifier has been discussed. However the design of multi-class classifier as well as issue of scalability has not been dealt with. This paper refines the design of the MACA based classifier proposed earlier and provides a detailed insight into the scalability analysis of the machine. Detailed experimental results are reported along with the analysis of its performance.

P.M.A. Sloot, B. Chopard, and A.G. Hoekstra (Eds.): ACRI 2004, LNCS 3305, pp. 660–669, 2004.
© Springer-Verlag Berlin Heidelberg 2004

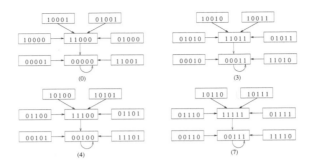

Fig. 1. State transition diagram of a 5-cell MACA. Four cyclic states 0, 3, 4, 7 are referred to as attractors and the corresponding inverted tree rooted on α ($\alpha = 0, 3, 4,$ 7) as α-basin.

2   Multiple Attractor CA (MACA)

A Cellular Automaton (CA) consists of a number of cells. In a 3-neighborhood dependency, the next state $q_i(t + 1)$ of a cell is assumed to be dependent only on itself and on its two neighbors (left and right), and is denoted as

$$q_i(t + 1) \; = \; f(q_{i-1}(t), q_i(t), q_{i+1}(t)) \tag{1}$$

where $q_i(t)$ represents the state of the ith cell at t^{th} instant of time. f is the next state function and referred to as the rule of the automata. Since f is a function of 3 variables, there are 2^{2^3} i.e., 256 possible next state functions (rules) for a CA cell. Out of 256 rules there are only 7 rules with XOR logic. The CA employing XOR rule is referred to as linear CA. The pattern classifier proposed in this paper employs a special class of linear CA referred to as MACA.

The state transition graph of an MACA consists of a number of cyclic and non-cyclic states. The set of non-cyclic states of an MACA forms inverted trees rooted at the cyclic states. The cyclic states with self loop are referred to as attractors. Fig. 1 depicts the state transition diagram of a 5-cell MACA with four attractors {00000(0), 00011(3), 00100(4), 00111(7)}. The states of a tree rooted at the cyclic state α forms the α-basin. The detailed characterization of MACA is available in [8,9]. A few fundamental results for an n-cell MACA having k number of attractor basins are next outlined.

Definition 1. *An m-bit field of an n-bit pattern set is said to be pseudo-exhaustive if all possible 2^m patterns appear in the set.*

Theorem 1. *In an n-cell MACA with $k = 2^m$ attractors, there exists m-bit positions at which the attractors generate pseudo-exhaustive 2^m patterns.*

3   Design of MACA Based Pattern Classifier

An n-bit MACA with k-attractor basins can be viewed as a natural classifier. It classifies a given set of patterns into k number of distinct classes, each class con-

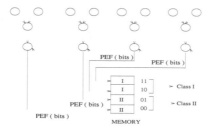

Fig. 2. MACA based classification strategy with 4 attractor basins classifying the elements into two classes. The PEF (Pseudo Exhaustive Field) of the attractor of a basin is extracted to determine the class. Also, the PEF of each attractor points to the memory location that stores the class information.

taining the set of states in the attractor basin. The following example illustrates an MACA based two class pattern classifier.

Example 1. *Let the MACA of Fig. 1 be employed to classify patterns into two classes (say I and II), where Class I is represented by one set of attractor basins (say [I]= {00100 and 00111} in Fig. 1) while Class II is represented by the rest of the basins (say [II] = {00000 and 00011}). All the patterns in the attractor basins [I] belong to Class I while rest of the patterns belong to Class II. As per Theorem 1, the pseudo-exhaustive field (PEF) will identify the class of the patterns uniquely. The PEF yields the address of the memory that stores the class information. Therefore, Class I attractors yield the memory address {10, 11}, while Class II will be identified by the memory address {00, 01} (Fig. 2). When the MACA is loaded with an input pattern $\mathcal{P}$, corresponding MACA identifies the PEF of the attractor basin where $\mathcal{P}$ belongs.*

The proposed pattern classifier is built out of the linear machine of MACA. Since any non-trivial classification function is non-linear in nature, the principle of realizing the non-linear function with multiple (piece-wise) linear functions is employed. Multiple (linear) MACAs are utilized to address the classification of benchmark data used to evaluate performance of a classifier in Section 4.

MACA Based Tree-Structured Classifier (MTSC)

Like decision tree classifiers, MACA based tree-structured classifiers are class discriminators which recursively partition the training set to get nodes belonging to a single class. Fig. 3 shows an MACA based tree-structured classifier elaborated next. Single or multiple nodes of the tree may form a leaf (node) representing a class, or it may be an intermediate node. A leaf node represents an MACA attractor basin that covers the set/subset of elements of only one class. By contrast, an intermediate node refers to an MACA attractor basin that covers the elements belonging to more than one class. In effect, an intermediate node represents the decision to build an MACA based classifier for the elements of multiple classes covered by the attractor basin of the earlier level. For example in Fig. 3,

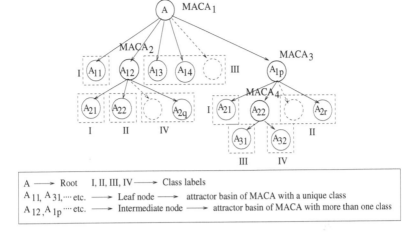

Fig. 3. Basic architecture of MACA based tree-structured pattern classifier

the node A_{12} is an intermediate node that represents a basin of MACA$_1$. The elements covered by this basin belong to multiple classes which are classified by MACA$_2$ having q number of basins - $A_{21}, A_{22}, \cdots, A_{2q}$.

Suppose, we want to design an MACA based pattern classifier to classify a training set $S = \{S_1, S_2, \cdots, S_K\}$ into K number of classes. First, an MACA with k $(k \geq K)$ number of attractor basins is generated. The training set S gets distributed into k attractor basins (nodes). Let, $\acute{S}$ be the set of elements in an attractor basin. If $\acute{S}$ belongs to only one class, then label that attractor basin as that class. Otherwise, this process is repeated recursively for each attractor basin (node) until all the patterns in each attractor basin belong to only one class. Fig. 3 represents an overview of the process. The above discussions can be formalized in the following algorithm.

Algorithm 1 MACA_Tree_Building
Input: Training set $S = \{S_1, S_2, \cdots, S_K\}$
Output: MACA Tree.
              Partition*(S, K);*
Partition*(S, K)*
Step 1: Generate an MACA with k number of attractor basins $(k \geq K)$.
Step 2: Evaluate the distribution of patterns in each attractor basin (node).
Step 3: If all the patterns ($\acute{S}$) of an attractor basin (node) belong to one
*   particular class, then label the attractor basin (leaf node) for that class.*
Step 4: Else, for the set of patterns ($\acute{S}$) of an attractor basin belonging to
* $\acute{K}$ number of classes, **Partition**$(\acute{S}, \acute{K})$.*
Step 5: Stop.

Details design of MACA tree generation is reported in [10]. The optimal MACA tree is evolved through the application of Genetic Algorithm (GA) recursively at each intermediate node. In the next section, we report extensive experimental results to validate the design of MACA tree to address classification problem.

4   Performance Analysis of MACA Based Classifier

To analyze the performance of MACA based tree-structured pattern classifier, the experiment has been performed on datasets available from http://www.ics.uci.edu/~mlearn/MLRepository.html. All the experiments are performed in SUN with Solaris 5.6, 350 MHz clock.

Modification of Dataset

To handle real data having categorical and/or continuous attributes, the dataset is suitably modified to fit the input characteristic of the proposed MACA based pattern classifier. The modification of each type is elaborated next.

Categorical Attribute

To perform classification task on categorical/discrete attribute, each attribute is converted into binary form as per the popular Thermometer Code. If a categorical attribute X takes k possible values $\{c_1, c_2, \cdots, c_k\}$, it is replaced by a $(k\text{-}1)$-dimensional vector $(d_1, d_2, \cdots, d_{k-1})$ such that

$$d_j = \begin{cases} 1, \text{ if } X = c_i \text{ and } j \leq i \\ 0, \text{ otherwise.} \end{cases} \tag{2}$$

for $i, j = 1, 2, \cdots, k - 1$. If $X = c_k$, the vector consists of all zeros. For example, if an attribute has four categories, then it is represented as 100, 110, 111, 000, where 100 is first category, 110 is second category, and so on. After conversion, each attribute is concatenated to form the final pattern representing a tuple having multiple attributes.

Continuous Attribute

For continuous-valued attribute, it is transformed into a categorical attribute by Data Discretization [11]. Discretization technique is used to reduce the number of values for a given continuous attribute by dividing the range of attribute into intervals. Interval labels are used to replace actual data values. Though detail information of data is lost in this process, the generalized data is more meaningful and easier to interpret [11]. The formal treatment for continuous attributes, as reported in [11], is briefly introduced next.

Suppose training set S is described in an instance space $\mathcal{L} = <\, attr_1, attr_2, \cdots, attr_i, \cdots, attr_n\, >$ where $attr_i$ is a continuous attribute. Let the possible value range of continuous attribute $attr_i$ is $(attrval_{i,min}, attrval_{i,max})$ and the

Table 1. Performance Analysis of MACA based Tree-Structured Classifier

Dataset	No of Intervals	Value of PEF	Classification Accuracy (%)	No of Nodes	Memory Overhead (KB)	Retrieval Time (ms)
Australian	4	2	84.11	53.16	18.07	9
		6	80.64	12.32	2.17	2
	16	2	89.19	137.57	35.06	19
		4	87.12	27.26	8.04	4
		4	88.17	34.69	29.78	10
		6	87.02	19.11	14.08	7
Diabetes	4	2	76.96	43.12	7.81	8
		4	75.91	33.71	6.94	8
	16	2	76.04	42.03	10.24	13
		6	74.84	24.43	9.28	9
	64	2	76.00	38.11	9.58	12
		6	73.12	21.04	6.75	7
DNA	NA	3	89.39	144.2	67.18	617
		4	86.45	124.3	50.86	494
		6	81.11	35.5	19.48	387
German	4	2	74.16	49.50	8.61	18
		6	70.67	21.38	5.85	19
	16	2	76.21	52.83	18.13	18
		6	71.84	34.03	11.24	20
	64	2	76.00	48.51	19.53	22
		4	75.97	32.16	8.42	21

real value that an example $\mathcal{E}$ takes at $attr_i$ is $attr_{i,\mathcal{E}}$, then the discretized value of $attr_{i,\mathcal{E}}$ is given by

$$Discretized(attr_{i,\mathcal{E}}) = \left(\frac{attr_{i,\mathcal{E}} - attrval_{i,min}}{attrval_{i,max} - attrval_{i,min} + 1}\right) \times \mathcal{D} \qquad (3)$$

where $\mathcal{D}$ is the number of intervals. The above relation is a simple linear discretization scheme. Other discretization schemes such as scalar quantization [11] can also be used. If a priori knowledge on the value distribution of the attributes is available, then a knowledge-based discretization [11] can be more helpful.

The experimental results are presented in Tables 1 - 5. Subsequent discussions analyze the results presented in these tables in respect of classification accuracy and memory overhead.

4.1 Optimum Value of PEF and $\mathcal{D}$

The value of PEF indicates the number of pseudo-exhaustive bits of an n-cell MACA and the value of $\mathcal{D}$ specifies the number of intervals of the continuous attributes. To identify the desired values of both PEF and $\mathcal{D}$, we carry out

Table 2. Performance Analysis of MACA based Tree-Structured Classifier (Cont^n.)

Dataset	No of Intervals	Value of PEF	Classification Accuracy (%)	No of Nodes	Memory Overhead (KB)	Retrieval Time (ms)
Heart	4	2	77.32	39.14	9.25	21
		4	76.02	19.62	7.48	19
	16	2	87.31	29.81	7.34	20
		6	76.90	8.45	3.08	18
	64	2	81.54	30.51	7.11	19
		4	78.25	11.06	4.73	19
Satimage	4	2	86.34	581.02	681.07	5714
		6	81.78	81.60	121.67	5572
	16	2	89.02	690.21	743.45	6081
		4	87.64	199.20	222.74	4943
	64	4	86.93	197.36	886.51	6625
		6	82.49	76.94	102.63	4539
Shuttle	16	2	65.58	87.80	127.62	9716
		4	65.58	25.91	8.39	1655
		6	65.58	19.48	9.19	1594
	64	2	97.22	160.01	180.78	12873
		4	93.13	47.20	55.17	6633
		6	91.18	28.46	37.36	5776

extensive experiments on dataset available in http://www. ics.uci.edu/~mlearn/ MLRepository.html.

Tables 1-3 represent the performance of MACA based tree-structured pattern classifier (MTSC) for different values of PEF and $\mathcal{D}$. Columns II and III of Tables 1-3 represent the number of intervals ($\mathcal{D}$) and the value of PEF, while Columns IV to VII depict the classification accuracy, number of intermediate nodes (number of MACAs), memory overhead to implement MACA tree, and the retrieval time respectively of the MACA tree.

The results reported in Tables 1-3 establish the following facts:

1. For a fixed value of PEF, as the value of $\mathcal{D}$ increases, the classification accuracy also increases.
2. For a fixed value of $\mathcal{D}$, as the value of PEF increases, the classification accuracy decreases slowly. But, the memory overhead, number of intermediate nodes, and the retrieval time significantly reduce.

From the extensive experimentations of different values of $\mathcal{D}$ and PEF, we have observed that the optimum efficiency, - that is, higher classification accuracy with lower memory overhead and lower retrieval time, of the MACA based tree-structured classifier is achieved with $\mathcal{D} = 16$ and PEF $= 4$. So, the classification accuracy and memory overhead of MACA based classifier are compared with existing schemes considering $\mathcal{D} = 16$ and PEF $= 4$.

Table 3. Performance Analysis of MACA based Tree-Structured Classifier (Cont^n.)

Dataset	No of Intervals	Value of PEF	Classification Accuracy (%)	No of Nodes	Memory Overhead (KB)	Retrieval Time (ms)
Letter	16	4	89.97	1634.03	866.20	16173
		6	88.26	524.62	354.11	5633
		8	79.09	232.72	287.96	2418
	64	4	88.32	1463.85	1783.42	13156
		6	88.01	753.11	1641.52	12135
		8	86.48	540.89	1488.18	14214
Vehicle	16	2	79.57	103.62	51.27	32
		4	79.35	50.82	29.83	28
		6	76.08	44.32	23.61	29
	64	2	79.91	112.48	62.37	39
		4	79.32	51.18	33.59	43
		6	77.03	46.31	26.11	37
Segment	16	2	90.64	98.46	61.09	72
		4	88.01	39.71	24.51	58
		6	85.32	18.20	19.66	59
	64	2	90.87	107.24	72.40	79
		4	87.02	44.92	33.01	81
		6	82.09	21.71	23.88	72

4.2 Classification Accuracy

Classification accuracy is defined as the percentage of test samples that are correctly classified. Table 4 compares the classification accuracy of MACA based pattern classifiers with that of different classification algorithms namely bayesian [2], MLP (Multilayer Perceptron) [3], C4.5 [4] etc.

The experimental results of Table 4 clearly establish the fact that for most of the example datasets, the classification accuracy of MACA based tree-structured classifier is higher than that of different classification algorithms reported in published literature [2,3,4].

4.3 Memory Overhead

The memory overhead required to implement different classification algorithms is evaluated for the sake of comparison. Table 4 reports the comparison of memory overhead of different classification algorithms in terms of KByte. The results in Table 4 clearly establish the fact that the memory overhead to implement the proposed MACA based classifier is substantially smaller compared to that of bayesian classifier and C4.5 [2,4]. The memory overhead of MTSC is very small since for this classifier the overhead is independent of the size of the datasets.

Table 4. Classification Accuracy and Memory Overhead of Different Algorithms

Dataset	Classification Accuracy				Memory Overhead			
	Bayesian	C4.5	MLP	MTSC	Bayesian	C4.5	MLP	MTSC
monk1	99.9	100	100	98.65	1.7	2.77	0.35	2.03
monk3	92.12	96.3	76.58	98.10	1.7	2.38	0.36	2.84
crx	83.14	84.5	74.29	86.47	22	24.35	2.25	8.67
labor-neg	83.07	82.4	89.03	88.27	2.4	3.44	2.56	2.04
vote	92.37	94.8	90.87	95.91	13	14.35	2.66	7.69
hypo	98.18	99.4	94.13	99.06	213	214.54	6.32	57.62
Australian	83.4	85.8	84.7	87.12	19	37.85	1.93	8.04
Diabetes	72.9	74.2	75.3	75.99	14	27.15	0.44	9.96
DNA	90.3	93.3	91.4	86.45	1000	1067.96	37.22	50.86
German	66.79	67.4	67.12	75.99	49	99.31	13.64	17.42
Heart	80.12	79.3	80.74	87.07	9.8	19.46	1.52	3.17
Satimage	85.4	85.2	86.2	87.64	669	709.72	11.33	222.74
Shuttle	99.9	99.9	99.6	93.13	1500	1513.57	0.71	55.17
Letter	87.4	86.6	67.2	88.26	766	1299.28	2.57	354.11
Vehicle	72.9	68.5	79.3	79.35	63.08	72.14	3.08	29.83
Segment	96.7	94.6	94.4	88.01	271.38	370.42	2.41	24.51

Table 5. Comparison of MACA based Tree-Structured Classifier and C4.5

Dataset	Classification Accuracy (%)		Number of Intermediate Nodes		Memory Overhead (KB)		Retrieval Time (ms)	
	MTSC	C4.5	MTSC	C4.5	MTSC	C4.5	MTSC	C4.5
Australian	87.12	85.8	27.26	35.5	8.04	37.85	4	461
Diabetes	75.99	74.2	34.23	39.67	9.96	27.15	10	1739
DNA	86.45	93.3	124.3	127	50.86	1067.96	494	655
German	75.99	67.4	49.83	134	17.42	99.31	19	1967
Heart	87.07	79.3	8.63	33.56	3.17	19.46	17	1819
Satimage	87.64	85.2	199.20	433	222.74	709.72	4943	2255
Shuttle	93.13	99.9	47.20	49	55.17	1513.57	6633	3985
Letter	88.26	86.6	524.62	2107	354.11	1299.28	5633	14352
Vehicle	79.35	68.5	50.82	139	29.83	72.14	28	1963
Segment	88.01	94.6	39.71	81.6	24.51	370.42	58	2508

4.4   Comparison Between MTSC and C4.5

Since MACA based tree-structured classifier (MTSC) exhibits the best performance among the classifiers proposed, detailed results are presented in Table 5, comparing each of the factors - number of intermediate nodes, retrieval time, classification accuracy and memory overhead with the most popular C4.5 algorithm. Table 5 shows that MTSC outperforms C4.5 in most of the criteria.

5   Conclusion

The paper presents the detailed design and analysis of MACA based pattern classification algorithm. Extensive experimental results have established the potential of MACA model for pattern classification. The excellent classification accuracy with low memory overhead and low retrieval time prove the superiority of the proposed classifier over that of the existing classification algorithms.

References

1. R. Agrawal, T. Imielinski, and A. Swami, "Database Mining: A Performance Perspective," *IEEE Transaction on Knowledge and Data Engineering*, vol. 5, December 1993.
2. P. Cheeseman and J. Stutz, "Bayesian Classification (AutoClass): Theory and Results," *In U. M. Fayyad, G. Piatetsky-Shapiro, P. Smith and R. Uthurusamy, editors, Advances in Knowledge Discovery and Data Mining, AAAI/MIT Press*, pp. 153–180, 1996.
3. J. Hertz, A. Krogh, and R. G. Palmer, "Introduction to the Theory of Neural Computation," *Santa Fe Institute Studies in the Sciences of Complexity, Addison Wesley*, 1991.
4. J. R. Quinlan, "C4.5: Programs for Machine Learning," *Morgan Kaufmann, CA*, 1993.
5. L. Breiman, J. H. Friedman, R. A. Olshen, and C. J. Stone, "Classification and Regression Trees," *Wadsworth, Belmont*, 1984.
6. M. Mehta, R. Agrawal, and J. Rissanen, "SLIQ: A Fast Scalable Classifier for Data Mining," *Proceedings of International Conference on Extending Database Technology, Avignon, France*, 1996.
7. J. Shafer, R. Agrawal, and M. Mehta, "SPRINT: A Scalable Parallel Classifier for Data Mining," *In 22nd VLDB Conference*, 1996.
8. N. Ganguly, P. Maji, S. Dhar, B. K. Sikdar, and P. P. Chaudhuri, "Evolving Cellular Automata as Pattern Classifier," *Proceedings of Fifth International Conference on Cellular Automata for Research and Industry, ACRI 2002, Switzerland*, pp. 56–68, October 2002.
9. P. Maji, C. Shaw, N. Ganguly, B. K. Sikdar, and P. P. Chaudhuri, "Theory and Application of Cellular Automata For Pattern Classification," *Fundamenta Informaticae*, 2003.
10. P. Maji, "Cellular Automata Evolution For Pattern Recognition," *Ph.D thesis, Jadavpur University*, 2004.
11. J. Han and M. Kamber, "Data Mining, Concepts and Techniques," *Morgan Kaufmann Publishers*, vol. ISBN : 1-55860-489-8, 2001.

Simulation and Experimental Investigation of Two Dimensional Cracks Propagation in Ceramic Materials

Jacek Bomba, Julita Czopor, and Marek Rybaczuk

Wroclaw University of Technology, Institute of Materials Science and Applied Mechanics,
ul. Smoluchowskiego 25, 50-370 Wrocław

Abstract. The paper presents the application of the Movable Cellular Automata (MCA) method for a simulation of 2D crack propagation in ceramic materials. The MCA method let us to simulate a movement of formation and cracks course for impossible to observe during an experiment. Ceramic sample was chosen to the research as an elastic-brittle material. During the study the simulation was done and the experiment was carried out with the same guidelines. The MCA model was correlated with experimental data. The simulation program generates data which allow to compute quantities such as an ultimate compressive strength and to show in the graphic form the moment of cracks initiation. Comparison of experimental and simulated results proves that Movable Cellular Automata method is suitable for modeling crack propagation in ceramic materials in two-dimensional system.

1 Introduction

One of aims of mechanics' research is to find a description of real physical objects consisted of elements called material particles. This particles interact and they are subjected to actions of external forces. Mathematical description should make possible to read all necessary data in every program step. It should let us register information about position, internal state etc. The program also allow us to observe micro and macro-cracks forming.

Cellular automata can be treated as the competitive method enabling numerical solutions of the same partial differential equations (see [1], [2]). The main difference consists of a description of inhomogeneities or variable boundary conditions. It is relatively easy to model growing defects in terms of cellular automata loosing their contact (interaction) with the neighboring ones. Cellular automata calculations resemble method of molecular dynamics however with all damping processes taken into account.

2 Description of Simulation Method

Movable Cellular Automata method was used for cracks propagation simulation. This method is based on two principles:

P.M.A. Sloot, B. Chopard, and A.G. Hoekstra (Eds.): ACRI 2004, LNCS 3305, pp. 670–677, 2004.
© Springer-Verlag Berlin Heidelberg 2004

– the state of simple automata
– the state of pair of automata.
The automaton state depends on its state in previous program step and the state of all its neighbors.

C++ program language was chosen to create a simulation tool.

2.1 Basis of Calculation

The entire specimen is divided into fragments (automata) described with individual equations of motion. Each cellular automaton may move or rotate due to interaction with other automata. To describe one of them we have to define parameters such as radius-vector - line joining the center of circle to point (0,0), linear velocity , angle of rotation , rotation speed   (see Fig 1 and Fig 2).

Defined values of radius vectors caused that cellular automata are in the hexagonal system. Coordinates are computed according to equation:

$$R^{ij} = \begin{cases} \left(2 \cdot \rho \cdot j; \sqrt{3}\rho \cdot i\right) & i = 2 \cdot k + 1 \\ \\ \left(2 \cdot \rho \cdot j + \rho; \sqrt{3}\rho \cdot i\right) & i = 2 \cdot k \end{cases} \tag{1}$$

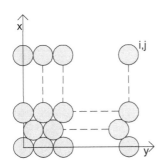

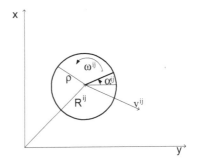

Fig. 1. Hexagonal system   **Fig. 2.** Cellular automaton parameters

2.2 Interactions

It is necessary to calculate a length of radius vector joining centers of two neighboring automata to check the interaction between them.

Pair of automata is connected if $jrj < 2^{1/2} + ln_{max}$. The parameter ln_{max} is the limiting value of displacement.

Each pair of automata satisfying this condition is described by special parameter $linkijkl$: $linkijkl = 1$ if pair is connected and $linkijkl = 0$ in the opposite case. The connected automata are treated as interacting whereas unconnected automata do not interact. In numerical simulations connectednes or interaction was assumed to nearest neighbors. This means that long range forces were excluded as depicted in fig 3 (see [3] for more details).

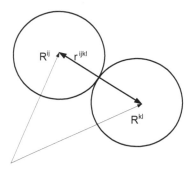

Fig. 3. Checking the interaction between automata

2.3 Internal Forces

One of main steps of simulation's algorithm is calculating force acting between automata. This force consists of such components: $F_p ijkl$ - central force (comes from volumetric deformation of two influenced automata) $fijkl$- viscous friction force proportional to the relative velocity of automata) $fijkl$- dry friction force(proportional to the thrust forces).

$$F^{ijkl} = F_P^{ijkl} + f_{dr}^{ijkl} + f^{ijkl} \tag{2}$$

- Central force

Central force is described by equation

$$F_P^{ijkl} = -P^{ijkl} \cdot S^{ijkl} \cdot n^{ijkl} \tag{3}$$

$Pijkl$ - pressure caused by volumetric strain of the automaton ij stays in connection with the automaton, $Sijkl$ -surface of connection, $nijkl$ – a unit vector in the direction of a vector joining both automata centers. Vector's $nijkl$ coordinates are computing on the basis of the equation:

$$n^{ijkl} = \frac{r^{ijkl}}{\left| r^{ijkl} \right|} \tag{4}$$

Equations of the other factors:

$$S^{ijkl} = a = \sqrt{\rho^2 - \left(\frac{\left|r^{ijkl}\right|}{2}\right)^2} \tag{5}$$

$$P^{ijkl} = \frac{1}{2}E_0\rho^2(\theta - \sin\theta) \text{ i } \theta = 2\cdot\arccos\left(\frac{\left|r^{ijkl}\right|}{2\rho}\right) \tag{6}$$

- Viscous friction force

Formulas for viscous friction forces assume forms

$$f_{dr}^{ijkl} = \begin{cases} -F_S^{ijkl}, & : \quad \left|F_S^{ijkl}\right| < \mu^{ijkl}\left|F_N^{ijkl}\right| \\ -\mu^{ijkl}\left|F_N^{ijkl}\right|, & : \quad \left|F_S^{ijkl}\right| \geq \mu^{ijkl}\left|F_N^{ijkl}\right| \end{cases} \tag{7}$$

where $F_s ijkl$- automata's kl and ij tangent component of impact forces $F_N ijkl$ - automata's kl and ij normal component of impact forces

$\mu ijkl$ - coefficient of dry friction between automata ij and kl.

If the force $f_{dr} ijkl$ is defined by the first equation then both automata stay in immobility in the direction of contact surface. In the opposite case automata are moving and the force is counteracting movements. All these rules are valid only in the case when automata exert an influence on themselves i.e. $|rijkl| < 2\rho$. If this condition is not fulfilled, automaton does not exert an influence on neighbor.

- Dry friction force

Two components determine dry friction force: normal and tangent in the direction of contact's surface (as depicted in 8). Equations of viscous friction force:

$$f_n^{ijkl} = -\eta_n \cdot v_n^{ijkl}$$
$$f_s^{ijkl} = -\eta_s \cdot v_s^{ijkl} \tag{8}$$

where $f_s ijkl$ - tangent component of viscous friction force,

$f_n ijkl$ -normal component of viscous friction force,

η_s - tangent coefficient of viscous friction between automata ij and kl,

ηn - normal coefficient of viscous friction between automata ij and kl,

$v_s ijkl$- tangent coefficient of relative velocity,

$v_n ijkl$ - normal coefficient of relative velocity.

$$v^{ijkl} = v^{kl} - v^{ij} \tag{9}$$

Program calculates all specified parameters for each pair of automata described by the parameter $linkijkl = 1$ and additionally takes the gravitational force into consideration.

2.4 Results of Simulations

During the simulation data are recorded in two files for every program step. Frames of animation are created on the basis of the first one. The special software written in POV-Ray[1] was used for creating graph of a function $\sigma=f(\varepsilon)$. Theoretical stress-strain plot for the brittle material is presented in fig. 4

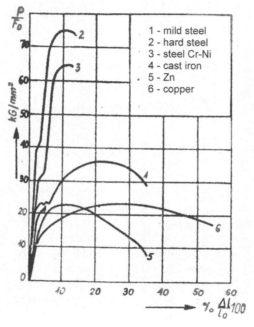

Fig. 4. Theoretical stress-strain plot [8]

3 Experiment

Ceramics specimens in lammelar form were investigated. Only compression tests were carried out. Hydraulic pulser MTS810 was used for the experiment. Special sample jaws presented in Fig. 5a was prepared. The upper machine jaw moved with speed 1 mm/s usually. Break of tested specimens take place after 15 s. Young's modulus was calculated on the basis of the stress-strain trace (Fig. 6) registered during experiment. The parameters of investigated specimens and received results are presented in tab. 1.

Thickness of specimens had an effect on results. Size of samples and jaws misfit caused measuring error.

---

[1] POV-Ray for Windows version 3.5

Table 1. Tests data

Nr	Width [mm]	High [mm]	Thickness [mm]	Ultimate compressive strength [MPa]	Young's modulus [MPa]
1	14.00	14.00	2.42	44	2.8*1e5
2	14.00	14.00	2.1	47	3.2*1e5
3	13.86	13.94	2.26	42	2.5*1e5

Fig. 5a. Sample placed between jaws   **Fig. 5b.** Broken sample

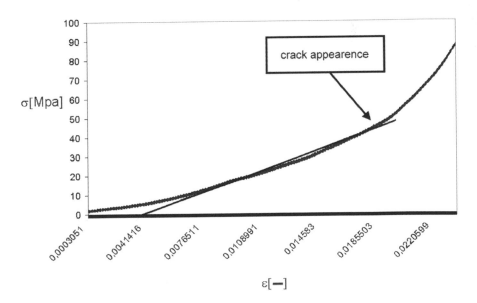

Fig. 6. Stress-strain diagram

Table 2. Mechanical proprietes

M	n	High [mm]	Young's modulus [MPa]	Poisson's ratio	Rigidity	Density	Coefficient of dry friction
13	11	16	2.7*1e5	0.1	2*1e4	4.27*1e -2	0.2

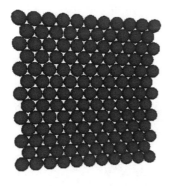

Fig. 7a. 1ˢᵗ frame of animation   **Fig. 7b.** Last frame of animation

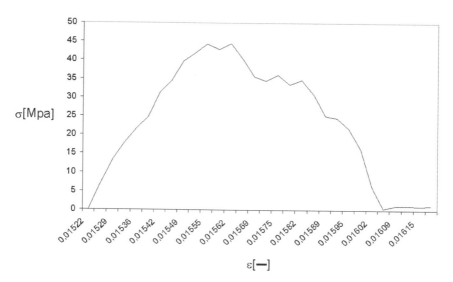

σ[Mpa]

ε[—]

Fig. 8. Simulation of stress-strain trace for investigated ceramics

4 Simulation

Computer experiment is usually started from the analyze of material physical
proprieties. Tab. 2 presents proprietes of chosen ceramic. It is possible to control the

number of automata describing the specimen. Increasing of automata' number and decreasing program step decrease leads to improvement in calculations accuracy.

The following presented results were created for sample divided into 143 elements. Fig. 7a and 7b show generated animation frames. The first one (fig. 7a) shows the moment of the simulation start. The second one (fig 7b.) is the sample frame after 13 seconds of the simulated experiment. Comparison of fig 5b and 7b shows similarity in crack shape and size received by experimental method and simulation. The crack appears on the edge and evolves into the interior of specimen, in accordance with theoretical description of ceramic materials.

Using the diagram in fig. 8 Young's modulus and compression strength Rm were evaluated. This outcomes differ from experimental results about:

9% -Young's modulus

14% - Rm

5 Conclusions

Within a framework of this research, analysis of cracking process were investigated. Computer simulations with use of the MCA method were realized. Findings of simulation for small and flat samples were presented and compared to experimental results.

Analysis of investigated calculations shows effectiveness of chosen method as a tool for cracks propagation modeling. Obtained results let us suppose that consideration of farther research is possible and promising.

References

1. Psakhie, Horie, Smolin, Dmitrie, Shilko, Alekseev: Movable Cellular Automata Method As a New Technique to Simulate Powder Metallurgy Materials, Proceedings of Deformation and Fracture in Structural PM Materials, SAS Bratislava, (1996).
2. Krzysztof Kulakowski: Cellular automata, OEN AGH Krakw (2002), (in Polish).
3. Landau L.D., Lipshitz E.M. :Elasticity theory, PWN, Warsaw (1993), (in Polish).
4. Rybaczuk M., Stoppel P.: The fractal growth of fatigue defects in materials, Int. Journal of Fracture, Vol 103, pp. 71-94, (2000).
5. Walczak J.: Materials strength and foundations of elasticity and plasticity theory Vol I Warsaw (1978), (in Polish)

Cellular Automata in the Hyperbolic Plane: Proposal for a New Environment

Kamel Chelghoum, Maurice Margenstern, Benoît Martin, and Isabelle Pecci

LITA, University of Metz, Île du Saulcy, 57045 Metz, Cedex 01, France
{chelghoum, margens, martin, pecci}@sciences.univ-metz.fr

Abstract. In this paper, we deal with new environment to visualise and to interact with cellular automata implemented in a grid of the hyperbolic plane. We use two kinds of tiling: the ternary *heptagrid* and the rectangular *pentagrid*. We show that both grids have the same spanning tree: the same numbering with maximal Fibonacci numbers can be used to identify all tiles. We give all the materials to compute the neighbourhood of any tile in the *heptagrid* or in the *pentagrid*. Then we propose visualisation and interaction techniques to interact with cellular automata which are grounded in these two grids.

1 Introduction

Cellular automata are used in a lot of fields, especially in industrial applications, in order to simulate reaction diffusion phenomena. In most of these cases, we are able to perform measures before the phenomena and after it happened, but measures during the process it-self are usually out of reach. Cellular automata turned out to be an efficient way for trying to understand what happens during the phenomenon, thanks to their great power of simulation. In these simulations, the initial configuration of the cellular automaton and the states of the cells during the process are discretisations of the situation before and during the event. In Euclidean geometry this raises no problem and usually no attention is given to this issue.

The situation is very different in the hyperbolic plane. Hyperbolic geometry is more and more used for solving more easily complex problems. This is the main reason to use the tiling of the hyperbolic plane to implement and manipulate automata cellular. We refer the reader to [7] [8] for introductory material on hyperbolic geometry. In order to fix things and to spare space, we shall use Poincaré's disc model of the hyperbolic plane. The open unit disc U of the Euclidean plane constitutes the points of the hyperbolic plane IH^2. The border of U, ∂U is the set of points at infinity. Lines are the trace in U of its diameters or the trace in U of circles which are orthogonal to ∂U.

In this paper, we present a new environment to visualise and to interact with cellular automata implemented in the rectangular *pentagrid* and similarly in the ternary *heptagrid* on the hyperbolic plane. For cellular automata being grounded on a *polygrid* of the hyperbolic plane, a polygon represents a cell. The problem of initialising

P.M.A. Sloot, B. Chopard, and A.G. Hoekstra (Eds.): ACRI 2004, LNCS 3305, pp. 678–687, 2004.

cellular automata based on locating points on the *polygrid* is already studied and algorithms are given in [1] for the *pentagrid* and in [2] for the *heptagrid*. Our goal is to compute the neighbours of a cell and to show the state of each cell of the cellular automaton. In section 2, we shortly recall the splitting method for the rectangular *pentagrid* and we apply it for the ternary *heptagrid*. Then, in section 3, we propose algorithms to find direct neighbours of a cell using the maximal Fibonacci representation. Thanks to this neighbourhood, we can write now algorithms for implementing cellular automata in the both grids of the hyperbolic plane. Thus, in section 4, we propose algorithms to visualise and to interact with them.

2 Splitting the Plane

Recall that in the theory of tilings, a particular case consists in considering a polygon P and then, all the reflections of P in its sides and, recursively, of the images in their sides: this is called a *tessellation* of P. We say that the obtained polygons are generated by P. Of course, we assume that we have the tiling property: two distinct polygons being generated by P have non intersecting interiors and any point of the plane is in the closure of at least one polygon of the set. In this case, we say that the tiling is generated by P; we shall also say that the tiling is the grid defined by P.

The rectangular *pentagrid* is defined as the tiling which is generated from a central regular pentagon with an interior angle of $\pi/2$ while the ternary *heptagrid* is generated from a central regular heptagon with an interior angle of $2\pi/3$. Following the general method [5], the plane is split into independent basic regions R_i, five for the *pentagrid* and seven for the *heptagrid*, see figure 1. Each basic region has a leading polygon which is the reflection of the central polygon into the common side.

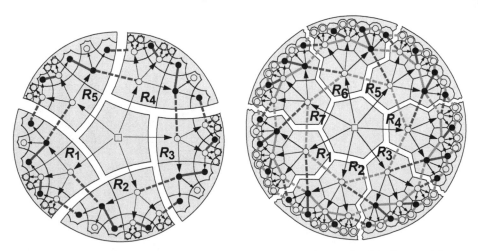

Fig. 1. Tiling tree T and neighbourhood graph G for the *pentagrid* and the *heptagrid*.

As it was first shown in [4], the splitting defined above generates a tree: nodes are associated with the polygons and arcs denote the reflections. This tiling tree T is illustrated with arrows in figure 1. There are two simple rules for generating the sons of a node. One rule applies to 3-nodes, in white in the tree, and the other rule applies to 2-nodes, in black in the tree [4]:

- a 3-node has three sons: to left, a 2-node and, in the middle and to right in both cases, 3-nodes.
- a 2-node has 2 sons: to left a 2-node, to right a 3-node.

These rules are applied for splitting the *heptagrid* and for splitting the *pentagrid*. They generate the same spanning tree for the basic regions of both grids. To complete the tiling tree, the main node which corresponds to the central polygon and represented by a white square has arcs which connect it with the leading polygon of each basic region R_i. Notice that this tree is a spanning tree of the neighbourhood graph G. It is not difficult to restore that dual graph from this tree by defining additional connections represented in bold lines and dotted lines in figure 1.

3   Cellular Automata in the Hyperbolic Plane

Initialising a cellular automaton and locating a cell and its neighbours in the hyperbolic plane is not that trivial as it is in the Euclidean case. We focus now in this problem of locating a cell and its neighbours. Required information can be extracted from the Fibonacci representations attached to the polygons, hence to the cells of the automaton.

3.1   Fibonacci Numbering

In [3], a new ingredient is brought. Numbering the nodes of the tree which is obtained from the splitting, we use what is called the standard Fibonacci representation of the positive integers. Indeed, it is well known that any positive number n can be written as $n = \overline{w}$, which means:

$$w = (a_k\, a_{k-1} \ldots a_1) \text{ with } a_i \in \{0,1\}, \quad \overline{w} = \sum_{i=1}^{k} a_i.f_i \text{ with } \begin{cases} f_0 = f_1 = 1 \\ f_n = f_{n-2} + f_{n-1} \ \forall n \geq 2 \end{cases}$$

This representation is not unique, as an example: $(111) = (1001)$. To obtain the uniqueness, we decide that if $a_i = 1$ then $a_{i+1} = 0$, for all i in $\{1..k-1\}$. It is the maximal Fibonacci representation with respect to the lexicographical order. Thus, there are two simple rules for generating the Fibonacci representation:

$$
\begin{array}{ll}
\begin{array}{l} \text{3-node} \\ w = (a_k..a_1) \end{array} &
\left\{
\begin{array}{lll}
\text{leftmost son (2-node)} & : w' = (a_k..a_1\, 0\, 0) - 1 & \text{rule } ① \\
\text{middle son (3-node)} & : w' = (a_k..a_1\, 0\, 0) & \text{rule } ② \\
\text{rightmost son (3-node)} & : w' = (a_k..a_1\, 0\, 1) & \text{rule } ③
\end{array}
\right.
\end{array}
$$

$$
\begin{array}{ll}
\begin{array}{l} \text{2-node} \\ w = (a'_p..a'_1) \end{array} &
\left\{
\begin{array}{lll}
\text{left-hand son (2-node)} & : w' = (a'_p..a'_1\, 0\, 0) & \text{rule } ④ \\
\text{right-hand son (3-node)} & : w' = (a'_p..a'_1\, 0\, 1) & \text{rule } ⑤
\end{array}
\right.
\end{array}
$$

The corresponding Fibonacci representations are shown figure 2 for a basic region R_i. It is a very convenient way to number the nodes of the tree as pointed out by the above rules. For example, it is easy to determine the type of a node n numbered w: we can note $w = u1(0)^p$ with $p \geq 0$. If p is odd, we know that w is a 2-node. In the contrary, if p is even, n is a 3-node.

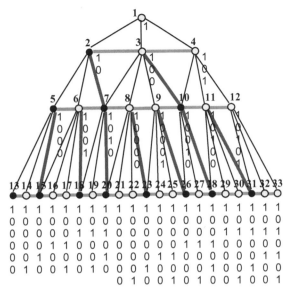

Fig. 2. Fibonacci numbering for a basic region R_i.

The maximal Fibonacci representation gives a coordinate for all polygons of the basic regions. By extension, we define 0 to be the coordinate of the central polygon. Next numbering the basic regions from 1 up to $nbSides$ (five for the *pentagrid* and seven for the *heptagrid*), counter clockwise, we obtain the coordinate of a polygon as a couple (r, w) with r being the basic region containing the polygon and w being a maximal Fibonacci representation of a positive number.

3.2 Neighbourhood Computation

The immediate neighbours of a polygon p are the polygons which are obtained by reflection of p in one of its sides. In previous works, we obtained the following theorem: "there is a linear algorithm to compute the path from a node of the spanning tree of a basic region to its root as a list of coordinates. There is also a linear algorithm to compute the coordinates of the immediate neighbours of a polygon from its coordinates".

To define the neighbours of a polygon, we introduce functions $Son_i(c)$ and $Side_i(c)$ to explore the tiling tree and the neighbourhood graph without any additional data structures. We note c the coordinate of the polygon and i the number of a side. Thus, $Son_i(c)$ is the son of c adjacent to side i and $Side_i(c)$ is the number of the side such as $c = Son_{Side_i(c)}(Son_i(c))$. For $Son_i(c)$, $Side_i(c)$ is the number of the side to reach c.

The sides of a polygon are numbered from 1 to $nbSides$. For a polygon, this numbering is unique and is a consequence of the reflections used for the splitting: the side numbered *nbSides* is the parent side. It is the side which is adjacent with its parent. Then, the other sides are numbered counter clockwise from this parent side from 1 to *nbSides*-1. For the central polygon, side 1 indicates region 1 and so on. Figure 3 shows functions *Son* and *Side* for the *heptagrid* by using the following functions *inc* and *pred*:

$$\begin{cases} inc(nbSides) = 1 \\ inc(i) = i+1 \text{ with } i \in [1..nbSides-1] \end{cases} \qquad \begin{cases} pred(1) = nbSides \\ pred(i) = i-1 \text{ with } i \in [2..nbSides] \end{cases}$$

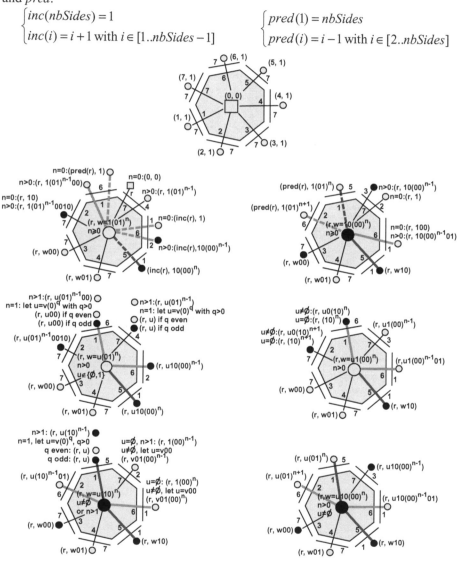

Fig. 3. The neighbourhood of a heptagon of the *heptagrid*.

We obtain the corresponding neighbourhood of the *pentagrid* just by removing the light seams. Then side 7 becomes side 5 and we number the sides counter clockwise from 1 to 4 starting from side 5.

4 Visualisation and Interaction Techniques

For cellular automata being grounded on the hyperbolic plane, a polygon represents a cell. The Fibonacci numbering allows us to compute the coordinates of the immediate neighbours of a cell, which is the starting point of an implementation of cellular automata in the *pentagrid* or the *heptagrid*. However, our goal is to use the tiling as a display to show the state of each cell too. For this, many techniques can be used: different colours, values ... We propose to dissociate the polygon of the display from the cell which is displayed in. In this case, the tiling tree T is viewed as the display and the neighbourhood graph G is viewed as the cellular automaton. By bringing a cell to the centre of the tiling, user focuses on a specific cell. We note that this action is not a scaling in the hyperbolic plane but a shift of the cells. The distortion of the mapping between the hyperbolic plane and the Poincaré's disc gives the feeling of a zoom.

By this way, some cells not yet visible can appear, some visible cells can disappear, some cells become more important while other become less important ... Of course, in all cases, the neighbourhood of the cells must be kept. In this paper, we propose a technique to associate any cells to the main polygon of the tiling while keeping the neighbourhood. We will call the cell displayed in the central polygon, the *main cell*.

When the tiling is displayed, each polygon must be computed only one time. For this, we use tiling tree T. In addition, the height of T can be parameterised to show more or less polygons. Each polygon p of T is called "receiver" (figure 4). As the computation is done from the root of the tree, we are sure that the polygon computed before p is its father called $Son_7(p)$ for the *heptagrid* ($Son_5(p)$ for the *pentagrid*).

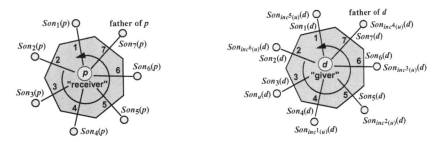

Fig. 4. A receiver and a giver for the *heptagrid*.

For each receiver p, we must compute its associated cell. Thus, concurrently to the visit of T, graph G is visited too. Therefore, thanks to G, we can reach cell d which is attached to receiver p. Each polygon d of G is called "giver" (figure 4). We know that d is the giver for polygon p: cell d will be displayed in polygon p. To preserve the neighbourhood of the cell, the sons of d must be displayed in the sons of p. We have to compute which son Son_i of d with $i \in \{1..nbSides\}$ will be attached to Son_j of p with $j \in \{1..nbSides\}$. We need one additional information: we choose to indicate the giver for the father of p called $Son_{nbSides}(p)$. It is necessarily a son of d, we denote it by

$Son_u(d)$ with $u \in \{1..nbSides\}$. Now, we take the givers and the receivers counter clockwise from $Son_u(d)$ and $Son_{nbSides}(p)$ respectively:

for all i in $\{1..nbSides\}$, the giver for $Son_i(p)$ is $Son_{inc^i(u)}(d)$

The function inc^i is an extension of the previous function inc:

for all u in $\{1..nbSides\}$ $inc^0(u) = u$

$$inc^i(u) = inc(inc^{i-1}(u)) \text{ with } i > 1$$

In addition, we know that from the point of view of $Son_{inc^i(u)}(d)$, the giver for p is obtained by side $Side_{inc^i(u)}(d)$. Figure 4 shows giver d for a receiver p with $Son_3(d)$ the giver for the father of p. The solution is simpler because, in T, when a receiver p is reached, we come from $Son_{nbSides}(p)$ and we have only two or three sons to compute. The type of p must be taken into account:

- 2-nodes: we just have to compute $Son_i(p)$ for all i in $\{2..3\}$ for the *pentagrid* and $Son_i(p)$ for all i in $\{3..4\}$ for the *heptagrid*. The others are seams.
- 3-nodes: we just have to compute $Son_i(p)$ for all i in $\{1..3\}$ for the *pentagrid* and $Son_i(p)$ for all i in $\{2..4\}$ for the *heptagrid*. The others are seams.

The following algorithm applies to the *heptagrid* and associates a heptagon p (2-node or 3-node) to cell d knowing u, the side to reach the giver for the father of p from d. The computation goes on recursively with all sons until a required *level* is reached.

```
Algorithm for Walk
  input
  level: depth to compute (at least 1)
      p: heptagon to display (the receiver)
      d: cell attached to p (the giver)
      u: side of d to reach the giver for the father of p

  Put cell d in heptagon p
  if (level > 1)
      // it is not the last level … we continue
      if is3Node(p)
      then firstSon := 2 //3-node: sons from 2 to 4
      else firstSon := 3 //2-node: sons from 3 to 4
      fi

      // heptagon Son_i (p) will receive cell Son_inc^i(u) (d)
      // Side_inc^i(u) (d) is the side to reach Son_inc^i(u) (d)
      for i from firstSon to 4 do
          Walk (level-1, Son_i(p), Son_inc^i(u) (d), Side_inc^i(u) (d))
      rof
  fi
```

To complete the display of the tiling, we need an algorithm to initiate the display of each basic region R_i and to manage the central heptagon. So, the next algorithm associates the central heptagon to cell *mainCell*. To compute all basic regions R_i, we need to know the giver for one leading heptagon. We choose to indicate *side1*, the side of *mainCell* to be used to reach the cell associated to the leading heptagon of region R_l. The computation goes on until a required *level* is reached.

```
Algorithm for Refresh
 input
      level : depth to compute(at least one)
  mainCell : cell associated to central heptagon (0,0)
     side1 : side of mainCell to reach the giver of the
             leading heptagon of region 1

  Put cell mainCell in the central heptagon
  if (level > 1)
      // it is not the last level … we fill basic regions
      // Son_i((0,0)) receives the cell Son_inc^i-1_(u)(mainCell)
      for i from 1 to 7 do
        Walk (level-1,
              Son_i( (0, 0) ),           // in tree T
              Son_inc^i-1_(u)(mainCell),
              Side_inc^i-1_(u)(mainCell)) // in graph G
      rof
  fi
```

Figure 5 shows two different points of view of one cellular automaton with the same depth of display: we are focused on different cells, $(0, 0)$ and $(5, 3)$. User obtains a zooming effect: the *polygrid* is mainly occupied by the neighbourhood of the cell being focused. Thus, cells not yet visible appear and some visible cells disappear.

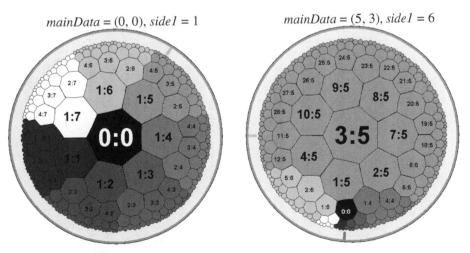

mainData = $(0, 0)$, *side1* = 1   *mainData* = $(5, 3)$, *side1* = 6

Fig. 5. Several visualisations of the same cellular automata. A cell is displayed with a colour to show its state and its coordinate (r, w) is displayed as $\overline{w} : r$.

We provide an interactive environment to use this algorithm for visualisation and to interact with the hyperbolic plane. Thanks to the algorithms to locale points, see [2], user can directly select a cell in the Poincaré's disc to bring it up in the central polygon. He can also use a simplified interaction based on a vector of displacement V provided by a movement of 2D device like a mouse. A new specific device is even manufacturing for this purpose [6]. This vector is interpreted as a zoom $\{src::dest\}$ which brings up the cell of the leading polygon of basic region src into the central polygon and brings down the cell of the central polygon into the leading polygon of basic region $dest$ (see figure 6). For example, if user gives a vector between $2\pi/7$ and $4\pi/7$, it will be interpreted as a zoom $\{3::6\}$, the leading polygon of region 3 will go in the central polygon and the central polygon will go in the leading of region 6. By this way, user accesses to a restrictive set of displacements but the dialogue is highly interactive and simple to use.

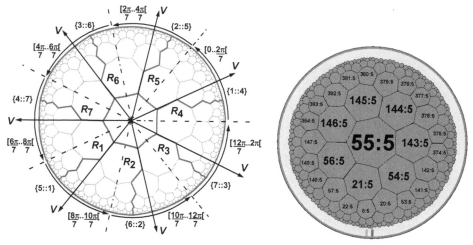

Fig. 6. Interaction technique for zooming and compass metaphor.

Unfortunately, after some zooming, it is possible to get lost like in all tools based on hyperbolic geometry: user needs help to get one's bearing. We propose to solve this by using the metaphor of the compass: for example a reference always indicates the location of cell $(0, 0)$, the centre of the cellular automaton. Of course, this can be done only when cell $(0, 0)$ is not in the central polygon.We can see it in figure 5 with the dark mark in the border. The computation of this reference is easy by using the algorithm to locate cells which computes the polygon to which a cell is attached. But more generally, our goal is to extend the compass. We want:

- To give the user the possibility to put and remove references, to remember a way, to focus on some cells ...
- To use references to attract the attention of user, to inform about important places. This can be results of requests, of active parts in the working of the CA ...

These references will be displayed in different colors, icons ... Figure 5 shows two references with different colors, one in light gray for cell (5, 11) and one in dark gray for (0, 0). The most important thing is to imagine the importance of the reference when the cell is not visible like in figure 6 where cell (5, 55) is in the central polygon. Cell (0, 0) is no longer visible but user can access it by a minimum of zooms thanks to the dark gray reference. By extension, user can select directly the reference to go to the cell which is referenced.

5 Conclusion

In this paper we provide all the materials to ground and compare cellular automata in the rectangular *pentagrid* and the ternary *heptagrid* of the hyperbolic plane. In particular, we describe the neighbourhood computation with the Fibonacci numbering and an interactive environment for visualisation and interaction. By using the "fisheye" effect of the Poincaré's disc, this environment allows user to concentrate on a part of a snapshot from a cellular automaton. The introduction of the compass avoids any loss of reference during this interaction. In future development, we hope to enhance our environment to provide tools to follow and to better understand the evolution of the cellular automaton during a period of time. On another hand, we can note that the ternary *heptagrid* introduces a very important and useful feature: the connection between neighbours. As suggested by the content of [9], this would have interesting consequences in complexity issues.

References

1. K. Chelghoum, M. Margenstern, B. Martin et I. Pecci. Initialising Cellular Automata in the Hyperbolic Plane. IEICE Transactions on Information and Systems, Special Section on Cellular Automata, vol. E87-D, No3, 677-686, March, 2004.
2. K. Chelghoum, M. Margenstern, B. Martin, I. Pecci. Tools for implementing cellular automata in grid {7,3} of the hyperbolic plane. DMCS, Turku, July, 2004.
3. M. Margenstern. New tools for Cellular Automata in the Hyperbolic Plane, Journal of Universal Computer Science, vol 6, issue 12, 1226-1252, 2000.
4. M. Margenstern, K. Morita. NP-problems are tractable in the space of cellular automata in the hyperbolic plane, Theoretical Computer Science, 259, 99-128, 2001.
5. M. Margenstern. Cellular Automata and Combinatoric Tilings in Hyperbolic Spaces, a survey, Lecture Notes of Computer Sciences, 2731, (2003), 48-72, (proceedings of DMTCS'2003, Dijon, July, 7-12, 2003, invited talk).
6. B. Martin. TrackMouse: a 4D solution for interacting with two cursors. Accepted in IHM'04, Namur, Belgique, September, 2004.
7. H. Meschkowski. Non-Euclidean geometry, translated by A. Shenitzer, Academic Press, New-York, 1964.
8. A. Ramsey, R. D. Richtmyer. Introduction to hyperbolic geometry, Springer, Berlin, 1995.
9. T. Worsch. Simulations Between Cellular Automata on Trees Extended by Horizontal Edges, Fundamenta Informaticae, vol. 58, No3, 241-260, 2004.

Algebraic Properties of Cellular Automata: The Basis for Composition Technique*

Olga Bandman

Supercomputer Software Department
ICMMG, Siberian Branch Russian Academy of Sciences
Pr. Lavrentieva, 6, Novosibirsk, 630090, Russia
bandman@ssd.sscc.ru

Abstract. An extended class of Cellular Automata (CA), in which arbitrary transition functions are allowed, are considered as a model for spatial dynamic simulation. CA are represented as operators over a set of cellular arrays, where binary operations (superposition, addition and multiplication) are defined. The algebraic properties of the operations are studied. The aim of the investigation is to create a formal basis for the CA composition methods, which are also presented in brief.

1   Introduction

Nowadays application of CA for the spatial dynamics simulation attracts much interest. By the present time a large amount of CA-models of natural processes are proposed and well studied [1]. The most known are CA models of diffusion, Gas-Lattice, phase-separation, snow flakes formation, stripes formation, etc. An important aim of those simulations is to study the behavioral properties of the processes. Such studies would be more efficient if some dependence between the properties of CA-transition functions and those of the evolution progress were known. Unfortunately, it is unlikely that such a knowledge for a general case may be available. In other words, the problem of synthesis of a CA, whose evolution follows some prescribed behavioral properties is stiff. The only way to approach it is to perform case study for CA of typical processes and to develop methods for making them functioning in common. This idea has been already used in a number of methods for simulation of complex phenomena, the most successful being intended for the reaction-diffusion simulation [2,3].

A similar problem exists in mathematical physics, where a set of typical functions and differential operators, simulating convection, diffusion, reaction, wave propagation etc., are composed to represent complex processes. The same strategy may be used relative to the composed CA systems. The problem now is seen from far away. In order to approach it, composition methods of CA are needed. Hence, mathematical operations on CA should be available. In the paper

---

* Supported by Presidium of Russian Academy of Sciences, Basic Research Program
  N 17-6 (2004)

P.M.A. Sloot, B. Chopard, and A.G. Hoekstra (Eds.): ACRI 2004, LNCS 3305, pp. 688–697, 2004.

an attempt is made to define a set of such operations and to study their properties. Taking into account the diversity of representation forms of spatial dynamics (molecular kinetics, differential equations, nonlinear functions, probabilistic functions) to be simulated by CA, an extended concept of CA is considered: the alphabet is extended to the real number set, and the arbitrary transition functions including stochastic ones are allowed. To capture all above extensions, the Parallel Substitution Algorithm formalism [5] is used.

The paper is divided into five sections. The second section contains formal definitions of the used concepts. In the third and in the fourth sections algebraic properties of cellular arrays and CA sets are defined and analyzed. The last section is intended for presenting some composition techniques.

2 Formal Definitions of Used Concepts

Cellular Automata under consideration are intended for processing spatially distributed functions further represented by *cellular arrays*. A cellular array Ω is a finite set of pairs (u, m) called *cells*: $\Omega = \{(u, m) : u \in A, m \in M\}$, where u is a *cell state variable* with the domain A, referred to as *alphabet*, m is a *cell name* from a discrete *naming set* M. Further, in the examples, the finite naming sets are used, whose elements are integer vectors, representing coordinates of a Cartesian space. For example, in a 2D case $M = \{(i, j) : i, j = 0, 1, \ldots, N\}$. In abstract definitions a countable naming set is considered, a notion m instead of (i, j) being used to be more concise and to show that any other kind of naming set is also permitted. To indicate to the state of a cell named m both notations $u(m)$ and u_m are used.

There is no constraint imposed on the alphabet A. The following cases are further used: $A_s = \{a, b, c, \ldots, n\}$ – a finite set of symbols, $A_B = \{0, 1\}$ – Boolean alphabet, $A_q = \{0, 1/q, \ldots, 1\}$ – a finite set of rational numbers, and $A_R = (0, 1)$ – the set of real numbers in the closed interval. Symbols from the second part of the latin alphabet $\{v, u, x, y, \ldots, z\}$ denote state variables. Such an extended concept of an alphabet is dictated by the aim of the study which is to combine different kind of cellular automata for simulating complex natural phenomena.

On the naming set M, a mapping $\phi : M \to M$, called a *naming function*, is defined. In the 2D set $M = \{(i, j)\}$ naming functions are usually given in the form of shifts $\phi(i, j) = (i + a, j + b)$, a, b being integers not exceeding a fixed r, called a *radius of neighborhood*. A set of naming functions

$$\Gamma(m) = \{\phi_0(m), \ldots, \phi_i(m), \ldots, \phi_n(m)\}, \quad \phi_0(m) = m, \tag{1}$$

referred to as a *template* , determines the structure of local interactions between cells. A template $\Gamma(m)$ associates a name $m \in M$ with a subset of cells

$$S(m) = \{(u_0, \phi_0(m)), \ldots, (u_i, \phi_i(m)), \ldots, (u_n, \phi_n(m))\}, \tag{2}$$

called a *local configuration*. The cell states from $S(m)$ form a *local configuration state* $U(m) = \{u_0, \ldots, u_n\}$. If cell interactions are weighted, then a weight value $w_i \in \mathbf{R}$ is associated with each $\phi_i(m)$, forming a set $W = \{w_0, \ldots, w_n\}$.

A transition from $\Omega(t)$ to $\Omega(t+1)$ is the result of computing a *global transition function* $\Phi(\Omega)$, which is given by a *parallel substitution system* $\Phi = \{\Phi_1 \ldots, \Phi_k, \ldots, \Phi_l\}$ [5], where

$$\Phi_k : \; S_k(m) \to S'_k(m), \quad \Gamma'_k(m) \subseteq \Gamma^{(}_k m), \quad k = 0, \ldots, l, \tag{3}$$

$\Gamma_k(m), \Gamma'_k(m)$ being the underlying templates for $S_k(m), S'_k(m)$, respectively, and $S'_k(m) = \{(u'_i, \phi'_i(m) : \phi'_i(m) \in \Gamma'_k\}$ is the *next state local configuration*. The substitution Φ_k is applicable to a cell (u_m, m), if $S_k(m) \subseteq \Omega(t)$, otherwise it is not. All $\Phi_k \in \Phi$ are applied to $\Omega(t)$ in parallel. An application of Φ_k replaces the states in cells from $S_k(m)$ by those given in the $S'_k(m)$, which are obtained as a function $u'_m = f_k(U(m))$, which is allowed to be of any kind: a Boolean function if $A = A_B$, a real function if $A = A_R$ or $A = A_q$. In the latter case u'_m may occur between two values of A_q. In that case u'_m is represented as $u''_m + r'_m$, where $u''_m \in A_q$ and $r'(m) < 1/q$ is a residue which is added to the state u_m on the next iteration, i.e. $r_m(t+1) = r'(t)$, providing a good accuracy of discrete computations. So, the *cell transition function* is as follows.

$$f_k(U(m), r(m)) = u'_m + r'_m. \tag{4}$$

When u'_i occurs to be beyond the interval (0,1) the alphabet should be renormalized (if it is not possible, then the process under simulation is unstable).

There are three modes of CA functioning: 1) *synchronous* mode when all cells compute their next states in parallel and transit to the next state at once at time steps $t = 0, 1, \ldots$, changing the global cellular array state; 2) *n-step synchronous*, where each iteration is executed by n sequential steps; and 3) *asynchronous* mode, when the cells execute their transitions sequentially in a certain order. Of course, simulation on an ordinary computer is performed in a quasiparallel mode. In all cases transition to the next global state, $\Omega(t+1) = \Phi(\Omega(t))$ is considered as *an iteration*. The sequence of cellular arrays, $\Omega(0), \Omega(1), \ldots, \Omega(t), \ldots, \Omega(T)$, obtained by iterative application of Φ to the initial array $\Omega(0)$, is called *CA evolution*. The time T indicates the termination step.

With the above notions CA is defined as a pair

$$\Theta = (\Omega(0), \Phi)$$

together with the indication to the mode of operation. A set of cellular arrays characterized by the same pair (A, M) is further denoted by $\Upsilon(A, M)$. All CA acting on $\Upsilon(A, M)$ form a set $\Xi(A, M)$.

Since Boolean and real alphabets are allowed to be used in common in one and the same simulation process, some transformations of $\Omega \in \Upsilon(A_R, M)$ and $\Omega \in \Upsilon(A_q, M)$ to $\Omega \in \Upsilon(A_B, M)$ and vice versa are required, which are as follows.

1. *Averaging* $(Av(\Omega))$ is transformation of $\Omega_1 \in \Upsilon(A_B, M)$ to $\Omega_2 \in \Upsilon(A_q, M)$. Let $\Omega_1 = \{(v_1, m) : v_1 \in \{0,1\}, m \in M\}$, and $\Omega_2 = \{(v_2, m) : v_2 \in A_q, |A_q| = q + 1\}$, then

$$v_2(m) = \langle v_1(m) \rangle = \frac{1}{q} \sum_{k=0}^{q} v_1(\psi_k(m)), \quad \forall m \in M, \tag{5}$$

i.e. v_2 is a mean state value taken over the *averaging area* $Av_q(m) \subset M$, $|Av(m)| = q,$.

$$Av(m) = \{\psi_0(m), \psi_1(m), \ldots, \psi_q(m)\}, \quad \forall m \in M. \tag{6}$$

2. *Boolean discretization* $(Disc(\Omega))$ is transformation of $\Omega_1 \in \Upsilon(A_R, M)$ to $\Omega_2 \in \Upsilon(A_B, M)$. Let $\Omega_1 = \{(v_1, m) : v_1 \in A_R, \ m \in M\}$ and $\Omega_2 = \{(v_2, m) : v_2 \in \{0, 1\}, m \in M\}$, then for all $m \in M$

$$v_2(m) = \begin{cases} 1 & \text{with probability } \pi = v_1, \\ 0 & \text{otherwise} \end{cases} \tag{7}$$

Boolean discretization approximates a real array by a Boolean one, approximation accuracy having been studied in [4].

Taking into account that $A_q \subset A_R$, two transformations are in the following relationship:

$$\begin{array}{ll} Disc(\Omega(A_B, M)) = \Omega(A_B, M), & Av(\Omega(A_R, M)) = \Omega(A_R, M), \\ Av(Disk(\Omega(A_R, M)) = \Omega(A_q, M), & Disc(Av(\Omega(A_B, M)) = \Omega(A_B, M), \end{array} \tag{8}$$

where $\Omega(A_B, M) \in \Upsilon(A_B, M), \Omega(A_R, M) \in \Upsilon(A_R, M)$.

3 Algebraic Properties of Cellular Arrays

All operations from the set theory (union, intersection, equivalence relations, etc.) are allowed on the set of cellular arrays $\Upsilon(A, M)$. However, since the class of CA under consideration is intended for the spatial dynamics simulation, where functions obey conventional arithmetic laws, the corresponding operations are also to be defined. It is done so as to follow arithmetic rules on cell-by-cell averaged state values.

Cellular array addition is a binary operation on $\Upsilon'(A, M) = \Upsilon(A_B, M) \cup \Upsilon(A_R, M)$.

$$\Omega_3 = \Omega_1 \oplus \Omega_2, \quad \text{if } \langle v_3(m) \rangle = \langle v_1(m) \rangle + \langle v_2(m) \rangle \quad \forall m \in M, \tag{9}$$

where $\langle v(m) \rangle$ are computed according to (5) for a certain q. Using cellular array properties (8), the addition may be performed in a number of ways, depending on the state alphabets of the items and of the sum. When all of them have as alphabets A_q or A_R, then according to (9), $\oplus$ turns into the ordinary arithmetic cell-by-cell addition. When $\Omega_1 \in \Upsilon(A_B, M)$ $\Omega_2 \in \Upsilon(A_R, M)$ and a Boolean result is wanted, then the following formula may be used.

$$v_3(m) = \begin{cases} 1 & \text{if } v_1(m) = 0, \text{ with probability } \pi_1(m) \\ v_1(m) & \text{otherwise} \end{cases}, \tag{10}$$

where $\pi_1(m) = v_2(m)/(1 - \langle v_1(m) \rangle)$ [3].

A cellular array *subtraction* is also defined. When both operands are in $\Upsilon(A_R, M)$ the difference is computed by (9) with "+" changed to "-". When

$\Omega_1 \in \Upsilon(A_B, M)$, and $\Omega_2 \in \Upsilon(A_R, M)$ and a Boolean result is wanted, the difference is obtained as follows.

$$v_3(m) = \begin{cases} 0 & \text{if } v_1(m) = 1, \text{ with probability } \pi_2(m) \\ v_1(m) & \text{otherwise,} \end{cases} \tag{11}$$

where $\pi_2(m) = v_2(m)/\langle v_1(m) \rangle$ [3].

Since addition and subtraction are defined on the set $\Upsilon'(A, M)$ with the values in the interval $(0,1)$, the condition $0 \leq v_3(m) \leq 1$ should be satisfied for all $v_3(m) \in \Omega$. If it is not so, the alphabet is to be renormalized.

Cellular array multiplication is also defined on $\Upsilon'(A, M)$. Let $\Omega_k = \{(v_k, m)\}$, $k = 1, 2, 3$, then

$$\Omega_3 = \Omega_1 \otimes \Omega_2 \quad \text{if} \quad \langle v_3, m \rangle = \langle v_1(m) \rangle \times \langle v_2(m) \rangle \quad \forall m \in M. \tag{12}$$

Similar to the cellular array addition, several techniques may be used to perform multiplication, depending on the alphabet types of the items and the result to be obtained. The simplest way is to use all of them in the averaged form, executing Boolean discretization on the result, if the latter is required to be Boolean.

The following relations are valid on $\Upsilon'(A, M)$.

$$\Omega_1 < \Omega_2 \text{ if } \langle v_1(m) \rangle \leq \langle v_2(m) \rangle \quad \forall m \in M,$$
$$\Omega_1 > \Omega_2 \text{ if } \langle v_1(m) \rangle \geq \langle v_2(m) \rangle \quad \forall m \in M,$$

which induce on $\Upsilon'(A, M)$ a partial order with the following properties:

$$\Omega_1 \oplus \Omega_2 \geq \Omega_1, \quad \Omega_1 \oplus \Omega_2 \geq \Omega_2,$$
$$\Omega_1 \otimes \Omega_2 \leq \Omega_1, \quad \Omega_1 \otimes \Omega_2 \leq \Omega_2. \tag{13}$$

So, the set $\Upsilon'(A, M)$ forms an algebraic lattice, containing two neutral elements: a ZERO $\Omega = \{(0, m) : \forall m \in M\} = \mathbf{0}$, such that for any $\Omega \in \Upsilon : \Omega \oplus \mathbf{0} = \Omega\}$; and a ONE $\Omega = \{(1, m) : \forall m \in M\} = \mathbf{1}$, such that for any $\Omega \in \Upsilon : \Omega \otimes \mathbf{1} = \Omega$. The cellular array addition and multiplication are associative and commutative, the multiplication being distributive relative to the addition. However, since the inverse relative to ONE and ZERO are not defined, the set $\Upsilon'(A, M)$ with $\oplus$ and $\otimes$ may not be regarded as a classic algebraic system.

4   Algebraic Properties of Cellular Automata

In order that the algebraic properties of CA be studied, let us consider a set of global transition functions (3) defined on $\Upsilon(A, M)$ as a set of operators

$$\Sigma = \{\Phi : \Upsilon(A, M) \Rightarrow \Upsilon(A, M)\}$$

and the pair $(\Upsilon(A, M), \Sigma)$ as a representation of the CA set $\Xi(A, M)$. Each $\Phi \in \Sigma$ is then a closure operator on the set of cellular arrays appearing in the evolution sequences of $\Theta = (\Omega(A, M), \Phi)$.

Due to its substitution character, the operator Φ is not distributive relative to the addition and multiplication defined on $\Upsilon(A, M)$. Moreover, it is not distributive relative to the union and the intersection of Boolean cellular arrays, i.e.

$$
\begin{aligned}
\Phi(\Omega_1 \cup \Omega_2) &\neq \Phi((\Omega_1) \cup \Phi(\Omega_2)), \quad \forall \Omega_1, \Omega_2 \in \Upsilon(A_B, M), \\
\Phi(\Omega_1 \cap \Omega_2) &\neq \Phi((\Omega_1) \cap \Phi(\Omega_2)), \quad \forall \Omega_1, \Omega_2 \in \Upsilon(A_B, M).
\end{aligned}
\tag{14}
$$

In order that common functioning of several CA be studied, the following binary operations are defined on the set $\Xi(A, M)$.

Superposition of CA. Let $\Theta_1, \Theta_2 \in \Xi(A, M)$, then a CA $\Theta_3 = \Theta_2(\Theta_1)$ is a superposition of Θ_1 and Θ_2, if $\Phi_3 = \Phi_2(\Phi_1(\Omega(A, M))$. The CA-superposition is neither commutative nor associative, i.e. if $\Phi_1 \neq \Phi_2 \neq \Phi_3$, then

$$
\begin{aligned}
\Phi_2(\Phi_1(\Omega)) &\neq \Phi_1(\Phi_2(\Omega)), \\
\Phi_3(\Phi_2(\Phi_1(\Omega))) &\neq (\Phi_3(\Phi_2))(\Phi_1(\Omega)).
\end{aligned}
\tag{15}
$$

Nevertheless, the iterative CA functioning during which a long sequence of repetitive applications $\Phi_1(\Phi_2(\Phi_1(\Phi_2, \ldots,)))$ is performed, makes the evolution independent of the CA being the first. Of course the superposition of the same CA is commutative and represents the CA evolution steps. All kinds of the combined superposition of the form $\Theta = \Theta_1^n(\Theta_2^s)$, n, s being natural numbers, are allowed. Moreover, n, s, may be related by a functional dependence.

CA addition. Let $\Theta_1, \Theta_2 \in \Xi(A, M)$. A CA $\Theta_3 = \Theta_1 \oplus \Theta_2$ is the sum of Θ_1 and Θ_2 if for any $\Omega \in \Upsilon(A, M)$ $\Phi_3(\Omega) = \Phi_1(\Omega) \oplus \Phi_2(\Omega)$. In the general case it is not possible to construct a single substitution Φ_3 when Φ_1, Φ_2 are given. Hence, each iteration of Θ_3 should be performed in three steps:

$$
\begin{aligned}
\Omega_1(t+1) &= \Phi_1(\Omega(t)), \\
\Omega_2(t+1) &= \Phi_2(\Omega(t)), \\
\Omega_3(t+1) &= \Omega_1(t+1) \oplus \Omega_2(t+1),
\end{aligned}
$$

the two first steps being allowed to be performed in parallel.

CA multiplication. The operation is similar to the addition. All the above said about the CA addition is valid for the CA-multiplication with the replacement of " $\oplus$ " by " $\otimes$ ".

Since the CA-addition and the CA-multiplication are the operations on the resulting at each iteration cellular arrays at each-iteration, they inherit the corresponding algebraic properties of the cellular array operations, i.e. they are commutative and associative, the multiplication being distributive relative to the addition.

$$
\begin{aligned}
\Theta_1 \oplus \Theta_2 &= \Theta_2 \oplus \Theta_1, \\
\Theta_1 \otimes \Theta_2 &= \Theta_2 \otimes \Theta_1, \\
\Theta_1 \oplus (\Theta_2 \oplus \Theta_3) &= (\Theta_1 \oplus \Theta_2) \oplus \Theta_3. \\
\Theta_1 \otimes (\Theta_2 \otimes \Theta_3) &= (\Theta_1 \otimes \Theta_2) \otimes \Theta_3. \\
\Theta_1 \otimes (\Theta_2 \oplus \Theta_3) &= \Theta_1 \otimes \Theta_2 \oplus \Theta_1 \otimes \Theta_3.
\end{aligned}
\tag{16}
$$

Superposition is not distributive relative to the CA addition and the CA multiplication, i.e.

$$
\Theta_1(\Theta_2 \oplus \Theta_3) \neq \Theta_1(\Theta_2) \oplus \Theta_1(\Theta_3).
\tag{17}
$$

As distinct from the cellular array set $\Upsilon(A, M)$ the set $\Xi(A, M)$ is not a partial ordered one, having no neutral elements, because no order can be defined on $\Xi(A, M)$ without imposing constraints onto Φ.

Example 1. A chemical reaction of CO oxidation over platinum metals, studied by means of a number of kinetic and continuous models [9,10], is represented by the superposition of elementary substitutions as follows. The cellular array $\Omega(A, M)$ corresponds to a metallic plate each site on it being named by $(i, j) \in M$. The alphabet contains three symbols $A = \{a, b, 0\}$, so that $(a, (i, j)), (b, (i, j))$, and $(0, (i, j))$ are cells corresponding to the sites occupied by the molecules of CO, O or being empty, respectively. In the initial array cell states a and b are randomly distributed according to given partial pressure of CO and O_2 in the gas above the plate. The reaction mechanism consists of the following elementary molecular actions.

1) Adsorption of CO from the gas: if a cell is empty, it becomes occupied by a CO molecule with probability π_a.

2) Adsorption of O_2 from the gas: if two neighboring cells are empty, each becomes occupied by a molecule of oxygen with probability π_b.

3) Reaction of oxidation of CO (CO+0 $\rightarrow$ CO_2): if two different molecules CO and O occur to be neighbors, then the molecule CO_2, formed by the reaction, transits to the gas and both cells become empty.

4) Diffusion of CO: if a CO molecule has an empty neighbor, it moves there with probability π_d, depending of the temperature.

The above actions are transformed to a parallel substitution system as follows:

$$
\begin{aligned}
&\Phi_1(\pi_a): \; \{(0, (i, j))\} \rightarrow \{(a, (i, j))\}, \\
&\Phi_2(\pi_b): \; \{(0, (i, j))(0, (i + k, j + l))\} \rightarrow \{(b, (i, j)), (b, (i + k, j + l))\}, \\
&\Phi_3: \qquad \{(a, (i, j))(b, (i + k, j + l))\} \rightarrow \{(0, (i, j)), (0, (i + k, j + l))\}, \\
&\Phi_4(\pi_d): \; \{(0, (i, j)), (a, (i + k, j + l))\} \rightarrow \{(a, (i, j)), (0, (i + k, j + l))\}.
\end{aligned}
\tag{18}
$$

In (18), the notion $\Phi(\pi)$ means that Φ is applied to Ω with probability π, the pair (k, l), which determines one of the four neighbors of a cell, is chosen out of the set $\{(0, 1), (1, 0), (0, -1)(-1, 0)\}$ with equal probability. In [10], the process is simulated in asynchronous mode, (the method being called by the authors as Monte Carlo simulation), the global transition function of the CA being the following superposition: $\Phi = \Phi_4^h(\Phi_1(\Phi_2(\Phi_3)))$. The transition function Φ_4, which simulates diffusion, is applied h times, h depending on the temperature of the process.

5   The CA Composition Methods

The algebraic properties of CA underlie the basis of the CA composition techniques. Let us partition the whole scope of CA composition methods into two groups: 1) disjoint (trivial) composition, and 2) shared variables composition.

Disjoint composition is a cooperative functioning of two CA, whose transition rules are defined on separate cellular arrays. So, they evolve independently, interacting only at the start and the termination. There are two forms of disjoint composition: sequential and parallel.

Sequential disjoint composition is a superposition of the form

$$\Theta_3 = \Theta_2^{T_2}(\Theta_1^{T_1}),$$

where T_1 and T_2 are termination times of Θ_1 and Θ_2 evolution, respectively. The evolution of Θ_3 terminates at $T_3 = T_1 + T_2$, Θ_2 starting when Θ_1 terminates, $\Phi_3 = \Phi_2^{T_2}(\Phi_1^{T_1})$. It should be noted that the time steps of Θ_1 and Θ_2 are allowed to be different, and Θ_2 starts only after Θ_1 has terminated. The composition is useful, especially, in pipelined systems executing a fine-grained parallel cellular computation or image processing.

Parallel disjoint composition is the independent evolution of two CA, the total result being then obtained by performing one of the binary operations over the terminal arrays, i.e.

$$\Theta_3 = \Theta_1^T \Diamond \Theta_2^T,$$

where the simbol $\Diamond$ defines any of binary operations on $\Upsilon(A, M)$, i.e. $\Omega_3 = \Omega_1(T_1) \Diamond \Omega_2(T_2)$. In this form of composition, the component CA may have different alphabets and different timings, hence, they need a synchronization signal to start "$\Diamond$" operation.

Shared variables compositioon. A CA Θ is a shared variable composition of Θ_1 and Θ_2,

$$\Theta = \Theta_1 \square \Theta_2$$

if Φ_1 contains in the left-hand side of $S_1(m)$ some cells from Ω_2 and, similarly, Φ_2 contains in the left-hand-side of $S_2(m)$ some cells from Ω_1. By partitioning the local configurations (3) into two subsets each belonging to Ω_1 or to Ω_2, substitutions (8) take the following form:

$$\begin{aligned} \Phi_1: \quad & S_{11}(m) \cup S_{12}(m) \rightarrow S_1'(m), \\ \Phi_2: \quad & S_{22}(m) \cup S_{21}(m) \rightarrow S_2'(m), \end{aligned} \tag{19}$$

where $S_{11}(m), S_{21}(m) \in \Omega_1$, $S_{22}(m), S_{12}(m) \in \Omega_2$. The composition may be regarded as two CA: $\Theta_1 = (\Phi_1, \Omega)$ and $\Theta_2 = (\Phi_2, \Omega)$, which evolve under common timing on a common $\Omega = \Omega_1 \cup \Omega_2$ under the global transition function $\Phi = \{\Phi_1, \Phi_2\}$.

A shared variable composition is called *unidirectional* if S_{12} or S_{21} is empty, otherwise the composition is *biderectional*. The composition is useful in all those cases, when a process with two or more species is under simulation. That is the case when reaction-diffusion spatial dynamics is investigated, where diffusion components are independent while reaction functions depend on all or several species taking part in the process. In conventional mathematics, such phenomena are usually represented by a PDE system.

Example 2. A soliton-like 1D process is simulated by superposition of two CA. A Boolean parity totalistic CA $\Theta_1 = (\Phi_1, \Omega_1)$ with $A_1 = \{0, 1\}$, $M = 0, 1, \ldots, N$ simulates movements of "particles" [9], while Θ_2 averages the results

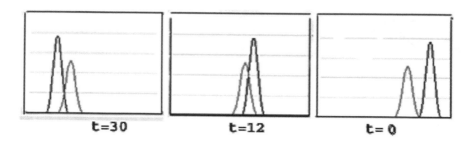

Fig. 1. Three snapshots of the unidirectional composition, simulating a soliton-like process

to make them observable in the form of moving waves. The transition function Φ_1 is as follows.

$$\Phi_1 : \ \{(u_{i+k}, i+k) : k = -r, \ldots, 0, \ldots, r\} \to (u'_i, i)$$

with

$$u'_i = \begin{cases} 1, & \text{if } \sum_{k=-r}^{r} u_{i+k} \text{ is even, but not } 0 \\ 0, & \text{otherwise} \end{cases} \tag{20}$$

The transition function Φ_1 is applied to Ω in an ordered asynchronous mode. This means, that u'_i are computed sequentially in the cells named $0, 1, \ldots, N$. Hence, at the time when (20) is applied to the cell (u, i), the first $(i + 1)$ items of the sum occur to be in the next states. The soliton-like behavior may be obtained only with initial patterns (referred to as "particles") satisfying certain conditions [9]. In the example two "particles" are used: "11011" and "10001001", r=5. The first has the displacement $d = 7$ cells to the left with a period $p = 2$. The second has $d = 12$ to the left, and $p = 6$. So, each six iterations the distance between the particles diminishes by nine cells. During 12th to the 24th iterations the particles are superimposed, and on the 30th – the first "particle" is ahead, as it is shown in the following states of $\Omega_1(t)$:

$t = 0 :$ 00000000000000000 ... 00**10001001**00000000000000000000**1101100**
$t = 6 :$ 00000 ... 00**10001001**0000000000**11011**00000000000000000000000000
$t = 30 :$ 000000000000000000000**11011**00001**0001001** ... 000000000000000
$t = 36 :$ **011011**00000000000000**10001001**0000000 ... 000000000000000

If "particles" are wanted to be observed each six iterations, being alike continuous waves, the CA Θ_2 should be used, whose transition function takes its variables from the cells of Ω_1. So a unidirectional shared variable composition should be used: $\Theta = \Theta_2^2 \diamond \Theta_1^6$, where Θ_2 is a CA which performs averaging with a radius $R = 4$. Hence, its alphabet is A_9. To achieve a good smoothness Θ_2 is applied twice. The boundary conditions are periodic, and the two particles run around from right to left, the velocity of the first particle being larger, than that of the second one (Fig.1).

6   Conclusion

Since the construction of transition rules for the CA simulation of complex phemomena is a hard task and sometimes impossible, the idea of doing so by composing simple ones seems to be fruitful. So, the theoretical basis for the CA composition techniques is important, because it allows one to widen the range of CA application for the spatial dynamics simulation. In this paper an attempt is made to approach the problem by studying the algebraic properties of cellular arrays and cellular automata.

References

1. Wolfram S.: A New Kind of Science. - Wolfram Media Inc., Champaign, Ill., USA.(2002) 1200 pp.
2. Weimar J.R.: Cellular Automata for Reaction-Diffusion Systems. Parallel Computing, vol.23,N 11 (1999) 1699-1715.
3. Bandman O.: Simulation Spatial Dynamics by Probabilistic Cellular Automata. Lecture Notes in Computer Science, vol.2493 (2002) 10-19.
4. Bandman.O.: Accuracy and Stability of Spatial Dynamics Simulation by Cellular Automata. Lecture Notes in Computer Science, vol.2766 (2003) 20-34.
5. S. Achasova S., Bandman O., Markova V., and S. Piskunov: Parallel Substitution Algorithm. Theory and Application. - World Scientific, Singapoore (1994) 180 pp.
6. Toffolli T.,and Margolus N.: Cellular Automata Machines.- MIT Press, USA (1987) 280 pp.210.
7. Malinetski G.G., and Stepantsov M.E.: Modelling diffusive processes by cellular automata with Margolus neighborhood. Zh. Vychislitelnoy matematiki i matematicheskoy phiziki, vol.36, N 6 (1998) 1017-1021.
8. Schlogl F.: Chemical reaction models for non-equilibrium phase transitions. Zh.Physik, vol.253 (1972) 147-161.
9. Weimar J.R.: Coupling Microscopic and Macroscopic Cellular Automata. Parallel Computing, vol.27 (20-01) 601-611.
10. Latkin E.I., Elokhin V.I. and Gorodetskii.: Spiral cocentration waves in the Monte-Carlo Model of CO oxidation over PD(110) caused by synchronization via CO_{ads} diffusion between separate parts of catalitic surface. Chemical Engineering Journal, vol.91 (2003) 123-131.
11. Park J.K., Steiglitz K., and Thurston W.P.: Soliton-like behavior in automata. Physica D, vol.19 (1986) 423-432.

DSCA Implementation of 3D Self-Replicating Structures

André Stauffer, Daniel Mange, Enrico Petraglio, and Fabien Vannel

Logic Systems Laboratory, Swiss Federal Institute of Technology,
IN-Ecublens, CH-1015 Lausanne, Switzerland.
andre.stauffer@epfl.ch, lslwww.epfl.ch.

Abstract. After a survey of some realizations of self-replicating machines, this paper presents the construction based self-replication of 3D structures. This self-replication process is achieved by translation and transcription of a configuration information in a three-dimensional data and signals cellular automaton (DSCA). The specifications and the design of the basic three-dimensional cell of the automaton results in a new and straightforward methodology for the self-replication of 3D computing machines of any dimensions.

1   Introduction

In the history of non trivial self-replicating machines, there are mainly two different approaches: (1) the self-replication based on inspection, and (2) the self-replication based on construction.

Using *inspection* in order to implement self-replicating structures was the approach chosen by a few researchers. Morita and Imai [1] present configurations named worms and loops able to self-replicate by using a shape-encoding method. Ibanez and al. [2] describe also a self-inspecting loop capable of self-replication. In these works, the data are only used in an uninterpreted way called transcription. It is accomplished by duplication of signals at the periphery of the structure.

Using *construction* in order to self-replicate structures was the way von Neumann [3] conceived to solve the problem. It was Langton [4] who realized the first practical implementation of the process. In these approaches, the information is successively used in two different modes, interpreted and uninterpreted. First, in the interpreted mode or translation, the signals are executed as they reach the periphery in order to construct the replicated structure. After, in the uninterpreted mode or transcription, the signals are copied in the replicated structure.

The main goal of this paper is to carry out construction in order to self-replicate 3D structures. This self-replication process is achieved in a three-dimensional data and signals cellular automaton (DSCA) [5]. The fundamentals of this three-dimensional, seven-neighbor DSCA are defined in Section 2. Section 3 presents the specifications of the basic cell of the automaton. The design of this cell is described in Section 4. Section 5 will conclude by opening new avenues based on the self-replication of 3D universal structures.

P.M.A. Sloot, B. Chopard, and A.G. Hoekstra (Eds.): ACRI 2004, LNCS 3305, pp. 698–708, 2004.

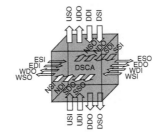

Fig. 1. Basic cell of the three-dimensional seven-neighbor DSCA.

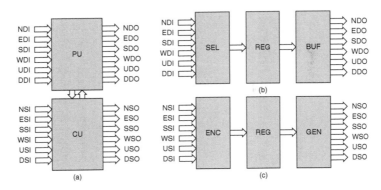

Fig. 2. DSCA cell. (a) Processing unit PU and control unit CU. (b) Detailed architecture of PU. (c) Detailed architecture of CU.

2   Data and Signals Cellular Automaton

Data and signals cellular automata (DSCA) were originally conceived to provide a formal framework for designing growing structures [6], [7]. Such an automaton is made up of an array of cells, each of which is implemented as a digital system processing both data and signals in discrete time steps. The cellular array (grid) is n-dimensional, where $n = 1, 2, 3$ is used in practice.

In growing structures, the data and the signals represents two different types of information. The *data* constitute the information that travels through the grown structure. The *signals* constitute the information that controls the growth of the structure.

The basic cell of a three-dimensional seven-neighbor DSCA works with the northward (N), eastward (E), southward (S), westward (W), upward (U) and downward (D) directed data (D) and signals (S) (Figure 1). The cell computes its digital outputs O from its digital inputs I. These data and signals outputs are not necessarily identical for all the neighboring cells.

Each cell of the automaton is designed as a *digital system*, resulting from the interconnection of a data processing unit PU and a control unit CU (Figure 2a). In this digital system, the *processing unit* handles the data. It is made up of

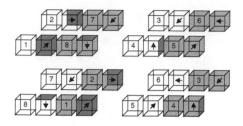

Fig. 3. The minimal 3D structure composed of $2 \times 2 \times 2$ cells. Each cell is represented as a cluster of four cubes.

Fig. 4. 3D graphical representations. (a) Nature of the data. (b) Status of the data.

input selectors SEL, data registers REG, and output buffers BUF (Figure 2b). The *control unit* of the digital system computes the signals. It combines input encoders ENC, control registers REG, and output generators GEN (Figure 2c).

3   Cell Specifications

The minimal 3D structure is made up of eight cells organized as the $2 \times 2 \times 2$ array represented in Figure 3. Each cell of the array comprises four data expressed in small cubes. As we will see later, the two data to the left are mobile and constitute the genotype of the cell, while the two data to the right are fixed and define the phenotype of the cell. Each of these data is either a code or a flag. The code data is used for configuring the structure whereas the flag data is indispensable for constructing the skeleton of the structure, i.e. defining the information path. Figures 4 summarizes the 3D graphical representations of the data.

In order to show the construction of our 3D minimal self-replicating structure, we introduce 2D graphical representations. In Figure 5, the eight cells of the minimal structure are organized as two levels $L = 1$ and $L = 2$ of two rows by two columns. Each cell is able to store in its four memory positions four configuration data. The original configuration is a string of 16 data moving counterclockwise by one data at each time step ($t = 0, 1, 2, ...$).

The 2D graphical representations as well as the hexadecimal representations of the data composing the configuration string are detailed in Figure 6. They are either *empty data* (0), *code data* (from 1 to E) or *flag data* (from 1 to 9 in addition to F). The code data will be used to define the functionality of the structure. The flag data will be used to build the connections between the cells of the structure and to create branches for self-replication. Furthermore, each data is given a status and will eventually be a *mobile data*, indefinitely moving

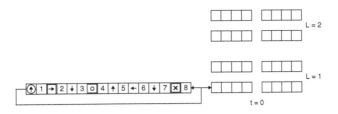

Fig. 5. The minimal structure ($2 \times 2 \times 2$ cells) with its configuration string at the start ($t = 0$).

☐ : empty data (0)	C : code data (1 ... E)	- : mobile data
- : don't care data (1 ... F)	F : flag data (1 ... 9, F)	▨ : fixed data

↑ : north connection flag (1)	← : west connection flag (4)	→ : north branch and east connection flag (7)
→ : east connection flag (2)	○ : up connection flag (5)	○ : east branch and up connection flag (8)
↓ : south connection flag (3)	✕ : down connection flag (6)	✕ : up branch and down connection flag (9)
		⊕ : branch activation and north connection flag (F)

Fig. 6. 2D graphical and hexadecimal representations of the data.

around the structure, or a *fixed data*, definitely trapped in a memory position of a cell.

At each time step, a data of the original configuration string is shifted from right to left and simultaneously stored in the lower leftmost cell (Figure 5). Note that the first, third, ... data of the string (i.e. each odd data) is always a flag F, while the second, fourth, ... data (i.e. each even data) is always a code C. The construction of the structure, i.e. storing the fixed data and defining the paths for mobile data, depends on two major patterns (Figure 7).

- If the two, three or four rightmost memory positions of a cell are empty (blank squares), the data are shifted by one position to the right (shift data).
- If the rightmost memory position is empty, the data are shifted by one position to the right (load data). In this situation, the rightmost F' and C' data are trapped in the cell (fixed data), and a new connection is established from the second leftmost position toward the northward, eastward, southward, westward, upward or downward cell, depending on the fixed flag information ($F' = 1$ or F, 2 or 7, 3, 4, 5 or 8, 6 or 9).

Applying the memory patterns of Figure 7 to our original configuration string, we get two data trapped in a cell and a new connection toward another cell of the structure every four time steps (Figure 8). At time $t = 32$, 32 data, i.e. twice the contents of the original configuration, have been stored in the 32 memory positions of the structure. 16 data are fixed data, forming the phenotype of the final structure, and the 16 remaining ones are mobile data, composing a copy of the original configuration, i.e. the genotype. Both *translation* (i.e. con-

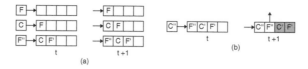

Fig. 7. Memory patterns for constructing a structure. (a) Shift data. (b) Load data.

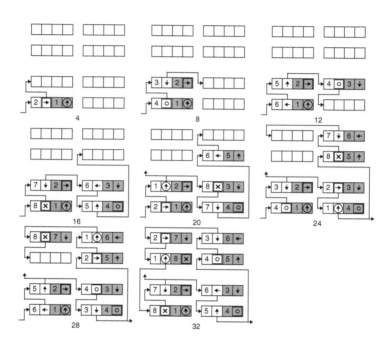

Fig. 8. Constructing the minimal structure ($t = 4$: north path, $t = 8$: east path, $t = 12$: south path, $t = 16$: up path, $t = 20$: north path ($L = 2$) and north branch ($L = 1$), $t = 24$: west path ($L = 2$) and east branch ($L = 1$), $t = 28$: south path, $t = 32$: down path and structure completion).

struction of the structure) and *transcription* (i.e. copy of the configuration) have been therefore achieved.

In order to self-replicate, the original structure is able to trigger the construction of three copies, nothward, eastward and upward. At time $t = 19$, the pattern of data initiates the construction of the northward structure. In this pattern, the lower level upper leftmost cell is characterized by two specific flags, i.e. a fixed flag indicating a north branch ($F = 7$) and the branch activation flag ($F = F$). This pattern is visible in Figure 9a (third row). The new path to the northward structure starts from the second leftmost memory position (Figure 8). At time $t = 23$ and $t = 47$, the patterns corresponding to the third row of the eastward and upward signals in Figure 9b and e initiate self-replication of the

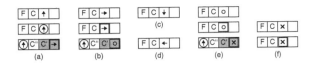

Fig. 9. Patterns of data triggering the path signals. (a) Northward. (b) Eastward. (c) Southward. (d) Westward. (e) Upward. (f) Downward.

structure to the east and to the top respectively. The other patterns are needed for constructing the inner paths of the structure.

The self-replicating structure in Figure 10 is an example of a non minimal four-column, three-rows and three-level structure. All the non minimal structures can be realized according to this implementation which keeps the number of column even in order to properly close the data path. These non minimal structures involve a new flag (Figure 11) and two more construction patterns (Figure 12).

4   Cell Design

The processing unit of our cell performs the shift data and load data operations represented in Figure 7. The control unit of our cell produces the signals implied in the construction of the connections between the cells of the structure (Figures 9 and 12). The resources needed in order to do it define the architecture of the cell (Figure 13). The processing unit involves the following ones:

- Two 4-bit genotypic registers GA3:0 and GB3:0 for the propagation of the configuration data.
- Two 4-bit phenotypic registers PA3:0 and PB3:0 for the memorization of the configuration data.
- A 6-input multiplexer DIMUX for the selection of one of the six data input lines, $NDI3:0$, $EDI3:0$, $SDI3:0$, $WDI3:0$, $UDI3:0$, or $DDI3:0$.
- A buffer DOBUF to enable the data output $DO3:0$.

The control unit consists of three resources:

- A 4-bit data input register I3:0 for the memorization of the selection operated by the multiplexer DIMUX.
- A signal inputs SI encoder ENC.
- A signal outputs SO generator GEN.

The genotypic registers GA3:0 and GB3:0 always propagate the data DI selected by the multiplexer DIMUX (Figure 14), while the phenotypic registers PA3:0 and PB3:0 perform a hold operation or a load operation according to the control variable LDP (Figure 15). When equal to 1 this control variable expresses that the phenotypic register PB3:0 contains an empty data:

$$LDP = PB3'.PB2'.PB1'.PB0' \tag{1}$$

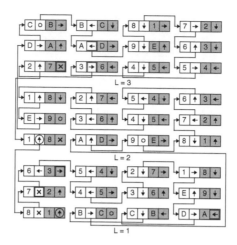

Fig. 10. Example of a non minimal structure ($4 \times 3 \times 3$ cells).

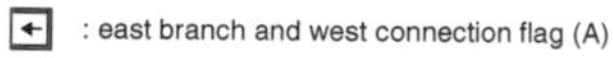

Fig. 11. 2D graphical and hexadecimal representations of the additional data.

Fig. 12. Additional patterns of data triggering the path signals. (a) Westward. (b) Eastward.

The selection realized by the data input multiplexer DIMUX is specified in the operation table of Figure 16.

The operations of the data output buffer DOBUF implies the control variable ENO (Figure 17). When equal to 1 this control variable expresses that the phenotypic register PB3:0 contains a flag data:

$$ENO = PB3 + PB2 + PB1 + PB0 \qquad (2)$$

According to the control variable LDI, the data input register I3:0 performs a hold or a load operation (Figure 18). The load operation ($LDI = 1$) is achieved every time that there is at least one input signal equal to 1:

$$LDI = NSI + ESI + SSI + WSI + USI + DSI \qquad (3)$$

The encoder ENC operates a priority coding of the input signals according to the truth table of Figure 19. In this table, the variables $D3:0$ define the state to be loaded in the input register I3:0, while the variable ID reflects the state corresponding to the selection of the downward data $DDI3:0$:

$$ID = I3.I2.I1'.I0 \qquad (4)$$

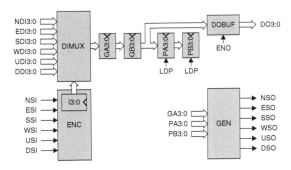

Fig. 13. Detailed architecture of the 3D structure cell.

operation	description
LOAD	GA <= DI
	GB <= GA

Fig. 14. Operation table of the genotypic registers GA3:0 and GB3:0.

operation	description	LDP
HOLD	PA <= PA	0
	PB <= PB	
LOAD	PA <= GB	1
	PB <= PA	

Fig. 15. Operation table of the phenotypic registers PA3:0 and PB3:0.

operation	description	I3:0
ZERO	DI = 0	0 0 0 0
SELECT NDI	DI = NDI	1 0 0 0
SELECT EDI	DI = EDI	1 0 0 1
SELECT SDI	DI = SDI	1 0 1 0
SELECT WDI	DI = WDI	1 0 1 1
SELECT UDI	DI = UDI	1 1 0 0
SELECT DDI	DI = DDI	1 1 0 1

Fig. 16. Operation table of the data input multiplexer DIMUX.

After simplification, the variables $D3 : 0$ verify the relations:

$$D3 = 1 \tag{5}$$

$$
\begin{aligned}
D2 = &\ ID \\
&+ ID'.DSI \\
&+ ID'.DSI'.NSI'.ESI'.USI
\end{aligned}
\tag{6}
$$

$$
\begin{aligned}
D1 = &\ ID'.SSI \\
&+ ID'.WSI
\end{aligned}
\tag{7}
$$

$$
\begin{aligned}
D0 = &\ ID \\
&+ ID'.DSI \\
&+ ID'.DSI'.NSI'.ESI \\
&+ ID'.WSI
\end{aligned}
\tag{8}
$$

operation	description	ENO
ZERO	DO = 0	0
TRUE	DO = GB	1

Fig. 17. Operation table of the data output buffer DOBUF.

operation	description	LDI
HOLD	I <= I	0
LOAD	I <= D	1

Fig. 18. Operation table of the data input register I3:0.

ID	DSI	NSI	ESI	USI	SSI	WSI	D3:0
1	-	-	-	-	-	-	1 1 0 1
0	1	-	-	-	-	-	1 1 0 1
0	0	1	-	-	-	-	1 0 0 0
0	0	0	1	-	-	-	1 0 0 1
0	0	0	0	1	-	-	1 1 0 0
0	-	-	-	-	1	-	1 0 1 0
0	-	-	-	-	-	1	1 0 1 1

Fig. 19. Truth table of the encoder ENC.

The generator GEN implements the output signals implied in the construction of the connections according to the patterns of Figures 9 and 12. The equations of these signals translate the code data and flag data memorized in the phenotypic register PA3:0 and the genotypic registers GA3:0 and GB3:0:

$$NSO = PBZ.PA3'.PA2'.PA1'.PA0$$
$$+ PBZ.PA3.PA2.PA1.PA0$$
$$+ GAF.PB3'.PB2.PB1.PB0 \tag{9}$$

$$ESO = PBZ.PA3'.PA2'.PA1.PA0'$$
$$+ PBZ.PA3'.PA2.PA1.PA0$$
$$+ GAF.PB3.PB2'.PB1'.PB0'$$
$$+ GAF.PB3.PB2'.PB1.PB0' \tag{10}$$

$$SSO = PBZ.PA3'.PA2'.PA1.PA0 \tag{11}$$

$$WSO = PBZ.PA3'.PA2.PA1'.PA0'$$
$$+ PBZ.PA3.PA2'.PA1.PA0' \tag{12}$$

$$USO = PBZ.PA3'.PA2.PA1'.PA0$$
$$+ PBZ.PA3.PA2'.PA1'.PA0'$$
$$+ GAF.PB3.PB2'.PB1'.PB0 \tag{13}$$

$$DSO = PBZ.PA3'.PA2.PA1.PA0'$$
$$+ PBZ.PA3.PA2'.PA1'.PA0 \tag{14}$$

In the preceding relations, the variables PBZ and GAF correspond respectively to an empty data (0) in the phenotypic register PB3:0 and to a branch activation and north connection flag (F) in the genotypic register GA3:0:

$$PBZ = PB3'.PB2'.PB1'.PB0' \qquad (15)$$

$$GAF = GA3.GA2.GA1.GA0 \qquad (16)$$

5 Conclusion

Several years before the publication of the historical paper by Crick and Watson [8] revealing the existence and the detailed architecture of the DNA double helix, von Neumann was already able to point out that self-replication was a two-mode process able to both interpret (translation mode) and copy (transcription mode) a one-dimensional description, the configuration string. Self-replication will allow not only to grow, but also to repair complete 3D structures. Self-replication is now considered as a central mechanism indispensable for those circuits which will be implemented through the nascent field of nanotechnologies [9] [10].

A first field of application of the self-replication of 3D structures is quite naturally the classical self-replicating automata, such as three-dimensional reversible automata [11] or asynchronous cellular automata [12].

A second, and possibly more important field of application is Embryonics, where artificial multicellular organisms are based on the growth of a cluster of cells, themselves produced by cellular division [13] [14].

Other possible open avenues are about the evolution of such structures and/or their capability of carrying out massive parallel computation [15].

References

1. K. Morita and K. Imai. Logical universality and self-reproduction in reversible cellular automata. In T. Higuchi, M. Iwata, and W. Liu (Eds.), Proceedings of The First International Conference on Evolvable Systems: From Biology to Hardware (ICES96). Lecture Notes in Computer Science, pp.152–166, Springer-Verlag, Heidelberg, 1997.
2. J. Ibanez, D. Anabitarte, I. Azpeitia, O. Barrera, A. Barrutieta, H. Blanco, and F. Echarte. Self-inspection based reproduction in cellular automata. In A. Moreno, J.J. Merelo, and P. Chacon (Eds.), Proceedings of the European Conference on Artificial Life (ECAL95). Advances in Artificial Life, Springer-Verlag, Heidelberg, 1995.
3. J. von Neumann. Theory of Self-Reproducing Automata. University of Illinois Press, Illinois, 1966. Edited and completed by A. W. Burks.
4. C. Langton. Self-reproduction in cellular automata. Physica D, vol.10, pp.135–144, 1984.
5. A. Stauffer and M. Sipper. The data-and-signals cellular automaton and its application to growing structures. Artificial Life, vol.10, no.4, pp.463–477, 2004.
6. A. Stauffer and M. Sipper. Data and signals: A new kind of cellular automaton for growing systems. In J. Lohn, R. Zebulum, J. Steincamp, D. Keymeulen, A. Stoica, and M. I. Ferguson (Eds.), Proceedings of the 2003 NASA/DOD Conference on Evolvable Hardware, pp.235–241, IEEE Computer Society, Los Alamitos CA, 2003.

7. A. Stauffer and M. Sipper. Biomorphs Implemented as a Data and Signals Cellular Automaton. In W. Banzhaf, T. Christaller, P. Dittrich, J. T. Kin, and J. Ziegler (Eds.), Advances in Artificial Life: Proceedings of the 7th European Conference on Artificial Life (ECAL 2003). Lecture Notes in Artificial Intelligence, 2801:724–732, Springer-Verlag, Berlin Heidelberg, 2003.
8. J. D. Watson and F. H. C. Crick. A structure for desoxyribose nucleid acid. Nature, vol.171, pp.737–738, 1953.
9. M. C. Roco and W. S. Bainbridge. Converging technologies for improving human performance. Nanotechnology, biotechnology, information technology and cognitive science. NSF/DOC - sponsored report, Arlington VA, 2002.
10. K. E. Drexler. Nanosystems: Molecular Machinery, Manufacturing, and Computation. John Wiley, New York, 1992.
11. K. Imai, T. Hori, and K. Morita. Self-reproduction in three-dimensional reversible cellular space. Artificial Life, vol.8, no.2, pp.155–174, 2002.
12. C. L. Nehaniv. Self-reproduction in asynchronous cellular automaton. In A. Stoica, J. Lohn, R. Katz, D. Keymeulen and, R. S. Zebulum (Eds.), Proceedings of the 2002 NASA/DOD Workshop on Evolvable Hardware, pp.201–209, IEEE Computer Society, Los Alamitos CA, 2002.
13. N. J. Macias and L. J. K. Durbeck. Self-assembling circuits with autonomous fault handling. In A. Stoica, J. Lohn, R. Katz, D. Keymeulen and, R. S. Zebulum (Eds.), Proceedings of the 2002 NASA/DOD Workshop on Evolvable Hardware, pp.46–55, IEEE Computer Society, Los Alamitos CA, 2002.
14. D. Mange, M. Sipper, A. Stauffer, and G. Tempesti. Toward robust integrated circuits: The Embryonics approach. Proceedings of the IEEE, vol.88, no.4, pp.516–541, April 2000.
15. H.-H. Chou and J. A. Reggia. Problem solving during artificial selection of self-replicating loops. Physica D, vol.115, no.3-4, pp.293–312, 1998.

Calculation of the Critical Point for Two-Layer Ising and Potts Models Using Cellular Automata

Yazdan Asgari[1], Mehrdad Ghaemi[2,3], and Mohammad Ghasem Mahjani[1]

[1] Department of Chemistry, K.N.Toosi University of Technology, P.O.Box 16315-1618,
Tehran, Iran
yazdan1130@hotmail.com, mahjani@kntu.ac.ir
[2] Department of chemistry, Teacher Training University, Tehran, Iran
ghaemi@saba.tmu.ac.ir
[3] Atomic Energy Organization of Iran, Deputy in Nuclear Fuel Production, Tehran, Iran

Abstract. The critical points of the two-layer Ising and Potts models for square lattice have been calculated with high precision using probabilistic cellular automata (PCA) with Glauber alghorithm. The critical temperature is calculated for the isotropic and symmetric case ($K_x=K_y=K_z=K$), where K_x and K_y are the nearest-neighbor interactions within each layer in the x and y directions, respectively, and K_z is the interlayer coupling. The obtained results are 0.310 and 0.726 for two-layer Ising and Potts models, respectively, that are in good agreement with the accurate values reported by others.

Introduction

For many years, the lattice statistics has been the subject of intense research interests. Although, at zero magnetic field, there is an exact solution for the 2-dimensional (2-D) Ising model [1,2], however, there is no such a solution for the two-layer Ising and Potts models. The Potts models are the general extension of the Ising model with q-state spin lattice i.e., the Potts model with $q = 2$ is equivalent to the Ising model. Although we do not know the exact solution of the two-dimensional Potts model at present time, a large amount of the numerical information has been accumulated for the critical properties of the various Potts models. For further information, see the excellent review written by Wu [3] or the references given by him.

The two-layer Ising model, as a simple generalization of the 2-D Ising model and also as an intermediate model between the 2-D and 3-D Ising models, has long been studied [4-7] and several approximation methods have been applied to this model [8-14]. In the absence of exact solution, simulation methods such as Monte Carlo [15] are most important tools for computation of the critical properties of the various Ising and Potts models.

In addition to the Monte Carlo method, it was proposed that the Cellular Automata (CA) could be a good candidate to simulate the Ising models [16]. In the last two decade a large amount of works were done for describing Ising models by the CA approach and a great number of papers and excellent reviews were published [17-22].

P.M.A. Sloot, B. Chopard, and A.G. Hoekstra (Eds.): ACRI 2004, LNCS 3305, pp. 709–718, 2004.
© Springer-Verlag Berlin Heidelberg 2004

Most of the works that have been done until now are focused on the qualitative description of various Ising and Potts models or to introduce a faster algorithm. For example, the Q2R automaton as a fast algorithm was suggested which has been studied extensively [22-27]. It was so fast, because no random numbers must be generated at each step. But in the probabilistic CA, like Metropolis algorithm [28], generation of the random number causes to reduce the speed of calculation, even though it is more realistic for describing the Ising model.

In this article, at the first section we have used probabilistic CA with Glauber algorithm [29] for calculating the critical temperature of the two-layer symmetric Ising model on the square grid. We used a large lattice size (2500 × 2500) in simulation in order to reduce the finite size effects. It is shown that our results are in a good agreement with those obtained from the best numerical methods. In section 2 we have extended the method to the two-layer symmetric 3-state Potts model. The importance of this section is due to the fact that there is no well tabulated data for such a model.

1 Two-Layer Ising Model

Consider a two-layer square lattice with the periodic boundary condition, each layer with p rows and r columns. Each layer has then $r \times p$ sites and the number of the sites in the lattice is $2 \times r \times p = N$. We consider the next nearest neighbor interactions as well, so the number of neighbor for each site is 5. In the two-layer Ising model, for any site we define a spin variable $\sigma^{1(2)}(i, j) = \pm 1$ in such a way that $i = 1,...,r$ and $j = 1,..., p$ where superscript 1(2) denotes the layer number. We include the periodic boundary condition as

$$\sigma^{1(2)}(i + r, j) = \sigma^{1(2)}(i, j) \tag{1}$$

$$\sigma^{1(2)}(i, j + p) = \sigma^{1(2)}(i, j) \tag{2}$$

The configuration energy for this model may be defined as [14]

$$\frac{E(\sigma)}{kT} = -\sum_{i=1}^{r,*} \sum_{j=1}^{p,*} \sum_{n=1}^{2} \{K_x \sigma^n(i, j)\sigma^n(i+1, j) +$$

$$K_y \sigma^n(i, j)\sigma^n(i, j+1)\} - K_z \sum_{i=1}^{r} \sum_{j=1}^{p} \sigma^1(i, j)\sigma^2(i, j) \tag{3}$$

where * indicates the periodic boundary conditions (eqs 1,2), and K_x and K_y are the nearest-neighbor interactions within each layer in the x and y directions, respectively, and K_z is the interlayer coupling. Therefore, the configuration energy per spin is

$$e = \frac{E(\sigma)}{kTN} \tag{4}$$

The average magnetization of the lattice for this model can be defined as [15]

$$\langle M \rangle = \left\langle \sum_{i=1}^{r,*} \sum_{j=1}^{p,*} \sum_{n=1}^{2} \sigma^n(i,j) \right\rangle \tag{5}$$

and the average magnetization per spin is

$$\langle m \rangle = \frac{\langle M \rangle}{N} \tag{6}$$

The magnetic susceptibility per spin (χ) and specific heat per spin (C) is defined as [15]

$$\frac{\partial <M>}{\partial \beta} = \beta(<M^2> - <M>^2) \tag{7}$$

$$\chi = \frac{\beta}{N}\left(\left\langle M^2 \right\rangle - \langle M \rangle^2\right) = \beta N\left(\left\langle m^2 \right\rangle - \langle m \rangle^2\right) \tag{8}$$

$$C = \frac{k\beta^2}{N}\left(\left\langle E^2 \right\rangle - \langle E \rangle^2\right) = k\beta^2 N\left(\left\langle e^2 \right\rangle - \langle e \rangle^2\right) \tag{9}$$

where $\beta = \dfrac{1}{kT}$.

1.1   Method

In the present work, we considered the isotropic ferromagnetic and symmetric case i.e. $K_x = K_y = K_z = K \geq 0$. We have used a two-layer square lattice with 2500×2500 sites in each layer with the periodic boundary condition. The Glauber method [29] was used with checkerboard approach to update sites. For this purpose the surfaces of two layers are checkered same as each others. For updating the lattice, we use following procedure: after updating the first layer, the second layer could be updated. The updating of the spins is based on the probabilistic rules. The probability that the spin of one site will be up (p_i^+) is calculated from [30]

$$p_i^+ = \frac{e^{-\beta E_i^+}}{e^{-\beta E_i^+} + e^{-\beta E_i^-}} \tag{10}$$

where

$$E_i^{\pm} = -K\{\sigma^n(i,j)\sigma^n(i+1,j) + \sigma^n(i,j)\sigma^n(i-1,j) + \sigma^n(i,j)\sigma^n(i,j+1)$$
$$+ \sigma^n(i,j)\sigma^n(i,j-1) + \sigma^n(i,j)\sigma^{n'}(i,j)\} \tag{11}$$

and

$$\sigma^n(i,j) = +1 \text{ for } E_i^+$$
$$\sigma^n(i,j) = -1 \text{ for } E_i^- \tag{12}$$

and $\sigma^{n'}(i,j)$ is the neighboring site (i,j) in the other layer. Hence, the probability that the spin to be down is

$$p_i^- = 1 - p_i^+ \tag{13}$$

The approach is as follow: first a random number is generated. If it is less than p_i^+, the spin of the site (i,j) is up, otherwise (it means that random number is greater than p_i^+), it will be down.

When we start CA with the homogeneous initial state (namely, all sites have spin up or +1), before the critical point (K_c), the magnetization per spin (m) will decay rapidly to zero and fluctuate around it. After the critical point, m will approach to a nonzero point and fluctuate around it; and with increasing of K, the magnetization per spin will increase. But at the critical point, m will decay very slowly to the zero point and the fluctuation of the system will reach to a maximum. For each K, the time that m reaches to the special point and starts to fluctuate around it is called the relaxation time (τ). On the other words, the relaxation time is the time that the system is thermalized. The value of τ can be obtained from the graph of m vs. t (Fig. 1). One can see from these graphs that the relaxation time increases before critical point and reaches to a maximum at K_c, but after the critical point, τ decreases rapidly. So, in the critical point, the system last a long time to stabilized. Hence, the critical point may be obtained from the graph of τ vs. K (Fig. 2). The obtained critical point from this graph is 0.310 for the two-layer Ising model.

In our approach, we have calculated the thermodynamic quantities after thermalization of the lattice. In other words, first we let the system reaches to a stable state after some time step $(t=\tau)$, and then to be updated up to the end of the automata $(t=50000)$. For example to calculate the average value of magnetization per spin $(<m>)$, one should add all values of m from the relaxation time up to the end of the automata (or end of the time step) and divide the result to number of steps. The other way for calculation of the critical point is the usage of $<m>$. By drawing the graph of $<m>$ vs. K, we may also obtain K_c. Fig. 3 shows the results of such calculation. As it is seen, before critical point $(K<K_c)$, $<m>=0$ and after that $(K> K_c)$, $<m>\neq 0$. The obtained values of the critical point from this approach is K_c =0.310 for the two-layer Ising model.

For calculation of χ for each K, first we have calculated the value of $(m-<m>)^2$ in each time step. Then these values are averaged in a some way explained above. According to eq. 8 this average could be used for computation of χ. Using eq. 9 for calculation of the specific heat (C), we have done it in a same way described above. Figures 4 and 5 show the graphs of χ vs. K and C vs. K, respectively, for the two-layer Ising model. These graphs are the other ways for obtaining the critical point. The maximum of these graphs indicates the critical point. The obtained value for K_c from these graphs is 0.310 for the two-layer Ising model.

2   Two-Layer Potts Model

Consider a two-layer square lattice with the periodic boundary condition, each layer with p rows and r columns. Each layer has then $r\times p$ sites and number of sites in the lattice is $2\times r\times p = N$. We consider the next nearest neighbor interactions as well, so

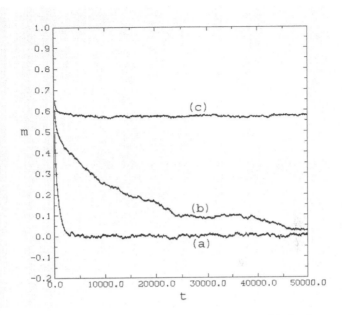

Fig. 1. The magnetization versus time in the two-layer Ising model. for 3 states. a: K=0.304 ($K<K_c$), τ =3500. b: K=0.310 ($K=K_c$), τ =46000. c: K=0.313 ($K>K_c$), τ =4000. (each layer has 2500× 2500 sites, start from homogeneous initial state "all +1", time steps = 50000)

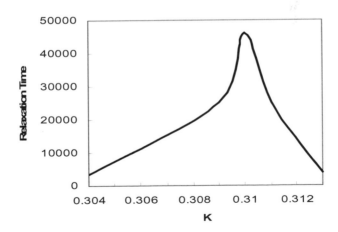

Fig. 2. The relaxation time obtained from Figure 1 versus K for the two-layer Ising model. The maximum appears at $K=K_c$

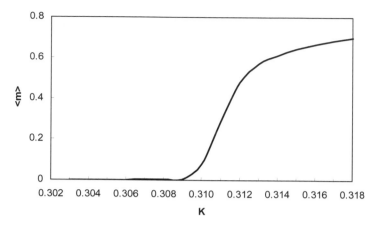

Fig. 3. $<m>$ versus coupling coefficient (K) for the two-layer Ising model. The average value for each K is calculated after its relaxation time. (data are the results for the lattice that each layer has 2500×2500 sites, starting from the homogeneous initial state with all $+1$, time steps = 50000)

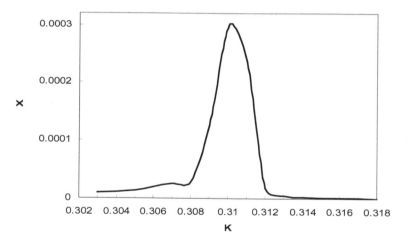

Fig. 4. Magnetization susceptibility per spin (χ) versus K for the two-layer Ising model. (The calculated data are the results for the lattice for which each layer has 2500×2500 sites, starting from the homogeneous initial state with all spins up, time steps = 50000)

the number of neighbor for each site is 5. For any site we define a spin variable $\sigma^{1(2)}(i, j) = 0, \pm 1$ so that $i = 1, ...r$ and $j = 1, ..., p$. The configuration energy of the standard 3-state Potts model is given by [3],

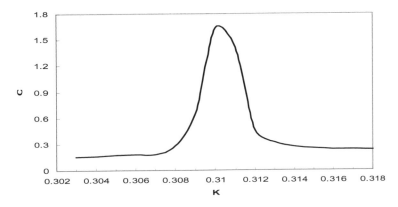

Fig. 5. Specific Heat per spin (*C*) versus *K* for the two-layer Ising model. (The calculated data are the results for the lattice for which each layer has 2500× 2500 sites, starting from the homogeneous initial state with all spins up, time steps = 50000)

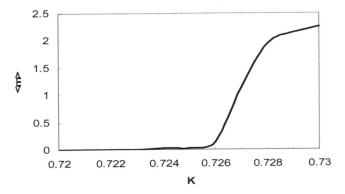

Fig. 6. <*m*> versus coupling coefficient (*K*) for the two-layer Potts model. (The calculated data are for the lattice that each layer has 1500× 1500 sites, starting from the homogeneous initial state with all spins up, time steps = 50000)

$$\frac{E(\sigma)}{kT} = \sum_{i=1}^{r,*} \sum_{j=1}^{p,*} \sum_{n=1}^{2} -\{K_x \delta_{\sigma^n(i,j),\sigma^n(i+1,j)} + K_y \delta_{\sigma^n(i,j),\sigma^n(i,j+1)}$$

$$+ K_z \delta_{\sigma^1(i,j),\sigma^2(i,j)}\} \qquad (14)$$

where

$$\delta_{i,j} = 1 \ \text{ for } i = j$$

$$\delta_{i,j} = 0 \ \text{ for } i \neq j \qquad (15)$$

Other quantities are obtained from the equations 4-9.

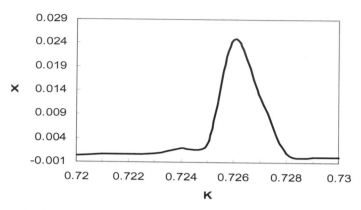

Fig. 7. Magnetization susceptibility per spin (χ) versus K for the two-layer Potts model. (The calculated data are for the lattice that each layer has 1500×1500 sites, starting from the homogeneous initial state with all spins up, time steps = 50000)

2.1 Method

For quantitative computation of the two-layer Potts model, we have considered the isotropic ferromagnetic and symmetric case which $K_x = K_y = K_z = K \geq 0$. We have used a two-layer square lattice that each layer has 1500×1500 sites with periodic boundary condition. Each site can have a value of the spin up (+1), down (-1) or zero (0). We used the Glauber method with checkerboard approach similar to the Ising model for updating the sites of the 3-state Potts model. The probability that the spin of one site will be up (p_i^+) is calculated from

$$p_i^+ = \frac{e^{-\beta E_i^+}}{e^{-\beta E_i^+} + e^{-\beta E_i^-} + e^{-\beta E_i^0}} \tag{16}$$

and, the probability that the spin to be down is

$$p_i^- = \frac{e^{-\beta E_i^-}}{e^{-\beta E_i^+} + e^{-\beta E_i^-} + e^{-\beta E_i^0}} \tag{17}$$

Hence, the probability that the spin to be in zero state is

$$p_i^0 = 1 - (p_i^+ + p_i^-) \tag{18}$$

where

$$E_i^{\pm,0} = -K_x \{ \delta_{\sigma^n(i,j),\sigma^n(i+1,j)} + \delta_{\sigma^n(i,j),\sigma^n(i-1,j)} \} - K_y \{ \delta_{\sigma^n(i,j),\sigma^n(i,j+1)} + \delta_{\sigma^n(i,j),\sigma^n(i,j-1)} \}$$

$$- K_z \{ \delta_{\sigma^n(i,j),\sigma^{n'}(i,j)} \} \tag{19}$$

and

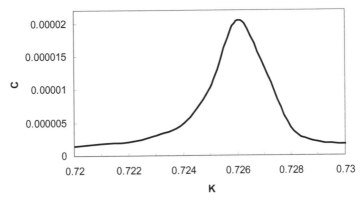

Fig. 8. Specific Heat per spin (C) versus K for the two-layer Potts model. (The calculated data are for the lattice that each layer has 1500×1500 sites, starting from the homogeneous initial state with all spins up, time steps $= 50000$)

$$\sigma^n(i, j) = +1 \text{ for } E_i^+$$
$$\sigma^n(i, j) = -1 \text{ for } E_i^-$$
$$\sigma^n(i, j) = 0 \text{ for } E_i^0 \tag{20}$$

The calculation steps are similar to the two-layer Ising model. Figure 6 shows the graph of $<m>$ vs. K for the two-layer Potts model. Figure 7 and 8 are the graphs for χ and C vs. K, respectively. The obtained value of K_c for the two-layer Potts model is 0.726. It is obvious that the value obtained from these figures, are in agreement.

3 Conclusion

It was demonstrated that the high precision calculation of the critical point can be done by the CA. For obtaining the fourth and further digits after the decimal point by the CA, one must use a larger lattice and since the relaxation time is large near the critical point, the numbers of time steps must be increased. For example, in order to compute the fourth digit of K_c in the two-layer Ising model, it is sufficient to increase the number of time step up to 300000 steps and draw the graph $<m>$ vs. K. The calculated K_c is 0.3108 that is in good agreement with other numerical method [14].

Although the extension of numerical methods for calculation of the critical properties of the two-layer 3-state Potts model is a difficult task, but such extension is easy in cellular automata approach. The importance of this approach is due to the fact that there is no well tabulated data for the two-layer Potts model.

Acknowledgment. We acknowledge Prof. G. A. Parsafar for his useful comment.

References

1. Huang, K.: Statistical mechanics. John Wiley and Sons, 2nd Edition, (1987)
2. Onsager, L.: Phys. Rev. (1944) 65, 117
3. Wu, F.Y.: Rev. Mod. Phys. (1982) 54, 235
4. Ballentine, L.E.: Physica, (1964) 30, 1231
5. Allan, G.A.T.: Phys. Rev. B. (1970) 1, 352
6. Binder, K.: Thin Solid Films. (1974) 20, 367
7. Oitmaa, J., Enting, G.: J. Phys. A. (1975) 8, 1097
8. Wosiek, J.: Phys. Rev. B. (1994) 49, 15023
9. Angelini, L., Carappo, D., Pellicoro, M., Villani, M.: Physica A. (1995) 19, 447
10. Horiguchi, T., Lipowski, A., Tsushima, N.: Physica A. (1996) 224, 626
11. Angelini, L., Carappo, D., Pellicoro, M., Villani, M.: Physica A. (1997) 237, 320
12. Lipowski, A., Suzuki, M.: Physica A. (1998) 250, 373
13. Li, Z.B., Shuai, Z., Wang, Q., Luo, H.J., Schulke, L.: J. Phys. A. (2001) 34, 6069-6079
14. Ghaemi, M., Ghannadi, M., Mirza, B.: J. Phys. Chem. B. (2003) 107, 829-831
15. Newman, M.E., Barkema, G.T.: Monte Carlo Methods in Statistical Physics. Oxford University Press Inc., New York, Reprinted. (2001) Chap. 3-4.
16. Domany, E., Kinzel, W.: Phys. Rev. Let. (1984) 53, 4, 311-314
17. MacIsaac, A.B.: J. Phys. A. (1990) 23, 899-903
18. Creutz, M.: Annals of physics. (1986) 167, 62-76
19. Toffoli, T., Margolus, N.: Physica D. (1990) 45, 229-253
20. Kinzel, W.: Z. Phys. B. (1985) 58, 229-244
21. Aktekin, N.: Annal Review of computational Physics VII. Edited by Staufer, D., World Scientific Publishing Company (1999) 1-23
22. Vichniac, G.: Physica D10. (1984) 96-115
23. Pomeau, Y.: J. Phys. A. (1984) 17, 415
24. Herrmann, H.J.: J. Stat. Phys. (1986) 45, 145
25. Glotzer, S.C., Stauffer, D., Sastry, S.: Physica 164A (1990) 1
26. Moukarzel, C., Parga, N.: J. Phys. A. (1989) 22, 943
27. Jan, N.: J. Physique. (1990) 51, 201
28. Metropolis, N., Rosenbluth, A.W., Rosenbluth, M.N., Teller, A.H., Teller, E.: J. Chem. Phys. (1953) 21, 1087
29. Glauber, R.J.: J. Math. Phys. (1963) 4, 294
30. Hedet, B., Herrmann, H.J.: J. Phys. A. (1991) 24, L691-L697

Directed Ligand Passage over the Surface of Diffusion-Controlled Enzymes: A Cellular Automata Model

Mehrdad Ghaemi[1,2], Nasrollah Rezaei-Ghaleh[3], and Mohammad-Nabi Sarbolouki[3]

[1] Atomic Energy Organization of Iran, Deputy in Nuclear Fuel Production, Tehran, Iran
[2] Department of Chemistry, Tarbiat Moalem University, Tehran, Iran
ghaemi@saba.tmu.ac.ir
[3] Institue of Biochemistry and Biophysics, Tehran University, P.O. Box: 13145-1384, Tehran, Iran

Abstract. The rate-limiting step of some enzymatic reactions is a physical step, i.e. diffusion. The efficiency of such reactions can be improved through an increase in the arrival rate of the substrate molecules, e.g. by a directed passage of substrate (ligand) to active site after its random encounter with the enzyme surface. Herein, we introduce a cellular automata model simulating the ligand passage over the protein surface to its destined active site. The system is simulated using the lattice gas automata with probabilistic transition rules. Different distributions of amino acids over the protein surface are examined. For each distribution, the hydration pattern is achieved and the mean number of iteration steps needed for the ligand to arrive at the active site calculated. Comparison of results indicates that the rate at which ligand arrives at the active site is clearly affected by the distribution of amino acids outside the active side. Such a process can facilitate the ligand diffusion towards the active site thereby enhancing the efficiency of the enzyme action.

1 Introduction

The chemical machinery of many enzymes (proteins which act as catalysts of biochemical reactions) is so optimized that whenever a substrate molecule arrives at the active site of the enzyme and the enzyme-substrate complex is formed, the complex goes on the way to form the product instead of dissociating back to enzyme and substrate molecules. Under such conditions, the enzymes function at rates that depend on the diffusion-limited association of their substrates with the active site [1]. According to the Smulochowski equation, the maximum rate constant for the enzyme-substrate encounter in a solution is $k_{collision} = 4\pi Da$, where D is the relative translational diffusion coefficient of enzyme and ligand molecules and a is the sum of their effective radii [2]. For typical values of D and a, $k_{collision}$ is of the order of 10^9-10^{10} $M^{-1}S^{-1}$ [3]. To account for any change in the diffusional encounter due to electrostatic interaction between the enzyme and substrate molecules, the Smulochowski equation is modified by introducing a dimensionless factor, f, [4] which does not however exceed 10 even for very favorable interactions [5]. Furthermore, regarding that only a small fraction of the enzyme surface is involved in the reaction, the Smulochowski

P.M.A. Sloot, B. Chopard, and A.G. Hoekstra (Eds.): ACRI 2004, LNCS 3305, pp. 719–724, 2004.
© Springer-Verlag Berlin Heidelberg 2004

equation should be modified further [6], then for typical enzymes, $k_{association}$ is not expected to exceed the value of 10^4-10^5 $M^{-1}S^{-1}$ [7]. However, the association rate constants frequently exceed this theoretical limit [3]. Many models have been suggested to explain this discrepancy [8-10]. Herein, this problem is dealt with using a cellular automata model of ligand passage on the surface of enzyme molecules. It will be shown that the motion of ligand molecule on the surface of enzyme molecule is affected by different distributions of amino acid residues lying outside the active side of the enzyme; thereby their distribution may greatly facilitate arrival of the substrate molecule at the active site.   This means that the effective area for the reaction may be larger than those considered merely based on geometrical assessment of the active site.

2 Method

In order to provide a simple representation of enzyme surfaces, a 27*27 grid of square cells with periodic boundary conditions was created (This is at the same order of magnitude as the number of amino acid residues occurring on the enzyme surfaces). The hydropathic profile of enzyme surfaces was represented assigning each cell an integer number between 0 and 8, corresponding to the hydropathic indices of amino acid residues occurring in those cells. The hydropathic indices were adopted from Kyte and Doolittle [11], then ranked from the most hydrophobic residues to the most hydrophilic ones in 9 scales, 0-8, i.e. 0 corresponds to the most hydrophobic residue- isoleucine- and 8 corresponds to the most hydrophilic one- arginine. Configuration of the entire system was then defined by the state values of all cells in the grid. Four configurations were examined in this study (Fig.1): A- a uniform configuration with all cells adopting a value of 4, i.e. occupied with a residue neither hydrophobic nor hydrophilic. The mean hydropathic index of this configuration is clearly 4 and its variance is zero. B- a random configuration with cells adopting numbers generated by a non- biased random method. This configuration has the same mean hydropathic index as the A configuration but displays a non-zero variance around the same mean. C- a configuration like A except that cells in diagonal, vertical and horizontal lines crossing the center of the grid adopt a value of 8, i.e. occupied with the most hydrophilic residues.

D- a configuration like B except that cells in diagonal, vertical and horizontal lines crossing the center of the grid adopt a value of 8. The C and D configurations have the same mean hydropathic indices but show different non-zero variances around the same mean.

For each configuration mentioned above, water molecules were allowed to move around on the surface of grid and create a specific hydration pattern characteristic to that configuration. At first, each cell in the grid was assigned a random integer number between 0 and 99 indicating the number of water molecules, which exist in its vicinity. Then, the grid was partitioned into 81 3*3 blocks. At each step, the numbers of water molecules in each block were first added and then redistributed randomly among its 9 cells according to their hydropathic indices, i.e. the probability with which a water molecule occurs in a cell is directly proportional to its hydropathic index. Between steps, the blocks were displaced one cell toward the lower right

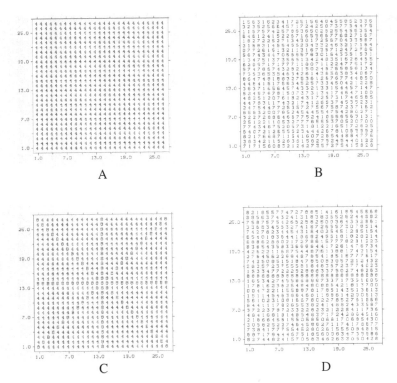

Fig. 1. Examined configurations of the entire system; See the text for a precise definition of each configuration.

direction. Iterations were continued until an almost constant hydration pattern was produced. It was judged qualitatively according to graphical views of the system and achieved typically after 50 iterations.

To assess the effect of each configuration with its characteristic hydration pattern on the rate at which substrate molecule arrives in the active site, we placed the substrate (ligand) molecule at the corner and the active site at the center of the grid and simulated the ligand motion over the surface of the grid. The ligand molecule could either be stationary or move along one of the four directions (up, down, right, left) with the same velocity (1 cell/iteration). Initially, the ligand molecule was assumed to be stationary. Then, it was allowed to move around on the surface of the grid according to the scheme presented by Boon et al. [12]. At each iteration, the ligand molecule first would take propagation according to its directed velocity. Then, during the subsequent redistribution step, the ligand molecule arrived in a new cell would lose its previous velocity thereby making its next decision merely on the basis of the local hydration pattern in its neighborhood: The probability with which the ligand molecule would adopt a specific directed velocity hence displace into a specific cell was directly proportional to the number of water molecules occurring in that cell. The system was iterated 5000 times for each configuration -at each iteration, different sets of random numbers were generated- and the average number of iterations needed for the ligand molecule to reach at the active site was calculated for them.

3 Results and Discussion

The hydration patterns, achieved for each of four configurations, are illustrated in Fig. 2. As expected, the distribution of water molecules over the grid obeys the hydropathic profile of each configuration. It is uniform in the case of configuration A and random in configuration B. In C and D configurations, the cells occurring on the diagonal, vertical and horizontal lines display more water molecules.

The average numbers of iterations required for the substrate to arrive at the active site were 2142, 2424, 1778 and 1984 for A, B, C and D configurations, respectively. It was significantly lower for configurations with specified diagonal, vertical and horizontal paths (C and D) than their counterpart configurations (A and B, respectively). A less prominent difference was observed between configurations with the same mean but different variances of hydropathic indices. The configurations with higher variances (B and D) showed higher average numbers of iterations required for the substrate to arrive at the active site than those with lower variances (A and C,

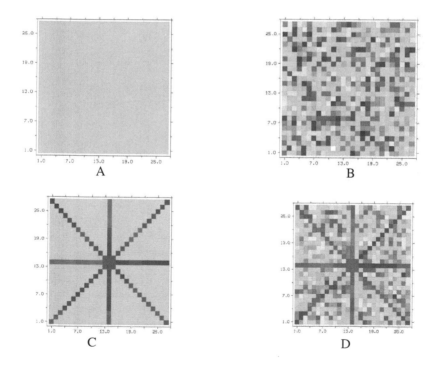

Fig. 2. Hydration patterns achieved for each examined configuration (A, B, C and D). The number of water molecules in each cell varies between 0 (dark red) and 99 molecules (dark blue). The intermediate numbers have been shown with colors of the spectrum between red and blue.

respectively). These results support the idea that the hydropathic profile of enzyme surfaces away from the active site modifies the rate at which ligand arrives at the active site. Such an effect can be prominent for a chemically perfect enzyme, where the enzyme activity is diffusion-controlled.

The subject of ligand passage over the surface of proteins towards the active site has been extensively addressed in the literature. According to the current view, the ligand molecule temporarily resides in the vicinity of the protein surface after its encounter with the surface. Then, the ligand undergoes a two-dimensional walk toward the active site. It is generally believed that a two-dimensional surface diffusion to the active site can enhance the rate of a diffusion-controlled reaction [13]. Several models of two-dimensional surface diffusion have been presented. The directed passage of ligand toward the active site, as suggested by some of these models, enhances the rate of diffusion-controlled reactions even further. Some models suggest that the electrostatic field experienced by the ligand on the surface of protein may guide it toward the active site [14-15]. Some other models present the van der Waals interactions as the prominent force directing the ligand over the protein surfaces [10]. However, considering the effect of protein side chains on their vicinal water structure and the resultant changes on the local viscosity and diffusion coefficient, the ligand passage over the protein surface can be regarded as an anisotropic two-dimensional diffusion process. This anisotropy may provide preferred pathways for the ligand to arrive at the active site more rapidly. Using this approach, Kier et al. [16] have examined the ligand passage over hydrodynamic landscape of the protein by simulation via a cellular automata model. We hereby used a different cellular automata model to examine whether the hydropathic profile of protein surface can affect the rate at which the ligand arrives at the active site. The results presented here clearly indicate that the hydropathic profile of proteins can facilitate the ligand diffusion under some conditions. This is in accord with results obtained by Kier et al [16]. It can be interpreted that the existence of the preferred paths for ligand diffusion nearly converts a two-dimensional walk to a rather more efficient one-dimensional one. Indeed, in C and D configurations, the ligand molecule has spent most of its time within the preferred pathways moving toward or away from the active site. In comparison with the model presented by Kier et al. [16], our model may be judged to be simpler and more realistic. In addition, our model, due to its flexibility, may be more simply improved through the implementation of e.g. surface charge effects or detailed surface geometry. Such improvements are our current concerns regarding the model.

The activity of diffusion-controlled enzymes, which are chemically perfect, is limited by the physical step of ligand diffusion to the active site. It may be that such enzymes, through their evolution, have searched for ways to facilitate the ligand diffusion toward their active sites. The hydropathic profiles of the surfaces of such enzymes, when compared with other enzymes and/or among their variants, may provide some evidences regarding the existence of preferred profiles for ligand diffusion. Modification of these profiles lead to subtle changes in the activity of diffusion-controlled enzymes. Hence, the view presented in this study may provide some more reasonable tools for protein design and site-directed mutagenesis.

4 Conclusion

The presented cellular automata model of directed ligand passage over the surface of enzymes clearly shows that the hydropathic profile of enzyme surfaces can increase the rate at which the ligand molecule arrives in the enzyme active site. Such enhancing effect may be of functional importance in the case of enzymes with diffusion-controlled activity.

References

1. Fersht, A.: Enzyme structure and mechanism. Freeman, New York (1985)
2. DeLisi, C.: The biophysics of ligand-receptor interactions. Q. Rev. biophys. 13 (1980) 201-230
3. Camacho, C.J., Weng, Z., Vajda, S., DeLisi, C.: Free energy landscapes of encounter complexes in protein-protein association. Biophys. J. 76 (1999) 1166-1178
4. von Hippel, P.H., Berg, O.G.: Facilitated target location in biological systems. J. Biol. Chem. 264 (1989) 675-678
5. Noyes, R.M.: Effects of diffusion rates on chemical kinetics. Prog. React. Kinet. 1 (1961) 129-160
6. Janin, J.: The kinetics of protein-protein recognition. Proteins: Struct. Funct. Genet. 28 (1997) 153-161
7. Schreiber, G., Fersht, A.R.: Rapid, electrostatically assisted association of proteins. Nature Struct. Biol. 3 (1996) 427-431
8. Berg, H.C., Purcell, E.M.: Physics of chemoreception, Biophys. J. 20 (1977) 193-215
9. Hasinoff, B.B.: Kinetics of acetylcholine binding to electric eel acetylcholine esterase in glycerol/water solvents of increased viscosity. Biochim. Biophys. Acta. 704 (1982) 52-58
10. Chou, K.C., Zhou, G.P.: Role of the protein outside active site on the diffusion-controlled reaction of enzyme. J. Am. Chem. Soc. 104 (1982) 1409-1413
11. Kyte, J., Doolittle, R.F.: A simple method for displaying the hydrophobic character of a protein. J. Mol. Biol. 157 (1982) 105-132
12. Boon, J.P., Dab, D., Kapral, R., Lawniczak, A.: Lattice gas automata for reactive systems. Physics Reports 273 (1996) 55-147
13. Welch, G.R.: The enzymatic basis of information processing in the living cell. Biosystems 38 (1996) 147-153
14. Radic, Z., Kirchhoff P.D., Quinin, D.M., McCommon, J.A., Taylor, P.: Electrostatic influence on kinetics of ligand binding to acetylcholinesterase. J. Biol. Chem. 272 (1997) 23265-23277
15. Wade, R.C., Gabdoulline, R.R., Ludeman, S.K., Lounnas, V.: Electrostatic steering and ionic tethering in enzyme-ligand binding: insights from simulations. Proc. Natl. Acad. Sci. U.S.A. 95 (1998) 5942-5949
16. Kier, L.B., Cheng, C.K., Testa, B.: A cellular automata model of ligand passage over a protein hydrodynamic landscape. J. Theor. Biol. 215 (2002) 415-426

An Evolutionary Approach for Modelling Lava Flows Through Cellular Automata

William Spataro[1], Donato D'Ambrosio[1], Rocco Rongo[2], and Giuseppe A. Trunfio[1]

[1]University of Calabria, Department of Mathematics & High Performance Computing Center, Arcavacata, 87036 Rende (CS), Italy
{spataro, d.dambrosio, trunfio}@unical.it
[2]University of Calabria, Department of Earth Sciences, Arcavacata, 87036 Rende (CS), Italy
rongo@unical.it

Abstract. A Master-Slave Genetic Algorithm is applied to evolve a two-dimensional Cellular Automata model for lava flow simulation. The 2002 Etnean Linguaglossa case study is considered for model calibration. A quantitative measure for the evaluation of the simulations result with respect to the real event is defined and employed as fitness function.

1 Introduction

Cellular Automata (CA) came to the attention of the Scientific Community as a powerful tool for the simulation of fluid-dynamics processes.

CA [1] are dynamical systems, discrete in space and time. They can be thought as a regular n-dimensional lattice of sites or, equivalently, as an n-dimensional space (called cellular space) partitioned in cells of uniform size (e.g. square or hexagonal for $n=2$), each one embedding an identical finite automaton. The cell state changes by means of the finite automaton transition function, which defines local rules of evolution for the system. In fact, its input is constituted by the states of a small set of cells that, usually, includes the cell itself (called central cell) and a little number of neighbouring ones. The CA initial configuration is defined by the finite automata states at time $t=0$. The overall global behaviour of the system emerges, step by step, as a consequence of the simultaneous application of the transition function to each cell of the cellular space.

The classes of CA known as Lattice Gas Automata and Lattice Boltzmann Models [2,3,4,5,6] were proposed in order to study fluid dynamics and applied, with notably results, to the simulation of turbulent phenomena. However, their applications do not include, in general, phenomena evolving on macroscopic space scales.

After the development of Lattice Gas Models and before the definition of Lattice Boltzmann Models, a CA based empirical method was proposed by Di Gregorio and his research group to model the dynamics of macroscopic spatially extended systems; the first application of such a method concerned the simulation of lava flows [7]. Subsequently, the Di Gregorio empirical method was applied effectively for modelling and simulating different complex macroscopic phenomena [8,9,10].

P.M.A. Sloot, B. Chopard, and A.G. Hoekstra (Eds.): ACRI 2004, LNCS 3305, pp. 725–734, 2004.

2 The Di Gregorio Empirical Method for Surface Flows Modelling

The Di Gregorio empirical method share with Lattice Boltzmann Models the characteristic of having a huge number of states for the cell and, thus, a transition function that cannot be conveniently expressed as a look-up table. It is expressed in algorithmic terms and, as for Lattice Boltzmann Models, it operates in order to lead the equilibrium condition in the local context of the cell neighbourhood. The following considerations introduce an extended CA definition that better fits to the modelling of complex macroscopic surface flows phenomena.

2.1 Parameters

A spatial correspondence between CA cells and the region where the phenomenon evolves must be fixed. In fact, when dealing with surface flows (e.g. debris flows), Digital Elevation Models (DEMs) impose a prefixed (macroscopic) detail. As a consequence, the CA cell size must be accordingly fixed. Analogously, the CA clock must be determined in order to define a temporal correspondence between the simulated and the real phenomenon.

Once set, the dimension of the cell and the CA clock are defined as parameters, since their values are assumed constant in the overall CA simulation. It is worth to note that, however, while the cell dimension can be fixed "a priori" on the basis of the detail of the digital topographic map, an exact assessment of the time step can be given only "a posteriori", by analysing the overall behaviour of the system.

Moreover, other physical and/or empirical parameters can be considered in order to define the required links between the CA framework and the considered phenomenon. Examples of such parameters are discussed in section 4.

2.2 Substates

The state of the cell must account for all the characteristics which are assumed to be relevant to the evolution of the system. For a more clear representation of the problem, each characteristic corresponds to a "substate", which must form a finite set of values. Let Q_i be the ith substate; the set of the substates of the cell is defined as:

$$S = \{Q_1, Q_2, \dots, Q_s\} \tag{1}$$

The set Q of all possible state values for the cell is given by the Cartesian product:

$$Q = Q_1 \times Q_2 \times \dots \times Q_s \tag{2}$$

The value of each substate is considered always constant inside the cell (as usually occurs for the altitude inside DEMs). As a consequence, the maps in case needed for the problem representation, must be sufficiently accurate so that the resulting CA cell size is adequate to appropriately describe the features of the considered phenomenon.

Eventually, this approach permits to describe three-dimensional surface flows through bi-dimensional models by including the third dimension among cell substates.

2.3 Elementary Processes

The CA transition function, σ, must account for all processes which are responsible for the cell state changes that are considered relevant for the correct system's evolution. So, as the set Q of states is split in substates, even the transition function can be decomposed in "elementary processes". The system's evolution is obtained by applying the elementary processes to each CA cell, according to a defined order. This assumption is not justified "a priori", and must be empirically verified in the simulation phase.

2.4 External Influences

In some cases a kind of input from the "external world" must be considered to account for influences that cannot be naturally described in terms of local rules (e.g. the location of the detachment area of a landslide) or for some kind of probabilistic approach to the phenomenon.

2.5 Extended CA Formal Definition

The above considerations lead to an extended definition of CA for macroscopic surface flows phenomena [11]:

$$A =< R, E, Q, X, P, \sigma, \gamma >$$ (3)

where:

- $R=\{(x,y) \in \mathbf{Z}^2, x=-l_x,\ldots,0,\ldots,l_x; y=-l_y,\ldots,0,\ldots,l_y\}$ is the set of points, with integer coordinates, of the finite region where the phenomenon evolves.
- $E=\{E_1 \cup E_2 \cup \ldots \cup E_r\}$ is the set of cells which undergo to the influences of the "external world"; r external influences are here considered, each one defines a subregion E_i ($i=1,2,\ldots,r$) of the cellular space, where the influence is active.
- X is the neighbourhood index. It defines the coordinates of neighbouring cells with respect to the central one.
- $Q=Q_1 \times Q_2 \times \ldots \times Q_s$ is the set of the state values; it is specified by the Cartesian product of the finite sets of the values of the s substates $Q_1, Q_2, \ldots, Q_s$.
- P is the finite set of parameters which affect the transition function.
- $\sigma: S^{\#X} \rightarrow S$ is the deterministic state transition function. It is specified by the ordered set of elementary processes in order of application.
- $\gamma=\{\gamma_1, \gamma_2, \ldots, \gamma_r\}$ is the finite set of functions that define the external influences to the cells of E; γ_i: $\mathbf{N} \times E_i \times Q \rightarrow Q$ ($i=1,2,\ldots,r$), where $\mathbf{N}$ is the set of natural numbers, here referred to the CA steps.

2.6 Macroscopic Surface Flows Modelling

Surface flows (e.g. lava flows, debris flows, etc) belong to those phenomena that can naturally be described in terms of local interactions. In fact, by opportunely discreetizing the surface on which the phenomenon evolves, the dynamics of the system can be described in terms of flows of some quantity (e.g. lava, debris, etc) from one cell to neighbouring ones. Moreover, as previously stated, the fact that the cell dimension is constant throughout the cellular space, permits to consider characteristics of the cell (i.e. substates), typically expressed in terms of volume (e.g. lava volume), in terms of thickness.

These simple assumptions permit to adopt a straightforward but efficacious strategy that consists in the outflow computation in order to minimize the local non-equilibrium conditions.

The Minimisation Algorithm of the Differences. The determination of the outflows from the central cell towards the neighbourhood is based on the Di Gregorio "minimisation algorithm of the differences", well described in [11]. In the local context of the CA cell, the algorithm computes the outflows in order to minimise the differences of "certain quantities" in the neighbourhood. It is based on the following assumptions:

- two parts of the considered quantity must be identified in the central cell: these are the unmovable part, $u(0)$, and the mobile part, m;
- only m can be distributed to the adjacent cells. Let $f(a,b)$ denote the flow from cell a to cell b; m can be written as:

$$m = \sum_{i=0}^{\#X} f(0,i) \qquad (4)$$

where $f(0,0)$ is the part which is not distributed;

- the quantities in the adjacent cells, $u(i)$ ($i=1,2,...,\#X$) are considered unmovable;
- let $c(i)=u(i)+f(0,i)$ ($i=0,1,...,\#X$) be the new quantity content in the ith neighbouring cell after the distribution; let c_{min} be the minimum value of $c(i)$ ($i=0,1,...,\#X$). The outflows are computed in order to minimise the following expression:

$$\sum_{i=0}^{\#X} (c(i) - c_{min}) \qquad (5)$$

This represents the condition of maximum possible equilibrium for the considered quantity in the neighbourhood, according to the principle of hydrostatic equilibrium [11]. Moreover, a relaxation rate $r_r \in [0,1]$ can be introduced, denoting that such conditions may not be reached in a single CA step; the obtained values of outflows are therefore multiplied by r_r (if $r_r=1$, no relaxation is induced; if $r_r=0$, there will be no outflows towards the neighbourhood).

Eventually, the simultaneous application of the minimization principle to each cell gives rise to the global equilibrium of the system [11].

3 Genetic Algorithms

When dealing with Di Gregorio based models for macroscopic surface flows, a proper calibration phase might be needed to properly fit the set of parameters (which not always correspond to actual physical ones, nor do their values strictly need to have a physical meaning) that define the required links with the considered phenomenon.

However, regarding the CA modelling of natural complex phenomena, no standardised optimisation techniques do exist, and the calibration phase is often performed "manually" [12]. An alternative solution is offered by Genetic Algorithms.

Genetic Algorithms (GAs) are general-purpose search algorithms inspired from genetics and natural selection [13]. GAs simulate the evolution of a population of candidate solutions of a specific search problem by favouring the reproduction of the most appropriate individuals (or genotype). Genotypes are represented by a given data structure, e.g. bit strings, where each element is called gene. In order to find a proper solution, the GA must investigate the so-called search space, defined as the set of all possible values that the genotype can assume. Evaluation of individuals is performed by choosing a suitable fitness function, which determines the "goodness" of the individual in solving the given search problem. The basic idea is that better individuals (i.e. characterised by higher fitness) can be obtained over time by combining and mutating partial solutions.

The evolution of the (randomly generated) population is typically obtained by the application of simple random operators. The "selection" operator, which represents a metaphor of Darwinian Natural Selection, chooses individuals that undergo "reproduction" by means of "genetic" operators, to form a new population. Classical genetic operators are "crossover" and "mutation": they represent a metaphor of sexual reproduction and of genetic mutation, respectively. According to a prefixed probability, pairs of genotypes produce offspring via crossover, receiving components from each parent. Then, according to a prefixed and usually small probability, each gene of the offspring is subject to mutation. The mutation operator simply changes the gene value with another one, randomly chosen within those allowed.

Eventually, it is worth to note that any change that actually increases the individual's fitness will be more likely to be preserved over the selection process, thus obtaining better generations, as stated by the fundamental theorem of genetic algorithms [13]. An exhaustive overview of GAs can be found in [14].

The following section briefly describes the model SCIARA for the simulation of lava flows and its calibration through GAs.

4 Evolving the SCIARA CA Model for Lava Flows Simulation

Lava flows belong to the class of complex macroscopic phenomena, which are usually hard to model through differential equations systems [11]. At the contrary, by considering the Di Gregorio based CA approach, their modelling can result quite simple, as shown in the following section.

4.1 The SCIARA CA Model

SCIARA [9] is a CA based model for lava flows simulation, in the past successfully applied to real cases occurred in the Etnean area. The main SCIARA characteristics can be summarised by the following points:

Table 1. List of parameters of the model SCIARA

SCIARA parameters	Description
$P_1=c$	Time corresponding to a CA step
$P_2=T_{vent}$	Lava temperature at vents
$P_3=T_{sol}$	Lava solidification temperature
$P_4=T_{int}$	Lava intermediate temperature (see Fig. 1)
$P_5=v_{vent}$	Lava adherence value at vents
$P_6=v_{sol}$	Lava adherence at solidification temperature
$P_7=v_{int}$	Lava adherence at intermediate temperature
$P_8=C$	Cooling parameter, related to temperature drop

- it is a bi-dimensional model based on hexagonal cells;
- the cell neighbourhood is composed by the cell itself and the six adjacent ones;
- the model substates are Q_a, Q_t, Q_f^6 and Q_T for altitude, lava thickness, cell lava flows from the central cell towards the six adjacent ones and temperature, respectively;
- lava feeding is modelled as an external influence by specifying cells which behave as vents;
- lava flows are computed by applying the Di Gregorio minimisation algorithm;
- lava temperature drop is modelled by applying the irradiation equation;
- lava viscosity varies according to lava temperature; it is modelled in terms of adherence, which specifies the amount of lava that cannot flow out of the cell;
- solidification process depends on lava temperature; it is trivially modelled by adding solidified lava thickness to the cell altitude.

The model parameters are listed in Table 1; the elementary processes of the transition function are briefly described in the following sections in order of application.

Lava Flows. Lava rheological resistance increases as temperature decreases; consequently, a certain amount of lava, i.e. the lava adherence v, cannot flow out from the central cell towards any neighbouring ones. As shown in Fig. 1, it is obtained by means of a piecewise linear function [9] that approximates the equation

$$v = k_1 e^{-k_2 T} \tag{6}$$

where $T \in Q_T$ is the cell lava temperature, while k_1 and k_2 are parameters depending on lava rheological properties [15].

Let $a \in Q_a$ and $t \in Q_t$ be the cell altitude and cell lava thickness, respectively; in order to compute lava outflows from the central cell towards its neighbouring ones, the Di Gregorio minimisation algorithm is applied to the following quantities: $u(0)=a(0)+v$; $m=t(0)-v$; $u(i)=a(i)+t(i)$ $(i=1,2,\dots,6)$.

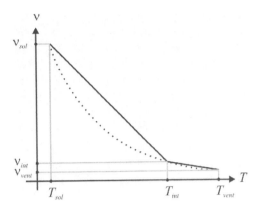

Fig. 1. In black the SCIARA adherence function. It approximates the eq. (6), shown in the graphic as a dotted line. T is the lava temperature, v the lava adherence. The subscripts *sol*, *int* and *vent* indicate solidification, intermediate and vent values, respectively

Eventually, a relaxation rate factor, related to the CA clock c, is considered in order to obtain the local equilibrium condition in the correct number of CA steps [9].

Temperature Variation. A two step process determines the new cell temperature. In the first one, the cell temperature is obtained as weighted average of residual lava inside the cell and lava inflows from neighbouring ones:

$$T_{av} = \left(t_r \times T(0) + \sum_{i=1}^{6} f(i,0) \times T(i) \right) \Big/ \left(t_r + \sum_{i=1}^{6} f(i,0) \right) \qquad (7)$$

where $t_r \in Q_t$ is the residual lava thickness inside the central cell after the outflows distribution, $T \in Q_T$ is the lava temperature and $f(i,0)$ the lava inflow from the ith neighbouring cell. Note that $f(i,0)$ is equal to the lava outflow from the ith neighbouring cell towards the central one, computed by means of the minimisation algorithm.

The final step updates the previous calculated temperature by considering thermal energy loss due to lava surface irradiation:

$$T = T_{av} \Big/ \sqrt[3]{1 + \left(T_{av}^3 CA/V \right)} \qquad (8)$$

where C is a parameter depending on lava rheology, A is the surface area of the cell, and V the lava volume [9].

Lava Solidification. When the lava temperature drops below the threshold T_{sol}, lava solidifies. Consequently, cell altitude increases by an amount equal to lava thickness and new lava thickness is set to zero.

4.2 SCIARA Parameters Calibration Through Genetic Algorithms

In this work, GAs were employed for the SCIARA parameters optimisation by considering a real event occurred on Mt. Etna (Sicily, Italy) in 2002. The event involved two main lava bodies. Calibration was performed on the part which interested the NW flank of the volcano, with lava generated by a fracture between 2500 m a.s.l. and 1900 m a.s.l., near the 1809 fracture and pointing towards the town of Linguaglossa.

The CA parameters to be optimised (Table 1) were encoded into the GA genotype as bit strings (8 bits were used for the encoding of each parameter), and populations of 100 individuals were considered. Previous empirical attempts of simulation of the same case-study, manually performed by iteratively assigning reasonable values to the model parameters, helped in hypothesising the ranges $[a_i,b_i]$ $(i=1,2,...,8)$ within which the values of the CA parameters P_i are allowed to vary. These ranges define the search space S for the GA:

$$S = [a_1,b_1] \times [a_2,b_2] \times \cdots \times [a_8,b_8] = [30,120] \times [1350,1400] \times$$
$$\times [1050,1200] \times [1250,1340] \times [0.1,1] \times [7,15] \times [1.1,3] \times [10^{-17},10^{-13}] \quad (9)$$

The adopted GA is a steady-state elitist model, as at each step only the worst individuals are replaced (in our case, the worst 32). The remaining (68) individuals required to form the new population, are copied from the old one, choosing the best. In order to select the individuals to be reproduced, the "binary-tournament without replacement" selection operator was utilised. It consists of a series of "tournaments" in which two individuals are selected at random, and the winner is chosen according to a prefixed probability, which must be set greater for the fittest individual. In our case, this probability is equal to 0.6. Moreover, as the variation without replacement was adopted, the individuals cannot be selected more than once. Finally, employed genetic operators are classic Holland's crossover and mutation with probability of 0.8 and 1/64 (in order to have one bit mutated for each individual), respectively.

In general, in order to apply a simulation model for reliably predictive purposes, calibration has to be performed by comparing simulations with actual case studies. The choice of an appropriate fitness function is essential to evaluate the goodness of a given simulation. In the present study, a fitness functions, e_1, which simply compares the extent of actual and simulated events (in terms of affected area) was considered. Let R and S be the regions affected by the real and simulated event, respectively; let $m(A)$ denote the measure of the set A. The function e_1 is defined as:

$$e_1 = \sqrt{\frac{m(R \cap S)}{m(R \cup S)}} \quad (10)$$

Note that $e_1 \in [0,1]$. Its value is 0 if the real and simulated events are completely disjoint, being $m(R \cap S)=0$; it is 1 in case of perfect overlap, being $m(R \cap S)= m(R \cup S)$. Thus, the goal for the GA is to find a set of CA parameters that maximise e_1.

4.3 Parallel Implementation and Experimental Results

Aiming to speed up experiments execution time, a Master-Slave GA [16] was applied in a parallel computer environment: a processor (the master) executes the GA steps (selection, population replacement, crossover and mutation), while several others (the slaves) evaluate the individual's fitness. D'Ambrosio et al. [17] obtained a linear speed-up of the considered Master-Slave GA on a Beowulf Linux Cluster with 16 1.4 GHz Pentium 4 processors for the calibration of a CA model for debris flows simulation. Linear speed-up permits to reduce execution time of a factor equal to the number of processing nodes. In this work, calibration experiments were performed on a Linux

Cluster composed by a master mono-processor node and 8 bi-processor slave nodes. All processors are 3GHz Intel Xeon, with an overall 34 GB RAM memory, connected by a GigaBit LAN Ethernet.

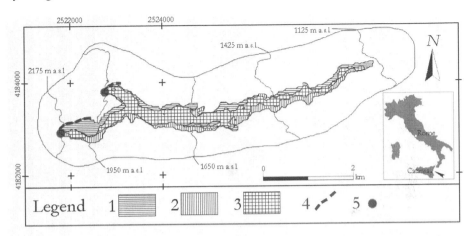

Fig. 2. Comparison between the real and the simulated 2002 Linguaglossa lava flow at Mt. Etna. Key: 1) area affected by real lava flow; 2) area affected by simulated lava flow; 3) area affected by both cases; 4) fractures of real lava flows; 5) SCIARA emission points

Four GA runs of 100 steps were carried out, each one with different initial population. As a whole, the GA optimisation lasted less than 4 days (on a sequential machine, the same experiment would had lasted more than 2 months). The CA parameters corresponding to the best-evolved individual, whose fitness value resulted in e_1=0.65, are: c=117.2 s, T_{vent}=1380.9 °K, T_{sol}=1074.7 °K, T_{int}=1302.6 °K, v_{vent}=0.83 m, v_{sol}=7.03 m, v_{int}=2.93 m, C=4.02·10^{-16} m°K^{-3}. The related simulation is shown in Fig. 2.

5 Discussion

We proposed the application of a Master Slave GA to the calibration of the CA model SCIARA for lava flows simulation, by considering the 2002 Linguaglossa (Sicily, Italy) case study.

Results demonstrated GAs reliability and, consequently, the SCIARA efficacy in the simulation of Etnean lava flows. From a qualitative point of view, the simulation carried out by considering CA parameters corresponding to the best evolved individual, does not differ significantly from the real case. From a quantitative point of view, the overlapping between the real and simulated event (in terms of e_1) is significantly greater than those previously obtained without applying GAs on the same case-study.

However, further improvements could be achieved. In fact, as shown in Fig. 2, real lava emission points were generated by a fracture, while simulations were carried out by considering only two lava vents. This could justify the limited overlapping between the real and simulated event near lava sources. Moreover, the adoption of a more reliable topographic map could sensibly improve the model calibration. Among future developments, a thorough investigation of these problems will be addressed.

References

1. von Neumann, J.: Theory of self reproducing automata. University of Illinois Press, Urbana (1966)
2. Hardy, J., Pomeau, Y., de Pazzis, G.: Thermodynamics and hydrodynamics for a modeled fluid. Journal of Mathematical Physics A 13 (1976) 1949-1961
3. Higuera, F., Jimenez, J.: Boltzmann approach to lattice gas simulations. Europhysics Letters 9 (1989) 663-668
4. McNamara, G.R., Zanetti, G.: Use of the Boltzmann equation to simulate lattice-gas automata. Physical Review Letters 61 (1988) 2332-2335
5. Chopard, B., Droz, M.: Cellular Automata Modeling of Physical Systems, Cambridge University Press (1998)
6. Succi, S.: The Lattice Boltzmann Equation for Fluid Dynamics and Beyond. Oxford University Press (2004)
7. Crisci, G.M., Di Gregorio, S., Ranieri, G.A.: A Cellular space model of basaltic lava flow. Proceedings of International Conference "Applied Modelling and Simulation 82", Paris, France, July 1-3, Vol. 11 (1982) 65-67
8. Iovine, G., Di Gregorio, S., Lupiano V.: Debris-flow susceptibility assessment through cellular automata modeling: an example from 15-16 December 1999 disaster at Cervinara and San Martino Valle Caudina (Campania, southern Italy). Natural Hazards and Earth System Sciences 3 (2003) 457-468
9. Crisci G.M., Rongo, R., Di Gregorio, S., Spataro, W.: The simulation model SCIARA: the 1991 and 2001 lava flows at Mount Etna. Journal of Volcanology and Geothermal Research 132 (2004) 253-267
10. Di Gregorio, S., Serra, R., Villani, M.: A Cellular Automata Model of Soil Bioremediation. Complex Systems 11 (1997) 31-54
11. Di Gregorio, S., Serra, R.: An empirical method for modelling and simulating some complex macroscopic phenomena by cellular automata. Future Generation Computer Systems 16 (1999) 259-271
12. D'Ambrosio, D., Di Gregorio, S., Iovine G.: Simulating debris flows through a hexagonal cellular automata model: Sciddica S3-hex. Natural Hazards and Earth System Sciences 3 (2003) 545-559
13. Holland, J.H.: Adaptation in Natural and Artificial Systems. University of Michigan Press, Ann Arbor (1975)
14. Mitchell, M.: An Introduction to Genetic Algorithms. MIT Press, Cambridge, Massachusetts (1996)
15. Park, S., Iversen, J.D.: Dynamics of lava flow: Thickness growth characteristics of steady two-dimensional flows. Geophysical Research Letters 11 (1984) 641-644
16. Alba, E., Tomassini, M.: Parallelism and evolutionary algorithms. IEEE Transactions on Evolutionary Computation, 6 (2002) 443-462
17. D'Ambrosio, D., Spataro, W., Iovine, G.: Parallel genetic algorithms for optimising cellular automata models of natural complex phenomena: an application to debris-flows. Computer & Geosciences (in press)

CAME&L – Cellular Automata Modeling Environment & Library

Lev Naumov

Saint-Peterburg State University of Information Technologies, Mechanics and Optics,
Computer Technologies Department,
197101 Sablinskaya st. 14, Saint-Peterburg, Russia
levnaumov@mail.ru
http://camel.ifmo.ru

Abstract. New software for distributed parallel computations is presented. It is desired to be universal, easy-to-use, featureful and extensible workspace for cellular automata studying and complicated scientific computations. The idea is to represent each automaton by the set of components of four types (grid, datum, metrics and rules). Either of types is to implement its own part of functionality and combining allows to build different automata for arbitrary tasks. Class of systems that could be modeled with the help of introduced project is even wider than "cellular automata". Project has rather long list of features and abilities, which mark it out the set of existing software of this kind.

1 Introduction

Cellular automaton is specific parallel architecture [1–3]. So if it is wanted to get some benefits from using it automaton is to be implemented on specialized hardware platform (like CAM [1]) or, at least, with the help of particular software.

Multifunctional software environment for solving problems basing on cellular automata will allow to use computers as an assembly for physical, chemical, biological or other kinds of experiments (actually real specimens of such assemblies can be very expensive) or as a tool for execution, visualization and analysis of parallel computations.

Trying to use or reading descriptions of near 20 existing products for cellular automata modeling (CAM Simulator, CAMEL, CANL, CAPow, CASim, CAT/CAR, CDL, CDM/SLANG, CelLab, CELLAS/FUNDEF, Cellsim, Cellular/Cellang, CEPROL, DDLab, HICAL, LCAU, Mirek's Cellebration, SCARLET, WinCA) showed that there are rather significant common shortcomings:

- *Existing products put limitations on automata that can be modeled.* Dimension of the grid, possible cells neighborhood or amount of cells states are commonly predefined. For example, for tasks of language recognition [4, 5] cells are to store strings in cells. Only specialized programs, developed for definite tasks, allow this.

P.M.A. Sloot, B. Chopard, and A.G. Hoekstra (Eds.): ACRI 2004, LNCS 3305, pp. 735–744, 2004.
© Springer-Verlag Berlin Heidelberg 2004

- *Majority of existing products do not support contemporary technologies* like cluster computations and multiprocessor computations. Such software just "simulate" cellular automata but do not actually "use" them.
- *Products have different languages (sometimes complicated) for cellular automata description.* So such languages increase amount of things that researcher have to study before using software.
- *Majority of existing products do not satisfy modern requirements to user interface* and do not use features that now are ordinary.

So, it was decided to develop software, which will keep from these shortcomings in the following way (in the same order):

- No limitations to cellular automata that can be used. Actually the class of basic abstractions is even wide then "cellular automaton", because basic properties (locality of the rules, similarity of the system everywhere and assignment of new cells states at the end of timestep) [1], can be, optionally, not satisfied.
- Support of distributed cluster computations (with ability of cluster arrangement via Internet), computations on multiprocessor platform and also on personal computer with single processor.
- Knowledge of C++ is to be enough for implementing arbitrary cellular experiment. This can sound strange, because ability to use C++ can be thought to be too complicated skill, but everybody who is going to create cluster and perform computations on it (with Globus [6], for example), is to be familiar with programming. It has to be also possible to extend set of automata description languages (with the help of C++ again).
- Handy user interface with the support of many useful features.

This project got name "Cellular Automata Modeling Environment & Library", "CAME&L" abbreviated[1].

2   CAME&L Software

CAME&L project is desired to be universal, easy-to-use, featureful and extensible workspace for cellular automata studying and complicated scientific computations.

This software is developed for workstations with operating system from Windows NT family. This can be considered among both, advantages and disadvantages, but firstly there are much more good quality parallel computations products for UNIX/Linux and secondly ideas of CAME&L are independent of operating system.

---

[1] By twist of fate, as was mentioned above, there is one more project called "CAMEL". Its authors are D. Talia and G. Spezzano. But in this case such abbreviation comes from "Cellular Automata environMent for systEms modeLing". The author learned about such awkward coincidence after his project was already started and it was decided to keep similar name. After small discussion with Mr. Talia, an ampersand appeared in the logo of introduced project. Moreover, project of D. Talia and G. Spezzano was renamed to "CAMELOT" (of course, it was not concerned with the appearing of CAME&L). So author wants to take advantage and make excuses for the same name of two such different projects.

Project source code, which is not related to user interface, is written in ANSI C++, so it can be ported to Linux or another operating system.

Software consists of three main parts:

- Environment – application with rich and friendly user interface for researching cellular automata (Fig. 1). Basic abstraction, in terms of which environment functions, is "experiment" – computational task. Here "experiment" is synonym of term "document". Environment contains tools for computations control, studying and analysis, cluster arrangement, workstations management and many others.

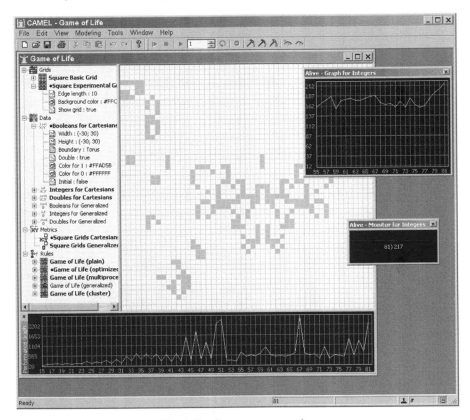

Fig. 1. Environments screenshot

- Cellular Automata Development Library (CADLib abbreviated) – C++ class library, which is designed to present an easy-to-use and rich set of instrument for researchers. It is provided for reusing and enlarging for specific problems solving. Library also contains useful functions, macrodefinitions and constants to make development of, so named, "components" (next part of software) easier.
- Components – bricks, from which all experiments are built. In fact, any component is a dynamic-link library, which contains functions and classes, developed with the help of CADLib. Component is to provide definite part of cellular automatons

functionality and necessary analysis. CADLib makes development of all formal, common, non-specific functions of component trivial.

Now last two parts of software will be discussed in the reverse order. Features and abilities of the firs part will be described in the features list afterwards.

3 Components

Components may be used in different combinations to add arbitrary functionality to the experiment. There are five possible types of components: grids, metrics, datum, rules and analyzers. Description of their functions follows:

- Grid – implements visualization of grid and cells navigation. It is not the same as set G from cellular automatons formal definition [7], because it does not actually store cells states. This component's main task is drawing and interacting with user.
- Metrics – provides the relationship of neighborhood, coordinates for any cell and distance function, which allows calculating remoteness between each pair of cells. It is not actually set N (neighborhood) from cellular automatons formal definition [7], but very similar. At least, it allows to retrieve elements from set N. This component also provides abilities, which do not refer this set. Implementation of metrics as a separate component (not providing grid or datum components with functions, implemented by metrics) allows, for example, to use non-standard coordinates systems, like generalized coordinates [7].
- Datum – maintains cells states storage, exchange and some aspects of data visualization (namely it provides accordance between cells state and color, which is to be used for its displaying). So this component unites functions of sets G (grid) and Z (set of possible states) from cellular automatons formal definition [7].
- Rules – fully describes computations and controls the iteration. In the introduced project "rules" and "transition function" are not synonyms. This component defines the method of parallelization, method of computations optimization (if used) and, possibly, many other aspects and transition function. But single rules component may represent a parser of language for transition functions description (like CARPET [8], for example) and work with arbitrary transition functions (not with only one). However, from the opposite side, it would be better (but not necessary) to implement different rules components for various computational platforms (cluster variant, multiprocessor variant and variant for single processor). This component also allows
  - o to handle experiments starting;
  - o to determine and handle experiments finishing;
  - o to define special tools for checking or changing something in the experiment;
  - o to define important experiments properties for further studying with analyzer components (see bellow).
- Analyzer – allows to keep an eye on definite properties of the experiment, draw graphs, create reports, monitor values and all of this kind. For example on Fig. 1 there are tree analyzers, which allow researcher to track important automatons parameter. First displays graph of the amount of "alive cells" in Conway's game of

Life. This value was announced in rules component as analyzable parameter and can be studied while experimenting. Second is simple monitor of the current value of the same parameter. Third is graph of systems performance: the time, required for each iteration, in milliseconds. This is standard analyzer, which is available always, for any experiment.

First three components totally define the cellular automaton without the task it is to solve. Absence of the definition of transition function allows to name it "functionless". Nevertheless these three components are enough to begin working with automaton, using the environment.

Addition of fourth component to the union of first three components will form cellular automaton that can took part in the experiment. Usage of analyzers is, obviously, optional.

Only one component of each of first four types can participate in the experiment, but unlimited amount of analyzers can be used.

Each component has special user interface: set of available parameters, which allows tuning the component for corresponding task or for accordance to users aesthetic predilection.

It could be seen on Fig. 1 that each document inside the environment is viewed in window, which is divided in two parts: right – for grids visualization and left – for displaying the tree of installed components with their parameters (analyzers are not listed here, there is another way for their addition to the experiment). Selected components are marked with small circle before its name.

Of course, each component is to work in tandem with some components (not alone). But it cannot be compatible with all developed components. So components are to describe their properties and properties of components, they are able to cooperate with. For description of these properties special language of logical expressions is used.

Components compatibility is visualized on tree of installed components. All components, that are compatible with already selected, are shown with bold font.

Information about component, about its parameters and also about properties, which it "realizes" and "requires", can be viewed with components manager (Fig. 2), tool for installing and removing components. This tool is built in the environment.

4 Cellular Automata Development Library

In the ideology of CADLib terms "user", "developer" and "researcher" become identical.

Main purpose of this library is to provide basic classes for all types of components and to make components development as easy, agile and obvious as possible.

Class hierarchy chart of the library is shown on Fig. 3. Boxes with dotted boundary lines show class templates. Boxes, which are filled with gray color, correspond to classes of components, which are provided with the environment. They are not actually members of CADLib, but their place in the hierarchy is to be shown and understood.

Fig. 2. Components manager screenshot

Basic class of all components is called CAComponent. Its descendants CAGrid, CAMetrics, CADatum, CARules and CAAnalyzer are basic classes for five mentioned types of components. Some of these classes also have descendants for developing more specialized components.

For example, development of user datum component, which supports specialized data type, may result in several lines of code with the help of templates CABasic-CrtsData and CABasicGenData. Creation of new analyzer is also quite simple. Writing of user rules is also not complicated and became obvious because of variety of sample rules components. In most cases there is a need to change only several lines of code in the source code of the examples to get rules for user cellular automaton.

Development of new grids and metrics are the most difficult cases. These components are too universal and their behavior is unsuspected for CADLib so it could not help user anyhow. However the fact is that the need of new components of any type, except rules, will rise rarely.

Besides components classes, CADLib also contains parameter classes. Parameters are actually values of some type. These classes are used for implementing components user interface (not the appearance, but the points of tuning).

Querying of parameters values is performed with the help of special dialogs. Classes, which implement these dialogs, are also included in the library. These classes (CDlg's descendants) are only CADLib members, which are not ANSI C++ classes, because they contain user interface implementation[2].

There are some more classes in CADLib, but their overview is outside the examination.

As was mentioned above, each component is to be represented by dynamic-link library. Component's library is to contain four objects:

- Component's class implementation.
- Creation function, which is used for components initiation.

---

[2] These classes have members of MFC (Microsoft Foundation Classes) library as ancestors.

- Destruction function, which is used for components annihilation.
- Authentication function, which is used to determine
  o if library really contains ✦CAME&L component;
  o type of the component (it was decided not to use RTTI [9] at all);
  o version of framework, for which component was developed.

  CADLib gives macrodefinitions, which allows to add last three functions to the library with three small lines of code.

5 Features of ✦CAME&L Project

Most significant features, which advantageously distinguish ✦CAME&L from other project, developed for similar problems, listed below. It is impossible to separate environment's features from library's ar component's, so they will be enumerated as mixture:

- There are no limitations on cellular automata, which can be used. The fact that each automaton is represented by the set of components allows to develop arbitrary system. It is possible even to overcome basic properties of cellular automata [1, 7]. In addition, each component can be tuned using parameters. Important note is that the main accent of ✦CAME&L was made to the universality (lattice gas, language recognition, phase unwrapping everything is possible). It is the main tendency in software developing now: it is possible to loose a little bit in the performance, but do not constrict the spectrum abilities (the popularity of programming language Java is the best proof of last words).
- Environment represents multi-document interface and provides ability to implement interactions between cellular automata. This may be useful, for example, when solving tasks of modeling crystals with some dissemination. In this case the dissemination can be realized with one automaton (if it is needed) and the rest of crystal – with another automaton. Automata interact to determine what to do on the boundary of the dissemination.
- It is possible to perform parallel computations on multiprocessor computers and on clusters.
- Roles of workstations involved in computational cluster can be totally controlled, user may describe parallelization and distribution of the task. Cluster can also involve workstations via Internet.
- Software uses novel specialized fast, reliable and featureful networking protocol for parallel cluster computing, Commands Transfer Protocol (CTP) [10, 11]. So project does not use MPI, PVM or any other standard library for these purposes. Necessary functionality is built in the protocol.

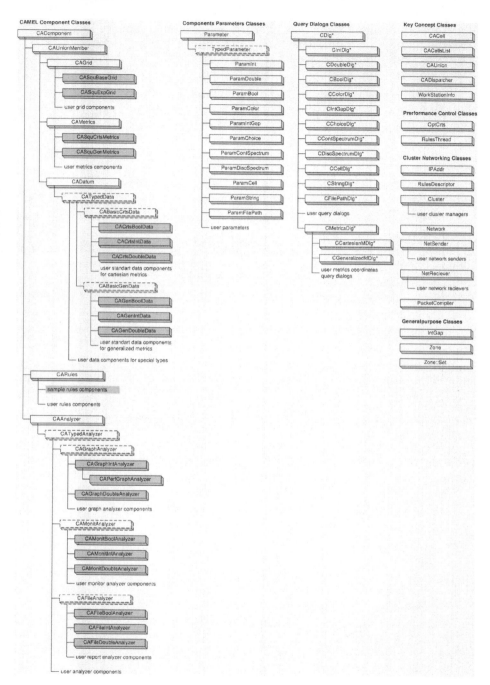

Fig. 3. CADLib class hierarchy chart

- Important fact about whole ⚡CAME&L project is that there is now dark, unclear "key points". Exterior developers wrote no crucial parts of source code[3].
- Environment has handy user interface that supports, for example
  undo-redo functionality;
  clipboard operations;
  rich set of printing functions;
  picture storing functions (for illustrating papers);
  many other functions.
- Environment stores data in XML format (CML files), which is advantageous for information exchange. Cells states data may be, optionally, compressed inside CML file using BZip2 algorithm. This ability decreases files size in thousands times.
- Environment has rich toolkit to control, study and analyze the experiment.
- There is an ability to build graphs of computations performance, so it is possible to tune the system to the optimal throughput.
- Implementation of metrics as a separate automatons component allows, for example, to use non-standard coordinates systems, like generalized coordinates [7].
- Software is provided with a lot of examples of different components, which can be used for users tasks solving or as a basis of new users components.

So, here is the list of main abilities of the project. Some other existing environments for cellular computations possess some of them, but the majority is novel. The idea to assemble all these features inside one project provoked ⚡CAME&L to appear.

The development and testing of this project is now in progress, but it is planed to publish the release rather soon. The best ways to learn more about current state of the project or to get this software are

- to contact the author (e-mail and address were given in the beginning of the paper);
- to visit http://camel.ifmo.ru.

References

1. Toffoli, T., Margolus, N.: Cellular Automata Machines. Mir (World), Moscow (1991)
2. Sarkar, P.: A Brief History of Cellular Automata // ACM Computing Surveys, Vol. 32. N1. (2000)
3. Von Neumann, J.: Theory of Self-Reproducing Automata. University of Illinois Press (1966)
4. Worsch, T.: Linear Time Language Recognition on Cellular Automata with Restricted Communication // Tech. Report 25/98 of the Department of Informatics, University of Karlsruhe (1998)

---

[3] Only several graphical user interface open source components were taken over. References could be found.

5. Buchholtz, T., Klein, A., Kutrib, M., Real-Time Language Recognition by Alternating Cellular Automata // IFIG Research Report 9904 (1999)
6. Foster, I., Kesselman, C.: Globus: A Metacomputing Infrastructure Toolkit (2002)
7. Naumov, L.: Generalized Coordinates for Cellular Automata Grids // Computational Science – ICCS 2003. Part 2. Springer-Verlag. (2003)
8. Spezzano, G., Talia, D., Designing Parallel Models of Soil Contamination by the CARPET Language (1998)
9. Stroustrup, B., The C++ Programming Language. Addison-Wesley Publishing Company (1991)
10. Naumov, L., Commands Transfer Protocol – Networking Protocol for Cluster Computations, in preparation (2004)
11. Naumov, L., Commands Transfer Protocol – New Networking Protocol for Distributed and Parallel Computations
    //http://www.codeproject.com/internet/ctp.asp (2004)

SAT-Based Analysis of Cellular Automata

Massimo D'Antonio and Giorgio Delzanno

Dipartimento di Informatica e Scienze dell'Informazione
Università di Genova, via Dodecaneso 35, 16146 Genova, Italy
giorgio@disi.unige.it

Abstract. In the last decade there has been a dramatic speed-up for algorithms solving the Satisfiability (SAT) problem for propositional formulas, a well known NP-complete problem. In this paper we will investigate the applicability of modern SAT *solvers* to the qualitative analysis of Cellular Automata. For this purpose we have defined an encoding of the *evolution* of Cellular Automata into formulas in propositional logic. The resulting formula can be used to test *forward* and *inverse reachability* problems for the original Cellular Automata in a modular way. In the paper we will report on experimental results obtained by applying the SAT-solver zChaff to reachability problems for classical examples of Cellular Automata like the Firing Squad Synchronization Problem.

1 Introduction

Several tools have been used to animate specifications of Cellular Automata (CAs) e.g., for traffic and artificial life processes simulation (for a survey, see e.g., [15]). Simulation amounts to compute all configurations reachable from an initial one, a simple problem for a *deterministic* CA. Differently from plain simulation, a *qualitative analysis* of the behavior of a CA can be a hard problem to solve. Problems like reachability of a subconfiguration or existence of a predecessor configuration have been shown to be exponentially hard in the worst case [4,13,14]. In recent years practical solutions to large instances of known NP-complete problems like Satisfiability (SAT) of propositional formulas have been made possible by the application of specialized search algorithms and pruning heuristics. Since 1991 the problems solvable by SAT solvers have grown from 100 to 10,000 variables. On the basis of these results, researchers from various communities have started encoding real-world problems into SAT. This has lead to breakthroughs in planning and model-checking of hardware circuits [1]. The connection between the complexity of some interesting problems for CAs and SAT (see e.g. [4]) suggests us a possible new application of all these technologies.

In this paper we will investigate the applicability of SAT solvers to the *qualitative analysis* of CAs. Specifically, following the *Bounded Model Checking* (BMC) paradigm introduced in [1], we will define a *polynomial time* encoding of a *bounded number* of evolution steps of a CA into a formula in *propositional logic*. Our encoding allows us to specify in a *declarative* and *modular way* several decision problems for CAs like forward and backward (inverse) reachability

P.M.A. Sloot, B. Chopard, and A.G. Hoekstra (Eds.): ACRI 2004, LNCS 3305, pp. 745–754, 2004.

as a satisfiability problem. As a conceptual contribution, we obtain an effective method for the analysis of CAs in which we can plug in SAT modern solvers like [5,6,11,9]. As a preliminary experiment, we have studied several reachability problems for Mazoyer's solution to the Firing Squad Synchronization Problem [7]. In this example the length of the evolution (the diameter of the model in the terminology of BMC) leading to a successful final configuration depends on the dimension of the cellular space. For this reason, this problem is adequate to check qualitative problems that can be encoded as *bounded reachability*, e.g., checking if the final solution is the correct one, computing predecessor configurations, computing alternative initial configurations leading to the same solution, etc. We will use this case-study to test the performance of zChaff [9]. zChaff can handle problems with up to 10^6 propositional variables. In our setting zChaff returns interesting results for problems of reasonable size (e.g. cellular spaces with 70 cells and evolution of 140 steps). Some built-in heuristics of zChaff however turned out to be inadequate for CA-problems like inverse reachability. We believe that specialization of SAT-solving algorithms to problems formulated on CAs could be an interesting future direction of research.

Plan of the Paper. In Section 2 we will give some preliminary notions on Cellular Automata and the SAT problem. In Sections 3 and 4 we will define an encoding of the evolution of a CA and of its qualitative problems into a SAT formula. In Section 5 we will discuss experimental results obtained by using the SAT solver zChaff. In Section 6 we will discuss related works and future directions of our research.

2   Preliminaries

Cellular Automata. A d-CA $\mathcal{A}$ is a tuple $\langle d, S, N, \delta \rangle$, where $d \in \mathbb{N}$ is the dimension of the cellular space ($\mathbb{Z}^d$); S is the finite set of states of $\mathcal{A}$; $N \subseteq \mathbb{Z}^d$ is the *neighborhood* of $\mathcal{A}$, with cardinality n; $\delta : S^{n+1} \to S$ is the transition rule of $\mathcal{A}$. The definition of δ takes into account the cell and its neighborhood. A *configuration* is defined as a function $c : \mathbb{Z}^d \to S$ that assigns a state to each cell of the cellular space. We will use $\mathcal{C}$ to denote the set of configurations. The *global evolution function* $G_{\mathcal{A}}$ associated to $\mathcal{A}$ is a transformation from configurations to configurations such that

$$G_{\mathcal{A}}(c)(\boldsymbol{i}) = \delta(\langle c(\boldsymbol{i}), c(\boldsymbol{i} + \boldsymbol{v}_1), ..., c(\boldsymbol{i} + \boldsymbol{v}_n) \rangle) \text{ for any } c \in \mathcal{C}, \ \boldsymbol{i} \in \mathbb{Z}^d.$$

Given an initial configuration c_0, the evolution of $\mathcal{A}$, written $Ev^{\mathcal{A}}(c_0)$, is a sequence $\{c_t\}_{t \geq 0}$ of configurations such that $c_{t+1} = G_{\mathcal{A}}(c_t)$ for any $t \geq 0$. A configuration c' is *reachable* in k steps from configuration c_0 if there exists an evolution $\{c_t\}_{t \geq 0}$ such that $c' = c_k$. A configuration c' is *reachable* from c_0 if it is reachable in $k \geq 0$ steps.

The Satisfiability Problem. The Satisfiability problem (SAT) is a decision problem considered in complexity theory. An instance of the problem is defined by a Boolean expression written using only the connectives $\wedge$ (*and*), $\vee$ (*or*), $\neg$ (*not*), and propositional variables. The question is: given the expression, is there some assignment of *true* and *false* values to the variables that will make the entire expression true? In mathematics, a formula of propositional logic is said to be satisfiable if truth-values can be assigned to its free variables in a way that makes the formula true. The class of satisfiable propositional formulae is NP-complete, as is that of its variant 3-Satisfiability (3SAT). This means that the best known algorithm that solves this problem has worst case exponential time complexity unless the complexity class P is equal to NP. Other variants, such as 2-Satisfiability and Horn-satisfiability, can be solved by efficient algorithms.

Qualitative Analysis of CAs. Several decision problems related to the computational interpretation of the evolution of CAs are hard or impossible to solve. The hardest problems are often related to the inverse exploration of the configuration space of a CA. This because configurations might have a *branching past*. For instance, the Predecessor Existence Problem

(PEP) Given a d-CA $\mathcal{A}$ and $x \in \mathcal{C}$, $\exists y \in \mathcal{C}$ such that $x = G_{\mathcal{A}}(y)$?

is NP-complete for d-CAs with $d > 1$ (see [12]). The proof of NP-completeness can be given via a reduction from 3SAT. In this paper we are interested however in the inverse reduction (i.e. from CA to SAT), our goal being the definition of an effective method for the analysis of CAs.

3   From Cellular Automata to Propositional Logic

In this section we will describe how to represent a finite number of evolution steps of a CA in propositional logic. The resulting formula will be used later to specify several different qualitative analyses of a CA.

Configurations. Given a CA $\mathcal{A}$, we first represent its set of states $S = \{s_1, \ldots, s_n\}$ using a binary encoding over $m = \lceil log_2 n \rceil$ bits of a given choice of ordering numbers. Let us call $S' = \{w_1, \ldots, w_n\}$ be the resulting set of binary representations, where each $w_i \in \{0, 1\}^m$ (sequence of m bits). Every state represented in binary can be naturally encoded as a propositional formula as follows. Let ℓ be a label and w a sequence of m bits $b_1 \ldots b_m$. Furthermore, let . be an operator for concatenating labels. Then, we define the formula encoding as follows:

$$Cod_w(w, \ell) \doteq \bigwedge_{i=1}^{m} Cod_b(b_i, i.\ell) \quad \text{where} \quad Cod_b(b, \ell) \doteq \begin{cases} x_\ell \; if \; b = 1 \\ \neg x_\ell \; if \; b = 0 \end{cases}$$

Let us assume that the cellular space is linearized into the range $1, \ldots, N$. Then, a configuration is simply a tuple $c = \langle\langle 1, w_1'\rangle, \ldots, \langle N, w_N'\rangle\rangle$, where $w_i' \in S'$. The encoding of c at instant t is defined then as follows:

$$Cod_c(c, t) \doteq Cod_w(w_1', 1.t) \wedge \ldots \wedge Cod_w(w_N', N.t)$$

Thus, $Cod_c(c, t)$ gives rise to a conjunction of *literals* over the set of predicate symbols $x_{b.p.t}$ where $b \in \{1, \ldots, m\}$, $p \in \{1, \ldots, N\}$.

Transition Rules. A CA local rule is usually given in form of a table: each row is a transition rule for a generic cell in function of its state and one possible global state of the neighborhood. Let us call $\mathcal{R}_p$ the set of rows of the table relative to a cell in position p. Let us assume that the neighborhood is $v_1, \ldots, v_n$. Let $R \in \mathcal{R}_p$ be a rule that, at time t, operates on the neighborhood of a cell p, namely $\langle\langle p, w\rangle, \langle p + v_1, w_1\rangle, \ldots, \langle p + v_n, w_n\rangle\rangle$, and that updates its state into w'. Then, the encoding of R is the formula

$$Cod_r(R, p, t) \doteq Cod_w(w, p.t) \wedge \bigwedge_{i=1}^{n} Cod_w(w_i, (p + v_i).t) \wedge Cod_w(w', p.(t+1))$$

We can extend this encoding to $\mathcal{R}_p$ in the natural way:

$$Cod_R(\mathcal{R}_p, t) \doteq \bigvee_{R \in \mathcal{R}_p} Cod_r(R, p, t)$$

Using this disjunctive formula we can express one evolution step without having to specify the initial configuration (we let open all possible choices of rules in $\mathcal{R}_p$).

CA-Evolution. Specifically, the formula $Ev^{\mathcal{A}}(N, k)$ that describes all possible evolutions in k steps of a CA with N cells is defined as follows

$$Ev^{\mathcal{A}}(N, k) \doteq \bigwedge_{t=0}^{k-1} \bigwedge_{i=1}^{N} Cod_R(\mathcal{R}_i, t)$$

The following properties formalize the connection between the evolution of a CA and the formula $Ev^{\mathcal{A}}(N, k)$.

Proposition 1. *Given a CA $\mathcal{A}$, every assignment ρ that satisfies the propositional formula $Ev^{\mathcal{A}}(N, k)$ represents a possible evolution $\{c_t\}_{t \geq 0}$ of $\mathcal{A}$ such that ρ satisfies $Cod(c_t, t)$ for any $t \geq 0$.*

As a consequence, we have the following link between k-reachability and satisfiability of $Ev^{\mathcal{A}}(N, k)$.

Theorem 1. *Given a CA $\mathcal{A}$ and two configurations c and c', c' is reachable in k-steps from c if and only if the formula*

$$REACH_k \doteq Cod_c(c, 0) \wedge Ev^{\mathcal{A}}(N, k) \wedge Cod_c(c', k) \tag{1}$$

is satisfiable.

As a final remark, it is easy to check that the size of the encoding is polynomial in the size of the cellular space, size of the neighborhood and in the number of steps taken into consideration.

4   SAT-Based Qualitative Reasoning

The formula $Ev^{\mathcal{A}}(N, k)$ represents an encoding of all possible CA-evolutions of length k independently from any initial or target configuration. This property allows us to encode in a modular way several interesting properties of CAs in terms of satisfiability of a propositional formula. In the rest of the section we will discuss some examples.

Reachability. By solving of the formula (1) we can decide whether c' is reachable in k-steps from c. To compute all configurations reachable in at most k-steps we first solve the satisfiability problem for the formula

$$CREACH_k \; \doteq \; Cod_c(c, 0) \wedge Ev^{\mathcal{A}}(N, k)$$

and then extract the configurations c_t for $0 \leq t \leq k$ from the resulting satisfying assignment ρ.

$(C)REACH_k$ can be refined in order to be satisfiable only if the evolution is acyclic, i.e. the assignment to predicates at time t is distinct from all assignments at time $t' < t$ for any pair of values of t and t' between 0 and k. Thus, for finite CA we can explore all the reachable configurations by *iterative deepening* on k until the acyclicity test fails.

Inverse Reachability With our encoding it's easy to encode the *inverse* reachability problems in terms of reachability. For instance, given a (sub)configuration c and a configuration c', we can decide whether c' is a predecessor in k-steps of c by solving the satisfiability problem for the formula

$$PREP_k \; \doteq \; Cod_c(c', 0) \wedge Ev^{\mathcal{A}}(N, k) \wedge Cod_c(c, k)$$

So we can find a solution for the Predecessor Existence Problem (PEP) solving the formula $PREP_1$. Finally, as for forward reachability, we can also *compute* a possible trace in the CA-evolution (and the corresponding initial state) of k steps that leads to an encoded configuration c at time k. We first solve the satisfiability problem for the formula

$$IREACH_k \; \doteq \; Ev^{\mathcal{A}}(N, k) \wedge Cod_c(c, k)$$

and then extract the configurations c_t for $0 \leq t \leq k$ from the resulting satisfying assignment ρ. In order to find the set of all predecessors of a configuration c we can use the following procedure: (1) set F to $IREACH_1$; (2) solve the satisfiability problem for the formula F (that gives us as a result *one* possible predecessor); (3) if the problem is unsatisfiable exit the procedure, otherwise (4) extract the formula G corresponding to the computed predecessor, set F to $F \wedge \neg G$ and go back to (2).

4.1   Goal-Driven SAT-Encoding

Inverse reachability is the more difficult problem among the one listed in the previous section. This is due to the non-determinism in the computation of the preimage of a given configuration. To reduce the complexity of the SAT-solving procedure we can try to reduce the size of the SAT-formula encoding the CA-evolution and specialize it to the goal we are looking for. For example we can apply a version of the *cone of influence* introduced in [1] to statically compute the set of variables that influence the evolution of a cell, if we want to study its final or initial state. To limit the number of variables in the SAT-formula, we can also exploit the fact that *boundary* cells never change state. Thus, we only need to encode boundary cells at time zero and refer to this encoding in every step of the construction of the SAT-formula. This optimization preserves the correctness of the encoding. In the following section we will discuss a practical evaluation of the proposed SAT-based methodology and related heuristics/optimizations.

5   Experimental Results

In order to test the effectiveness of the SAT-based analysis we have performed several experiments using the SAT-solver zChaff [9]. The input for zChaff is a CNF-formula written in DIMACS format. By using the structure-preserving algorithm of [10], we have built a front end to put the formula resulting from the encoding of a CA-evolution in CNF. The algorithm makes use of a polynomial number of auxiliary variables (one per each row of a CA-table). All experiments are performed on a Pentium4 2 GHz, with 1GB of RAM.

5.1   Tested Example

As main example we have considered a solution to the Firing Squad Synchronization Problem (FSSP). Mazoyer [7] has given a six-state (plus a cell for the boundary of the cellular space) minimal time solution defined via 120 interesting rows.

5.2   Tested Properties

In Table 1 we illustrate the type of reachability properties we have tested on FSSP. Specifically, we have considered reachability problems in which either the initial and final configuration are completely encoded or part of them are left unconstrained. For instance, $I^{-n} + F$ denotes a reachability problem in which n cells of the initial configuration are left unconstrained (i.e. we considered a subconfiguration of the initial configuration); F denotes a problem in which only the final state is encoded. The properties $nF + B$ and $F + B + nL$ listed in Table 1 are related to special tricks we used to exploit an heuristic called VSIDS of zChaff [9]. The heuristic VSIDS is used to choose a starting variable for the resolution algorithm between those that appear most frequently in the formula. In order to force the SAT-solver to choose the variables that encode a certain configuration, we can either put n-copies of this encoding (like properties $nF + B$) or put n-copies of the step of the formula representing the evolution that contains these variables (like property $F + B + nL$). This way when computing predecessors of

Table 1. List of reachability properties considered in the experiments.

Added to $Ev^{\mathcal{A}}$	Description
I	Initial configuration (i.e. $CREACH$).
I^{-n}	Initial subconfiguration in which n cells are unconstrained.
F	Final configuration (i.e. $IREACH$)
F^1	One cell of the final configuration.
$I + F$	Initial and final configuration (i.e. $REACH$).
$F + B$	Final configuration and boundary cells.
$I^{-n} + F$	Initial configuration without n cells and a final configuration.
$F^1 + B$	Only one cell of the final configuration and boundary cells
$nF + B$	Final configuration with n-copies of formula F.
$F + B + nL$	$F + B$ and n-copies of the last step of the evolution formula.

a configuration we force the SAT-solver to choose the variables that encode the final configuration, i.e., those with the smaller number of occurrences in $Ev^{\mathcal{A}}$ but with trivial truth assignment.

5.3   Experimental Evaluation

All the experiments require a preliminary compilation phase in which the SAT-formula is built up starting from a CA rule table. The time required for the biggest example is around 20 minutes due to the huge size of the resulting output. In the following we will focus however on the performance of the solver on SAT-formula of different size and on properties taken from Table 1.

$I + F$ and $I^{-n} + F$ **Properties [Table 2].** For this kind of problems, the size of the formulas that zChaff manages to solve scales up smoothly to formulas with one million variables. We considered then problems of the form $I^{-n} + F$. Since there might be several initial states (legal or illegal) containing the subconfiguration I^{-n} and leading to the same final state F, the resulting SAT problem becomes more difficult. As expected, on this new kind of problems the performance of zChaff decreases with the number of cells n removed from I.

I and I^{-n} **Properties [Table 3].** In a second series of experiments we have tested I-like properties that can be used to *compute* reachable states. Unexpectedly, the behavior of zChaff is quite irregular with respect to the growth of the size of the SAT formulas. The average of the execution times tends to grow exponentially with the number of cells removed from the initial configuration until the problem becomes trivial (i.e. when we do not have neither I nor F). Other examples we tested in [2] did not suffer from this anomaly.

F **Properties [Table 4].** In the third series of experiments we have considered different types of F-like properties that can be used to compute *predecessor configurations*, one configuration by step, of a given final configuration. This is a hard problem in general. As expected, we had to reduce the size of the

Table 2. Experiments on $I + F$-like problems.

Problem	#Cells	#Steps	Input(MB)	#Vars	#Clauses	ExTime
$I + F$	15	28	12.18	51708	655713	3s
$I + F$	29	56	51.76	199842	2535241	13s
$I + F$	40	78	101.8	383883	4870563	25s
$I + F$	50	98	165.57	602853	7649203	39s
$I + F$	70	138	340.21	1118393	15079683	1m 22s
$I^{-1} + F$	15	28	12.18	51708	655710	3s
$I^{-2} + F$	15	28	12.18	51708	655707	69s
$I^{-3} + F$	15	28	12.18	51708	655704	65s
$I^{-4} + F$	15	28	12.18	51708	655701	30m53s

Table 3. Experiments on I and I^{-n} problems.

Problem	#Cells	#Steps	Input(MB)	#Vars	#Clauses	ExTime
I	15	28	12.18	51708	655668	3s
I	29	56	51.76	199842	2535154	13s
I	50	98	165.57	602853	7649053	40s
I	70	138	340.21	1118393	15079473	1m 06s
I^{-1}	15	28	12.18	51708	655665	3s
I^{-2}	15	28	12.18	51708	655662	7m 21s
I^{-3}	15	28	12.18	51708	655659	4s
I^{-4}	15	28	12.18	51708	655656	10s
I^{-5}	15	28	12.18	51708	655653	3m 22s
I^{-7}	15	28	12.18	51708	655647	35m 36s

SAT-formulas in order to get reasonable execution times. For a cellular space of dimension 10 it takes about $9m$ to solve the problem F. Adding a constraint on the boundary cells, i.e. property $F + B$, we dramatically decrease the execution time ($2m$). The execution time further improves when forcing zChaff to select the variables occurring in F with the trick discussed at the beginning of this section. Specifically, when duplicating the last step of the formula Ev^A zChaff takes $35s$ to solve the same problem Similar results are obtained by simply copying F 10 times in the input formula given to zChaff. Tuning the heuristics might be difficult (without modifying the code of zChaff) as shown by further experiments (like $400F + B$) where the performance gets worse again.

F^1 **Properties [Table 5].** In order to study the effectiveness of the cone of influence reduction we have also considered $F^1 + B$ properties. The use of this reduction alone does not improve much the execution time. However, when coupled with the n-copy of the last step of Ev^A (to force the selection of variables in F) then it seems to work (see $F^1 + B + 10L$ with and without C.o.I. in Table

Table 4. Experiments on F-like problems.

Problem	#Cells	#Steps	Input(MB)	#Vars	#Clauses	ExTime
F	10	18	5	22173	281010	9m 40s
$F + B$	10	18	5	22173	281013	2m 27s
$F + B + 2L$	10	18	5	22173	296623	35s
$10F + B$	10	18	5	22173	281043	39s
$400F + B$	10	18	5	22173	292983	1m 50s

Table 5. Experiments on F^1-like problems.

C.o.I.=Reduction of the SAT-formula via the Cone of Influence

Problem	C.o.I.	#Cells	#Steps	Input(MB)	#Vars	#Clauses	ExTime
$F^1 + B$		10	18	5	22173	280987	1m 48s
$F^1 + B$	$\sqrt{}$	10	18	4	16773	241961	1m 59s
$F^1 + B + 10L$		10	18	5	22173	296605	2m 05s
$F^1 + B + 10L$	$\sqrt{}$	10	18	4	16773	257561	1m 40s
$F^1 + B + 30L$		10	18	5	22173	330962	54s
$F^1 + B + 30L$	$\sqrt{}$	10	18	4	16773	288791	59s
$100F^1 + B$		10	18	4	22173	281283	2m20s
$100F^1 + B$	$\sqrt{}$	10	18	4	16773	241961	2m

5). Copying the formula F does not seem to work well in this examples. Again tuning the parameters used in heuristic like the number of copies n in $\dots + nL$ might be difficult by simply using zChaff as a black box.

5.4 Other Examples

In another series of experiments we have randomly generated a 1-CA with 4096 table rows (16 states and nearest-neighbor) and tested on it I-properties of increasing size. The aim here was to reach the limit of zChaff w.r.t. number of variables and clauses generated by the encoding on an easy problem. zChaff gets in trouble when the formula has more than one million variables and about 20 millions of clauses (15 cells, 20 steps), while it can handle problems with 17 millions clauses (15 cells, 17 steps) and 1 million of variables. This kind of analysis can be useful to evaluate the size of CAs we can handle with non-specialized SAT solvers.

6 Conclusions and Related Work

Although several CAs programming and simulation tools have been developed (see e.g. the survey of [15]), we are not aware of general frameworks for performing qualitative analysis of CAs automatically. In this paper we have proposed a SAT-based methodology for attacking this problem. One of the advantages of the proposed method is that, once the encoding of the CA-evolution has been computed, several different reachability problems can be formulated as simple propositional queries to a SAT-solver. The formula encoding the evolution can then be reused in a modular way. Hard problems like inverse reachability can be attacked then by using modern SAT-solvers like zChaff that seems to perform well on problems with millions of variables and clauses. Although this seems a new approach for checking properties of CAs, SAT technology is widely used for computer aided verification of hardware and software design [1]. In our preliminary experiments we have obtained interesting results for CAs of reasonable size (e.g. 70 cells, 140 steps, 120 rule rows). We believe that it might be possible to manage larger problems by a specialization of the SAT-solving algorithm (and, especially, of its heuristics) that could benefit from structural properties of CAs. This might be an interesting future direction for our research.

References

1. A. Biere, E.M. Clarke, R. Raimi, Y. Zhu. *Verifiying Safety Properties of a Power PC Microprocessor Using Symbolic Model Checking without BDDs*, CAV '99, Lecture Notes in Computer Science, 60-71, 1999.
2. M. D'Antonio. *Analisi SAT-based di Automi Cellulari*, Tesi di laurea, Dip. di Informatica e Scienze dell'Informazione, Università di Genova, Marzo 2004.
3. M. Davis, H. Putnam. *A computing procedure for quantification theory*, Journal of the Association for Computing Machinery, 7:201-215, 1960.
4. F. Green. *NP-Complete Problems in Cellular Automata*, Complex Systems, 1:453-474, 1987.
5. J. Groote, J. Warners *The propositional formula checker HeerHugo*, Journal of Automated Reasoning, 24(1-2):101-125, 2000.
6. The ICS home page: http://www.icansolve.com
7. J. Mazoyer. *A six-state minimal time solution to the firing squad synchronization problem*, Theoretical Computer Science, 50(2):183-240, Elsevier, 1987.
8. E.F. Moore. *Sequential machines* in: E.F. Moore *Selected Papers*, Addison-Wesley, Reading, 1964.
9. M.W. Moskewicz, C.F. Madigan, Y. Zhao, L. Zhang, S. Malik. *Chaff: Engineering an Efficient SAT Solver*, Proceedings of the 38th Design Automation Conference (DAC'01), 2001.
10. D. A. Plaisted and S. Greenbaum. *A Structure Preserving Clause Form Translation* Journal of Symbolic Computation, 2(3):293-304, 1986.
11. The SIMO web page: http://www.mrg.dist.unige.it/ sim/simo/
12. K. Sutner. *On the computational complexity of finite cellular automata*, JCSS, 50(1):87-97, 1995.
13. S. Wolfram. *Universality and complexity in cellular automata*, Physica D, 10:1-35, 1984.
14. S. Wolfram. *Computation Theory of Cellular Automata*, Communications in Mathematical Physics, 96:15-57, November 1984.
15. T. Worsch. *Programming Environments for Cellular Automata*, Technical report 37/96, Universitat Karlsruhe, Fakultat fur Informatik, 1996.

The Kernel Hopfield Memory Network

Cristina García and José Alí Moreno

Laboratorio de Computación Emergente,
Facultades de Ciencias e Ingeniería,
Universidad Central de Venezuela.
{cgarcia, jose}@neurona.ciens.ucv.ve
http://neurona.ciens.ucv.ve/laboratorio

Abstract. The kernel theory drawn from the work on learning machines is applied to the Hopfield neural network. This provides a new insight into the workings of the neural network as associative memory. The kernel "trick" defines an embedding of memory patterns into (higher or infinite dimensional) memory feature vectors and the training of the network is carried out in this feature space. The generalization of the network by using the kernel theory improves its performance in three aspects. First, an adequate kernel selection enables the satisfaction of the condition that any set of memory patterns be attractors of the network dynamics. Second, the basins of attraction of the memory patterns are enhanced improving the recall capacity. Third, since the memory patterns are mapped into a higher dimensional feature space the memory capacity density is effectively increased. These aspects are experimentally demonstrated on sets of random memory patterns.

1 Introduction

The Hopfield neural net (HNN) [1] is one of the most profusely studied neural network models [2,3]. Research interest has mainly been focused on properties of the network when implementing autoassociative content addressable memories. Issues like the capacity of the network, its learning rules and learning dynamics as well as the dynamics of pattern retrieval have been exhaustively studied [4, 5,6,7,8,9,10]. This solid theoretic background together with its characteristics of emergent computation machine makes this model a very attractive object of study. The purpose of this paper is to present a new insight on the workings of this neural model with the application of the theory of Mercer kernels [11].

The Hopfield neural model consists on a network of N two state ($S_i = \pm 1$) neurons or processing units fully connected to each other through synaptic weights w_{ij}. It conforms a dynamical system that evolves in discrete time according to a relaxation dynamics. When used as an autoassociative memory it is able to retrieve a previously learnt memory pattern from an example which is similar to, or a noisy version of one of the memories. A pattern is represented in the network by associating each of its components to one of the processing units of the HNN. Memory recall proceeds by initially clamping the neurons to a starting pattern $\boldsymbol{S}(t = 0)$. Then allowing the state of the network to evolve

P.M.A. Sloot, B. Chopard, and A.G. Hoekstra (Eds.): ACRI 2004, LNCS 3305, pp. 755–764, 2004.
© Springer-Verlag Berlin Heidelberg 2004

in time according to the dynamical rule towards the nearest attractor state, a fix point of the dynamics. In consequence for the network to perform properly as an autoassociative memory, the activity pattern of the attractor state must correspond to a memory pattern. When this is the case it is said that $S(t = 0)$ lies in the basin of attraction of the corresponding memory pattern. Hence the purpose of a learning algorithm for the HNN is to find a synaptic weight matrix w_{ij} such that given p memory patterns, they become fixed points of the dynamics and that patterns resulting from small deviations of the memories be in their basin of attraction.

Large basins of attraction imply that the output activity of the processing units must be robust against deviations of the inputs from the memory patterns used in training. This is accounted for in the network by training the processing units so as to maximize a stability operative criterion. The Adatron learning rule, a perceptron like algorithm proposed in the statistical mechanics literature [7], implements this maximum stability criterion. Hence learning in a HNN reduces to the training of the N processing units with the Adatron algorithm so that each one of them attain the maximum stability condition. It is noteworthy that the procedure is fully local, each processing unit is trained individually and the applied learning rule only depends on local information to the processing unit. Recently [12] the Adatron algorithm has been generalized with the incorporation of the kernel trick. In this way the implementation simplicity of the Adatron is enhanced with the capability of working in a high dimensional nonlinear feature space. The result is that each processing unit becomes a kernel machine with maximum stability in a feature space. This is equivalent to a nonlinear stability condition in input memory space.

The basic idea behind kernel machines is that under certain conditions the kernel function can be interpreted as an inner product in a high dimensional Hilbert space (feature space). This idea commonly known as the "kernel trick" has been used extensively in generating non-linear versions of conventional linear supervised and unsupervised learning algorithms [11]. In the present case, the application of this procedure to the HNN defines an embedding of memory patterns into (higher or infinite dimensional) memory feature vectors allowing the training of the network to be carried out in the feature space. We refer to this enhanced neural model as kernel-HNN. The result is that the performance of the network is improved in three aspects. First, the condition that any set of memory patterns be attractors of the network dynamics can be readily met by the selection of an adequate kernel. Second, since the training procedure produces optimal stability conditions on the processing units, the basins of attraction of the memory patterns are increased improving the capacity of recall of the network. Third, the fact that the memory patterns are mapped into a higher dimensional feature space effectively enlarges the memory capacity density.

Experimental simulation runs on a kernel-HNN trained with a set of uncorrelated random memory patterns for different memory loads and several kernel functions are carried out. The experimental results show a significant performance gain in the pattern retrieval dynamics with respect to the linear HNN model. Qualitative measures of the increase of the basins of attraction are reported. The organization of the paper is as follows: in section 2 an introduction to the the formalism of the HNN model is presented; in section 3, the Kernel extension of the Adatron learning algorithm is described and in section 4 the kernel-HNN model introduced; in section 5 the experiments and results are discussed and, in section 6, the conclusions are presented.

2   The Hopfield Associative Memory Network

The HNN consists on a network of N two state ($S_i = \pm 1$) processing units fully connected to each other through a matrix of synaptic weights w_{ij}, with no self coupling ($w_{ii} = 0$). The exclusion of the self coupling terms enlarge the basins of attraction [9]. The dynamics of such a system is taken to be a simple zero-temperature Monte Carlo process

$$S_i(t+1) = sign(\sum_j w_{ij}S_j(t)) = sign\left(\langle \boldsymbol{w}_i \cdot \boldsymbol{S}(t)\rangle\right) \tag{1}$$

where $\boldsymbol{S}(t)$ is the vector of activities of network at time t, $\boldsymbol{w}_i$ the weight vector of the ith processing unit and the brackets denotes dot product. The update of the network can be performed either asynchronously or in parallel.

It is interesting to note that the HNN model shows several conceptual similarities with Cellular Automata (CA) models. The HNN model implements a sort of learning binary CA with a fully extended neighborhood. The synaptic weight matrix, "learned", in the present case, from the memory patterns define the transition rule in (1). The resulting dynamics of the model show much of the emergent behavior evident in CA models.

The configuration of synaptic weights is adjusted by a learning algorithm such that, the given p memory patterns

$$\boldsymbol{Y}^\nu = (y_1^\nu, \ldots, y_N^\nu)^T, \quad y_i^\nu = \pm 1, \quad \nu = 1, \ldots, p \tag{2}$$

become locally stable fix points of the dynamics. That is, the set of inequalities

$$y_i^\nu h_i^\nu = y_i^\nu \sum_j w_{ij}\, y_j^\nu \geq c > 0 \tag{3}$$

must be satisfied for every memory pattern ν and processing unit i. Since the diagonal elements of the weight matrix are null, the above set of inequalities decouple and each processing unit can be treated independently. We can then consider the case for one processing unit only, say $i = 1$, and omit the index i in the following. The condition for the stability of the memories is then written

$$y^\nu h^\nu = y^\nu \sum_j w_j\, y_j^\nu = \gamma^\nu \geq c > 0 \tag{4}$$

where w_j denotes the jth component of the weight vector of a linear processing unit with component $w_i = 0$ (i is the index of the processing unit). In consequence the training phase of the HNN can be carried out by perceptronlike learning algorithms applied independently on each processing unit. The associative memory network will be properly trained when each of the processing units satisfy the stability condition. In another case the recall dynamics will be unstable and converge to a pattern of activities different from a memory.

Fulfillment of inequality (4) is a necessary condition for the HNN to operate as an associative memory but in addition large basins of attraction are desirable for each memory pattern. Thus the fix points should be stable against many component inversions of the activity patterns of the network in its time evolution. In [6,7] it has been argued that it is desirable that the stabilities γ^ν in (4) should be large relative to the magnitudes of the synaptic weights. A normalized measure of stability for the processing units, the stability coefficient, is then defined as:

$$\hat{\gamma} = \min_\nu(\hat{\gamma}^\nu) \quad \hat{\gamma}^\nu = \frac{\gamma^\nu}{||\boldsymbol{w}||} = \frac{y^\nu \sum_j w_j \, y_j^\nu}{||\boldsymbol{w}||} \tag{5}$$

The Adatron algorithm is a learning algorithm which attains optimal normalized stability, i.e. a configuration of weights with maximum stability coefficient for a set of arbitrary memory patterns.

3   The Kernel Trick in the Adatron Algorithm

The basic idea behind the Adatron algorithm of Anlauf and Biehl [7] is to induce a configuration of synaptic weights that maximize the normalized stability of the processing unit (5). They assume a scale for the weight vectors where the positive constant c in relation (4) is unity. In this way the algorithm is derived from the problem of minimizing the norm of the weight vector subject to the restrictions that the stability conditions of the memory patterns be greater or equal to unity:

$$minimize \; \frac{1}{2}||\boldsymbol{w}||^2 \quad s.t. \; \gamma^\nu = y^\nu \sum_j w_j \, y_j^\nu \geq 1 \quad \forall \nu = 1, \ldots, p \tag{6}$$

In the dual formulation of this optimization problem they show that the solution has the form:

$$\boldsymbol{w}_j = \frac{1}{N} \sum_{\nu=1}^p \alpha_\nu \, y_j^\nu \boldsymbol{Y}^\nu \tag{7}$$

where the α_ν are positive Lagrange multipliers which can be interpreted as a measure of the information contribution that each memory pattern does to the synaptic weights. These dual variables are learned, from a *tabula rasa* initialization, by an iterative procedure where the memory patterns are presented repeatedly and the following corrections are applied for each memory:

$$\delta\alpha_\nu = \max\{-\alpha_\nu, \lambda(1 - \gamma^\nu)\} \tag{8}$$

where λ is a suitable learning rate. The learning is done when the minimum stability condition (4) equals unity.

The algorithm is presented with theoretical guaranties of convergence to the optimal solution and of a rate of convergence exponentially fast in the number of iterations, provided that a solution exists. An enhanced version of the algorithm with the application of the kernel trick has been presented [12]. In this way the learning proceeds in a high-dimensional memory feature space providing a non-linear version of the conventional linear perceptronlike learning algorithm.

A symmetric function $K(\boldsymbol{x}, \boldsymbol{y})$ is a kernel if it fulfills Mercer's condition, i.e. the function K is (semi) positive definite. When this is the case there exists a mapping ϕ such that it is possible to write $K(\boldsymbol{x}, \boldsymbol{y}) = \langle \phi(\boldsymbol{x}) \cdot \phi(\boldsymbol{y}) \rangle$. The kernel represents a dot product on a feature space F into which the original vectors are mapped. In this way a kernel function defines an embedding of memory patterns into (high or infinite dimensional) feature vectors and allows the algorithm to be carried out in this space without the need of representing it explicitly.

Summarizing, in [12] is shown that the learning rule given in expression (8) remains invariant when considering learning in feature space and the activity on each processing unit of the network is given by

$$S_i(t+1) = sign\left(\sum_{\nu=1}^{p} \alpha_\nu \, y_i^\nu K(\boldsymbol{Y}^\nu, \boldsymbol{S}(t))\right) \tag{9}$$

Where $K(\boldsymbol{Y}^\nu, \boldsymbol{S})$ is the kernel function and the α_ν are the Lagrange multipliers.

By introducing Kernels into the algorithm the measure of stability of the processing units is maximized in memory feature space. That is, the inequalities in (4) become nonlinear in input memory space. This allows that, with a suitable kernel choice, sets of memory patterns for which the conditions (4) could not be fulfilled in input memory space do satisfy them in memory feature space.

In the literature [11] the most common used kernels are the linear, polynomial, and Gaussian kernels shown in relation (10). The linear kernel is the simple dot product in input space whereas the other kernel functions represent dot products in arbitrary feature space.

$$\begin{aligned}
K_L(\boldsymbol{Y}, \boldsymbol{S}) &= \langle \boldsymbol{Y} \cdot \boldsymbol{S} \rangle \\
K_P(\boldsymbol{Y}, \boldsymbol{S}) &= (\langle \boldsymbol{Y} \cdot \boldsymbol{S} \rangle + b)^n \\
K_G(\boldsymbol{Y}, \boldsymbol{S}) &= \exp(-||\boldsymbol{Y} - \boldsymbol{S}||^2/\sigma^2)
\end{aligned} \tag{10}$$

In this work, experiments with the above three types of kernel functions are carried out.

4 Kernel Hopfield Network

It is clear that expression (9) is a generalization of the dynamic equation in (1) defining the dual representation of the dynamic of the HNN in feature space. A similar generalized expression for the synaptic weights equivalent to relation (7), as a linear combination of the transforms of the memory patterns in feature space is not provided by the formalism. The reason for this is simply that the explicit mapping of the input memories into feature space is not known. Nevertheless rewriting the definitions (10) of the kernel functions in terms of the products of components of the involved vectors in input space an expression equivalent to (7) for the weight vectors can be given as a generalized product of functions of the memory components. It is shown in [11] that for the polynomial kernel this is readily done. As an example let us consider a simple polynomial kernel with $n = 2$. Equation (9) can be written

$$S_i(t+1) = sign\left(\sum_{\nu=1}^{p} \alpha_\nu \, y_i^\nu \left(\langle \boldsymbol{Y}^\nu \cdot \boldsymbol{S}(t)\rangle + b\right)^2\right)$$

$$= sign\left(\sum_{\nu=1}^{p} \alpha_\nu \, y_i^\nu \left(\sum_{k=1}^{N}\sum_{j=1}^{N} y_k^\nu y_j^\nu S_k S_j + 2b\sum_{k=1}^{N} y_k^\nu S_k + b^2\right)\right) \quad (11)$$

$$= sign\left(\sum_{\nu=1}^{p} \alpha_\nu \, y_i^\nu \left(\sum_{k=1}^{N}\sum_{j=1}^{N} y_k^\nu y_j^\nu S_k S_j + \sum_{k=1}^{N} \sqrt{2b} \, y_k^\nu \sqrt{2b} \, S_k + b^2\right)\right)$$

It can be appreciated that the argument of the function $sign$ in the last line of expression (11) is a generalized inner product of feature vectors with components up to second order in S_k and y_k^ν. From this generalized product a term depending on the memory patterns and of similar form as expression (7) can be extracted. The writing of an equivalent expression for the Gaussian kernel is a more involved procedure that takes us out of the scope of this paper, but in general one such expression can be written.

   In conclusion the kernel trick allows a straightforward generalization of the Hopfield network to a to higher dimensional feature space. The main advantage of this procedure is that in principle all processing units can be trained to optimal stability. Such a network of fully optimal processing units show several important improvements that can be experimentally verified: larger memory capacity, increased capacity of memory recall and bigger basins of attraction.

5   Experiments and Results

In order to investigate the kernel-HNN in a systematic fashion a statistical analysis of several simulations were carried out. A $N = 100$ processing unit network was trained with the kernel-Adatron algorithm on several memory loads. Three kinds of kernel functions were investigated: linear, polynomial with $b = 0.1$ and $n = 2$; and Gaussian kernel. The parameter value of the Gaussian was established experimentally. For every trained network, experiments on the recovery of each memory pattern contaminated with a given percentage of random noise were repeated 50 times. The dynamic of the network is synchronous in the one step memory recall experiment. In the other experiments an asynchronous dynamics was applied.

5.1   Experiments on the Capacity of Memory Recall

In these experiments the fraction of correctly recovered memory patterns were measured as a function of the magnitude of the initial distortion of the memories (random noise contamination) for various values of the loading parameter ($\alpha = p/N$). The experiments were carried out for the three kernel types and the results are depicted in the following figures.

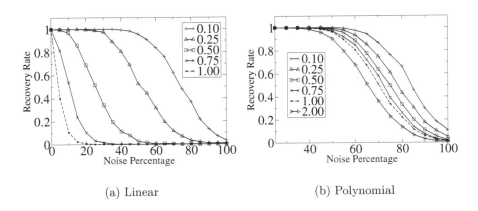

(a) Linear   (b) Polynomial

Fig. 1. Fraction of correctly recovered patterns as a function of the noise contamination of the input stimuli for different kernel networks: (a) Linear (b) Polynomial, with different values of the memory loading parameter: 0.10, 0.25, 0.5, 0.75, 1.0 and 2.0 (polynomial only)

In figure 1 the results for the linear and polynomial kernels are shown. It can be seen that while for both kernels the basins of attraction shrink with increasing values of the loading parameter, this effect is more pronounced for the linear kernel. Already for loading parameter 0.75 the linear network barely supports a slight contamination of the input stimulus. This is the typical behavior of standard linear Hopfield Networks [9]. In contrast the polynomial network is highly resistant to contamination. In this case a moderate decrease of the basins of attraction with increasing values of memory loading is perceived but they remain robust for loading parameter values as high as 2. The network is tolerant to input contaminations as big as 40% for the highest memory load of 2.0. This is indicative of the presence of large basins of attraction.

Figure 2 show the results for a network with Gaussian kernel. In this case two different experiments were carried out. The first one, for the sake of establishing an adequate value of the kernel parameter. The fraction of correctly recovered memory patterns, in one dynamical step, are measured as a function of the parameter of the Gaussian for various values of the memory loading parameter $\alpha = p/N$ (0.25, 0.5, 0.75). The experiments measure a sort of direct basin of at-

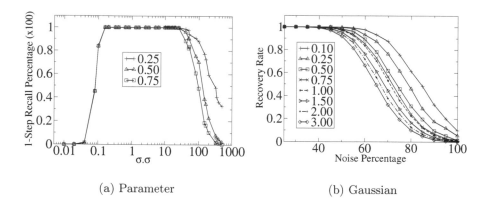

(a) Parameter   (b) Gaussian

Fig. 2. (a) Fraction of correctly recognized patterns in one dynamical step as a function of the parameter of the Gaussian kernel, for three values of the memory loading parameter: 0.25, 0.5 and 0.75. (b) Fraction of correctly recovered patterns in a Gaussian network as a function of the noise contamination of the input stimuli, for eight values of the memory loading parameter: 0.10, 0.25, 0.5, 0.75, 1.0, 1.5, 2.0 and 3.0

traction of the memories. The kernel parameter is swept over several orders of magnitude and the recall experiment is repeated 100 times for each memory. It can be appreciated that the direct basins of attraction suffer a slight degradation with memory loading but remain essentially invariant over a broad range (three orders of magnitude) of parameter values. Since greater parameter values produce sparser dual representations, the results suggest that a reasonable good choice for the value of this parameter is $\sigma^2 = 25$. This value is used in the remaining experiments.

In the experiments of memory recall it can again be appreciated that the basins of attraction of the Gaussian network decrease in a moderate way with increasing values of memory loading but remain robust for loading parameter values as high as 3. The Gaussian network results are also evidence for the presence of large basins of attraction.

5.2   Normalized Stability Coefficients

In figure 3 histograms of the distribution of the normalized stability coefficients for the three studied kernel networks and two values of memory loading parameter (0.25 and 1.0) are depicted. In each case the stability coefficients are normalized by their respective average values so that the curves are centered at unity. It can be appreciated that the histograms for the linear network are considerably broader than those of the other networks much narrower. As the value of the loading parameter is increased the shape of the histogram of the linear network is very much altered and the broadening seems to grow. In contrast the shape of the histograms of the polynomial and Gaussian networks remain essentially unaltered. These facts reflect, the detrimental effect of the increase in the values of the loading parameter on the distribution of stability coefficients of the linear network and the contrasting robustness of the distribution for the other kernel networks.

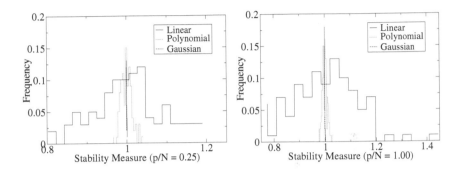

Fig. 3. Histogram of the distribution of normalized stability coefficients for the three kernel networks: Linear, Polynomial and Gaussian for two values of the memory loading parameter: 0.25 and 1.0

Summarizing, this series of experiments and observations clearly show that the kernel HNN model is superior to the standard linear model in several aspects: increased memory capacity, larger basins of attraction and hence a great robustness to noise contamination of the stimuli patterns.

6   Conclusions

We have presented a generalization of the Hopfield auto-associative memory network taking advantage of the kernel trick already well known in the Machine Learning literature. It is experimentally shown the kernel-Hopfield networks are clearly superior in performance to the standard linear model. Important observables of these models like memory capacity, recall capacity, noise tolerance and size of the basins of attraction are clearly improved by the introduction of the kernel formalism. That is, of an implicit mapping of the network to a higher dimensional feature space. In this generalization procedure the learning algorithm of the network remains in its simple form as it is applied to linear networks. This means that the training complexity is by no means affected by the generalization. This results stimulate the conduction of further theoretical and experimental work on the model.

References

1. Hopfield, J.: Neural networks and physical systems with emergent collective computational abilities. Proc. Natl. Acad. Sci. USA **79** (1982) 2554
2. Muller, B., Reinhardt, J.: Neural Networks. An Introduction. Springer-Verlag, Berlin (1990)
3. Hertz, J., Krogh, A., Palmer, R.: Introduction to the Theory of Neural Computation. Addison-Wesley, Redwood City, CA (1991)
4. Personnaz, L., Guyon, I., Dreyfus, J.: Collective computational properties of neural networks: new learning mechanisms. J. Physique Lett. **16** (1985) 1359
5. Diederich, S., Opper, M.: Learning of correlated patterns in spin-glass networks by local learning rules. Phys. Rev. Lett. **58** (1987) 949
6. Krauth, W., Mezard, M.: Learning algorithms with optimal stability in neural networks. J. Phys. A **20** (1987) 1745
7. Anlauf, J., Biehl, M.: The adatron - an adaptive perceptron algorithm. Europhysics Letters **10** (1989) 687–692
8. Opper, M.: Learning times of neural networks: exact solution for a perceptron algorithm. Phys. Rev. A **38** (1988) 3824
9. Gardner, E.: The space of interactions in neural network models. J. Phys. A **21** (1988) 257
10. Gardner, E., Derrida, B.: Optimal storage properties of neural network models. J. Phys. A **21** (1988) 271
11. Cristianini, N., Shawe-Taylor, J.: An Introduction to Support Vector Machines. Cambridge University Press (2000)
12. Friest, T., Campbell, C., Cristianini, N.: The kernel-adatron: A fast and simple learning procedure for support vector machines. In: Proceedings of the Fifteenth International Conference on Machine Learning. Morgan-Kaufmann, San Francisco, CA (1998)

Timescale Separated Pollination-Colonisation Models

J.A. Stewart-Cox[1], N.F. Britton[1], and M. Mogie[2]

[1] Department Mathematical Sciences, University of Bath, BA2 7AY.
[2] Department of Biology and Biochemistry, University of Bath, BA2 7AY.

Abstract. In flowering plant species con-specifics of distinct type may cross-pollinate. The type of offspring that result depends on both the pollen donor and the parent that produces the seed. Within a cellular automaton framework, this process fundamentally requires consideration of triplets of cells: a pollen donor, a seed producer, and a empty cell to be colonised. Such a triplet process cannot be captured by the standard second order analytical tool of pair approximation. We propose a general cellular automaton model for an arbitrary number of inter-pollinating con-specifics. Time scale separation between the dynamics of distinct pollination and colonisation processes permits aggregation of variables in mean field and pair approximation characterisations. The aggregated pair approximation successfully captures the triplet processes at work in the cellular automaton model.

1 Introduction

Continuous time probabilistic cellular automata are a useful tool for modelling the spread and interaction of terrestrial plant species. Because plants are typically sessile, it is reasonable to build cellular automata models on the level of the individual, see Iwasa (2000) for examples. Useful tools for analysing cellular automaton behaviour are mean field and pair approximation characterisations, which are systems of ordinary differential equations constructed to track densities of cells. The mean field ignores the role of space in the cellular automaton, and often fails to correspond well with simulations. The pair approximation is a second order approximation which concentrates on local interactions between cells and can provide an analytically tractable characterisation which predicts important aspects of a cellular automaton's behaviour (Iwasa 2000, Satō & Iwasa (2000). Familiarity with obtaining mean field and pair approximations will prove invaluable to understanding our modelling procedure.

In biological systems of two or more con-specifics, one or more of the types may produce fertile offspring when pollinated by another type. An example is gynodioecy: a system of female and hermaphrodite con-specifics. Both types can only produce offspring when pollinated by the hermaphrodite type. In such examples the colonisation of an empty cell requires consideration not only of neighbouring occupied cells but of whether or not those cells have received pollen and who the pollen came from. Thus colonisation is fundamentally a process involving

P.M.A. Sloot, B. Chopard, and A.G. Hoekstra (Eds.): ACRI 2004, LNCS 3305, pp. 765–774, 2004.
© Springer-Verlag Berlin Heidelberg 2004

triplets of cells, which cannot be incorporated in a standard pair approximation. Although mean field characterisation may be possible: Carrillo et al. (2002) treat a system of sexuals and asexuals. The problem here is a general problem of obtaining second order approximations for cellular automaton on which processes involve triplets. We present a resolution of this problem for a class of ecological models which feature inter-pollinating con-specifics, and subsequently discuss how this solution could be interpreted for applications in other fields

In this article we consider a one-individual-per-cell cellular automaton model for N con-specifics. We establish separate pollination and colonisation processes for the model. We assume that colonisation and death are slow seasonal processes and by contrast pollen distribution and expiry is a fast within season process. These assumptions about the time-scales of the two processes permit aggregation of variables which allow us to analyse a simpler aggregated mean field and pair approximations which correspond well to the complete characterisations. The generalised procedure is followed by an example for a single species.

2   Modelling

We construct a cellular automata model with a neighbourhood size of z. For each con-specific we require a family of unpollinated and pollinated cell states. Our cell states are: O - Empty; X_i^j - Occupied with con-specific i pollen-status j, for all $i \in \{1, \ldots, N\}$, $j \in \{0, \ldots, N\}$. Pollen-status indicates which con-specific's pollen is currently present in the cell. Pollen-status 0 indicates the con-specific is unpollinated. We denote the set of all $N(N+1)+1$ cell states $\mathcal{X} = \{O, X_1^0, \ldots, X_N^N\}$. Our pollination process consists in supposing that $X_j^\bullet$ cells (where $\bullet$ denotes pollen-status is not important) can set the pollen-status of neighbouring unpollinated cells to j, so for example X_i^0 cells become X_i^j cells. This occurs at rates p_{ij}/ϵ for all $i, j \in \{1, \ldots, N\}$, where ϵ is our small, positive time separation parameter. In counterpoint to the pollination process we assume that pollen expires rapidly and that X_j^i cells revert to state X_j^0 at rate e_i/ϵ. Pollinated X_j^k cells ($k > 0$) colonise neighbouring empty cells, so O cells are switched to state X_i^0. This colonisation process occurs at rates b_{ijk} for $i, j, k \in \{1, \ldots, N\}$. $X_i^\bullet$ cells switch to state O at death rate d_i. To pursue our time separation assumptions we follow the aggregation of variables technique suggested by Auger & Bravo de la Parra (2000), providing first the complete characterisations and then obtaining equilibria for the fast dynamics before presenting the aggregated characterisations.

2.1   Complete Mean Field and Pair Approximation

The mean field characterisation is composed by constructing cell density equations and then approximating neighbour probabilities to close moments. In order to construct the cell density equations we must define the densities of each cell type: ρ_O and $\rho_{X_i^j}$ for $i \in \{1, \ldots, N\}$, $j \in \{0, \ldots, N\}$. We define: $\rho_O + \sum_{i=1}^N \sum_{j=0}^N \rho_{X_i^j} = 1$. For convenience we also make use of the standard

Table 1. Cell density equations for complete mean field and pair approximation characterisations

$$\epsilon \frac{d\rho_{X_i^0}}{dt} = \underbrace{-\rho_{X_i^0}\sum_{j=1,k=0}^{N} p_{ij}\, q_{X_j^k/X_i^0}}_{\text{pollination}} + \underbrace{\sum_{j=1}^{N} e_j \rho_{X_i^j}}_{\text{pollen expiry}} + \epsilon\Big[\underbrace{-d_i\rho_{X_i^0}}_{\text{death}} + \underbrace{\sum_{j,k=0}^{N} b_{ijk}\rho_O\, q_{X_j^k/O}}_{\text{colonisation}}\Big]$$

$$\epsilon \frac{d\rho_{X_i^j}}{dt} = +\rho_{X_i^0}\sum_{k=0}^{N} p_{ij}\, q_{X_j^k/X_i^0} - e_j\rho_{X_i^j} + \epsilon\Big[-d_i\rho_{X_i^j}\Big]$$

notation $q_{\sigma/\sigma'}$ to denote the probability that a randomly chosen neighbour of a cell in state σ' is in state σ. The terms of the the cell density equations are determined by considering the processes on the cellular automata described above. So for example the pollination process causes a loss to $\rho_{X_i^0}$ determined by: the probability that X_i^0 cells have occupied neighbouring cells; the pollination rates from those occupied cells. We must sum over all possible neighbours so the loss is given by: $\rho_{X_i^0}\sum_{j=1}^{N}(p_{ij}/\epsilon)\sum_{k=0}^{N} q_{X_j^k/X_i^0}$. By similar considerations we obtain all other terms of the cell density equations for unpollinated and pollinated states in Table 1. The rate of change of empty cells can be retrieved since the cell densities have unit sum. To obtain the mean field characterisation we apply the approximation:

$$q_{\sigma'/\sigma} \approx \rho_\sigma. \tag{1}$$

The pair approximation is composed by constructing cell-pair density equations, considering these together with the cell density equations in Table 1, and closing moments by approximating cell-pair neighbour probabilities. We define cell-pair densities: $\rho_{\sigma\sigma'}$ where $\sigma, \sigma' \in \mathcal{X}$. The following relationships hold: $\rho_{\sigma\sigma'} = \rho_{\sigma'\sigma}$ and $\rho_{\sigma O} + \sum_{k,n=1}^{N} \rho_{\sigma X_k^n} = \rho_\sigma$. To establish the linearly independent cell-pair density equations there are five sorts of pairs which we need to consider: OX_i^0; OX_i^j; $X_i^0 X_k^0$; $X_i^0 X_k^m$; and $X_i^j X_k^m$, where $j > i$, $m > k$ and $i,j,k,m \in \{1,\ldots,N\}$. We pursue the same considerations as with the cell density equations. However, we must now respect whether a process is: proximal - between the cells in the pair; distal - between one cell in the pair and a non pair cell in the neighbourhood. We require the notation $q_{\sigma/\sigma'\sigma''}$ denoting the probability that the σ' cell in a $\sigma'\sigma''$ pair has a randomly chosen neighbour in state σ. The pair approximation treats all configurations of triplets as equivalent, Satō & Iwasa (2000) give details. As an example consider the rate at which an $X_j^\bullet$ cells pollinate the X_i^0 cells of $X_i^0 X_j^\bullet$ cell-pairs, this process occurs at the following rates:

$$\text{proximally}: \frac{1}{z}\frac{p_{ij}}{\epsilon}\rho_{X_i^0 X_j^\bullet}; \quad \text{distally}: \left(\frac{z-1}{z}\right)\frac{p_{ij}}{\epsilon}\rho_{X_i^0 X_j^\bullet}\sum_{k=0}^{N} q_{X_j^k/X_i^0 X_j^\bullet}.$$

Recall z is the neighbourhood size in the cellular automata. The proximal and distal expressions are combined in the terms of the cell-pair density equations which are given for the five sorts of cell-pairs in Table 2. In total we obtain $\frac{1}{2}N(N+1)(N(N+1)+1)$ linearly independent cell-pair density equations. Taking the equations of Tables 1 and 2 together we obtain the pair approximation by taking:

$$q_{\sigma/\sigma'} = \frac{\rho_{\sigma\sigma'}}{\rho_\sigma}, \text{ and } q_{\sigma/\sigma'\sigma''} \approx q_{\sigma/\sigma'}, \tag{2}$$

Notice that because we close moments at a higher order $q_{\sigma/\sigma'}$ has a different approximation depending on which characterisation we are considering.

2.2   Fast Equilibria

We define a fast timescale $\tau = t/\epsilon$, and we define the aggregated variables:

$$\rho_{X_i} = \sum_{j=0}^{N} \rho_{X_i^j}, \text{ and } \rho_{\sigma X_i} = \sum_{j=0}^{N} \rho_{\sigma X_i^j} \text{ for } \sigma \in \mathcal{X} \cup \{X_1, \ldots, X_N\}. \tag{3}$$

The aggregated variables are the densities and pair densities of con-specific types. Notice that because of cancellation of terms: $d\rho_{X_i}/d\tau = \sum_{j=0}^{N} d\rho_{X_i^j}/d\tau = O(\epsilon)$ and $d\rho_{\sigma X_i}/d\tau = \sum_{j=0}^{N} d\rho_{\sigma X_i^j}/d\tau = O(\epsilon)$, and so on the fast timescale we do not expect changes in the aggregated variables. We obtain the fast equilibria by substituting in the fast time-scale, neglecting terms of order ϵ, and finding the equilibria of the consequent fast system. The coupling between the equations of the complete characterisations is severed, resulting in N independent fast systems which we can examine for equilibria separately. For con-specific X_i the fast dynamics of the density equations are given as follows for $j \in \{1, \ldots, N\}$:

$$\frac{d\rho_{X_i^j}}{d\tau} = +\rho_{X_i^0} \sum_{k=0}^{N} p_{ij} \, q_{X_j^k/X_i^0} - e_j \rho_{X_i^j}. \tag{4}$$

Note that we can retrieve the case $j = 0$ utilising 3. We form the fast mean field with 1. For con-specific X_i the fast dynamics of the pair-density equations are given as follows for $j, k \in \{1, \ldots, N\}$:

$$\frac{d\rho_{X_i^j X_k}}{d\tau} = \rho_{X_i^0 X_k} p_{ij} \left(\frac{\delta_{jk}}{z} + \left(\frac{z-1}{z} \right) q_{X_j/X_i^0 X_k} \right) - e_j \rho_{X_i^j X_k}. \tag{5}$$

Again we can retrieve the cases where $j = 0$ by utilising 3. We form the fast pair approximation taking 4 and 5 together and applying 2. If the mean field and the pair approximation fast dynamics have a single globally attracting equilibrium for all N uncoupled fast systems then it is reasonable to proceed with the aggregation process. Only in this case can we be confident that branch-switching between two or more fast equilibria does not occur on the slow timescale for the complete dynamics. From here on we therefore assume we can find such equilibria. We denote the mean field fast equilibrium by: $\tilde{\rho}_{X_i}^{MF} = (\tilde{\rho}_{X_i^1}, \ldots, \tilde{\rho}_{X_i^N})$, and the pair approximation fast equilibrium by: $\tilde{\rho}_{X_i}^{PA} = (\tilde{\rho}_{X_i^1}, \ldots, \tilde{\rho}_{X_i^N}, \tilde{\rho}_{X_i^1 X_1}, \ldots, \tilde{\rho}_{X_i^N X_1}, \ldots, \tilde{\rho}_{X_i^N X_N})$.

Table 2. Complete cell-pair density equations, the below equations are required for all $i, j, k, m \in \{1, \dots, N\}$. Note δ_{ij} used below is the Kronecker delta.

$$
\epsilon \frac{d\rho_{OX_i^0}}{dt} = \underbrace{-\left(\frac{z-1}{z}\right) \rho_{OX_i^0} \sum_{j=1,k=0}^{N} p_{ij} q_{X_j^k/X_i^0 O}}_{\text{pollination}} + \underbrace{\sum_{j=1}^{N} e_j \rho_{OX_i^j}}_{\text{pollen expiry}} + \epsilon \left[\underbrace{\sum_{j=1,k=0}^{N} d_j \rho_{X_j^k X_i^0}}_{\text{death}} \right.
$$

$$
\underbrace{+ d_i \rho_{OX_i^0}}_{\text{death}} + \underbrace{\left. \left(\frac{z-1}{z}\right) \sum_{j,k=1}^{N} \left(b_{ijk} \rho_{OO} q_{X_j^k/OO} - \sum_{m=0}^{N} b_{mjk} \rho_{OX_i^0} q_{X_k^m/OX_i^0} \right) \right]}_{\text{colonisation}}
$$

$$
\epsilon \frac{d\rho_{OX_i^j}}{dt} = \left(\frac{z-1}{z}\right) \rho_{OX_i^0} \sum_{k=0}^{N} p_{ij} q_{X_j^k/X_i^0 O} - e_j \rho_{OX_i^j} + \epsilon \left[\sum_{k=1,m=0}^{N} d_j \rho_{X_k^m X_i^j} \right.
$$

$$
\left. - d_i \rho_{OX_i^j} - \rho_{OX_i^j} \sum_{k=1}^{N} \left(\frac{b_{kij}}{z} + \left(\frac{z-1}{z}\right) \sum_{m,n=1}^{N} b_{kmn} q_{X_m^n/OX_i^j} \right) \right]
$$

$$
\epsilon \frac{d\rho_{X_i^0 X_j^0}}{dt} = -\left(\frac{z-1}{z}\right) \rho_{X_i^0 X_j^0} \sum_{k=1,m=0}^{N} (p_{ik} + p_{jk}) q_{X_k^m/X_i^0 X_j^0}
$$

$$
+ \sum_{k=1}^{N} e_k \left(\rho_{X_i^k X_j^0} + \rho_{X_i^0 X_j^k} \right) + \epsilon \left[-(d_i + d_j) \rho_{X_i^0 X_j^0} \right.
$$

$$
\left. + \left(\frac{z-1}{z}\right) \sum_{k,m=1}^{N} \left(b_{ikm} \rho_{OX_i^0} q_{X_k^m/OX_j^0} + b_{jkm} \rho_{OX_j^0} q_{X_k^m/OX_i^0} \right) \right]
$$

$$
\epsilon \frac{d\rho_{X_i^0 X_j^k}}{dt} = \rho_{X_i^0 X_j^k} \left(\frac{p_{ij}}{z} + \left(1 - \frac{1}{z}\right) \sum_{m=1,n=0}^{N} p_{im} q_{X_m^n/X_i^0 X_j^k} \right)
$$

$$
+ \rho_{X_i^0 X_j^0} \left(\frac{z-1}{z}\right) \sum_{m=0}^{N} p_{jk} q_{X_k^m/X_j^0 X_i^0} - e_k \rho_{X_i^0 X_j^k} + \sum_{m=1}^{N} e_m \rho_{X_i^m X_j^k}
$$

$$
+ \epsilon \left[-(d_i + d_j) \rho_{X_i^0 X_j^k} + \rho_{OX_j^k} \left(\frac{b_{ijk}}{z} + \left(\frac{z-1}{z}\right) \sum_{m,n=1}^{N} b_{imn} q_{X_m^n/OX_j^k} \right) \right]
$$

$$
\epsilon \frac{d\rho_{X_i^j X_k^m}}{dt} = \rho_{X_i^0 X_k^m} p_{ij} \left(\frac{\delta_{jk}}{z} + \left(1 - \frac{1}{z}\right) \sum_{n=0}^{N} q_{X_j^n/X_i^0 X_k^m} \right)
$$

$$
+ \rho_{X_i^j X_k^0} \frac{p_{km}}{\epsilon} \left(\frac{\delta_{im}}{z} + \left(1 - \frac{1}{z}\right) \sum_{n=0}^{N} q_{X_m^n/X_k^0 X_i^j} \right) - (e_j + e_m) \rho_{X_i^j X_k^m}
$$

$$
+ \epsilon \left[-(d_i + d_k) \rho_{X_i^j X_k^m} \right]
$$

2.3   Aggregated Mean Field and Pair Approximation

We take as our aggregated cell and cell-pair density equations the first term of the outer asymptotic expansion of the complete cell and cell-pair density equations around the equilibria $\tilde{\rho}_{X_i}^{\text{MF}}$ or $\tilde{\rho}_{X_i}^{\text{PA}}$ as $\epsilon \to 0$. We obtain N linearly independent cell density equations which appear as follows for $i \in \{1, \dots, N\}$:

$$\frac{d\rho_{X_i}}{dt} = \sum_{j=1}^{N} \sum_{k=1}^{N} b_{ijk} \rho_O \tilde{q}_{X_j^k/O} - d_i \rho_{X_i}, \tag{6}$$

where for the mean field we use $\tilde{q}_{X_j^k/O} = \tilde{\rho}_{X_i^j}$, and for the pair approximation $\tilde{q}_{X_j^k/O} = \tilde{\rho}_{OX_i^j}/\tilde{\rho}_O$. We obtain N linearly independent empty-occupied cell-pair density equations which appear for $i \in \{1, \dots, N\}$:

$$\begin{aligned}
\frac{d\rho_{OX_i}}{dt} = {} & \left(\frac{z-1}{z}\right) \sum_{j,k=1}^{N} \frac{\tilde{\rho}_{OX_j^k}}{\rho_O} \left(b_{ijk}\rho_{OO} - \sum_{m=1}^{N} b_{mjk}\rho_{OX_i}\right) \\
& - \frac{1}{z}\rho_{OX_i} \sum_{k,j=1}^{N} b_{kij}\tilde{\rho}_{X_i^j} - d_i \rho_{OX_i} + \sum_{j=1}^{N} d_j \rho_{X_i X_j},
\end{aligned} \tag{7}$$

along with $\frac{1}{2}N(N-1)$ linearly independent occupied-occupied cell-pair density equations which appear for $i < j$ with $i, j \in \{1, \dots, N\}$:

$$\begin{aligned}
\frac{d\rho_{X_i X_j}}{dt} = {} & \rho_{OX_i}\left(\sum_{k=1}^{N} \frac{b_{jik}}{z} + \left(\frac{z-1}{z}\right) \sum_{k,m=1}^{N} b_{jkm}\frac{\tilde{\rho}_{OX_k^m}}{\rho_O}\right) \\
& + \rho_{OX_j}\left(\sum_{k=1}^{N} \frac{b_{ijk}}{z} + \left(\frac{z-1}{z}\right) \sum_{k,m=1}^{N} b_{ikm}\frac{\tilde{\rho}_{OX_k^m}}{\rho_O}\right) - (d_i + d_j)\rho_{X_i X_j}.
\end{aligned} \tag{8}$$

The dynamics of the aggregated systems are a good approximation of the dynamics of the complete systems after an initial short time period so long as ϵ is small and the aggregated system is structurally stable (Auger & Bravo de la Parra 2000). We require the initial short time period since the aggregated models will not accept arbitrary initial conditions.

The procedure for obtaining aggregated mean field and pair approximation characterisations for a cellular automaton with distinct pollination and colonisation processes has been outlined above in complete generality. For specific biological systems we may find there are i, j where $p_{ij} = 0$ in which case we can remove the cell state X_i^j, since pollination of con-specific i by con-specific j cannot occur. Similarly if $b_{ijk} = 0$ for all $i \in \{1, \dots, N\}$ we can remove cell state X_j^k because it is not a fertile state and so is irrelevant to the colonisation dynamics.

3   Application to Single Species

3.1   Complete Mean Field and Pair Approximation

As an illustration, we now apply our technique to a single species pollen limitation model. Since all subscripts are 1 we drop them. Our cells types are therefore: O - Empty; X^0 - Occupied unpollinated; X^1 - Occupied pollinated, the pollination rate is p/ϵ and the colonisation rate is b. We fix pollen expiry at $1/\epsilon$ and assume the death process is unitary. Since at most recovering parameters e_1 and d_1 would involve scaling time and either p or b. Our complete cell density equations are:

$$\epsilon\frac{d\rho_{X^0}}{dt} = -p(q_{X^0/X^0} + q_{X^1/X^0})\rho_{X^0} + \rho_{X^1} + \epsilon[-\rho_{X^0} + bq_{X^1/O}\rho_O],$$

$$\epsilon\frac{d\rho_{X^1}}{dt} = +p(q_{X^0/X^0} + q_{X^1/X^0})\rho_{X^0} - \rho_{X^1} + \epsilon[-\rho_{X^1}], \qquad (9)$$

To form the mean field we close moments with the approximation 1. The cell-pair density equations appear as follows:

$$\epsilon\frac{d\rho_{OX^0}}{dt} = -p(\tfrac{z-1}{z})(q_{X^0/X^0O} + q_{X^1/X^0O})\rho_{OX^0} + \rho_{OX^1} + \epsilon[\rho_{X^0X^0} + \rho_{X^1X^0}$$
$$-\rho_{OX^0} - b(\tfrac{z-1}{z})q_{X^1/OX^0}\rho_{OX^0} + b(\tfrac{z-1}{z})q_{X^1/OO}\rho_{OO}],$$

$$\epsilon\frac{d\rho_{OX^1}}{dt} = p(\tfrac{z-1}{z})(q_{X^0/X^0O} + q_{X^1/X^0O})\rho_{OX^0} - \rho_{OX^1} + \epsilon[\rho_{X^0X^1} + \rho_{X^1X^1}$$
$$-\rho_{OX^1} - b(\tfrac{1}{z} + (\tfrac{z-1}{z})q_{X^1/OX^1})\rho_{OX^1}],$$

$$\epsilon\frac{d\rho_{X^0X^1}}{dt} = -p(\tfrac{1}{z} + (\tfrac{z-1}{z})(q_{X^0/X^0O} + q_{X^1/X^0X^1}))\rho_{X^0X^1}$$
$$+p(\tfrac{z-1}{z})(q_{X^0/X^0X^0} + q_{X^1/X^0X^0})\rho_{X^0X^0} + \rho_{X^1X^1} - \rho_{X^0X^1}$$
$$+\epsilon[-2\rho_{X^0X^1} + b(\tfrac{1}{z} + (\tfrac{z-1}{z})q_{X^1/OX^1})\rho_{OX^1}], \qquad (10)$$

To form the pair approximation we close moments by taking 2.

3.2   Fast Equilibria

We define the aggregated variables: $\rho_X = \rho_{X^0} + \rho_{X^1}$; and $\rho_{\sigma X} = \rho_{\sigma X^0} + \rho_{\sigma X^1}$ for $\sigma \in \{O, X^0, X^1, X\}$. We obtain the fast dynamics for the cell density and cell-pair density equations on the fast timescale $\tau = t/\epsilon$:

$$\frac{d\rho_{X^1}}{d\tau} = p\rho_X q_{X/X^0} - \rho_{X^1},$$

$$\frac{d\rho_{X^1X}}{d\tau} = p(\tfrac{1}{z} + (\tfrac{z-1}{z})q_{B/X^0X})\rho_{X^0X} - \rho_{X^1X}. \qquad (11)$$

The mean field system has one globally asymptotically stable equilibrium:

$$\tilde{\rho}_{X^1} = \frac{p\rho_X^2}{1 + p\rho_X}, \qquad (12)$$

The pair approximation also has one globally asymptotically stable equilibrium:

$$\tilde{\rho}_{X^1} = \frac{(p+z)\rho_X + zp\rho_{XX}}{2(p+1)} - \sqrt{\left(\frac{(p+z)\rho_X + pz\rho_{XX}}{2(p+1)}\right)^2 - \frac{pz\rho_X\rho_{XX}}{p+1}},$$

$$\tilde{\rho}_{X^1X} = \rho_{XX} - \frac{\tilde{\rho}_{X^1}}{p}. \tag{13}$$

3.3   Analysis of Aggregated Mean Field

We take as our aggregated mean field the first term of the outer asymptotic expansion about $\tilde{\rho}_{X^1}$ from 12 of the complete mean field 9 as $\epsilon \to 0$:

$$\frac{d\rho_X}{dt} = \rho_X \left(\frac{bp\rho_X(1-\rho_X)}{1+p\rho_X} - 1\right), \tag{14}$$

Equation 14 has an equilibrium at $\rho_X = 0$ and also two non-trivial equilibria:

$$\hat{\rho}_X^{\pm} = \frac{b-1}{2b} \pm \sqrt{\left(\frac{1-b}{2b}\right)^2 - \frac{1}{pb}}. \tag{15}$$

We find $\hat{\rho}_X^+$ is stable and attracting and $\hat{\rho}_X^-$ is unstable. We see that $\hat{\rho}_X^-$ is a threshold population density below which extinction is predicted. This is a typical arrangement for models with pollen-limited colonisation. So long as $b > 1$ this model has a finite bifurcation point at $p_{CRIT} = 4b/(1-b)^2$. For $p < p_{CRIT}$ the two non-trivial equilibria disappear, and the model predicts extinction for all initial conditions.

3.4   Analysis of Aggregated Pair Approximation

We take as our aggregated pair approximation the first term of the outer asymptotic expansion about $(\tilde{\rho}_{X^1}, \tilde{\rho}_{X^1X})$ from 13 of the complete pair approximation 10 as $\epsilon \to 0$:

$$\frac{d\rho_X}{dt} = b\tilde{\rho}_{OX^1} - \rho_X,$$

$$\frac{d\rho_{XX}}{dt} = 2b(\tfrac{1}{z}(1-\rho_X) + (\tfrac{z-1}{z})(\rho_X - \rho_{XX}))\frac{\tilde{\rho}_{OX^1}}{1-\rho_X} - 2\rho_{XX}, \tag{16}$$

where:

$$\tilde{\rho}_{OX^1} = \tilde{\rho}_{X^1} - \tilde{\rho}_{X^1X} = \frac{p+1}{p}\tilde{\rho}_{X^1} - \rho_{XX},$$

and $\tilde{\rho}_{X^1}$ is given in 13. Since all cell-pair densities must be positive: $2\rho_X - 1 \le \rho_{XX} \le \rho_X$, so our region of interest $\triangle$ on the (ρ_X, ρ_{XX})-plane is the triangle with vertices $(0,0)$, $(1/2, 0)$ and $(1,1)$. It is straight-forward to demonstrate that $\triangle$ is invariant under 16. Considering $\dot{\rho}_X = 0$ we obtain two linear nullclines which we write: $\rho_{XX} = f_X^{\pm}(\rho_X) = \alpha^{\pm}\rho_X$. Up to two non-trivial equilibria may occur in $\triangle$ corresponding to intersections of $f_X^{\pm}$ and the nullcline specified by $\dot{\rho}_{XX} = 0$. We can compute the non-trivial equilibria $\hat{\rho}_X^{\pm}$ directly:

$$\hat{\rho}_X^{\pm} = \frac{1 - z\alpha^{\pm}}{2 - z - \alpha^{\pm}}, \tag{17}$$

For $b > z/(z-1)$ this model undergoes a saddle-node bifurcation at $p = p_{SN}$ which occurs when $f_X^+ = f_X^-$. Also the model undergoes a transcritical bifurcation at $p = p_{TC}$ when $\alpha^- = 1/z$, at this point $\hat{\rho}_X^- = 0$.

$$p_{SN} = \frac{4bz(z-1)}{(b(z-1)-z)^2}, \text{ and } p_{TC} = \frac{bz^3}{(b(z-1)-z)^2}. \tag{18}$$

It is straight forward to see that $p_{SN} < p_{TC}$ so long as $z > 2$. So (b,p)-parameter space is divided into three regions: For $p < p_{SN}$ the two non-trivial equilibria disappear, and the model predicts extinction for all initial conditions. For $p_{SN} \leq p < p_{TC}$ the (ρ_X, ρ_{XX}) phase-plane is divided into survival and extinction zones by the stable manifold of the unstable equilibrium $\hat{\rho}_X^-$, see Figure 1(a). For $p \geq p_{TC}$ we find $\hat{\rho}_X^- < 0$ and the model predicts survival for all initial conditions in the interior of $\triangle$. Figure 1(b) illustrates these regions.

The pair approximation identifies two phenomena which the mean field cannot detect. The first is the importance of spatial configuration for population survival. Figure 1(a) indicates that when survival is conditional on initial conditions, there is a threshold population density below which extinction is certain. Above this density survival is subject to configurational constraints: If the population is too sparse (ρ_{XX} is low) or if the population is too clustered (ρ_{XX} is high) extinction is possible for initial population densities in excess of the threshold density. The second phenomena is the region of parameter space where population survival is unconditional, see Figure 1(b). This region is not too remote for small neighbourhood sizes, and is attainable for species which produce a lot of pollen and set a lot of seed. Invasion is possible from arbitrarily low initial

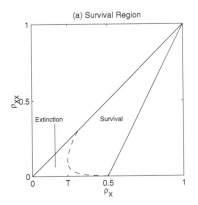
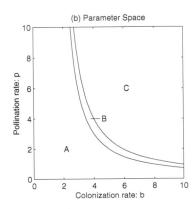

Fig. 1. Parameters $b = 3.9$, $p = 3.2$, $z = 4$. (a) The survival and extinction regions of the phase plane for the aggregated pair approximation, T marks the threshold population density. (b) Parameter space for the aggregated pair approximation is divided into three regions: A - $p < p_{SN}$; B - $p \in [p_{SN}, p_{TC})$; C - $p \geq p_{TC}$.

population densities, which contrasts with the predictions of pollen limitation models which are non-spatial (the mean field model 14 for example) and with diffusional models (Lewis & Kareiva 1993).

4   Discussion

The techniques detailed in this paper provide a method for obtaining pair approximation results for systems of plant con-specifics with complicated pollination interactions. The procedure, however, has applications to a more general class of cellular automata problems. Here requiring information about pollen donors makes colonisation a process fundamentally involving triplets of cells. Such triplet processes cannot be effectively captured by pair approximation methods. Our solution is to let cells record information about the constitution of their neighbourhood. To do this each cell type must be split into sub-types, each representing the presence of different types of neighbouring cells. A fast signalling process between cells adjusts the sub-type of a cell to suit its neighbourhood. In our models we call this process pollination, but in general the signalling process need not have a phenomenological parallel. We can translate triplet processes involving cell types into pair processes involving cell sub-types, and thus capture these processes with a pair approximation. Since there are many sub-types for each cell type, this pair approximation may have a large dimension. However, by applying perturbation methods we can aggregate variables and reduce the dimension of the approximation, whilst retaining a good correspondence with the original cellular automaton model.

References

Auger, P. & Bravo de la Parra, R. (2000), 'Methods of aggregation of variables in population dynamics', *C.R. Acad. Sci. Paris, Sciences de la vie / Life Sciences* (323), 665–674.

Carrillo, C., Britton, N. & Mogie, M. (2002), 'Coexistence of sexual and asexual con-specifics: A cellular automaton model', *Journal of Theoretical Biology* 217, 275–285.

Iwasa, Y. (2000), Lattice models and pair approximations in ecology, in U. Dieckmann, R. Law & J.A.J. Metz, eds, 'The Geometry of Ecological Interactions', Cambridge Studies in Adaptive Dynamics, Cambridge University Press, chapter 13, pp. 227–251.

Lewis, M. & Kareiva, P. (1993), 'Allee dynamics and the spread of invading organisms', *Theoretical Population Biology* **43**, 141–158.

Satō, K. & Iwasa, Y. (2000), Pair approximations, in U. Dieckmann, R. Law & J.A.J. Metz, eds, 'The Geometry of Ecological Interactions', *Cambridge Studies in Adaptive Dynamics*, Cambridge University Press, chapter 18, pp. 341–358.

Characterization of a Class of Complemented Group Cellular Automata

Debdeep Mukhopadhyay* and Dipanwita Roy Chowdhury**

Indian Institute of Technology, Kharagpur, India
debdeep@vlsi.iitkgp.ernet.in, drc@cse.iitkgp.ernet.in

Abstract. The present paper characterizes a specific class of complemented group cellular automata (CA). The CA rule referred to as the fundamental transformation divides the entire state space into smaller spaces of equal lengths. Some interesting properties of this particular Cellular Automata have been analyzed. The relations developed promise the development of agreement theorems which shall be useful in constructing key agreement algorithms.

1 Introduction

Cellular Automata (CA) was first introduced by *J. von Neumann* for modeling self-reproducible configurations. Research in the field of CA was initiated as early as 1950. *Wolfram* [1] suggested simplification of the Cellular Automata with local interconnections. The CA structure he proposed consists of cells, each having only two states with uniform 3-neighborhood connections. Various researcher's like ([2,3,4,5]) have carried out extensive study in the modeling of CA and finding out better applications of the automata. Later *Das et al* [6] proposed a versatile matrix algebraic tool for the analysis of state transition of CA with linear next-state functions. The VLSI era has ushered in a new phase of activities into the research of linear machines, and specially the local neighborhood CA structures. The VLSI design community prefer simple, regular, modular and cascadable structures with local interconnections. Tha CA provides a wonderful solution in all these respects [7]. Also another advantage of CA is a class of machines constructed by inverting the linear state functions.

With the ever increasing growth of data communication, the need for security and privacy has become a necessity. CA based pseudorandom generator has been studied in ([8,9,10,11,12,13]). Quality of randomness has been evaluated as per the criterion set by Knuth[14]. The advent of wireless communication and other handheld devices like Personal Digital Assistants and smart cards have made the implementation of cryptosystems a major issue. One important aspect of modern day ciphers is the scope for hardware sharing between the encryption and

---

* Debdeep Mukhopadhyay is a Phd student in the Department of Computer Sc. and Engg, IIT Kharagpur.
** Dipanwita Roy Chowdhury is Associate Professor in the Department of Computer Sc. and Engg, IIT Kharagpur.

P.M.A. Sloot, B. Chopard, and A.G. Hoekstra (Eds.): ACRI 2004, LNCS 3305, pp. 775–784, 2004.

decryption algorithms. The Cellular Automata can be programmed to perform both the operations without using any dedicated hardware.

In this paper a new class of complemented group CA has been explored. The function determining the state transition of the CA is referred to as the *fundamental transformation*. The relationship between the cyclic subspaces has been established. It can be proved that the state space is divided into cycles which are seemingly unrelated. But the apparent independence of the state transitions of the fundamental transformations does not allow for the transition of states from one cycle to the other. This leads to serious worries in applications like encryption and key agreement where the entire state is to be effectively used. No reported literature has provided a relation between the state transition cycles. The present paper develops new rules which govern the transition between the cycles. These properties promise the CA to function as a core of a CA based cryptographic algorithm.

The outline of the paper is as follows: *Section 2* details the characterization of the complemented CA. The state spaces of the fundamental transformations are related in *section 3*. *Section 4* sketches a possible application of the existing properties. The work is concluded in *section 5*.

2   Fundamental Transformations and Its State Spaces

A *Cellular Automata (CA)* consists of a number of cells arranged in a regular manner, where the state transitions of each cell depends on the states of its neighbors. The next state of a particular cell is assumed to depend only on itself and on its two neighbors (3-neighborhood dependency). The state x of the ith cell at time $(t+1)$ is denoted as $x_{t+1}^i = f(x_t^{i-1}, x_t^i, x_t^{i+1})$, where x_t^i denotes the state of the ith cell at time t and f is the next state function called the rule of the automata [1]. Since f is a function of 3 variables, there are 2^{2^3} or 256 possible next state functions. The decimal equivalent of the output column in the truth table of the function is denoted as the rule number. The next state function for three different rules are noted below:

$$\text{Rule } 90 \ : \quad x_{t+1}^i = x_t^{i-1} \oplus x_t^{i+1}$$
$$\text{Rule } 150 : x_{t+1}^i = x_t^{i-1} \oplus x_t^i \oplus x_t^{i+1}$$
$$\text{Rule } 153 : \quad x_{t+1}^i = \overline{x_t^i \oplus x_t^{i+1}}$$

One of the rules of fundamental transformations $(\overline{T})$ is the rule 153, [7]. The rule 153 represented as $(\overline{x^0 \oplus x^1})$, is the additive complement of rule 102 represented as $(x^0 \oplus x^1)$. It is known that if a cellular automata with rule 153 is fed with an initial seed of X, then the cellular automata produces an output $\overline{T}(X) = T(X) + IF$, where I is a unit matrix and F is all one vector. Hence, we have $X, \overline{T}(X)$ and $\overline{T}^2(X)$ members of the same cycle. Physically, an n-cell uniform CA having rule 153 evolves with equal number of cyclic states.

The following existing lemmas are cited without proof for convenience.

Lemma 1. *[15] If R is a space generated by a linear operator G (say), then the space can be decomposed into cyclic subspaces*

$$R = I_1 + I_2 + \ldots + I_t$$

such that the minimal polynomial of each of these cyclic subspace is a power of an irreducible polynomial.

Lemma 2. *[16] If the degree of an irreducible polynomial is m, then the period of this polynomial is $(2^m - 1)$.*

Lemma 3. *[17] If the period of an irreducible polynomial $p(x)$ is k then the period of $[p(x)]^j$ is kq^r, where $q^{r-1} < j \leq q^r$, q being the modulus.*

Theorem 1. *The CA having rule T and number of cells ranging from $(2^{k-1}+1)$ to 2^k have maximum cycle length of $m = 2^k$.*

Proof. Let us consider the cycle structure of $Y = T(X)$, where T is the nxn matrix of rule 102.

$$T = \begin{bmatrix} 1 & 1 & 0 & . & . & 0 \\ 0 & 1 & 1 & . & . & 0 \\ 0 & 0 & 1 & 1 & . & 0 \\ . & . & . & . & . & . \\ . & . & . & . & . & . \\ 0 & 0 & 0 & 0 & . & 1 \end{bmatrix}$$

For the linear CA having characteristic matrix T, R is the space generated by the linear operator T. The characteristic polynomial of an n-cell CA is given by $p(x) = (x + 1)^n = [p_1(x)]^n$, where $p_1(x) = (1 + x)$. Thus according to *Lemma 1*, $p_2(x)$ is responsible for a cyclic subspace. Period of $p_1(x)=(1 + x)$ is $k = 2^1 - 1 = 1$. Period of $p_2(x)$ can be found by *Lemma 3*. In this case, the modulus $q=2$ and $k = 1$. So the period of $p_2(x)$ is 2^r for an n-cell CA where,
$2^{r-1} < n \leq 2^r$
or, $\lceil log(n) \rceil \leq r < \lceil log(n) \rceil + 1$. So, the maximum cycle length of the CA is always some power of 2.

Let, n be the number of cells of the CA with rule T. From the inequality $2^{r-1} < n \leq 2^r$, if n is of the form 2^k, $2^{r-1} < 2^k \leq 2^r$. Thus, $k=r$ and the length of the linear machine is $2^{log n}$. If, n is of the form $2^k + 1$, $2^{r-1} < (2^k + 1) \leq 2^r$. Thus $r > k$. As the period is a power of 2, the period is 2^{k+1}. The maximum size of a CA that evolves cycle length of 2^k is 2^k. Thus the maximum size of the CA that evolves cycle length of 2^{k-1} is 2^{k-1}.

Thus, if the number of cells range from $2^{k-1} + 1$ to 2^k the maximum cycle length is 2^k.

For the sake of simplicity let the global state of a CA be simply represented as X rather than $f_t(x)$.

Theorem 2. *If $\overline{T}^p$ denotes p times application of the complemented CA operator $\overline{T}$, then,*

$$\overline{T}^p(X) = (I \oplus T \oplus T^2 \oplus \ldots \oplus T^{p-1}).F \oplus T^p.(X) \tag{1}$$

where T is the matrix of the corresponding non-complemented CA.

Proof. By definition (as stated in the preliminaries),

$$\overline{T}.(X) = F \oplus T.(X)$$
$$\overline{T}^2.(X) = F \oplus T[F \oplus T.(X)] = [I \oplus T]F \oplus T^2.(X)$$
$$\text{Thus, } \overline{T}^p.(X) = [I \oplus T \oplus T^2 \oplus \ldots \oplus T^{p-1}]F \oplus T^p.(X).$$

Hence, $\overline{T}^p$ is expressible in terms of powers of T (the corresponding non-complemented version of the rule).

Inorder to evaluate the cycle structure of the complemented CA with rule $\overline{T}$ the following lemmas are required.

Lemma 4. *If for the linear CA characterized by operator T, the maximum cycle length is k then the length of the cycles formed by the complemented CA is nk, where n is a natural number.*

Proof. Let, the length of the complemented CA be $nk + r$, where $r < k$.
  Thus, $\overline{T}^{nk+r}(X) = X$ and $T^{nk} = I$.
  Hence, $X = T^{nk+r}(X) + [I + T + T^2 + \ldots + T^{nk+r-1}]F$
    $= T^r(X) + [I+T+T^2+\ldots+T^{nk-1}]F+T^{nk}[I+T+T^2+\ldots+T^{r-1}]F$
or, $(I + T^r)X = [I + T + T^2 + \ldots + T^{nk-1}]F + T^{nk}[I + T + T^2 + \ldots + T^{r-1}]F$
or, $(I + T)(I + T^r)X = (I + T)[I + T + T^2 + \ldots + T^{nk-1}]F + (I + T)[I + T + T^2 + \ldots + T^{r-1}]F$
or, $(I + T^r)(I + T)X = (I + T^{nk})F + (I + T^r)F$
or, $(I + T^r)[(I + T)X + IF] = 0$.
  If, $(I + T^r) \neq 0$, for solution of X to exist
rank$(I + T)$=rank$(I + T, F)$.
  But the lower row of $I + T$ is zero, so the rank is less than n, the order of the matrix T. But F is an all one vector, so the ranks cannot be equal. Thus, $(I + T^r)$=0. Since $r < k$, hence this is not possible. Thus we arrive at a contradiction. Thus the maximal cycle length is nk, where n is a natural number.

Lemma 5. *If for the linear CA characterized by operator T, there exists a cycle of length k then in the complemented CA characterized by $\overline{T}$ there will exist a cycle of length k or $2k$.*

Proof. Let X be the current state. The state of the complemented CA after m cycles is given by $\overline{T}^m(X) = [I+T+T^2+\ldots T^{m-1}]F+T^m(X)$. If k is the order of the group generated by T, then $T^k = I$. Now to show $\overline{T}$ also generates a group it is needed to show that there exists an $m = k'$ such that $[I+T+T^2+\ldots+T^{k'-1}] = 0$ and $T^{k'} = I$.
For $k' = 2k$,

$$I + T + T^2 + T^3 + \ldots + T^{k-1} + T^k + T^{k+1} + \ldots + T^{2k-1}$$

$$= [I + T + T^2 + T^3 + \ldots T^{k-1}] + [I + T + T^2 + T^3 + \ldots T^{k-1}]T^k$$

$$=[I + T + T^2 + T^3 + \dots T^{k-1}][I + T^k]$$
$$=0, since T^k = I.$$

Also, $T^{2k} = (T^k)^2 = I$. So, the length of the cycles generated by $\overline{T}$ is less than or equal to $2k$. Thus combining with the previous lemma, the cycle length of the complemented CA is either k or $2k$.

Next, the condition for determining whether the order is k or $2k$ is stated. If, both the linear CA (T) and the complemented CA ($\overline{T}$) have length k, then $\overline{T}^k(X)=[I + T + T^2 + \dots T^{k-1}]F + T^k(X) = Y + T^k(X)$. Thus, $Y = 0$, since both $\overline{T}^k(X) = T^k(X) = X$.

In other words the length of the state transition of $\overline{T}$ will have length $2k$ when $Y \neq 0$, otherwise the length is k.

Theorem 3. *If the number of cells is not a power of 2, $Y = 0$. But if the number of cells is a power of 2, $Y \neq 0$.*

Theorem 4. *The length of cycle for an n-cell CA, having rule $\overline{T}$, is*

$$l = \begin{cases} 2 & n=2 \\ 2^{\lfloor logn \rfloor + 1} & n>2 \end{cases} \tag{2}$$

Proof. The result is trivial for $n = 2$. Using the result that if the number of cells range from $2^{k-1}+1$ to 2^k the cycle length is 2^k, the following table is constructed (*Table 1*).

Table 1. Maximum Cycle Length

Range for the number of cells	Maximum Cycle Length
2	2
3 − 4	4
5 − 8	8
9 − 16	16
17 − 32	32
$\vdots$	$\vdots$
$(2^{n-1} + 1) - (2^n)$	2^n

Thus, length of the cycles generated by the linear CA is $2^{\lceil log(n) \rceil}$.

From theorem 8 if the number of cells is not a power of 2, $Y = 0$. Then if the length of the linear CA is k, so is that of the complemented CA. But if the number of cells is a power of 2 $Y \neq 0$. Thus, the length of the complemented CA is $2k$. Now,

$$\lceil log(n) \rceil = \begin{cases} \lfloor log(n) \rfloor + 1, n \neq 2^k \\ \lfloor log(n) \rfloor, \quad n = 2^k \end{cases} \tag{3}$$

Thus, the length of an n-cell complemented CA $(n > 2)$ is formulated by

$$l = \begin{cases} 2^{\lceil log(n)\rceil} & = 2^{\lfloor log(n)\rfloor+1} \ n \neq 2^k \\ 2.2^{\lceil log(n)\rceil} & = 2^{\lfloor log(n)\rfloor+1} \ n = 2^k \end{cases} \tag{4}$$

This completes the proof for $n > 2$.

Based upon the above fundamentals the following theorems have been developed. Both $\oplus$ and $+$ denote the exor operation.

The figure 1 shows the cycles generated by the finite states in a CA with rule 153. The cycles are shown for a 5-bit CA, length of each being 8. The total 32 states are thus divided in 4 non-intersecting (non-overlapping) cycles. The following theorems find out an inter-relationship between these cycles. The objective is to find out a new set of rules which can help elements to migrate from any position of the state space to another. The relation between the state spaces is hence searched for in the present paper.

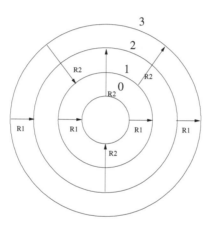

Fig. 1. Cycles of a complementary CA and the interconnecting rules

3 Relation Between the State Spaces of Fundamental Transformations

Theorem 5. *Every element, X of a cycle generated by CA with rule $\overline{T}$ when mapped by the rule, $X \oplus \overline{T}(X) \oplus \overline{T}^2(X)$, also lie in a cycle.*

Proof. Given $X, \overline{T}(X), \overline{T}^2(X)$ and $\overline{T}^3(X)$ are members of the same cycle. In the following equations, $+$ means simple exor operation.

$$\overline{T}(X) = T(X) + IF \tag{5}$$
$$\overline{T}^2(X) = T^2(X) + (I+T)F \tag{6}$$

Let the rule map X to an element ϵ_1, such that:
$$\epsilon_1 = X \oplus \overline{T}(X) \oplus \overline{T}^2(X).$$

$$or, \epsilon_1 = X + T(X) + T^2(X) + TF \tag{7}$$

The same rule when applied on the next element, $\overline{T}(X)$ we have,
$$\epsilon_2 = [T(X) + IF] \oplus [T^2(X) + (I+T)F] \oplus [T^3(X) + (I+T+T^2)F]$$
or, $\epsilon_2 = \overline{T}(X + T(X) + T^2(X) + TF)$
$$\epsilon_2 = \overline{T}(\epsilon_1)$$
Therefore, ϵ_1 and ϵ_2 are concyclic.

Theorem 6. *If X, $\overline{T}(X)$, $\overline{T}^2(X), \ldots$ lie in one cycle, then $X \oplus \overline{T}(X) \oplus \overline{T}^2(X)$, $\overline{T}(X) \oplus \overline{T}^2(X) \oplus \overline{T}^3(X), \ldots$ lie on another non-intersecting cycle.*

Proof. From, theorem 5, $\epsilon_2 = \overline{T}(\epsilon_1)$, as they are members of the same cycle.

To prove that ϵ_1 and X do not belong to the same cycle, it is required to prove that no λ exists such that, $\epsilon_1 = \overline{T}^\lambda(X)$.

In other words, there does not exist any λ such that, $X + T(X) + T^2(X) + TF = \overline{T}^\lambda(X) = T^\lambda(X) + [I + T + \ldots + T^{\lambda-1}]F$. We prove the theorem by contradiction.

Case1: Let λ exist and be even.

$LHS = X + T(X) + T^2(X) + TF =$

$$(I + T + T^2)(X) + TF = \begin{bmatrix} \cdots \cdots \cdots \\ \cdots\ 1\ \ 1\ \ 1 \\ \cdots \cdots\ 1\ \ 1 \\ 0\ \ 0\ \cdots\ 1 \end{bmatrix} \begin{bmatrix} x^0 \\ \cdot \\ \cdot \\ x^{n-1} \end{bmatrix} + \begin{bmatrix} \cdot \\ 0 \\ 0 \\ 1 \end{bmatrix} = \begin{bmatrix} \cdot \\ \cdot \\ \cdot \\ \overline{x}^{n-1} \end{bmatrix}$$

$$RHS = T^\lambda(X) + [I + T + \ldots + T^{\lambda-1}]F = \begin{bmatrix} \cdots \cdots \cdots \\ \cdots \cdots \cdots \\ \cdots \cdots \cdots \\ 0\ \ 0\ \cdots\ 1 \end{bmatrix} \begin{bmatrix} x^0 \\ \cdot \\ \cdot \\ x^{n-1} \end{bmatrix} +$$

$$\left(\begin{bmatrix} \cdots \cdots \cdots \\ \cdots \cdots \cdots \\ \cdots \cdots \cdots \\ 0\ \ 0\ \cdots\ 1 \end{bmatrix} + \ldots + (\text{even number of terms}) + \begin{bmatrix} \cdots \cdots \cdots \\ \cdots \cdots \cdots \\ \cdots \cdots \cdots \\ 0\ \ 0\ \cdots\ 1 \end{bmatrix} \right) F$$

$$= \begin{bmatrix} \cdots \cdots \cdots \\ \cdots \cdots \cdots \\ \cdots \cdots \cdots \\ 0\ \ 0\ \cdots\ 1 \end{bmatrix} \begin{bmatrix} x^0 \\ \cdot \\ \cdot \\ x^{n-1} \end{bmatrix} + \begin{bmatrix} \cdot \\ \cdot \\ \cdot \\ 0 \end{bmatrix} = \begin{bmatrix} \cdot \\ \cdot \\ \cdot \\ x^{n-1} \end{bmatrix}$$

Hence, we have a contradiction, that is $x^{n-1} = \overline{x^{n-1}}$.

Case2: Let λ be odd. It may be observed from the evolution of the CA that the 0th bit of $T^\lambda(X)$ can be represented as
$(x^0 + x^1) + \binom{\lambda-1}{1}(x^1 + x^2) + \binom{\lambda-1}{2}(x^2 + x^3) + \ldots + (x^{\lambda-1} + x^\lambda)$

Hence, if λ is 4n+1, the 0th bit of $T^\lambda(X)$ depends on x^0, x^1 but not x^2. If, λ is 4n+3, the 0th bit of $T^\lambda(X)$ depends on x^0, x^1 and x^2. Also, if λ is 4n+1, the 0th bit of $[I + T + \ldots + T^{\lambda-1}](X)$ depends upon x^0. If λ is 4n+3, the 0th bit of $[I + T + \ldots + T^{\lambda-1}](X)$ depends upon x^0, x^1, x^2.

Hence, we have for $\lambda = 4n + 1$,

$$
\begin{bmatrix} \cdots\cdots\cdots \\ \cdots\ 1\ 1\ 1 \\ \cdots\cdots\ 1\ 1 \\ 0\ \ 0\ \cdots\ 1 \end{bmatrix}
\begin{bmatrix} x^0 \\ \cdot \\ \cdot \\ x^{n-1} \end{bmatrix}
+
\begin{bmatrix} \cdot \\ 0 \\ 0 \\ 1 \end{bmatrix}
=
\begin{bmatrix} \cdots\cdots\cdots \\ \cdots\ 1\ 1\ 0 \\ \cdots\cdots\ 1\ 1 \\ 0\ \ 0\ \cdots\ 1 \end{bmatrix}
\begin{bmatrix} x^0 \\ \cdot \\ \cdot \\ x^{n-1} \end{bmatrix}
+
\begin{bmatrix} \cdot \\ 1 \\ 1 \\ 1 \end{bmatrix}
$$

Hence, we have a contradiction, that is
$(x^{n-2} + x^{n-1}) = \overline{(x^{n-2} + x^{n-1})}$.

Similarly, we have for $\lambda = 4n + 3$,

$$
\begin{bmatrix} \cdots\cdots\cdots \\ \cdots\ 1\ 1\ 1 \\ \cdots\cdots\ 1\ 1 \\ 0\ \ 0\ \cdots\ 1 \end{bmatrix}
\begin{bmatrix} x^0 \\ \cdot \\ \cdot \\ x^{n-1} \end{bmatrix}
+
\begin{bmatrix} \cdot \\ 0 \\ 0 \\ 1 \end{bmatrix}
=
\begin{bmatrix} \cdots\cdots\cdots \\ \cdots\ 1\ 1\ 1 \\ \cdots\cdots\ 1\ 1 \\ 0\ \ 0\ \cdots\ 1 \end{bmatrix}
\begin{bmatrix} x^0 \\ \cdot \\ \cdot \\ x^{n-1} \end{bmatrix}
+
\begin{bmatrix} \cdot \\ 1 \\ 0 \\ 1 \end{bmatrix}
$$

Hence, we have a contradiction, that is
$(x^{n-3} + x^{n-2} + x^{n-1}) = \overline{(x^{n-3} + x^{n-2} + x^{n-1})}$. This completes the proof.

Corollary 1. $X + \overline{T}(X) + \overline{T}^2(X), X + \overline{T}(X) + \overline{T}^3(X)$, *construct non-intersecting cycles.*

Construction of rules: The following operations are defined as rules:

$$R1(X) = X + \overline{T}(X) + \overline{T}^2(X) \tag{8}$$
$$and,\ R2(X) = X + \overline{T}(X) + \overline{T}^3(X) \tag{9}$$

Corollary 2. *R1 and R2 are commutative i.e R1R2(X)=R2R1(X). Applying, the rules on X shows that both the operations produce the same result.*

Corollary 3. $R1(\overline{T}^a(X)) = \overline{T}^a(R1(X))$, *where a is any index.*

Corollary 4. $\overline{T}^a R1R2(\overline{T}^b(X)) = \overline{T}^b R2R1(\overline{T}^a(X))$, *where a and b are indices.*

Corollary 5.
$$R1(a+b) = R1(a) + R1(b) + TF$$
$$R2(a+b) = R2(a) + R2(b) + (T+T^2)F$$

The rules are used to migrate from one cyclic subspace generated by $\overline{T}$ to another. The inter-relations promise the development of CA-based algorithms used in encryption. A possible application is outlined in the next section.

4   A Possible Application

Key agreement protocols are mechanisms which establish the keys before the onset of private key algorithms. The private key algorithms are used for bulk data encryption. The shared key or secret is derived by two or more parties as a function of the information provided by each party. Ideally the key should

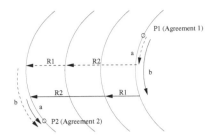

Fig. 2. Agreement Property of the State Spaces

not be derivable by either of the parties alone. Such partial key algorithms thus establish key on the fly. Key freshness is important, that is the key should change frequently. Thus less data is encrypted by the same key, thus the eavesdropper has lesser probability of success. Further the amount of damage done due to the revelation of a key is reduced if the key is frequently changed.

Recently many researchers have identified the CA as the core of security algorithms [18,19]. But an essential requirement is that the cycle length of the CA has to be small, so that ciphering (or deciphering) is performed at the expense of few clock cycles. Moreover the length of the machines has to be equal so that the number of cycles required to encrypt or decrypt is predecided. The specific class of the complemented group CA dealt with in this paper (fundamental transformations) exhibit an interesting agreement property. The figure 2 shows the state space cycles (as described for a Cellular Automata employing the fundamental transformations). P1 is an initial point of agreement of two parties. After the initial agreement both takes up different paths (as shown by the dashed and the solid lines). It is certain from the above theorems and corollaries both the paths converge again at P2 which is the second point of collision or agreement. This property promises the development of an efficient agreement protocol using Cellular Automata. However for the development of a security protocol the security aspect needs to be thoroughly investigated and is not the objective of the current paper.

5   Conclusion

The present paper investigates the state spaces of the fundamental transformations of a cellular automata. New properties have been proved which relate the state spaces of the cellular automata. The properties help to use the entire state space. The new relations promise the development of new encryption and key distribution protocols.

References

[1] S. Wolfram, "Statistical mechanics of cellular automata", *Rev. Mod. Phys.* vol. 55, no. 3, pp. 601–644, July 1983.

[2] J. Thatcher, "Universality in von Neumann cellular model," Tech. Rep. 03105-30-T, ORA, University of Michigan, 1964.

[3] Ch. Lee, "Synthesis of a cellular universal machine using 29-state model of von Neumann," in *The University of Michigan Engineering Summer Conferences*, 1964.

[4] E. F. Codd, *Cellular Automata*, Academic Press Inc., 1968.

[5] F.C. Hennie, *Iterative Arrays of Logical Circuits*, Academic, Nework, London, 1961.

[6] A.K. Das and P.P. Chaudhuri, "Efficient characterization of cellular automata," in *Proc. IEE (Part E)*, January 1964, vol. 137, pp. 81–87.

[7] P. Pal Chaudhuri, D. Roy Chowdhury, Sukumar Nandi, and Santanu Chattopadhyay, *Additive Cellular Automata Theory and its Application*, vol. 1, chapter 4, pp. 200–300, IEEE Computer Society Press, 1997.

[8] Ph. Tsalides, "Cellular Automata based Built-In Self-Test Structures for VLSI Systems," *Elect. Lett.*, vol. 26, no. 17, pp. 1350–1352, 1990.

[9] Ph. Tsalides, T. A. York, and A. Thanailakis, "Pseudo-random Number Generators for VLSI Systems based on Linear Cellular Automata," *IEE Proc. E. Comput. Digit. Tech.*, vol. 138, no. 4, pp. 241–249, 1991.

[10] P. D. Hortensius et al., "Cellular automata based pseudo-random number generators for built-in self-test," vol. 8, no. 8, pp. 842–859, August 1989.

[11] D. Roy Chowdhury, *Theory and Applications of Additive Cellular Automata for Reliable and Testable VLSI Circuit Design*, Ph.D. thesis, I.I.T. Kharagpur, India, 1992.

[12] D. Roy Chowdhury and P. Pal Chaudhuri, "Parallel memory testing: a BIST approach," in *Proc. 3rd Intl. Workshop on VLSI Design*. Bangalore, India, 1989, pp. 373–377.

[13] A. K. Das, *Additive Cellular Automata: Theory and Application as a Built-in Self-test Structure*, Ph.D. thesis, I.I.T. Kharagpur, India, 1990.

[14] D. E. Knuth, *The Art of Computer Programming – Seminumerical Algorithms*, Addison-Wesley, 1981.

[15] F. R. Gantmatcher, *The Theory of Matrices*, Vol 11, Chelsea Publishing Co., NY., 1959.

[16] S. W. Golomb, *Shift Register Sequences*, Holden Day, 1967.

[17] B. Elspas, "The theory of autonomos linear sequential networks," *TRE Trans. on Circuits*, vol. CT-6, no. 1, pp. 45–60, March 1959.

[18] Subhayan Sen, Chandrama Shaw, D. Roy Chowdhury, Niloy Ganguly, and P. Pal Chaudhuri, "Cellular automata based cryptosystem (cac)," in *Proc. of ICICS 2002*. Singapore, December 2002, pp. 303–314.

[19] Monalisa Mukherjee, Niloy Ganguly, and P. Pal Chaudhuri, "Cellular automata based authentication (caa)," in *Proceedings of ACRI 2002*. Geneva, Switzerland, October 2002, pp. 259–269.

[20] P. Pal Chaudhury, D. Roy Chowdhury, I. Sengupta, "Ca-based byte error correcting code," in *IEEE Transactions on Computers*. 1995, pp. 371–382, IEEE.

[21] P. Pal Chaudhury, S. Chakraborty, D. Roy Chowdhury, "Theory and application of nongroup cellular automata for synthesis of easily testable finite state machines," in *IEEE Transactions on Computers*. 1996, pp. 769–781, IEEE.

Block Encryption Using Reversible Cellular Automata

Marcin Seredynski[1,2] and Pascal Bouvry[2]

[1] Polish-Japanese Institute of Information Technology, Research Center
Koszykowa 86, 02-008 Warsaw, Poland
seredynski@acn.waw.pl
[2] Luxembourg University of Applied Sciences
6, rue Coudenhove Kalergi, L-1359, Luxembourg-Kirchberg, Luxembourg
pascal.bouvry@univ.lu

Abstract. Cellular automata (CA) are highly parallel and discrete dynamical systems, whose behavior is completely specified in terms of a local relation. They were successfully applied for simulation of biological systems and physical phenomena and recently to design parallel and distributed algorithms for solving task density and synchronization problems. In this paper CA are applied to construct cryptography algorithms. A new encryption concept based on one dimensional, uniform and reversible CA is proposed. A class of CA with rules specifically constructed to be reversible is used.

1 Introduction

Since the development of computers there has been strong demand for means to protect information and to provide various security services. The main aspects of information security are privacy, data integrity, authentication, and non-repudiation. This paper deals with encryption that is transformation of the message (plaintext) in to ciphertext and the opposite process that is decryption. These two complementary operations satisfy the demand of privacy. Cryptographic techniques are divided into two categories [5]: symmetric-key and public key. If both sender and receiver use the same key, or it is easy to obtain one form another then the system is referred to as symmetric key encryption. If the sender and receiver each uses different key, ant it is computationally infeasible to determine one form another without knowing some additional secret information then the system is referred to as a public key encryption. There are two classes of symmetric-key encryption schemes: block ciphers and stream ciphers. A block cipher breaks up the message into blocks of the fixed length and encrypts one block at a time. A stream cipher is one that encrypts data stream one bit or one byte at a time.

Good overview of all major cryptography techniques can be found in [5]. Description of block ciphers including AES cipher is presented in [8]. This paper deals with symmetric-key block encryption. CA have been used so far in both symmetric-key and public-key cryptography. CA-based public cipher was proposed by Guan [2]. Stream CA-based encryption algorithm was first proposed by Wolfram [13] and later it was developed by Tommassini et al. [10], and recently by Seredynski et al. [6]. Block cipher using reversible and irreversible rules was proposed by Gutowitz [3].

P.M.A. Sloot, B. Chopard, and A.G. Hoekstra (Eds.): ACRI 2004, LNCS 3305, pp. 785–792, 2004.
© Springer-Verlag Berlin Heidelberg 2004

This paper presents a new encryption concept based on a class of reversible rules specially designed to be reversible.

The paper is organized as follows. The next section defines elementary and reversible CA. Section 3 presents the idea how a particular class of reversible CA can be used for block encryption. Experiment results are presented in section 4. Section 5 concludes the paper.

2 Cellular Automata

2.1 Elementary Cellular Automata

One-dimensional CA is an array of cells. Each cell is assigned a value over some state alphabet. CA is defined by four parameters: size, initial state, neighborhood, rule and boundary conditions. Size defines number of cells. All cells update its value synchronously in discrete time steps accordingly to some rule. Such rule is based on the state of the cell itself and its neighborhood:

$$s_i^{t+1} = R(s_{i-r}^t, ..., s_{i-1}^t, s_i^t, s_{i+1}^t, ..., s_{i+r}^t), \tag{1}$$

where s_i^t is a value of i-th cell (the state of a cell) in step t and r is a radius of the neighborhood. When dealing with finite CA, cyclic boundary conditions are usually applied which means that CA can be treated as a ring. Changing values of all cells in step t is called CA iteration. Before the first iteration can take place some initial values must be assigned to all cells. This is called the initial state of CA. By updating values in all cells, the initial state is transformed into a new configuration. When each cell updates its state according to the same rule, CA is said to be uniform. Otherwise it is called non-uniform CA. The total number of rules for radius r neighborhood is 2^n, where $n = 2^{2*r+1}$. In this paper one-dimensional, uniform CA defined over binary state alphabet (cells can be either in state 0 or 1) with neighborhood size two and three is used.

2.2 Reversible Cellular Automata

By applying a rule to each cell s_i of the configuration q_t a new configuration q_{t+1} is obtained. This transformation can also be defined by a global transition function, which as an input takes configuration q_t and results in a successive configuration q_{t+1}. A CA is reversible if and only if the global transition function is one-to-one that is if every configuration not only has one successor but also has one predecessor.

Reversible rules that could by useful in cryptography should meet the following criteria: they should be numerous and they should exhibit complex behavior. When analyzing elementary CA it turns out that only a small number of rules have the property of being reversible. For example, among all 256 radius 1 CA of only six are reversible. This is why class of CA with rules specially created to be reversible is considered. Different reversible CA classes are presented in [9]. This paper presents the idea of using reversible CA class presented by Wolfram [12]. In this class rule depends not on one but on two steps back:

$$s_i^{t+1} = R(s_{i-r}^t, ..., s_{i-1}^t, s_i^t, s_i^{t-1}, s_{i+1}^t, ..., s_{i+r}^t). \tag{2}$$

In the elementary CA value s_i^{t+1} of i-th cell in configuration $t+1$ depends on the value of the state of itself and r of its neighbors in configuration t. In this reversible class additional dependency is added: the value of the central cell s_i^{t-1} in step t-1 is considered. Such a rule can be simply constructed by taking elementary CA rule and adding dependency on two steps back. Example of such rule definition is shown on Fig. 1.

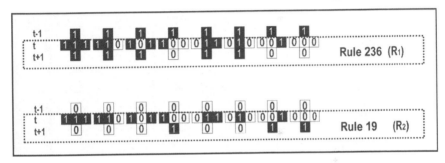

Fig. 1. Reversible rule 236/19

Definition of the rule is now composed of two elementary rules. The first one is defining state transition in case when in step t-1 cell was in a state 1, and the second one when the cell was in the state 0. Figure 1 gives an example of two elementary rules: 236 and rule 19. These two rules are complementary to each other. Knowing one value it is possible to calculate the second one using the following formula:

$$R_2 = 2^d - R_1 - 1, \tag{3}$$

where $d = 2^{2*r+1}$, and r is radius of the neighborhood. Since a reversible rule depends now on two steps back, an initial configuration must be composed of two successive configurations q_0 and q_1. The same rule is used in forward and backward iteration.

3 The Idea of Using Reversible CA for Encryption

First encryption and decryption algorithm of a single plaintext block is shown. When using reversible CA described in the previous section, plaintext is encoded as part of initial state of a CA (q_1). Configuration q_0 is set up with some random data. Both configurations form an initial state of CA. Encryption is done by forward iteration of CA by fixed number of steps according to some reversible rule. This process is shown on Fig. 2.

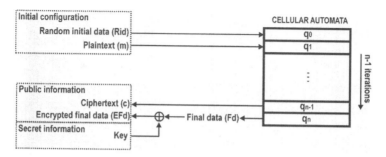

Fig. 2. Single block encryption using reversible cellular automata

Configuration q_{n-1} is a ciphertext. The rule used during encryption is a secret *key* of that transformation. There are two options on how to treat configuration q_n (called final data) generated by the encryption process. The most secure one assumes that this information is kept secret, which means that configuration q_n becomes a part of the key. The disadvantage of this option is that the *key* changes with each encryption. This is because now the *key* is a function of a rule, plaintext and some initial data (Rid). In the second option the final configuration q_n is encrypted using Vernam encryption algorithm. This is done by applying logical bitwise operation XOR ($\oplus$) on the final configuration q_n and selected bits of the *key*.

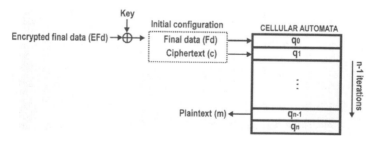

Fig. 3. Single block decryption using reversible cellular automata

Decryption algorithm is shown on Fig. 3. The same operations as in encryption are used in reverse order. Initial state is composed of the final data and the ciphertext. To obtain final data for the decryption, XOR operation must be applied first to encrypted final data and the *key*. Next, CA is iterated for the same number of steps as during encryption with use of the same secret rule.

In practice plaintext is divided into many fixed size blocks. Each block is encrypted separately. Typical block size for encryption algorithms is 64 or 128 bits. The algorithm for successive blocks encryption is shown on the Fig. 4.

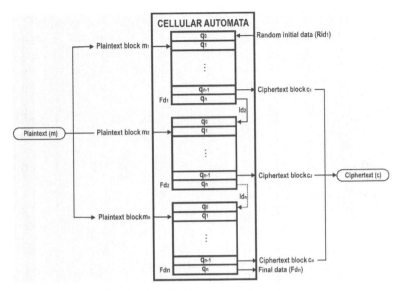

Fig. 4. Multiple block encryption scheme

Plaintext is divided into n fixed size blocks. For the encryption of the first plaintext block random initial data is used. For the blocks number 2..n initial data is taken from the encryption of the previous block. Final data generated by the encryption of the i-th plaintext block is used for the encryption of the $i+1$ block. Final data produced by the encryption of the last plaintext block can be either encrypted using XOR operation or kept secret.

4   Experiments

Desirable property of any encryption algorithm is that a small change in either plaintext or the key should result in a significant change in the ciphertext. Changing value of one randomly chosen bit in the plaintext or in the key should produce change of nearly half of the values of the ciphertext. This is so called *avalanche property*. It was introduced by H. Feistel in 1973 [1]. Later Kam and Davida gave the concept of *completeness* [4]. It says that for every possible key value, every output bit of the ciphertext must depends upon all input bits of the plaintext and not just a proper subset of the input bits. The concepts of completeness and the avalanche effect was combined by Webster and Tavares. They defined so called *strict avalanche criterion* (SAC) [11]. According to this property, each output bit should change with a probability of one half whenever a single input bit is complemented.

Number of iterations needed to achieve this property depends on the radius of the rule and the size of CA. We have tested 32 and 64 cell CA. For each size radius 2 and radius 3 rules were used. The following results are based on 10000 experiments for each parameters set (CA size/radius/iteration number). For each experiment random initial conditions and random rules were used.

The following figures show dependency between number of iterations and percentage of states changed after one bit was changed either in the plaintext or in the ciphertext. Fig. 5 shows that dependency for 32 cell radius 2 CA while Fig. 6 shows it for 64 cell radius 3 CA.

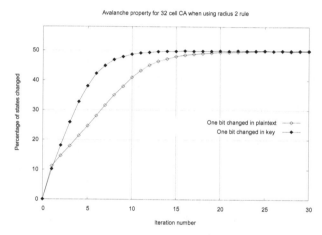

Fig. 5. Avalanche property for 32 cell CA and radius 2 rule

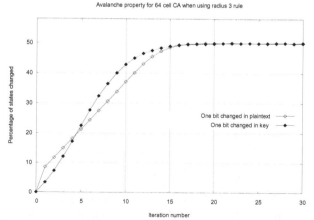

Fig. 6. Avalanche property for 64 cell CA and radius 3 rule

Table 1. Result for one random bit changed in the plaintext

	radius 2	radius 3
32 cells CA	19	8
64 cells CA	38	17

Table 2. Result for one random bit changed in the ciphertext

	radius 2	radius 3
32 cells CA	12	20
64 cells CA	11	16

Table 1 shows number of iteration needed to achieve the state in which over 49 % of cells change its value after changing one bit in the plaintext. Results are shown for 32 and 64 cell CA with neighborhood size 2 and 3.

Number of iteration needed to achieve the same result after changing one bit in the ciphertext is shown in Table 2.

After iterating CA for number of steps given in Table 1 and Table 2 strict avalanche effect is achieved. On average nearly half of cells are changed. The probability that a single cell is going to change it's value after that number of iterations is around 0.5. The example for 64 cell CA with radius 3 neighborhood is shown on the Fig. 7.

For the other parameters the result is similar (0.48 - 0.52 interval).

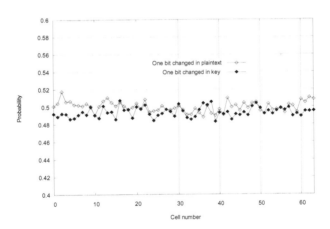

Fig. 7. Probability of cell state value change

5 Algorithm Properties

Our reversible CA-based algorithm works in a mode that is similar to CBC mode in terms of achieved result. The same plaintext block that appears in the whole plaintext more than once produces different block of ciphertext. This is because encryption of each plaintext block starts with some initial data from the encryption of the previous block. In DES like ciphers there is still problem with encryption (using the same key) of the same plaintext more than once, or when two encrypted plaintext begin with the same information. In the first case the same ciphertext will be produced, while in the second case both plaintext will be encrypted the same way until the first difference is reached. It is possible to overcome this problem with encryption of some random data block (called initialization vector) first. In the proposed cipher encrypting the same plaintext with the same key will always result in a different ciphertext. This is achieved because of use of randomly generated data in the first phase of each encryption session. This data needs not to be remembered.

6   Conclusions

In this paper we have proposed a new encryption concept based on reversible CA. It ensures that strict avalanche criterion is achieved. Encryption using a single reversible CA does not provide enough security. Multiple reversible CA should be used for encryption of a single plaintext block. Detailed description of a block cipher based on this concept can be found in [7].

References

1. Feistel, H.: Cryptography and Computer Privacy, Scientific American 228(5). (1973) 15-23
2. Guan, P.: Cellular Automaton Public-Key Cryptosystem. Complex Systems 1 (1987) 51-56
3. Gutowitz, H.: Cryptography with Dynamical Systems, manuscript
4. Kam, J., Davida, G.: Structured Design of Substitution-Permutation Encryption Networks, IEEE Transactions on Computers. C-28(10). (1979) 747-753
5. Menezes, A., van Oorschot, P., Vanstone, S.: Handbook of Applied Cryptography, CRC Press (1996)
6. Seredynski, F., Bouvry, P., Zomaya, A.Y.: Cellular Programming and Symmetric Key Cryptography Systems. In: E.Cantú-Paz et al. (eds.): Genetic and Evolutionary Computation – GECCO 2003. LNCS 2724. Part II. Springer (2003) 1369-1381
7. Seredynski, M., Pienkosz, K., Bouvry, P.: Reversible Cellular Automata Based Encryption, IFIP International Conference on Network and Parallel Computing (NPC 2004), Wuhan, China, 18-20.10.2004. LNCS. Springer, (2004) (to appear)
8. Stallings, W.: Cryptography and Network Security, 3rd ed, Prentice Hall. (2003)
9. Toffoli, T., Margolus, N.: Invertible cellular automata: a review. Physica D 666. North-Holland, Amsterdam (1997)
10. Tomassini, M., Perrenoud, M.: Stream Ciphers with One and Two-Dimensional Cellular Automata. In: M. Schoenauer et al. (eds.): Parallel Problem Solving from Nature – PPSN VI. LNCS 1917. Springer (2000) 722-731
11. Webster, A.F., Tavares, S.E.: On the Design of S-Boxes, Advances in Cryptology : Crypto '85 Proceedings. Springer. LNCS 218. Springer (1985) 523-534
12. Wolfram, S.: A New Kind of Science, Wolfram Media (2002) 435-441
13. Wolfram, S.: Cryptography with Cellular Automata in Advances in Cryptology : Crypto '85Proceedings. LNCS 218. Springer (1985) 429-432

Cellular Model of Complex Porous Media Application to Permeability Determination*

André Chambarel, Hervé Bolvin, and Evelyne Ferry

UMR A 1114 Climate-Soil-Environment
Faculté des Sciences – 33 rue Louis Pasteur
F-84000 Avignon (France)
andre.chambarel@univ-avignon.fr

Abstract. In soil science we need complex porous media models. Usually these media present discontinuous characteristics with random space distribution. So we propose to study a medium based on a cellular model. In this work we represent the soil as a compact matter associated with vacuum areas. Under these conditions we study the flux of water through this medium. We formulate the hypothesis that it is composed of a mixture of two different permeability values. The medium is discretized with tetrahedral cells and we dedicate permeability to each cell with a random space distribution. We associate to each cell an inner and an outer physical law and we test the flux of water through this medium. So we introduce a physical consideration in a cellular model. We also present a study for several scales of the problem.

1 Introduction

Many models of flux through porous media are based on partial differential equations [1]. There results that these models based on the resolution of a partial differential problem become inefficient because we have non-derivable functions [2] [3] in the case of such a complex porous medium as a soil. Stochastic approaches based on the resolution of partial differential problems notably pose the questions of the continuity of the functions representing the medium's physical properties. To solve this problem, discretized approaches based on a cellular model are used. We can find in bibliographies for example LBM and LBA [4] [5] methods based on the statistical mechanics. We propose a cellular model of complex porous media by the introduction of two laws:

- an inner law for the filtration model through the cell,
- an outer law for communication with the connected cells.

As an example, we propose the Darcy law for filtration inner law; other laws are possible [2]. We study the case of a saturated medium, so as to preserve the flux balance through the sides of the tetrahedral cells.

---

* This work was supported by French National Program in Hydrology (PNRH/ACI).

P.M.A. Sloot, B. Chopard, and A.G. Hoekstra (Eds.): ACRI 2004, LNCS 3305, pp. 793–802, 2004.

2 Theoretical Approach

If V is the local velocity and Q_v a source term, the conservative law of the flow in domain (Ω) can be written:

$$\oint_{\Gamma(\Omega)} \vec{V}.\vec{n}.dS + \int_{(\Omega)} Q_v.dv = 0 \tag{1}$$

Through the application of Green's theorem, we obtain:

$$\int_{(\Omega)} div\,\vec{V}.dv + \int_{(\Omega)} Q_v.dv = 0 \tag{2}$$

The application of Green's theorem is possible if velocity V is derivable and if pressure P is a continuous function. Under these conditions we obtain:

$$\begin{aligned} div\,\vec{V} + Q_v &= 0 \qquad in\ (\Omega) \\ \vec{V} &= -K.\overrightarrow{grad}\ P \qquad Darcy\ law \end{aligned} \tag{3}$$

The usual boundary conditions in our problem are:

$$\vec{V}.\vec{n} = -K.\frac{\partial P}{\partial n} = \left(\frac{d\phi}{dS}\right)_\Gamma \qquad on\ (\Gamma_1) \tag{4}$$

$$P = P_\Gamma \quad on\ (\Gamma_2)\ and\ \Gamma_1 \bigcup \Gamma_2 = \Gamma(\Omega)$$

This approach is based on the continuous and derivable functions. In the case of complex property K, the validity of Green's theorem (2) is not obvious in regard to the partial differential model. It is in this context that we propose our approach.

2.1 The Principle

We build a set of physical, mathematical and numerical models. We divide domain (Ω) in sub-domains (Ω_i) called cells. So we have:

$$(\Omega) = \bigcup (\Omega_i) \quad and \quad (\Omega_i) \bigcap (\Omega_j) = \varnothing\ (i \neq j) \tag{5}$$

By introduction of the inner law, the mathematical model for each cell (Ω_i) becomes:

$$\begin{aligned} \vec{V} &= -K_i.\overrightarrow{grad}\ P \\ div\,\vec{V} + Q_v &= 0 \qquad in\ (\Omega_i)\ \ i = 1..n \end{aligned} \tag{6}$$

Here we do not consider a volumic source. So the variational formulation of the problem for the full domain can be written:

$$\sum_i \int_{(\Omega_i)} \delta P.div(K_i.\overrightarrow{grad}\ P).d\Omega_i = 0 \tag{7}$$

With Green's theorem we obtain the classical expression:

$$\sum_i \int_{(\Omega_i)} \overrightarrow{grad}\,\delta P.K_i.\overrightarrow{grad}\,P.d\Omega_i - \sum_i \int_{(\Gamma_i)} \delta P.K_i.\frac{\partial P}{\partial n}.d\Gamma_i = 0 \qquad (8)$$

In the second integral in formula (8), it is possible to introduce the outer law for each side of the cells. For this reason this method differs from the finite element formulation. Under this condition and for the inner sides, these terms are zero. For the other sides associated with the outer boundary of (Ω) it depends on the applied boundary conditions. So we can see that this variational formulation contains the two laws of the cellular model. In fact scalar field P is computed with a technique similar to the finite element method [6].

2.2 The Numerical Model

For the numerical model we choose a medium (a soil for example) made up of compact matter and a few vacuum areas. So we consider a mixture of two media with respective permeability values:

- K_1 low dimensionless value for compact matter
- K_2 high dimensionless value for vacuum

To build this mixture we introduce in medium 1 a small volumetric ratio α of medium 2. Under these conditions we can study the 3D flow through a cubic cavity to which we apply a unit difference of pressure between two opposite sides. The other sides are waterproof [7].

In each cell we use a linear approximation of the pressure by using the vertex of the tetrahedral cells as nodal interpolation. So the pressure is a continuous function in full domain (Ω).

So it is possible to transform the variational formulation into a linear system with the nodal value of the pressure. For resolution of this, we use a classical sky-line storage associated with a direct (L) (U) method [6].

3 Numerical Study

Tests are performed in the cubic cavity and we compute the following flux through entrance surface (S):

$$\phi = \int_{(S)} \overrightarrow{V}.\vec{n}.dS = - \int_{(S)} K_n.\overrightarrow{grad}\,P.\vec{n}.dS \qquad (9)$$

We define an equivalent permeability coefficient K_{eq} by formula (10):

$$\phi = K_{eq}.(P_2 - P_1) \qquad (10)$$

The exact solution in a homogeneous medium with property K is:

$$P = -K.(1-x) \quad and \quad \phi = K \qquad (11)$$

For an α-value we build 1000 successive random space distributions of $(K_1\text{-}K_2)$ in each test. So we obtain a probability accuracy of 0.1%.

3.1 The 3D-Model

To do so, we construct a cubic volume of normalized length side, and we apply a unit-difference of pressure between two opposite faces. A random α-distribution $(K_1\text{-}K_2)$ of element property of the mixture is done. Calculations of the corresponding flux and the equivalent permeability are carried out. For the cubic volume, we build a regular meshing [2] with a number of cells 40,000–320,000. In Figure 1, we can see the meshing of the cube.

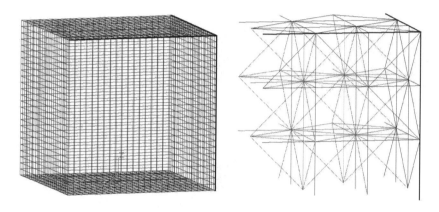

Fig. 1. The meshing.

In a first approach the K_1 and K_2-values present a ratio of 10^6. It is possible to find these values in porous media. In Figure 2 we note a percolation-like effect close to 3.5-4 % [8] [9] [10]. It is interesting to study this transition flow more specifically.

We note a very large scale of flux values. So we use a logarithmic scale for the data analysis. Figures 3 show profiles of log (ϕ) respectively for α-values of 3, 3.5 and 4%. We notice the cohabitation of very distinct regimes of the flux in the shape of two different gaussian curves. The theorem of the central limit shows the presence of two probability laws for flow through the cavity.

After analysis of the post-processing iso-values of P, the left curve merely corresponds to a diffusive flux while the right curve corresponds to the presence of a preferential flow area (Figure 4). This set of curves shows the transition between a merely diffusive regime and a regime of preferential flow. Beyond 4%, the flow essentially translates in the shape of a preferential flow, and beyond 3%, the flow is practically always a diffusive phenomenon. In fact the corresponding probability becomes very weak, but it is not equivalent to zero.

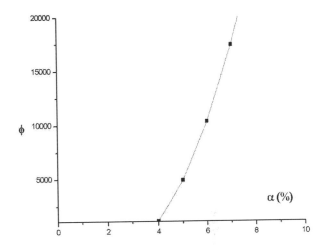

Fig. 2. Flux evolution according to volumetric ratio.

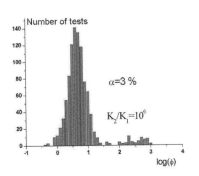

Fig. 3a. Gaussian profile (α=3 %)

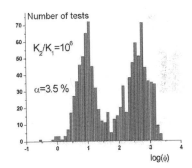

Fig. 3b. Gaussian profile (α=3.5 %)

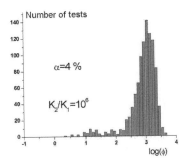

Fig. 3c. Gaussian profile (α=4 %)

It can also be interpreted physically. Indeed, in the case of a merely diffusive flow, elements (K_2) distribute themselves more or less regularly, while the preferential flow corresponds to agglomerates of elements putting the two faces of the cube in quasi-communication. The illustrations presented in Figure 4 show the large diversity of the flows.

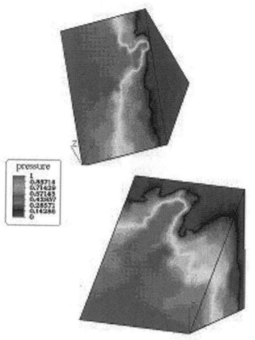

Fig. 4. Preferential flow.

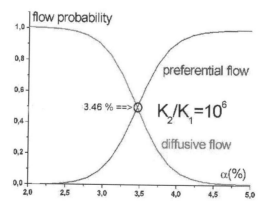

Fig. 5. Transition flow.

We notice that the introduction of some high permeability cells in a medium that is relatively weak, introduces a very important disruption. In the transition area, we observe a chaotic behaviour of the iso-pressure surfaces, therefore of the filtration speed, notably in the case of a preferential flow. Beyond the percolation area, the flux becomes regular with only one gaussian distribution (Figures 6).

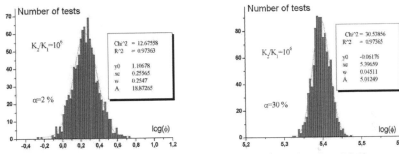

Fig. 6. Flux distribution for volumetric ratios $\alpha = 2\ \%$ and $\alpha = 30\ \%$.

3.2 Normal Flow

Figures 6 present the permeability probability law respectively for an α-ratio below and beyond the transition threshold [11]. We notice in both cases a log-normal distribution for permeability with a correlation coefficient greater than 0.97.

So we obtain the empirical law used by hydro-geologists [2]. We establish that a soil with a log-normal distribution of permeability can be modelized by a mixture of several media with constant permeability. We can thus deduce that the physical approach of soil permeability is more realistic with our model.

3.3 Other Cases

Now we can study the problem for different values of ratio K_2/K_1, which corresponds to different physical problems. It is interesting to examine the nature of the flow in the area of a transition threshold of 3.5%. Figures 7 present the distribution of the fluxes for ratios 10^9, 10^6 and 10^5. We notice the increasing proximity of the two regimes of flux, then their fusion when ratio K_2/K_1 becomes lower than 10^6, also the progressive disappearance of the preferential flow. In fact we hereby demonstrate that we have a critical value of ratio K_2/K_1 below which we cannot distinguish two distinctive flows. The proximity of the two values of K does not allow us to work out the nature of the flow anymore, and in particular, the concept of preferential flow disappears. This phenomenon can exist in porous media and electrical conduction whereas the thermal model is at the frontier of this peculiarity. Above the limit value of K_2/K_1 we notice that fluxes inferior to 1 disappear.

Figures 7 show the evolution of the flux distribution according to ratio K_2/K_1. The left gaussian curve is set at flux ϕ_0 and the right gaussian curve comes closer when the preceding ratio decreases. Both curves coincide if the ratio is lower than the following critical value:

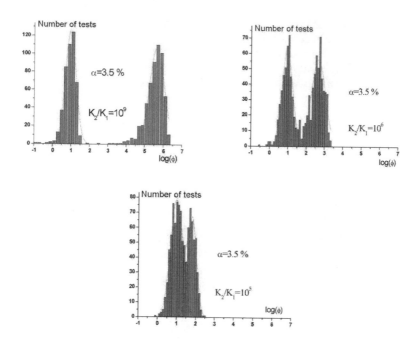

Fig. 7. Evolution of the flux distribution according to ratio K_2/K_1.

$$\frac{K_2}{K_1} = 14638 \pm 3\%$$

We notice a linear law in Figure 8. We can write:

$$\log\left(\frac{K_2}{K_1}\right) = a.\log\left(\frac{\phi}{\phi_0}\right) + b \quad with \quad a \approx 1$$

$$\frac{K_2}{K_1} = \left(\frac{K_2}{K_1}\right)_{critical} . \frac{\phi}{\phi_0}$$

As regards the physical problem, these are the situations that we may come across. We can mention the example of the porous environment met in soil science, an environment which is constituted of earth and cavities [1]. The doping of the semiconductors is another example in the domain of electric conductivity [10]. Another qualitative example concerns the cardiac muscle. Indeed, if some cells of the heart present abnormal electric conductivity, some important unrests of the rhythm appear. A few sick cells destroyed by the surgeon will allow the patient's heart to go back to normal [13].

For electrostatic problems, where K_2/K_1 ratio is at a maximum of 81, the probability of two regimes is not detectable. This is what is noted in practice [14].

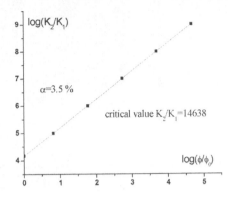

Fig. 8. Evolution of ratio K_2/K_1.

4   Conclusion

In this study, the finite element method is used in a specific approach. It facilitates the construction of a numerical model without being representative of the approximate solution of the partial differential equations. The mathematical model is only a temporary support permitting the elaboration of a weak formulation. The consistency of this approach resides in the fact that the weak formulation preserves, in a rigorous way, the physical principle that allowed the constitution of the mathematical model. In the examples concerned, we have used a vector model with a conservative flux. This approach applies particularly well to a survey of surroundings with complex physical properties that notably present strong discontinuity. The interest is reinforced in the particular case of percolation phenomena. This method allows a new approach of the survey of the porous media's complex features. In the latter case, we used the Darcy model. Many authors agree and say that this model does not give entire satisfaction, but our approach confers a new interest to the Darcy model. However, it is clear that the approach used in this work does not limit itself to this type of models. Besides, for convenience reasons, some spatial correlations permit to take in account a more realistic shape of the properties of porous media. To speak only of the porous media, we can apply the same process to Richard's equation used, in particular, for unsaturated porous media. In a more general way, many physical models based on a balance between conservative and non conservative fluxes can be studied thanks to this method.

Acknowledgment. The authors would like to thank Ralph Beisson for his contribution to the English composition of this paper.

References

1. Le Tong E., Anguy Y., Ehrlich R., Ahmadi A.: Evaluation of Porous Microstructures Generated in a Stochastic Manner from Thin Section Data. Image Analysis & Stereology, Vol. 202, Supp. 1 (2000) 425-431
2. Birkholzer J., Tsang C.F.: Flow Channeling in Unsatured Porous Media of Strong Heterogeneity. Proceedings of the first GAMM-seminar at ICA Stuttgart (October 12-13, 1995)
3. Mauri G., Bandini S., Pavesi G.: Parallel Generation of Percolation Beds Based on Stochastic Cellular Automata. 6th International Conference, PACT 2001, Novosibirsk, Russia (September 3-7, 2001)
4. Koponen A., Kandhai D., Hellén E., Alava M., Hoekstra A., Kataja M., Niskanen, K., Sloot P., and Timonen J.: Permeability of Three-Dimensional Random Fiber Webs. Phys. Rev. Lett. Vol.80 (4) (1998) 716–719
5. Kandhai D., Hlushkou D., Hoekstra A., Sloot P. M. A., Van As H. and Tallarek U. : Influence of Stagnant Zones on Transient and Asymptotic Dispersion in Macroscopically Homogeneous Porous Media. Phys. Rev. Lett., Vol.88 (2002) 234501-1 – 234501-4.
6. Dhatt G., Touzot .G : Une Présentation de la Méthode des Eléments Finis (in French). Editions Maloine S.A., Paris (1981)
7. Chambarel A., Bolvin H.: Numerical Model of Complex Porous Media. Proceedings of IMECE 2002, ASME International Mechanical Engineering Congress, New Orleans, Louisiana (November 17-22, 2002)
8. Bandman O.: A Hybrid Approach to Reaction-Diffusion Processes Simulation. Proceeding of 6th International Conference, PACT 2001, Novosibirsk, Russia (September 3-7, 2001)
9. Grimmet G.: Percolation. North Holland (1989)
10. Kirkpatrick S.: Percolation and Conduction. Rev. Mod. Phys., Vol. 45 (1971) 574-588.
11. Gelhar L.W., Axness C.L.: Three Dimensional Stochastic Analysis of Macrodispersion in Aquifers. Water Resour. Res., Vol. 19 (1983) 161
12. Wen H.J., Prietsch M., Bauer A., Cuberes M.T., Manke I., Kaindl G.: p+-Doping of Si by Al Diffusion upon Annealing Al/n-Si(111)7 7. Appl. Phys. Lett., Vol. 66 (1995) 3010
13. Cascio W.E., Johnson T.A., Gettes L.S.: Electrophysiologic Changes in Ventricular Myocardium: Influence of Ionic, Metabolic and Energetic Changes. J. Cardiovasc. Electrophysiol. Vol. 6 (1995) 1039-1062
14. Tabbagh C., Camerlinck C., Cosenza P.: Numerical Modelling for Investigating the Physical Meaning of the Relationship between Relative Dielectric Permittivity and Water Content of Soils. Water Resour. Res., Vol. 36 (9) (2000) 2771-2776

Improved Cell-DEVS Model Definition in CD++

Alejandro López[1] and Gabriel Wainer[2]

[1]Computer Science Department. Universidad de Buenos Aires
Ciudad Universitaria (1428). Buenos Aires. Argentina.
[2]Department of Systems and Computer Engineering. Carleton University
1125 Colonel By Dr. Ottawa, ON. K1S 5B6. Canada.

Abstract. We describe two improvements made to CD++, a tool for modeling and simulation of cellular models based on the Cell-DEVS formalism. The modifications described in this work remove some limitations existing in the previous implementation. These modifications allow the cells to use multiple state variables and multiple ports for inter-cell communication. The cellular model specification language has been extended to cover these cases, making CD++ a more powerful tool.

1 Introduction

The Cell-DEVS formalism [1] was defined as an extension to Cellular Automata combined with DEVS (Discrete Event systems Specification) [2], a formalism for specification of discrete-event models. The DEVS formalism provides a framework for the construction of hierarchical modular models, allowing for model reuse, reducing development and testing times. In DEVS, basic models (called **atomic**) are specified as black boxes, and several DEVS models can be integrated together forming a hierarchical structural model (called **coupled**). DEVS not only proposes a framework for model construction, but also defines an abstract simulation mechanism that is independent of the model itself. A DEVS atomic model defined as:

$$DEVS = < X, Y, S, \delta_{ext}, \delta_{int}, \lambda, ta>$$

In the absence of external events, a DEVS model will remain in state $s \in S$ during $ta(s)$. Transitions that occur due to the expiration of $ta(s)$ are called internal transitions. When an internal transition takes place, the system outputs the value $\lambda(s) \in Y$, and changes to the state defined by $\delta_{int}(s)$. Upon reception of an external event, $\delta_{ext}(s, e, x)$ is activated using the input value $x \in X$, the current state s and the time elapsed since the last transition e. Coupled models are defined as:

$$DN = < X, Y, D, \{M_i\}, \{I_i\}, \{Z_{ij}\}>$$

Coupled models consist of a set of basic models (Mi, atomic or coupled) connected through the models' interfaces. Component identifications are stored into an index (D). A translation function (Zij) is defined by using an index of influencees created for each model (Ii). The function defines which outputs of model Mi are connected to inputs in model Mj.

P.M.A. Sloot, B. Chopard, and A.G. Hoekstra (Eds.): ACRI 2004, LNCS 3305, pp. 803–812, 2004.

Cell-DEVS defines a cell as a DEVS atomic model and a cell space as a coupled model. Each cell of a Cell-DEVS model holds a state variable and a computing function, which updates the cell state by using its present state and its neighborhood. A Cell-DEVS atomic model is defined as:

$$TDC = < X, Y, S, N, delay, d, \delta_{INT}, \delta_{EXT}, \tau, \lambda, D >$$

A cell uses a set of N input values to compute its future state, which is obtained by applying the local function τ. A delay function is associated with each cell, after which, the new state value is sent out. There are two types of delays: inertial and transport. When a transport delay is used, every value scheduled for output will be transmitted. Inertial delays use a preemptive policy: any previous scheduled output will be preempted unless its value is the same as the new computed one. After the basic behavior for a cell is defined, a complete cell space can be built as a coupled Cell-DEVS:

$$GCC = < Xlist, Ylist, I, X, Y, n, \{t_1,...,t_n\}, N, C, B, Z >$$

A coupled Cell-DEVS is composed of an array of atomic cells (C), each of which is connected to the cells in the neighborhood (N). The border cells (B) can have a different behavior than the rest of the space. The Z function defines the internal and external coupling of cells in the model. This function translates the outputs of mth output port in cell C_{ij} into values for the mth input port of cell C_{kl}. Each output port will correspond to one neighbor and each input port will be associated with one cell in the inverse neighborhood. The Xlist and Ylist are used for defining the coupling with external models.

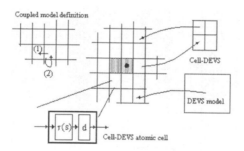

Fig. 1. Informal definition of a Cell-DEVS model [3]

Using Cell-DEVS has different advantages. First, we have asynchronous model execution, which, as showed in [3], results in improved execution times. Timing constructions permit defining complex conditions for the cells in a simple fashion, as showed in [4, 5]. As DEVS models are closed under coupling, seamless integration with other types of models in different formalisms is possible. The independent simulation mechanisms permit these models to be executed interchangeably in single-processor, parallel or real-time simulators without any changes.

The CD++ tool [6] was created for the simulation of DEVS and Cell-DEVS models based on the formal specifications in [1]. This version of the tool and the formalism was used to study a variety of models including traffic, forest fires, biological systems and experiments in chemistry [4, 5, 7, 8]. While developing these models, we found that Cell-DEVS formal specifications and CD++ implementation lacked on expressiveness when defining very complex applications. We were able to solve some of these problems with the n-dimensional Cell-DEVS definition presented in [9], which permitted us to store different state variables in each dimension of a cell space. Nevertheless, as this organization require extra work from the modelers, and is time-consuming, we decided to add new facilities to CD++. We will show how to define different state variables for each cell, and to declare and use multiple inter-cell ports to communicate with the neighbors, which permitted to improve the definition of complex models.

Other cellular automata languages as CARPET [10] and Cellang [11] include these features which are new to CD++. However, these languages use different approaches from the one used in CD++. CARPET is a procedural language while CD++ is logical (as Prolog is) and Cellang is a mix. With the new extensions to CD++, it is leveraged in capabilities to these two languages.

2 The CD++ Toolkit

CD++ [6] is a tool built to implement DEVS and Cell-DEVS theory. The tool allows defining models according to the specifications introduced in the previous section. DEVS atomic models can be incorporated into a class hierarchy in C++, while coupled models are defined using a built-in specification language. The tool also includes an interpreter for a specification language that allows describing Cell-DEVS models.

The behavior specification of a Cell-DEVS atomic model is defined using a set of rules, each indicating the future value for the cell's state if a precondition is satisfied. The local computing function evaluates the first rule, and if the precondition does not hold, the following rules are evaluated until one of them is satisfied or there are no more rules. The behavior of the local computing function is defined using a set of rules with the form: VALUE DELAY { CONDITION }. These indicate that when the CONDITION is satisfied, the state of the cell changes to the designated VALUE, and its output is DELAYed for the specified time. The main operators available to define rules and delays include: boolean, comparison, arithmetic, neighborhood values, time, conditionals, angle conversion, pseudo-random numbers, error rounding and constants (i.e., gravitation, acceleration, light, Planck, etc.) [12].

```
[ex]
width : 20      height : 40      border : wrapped
neighbors : (-1,-1) (-1,0) (-1,1) (0,-1)  (0,0)  (0,1)
neighbors : (1,-1)  (1,0)  (1,1)
localtransition : tau-function

[tau-function]
rule: 1 100 {(0,0)=1 and (truecount=8 or truecount=10)}
rule: 1 200 {(0,0) = 0 and truecount >= 10 }
rule: (0,0) 150 { t }
```

Fig. 2. A Cell-DEVS specification in CD++

Figure 2 shows the specification of a Cell-DEVS model in CD++. The specification follows Cell-DEVS coupled model's formal definitions. In this case, *Xlist = Ylist* = { ∅ }. The set {*m*, *n*} is defined by *width-height*, which specifies the size of the cell space (in this example, *m*=20, *n*=40). The *N* set is defined by the lines starting with the *neighbors* keyword. The border *B* is wrapped. Using this information, the tool builds a cell space, and the *Z* translation function following Cell-DEVS specifications. The local computing function executes very simple rules. The first one indicates that, whenever a cell state is 1 and the sum of the state values in *N* is 8 or 10, the cell state remain in 1. This state change is spread to the neighboring cells after 100 ms. The second rule states that, whenever a cell state is 0 and the sum of the inputs is larger or equal to 10, the cell value changes to 1. In any other case (*t* = true), the result remains unchanged, and it is spread to the neighbors after 150 ms.

3   Expanding CD++ Architecture

CD++ only supported one state variable per cell. To work around this problem, modelers usually defined extra planes in their cell space, creating as many layers as state variables needed. For instance, when one state variable was needed in a planar cell space, the solution was to create a three-dimensional cell space with two planar layers [7]. State variables are declared as follows:

```
StateVariables: pend temp vol
StateValues: 3.4 22 -5.2
InitialVariablesValue: initial.var
```

The first line declares the list of state variables for every cell, the second one the default initial values, and the last one provides the name of a file where the initial values for some particular cells are stored, using the following format:

```
(0,0,1) = 2.8 21.5 -6.7
(2,3,7) = 6 20.1 8
```

The values are assigned to the state variables following the order in which they are listed in the sentence *StateVariables*. Here, the first line assigns 2.8 to *pend*, 21.5 to *temp*, and -6.7 to *vol* in the cell (0,0,1). The second line will assign respectively the values 6, 20.1 and 8, to the variables *pend*, *temp* and *vol* in the cell (2,3,7).

State variables can be referenced from within the rules that define the cells' behavior by using its name preceded by a **$**.

```
rule: {(0,0,0)+$pend} 10 { (0,0,0)>4.5 and $vol<22.3 }
```

The identifier ':=' is used to assign values to a state variable. Assignments must be placed in a new section in the rules (a list of assignments, separated by semi-colons).

```
% <value> [ { <assignments> } ] <delay> <condition>
rule: { (0,0,0)+1 } { $temp:=$vol/2; $pend:=(0,1,0); }
            10 { (0,1,0) > 5.5 }
```

In the example, if the condition *(0,1,0)>5.5* is true, the variable *temp* will be assigned half of *vol* value, and *pend* will be assigned the value of the neighbor cell (0,1,0). These assignments are executed immediately (they are not delayed).

A second limitation was that the previous implementation of CD++ only used one port for inputs (*neighborChange*) and one for outputs (*out*), which are automatically created with the cell. The use of different I/O ports provides a more flexible definition of the cell behavior, as the rules can react in different ways according to inputs arriving in different ports. Therefore, our second extension supports the use of multiple I/O ports, which are defined as follows:

```
NeighborPorts: alarm weight number
```

The input and output ports share the names, making possible to automatically create the translation function: an output from a cell will influence exclusively the input port with the same name in every cell in its neighborhood. When a cell outputs a value through one of the ports, it will be received by all its neighbors through the input ports with the same name. A cell can read the value sent by one of its neighbors, specifying both the cell and port name, separated by a tilde (~), as follows:

```
rule : 1 100 { (0,1)~alarm != 0 }
```

In this case, if the cell receives an input in the *alarm* port from the cell to the right, and that value is not 0, the cell status will change to 1, and this change will be sent through the default output port 100 ms after. As one might need to output values through many ports at the same time, the assignment can be used as many times as needed (each followed by a semi-colon), as follows:

```
% <port_assigns> [ <assignments> ] <delay> <condition>
rule: { ~alarm := 1; ~weight := (0,-1)~weight; } 100
          { (0,1)~number > 50 }
```

In this example, if we receive a value larger than 50 in the port *number* on the cell to the right, we wait 100 ms, we generate an output of 1 in the *alarm* port, and we copy the *weight* value received from the cell to the left to the *weight* output port.

The rules defining the models are translated into an executable definition. Each of the rules is represented with a structure <value, assignations, delay, condition>, each represented by a tree. Rules are evaluated recursively form the tree that represents the condition. If the result of the evaluation is *True*, it then evaluates the trees corresponding to the value and the delay, and the result of these evaluations are the values used by the cell. The complete language grammar and details about the tool implementation are described in [13].

4 Using the Extensions in a Model of Fire Spread

In [14], we described a fire model using Cell-DEVS. Figure 3 represents the specification of this model in CD++.

```
[ForestFire]
dim : (100,100,2)     border : nowrapped
neighbors : (-1,0,0) (0,-1,0) (1,0,0)
neighbors : (0,1,0)(0,0,0)(0,0,-1)(0,0,1)
zone : ti { (0,0,1)..(99,99,1) }
localTransition : FireBehavior

[ti]
rule:{ time/100 } 1 { cellpos(2)=1 AND (0,0,-1)>=573
             AND (0,0,0) = 1.0 }

[FireBehavior]
rule: {#unburned} 1 {(0,0,0)<300 AND (0,0,0)!=26
     AND (#unburned>(0,0,0) OR time<=20)} %Unburned
rule: {#burning} 1 {cellpos(2)=0 AND ( ((0,0,0) >
     #burning AND (0,0,0)>333) OR (#burning> (0,0,0)
         AND (0,0,0)>=573) ) AND (0,0,0)!=209 } %Burning
rule: {26} 1 { (0,0,0)<=60 AND (0,0,0)!=26 AND
          (0,0,0)>#burning } %Burned
rule : { (0,0,0) } 1 { t }    %Stay Burned or constant

#BeginMacro(unburned)
(0.98689 * (0,0,0) + 0.0031 * ( (0,-1,0) + (0,1,0) +
(1,0,0) + (-1,0,0) ) + 0.213 )
#EndMacro

#BeginMacro(burning)
(0.98689*(0,0,0)+.0031*((0,-1,0)+(0,1,0)+(1,0,0)+
   (-1,0,0))+2.74*exp(-.19*((time+1)*.01-(0,0,1))))+.213)
#EndMacro
```

Fig. 3. Fire spread model specification.

We first define the Cell-DEVS coupled model (including neighborhood, dimension, etc.). Then, the *ti* rules show how to store ignition times: if a cell in plane 0 starts to burn, we record the current simulation time in plane 1. To make this happen, we include a clause specifying to identify the layer in which the current cell is located (*cellpos(2)=x*). Then, we show the rules used to compute the cells' temperatures. The model specification was simplified using macros containing rules corresponding to the temperature calculus when the cell is in unburned or burning phase.

As described in Figure 4, we used two planes representing the different variables in our model. The first plane stores the cell's temperature. The second plane stores the ignition time of the cells in the propagation plane.

In the example, we need n x m x 2 cells (double the size of simulated field). Using the new simulator, the *temperature* is stored as the cell's value and the *ignition time* in a state variable (*temperature* is stored in the cell's value because it must be passed to the neighbor cells, while the *ti* value is only used internally to the cell). The first step

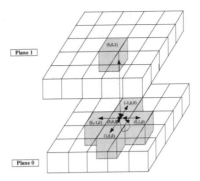

Fig. 4. Cell's neighborhood specification

was to add a state variable *ti*, to remove the higher layer of cells and to replace all the references to this layer by references to the state variable. The original *burning* and *ti* rules in Figure 5 were replaced as follows:

```
rule: {#burning} 1 {((0,0)>#burning AND (0,0)>333) OR
      (#burning>(0,0) AND (0,0)>=573) AND (0,0)!=209}

rule : { (0,0) } { $ti := time/100; } 1 { (0,0)>=573
      AND $ti = 1.0 }
```

The direct translation has a problem: in some cases, both conditions can be true at the same time. For instance, when $ti = 1.0$, $(0,0) >= 573$ and #burning > $(0,0)$, both rules apply. In order to solve this problem, the *burning* rule was factorized into two simpler rules, as follows:

```
rule : { #burning } 1 { (0,0) > #burning AND (0,0)> 333
      AND (0,0) != 209 }
rule : { #burning } 1 { #burning > (0,0) AND (0,0)>=
      573 AND (0,0)!= 209 }
```

We can see that in both rules we need $(0,0) != 209$, and $(0,0) > 333$ and $(0,0) \geq 333$ $\Rightarrow (0,0) \neq 209$. Hence, $(0,0) != 209$ is redundant, and so it can be removed. Rule *ti* overlaps with the second part of the rule *burning*, so they were merged. To shorten the execution time, the number of rules was reduced and the clauses in the rules' condition reordered. The two rules were merged in one rule that will assign the new value to $ti depending on $ti's original value:

```
rule : { #burning } 1 { (0,0)> 333 AND  ( (0,0)< 573 OR
      $ti != 1.0) AND (0,0)>#burning }
rule : { #burning }{ $ti := if($ti = 1.0, time/100,
      $ti); } 1{ (0,0)>=573 AND #burning>=(0,0) }
rule : { #burning } { $ti := time / 100; } 1 { $ti=1.0
      AND (0,0)>=573 AND #burning<(0,0) }
```

A second step optimization is based on the fact that CD++ is capable of using short-cut evaluation (in the same style as the C programming language). When the left expression of an **and** operation evaluates to false, the whole operation will evaluate to *false*, so it is useless to evaluate the right expression. Similarly, when the left expression of an **or** operation evaluates to *true*, the whole operation will evaluate to true, and so there is no need to evaluate the right expression of the operation. By simply reordering the operations and their parameters, we can save execution time. The idea is to execute the simplest conditions first, while leaving the more complex ones to the end.

```
%Unburned
rule : { #macro(unburned) } 1
         { (0,0) != 209 AND (0,0) < 573 AND
         ( time <= 20 OR #macro(unburned) > (0,0) ) }
%Burning and ti
rule : { #macro(burning) } 1
         { (0,0) > 333 AND ( (0,0) < 573 OR $ti != 1.0 )
         AND (0,0) > #macro(burning) }
rule : { #macro(burning) }
         { $ti := if($ti = 1.0, time / 100, $ti); } 1
         { (0,0) >= 573 AND #macro(burning) >= (0,0) }
rule : { #macro(burning) } { $ti := time / 100; } 1
         { $ti = 1.0 AND (0,0) >= 573 AND
         #macro(burning) < (0,0) }
%Burned
rule : { 209 } 100
         { (0,0) != 209 AND (0,0) <= 333 AND
         (0,0) > #macro(burning) }
%Stay Burned or constant
rule : { (0,0) } 1 { t }
```

In the FireSpread model the cells can be in one of four phases: inactive, unburned, burning and burned. An unburned cell's temperature is lower than 573 degrees. A cell starts burning at 573 degrees and its temperature increases for a while and then start decreasing as the fuel mass is consumed. When the temperature gets lower than 333 degrees, the cell enters the burned phase. In the simulation this is signaled by a constant temperature of 209 degrees.

The first rule applies to unburned cells, whose temperature in the next step will be higher than its current one or the simulation time is smaller than twenty (transient period). The second rule is based on the same principles but applies to burning cells. The third rule is used when the cells start burning to modify the temperature and the ignition time (depending on its value). Fourth rule updates the ignition time and the temperature of burning cells when their temperature is decreasing. The fifth rule sets the burned flag (temperature equals 209 degrees) when a burning cell crosses down the 333-degrees threshold, and the sixth rule keeps the burned cells constant.

This problem can also be solved using multiple ports to replace the extra plane. When we use multiple ports we do not need to store internally the values, but to transmit them through the ports. So, there is not need to set values, but just send them out though the port. In this case, two ports are declared: temp and ti. The port temp exports the cell s temperature (the old lower layer), while the port ti exports the ignition time (the higher layer).

```
%Unburned
rule : { ~temp := #unburned; } 1
        { (0,0)~temp!=209 AND (0,0)~temp<573 AND
          (time<=20 OR #unburned>(0,0)~temp ) }
%Burning and ti
rule : { ~temp := #burning; } 1 { (0,0)~temp>333 AND
        ( (0,0)~temp<573 OR (0,0)~ti!=1.0 ) AND
        (0,0)~temp > #burning }
rule : { #burning } 1
        { (0,0)> 333 AND ( (0,0)< 573 OR $ti != 1.0) AND
        (0,0)>#burning }
rule : { #burning }
        { $ti := if($ti = 1.0, time/100, $ti); } 1
        { (0,0)>=573 AND #burning>=(0,0) }
rule : { #burning } { $ti := time / 100; } 1
        { $ti=1.0 AND (0,0)>=573 AND #burning<(0,0) }
%Burned
rule : { ~temp := 209; } 100
        { (0,0)~temp > #macro(burning) AND
        (0,0)~temp <= 333 AND (0,0)~temp != 209 }
%Stay Burned or constant
rule : { } 1 { t }
```

This model behaves exactly the same as the previous one. As the initial value for both ports is the same and this model needs different values, it can solved by assigning negative initial value that will never appear during the simulation and adding two rules that generate the real initial state when the cell has this special values.

5 Conclusions

A new implementation of CD++ was presented, which allows using state variables and multiple neighbor ports in each cell of a cellular model. These new features add great power to the specification language to the simulator, simplifying the modeling task.

Cell-DEVS simplifies the construction of complex cellular models by allowing simple and intuitive model specification. The CD++ logic rules facilitate the debugging phase and, consequently, reduces development time. Complex model modifications can now be easily and quickly integrated to the current model of fire spread even by a non-computer specialist.

Models can now be written more clearly, and their simulation consume less memory and file descriptors (than those models with extra cell layers), which allow for larger cell spaces to be simulated.

References

1. Wainer, G.; Giambiasi, N., 2000. "Timed Cell-DEVS: modelling and simulation of cell spaces". *Discrete Event Modeling & Simulation: Enabling Future Technologies*, to be published by Springer-Verlag.
2. Zeigler, B.; Kim, T.; Praehofer, H. "Theory of Modeling and Simulation: Integrating Discrete Event and Continuous Complex Dynamic Systems". Academic Press. 2000.
3. Wainer, G.; Giambiasi, N. "Application of the Cell-DEVS paradigm for cell spaces modeling and simulation.". *Simulation*; Vol. 76, No. 1. January 2001.
4. Ameghino, J.; Troccoli, A.; Wainer, G. "Modeling and simulation of complex physical systems using Cell-DEVS". *Proceedings of 34th IEEE/SCS Annual Simulation Symposium*. Seattle, U.S.A. 2001.
5. Muzy, A.; Wainer, G.; Innocenti, E.; Aiello, A.; Santucci, J.-F. "Dynamic and discrete quantization for simulation time improvement: fire spreading application using the CD++ tool". *Proceedings of 2002 Winter Simulation Conference*. San Diego, U.S.A. 2002.
6. Wainer, G. "CD++: a toolkit to define discrete-event models". *Software, Practice and Experience*. Wiley. Vol. 32, No.3. pp. 1261-1306. November 2002.
7. Ameghino, J.; Wainer, G. "Application of the Cell-DEVS paradigm using CD++". *Proceedings of the 32nd SCS Summer Computer Simulation Conference*. Vancouver, Canada. 2000.
8. Ameghino, J.; Troccoli, A.; Wainer, G. "Applying Cell-DEVS Models of Complex Systems". *Proceedings of Summer Simulation Multiconference*. Montreal, QC. Canada. 2003.
9. Wainer, G.; Giambiasi, N. "N-dimensional Cell-DEVS". *Discrete Events Systems: Theory and Applications*, Kluwer, Vol. 12 N° 1, January 2002. pp 135-157.
10. Spezzano, G.; Talia, D. "CARPET: A Programming Language for Parallel Cellular Processing". In *Proceedings of the European School on Parallel Programming Environments for HPC'96*. April 1996.
11. Eckart, D. "A Cellular Automata Simulation System". SIGPLAN Notices, 26(8):80--85, August 1991.
12. D. Rodríguez, G. Wainer. "New Extensions to the CD++ tool". In *Proceedings of SCS Summer Multiconference on Computer Simulation*. 1-7. 1999.
13. López, A.; Wainer, G. "Extending CD++ for Cell-DEVS model definition". Technical Report SCE-04-11. Dept. of Systems and Computer Engineering. Carleton University. 2004.
14. Muzy, A.; Wainer, G.; Innocenti, E.; Aiello, A.; Santucci, J.F. "Cellular Discrete-event modeling and simulation of fire spreading across a fuel bed". Accepted for publication in Simulation: Transactions of the Society for Modeling and Simulation International (Accepted: September 2003).

Characterization of Reachable/Nonreachable Cellular Automata States

Sukanta Das[1], Biplab K. Sikdar[2], and P. Pal Chaudhuri[3]

[1] Department of Information Technology, Bengal Engineering College (D U),
Howrah, India 711103 sukd@cs.becs.ac.in
[2] Department of Computer Science & Technology, Bengal Engineering College (D U),
Howrah, India 711103 biplab@cs.becs.ac.in
[3] Flat E4, Block H30, Murchhana Housing, Kolkata - 94, India palchau@vsnl.net

Abstract. This paper reports characterization of reachable/nonreachable states of 3-neighborhood non-homogeneous Cellular Automata (CA). An efficient scheme to identify nonreachable states in $O(n)$ time is proposed. It also computes the number of such states in $O(n)$ time. The reported characterization of nonreachable states provides the theoretical background to identify and synthesize a reversible CA in linear time.

1 Introduction

The study of homogeneous structure of cellular automata (CA) was first initiated by J. von Neumann [1]. Since then the CA has been used for modeling physical systems [2,3]. Stephen Wolfram [2] proposed a simplified structure, each CA cell having only two states, with uniform 3-neighborhood interconnection. It is hard to assume that the interacting objects in a dynamical system obey the same interconnection structure (local rule) during its evolution. For such systems, an effective modeling tool can be the non-homogeneous CA (*hybrid CA*).

Characterization of a specific class of hybrid CA has been proposed in [3] for a number of applications in $VLSI$ domain. However, it is limited only to a specific class of CA referred to as linear/additive CA. It limits the search space while modeling a solution. Further, the CA researchers put emphasis to adopt nonlinear CA as the generalized modeling tool [4,6]. However, available results on characterization of nonlinear hybrid CA are too insignificant. In this work, we report an analysis to characterize the reachable/nonreachable states of a CA and to identify the special type of CA having only reachable states. Wolfram proposes a method to check the nonreachability condition of a state in a uniform CA [5]. Wuensche proposes a method [6] to compute the predecessors of a CA state that further can be extended to check its nonreachability condition. However, the complexity of this approach is not estimated.

The current work, targeting characterization of states of a nonlinear hybrid CA, reports the simple linear time solutions for the above mentioned problems. The major contributions of this work are (i) characterization of nonreachable states of hybrid CA in $O(n)$ time, (ii) identification of all the nonreachable

P.M.A. Sloot, B. Chopard, and A.G. Hoekstra (Eds.): ACRI 2004, LNCS 3305, pp. 813–822, 2004.
© Springer-Verlag Berlin Heidelberg 2004

states of a given CA, (iii) computation of the number of nonreachable states in $O(n)$ time, and (iv) a linear time solution to identify and synthesize the reversible or group CA.

The introduction to CA is provided in *Section 2*. *Section 3* reports characterization of reachable/nonreachable states. Characterization and synthesis of a reversible CA are presented in *Section 4*.

2   Cellular Automata

Each cell of a CA consists of a discrete variable. The value of it at time t is defined as the present states of the cell. The next state of a cell at $(t+1)$ is evaluated from the present state of the cell and in its *neighborhood*. In this work, we concentrate on 3-neighborhood one dimensional CA, each cell having two states - 0 or 1; where the next state S_t^{t+1} of a cell depends only on the present states S_i^t, S_{i-1}^t, and S_{i+1}^t of itself, its *left*, and *right* neighbors respectively. That is,

$$S_i^{t+1} = f_i(S_{i-1}^t, S_i^t, S_{i+1}^t) \tag{1}$$

where f_i is the *next state function* for cell i.

The collection of states of the cells at time t is the state $\mathcal{S}^t = (S_1^t, S_2^t, \cdots, S_n^t)$ of a CA at t. Therefore, the next state of the CA is determined as

$$\mathcal{S}^{t+1} = (f_1(S_0^t, S_1^t, S_2^t), f_2(S_1^t, S_2^t, S_3^t), \cdots, f_n(S_{n-1}^t, S_n^t, S_{n+1}^t)) \tag{2}$$

If $S_0^t = 0$ and $S_{n+1}^t = 0$, then the CA is a *null boundary CA*.

If f_i is expressed in the form of a truth table, then the decimal equivalent of its output is referred to as the 'Rule' $\mathcal{R}_i$ [2]. Three such rules 90, 150, and 75 are illustrated in *Table 1*. The first row lists the possible 2^3 (8) combinations of the present states of $(i-1)^{th}$, i^{th} and $(i+1)^{th}$ cells at time t. In a two state 3-neighborhood CA, there can be 256 rules.

Table 1. Truth Table for Rule 90, 150 and 75

PS :	111	110	101	100	011	010	001	000	Rule
(RMT)	(7)	(6)	(5)	(4)	(3)	(2)	(1)	(0)	
(i) NS :	0	1	0	1	1	0	1	0	90
(ii) NS :	1	0	0	1	0	1	1	0	150
(iii) NS :	0	1	0	0	1	0	1	1	75

Note: PS, RMT and NS stand for Present State, Rule Min Term and Next State.

The next state logics for the rules 90 and 150 employ XOR function. There are only 14 rules with $XOR/XNOR$ logic and are referred to as linear/additive rules. Other rules (say, 75) are non-linear rules.

The set of rules that configures the cells of an $n-$cell CA is called rule vector $\mathcal{R} =< \mathcal{R}_1, \mathcal{R}_2, \cdots, \mathcal{R}_i, \cdots, \mathcal{R}_n >$. If all $\mathcal{R}_i$s $(i = 1, 2, \cdots, n)$ are linear/additive, the CA is a linear/additive CA, otherwise it is a nonlinear CA. Moreover, if $\mathcal{R}_1 = \mathcal{R}_2 = \cdots = \mathcal{R}_n$, then it is a homogeneous or *uniform* CA; otherwise the CA is called non-homogeneous or *hybrid*. An analytical framework to characterize CA rules (linear/additive or non-linear) is reported in the subsequent discussions.

Definition 1. *A rule is* **Balanced** *if it contains equal number of 1s and 0s in its 8−bit binary representation; otherwise it is an* **Unbalanced** *rule.*

The rules shown in *Table 1* are balanced. Each of the rules has four 1s and four 0s in its 8-bit binary representation. On the other hand, rule 171 with five 1s in its 8-bit representation (10101011) is an unbalanced rule.

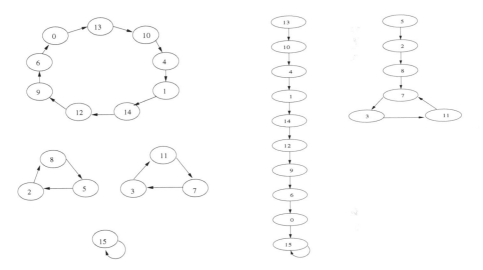

Fig. 1. A group CA with rule vector $< 105, 177, 170, 75 >$

Fig. 2. A non-group CA with rule vector $< 105, 177, 171, 75 >$

Rule Min Term (RMT): The set of present states (1st row of *Table 1*) can be viewed as the *Min Term* of a 3-variable $(S_{i-1}^t, S_i^t, S_{i+1}^t)$ switching function. Therefore, each column of the first row of *Table 1* is referred to as the **Rule Min Term** (RMT). The column 011 in the truth table (*Table 1*) is the 3rd RMT. The next states corresponding to this RMT are 1 for Rule 90 and 75, and 0 for Rule 150. The proposed characterization is based on the analysis of the RMTs of the CA rules.

A reversible CA (also called *group* CA) contains only cyclic states (*Fig.1*) – that is, each state is reachable from some other states of the CA. Whereas, an irreversible CA (also called *non − group* CA) contains both cyclic and non-cyclic states (*Fig.2*). There are a number of states in a non-group CA that are *nonreachable* (5 and 13 of *Fig.2*) – that is without having a predecessor. Further, in a non-group CA, some states may have more than one predecessors. For example, the states 15 and 7 of *Fig.2* have more than one predecessors.

3 Characterization of Nonreachable States

To characterize a CA state S we adopt an approach to find its predecessor. The scheme first evaluates a condition (say C) assuming that the given state S is reachable. The condition C is so framed that the true value of C implies, the CA state S can not have a predecessor and, therefore, S is nonreachable.

Let us consider the $CA < 105, 177, 171, 65 >$ and a state 1101 (13). Assume that 13 is a reachable state. Therefore, it should have predecessor state(s). Consider, S_p is one of the immediate predecessors of 13. That is, the state transition $S_p - > 1101(13)$ follows the RMTs of the rules noted in *Table 2*. As we are considering null-boundary CA, some of the RMTs of rule 105 and 65 are set to don't care (d). For example, the RMTs 7, 6, 5 & 4 of rule 105 are don't cares.

To get the first bit (MSB) '1' of 1101 from S_p, the left most cell of the CA have to follow either 0th or 3rd RMT, as the 0th and 3rd RMT of rule 105 can result in 1 (*Table 2*). It indicates that the two MSBs of S_p are either 00 or 11. We denote these two effective RMTs as $S_1 = \{0, 3\}$.

The candidate RMTs that can generate the 2nd MSB of $S = 1101$ are 0, 1, 6 and 7 (*Table 3*) of the rule 177. However, the 1st and 6th RMTs result in 0. Therefore, the 2nd MSB (1) of 1101 should effectively be reached from S_p following any one of the RMTs of set $S_2 = \{0, 7\}$. Similarly, $S_3 = \{6\}$ – that is, RMT 6 of the 3rd cell rule (171) is effective for the transition S_p to 1101. Once the RMT 6 is identified for the 3rd cell, it signifies the 3rd and 4th (LSB) bit of S_p are 1 and 0 respectively. Therefore, the 4th and 5th RMTs for the rule 65 may be effective. As the 5th RMT is *don't care* and since the value of RMT 4 is 0 (*Table 2*), the LSB (1) of 1101 can't be generated from S_p. Therefore, the assumption is wrong – that is, S_p does not exist and hence 1101 is a nonreachable state.

Table 2. Binary values of the CA, $< 105, 177, 171, 65 >$

RMT	111	110	101	100	011	010	001	000	Rule
	(7)	(6)	(5)	(4)	(3)	(2)	(1)	(0)	
Firstcell	d	d	d	d	1	0	0	1	105
Secondcell	1	0	1	1	0	0	0	1	177
Thirdcell	1	0	1	0	1	0	1	1	171
Fourthcell	d	1	d	0	d	0	d	1	65

Table 3. Transition of RMTs

RMT at i^{th} rule	RMTs at $(i+1)^{th}$ rule
0 or 4	0, 1
1 or 5	2, 3
2 or 6	4, 5
3 or 7	6, 7

The above discussion reports that to check the existence of predecessor of a CA state S_t, we should identify (i) the set of RMTs (S'_{i+1}) for each CA cell rule $\mathcal{R}_{i+1}$ on which the cell ($i + 1$) can change its state, and (ii) the set S''_{i+1} containing the RMTs which generate the $(i+1)^{th}$ bit of S_t. Table 3 gives the set of RMTs (S'_{i+1}) at $(i+1)^{th}$ cell rule on which the cell can change its state for an RMT chosen at the ith cell rule for state change. If the selected RMT of the ith

rule is k, then $(i+1)^{th}$ cell is to be changed following either the RMT $2k$ mod 8 or $(2k+1)$ mod 8. While $S_i = S_i' \cap S_i'' = \phi$, for any i, the S_t is nonreachable.

For the current example, $S_1' = \{0,1,2,3\}$ and $S_1'' = \{0,3\}$ (to satisfy $\mathcal{S}_p->$ 1101). So, $S_1 = S_1' \cap S_1'' = \{0,3\}$. Similarly, $S_2' = \{0,1,6,7\}$ and $S_2'' = \{0,4,5,7\}$. That is, $S_2 = S_2' \cap S_2'' = \{0,1,6,7\} \cap \{0,4,5,7\} = \{0,7\}$. The $S_3' = \{0,1,6,7\}$ and $S_3'' = \{2,4,6\}$. Therefore, $S_3 = S_3' \cap S_3'' = \{0,1,6,7\} \cap \{2,4,6\} = \{6\}$. Finally, for the last cell $S_4' = \{4\}$ and $S_4'' = \{0,6\}$. It results in $S_4 = S_4' \cap S_4'' = \{4\} \cap \{0,6\} = \phi$. The complete algorithm to test the reachability condition of a CA state is presented next.

Algorithm 1. *FindNonReachable*
Input: *Rule[n][8], state[n], n.* **Output:** 1 if nonreachable; 0 otherwise
Step 1: *Find S_1 where $Rule[1][j] = state[1]$, $j = 1,2,3,4$.*
    If $S_1 = \phi$, return 1 as the state is not reachable.
Step 2: *For $i = 2$ to $n-1$*
    (a) *Find S_i' such that if $k \in S_{i-1}$, $((2k)$ mod $8)$ and $((2k+1)$ mod $8)$ are in S_i'.*
    (b) *Find S_i'', where $S_i'' = \{j\}$ and $Rule[i][j] = state[j]$, $j = 0, \cdots, 7$.*
    (c) *Find $S_i = S_i' \cap S_i''$.*
    (d) *If $S_i = \phi$, return 1 as the state is nonreachable.*
Step 3:
    (a) *Find S_n' such that if $k \in S_{n-1}$, $((2k)$ mod $8)$ and $((2k+1)$ mod $8)$ are in S_n'.*
    (b) *Find S_n'', where $S_n'' = \{j\}$ and $Rule[i][j] = state[j]$, $j = 0,2,4,6$.*
    (c) *Find $S_n = S_n' \cap S_n''$.*
    (d) *If $S_n = \phi$, return 1 as the state is not reachable.*
Step 4: *The state is reachable. Return 0.*

Algorithm 1 contains only a single loop (*Step 2*). In each iteration, it demands constant, (say T) time unit. Therefore, the computation time to test the reachability condition of a state is $T * n$ – that is, $O(n)$.

3.1   Identifying the Nonreachable States

To find the list of all nonreachable states of a given CA, a recursive algorithm is proposed. It traverses all possible paths of a tree referred to as the *Reachability Tree*.

Reachability Tree: Each node of a reachability tree (*Fig.3*) can have maximum 2 outgoing edges – 0-edge (left edge) and 1-edge (right edge). For an $n-$cell CA, its number of levels is $(n+1)$. The number of leaf nodes denotes the number of reachable states. A sequence of edges from the root to a leaf node, representing an $n-$bit binary string, is a reachable state.

Fig.3 is the reachability tree for a CA with rule vector $< 105, 129, 171, 65 >$. The RMT values of a rule for which we follow an edge are noted in bracket. For example, as the $RMTs$ 1 & 2 are 0 and $RMTs$ 0 & 3 are 1 for the 1st rule (105), the corresponding $RMTs$ are noted in 0-edge and 1-edge respectively. Similarly, if the 1st bit of the next state is determined by RMT 1 or 2, then the 2nd bit of the next state is to be generated following the $RMTs$ 2, 3, 4 or 5 of the rule 129 (*Table 3*). The RMT values of all these 4 for rule 129 are 0. These $RMTs$

Table 4. Binary values of the CA, $< 105, 129, 171, 65 >$

RMT	111	110	101	100	011	010	001	000	Rule
	(7)	(6)	(5)	(4)	(3)	(2)	(1)	(0)	
Cell 1	d	d	d	d	1	0	0	1	105
Cell 2	1	0	0	0	0	0	0	1	129
Cell 3	1	0	1	0	1	0	1	1	171
Cell 4	d	1	d	0	d	0	d	1	65

are noted against the 0-edge of the 2nd node. Hence, there is no 1-edge (dotted line) for this node. It signifies – the states started with 01 are nonreachable.

3.2   Finding List of Nonreachable States

To find the complete set of nonreachable states, we construct the reachability tree for a CA. For a terminated path (length$< n$), the proposed scheme reports all the states that follow the path as nonreachable. For example, the $2^{4-2} = 4$ states 0100, 0101, 0110 and 0111 of the CA $< 105, 129, 171, 65 >$ (*Fig.3*) started with 01, are nonreachable.

The complexity of the scheme depends on the number of nodes in the reachability tree. The best case is – all the states, except one, of an $n-$cell non-group CA are the nonreachable. For such cases, each node except the leaf nodes of the reachability tree is having exactly one outgoing edge. Therefore, the number of nodes in the tree is n. Hence, the complexity is $O(n)$. In the worst case, all the states of an $n-$cell CA are reachable. For such a case, the reachability tree is a complete binary tree. The number of nodes in the tree is $2^{n+1}-1$. Therefore, the complexity is $O(2^n)$. However, in average case, the number of reachable states of an $n-$cell non-group CA is $m < 2^n$. Since to identify a reachable state, the algorithm demands $O(n)$ time, the complexity is $O(mn)$.

4   Group CA

The following theorems characterize a group CA.

Theorem 1. *The reachability tree of a group CA is balanced.*

Proof. Since all states of a group CA are reachable, the number of leaf nodes in the reachability tree of such an $n-$cell CA is 2^n. Therefore, the tree is balanced as it is a binary tree with $(n + 1)$ levels.

Theorem 2. *The reachability tree for a 3-neighborhood CA is balanced if each edge of the tree follows exactly two $RMTs$ of a rule.*

Proof. Let us consider, an intermediate edge e_i of the reachability tree that follows single RMT (k) of a rule. Therefore, the following two cases may arise:
(i) the e_i is the predecessor of the edge e_l connecting a leaf node (leaf edge) – therefore, each of the next edge should follow either $2k \bmod 8$ or from

$(2k+1)$ *mod* 8. But $(2k+1)$ *mod* 8 does not exit since the CA is a null boundary and the next edge is the leaf edge e_l. Hence the tree is unbalanced.

(*ii*) the e_i is any intermediate edge – for this case, the very next edges of the edge e_i should follow RMT $2k$ *mod* 8 or RMT $(2k+1)$ *mod* 8. If both the RMTs result in the same value for that particular rule, the tree becomes unbalanced. Otherwise, there exists two edges and each follows a single RMT. This consideration is true for all the nodes until we reach to the predecessor of a leaf node. That is, the tree may remain balanced up to the predecessor of leaf nodes. For that case, there are a number of edges, whose next edge is the leaf, follow a single RMT. Hence the tree is unbalanced.

The reachability tree, as shown in *Fig.3*, is unbalanced. The 0-edge at level 1 follows four RMTs. On other hand, the reachability tree of *Fig.4* depicts a balanced tree.

4.1   Identification of Group CA

Since the reachability tree for a group CA is balanced, there are 2^i number of nodes at the ith level. However, only $^8C_2 = 28$ combinations of RMTs (taking exactly two RMTs in a combination) are possible. Further, the RMTs 0 and 4 of a rule are equivalent since these two result in the same set of RMTs (0 and 1) for the next level (*Table 3*). Similarly, RMTs 1 & 5, 2 & 6, and 3 & 7 are equivalent. Therefore, number of possible nodes in the reachability tree at any level is $^4C_2 = 6$.

The following algorithm scans a CA rule vector from left to right and notes an edge in the reachability tree, having $<> 2$ RMTs. If such an edge exists, the CA is non-group.

Algorithm 2. CheckGroup
Input: n, $Rule[n][8]$. **Output**: group or non-group.
Step 1: *Find (a)* $S[1] = \{j\}$, *where* $Rule[1][j] = 0$ *and* $1 \le j \le 3$, *(b)* $S[2] = \{j\}$, *where* $Rule[1][j] = 1$.
　　Set nos := 2. *If* $|S[1]| \ne |S[2]|$, *then*
　　　report the CA *as non-group and exit.*
Step 2: *For* $i = 2$ *to* $n - 1$
　　2.1 *For* $j = 1$ *to nos*
　　Determine 4 RMTs for the next level using Table 3 *of* $S[j]$.
　　Distribute these 4 RMTs into $S'[2j]$ *and* $S'[2j+1]$, *such that* $S'[2j]$ *and* $S'[2j+1]$ *contain the RMTs that are 0 and 1 respectively for* $Rule_i$.
　　If $|S'[2j]| \ne |S'[2j+1]|$, *then report the* CA *as non-group and exit.*
　　2.2 *Replace RMTs 4, 5, 6 and 7 by 0, 1, 2 and 3 respectively for each* $S'[k]$.
　　2.3 *If* $|S'[k]|$ *becomes 1, report the* CA *as non-group and exit.*
　　2.4 *Remove duplicate sets from* S' *and assign the sets of* S' *to* S.
　　2.5 *nop* := *number of sets in* S.
Step 3: *For* $j = 1$ *to nos*
　　Determine next 4 RMTs of $S[j]$, *of which 2 are invalid since it is the last rule.*
　　If both RMTs are 0 or 1 for the rule, then report the CA *as non-group and exit.*
Step 4: *Report the* CA *as group.*

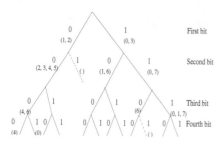

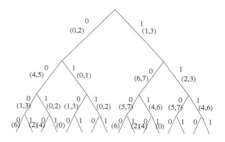

Fig. 3. Reachability Tree for the CA $< 105, 129, 171, 65 >$.

Fig. 4. Reachability tree for the CA $< 90, 15, 85, 31 >$.

Table 5. Binary values of the CA, $< 90, 15, 85, 31 >$

RMT	111	110	101	100	011	010	001	000	Rule
	(7)	(6)	(5)	(4)	(3)	(2)	(1)	(0)	
First cell	d	d	d	d	1	0	1	0	90
Second cell	0	0	0	0	1	1	1	1	15
Third cell	0	1	0	1	0	1	0	1	85
Fourth cell	d	0	d	0	d	1	d	1	31

Example 1. Let consider the $CA < 90, 15, 85, 31 >$ of *Table 5*. From *Step 1* of *Algorithm 2*, we get $S[1] = \{0, 2\}$ and $S[2] = \{1, 3\}$.

In *Step 2*, when $i = 2$ we obtain –

$S'[1] = \{4, 5\}$, $S'[2] = \{0, 1\}$, $S'[3] = \{6, 7\}$ and $S'[4] = \{2, 3\}$.

Since each set of S' contains exactly 2 RMTs, decision at this stage is the CA is nongroup. Now S' can be modified as

$S'[1] = \{0, 1\}$, $S'[2] = \{0, 1\}$, $S'[3] = \{2, 3\}$ and $S'[4] = \{2, 3\}$.

Here each set of S' contains exactly 2 RMTs, so S' is reduced removing the duplicates and assigned to S. Therefore, $S[1] = \{0, 1\}$ and $S[2] = \{2, 3\}$.

When $i = 3$, $S'[1] = \{1, 3\}$, $S'[2] = \{0, 2\}$, $S'[3] = \{5, 7\}$ and $S'[4] = \{4, 6\}$.

Hence the modified S': $S'[1] = \{1, 3\}$, $S'[2] = \{0, 2\}$, $S'[3] = \{1, 3\}$ and $S'[4] = \{0, 2\}$. Further, assigning reduced S' to S, we get $S[1] = \{1, 3\}$ and $S[2] = \{0, 2\}$.

Now *Step 3* results in $S'[1] = \{2\}$, $S'[2] = \{6\}$, $S'[3] = \{0\}$ and $S'[4] = \{4\}$. Each set of S' contains a single RMT, that is, number of 0s and 1s in RMTs $\{2, 6\}$ and $\{0, 4\}$ are the same. So, the CA is a group (*Step 4*). The reachability tree (*Fig.4*) also shows that the CA is a group as the tree is balanced.

Algorithm 2 is having the main loop in *Step 2*. It contains a subloop with expected number of iterations depends on *nos*. The maximum value of *nos* is a constant (6). Therefore, the execution time of the algorithm only depends on n. Hence the complexity is $O(n)$.

4.2   Synthesizing a Group CA

The following algorithm synthesizes the rule vector for a group CA in such a way that the reachability tree for the CA is balanced.

Algorithm 3. SynthesizeGroup

Input: n. **Output**: An $n-$cell group CA.

Step 1: *Distribute two 0s and two 1s arbitrarily in first 4 RMT.*
Consider, $S[1] = \{j\}$ for $Rule[1][j] = 0$ and $S[2] = \{j\}$ for $Rule[1][j] = 1$ $(1 \leq j \leq 3)$.
  Set nos := 2

Step 2: *For $i = 2$ to $n - 1$*
  2.1 *For $j = 1$ to nos*
    Determine 4 RMTs for the next level using Table 3 of $S[j]$.
    Distribute two 0s and two 1s arbitrarily in these 4 RMTs. If there are RMTs
0 and 4, 1 and 5, 2 and 6, or 3 and 7 simultaneously in those 4 RMTs, 0 and 1 are
to be distributed in such a way that those RMT pairs are not 0 or 1 simultaneously.
    Suppose that $S'[2j]$ and $S'[2j+1]$ contain RMTs that are 0 and 1 respectively.
  2.2 *Replace RMTs 4, 5, 6 and 7 by 0, 1, 2 and 3 respectively for each $S'[k]$.*
  2.3 *Remove duplicate sets from S' and assign the sets of S' to S.*
  2.4 *nop := number of sets in S.*

Step 3: *For $j = 1$ to nos*
  Determine next 4 RMTs of $S[j]$, of which 2 are invalid since it is last rule.
  Distribute 0 and 1 randomly in two RMTs.

Step 4: *Report the CA as an $n-$cell group CA.*

The complexity of the algorithm is obviously $O(n)$.

4.3   Computation of the Number of Nonreachable States

The following algorithm is the generalization of *Algorithm 2* that computes the number of nonreachable states in a CA.

Algorithm 4. CalNonReachable

Input: n, $Rule[n][8]$. **Output**: number of nonreachable states.

Step 1: *Find $S[1] = \{j\}$, where $Rule[1][j] = 0$ and $1 \leq j \leq 3$.*
  Similarly find $S[2] = \{j\}$, where $Rule[1][j] = 1$.
  If $S[i] = \phi$, Nonreachable $:= 2^{n-1}$, oldWeight[1] $:= 2^{n-1}$ and nos := 1, where
$i = 1, 2$.
  Otherwise oldWeight[1] $:=$ oldWeight[2] $:= 2^{n-1}$ and nos := 2

Step 2: *For $i = 2$ to $n - 1$*
  2.1 *For $j = 1$ to nos*
    Determine RMTs for the next level using Table 3 and $S[j]$.
    Distribute these RMTs into $S'[2j]$ and $S'[2j+1]$, such that $S'[2j-1]$ and $S'[2j]$
contain those RMTs that are 0 and 1 respectively for $Rule_i$.
    Set newWeight[2j-1] := newWeight[2j] := oldWeight[j]/2.
    If $S'[k] = \phi$, Nonreachable := Nonreachable + newWeight[k], where $k = 2j - 1, 2j$.
  2.2 *Replace RMTs 4, 5, 6 and 7 by 0, 1, 2 and 3 respectively for each $S'[k]$.*

2.3 If $S'[k] = S'[k']$ for any k', then set $oldWeight[k] := newWeight[k] + newWeight[k']$; otherwise set $oldWeight[k] := newWeight[k]$.

2.4 $nop :=$ number of sets in S.

Step 3: For $j = 1$ to nos

Determine next RMTs of $S[j]$, of which 2 are invalid since it is last rule.

Distribute these RMTs into $S'[2j]$ and $S'[2j+1]$, such that $S'[2j-1]$ and $S'[2j]$ contain those RMTs that are 0 and 1 respectively for $Rule_n$.

If $S'[k] = \phi$, Nonreachable $:=$ Nonreachable $+oldWeight[k]/2$, where $k = 2j-1, 2j$.

Step 4: Report the value of Nonreachable as the number of nonreachable states.

Algorithm 4 contains the main loop that depends on n and the subloop dependent on nos. The maximum value of nos is 6. Therefore, the complexity of the algorithm is $O(n)$.

5   Conclusion

This work presents characterization of reachable/nonreachable states of a 3-neighborhood hybrid CA. The characterization enables the design of linear time solution to identify and synthesize reversible or group CA.

References

1. J. V. Neumann. 'The Theory of Self Reproducing Automata' A. W. Burks, Ed. University of Illinois Press, Urbana and London, 1966.
2. S. Wolfram. 'Theory and application of cellular automata', World Scientific, 1986.
3. P Pal Chaudhuri, D.Roy Choudhury, S. Nandi and S. Chattopadhyay. 'Additive Cellular Automata Theory and Applications', IEEE Computer Society Press, USA.
4. Sukanta Das, Anirban Kundu, Subhayan Sen, Biplab K Sikdar, P Pal Chaudhuri. 'Non-Linear Cellular Automata Based PRPG Design (Without Prohibited Pattern Set) In Linear Time Complexity', Asian Test Conference, 2003.
5. S. Wolfram, Oliver Martin and Andrew M. Odlyzko. 'Algebraic Properties of Cellular Automata' Communications in Mathematical Physics, vol. 93, pages 219-258, March 1984.
6. Andrew Wuensche 'Attractor Basins of Discrete Networks', Cognitive Science Research Paper, The University of Sussex, 1997.

Building Classifier Cellular Automata

Peter Kokol, Petra Povalej, Mitja Lenič, and Gregor Štiglic

University of Maribor, FERI, Laboratory for system design, Smetanova ulica 17,
2000 Maribor, Slovenia
{kokol, petra.povalej, mitja.lenic, gregor.stiglic}@uni-mb.si

Abstract. Ensembles of classifiers have the ability to boost classification accuracy comparing to single classifiers and are a commonly used method in the field of machine learning. However in some cases ensemble construction algorithms do not improve the classification accuracy. Mostly ensembles are constructed using specific machine learning method or a combination of methods, the drawback being that the combination of methods or selection of the appropriate method for a specific problem must be made by the user. To overcome this problem we in-vented a novel approach where an ensemble of classifiers is constructed by a self-organizing system applying cellular automata (CA). First results are promising and show that in the iterative process of combining classifiers in the CA, a combination of methods can occur, that leads to superior accuracy.

1 Introduction

A large variety of problems arising in engineering, physics, chemistry and economics can be formulated as classification problems [1, 2, 8]. Although classification represents only a small part of the machine learning field, there are a lot of methods available. To develop a general method that at the same time exposes different aspects of a problem and produces "optimal" solution is unfortunately impossible, due to the so called "no free lunch" theorem [6]. Therefore a standard local optimization technique is to use multi-starts, by trying different starting points and running the processes of classification independently from each other and selecting the best result from all trials. Moreover ensembles [4] of classifiers are often used since they have the ability to boost classification accuracy comparing to single classifiers. However, single classifiers just like ensembles of classifiers can often find solutions near local optima, but are not so successful in global exploration of search space. Therefore different popular methods for global exploration of the search space are used, like simulated annealing, genetic algorithms and lately also a theory of self-organization systems that could gain some diversity leading to possible better solutions.

During the last few years, the scientific area of self-organizing systems became very popular. The field seeks general rules about the growth and evolution of systemic structure, the forms it might take, and finally methods that predict the future organization that will result from changes made to the underlying components. A lot

P.M.A. Sloot, B. Chopard, and A.G. Hoekstra (Eds.): ACRI 2004, LNCS 3305, pp. 823–830, 2004.

of work in this field has been done using Cellular Automata (CA), Boolean Networks, with Alife, Genetic Algorithms, Neural Networks and similar techniques. In this paper we propose a new method for nonlinear ensembles of classifiers that exploit the ability of self-organization applying CA in search for an optimal solution. The aim is to combine different single classifiers in an ensemble represented by a CA. We show how improved accuracy can be obtained by interaction of neighborhood cells containing different kind of classifiers.

The paper is organized as follows. In Sec. 2 and 3 the process of classification and the basics of CA is shortly introduced. In Sec. 4 we discuss how to design a CA as classifier. Sec. 5 presents experiment setup and in Sec. 6 first results are discussed.

2   Classifier Systems and Classification

As mentioned before in this research we are focused on solving classification tasks. Classification is a process in which each sample is assigned with a predefined class. Classifier systems were introduced in 1978 by Holland as a machine learning methodology, which can be taught of syntactically simple rules.

For learning a classifier a training set, which consists of training samples, is used. Every training sample is completely described by a set of attributes (sample properties) and class (decision). After learning a classifier a testing set is used to evaluate its quality. The testing set consists of testing samples described with the same attributes as training samples except that testing samples are not included in the training set. In general the accuracy of classifying unseen testing samples can be used for predicting the efficiency of applying the classifier into practice.

3   Cellular Automata

CA are massively parallel systems [3] obtained by composition of myriads of simple agents interacting locally, i.e. with their closest neighbors. In spite of their simplicity, the dynamics of CA is potentially very rich, and ranges from attracting stable configurations to spatio-temporal chaotic features and pseudo-random generation abilities. Those abilities enable the diversity that can possibly overcome local optima by solving engineering problems. Moreover, from the computational viewpoint, they are universal, one could say, as powerful as Turing machines and, thus, classical Von Neumann architectures. These structural and dynamical features make them very powerful: fast CA-based algorithms are developed to solve engineering problems in cryptography and microelectronics for instance, and theoretical CA-based models are built in ecology, biology, physics and image-processing. On the other hand, these powerful features make CA difficult to analyze - almost all long-term behavioral properties of dynamical systems, and cellular automata in particular, are unpredictable. However in this paper the aim was not to analyze the process of CA rather to use it for superior classification tasks.

4   Cellular Automata as a Classifier

Our novel idea is to exploit benefits of self-organization abilities of cellular automata in classification and its possible use in the extraction of new knowledge. Our first task was to define the basic elements (content of the cells) and transaction rules that would result in a learning ability of cellular automata and representing gained classification knowledge in its structure. Most obvious choice is to define a cell in the classification cellular automata (CCA) as a classifier. In a simplified view we can look at cellular automata as on an ensemble of classifiers. In each cell we have to build a classifier that has different and eventually better abilities than already produced ones. Contrary if all cells would have the same classifier there would be no diversity and it would be quite unreasonable to use any trans-action rules on such automata, because all cells would classify in the same way. Thus we must ensure the most possible diversity of classifiers used in different automata's cells to benefit from the idea of CCA.

4.1   Initializing Automata

The most desirable initial situation in a CCA is having a unique classifier in each of its cells. We can ensure that by using different methods but the problem is (especially when the CCA has a lot of cells) that the number of different methods is limited. Nevertheless, even if there is only one method available we can still use so called fine-tuning. Namely, almost all machine-learning methods used for classification have multiple parameters that affect classification. Therefore with changing those parameters different classifiers can be obtained. Parameters can be randomly selected or defined by using for example evolutionary algorithms for determining most appropriate parameters. An-other possibility is by changing expected probability distributions of input samples, which may also result in different classifiers, even by using the same machine learning method with the same parameters. Still another approach is the feature reduction/selection. That technique is recommended when a lot of features are presented.

4.2   Transaction Rules

Transaction rules must be defined in such a way to enforce the learning process that should lead to generalization abilities of the CCA. Successful cells should therefore be rewarded, but on the other hand cells with not so good classifiers shouldn't be punished too much, to preserve the diversity of the CCA. Each classifier in a cell can classify a single learning sample or can generate unknown tag to signal that it cannot assign any class to current sample. From the transaction rules point of view a classification result can have three outcomes: same class as the learning sample, different class or cannot classify. Cannot classify tag plays important role when combining partial classifiers that are not defined on the whole learning set. In that case CCA becomes a classifier system i.e. when using *if-then* rules in CCAs cells. Therefore a cell with unknown classification for current learning sample should be treated differently as misclassification. Beside the cells classification ability also the neighborhood plays a very important role in the self-organization ability of a CCA. Transaction rules depend on the specific neighborhood state to calculate new cell's state. In general we want to group classifiers that support similar hypothesis and have therefore similar classification on learning samples. Even if sample is wrongly classified, the neighborhood can support a cell classifier by preventing its elimination from automata. With that transaction rule we encourage creation of decision centers for a specific class and in this way we can overcome the problem of noisy learning samples – another CCAs advantage.

4.3 Learning Algorithm

```
Input: training set with N training samples
   Number of iterations: t=1,2,...T
   For t=1,2...T:
      -  choose a learning sample I
      -  fill the automaton
      -  each cell in automaton classifies the learning
         sample I
      -  change cells energy according to the transac-
         tion rules
      -  a cell with energy bellow zero does not survive
   Output: CCA with highest classification accuracy on
   the training set
```

Once the CCAs classifier diversity is ensured, transaction rules are continuously applied. Beside its classifier information, each cell contains also statistical information about its successfulness in a form of cell's energy. Transaction rules can increase or decrease energy level dependent on the successfulness of classification and cells neighbors. If energy drops below zero the cell is terminated. New cell can be created dependent on learning algorithm parameters with its initial energy state and a classifier used from pool of classifiers or newly generated classifier dependent on neighborhood classification abilities and modifying expected probability distribution and/or used features. When using second approach we create local boosting algorithm to assure that misclassified samples are correctly classified by the new cell. Of course if cell is too different from the neighborhood it will decently die out and the classifier will be returned to the pool. The learning of a CCA is done incrementally by supplying samples from the learning set. Transaction rules are executed first on the whole CCA with a single sample and then continued with the next until the whole problem is learned by using all samples - that is a similar technique than used in neural networks [5, 7]. Transaction rules do not directly imply learning, but the iteration of those rules creates the self-organizing ability. Of course this ability depends on classifiers used in CCAs cells, and its geometry. Stopping criteria can be determined by defining fixed number of iterations or by monitoring accuracy.

4.4 Inference Algorithm

```
Input: a sample for classification
   Number of iterations: t=1,2,...V
   For t=1,2...V
      -   each cell in automaton classifies the sample
      -   change cells energy according to the transac-
          tion rules
      -   each cell with energy bellow zero does not sur-
          vive
   Classify the sample according to the weighted voting
   of the survived cells
Output: class of the input sample
```

Inference algorithm differs from learning algorithm, because it does not use self-organization. Simplest way to pro-duce single classification would be to use the majority of the cell voting. On the other hand some votes can be very weak from the transaction rule point of view. If transaction rules are applied using only neighborhood majority vote as sample class those weak cells can be eliminated. After several irritations of transaction rules only cells with strong structural support survive on which majority voting can be executed. Weighted voting algorithm can be used by exploiting energy state of classifier in a cell.

5 Experiment Setup and Results

To test the presented idea of the CCA we implemented simple cellular automata and used simple *if-then* rules in the cells. Rule form is as follows:

if (*attribute≤value*) **then** *decision* ;

where *decision* is a class of a current sample.

The following transaction rules were used:
- If a cell has the same classification as the sample class:
  - if majority neighbourhood vote is the same as learning sample class the increase cell's energy
  - if majority neighbourhood vote differs the dramatically increase energy of the cell;

- If a cell classification differs from the learning sample class
  - if neighbourhood majority vote is the same as learning sample class then decrease energy of the cell
  - if neighbourhood majority class is the same as the cell class then slightly decrease energy of cell;
- If a cell cannot classify learning sample then leave the energy state of the cell unchanged.

Through all iterations all cells use one point of energy (to live). If the energy level of a cell drops below zero the cell is terminated.

The presented CA Simple approach was tested on five databases from UCI repository. We compared the results with the following commonly used methods for decision tree induction that are able to use more complex conditions as our CA Simple:

- greedy decision tree induction based on different purity measures (Quinlan's ID3, C4.5, C5 and Decrain),
- genetically induced decision trees – a hybrid between genetic algorithms and decision trees (Vedec) and
- boosting of decision trees – a method for generating an ensemble of classifiers by successive re-weighting of the training instances. AdaBoost algorithm, introduced by Freund and Schapire was used.

The predicting power of induced classifiers was evaluated on the basis of average accuracy (Eq. 1) and average class accuracy (Eq. 2).

$$accuracy = \frac{num \ of \ correctly \ classified \ objects}{num. \ of \ all \ objects} \tag{1}$$

$$accuracy_c = \frac{num \ of \ correctly \ classified \ objects \ in \ class \ c}{num. \ of \ all \ objects \ in \ class \ c}$$

$$\tag{2}$$

$$average \ class \ accuracy = \frac{\sum_c accuracy_c}{num. \ of \ classes}$$

Table 1. Accuracy of the induced classifiers on the test sets.

Dataset	C 4.5	C5	C5 Boost	ID3	Decrain ID3	Vedec	CA Simple
BreastCancer	96.4	95.3	96.6	92.7	95.7	96.1	97.4
GlassType	71.8	83.6	92.7	69.1	83.6	87.3	81.8
Hepatitis	80.8	82.7	82.7	78.8	82.7	78.8	86.5
Iris	97.0	94.0	94.0	94.0	94.0	96.0	96.0
Pima	76.2	75.8	81.3	70.7	76.6	77.3	75.7

Table 1 shows the results in the terms of the CCAs total accuracy on unseen cases compared to some very popular decision trees approaches. We can see that even this very simple CCA can outperform more prominent methods. The average class accuracy is presented in Table 2 which once again shows that the simple CCA performed best on two databases. Even in all other cases the results are comparable with the results obtained with other approaches in the terms of total accuracy and also in average class accuracy. That shows that the ability of self-organization, is very promising and that more elaborate CCAs can produce even better results.

Table 2. Average class accuracy of induced classifiers on the test sets.

Dataset			C5		Decrain		CA
	C 4.5	C5	Boost	ID3	ID3	Vedec	Simple
BreastCancer	94.4	95.0	96.7	90.2	96.1	96.8	98.1
GlassType	80.1	82.3	93.1	69.2	83.5	86.0	78.8
Hepatitis	58.7	59.8	59.8	63.7	59.8	75.7	50.0
Iris	94.2	94.2	94.2	94.2	94.2	96.1	96.1
Pima	73.0	70.5	79.2	66.1	70.4	76.0	72.0

6 Concluding Remarks and Future Work

The aim of this paper was to present the use of self-organization ability of cellular automata in classification. This way we combined classifiers in an ensemble that is eventually better than individual classifiers or traditional ensembles generated by boosting or bagging methods. We empirically showed that even a very simple CCA can give superior results as more complex classifiers or ensembles of those classifiers. This is very promising and taking into account the simplicity of the tested CCA we can foresee a lot of room for improvements. The advantages of the resulting self-organizing structure of cells in CCA is the problem independency, robustness to noise and no need for the user input. The important research direction in the future are to analyze the resulting self-organized structure, impact of transaction rules on classification accuracy, introduction of other social aspect for cells survival and enlarging the classifier diversity by more complex cells classifiers.

References

1. Coello, C.A.C.: Self-Adaptive Penalties for GA-based Optimization, 1999 Congress on Evolutionary Computation, Washing-ton D.C., Vol. 1, IEEE Service Center (1999) 573-580.
2. Dieterich, T.G.: Ensemble Methods in Machine Learning. In J. Kittler and F. Roli (Ed.) First International Workshop on Multiple Classifier Systems, Lecture Notes in Computer Science (2000) 1-15. New York: Springer Verlag.

3. Flocchini, P., Geurts, F., Santoro, N.: Compositional experimental analysis of cellular automata: Attraction properties and logic disjunction. Technical Report TR-96-31, School of Computer Science, Carleton University (1996)
4. Freund, Y., Schapire, R. E.: Experiments with a new boosting algorithm, In Proceedings Thirteenth International Conference on Machine Learning, Morgan Kaufman, San Francisco (1996) 148-156.
5. Lenič, M., Kokol, P.: Combining classifiers with multimethod approach, In Proceedings Second international conference on Hybrid Intelligent Systems, Santiago de Chile, December 1-4, 2002. IOS Press (2002) 374-383.
6. Kirkpatrick, S., Jr., C. G., Vecchi, M.: Optimization by simulated annealing. Science, (1983) 220.
7. Towel, G., Shavlik, J: The Extraction of Refined Rules From Knowledge Based Neural Networks. Machine Learning (1993) 131, 71-101.
8. Zorman, M., Podgorelec, V., Kokol, P., Peterson, M., Sprogar, M., Ojstersek, M: Finding the right decision tree's induction strategy for a hard real world problem. International Journal of Medical Informatics (2001) 63, Issues 1-2, 109-121

On Evolutionary 3-Person Prisoner's Dilemma Games on 2-D Lattice

László Gulyás[1] and Tadeusz Płatkowski[2]

[1] Computer and Automation Research Institute,
Hungarian Academy of Sciences,
1111, Kende u. 13-17, Budapest, Hungary
[2] Warsaw University, Dept. of Mathematics, Informatics and Mechanics,
02-957 Warsaw, Banacha 2, Poland

Abstract. We investigate a system of interacting agents which play 3-person Prisoner's Dilemma game on a regular 2-dimensional lattice. The agents can choose between All-D, All-C, and TFT strategies. The peculiar structure of 3-person interactions gives rise to two different TFT strategies, which have different influence on the temporal evolution of the system. We introduce a formal setting for the relevant cellular automaton with the 3-person interactions, compare different TFT strategies, and discuss various properties of the 3-person games on the lattice.

1 Introduction

In many scientific disciplines, which investigate macroscopic systems of entities (individuals, agents) with microscopic interactions, the theoretical description of such systems is based on binary contests. The multi-player game theory is, both mathematically and conceptually, much more complicated than the theory for two-player games; quantitative considerations of multi-player interactions started only recently. However, in the real world the multi-player contests, in which more than two players are in conflict, are common. Such interactions are important in the biological world as well as in the economy or for the description of human behavior. The payoffs from such multi-player contests can be different from binary ones. In the former case all the players take part in one, simultaneous contest. In symmetric contests the payoff of each player depends on the number of other players who use specific strategies allowed in the game. Such multi-player contests can significantly change the time evolution and the equilibrium properties of emerging stationary states of the population.

One of the most popular and important for applications games is the Prisoner's Dilemma (PD) game. It has been studied for many years as a paradigm for the evolution of cooperation in social, biological and other contexts, cf. e.g. Hoffman 2000 for recent review. The multi-person PD has been also studied in various contexts, cf. e.g. Schweitzer et al. 2002, and references cited therein.

We investigate the system of interacting agents playing iterative three-person PD games on a regular 2D lattice, with opponents from their first order von Neumann neighborhood.

P.M.A. Sloot, B. Chopard, and A.G. Hoekstra (Eds.): ACRI 2004, LNCS 3305, pp. 831–840, 2004.
© Springer-Verlag Berlin Heidelberg 2004

In this note we concentrate on the case with only 3 strategies available for each agent: All-C (always cooperate), All-D (always defect), and TFT (Tit For Tat: Play C in the first iteration, then repeat the action of the opponents).

An interesting feature of 3-person interactions is that they give rise to two different types of TFT strategies, which we call TFT-1 (optimistic/naive Tit For Tat) and TFT-2 (pessimistic/sceptic Tit For Tat). In TFT-1 the agents respond C if one opponent played C and another one played D, whereas in TFT-2 they respond D in the same situation (and C for CC actions, D for DD actions of the opponents). Thus, we shall study and compare the time behavior of two systems:

I. All-C, TFT-1, All-D,
II. All-C, TFT-2, All-D.

We compare results for various realizations of the payoff matrix for 3-person PD, and for both TFT strategies. We investigate the emergence of cooperation for different realizations of the considered games.

In the next section we introduce the spatial structure, interaction neighborhood and dynamics for the proposed cellular automaton, then we discuss results of simulations and some generalizations.

2   The Model

2.1   3-Person PD Games

We define the stage 3-person PD game as the one-shot simultaneous contest between three indistinguishable agents, each playing one of two admissible *actions* : C (*cooperate*), or D (*defect*). The players receive payoffs, which depend on their actions as well as on the number (but not the ordering) of defectors (or cooperators) in this group.

It follows that the payoff matrix for each player has 6 values, which form a 6-parameter vector, which we call the payoff vector PV of the stage 3-person PD game:

$$(R, S', S'', T'', T', P)$$

where R, S', S'' are the payoffs of cooperator if the opponents played CC, CD (=DC), DD, respectively, and T'', T', P are the relevant payoffs for defector if the opponents played CC, CD (=DC), DD, respectively. This notation generalizes the standard notation for the 2-person PD, where R corresponds to Reward, S to Sucker, T to Temptation, and P to Punishment strategy, with $T > R > P > S$, and $2R > T + S$.

We shall consider iterated 3-person PD games, in which each stage game between the same three agents is played (at one time step or round) a certain finite number of times, NI. This leads to considerations of strategies rather than actions for the players.

As discussed in the introduction, agents can choose between the following strategies: All-C, All-D, and one of the two types of the Tit-For-Tat strategies:

Naive Tit-For-Tat, and Sceptic Tit-For-Tat, which are defined for the 3-person interactions, in which three agents have to choose simultaneously one of the two actions: cooperate or defect, at each time step of the game.

In general the parameters of the payoff vector may belong to some intervals, as long as the essence of the PD game is preserved, cf. Yao and Paul 1994, and Schweitzer et al. 2002 for a discussion of admissible numerical values of the payoffs for general n-person games. We note that usually the setting and payoffs of the underlying 2-person games is used in this context, and the payoff of the agent in the 3-person (n-person in general) game is calculated as the accumulated (and/or averaged) payoff of two (n-1 in general) 2-person games, that would be played independently, at the same time. We refer to this case as to the "Average Payoffs" case.

In this note the numerical values for the Average Payoffs case are defined on the basis of the underlying 2-person PD game with the payoffs: 3 (0) for C if the opponent plays C (D), 5 (1) for D if the opponent plays C (D), cf. Axelrod 1999. Thus, the vector

$$(R, S', S'', T'', T', P) = (3.0,\ 1.5,\ 0.0,\ 5.0,\ 3.0,\ 1.0)$$

is the payoff vector in the Average Payoffs case.

2.2   Spatial Structure of Interactions

The agents are located in the nodes of a regular, square, finite 2-D lattice. Each cell of the lattice is identified with one agent, and periodic boundary conditions are imposed.

The agents interact (play) only locally, i.e. with oponents in their neighborhood. In this note we use the von Neumann closest neighborhood (size 1 vN neighborhood). Let us consider the following spatial arrangement (the agents are denoted by their numbers) for the square lattice:

$$
\begin{array}{cccccc}
1 & 2 & 3 & \mathbf{4} & 5 & 6 \\
7 & 8 & \mathbf{9} & \mathbf{10} & \mathbf{11} & 12 \\
13 & \mathbf{14} & \mathbf{15} & \mathbf{16} & \mathbf{17} & \mathbf{18} \\
19 & 20 & \mathbf{21} & \mathbf{22} & \mathbf{23} & 24 \\
25 & 26 & 27 & \mathbf{28} & 29 & 30 \\
31 & 32 & 33 & 34 & 35 & 36
\end{array}
$$

Fig. 1. Interaction neighborhood of agent no. 16, agents are denoted by their numbers. Only the relevant part of the lattice is shown.

We are interested in the number of stage games played by agent no. 16. The size 1 vN neighborhood of agent 16 contains the agents: 10, 15, 17, and 22. Agent 16 initiates the following six games: (16, 10, 15) (16, 10, 17) (16, 10, 22) (16, 15,

17) (16, 15, 2) (16, 17, 22), cf. Fig. 1. These are called the first hand games of agent 16.

However, agent 16 plays not only with its closest neighbors, but also with other agents, since it gets challenged by agents in their size 1 vN neighborhood (since these are the agents whose size 1 vN neighborhood includes agent 16). Thus, agent 16 is also involved in the following – second hand – games: (the first member of the triple is always the challenger, i.e. the agent that initiates the game; the order of the last two members is arbitrary.) (17, 11, 16), (17, 16, 18), (17, 16, 2), (10, 4, 16), (10, 9, 16), (10, 11, 16), (15, 14, 16), (15, 9, 16), (15, 16, 21), (22, 16, 21), (22, 16, 23), (22, 16, 28).

In sum, agent 16 plays 18 games. It initiates 6 games itself, and accepts three challenges from each of its neighbors. Moreover, it never plays the same game (i.e., with exactly the same participants) twice in a round. However, it plays more than once with the same opponents, except that the 'third party' is different in such games; the 'additional' (third) players come from the size 2 vN neighborhood. Note that the frequency of games decays with distance. For example, agent 16 plays 6 times with each of its neighbors (10, 15, 17, and 22), twice with the agents in its size one Moore neighborhood, that are not in its size 1 vN neighborhood (9, 11, 21, and 23). Finally, it plays only once with the agents in the 'farthest poles' of its size 2 vN neighborhood (4, 14, 18, and 28), cf. Fig. 1.

2.3 Description of the Algorithm

Let's introduce the following terminology: an agent 'acts' when it has the opportunity to start a game. When the acting agent starts a game, we say that it 'challenges' two of its neighbors to play. Furthermore, we will use the term round to denote one time-step of the simulation, when each agent has the chance to act once (in randomized order). A game consists of a certain number of iterations of the basic stage game.

Using this terminology, the model's algorithm can be described as follows. In each round,

1. Each agent gets to act once, in a randomized order (randomization is done at the beginning of each round).
2. When an agent 'acts', it creates a list of all unordered pairs of its neighbors (i.e., from the agents in its size 1 vN neighborhood), and challenges each of these pairs. The challenged agents always accept the challenge, and the three agents play a game.
3. During these games, all participants receive payoffs, independent of their position (i.e., whether they are challenged or challenging).
4. When each agent had the chance to 'act', they each adapt. Adaptation is done in the same randomized order as above, but using double buffering, so agents adapting first will not corrupt the adaptation process of those coming later in the line. Adaptation is done by observing the performance (average accumulated payoff) of all opponents in the round, independent of whether it

was the given agent who initiated the play or it was challenged. 'First hand' and 'second hand' games are treated equally, the adaptation neighborhood of the agents is the same as their interaction neighborhood, as exemplified in Fig. 1.

3 Results

3.1 TFT-1 Versus TFT-2

First we compared, for the same initial conditions, the final states of two systems:

I.   All-C, TFT-1, All-D,
II. All-C, TFT-2, All-D,

for the Average Payoffs case. Initial configurations were created randomly, with 1/3 proportion of each of admissible strategy in both considered cases. Simulations were performed for various system sizes (typically 25 x 25) and number of iterations (in the range from 4 to 100) in each round.

In general in the system I All-D emerges as the unique strategy of all agents in the final (i.e. after sufficiently many time steps) state, whereas in the system II TFT-2 (i.e. the sceptic Tit For Tat) wins in most of the cases. Thus, when comparing both TFT strategies one can say that being sceptic rather than naive furthers cooperation in the system.

To get more insight into the behavior of TFT strategies we also carried out simulations for the following system:

III. All-C, TFT-1, TFT-2, All-D,

i.e. with four strategies. Initial configurations were created randomly, with 1/4 proportion of each strategy. In most of the cases, the finally evolving state has been composed of TFT strategies and – for some initial configurations – All-C strategy. Thus, the presence of two TFT strategies prevented invasion of defection.

Then we manipulated the system by raising the payoff P, i.e. increasing the individual profit from three simultaneous defections. It turned out that still All-D can be expulsed from the final state if the number NI of iterations in each round was big enough. Analogous "interplay" between payoffs for simultaneous defection and NI has been found for the system II. A more detailed study of the dependence of finally evolving states on the structure of payoffs will be reported elsewhere.

3.2 Quasi-Periodic Structures of Cooperation

We observed, for the payoff vector

$$(R, S', S'', T'', T', P) = (3.0, 1.5, 0.0, 5.0, 3.0, P), \quad P \in [0, 1],$$

			T		
1	2	3	4	5	**T**
7	8	9	10	11	12	**T**
13	**T**	15	16	17	18
19	20	**T**	22	23	24
25	26	27	**T**	29	30
31	32	33	34	35	36

Fig. 2. Spatial configuration after the first step, when in the zeroth step only agents 11 and 16 played TFT-1, all the others played All-D. **T** stands for TFT-1, all the other indicated agents play All-D.

		T			
1	**T**	3	4	5	6
T	8	9	10	11	12
T	13	14	15	16	17	18
19	20	21	22	23	24	**T**
25	26	27	28	29	**T**
31	32	33	34	**T**	36
			T		

Fig. 3. Spatial configuration after the second step, zeroth step and notation are as in Fig. 2. Note that some of the "after-the-second-step" TFT-1 players are not displayed.

propagation of regular patterns, lines, of TFT-1 players in the otherwise uniform sea of All-D players for various initial configurations with 33 % All-C, 33% TFT-1, and 34% of All-D. Such patterns, which we call "waves", are more frequent in larger worlds, for larger values of NI, and for lower values of P.

To get some idea about the generation of "waves" let's assume that the TFT-1 players are placed at positions 16 and 11. Below we show that this setup yields 6 TFT-1 players, 2 sets of 'diagonally adjacent' TFT-1 players (at 14, 21, and 28; and symmetrically, at 6 and at two of its diagonal neighbors, outside of Figure 1), and that in the next step such a structure generates another pair of "diagonal lines" of TFT-1 players, cf. Figs. 2 and 3. To this end we calculate the payoffs of a number of important game settings. First, let's calculate the payoff of a TFT-1 player, playing with two All-D opponents. In the first play, 'our' player cooperates, and receives 0 payoff. Since in this, and in all the following rounds the opponents play D, in the remaining games 'our' player plays D and receives payoff 1. This yields

$$PO(\text{TFT-1, All-D, All-D}) = 0 + (NI - 1) * 1 \tag{1}$$

Based on similar arguments we get (in our notation, the order of the last two members of the triple is arbitrary, given the fact that our payoff matrix assigns the same values to CD and DC situations):

$$PO(\text{TFT-1}, \text{TFT-1}, \text{All-D}) = 1.5 + (NI - 1) * 1.5 \tag{2}$$

$$PO(\text{All-D}, \text{All-D}, \text{All-D}) = NI * 1 \tag{3}$$

$$PO(\text{All-D}, \text{TFT-1}, \text{All-D}) = 3 + (NI - 1) * 1 \tag{4}$$

$$PO(\text{All-D}, \text{TFT-1}, \text{TFT-1}) = 5 * NI \tag{5}$$

Now, let's turn back to our imaginary setting with TFT-1 at 16 and 11, and All-D in all other places. Agent 16 plays 18 games, twice with 11 involved (a TFT-1, TFT-1, All-D situation), and 16 times with two All-D opponents. Therefore, from (1) and (2) it follows that the payoff of agent 16 will be:

$$PO(16) = 2 * (1.5 + (NI - 1) * 1.5) + 16 * (NI - 1) = 19 * NI - 16$$

However, adaptation is based on the average payoff of agents, which average is taken over the number of plays the agent played, in our case $18 * NI$. The average payoff of agent 16 is the following: $APO(16) = \frac{19*NI-16}{18*NI}$.

Let's now turn towards the neighboring All-D players (i.e., 10 and 17). They play an All-D, TFT-1, TFT-1 game once; ten times an All-D, TFT-1, All-D game, and seven times an All-D, All-D, All-D game. This yields the payoffs:

$$PO(10, 17) = 1 * 5 * NI + 10 * (3 + NI - 1) + 7 * NI = 22 * NI + 20, \text{ and}$$
$APO(10, 17) = \frac{22*NI+20}{18*NI}$.

Obviously, APO(10, 17) is greater than APO(16), and thus, agent 16 will adapt the All-D strategy. However, some All-D players will be worse off than their TFT-1 opponent, so they will change to TFT-1. To see this, let's turn towards agent 21 (or 6). It plays two games with 16, and none with 11. Therefore, the rest of its 16 games are with All-D opponents. This yields the following payoffs:

$$PO(21) = 2 * (3 + NI - 1) + 16 * NI = 4 + 18 * NI, \text{ and } APO(21) = \frac{18*NI+4}{18*NI}.$$

On the other hand, agent 28 (and 14) plays once with agent 16, and zero times with 11. Therefore, they play one All-D, TFT-1, All-D game, and 17 All-D, All-D, All-D games. That is, they have the following payoffs:

$$PO(28, 14) = 3 + NI - 1 + 17 * NI = 18 * NI + 2, \text{ and } APO(28, 14) = \frac{18*NI+2}{18*NI}.$$

In Fig. 4 we plot these (average) payoffs against various values of parameter NI. For completness note that agents 15 and 22 play three games with agent 16, and none with 11. Therefore, they play 3 All-D, TFT-1, All-D games, and 15 All-D, All-D, All-D games. Their payoff is then:

$$PO(15, 22) = 3 * (3 + NI - 1) + 15 * NI = 6 + 18 * NI, \text{ and } APO(15, 22) = \frac{18*NI+6}{18*NI}$$

We note that other similar initial configurations of e.g. two "close" TFT-1 players in the sea of All-D players do not generate waves of TFT-1. This is for example the case of (10, 16) or (15, 17) or (11, 21) initial TFT-1 players surrounded by All-D ones. We also note that in larger systems the initial (random) configuration is more likely to yield two 'diagonally adjacent' TFT-1 players in a "neighborhood" of All-D agents. Analogous analysis of the next steps of the evolution yields the following observation: parallel 'lines' of diagonally adjacent TFT-1 players in a sufficiently large All-D neighborhood (i.e., the parallel 'lines' are at least two cells apart) yield perpendicular 'lines' formed by three TFT-1

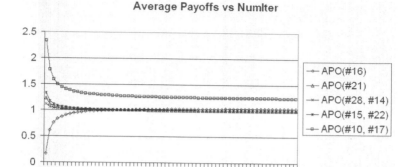

Fig. 4. Average payoffs versus values of NI

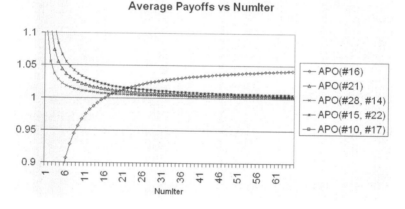

Fig. 5. Average payoffs versus values of NI

players at both ends of each line. The operation of this 'rule' is illustrated on Figure 6, where letters denote TFT-1 players. Note that cooperators in the second step form a true subset of those playing TFT-1 in the 6th step. Thus, both F's and B's denote the latter. Figure 6 provides a suggestion of the explanation for the evolution of the 'waves' observed. It is important to notice, however, that since the model operates with periodic boundary conditions, the expanding 'lines' will sooner or later overlap. Such overlaps cause interferences and give rise to more irregular shapes than simple lines.

Notes and Comments. We presented the mathematical formalism and some results of simulations for the 2-D cellular automaton describing the spatially extended system of agents playing 3-person PD games with a general payoffs matrix. We discussed the structure of the local interactions in the system, and

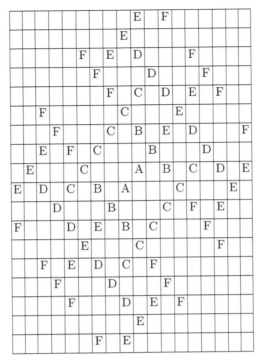

Fig. 6. Evolution of "waves". Letters denote TFT-1 players. A's, B's,... stand for cooperation in the first, second,... step. Cooperators in the 6th step are those denoted by F and B).

compared performance of two different TFT strategies which can be defined for such games, in the presence of All-C and All-D strategies.

There are many ways to generalize the proposed model, and to include different types of effects, some of them peculiar for multi-person interactions, cf. Platkowski 2004 for the replicator equations approach to mixed games.

The model investigated in this paper is – except the choice of initial conditions – deterministic. In a more general setting one can study effects of noise, adaptation abilities or idiosyncratic behavior of agents, as well as more irregular networks, e.g. those with rewirings, cf. Gulyás 2004.

One can also study the influence of memory of agents and possibilities of accumulation of payoffs on the choice of actions, strategy oriented rules of action choice rather than the agent oriented rules, influence of network structure (Gulyás and Dugundji 2003), etc. Study of robustness of final states with respect to changes of the payoffs matrix could also be of interest.

References

Yao, X., Paul, J.D.: An experimental study of n-person iterated prisoner's dilemma games. Informatica **18** (1994) 435–450

Axelrod, R.: The Complexity of Cooperation: Agent-Based Models of Competition and Collaboration. University Press, Princeton, New Jersey 1999.

Hoffmann, R.: Twenty years on: The evolution of cooperation revisited. Journal of Artificial Societies and Social Simulation. **3** (2) (2000)

Schweitzer, F., Behera, L., Muhlenbein, H.: Evolution of cooperation in a Spatial Prisoner's Dilemma. Advances in Complex Systems. **5** (2 and 3) (2002) 269–299

Platkowski, T.: Evolution of Populations Playing Mixed Multiplayer Games. Mathematical and Computer Modelling. **39** (2004) 981–989

Gulyás, L.: Understanding Emergent Social Phenomena: Methods, Tools, and Applications for Agent-Based Modeling. Ph.D. Thesis, Lorand Eotvos University, Budapest, Hungary, 2004.

Gulyás, L. and Dugundji, E. R.: Discrete Choice on Networks: An Agent-Based Approach. In Proceedings of North American Association for Computational Social and Organizational Science Conference (NAACSOS 2003), June 22-25, 2003, Omni William Penn, Pittsburgh, PA. 2003.

Optimizing the Behavior of a Moving Creature in Software and in Hardware

Mathias Halbach, Wolfgang Heenes, Rolf Hoffmann, and Jan Tisje

TU Darmstadt, FB Informatik, FG Rechnerarchitektur
Hochschulstraße 10, D-64289 Darmstadt
Phone +49 6151 16 {3713, 3606}, Fax +49 6151 16 5410
{halbach, heenes, hoffmann}@ra.informatik.tu-darmstadt.de

Abstract. We have investigated a problem where the goal is to find automatically the best rule for a cell in the cellular automata model. The cells are either of type OBSTACLE, EMPTY or CREATURE. Only CREATURE can move around in the cell space in one changeable direction and can perform four actions: if the path to the next cell is blocked turn left or right, if the path is free, i. e. the neighbor cell is of type EMPTY: move ahead and simultaneously turn left or right. The task of the creature is to cross all empty cells with a minimum number of steps. The behavior was modeled using a variable state machine represented by a state table. Input to the state table is the neighbors state in front of its moving direction.

All combinations of the state table which do not expect a trivial or bad behavior were considered in software and in hardware in order to find out the best behavior. The best four-state algorithm allows the creature to cross 97 % empty cells on average over the given initial configurations. As software simulation, optimization and learning methods are very time consuming, parallel hardware is a promising solution. We described this model in Verilog HDL. A hardware synthesizing tool transforms the description into a configuration file which was loaded into a field programmable gate array (FPGA). Hardware implementation offers a significant speed up of many thousands compared to software.

1   Introduction

We are presenting results of the project "Behavior of Artificial Creature and their Simulation under Massively Parallel Hardware". The general goal of the project is the design of a massively parallel model which allows describing many moving and learning creatures in artificial worlds. The simulation of such models is very time consuming and therefore the model should be massively parallel in such a way that it can efficiently be supported by special hardware or multiprocessor systems. There are many fields of applications for such artificial worlds:

- Computational worlds: Creatures are considered as active moving objects. Passive objects contain data. Creatures are programmed or are able to learn to solve a complex algorithmic problem.
- Synthetic worlds: Games, genetic art, optimization of the behavior of the creatures to reach global goals, social behavior, self organization.

P.M.A. Sloot, B. Chopard, and A.G. Hoekstra (Eds.): ACRI 2004, LNCS 3305, pp. 841–850, 2004.

2   Previous Work

Cellular Automata (CA). The popular CA model dates back to J. von Neumann. Well known is the self replication rule of Von Neumann and Conways rule of LIFE. In our group the language CDL [6] was defined to describe such rules in an easy and concise way. CDL was enhanced to CDL++ [8] in order to describe moving objects and features to resolve conflict situations. A number of FPGA-based configurable special processor were developed to support the CA model in hardware (CEPRA family) [7]. We have shown that CA can efficiently be implemented in FPGA logic reaching speed-ups up to thousands compared to software implementations on a PC [9][10].

Global Cellular Automata (GCA). [3, etc.] For the simulation of artificial worlds direct communication between arbitrary cells should be available. The CA model offers only local communication. Global communication between remote cells has to be emulated step by step through local communication. A new massively parallel model called GCA was defined, which allows direct access to any remote cell. The model is more complex than the CA, but it can still be computed in a synchronous parallel way like the CA because there are no write conflicts. As the model allows long distance communication it is better suited for complex Artificial Life problems. This model will not be used for the presented problem but is well suited for problems where creatures can move and communicate over long distances in one time step.

Other Work. This work is related to the general research field Artificial Life. Steven Levy gives in his book [5] an overview over this field. Thomas Ray [4], an American environmentalist and bio-scientist has developed a simulation program allowing the simulation of artificial individuals. The individuals are able to mutate and they survive only if they have certain fitness. He developed the language TIERRA to describe the behavior of the individuals by simple programs based on 32 different instructions. Individuals are able to learn and to use program parts from other individuals.

There is a lot of other relevant work which will not be discussed here in detail, like Genetic Algorithms, Neural Networks, Classifier Systems, and Rule Based Learning Models. The task to find a path to all cells is also related to space filling curves like the Hilbert curve and to the snake tiling problem [11]. In [12] an agent learns smart behavior which is stored in a FSM table using a reinforcement learning procedure.

3   The Problem: Optimal Algorithm for Checking the Environment

We have studied a simplified problem in order to perceive the open questions and to find some first solutions in the context of learning creatures. The problem is defined as follows.

Consider a two-dimensional grid of cells. A cell can be of the type empty or of the composed type "object". There are two kinds of objects scattered in the space: obstacles and creatures. Border cells are also modeled as obstacles.

All these objects act according to a given set of rules which are as follows:

Creature is variable in nature, it can move within the space from one place to other but a creature cannot go to a cell where a border cell or an obstacle is placed. At any time the creature can look in a certain direction one cell ahead and it will move in that direction if possible.

The actions. The creature may perform four different actions.

R   turn right

L   turn left

Rm   (Right Move) move forward and simultaneously turn right

Lm   (Left Move) move forward and simultaneously turn left

If the path (one cell ahead) is not free because of obstacle or border, either action R or L will be performed. If the path is free, either action Rm or Lm is performed (fig. 1).

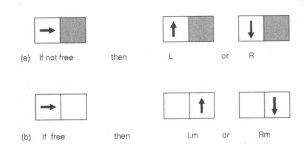

(a) if not free   then   L   or   R

(b) if free   then   Lm or   Rm

Fig. 1. The actions of the creature

Initial configuration. At the beginning the creature is placed in a certain start position with a start direction. Also at the beginning the number and the placement of the obstacles will be given.

Goal. The goal is to find an optimal and simple local algorithm for the creature to cross a maximum number of empty cells with a minimum number of time steps for a given set of initial configurations.

3.1   The Model of Moving Creature

To keep the problem simple, the moving of the creature is emulated in the CA model according to the following rules (in simplified pseudo code; only the changing values are printed). The type of a cell is EMPTY, CREATURE or OBSTACLE. The border cells are of type OBSTACLE. The center cell is called I.

Rule for I.Type = EMPTY
(a1) {CASE Free}
    if (Neighbor.Type = CREATURE) and (Neighbor.Direction points to I)
    then
        I.Type := CREATURE //create (move by copy)
        I.Direction := TurnRight/Left(Neighbor.Direction) //new direction

Rule for I.Type = CREATURE
(a2) {CASE Free}
    if (ahead Neighbor.Type= EMPTY) then I.Type:= EMPTY //delete
(b) {CASE not free}
        I.Direction := TurnRight/Left(I.Direction) //only turn R, L

In case a1, a2 where a creature can move in its direction, it changes its own type to EMPTY (case a2) and at the same time a new creature will be created by the empty cell ahead (case a1). In case b where the cell cannot move, it will only turn right or left.

3.2 Creature with Intelligence

The behavior of the creature can be either fixed or variable. We have experimented with a variable behavior in order to find optimal solutions for our problem. In our first approach we use a variable state machine for that purpose. The state machine can also be seen as control logic, intelligence or brain of the creature.

To study the basic problems with variable behavior (fig. 2) we reduced the intelligence to a minimum. The intelligence is stored in a state machine with two state tables called *TableFree* and *TableNotFree*. Input to the tables is the state S which is either 0 or 1 (if the brain is modeled with two states). *TableFree* is selected if the creature is able to move (condition *CreatureCanMove*) and *TableNotFree* is selected if the creature cannot move because an obstacle or border is in front.

There are totally 256 different two-state algorithms, because each table consists of four bit. The tables can be concatenated to one table with 8 bit information. These 8 bit can be represented as a number. E. g. the algorithm 57 shown in fig. 2 is abbreviated 0R1L-1R0L. The number 57 is the decimal equivalent to 0011-1001, where R is coded with 0 and L is coded with 1. The first part 0R1L is the line by line contents of *TableNotFree*, the second part is the line by line contents of *TableFree*. The second part can also be written as 1Rm0Lm, where Lm means: turn left and move, Rm means: turn right and move. The algorithm can be represented clearer as a state graph (fig. 2(c)).

3.3 Finding the Optimal Behavior

We have investigated two-state and four-state behaviors. The two-state table contains 8 bit of information. Each code corresponds to a certain algorithm.

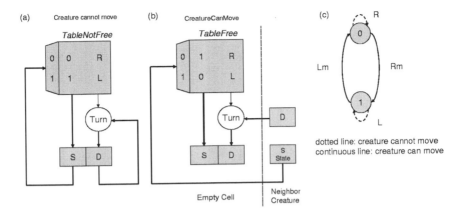

Fig. 2. Table driven state machine (a, b); two-state algorithm 57 as state graph (c)

Input to the state-machine algorithm is the old control state S and the signal X=*CreatureCanMove*. Output is Y=L/R. In case of X=*true* the creature turns left or right and moves forward, in case X=*false* the creature turns left or right without moving.

The creature can learn and optimize the algorithm by itself. Before implementing the procedure in hardware we used a software simulation which tried out all possible algorithms by enumeration and evaluated them.

> *for all algorithms do*
> > *for all configurations do*
> > > *count the cells which are crossed*
> > *compute the percentage of cells which are crossed related to all cells on average.*

All algorithms were tested for the following five configurations (fig. 3).

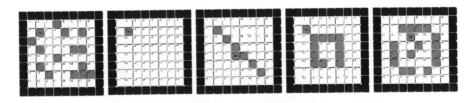

Fig. 3. The initial configurations 1 to 5 from left to right

In order to reduce simulation time, algorithms (tables) were deleted in advance if not all possible states are used. Also the further simulation was aborted when a path turned out to be a loop or the number of crossed cells did not increase after a certain time.

Two-State Algorithms. The best average algorithms found are algorithm 57 with 61 % crossed cells and algorithm 108 with 60 % crossed cells (table 1). The number of time steps (generations) was big enough that no improvement over time was possible. It can be realized, that no two-state algorithm exists, which is able to cross all cells for all these configurations. Therefore the "capacity of intelligence" (COI) has to be increased for better results. In our model the COI was defined as the number of bits used in the state tables.

Table 1. Algorithm 57 = 0R1L 1R0L and Algorithm 108 = 0L1R 1L0R (two states)

crossed cells	config. 1	config. 2	config. 3	config. 4	config. 5	% average
maximum	50	64	58	53	48	
algorithm 57	50	22	28	34	34	61%
algorithm 108	50	28	10	36	41	60%

Another result of the analysis is that only 144 of the 256 algorithms are real two-state algorithms, where both states are reached or used. Before simulation an algorithm can formally check the bit pattern if it is a real two-state algorithm or if it is trivial. By this technique the simulation time was significantly reduced. Only 19 of the 144 algorithms allow the creature to cross 42 − 61 % of the empty cells. Many of the algorithms yield bad or unacceptable results mainly because they cyclically cross the same cells in a loop without any improvement after having visited a certain number of cells.

Four-State Algorithms. As expected the four-state algorithms lead to better results. The algorithms with four states, one input and one output can be represented by a 24 bit table, meaning that 2^{24} different algorithm have to be checked.

The five best algorithms found are:

- A: Algorithm 0944085 = 0R1L2R3R 1L3L1R2L
- B: Algorithm 8260210 = 1L3L2R0R 2L0L3R1R
- C: Algorithm 2010316 = 0R3L2L1R 3R1L0L2R
- D: Algorithm 2009329 = 0R3L2L1R 2R1L3R0L
- E: Algorithm 9825748 = 2R2L1L3R 3R3L1R2R

For each algorithm a number of equivalent algorithms were found, which only differ by the state encoding. However, the initial state is always state 0. The state graphs for the algorithms A and B are shown in fig. 4.

Algorithm A is not able to reach all cells of the configuration 2 and 3. Algorithm B is not able to reach all cells of the configuration 4, even if the number of generations (computation steps in the CA model) is very high (tested for 40 000). Algorithms C and D are not able to reach all cells of the configuration 2 and 4. Algorithm E is not able to reach all cells of the configuration 1, 2, 3, and 4. Only the algorithm B is able to reach all cells of the empty configuration 2 of size 8 × 8.

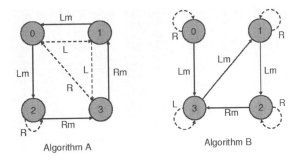

Fig. 4. The best four-state algorithms

Table 2. Four-state Algorithms

crossed cells	config. 1	config. 2	config. 3	config. 4	config. 5	% average
maximum	50	64	58	53	48	
algorithm A	50	60	56	53	48	97 %
algorithm B	50	64	58	50	48	97 %
algorithm C	50	60	58	48	48	96 %
algorithm D	50	60	58	47	48	95 %
algorithm E	48	60	47	48	48	91 %

Note that the performance of the algorithm strongly depends on the starting position and starting direction of the creature, the size of the field and on the number and arrangement of the obstacles.

Another criterion for the performance of the algorithms is the speed, meaning how fast the cells are crossed. The diagram fig. 5 shows the number of crossed cells vs. the number of generations for the configuration 1. We would expect from the best algorithm that only k generations are necessary, where k is the number of empty cells. This lowest bound of k could only be reached if the creature could also move straight forward without turning, which is not the case here. So the lower bound in our case is larger than k, but is guessed not to be larger than $2k$ (upper bound). The lower bound could not be reached with the four-state algorithm because of three reasons: (1) The creature cannot move straight forward directly, and (2) the creature sometimes turns too often on a site in order to find a free way and (3) already crossed cells are crossed repeatedly which is due to the limited capacity of intelligence (number of states).

Figure 5 shows for the first configuration with many scattered obstacles that the five algorithms differ in their speed. Algorithm E is the fastest, but it is not able to cross all cells. Algorithm B is slower than E, but it can cross all cells. The other algorithms are even slower and cannot cross all cells.

For the second (empty) configuration around three steps (generations) are necessary to find a new empty cell which was not crossed before. So the number of crossed cells grows almost linear, with slight differences between the five algorithms.

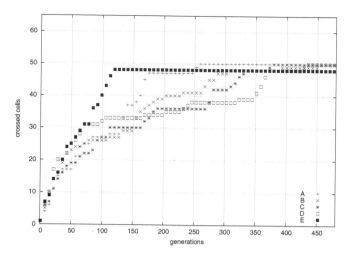

Fig. 5. The speed of the algorithms for the first configuration

The optimizations needed minutes to days on a regular PC, depending on the field size, number of initial configurations, and the capacity of intelligence. In order to speed up the optimizations significantly, the problem was mapped into programmable FPGA logic.

3.4   Implementation in Hardware

One of our goals is to speed up the computation by means of special hardware using field programmable gate arrays (FPGA). In our case the hardware for the cell field was described in the hardware description language Verilog and synthesized into basic logic, which can be loaded into a FPGA. Figure 6 shows the logic in principal of a cell with connections to the horizontal neighbor cells. The connections to the vertical neighbors are left out for clarity and have to be completed. This logic represents the behavior of a cell for the different types (T = CREATURE, EMPTY) and the direction D of a creature.

The rule is described by a logical function. The cell state contains the direction, type, and control state. The control state *cstate* controls the actual behavior. It changes its state depending on its old state, the condition *Icanmove*, and the table *tableNextcstate* which holds the behavior. The new direction of the creature depends on *cstate* and *tableAction*. The behavior of the creature, represented by the actual state and the tables *tableNextcstate* and *tableAction* is automatically modified in the hardware in order to yield an optimum.

We used the Altera chip EPF10K70RC240-4 and the MAX+plus II Tools for the synthesis. The parallel implementation of 16 kernel cells in the FPGA needs 784 logic cells, which is 20 % of all the total amount of cells. The maximum clock frequency which was achieved is around 20 MHz for this chip. This means that in every clock cycle 16 cells can be updated. The recent technology of Altera FPGA device EP2S180 offers 179 400 logic elements operating at a clock

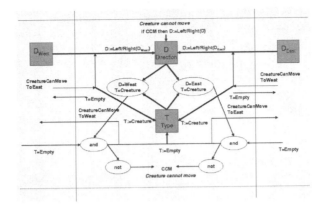

Fig. 6. The principal logic of a cell

frequency around 400 MHz. This device is large enough to hold a cell array of size $60 \times 60 = 3\,600$. The time to update one generation in hardware will be $1/400$ MHz $= 2.5$ ns. The software simulation needs around 25 cycles to update one cell. The time to update $3\,600$ cells is $25 \times 3\,600/2$ GHz $= 45$ μs, assuming an operating clock frequency of 2 GHz for a PC. Thus the speed-up gained by the use of the recent FPGA logic technology will be around $18\,000$ to find out the best algorithm. With a storage of all results and a resulting clock rate of 350 MHz the speed-up is around $15\,750$.

4   Conclusion and Future Work

We implemented a learning moving creature both in software and in hardware. The creature has the task to cross as many as possible empty cells using a local algorithm. This algorithm can be seen as the brain of the creature which implements a certain behavior. A variable state machine was used for the hardware and software implementation of the algorithm. The synthesized hardware allows to work massively parallel yielding to speed-ups of many thousands compared to software simulation on a PC.

All 256 two-state algorithms and all 2^{14} four-state algorithms have been investigated systematically. Only one four-state algorithm was found, which is able to cross all cells of the 8×8 empty configuration 2. The best algorithms A and B cross 97 % of the cells on average.

The goal is to discover better algorithms using a higher capacity of intelligence. The capacity intelligence can be enhanced by increasing the number of states, the number of inputs from the environment or the number and type of outputs (actions).

There is a lot of interesting future work to do, like:

- Find efficient and robust behaviors for a higher capacity of intelligence.
- Analyze and evaluate the performance of the algorithms.
- Speeding up the optimizing procedures.
- Use more complex worlds and tasks.
- Improve the hardware architectures.

References

1. Epstein, J.M., Axtell, R.: Growing artificial societies – social science from the bottom up. Brooking Institution Press, Washington D. C. (1996)
2. Dascalu, M., Franti, E., Stefan, G.: Modeling production with artificial societies: the emergence of social structure. In: Cellular Automata Research Towards Industry. (1998)
3. Hoffmann, R., Völkmann, K.P., Waldschmidt, S., Heenes, W.: Global Cellular Automata, A Flexible Parallel Model. In: 6th International Conference on Parallel Computing Technologies PaCT2001. Lecture Notes in Computer Science (LNCS 2127), Springer (2001)
4. Ray, T.: An Approach to the Synthesis of Life. In: Artificial Life II. (1991)
5. Levy, S.: KL – Künstliches Leben aus dem Computer. Droemer Knaur (1993) translation from the English, 'Artificial Life' (1992).
6. Hochberger, C.: CDL – Eine Sprache für die Zellularverarbeitung auf verschiedenen Zielplattformen. PhD thesis, Darmstädter Dissertation D17 (1998)
7. Hoffmann, R., Ulmann, B., Völkmann, K.P., Waldschmidt, S.: A Stream Processor Architecture Based on the Configurable CEPRA-S. In: FPL 2000. LNCS 1896, Springer (2000)
8. Hochberger, C., Hoffmann, R., Waldschmidt, S.: CDL++ for the Description of Moving Objects in Cellular Automata. In: PaCT99, Par. Comp. Technologies. LNCS 1662, Springer (1999)
9. Halbach, M., Hoffmann, R., Röder, P.: FPGA Implementation of Cellular Automata Compared to Software Implementation. In: PASA Workshop. ARCS, Augsburg (2004)
10. Halbach, M., Hoffmann, R.: Implementing Cellular Automata in FPGA Logic. In: International Parallel & Distributed Processing Symposium (IPDPS), Workshop on Massively Parallel Processing (WMPP), Santa Fe, NM, IEEE Computer Society (2004)
11. Kari, J.: Infinite snake tiling problems. In: DLT'2002, Developments in Language Theory. Lecture Notes in Computer Science, Springer (2002)
12. Mesot, B., Sanchez, E., Pena, C.A., Perez-Uribe, A.: SOS++: Finding Smart Behaviors Using Learning and Evolution. In Standish, Abbass, Bedau, eds.: Artificial Life VIII, MIT Press (2002) pp. 264

A Generalized Rapid Development Environment for Cellular Automata Based Simulations

Ivan Blecic[1], Arnaldo Cecchini[2], and Giuseppe A. Trunfio[3]

[1] Università IUAV di Venezia, Dept. of Planning, Venezia, Italy
ivan@iuav.it
[2] Faculty of Architecture in Alghero - University of Sassari, Alghero, Italy,
cecchini@uniss.it
[3] University of Calabria, Center of High-Performance Computing, Rende (CS), Italy
trunfio@unical.it

Abstract. Cellular Automata (CA) are widely applied in variety of fields, and this made generalised simulation environments become increasingly important for the development of CA-based scientific applications. In this paper we discuss the fact that many real phenomena require strong relaxation of classical CA assumptions in order to be adequately modelled, and that brings about limitations of existing modelling and simulation environments, often based on insufficiently generalised CA formulations. These considerations have induced us to develop a modelling environment based on a largely generalised CA formulation. The environment has proven to be particularly suitable for modelling and simulation of spatial urban, territorial and environmentally-oriented phenomena.

1 Introduction

In the recent years, cellular automata approach [1] has been successfully applied in different fields including ecology, biology, geology, medicine, urban studies, chaos theory and many others.

The interdisciplinary nature of CA-based modelling is an important challenge, resulting in an increasing demand for dedicated Problem Solving Environments (PSEs) suitable for supporting educational, research and industrial activities. The main objective of such software environments is to relieve the researcher from low-level operational and programming activities, allowing him/her to concentrate efforts on the modelling itself. Furthermore, the visualisation and data analysis features usually available in PSEs make the CA modelling-calibration-validation cycle much faster and effective. As a main consequence of all this, PSEs are of particular use in cases where an integration of different interdisciplinary knowledge is required, which in CA modelling of real systems typically corresponds to the involvement of researchers from various scientific areas, and not only computer scientist.

As pointed out by Worsh [2], there exist a number of software packages for CA-based simulations. Some of these implement variations and generalisations of the

P.M.A. Sloot, B. Chopard, and A.G. Hoekstra (Eds.): ACRI 2004, LNCS 3305, pp. 851–860, 2004.

classical definition of CA, which have proven to be useful for modelling of real phenomena. On the other hand, many studies related to the application of CAs to the simulation of dynamic processes in geography [3], [4], have stressed the necessity of a stronger relaxation of classical CA assumptions with respect to those usually implemented in available CA environments.

First of all, even if great majority of CA applications successfully adopt a strict local neighbourhoods, spatial interactions in geographical phenomena can often take place over greater distances. Hence, the CA model presented hereby is partially based on the notion of *proximal* space, deriving from research in 'cellular geography' [5] which set the basis for the so called *geo-algebra* approach proposed by Takeyama and Coucleis [6]. In this later work, the relaxation of some of the main assumptions of the classical CA theory has been suggested: namely, the spatial regularity of the lattice and the homogeneity of the cells' neighbourhoods. Thus, in *geo-algebra* every cell has a different neighbourhood, defined by relations of *nearness* between spatial entities (i.e. cells), where *nearness* can means both topological relation or generic "behavioural" (e.g. functional) influence. Following the described approach, in the present work we define neighbourhoods as generic sets of cells whose state can influence, in some way, the variation of the current cell's state. Another relaxation we have adopted regards the temporal stationariness of neighbourhoods which, differently from classical CAs, can change with time.

In comparison with the most CA models, we have introduced a further variation inspired by the observation that simulation of complex systems is often founded on the interaction between quite different sub-systems. Such modelling might require different sub-systems' dynamic be based on knowledge from different disciplines, and can require different spatial and temporal granularity. Thus, likewise in [7], it appears useful and effective to organise the 2D-physical domain in more distinct *layers*. Cells can have both a *horizontal neighborhood*, a subset of cells belonging to the same layer, as well as several *vertical neighborhoods* with cells belonging to other layers.

Moreover, with respect to the classical CA formulation, the proposed model includes many of the well known generalisations and modifications (e.g. [8]), such as parametric dependence of transition rules, which simplify global steering of CA (i.e. global-to-local influence), and cell states decomposition in sub-states.

Another relevant issue is the integration and interoperability of available geographical data infrastructures with CA environments. The integration of CA engines into existing GIS systems has been proposed (e.g. loose coupling based on the Remote Procedure Call paradigm or other proprietary protocols) [9], [10]. However, for the hereby proposed CA reference model, loose coupling with proprietary GIS is hard to obtain both for the required flexibility, especially in the modelling phase, and due to low computational efficiency. Therefore, we have opted for the development "from scratch" of a programmable simulation environment. The software, based on the generalised reference model illustrated in the next paragraph, has limited GIS-like functionalities and can support a wide variety of hypothetical as well as real applications.

2 Model Formalisation

The Cellular Automaton (CA) is defined as:

$$AC =< P_G, \mathbf{f}_G, L >$$ (1)

where:

- $P_G = P_G^{(1)} \times P_G^{(2)} \times \cdots \times P_G^{(g)}$ is the finite set of values assumed by the vector of global parameters;
- $\mathbf{f}_G = \{ f_G^{(1)}, f_G^{(2)}, \ldots, f_G^{(g)} \}$ is a vector of global parameters' updating functions;
- $L = \{ l_1, l_2, \cdots, l_n \}$ is a set of n cells layer.

A layer is defined as:

$$l_i =< C_i, P_{Li}, \mathbf{f}_{Li} >$$ (2)

where:

- C_i is a set of cells;
- $P_{Li} = P_{Li}^{(1)} \times P_{Li}^{(2)} \times \cdots \times P_{Li}^{(r)}$ is the finite set of values assumed by the vector of layer parameters;
- $\mathbf{f}_{Li} = \{ f_{Li}^{(1)}, f_{Li}^{(2)}, \ldots, f_{Li}^{(r)} \}$ is a vector of the layer parameters' updating functions.

A cell belonging to a layer l_i is defined as:

$$c_i =< S_i, P_{Ci}, \boldsymbol{\sigma}_i, \mathbf{f}_{Ci}, \phi_i, O_i >$$ (3)

where:

- $S_i = S_i^{(1)} \times S_i^{(2)} \times \cdots \times S_i^{(q)}$ is the finite set of values assumed by the cell state vector. Each scalar component of $\mathbf{s}_i \in S_i$ represents a cell sub-state.
- $P_{Ci} = P_{Ci}^{(1)} \times P_{Ci}^{(2)} \times \cdots \times P_{Ci}^{(m)}$ is the finite set of values assumed by the cell parameters vector.
- $\boldsymbol{\sigma}_i = \{ \sigma_i^{(1)}, \sigma_i^{(2)}, \ldots, \sigma_i^{(n)} \}$ is the vector of n neighbourhood functions defined as:

$$\sigma_i^{(k)}: \left[\ C_i \times (C_k)^{|C_k|} \times P_{Li} \times P_G \ \right] \to \wp(C_k), \quad k = 1 \ldots n$$ (4)

where $\wp(C_k)$ is the set of subsets belonging to C_k, and $|C_k|$ is the total number of cells of the k-th layer. Thus, $\sigma_i^{(k)}$ represents the neighbourhood of the cell c_i, as a subset of cells belonging to the k-th layer. In particular, we define *horizontal neighbourhood* of the cell $c \in C_i$ as a subset of C_i defined by a function $\sigma_i^{(i)}$. Likewise, we define *vertical neighbourhood* of the cell $c \in C_i$ as a subset of C_j defined by a function $\sigma_i^{(j)}$, where $j \neq i$.

- $\mathbf{f}_{Ci} = \{f_{Ci}^{(1)}, f_{Ci}^{(2)}, \ldots, f_{Ci}^{(m)}\}$ is a vector of local parameters' updating functions. Generally the vector $\mathbf{p}_i$ evolves according to the function $\mathbf{f}_{Ci}$ defined as:

$$\mathbf{f}_{Ci} : \prod_{\substack{k=1 \\ k \neq i}}^{n} (S_k)^{\left|\sigma_i^{(k)}\right|} \times P_G \times P_{Li} \times P_{Ci} \rightarrow P_{Ci} \tag{5}$$

where P_{Ci} is the set of values P_c related to the layer l_i and $|\sigma_i^{(k)}|$ represents the total number of cells belonging to the vertical neighbourhood $\sigma_i^{(k)}$, with $i \neq k$. Cell's parameters can, via updating functions, acquire information about cells belonging to other layers and therefore serve for its inclusion into vertical neighbourhood.

- ϕ_i is the *transition rule* of a generic cell belonging to layer l_i, and is defined as:

$$\phi_i : \left[(S_i)^{\left|\sigma_i^{(i)}\right|} \times P_G \times P_{Li} \times P_{Ci} \right] \rightarrow S_i \tag{6}$$

- O_i is a finite set of *geometrical objects*, characterised by an adequate graphical vector description (i.e. cells).

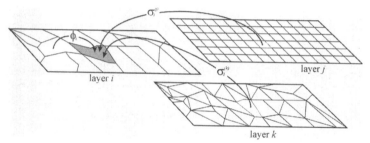

Fig. 1. Relations between cells and layers in the proposed model

The parameters' updating functions of a generic layer l_i are defined as:

$$\mathbf{f}_{Li} : \left[(S_i)^{|C_i|} \times P_{Li} \right] \rightarrow P_{Li} \tag{7}$$

where $|C_i|$ is the total number of layer's cells. Such definition permits the layer's parameters assume values depending on actual configuration of the whole layer, offering hence a possible mechanism for a global steering of the layer's evolution.

With regard to the k-th component $\mathbf{f}_G^{(k)}$ of global parameters' updating functions, the model includes both the possibility it be provided by an independent calculation model evolving in parallel with the cellular automaton, as well as to have $\mathbf{f}_G^{(k)}$ update the value of the global k-th parameter based on values assumed by other global parameters and all the layers' parameters:

$$\mathbf{f}_G^{(k)} : \prod_{k=1}^{n} P_{Lk} \times P_G \rightarrow P_G^{(k)} \tag{8}$$

Relations (5), (7) and (8), show us the possibility a layer's evolution is "controlled" based on the global configuration of other layers.

3   The Architecture of the Software Environment

CAGE (*Cellular Automata General Environment*) has been developed for an efficacious implementation of multi-layer cellular automata illustrated above. The fig. 3
shows a typical screen-shoot of the environment.

Internally, CAGE generates C++ source code according to the visual definition of
the CA structure and the flow-chart diagrams of transition rules. The later can also be
directly coded in a C-like language which comprises specific constructs and an extended library of predefined function. Furthermore, different scenario editing tools
are available, as well as simulation evolution monitoring and analysis features.

It can be seen from the fig. 2 that CAGE has a base class implementing the generalised CA described in the paragraph 2, which gets instanced as a specific model
object designed by the user. The environment should be coupled with a C++ compiler
in order to generate the so called CA kernel (the CA execution programme).

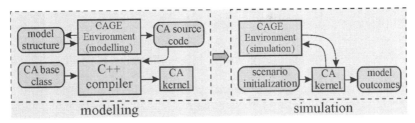

Fig. 2. Modelling and simulation in CAGE

Once the CA kernel is compiled, the environment can execute it as a child process.
The kernel reads the initial scenario data and starts the simulation. During the simulation the kernel constantly pushes back to the environment, via a named pipe inter-
process communication, the current state of the scenario for the real-time evolution
visualisation. If necessary, the kernel can be executed autonomously, avoiding thus
the overhead related to the communication with the environment.

3.1   Making the CA Structure

Within the environment, the CA structure can be designed via an efficacious and
user-friendly graphical interface (see fig. 3) where all components of the CA (layers,
parameters, sub-states, functions, neighbourhoods and graphical objects) are organised in a tree structure. Properties of elements can be inserted and modified through a
specific input forms. If a function (updating, transition or neighbourhood) gets selected, the software provides an adequate graphical (flow-chats diagram) or textual
(source code) representation.

The design of a CA passes through the specification of layers' space tessellation
and the type of neighbourhood. The space tessellation can be regular or irregular.
Regular tessellation (rectangular, triangular, hexagonal cells) is obtained automatically by the environment, while in case of irregular tessellation, the graphical objects

can be imported from a GIS database or manually designed in the environment. In case of regular tessellation, it is possible to use one of the classical horizontal neighbourhoods (Moore, Von Neumann, etc.). Otherwise, user can define a horizontal neighbourhood based on a specific query.

Per each parameter (global, layer's, cell's) and sub-state, it is required an alphanumeric identifier and the data type (integer, real, char). The parameters can be constant or variable function-based (thus updated during the simulation).

Per each function (of parameters, sub-states, neighbourhoods update), it is required an identifier, the execution frequency and probability, and a condition the execution is subordinated to. The definition of a transition rule or an updating function can be achieved through a visual design of the flow-chart diagram (see fig. 3). Normally, it is not necessary to code expressions directly, but simply to select functions, variables and conditions from the tree-structure these are organised in. Finally, CAGE will generate the source code of the designed flow-chart diagram.

3.2   The Rules Programming Language and the Standard Function Library

The creation of a CA requires the coding of transition rules, parameters' updating functions, and the neighbourhood queries. In CAGE, functions are coded in a C-like language enriched with specific constructs, library functions and operators. Available functions and operators are those frequently used in the CA development, and accept as arguments parameters, sub-states, graphical objects or constant values. The user can extend the library with his/her own functions. Besides a series of classical mathematical functions, the following are main available function "families":

-   *geometrical functions:* operate on and with graphical objects representing cells. For example, the function `dist(obj1, obj2)` returns the distance between two cells, while the function `perimeter(obj)` returns the length of the perimeter of a cell;

-   *aggregation functions:* return values related to sets of cells. For example, the function `NeighCell[lay].NEqVal(var, val)` returns the number of cells belonging to the neighbourhood of the current cell on layer *lay* whose variable *var* assumes the value *val*. Analogous sum, minimum, maximum, mean, etc. functions are available.

Furthermore, the language allows the use of particular geometric operators such as *"Contains"*, *"Intersect"* and *"Within"* permitting the formulation of logical propositions based on the cell's position in the space.

3.3   Query-Based Neighborhood Generation

The neighbourhood of a cell from i-th layer on k-th layer, defined by the function $\sigma_i^{(k)}$, is generally the result of a query on the sets of cells, where operators, as well as logical, mathematical and geometrical functions are used. The neighbourhood is not inevitably stationary with time, but can vary, since queries can be reiterated with given frequencies and probabilities. The function $\sigma_i^{(k)}$ can be specified through the definition of a logical proposition $p(c)$, which associates the value "true" to every cell, from the set c, that has to be included in the neighbourhood. The definition of this proposition can in CAGE be made in the specific form for conditions generation, using available library functions and operators. For example, with the use of function `dist(obj1, obj2)` and `area(obj1)` we can generate a neighbourhood made of all cells less that 200 units far from the current cell whose area is smaller that 2500 square units:

`dist(Obj,Cell[Lay].Obj)<200 and area(Cell[Lay].Obj)<2500`

where `Obj` is the graphical object of the current cell, while `Cell[Lay].Obj` is the target object of the cell candidate for the inclusion into the neighbourhood.

4 An Example of a Rapid Model Development

CAGE has already been used for the development of dynamic urban simulations [11]. Due to space restrictions, in this paper we will try to prove the efficacy of the modelling and simulation environment by presenting a conceptually simple prey-predator model with the use of multi-layer features. Since the pioneering studies by Lotka and the work of Volterra [12], many models have been proposed for prey-predator systems. Some are based on the standard differential equation approach by Lotka-Volterra, others on lattice-gas simulations and some more on CA.

In the model hereby described (see fig. 4), there are three sub-systems whose dynamics evolve in separate but interacting layers: *Grass*, *Prey* and *Predator*:

Grass Layer. This layer describes the evolution of the vegetation which is the food for prey. Each cell has a *Weight* sub-state representing the quantity of the available vegetation. The value of *Weight* grows asymptotically according to a regeneration rate defined as layer's parameter *RegenRate*. Probabilistically, a grassless cell can be inseminated by an adjacent cell.

Prey Layer. In this layer, each cell can "host" a prey, so the cell is defined by a sub-state *PreyStamina* (> 0 if the prey is present) which decreases continuously according to the rate given by the layer's parameter *PreyBasalMetabolism*. In fact, for each step of simulation, a prey has to be feed with grass, and this event changes the stamina value according to the layer's parameter *GrassToStaminaRate*. A vertical neighbourhood associates each cell of this layer to the corresponding cell from the *Grass* layer. Preys are characterised by a vision capacity (layer's parameter *PreyVisualRange*) which defines the vertical neighbourhood on the *Predator* layer. Each cell is characterised by an appeal according to sub-state *CellAppealPrey* which assumes value zero if there is a predator in its visual range, otherwise it assumes the value of the grass availability. The prey tends to move probabilistically toward more appealing cells. When two preys are within the same horizontal neighbourhoods and there is a vacant cell within the same neighbourhood, then a new prey is born, and its stamina is set to equal the mean stamina values of the two progenitors.

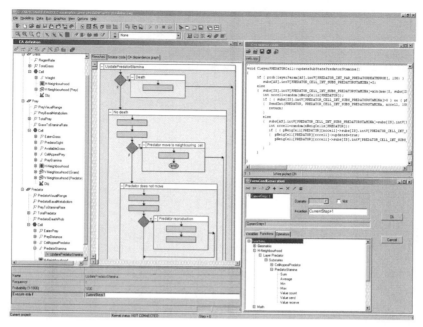

Fig. 3. A screen-shoot of the prey-predator model implemented in CAGE

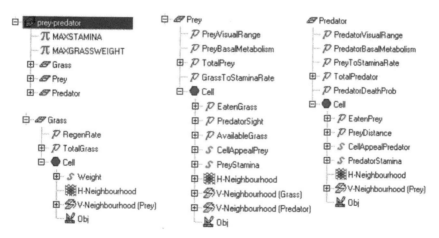

Fig. 4. Structure of the implemented prey-predator model in CAGE tree interface

Predator Layer. As with the *Prey* layer, each cell can "host" a predator characterised by a sub-state *PredatorStamina,* which continuously decreases according to
the layer's parameter *PredatorBasalMetabolism*. Predators are feed with preys, and
this increases the stamina according to the layer's parameter *PreyToStaminaRate*.
Predators as well are characterised by a vision capacity (layer's parameter *Predator-
VisualRange*) which defines the vertical neighbourhood with regard to the layer *Prey*.
Also, each cell is characterised by an appeal determined with the sub-state *CellAp-
pealPredator*, which is inversely proportional to the distance from the closest prey

within the visual range. Predators tend to move, in a probabilistic manner, towards more appealing cells. When two predators are within the same horizontal neighbourhood, and there exits a vacant cell, it gives birth to a new predator whose stamina is set to equal the mean stamina values of the two progenitors.

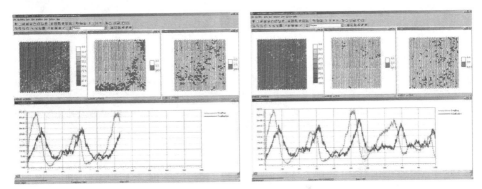

Fig. 5. CAGE screen shot during prey-predator simulation (step 340 and step 1000)

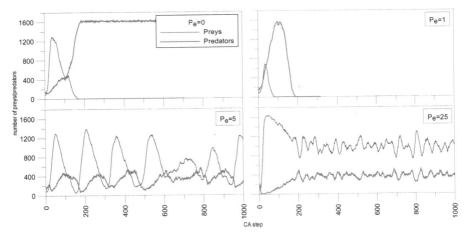

Fig. 6. Graphs obtained with the variation of the parameter *PreyToStaminaRate* (P_e), which represent the conversion "efficiency" of pray into predator's stamina

For the implementation of the above described the model structure in CAGE has been created (see fig. 4) and the transition rules, update functions and neighbourhood queries have been written (less than 50 lines of code in whole). The fig. 3 shows a screen-shoot of CAGE environment with the flow-chart diagram of the sub-state *PredatorStamina* update function. The used scenario was composed by three 38×44 hexagonal-cell layers with hex-apothem of 250. Fig. 5 shows two screen-shoots of the executed simulations with their respective three layers and the evolution of different populations of preys and predators. In fig. 6 we illustrate the results of some experimentations related to the sensibility of the system with regard to the value of the parameter *PredatorBasalMetabolism*. The constant value parameters were: *Regen-*

Rate=3, PreyBasalMetabolism=2, GrassToStaminaRate=5, PreyVisualRange=750, PredatorVisualRange=1000, PreyToStaminaRate=50, PredatorBasalMetabolism=0, 1, 5, 25.

5 Conclusions

We believe that CAGE software environment has proven to be suitable for rapid, easy and user-friendly development of CA-based simulation models. First real-case applications have shown that CAGE can result particularly useful both for educational useful as well as for research. Future developments will include the development of a parallel computing version of the kernel based on the *message-passing* paradigm.

References

1. von Neumann, J.: Theory of self reproducing automata. University of Illinois Press, Urbana (1966)
2. Worsch, T., Simulations of cellular automata, Fut. Gen. Comp. Syst. 16 (1999) : 157-170
3. Batty, M., Xie, Y., From cells to cities, Environ. Planning B (1994), 21.
4. Cecchini, A., Urban modelling by means of cellular automata: generalised urban automata with the help on-line (Augh) model. Environment and Planning (B), (1996) 23:721-732
5. Tobler, W., Cellular geography, in S. Gale & G. Olsson, Philosophy in Geography (pp. 379-386). Dordrecht: Reidel
6. Takeyama, M., Couclelis, H., Map dynamics: integrating cellular automata and GIS through Geo-Algebra, Intern. Journ. of Geogr. Inf. Science, (1997), 11:73-91
7. Bandini, S., Mauri, G.: Multilayered Cellular Automata. Theoretical Computer Science, 217 (1999) 99-113
8. Di Gregorio, S., Serra, R. An empirical method for modelling and simulating some complex macroscopic phenomena by cellular automata, Fut. Gen. Comp. Syst. 16 (1999) : 259-271
9. Wu, F.: GIS-based simulation as an exploratory analysis for space-time processes. J. Geograph. Syst. (1999) 1:199-218
10. Wagner, D., Cellular automata and geographic information systems, Env. and Plann. B, (1997), 24:219-234
11. Blecic I., Cecchini A., Prastacos P., Trunfio G.A., Verigos E. - Modeling Urban Dynamics with Cellular Automata: a Model of the City of Heraklion - 7th AGILE conference on Geographic Information Science, April 29th - May 1st 2004, Heraklion, Greece
12. Volterra, V., Mem. Accad. Nazionale Lincei 2 6 (1926) 31

Characterizing Configuration Spaces of Simple Threshold Cellular Automata

Predrag T. Tosic and Gul A. Agha

Open Systems Laboratory, Department of Computer Science
University of Illinois at Urbana-Champaign
Mailing address: Siebel Center for Computer Science,
201 N. Goodwin Ave., Urbana, IL 61801, USA
{p-tosic,agha}@cs.uiuc.edu

Abstract. We study herewith *the simple threshold cellular automata (CA)*, as perhaps the simplest broad class of *CA* with non-additive (that is, non-linear and non-affine) local update rules. We characterize all possible computations of the most interesting rule for such *CA*, namely, the *Majority (MAJ)* rule, both in the classical, parallel CA case, and in case of the corresponding sequential CA where the nodes update sequentially, one at a time. We compare and contrast the configuration spaces of arbitrary simple threshold automata in those two cases, and point out that some parallel threshold CA cannot be simulated by any of their sequential equivalents. We show that the temporal cycles exist only in case of (some) parallel simple threshold CA, but can never take place in sequential threshold CA. We also show that most threshold *CA* have very few fixed point configurations and few (if any) cycle configurations, and that, while the *MAJ* sequential and parallel *CA* may have many fixed points, nonetheless "almost all" configurations, in both parallel and sequential cases, are transient states. Finally, motivated by the contrasts between parallel and sequential simple threshold CA, we try to motivate the study of *genuinely asynchronous CA*.

1   Introduction and Motivation

Cellular automata (CA) were originally introduced as an abstract mathematical model of the behavior of biological systems capable of self-reproduction [15]. Subsequently, variants of *CA* have been extensively studied in a great variety of application domains, predominantly in the context of complex physical or biological systems and their dynamics (e.g., [20,21,22]). However, *CA* can also be viewed as an abstraction of massively parallel computers (e.g, [7]). Herein, we study a particular simple yet nontrivial class of *CA* from a computer science perspective. This class are the *threshold cellular automata.* In the context of such *CA,* we shall first compare and contrast the configuration spaces of the classical, concurrent *CA* and their sequential analogues. We will then pick a particular threshold node update rule, and fully characterize possible computations in both parallel and sequential cases for the one-dimensional automata.

Cellular automata CA are an abstract computational model of *fine-grain parallelism* [7], in that the elementary operations executed at each node are rather simple and hence comparable to the basic operations performed by the computer hardware. In a classical,

P.M.A. Sloot, B. Chopard, and A.G. Hoekstra (Eds.): ACRI 2004, LNCS 3305, pp. 861–870, 2004.

that is, concurrently executing *CA,* whether finite or infinite, all the nodes execute their operations *logically simultaneously:* the state of a node x_i at time step $t + 1$ is some simple function of the states (i) of the node x_i itself, and (ii) of a set of its pre-specified neighbors, at time t.

We consider herewith the sequential version of *CA,* heretofore abridged to *SCA,* and compare such sequential *CA* with the classical, *parallel (concurrent) CA.* In particular, we show that there are *1-D CA* with very simple node state update rules that cannot be simulated by any comparable *SCA,* irrespective of the node update ordering.

We also fully characterize the possible computations of the most interesting case of *threshold cellular automata,* namely, the *(S)CA* with the *Majority* node update rule.

An important remark is that we use the terms *parallel* and *concurrent* as synonyms throughout the paper. This is perhaps not the most standard convention, but we are not alone in not making the distinction between the two terms (cf. discussion in [16]). Moreover, by a *parallel* (equivalently, *concurrent*) *computation* we shall mean actions of several processing units that are carried out *logically* (if not necessarily *physically*) *simultaneously.* In particular, when referring to *parallel* or *concurrent* computation, we do assume a *perfect synchrony.*

2   Cellular Automata and Types of Their Configurations

We follow [7] and define classical (that is, synchronous and concurrent) *CA* in two steps: by first defining the notion of a *cellular space,* and subsequently that of a *cellular automaton* defined over an appropriate cellular space.

Definition 1: A *Cellular Space,* Γ, is an ordered pair (G, Q) where G is a regular graph (finite or infinite) with each node labeled with a distinct positive integer, and Q is a finite set of states that has at least two elements, one of which being the special *quiescent state,* denoted by 0.

We denote the set of integer labels of the nodes (vertices) in Γ by L.

Definition 2: A *Cellular Automaton (CA),* **A**, is an ordered triple (Γ, N, M) where Γ is a *cellular space,* N is a *fundamental neighborhood,* and M is a *finite state machine* such that the input alphabet of M is $Q^{|N|}$, and the local transition function (update rule) for each node is of the form $\delta : Q^{|N|+1} \rightarrow Q$ for *CA with memory,* and $\delta : Q^{|N|} \rightarrow Q$ for *memoryless CA.*

Some of our results pertain to a comparison and contrast between the classical, concurrent threshold CA and their sequential counterparts, the threshold SCA.

Definition 3: A *Sequential Cellular Automaton (SCA)* **S** is an ordered quadruple (Γ, N, M, s), where Γ, N and M are as in *Def. 2,* and s is a sequence, finite or infinite, all of whose elements are drawn from the set L of integers used in labeling the vertices of Γ. The sequence s is specifying the sequential ordering according to which an SCA's nodes update their states, one at a time.

However, when comparing and contrasting the concurrent threshold CA with their sequential counterparts, rather than making a comparison between a given CA with a *particular SCA,* we compare the parallel CA computations with the computations of the corresponding SCA for *all* possible sequences of node updates. To that end, the following convenient terminology is introduced:

Definition 4: A *Nondeterministic Interleavings Cellular Automaton (NICA)* **I** is defined to be the union of all sequential automata **S** whose first three components, Γ, N and M, are fixed. That is, $\mathbf{I} = \cup_s (\Gamma, N, M, s)$, where the meanings of Γ, N, M, and s are the same as before, and the union is taken over *all* (finite and infinite) sequences $s : \{1, 2, 3, ...\} \to L$ (where L is the set of integer labels of the nodes in Γ).

Since our goal is to characterize *all* possible computations of parallel and sequential threshold *CA,* a a *(discrete) dynamical system* view of *CA* will be useful. A *phase space* of a dynamical system is a (finite or infinite, as appropriate) directed graph where the vertices are the *global configurations* (or *global states*) of the system, and directed edges correspond to possible transitions from one global state to another. We now define the fundamental, qualitatively distinct types of (global) configurations that a classical (parallel) cellular automaton can find itself in.

Definition 5: A *fixed point (FP)* is a configuration in the phase space of a *CA* such that, once the *CA* reaches this configuration, it stays there forever. A *cycle configuration (CC)* is a state that, if once reached, will be revisited infinitely often with a fixed, finite period of 2 or greater. A *transient configuration (TC)* is a state that, once reached, is never going to be revisited again.

In particular, a FP is a special, degenerate case of CC with period 1. Due to their deterministic evolution, any configuration of a classical, parallel *CA* belongs to exactly one of these basic configuration types, i.e., it is a FP, a proper CC, or a TC.

On the other hand, if one considers a *sequential CA* so that *arbitrary* node update orderings are permitted, that is, if one considers a *NICA* automaton, then, given the underlying cellular space and the local update rule, the resulting phase space configurations, due to nondeterminism that results from different choices of possible sequences of node updates, are more complicated. In a particular *SCA,* a cycle configuration is any configuration revisited infinitely often - but the period between different consecutive visits, assuming an arbitrary sequence s of node updates, need not be fixed. We call a global configuration that is revisited only finitely many times (under a given ordering s) *quasi-cyclic.* Similarly, a *quasi-fixed point* is a *SCA* configuration such that, once the dynamics reaches this configuration, it stays there "for a while" (i.e., for some finite number of sequential node update steps), and then leaves. For example, a configuration of a *SCA* can be simultaneously a (quasi-)FP and a (quasi-)CC (see, e.g., the *XOR CA* vs. *XOR NICA* example in [19]). For simplicity, heretofore we shall refer to a configuration x of a *NICA* as a pseudo fixed point if there exists some infinite sequence of node updates s such that x is a FP in the usual sense when the corresponding *SCA's* nodes update according to ordering s. A global configuration of a *NICA* is a *proper* FP iff it is a fixed point of each corresponding *SCA,* that is, for every sequence of node updates s. Similarly, we consider a global configuration y to be a cycle state, if there exists an infinite sequence of node updates s' such that, if the corresponding *SCA's* nodes update according to s', y is a cycle state of period 2 or greater in the usual sense (see **Def. 5**). Thus, in general, a global configuration of a nondeterministic *NICA* automaton, for instance, can be simultaneously a (pseudo) FP, a CC and a TS (with respect to different node update sequences s).

Definition 6: A *1-D cellular automaton of radius r* $(r \geq 1)$ is a *CA* defined over a one-dimensional string of nodes, such that each node's next state depends on the current states of its neighbors to the left and right that are no more than r nodes away (and, in case of the *CA with memory*, on the current state of that node itself).

We fix the following conventions and terminology. Throughout, only *Boolean CA* and *SCA/NICA* are considered; in particular, the set of possible states of any node is $\{0, 1\}$. The terms "monotone symmetric" and "symmetric (linear) threshold" functions/update rules/automata are used interchangeably. Similarly, the terms "(global) dynamics" and "(global) computation" are used synonymously. Also, unless explicitly stated otherwise, automata *with memory* are assumed. The default *infinite* cellular space Γ is a two-way infinite line. The default *finite* Γ is a ring with an appropriate number of nodes[1]. The terms "phase space" and "configuration space" will be used synonymously, as well, and sometimes abridged to *PS*.

3   Properties of 1-D Simple Boolean Threshold CA and SCA

Herein, we compare and contrast the classical, concurrent *CA* with their sequential counterparts, *SCA* and *NICA*, in the context of the simplest (nonlinear) local update rules possible, viz., the *CA* in which the nodes locally update according to *linear threshold functions*. Moreover, we choose these threshold functions to be *symmetric*, so that the resulting *CA* are also *totalistic* (see, e.g., [7] or [21]). We show the fundamental difference in the configuration spaces, and therefore possible computations, in case of the classical, concurrent automata on one, and the sequential threshold cellular automata, on the other hand: while the former can have temporal cycles (of length two), the computations of the latter, under some mild additional conditions whose sole purpose is to ensure *some form of convergence*, necessarily *always* converge to a fixed point.

First, we need to define *threshold functions*, *simple threshold functions*, and the corresponding types of *(S)CA*.

Definition 7: A *Boolean-valued linear threshold function* of n inputs, $x_1, ..., x_n$, is any function of the form

$$f(x_1, ..., x_n) = \begin{cases} 1, & \text{if } \sum_i w_i \cdot x_i \geq \theta \\ 0, & \text{otherwise} \end{cases} \tag{1}$$

where θ is an appropriate *threshold constant*.

Definition 8: A *threshold cellular automaton* is a (parallel or sequential) cellular automaton such that its node update rule δ is a *Boolean-valued linear threshold function*.

Definition 9: A *simple* threshold *(S)CA* is an automaton whose local update rule δ is a monotone symmetric Boolean (threshold) function.

Throughout, whenever we say *a threshold automaton (threshold CA)*, we shall mean *simple threshold automaton (threshold CA)* - unless explicitly stated otherwise.

---

[1] It turns out, that circular boundary conditions are important for some of our technical results. Likewise, some results about the phase space properties of concurrent and sequential threshold *CA* may require (i) a certain minimal number of nodes and (ii) that the number of nodes be, e.g., even, divisible by four, or the like. Heretofore, we shall assume a sufficient number of nodes that "works" in the particular situation, without detailed elaborations.

Due to the nature of the node update rules, cyclic behavior intuitively should not be expected in these simple threshold automata. This is, generally, (almost) the case, as will be shown below. We argue that the importance of the results in this section largely stems from the following three factors: (i) the local update rules are the simplest nonlinear totalistic rules one can think of; (ii) given the rules, the cycles are not to be expected - yet they exist, and in the case of classical, parallel *CA only*; and, related to that observation, (iii) it is, for this class of *(S)CA*, the parallel *CA* that exhibit the more interesting behavior than any corresponding sequential *SCA* (and consequently also *NICA*), and, in particular, while there is nothing (qualitatively) among the possible sequential computations that is not present in the parallel case, the classical parallel threshold *CA* are capable of a particular qualitative behavior - namely, they may have nontrivial temporal cycles - that cannot be reproduced by *any* simple threshold *SCA* (and, therefore, also threshold *NICA*).

The results below hold for the two-way infinite *1-D CA,* as well as for the finite *CA* and *SCA* with sufficiently many nodes and circular boundary conditions.

Lemma 1:   (i) A 1-D classical (i.e., parallel) *CA* with $r = 1$ and the *Majority* update rule has (finite) temporal cycles in the phase space (*PS*). In contrast, (ii) *1-D Sequential CA* with $r = 1$ and the *Majority* update rule do not have any (finite) cycles in the phase space, *irrespective* of the sequential node update order ρ. ◇

Remark: In case of infinite sequential *SCA* as in the Lemma above, a nontrivial cycle configuration does not exist even in the limit. We also note that, in finite cases, ρ is an arbitrary sequence of an *SCA* nodes' indices, not necessarily a permutation. Thus, we may conclude that *NICA* with $\delta = MAJ$ and $r = 1$ are temporal cycle-free.

It turns out that, even if we consider local update rules δ other than the *MAJ* rule, yet restrict δ to *monotone symmetric Boolean functions,* such sequential *CA* still do not have any proper cycles.

Lemma 2:   For any *Monotone Symmetric Boolean 1-D Sequential CA* **S** with $r = 1$, and any sequential update order ρ, the phase space *PS(S)* of the automaton **S** is cycle-free. ◇

Similar results to those in *Lemmata 1-2* also hold for *1-D CA* with radius $r \geq 2$.

Theorem 1:   (i) *1-D (parallel) CA* with $r \geq 1$ and with the *Majority* node update rule have (finite) cycles in the phase space.   (ii) Any *1-D SCA* with $\delta = MAJ$ or any other monotone symmetric Boolean node update rule, $r \geq 1$ and any sequential order ρ of the node updates has a cycle-free phase space. ◇

Remarks: The claims of *Thm. 1* hold both for the finite *(S)CA* (provided that they have sufficiently many nodes, an even number of nodes in case of the *CA* with cycles, and assuming the circular boundary conditions in *part (i)*), and for the infinite *(S)CA.* We also observe that several variants of the result in *Theorem 1 (ii)* can be found in the literature. When the sequence of node updates of a finite *SCA* is periodic, with a single period a fixed permutation of the nodes, cycle-freeness of sequential *CA* and many other properties can be found in [8] and references therein. In [4], fixed permutation of node updates is also required, but the underlying cellular space Γ is allowed to be an arbitrary finite graph, and different nodes are allowed to compute *different* simple k-threshold functions.

As an immediate consequence of the results presented thus far, we have

Corollary 1:   For all $r \geq 1$,   there exists a *monotone symmetric CA* (that is, a *threshold automaton*) **A** such that **A** has finite temporal cycles in the phase space.

Some of the results for *(S)CA* with $\delta = MAJ$ do extend to some, but by no means all, other simple threshold *(S)CA* defined over the same cellular spaces. For instance, consider the k-threshold functions with $r = 2$. There are five nontrivial such functions, for $k \in \{1, 2, 3, 4, 5\}$. The 1-threshold function is Boolean *OR* function (in this case, on $2r + 1 = 5$ inputs), and the corresponding *CA* do not have temporal cycles; likewise with the "5-threshold" *CA,* that update according to Boolean *AND* on five inputs. However, in addition to *Majority* (i.e., 3-threshold), it is easy to show that 2-threshold (and therefore, by symmetry, also 4-threshold) such *CA* with $r = 2$ do have temporal two-cycles; e.g., in the 2-threshold case, for *CA* defined over an infinite line, $\{(1000)^{\omega}, (0010)^{\omega}\}$ is a two-cycle.

We now relate our results thus far to what has been already known about simple threshold *CA* and their phase space properties. In particular, the only recurrent types of configurations we have identified thus far are FPs (in the sequential case), and FPs and two-cycles, in the concurrent *CA* case. This is not a coincidence.

It turns out that the two-cycles in the *PS* of the parallel *CA* with $\delta = MAJ$ are actually the only type of (proper) temporal cycles such cellular automata can have. Indeed, for any *symmetric linear threshold update rule* δ, and any *finite* regular Cayley graph as the underlying cellular space, the following general result holds (see [7,8]):

Proposition 1:   Let a classical *CA* **A** $= (\Gamma, N, T)$ be such that Γ is finite and the underlying local rule of T is an elementary symmetric threshold function. Then for all configurations $C \in PS(\mathbf{A})$,   there exists $t \geq 0$ such that $T^{t+2}(C) = T^t(C)$.   ◇

In particular, this result implies that, in case of any finite simple threshold automaton, and for any starting configuration C_0, there are only two possible kinds of orbits: upon repeated iteration, after finitely many steps, the computation either converges to a fixed point configuration, or else it converges to a two-cycle[2].

We now specifically focus on $\delta = MAJ$ 1-D *CA,* with an emphasis on the infinite case, and completely characterize the configuration spaces of such threshold automata. In particular, in the $\Gamma = infinite\ line$ case, we show that the cycle configurations are rather rare, that fixed point configurations are quite numerous - yet still relatively rare in a sense to be discussed below, and that *almost all* configurations of these threshold automata are transient states.

We begin with some simple observations about the nature of various configurations in the *(S)CA* with $\delta = MAJ$ and $r = 1$. We shall subsequently generalize most of these results to arbitrary $r \geq 1$. We first recall that, for such *(S)CA* with $r = 1$, two adjacent nodes of the same value are stable. That is, 11 and 00 are stable sub-configurations. Consider now the starting sub-configuration $x_{i-1}x_i x_{i+1} = 101$. In the parallel case, at the next time step, $x_i \rightarrow 1$. Hence, no FP configuration of a parallel *CA* can contain 101 as a sub-configuration. In the sequential case, assuming fairness, x_i will eventually

---

[2] If one considers *threshold (S)CA* defined over infinite Γ, the only additional possibility is that such automaton's dynamic evolution altogether fails to converge; in that case, one can readily convince herself that the limit of such an infinite computation is a FP.

have to update. If, at that time, it is still the case that $x_{i-1} = x_{i+1} = 1$, then $x_i \to 1$, and $x_{i-1}x_ix_{i+1} \to 111$, which is stable. Else, at least one of x_{i-1}, x_{i+1} has already "flipped" into 0. Without loss of generality, let's assume $x_{i-1} = 0$. Then $x_{i-1}x_i = 00$, which is stable; so, in particular, $x_{i-1}x_ix_{i+1}$ will never go back to the original 101. By symmetry of $\delta = MAJ$ with respect to 0 and 1, the same line of reasoning applies to the sub-configuration $x_{i-1}x_ix_{i+1} = 010$. In particular, the following properties hold:

Lemma 3: A fixed point configuration of a *1D-(S)CA* with $\delta = $ *Majority* and $r = 1$ cannot contain sub-configurations 101 or 010. Similarly, a cycle configuration of such a *1D-(S)CA* cannot contain sub-configurations 00 or 11. ◇

Of course, we have already known that, in the sequential case, no cycle states exist, period. In case of the parallel threshold *CA*, by virtue of determinism, a complete characterization of each of the three basic types of configurations (FPs, CCs, TCs) is now almost immediate:

Lemma 4: The FPs of the *1D-(S)CA* with $\delta = MAJ$ and $r = 1$ are precisely of the form $(000^* + 111^*)^*$. The CCs of such *1D-CA* exist only in the concurrent case, and the temporal cycles are precisely of the form $\{(10)^*, (01)^*\}$. All other configurations are *transient states*, that is, TCs are precisely the configurations that contain both (i) 000^* or 111^* (or both), and (ii) 101 or 010 (or both) as their sub-configurations. In addition, the CCs in the parallel case become TCs in all corresponding sequential cases. ◇

Some generalizations to arbitrary (finite) rule radii r are now immediate. For instance, given any such $r \geq 1$, the finite sub-configurations 0^{r+1} and 1^{r+1} are stable with respect to $\delta = MAJ$ update rule applied either in parallel or sequentially; consequently, any configuration of the form $(0^{r+1}0^* + 1^{r+1}1^*)^*$, for both finite and infinite *(S)CA*, is a fixed point. This characterization, only with a considerably different notation, has been known for the case of configurations with *compact support* for a relatively long time; see, e.g., *Chapter 4* in [8]. On the other hand, fully characterizing CCs (and, consequently, also TCs) in case of finite or infinite (parallel) *CA* is more complicated than in the simplest case with $r = 1$. For example, for $r \geq 1$ odd, and $\Gamma = $ *infinite line*, $\{(10)^\omega, (01)^\omega\}$ is a two-cycle, whereas for $r \geq 2$ even, each of $(10)^\omega, (01)^\omega$ is a fixed point. However, for all $r \geq 1$, the corresponding (parallel) *CA* are guaranteed to have some temporal cycles, namely, given $r \geq 1$, the doubleton of states $\{(1^r0^r)^\omega, (0^r1^r)^\omega\}$ forms a temporal two-cycle.

Lemma 5: Given any (finite or infinite) threshold *(S)CA*, one of the following two properties always holds: either (i) this threshold automaton does not have proper cycles and cycle states; or (ii) if there are cycle states in the *PS* of this automaton, then none of those cycle states has any incoming transients. ◇

Moreover, if there are any (two-)cycles, the number of these temporal cycles and therefore of the cycle states is, statistically speaking, negligible:

Lemma 6: Given an infinite *MAJ CA* and a finite radius of the node update rules $r \geq 1$, among uncountably many ($2^{\aleph_0}$, to be precise) global configurations of such a *CA*, there are only finitely many (proper) cycle states. ◇

On the other hand, fixed points of some threshold automata are *much more numerous* than the CCs. The most striking are the *MAJ (S)CA* with their abundance of FPs. Namely, the cardinality of the set of FPs, in case of $\delta = MAJ$ and (countably) infinite cellular spaces, equals the cardinality of the entire PS:

Theorem 2: An infinite *1D-(S)CA* with $\delta = MAJ$ and any $r \geq 1$ has *uncountably many* fixed points. ◇

The above result is another evidence that "not all threshold *(S)CA* are born equal". It suffices to consider only 1D, infinite *CA* to see a rather dramatic difference. Namely, in contrast to the $\delta = MAJ$ *CA*, the *CA* with memory and with $\delta \in \{OR, AND\}$ (i) do not have any temporal cycles, and (ii) have *exactly two* FPs, namely, 0^ω and 1^ω. Other threshold *CA* may have temporal cycles, as we have already shown, but they still have only a finite number of FPs.

We have just argued that *1-D infinite MAJ (S)CA* have uncountably many FPs. However, these FPs are, when compared to the transient states, still but a few. To see this, let's assume that a "random" global configuration is obtained by "picking" each site's value to be either 0 or 1 at random, with equal probability, and so that assigning a value to one site is independent of the value assignment to any of the other sites. Then the following result holds:

Lemma 7: If a global configuration of an infinite threshold automaton is selected "at random", that is, by assigning each node's value independently and according to a toss of a fair coin, then, with probability 1, this randomly picked configuration will be a transient state. ◇

Moreover, the "unbiased randomness", while sufficient, is certainly not necessary. In particular, assigning bit values according to outcomes of tossing a coin with a fixed bias also yields transient states being of probability one.

Theorem 3: Let p be any real number such that $0 < p < 1$, and let the probability of a site in a global configuration of a threshold automaton being in state 1 be equal to p (so that the probability of this site's state being 0 is equal to $q = 1 - p$). If a global configuration of this threshold automaton is selected "at random" where the state of each node is an i.i.d. discrete random variable according to the probability distribution specified by p, then, with probability 1, this global configuration will be a transient state. ◇

In case of the finite threshold *(S)CA*, as the number of nodes, N, grows, the fraction of the total of 2^N global configurations that are TCs will also tend to grow. In particular, under the same assumptions as above, in the limit, as $N \to \infty$, the probability that a randomly picked configuration, C, is a transient state approaches 1:

$$lim_{N \to \infty} Pr(C \ is \ transient) = 1 \qquad (2)$$

Thus, a fairly complete characterization of the configuration spaces of threshold *(S)CA* over finite and infinite 1-D cellular spaces can be given. Under a simple and reasonable definition of what is meant by a "randomly chosen" global configuration in the infinite threshold *(S)CA* case, *almost every* configuration is a TC. However, when it comes to the number of fixed points, the striking contrast between $\delta = MAJ$ and all other threshold rules remains: in case of the infinite Γ, the former has uncountably many FPs, whereas all other simple threshold *(S)CA* have only finitely many FPs.

4   Conclusion

The theme of this work is the study of configuration space properties of simple threshold cellular automata, both when the nodes update synchronously in parallel, and when they update sequentially, one at a time.

Motivated by the well-known notion of the sequential interleaving semantics of concurrency, we apply the *"interleaving semantics"* metaphor to the parallel *CA* and thus motivate the study of sequential cellular automata, *SCA* and *NICA*, and the comparison and contrast between *SCA* and *NICA* on one, and the classical, concurrent *CA*, on the other hand [19]. We have shown that even in this simplistic context, the perfect synchrony of the classical *CA* node updates has some important implications, and that the sequential *CA* cannot capture certain aspects of their parallel counterparts' behavior. Hence, simple as they may be, the basic operations (local node updates) in classical *CA* cannot always be considered atomic. Thus we find it reasonable to consider a single local node update to be made of an ordered sequence of finer elementary operations: (1) fetching ("receiving"?) all the neighbors' values, (ii) updating one's own state according to the update rule δ, and (iii) making available ("sending"?) one's new state to the neighbors.

We also study in some detail perhaps the most interesting of all simple threshold rules, namely, the *Majority* rule. In particular, we characterize all three fundamental types of configurations (transient states, cycle states and fixed point states) in case of finite and infinite *1D-CA* with $\delta = MAJ$ for various finite rule radii $r \geq 1$. We show that CCs are, indeed, a rare exception in such *MAJ CA*, and that, for instance, the infinite *MAJ (S)CA* have uncountably many FPs, in a huge contrast to other simple threshold rules that have only a handful of FPs. We also show that, assuming a random configuration is chosen via independently assigning to each node its state value by tossing a (not necessarily fair) coin, it is very likely, for a sufficiently large number of the automaton's nodes, that this randomly chosen configuration is a TC.

Overall, we conclude that the class of simple threshold *CA*, *SCA*, and *NICA* is (i) relatively broad and interesting, and (ii) nonlinear (and non-affine), yet (iii) these automata's long-term behavior can be fully analytically characterized and predicted.

As for the future work, we envision a thorough study of *genuinely asynchronous CA* (*ACA*), where communication delays and lack of a global clock are captured. The *ACA* model we have in mind is motivated both by our results in *Section 3* herein, and the desire to make the cellular automata models more physically realistic. Initially, we plan to study in detail *(simple) threshold ACA*, and compare and contrast their properties with those of *(simple) threshold (S)CA*. Further down the road, such comparative study shall be extended to update rules δ more complex than the simple threshold functions, yet yielding global *ACA*, *SCA and parallel CA* behaviors that can be analytically characterized and, hopefully, also effectively predicted, and that would thus bring additional insights into the implications of various assumptions regarding the cellular automata operations' (a)synchrony.

Acknowledgments. The work presented herein was supported by the *DARPA IPTO TASK Program*, contract number *F30602-00-2-0586*.

References

1. W. Ross Ashby, "Design for a Brain", Wiley, 1960
2. C. Barrett and C. Reidys, "Elements of a theory of computer simulation I: sequential CA over random graphs", Applied Math. & Comput., vol. 98 (2-3), 1999
3. C. Barrett, H. Hunt, M. Marathe, S. S. Ravi, D. Rosenkrantz, R. Stearns, and P. Tosic, "Gardens of Eden and Fixed Points in Sequential Dynamical Systems", Discrete Math. & Theoretical Comp. Sci. Proc. AA (DM-CCG), July 2001
4. C. Barrett, H. B. Hunt III, M. V. Marathe, S. S. Ravi, D. J. Rosenkrantz, R. E. Stearns, " Reachability problems for sequential dynamical systems with threshold functions", TCS 1-3: 41-64, 2003
5. C. Barrett, H. Mortveit, and C. Reidys, "Elements of a theory of computer simulation II: sequential dynamical systems", Applied Math. & Comput. vol. 107(2-3), 2000
6. C. Barrett, H. Mortveit, and C. Reidys, "Elements of a theory of computer simulation III: equivalence of sequential dynamical systems", Appl. Math. & Comput. vol. 122(3), 2001
7. Max Garzon, "Models of Massive Parallelism: Analysis of Cellular Automata and Neural Networks", Springer, 1995
8. E. Goles, S. Martinez, "Neural and Automata Networks: Dynamical Behavior and Applications", Math. & Its Applications series (vol. 58), Kluwer, 1990
9. E. Goles, S. Martinez (eds.), "Cellular Automata and Complex Systems", Nonlinear Phenomena and Complex Systems series, Kluwer, 1999
10. T. E. Ingerson and R. L. Buvel, "Structure in asynchronous cellular automata", Physica D: Nonlinear Phenomena, vol. 10 (1-2), Jan. 1984
11. S. A. Kauffman, "Emergent properties in random complex automata", Physica D: Nonlinear Phenomena, vol. 10 (1-2), Jan. 1984
12. Robin Milner, "A Calculus of Communicating Systems", Lecture Notes Comp. Sci., Springer, Berlin, 1989
13. Robin Milner, "Calculi for synchrony and asynchrony", Theoretical Comp. Sci. 25, Elsevier, 1983
14. Robin Milner, "Communication and Concurrency", C. A. R. Hoare series ed., Prentice-Hall Int'l, 1989
15. John von Neumann, "Theory of Self-Reproducing Automata", edited and completed by A. W. Burks, Univ. of Illinois Press, Urbana, 1966
16. J. C. Reynolds, "Theories of Programming Languages", Cambridge Univ. Press, 1998
17. Ravi Sethi, "Programming Languages: Concepts & Constructs", 2nd ed., Addison-Wesley, 1996
18. K. Sutner, "Computation theory of cellular automata", MFCS98 Satellite Workshop on CA, Brno, Czech Rep., 1998
19. P. Tosic, G. Agha, "Concurrency vs. Sequential Interleavings in 1-D Cellular Automata", APDCM Workshop, Proc. IEEE IPDPS'04, Santa Fe, New Mexico, 2004
20. Stephen Wolfram "Twenty problems in the theory of CA", Physica Scripta 9, 1985
21. Stephen Wolfram (ed.), "Theory and applications of CA", World Scientific, Singapore, 1986
22. Stephen Wolfram, "Cellular Automata and Complexity (collected papers)", Addison-Wesley, 1994
23. Stephen Wolfram, "A New Kind of Science", Wolfram Media, Inc., 2002

Lattice Boltzmann Approach to Incompressible Fluidynamics Dimensional Investigation and Poiseuille Test*

Gianpiero Cattaneo, Alberto Dennunzio, and Fabio Farina

Università degli Studi di Milano–Bicocca,
Dipartimento di Informatica Sistemistica e Comunicazione, Milano, Italy
{cattang, dennunzio}@disco.unimib.it, fabio@fislab.disco.unimib.it

Abstract. The problem of fluid compressibility in the ordinary approach to lattice Boltzmann (LB) according to the BGK method is analyzed. A new velocity is introduced besides the usual one, linked to this later by a dimensionless mass density. The LBGK method based on this second velocity, with a suitable second order equilibrium distribution (different from the ordinary one), leads to the real Navier–Stokes equation of incompressible fluids under the steady mass density condition. This approach is compared with two well known methods one can found in literature. Finally, the role of the approach introduced here and of the ordinary one with respect to Poiseuille flow simulation is presented.

1 The Ordinary Lattice Boltzmann BGK Methods

The Lattice Boltzmann (LB) models we consider in this paper are based on the 2-D discreet hexagonal lattice space consisting of L cells in the horizontal direction and M cells in the vertical one. Each cell is connected to its 6 neighbors along the directions given by the unary vectors $e_i := \left(\cos\left(\frac{2\pi(i-1)}{6} \right), \sin\left(\frac{2\pi(i-1)}{6} \right) \right)$, $i \in \{1,2,3,4,5,6\}$. The vector e_0 corresponds to the central position of each cell. Let L_R be the horizontal size of the real experimental situation we want simulate by LB. Then the lattice cell spacing (distance between two adjacent cells in the lattice) is given by $l_0 = \frac{L_R}{L}$. The system evolves in discrete time steps of duration δt, the time that each particle takes to move with uniform velocity $v_p = \frac{l_0}{\delta t} = \frac{L_R}{L \cdot \delta t}$ along the e_i direction from one cell to the adjacent one. Thus, each vector $v_i = v_p \, e_i$ (for $i = 1, 2, \ldots 6$) represents the *velocity* of particles moving along the e_i direction.

A *state*, located in cell r at time t, is a 7–uple of *population densities* (also *particle populations*) $f(r, t) = \{f_i(r, t) : i = 0, \ldots, 6\}$, where each population density $f_i(r, t)$ is related to the link i and is expressed by a real number (implemented as floating point number in computer codes). These distributions

---

* This work has been supported by M.I.U.R. COFIN project "Formal Languages and Automata: Theory and Application"

P.M.A. Sloot, B. Chopard, and A.G. Hoekstra (Eds.): ACRI 2004, LNCS 3305, pp. 871–880, 2004.
© Springer-Verlag Berlin Heidelberg 2004

describe in details a unique distribution $f(\boldsymbol{r}, \boldsymbol{v}, t)$ in which the velocity variable $\boldsymbol{v}$ ranges over the discrete set $\{\boldsymbol{v}_i = v_p \boldsymbol{e}_i : i = 0, 1, \dots, 6\}$ according to $f(\boldsymbol{r}, \boldsymbol{v}_i, t) := f_i(\boldsymbol{r}, t)$. We stress that each distribution has the dimension $[\frac{1}{L^2}]$ by the following interpretation:

$$f_i(\boldsymbol{r}, t) = \frac{\mathcal{N}_i(\boldsymbol{r}, t)}{\delta S} \tag{1}$$

where $\mathcal{N}_i(\boldsymbol{r}, t)$ is the (mean) number of particles located at time t in site $\boldsymbol{r}$ with velocity $\boldsymbol{v}_i$ and δS is the elementary surface associated to each $\boldsymbol{r}$, that in the LB context can be identified with the lattice hexagonal area $S_0 = \frac{3}{2}\sqrt{3}\, l_0^2$. The particle distribution (irrespective of velocity) is defined as

$$n(\boldsymbol{r}, t) = \sum_{i=0}^{6} f_i(\boldsymbol{r}, t) \tag{2}$$

and then $n(\boldsymbol{r}, t)\delta S$ is the (mean) number of particles (irrespective of velocity) which at time t are locate in $\boldsymbol{r}$ (for the analogous concepts in the continuous case see [6, p. 495]). On the basis of these distributions the macroscopic *mass* and *momentum densities* are introduced according to the following definitions:

$$\rho(\boldsymbol{r}, t) = \sum_{i=0}^{6} f_i(\boldsymbol{r}, t) \cdot m_p \qquad \boldsymbol{q}(\boldsymbol{r}, t) = \sum_{i=1}^{6} f_i(\boldsymbol{r}, t) \cdot m_p \boldsymbol{v}_i \tag{3}$$

where the constant m_p represents the single particle mass and whose dimensions are $[\frac{M}{L^2}]$ and $[\frac{M}{LT}]$ respectively. Note that $n(\boldsymbol{r}, t) = \rho(\boldsymbol{r}, t)/m_p$. A mean *velocity* (since the corresponding dimension is $[\frac{L}{T}]$) of a particle at site $\boldsymbol{r}$ and time t is defined by (discrete version of the continuos case, see [6, p. 495]):

$$\boldsymbol{u}(\boldsymbol{r}, t) = \frac{1}{n(\boldsymbol{r}, t)} \sum_{i=1}^{6} f_i(\boldsymbol{r}, t) \cdot \boldsymbol{v}_i = \frac{\boldsymbol{q}(\boldsymbol{r}, t)}{\rho(\boldsymbol{r}, t)} \tag{4}$$

The time evolution of particle populations in the LB method consists of two steps:

- *Collision step*: the particles within a cell are redistributed among the six directions and the rest particles distribution. The original distribution $\boldsymbol{f}(\boldsymbol{r}, t) = \{f_i(\boldsymbol{r}, t) : i = 0, 1, \dots, 6\}$ is modified in $\boldsymbol{f}^*(\boldsymbol{r}, t) = \{f_i^*(\boldsymbol{r}, t) : i = 0, 1, \dots, 6\}$ applying an *instantaneous* transition formalized by the following equation:

$$f_i^*(\boldsymbol{r}, t) = f_i(\boldsymbol{r}, t) + \Omega_i(\boldsymbol{r}, t) \tag{5}$$

where the *collision operators* $\Omega_i(\boldsymbol{r}, t)$ must satisfy the following mass and momentum conservation laws:

$$\rho^*(\boldsymbol{r}, t) = \sum_{i=0}^{6} m_p f_i^*(\boldsymbol{r}, t) = \sum_{i=0}^{6} m_p f_i(\boldsymbol{r}, t) = \rho(\boldsymbol{r}, t) \tag{6a}$$

$$\boldsymbol{q}^*(\boldsymbol{r}, t) = \sum_{i=1}^{6} m_p f_i^*(\boldsymbol{r}, t)\boldsymbol{v}_i = \sum_{i=1}^{6} m_p f_i(\boldsymbol{r}, t)\boldsymbol{v}_i = \boldsymbol{q}(\boldsymbol{r}, t) \tag{6b}$$

Equivalently these conservation laws correspond to the following conditions on the collision operator:

$$\sum_{i=0}^{6} \Omega_i(\boldsymbol{r}, t) = 0 \quad \text{and} \quad \sum_{i=1}^{6} \Omega_i(\boldsymbol{r}, t) \boldsymbol{v}_i = 0 \tag{7}$$

- *Streaming step*: the particles move along their direction toward adjacent cells with a uniform motion described by the following equation:

$$f_i(\boldsymbol{r} + l_0 \, \boldsymbol{e}_i, t + \delta t) = f_i^*(\boldsymbol{r}, t) \tag{8}$$

The composition of the two steps formalized by Eqs. (5) and (8) leads to the *Lattice Boltzmann (LB) equation*:

$$f_i(\boldsymbol{r} + l_0 \, \boldsymbol{e}_i, t + \delta t) = f_i(\boldsymbol{r}, t) + \Omega_i(\boldsymbol{r}, t) \tag{9}$$

The usual BGK formulation consists of a particularly simple linearized version of the collision operator Ω_i around an equilibrium distribution f_i^{eq}:

$$\Omega_i(f_i(\boldsymbol{r}, t)) = \frac{1}{\tau} \left(f_i^{eq}(\boldsymbol{r}, t) - f_i(\boldsymbol{r}, t) \right) \tag{10}$$

where τ is the *relaxation time* of the model. Thus, the LB equation with the BGK collision operator (10) (the *evolution equation* of the LBGK method) is:

$$f_i(\boldsymbol{r} + l_0 \boldsymbol{e}_i, t + \delta t) = f_i(\boldsymbol{r}, t) + \frac{1}{\tau} \left(f_i^{eq}(\boldsymbol{r}, t) - f_i(\boldsymbol{r}, t) \right) \tag{11}$$

We stress that in the previous equation no choice is made for the equilibrium distribution f_i^{eq}, but applying to (10) the conservations conditions in the form (7) the equilibrium distribution must satisfy the constraints:

$$\sum_{i=0}^{6} f_i^{eq}(\boldsymbol{r}, t) \cdot m_p = \rho(\boldsymbol{r}, t) \quad \text{and} \quad \sum_{i=1}^{6} f_i^{eq}(\boldsymbol{r}, t) \cdot m_p \boldsymbol{v}_i = \rho(\boldsymbol{r}, t) \boldsymbol{u}(\boldsymbol{r}, t) \tag{12}$$

We obtain a specific LBGK model whenever a particular expression for the equilibrium distributions f_i^{eq} is considered. In general it is used a second order expansion with respect to the velocity (small velocity approximation, i.e., low Mach number) of the Maxwellian distribution at constant temperature, whose general expression is of the form:

$$f_i^{eq}(\boldsymbol{r}, t) = n(\boldsymbol{r}, t) \left[A + B \left(\frac{\boldsymbol{v}_i \cdot \boldsymbol{u}}{v_p^2} \right) + C \left(\frac{\boldsymbol{v}_i \cdot \boldsymbol{u}}{v_p^2} \right) + D \frac{\boldsymbol{u} \cdot \boldsymbol{u}}{v_p^2} \right] \tag{13a}$$

$$f_0^{eq}(\boldsymbol{r}, t) = n(\boldsymbol{r}, t) \left(A_0 + B_0 \cdot \frac{\boldsymbol{u} \cdot \boldsymbol{u}}{v_p^2} \right) \tag{13b}$$

where A, B, C, D and A_0, B_0 are dimensionless adjustable coefficients which must be determined. This is done applying to (13) the following two steps procedure:

(P1) by verifying the satisfaction of the mass and momentum conservation laws (12),

(P2) by matching the form of the momentum tensor of the ordinary LBGK method

$$\Pi^{(0)}_{\alpha\beta} = c_s^2 \rho \delta_{\alpha\beta} + \rho u_\alpha u_\beta \tag{14}$$

with the standard expression of hydrodynamics.

It is straightforward to prove that this procedure leads to the following equilibrium distribution of the so-called *ordinary LBGK* method (see for instance [1, 5]), determined except a constant parameter α:

$$f_i^{eq}(\boldsymbol{r}, t) = n\frac{1-\alpha}{6} + \frac{1}{3}n\left[\boldsymbol{e}_i \cdot \frac{\boldsymbol{u}}{v_p} + 2\left(\boldsymbol{e}_i \cdot \frac{\boldsymbol{u}}{v_p}\right)^2 - \frac{1}{2}\left(\frac{\boldsymbol{u} \cdot \boldsymbol{u}}{v_p^2}\right)\right] \tag{15a}$$

$$f_0^{eq}(\boldsymbol{r}, t) = n\left(\alpha - \frac{\boldsymbol{u} \cdot \boldsymbol{u}}{v_p^2}\right) \tag{15b}$$

The constant α is the *rest particles coefficient*, usually set to $\frac{2}{3}$ in order to obtain best numerical stability ([7, p. 203]). It can be proved that the dynamic evolution expressed by Eq. (11), applied to equilibrium distributions (13) which satisfy mass and momentum conservation laws (P1), is such that each distribution f_i, in the absence of external forcing, evolves toward f_i^{eq} with τ as the typical parameter of convergence which fixes the rate of approach to equilibrium. Furthermore, applying to the Eq. (11) a second order Chapman–Enskog expansion, continuous equation for mass and momentum can be obtained. Precisely, mass conservation leads to the continuity equation:

$$\partial_t \rho + \nabla \cdot (\rho \boldsymbol{u}) = 0 \tag{16}$$

Under the condition of *steady* mass density, $\partial_t \rho = 0$, (which implies that $\rho = \rho(\boldsymbol{r})$ is a function of spatial variables only), Eq. (16) assumes the form $\nabla \cdot (\rho \boldsymbol{u}) = 0$. Moreover, the momentum conservation is expressed as a *Navier–Stokes "like"* equation (like in the sense that it "is very similar to, but not exactly the same, as the momentum equation of Navier–Stokes equations" [8]):

$$\rho \, \partial_t(\boldsymbol{u}) + \rho \, (\boldsymbol{u} \cdot \nabla)(\boldsymbol{u}) = -\nabla p(\rho) + \nu \, \nabla^2(\rho \boldsymbol{u}) \tag{17}$$

where the *kinematic viscosity*, the *sound velocity*, and the *pressure* are defined by the equations

$$\nu = \frac{v_p^2}{4}\delta t\left(\tau - \frac{1}{2}\right) = \frac{L_R^2}{4L^2}\frac{1}{\delta t}\left(\tau - \frac{1}{2}\right) \tag{18a}$$

$$c_s^2 = \frac{1-\alpha}{2}v_p^2 \quad \text{and} \quad p(\rho) = \rho c_s^2 \tag{18b}$$

Of course, we have to take $\tau > \frac{1}{2}$ to get a positive viscosity. In the particular case of the *slow velocity limit* (that is under condition $\boldsymbol{u} \simeq 0$ which allows the approximations $\nabla \cdot (\rho\, \boldsymbol{u}) \simeq \rho\, \nabla \cdot \boldsymbol{u}$ and $\nabla^2 (\rho\, \boldsymbol{u}) \simeq \rho\, \nabla^2 \boldsymbol{u}$ and assuming that the density is everywhere different from 0, Eqs. (17) and (16) become:

$$\partial_t \boldsymbol{u} + (\boldsymbol{u} \cdot \nabla)\boldsymbol{u} = -\frac{1}{\rho(\boldsymbol{r})}\nabla p(\rho) + \nu\, \nabla^2 \boldsymbol{u} \tag{19a}$$

$$\nabla \cdot \boldsymbol{u} = 0 \tag{19b}$$

According to [8], when $\nabla \cdot (\rho \boldsymbol{u}) = \rho \nabla \cdot \boldsymbol{u} + (\nabla\rho) \cdot \boldsymbol{u}$ "is used to approximate [the incompressibility condition $\nabla \cdot \boldsymbol{u} = 0$], the term $(\nabla\rho) \cdot \boldsymbol{u}$ is neglected. This term represents a compressibility error."

Summarizing, in the ordinary LBGK method if the steady mass density $\partial_t \rho$ and the small Mach number $M \ll 1$ (equivalent to the small velocity limit) conditions are satisfied both the Navier–Stokes like equation (19a) hold and the condition for incompressible flow (19b) is satisfied exactly.

1.1   He and Luo Incompressible LB Model

As to the continuity equation (16), in [8] one can find the following statement: "As Frisch et al. [3] pointed out, if one uses the mass current $\boldsymbol{v} = \rho\boldsymbol{u}$ [in our notation $\boldsymbol{q} = \rho\,\boldsymbol{u}$] to represent the velocity, then in the steady state the continuity equation implies exactly $\nabla \cdot \boldsymbol{v} = 0$ [in our notation $\nabla \cdot \boldsymbol{q} = 0$]." But whatever be the possible consequences "achieved by rewriting the Navier–Stokes equation in terms of the momentum density rather than the velocity" [4], the quantity $\boldsymbol{q} = \rho\,\boldsymbol{u}$ unavoidable has the dimension of a momentum density (or mass current) and not of a velocity, and the condition $\nabla \cdot \boldsymbol{q} = 0$ has nothing to do with the incompressibility condition $\nabla \cdot \boldsymbol{u} = 0$ [2, (ii) of p. 11].

In a very interesting paper of He and Luo [4], a LBGK model for the incompressible Navier–Stokes equation is presented. This method is based on the second order equilibrium distribution function involving (also if not explicitly mentioned) the velocity (4) and whose form in the hexagonal lattice case is just given by (15). The main idea is that "in an incompressible fluid the density is (approximately) a constant, say ρ_0, and the density fluctuation $\delta\rho$, should be of the order $O(M^2)$ [with $M \approx |\boldsymbol{u}|/v_p$] in the limit $M \to 0$. If we explicitly substitute $\rho = \rho_0 + \delta\rho$ into the equilibrium distribution, f_i^{eq} [i.e., (15)], and neglect the terms proportional to $\delta\rho(\boldsymbol{u}/v_p)$, and $\delta\rho(\boldsymbol{u}/v_p)^2$, which are of the order $O(M^3)$ or higher," [4], then in the case of the hexagonal lattice and considering the (irrespective of velocity) distribution $n = \rho/m_p$, with $n = n_0 + \delta n$ ($n_0 = \rho_0/m_p$), the equilibrium distribution function (by a substitution) trivially becomes

$$f_i^{eq}(\boldsymbol{r}, t) = n\frac{1-\alpha}{6} + \frac{1}{3}n_0\left[\boldsymbol{e}_i \cdot \frac{\boldsymbol{u}}{v_p} + 2\left(\boldsymbol{e}_i \cdot \frac{\boldsymbol{u}}{v_p}\right)^2 - \frac{1}{2}\left(\frac{\boldsymbol{u} \cdot \boldsymbol{u}}{v_p^2}\right)\right] \tag{20a}$$

$$f_0^{eq}(\boldsymbol{r}, t) = n\alpha - n_0\frac{\boldsymbol{u} \cdot \boldsymbol{u}}{v_p^2} \tag{20b}$$

Let us stress that also in this equilibrium distribution, since it is obtained by a simple substitution into equation (15), the involved velocity is always the one defined by (4).

In the quoted paper [4], and this is a delicate point of the model, it is introduced a *local pressure distribution* function $p_i := c_s^2 m_p f_i$ (in our notation) which produces the "global" pressure of (18b) according to

$$p = c_s^2 \rho = \sum_i p_i \tag{21}$$

and in terms of which it is possible to reformulate both the evolution equation (11) and the equilibrium distribution (15) of the LBGK system. In particular, the equilibrium pressure is given by $p_i^{eq}(\boldsymbol{r}, t) := c_s^2 m_p f_i^{eq}(\boldsymbol{r}, t)$ and thus the involved velocity $\boldsymbol{u}$ is always the (4). Along this line of tough, in [4] it is claimed that "with the p–representation, [...] the velocity, $\boldsymbol{u}$, is given by $p_0 \boldsymbol{u} = \sum_i p_i \boldsymbol{v}_i$" (where $p_0 = c_s^2 \rho_0$) with the unpleasant consequence that $\boldsymbol{u} = \frac{m_p}{\rho_0} \sum_i f_i \boldsymbol{v}_i \neq \frac{m_p}{\rho} \sum_i f_i \boldsymbol{v}_i = (4) = \boldsymbol{u}$. Of course, under the identification $\rho_0 \simeq \rho = \rho_0 + \delta\rho$ (i.e., $\delta\rho \simeq 0$) we can make the approximation $\frac{m_p}{\rho_0} \sum_i f_i \boldsymbol{v}_i \simeq \boldsymbol{u}$, even if the left term define a velocity a priori different from $\boldsymbol{u}$, and so the adoption of the same symbol is in some sense a little bit misleading.

Owing to the identification of the above two velocities, it must be clear that, even if according to "a common practice [one] uses the pressure, p, as an independent variable" [4], the equilibrium distribution function (20) of the He and Luo approach can be applied in the range of validity corresponding to the strong assumption $\delta\rho \simeq 0$. Applying this condition to (21), it follows that also the pressure must be approximatively constant $p \simeq p_0$. But in some simulations (for instance in the case of Poiseuille flow, see Fig. 1) it is possible to have a relevant difference between p and p_0 which leads to suggest that an incompressible model holds outside the restrictive conditions of the He and Luo approach. In the next section we introduce another approach in which this difficulty is avoided.

2   Incompressible LB Method

Introducing a constant *reference density* ρ_0, in the formal context outlined in Sec. 1 we define the following *dimensionless* particle distribution (where, following [7], the caret symbol is used to denote dimensionless quantities):

$$\widehat{f}_i(\boldsymbol{r}, t) := \frac{m_p f_i(\boldsymbol{r}, t)}{\rho_0} \qquad \widehat{f}_i^{eq}(\boldsymbol{r}, t) := \frac{m_p f_i^{eq}(\boldsymbol{r}, t)}{\rho_0} \tag{22}$$

According to the interpretation of quantities $\mathcal{N}_i$ given in equation (1), $\mathcal{N}(\boldsymbol{r}, t) = \sum_{i=0}^{6} \mathcal{N}_i(\boldsymbol{r}, t)$. is the *total number* of particles in position $\boldsymbol{r}$ at time t. In simulations, we assume that the initial configuration $\mathcal{N}(\boldsymbol{r}, 0)$ at time $t = 0$ is uniformly distributed in the space, i.e., $\exists \mathcal{N}_0$ constant s.t. $\forall \boldsymbol{r}$, $\mathcal{N}(\boldsymbol{r}, 0) = \mathcal{N}_0$ and so, taking into account (1) and (3), we can express the mass distribution at time $t = 0$ as follows: $\rho(\boldsymbol{r}, 0) = \sum_{i=0}^{6} \frac{\mathcal{N}_i(\boldsymbol{r}, 0)}{\delta S} m_p = \frac{\mathcal{N}_0}{\delta S} m_p$. If this initial constant density is assumed as the reference density, $\rho_0 = \rho(\boldsymbol{r}, 0)$, we have that $\widehat{f}_i(\boldsymbol{r}, t) = \mathcal{N}_i(\boldsymbol{r}, t)/\mathcal{N}_0$, that is $\widehat{f}_i(\boldsymbol{r}, t)$ *represents the number of particles with* *velocity v_i at time t in the site r normalized with respect to the initial uniform distribution.* Furthermore, we can define the *normalized (dimensionless) density*:

$$\widehat{\rho}(r,t) := \sum_{i=0}^{6} \widehat{f}_i(r,t) = \frac{\rho(r,t)}{\rho_0} \tag{23}$$

Finally, a new quantity, whose dimension is of a velocity, is defined as follows:

$$v(r,t) := \widehat{\rho}(r,t) \cdot u(r,t) = \frac{1}{n_0} \sum_{i=1}^{6} f_i(r,t) \cdot v_i \tag{24}$$

where $n_0 = \rho_0/m_p$. If in the LBGK procedure outlined in Sec. 1 we take into account the velocity v of equation (24) instead of the ordinary velocity u of equation (4), the evolution equation (11) remains the same, but with a possible different equilibrium distribution which, if no confusion is likely, will be still denoted by f_i^{eq}. Moreover, the constraints (12) must be adapted to the new velocity obtaining the following relations:

$$\sum_{i=0}^{6} f_i^{eq}(r,t) \cdot m_p = \rho(r,t) \quad \text{and} \quad \sum_{i=1}^{6} f_i^{eq}(r,t) \cdot m_p v_i = \rho_0 v(r,t) \tag{25}$$

and the momentum tensor of the ordinary approach (14) must be substituted by $\Pi_{\alpha\beta}^{(0)} = c_s^2 \rho \delta_{\alpha\beta} + \rho_0 v_\alpha v_\beta$. Then, according to the previous constraints, the second order equilibrium distribution obtained by applying to (13) the two steps procedure (P1) and (P2) described in Sec. 1 is the following:

$$f_i^{eq}(r,t) = n\frac{1-\alpha}{6} + \frac{1}{3}n_0 \left[e_i \cdot \frac{v}{v_p} + 2\left(e_i \cdot \frac{v}{v_p}\right)^2 - \frac{1}{2}\left(\frac{v \cdot v}{v_p^2}\right) \right] \tag{26a}$$

$$f_0^{eq}(r,t) = n\,\alpha - n_0 \frac{v \cdot v}{v_p^2} \tag{26b}$$

We can observe that Eq. (20) is the same of Eq. (26) if one considers the velocity v instead of u. This fact can lead to the following new interpretation of the He and Luo method: the ordinary method based on the equilibrium distribution (15) and the one based on the equilibrium distribution (26) coincide when $v \simeq u$, corresponding to the approximation $\rho \simeq \rho_0$ (i.e., $\delta\rho \simeq 0$ according to [4]).

The importance of the now introduced method (velocity v) is due to the fact that it reduces the compressibility errors of the ordinary method (velocity u). This fact has a theoretical explanation. Since in this method the velocity of the fluid is v (= $\widehat{\rho}{\cdot}u$), Eq. (16) of mass conservation transforms into $\partial_t \rho + \rho_0 \nabla \cdot v = 0$. Hence, the condition of *steady* mass density $\partial_t \rho = 0$ is equivalent to $\nabla \cdot v = 0$, the incompressibility condition. Moreover, under this condition, and applying the usual Chapman–Enskog procedure, the momentum conservation equation assumes now the form of a real Navier-Stokes equation for incompressible flow

$$\partial_t v + (v \cdot \nabla) v = -\frac{1}{\rho_0}\nabla p + \nu \nabla^2 v \tag{27}$$

with $p = \widehat{\rho} \rho_0 c_s^2$; the sound velocity c_s and the kinematic viscosity ν are the same of (18b). Let us stress that this incompressible Navier–Stokes equation, differently from the (19a) of the ordinary compressible LB approach, is obtained *without the slow velocity limit assumption.*

2.1   The Zou et al. Incompressible LB Method

Introducing the dimensionless velocity $\widehat{v} = v/v_p$, from (26) it is possible to derive the following form of the dimensionless equilibrium distribution defined by equations (22):

$$\widehat{f}_i^{eq}(r, t) = \widehat{\rho} \frac{1 - \alpha}{6} + \frac{1}{3} \left[e_i \cdot \widehat{v} + 2 \left(e_i \cdot \widehat{v} \right)^2 - \frac{1}{2} \widehat{v} \cdot \widehat{v} \right] \tag{28a}$$

$$\widehat{f}_0^{eq}(r, t) = \widehat{\rho} \, \alpha - \widehat{v} \cdot \widehat{v} \tag{28b}$$

This is the hexagonal version of the square lattice equilibrium distribution (11) considered in [8], in which the symbols ρ and v correspond to our dimensionless mass density $\widehat{\rho}$ and normalized velocity $\widehat{v}$ respectively.

This put a problem in the interpretation of the incompressible method of [8] from the dimensional point of view. Indeed, as usual, in [8] no mention is done about the dimension of the involved quantity, if one excludes a generic claim that "the particle distribution function satisfies the [...] lattice Boltzmann equation with BGK collision operator written in physical unit," whatever be the meaning of the statement *physical unit* attributed to the particle distribution function. Of course, if one considers (28) (or the square lattice Eq. (11) in [8]) it turns out that quantities $\widehat{f}^{eq}$, $\widehat{\rho}$ and the square norm $||\widehat{v}||^2 = \widehat{v} \cdot \widehat{v}$ must have the same dimension (quantities without caret in [8]). The unique coherent possibility is that the involved quantities are all dimensionless (might this be the meaning of statement: "written in physical units"?). This clarification is done in order to avoid a possible misunderstanding due to the assertion by Zou et al. in [8] (quoted at the beginning of Sec. 1.1 and relative to Frisch et al.) that $v = \rho u$ is a mass current (i.e., momentum density), giving in this way the impression that the quantity denoted by them with the same symbol v is a mass current. This is contrary to the fact (as clearly described in this section) that the coherence of the whole theory is based on the relationship (24), $v = \widehat{\rho} u$, in which v is a velocity linked to the velocity u of the ordinary approach by the dimensionless mass density $\widehat{\rho}$.

3   Conclusions and Poiseuille Simulations

In this paper a LBGK method for incompressible flows is discussed from an explicit theoretical point of view: its premises are well declared, especially with respect to the role of the new velocity v, "modified" with respect to the velocity u of the ordinary approach according to Eq. (24). Moreover, the modified equilibrium distribution (26) is formally derived in an explicit way by the standard

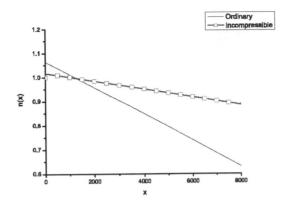

Fig. 1. Simulation results of density (pressure) linear decrease in ordinary (solid, with $n(x) = n_{in} - [n_{in}/L \cdot (\log n_{in} - \log n_{out})]\, x$) and incompressible (squared) cases.

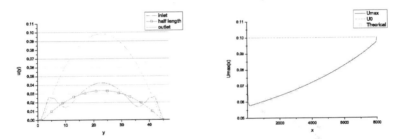

Fig. 2. Ordinary LB simulations: velocity profiles (left) and their peaks plotted as function of x (right), in agreement with the theoretical expectation $u_x(x,y) = \frac{1}{p_{in} - k\,x} \frac{c_s^2}{2\nu} \frac{p_{in} - p_{out}}{L}\, y\,(M - y)$

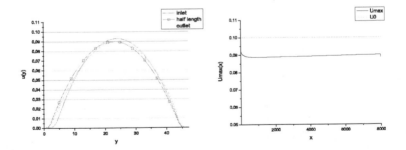

Fig. 3. Incompressible LB simulations: parabolic velocity profiles (left) and semi-stationary behavior of their peak (right)

procedure applied to v instead of to u. Finally, the difference between the standard and the dimensionless versions of the method is formally given. Differently from the Zou et al. approach [8], in Eq. (23) the role played by the reference constant density ρ_0 in the relationship between v and u is well clarified. This difference allows our method to derive the real Navier–Stokes equation for incompressible flow (27); moreover, this result is obtained under the only condition of steady mass density, differently from Eq. (15) of [8] in which the "global" (in particular also the velocity) steady flow condition is applied. Another withdraw of [8] with respect to the present approach is that there seems to be a theoretical jump in introducing the equilibrium distribution (26) (or the equivalent dimensionless version (28)), since its choice is not clearly motivated.

As to the second approach considered in this paper, the He and Luo one [4], its derivation (and formal motivation) is based on the velocity u of Eq. (4). In order to obtain the desired behavior, it is done the identification $v \simeq u$, and this assumption put a dramatic limitation of its applicability range since, once adopted the practice to use the pressure p as the independent variable of the method, the above identification implies the consequent identification $p \simeq p_0$. As pointed pout in Sec. 1.1, this approach can be more correctly considered a proof of the fact that under the condition $v \simeq u$ (equivalently, $p \simeq p_0$), the ordinary method and the incompressible one produce the same results.

The numerical results of simulations relative to the 2D–Poiseuille flow are presented in Fig. 1–Fig. 3. The system size is of $L \times M = 8000 \times 45$, whereas in [4] $L \times M = 17 \times 5$. Moreover, a constant inlet pressure p_{in} is fixed but, differently from [4], the outlet one p_{out} is free and obtained by simulations

References

[1] H. Chen, S. Chen, and W. Matthaeus, *Recovery of the Navier Stokes equation using a Lattice Gas Boltzmann method*, Physical Review A **45** (1992), 5339–5342.

[2] A. J. Chorin and Marsden J. E., *A mathematical introduction to fluid mechanics third edition*, Springer-Verlag, New York, 1993.

[3] U. Frisch, D. d'Humieres, B. Hasslacher, P. Lallemand, Y. Pomeau, and J.-P. Rivet, *Lattice gas hydrodynamics in two and three dimensions*, Complex Systems **1** (1987), 647–707.

[4] X. He and L. Luo, *Lattice Boltzmann model for the incompressible Navier-Stokes equation*, Journal of Statistical Physics **88** (1997), 927–944.

[5] Y. H. Qian, D. D'Humieres, and P. Lallemand, *Lattice BGK models for Navier-Stokes equation*, Europhysics Letters **17** (1992), 479–484.

[6] F. Reif, *Statistical and Thermal Physics*, McGraw–Hill, 1985.

[7] J. D. Sterling and S. Chen, *Stability analysis of Lattice Boltzmann methods*, Journal of Computational Physics **123** (1996), 196–206.

[8] Q. Zou, S. Hou, S. Chen, and G. Doolen, *An improved Lattice Boltzmann Model for time–independent flows*, Journal of Statistical Physics **81** (1995), 35–48.

Author Index

Lecture Notes in Computer Science

For information about Vols. 1–3180

please contact your bookseller or Springer